GERMAN-ENGLISH

SCIENCE DICTIONARY

"Every other author may aspire to praise; the lexicographer can only hope to escape reproach."

—Dr. Samuel Johnson

German-English
SCIENCE
DICTIONARY

LOUIS De VRIES
Formerly of Iowa State University

UPDATED AND EXPANDED BY

LEON JACOLEV, P.E.
Chemical Engineer and Technical Director
Associated Technical Services, Inc., Glen Ridge, N.J.

WITH THE ASSISTANCE OF

PHYLLIS L. BOLTON, M.A.

Fourth Edition

McGRAW-HILL BOOK COMPANY

New York St. Louis San Francisco Auckland Bogotá
Düsseldorf Johannesburg London Madrid Mexico
Montreal New Delhi Panama Paris São Paulo
Singapore Sydney Tokyo Toronto

Library of Congress Cataloging in Publication Data

De Vries, Louis, date.
German-English science dictionary.

Third ed. published in 1959 under title: German-
English science dictionary for students in chemistry,
physics, biology, agriculture, and related sciences.
1. Science—Dictionaries—German.   2. German
language—Dictionaries—English.   I. Jacolev, Leon.
II. Bolton, Phyllis L.   III. Title.
Q123.D4   1978   503   78-6465
ISBN 0-07-016602-1

5 6 7 8 9 10 11   BKP BKP   8 9 8 7 6 5 4 3

CONTENTS

PREFACE TO THE FOURTH EDITION

An attempt has been made in this new edition to update the terminologies of the traditional fields of science covered in the previous edition and introduce the essential terms of new branches of science and technology that have evolved during the past two decades since the Third Edition. The Fourth Edition introduces the newly specialized terminologies of nuclear science and engineering, computer science and data processing, solid state physics, molecular biology, genetics, automation, soil and environmental sciences, electronics, etc. The classic scientific disciplines of chemistry, physics, biology, bacteriology, medicine, botany, optics, geology, agriculture, astronomy, entomology, metallurgy, mechanics, etc., were updated by selected new terms, as well as new or modified meanings of old terms. Mathematics and statistics, essential to practically all fields of science and technology, received special attention.

Engineering and technology also contributed their important share of new terms, particularly since these fields often do not have Greek or Latin roots so common to pure science and so very helpful in grasping the meaning of new terms. The technologies have a highly vernacularized language and this new edition provides translations of many difficult German terms in chemical engineering, petroleum refining, polymers, mechanical and electrical engineering, metallurgy, etc., that have not yet found their way into the existing polytechnical dictionaries.

Obviously, the coverage of new terms, while relatively broad, is not exhaustive, in view of the multifaceted nature of the dictionary and certain limitations as to size. For the sake of expediency and, regretfully, some sacrifice of user convenience, the new terms have again been placed at the back and incorporated into the Addendum, thus more than doubling its previous size to some 7000 entries. The total number of entries in this new edition is close to 65,000.

Most of the new terms have been chosen from accumulated word lists compiled in the course of almost daily contact with German and English scientific and engineering literature in the process of editing, translating, and research during the past three decades. The compiler is especially grateful to the scores of bilingual scientists and engineers whose translations he was privileged to edit during his many years with Associated Technical Services, Inc.

Valuable assistance by Richard Van Emburgh, Translator and Editorial Assistant, Associated Technical Services, Inc., Glen Ridge, N.J., rendered in proofreading the typescript and page proofs is gratefully acknowledged.

Constructive comments, corrections (alas, there may be errors!), additions and suggestions for improvements are welcomed.

LEON JACOLEV

EXCERPT FROM THE PREFACE TO
THE SECOND EDITION

In order to make this work a real handbook for the translator, the following features have been included in the Appendix: Conversion Table, Atomic Table, Thermodynamic Symbols, Electric Units of Measure, Abbreviations of Periodicals, List of Measurements, and Geographic Names.

When using the book, the following principles should be kept in mind:

Nouns are shown by giving their genders: *m.* (masculine), *f.* (feminine), *n.* (neuter). Verbs are indicated by "to" before the English equivalents. Thus only adjectives, adverbs, prepositions, pronouns, and conjunctions are not identified.

The plurals of nouns are given with the exception of feminines ending in **-e, -heit, -keit, -schaft, -ung, -ei, -ie, -tät,** and **-tion,** all of which form their plurals by adding **-(e)n.**

Certain verbs and adjectives governing other cases besides the accusative have been noted by *(gen.)* or *(dat.)* immediately following the entry.

When adjectives may be used as adverbs, a frequent practice in German, only the adjectival form is given.

Forms of past participles and of strong verbs in the present and past tenses are translated by at least one equivalent; the infinitive is given in parentheses for additional meanings.

For the sake of compactness, self-explanatory compounds have been omitted. The student should therefore try to deduce independently the meaning of compound words instead of slavishly thumbing the dictionary.

Louis De Vries.

Ames, Iowa,
June, 1946.

PREFACE TO THE FIRST EDITION

Since coming to Iowa State College twenty-five years ago, the author has been more or less closely associated with students and instructors in practically all branches of science, translating with them the German literature in their respective fields and assisting candidates for advanced degrees in acquiring a reading knowledge of the language.

Research within the various departments of science has gradually developed during these years into complicated interdepartmental problems. No entomological vocabulary, for example, can today dissociate itself from the many aspects of biology in general; even the physical sciences are embraced. Terms must be included covering not only entomology and the sciences into which it enters, such as embryology, cytology, physiology, morphology, genetics, ecology, but also chemistry, physics, botany, and medicine, all of which enter into modern treatises on insects.

This situation made the need for a comprehensive dictionary more and more apparent, until the author was prevailed upon by his colleagues to compile for them and their students a suitable German-English Science Dictionary. This enormous task was accepted only with the assurance of close cooperation on the part of the science faculty. Each department began by submitting a list of the outstanding German texts, reference books, journals, dictionaries, encyclopedias, and glossaries from which information and specific word lists could be derived.

This work is the first dictionary of its kind. The number of sciences that had to be studied made imperative a selection of the words to be included in a small and handy dictionary. Not all the names of animals, plants, insects, or chemical compounds have been included, since each subject would make a dictionary of its own. This problem of selection has been simplified somewhat by the nature of the German language itself, which permits the compounding of words almost without restriction. These composite words, because of their compactness and conciseness, are especially adapted to the requirements of scientific literature and enlarge scientific vocabularies constantly. The first impulse of the average student, on encountering these compounds, is to look for the whole word in a dictionary. However, these words are always composed of short root stems, as noun and noun, noun and adjective, or adjective and adejective, with which the student, on reflection, will usually find himself familiar. The present work limits the number of compound terms but includes all basic information needed in finding meanings of compounds. It is, therefore, strongly recommended that the student try to deduce independently the meaning of every compound word instead of slavishly thumbing the dictionary.

This dictionary of 48,000 entries cannot, therefore, make a claim to completeness, and the author would be grateful if the users would send him any useful suggestions, with regard either to words that have been omitted or to incorrect meanings and equivalents.

Since this dictionary was compiled for students in science, the author has indicated nouns by giving their genders, *m.* (masculine), *f.* (feminine), *n.* (neuter); the verbs are recognized by "to" before the English equivalents; this leaves adjectives, adverbs, pronouns, and conjunctions without any identification. Forms of past participles and of strong verbs in the present and past tenses are translated by at least one equivalent; the infinitive is given in parentheses, in case other meanings are needed.

LOUIS DE VRIES

AMES, IOWA
April, 1939

SUGGESTIONS FOR TRANSLATORS

In this dictionary the student will find not only the interpretation of the German word, but he can also see for himself how verbs, nouns, adjectives, etc., are translated into English from the German sentence, which, especially in scientific German, may have a complicated structure.

The gender of every noun in the dictionary is indicated by *m.* (masculine), *f.* (feminine), or *n.* (neuter). The plurals are also indicated, except for the feminines ending in **-e, -heit, -keit, -schaft, -ung, -ei, -ie, -tät, and -tion,** all of which form their plurals by the addition of **-(e)n.**

Neither the nouns nor the verbs are listed by classes.

Verbs are indicated by the word *to* preceding the English equivalents. In the case of strong verbs, the vowel changes are shown; e.g., for **geben,** the forms **gab, gegeben, gibt** are indicated by **a, e, i,** and for **lassen,** the forms **liess, gelassen, lässt** are indicated by **ie, a, ä.** Verbs with prefixes may not show the vowel changes in all cases. In addition, the full forms of the third person singular and of the past participle are listed alphabetically, e.g., **nimmt (nehmen),** (he) takes, **nahm (nehmen),** (he) took, and **genommen (nehmen),** taken, with the infinitive given in parentheses to facilitate looking it up for further meanings and for idioms.

Idioms will generally be found under the key word.

VERBS

Since the verb almost always appears in scientific literature in the form of the third person singular or plural, a few general suggestions can be very helpful. If a verb ends in **-en,** the verb

xiii

and its subject are *plural*. If it does not end in **-en,** then, with very few exceptions, the verb and its subject are *singular*. For example, **sie haben, sie hatten, sie werden, sie wurden, sie sagen, sie sagten, sie geben, sie gaben** are all plural (they have, they had, they become, they became, they say, they said, they give, they gave); exception, **sie sind** (they are). On the other hand, **es hat, es ist, es sagt, es spaltet, es gibt, es bindet** are all singular (it has, it is, it says, it splits, it yields, it binds), for the ending of the third person singular in German, **-(e)t,** is equivalent to *-s* in English.

In the *past tense,* weak verbs end in **-te** in the third person singular [the English ending is generally *-(e)d*], while strong verbs have no ending. The plural endings are **-ten** for weak verbs and **-en** for strong verbs. Compare the following weak verbs in the singular: **es hatte, es sagte, es spaltete, es führte** (it had, it said, it split, it conducted) with the following strong verbs: **es war, es gab, es band** (it was, it yielded, it bound). Compare also the plural of the weak verbs **sie hatten** and **sie spalteten** (they had and they split) with the plural of the strong verbs **sie waren** and **sie gaben** (they were and they yielded).

As in English, most verbs in German are weak verbs. A list of the strong verbs that occur most frequently in scientific German is given below. The principal parts of verbs with separable or inseparable prefixes may be obtained from the stem verb. The third person singular is given only ·for verbs with a vowel change. Verbs that take **sein** as an auxiliary are indicated by **ist** with the past participle.

Infinitive	*3d Sing. Present*	*Past*	*Past Participle*
backen	**bäckt**	**buk**	**gebacken**
beginnen		**begann**	**begonnen**
beissen		**biss**	**gebissen**
bergen	**birgt**	**barg**	**geborgen**
bersten	**birst**	**barst**	**ist geborsten**
biegen		**bog**	**gebogen**

Infinitive	3d Sing. Present	Past	Past Participle
bieten		bot	geboten
binden		band	gebunden
bitten		bat	gebeten
blasen	bläst	blies	geblasen
bleiben		blieb	ist geblieben
braten	brät	briet	gebraten
brechen	bricht	brach	gebrochen
dringen		drang	ist gedrungen
empfehlen	empfiehlt	empfahl	empfohlen
erloschen	erlischt	erlosch	ist erloschen
essen	isst	ass	gegessen
fahren	fährt	fuhr	ist gefahren
fallen	fällt	fiel	ist gefallen
fangen	fängt	fing	gefangen
finden		fand	gefunden
flechten	flicht	flocht	geflochten
fliegen		flog	ist geflogen
fliessen		floss	ist geflossen
fressen	frisst	frass	gefressen
frieren		fror	gefroren
gären		gor	gegoren
geben	gibt	gab	gegeben
gedeihen		gedieh	ist gediehen
gehen		ging	ist gegangen
gelingen		gelang	ist gelungen
gelten	gilt	galt	gegolten
geschehen	geschieht	geschah	ist geschehen
gewinnen		gewann	gewonnen
giessen		goss	gegossen
gleichen		glich	geglichen
gleiten		glitt	ist geglitten
glimmen		glomm	geglommen
graben	gräbt	grub	gegraben
greifen		griff	gegriffen

Infinitive	3d Sing. Present	Past	Past Participle
halten	hält	hielt	gehalten
hangen	hängt	hing	gehangen
heben		hob	gehoben
heissen		hiess	geheissen
helfen	hilft	half	geholfen
klingen		klang	geklungen
kommen		kam	ist gekommen
kriechen		kroch	ist gekrochen
laden	lädt	lud	geladen
lassen	lässt	liess	gelassen
laufen	läuft	lief	ist gelaufen
leiden		litt	gelitten
leihen		lieh	geliehen
lesen	liest	las	gelesen
liegen		lag	gelegen
messen	misst	mass	gemessen
misslingen		misslang	ist misslungen
nehmen	nimmt	nahm	genommen
preisen		pries	gepriesen
quellen	quillt	quoll	ist gequollen
raten	rät	riet	geraten
reiben		rieb	gerieben
reissen		riss	gerissen
riechen		roch	gerochen
saugen		sog	gesogen
schaffen		schuf	geschaffen
scheiden		schied	(ist) geschieden
scheinen		schien	geschienen
scheren		schor	geschoren
schieben		schob	geschoben
schiessen		schoss	geschossen
schlafen	schläft	schlief	geschlafen
schlagen	schlägt	schlug	geschlagen
schleifen		schliff	geschliffen
schleissen		schliss	geschlissen

Infinitive	3d Sing. Present	Past	Past Participle
schliessen		schloss	geschlossen
schmelzen	schmilzt	schmolz	ist geschmolzen
schneiden		schnitt	geschnitten
schreiben		schrieb	geschrieben
schwellen	schwillt	schwoll	ist geschwollen
schwimmen		schwamm	ist geschwommen
schwinden		schwand	ist geschwunden
schwingen		schwang	geschwungen
sehen	sieht	sah	gesehen
sein	ist	war	ist gewesen
sieden		sott	gesotten
singen		sang	gesungen
sinken		sank	ist gesunken
sinnen		sann	gesonnen
sitzen		sass	gesessen
spinnen		spann	gesponnen
sprechen	spricht	sprach	gesprochen
springen		sprang	(ist) gesprungen
stechen	sticht	stach	gestochen
stehen		stand	gestanden
stehlen	stiehlt	stahl	gestohlen
steigen		stieg	ist gestiegen
sterben	stirbt	starb	ist gestorben
stossen	stösst	stiess	gestossen
streichen		strich	(ist) gestrichen
tragen	trägt	trug	getragen
treffen	trifft	traf	getroffen
treiben		trieb	getrieben
treten	tritt	trat	(ist) getreten
trinken		trank	getrunken
tun	tut	tat	getan
verderben	verdirbt	verdarb	(ist) verdorben
vergessen	vergisst	vergass	hat vergessen
verlieren		verlor	verloren
wachsen	wächst	wuchs	ist gewachsen

Infinitive	3d Sing. Present	Past	Past Participle
waschen	wäscht	wusch	gewaschen
weisen		wies	gewiesen
werden	wird	wurde	ist geworden
werfen	wirft	warf	geworfen
wiegen		wog	gewogen
ziehen		zog	(ist) gezogen
zwingen		zwang	gezwungen

Irregular Weak Verbs

brennen		brannte	gebrannt
bringen		brachte	gebracht
denken		dachte	gedacht
haben	hat	hatte	gehabt
kennen		kannte	gekannt
nennen		nannte	genannt
wenden	wendet	wandte	gewandt
wissen	weiss	wusste	gewusst

Auxiliaries

ist   sind   war   werden

Weak or strong verbs that do not take an object in the accusative case *and* that show motion or a change of state or condition have **sein** as an auxiliary. All others take **haben**.

er ist	he is	**es ist geschmolzen**	it melted, it has melted
sie sind	they are	**sie sind geschmolzen**	they melted, they have melted
er war	he was	**es war geschmolzen**	it had melted
sie waren	they were	**sie waren geschmolzen**	they had melted
er sei	he be, he were	**es sei geschmolzen**	it melted, it has (had) melted
er wäre	he were, he would be	**es wäre geschmolzen**	it had melted, it would have melted

er würde sein	he would be	es würde ge- schmolzen sein	it would have melted

1. *werden* as auxiliary:

es wird schmelzen	it will melt
sie werden schmelzen	they will melt

2. Meanings of **werden** as a verb:

All tenses of **werden** are used with adjectives and **nouns**, meaning to become, get, grow, turn; **werden zu** means to change to or become.

Das Lackmuspapier wird blau.	The litmus paper is turning (becomes) blue.
Er wird Lehrer.	He is going to become a teacher.
Es wurde blau.	It turned (became) blue.
Es ist blau geworden.	It turned (has turned) blue.
Es sei blau geworden.	It has (had) turned blue.
Es würde blau werden.	It would turn (become) blue.

3. **werden** as auxiliary of the passive:

All forms of **werden** (**worden** instead of **geworden**) are used with the past participle of transitive verbs to form the passive (in English, *to be* + past participle). Participles with inseparable prefixes (**zer-, ver-, ent-,** etc.) do not have the familiar **ge-** of the past participle.

Es wird von ihm geprüft.	It is (being) examined by him.
Sie werden geprüft.	They are (being) examined.
Es wurde erhitzt.	It was (being) heated.
Sie wurden erhitzt.	They were heated.
Es ist übernommen worden.	It was (has been) taken over.
Sie sind gebraucht worden.	They were (have been) used.
Es war verbraucht worden.	It had been spent.
Es wäre angenommen worden.	It would have been accepted.
Es wird angebracht werden.	It will be attached.
Es kann gebraucht werden.	It can be used.

Es soll gebraucht werden.   It is to be used.

Es musste gebraucht werden.   It had to be used.

Sie werden gefärbt und sichtbar.   They *are* stained and *become* visible.

The Subjunctive

Since the subjunctive is not so common in German scientific literature as it is in nonscientific literature, only a few forms are shown. The ending for the third person singular is **-e** (except **sei**), while the third person plural retains the **-en** ending.

Indicative		*Subjunctive*	
er ist	he is	**er sei**	he may (might) be
er hat	he has	**er habe**	he may (might) have
er war	he was	**er wäre**	he would be (were)
er war gegangen	he had gone	**er wäre gegangen**	he would have gone
er hatte	he had	**er hätte**	he would have (had)
er musste	he had to	**er müsste**	he would have to
er gab	he gave	**er gäbe**	he would give
es gab	there was	**es gäbe**	there would be
es musste geben	there had to be	**es müsste geben**	there would have to be
er machte	he made	**er machte**	he would make
er ging	he went	**er ginge**	he would go

Es drehte sich in einer Richtung, als hätten es (vom negativen Pol ausgehende) Teilchen getroffen. It turned in one direction, as if particles (coming from the negative pole) (would have) had struck it.

Ich möchte berichten, wie ich dazu kam . . . . I should like to report how I came to . . . .

Zunächst glaubte er, diese Strahlung werde von den Mineralien ausgesandt . . . . At first he thought this radiation was emitted by the minerals . . . .

Sie hatte die Überzeugung gehabt, die Energieemission des Urans müsse eine Eigenschaft sein, die mit dem Atom des Urans zusammenhänge. She had been convinced that the emission of energy by uranium would have to be a property which must (would) be connected with the uranium atom.

Das entspräche etwa einem Tröpfchen in einigen Litern Wasser. That would correspond approximately to a small drop in a few liters of water.

Und sei es auch nur um beliebig wenig . . . . And be it ever so slight . . . .

Um auch in dem Fall sicher zu gehen, da es sich als ungeeignet erwiese . . . . In order to be sure in this case, too, that it would prove unsuited . . . .

Ein Wasserglas würde . . . enthalten. A water glass would contain . . . .

Wir sähen eine Menge von Sauerstoffmolekülen. We would see a number of oxygen atoms.

NOUNS ARTICLES ADJECTIVES

Note two very important endings, **-es, -em,** which occur only in the singular. Therefore, if a German word ends in either **-s** or **-m,** that *word* or the noun it modifies is used in the singular.

When an adjective follows the article **der,** it will take the ending **-e** in the masculine nominative singular and in the nominative and accusative singular of the feminine and neuter. When an adjective follows the article **ein,** it has the ending **-er** in the masculine nominative singular, the ending **-e** in the nominative and accusative singular of the feminine, and the ending **-es** in the nominative and accusative singular of the neuter. In all other cases, both singular and plural, the ending for the adjective is **-en.** When no modifier precedes the adjective, it has the same endings as the article **der,** except in the genitive singular of the masculine and neuter, where it ends in **-en.**

	Masc.	*Fem.*	*Neuter*	*Plural*
the	der	die	das	die
of the	des	der	des	der
to or for the	dem	der	dem	den
the	den	die	das	die
a, an	ein	eine	ein	
(no)	(kein)	(keine)	(kein)	(keine)
of a	eines	einer	eines	
(of no)	(keines)	(keiner)	(keines)	(keiner)
to or for a	einem	einer	einem	
(to or for no)	(keinem)	(keiner)	(keinem)	(keinen)
a, an	einen	eine	ein	
(no)	(keinen)	(keine)	(kein)	(keine)
this	dieser	diese	dieses	diese
of this	dieses	dieser	dieses	dieser
to or for this	diesem	dieser	diesem	diesen
this	diesen	diese	dieses	diese

THE PARTICIPIAL-ADJECTIVE CONSTRUCTION

In order to read scientific German with any degree of facility and accuracy, it is absolutely essential to have a thorough knowledge of participial constructions. This mode of expression, because of its conciseness, is used extensively.

The following rule will usually give a good translation:

Translate (1) the article (with preposition, if any), (2) the noun (with adjective, if any), (3) the participle (with adverb, if any), (4) the intervening words or modifiers of the participle. The German order is usually 1-4-3-2. For best results, if the sentence is not too long, the participial phrase may be translated as a relative clause.

In the examples given here, the participial construction has been set off by parentheses.

With the *present participle:*

Sauerstoff besteht aus (paarweise ein Molekül *bildenden*)
Atomen. Oxygen consists of atoms (*which form*) *forming*
molecules in pairs.

In einer (viel Sauerstoff enthaltenden) Atmosphäre . . .
In an atmosphere (*which contains*) *containing* much oxygen . . .

With the *past participle*:

Zu dem (in einem Becherglas *aufgefangenen*) Filtrat gibt man
eine Lösung reinstem Kaliumhydroxyd. To the filtrate (*which
has been*) *collected* in a beaker, a solution of very pure potassium
hydroxide is added.

Man filtriert die (mit etwas Tierkohle *aufgekochte*) Flüssigkeit nach dem Erkalten durch Papier oder Asbest. After cooling,
one filters the liquid, (*which has been*) *boiled* with some animal
charcoal, through paper or asbestos.

With an adjective rather than a participle:

Das war in einem (im Vergleich zu dem Inhalt des Kessels
sehr *kleinen*) Raum. That was in a space *that was very small* in
comparison to the content of the tank.

Der (damals sehr *berühmte* und heute noch *wohlbekannte*)
Forscher war Robert Koch. The investigator, who was very
famous at that time and is still *well known* today, was Robert
Koch.

With a present participle preceded by zu, *to be*, this construction has future passive meaning:

eine (*zu lösende*) Aufgabe   a problem *to be solved*

In den (von uns morgen *auszuführenden*) Versuchen werden
wir zeigen, dass unsere Voraussetzung richtig war. We will

show, in the experiments *to be carried out* by us tomorrow, that our hypothesis was correct.

Sometimes one participial-adjective construction appears within another:

Es war in einem (mit den oben *beschriebenen* Gasen *gefüllten*) Kolben.   It was in a flask *filled* with the gases *described* above.

Sometimes the past participle is used as a noun: **das Gesagte, der Vertraute**:

Das (bei der Darstellung der Kohle) *Gesagte* war von grosser Bedeutung.   *The statement made* or *what was said* in the case of the preparation of carbon was of great importance.

Der (mit der andern Sprache) *Vertraute* lernt die chemische Terminologie viel schneller.   The one *familiar with* the other language learns the chemical terminology much more rapidly.

Other examples:

Es drehte sich, als hätten es (vom negative Pol *ausgehende*) **Teilchen getroffen.**   It turned as if particles *coming from* the negative pole had struck it.

Jetzt kennen wir die Ströme negativer Teilchen, die von der negativen Elektrode der (*uns nun wohlbekannten*) Vakuum-röhren ausgehen.   Now we know the streams of negative particles that come from the negative electrodes of the vacuum tubes now familiar to us.

Dann legte er etwas von dem (*zu untersuchenden*) Mineral auf die Platte.   Then he placed some of the mineral *to be tested* on the plate.

Zur grössten Überraschung erwies sich dieses Uranerz als vielmal radioaktiver als die (aus ihr *präparierten*) reinen Ver-bindungen.   To his very great surprise this uranium ore proved to be many times more radioactive than the pure compounds *prepared* from it.

Sie macht die Bahn der einzelnen (aus dem Radium *ausgeschleuderten*) Partikeln sichtbar.   It makes visible the path of the individual particles shot out of the radium.

. . . die Freisetzung von Energien, die alle (bisher im Laboratorium *erzeugten*) so weit übertraf . . . .   the liberation of energies which so far surpassed all (those) previously *produced* in the laboratory . . . .

Dann werden viele, (von gespaltenen Uranatomen *wegfliegende*) Neutronen entweichen.   Then many neutrons *flying out* from split atoms of uranium will escape.

Die leichten und schweren, (in der Natur *vorhandenen*) Atome werden in die stabileren Atome verwandelt.   The light and heavy atoms *present* in nature are converted into more stable atoms.

PRONOUNS

The Relative Pronoun

der

	Masc.	*Fem.*	*Neuter*	*Plural*
who, which, that	**der**	**die**	**das**	**die**
of whom, which, that	**dessen**	**deren**	**dessen**	**deren**
to or for whom, which	**dem**	**der**	**dem**	**denen**
whom, which, that	**den**	**die**	**das**	**die**

In German the relative clause is always preceded by a comma and always contains a relative pronoun (unlike English: the man (whom) I saw); the verb comes at the end.

Es gibt eine grosse Zahl von Elementen, *deren jede* sehr wichtig *ist*.   There is a larger number of elements, *each of which* is very important.

Es war Dalton, der den Atombegriff *schuf*.   It was Dalton *who* created the concept of the atom.

The Demonstrative Pronoun

The demonstrative pronoun is exactly the same as the relative pronoun above in form, and it may be translated as the one, this one, that one, these, those, he, she, it, they, his, her, their, etc. Unlike the relative pronoun, the demonstrative pronoun does *not* shift the verb to the end.

Der Professor der Chemie und *der* der Physik sind Brüder. The professor of chemistry and *the one* of physics are brothers.

Unter *denen*, die sich interessierten, war auch Marie Curie. Among *those* who were interested was Marie Curie.

Dem Verkauf dieser kleinen Probe ist *der* einer grossen Zahl gefolgt. The sale of this small sample was followed by *that* of a great number.

Mit der Pile kann man Neutronen erhalten, die viel intensiver sind als *die* mit dem Zyklotron erreichbaren. With a pile, neutrons can be obtained which are much more intensive than *those* obtainable with a cyclotron.

Aus *dem*, was wir gesagt haben . . . . From (*that* which) what we have said . . . .

WORD ORDER

The German sentence does not always begin with the subject. The sentence may start with the object.

Den Rest hielt man (lange) für ein Element. One considered the residue as an element (for a long time), *or* the residue was considered as an element (for a long time).

Die Ursachen solcher Krankheiten hat man lange gesucht. One has long sought the causes of such diseases *or* the causes of such diseases have long been sought.

Den Gegensatz zu den Säuren bilden solche Stoffe, die rotes Lackmus blau färben. Such materials, which color red litmus blue, constitute the contrast to the acids.

Vielleicht hat mancher Ausführungen über Atomenergie vermisst. Perhaps many a one has missed the discussions about atomic energy.

Be particularly careful with the dative: **dem, diesem, einem, der, den.**

Dem Zirkonium ist das Element 72 in seinen Eigenschaften so ähnlich, dass . . . . Element 72 is so similar in its properties to zirconium that . . . .

Einem allgemeinen Gesetz sind Erscheinungen verschiedenster Art unterworfen. Phenomena of the most varied type are subject to a common law.

Allen Beispielen ist gemein . . . . Common to all examples is . . . .

Dem ist immer so.	That is always true.
Wenn dem so ist.	If that be true.
Wie dem auch sei.	However that may be.
Dem sei wie ihm wolle.	Be that as it may.

In dependent word order the (finite) verb is transposed to the end of the clause or sentence. This type of word order is introduced by the relative pronoun **der, die, das, welcher, welche, welches,** or by a subordinating conjunction like **weil, als, da, wenn, da . . . .**

Er blieb zu Hause, *weil* **er sehr krank** *war.*

If a German sentence begins with the verb, and the second clause begins with **so** (sometimes **dann**) and shows the result of an action, then the translation will usually start with *if.*

Führt **man diesen Versuch mit Luft durch,** *so* **wird das Resultat nicht gut sein.** *If* we carry out this experiment with air, (*then*) the result will not be good.

Pumpte er **einen Teil der Luft aus,** *so* **vermochte der Funke überzuspringen.** *If* he pumped out a part of the air, (*then*) the spark could jump across.

Note the following sentences beginning with the verb:

Sehen wir uns das Vitamin C an.   Let us examine vitamin C.
Nehmen wir heute an . . . .   Let us assume today . . . .

For the third person singular the order is either normal or inverted.

Bemerkt sei noch . . . .   Let it also be noted . . . .
Hierzu sei noch folgendes bemerkt.   In addition, let the following also be noted.
t **sei die Temperatur.**   Let t be the temperature.

The last word in the sentence may be most necessary to complete the meaning of the statement. Therefore, always look right through to the end of the sentence for past participles, infinitives, and above all for separable prefixes. Note the following:

fangen, to *catch;* but **sie fangen** . . . **an,** they *begin*
kommen, to *come;* but **es kommt** . . . **vor,** it *occurs*
hören, to *hear;* but **es hört** . . . **auf,** it *stops, ceases*
bringen, to *bring;* but **sie bringen** . . . **um,** they *kill*
Doch *sehen wir von* **diesem graduellen Unterschied** *ab.*
But *we disregard* this gradual difference.
Er setzt **diese Säure aus ihren Salzen** *in Freiheit.*   *He (sets free) liberates* this acid from its salts.

Prepositional Compounds

damit dabei dadurch . . . dass

damit, with this; **dabei,** in this case; **dafür,** for this; **dazu,** to this; **darauf,** on this; **dadurch** . . . **dass,** by the fact that.
Da- is frequently replaced by **hier-**: **hierfür, hiermit, hierzu.**
These *prepositional compounds* are used in various ways:

Reference to a preceding action

Er hat *damit* **nichts zu tun.**   He has nothing to do *with this.*
Der Sauerstoff wirkt *darauf ein.*   Oxygen acts *upon this.*

Wir werden *hierauf* **zurückkommen.** We will come back *to this.*

Reference to a following action

With a following infinitive:

Wir sind weit *davon entfernt*, alle Grundbegriffe, *zu erklären*. We are far *removed from explaining* all basic ideas.

Er *beschränkte sich darauf*, alle diese Erscheinungen *zu beschreiben*. He *confined himself to describing* all these phenomena.

Ich möchte berichten, *wie ich dazu kam*, diese Beobachtungen *zu machen*. I should like to state *how I came to make* these observations.

Die freiwerdende Energie *wird* zweifellos *dahin wirken*, die Stücke wieder *zu trennen*. The energy liberated *will* undoubtedly *act to separate* the pieces again.

With a following **dass** . . . clause, the **dass** may be translated as "the fact that," or the verb of the **dass** clause may be translated as a present participle. In either case, the **da** of the prepositional compound is ignored, and only the preposition in it is translated.

Er *zweifelt* nicht *daran, dass* seine Erfindung erfolgreich sein wird. He does not *doubt that* his invention will be successful.

Die Berechnung der Grenzen *hängt davon ab, dass* der Unterschied zu gross ist. The calculation of the limits *depends on the fact that* the difference is too great.

Er *gehört* zu den Begründern der modernen Chemie *dadurch, dass* er neue Methoden in die Chemie einführte. He *belongs* among the founders of modern chemistry *through the fact that* he introduced new methods into chemistry.

Alle Anzeichen *führten darauf, dass* die Kathodenstrahlen aus negativ geladenen Partikeln bestehen müssten. All signs *indicated that* the cathode rays would have to consist of negatively charged particles.

Die Kathode *wird dadurch* negativ *aufgeladen, da* man einen

Überschuss von Elektronen in sie hineinpresst. The cathode *is* negatively *charged by forcing* an excess of electrons into it.

Der Enderfolg dieser Zufügung eines Neutrons *besteht* also *darin, dass* ein Element mit einer um 1 grösseren Atomnummer erzeugt wird. The end result of this addition of a neutron *consists*, therefore, *in producing* an element with an atomic number that is greater by 1.

The sentences below do not have a following infinitive clause or a dass . . . clause.

Weiter *hatte* man damals gar *keine Vorstellung davon, wie* es in solch einer Pile stattfinden musste. One *had no idea,* at that time, *of how* such a pile had to function.

Hätte jemand 1940 *die Meinung* der Techniker und Physiker *darüber gesammelt, ob es* denkbar *sei,* in fünf Jahren eine Atombombe herzustellen . . . . *If anyone had gathered the opinion* of engineers and physicists in 1940 *on the question of whether it was (would be)* conceivable to manufacture an atom bomb in five years . . . .

Alles hing davon ab, mit welcher Schnelligkeit der Prozess sich abspielen würde. *All depended on the speed with which* the process would take place.

Sie werden im ganzen Körper *dahin gehen, wohin* auch der stabile Phosphor geht. *They will go anywhere* in the body *that* the stable phosphorus goes.

Adverbs of Direction

durch . . . hindurch von . . . aus

Adverbs of direction often follow a noun governed by a preposition to make the statement expressed by the preposition more emphatic or definite.

. . . in der Richtung *auf* die geladene Platte *hin* . . . . . . in the direction *toward* the charged plate . . .

. . . *durch* eine Schicht schwarzen Papiers *hindurch* . . . . . . *through* a layer of black paper . . .

Ihre Geschwindigkeit geht *bis* 30,000 km in der Sekunde *herauf.*

Its velocity goes *up to* 30,000 km a second.

. . . so schlagen sie *aus* vielen Atomen Elektronen *heraus* . . .

. . . they drive electrons *from* many atoms . . .

Viele werden ganz *aus* der Maschine *heraus* entweichen.

Many will escape *from* the machine entirely.

es

The impersonal **es** is often used in German scientific literature. When the sentence begins with **es,** the reader should ask himself whether **es** should be translated by *it* or by *there,* or whether **es** should be replaced by the real subject of the sentence. Examine the following sentences.

Es ist interessant, dieses Problem zu untersuchen.   *It* is interesting to study this problem.

Es gibt eine Reihe von Fällen.   *There* is a series of cases.

Es muss noch ein anderes Buch geben.   *There* must be another book.

Es müssen neue Methoden versucht werden.   New methods must be tried.

Es sind dies neue Erscheinungen.   These are new phenomena.

gelingen

es gelingt	it is possible
es gelang	it was possible
es ist gelungen	it (has been) was possible
es war gelungen	it had been possible
es wird gelingen	it will be possible
es gelingt dem Forscher	the investigator succeeds (it is possible for the investigator)
es gelang ihnen	they succeeded (it was possible for them)
es ist ihm gelungen	he succeeded (it was possible for him)

es war ihr gelungen	she had succeeded
es wird dem Chemiker gelingen	the chemist will succeed (it will be possible for the chemist)

NOTE: **er gelangt,** he arrives at, reaches, attains
　　　sie gelangten, they arrived at, reached, attained

sich

Reflexive verbs are quite common in German.
The pronoun may be part of the verb:

Er hält sich **immer etwas Wasser** *bereit.*   He always *keeps* some water *in readiness.*
Das *bringt es mit sich.*   That *carries it with it.*

The reflexive verb is used in a passive sense:

Das *erklärt sich* **daraus, dass** . . .   That *is explained* from the fact that . . .
Der Blutzucker *erhöht sich.*   The blood sugar *is increased* (or increases).
Die Preise *haben sich gesenkt.*   The prices *have been lowered.*
Die Grenze *lässt sich* **oder** *liess sich* **leicht bestimmen.**   The margin *can be* or *could be* easily determined.

The Ending -er

In general, when a student detects the ending **-es,** he thinks of 's or of the possessive and is inclined to use the preposition *of,* but this does not hold true when he finds himself confronted with the ending **-er.**

The ending **-er** may indicate the comparative degree:

gross, grösser　　　schön, schöner

It may be the adjective ending after an **ein** word in the nominative masculine singular with no direct bearing on the translation:

mein guter Vater   my good father

The ending **-er** however occurs *most frequently* as the adjective ending of the genitive feminine singular or genitive plural and may then be translated by *of:*

Ein Gemisch *nicht identischer* Substanzen . . . . A mixture *of nonidentical* substances . . . .

Eine chemische Verbindung *zweier* Körper . . . . A chemical combination *of two* substances . . . .

Das Verhältnis *der schneller* verdampfenden Atomarten . . . . The ratio *of the more rapidly* evaporating atom varieties . . . .

Das Alter *einzelner geologischer* Schichten . . . . The age *of individual geological* strata . . . .

zu   um . . . **zu**

ohne . . . **zu   anstatt** . . . **zu**

Zu is too often overlooked or ignored. **Zu,** to, too, to be, or as a separable prefix of a verb at the end of a sentence.

Er *machte* das Fenster *zu.* He closed the window.

Notice **zu** in verbs with other separable prefixes:

Er fing an, dies Problem aus*zu*arbeiten. He began *to* work out this problem.

In English the infinitive clause begins with *to.*

Es ist interessant, die Entwicklung des Radios *zu* verfolgen. It is interesting *to* follow the development of radio.

Er ist noch *zu* jung, *um* seinen Eltern viel *zu* helfen. He is still *too* young (*in order*) *to* help his parents much.

Die *zu* lösende Aufgabe ist *zu* lang. The problem *to be* solved is *too* long.

Die an*zu*nehmende Grösse war *zu* wichtig, um übersehen *zu* werden. The magnitude *to be* assumed was *too* important *to* be overlooked.

Der Vater verliess das Haus *ohne* den Wagen *zu* nehmen. Father left home *without* taking the car.

Man braucht Natrium, *anstatt* mit Kalium *zu* arbeiten.
One uses sodium *instead of* working with potassium.

Es ist jetzt leicht, das Röhrchen zu*zu*schmelzen. It is now easy *to* seal the little tube.

TROUBLESOME WORDS

vor drei Tagen	three days *ago*
drei Tage lang	*for* three days
schon drei Tage lang	*for* the past three days
jahrelang	*for* years
seit drei Tagen	*for* three days
auf sechs Wochen	*for* six weeks (with the future)

da

Da kommt er. *There* he comes. (**da** followed by the verb.)

Da er heute nicht kommen kann . . . . *Since* he cannot come today . . . . (**da** with the verb at the end of the sentence.)

selbst

dieser Stoff selbst   this substance *itself*
selbst bei hohen Temperaturen   *even* at high temperatures

Note: With **selbst**, try *even* first.

derselben

As an adjective:

Alle Elemente derselben Gruppe . . . . All elements of the same group . . . .

As a pronoun, however:

Die organische Chemie ist noch jung, die eigentliche Geschichte *derselben* . . . . Organic chemistry is still young, the real history *of the latter* (or *its* real history) . . . .

Die Bücher sind lehrreich, aber der Stil *derselben* . . . .
The books are instructive, but the style *of the latter* (or *their* style) . . . .

erst

Er ist *erst* vier Jahre alt.   He is *only* four years old.

Ein *erst* kürzlich gefangenes Tier . . . .   An animal captured *only* recently . . . .

***Erst* bei 1200° . . . .**   *Only* at 1200° or *not until* the temperature reached 1200° . . . .

Das Wasser wird *erst* untersucht und dann *erst* . . . .   The water is *first* examined and *only* then (*not until* then) . . . .

   ***erst*,** only, not until, first.   (Note the order.)

indem

Indem is one word; translate it as *while, by,* etc.

***indem* wir . . . zerlegten . . .** *while* we broke down (or *by* breaking down . . .

***indem* man . . . schreibt . . .** *by* writing . . .

***indem* er noch sprach . . .** *while* he was still speaking . . .

however

Das Gebiet, *in dem* er arbeitete . . . .   The field *in which* he worked . . . .   (Note two words each.)

bei

Bei only rarely means "by."

bei den Metallen	*in* (*the case of*) metals
bei der Fabrik	*near* the factory
er war *bei* uns	he was *with* us, *at* our house
bei dieser Gelegenheit	*on* this occasion
bei diesen Worten	*at* these words
da*bei*	*in* this case, *on* this occasion
wo*bei*	*in* which case, *in* the case of which
bei denen	*in* (the case of) which, *with* which

man

The use of **man** in German is simply a way of avoiding the passive construction.

man bricht es	one breaks it, we break it, it is broken
man findet Bausteine	we find building blocks, building blocks are found
so hört man nichts mehr	thus nothing more is heard
man lernt viel	much is learned, we learn much
das Atom kann man spalten	the atom can be split
dies bekannte Wort versteht man selten	this well-known word is seldom understood
so entdeckt man die Metalle	thus metals are discovered
man kann das Atom zertrümmern	the atom can be split

Ja, doch, ja doch, denn, nur, wohl, wenn . . . auch, schon, ausser, ohne . . . zu, anstatt . . . zu, anstatt . . . dass, gar, mit

These emphatic adverbs in German often cannot be translated into English, but they often add force to another word or to the verb.

Eine Beschreibung drückt *ja nur* das in Worten aus, was . . . A description expresses *indeed* (*to be sure, of course*) in words *only* what . . . (**ja sogar,** indeed even)

Note the position (first) in clauses with **doch**:

Gibt es *doch* eine grosse Anzahl von Industrien, in denen . . . . There are *nevertheless* (*indeed, yet, surely*, etc.) a great many industries in which . . . .

***Doch* kann man in vielen Fällen grosse Veränderungen wahrnehmen im Falle, dass . . . .** *Yet* (*surely, indeed*, etc.) in many cases great changes can be noticed in case . . . .

Wenn der erwartete Erfolg *auch* nicht erreicht wurde, so . . . .
Even (if) *though* the expected success was not attained . . . .

schon—note the present perfect construction:

Das *wissen* wir *schon* lange.   We have known that for a long time.

Eine Woche *sitzt* er *schon* an seinem Arbeitstisch und wartet auf das gewünschte Resultat.   For a week he *has been sitting* at his work table, waiting for the desired result.

schon, already:

Schon **in seiner Jugend war er zu dieser Lösung gekommen.** He had *already* arrived at this solution in his youth.

ausser, in addition to, besides:

Der Chemiker muss *ausser* dem Stoff selbst und dessen Änderungen auch den Zustand des Stoffes in Betracht ziehen. The chemist must consider the condition of the material *in addition to* (*besides*) the material itself and its changes.

gar as adverb is used to intensify an adjective or adverb:

gar bald very soon	**eine gar liebliche Gegend** a most
gar nichts nothing at all	charming region
gar zu viel far too much	**gar in diesem Hause** in this very
gar zu selten very rarely	house

mit sometimes has the meaning of *also:*

Sie tragen *mit* dazu bei.   They *also* contribute.
Sie werden *mit* in Tätigkeit gesetzt.   They are *also* activated.

Prepositional Phrases

anstatt dass **er kam** ⎫
anstatt zu **kommen** ⎭ *instead of* (his) coming

ohne dass **er einen Grund hatte** ⎫
ohne **einen Grund** *zu* **haben** ⎭ *without* (his) having a reason

COMPOUND NOUNS

A compound noun is a word formed by the close union of two or more words whose meanings blend so thoroughly as to produce one single idea:

Dampfschiffahrt   steam navigation

Although a compound noun may consist of two or more words, it can, as a rule, have only two component elements, the *basal component*, which contains the more general idea, and the *modifying component*, which contains the more special meaning, e.g., **Zweig-eisenbahn** a branch railroad, **Spannungs-abfall** voltage drop. Each element can thus be either simple or compound. When a noun is thus a compound of two or more nouns, the final one in the compound is the *determining* one. It is the base of the noun and determines the gender, e.g., **die Spannung, der Abfall: der Spannungsabfall.**

In German there is no limit to the formation of compound nouns. Such compounds may consist of two or more nouns; but other combinations, with adjectives, adverbs, prepositions, and verb stems are also quite frequent.

Noun and adjective: **der Wert,** value, **gleich,** equal: **der Gleichwert,** equivalent (value).

Noun and adverb or preposition: **der Flug,** flight, **auf,** up: **der Aufflug,** ascent.

Noun and verb stem: **der Ofen,** furnace, **schmieden,** to forge: **der Schmiedeofen,** forging furnace.

Sometimes compound nouns have their components connected by **-s: Landeserzeugnis,** agricultural product; **Leitungsdraht,** conducting wire.

Sometimes the components are connected by **-n: Schraubengang** thread (pitch) of a screw.

A noun and an adjective may form a compound adjective: **das Blut,** blood, **arm,** poor: **blutarm,** anemic.

Two adjectives may also combine to form a compound adjective: **dunkel,** dark, **blau,** blue: **dunkelblau,** dark-blue.

GERMAN-ENGLISH
SCIENCE DICTIONARY

A

Aal, *m.*-e, eel; **-beere,** *f.* black currant (*Ribes nigrum*); **-glatt,** slippery as an eel **-mutter,** *f.* eelpout (*Zoarces viviparus*).

Aar, *m.*-e, eagle.

Aaronsstab, *m.* cuckoopint (*Arum maculatum*).

Aas, *n.*-es, carrion, carcass, fleshings, bait. **-blume,** *f.* carrion flower (*Stapelia asterias*).

aasen (mit etwas), to squander; Felle ~ to flesh hides.

Aasfliege, *f.*, carrion fly, dung fly; **-geier,** *m.* carrion vulture. **-geruch,** *m.*˙⁼e, cadaverous odor.

aasig, cadaverous, foul, dirty.

Aas-käfer, *m.*-, carrion beetle; **-seite,** *f.* flesh side (of a skin).

ab, off, down, away, from, since; ~ **und zu,** now and then, to and fro, off and on; **auf und ~,** up and down.

Abaka, *f.* Manila hemp, fiber; **-faser,** abaca fiber.

abänderlich, alterable.

Abänderlichkeit, *f.* alterability.

abändern, to alter, modify, change, vary, depart from, form a (new) variety.

Abänderung, *f.* modification, change, alteration, variation, transformation.

abänderungs-fähig, capable of modification, alterable; **-merkmale,** *n.pl.* characteristics of variation; **-spielraum,** *m.*˙⁼e, range of variation.

abarbeiten, to work off, overwork; sich ~, to work hard.

Abart, *f.*-en, variety, (sub)species, modification, variation.

abarten, to degenerate, vary, form a (new) variety.

abästen, to lop off, prune, trim, pollard.

abatmen, abätmen, to glow in a muffle, desiccate, anneal (superficially).

abätzen, to remove with caustics, corrode.

abbalgen, to skin, enucleate.

Abbau, *m.*-e, -ten, decomposition, disintegration, degradation, demolition, destruction, separation, analysis, degeneration, retrenchment, catabolism, dissimilation, breaking up, working (mine); ~ **vom Stock,** stoping.

abbauen, to decompose, disintegrate, remove, demolish, analyze, work (mines).

abbeissen, to bite off.

Abbeizdruckverfahren, *n.* printing of cloth by discharging the color.

abbeizen, to corrode, cauterize, scour, cleanse, taw (skins), dress, dip, pickle; **Metalle ~,** to remove the oxidized surface from metals; **Metallerze ~,** to scour, pickle, or dip metal ores.

Abbeizmittel, *n.*-, corrosive, pickling agent.

Abbeizung, *f.* corrosion, scouring, dipping, cleansing, pickling, dressing, tawing; ~ **der Wolle,** removal of wool by corrosion.

abbekommen, to get off, to get (one's share).

abbersten, to burst, spring, jump, fly off.

abberufen, to call away, recall.

abbestellen, to countermand, discontinue.

abbiegen, deflect, diverge, inflect, bend aside, branch off, deviate, take off layers.

Abbild, *n.* image, copy, likeness.

abbilden, to portray, copy, illustrate, describe, form an image.

abbildend, image-forming, reproductive, illustrative.

Abbildung 2 Abdeckung

Abbildung, *f.* illustration, drawing, copy, cut, diagram, figure; **konforme** ~, conformal representation.

Abbildungs-güte, *f.* definition, quality of image; **-struktur,** *f.* palimpsest texture; **-vermögen,** *n.* resolving power (of a microscope).

abbimsen, to rub off with pumice, fluff, buff (leather).

abbinden, to unbind, untie, loosen, block, detach, castrate, remove by ligature, tie up, set, wean; **langsam abbindender Zement,** *m.* slow-setting cement.

Abbindezeit, *f.* setting time (of cement).

Abbitte, *f.* apology.

abbitten, to apologize, beg pardon, deprecate.

Abblasehahn, *m.*̶e, blowoff cock.

abblasen, to blow off or away.

Abblaseventil, *n.* exhaust valve.

abblassen, to lose color, turn pale.

abblättern, to peel off, exfoliate, shed leaves, defoliate, desquamate, scale off, laminate, effloresce, spall.

Abblätterung, *f.* exfoliation. peeling off.

abbläuen, to blue, dye blue, lose blue color, wash out (of blue fabrics), beat.

abbleichen, to bleach, fade, finish bleaching, bleach thoroughly.

abblenden, to dim, turn off, screen off.

abblicken, to brighten, grow dull, tarnish, give the blick to.

abblitzen, to miss fire, meet with refusal, cease lightning.

abbluten, to bleed.

abborken, to peel (bark) off, excorticate.

abböschen, to slope, incline, slant.

Abbrand, *m.*̶e, consumption, residual metallic oxides, loss in thermal processing.

abbrauchen, to use up, wear out.

abbrauen, to brew well, finish brewing.

abbraunen, to lose brown color.

abbräunen, to brown thoroughly.

abbrausen, to cease fermenting, rinse off.

abbrechen, to break off, pick, pluck, interrupt, discontinue, stop short.

abbreiten, to flatten, stretch out.

abbremsen, to check, retard, apply the brake.

abbrennbar, combustible.

Abbrennbürste, *f.* sparking-contact brush, contact-breaking brush.

abbrennen, to burn off, cauterize, temper, dip, pickle, deflagrate, blaze off, sear, singe, finish firing (kilns); **Messing** ~, to pickle brass; **Metalle** ~, to refine metals.

Abbrenner, *m.* deflagrator.

Abbrennung, *f.* burning, deflagration.

abbringen, to remove, dissuade, divert.

abbröckeln, to scale off, chip off, flake off, crumble.

Abbruch, *m.*̶e, breaking off, damage, demolition, declivity, injury, detriment; **zum** ~ **gereichen,** to impair, do harm to.

Abbruchholz, *n.* broken wood, lumber from wrecked buildings.

abbrüchig, brittle, detrimental.

Abbruchlinie, *f.* line of cleavage.

abbrühen, to seethe, scald, parboil.

abbürsten, to brush off.

abdachen, to slant, slope, incline, dip unroof.

Abdachung, *f.* slope, declivity, unroofing.

abdämmen, to dam up, restrain, insulate.

Abdampf, *m.*̶e, exhaust steam; **mit** ~ **geheizter Vorwärmer,** exhaust-feed heater.

Abdampfdruckregler, *m.* exhaust-steam pressure regulator.

abdampfen, to evaporate; **die Mutterlauge** ~ **lassen,** to evaporate the mother liquor.

abdämpfen, to steam, damp (a tone), throttle, quench.

Abdampf-entöler, *m.* exhaust-steam oil separator; **-gefäss,** *n.* evaporating vessel; **-kapelle,** *f.* evaporating capsule; **-kondenswasserabscheider,** *m.* exhaust-steam separator; **-rückstand,** *m.* residue on evaporating; **-sammelstück,** *n.* exhaust-steam collector; **-stutzen,** *m.* exhaust hood; **-verflüssiger,** *m.* exhaust-steam collector; **vorrichtung,** *f.* evaporator.

Abdampfung, *f.* evaporation.

abdanken, to dismiss, retire.

abdarren, to (kiln-)dry malt, liquate.

Abdarrtemperatur, *f.* finishing temperature, brewing temperature.

abdecken, to uncover, skin, flay, strip, cover.

Abdeck-papier, *n.* carpet felt paper; **-platte,** *f.* cover plate; **-vorrichtung,** *f.* covering device.

Abdeckung, *f.* uncovering.

abdekantieren, to decant, draw off.

abdestillieren, to distill off.

abdichten, to make tight, calk, pack, render impervious, waterproof.

Abdichtung, *f.* packing, reaction of electrolytes on the cell wall.

abdicken, to boil down, inspissate, evaporate, thicken.

Abdomen, *n.* abdomen.

Abdominal-fuss, *m.* abdominal leg; **-typhus,** *m.* enteric (typhoid) fever.

abdorren, to wither.

abdörren, to dry up, parch, roast, desiccate thoroughly.

Abdörr-ofen, *m.* refining furnace; **-stein,** *m.* lead ore containing silver or copper.

Abdraht, *m.* turnings.

abdrängen, to push off or away, force out, squeeze out.

abdrehen, to turn off, remove by torsion, machine, unscrew, dress.

Abdreh-maschine, *f.* lathe, finishing machine; **-späne,** *m.pl.* turnings; **-spindel,** *f.* lathe spindle; **-stahl,** *m.* turning tool.

abdreschen, to thresh.

abdringen, to extort.

abdrosseln, to throttle.

Abdruck, *m.-̈e,* copy, impression, transfer, print, dendrolite, ichthyolite; **-lauge,** *f.* release (liquor); **-masse,** *f.* molding material, plaster of Paris.

abdrucken, to print.

abdrücken, to separate by pressing, mold, discharge (gun).

Abdrückschraube, *f.* set screw used to break a joint.

abduften, to lose smell, grow hazy or misty.

Abduktor, *m.* abductor (muscle).

abdunkeln, to darken, grow darker.

abdunsten, abdünsten, to evaporate, graduate; **die Salzsohle ~,** to graduate brine.

Abdunstung, Abdünstung, *f.* evaporation.

Abdünstungshaus, *n.* graduation house.

abduzieren, to abduct.

abeggen, to harrow off.

abeichen, to gauge, adjust, measure.

Abelmoschus-körner, *n.pl.* musk seed, amber seed; **-faser,** *f.* abelmosk fiber.

Abend, *m.-e,* evening, night; **-falter,** *m.* hawk moth; **-land,** *n.* occident; **-ländisch,** western, occidental; **-mahl,** *n.* supper

(Communion); **-pfauenauge,** *n.* eyed hawk moth; **-rot,** *n.* **-röte,** *f.* sunset sky.

abends, in the evening.

Abend-stille, *f.* evening calm; **-tau,** *m.* night dew; **-wärts,** to the west; **-wind,** *m.* evening wind; **-zeit,** *f.* night time.

Abenteuer, *n.-,* adventure.

abenteuerlich, adventurous, odd, strange.

aber, but, however.

Aberglaube, *m.* superstition.

abergläubisch, superstitious.

aberkennen, to dispossess, deprive.

abermalig, repeated, renewed, further.

abermals, once more.

abernten, to reap.

aberrant, abnormal, exceptional.

Aberration, *f.* aberration.

Aberraute, *f.* southernwood (*Artemisia abrotanum*).

aberregen, to de-energize.

aberwitzig, crazy.

abfachen, to classify, arrange, partition.

abfahren, to set out, depart, start.

Abfahrt, *f.-en,* departure, start.

Abfall, *m.-̈e,* falling off, decrease, waste, refuse, garbage, decline, declivity, by-products, cuttings, shavings, chippings, scrap, cass(i)e, residue; **-brennstoff,** *m.* waste or refuse fuel; **-dünger,** *m.* offal used as manure.

Abfalleisen, *n.* scrap iron.

abfallen, to fall off or away, degenerate, become emaciated, decrease, slope, desert, decline, droop, shed, incline, waste.

abfallend, deciduous, sloping.

Abfall-erzeugnis, *n.* waste product; **-grenze,** *f.* critical limit; **-gut,** *n.* waste washings, mud, fuel recovered from waste; **-holz,** *n.* waste wood.

Abfälleverwertung, *f.* utilization of waste.

abfällig, deciduous, disapproving.

Abfall-lauge, *f.* spent lye; **-marke,** *f.* off shade (in dyeing); **-moment,** *n.* breaking-down moment; **-produkt,** *n.* by-product; **-rohr,** *n.* draft tube, suction tube; **-säure,** *f.* residuary (recovered) acid; **-stoff,** *m.* waste material; **-vernichtungsanlage,** *f.* refuse destructor, incinerator; **-ware,** *f.* culls; **-wasser,** *n.* waste water.

abfalzen, to remove hair from skins.

abfangen, to catch, seize, intercept.

abfärben, to finish dying, lose col·r, fade, rub off, bleed (of dyes).

abfärbig, discolorable.

abfasern, to lose fibers, ravel out.

abfassen, to compose, draw up, write, catch, bend (of iron).

abfedern, to molt, pluck, cushion, spring, suspend on springs.

Abfegemittel, *n.-,* detergent.

abfegen, to sweep off, cleanse.

abfegend, detergent.

Abfegung, *f.* depuration.

abfeilen, to file off.

Abfeilicht, *n.* filings.

abfertigen, to dispatch, expedite, complete.

Abfertigung, *f.* readiness, completion, expedition.

Abfett, *n.-e,* fat skimmings, drain-oil scourings.

abfetten, to skim the fat (grease) off.

abfeuern, to fire off, discharge (a gun).

abfiltern, abfiltrieren, to strain, filter.

abfinden, to pay off, satisfy, compensate, indemnify; **sich mit etwas ~,** to put up with, reckon with, acquiesce in; **sich mit jemandem ~,** to reach an agreement with.

Abfindung, *f.* indemnification, settlement.

abfischen, to fish out.

abflachen, to level off, bevel, face.

Abflachung, beveling, rounding off.

abflammen, to grease, tallow (hides).

abflauen, to wash, scour, abate, slacken, lag, decrease, become weaker

abfleckecht, fast to rubbing. nonspotting.

abflecken, to stain.

abfleischen, to flesh, scrape (hides).

abfliegen, to fly off, dry and drop off, take off (of airplane).

abfliessen, to flow off, discharge; **~ unter Luftdruck,** to be drained by compressed air; **~ durch natürliches Gefälle,** to be drained by gravity.

abflöhen, to pick fleas off.

Abflug, *m.-̈e,* flying away, flight, take-off, matter carried off by draft of air.

Abfluss, *m.-̈e,* flowing off, discharge, drain, outlet; **-gebiet,** *n.* drainage (catchment) area; **-geschwindigkeit,** *f.* discharge velocity; **-graben,** *m.* drain ditch; **-kühler,** *m.* efflux condenser; **-leitung,** *f.* drainpipe;

-röhre, *f.* waste pipe, drain tube, gutter; **-vorgang,** *m.* process of discharge; **-wasser,** *n.* waste water.

abflusslos, lacking outlet; **abflusslose Wanne,** *f.* isolated basin.

Abfolge, *f.* (magmatic) origin.

abfordern, to demand.

abformen, to mold, shape, cast.

Abformmasse, *f.* molding compound.

abforsten, to clear, cut down (trees).

abfragen, to question, inquire, ascertain.

abfressen, to eat off, browse, corrode, consume, erode.

abfrieren, to be nipped by frost.

Abfuhr, *f.-en,* removal, elimination; **-dünger,** *m.* night soil.

abführen, to lead off, remove, purge, draw off, drain off, exhaust (steam); **Wärme ~,** to dissipate or remove heat.

abführend, purgative, efferent, excretory; **abführendes Brausepulver,** *n.* Seidlitz powder.

Abführ-gang, *m.-̈e,* secretory duct, efferent duct; **-mittel,** *n.* purgative, laxative.

Abführung, *f.* leading off, discharge, evacuation, removal.

Abführungs-gang, *m.* efferent duct; **-rohr,** *n.* discharge tube.

Abfüll-apparat, *m.-e,* filling device, emptying apparatus, racking apparatus; **-bütte,** *f.* racking square.

abfüllen, to draw off, decant, skim off, empty, rack, fill.

Abfüll-maschine, *f.* bottling machine; **-schlauch,** *m.* racking hose; **-trichter,** *m.* filling funnel; **-vorrichtung,** *f.* filling device, emptying contrivance.

abfurchen, to furrow off, divide by furrows.

Abfurchung, *f.* segmentation, division.

abfüttern, to feed, line, case.

Abgabe, *f.* giving off, delivery, emission, escape, evolution, loss, release, output, yield; **-satz,** *m.* rate of levy, yield.

Abgang, *m.-̈e,* departure, waste, loss, escape, sale; *pl.* tailings.

abgängig, missing, waste, declining, decrepit, salable, worn out.

Abgangsrohr, *n.-e,* waste pipe.

abgären, to ferment thoroughly, cease fermenting.

Abgasbrüden, *n.* blowoff vapors.

Abgase, *n.pl.* waste gases, exhaust gases; ~ der Hüttenbetriebe, metallurgical waste gases.

Abgas-speicherofen, *m.* regenerative-furnace recuperator; **vorwärmer,** *m.* waste-gas feed heater, economizer.

abgautschen, to couch (paper).

abgeätzt, corroded off.

abgeben, to deliver, give off, serve as, generate, yield, develop, lose, release, dispose of; sich ~ mit, to concern oneself with.

abgebrannt (abbrennen), calcined, deflagrated; **abgebrannte Metalle,** *n.pl.* refined metals.

abgebrochen (abbrechen), broken off; -blätterig, with abruptly terminating leaves.

abgebrüht, parboiled, hardened.

abgebunden (abbinden), removed, set.

abgedroschen (abdreschen), trite, commonplace, stale.

abgeebbt (abebben), dwindled, declined.

abgefeimt, cunning, crafty.

abgeflacht, flattened, oblate, beveled, shallow, flat.

abgeflammt, greased, tallowed.

abgefroren (abfrieren), frostbitten, nipped.

abgegossen (abgiessen), decanted, cast (in foundry).

abgegrenzt, delimited, circumscribed, separated, defined.

abgegriffen (abgreifen), worn (out), hackneyed.

abgehaart, hairless, glabrous.

abgehen, to go off, pass away, leave, proceed.

abgehoben (abheben), lifted off, withdrawn, separated, siphoned off.

abgeholzt, cut down, cleared.

abgekantet, subrounded, chamfered, beveled.

abgekürzt, condensed.

abgelagert, stabilized, mellow, mature.

abgelebt, worn out, decrepit.

abgelegen (abliegen), distant, matured, out-of-the-way, remote.

Abgelegenheit, *f.* remoteness, isolation.

abgeleitet, derived, run off.

abgelenkt, deflected, deviated.

abgelten, to discharge.

Abgeltung, *f.* discharge, compensation.

abgemergelt, worn out, emaciated.

abgemessen, measured, precise, formal.

Abgemessenheit, *f.* exactness, formality.

abgeneigt, disinclined.

abgenutzt, worn out, used up.

Abgeordnete, *m.* deputy, representative.

abgeplattet, flattened, oblate.

abgerahmt, skimmed.

abgerben, to tan, tan thoroughly.

abgerechnet, excepting, excepted.

abgerindet, excorciated.

abgerissen (abreissen), torn, ragged, abrupt.

abgerundet, rounded, obtuse, dished.

abgesackt, encysted, sacculated, sacked.

abgesäuert, acidulated, acidified.

Abgeschäumtes, *n.* skimmings, scum.

abgeschieden (abscheiden), departed, separated, secluded, retired.

abgeschlämmt, washed out, decanted.

abgeschliffen (abschleifen), polished, ground.

Abgeschliffenheit, *f.* polish.

abgeschlossen (abschliessen), secluded, settled, distinct, complete.

abgeschmackt, insipid, tasteless, absurd.

abgeschmolzen (abschmelzen), melted off.

abgeschnitten (abschneiden), cut off.

abgeschnürt, tied off, constricted; **abgeschnürtes Meeresbecken,** *n.* enclosed sea basin.

abgeschwefelt, desulphurized.

abgeschwelt, calcined.

abgesehen (von), apart (from), without regard to, neglecting, exclusive of, irrespective of; auf ihn ~, meant for him.

abgeseiht, strained, filtered.

abgesetzt, deposited, disposed of, deposed, settled.

abgesondert, separated.

abgespalten, split off.

abgespannt, weary, exhausted.

Abgespanntheit, *f.* exhaustion.

abgesperrt, separated, closed off.

abgestanden (abstehen), stale, decayed, brittle, rotten, sour. flat; **abgestandener Stahl,** *m.* perished steel.

abgestrichen (abstreichen), skimmed, scraped.

abgestumpft, neutralized, truncated, blunt, dull.

abgestutzt, truncated, trimmed.

abgetan (abtun), settled, disposed of.

abgetrieben (abtreiben), driven off, cleared.

abgewandt (abwenden), turned away, removed.

abgewinnen, to win (from), extract.

abgewischt, wiped off.

abgewogen (abwägen), weighed, considered.

abgewöhnen, to wean from, break a habit.

abgezogen (abziehen), drawn off, deducted, distilled, extracted.

abgiessen, to pour off, decant, cast (of founding).

abgiften, Wolle ~, to loosen wool by arsenic.

Abglanz, m. reflection, reflected glory.

abglätten, to smooth, polish.

abgleichen, to make even, equalize, level, balance, square, justify.

Abgleichverfahren, n. process of balancing.

abgleiten, to glide off, slide off.

abgliedern, to segment (joint) off, form laterally, organize lateral members.

Abgliederung, f. dismemberment, segmenting off, outgrowth, offshoot, lateral organization or formation.

abglühen, to make red-hot, anneal, cease glowing, mull (of wine).

abgraben, to dig off, drain, draw off, uproot.

abgraten, to remove the burr, trim.

abgreifen, to obtain, determine, read off.

abgrasen, to graze.

abgrenzbar, definable.

abgrenzen, to mark off, define, bound, set a limit, differentiate, separate.

Abgrenzung, f. demarcation, limit, division, border, boundary, scope.

Abgrund, m.ːe, abyss, precipice, chasm.

Abguss, m.ːe, pouring off, decanting, cast, mold, casting; -kasten, m. trap, gully.

abhaaren, to remove hair from, unhair, molt.

abhacken, to chop (cut) off.

abhalftern, to unhalter.

abhalten, to keep off, detain, prevent, hold (a meeting), protect from or against.

Abhaltung, f. hindrance, detention, prevention, holding, conducting.

abhandeln, to treat, discuss, negotiate, transact.

abhanden, lost, missing.

Abhandlung, f. treatise, paper, discourse, dissertation, essay, transaction.

Abhang, m.ːe, slope, declivity.

abhangen, to depend upon, hang down, slope, be suspended; das hängt von Ihnen ab, that depends on you; von etwas ~, to depend on, rest upon, be dependent or subject (to).

abhängen, to take down, disconnect.

abhängig, dependent, sloping, inclined, subject to.

Abhängige (Veränderliche), f. dependent, variable.

Abhängigkeit, f. dependence, declivity, relation(ship), function, slope; in ~ von . . . auftragen, to plot as a function of.

Abhangsfortsatz, m. clinoid process.

abhären, to lose hair.

abhärten, to harden, inure, temper.

abharzen, to collect resin from, tap trees.

abhauen, to cut off, hew down, lop, fell.

abhäuten, to skin, peel, abrade, excoriate, cast, scum.

abheben, to lift off, take off, contrast with, remove, skim off, part, siphon off, separate; den Abstrich ~, to remove the scum; das Hangende ~, to take off the top layer.

Abheber, m. pack parter.

abhebern, to siphon off.

abhelfen, to help, remedy, correct.

abhellen, to clarify.

abhetzen, to overwork, harass.

Abhieb, m.-e, cut.

Abhiebsfläche, f. cutting area.

Abhilfe, f. remedy, redress, relief.

Abhitze, f. waste heat; -kanal, m. waste-heat flue; -kessel, m. waste-heat boiler.

abhobeln, to plane off.

abhold, (dat.) averse, disinclined, unfavorable.

abholen, to fetch, call for, go to meet.

abholzen, to clear, cut down, prune.

abholzig, tapering (of tree trunks), thinly timbered.

Abholzung, f. clearing of timber, pruning of a tree, deforestation.

abhören, to hear, tune in.

Abhub, *m.*⸚e, remains, waste, scum, dross, draw.

abhülsen, to shell, peel, husk, hull.

Abiesöl, *n.*-e, abies oil.

Abietinsäure, *f.*-n, abietic acid; -äthylester, *n.* ethyl abietate.

abirren, to lose one's way.

abirrend, aberrant.

abjagen, to override, overdrive.

abkalken, to remove lime.

abkanten, to bevel, chamfer, round off, border, shear off.

abkappen, to top (trees), decapitate, lop.

Abkapselung, *f.* encystment, encapsulation.

abkarten, to prearrange, plan.

abkehren, to turn away, off, or aside, avert, divert, sweep, brush (off), renunciate.

abkeltern, to press.

abklappen, to lift the flap, swing out, let down, uncover.

abklären, to clarify, filter, decant, clear up, decolorize, boil off.

Abklärflasche, *f.* decanting flask.

Abklärung, *f.* clarification, filtration, decantation.

Abklärungsmittel, *n.*-, clarifying agent.

abklatschen, to stereotype, plagiarize, copy.

Abklatschpräparat, *n.*-e, impression preparation.

abklemmen, to pinch off.

abklingen, to die away, fade away (of sound).

abklopfen, to beat off, knock off, percuss, scale off.

abknallen, to blow off, explode, fire off.

abkneifen, to pinch off, nip off.

abknicken, to crack off, snap off.

abknistern, to decrepitate.

abknöpfen, to unbutton.

abkochbar, decoctible.

abkochecht, fast to boiling.

abkochen, to boil, decoct, scald, extract; langsam ⁓, to coddle, boil slowly; Seide ⁓, to ungum silk, wash out silk.

Abkochmittel, *n.*-, decoction medium.

Abkochung, *f.* decoction; ⁓ schleimgebender Pflanzen, decoction of gelatinous plants.

abkommen, to get off, be spared, discontinue, agree, deviate, become obsolete.

Abĸommen, *n.* agreement, arrangement.

Abkömmling, *m.*-e, derivative, descendant.

abköpfen, to top (trees), decapitate.

Abkratzeisen, *n.* scraper.

abkratzen, to scrape off.

Abkreiden, *n.* chalking (of protective coatings), flaking.

abkrücken, to rake off.

Abkühlapparat, *m.*-e, refrigerator, cooler.

abkühlen, to cool down, refrigerate, anneal.

Abkühler, *m.*-, refrigerator, annealer.

Abkühl-fass, *n.*⸚er, cooling (annealing) vat; -geschwindigkeit, *f.* cooling speed.

Abkühlung, *f.* cooling, refrigeration, chilling; ⁓ durch **Verflüssigung,** cooling by liquefaction.

Abkühlungs-fläche, *f.*-n, cooling surface; -mittel, *n.* cooling agent.

Abkühl-verlust, *m.*-e, loss due to cooling; -zeit, *f.* cooling period.

Abkunft, *f.*⸚e, origin, descent.

abkuppeln, to throw out (a clutch), disengage, disconnect.

abkürzen, to shorten, abbreviate, condense.

Abkürzung, *f.* abbreviation.

abladen, to unload, discharge, dump.

Ablage, *f.* place of deposit, warehouse.

ablagern, to deposit, store, season, settle.

Ablagerung, *f.* deposit, deposition, subsidence, sediment, storage, seasoning, sedimentation.

Ablaktation, *f.* ablactation, inarching, weaning.

Ablaktierung, *f.* inarching.

Ablängung, *f.* cutting into lengths.

Ablass, *m.*⸚e, drainage, blowoff, outlet, escape, delivery, discount.

ablassen, to let off, drain, decant, deduct, leave off, cease, anneal, fade, empty, tap.

Ablassen, *n.* discharging; ⁓ der **Schlacken,** tapping of the slags.

Ablass-hahn, *m.*⸚e, drain cock; -rohr, *n.* waste pipe; -schieber, drain-sluice valve; -schraube, *f.* drain plug.

Ablast, *m.*-en, complete failure of development (of an organ).

ablauern, to lie in wait for.

Ablauf, *m.*⸚e, running off, discharge, drain, sink, expiration (of time), result, lapse, start, course, issue; ⁓ der **Sole,** outlet of brine.

ablaufen, to run off, drain, expire, start, progress, happen, occur, terminate; **langsam ~,** to ooze; **die Waschflotte ~ lassen,** to discharge the liquor.

ablaufend, decurrent, decurring.

Ablauf-öl, *n.*-e, run oil, used oil, expressed oil; **-rinne,** *f.* sink, gutter, channel; **-rohr,** *n.* outlet tube; **-trichter,** *m.* draining funnel.

Ablauge, *f.* waste lye, spent liquor.

ablaugen, to lixiviate, wash off lye from, steep in lye, scour before drying.

abläutern, to clarify, refine, filter, purify, wash (ore).

Abläuterungs-vorrichtung, *f.* clarifying plant or apparatus; **-zeit,** *f.* clarifying (filtering) period.

Ableben, *n.* death, demise, decease.

ablecken, to lick off.

ablegen, to lay aside, take off, take (examinations).

Ableger, *m.*-, layer, slip, scion.

ablehnen, to decline, turn aside, refuse.

ablehren, to gauge, dress, true.

ableitbar, derivable.

ableiten, to derive, deduce, turn aside, remove, carry off, draw off, lead off, discharge, divert.

Ableiter, *m.*-, (electric) conductor.

Ableitung, *f.* derivation, deduction, derivative, grounding, branch circuit, differential coefficient; **~ der Wärme,** conduction of heat.

Ableitungs-gewebe, *n.*-, conducting tissue; **-kanal,** *m.* drain; **-mittel,** *n.* revulsive, derivative, antispastic; **-rinne,** *f.* drain channel, delivery duct, gutter.

ablenken, to turn aside, deviate, deflect, bend, refract, divert, fault.

Ablenkung, *f.* deviation, diversion, diffraction, deflection.

Ablenkungs-kraft, *f.* force of deflection; **-winkel,** *m.* angle of deflection.

ablesbar, readable.

Ablese-einrichtung, *f.* reading device; **-fehler,** *m.* error in reading.

ablesen, to read off, pick off, gather.

Ableser, *m.*-, reader, picker, gatherer, roll skinner.

Ablesevorrichtung, *f.* reading device.

ableugnen, to deny.

ablichten, to clear, reduce, shade, lighten.

abliefern, to deliver.

Ablieferung, *f.* delivery.

abliegen, to lie at a distance.

ablocken, to lure away.

ablohen, to bark.

ablöhnen, to pay off.

ablöschbar, temperable, quenchable, slakable.

ablöschen, to extinguish, slake (lime), quench.

Ablöschflüssigkeit, *f.* hardening liquid, quenching liquid.

ablösen, to loosen, amputate, scale off, detach, come loose, buy out, commute, relieve, dissolve, lose, eliminate.

Ablösen, *n.* frilling (of a layer of emulsion).

ablösend, resolvent, alternate (of shift).

Ablösung, *f.* detaching, commutation, elimination, relief (of shift).

Ablösungsfläche, *f.*-n, joint, jointing plane, plane of discontinuity.

ablöten, to unsolder.

Abluft, *f.*-e, foul air, waste air, outgoing air; **-kanal,** *m.* **-lutte,** *f.* exhaust air duct or exit.

ablüften, to air.

abmachen, to loosen, detach, arrange, conclude.

Abmachung, *f.* arrangement, settlement, agreement, contract.

abmagern, to become thin, emaciated.

abmähen, to mow off or down.

abmahnen, to dissuade (from).

abmaischen, to finish mashing.

abmarken, to demarcate.

abmatten, to fatigue, tire.

abmessbar, measurable.

abmessen, to measure off, fathom, survey.

Abmessung, *f.* measurement, dimension, survey, size.

abmildern, to moderate.

abmindern, to lessen, diminish.

abmontieren, to dismount, dismantle.

abmühen, sich ~, to exert oneself, toil.

abmustern, to lay off.

abnagen, to gnaw (off).

Abnahme, *f.* decrease, diminution, decay, acceptance. decline, sale, taking away, taper, decrement, subtraction, waning, loss; **-versuch,** *m.* acceptance test.

abnarben, to grain, buff, scrape.

abnehmbar, detachable, removable.

abnehmen, to take off, amputate, remove, decrease, decline, diminish, reduce, dismantle, subtract, skim, accept; **an Gewicht** ∼, to lose weight.

abnehmend, decreasing; **abnehmende Changierung,** *f.* decreasing stroke, traverse motion.

Abnehmer, *m.*-, buyer, purchaser, consumer.

Abneigung, *f.* declination, disinclination, antipathy, slope.

abnorm, abnormal, irregular.

Abnormität, *f.* abnormality, deformity.

abnötigen, to extort from.

abnutschen, to suck off.

Abnutzbarkeit, *f.* wear, wearing capacity.

abnutzen, abnützen, to wear out, use up.

Abnutzung, *f.* wear and tear, wasting, exploitation, utilization, abrasion.

Abnutzungs-erscheinung, *f.* appearance of attrition; -grösse, *f.* coefficient of wear; -satz, *m.* degree of deterioration.

Aböl, *n.* waste oil.

abölen, to oil.

Abonnement, *m.* subscription.

Abonnent, *m.*-en, subscriber.

abonnieren, to subscribe.

abordnen, to delegate.

Abort, *m.*-e, lavatory, toilet, failure (abortion).

Abortivei, *n.* blighted ovum, false conception.

Abortusbazillus, *m.* Bang's bacillus (*Brucella abortus*).

aboxydieren, to oxidize off.

abpalen, to shell (peas or beans).

abpälen, to pull off the hair, depilate.

abpassen, to fit, measure, adjust.

abpellen, to peel.

abpflücken, to pick, pluck, gather.

abpfropfen, to regraft.

abplaggen, to cut (remove) sod.

abplatten, to flatten, crush.

abprallen, to rebound, recoil, reverberate, bounce off.

Abprallung, *f.* rebound, reflection, resilience.

abpressen, to squeeze out of, couch.

Abpressmaschine, *f.* press.

Abproduckt, *n.*-e, waste product, by-product.

abpumpen, to pump, drain.

Abputz, *m.* plaster.

abputzen, to clean, cleanse, polish, plaster, wipe down.

abquetschen, to squeeze off, crush.

Abquickbeutel, *m.* filter bag.

abquicken, to purify, separate, refine; **abgetriebenes Silber** ∼, to wash refined silver cake.

abrahmen, to take the cream off, skim off.

abrammen, to ram, tamp.

Abrandkraut, *n.*-̈er, southernwood (*Artemisia abrotanum*).

abranken, to thin out, prune (grapevines).

abrasen, to cut (grass), remove (sod).

abraspeln, to rasp off.

abraten, to dissuade, warn.

abrauchen, to evaporate, vaporize, fume.

abräuchern, to fumigate, smoke.

Abrauchschale, *f.* evaporating dish.

Abraum, *m.* rubbish, trash, loppings, top layer over a mineral deposit.

abräumen, to clear off, remove, strip.

Abraum-salze, *n.pl.* abraum salts; -sprengung, *f.* stripping with explosives.

Abräumung, *f.* removal.

Abräumungsschlag, *m.*-̈e, final cutting.

abrechen, to rake off.

abrechnen, to deduct, settle, subtract.

Abrechnung, *f.* deduction, settlement.

Abrede, *f.* understanding, agreement; **in** ∼ **stellen,** to deny.

abreden, to dissuade.

Abreib, *m.* abrasion.

abreiben, to rub off, scour, grind.

Abreibung, *f.* rubbing off.

abreisen, to depart.

abreissen, to tear off, break away, detach, rupture, be interrupted.

Abreisszünder, *m.*-, friction igniter.

Abrichtelauge, *f.* weak caustic liquor.

abrichten, to train, fit, adjust, level, face.

Abrieb, *m.*-e, pieces broken off, dust, abrasion.

abrinden, to decorticate, bark, skin.

abringen, to wrest from.

Abriss, *m.*-e, sketch, design, draft, summary; -zone, *f.* zone of abscission.

abröschen, to air (paper).

abrollen, to roll off, uncoil, unwind.

abrosten, to rust off, corrode.

abrösten, to roast.

abröten, to dye red, lose red color.

abrücken, to move off, remove, move away from.

Abrufauftrag, *m.*̈e, make and hold, will-call order.

abrufen, to call off, call away.

abrunden, to round off, even up, curve.

abrupfen, to pluck off.

abrussecht, fast to rubbing, noncrocking.

abrüsten, to disarm, disassemble, take apart.

abrutschen, to slip off, slide.

absacken, to load, become encysted, sack, pack in bags.

Absackung, *f.* encystment, sacculation.

Absage, *f.* counterorder, refusal.

absagen, to break with, countermand, revoke, decline.

absägen, to saw off.

absalzen, to salt adequately.

absatteln, to unsaddle.

absättigen, to saturate, neutralize.

Absättigungsversuch, *m.*-e, saturation test.

Absatz, *m.*̈e, deposit, sediment, pause, stop, sale, heel, reduction, turnover, market, precipitate; **in Absätzen,** alternately, intermittently.

Absatz-gebiet, *m.* outlet, market; **-gebiets-verhältnisse,** *n.pl.* market conditions; **-gestein,** *n.* sedimentary (stratified) rock.

absätzig, inferior, intermittent.

absatzweise, interruptedly, intermittently, in batches.

absäuern, to acidulate, acidify.

Absauganlage, *f.* induced-draft installation.

absaugen, to suck off, filter with suction, withdraw.

Absauger, *m.*-, suction box, exhauster, hydroextractor, ejector.

Absaug-flasche, *f.* filtering flask; **-pumpe,** *f.* vacuum pump.

absäumen, to trim.

abschaben, to scrape off, grind off.

Abschabsel, *n.* scrapings, shavings.

abschaffen, to abolish, to do away with.

abschälen, to peel off, excoriate, strip, exfoliate.

abschalten, to cut out, turn off, detach, disconnect, arrest.

abschattieren, to shade off (color).

abschätzen, to estimate, appraise, tax, value, rate.

Abschaum *m.*̈e, skimmings, scum, refuse, dross.

abschäumen, to skim off.

abscheidbar, separable.

abscheiden, to separate, disengage, liberate, seclude, precipitate, deposit, refine, fare, eliminate, depart.

Abscheider, *m.*-, separator, deflector, extractor, skimmer.

Abscheidung, *f.* separation, elimination, secretion, precipitation, refining, deposit, sediment, excretion.

Abscheidungs-mittel, *n.*-, means of separation, precipitant; **-produkt,** *n.* secretion.

abscheren, to clip, shear off, cut off.

Abscherungs-beanspruchung, *f.* shearing strain; **-festigkeit,** *f.* shearing strength.

Abscheu, *m.* aversion, abhorrence, loathing.

abscheuern, to scour (off), erode, wear.

abscheulich, abominable, detestable.

abschichten, to separate into layers.

abschicken, to dispatch, send off.

Abschied, *m.*-e, departure, dismissal; ∼ **nehmen,** to say good-by.

abschiefern, to peel, scale off, exfoliate, laminate.

abschiessen, to fire, shoot off, fade.

abschilfern, to desquamate, excoriate, exfoliate.

abschirmen, to screen off, cover, protect.

Abschirmung, *f.* shielding.

abschlachten, to slaughter, butcher.

abschlacken, to remove slag from.

Abschlag, *m.*̈e, fragments, chips, loppings. reduction, deduction, installment.

abschlagen, to knock off, refuse, deny, chip, take to pieces, sieve, reject, turn off, abate, slough (thread).

abschlägig, negative.

Abschlagszahlung, *f.* installment, part payment.

abschlämmen, to wash. elutriate, decant.

abschleifen, to grind off, sharpen, rub down, furbish, finish, polish, wear out.

Abschleifung, *f.* attrition, grinding off, sharpening.

abschleimen, to clarify.

abschleppen, to carry off.

Abschleudermaschine, *f.* centrifuge.

abschleudern, to throw off, centrifuge.

abschlichten, to plane, polish, smooth.

abschliessbar, capable of being closed or sealed.

abschliessen, to shut off, occlude, close, conclude, end, separate, seclude, terminate, complete, seal.

abschliessend, conclusive, final, positive, in closing, definite.

Abschliessung, *f.* occlusion, shutting off.

Abschluss, *m.*-̈e, conclusion, agreement, end, cutoff, closing; **-blende,** *f.* front diaphragm (of camera); **-hahn,** *m.* stopcock.

Abschmelzdraht, *m.*-̈e, safety fuse, fuse wire.

abschmelzen, to melt off, fuse.

Abschmelz-sicherung, *f.* safety cutout, electric fuse.

abschmieren, to grease, lubricate.

abschmirgeln, to rub (grind) with emery, machine by means of emery wheel.

abschmutzen, to soil.

Abschmutz-makulatur, *f.* offset (paper); **-papier,** *n.* maculature, blotting paper.

abschneiden, to cut off, lop off, amputate, truncate, secrete, part, clip, isolate, deprive of; **gut** ∼, to show up well, fare well.

Abschnitt, *m.*-e, cutting, part, segment, portion, section, intercept, period, era, paragraph; **neue Abschnitte,** shavings, waste paper.

Abschnitzel, *n.*-, shred, chip, cutting, segment, clipping, paring.

abschnüren, to tie off, constrict.

Abschnürung, *f.* abscission, abstriction, constriction, segmentation, marking off.

abschöpfen, to skim off, ladle out, scum.

abschrägen, to bevel, slant, slope, plane, chamfer.

Abschrägung, *f.* slope, slant, bezel.

abschrauben, to screw off, unscrew.

abschrecken, to frighten off, chill, quench.

abschreckend, deterrent.

Abschreckung, *f.* chilling, intimidation, quenching.

Abschreckungsmittel, *n.* deterrent, repulsive agent.

abschreiben, to copy, revoke, write off, plagiarize, depreciate.

Abschreibung, *f.* amount written off, depreciation, amortization.

abschreiten, to step off.

Abschrift, *f.*-en, copy, summary, transcript.

abschroten, to clip, hew.

abschruppen, to rough-turn on lathe, plane off.

abschülfern, to scale off.

abschuppen, to scale off, peel off, laminate.

abschürfen, to gall, rub off the skin.

abschüssig, steep, precipitous, slanting.

Abschüssigkeit, *f.* declivity, steepness.

abschütteln, to shake off.

abschütten, to pour out of, decant.

abschwächen, to weaken, diminish, decrease, mitigate, reduce, soften, level off.

Abschwächer, *m.* reducer, reducing medium.

Abschwächung, *f.* weakening, reduction.

abschwärmen, to leave in swarms, cease swarming.

abschwarten, to bark, decorticate, square.

abschwefeln, to desulphurize, impregnate with sulphur, calcine.

abschweifen, to deviate, digress.

Abschweifung, *f.* deviation, digression.

abschwelen, to calcine, roast, carbonize (distill) under vacuum.

abschwemmen, to wash (away), float, elutriate.

abschwenken, to rinse off.

abschwingen, to shake off, centrifuge, winnow, hydroextract.

abschwitzen, to sweat out, depilate.

abschwören, to abjure.

Abscissenachse, *f.* abscissa axis.

absehbar, within sight, perceivable, observable, conceivable, imaginable, visible; **in absehbarer Zeit,** before long.

absehen, to sight, perceive, neglect, let alone; ∼ **von,** to exclude, disregard, let alone; **abgesehen auf,** meant (intended) for; **abgesehen von,** without mentioning, aside from, irrespective of.

Absehlinie, *f.* line of collimation.

Abseide, *f.* floss silk.

abseifen, to clean with soap.

Abseifen der Schweissnähte, air test with soap and water on welds of pressure vessels.

abseigern, to liquate, separate by fusion, plumb.

Abseihbier, *n.* drawings.

abseihen, to filter, decant, percolate, strain.

Abseihung, *f.* filtration, decantation.

abseits, aside, apart.

absenden, to send (off), ship, despatch, mail.

absengen, to singe off.

absenken, to lower, plant layers, sink, settle, subside.

Absenker, *m.* layer, shoot.

Absenkung, *f.* lowering, layering, slope, settlement, subsidence.

Absetz-becken, *n.* settling basin; **-behälter,** *m.* straining chamber, thickener, draining tank; **-bottich,** *m.* settling vat.

absetzen, to deposit, precipitate, interrupt, sell, dispose of, thicken, displace, settle, wean, contrast; ∼**lassen,** to settle.

Absetzung, *f.* deposition, precipitation, sediment, settling.

Absetzzeit, *f.* settling time.

Absicht, *f.* intention, purpose; **mit** ∼, intentionally.

absichtlich, intentional.

absieben, to sieve, sift off, screen, riddle.

absieden, to boil, decoct, extract by boiling.

absinken, to sink down, decrease, descend.

Absinth, *m.* wormwood, absinthe.

Absitz-dauer, *f.* time needed for precipitation or settling; **-rohr,** *m.* deposition tube, settling cylinder.

absitzen, to settle, dismount; ∼ **lassen,** to allow to settle.

absolut, absolute; **absolute Öle,** *n.pl.* essential oils.

absoluttrocken (Gewicht), bone dry.

absondern, to separate, detach, isolate, secrete, excrete, insulate, abstract, differentiate, extract, segregate.

absondernd, secreting, excreting, secretory.

absonderlich, special, unusual, extraordinary, queer, odd.

Absonderliche, das ∼, the singular, strange (thing).

Absonderung, *f.* separation, secretion, excretion, structure, division.

Absonderungs-drüse, *f.*-**n,** secretory gland; **-flüssigkeit,** *f.* secretory fluid, secretion; **-organ,** *n.* secretory organ; **-stoff,** *m.* secreted material; **-vermögen,** *n.* secretory power; **-vorgang,** *m.* process of secretion; **-werkzeug,** *n.* secretory organ.

Absorbens, *n.* absorbent.

absorbierbar, absorbable.

absorbieren, to absorb, occlude.

absorbierend, absorbent.

Absorbierung, *f.* absorbing, absorption.

absorptions-fähig, capable of absorbing, absorbent; **-fähigkeit,** *f.* absorptive power; **-flüssigkeit,** *f.* absorption liquid; **-gefäss,** *n.* absorption vessel; **-gewebe,** *n.* absorbing tissue; **-kraft,** *f.* absorptive power.

Absorptions-mittel, *n.* absorbent; **-röhre,** *f.* absorption tube; **-schlange,** *f.* absorption coil; **-streifen,** *m.* absorption band; **-turn,** *m.* reaction tower; **-verbindung,** *f.* absorption compound; **-vermögen,** *n.* absorptive power.

abspalten, to split off, cleave off, separate.

Abspaltung, *f.* splitting off, cleavage, separation, segregation, elimination.

abspannen, to ease (the mind), relax, unharness; **abgespannt,** weary, fatigued, released.

Abspanner, *m.* step-down transformer.

Abspannung, *f.* relaxation, fatigue, exhaustion, slackening, asthenia.

abspenstig machen, to estrange, entice away, unsettle.

absperren, to shut off, confine, isolate.

absperrend, confining.

Absperr-flüssigkeit, *f.* confining liquid, sealing fluid; **-hahn,** *m.* stopcock; **-schieber,** *m.* slide (gate) valve; **-sunk,** *m.* suction wave.

Absperrung, *f.* shutting off, separation.

Absperrvorrichtung, *f.* isolating device (valve, gate).

abspiegeln, to reflect.

abspielen, to play, occur, happen, take place.

absplittern, to splinter off.

absprechen, to dispute, deny, deprive.

absprechend, positive, adverse.

abspreizen, to spread away, stay, prop, support.

absprengen, to blast off, drive off, sprinkle.

Absprenger, *m.* cutter.

abspringen, to leap off, rebound, crack.

abspringend, in contrast, desultory.

abspritzen, to wash down (with a hose), spray, wash off.

Absprung, *m.* leaping off, offshoot, reflection.

abspulen, to wind off.

abspülen, to wash off, flush, rinse, scour away.

Abspülung, *f.* washing off.

abstammen, to descend, be derived.

Abstammung, *f.* descent, derivation, origin.

Abstand, *m.*⁝e, distance, clearance, interval, difference, renunciation; **in gleichen Abständen von einander,** spaced equidistantly; ~ **nehmen,** to desist (from), object to.

Abstand(s)-messer, *m.* position finder; **-gleich,** equidistant.

abständig, decayed, deteriorated, declining.

abstatten, to render (a visit, report).

abstäubecht, noncrocking (of colors).

abstauben, to dust off.

abstechen, to drain, run off, tap, cut off; **von etwas** ~, to contrast with something.

Abstecher, *m.*-, digression, excursion, tapper.

abstecken, to mark out, stake out.

Absteckpfahl, *m.*⁝e, surveying rod.

abstehen, to get stale, decompose, stand off, refrain from, stay away from, stand clean of, desist; **gleichweit** ~, to be at equal distance; **abgestanden,** stale, flat, dead.

abstehend, spreading, distant.

absteifen, to prop, support, stiffen.

absteigen, to descend, come from, fall, dismount.

abstellen, to disconnect, shut off, turn off, abolish, put out of commission.

Abstell-hahn, *m.*⁝e, stopcock; **-vorrichtung,** *f.* cutoff device.

absterben, to die, expire, fade, wither, decay, be benumbed, become opaque.

Abstich, *m.*-e, drawing, running, tapping (of liquid or molten metal); **-loch,** *n.* taphole.

abstimmen, to vote, tune, balance, synchronize.

Abstimmspule, *f.* tuning coil.

Abstimmung, *f.* vote, voting, tuning.

abstinent, totally abstinent.

abstoppen, to close, stop up.

abstossen, to repel, cast off, sell, scrape, bump (of railroad car), hump.

abstossend, repulsive, repelling.

Abstossung, *f.* repulsion, casting off.

abstrahieren, to abstract.

Abstrahlung, *f.* radiation.

Abstrebekraft, *f.*⁝e, centrifugal force.

abstreichen, to wipe or scrape off.

Abstreich-löffel, *n.* skimming ladle, scummer; **-messer,** *m.* raspatory, lint ductor.

abstreifen, to strip off, skin, divest of.

Abstreifer, *m.*-, ingot stripper, skimmer.

Abstreifmesser, *n.*-, doctor blade.

abstreiten, to dispute, contest, deny.

Abstrich, *m.*-e, deduction, skim, dross, smear (of microscopic preparation); **-blei,** *n.* crude litharge, lead scum.

abströmen, to flow off.

abstufen, to graduate, shade off, step off.

Abstufung, *f.* gradation, shading.

abstumpfen, to blunt, dull, deaden, weaken, neutralize, truncate; **abgestumpft,** truncated, neutralized.

Abstumpfung, *f.* neutralization, truncation.

Abstumpfungsfläche, *f.* truncating face.

Absturz, *m.*⁝e, sudden fall, precipice, crash (of airplane); **-bauwerk,** *n.* drop structure.

abstürzen, to hurl down, fall down, plunge, crash (of plane).

abstutzen, to clip, cut short.

absuchen, to work a field, search and take.

Absud, *m.*-e, decoction, extract, mordant.

absüssen, to sweeten, wash a precipitate, edulcorate.

Absüsspindel, *f.*-n, hydrometer, sweet-water spindle.

Absynth, *m.* wormwood.

Abszess, *m.*-e, abscess.

Abszisse, *f.* abscissa.

abtasten, to palpate, feel out, make contact with, investigate by feel, find, move about.

abtauen, to thaw off, defrost, melt.

Abteil, *m.*-e, compartment.

abteilen, to divide, classify.

Abteilung, *f.* division, compartment.

abteufen, to sink, bore (a shaft).

abthun (abtun), to take off, cast off, kill, settle.

Abtitrierungspunkt, *m.*-e, end point.

abtönen, to tone down.

abtöten, to kill, destroy.

Abtrag, *m.* excavation, cutting, payment.

abtragen, to carry off, wear out, excavate, demolish.

abtragend, abrasive.

abträglich, injurious.

Abtragung, *f.* denudation.

Abtragungsgebiet, *n.* area of erosion.

Abtreibe-herd, *m.*-e, refining hearth; -kupelle, *f.* refining cupel; -kolonne, *f.* exhausting column; -mittel, *n.* abortifacient, purge, expulsive agent; -ofen, *m.* refining furnace.

abtreiben, to drive off, expel, fell (trees), clear (woods), refine, cupel, abort, exhaust.

abtreibend, abortive.

Abtreibung, *f.* driving off.

abtrennbar, separable.

abtrennen, to separate, cut off.

abtreten, to tread on, wear down, surrender, cede.

Abtretung, *f.* surrender, withdrawal, transfer.

Abtrieb, *m.*-e, felling trees, timber cut down, clearing, stripping, run.

Abtriebs-ertrag, *m.* final yield (of timber); -fläche, *f.* clear-felled area; -schlag, *m.* recent cutting.

abtriefen, to trickle down.

Abtrift, *f.*-e, drift, leeway.

Abtritt, *m.* withdrawal, exit, privy.

Abtritts-dünger, *m.* fertilizer from cesspools; -grube, *f.* cesspool.

abtrocknen, to dry off.

abtröpfeln, abtropfen, to drip off, drain dry.

Abtropf-brett, *n.*-er, draining board; -gestell, *n.* draining rack; -kasten, *m.* draining tank; -pfanne, *f.* list pot; -schale, *f.* draining dish.

abtrünnig, faithless, disloyal.

abtun, to take off, abolish, settle.

abwägen, to weigh off, ponder, consider.

abwällen, to boil gently.

abwalzen, to roll down, compact with roller.

abwälzen, to roll off, shift off.

abwandeln, to vary, alter.

abwandern, to move away.

Abwandlung, *f.* modification, variation.

Abwärme, *f.* waste heat.

abwarten, to wait for; abwartende Haltung, *f.* attitude of reserve.

abwärts, downward; -bewegung, *f.* downward motion; -krümmung, *f.* epinasty; -transformator, *m.* step-down transformer.

abwaschen, to wash off, cleanse, rinse.

Abwaschung, *f.* washing.

Abwasser, *n.*-, waste water, sewage, back water, white water; -anlage, *f.* -betrieb, *m.* sewage-disposal plant; -desinfektion, *f.* disinfection of sewage; -klärtrichter, *m.* save-all tray.

abwechseln, to vary, alternate, fluctuate.

abwechselnd, alternating, intermittent, variable.

Abwechselung, *f.* change, variation.

Abweg, *m.*-e, byway, wrong way.

Abwehr, *f.* defense; -bewegung, *f.* defensive movement.

abwehren, to ward off, prevent, protect.

Abwehr-ferment, *n.*-e, protective ferment, defensive enzymes; -mittel, *n.* prophylactic.

abweichen, to macerate, decline, depart, soak, soften, deviate, vary, diverge, differ, deflect.

abweichend, divergent, deviating, varying, imperfect (of paper).

Abweichung, *f.* deviation, variation, aberration, anomaly, discrepancy, divergence, difference.

abweisen, to refuse, dismiss, reject, repel.

abweissen, to whiten.

abwelken, to wither, shrivel, dry, fade.

abwenden, to turn off, avert.

abwendig machen, to alienate, estrange.

abwerfen, to throw off, shed, yield, discard.

Abwerfofen, *m.*-̈, refining furnace.

abwesend, absent.

Abwesenheit, *f.* absence.

abwickelbar, evolvable.

abwickeln, to unroll, unwind, develop, rectify, settle, perform.

Abwickelspule, *f.* feed reel.

abwiegen, to weigh out.

Abwind, *m.* down current, downdraft.

abwinden, to unwind.

abwirtschaften, to ruin

abwischen, to wipe off.

Abwitterung, *f.* weathering, disintegration.

Abwitterungshalde, *f.* a disintegrated slope.

Abwurf, *m.*⁼e, throwing off, refuse, rough cast.

abzählbar, countable.

abzahlen, to pay off.

abzählen, to count (off).

abzapfen, to draw off, tap, let blood.

abzäunen, to fence in or off.

abzehren, to waste away, become emaciated.

Abzehrung, *f.* wasting away, consumption; rillenförmige ∼, grooving produced by corrosion.

Abzeichen, *n.*-, mark, sign.

abzeichnen, to mark off, sketch, copy.

Abzieh-bild, *n.*-er, transfer picture, design, decalcomania, metachromotype; -blase, *f.* still, retort.

abziehen, to draw off, remove, decant, subtract, depart, leave, skim, rack, strip, scrape, escape, siphon, drain off.

Abziehen, *n.* honing.

Abzieher, *m.* abductor muscle.

Abzieh-halle, *f.* racking room; -kolben, *m.* retort; -mittel, *n.* stripping agent; -muskel, *m.* abductor (muscle); -papier, *n.* pottery tissue, proof(ing) paper; -stein, *m.* hone, grindstone.

Abziehung, *f.* subtraction, deduction.

Abziehzünder, *m.* friction lighter.

abzirkeln, to measure with (a compass or) dividers.

Abzug, *m.*⁼e, hood, outlet, drainage, drawing off, deduction, print, proof sheet, copy, rebate, exhaust, scum, discharge, positive (in photography).

abzüglich, less, deducting, minus.

Abzugs-blei, *n.* lead obtained by the melting of scoria; -bogen, *m.* proof sheet, firing spring; -dampf, *m.* exhaust steam; -dose, *f.* junction box; -gas, *n.* chimney gas; -graben, *m.* sewer; -kanal, *m.* drain; -klappe, *f.* trap; -papier, *n.* duplicating paper, proofing paper; -raum, *m.* room equipped with hoods; -rohr, *n.* drain pipe, delivery tube; -schalter, *m.* firing connector.

Abzweig, *m.* branch.

abzweigen, to detach, branch off, lop off branches.

Abzweig-leitung, *f.* branch line; -muffe, *f.* branch T, branch box; -reaktanzspule, *f.* feeder reactor; -stromkreis, *m.* derived circuit.

Abzweigung, *f.* detaching, offshoot, branching, ramification.

abzwicken, to pinch off (wire, etc.).

abzwingen, to extort.

Abzwirnen, *n.* (über Kopf) upstroke twisting.

Aca . . . , see AKA . . . ; Acc . . . , see AKZ . . . or AKK . . . ; Ace . . . , see AZE . . .

Acajou, *m.* acajou, cashew.

Acceleren, *f.pl.* accelerators.

accessorisch, accessory.

Accra-copalensäure, *f.* accra-copalenic acid; -copalinsäure, *f.* accra-copalinic acid; -copalsäure, *f.* accra-copalic acid.

Aceanthren, *n.* aceanthrene.

Acenaphten, *n.* acenaphthene.

Acenaphtylen, *n.* acenaphthylene.

Acetaldehyd, *n.* acetic aldehyde.

Acetatlösung, *f.* acetate solution.

Acetessig-äther, *m.* acetoacetic acid; -säure, *f.* acetoacetic acid; -ester, *m.* acetoacetic ester.

Acetindruck, *m.*⁼e, acetin printing.

acetisch, acetic.

Acetonlösung, *f.* acetone solution.

Acetopersäure, *f.* peracetic acid.

Acetsäure, *f.* acetic acid.

Acetylen-anlage, *f.* acetylene-gas generating plant; -bindung, *f.* acetylene linkage; -reihe, *f.* acetylene series.

Acetylharnstoff, *m.*-e, acetyluria.

acetylierbar, acetylable, capable of being acetylated.

acetylieren, to acetylate.

Acetyl-säure, *f.* acetic acid; -schwefelsäure, *f.* acetylsulphuric acid.

Achat, *n.* agate; in ∼ verwandeln, to agatize.

achat-ähnlich, agatelike; -artig, agatelike; -glätte, *f.* flint glazing; -haltig, agatiferous; -marmorpapier, *n.* marbled papers; -mörser, *m.* agate mortar; -porzellan, *n.* agateware; -schleifer, *m.* agate grinder; -tulpe, *f.* agate.

Achillenöl, *n.*-e, Achillea oil.

achromatisch, achromatic.

Achse, *f.* axis, axle, shaft, spindle.

Achsel, *f.*-**n,** shoulder, axilla, axil; -**bein,** *n.* shoulder blade; -**blütig,** axilliflorous; -**bogen,** *m.* axillary arch; -**drüse,** *f.* axillary gland; -**falte,** *f.* axillary fold; -**federn,** *f.pl.* axillaries; -**furche,** *f.* axillary groove; -**gelenk,** *n.* shoulder joint; -**grube,** *f.* armpit, axilla.

Achsel-höhle, *f.* armpit, axilla; -**knopse,** *f.* axillary bud; -**spross,** *m.* axillary shoot; -**ständig,** axillary; -**versprossung,** *f.* ecblastesis, appearance of buds within a flower.

Achsen-becher, *m.* hypanthium, enlargement of the torus; -**bürtig,** arising from the axis; -**cylinder,** *m.* axis cylinder; -**cylinderfortsatz,** *m.* axon, axis cylinder process; -**drehung,** *f.* rotation.

Achsen-ebene, *f.* plane of optical axes; -**faden,** *m.* central filament, axis cylinder; -**fadenranker,** *m.* axial tendril climber; -**höhlenwirbel,** *m.* axillary whorl; -**knospenanlage,** *f.* axillary bud primordium; -**kreuz,** *n.* system of coordinates; -**lager,** *m.* axle bearing, bearings; -**los,** anaxial; -**schlauch,** *m.* axial tube; -**schnitte,** *m.pl.* axial intercepts.

Achsen-skelett, *n.* chordoskeleton; -**strang,** *m.* dorsal chord, notochord; -**substanz,** *f.* axial substance; -**symmetrisch,** axially symmetrical; -**verhältnis,** *n.* axial ratio; -**winkel,** *m.* angle of the axis.

achsial, axial.

achsig, achsrecht, axial, axiferous.

achsparallel, concentric.

Achsstand, *m.* wheel base.

acht, eight.

Acht, *f.* attention, consideration, care; ausser ∼ lassen, to disregard, neglect; sich in ∼ nehmen, to be on one's guard.

achtbar, respectable, honorable.

achtbasisch, octabasic.

achte, eighth.

Achteck, *n.*-**e,** octagon.

achteckig, octagonal.

Achtel, *n.* eighth.

achten, to esteem, respect, pay attention.

ächten, to outlaw, proscribe.

Achtender, *m.* stag of eight points.

achtenswert, worthy of esteem.

Achter, *m.*-, figure 8; -**figur,** *f.* figure 8.

achterlei, of eight kinds.

acht-fach, eightfold; -**fältig,** eightfold; -**flach,** *n.* octahedron; -**flächig,** octahedral; -**füssler,** *m.* octopod.

achtgeben, to pay attention.

acht-gliedrig, eight-membered; -**kantig,** octagonal; -**klauig,** octodactylous.

achtlos, negligent, unmindful.

achtmal, eight times.

achtsam, careful.

achttägig, weekly.

Achtung, *f.* attention, esteem, respect.

Ächtung, *f.* outlawing.

achtungsvoll, respectful.

achtwertig, octavalent.

achtzehn, eighteen.

achtzig, eighty.

ächzen, to groan.

Aci . . . , see Azi . . .

acidifizieren, to acidify.

Acidität, *f.* acidity.

acidylieren, to acylate.

Acker, *m.*-, field, land, soil; -**bau,** *m.* field culture, agriculture; -**bautechnik,** *f.* science of agriculture; -**beere,** *f.* dewberry, bramble (*Rubus caesius*); -**boden,** *m.* arable (surface) soil; -**erde,** *f.* arable soil, earth; -**bohne,** *f.* field bean (*Vicia faba*); -**brachweide,** *f.* fallow pasture; -**distel,** *f.* Canada thistle (*Cirsium arvense*); -**doppen,** *f.pl.* acorn cups; -**ehrenpreis,** *m.* speedwell (*Veronica officinalis*).

Ackerei, *f.* tillage of land.

Acker-eule, *f.* turnip dart moth; -**fuchsschwanz,** *m.* field foxtail grass (*Alopecurus agrestis*); -**furche,** *f.* furrow; -**futterpflanze,** *f.* forage plant; -**gänsedistel,** *f.* corn sow thistle (*Sonchus arvensis*); -**gare,** *f.* favorable condition for cultivation; -**gauchheil,** *m.* pimpernel (*Anagallis arvensis*); -**gunsel,** *m.* ground pine (*Ajuga chamaepytis*).

Acker-hahnenfuss, *m.* buttercup, corn crowfoot (*Ranunculus arvensis*); -**hornkraut,** *n.* chickweed (*Cerastium arvense*); -**kamille,** *f.* field camomile (*Anthemis arvensis*); -**kratzdistel,** *f.* horse thistle (*Cirsium arvense*); -**krume,** *f.* surface soil; -**krummhals,** *m.* wild bugloss (*Lycopsis arvensis*); -**mennig,** *m.* agrimony (*Agrimonia eupatoria*); -**minze,** *f.* mint (*Mentha arvensis*).

ackern, to till, cultivate, plow.

Acker-rade, *f.* corn cockle (*Agrostemma githago*); -**rettich,** *m.* wild radish (*Raphanus raphanistrum*); -**röte,** *f.* field madder (*Sherardia arvensis*); -**salat,** *m.* lamb's-lettuce (*Valerianella olitoria*); -**schachtelhalm,** *m.* field horsetail (*Equisetum* *arvense);* **-senf,** *m.* charlock (*Sinapis arvensis*).

Acker-skabiose, *f.* field scabious (*Knautia arvensis*); **-spergel,** *m.* corn spurry (*Spergula arvensis*); **-steinsame,** *f.* corn gromwell (*Lithospermum arvense*); **-trespe,** *f.* field brome grass (*Bromus arvensis*); **-veilchen,** *n.* pansy, heartsease (*Viola tricolor*); **-winde,** *f.* (lesser) bindweed, (*Convolvulus arvensis*); cornbind, morning-glory; **-wolfsauge,** *f.* wild bugloss (*Lycopsis arvensis.*)

Aco . . . , Acro . . . , Act . . . , Acu . . . , see **Ak . . .**

Aconit, *n.* aconite.

acrogen, acrogenous, conidium-like, growing at the apex.

Acroreiz, *m.* formative stimulus.

acyclisch, acyclic.

acylieren, acylate.

Adams-apfel, *m.* Adam's apple, grapefruit, shaddock; **-nadel,** *f.* Adam's needle (Yucca).

Adaptationsfähigkeit, *f.* adaptability.

adäquat, adequate.

Addend, *m.* addendum.

addieren, to add.

Addition, *f.* addition.

additionsfähig, addierbar, additive.

additiv, additive, cumulative.

Adduktoreneindruck, *m.* adductor impression, scar.

Adel, *m.* nobility.

adelig, noble.

adeln, to ennoble, dignify, exalt.

Ader, *f.-n,* vein, grain of wood; **-blättrig,** inophyllous, with threadlike veins in leaf.

Aderchen, *n.* small vein.

Ader-flügler, *m.pl.* Hymenoptera; **-geflecht,** *n.* vascular or chorioid plexus; **-haut,** *f.* chorioid membrane; **-häutchen,** *n.* chorion; **-hautspanner,** *m.* ciliary (tensor) muscle; **-hautstroma,** *n.* stroma of chorioid; **-holz,** *n.* wood cut along the grain.

aderig, veined, streaked, venous, vascular.

Ader-knoten, *m.-,* varicose vein; **-lass,** *m.* venesection.

adern, to vein, mark with veins.

Ader-netz, *n.* venous network; **-netzschlagader,** *f.* choroid artery; **-reich,** veined, rich in veins; **-schlag,** *m.* pulse beat.

Aderung, *f.* venation.

Aderwasser, *n.* (blood) serum, lymph.

adhärieren, to adhere.

Adhäsion, *f.* adhesion, adherence.

Adhäsionsfähigkeit, *f.* adhesive power.

adhäsiv, adhesive.

Adiabate, *f.* adiabatic graph or curve.

adiabatisch, adiabatic.

Adiowansamen, *m.* ajowan fruit.

adipid, fat.

adipidieren, to grease.

Adipinsäure, *f.* adipic acid.

adipös, adipose.

adjustieren, to adjust, test, gauge, regulate.

Adler, *m.* eagle; **-farn,** *m.* brake (*Pteris aquilina*); **-holz,** *n.* eaglewood (aloeswood) (*Aquilaria agallocha*); **-nase,** *f.* aquiline nose; **-vitriol,** *m.* eagle (Salzburg) vitriol.

adlig, noble.

Adonisröschen, *n.* pheasant's eye (*Adonis annua*).

adoptieren, to adopt.

adoucieren, to anneal, temper, soften.

Adoucier-gefäss, *n.* annealing pot; **-ofen,** *m.* annealing furnace.

Adressant, *m.* writer, sender.

Adressat, *m.* person addressed, consignee.

Adressbuch, *n.-ᵉer,* directory.

Adresse, *f.* address, direction.

adressieren, to address, consign.

adrett, adroit, smart.

adrig, veined, venous.

Adsorbens, *n.* adsorbent.

adsorbierbar, adsorbable.

adsorbieren, to adsorb.

Adsorptions-fähigkeit, *f.* adsorption capacity; **-haut** *f.* adsorbed film; **-schicht,** *f.* adsorbed layer; **-vermögen,** *n.* adsorption capacity; **-vorgang,** *m.* adsorption effect.

adstringierend, astringent; **adstringierendes Mittel,** astringent.

Adular, *m.* adularia, moonstone.

Adventiv-fieder, *f.* accessory plumage; **-keim,** *m.* adventitious embryo; **-knospe,** *f.* adventitious bud; **-spross,** *m.* adventitious shoot; **-wurzel,** *f.* adventitious root; **-wurzelbildung,** *f.* adventitious root formation, radication.

Advokat, *m.-en,* lawyer.

Ae . . . , see also **Ä . . .**

Aequationsteilung, *f.* equal longitudinal division.

Aequatorial-ebene, *f.* equatorial plane; **-platte,** *f.* equatorial plate.

Aeroben, *pl.* aerobic bacteria.

aerobiontisch, aerobisch, aerobic.

Aerobisřnus, *m.* aerobism.

Aerodynamik, *f.* aerodynamics.

aerogen, conveyed by air, grown in air.

Aeroplan, *m.* airplane.

aerostatisch, aerostatic.

Affe, *m.*-n, ape, monkey.

Affekt, *m.*-e, passion, emotion.

affektieren, to affect, pretend.

äffen, to ape, mock.

Affenbrotbaum, *m.* baobab tree (*Adansonia digitata*).

Affiche, *f.* poster, bill.

affig, apish, foolish.

affinieren, to refine.

Affinität, *f.* affinity.

Affinitäts-einheit, *f.* unit of affinity; **-lehre,** *f.* doctrine of affinity; **-rest,** *m.* residual affinity; **-richtung,** *f.* direction of affinity.

Affinivalenz, *f.* valence, atomicity.

affizieren, to affect, touch.

Affodill, *m.* asphodel.

After, *m.* anus; **-anhang,** *m.* anal appendage; **-asseln,** *f.pl.* Anisopoda; **-bein,** *n.* spurious (pseudo) leg; **-bildung,** *f.* malformation, secondary growth; **-blatt,** *n.* stipule; **-blätterig,** stipulate; **-blattläuse,** *f.pl.* Phylloxeridae; **-borste,** *f.* anal bristle; **-darm,** *m.* rectum.

After-decke, *f.* a caudal shield (pygidium); **-dolde,** *f.* cyme; **-drüse,** *f.* anal gland; **-feld,** *n.* periproct, peripygium; **-flosse,** *f.* anal fin; **-flügel,** *m.* false wing; **-flur,** *f.* pteryla ani; **-furche,** *f.* anal groove; **-füsse,** *m.pl.* spurious legs, pleopods; **-geburt,** *f.* afterbirth.

After-gewebe, *n.* heteroplastic tissue; **-griffel,** *m.* anal spine; **-grube,** *f.* anal cavity, groove; **-haut,** *f.* membrane at the anus, false membrane; **-kegel,** *m.* conoid; **-klappen,** *f.pl.* cerci; **-klaue,** *f.* pseudoclaw; **-kohle,** *f.* slack coal; **-kralle,** *f.* pseudoclaw; **-krebse,** *m.pl.* Hippidae.

After-kristall, *m.* pseudomorphous crystal; **-kugel,** *f.* spheroid; **-lücke,** *f.* periproct; **-moos,** *n.* alga; **-öffnung,** *f.* anal opening; **-raupe,** *f.* pseudocaterpillar; **-schaft,**

m. aftershaft; **-schirm,** *m.* cyme; **-schliesser,** *m.* anal sphincter; **-schörl,** *m.* axinite.

After-schwanz, *m.* anal tail; **-silber,** *n.* silver containing dross; **-sipho,** *m.* anal siphon; **-skorpion,** *m.* pseudoscorpion; **-spitzchen,** *n.* anal spike; **-stück,** *n.* anal segment, posterior part; **-verschiebung,** *f.* anal displacement.

Agar-Agar, *n.* agar-agar.

Agarizin, *n.* agaricine.

Agathendisäure, *f.* agathic acid.

Agens, *n.* agent, principle.

Agentur, *f.* agency.

Agenzien, *m.pl.* agents.

agglomerieren, to agglomerate.

Agglutinationserscheinung, *f.* agglutination phenomenon.

agglutinieren, to agglutinate.

Aggregat, *n.* aggregate; **-zustand,** *m.* state of aggregation, average.

aggressiv, aggressive, corrosive.

Agio, *n.* premium (on exchange of money).

Agitation, *f.* agitation.

agitatorisch, agitative.

agitieren, to agitate.

Aglei, *f.* columbine (Aquilegia).

Agrarier, *m.* agrarian.

Agrikultur, *f.* agriculture.

Agtstein, *m.* amber.

Ahlbeere, *f.* black current (*Ribes nigrum*).

Ahlborste, *f.* subulate bristle.

Ahle, *f.* awl, punch, bodkin, broach.

Ahlkirsche, *f.* bird cherry (*Prunus padus*).

Ahn(e), *m.* ancestor, grandfather.

Ahne, *f.* awn, chaff.

ähneln, to resemble, be similar.

ahnen, to anticipate, guess, surmise, foresee.

Ahnen-keimplasma, *n.* germ plasm; **-plasma,** *n.* germ plasm; **-reihe,** *f.* line of ancestors; **-tafel,** *f.* genealogical table or tree, pedigree.

Ahnherr, *m.* ancestor.

ähnlich (*dat.*), similar, resembling, like, analogous; ∼ **wie,** just like.

Ähnlichkeit, *f.* similarity, resemblance, likeness.

Ähnlichkeits-ansatz, *m.* **-prinzip,** *n.* **-theorem,** *n.* dimensional analysis.

Ähnlichkeits-gesetz, *n.* law of similitude.

Ahnung, *f.* presentiment, anticipation.

ahnungs-los, unsuspecting; **-voll,** full of misgivings, ominous.

Ahorn, *m.* maple (tree); **-gewächse,** *n.pl.* Aceraceae; **-maser,** *f.* bird's-eye maple; **-melasse,** *f.* maple sirup; **-saft,** *m.* maple sap, juice; **-säure,** *f.* aceric acid; **-zucker,** *m.* maple sugar.

Ährchen, *m.* spikelet; **-achse,** *f.* pedicel; **-blumig,** bearing spikelets; **-spindel,** *f.* rachilla.

Ähre, *f.* ear, spike.

Ähren-dolde, *f.* spikelike umbel; **-feld,** *n.* field of grain in the ear; **-förmig,** spicate(d); **-frucht,** *f.* cereal, grain; **-gräser,** *n.pl.* cereals; **-köpfchen,** *n.* head-shaped spike; **-rispe,** *f.* spikelike panicle; **-spitze,** *f.* awn, glume, beard; **-tragend,** spicate(d); **-traube,** *f.* spikelike cluster, raceme.

Aich . . . , see Eich . . .

Aichamt, *n.* gauging office.

aichen, to measure, standardize, gauge.

ajustieren, to adjust.

Akademie, *f.* academy.

Akajou, *m.* acajou, cashew.

Akaridentod, *m.* acaricide.

Akaroidharz, *n.* acaroid resin, yellow balsam.

Akaschu, *m.* acajou, cashew.

Akazie, *f.* (falsche, unechte), acacia, common locust tree (*Robinia pseudoacacia*).

Akaziengummi, *n.* gum arabic.

Akazin, *n.* gum arabic.

Akeeöl, *n.* akee oil.

Akelei, *f.* columbine (Aquilegia).

akklimatisieren, to acclimate.

Akkommodations-breite, *f.* amplitude, extent of accommodation; **-leistung,** *f.* capacity for adaptation.

akkommodieren, to accommodate.

Akkord, *m.* agreement, contract; **-arbeit,** *f.* piecework, job work.

akkordieren, to arrange, agree with.

Akkumulator, *m.*-en, accumulator, storage battery.

akkumulieren, to accumulate.

akkurat, accurate, exact.

Akonitin, *n.* aconitine.

Akonit-knolle, *f.* aconite bulb or tuber; **-säure,** *f.* aconitic acid.

Akridin, *n.* acridine.

Akrylsäure, *f.* acrylic acid.

Akt, *m.*-e, act, action, deed, process.

Akte, *f.* deed, document.

Aktendeckel, *m.* folder.

Aktie, *f.* share (stock).

Aktiengesellschaft, *f.* joint-stock company.

Aktinienmundschlitz, *m.* actinian mouth (medusa).

aktinisch, actinic.

Aktinismus, *m.* actinism.

Aktinomyzes, Actinomyces.

Aktionär, *m.*-e, shareholder, stockholder.

Aktions-bereich, *n.* cruising radius; **-linie,** *f.* line of action; **-radius,** *m.* radius of action; **-strom,** *m.* action current.

aktiv, active, effective.

Aktiva, *n.pl.* assets.

Aktivator, *m.* accelerator.

Aktiven, *n.pl.* assets.

aktivieren, to activate, realize.

Aktivierung, *f.* activation.

Aktivität, *f.* activity.

aktuell, actual, present, important.

Akustik, *f.* acoustics.

akut, acute.

Akzelerator, *m.* accelerator.

Akzent, *m.* accent.

akzentuieren, to accentuate.

akzeptieren, to accept.

akzessorisch, accessory.

Akzidenz, *f.* display work, job (in printing).

Akzidenzien, *pl.* fluctuating or casual emoluments, perquisites.

Akzise, *f.* excise.

Alabaster, *m.* alabaster; **-gips,** *m.* gypseous alabaster, plaster of Paris.

Alant, *m.* elecampane (*Inula*); **-beere,** *f.* black currant; **-wurzel,** *f.* elecampane root.

alarmieren, to alarm.

Alarzelle, *f.* alar cell.

Alaun, *m.* alum; **-artig,** aluminous; **-auflöser,** *m.* dissolving chest; **-beize,** *f.* aluming, aluminous mordant.

alaunen, to alum.

Alaun-erde, *f.* alum earth, alumina; **-erdehaltig, alaunig,** aluminous, aluminiferous; **-erdesulfat,** *n.* aluminum sulphate; **-festigkeit,** *f.* alum resistance; **-förmig,** aluminiform; **-gar,** alumed, tawed, steeped, dressed with alum; **-gerberei,** *f.* tawing; **-haltig,** aluminous.

Alaun-hütte, *f.* alum works; **-karmin,** *m.* carmini alum; **-kies,** *m.* aluminous pyrites; **-mehl,** *n.* powdered alum; **-sauer,** aluminate (of); **-schiefer,** *m.* alum schist (shale, slate); **-siederei,** *f.* alum works; **-stein,** *m.* alunite; **-wurzel,** *f.* alumroot.

alaunt, steeped in alum, aluminated.

Albinismus, *m.* albin(o)ism.

Albumin, *n.* albumin; **-artig,** albuminoid; **-gehalt,** *m.* albumin content; **-stoff,** *m.* protein, albuminous substance.

Älchen, *n.* nematode, small eel; **-krätze,** *f.* nematode scab (gall).

Alchimie, Alchemie, *f.* alchemy.

Aldehyd, *m.* aldehyde; **-haltig,** containing aldehyde.

Aleppobeule, *f.* Aleppo boil.

Aleuronkorn, *n.* aleuron grain.

Alfa, *f.* esparto grass (*Stipa tenacissima*).

Alge, *f.* alga, seaweed.

algebraisch, algebraic.

Algen-pilz, *m.* Phycomycete; **-zone,** *f.* algal layer of lichens.

aliphatisch, aliphatic.

alitieren, to alite (steel).

Alkalescenz, *f.* alkalinity.

Alkali, *n.* alkali; **-artig,** alkaloid; **-beständig,** resistant to alkalies; **-bildend,** alkaligenous; **-echt,** fast to alkali; **-gehalt,** *m.* alkali content; **-halogenid,** *n.* alkali halide; **-lauge,** *f.* alkali liquor, lye; **-metrisch,** alkalimetric.

Alkalinität, *f.* alkalinity.

Alkalirückstand, *m.*⸗e, alkali residue.

alkalisch, alkaline, basic.

alkalisierbar, alkalizable.

alkalisieren, to render alkaline.

Alkalität, Alkalizität, *f.* alkalinity.

Alkaloid, *n.* alkaloid; **-artig,** alkaloidisch, alkaloid.

Alkanna, *f.* Alkanna, alkanet; **-wurzel,** *f.* alkanet.

Alkohol, *m.*-e, alcohol; **-artig,** alcohollike, alcoholic; **-artigkeit,** *f.* alcoholicity; **-auszug,** *m.* alcoholic extract; **-dampf,** *m.* alcohol vapor; **-frei,** nonalcoholic; **-gärung,** *f.* alcoholic fermentation; **-gehalt,** *m.* alcohol content; **-haltig,** alcoholic.

alkoholisch, alcoholic; **-wässerig,** aqueous alcoholic.

alkoholisierbar, alcoholizable.

alkoholisieren, to alcoholize.

alkohol-löslich, soluble in alcohol; **-lösung,** *f.* alcohol liquor; **-messer,** *m.* alcoholometer; **-reich,** rich in alcohol; **-vergällung,** *f.* denaturation of alcohol; **-vergärung,** *f.* alcoholic fermentation.

Alkoholyse, *f.* alcoholysis.

Alkoholzusatz, *m.* addition of alcohol.

Alkoven, *m.* alcove, recess.

alkylieren, to alkylate.

Alkylierungsmittel, *n.* alkylating agent.

Alkylrest, *m.* alkyl residue.

all, all, every, any; **vor allem,** above all, especially, mainly, chiefly; **trotz alledem,** for all that, nevertheless.

Allantoisgang, *m.* allantoic duct.

allassotonische Bewegung, *f.* change due to reduction in cell turgor.

allbekannt, notorious, well-known.

allda, alldort, there.

Allee, *f.* avenue, alley.

allein, alone, only, but.

alleinhemmende Dosis, *f.* inhibition dosage.

alleinig, exclusive, sole, unique.

alleinstehend, isolated.

Allelen Verhältnis, allelomorphic relationship.

allemal, always, every time, invariably; **ein für ∼,** once for all.

allenfalls, if need be, perhaps, at best; **∼ auch,** eventually.

allenthalben, everywhere, from all sides.

aller-best, best of all, very best; **-dings,** to be sure, it is true, of course, by all means.

allererst, first of all; **zu ∼,** first and foremost.

aller-feinst, very fine; **-geringst,** smallest, infinitesimal; **-grösst,** greatest of all, very greatest; **-grösstenteils,** for the greatest part; **-hand,** all kinds of, various; **-höchst,** highest of all; **-jüngst,** very recent; **-lei,** all kinds of, diverse; **-letzt,** very last, ultimate; **-liebst,** most charming.

Aller-mannsharnisch, *m.* serpent's garlic (*Allium victoriale*); **-merkwürdigst,** most noteworthy, most extraordinary.

alles, *n.* all, everything; **vor allem,** before all, above all, chiefly, primarily, mainly; **∼ in allem,** all in all; **das ∼,** all that; **was ∼,** whatever; **wer ∼,** whoever.

allesamt, all together, in a body.

Allesfresser, *m.* pantophagist.

all-fällig, eventually, in all cases; **-gegenwärtig,** omnipresent; **-geläufig,** generally known; **-gemach,** gradually, little by little.

allgemein, general, common, universal; **im allgemeinen,** generally.

allgemein-angenommen, commonly accepted; **-befinden,** n. general conditions.

Allgemeines, n. general information.

allgemein-gewaltig, omnipotent; **-gültig,** universally approved; **-gültigkeit,** f. universal validity; **-heit,** f. generality, universality; **-machen,** to generalize; **-reaktion,** f. general reaction; **-verständlich,** popular, generally intelligible; **-wirkung,** f. general effect; **-wohl,** n. common welfare.

allgültig, universally valid or approved.

alliieren, to ally.

all-jährlich, yearly, annual; **-mächtig,** omnipotent; **-mählich,** gradual, by degrees; **-monatlich,** once a month, monthly.

allogam, allogametic.

Alloisomerie, f. alloisomerism.

Allomerie, f. allomerism.

allomorph, allomorphic.

Allonge, f. adapter, extension.

allopathisch, allopathic.

Alloschleimsäure, f. allomucic acid.

allotrop, allotropic.

Allotropie, f. allotropism, allotropy.

allotropisch, allotropic.

Alloxurbase, f. alloxur base, purine base.

Allozimtsäure, f. allocinnamic acid.

allseitig, on all sides, universal, versatile; **~ symmetrisch,** homaxonic.

All-seitlage, f. ability to present any surface; **-seitwendig,** multilateral; **-täglich,** daily, commonplace; **-umfassend,** all-embracing; **-verbreitet,** widespread, widely distributed; **-wissend,** omniscient; **-wöchentlich,** weekly.

Allyljodid, n. allyl iodide.

All-zeichner, m. pantograph; **-zeugung,** f. pangenesis.

allzu . . . , much too . . . ; **-mal,** altogether; **-meist,** all too frequently; **-viel,** too much.

Alm, f. alpine pasture.

Alm, n. aluminum.

Almanach, m. almanac.

Almenrausch, m. alpine rose (Rhododendron).

Almosen, n. alms.

Aloe, f. aloe(s); **-haltig,** alvetic; **-hanf,** m. aloe hemp; **-tinsäure,** f. alvetic acid.

Alpaka, n. alpaca (an alloy), alpax.

Alpdrücken, n. nightmare.

Alpen-aster, f. alpine aster (Aster alpinus); **-glöckchen,** n. alpine soldanel (Soldanella alpina); **-glühen,** n. alpenglow; **-nelke,** f. alpine pink (Dianthus alpinus); **-rebe,** f. alpine clematis (Clematis alpina); **-rose,** f. alpine rose (Rhododendron).

Alpen-salamander (schwarzer), Alpine salamander (Salamandra atra); **-sinau,** m. alpine alchemil (Alchemilla alpina); **-stock,** m. climbing pole; **-veilchen,** n. cyclamen; **-vorland,** n. foothills of the Alps.

alphabetisch, alphabetical.

Alphamilchsäure, f. α lactic acid.

Alpranken, f.pl. bittersweet (Solanum dulcamara).

Alquifoux, n. alquifou, potter's lead.

Alraun, m. mandrake; **-wurzel,** f. Atropa mandragora.

als, when, than, as, like, for, but; **-bald,** immediately; **-dann,** then, thereupon; **~ ob, ~ wenn,** as if, as though; **sowohl . . . ~ auch,** as well . . . as.

also, thus, therefore, consequently, accordingly, and so.

alt, old, aged, ancient; **-bekannt,** long known, well known; **-bewährt,** approved, well tested; **-angesehen,** old and respected.

Altar, m.-e, altar.

altbacken, stale.

Alte, f. old woman.

Alteisen, n. scrap iron, junk.

Alter, m. old man.

Alter, n. (old) age.

älter, older.

Alterantia, n.pl. alterative.

alterfahren, old, experienced.

alterieren, to alter, excite.

altern, to age, grow old, season.

Alternative, f. alternative.

alternieren, to alternate.

alternierend, alternating, alternate.

alters, seit ~ her, since olden times.

Alters-abstufung, f. age gradation; **-bestimmung,** f. determination of age; **-entartung,** f. senile decay, degeneration; **-erscheinung,** f. appearance or manifestation of age; **-folge,** f. order of succession, seniority.

Alters-genosse, *f.* contemporary; **-schwach,** decrepit; **-schwäche,** *f.* senility, decrepitude; **-stufe,** *f.* stage or order of age; **-tod,** *m.* death due to age; **-veränderung,** *f.* senile change; **-vorsprung,** *m.* start in age.

Altertum, *n.* "er, antiquity.

altertümlich, ancient, antique.

Altertums-forscher, *m.***-,** archaeologist; **-kunde,** *f.* archaeology.

Alterung, *f.* aging, seasoning.

Alterungshärtung, *f.* hardening caused by age.

ältest, oldest.

Althee, *f.* marsh mallow; **-wurzel,** *f.* althaca.

althiebiges Holz, *n.* old growth, mature timber.

Altholz, *n.* mature timber; **-bestand,** *m* stand of mature timber; **-stamm,** *m.* veteran tree.

altklug, precocious.

Altkultur, *f.* aging culture.

ältlich, elderly.

Altmalz, *n.* old malt.

altmodisch, old-fashioned.

Altpapier, *n.* waste paper.

Alttier, *n.* hind.

Altwasser, *n.* old bed of a river; **-fauna,** *f.* fauna of old river bed.

Altweibersommer, *m.* Indian summer.

Aluchiharz, *n.* aluchi (aconchi) resin.

Aluminium, *n.* aluminum; **-draht,** *m.* aluminum wire; **-halter,** *m.* aluminum holder; **-haltig,** containing aluminum; **-hydrat,** **-hydroxyd,** *n.* aluminum hydroxide (hydrate); **-kaliumsulfat,** *n.* aluminum potassium sulphate; **-legierung,** *f.* aluminum alloy.

Aluminothermie, *f.* aluminothermics.

Alunit, *m.* alunite.

Alveolar-gang, *m.* alveolar duct, passage; **-schicht,** *f.* alveolar layer.

am (an dem), at the, on the, to the; ∼ **besten,** (at) best.

amalgamieren, to amalgamate.

Amalgamierwerk, *n.* amalgamating mill.

Amarant, *m.* amaranth; **-holz,** *n.* purplewood.

Amateur, *m.* amateur.

Amazonenstein, *m.* amazonite.

Amber, *m.* amber; **-baum,** *m.* sweet gum (*Liquidambar styraciflua*); **-fett, -harz,** *n.*

ambreine; **-kraut,** *n.* cat thyme (*Teucrium marum*).

Amboss, *m.* incus, anvil; **-bucht,** *f.* incudal fossa; **-falte,** *f.* incudal fold; **-stiel,** *m.* process of incus.

Ambra, *m.f.n.* amber; **gelber** ∼, ordinary amber; **grauer** ∼, ambergris.

Ambra-fett, *n.* ambrein; **-holz,** *n.* yellow sandalwood.

Ambrosia, *f.* ambrosia.

Ambulacral-felder, *n.pl.* ambulacra; **-füsschen,** *n.pl.* ambulacral feet, tube feet; **-gefässystem,** *n.* ambulacral system.

ambulant, itinerant, moving about.

Ambulanz, *f.* ambulance.

Ameisen, *f.pl.* ants; **-aldehyd,** *n.* formaldehyde; **-äther,** *m.* formic ether, ethyl formate; **-bär,** *m.* anteater; **-ei,** *n.* ant's egg; **-fresser,** *m.* anteater; **-haufen,** *m.* ant hill; **-löwe,** *m.* ant lion (Myrmeleon); **-pflanze,** *f.* ant plant, plant harboring ants; **-geist,** *m.* **-spiritus,** *m.* spirit of ants.

Ameisen-säure, *f.* formic acid; **ameisensaures Natrium.** **-Natron,** *n.* sodium formate.

Ametall, *n.* nonmetal.

Amethyst, *m.* amethyst.

Amiant, *m.* amianthus; **-artig,** amiantine.

Amid, *n.***-e,** amide; **-gruppe,** *f.* amido group.

amidieren, to amidate.

Aminierung, *f.* amination.

Amido-, amino-.

Amidsäure, *f.* amid (amic) acid.

aminartig, aminelike.

Aminosäure, *f.* amino acid.

Aminsäure, *f.* amino (amic) acid.

Amme, *f.* nurse, asexual organism.

Ammen-generation, *f.* asexual generation; **-zeugung,** *f.* asexual reproduction.

Ammer, *f.* bunting, yellowhammer.

Ammon, *m.* ammonia.

Ammoniak, *n.* ammonia; **-alaun,** *n.* ammonia alum.

ammoniakalisch, ammoniacal.

ammoniakbindend, combining with ammonia.

ammoniakhaltig, ammoniacal.

Ammoniak-salpeter, *m.* ammonium nitrate; **-weinstein,** *m.* ammoniated potassium tartrate.

Ammonium-chlorid, *n.* ammonium chloride; **-karbonat,** *n.* ammonium carbonate; **-rest,**

m. ammonium radical; **-sulfhydrat,** *n.* ammonium hydrosulphide; **verbindung,** *f.* ammonium compound.

Ammon-salpeter, *m.* ammonium nitrate; **-salze,** *n.pl.* salts of ammonium.

Ammonshorn, *n.* ammonite.

Ammon-sulfatsalpeter, *m.* ammonium sulphate nitrate.

Amniossäure, *f.* amniotic acid, allantoin.

Amöbe, *f. (pl.* Amöben) amoeba.

Amöbina, *f.* amoeba (a protozoan).

amorph, amorphous.

Ampel, *f.* hanging lamp.

Amperemeter, *m. & n.* ammeter.

Ampfer, *m.* dock, sorrel.

Amphibie, *f.* amphibium.

Amphibienschnecken, *f.pl.* Succineidae.

Ampulle, *f.* ampulla, phial, ampoule.

amputieren, to amputate.

Amsel, *f.* blackbird, ouzel (*Turdus merula*).

Amstelkraut, *n.* meadow rue (*Thalictrum aquilegifolium*).

Amt, *n.:-*er, office, appointment, post, service, board, court; **ein ~ versehen,** to officiate; **ein ~ bekleiden,** to hold an office.

amtieren, to hold office.

amtlich, official.

Amtmann, *m.:-*er, magistrate.

Amts-blatt, *n.:-*er, official gazette; **-führung,** *f.* administration; **-handlung,** *f.* official act.

amüsant, amusing.

müsieren, to amuse.

myl-acetat, *n.* amyl acetate; **-alkohol,** *m.* **oxydhydrat,** *n.* amyl alcohol.

Amylolyse, *f.* amylolysis.

an, at, on, against, as far as, up to, by, along, near to, about, in respect to, by way of; **~ sich, ~ und für sich,** in itself, in themselves.

anaerob, anaerobic.

Anaeroben, *pl.* anaerobic bacteria; **-kolben,** *m.* anaerobic flask; **-kultur,** *f.* culture of anaerobes; **-züchtung,** *f.* culture of anaerobes.

Anal-ader, *f.* anal vein; **-anhang,** *m.* anal appendage; **-drüse,** *f.* anal gland; **-fach,** *n.* anal cell (of wing); **-feld,** *n.* anal field; **-gegend,** *f.* anal region; **-gelenkstücke,** *n.pl.* pteralia.

analog, analogous, similar.

Analogie, *f.* analogy, similarity.

Analphabet, *m.* illiterate.

Analrand, *m.* anal rim.

Analysator, *m.* analyzer.

Analyse, *f.* analysis.

analysen-fertig, ready for analysis; **-formel,** *f.* empirical formula; **-gang,** *m.* course of analysis; **-gewicht,** *n.* analytical weight; **-trichter,** *m.* analytical funnel; **-waage,** *f.* analytical balance.

analysieren, to analyze.

Analytiker, *m.* analyst.

analytisch, analytical.

Anämie, anemia.

Ananas, *f.* pineapple; **-galle,** *f.* pineapple-like gall (from Chermes).

Anaphylaxe, *f.* anaphylaxis.

anarbeiten, to join, add to; **gegen jemand ~,** to counteract, oppose.

Anästhesie, *f.* anesthesia.

anästhetisch, anesthetic.

Anatas, *m.* anatase, octahedrite.

Anatom, *m.* anatomist.

Anatomie, *f.* anatomy.

anatomisch, anatomical.

anätzen, to corrode superficially.

anbacken, to bake on, bake slightly, stick on, adhere.

anbahnen, to pave (prepare) the way for.

Anbau, *m.-e,* cultivation, culture, addition (to building), colony, settlement.

anbauen, to grow, cultivate, build on, add.

Anbau-fähigkeit, *f.* possibility of cultivation; **-gebiet,** *n.* area for cultivation; **-stoffwechsel,** anabolism; **-wert,** *m.* cultivation value; **-würdigkeit,** *f.* worthiness of cultivation.

Anbeginn, *m.* first beginning; **von ~,** from the (very) first.

anbehalten, to keep on.

anbei, herewith.

anbeissen, to bite at.

anbeizen, to mordant.

anbelangen, to concern, relate to.

anbellen, to bark at.

anbequemen, sich, to accommodate oneself to, adapt oneself.

anberaumen, to appoint, assign (a date).

anbeten, to adore, worship.

Anbetracht, *m.* consideration; **in ~ des,** considering the.

anbetreffen, to concern.

anbieten, to offer, tender.

anbinden, to tie, bind.

anblaken, to blacken.

anblasen, to blow at, turn on the blast, start up, affix to.

anbläuen, to blue, color blue.

Anblick, *m.* sight, aspect, view, contemplation.

anblicken, to look at.

anbluten, to bleed, run (of colors).

Anbohrapparat, *m.* boring rig, drill rig.

anbohren, to begin to bore, drill, perforate.

anbräunen, to brown.

anbrechen, to open, broach, begin, dawn.

anbrennen, to catch fire, begin to burn, scorch, set fire to.

anbringen, to put, place, employ, install, attach, bring about, fit, establish, mount, fix, dispose of, sell, lodge a complaint; **angebracht,** fitting, suitable.

Anbruch, *m.*-e, decay, fracture, daybreak.

anbrüchig, decaying, putrescent, spoiled, rotten.

Anbrüchigkeit, *f.* rottenness, putridity, putrescence.

anbrühen, to scald, infuse, steep.

Anchovis, *f.* anchovy.

Anchusasäure, *f.* anchusic acid.

Andacht, *f.* devotion.

andächtig, devout, attentive.

andampfen, to precipitate by evaporation.

andauern, to last, continue.

andauernd, lasting, continuous, steady, permanent.

Andenken, *m.*-, remembrance, memory.

Andentanne, *f.* araucaria.

ander, other, another, different, else, second, next; **alles andere,** everything else; **ein anderer,** somebody else; **nichts anderes als,** nothing but; **unter anderem,** among other things.

anderartig, different, heterogeneous.

änderbar, changeable.

Änderbarkeit, *f.* changeability.

andererseits, otherwise.

ändern, to change, alter, rectify, amend.

andern-falls, else, otherwise; **-orts,** elsewhere; **-teils,** on the other hand.

anders, otherwise, differently; **wenn ~,** if indeed, provided that; **wenn ~ nicht,** unless; **~ artig,** differently.

andersdenkend, dissenting.

anderseits, on the other hand, moreover.

Anders-sein, *n.* difference, being different, deviation; **wertig,** of another valence; **-wo,** elsewhere; **-woher,** from elsewhere; **-wohin,** to some other place.

anderthalb, sesqui-, one and a half; **-fach,** one and a half times.

Änderung, *f.* change, alteration, improvement, amendment, correction.

Änderungsgeschwindigkeit, *f.* speed, rate of change.

anderwärts, elsewhere.

anderweitig, in another place or way, otherwise.

andeuten, to indicate, intimate, suggest, signify, hint, imply.

Andeutung, *f.* indication.

andeutungsweise, by way of suggestion.

Andorn, *m.* horehound (*Marrubium vulgare*).

andorren, to adhere to in drying.

Andrang, *m.* rush, crowd, congestion.

andrehen, to turn on, twist on, screw on.

Andrehkurbel, *f.* starting handle.

andringen, to press, rush.

andrücken, to press on or against.

andunkeln, to darken, begin to grow dark.

aneignen, to acquire, appropriate, assimilate.

aneinander, on each other, together; **-fügen,** to join; **-lagerung,** *f.* apposition (side by side), arrangement, juxtaposition; **-liegend,** accumbent, lying against one another; **-schliessen,** to join.

anekeln, to disgust.

aneliotrop, nonsensitive to light.

Anemone, *f.* wood anemone.

Anemonin, *n.* anemonine.

Anemonkampfer, *m.* anemonine.

anempfehlen, to recommend.

anerbieten, to offer, tender.

anerkannt, acknowledged.

anerkennbar, recognizable.

anerkennen, to acknowledge, recognize, admit, appreciate, accept.

anerkennenswert, worthy of appreciation.

Anerkennung, *f.* recognition, appreciation.

Aneth, *n.* dill, anethum.

Anethol, *n.* anethol, anis camphor.

anfächeln, to fan.

anfachen, to blow, kindle, fan.

anfahren, to carry to, run against, approach, arrive, rebuke, address angrily, snub, start, speed up, set in motion.

Anfahren, *n.* start.

Anfahrt, *f.* arrival.

Anfall, *m.*ᵉe, attack, fit, stroke, thrust, amount collected, revenue, yield.

anfallen, to fall, assail, attack, accumulate in falling, result, be given off, accrue, yield, obtain.

anfallend, aggressive.

anfällig, contagious, susceptible.

Anfälligkeit, *f.* susceptibility.

Anfang, *m.*ᵉe, beginning, origin, outset.

anfangen, to begin, commence, do; (ein Produkt) **mit dem er nichts anzufangen wusste,** with which he could do nothing.

Anfänger, *m.*-, beginner.

anfänglich, incipient, initial, original.

anfangs, at the beginning, originally, in initial condition, at first.

Anfangs-buchstabe, *m.* initial, capital (letter); **-darm,** *m.* embryonic intestinal tract; **-geschwindigkeit,** *f.* initial velocity; **-gesellschaften,** *f.pl.* initial stages of associations; **-gründe,** *m.pl.* elements, rudiments; **-kammer,** *f.* primordial or initial chamber; **-punkt,** *m.* starting point; **-spannung,** *f.* initial voltage, initial strain; **-teil,** *m.* base or lamella; **-wachstum,** *n.* early growth, initial growth; **-zustand,** *m.* initial state, original condition.

Anfärbbarkeit, *f.* dye affinity, dye adsorption.

anfärben, to color, tinge, dye.

Anfärb(e)vermögen, *n.* dye affinity, dye adsorption.

anfassen, to seize, handle.

anfaulen, to begin to rot.

Anfaulen, *n.* incipient decay, putrescence.

anfaulend, putrescent.

anfechtbar, contestable, vulnerable.

anfechten, to combat, attack, disturb.

anfertigen, to make, manufacture, (ready) prepare.

Anfertigung, *f.* making, manufacture, production, composition, preparation, parcel.

anfetten, to grease.

anfeuchten, to moisten, damp, wet.

Anfeuchtung, *f.* damping, wetting.

anfeuern, to light, fire, prime, inflame, incite, excite.

Anfeuerung, *f.* lighting, priming.

anfing (anfangen), began.

anfirnissen, to varnish.

anflehen, to implore, supplicate.

anflicken, to patch on.

anfliegen, to fly on, effloresce, spring up spontaneously; **angeflogen,** incrusted.

Anflug, *m.*ᵉe, approach, incrustation, film, coating, efflorescence, copse, tinge, flyspeck, superficial layer, slight attack, smattering, flying (against), young wood, seeds disseminated by wind.

Anflugstelle, *f.* landing place (of insects).

Anfluss, *m.* onflow, alluvium, afflux.

anfordern, to demand, require, claim.

Anforderung, *f.* claim, demand, requirement; ~ **stellen,** to set a requirement (standard).

Anfrage, *f.*-n, inquiry, demand.

anfragen, to inquire.

Anfrass, *m.* superficial corrosion, pitting, staining.

anfressen, to corrode, eat at, attack.

Anfressung, *f.* corrosion, erosion, attack.

anfrieren, to freeze on.

anfrischen, to freshen, refresh, revive, animate, reduce, varnish.

Anfrischherd, *m.* refining furnace.

Anfrischung, *f.* freshening.

anfügen, to join, attach, annex, affix.

anfühlen, to feel, touch, handle.

Anfuhr, *f.* conveying, supply, transporting.

anführen, to lead, adduce, advance, quote, mention, delude, deceive; **sich** ~ **lassen,** to be made a dupe of.

Anführer, *m.* leader.

Anführung, *f.* leadership, quotation, allegation.

Anführungszeichen, *n.pl.* quotation marks.

anfüllen, to fill (up).

Angabe, *f.* declaration, statement, information, indication, estimate, specification.

Angaben, *pl.* data, details.

angängig, admissible, feasible, practicable.

angänglich, admissible, feasible, practicable, specifiable, determinable.

angeätzt, slightly corroded.

angebbar, that can be estimated, assignable.

angeben, to state, declare, quote, tell, specify, indicate, accuse, yield, give.

angeblich, as stated, alleged.

angeboren, inborn, congenital, innate.

Angebot, *n.* offer, bid, supply, quotation.

angebracht (anbringen), applicable, fitting, well timed, timely, suitable, arranged; ~ **sein,** to be in place.

angebrannt (anbrennen), burnt, fire scarred, scorched.

angebunden (anbinden), tied up; **kurz** ~ **sein,** to be blunt, abrupt.

angedeihen lassen, to grant, give.

angedrückt, appressed, adpressed, squeezed.

angefasst (anfassen), treated, tackled.

angefeuchtet, moistened, humidified.

angeflogen (anfliegen), self-sown, spontaneous (growth), incrusted, covered with a film.

angefressen, superficially corroded.

angeführt, cited, imposed upon, led.

angegangen (angehen), slightly decayed or putrid.

angeglüht, brought to red heat.

angegriffen (angreifen), attacked, corroded, affected; ~ **aussehen,** to look poor.

Angehäufe, *n.* heap, aggregate.

angeheitert, tipsy.

angehen, to begin, take root, catch fire, decay, attack, be feasible, approach, con cern; **soweit es angeht,** as far as it is possible; **das geht an,** that will do.

angehender Baum, young tree.

angehören, to belong (to), (ap)pertain (to), be related (to), be classified among.

angehörig, (*dat.*) belonging, related.

Angehörige, -n, *pl.* relatives, relations.

Angel, *f.*-n, cardo, hinge, fishhook, pivot.

angelagert, attached.

angelangen, to arrive.

angelassen, annealed.

angelaufen, coated, tarnished.

Angelborste, *f.* glochidium.

angelegen (anliegen), adjacent, important; **sich etwas** ~ **sein lassen,** to interest oneself in something.

Angelegenheit, *f.* concern, affair, matter.

angelegentlich, earnest, urgent, pressing.

Angelglied, *n.* cardo (maxilla), the first joint of the maxilla.

Angelhaken, *m.* fishhook.

Angelika, *f.* angelica.

Angelikasäure, *f.* angelic acid.

angeln, to fish.

Angelpunkt, *m.* pivot, cardinal point.

Angelschnur, *f.* fishing line.

Angelstück, *n.* cardo (maxilla).

angemessen, (*dat.*) appropriate, suitable, adequate, proper.

angenähert, approached, drawn near, approximate.

angenehm, (*dat.*) pleasant, agreeable, desirable.

angenommen (annehmen), assumed, fictitious.

angeordnet, arranged.

angepasst, adapted, adjusted, appropriate.

Angepasstsein, *n.* adaptation.

Anger, *m.* lawn, meadow, pasture ground.

angereichert, enriched, concentrated.

angesammelt, accumulated.

angesäuert, acidified.

angeschimmelt, grown moldy.

angeschmolzen (anschmelzen), fused, welded.

angeschwemmt, alluvial.

angesehen, distinguished, prominent, esteemed, respected.

angesessen (sitzen), settled, resident.

angesetzt, attached.

Angesicht, *n.*-er, face, countenance; **von** ~, by sight; **von** ~ **zu** ~, face to face.

angesichts, in the face of, considering.

angespült, alluvial.

angestammt, hereditary.

Angestellte(r), *m.* employee, official.

angestrengt, intense, strenuous.

angetrieben (antreiben), worked, moved.

angetroffen (antreffen), met, found.

angetrunken, tipsy.

angewachsen, coherent, adnate.

angewandt (anwenden), applied, employed, practical.

angewiesen, dependent on, assigned, pointed out, referred to.

angewöhnen, to accustom; **sich** ∼, to become accustomed to.

angezeigt, indicated, advisable.

angezogen (anziehen), attracted, drawn.

angiessen, to pour on, cast on, moisten.

angleichen, to assimilate.

angliedern, to attach, join on, append.

Angliederung, *f.* annexing, affiliation, linkage, articulation, coalition.

anglühen, to begin to glow.

angreifbar, attackable, assailable.

Angreifbarkeit, *f.* attackability, effectiveness.

angreifen, to attack, corrode, seize on, act on, affect, touch, be attached, strain, fatigue; **angegriffen aussehen,** to look poor.

Angreifer, *m.* aggressor.

angrenzen, to border on, adjoin.

angrenzend, adjacent, adjoining.

Angrenzer, *m.* neighbor.

Angriff, *m.*-e, attack, action, corrosion, assault, undertaking, handling; **in** ∼ **nehmen,** to take in hand, attend to, begin, tackle.

Angriffs-einrichtung, *f.* adaptation for defense; **-punkt,** *m.* point of attack or application, working point; **-stelle,** *f.* point of application; **-stellung,** *f.* position, posture (ready for attack); **-tüchtigkeit,** *f.* pathogenicity, virulence; **-waffe,** *f.* weapon for offense; **-weise,** aggressively, by way of attack.

angrinsen, to grin at.

Angst, *f.*ᵉe, anxiety, fright.

ängstigen, to alarm, frighten; **sich** ∼, to be alarmed.

ängstlich, anxious, uneasy, scrupulous.

Ängstlichkeit, *f.* anxiety.

Angstschweiss, *m.* cold sweat.

angstvoll, fearful.

Anguss, *m.* any appendage on casting, sullage piece, feeding head, pouring on; **-farbe,** *f.* colored glazing clay.

anhaben, to have on; **jemanden etwas** ∼, to find something against someone.

anhaften, (*dat.*) to adhere, stick, accompany.

anhaken, to hook on.

Anhalt, *m.* basis, support, hold, pause.

anhalten, to stop, hold, stay, halt, encourage, urge, check, persist, endure, continue.

anhaltend, continuous, persistent, lasting.

Anhaltspunkt, *m.*-e, stopping point, station, essential point, evidence, criterion, clue; **keinen** ∼ **liefern,** to afford no clue.

Anhaltungsmittel, *n.* astringent, remedy.

Anhang, *m.*ᵉe, addition, appendage, supplement, followers, apophysis, appendix.

anhangen, to hang on, adhere.

anhängen, to append, tag, attach, add.

anhangend, adhering, adhesive.

Anhänger, *m.*-, follower, adherent, appendage, tag.

Anhängewagen, *m.* trailer.

anhängig, adhering, annexed.

anhänglich, attached, devoted.

Anhänglichkeit, *f.* attachment, affection.

Anhangsdrüse, *f.* appendicular gland.

Anhängsel, *n.*-, appendage.

Anhangs-gebilde, *n.* appendage; **-kraft,** *f.* adhesive force; **-leiste,** *f.* appendicular ridge; **-muskel,** *m.* suspensor muscle; **-teil,** *m.* base, proximal portion of barbule.

Anhau, *m.* the first cutting of wood in a forest.

Anhauch, *m.*-e, breathing on, afflation.

anhauchen, to breathe upon, tinge.

anhauen, to make the first cut.

anhäufen, to accumulate, aggregate, heap up.

Anhäufung, *f.* accumulation, aggregation, infiltration, agglomeration, cluster.

anheben, to begin, lift, raise, hoist.

anheften, to fasten to, attach, affix.

Anheftungs-linie, *f.* line of junction; **-punkt,** *m.* point of attachment; **-stelle,** *f.* place of attachment; **-stiel,** *m.* peduncle of attachment; **-trieb,** *m.* stereotropism, a definite direction toward the substratum (Loeb).

anheilen, to heal on.

anheimeln, to remind of home.

anheim-fallen, to fall to, devolve (on); **-geben,** to submit, suggest; **-stellen,** to suggest, submit, leave to a person.

anheischig, pledged, bound.

anheizen, to begin to heat, heat up.

anher, hither(to).

Anhieb, *m.*-e, first cutting, first blow.

Anhöhe, *f.*-n, elevation, hill, rising ground.

anhören, to listen to, hear.

Anhub, *m.* lift.

Anhubsmoment, *n.* initial stroke, upstroke.

anhydrisch, anhydrous.

anhydrisieren, to render anhydrous, dehydrate.

Anhydrisierungsmittel, *n.* dehydrating agent.

Anhydroxyd, *n.* anhydride, anhydrous oxide.

Anilid, *n.*-e, anilide.

Anilin, *n.* aniline; **-dampf,** *m.* aniline vapor; **-farbe,** *f.* aniline color, dye; **-farbstoff,** *m.* aniline dye; **-vergiftung,** *f.* aniline poisoning.

animalisch, animal.

Anime-gummi, -harz, *n.* animé gum, animé resin.

animieren, to animate.

Animosität, *f.* animosity.

Anion, *n.* anion.

Anis, *m.* anise, aniseed; **-geist,** *m.* spirit of anise; **-kerbel,** *m.* sweet cicely; **-ol,** *n.* anisol, anise oil; **-öl,** *n.* aniseed oil; **-samen,** *m.* aniseed; **-säure,** *f.* anisic acid.

anklammern, to cling to, attach to, by means of clips.

anisotropisch, anisotropic.

ankämpfen (gegen etwas), to struggle (against something).

Ankauf, *m.*⁼e, purchase, buying.

ankaufen, to buy.

Ankaufspreis, *m.*-e, purchase price, cost.

Anker, *m.*-, anchor, armature; **-förmig,** anchor-shaped; **-haar,** *m.* anchor hair; **-klette,** *f.* bur with attachments for anchoring; **-platte,** *f.* anchor plate, tie plate; **-spule,** *f.* armature coil; **-strom,** *m.* armature current; **-welle,** *f.* armature shaft; **-wicklung,** *f.* armature winding.

ankern, to anchor.

Ankerspannung, *f.* armature voltage.

anketten, to chain.

ankitten, to fasten with cement, cement.

anklagen, to accuse, charge.

Anklang, *m.* accord, approval.

ankleben, to stick on, glue on, paste on, agglutinate, adhere.

anklebend, adhesive, agglutinative.

ankleiden, to dress.

anklingeln, to call by telephone.

anklopfen, to knock.

anknöpfen, to button.

anknüpfen, to fasten, knot, join, connect, enter into, start from, pursue (a discussion), touch upon.

Anknüpfungspunkt, *m.*-e, point of contact, starting point.

ankochen, to begin to boil.

ankohlen, to char partly.

ankommen, to arrive, approach, succeed, commence fermenting, be important, depend; **es kommt darauf an,** it is of importance, the question is, it depends on; **bei etwas gut ∼,** to come off well.

Ankömmling, *m.*-e, arrival, newcomer, invader, new product.

ankörnen, to center punch.

ankreiden, to chalk up.

Ankultur, *f.* young culture.

ankünden, to announce, publish.

ankündigen, to announce, publish.

Ankündigung, *f.* announcement, notification, prospectus.

Ankunft, *f.*⁼e, arrival.

ankuppeln, to couple (on).

ankurbeln, to crank, put into gear, start.

Anlage, *f.* establishment, installation, enclosure, plant, construction, outline, arrangement, investment, tax, attached paper, tendency, primordium, rudiment, character, meristem, "Anlage," putting on, laying on, predisposition, aptitude, talent; **∼ zu etwas haben,** to be predisposed to, have talent for.

Anlagen, *f.pl.* park; **-kombination,** *f.* combination of tendencies; **-kosten,** *f.pl.* installation expense; **-umordnung,** *f.* rearrangement of "Anlagen" (hereditary factors).

anlagern, to accumulate, heap up, attach.

Anlagerung, *f.* accumulation, apposition, association, deposit, addition.

Anlagerungsverbindung, *f.* addition compound.

Anlage-substanz, *f.* basic substance; **-teil,** *n.* equipment; **-teilchen,** *n.* basic particle; **-typus,** *m.* genotype.

anlangen, to arrive, concern.

anlangend, concerning, as for.

anlaschen, to blaze (a tree), lash.

Anlass, *m.*⁼e, occasion, motive, inducement, cause, starting; **∼ geben,** to occasion, cause, give rise to; **allen ∼ dazu haben,** to have every reason for.

anlassen, to start up, let in, anneal, temper, draw, turn on, appear, put on.

Anlasser, *m.* starter.

Anlass-farbe, *f.* tempering color, oxidation tint; **-kurve,** *f.* annealing curve.

anlässlich, occasionally, on the occasion of.

Anlasswirkung, *f.* annealing effect, temper (drawing) effect.

Anlauf, *m.*ᴗe, swelling, slope, incline, batter, start, onset, run, attack, crowd, tarnish.

anlaufen, to begin to run, become coated, moldy, tarnish, swell, increase, start, crowd.

Anlauf-farbe, *f.* tempering color (tarnish); **-rad,** *n.* landing wheel.

anlegen, to apply, lay or put on, establish, invest, construct, put against, take aim, plot (curve).

Anlegung, *f.* application, inception, disposition, investment.

Anlegungsperiode, *f.* formative period.

Anlehen, *m.*-, loan.

anlehnen, to lean against, rest, find support, leave the door ajar.

Ahlehnung, *f.* leaning, support, leaning upon; **in ~ an,** depending on, with reference to.

Anleihe, *f.* loan.

anleimen, to glue on.

anleiten, to conduct, lead, guide, instruct.

Anleitung, *f.* conducting, guidance, instruction, introduction.

anlernen, to break in.

anliegen, to lie close, be adjacent, join, fit well, concern, entreat; **angelegen,** important, interesting.

Anliegen, *n.* request, wish.

anliegend, accumbent, appressed.

anlocken, to allure, entice.

Anlockungs-mittel, *m.* lure, decoy, bait; **-stellung,** *f.* position used to allure.

anlöten, to solder on.

anmachen, to attach, light (a fire), slake (lime), mix, temper, adulterate, fasten on; **irgend etwas ~,** to enrich anything, fasten something.

anmalen, to paint.

anmassen, to assume, usurp.

anmelden, to announce, advertise, declare, register.

Anmeldung, *f.* announcement, application.

anmengen, to mix, blend, temper.

anmerken, to note, write down, designate.

Anmerkung, *f.* remark, note, comment.

anmischen, to mix.

anmoorig, partly peat and partly mineral.

Anmut, *f.* grace, charm.

anmuten, (*dat.*) to demand, expect, ask, impute.

annähern, to approach, approximate, bring or draw near.

annähernd, approximate, approaching.

Annäherung, *f.* approximation, approach.

Annäherungs-grad, *m.* degree of approximation; **-weise,** approximately.

Annahme, *f.* acceptance, adoption, assumption, hypothesis, supposition; **alles spricht für die ~,** there is every indication to believe.

annässen, to moisten a little, dampen.

annehmbar, acceptable, reasonable.

annehmlich, acceptable, assumed.

Annehmlichkeit, *f.* comfort, convenience.

annehmen, to accept, assume, suppose, take, adopt, take up; **sich ~,** (*gen.*) to take charge; **angenommen,** assumed.

Annehmung, *f.* assumption.

annektieren, to annex.

annetzen, to moisten.

annieten, to rivet on.

Anno, in the year.

Annonce, *f.* advertisement.

annoncieren, to advertise, announce.

Anode, *f.* anode.

Anoden-batterie, *f.* B battery; **-spannung,** *f.* anode potential.

anölen, to oil, grease, lubricate.

anomal, anomalous.

Anon, *n.* cyclohexanone.

anonym, anonymous.

anordnen, to arrange, regulate, order.

Anordnung, *f.* arrangement, order, regulation, direction, instruction, pattern, layout, disposition; **räumliche ~,** configuration.

anorganisch, inorganic.

anormal, abnormal.

anoxydieren, to oxidize.

anpacken, to seize, grasp, take hold of.

anpassen, to adapt, fit, suit, adjust; **angepasst,** adjusted.

anpassend, suitable, fit.

Anpassung, *f.* adjustment, adaptation, accommodation; **biversale** ~, adaptation in two directions.

Anpassungs-erscheinung, *f.* adaptation phenomenon, mimicry; **-fähigkeit,** *f.* adaptability; **-gepräge,** *n.* adaptation stamp or feature; **-merkmal,** *n.* adaptive characteristic; **-notwendigkeit,** *f.* necessity for adaptation; **-produkt,** *n.* product of adaptation; **-vermögen,** *n.* adaptability; **-wechsel,** *m.* change in adaptation.

anpflanzen, to plant, cultivate.

Anpflanzung, *f.* planting, plantation, cultivation.

anpfropfen, to inoculate or graft on.

anpinseln, to daub.

anplätzen, to blaze (a tree).

anpochen, to knock.

Anprall, *m.* impact, contusion, collision.

anprallen, to strike or bound against.

anpreisen, to commend, extol, puff up, praise.

anprobieren, to try on.

anpudern, to powder.

anputzen, to dress up, decorate.

anquicken, to amalgamate.

Anquick-fass, *n.* amalgamating vat; **-silber,** *n.* amalgam of silver.

anranken, to fasten with tendrils.

anraten, to advise, recommend, counsel.

anrauchen, to (blacken with) smoke.

anräuchern, to fumigate.

Anräucherung, *f.* fumigation.

anrechnen, to charge, attribute, impute.

Anrecht, *n.* title, right, claim.

Anrede, *f.* address, speech.

anreden, to address, speak to.

anregbar, capable of being excited, stimulated.

anregen, to excite, stimulate, activate, interest, suggest, mention, incite, effect.

anregend, exciting, stimulating, interesting, inciting.

Anregung, *f.* stimulation, impulse, suggestion, excitation, progress; **auf** ~ **von,** at the instigation of.

Anregungs-mittel, *n.* stimulant; **-spanning,** *f.* excitation potential.

anreiben, to rub against, grind.

anreichern, to enrich, strengthen, concentrate, carburize.

Anreicherung, *f.* enrichment, concentration.

anreihen, to form in a row, arrange in a series, add.

anreissen, to begin to tear, cut into, trace, mark, draw, plot.

Anreiz, *m.* stimulus, impulse.

anreizen, to stimulate, instigate, irritate.

anrennen, to run against, attack.

anrichten, to prepare, perform, dress, produce, serve, cause.

Anrichter, *m.* assayer, dresser.

Anriss, *m.* crack, flaw, initial tear.

anrosten, to begin to rust.

anrücken, to approach.

Anruf, *m.*-e, telephone call, appeal.

anrufen, to call, call (ring) up, appeal to.

anrühren, to touch, stir, mix, grind.

anrussen, to cover with soot or carbon black.

ans (an das), to the.

Ansaatstärke, *f.* rate of seeding.

ansäen, to sow.

Ansage, *f.* announcement, notification.

ansagen, to announce.

ansalzen, to salt a little.

ansammeln, to collect, gather, accumulate.

Ansammlung, *f.* collection, accumulation, heap, crowd, aggregation, mass.

ansässig, resident; ~**sein,** to reside.

Ansatz, *m.*-e, deposit, appendage, apophysis, annex, tendency, expression, formulation, evolution, statement, charge, evaluation, equation, incrustation, sedimentary deposit, attachment, insertion, germ, spore (of a plant), epiphysis, setting of seed, ingredient, sediment; **seitlicher** ~, side arm.

Ansatz-bad, *n.*-er, initial bath; **-fähigkeit,** *f.* ability to set seed, take root; **-frei,** deposit-free, unincrusted; **-punkt,** *m.* starting point, point of insertion; **-rohr,** *n.* attached tube; **-schraube,** *f.* setscrew; **-stelle,** *f.* place of attachment; **-stück,** *n.* attached part.

ansäuern, to acidify, acidulate, leaven, sour.

Ansäuerung, *f.* acidification, acidulation.

Ansaugen, *n.* suction, adsorption.

Ansaug-heber, *m.* siphon; **-hub,** *m.* suction stroke; **-leitung,** *f.* induction manifold; **-rohr,** *n.* suction tube, induction pipe.

Ansaugung, *f.* suction, adsorption.

anschaffen, to supply, provide, purchase.

anschalmen, to blaze (a tree).

anschauen, to look at, view, contemplate.

anschaulich, clear, plain, evident, obvious.

Anschauung, *f.* mode of viewing, view, observation, perception, contemplation; zu der ~ kommen, to bring to the conclusion.

Anschauungs-material, *n.* illustrative material; -weise, *f.* point of view.

Anschein, *m.* appearance, semblance, likelihood, impression.

anscheinen, appear, shine upon.

anscheinend, apparent.

anschichten, to pile in layers, stratify.

anschicken, sich, to prepare, set about doing.

anschieben, to push, shove.

Anschieber, *m.* lengthening piece.

anschiessen, to shoot, rush, crystallize.

Anschiessgefäss, *n.* crystallizing vessel.

anschimmeln, to begin to mold.

anschirren, to harness.

Anschlag, *m.*⁼e, stroke, placard, estimate, poster, plan, plot, stop, valuation, price.

anschlagen, to strike at, mark, affix, estimate; die Nahrung schlägt an, the food agrees with.

anschlägig, ingenious.

Anschlag-wert, *m.*-e, estimated value; -winkel, *m.* back or try square.

anschlämmen, to elutriate, deposit, suspend, fill with mud.

anschleifen, to begin to grind, polish.

anschliessen, to fasten (on), attach, annex, connect, join, fit, conform (to), agree with, follow.

Anschluss, *m.*⁼e, joining, junction, connection, coupling, enclosure, annexation; -leiter, *m.* lead (terminal); -stück, *n.* nipple, gooseneck; -zelle, *f.* hypophysis.

anschmauchen, to smoke.

anschmelzen, to melt or fuse on, begin to melt.

anschmieden, to fasten by forging.

anschmiegen, to press closely, cling (to).

anschmieren, to besmear, adulterate, cheat.

anschmutzen, to soil.

anschnallen, to buckle on.

Anschnallgurt, *m.* safety belt.

anschneiden, to begin to cut, start, spot (a surface), raise (a question), notch.

Anschnitt, *m.* first cut, chamfer, bevel.

anschoppen, to choke, obstruct, stop up.

Anschovis, *f.* anchovy.

anschrauben, to screw on, bolt on.

anschreiben, to write down, note down; ~ lassen, to take on credit.

anschreien, to call at, cry at.

Anschrift, *f.* address.

anschüren, to stir up, kindle.

Anschuss, *m.*⁼e, crystallization.

anschütten, to pour against, store up, fill up

anschwängern, to saturate, impregnate.

Anschwängerung, *f.* impregnation.

anschwänzen, to sprinkle, sparge; die Treber ~, to sparge the draff.

anschwärmen, to begin to swarm.

anschwärzen, to blacken, slander.

anschwefeln, to fumigate with sulphur.

anschweissen, to weld on.

anschwellen, to swell (up or out), increase.

Anschwellung, *f.* swelling, tumor, intumescence.

anschwemmen, to float on, deposit.

anschwöden, to paint (hides) with lime.

ansehen, to look at, face, view, regard, consider; angesehen, prominent.

Ansehen, *n.* appearance, exterior, reputation.

ansehnlich, handsome, considerable, important, conspicuous.

ansetzbar, attachable.

ansetzen, to crystallize, be deposited, set on, incrustate, apply, attach, prepare, mix, form, produce, establish, try, join, fasten, lay on, granulate, build up.

Ansetzung, *f.* application, crystallization.

Ansetzungsstelle, *f.* place of attachment.

Ansicht, *f.*-en, view, inspection, opinion, look-down (paper); sich einer ~ anschliessen, to agree with an opinion.

ansichtig werden, (*gen.*) to catch sight of.

ansiedeln, to colonize, settle.

ansieden, to boil, scorify, blanch, taw, mordant.

Ansiede-probe, *f.* scorification test; -scherben, *m.* scorifier.

Ansiedler, *m.* epoikophyte, settler, colonist.

ansinnen, to expect, demand of.

ansintern, to sinter, form stalactites.

ansitzen, to be attached to.

anspannen, to strain, stretch, hitch.

Anspanner, *m.* tensor muscle.

Anspannung, *f.* tension, strain, exertion.

anspielen, to begin to play, hint, allude.

Anspielung, *f.* reference.

anspinnen, to enclose (in a cocoon), contrive, plot, string up.

Anspinnwalze, *f.* doffing (waste) roller.

anspitzen, to point, sharpen.

Ansporn, *m.* incitement, spur.

anspornen, to incite, to spur.

Ansprache, *f.* address, speech.

ansprechen, to speak to, address, beg, ask for, claim, compute, accost, request, call; ~ **als,** to mention as.

ansprechend, pleasing.

anspritzen, to besprinkle.

Anspruch, *m.*⸚e, claim, demand, consideration, application, pretension; in ~ **nehmen,** to engage, engross, claim, require.

anspruchs-los, unassuming, unpretending; **-losigkeit,** *f.* unpretentiousness; **-voll,** pretentious, exacting, assuming.

anspülen, to wash, deposit.

anstählen, to steel, point with steel.

Anstalt, *f.***-en,** preparation, arrangement, institution, establishment, plant.

Anstand, *m.* behavior, propriety, delay, hesitation, stand.

anständig, becoming, decent, suitable, presentable, proper.

Anständigkeit, *f.* decency, propriety.

anstandshalber, for decency's sake.

anstandslos, unhesitating.

anstarren, to stare at.

anstatt, instead of.

anstäuben, to cover with dust, powder.

anstauchen, to upset.

anstaunen, to gaze at.

Anstauung, *f.* swell, damming up (of water).

anstechen, to pierce, puncture, open, to tap (a vessel).

anstecken, to fasten, infect, stick on, light (fire), communicate (disease).

ansteckend, infectious, contagious.

Ansteckung, *f.* infection, contagion.

Ansteckungs-quelle, *f.* source of infection; **-stoff,** *m.* virus, infectious matter; **-vermögen,** *n.* pathogenicity.

anstehen, to be contiguous, near or next, be becoming, be deferred, hesitate, crop out.

anstehend, cropping out, occurring; **anstehender Talk,** *m.* naturally occurring talc; **anstehendes Gestein,** *n.* solid rock.

ansteigen, to mount, rise, ascend, increase.

Anstellbottich, *m.* starting tub (brewing).

anstellen, to appoint, institute, perform, make, install, start, prepare, pitch, employ.

anstellen, sich, behave, pretend.

Anstellen, *n.* opening.

Ansteller, *m.* employer.

anstellbar, adjustable.

Anstellhefe, *f.* starting yeast.

anstellig, skillful, handy.

Anstell-temperatur, *f.* pitching (starting) temperature; **-winkel,** *m.* angle of attack.

Anstellung, *f.* appointment, placing, position.

Anstich, *m.* worm bite (of fruit), canker, broaching (of cask); **-methode,** *f.* puncture method.

Anstieg, *m.***-e,** ascent, rise, increase.

anstieren, to stare at.

anstiften, to cause, provoke, instigate.

anstocken, to become moldy.

Anstoss, *m.*⸚e, shock, collision, impulse, impetus, offense, incentive.

anstossen, to strike against, join, crush, collide, impinge upon, offend, strike, be adjacent, stumble, stammer; **mit der Zunge** ~, to stutter; **gegen etwas** ~, to give offense to.

anstossend, impulsive, adjacent, contiguous.

anstössig, offensive, unpleasant.

Anstrebkraft, *f.*⸚e, centripetal force.

anstreben, to aspire to, strive for.

anstreichen, to paint, color, varnish, mark, underline.

anstrengen, to stretch, strain, exert.

Anstrengung, *f.* exertion, application, trouble, effort.

Anstrich, *m.***-e,** painting, coloring, air, appearance, coat of paint; **vorübergehender** ~, first coat.

anstücken, to piece on, joint, connect.

Ansturm, *m.* assault.

ansuchen, to apply, solicit.

Ansud, *m.* (ansieden), scorifying.

ansummen, to sum up.

ansüssen, to sweeten.

antasten, to touch, attack.

anteeren, to tar.

anteigen, to convert into paste, premix.

Anteil, *m.* portion, share, interest, sympathy, constituent, fraction.

anteillos, indifferent.

antemetisch, antiemetic.

Antenne, *f.* feeler, antenna, tentacle, aerial.

Antennen, *f.pl.* hairs, appendages that receive and stimulate; **-drüse,** *f.* antennal gland; **-schuppen,** *f.pl.* scales of antenna; **-stamm,** *m.* antennal peduncle; **-stiel,** *m.* peduncle of antenna.

Anthere, *f.* anther.

Antheren-brand, *m.* anther smut, blight; **-fach,** *n.* anther sac, locule; **-hälfte,** *f.* theca; **-röhre,** *f.* anther tube.

Antheridium-kopf, *m.* spermatogenous cell; **-stand,** *m.* antheridiophore; **-stift,** *m.* antheridium cuspid.

Anthracen, *n.* **Anthrazen,** *n.* anthracene.

Anthrachinolin, *n.* anthraquinoline.

Anthrachinon, *n.* anthraquinone.

Anthrax, *m.* anthrax.

Anthrazit, *n.* anthracite; **-artig,** anthracoid, anthracitic.

Anthroesäure, *f.* anthroic acid.

Antichlor, *n.* antichlorine.

anticipierter Trieb, *m.* prolepsis.

Antifermentativ, *n.* enzyme inhibiting.

Antiformin, *n.* antiformin (trade name).

antik, antique.

Antikatalysator, *m.* anticatalyzer.

Antiklopfmittel, *n.* antiknock agent.

Antikörper, *m.*-, antibody, antisubstance.

Antilope, *f.* antelope.

Antilyssaserum, *n.* antirabic serum.

Antimon, *n.* antimony; **-arsen,** *n.* allemontite; **-artig,** like antimony, antimonial; **-blei,** *n.* lead-antimony alloy; **-bleiblende,** *f.* boulangerite; **-blende,** *f.* kermisite; **-blüte,** *f.* antimony bloom; **-butter,** *f.* butter of antimony; **-glanz,** *m.* bournonite.

Antimon-halogen, *n.* antimony halide; **-haltig,** containing antimony, antimonial.

antimonig, antimonisch, antimonial.

Antimonigsäureanhydrid, *n.* antimony trioxide.

Antimon-kermes, *m.&n.* kermes mineral; **-nickel,** *n.* breithauptite; **-nickelglanz,** *m.* ullmannite; **-oxychlorid,** *n.* antimony oxychloride; **-sauer,** antimonate of; **-silberblende,** *f.* pyrargyrite; **-verbindung,** *f.* antimony compound; **-zinnober,** *m.* kermisite.

Antipathie, *f.* antipathy.

antipodisch, antipodal, opposite.

Antiquar, *m.* secondhand bookseller.

Antiquariat, *n.* second-hand bookstore.

antiquarisch, second-hand (books).

antiseptisch, antiseptic.

antiskorbutisch, antiscorbutic.

Antitoxinverbindung, *f.* antitoxin combination.

Antlitz, *n.* face, countenance.

Antoniusfeuer, *n.* St. Anthony's fire, erysipelas.

Antenskraut, *n.* willow herb (*Chamaenerion angustifolium*).

Antorbitalfortsatz, *m.* preorbital process.

Antrag, *m.*ᵘe, proposition, proposal.

antragen, to carry up, lay on, propose, offer, motion.

anträufeln, to drip (on).

antreffen, to meet with, hit upon, find, come across.

antreiben, to drive on, against, in, incite, urge on, force (plants), influence, affect.

antreten, to set out on, enter on, tread down.

Antrieb, *m.*-e, impulse, inducement, motive, drive; **mit ~ von oben,** top driven; **-scheibe,** *f.* driving pulley.

Antriebs-mittel, *n.* incentive; **-welle,** *f.* driving shaft.

Antritt, *m.* beginning, entrance, setting out, first step, installation.

Antrittsvorlesung, *f.* inaugural lecture.

antrocknen, to begin to dry.

antun, to put on, do to, inflict violence.

Antwort, *f.*-en, answer, reply.

anvertrauen, to entrust, confide.

anverwandt, related, allied.

anvisieren, to sight (at).

Anwachs, *m.* growth, increase, swelling.

anwachsen, to grow to or together, adhere, adnate, take root, increase, enlarge.

Anwachsstreifen, *m.pl.* lines of growth.

Anwalt, *m.* attorney, lawyer.

anwandeln, to befall, seize, come over.

Anwandlung, *f.* attack, fit.

anwärmen, to heat.

Anwartschaft, *f.* expectancy, prospect.

anwässern, to moisten (a little).

anwehen, to blow upon.

anweichen, to soak slightly, soften.

anweisen, to direct, instruct, show, assign, mark, point out, refer to.

anweissen, to whitewash.

Anweisung, *f.* direction, instruction, money order, check, draft, assignment, method, advice.

anwelken, to begin to wilt.

anwendbar, applicable, available, practical, feasible, usable.

Anwendbarkeit, *f.* applicability, practicability, feasibility.

anwenden, to employ, apply, make use of, use; **angewandt,** applied, employed.

Anwendung, *f.* application, employment, use; ∼ **finden, zur** ∼ **kommen,** to be used.

Anwendungs-bereich, *m.* range of application; **-weise,** *f.* mode of application.

anwerfen, to throw on, crank (an engine).

Anwesen, *n.* estate.

anwesend, present.

Anwesenheit, *f.* presence.

anwidern, to disgust.

Anwittern, to effloresce.

Anwohner, *m.* neighbor.

Anwuchs, *m.* growth, increase.

Anwurf, *m.* plastering, patch; **-kurbel,** *f.* starting crank.

anwürgen, to grip, pull (a screw) tight.

Anwurzeln, to take root.

Anzahl, *f.* number, quantity.

anzahlen, to pay on account.

anzapfen, to tap, box (trees).

Anzeichen, *n.* mark, sign, indication, symptom.

anzeichnen, to mark.

Anzeige, *f.* information, notice, advertisement, sign, announcement, wedding (paper); **-mittel,** *n.* indicator.

anzeigen, to advertise, notify, announce, advise, indicate, inform, report, imply.

Anzeigengebühren, *f.pl.* advertising rates.

Anzeiger, *m.*-, indicator, pointer, exponent, informer; **-blatt,** *n.* instruction sheet; **-feder,** *f.* indicator spring.

Anzeigevorrichtung, *f.* indicating device.

anzetteln, to frame, plot, warp.

anziehen, to put on, draw, pull, attract, absorb, tighten, stretch, raise, grow, take effect, (prices) improve, look up.

anziehend, attractive, alluring, astringent.

Anzieher, *m.* adductor muscle.

Anziehung, *f.* attraction, gravitation, adhesion, adduction.

Anziehungs-kraft, *f.*⁼e, attractive power, attraction; **-wirkung,** *f.* attraction effect.

anzinnen, to tin, coat with tin.

Anzucht, *f.* raising, breeding, cultivation, culture.

anzuckern, to sprinkle with sugar.

Anzug, *m.*⁼e, clothes, clothing, approach, slope, going into, entrance.

anzüglich, suggestive, offensive.

Anzüglichkeit, *f.* suggestiveness.

Anzugsmoment, *n.* initial torque.

anzünden, to kindle, light, ignite.

Anzünder, *m.* lighter, igniter.

anzweifeln, to doubt.

Aorta, *f.* aorta.

Aorten-ast, *m.* branch of aorta; **-bogen,** *m.* aortic arch; **-gabelung,** *f.* aortic bifurcation; **-geflecht,** *n.* aortic plexus; **-kammer,** *f.* left ventricle; **-klappe,** *f.* aortic valve. **-riss,** *m.* rupture of aorta; **-stamm,** *m*; trunk of aorta; **-wand,** *f.* wall of aorta.

Aouaraöl, *n.* African palm oil.

apart, singular, odd, cute, remarkable.

Apathie, *f.* apathy.

Apatitkristall, *m.* crystal of apatite or phosphorite.

Apfel, *m.*⁼, apple; **-äther,** *m.* malic ether, ethyl malate.

Apfelbaum, *m.*⁼e, apple tree; **wilder** ∼, crab tree.

Apfel-beere, *f.* chokeberry (*Pyrus arbutifolia*); **-blattsauger,** *m. Psylla malis;* **-blutlaus,** *f. Eriosoma lanigera;* **-branntwein,** *m.* apple brandy, applejack; **-dorn,** *m.* crab tree; **-förmig,** pomiform; **-frucht,** *f.* pome; **-gehäuse,** *n.* apple core; **-herz,** *n.* apple core; **-langtrieb,** *m.* long shoot on the apple tree.

Apfel-most, *m.* cider (sweet, unfermented); **-mus,** *n.* applesauce; **-salbe,** *f.* pomatum; **-sauer,** malate of; **-säure,** *f.* malic acid; **-schimmel,** *m.* dapple-gray horse; **-schorf,** *m.* apple scab; **-sine,** *f.* (sweet) orange.

Apfelsinen-einwickelpapier, *n.* orange wrapper; **-saft,** *m.* orange juice; **-schalenöl,** *n.* essence of orange.

Apfel-wein, *m.* cider; **-wickler,** *m.* codling moth (*Carpocapsa pomonella*).

Aphel, *m.* aphelion.

aphlogistisch, aphlogistic.

Apikal-öffnung, *f.* apical pore: **-rand,** *m.* apical margin, border.

aplanatisch, aplanatic.

Apochinin, *n.* apoquinine.

apochromatisch, apochromatic.

Apogluzinsäure, *f.* apoglucic acid.

Apokamphersäure, *f.* apocamphoric acid.

Apotheke, *f.* apothecary's shop, chemist's shop, drugstore, pharmacy.

Apotheker, *m.*-, pharmacist; **-buch,** *n.* dispensatory; **-gewicht,** *n.* apothecaries' weight; **-waren,** *f.pl.* drugs.

Apparat, *m.*-e, apparatus, contrivance; **-brett,** *n.* instrument board; **-tisch,** *m.* worktable.

apparativ, by means of apparatus.

Apparatur, *f.* device, equipment.

Appell, *m.*-e, roll call, appeal.

appellieren, to appeal to.

Appetit, *m.* appetite.

appetitlich, appetizing.

applizieren, to apply.

apportieren, to retrieve.

Appositionswachstum, *n.* growth by apposition.

appretieren, to dress, finish (cloth).

Appretur, *f.* finish (of cloth); **-echt,** fast to finishing; **-körper,** *m.* loading (agent) filler; **-masse,** *f.* sizing material; **-mittel,** *n.* finishing (sizing).

approbieren, to approve.

Aprikose, *f.* apricot.

April-blume, *f.* wood anemone (*Anemone nemorosa*); **-pflanze,** *f.* a spring plant.

Apsis, *f.* apse.

Apteren, *pl.* aptera.

apyrisch, apyrous, incombustible, fireproof.

Aquarell, *n.* water-color painting; **-farbe,** *f.* water color.

Äquator, *m.* equator.

Aquavit, *m.* aqua vitae, brandy, spirit(s).

Äquinoktium, *n.* equinox.

äquivalent, equivalent; **-verhältnis,** *n.* ratio of equivalents.

Äquivalenz, *f.* equivalence, **-punkt,** *m.* end point.

Ära, *f.* era.

Arabin, *n.* arabin; **-gummi,** *n.* gum arabic

arabisches Gummi, *n.* gum arabic.

Arachinsäure, *f.* arachidic acid.

Aräometer, *n.* areometer, hydrometer.

Arbeit, *f.* **-en,** employment, work, labor, fermentation, working, task, job, workmanship, report, investigation, process, energy, effort.

arbeiten, to work, ferment, perform, make.

Arbeiter, *m.*-, worker, laborer, workman; **-ameise,** *f.* worker ant.

Arbeit-geber, *m.*-, employer; **-nehmer,** *m.* employee.

Arbeitsabstand, *m.*-e, working distance.

arbeitsam, industrious, laborious.

Arbeitsamkeit, *f.* industry, diligence.

Arbeits-äquivalent, *n.* mechanical equivalent; **-aufwand,** *m.* expenditure of work; **-einheit,** *f.* unit of work, erg; **-einstellung,** *f.* strike; **-fähig,** capable of work, able-bodied; **-festigkeit,** *f.* fatigue (limit) strength; **-fugen,** *f.pl.* expansion joints; **-gang,** *m.* operation; **-gruppe,** *f.* group of workers; **-hyperplasia,** *f.* active hyperplasia.

Arbeits-leistung, *f.* performance, efficiency; **-los,** without work, unemployed; **-okular,** *n.* working eyepiece; **-sparend,** labor-saving; **-strom-element,** *n.* open-circuit cell; **-stube,** *f.* workroom; **-teilung,** *f.* division of labor; **-tüchtigkeit,** *f.* fitness, capacity for work; **-vermögen,** *n.* capacity for work, kinetic energy; **-vorgabe,** *f.* suggested work, procedure; **-zimmer,** *n.* workroom.

archäisch, archaic.

Arche, *f.* ark.

Archegoniatentypus, *m.* type of plant having archegonia.

Archegonium-polster, *n.* archegoniophore; **-trager,** *m.* archegonium receptacle, torus.

Architekt, *m.*-e, architect.

Archiv, *n.*-e, record office, (*pl.*) records, archives.

Areal, *n.* area; **-verschiebung,** *f.* shifting in location.

Arekanuss, *f.* areca nut, betel nut.

Arg, *n.* harm, malice.

arg, evil, bad, strong, awful, severe, tremendous, hard.

Ärger, *m.* vexation, anger.

ärgerlich, irritable, angry, vexatious.

ärgern, to annoy, vex; **sich über etwas ~,** to lose one's temper at.

Ärgernis, *n.* vexation.

Arglist, *f.* cunning.

arglistig, crafty, cunning.

arglos, harmless, innocent, unsuspecting.

Arglosigkeit, *f.* harmlessness.

Argwohn, *m.* suspicion.

argwöhnen, to suspect.

argwöhnisch, suspicious.

Aristokrat, *m.* aristocrat.

Arithmetik, *f.* arithmetic.

arithmetisch, arithmetical; **arithmetische Reihe,** *f.* arithmetical progression.

arktisch, arctic.

Arm, *m.*-e, arm, branch, cross bar, horn.

arm, poor, low, lean, low grade.

Armatur, *f.* armature, fittings, mountings.

Armbein, *n.* arm bone, humerus; **-höcker,** *m.* deltoid tuberosity; **-kopf,** *m.* head of humerus; **-narbe,** *f.* tubercle of humerus.

Arm-beuge, *f.* bend of elbow; **-biege,** *f.* bend of elbow; **-binde,** *f.* sling; **-blei,** *n.* refined lead; **-decken,** *f.-pl.* secondary coverts.

Armee, *f.* army.

Ärmel, *m.*-, sleeve; **-kanal,** *m.* the English Channel.

Arm-flosser, *m.pl.* Pediculati; **-förmig,** brachial, brachiate; **-füsser,** *m.pl.* Brachiopoda; **-geflecht,** *n.* brachial plexus; **-gelenk,** *n.* elbow joint; **-gerüst,** *n.* loop; **-grube,** *f.* axil, armpit.

armhaarig, with poor growth of hair, without much hair.

Arm-heber, *m.* deltoid muscle; **-höcker,** *m.* olecranon; **-höhle,** *f.* armpit, axilla.

armieren, to arm, equip.

Arm-kiemer, *m.pl.* Brachiopoda; **-knochen,** *m.* arm bone, humerus.

Armkreuz, *n.* spider; **~ -Ringe,** *m.pl.* backing wire(s), ring plates.

Armleuchteralge, *f.* stonewort, fetid chara (Chara).

ärmlich, poor.

Armoxyde, *n.pl.* refining skimmings.

Arm-nervengeflecht, *n.* brachial plexus; **-palisadenzelle,** *f.* arm palisade cell; **-rand,**

m. bend or border of wing; **-röhre,** *f.* humerus; **-schiene,** *f.* arm splint, radius; **-schwingen,** *f.pl.* secondaries.

armselig, poor, miserable, wretched.

Armskelett, *n.* skeleton of the arms.

armspannig, few barred.

Arm-speiche, *f.* radius; **-spindel,** *f.* radius; **-stütze,** *f.* arm rest; **-stern,** *m.* spider.

armtreiben, to concentrate.

Armut, *f.* poverty.

Arnika-blüten, *f.pl.* arnica flowers; **-wurzel,** *f.* arnica root.

Arom(a), *n.* aroma.

aromatisch, aromatic.

aromatisieren, to aromatize.

Aron, *m.* arum; **-gewächse,** *n.pl.* Araceae.

Arons-stab, *m.* cuckoopint, wake-robin (*Arum maculatum*); **-stärke,** *f.* arum starch.

Arrak, *m.* arrack.

Arrest, *m.* arrest.

arretieren, to arrest, lock up.

Arretierung, *f.* arrest, apprehension, stop, locking device.

arrodieren, to erode.

Arrosion, *f.* erosion.

Arrow-mehl, *n.* arrowroot flour; **-root,** *n.* arrowroot (*Maranta arundinacea*).

Arsch, *m.* buttocks.

Arsen, *n.* arsenic; **gelbe -blende,** *f.* orpiment; **rote -blende,** *f.* realgar.

Arsen-dampf, *m.*-e, arsenic vapor; **-erz,** *n.* arsenic ore; **-fahlerz,** *n.* tennantite; **-führend,** arseniferous; **-haltig,** arsenical.

arsenig, arsenious; **-sauer,** arsenite of.

Arsenik, *m.* arsenic.

Arsenikalfahlerz, *n.* tennantite, gray copper ore.

Arsenik-blüte, *f.* arsenic bloom, arsenolite; **-salz,** *n.* salt of arsenic; **-sinter,** *m.* scorodite; **-spiegel,** *m.* arsenic mirror; **-spiessglanz,** *m.* allemonite.

Arsen-kies, *m.* leucopyrite, arsenical pyrites; **-legierung,** *f.* arsenic alloy; **-säure,** *f.* arsenic acid; **-verbindung,** *f.* arsenic compound.

Arsinigsäure, *f.* arsinic acid, arsinous acid.

Arsinsäure, *f.* arsinic acid, arsonic acid.

Art, *f.*-en, manner, way, race, breed, kind, sort, bit, species, variety, nature; **-anfang,** *m.* beginning of the species; **-bastard,** *m.* species hybrid; **-bastardierung,** *f.* species hybridization; **-begrenzung,** *f.* limitation of a species; **-begriff,** *m.* species concept; **-bild,** *n.* image of species; **-bildung,** *f.* formation of species; **-eigen,** peculiar to the species, characteristic, authentic; **-eigenschaft,** *f.* species characteristic.

arten, to be of a certain quality or kind or form; **geartet,** of a certain nature disposed; **nach . . . arten,** to resemble, take after . . .

Art(en)genossenschaften, *f.pl.* species associations, groups.

Artenwandel, *m.* species change.

Arterie, *f.* artery.

arteriell, arterial.

Arterien-ast, *m.* arterial branch; **-gang,** *m.* arterial passage; **-kammer,** *f.* left ventricle; **-scheide,** *f.* sheath of artery; **-stiel,** *m.* arterial stem, stalk, trunk; **-verzweigung,** *f.* arterial ramification.

artesisch, artesian.

artfremd, foreign to the species, heterogeneous.

Artgleichheit, *f.* identity (of species).

artig, good, polite, well-behaved.

. . . **artig,** resembling, like; **gleich-,** of the same kind; **silber-,** like silver.

Artigkeit, *f.* good behavior.

Artikel, *m.*-, article, goods, commodity.

Artikulationsfläche, *f.* articular surface.

artikulieren, to articulate.

Artischocke, *f.* artichoke.

Art-kreuzung, *f.* hybridization between species; **-merkmal,** *n.* characteristic of a species; **-verband,** *m.* union, grouping of species; **-wärme,** *f.* specific heat.

Arznei, *f.* medicine, drug; **-fläschchen,** small medicine bottle; **-gabe,** *f.* dose; **-kräftig,** medicinal, therapeutic, curative; **-kunde,** *f.* pharmaceutics; **-mittel,** *n.pl.* remedies, drugs; **-mittellehre,** *f.* pharmacology; **-mittelträger,** *m.* excipient; **-pflanze,** *f.* medicinal plant; **-verordnung,** *f.* prescription; **-ware,** *f.* drug.

Arzt, *m.*-e, physician, doctor.

ärztlich, medical.

Asant, *m.* asafetida.

Asarumkampfer, *m.* asaron, asarum camphor.

Asbest, *m.* asbestos; **-artig,** asbestic, asbestiform, asbestoid; **-aufschlämmung,** *f.* asbestos slime, milk suspension; **-flocken,** *f.pl.* asbestos flakes, wool; **-pappe,** *f.* asbestos board; **-pflanze,** *f.* milkweed (As-clepias); **-schirm,** *m.* asbestos screen; **-schnur,** *f.* asbestos twine.

aschbleich, ashy pale.

Asche, *f.* ash; **-frei,** free from ash, ash free.

aschen, to ash or wash (the mold).

Aschen-bestandteil, *m.* ash constituent; **-bestimmung,** *f.* ash determination; **-dünger,** *m.* cinereal manure; **-ermittlung,** *f.* ash determination; **-fall,** *m.* ashpan; **-gehalt,** *m.* ash content; **-lauge,** *f.* lye from ashes; **-pflanze,** *f.* Cineraria; **-raum,** *m.* ashpit; **-salz,** *n.* alkali; **-trecker,** *m.* tourmaline; **-zieher,** *m.* tourmaline.

Äscher, *m.* tanner's pit, slack-lime pit, ash cistern.

aschereich, rich in ash.

äschern, to ash.

aschfarben, ash color.

aschig, ashy, ciner(ac)eous.

Aschlauch, *m.* eschalot, shallot (*Allium ascalonicum*).

Äsculin (Äskulin), *n.* esculin.

aseptisch, aseptic.

Askomyzeten, *pl.* Ascomycetes.

Äskulin (Äsculin), *n.* esculin.

Asparaginsäure, *f.* aspartic acid.

Aspe, *f.* aspen tree.

Aspergillusmykose, *f.* aspergillary mycosis.

Asphalt-beton, *m.* asphalt concrete; **-klee,** *m. Psoralea bituminosa;* **-lack,** *m.* asphalt varnish; **-pflaster,** *n.* asphalt pavement; **-stein,** *m.* crude asphalt, asphalt block.

Asphodill, *m.* asphodel (Affodill).

aspirieren, to aspire, aspirate.

Aspirin, aspirin.

asporagen, nonsporing.

ass (essen), ate.

Assaipalme, *f.* Euterpe (a palm).

Assanierung, *f.* sanitation.

assekurieren, to insure.

Assel, *f.* wood louse.

Asseln, *f.pl.* Isopoda.

Asselspinnen, *f.pl.* Pantopoda, Pycnogonida.

Assimilations-apparat, *m.* digestive organs; **-wurzel,** *f.* assimilating root.

assimilatorisch, assimilatory.

assimilierbar, assimilable.

Assimilierbarkeit, *f.* assimilability.

assimilieren, to assimilate.

Assistent, *m.*-en, assistant.

assortieren, to (as)sort.

assouplieren, to render pliable.

Assoziationsfasern, *f.pl.* associative (correlating) fibers.

assoziieren, to associate.

Ast, *m.* ⁼e, branch, knot (in wood), protuberance; **-anlage,** *f.* branch primordium.

astatisch, astatic.

Ast-bildung, *f.* branch formation; **-blatt,** *n.* branch leaf.

Aster, *f.* aster.

Ast-fänger, *m.* knotter; **-fäule,** *f.* branch rot; **-frei,** free of knots, branchless.

ästhetisch, esthetic.

Astholz, *n.* branch wood, loppings.

ästig, branchy, ramified, knotted.

Astigmatismus, *m.* astigmatism.

Ast-loch, *n.* knothole; **-los,** branchless; **-ranke,** *f.* branch tendril; **-rein,** clear of branches; **-reinigung,** *f.* pruning.

Astronom, *m.***-en,** astronomer.

Astronomie, *f.* astronomy.

ast-ständig, ramous; **-stielig,** cladodial; **-streu,** *f* branch litter.

Ästung, *f.* pruning.

Astwerk, *n.* branches, boughs.

Äsung, *f.* pasture, grazing.

Asyl, *n.***-e,** sanctuary, asylum.

asymmetrisch, asymmetric(al).

asymptotisch, asymptotic.

Aszese, *f.* asceticism.

Atavismus, *m.* atavism.

Atem, *m.* breath, breathing, respiration.

atembar, respirable, breathable.

Atem-bewegung, *f.* respiratory movement; **-einsatz,** *m.* drum (mask); **-höhle,** *f.* air chamber, stomatal chamber; **-holen,** *n.* respiration; **-löcher,** *n.pl.* spiracles, stigmata, stomata; **-los,** breathless; **-not,** *f.* shortness of breath; **-öffnung,** *f.* stomate; **-organ,** *n.* respiratory tube; **-pause,** *f.* breathing pause, breathing time.

Atem-rohr, *n.* respiratory tube; **-röhre,** *f.* respiratory tube, incurrent or exhalant siphon; **-stillstand,** *m.* cessation of respiration; **-wurzel,** *f.* respiratory root, pneumatophore; **-zug,** *m.* breath, inspiration, respiration.

Äthal, *n.* ethal, cetyl alcohol.

Äthan, *n.* ethane, ethyl hydride.

Äther, *m.* ether; **-artig,** ethereal; **-bildung,** *f.* ether formation.

ätherisch, ethereal, volatile, essential.

Äther-schwefelsäure, *f.* ethylsulphuric acid; **-schwingung,** *f.* vibration of the ether; **-wellen,** *f.pl.* ether waves.

Äthiden, *n.* ethydene.

Athionsäure, *f.* ethionic acid.

Äthylalkohol, *m.* ethyl alcohol.

Äthylen, *n.* ethylene; **-reihe,** *f.* ethylene series.

Äthyl-gruppe, *f.* ethyl group; **-reihe,** *f.* ethyl series; **-zinnsäure,** *f.* ethylstannic acid.

Ätiologie, *f.* etiology.

Atlas, *m.* atlas, satin; **-artig,** satined; **-beere,** *f.* serviceberry (*Pirus* or *Sorbus torminalis*); **-bogen,** *m.* arch of the atlas; **-erz,** *n.* fibrous malachite; **-flügel,** *m.* wing of the atlas; **-holz,** *n.* satinwood (*Chloroxylon swietenia*); **-papier,** *n.* glazed paper; **-spat,** *m.* satin spar.

Atlerberg-Grenzen, *f.pl.* Atlerberg limits, consistency limits (of sail).

atmen, to breathe, inhale.

Atmen, *n.* breathing, respiration, breath.

Atmosphäre, *f.* atmosphere.

Atmosphärendruck, *m.***-e,** atmospheric pressure.

Atmosphärilien, *pl.* atmospheric, atmospheric influences.

Atmung, *f.* breathing, respiration.

Atmungs-darm, *m.* respiratory intestinal tube; **-einrichtung,** *f.* provision for respiration; **-grösse,** *f.* respiration quotient; **-kohlensäure,** *f.* carbon dioxide of respiration; **-nahrungsmittel,** *n.* respiratory food substance; **-schleimhaut,** *f.* respiratory mucous membrane; **-stoffwechsel,** *m.* respiratory exchange; **-weg,** *m.* respiratory duct, passage; **-werkzeug,** *n.* respiratory apparatus, organ; **-zentrum,** *n.* respiratory center.

Atom, *n.***-e,** atom; **-ähnlich,** atomlike; **-artig,** atomic; **-begriff,** *m.* conception of the atom; **-bewegung,** *f.* atomic motion; **-bindungsvermögen,** *n.* valence, atomic combining power; **-bomb, -bombe,** *f.* atom bomb; **-gewicht,** *n.* atomic weight; **-gewichtafel,** *f.* table of atomic weights; **-gruppe,** *f.* group of atoms; **-haltig,** atomic.

Atomismus, *m.* atomism.

Atomizität, *f.* atomicity.

Atom-kern, *m.* atomic nucleus; **-verkettung,** *f.* atomic linkage; **-verschiebung,** *f.* atomic displacement; **-wärme,** *f.* atomic heat;

-wertigkeit, *f.* atomic valence; **-zahl,** *f.* atomic number.

atoxisch, nontoxic.

Atramentstein, *m.***-e,** inkstone, native copperas.

Atrioventricularöffnung, *f.* auriculo- (atrio-) ventricular orifice.

Atropasäure, *f.* atropic acid.

attenuieren, to attenuate.

Attest, *n.***-e,** certificate.

Attich, *m.* dwarf elder (*Sambucus ebulus*).

Attraktionssphäre, *f.* sphere of attraction.

Attrappe, *f.* trap.

atypisch, atypical, nontypical.

Ätze, *f.* corrosion, etch, etching, mordant cauterization, aqua fortis.

Ätz-alkali, *n.* caustic alkali; **-alkalisch,** caustic (alkaline).

ätzbar, corrodible, dischargeable.

Ätz-baryt, *m.* barium hydroxide; **-druck,** *m.* engraving.

ätzen, to corrode, etch, eat, cauterize.

ätzend, corrosive, mordant, caustic.

Ätz-kali, *n.* caustic potash, hydroxide of potassium; **-kalk,** *m.* caustic, unslaked lime, quicklime; **gelöschter** ~, slaked lime.

Ätz-kunst, *f.* art of etching; **-lauge,** *f.* caustic-soda solution; **-mittel,** *n.* caustic; **-natron,** *n.* caustic soda, sodium hydroxide; **-natronlauge,** *f.* caustic soda solution; **-stoff,** *m.* corrosive; **-sublimat,** *n.* corrosive sublimate; **-wasser,** *n.* nitric acid, aqua fortis; **-wirkung,** *f.* corrosive action.

Auboden, *m.* alluvial soil, fertile pasture or meadow.

auch, also, too, likewise, indeed, even; ~ **nicht,** neither; **wenn** ~, even if, even though; **so . . .** ~, however; **so reich er** ~ **ist,** however rich he may be.

Audienz, *f.* audience.

Audionröhre, *f.* detector tube.

Aue, *f.* small island, green meadow, ewe.

Auer-brenner, *m.* Welsbach burner; **-hahn,** *m.* heath cock (Capercaillie); **-henne,** *f.* heath (mountain) hen; **-huhn,** *n.* heath (mountain) hen; **-ochs,** *m.* ure-ox.

auf, on, upon, open, at, about, in(to), up, upward; ~ **dass,** in order that; ~ **einmal,** at once, suddenly; ~ **und ab,** up and down, to and fro; **aufs äusserste,** to the utmost; ~ **das hin,** on the strength of that; ~ **und davon,** (to be) gone; ~ **und nieder,** up and down; ~ **und über,** up to and beyond.

aufarbeiten, to work up, off, finish a task, recover, recondition, elaborate, utilize, stack.

Aufästung, *f.* pruning.

aufatmen, to breathe again or freely.

aufätzen, to open by caustics.

Aufbau, *m.***-e,** building, synthesis, erection.

Aufbauchung, *f.* fluffiness, bellying.

aufbauen, to build up, synthesize, erect, base on.

aufbäumen, to climb up, perch, rear, struggle against.

aufbauschen, to puff up.

aufbereiten, to convert, prepare, dress, concentrate, refine, upgrade, separate.

Aufbereitung, *f.* refining, separation.

Aufbereitungsanlage, *f.* upgrading plant, screen room.

aufbersten, to burst, crack.

aufbessern, to improve, ameliorate.

aufbewahren, to keep, save, preserve.

Aufbewahrung, *f.* keeping, preservation, storage.

Aufbewahrungsort, *m.* depository.

aufbiegen, to bend up, open, unfold.

aufbieten, to call out, summon, strain.

aufbinden, to untie, loosen, tie up.

aufblähen, to swell, inflate, puff up, expand.

aufblasen, to blow up, inflate, distend.

aufblättern, to unfold the leaves, exfoliate.

Aufblätterung, *f.* desquamation, exfoliation.

aufbleiben, to stay open, sit up (not go to bed).

Aufblick, *m.***-e,** upward glance, fulguration.

aufblicken, to look up, brighten.

aufblitzen, to flash.

aufblühen, to blossom, unfold.

Aufblühzeit, *f.* time of blossoming, efflorescence.

aufbohren, to bore open.

aufbrauchen, to use up, consume.

aufbrausen, to effervesce, roar, get into a rage, ferment, bubbling up.

aufbrausend, effervescent.

aufbrechen, to break open, open.

aufbrennen, to burn up, consume by burning, refine (metals).

aufbringen, to bring (up), lift (up), introduce, raise, provoke, muster.

Aufbruch, *m.* breaking up, departure.

aufbrühen, to scald.

aufbürden, to burden, impose, put (blame) upon, charge with.

aufdampfen, to evaporate.

aufdecken, to uncover, disclose, reveal.

aufdeuten, to point to,

aufdocken, to wind up, bundle.

Aufdornprobe, *f.* drifting test.

aufdörren, aufdarren, to dry, desiccate.

aufdrängen, to push open, obtrude, force upon, overwhelm.

aufdrehen, to unscrew, untwist, turn on, fan, shuffle.

aufdringen, to press up, strive up.

aufdringlich, importunate.

Aufdringlichkeit, *f.* obtrusiveness, importunity.

Aufdruck, *m.* printing, print, upward pressure.

aufdrucken, to imprint.

aufdrücken, to impress, stamp on.

aufduften, to give forth fragrance.

aufdunsten, to evaporate.

aufeinander, one upon (after) another; **-folge,** *f.* succession, series; **-folgen,** to succeed one another; **-folgend,** successive; **-legen,** *n.* superposition, series of layers.

Aufenthalt, *m.* stay, sojourn, residence.

Aufenthaltsort, *m.* place of stay, retreat.

auferlegen, to impose, inflict.

aufessen, to eat up.

auffädeln, to thread, string.

auffahren, to mount, rise up, drive up, start up.

Auffahrt, *f.*-en, ascent.

auffallen, to be noticeable, surprise, attract attention, fall, or strike upon.

auffallend, striking, remarkable, surprising, noteworthy, strange; **auffallendes Licht,** *n.* incident light.

auffällig, conspicuous, striking.

auffalten, to unfold, fold.

Auffangbarke, *f.* magma tank.

Auffangeglas, *n.*-er, objective lens.

auffangen, to collect, gather, intercept, catch, interrupt.

Auffänger, *m.* receiver (vessel).

Auffangschale, *f.* collecting dish.

auffärben, to color again, dye anew, lift, top, neutralize.

Auffärbung, *f.* dyeing white, bluing.

auffasern, to unravel, separate into fibers.

auffassen, to conceive, perceive, comprehend, interpret, take up, catch up, understand, take in.

Auffassung, *f.* conception, apprehension, comprehension.

Auffassungskraft, *f.*-e, perceptive faculty.

auffeuchten, to moisten, wet again.

auffinden, to discover, find out, detect.

auffischen, to fish up, pick up.

aufflackern, to flare, deflagrate.

aufflammen, to burst into flames, deflagrate.

auffliegen, to fly up, rise, blow up, explode.

Aufflug, *m.*-e, ascent.

auffordern, to ask, invite, summon, challenge.

Aufforderung, *f.* request, demand, invitation.

aufforsten, to afforest.

Aufforstung, *f.* afforestation, reforestation.

auffressen, to eat up, corrode.

auffrieren, to burst with frost.

Auffrieren, *n.* frost lifting, heaving.

auffrischen, to freshen (up), revive, renew.

Auffrischen, *n*, freshening, regeneration.

aufführen, to build, erect, raise, perform, quote, enter (on account), specify, lead (a mob), list, state, tabulate, summarize, enumerate, present, offer.

auffüllen, to fill up, refill, backfill, make.

auffüttern, to feed up, rear.

Aufgabe, *f.* task, problem, lesson, giving up, delivery; **-trichter,** *m.* feeding hopper.

Aufgabengebiet, *n.* field, scope.

Aufgabevorrichtung, *f.* feeder.

Aufgang, *m.* rising, ascent, upstroke, growth.

aufgären, to ferment.

aufgeben, to give up, deliver, propose, impose, charge.

aufgebläht, inflated.

aufgeblasen, puffed up, arrogant; **aufgeblasenes Leimkraut,** *n.* bladder campion (*Silene inflata*).

Aufgeblasenheit, *f.* conceit, arrogance.

Aufgebot, *n.*-e, public notice, summons, levy, bans, exertion.

aufgebracht (aufbringen), angry.

aufgedunsen, swollen.

aufgehen, to go up, rise, swell, ferment, appear, spring up, open, come open, unfold, be consumed, be merged, be absorbed, come up, shoot up, germinate, spring up, sprout.

aufgehoben (aufheben), abolished, liberated.

aufgeklärt, enlightened.

aufgeknäult, wound (into balls), entangled, entwined.

Aufgeld, *n.*-er, extra charge, premium.

aufgelegt, imposed, disposed, inclined.

aufgenommen (aufnehmen), taken up, received.

aufgeräumt, in high spirits.

aufgeschlossen (aufschliessen), decomposed.

aufgeschmolzen, (aufschmelzen), melted.

aufgesogen (aufsaugen), sucked up, drawn up.

aufgespeichert, latent, stored.

aufgestellt, put up, established, made.

aufgetaucht, emerged.

aufgetaut, thawed out.

Aufgetriebenheit, *f.* inflation, turgidity, distention, intumescence.

aufgewachsen, adnate, attached, grown up.

aufgeweckt, lively, clever.

aufgezogen (aufziehen), drawn up, raised.

aufgezwungen (aufzwingen), forced, imposed on.

aufgichten, to charge.

aufgiessen, to pour upon, infuse.

aufgischen, to ferment, bubble over.

aufgliedern, to classify, arrange, dismember.

aufgraben, to dig up.

aufgreifen, to take, snatch up, catch on.

Aufguss, *m.* infusion.

Aufgusstierchen, *n.pl.* Infusoria.

aufhacken, to cut up.

aufhaken, to unhook.

aufhalten, to hold up or open, support, stop, detain, criticize; **sich ~,** stay.

Aufhänge-band, *n.* suspensory ligament; **-muskel,** *m.* levator muscle.

aufhängen, to hang (up), suspend.

Aufhänger, *m.* hanger, rack, dryworker, loftsman.

Aufhängung, *f.* suspension.

aufhauen, to cut up, hit upward.

aufhäufen, to heap up, pile up, accumulate.

Aufhäufung, *f.* accumulation.

aufheben, to lift up, raise, pick up, lay up, preserve, break up, abolish, stop, balance, counteract, neutralize, reduce a fraction, increase, remove, cancel, annul, invalidate (a patent), compensate.

Aufheber, *m.* levator muscle.

Aufhebung, *f.* lifting up, nullification, counter action, suppression, neutralizing.

aufheitern, to brighten up, clear.

aufhelfen, to help up.

aufhellen, to clear up, clarify, elucidate.

Aufhellungs-dauer, *f.* period of illumination; **-mittel,** *n.* clearing agent.

aufhetzen, to incite, instigate, stir up.

aufholen, to fetch, draw up, haul up.

aufhorchen, to listen carefully.

aufhören, to cease, stop, discontinue, end, desist from.

aufjagen, to start, raise.

aufjauchzen, to shout with joy.

aufkaufen, to buy up, corner.

aufkeimen, to bud, germinate.

aufkippen, to tilt up.

aufkitten, to cement on.

aufklaftern, to pile up, cord (wood).

aufklappbar, capable of opening, folding.

aufklappen, to open.

aufklären, to clarify, clear up, elucidate, enlighten, explain, inform.

Aufklärer, *m.* scout.

Aufklärung, *f.* information, explanation, elucidation, clearing up, enlightenment, investigation, determination.

aufkleben, to paste on, affix.

aufklinken, to unlatch.

aufknacken, to crack open.

aufknöpfen, to unbutton.

aufknüpfen, to tie up.

aufkochen, to boil up, warm up, boil again.

aufkohlen, to (re)carburize, cement.

aufkommen, to come up, get up, grow, come into use, convalesce, thrive.

aufkratzen, to scratch (up).

aufkräusen, to form a head (beer).

aufkühlen, to aerate, cool.

aufkündigen, to give warning of, give notice of.

auflachen, to burst into a laugh.

Aufladegeschwindigkeit, *f.* rate of charging (electricity).

aufladen, to load, charge.

Aufladung, *f.* charging, top charge.

Auflage, *f.* edition, printing, levy, duty, tax, superimposed layer, medium (filter); **-fläche,** *f.* bearing-surface area; **-humus,** *m.* superficial layer of humus deposit.

Auflager, *n.*-, bearing, support.

auflagern, to store (up), mount on (bearings).

Auflagerung, *f.* stratification, deposition.

Auflagerungsschicht, *f.*-en, stratified or deposited layer.

auflassen, to leave open.

Auflast, *f.*-en, load, surcharge.

Auflauf, *m.*ʺe, swelling, puff, crowd, forward end.

auflaufen, to run up, increase, rise, swell.

Auflaufen, *n.* rising, germination.

Auflaufrahmen, *m.* deckle frame.

Aufläufer, *m.*-, (Einzelfaden) wrap (single filament).

aufleben, to revive.

auflecken, to lick up.

auflegen, to lay on or up, apply, impose, publish; **aufgelegt,** disposed, inclined.

Auflegeschuss, *m.*ʺe, mudcapping.

auflehnen, to lean upon; **sich** ~, rebel against.

auflesen, to pick up, gather.

aufleuchten, to flash up, light up, shine.

aufliegen, to lie (on), rest (on), weigh (on), be incumbent (on).

aufliegend, incumbent, adnate.

auflockern, to loosen (up), relax, disaggregate.

Auflockerung, *f.* loosening, relaxation.

auflodern, to flare up.

auflösbar, soluble.

Auflösbarkeit, *f.* solubility.

auflösen, to dissolve, liquefy, loosen, untie, undo, resolve, decompose, disintegrate, solve, analyze.

auflösend, solvent, dissolvent.

auflöslich, soluble.

Auflöslichkeit, *f.* solubility.

Auflösung, *f.* solution, dissolving, resolution, decomposition, disintegration, dissolution, analysis.

auflösungs-fähig, soluble; **-geschwindigkeit,** *f.* velocity of dissolution; **-grenze,** *f.* limit of resolution; **-kraft,** *f.* dissolving, resolving power; **-mittel,** *n.* solvent; **-vermögen,** *n.* resolving dissolvent power; **-wärme,** *f.* heat of solution.

auflöten, to solder on, unsolder.

aufmachen, to open, undo, put up, make up; **sich** ~, get up, rise.

aufmaischen, to mash.

aufmerken, to pay attention, attend.

aufmerksam, attentive, courteous, observant; ~ **machen,** to call (one's) attention (to).

Aufmerksamkeit, *f.* attention, attentiveness, courtesy.

aufmuntern, to awake, arouse, encourage.

Aufnahme, *f.*-n, taking up, assimilation, absorption, dissolving, reception, fashion, survey, sketch, admittance, photograph, exposure, shot, admission, view; **-apparat,** *m.* recording instrument; **-fähig,** absorbable, admissible; **-fähigkeit,** *f.* receptivity; **-filter,** *m.* taking filter; **-finden,** to be listed or considered; **-gerät,** *n.* **-kammer,** *f.* camera; **-spule,** *f.* take-up spool; **-vermögen,** *n.* capacity.

aufnehmbar, receivable.

aufnehmen, to raise, lift up, pick up, catch, take up, absorb, dissolve, admit, receive, photograph, hold, assume, part, separate, borrow, resume; **mit** ~ **in,** to embody in.

Aufnehmer, *m.* receiver.

aufnötigen, to force upon.

aufopfern, to offer up, sacrifice, give up.

aufpacken, to pack up.

aufpassen, to be watching, fit on.

Aufpfropfung, *f.* grafting upon.

aufplatzen, to burst open, explode, split.

Aufplatzen, *n.* bursting, dehiscence.

aufprägen, to imprint, impress on, give, import.

Aufprall, *m.* bound, rebounding.

aufprallen, to rebound, bounce, strike.

aufpumpen, to pump up, inflate (tires).

aufputzen, to trim up, clean up, polish.

aufquellen, to swell, swell out, well up, soak, steep, expand.

Aufquellung, *f.* swelling.

aufraffen, to rake up, collect.

aufragen, to tower up.

aufranken, to climb.

aufrauhen, to roughen, nap.

aufräumen, to remove, clear away, clear; **aufgeräumt,** cheerful, in good humor.

aufrechnen, to count (up).

aufrecht, upright, erect.

Aufrecht(er)haltung, f. maintenance, support.

aufregen, to excite, stimulate, irritate, agitate, rouse, alarm, disturb.

aufregend, irritant, stimulant, exciting.

Aufregungsmittel, n.-, irritant, stimulant.

aufreiben, to rub sore, gall, destroy; **sich ~,** to worry, wear out, exhaust.

aufreihen, to string, thread.

aufreissen, to tear up or open, crack, split, draw, design.

aufreizen, to incite, stir.

aufrichtbar, erectile.

aufrichten, to raise, set up, erect, comfort.

aufrichtig, sincere, upright.

Aufrichtigkeit, f. sincerity, uprightness.

Aufrichtung, f. erection.

aufriegeln, to unbolt.

Aufriss, m.-e, elevation, sketch.

aufrollen, to roll up, unroll, turn; **sich aufrollend, aufgerollt,** to convolute, spiral.

Aufrollen, n. curling.

Aufrollseite, f. reeling end.

Aufrollung, f. convolution, winding up.

Aufrollungswalze, f. delivery reel, receiving reel.

aufrücken, to move up, be promoted.

Aufruf, m.-e, call, summons.

Aufruhr, m. tumult, riot, uproar.

aufrühren, to stir up, rebel.

Aufrührer, m. stirrer, agitator.

aufrunden, to approximate, round off upward.

aufrütteln, to shake, stir up, rouse.

aufsagen, to recite, rescind, give warning, repeat.

aufsammeln, to collect, gather.

aufsässig, rebellious, refractory.

Aufsättigung, f. saturation.

Aufsatz, m.̈-e, headpiece, top, service (of china), essay, treatise, attachment; **-farbe,** f. topping color; **-schlüssel,** m. socket wrench.

aufsäuern, to acidify again.

aufsaugbar, absorbable, absorbent.

Aufsaugbarkeit, f. absorbability.

Aufsaugeflüssigkeit, f. absorption liquid.

aufsaugen, to suck up, absorb.

aufsaugend, absorbent; **aufsaugendes Mittel,** n. absorbent.

Aufsauger, m. absorber.

Aufsaugung, f. absorption.

Aufsaugungs-fähigkeit, f. absorptive ability; **-vermögen,** n. ability to absorb.

aufschauen, to lock up.

aufschäumen, to foam up, froth, effervesce.

aufscheuchen, to scare up.

aufscheuern, to scour, rub sore.

aufschichten, to pile, arrange in layers, stratify, film.

Aufschichtung, f. stratification.

aufschieben, to put off, postpone, push open.

aufschiessen, to shoot up, spring up.

Aufschlag, m.̈-e, impact, percussion, advance, increase, cuff, facing, application, seedlings (forest).

aufschlagen, to open, set up, erect, raise, apply, strike, look up, brush (out), patch, poach.

Aufschlagzünder, m.-, percussion fuse.

aufschlämmen, to suspend, make into a paste, triturate.

Aufschlämmung, f. suspension.

aufschleifen, to grind on.

aufschlemmen, to suspend.

Aufschliessarbeit, f.-en, task of decomposition, opening up (of a pit).

aufschliessbar, capable of being decomposed.

aufschliessen, to decompose, open up, break up, disintegrate, unlock, disclose, explain.

Aufschliessen, n. decomposition, hydrolysis.

Aufschliessmischung, f. decomposition mixture.

Aufschliessung, f. decomposition, hydrolysis, disintegration.

Aufschliessungsvermögen, n. ability to make available, decompose.

aufschlitzen, to slit, rip up.

Aufschluss, m.̈-e, decomposition, information, explanation, disclosure, solution, treatment, digestion, criterion.

aufschmelzen, to melt on, fuse on.

aufschnappen, to snap up, pick up.

aufschneiden, to cut open, dissect, brag, boast.

Aufschneidung, *f.* dissection.

Aufschnitt, *m.*⁼e, cutting open, cut, incision, sliced cold meat, cold cut.

aufschnüren, to untie.

aufschraubbar, capable of being unscrewed.

aufschrauben, to screw on, screw up, unscrew.

aufschrecken, to startle, become startled.

aufschreiben, to write down, enter.

aufschreien, to scream, cry out.

Aufschrift, *f.*-en, address, inscription, label.

Aufschub, *m.*⁼e, adjournment, delay.

aufschürzen, to tuck up.

aufschütteln, to shake (up).

aufschütten, to pour, put on, store up, charge.

Aufschüttung, *f.* pouring, putting on, charging, storage, embankment, deposition, mound, elevation.

aufschweissen, to weld on, fuse, build up.

aufschwellen, to swell up, tumefy, inflate.

aufschwemmen, to float or wash upon, deposit, swell up, bloat.

Aufschwemmung, *f.* suspension, depositing, swelling, bloating.

aufschwingen, to rise, soar up.

Aufschwung, *m.* growth, advance, rise, flight.

Aufsehen, *n.* looking up, surprise, sensation.

Aufseher, *m.*-, overseer, inspector, foreman.

aufsein, to be up, open.

aufsetzbar, fit to be put on, capable of being put on.

aufsetzen, to set up, put up, draw up, affix.

Aufsetzkasten, *m.* jigger (in dyeing).

Aufsicht, *f.* inspection, superintendence, supervision.

Aufsichtsfarbe, *f.*-n, reflected color.

aufsieden, to boil up.

aufsitzen, to sit up, perch, roost, mount; **aufsitzende Blüten,** sessile flowers.

aufspalten, to split (up), cleave, burst, depolymerize, follow Mendel's law.

Aufspaltung, *f.* splitting up, cleavage, decomposition, analysis.

aufspannen, to stretch, spread, fix, clamp.

Aufspanner, *m.*-, step-up transformer.

aufsparen, to save, reserve.

aufspeichern, to store, accumulate, lay in.

Aufspeicherung, *f.* storage, accumulation.

aufsperren, to open wide, gape.

aufspiessen, to put on a spit.

aufsprengen, to blow up, burst open.

aufspriessen, to sprout, germinate.

aufspringen, to spring up, crack open, split, burst open, chap, rebound.

aufspringend, dehiscent.

aufspritzen, to squirt up, sprinkle on.

aufsprudeln, to bubble up, boil up.

aufspulen, to wind up.

aufspunden, aufspünden, to unbung.

aufspüren, to trace, track, hunt out, find.

aufstacheln, to goad.

Aufstand, *m.*⁼e, insurrection, revolt, rebellion.

aufständisch, rebellious.

aufstapeln, to pile, stack, store, heap up.

aufstechen, to prick open, lance, puncture.

Aufsteck-blende, *f.* slip-on stop, lens cover; **-dorn,** *m.* arbor; **-glas,** *n.* supplementary slip-on lens segment; **-halter,** *m.* arbor; **-rabensenker,** *m.* spot facer; **-reibahle,** *f.* shell reamer; **-senker,** *m.* shell drill.

aufstehen, to stand open, stand up, rise.

aufsteigen, to mount, rise, ascend, increase, swell, bubble up, boil.

aufsteigend, ascending.

aufstellen, to set up, put up, prepare, arrange, erect, advance, draw up, formulate, establish, assemble.

Aufstellung, *f.* setting up, erection, formulation, statement, arrangement, table.

aufstemmen, to lean on, pry open.

Aufstieg, *m.*-e, ascent, step, rise.

aufstöbern, to discover, ferret out.

aufstören, to rouse up.

aufstossen, to push open or up, ferment, chance (upon).

aufstreben, to aspire.

aufstreichen, to spread on, brush on.

aufstreuen, to strew, sprinkle.

Aufstrich, *m.*-e, spreading or brushing on or up, stroke, auction, coat, smear.

aufstülpen, to clap on.

aufstützen, to support, prop up.

aufsuchen, to seek after, track, search for.

auftauchen, to rise, emerge, spring up.

auftauen, to thaw, melt.

aufteilen, to distribute, allot.

Aufteilung, *f.* division, distribution, disintegration.

auftischen, to serve up.

Auftrag, *m.*⸚e, commission, charge, putting on, coat(ing), embankment, order, behalf.

Auftragsführung, *f.* carrying out of, construction, order.

auftragen, to serve up, lay on, apply, wear out, incorporate, add, diagram.

aufträufeln, to drop on, drip on.

auftraufen, to drop on, drip on.

auftreffen, to strike upon, impinge on.

auftreiben, to shoot up, blow, swell, distend, inflate, drive up, procure, sublime.

auftrennen, to undo, rip open.

auftreten, to appear, step forth, enter, crop up, accrue, experience, occur, proceed.

Auftreten, *n.* appearance, entrance, occurrence, behavior.

Auftrieb, *m.*-e, buoyancy, uplift, plankton, aerenchyma, small organisms floating on the surface of ocean.

Auftriebs-beiwert, *m.* coefficient of lift; **-erhöhung,** *f.* increase of lift; **-kraft,** *f.* buoyancy.

Auftritt, *m.*-e, appearance, step, scene.

auftrocknen, to dry up.

auftun, to open, become visible.

auftürmen, to heap up, accumulate.

aufvulkanisieren, to start to vulcanize.

aufwachen, to awake, wake up.

aufwachsen, to grow up.

aufwallen, to bubble (up), boil (up), flush.

Aufwallung, *f.* bubbling, emotion, ebullition, effervescence, flush.

aufwalzen, to roll on or out, plate, put on rollers, produce "clad" materials, expand.

Aufwand, *m.*⸚e, expenditure, expense, display, consumption, requirement, loss.

aufwärmen, to warm (up).

aufwarten, to wait on, pay respects to.

aufwärts, upward; **-gekrümmt,** bent upward; **-transformator,** *m.* step-up transformer; **-transport,** *m.* upward translocation.

Aurwartung, *f.* attendance.

aufwaschen, to wash.

aufwecken, to rouse, awaken.

aufweichen, to soften, mollify, soak, open by fomentation.

aufweichend, emollient.

aufweisen, to exhibit, show, produce, point to, have.

aufweiten, to widen, expand, ream.

aufwenden, to spend, devote, employ.

Aufwendung, *f.* employment, expenditure.

aufwerfen, to throw up on, open, dig, construct, proclaim, put, pose, raise (a question).

aufwerten, to appreciate, assign higher value, re-evaluate.

aufwickeln, to wind (up), unwind, reel.

Aufwickelspule, *f.* take-up reel, winding spool.

aufwiegen, to counterbalance, compensate.

Aufwind, *m.* up current.

aufwinden, to wind up, hoist.

aufwirbeln, to whirl up.

aufwischen, to wipe up.

Aufwuchs, *m.* growing up, growth.

aufwühlen, to turn up, root up, excite.

aufzählen, to count up, enumerate.

Aufzählungsreihe, *f.*-n, frequency distribution.

aufzehren, to consume, absorb, eat up.

Aufzehrung, *f.* consumption, absorption.

aufzeichnen, to record, draw, sketch, note.

Aufzeichnung, *f.* design, record, sketch, note.

aufzeigen, to exhibit.

Aufzelle, *f.* cell that gives rise to the periblem.

Aufziehbrücke, *f.* drawbridge, rouser (brewing).

aufziehen, to draw (up), raise (up), wind (up), open, cultivate, educate, rear, mature, mount, appear, be absorbed (of dyes).

Aufzieher, *m.* levator muscle.

Aufziehkarton, *m.* mounting board.

aufzischen, to fizz.

Aufzucht, *f.* breeding, rearing, bringing up.

Aufzug, *m.*⸚e, elevator, hoist, act, procession; **-leine,** *f.* rip cord.

aufzwängen, aufzwingen, to force upon.

Augapfel, *m.* eyeball; **-bindehaut,** *f.* ocular conjunctiva; **-fläche,** *f.* surface of eyeball;

-gefässhaut, *f.* choroid; -haut, *f.* sclera; -höhle, *f.* eye socket; -wand, *f.* wall of eyeball.

Auge, *n.*-n, eye, bud; ins ~ fassen, to fix one's eye upon something, watch, look at, keep an eye on; die Augen betreffend, ocular, ophthalmic; ~ auf etwas haben, to have something in view; die Augen gehen mir auf, I begin to see now; in die Augen fallend, striking, conspicuous; unbewaffnetes ~, naked eye; vor Augen führen, to visualize, point out, demonstrate.

äugeln, to bud, graft.

Augen-abstand, *m.* interoculary distance; -achat, *m.* cat's-eye; -achse, *f.* axis of eye; -ader, *f.* ophthalmic vessel, vein; -aderhaut, *f.* choroid; -anlage, *n.* primordium of eye or bud; -arzt, *m.* oculist; -ast, *m.* ocular branch; -becher, *m.* optic cup; -becherspalte, *f.* choroidal fissure of the cup.

Augen-becherstiel, *m.* optic (cup) stalk; -bindehaut, *f.* ocular conjunctiva; -bläschen, *m.* eye vesicle; -blase, *f.* optic vesicle; -blasenausstülpung, *f.* optic (vesicle) evagination; -blasenstiel, *m.* optic pedicle, stalk; -blick, *m.* moment, instant; -blicklich, instantaneous, immediate, momentary; -blinzeln, *n.* blinking; -bogen, *m.* iris.

Augen-braue, *f.* eyebrow; -brauenbogen, *m.* superciliary arch, orbital curve; -brauenkreuz, *n.* eyebrow cross (meeting of hair lines); -brauenrunzler, *m.* corrugator muscle, supercilium; -brücke, *f.* front or face (Diptera); -dach, *n.* roof of orbit; -decke, *f.* nictitating membrane; -deckel, *m.* eyelid; -drehpunktsabstand, *m.* distance between the points of rotation of the eyes; -drüse, *f.* lachrymal, ocular gland.

Augen-entzündung, *f.* inflammation of the eye; -fällig, conspicuous, evident; -farbe, *f.* color of the eye; -faserhaut, *f.* fibrous tunic of eye; -fehler, *m.* visual error; -feld, *n.* field of vision; -fleck, *m.* optic, eyespot, stigma, ocellus; -fleckig, ocellated; -fliegen, *f.pl.* Dorylaidae, Pipunculidae.

Augenflüssigkeit, *f.* (ocular) humor; glasartige ~, vitreous humor; wasserartige ~, aqueous humor.

Augen-glas, *n.* eyeglass; -gefässhaut, *f.* choroid; -grübchen, *n.* orbital cavity; -hintergrund, *m.* back of the eye; -höhle, *f.* eye socket, orbital cavity.

Augenhöhlen-bogen, *m.* superciliary arch, ridge; -dach, *n.* roof of orbital cavity;

-drüse, *f.* orbital zygomatic gland; -loch, *n.* orbital foramen; -rand, *m.* orbital margin.

Augen-hornhaut, *f.* cornea; -kammer, *f.* chamber of the eye; -kammerwasser, *n.* aqueous humor; -kapsel, *f.* capsule of the eye; -keil, *m.* ommatidium; -klappe, *f.* eyelid; -klappenrand, *m.* margin of the eyelid; -klinik, eye clinic; -knorpel, *m.* tarsal (eye) cartilage.

Augen-knoten, *m.* ophthalmic ganglion; -kreis, *m.* orbit, orbital circle; -kugel, *f.* eyeball; -leiden, *n.* eye complaint; -leiste, *f.* canthus; -licht, *n.* eyesight.

Augenlid, *n.* eyelid; -bindehaut, *f.* palpebral (conjunctiva) membrane; -drüse, *f.* gland of eyelid; -fläche, *f.* surface of eyelid; -haare, *n.pl.* eyelashes; -rand, *m.* palpebral margin; -spalte, *f.* palpebral fissure; -winkel, *m.* canthus.

Augen-linse, *f.* crystalline lens; -loch, *n.* pupil, orbital cavity; -marmor, *m.* eyespotted marble; -mass, *n.* estimate by the eye; -merk, *n.* object in view, aim, mark; -nagel, *m.* unguis; -nasenrinne, *f.* orbitonasal groove; -nerv, *m.* optic nerve; -nichts, *n.* zinc oxide (sublimated); -pfropfen, *n.* bud grafting.

Augen-pinsel, *m.* eye brush; -pol, *m.* ocular pole; -punkt, *m.* visual point; -reizstoff, *m.* tear gas; -ring, *m.* circumorbital ring; -rollmuskel, *m.* trochlear muscle; -rücken, *m.* eye ridge, eyebrow; -scheide, *f.* ophthalmotheca; -schein, *m.* appearance examination; -scheinlich, apparent, evident.

Augen-schild, *m.* ocular plate; -schläfengrube, *f.* orbitotemporal fossa; -schleim, *m.* mucus of the eye; -schmalz, *n.* sebaceous humor; -schützer, *m.* goggles; -schwarz, *n.* retinal pigment; -spalte, *f.* sphenoidal cleft, orbital fissure; -spross, *m.* brow beam of the antlers; -ständig, inocular position (of antenna); -stellung, *f.* position of the eye; -stern, *m.* pupil; -stiel, *m.* optic peduncle, eyestalk.

Augen-täuschung, *f.* optical illusion; -trost, *m.* eyebright (*Euphrasia officinalis*); -wasser, *n.* eyewater; -weide, *f.* delight of the eyes; -weiss, *n.* sclera, sclerotica, white of the eye; -welle, *f.* optic axis; -wimper, *f.* eyelash; -windung, *f.* frontal convolution; -wirbel, *m.* eyebrow whorl; -wulst, *f.* optic swelling.

Augen-wurzel, *f.* wood anemone, (*Anemone nemorosa*); -zahn, *m.* eye (canine) tooth; -zeuge, *m.* eyewitness; -zeugnis, *n.* ocular proof; -zirkel, *m.* iris.

augit-artig, -haltig, augitic.

Aula, *f.* great hall.

Aurichlorid, *n.* auric chloride.

Auricularhöcker, *m.* auricular hillock.

Aurikel, *f.* bear's ear, French (mountain) cowslip (*Primula auricula*).

Auri-pigment, *n.* orpiment; -verbindung, *f.* auric compound.

Auro-chlorid, *n.* aurous chloride; -chlorwasserstoffsäure, *f.* chloroauric acid; -verbindung, *f.* aurous compound.

Aurochs, *m.* European bison.

aus, out of, from, off, away from, done.

ausarbeiten, to work out, prepare, finish (off), perfect, elaborate, make up, draft.

Ausarbeitung, *f.* elaboration.

ausarten, to degenerate, deteriorate.

Ausartung, *f.* degeneration.

ausasten, to trim, clear of branches.

ausäthern, to extract with ether.

ausatmen, to breathe forth, exhale, expire, die.

Ausatmung, *f.* expiration, exhalation.

ausätzen, cauterize, destroy by caustics.

ausbaggern, to dredge, excavate, dig out.

Ausbaggerungsfläche, *f.* dredge area.

ausbalanzieren, to equilibrate, balance.

Ausbau, *m.*-e, completion, development, extension, disassembly, enlargement.

ausbauchen, to swell, bulge out, hollow out, emboss, belly out.

Ausbauchung, *f.* swelling, bulging, protuberance, expansion.

ausbauen, to complete, improve, exhaust, develop, enlarge, extend.

ausbauend, expanding, formative.

ausbedingen, to stipulate, reserve.

ausbeizen, to remove with corrosive.

ausbessern, to mend, repair, restore, replant, correct, improve, reline.

ausbeulen, to swell, bulge, round out, flatten.

Ausbeute, *f.* gain, produce, yield, output, profit, crop, production.

ausbeuten, to make the best of, turn to account, exploit, cultivate.

Ausbeutung, *f.* exploitation, cultivation.

ausbiegen, to turn out, avoid, bend out.

ausbieten, to offer.

ausbilden, to form, develop, improve, perfect, educate.

Ausbildung, *f.* formation, cultivation, development, education, improvement.

Ausbiss, *m.*-e, outcrop.

ausbitten, to ask for, request, insist upon, invite.

Ausblase-dampf, *m.*-e, exhaust steam; -hahn, *m.* blowoff cock.

ausblasen, to blow out, blow off, dust off, shut down, exhaust.

Ausblassen, *n.* decoloration.

ausbleiben, to stay away, be absent, fail to appear.

Ausbleiben, *n.* absence, nonappearance, nonarrival.

ausbleichen, to bleach out, fade.

Ausbleichung, *f.* fading, bleaching out.

Ausbleichverfahren, *n.*-, bleaching-out method.

ausbleien, to line with lead.

ausblenden, to shield (of radio).

Ausblendung, *f.* scattering (of rays).

Ausblick, *m.*-e, outlook, prospect.

ausblühen, to cease blooming, effloresce.

Ausblühung, *f.* efflorescence.

ausbohren, to bore out, drill.

ausbraten, to roast well.

ausbrechen, to break out or off, cut off, prune, vomit, shell, extract, force out.

ausbreiten, to spread out, expand, display.

Ausbreiteprobe, *f.* flow test.

Ausbreitung, *f.* spreading out, extension, propagation, diffusion.

Ausbreitungs-gebiet, *n.*-e, area of spreading, regional spread; -geschwindigkeit, ,. velocity of propagation, speed of spreading, migration; -grenzen, geographical range; -herd, *m.* center of spreading distribution; -hindernis, *n.* distribution barrier; -mittel, *n.* means, agency oi distribution.

Ausbrennen, *n.* erosion (of gun barrel).

ausbrennen, to burn or blow (out), cauterize, parch.

ausbringen, to bring out, obtain, yield, put out.

Ausbruch, *m.*-e, break, explosion, eruption, rash.

ausbrühen, to scald.

ausbrüten, to incubate.

ausbuchten, to bend out, bow out; **ausgebuchtet,** sinuated.

Ausbuchtung, *f.* protrusion, dilation, excavation.

ausbügeln, to iron out.

ausdampfen, to evaporate, cease steaming.

ausdämpfen, to steam, expel by steam, evaporate.

Ausdampfung, *f.* evaporation.

Ausdauer, *f.* perseverance, endurance.

ausdauern, to persevere, hold out, endure, be perennial.

ausdauernd, perennial, lasting.

ausdehnbar, expansible, extensible.

ausdehnen, to expand, stretch, extend, distend, dilate; **ausgedehnt,** extensive, expanded.

Ausdehnung, *f.* expansion, extension, dilation, distention, dimension, deformation.

Ausdehnungs-änderung, *f.* alteration in expansion; **-vermögen,** *n.* expansive force; **-zahl,** *f.* expansion coefficient.

ausdenken, to imagine, devise, conceive.

ausdeuten, to explain, interpret.

ausdörren, to dry up, desiccate, season (timber).

ausdrehen, to turn (out or off).

ausdreschen, to thresh (thrash) out.

ausdringen, to penetrate.

Ausdruck, *m.*ᐨe, saying, expression; zum ∼ **kommen,** to be manifested (in), expressed, revealed; zum ∼ **bringen,** to express.

ausdrucken, to finish printing, print in full.

ausdrücken, to express, press out, squeeze out.

ausdrücklich, express, explicit, intentional.

Ausdrucks-form, *f.*-en, manner of expression; **-los,** void of expression; **-mittel,** *n.* means of expression; **-voll,** expressive.

ausdünnen, to thin (out).

Ausdunst, *m.*ᐨe, evaporation, exhalation, expiration, perspiration.

Ausdünstbarkeit, *f.* evaporability, perspirability.

ausdunsten, ausdünsten, transpire, perspire, evaporate.

Ausdunstung, Ausdünstung, *f.* perspiration, exhalation, evaporation.

auseinander, apart, asunder, separately; **-bringen,** to separate; **-fahren,** to move apart, diverge; **-falten,** to unfold; **-gehen,** to separate, diverge, differ, break up; **-halten,** to keep apart, distinguish between; **-hebung,** *f.* apostasis; **-jagen,** to scatter; **-laufend,** divergent; **-nehmen,** to take to pieces, strip, dismantle.

auseinander-setzen, to explain, analyze, put apart, **-setzung,** *f.* exposition, explanation, altercation, argument; **-stieben,** to scatter.

auserkoren, chosen, selected.

auserlesen, picked, selected, exquisite.

ausersehen, to choose, select, single out.

auserwählt, chosen, selected.

ausfahren, to drive out, set out, export, carry out, ship.

Ausfahrt, *f.*-en, drive, driveway, excursion.

Ausfall, *m.*ᐨe, falling (out or off), precipitation, precipitate, result, deficiency, deficit, attack, prolapse, shedding, failure.

ausfallen, to fall or come out, precipitate, deposit, dislocate, turn out.

Ausfallen, *n.* precipitation.

ausfällen, to precipitate, separate.

Ausfalls-erscheinung, *f.* pathological deficiency (atrophy); **-muster,** *m.* outturn.

Ausfällung, *f.* precipitation.

Ausfallwinkel, *m.*-, angle of reflection

ausfärben, to extract color, dye, pale.

Ausfärbvorrichtung, *f.* color extractor.

ausfasern, to unravel.

ausfaulen, to rot out.

ausfechten, to fight out.

ausfegen, to sweep out.

ausfertigen, to dispatch, draw up, make out, copy.

ausfeuern, to burn out, warm, heat.

ausfinden, to find out, discover.

ausfindig machen, to find out, discover.

ausfleischen, to flesh (hides).

ausflicken, to patch, reline, repair.

ausfliegen, to fly out, leave home.

ausfliessen, to flow out, discharge, emanate, ooze out.

ausflocken, to separate in flakes or flocks, flocculate.

Ausflocken, *n.* flocculation.

Ausflucht, *f.*ᐨe, subterfuge, excuse, evasion.

Ausflug, *m.*ᐨe, flight, excursion.

Ausfluss, *m.*ᐨe, outflow, discharge, secretion, flux, efflux, emission, emanation, effluence; **-loch,** *n.* **-öffnung,** *f.* outlet.

ausfolgen, to deliver up.

ausformen, to convert, shape.

ausforschen, to find out, search out, investigate.

ausfragen, to question.

ausfräsen, to countersink.

Ausfräsung, *f.* recess, cavity (milled).

ausfressen, to corrode, eat up, eat out.

ausfrieren, to congeal, freeze out, freeze (up) thoroughly.

Ausfuhr, *f.*-en, export; -bewilligung, *f.* export permit.

ausführbar, practicable, feasible, exportable.

ausführen, to carry out, execute, purge, enlarge on, perform, export, lead out, erect, evacuate.

Ausführgang, *m.*-e, excretory duct.

ausführlich, full, circumstantial, detailed, minutely, completely.

Ausführlichkeit, *f.* minuteness of detail, copiousness, completeness.

Ausfuhrröhre, *f.* excurrent canal.

Ausführung, *f.* carrying out, erection, excretion, evacuation, exposition, finish, style, design, pattern, method, performance, construction, execution, idea put forward or worked out.

Ausführungs-bestimmung, *f.* regulation for exportation, execution or carrying out; -gang, *m.* excretory duct; -mittel, *n.* purgative; -spalte, *f.* a leading-out split; crevice, pore.

Ausfuhrweg, *m.*-e, duct.

ausfüllen, to fill (up), empty, complete.

Ausfüll-masse, *f.* filling, stuffing, packing; -stoff, *m.* packing material.

Ausfüllungsmasse, *f.* filling, intermediary tissue, redundant tissue.

ausfuttern, ausfüttern, to line, coat, feed, fatten.

Ausfütterung, *f.* lining, fettling.

Ausgabe, *f.* expense, expenditure, edition, issue, delivery.

Ausgang, *m.*-e, going out, departure, starting point, exit, outlet, ending, end, result, termination.

Ausgangs-form, *f.*-en, initial, original form; -gestein, *n.* parent rock; -material, *n.* initial material, raw material; -punkt, *m.* starting point; -stoff, *m.* raw material, ingredient, component part.

ausgären, to cease fermenting, ferment sufficiently, throw off (by fermentation), weld (steel).

ausgeartet, degenerate.

ausgebaut, exhausted, completed.

ausgeben, to spend, yield, produce, give out, publish, issue.

ausgebildet, trained, schooled, skilled, fully developed, perfected, accomplished.

ausgeblasen, exhausted.

ausgebreitet, diffuse, scattered, prostrate.

ausgebuchtet, emarginated, pouched.

Ausgeburt, *f.* offspring, production.

ausgedehnt, extensive, wide, spread.

ausgefranst, laciniate, fringed.

ausgeführt, carried out, explained.

ausgeglichen (ausgleichen), balanced.

ausgehen, to go out, proceed, emanate, come off, fail, stop, wither, begin, ferment, fade, start out; **auf etwas ~,** to aim at something.

ausgehend, outgoing, proceeding, deduced, salient (of an angle).

ausgekocht, extracted.

ausgelassen, gay, unrestrained.

ausgemacht, certain, sure, settled.

ausgenommen, (ausnehmen), except, save, barring.

ausgeprägt, distinct, pronounced, strongly marked, delineated, defined, stamped, decided.

ausgerandet, crenate, emarginated.

ausgerben, to tan, weld (steel).

ausgereift, matured.

ausgerottet, exterminated.

ausgerückt, out of gear.

ausgeschaltet, disconnected.

ausgeschieden (ausscheiden), separated, eliminated, precipitated.

ausgeschlossen (ausschliessen), excluded, out of the question, impossible.

ausgeschmolzen (ausschmelzen), melted out.

ausgeschweift, sinuous, incised.

ausgespreizt, divergent.

ausgesprochen (aussprechen), pronounced, marked, decided, outspoken, strongly, very (exceptionally) well.

ausgestalten, to shape.

Ausgestaltung, *f.* putting into shape, development, formation, morphosis.

ausgestochen (ausstechen), scrobiculate.

ausgestorben, extinct.

ausgesucht, exquisite, choice.

ausgewogen (auswiegen), spread, inflated, weighed, calibrated.

ausgezeichnet, excellent, distinguished, exceptionally well, azeotropic (of a point), superb.

ausgezogen (ausziehen), drawn out, extracted, abstracted, solid or continuous (of a line).

ausgiebig, productive, fertile, abundant, yielding, extensive, freely, generous.

Ausgiebigkeit, *f.* productiveness, richness, fertility, abundance, spreading or covering, power (coatings).

ausgiessen, to pour out, discharge, run out, fill up, put out.

Ausgiessung, *f.* effusion, pouring out.

ausgipfeln, to lop, top (trees).

Ausgleich, *m.* equalization, adjustment, settlement, compensation; **-getriebe,** *n.* differential.

ausgleichen, to equalize, adjust, compensate, balance, level, settle, arrange, assimilate, balance.

Ausgleichspannung, *f.* compensating voltage.

Ausgleichung, *f.* equalization, compensation, adjustment.

Ausgleichungs-möglichkeit, *f.* possibility of equalization; **-strömung,** *f.* compensatory current; **-zeit,** *f.* regulation period.

ausgleiten, to slip.

ausgliedern, to segment (joint) off, form laterally, organize lateral members.

Ausgliederung, *f.* segmenting, outgrowth, offshoot.

ausglühen, to heat (thoroughly), ignite, anneal, calcine, cease glowing.

ausgraben, to dig (out), excavate, exhume, engrave.

Ausguck, *m.* lookout.

Ausguss, *m.*ᵉe, pouring out, drain, sink, effusion, spout, lookout, gutter; **-leitung,** *f.* discharge pipe; **-masse,** *f.* compound; **-mörser,** *m.* mortar with a lip.

aushagern, to emaciate, impoverish.

aushalten, to endure, bear, stand, suffer, last, hold out.

aushändigen, to hand over, turn over.

Aushang, *m.*ᵉe, placard.

aushängen, to hang out.

Aushängeschild, *n.*-er, signboard, sign.

ausharren, to persevere, hold out, persist.

Aushärtung, *f.* tempering.

aushauchen, to exhale, breathe, expire.

Aushauchmuskel, *m.* expiratory muscle.

Aushauchung, *f.* expiration, exhalation.

aushauen, to lop (a tree), clear (the wood), cull, carve.

ausheben, to lift out, draw out, select, dislocate, recruit, remove.

aushebern, to siphon out.

aushecken, to hatch, devise.

ausheilen, to heal up.

aushelfen, to aid, help out, assist.

Aushieb, *m.* cutting (of woods).

Aushilfe, *f.* assistance.

Aushilfs-mittel, *n.*-, makeshift, remedy; **-weise,** temporarily, as makeshift.

aushöhlen, to hollow out, excavate.

aushorchen, to listen, auscultate.

Aushub, *m.*ᵉe, excavated material.

aushülsen, to hull, husk, shell, peel.

aushusten, to expectorate, cough out.

ausjäten, to weed out.

auskalten, to cool (thoroughly), chill.

auskaufen, to buy out.

auskehlen, to flute, channel, groove.

auskehren, to sweep out.

auskeilen, to crop out, peter out, wedge out, pinch out.

auskeimen, to germinate, cease germinating.

auskerben, to notch, indent; **ausgekerbt,** crenated.

auskitten, to cement.

auskleiden, to undress, disguise, line, coat, equip.

Auskleidung, *f.* lining, disguise.

ausklingen, to die away (sound).

Ausklinken, *n.* release.

ausklopfen, to beat out.

auskochen, to boil (out), decoct, extract by boiling, clean by boiling, scour, blow out (of a mine); **ausgekocht,** extracted.

Auskochung, *f.* decoction, boiling out.

auskohlen, to carbonize (wool).

auskommen, to come out, sprout, manage, be sufficient, get by, use.

auskörnen, to shake out the grains, thrash, gin (cotton).

auskosten, to taste thoroughly.

Auskragung, *f.* projection.

auskratzen, to scratch out, erase.

auskriechen, to come, creep (out of shell).

auskristallisieren, to crystallize (out), form crystals.

auskrücken, to rake out, draw.

auskühlen, to cool thoroughly.

Auskunft, *f.* information.

Auskunftsmittel, *n.* expedient, resource.

Auskunfttätigkeit, *f.* information service.

auskuppeln, to disconnect, disengage.

auskurbeln, to wind.

auslachen, to laugh at.

ausladen, to unload, discharge.

Auslage, *f.*-n, outlay, advance, expense, display; show window.

Ausland, *n.* foreign country.

Ausländer, *m.* foreigner, alien.

ausländisch, foreign, exotic.

Auslass, *m.*:-e, outlet.

auslassen, to omit, let out, emit, discharge, melt, render, **sich** ~, express oneself; **sich über etwas** ~, to express one's thoughts on; **ausgelassen,** let out, unrestrained.

Auslassröhre, *f.* outlet pipe, discharge pipe.

auslauben, to thin out (foliage), prune.

Auslauf, *m.*:-e, running out, outflow, outlet, mouth, offshoot, continuation, projection.

auslaufen, to set out, run out, leak, cease running, spread.

Ausläufer, *m.*-, runner, stolon, offshoot, branch, process, ramification.

ausläufertreibend, stoloniferous.

Ausläuferwurzelstock, *m.* rhizome.

Auslauf-flasche, *f.* overflow flask; **-spitze,** *f.* discharge tip.

auslaugen, to leach (out), lixiviate, extract, wash (out), steep in lye, buck (in lye).

Auslauger, *m.* extraction apparatus.

Auslaugung, *f.* lixiviation, extraction.

Auslaugungszone, *f.* leached zone.

ausleben, sich, to live a full life.

ausleeren, to empty (out), evacuate, drain, purge, void.

Ausleerungen, *f.pl.* excretion, evacuation.

Ausleerungsmittel, *n.* evacuant, purgative.

auslegen, to lay out, display, inlay. veneer, interpret, explain, pay.

Ausleger, *m.* jib, crane beam.

Auslese, *f.* selection, choice (wine)

auslesen, to select.

Auslesestämmchen, *n.pl.* selected stems to leave (in thinning).

auslichten, to thin a forest, prune, lop (trees).

ausliefern, to deliver up.

Auslieferung, *f.* delivery, giving up.

auslöffeln, to empty (with spoon).

auslösbar, removable, soluble.

auslöschen, to extinguish, put out, blot out.

Auslösch-phänomen, *n.* -zeichen, *n.* Schultz-Charlton's sign in scarlet fever.

Auslöschung, *f.* extinction, effacement.

Auslöschungsschiefe, *f.* extinction angle.

auslösen, to dissolve (out), release, extirpate, loosen, uncouple, disengage, cause. have.

Auslösung, *f.* extirpation, dissolution, release.

auslüften, to air, ventilate.

ausmachen, to take out, remove, put out, make up, amount to, shell, gut, end, settle, matter, constitute; **ausgemacht,** settled.

ausmachend, constituent.

ausmalen, to paint, color, sketch, describe.

Ausmass, *n.*-e, extent, scale, measure, plan, size, dimension.

Ausmauerung, *f.* brickwork, lining.

ausmergeln, to enervate, exhaust, make lean.

ausmerzen, to reject, suppress, eliminate.

ausmessen, to measure (out), gauge, survey.

ausmisten, to clear out dung.

ausmitteln, to find out, ascertain, take the average of.

ausmittig, eccentric.

ausmünden, to open (into), end.

Ausmündung, *f.* mouth, outlet, orifice.

Ausnahme, *f.* exception; **-erscheinung,** *f.* **-fall,** *m.* exceptional case.

ausnahms-los, invariably, without exception; **-weise,** exceptionally.

ausnehmen, to empty, take out, draw, except, exclude, choose; **sich** ~, look, appear.

ausnehmend, exceeding, uncommon.

ausnutzbar, utilizable.

ausnutzen, to utilize, exploit, work, make the most of, turn to account.

Ausnutzung, *f.* using up, utilization, exploitation, efficiency.

Ausnutzungskoeffizient, *m.* utilization coefficient.

auspacken, to unpack.

Auspflanzung, *f.* transplantation, planting.

ausphotometrieren, to evaluate or record photometrically.

auspichen, to pitch (casks).

auspinseln, to paint out, blot out.

ausprägen, to press out, express, project, impress; **sich ~,** to mark distinctly.

auspressen, to press (out), squeeze.

ausproben, ausprobieren, to try (out), test (thoroughly).

Auspuff, *m.* exhaust; **-gas,** *n.* exhaust gas; **-klappe,** *f.* exhaust valve; **-rohr,** *n.* exhaust pipe; **-topf,** *m.* muffler.

auspumpen, to pump out, exhaust.

ausputzen, to clean (out), decorate, dress up, prune, trim, nip off.

ausquetschen, to squeeze out, flow out laterally.

ausradieren, to erase.

Ausrandung, *f.* emargination.

ausrangieren, to put away, discard.

ausranken, to send out tendrils.

ausräuchern, to fumigate, smoke (out).

Ausräucherung, *f.* fumigation, smoking.

ausräumen, to clear out, clean out, empty, ream, broach, rake out.

ausrechen, to rake out.

ausrechnen, to calculate, compute.

ausrecken, to stretch out, extend.

Ausrede, *f.* evasion, excuse, utterance, subterfuge.

ausreden, to finish speaking, utter, express, dissuade.

ausreiben, to rub out, clean.

ausreichen, to suffice, do, last.

ausreichend, adequate, sufficient.

ausreichern, to enrich.

ausreinigen, to clean (out).

ausreissen, to tear out, pull out, run away.

ausrenken, to sprain, dislocate.

ausreuten, to extirpate, root out.

ausrichten, to straighten (out), succeed, adjust, give, perform, do, discover.

Ausrichtung, *f.* straightening, adjustment, performance, orientation.

ausringen, to wring out.

ausroden, to root out, grub up, hew down.

Ausrollgrenze, *f.* plastic limit.

ausrotten, to root out, extirpate, exterminate, destroy, stamp out.

ausrücken, to disengage, ungear, uncouple, move out.

Ausrücker, *m.* disengaging (gear) lever.

Ausrück-hebel, *m.* disengaging lever, lifter; **-vorrichtung,** *f.* disengaging gear, shifting device.

ausrufen, to exclaim, cry out, call out.

Ausrufung, *f.* outcry, exclamation, proclamation.

ausruhen, to rest, repose.

ausrupfen, to pull or pluck out.

ausrüsten, to furnish, fit out, equip, supply, remove forms.

Ausrüstung, *f.* equipment, outfit, finishing.

Aussaat, *f.* sowing, inoculation, insemination, seed.

aussäckeln, aussacken, to empty a bag.

aussäen, to sow seed, inoculate, disseminate.

Aussage, *f.* assertion, declaration, statement.

aussagen, to assert, affirm, state, express, depose.

aussaigern, to segregate, liquate.

aussalzbar, capable of being salted out.

aussalzen, to salt out, separate by addition of salt.

Aussalzung, *f.* salting out.

Aussatz, *m.* leprosy, scurf.

aussätzig, leprous.

aussäuern, to extract (remove) the acid(ity)

aussaugen, to suck out, suck dry, exhaust, drain.

Aussauger, *m.* parasitical plant, sucker.

Aussäungsvorrichtung, *f.* device for seeding.

ausschachten, to excavate.

ausschalten, to eliminate, cut out, switch off, put out, remove, take out, exclude, avoid, disconnect.

Ausschalter, *m.* cutout, circuit breaker, switch.

Ausschaltung, *f.* elimination, removal, bypass, disconnecting.

ausschärfen, to neutralize, deaden.

ausschauen nach, to look out for.

ausscheiden, to separate, crystallize, liberate, eliminate, precipitate, secrete, excrete, exclude.

Ausscheidung, *f.* secretion, elimination, excretion, separation, precipitation, withdrawal, secession, extraction.

Ausscheidungs-bekämpfung, *f.* by-product competition; **-mittel,** *n.* separating agent, precipitant.

ausschenken, to pour out.

ausschiessen, to cast out, reject, discharge, sprout forth.

ausschirren, to unharness, ungear.

ausschlachten, to cut up for sale (meat), utilize, capitalize on.

ausschlacken, to clear of dross or clinker.

Ausschlag, *m.*-e, throw, deflection, divergence, plot, efflorescence, sprout, shoot, breaking out, exanthem, rash, eruption, vibration; ~ **geben,** to decide; **-gebend,** decisive, telling, determinative.

Ausschlag-bütte, *f.* underback; **-eisen,** *n.* punch, pounding tool (for ore).

ausschlagen, to knock, line, cover, refuse, break out, effloresce, turn, bud, strike out, punch out, remove, turn out, produce suckers, shoot forth, sprout, leaf out, decline.

Ausschlag-fähigkeit, *f.* power of sprouting; **-schuppe,** *f.* ramentum, thin scale of epidermis; **-wald,** *m.* coppice wood, sprout land; **-winkel,** *m.* angle of deflection.

ausschlämmen, to wash out, dredge.

ausschleifen, to grind, whet.

Ausschleudermaschine, *f.* centrifuge.

ausschleudern, to hurl forth, centrifuge.

ausschliessen, to shut out, exclude, sort, except; **ausgeschlossen,** out of the question.

ausschliesslich, exclusive, except.

Ausschliessung, *f.* exclusion.

ausschlüpfen, to slip out, hatch out.

Ausschluss, *m.* exclusion, exception.

ausschmelzen, to melt out, render dry.

ausschmieren, to smear, oil, grease, copy, cheat.

ausschneiden, to cut out, extirpate, lop, excise, prune, channel.

Ausschnitt, *m.*-e, cutting out, cut, indentation, notch, sector, section, part.

ausschöpfen, to scoop out, drain.

Ausschöpfkelle, *f.* ladle, scoop.

ausschreiben, to write out, summon, appoint, impose.

Ausschreitung, *f.* excess, transgression.

ausschrumpfen, to outshrink.

Ausschubdruck, *m.* squeezing-out pressure.

Ausschurfwirkung, *f.* abrading (action) effect.

Ausschuss, *m.*-e, refuse, waste, cull, committee, shoot, damaged goods, best part, spoilage, broke(s), offcuts, retree; **-fahrer,** *m.* broke hustler (paper manufacturing).

ausschütteln, to shake out, extract.

ausschwefeln, to fumigate with sulphur.

ausschweifen, to indent, stray, splay out, be dissolute; **ausgeschweift,** sinuated, imbricate(d).

ausschweifend, excessive, dissolute.

ausschweissen, to weld out, clean iron (by welding), bleed.

ausschwemmen, to wash out, scour, sluice.

ausschwenken, to whirl, centrifuge, shake.

Ausschwenkmaschine, *f.* centrifugal.

Ausschwingmaschine, *f.* centrifuge.

ausschwirren, to whiz, centrifuge, hydroextract.

ausschwitzen, to sweat, exude, cease sweating.

aussehen, to look, appear, seem, look out.

Aussehen, *n.* appearance, look, make up.

ausseigern, to segregate, liquate.

aussen, out, outside, outward(ly), abroad, without, exterior; **nach** ~, externally; **nach** ~ **hin,** toward the outside.

Aussen-ast, *m.*-e, exopodite; **-besatzbeutel,** *m.* external tamping bag.

aussenden, to emit, send out, transmit.

Aussendrüse, *f.* external gland.

Aussendung, *f.* sending out, giving forth, emission, radiation, exuding.

Aussen-fahne, *f.* outer vane, web; **-faktor,** *m.* external factor; **-falte,** *f.* external fold; **-fläche,** *f.* external surface; **-haut,** *f.* outer membrane, epidermis; **-hautdichtung,** *f.* membrane waterproofing; **-hülle,** *f.* outer cover, excipulum, involucre; **-keimig,** exorrhizal; **-kelch,** *m.* outer calyx; **-knospung,** *f.* extra gemmation.

Aussen-lade, *f.* paraglossa, galea of maxilla, lobus externus; **-leitung,** *f.* outer circuit; **-lippe,** *f.* outer lip; **-luft,** *f.* external air, atmosphere; **-rand,** *m.* outer margin, outer lip; **-rinde,** *f.* outer layer of bark, periderm; **-schmarotzer,** *m.* ectoparasite; **-seite,** *f.* outside; **-taster,** *m.* outside calipers; **-wäsche,** *f.* pressure wash.

Aussen-welt, *f.* environment; **-wendig,** turning outward, ventral, evaginate; **-wendigkeit,** *f.* exotropism (turning outward); **-winkel,** *m.* exterior angle; **-zehe,** *f.* outer toe.

ausser, outside of, out of, aside from, beside(s), in addition to, save, except, unless; ∼ **acht,** out of consideration.

ausserachsig, eccentric.

ausserdem, besides, moreover, over and above.

äusser, outward, outer, exterior, external; **äussere Anpassung,** *f.* ecological adaptation; **äusseres Ohr,** *n.* auricle.

Äussere, *n.* outside, exterior, outside appearance.

aussergewöhnlich, extraordinary, unusual.

ausserhalb, outside, beyond.

äusserlich, outer, external, apparent, superficial, extrinsic, outward.

Äusserlichkeit, *f.* formality.

aussermittig, eccentric.

äussern, to manifest, utter, express; **sich** ∼, to make itself felt, get in.

ausserordentlich, extraordinary, unusual, remarkable, extreme, special.

äusserst, extreme, exceeding, utmost, outermost, very.

ausserstande, unable.

Äusserung, *f.* manifestation, expression, characteristic, exhibition, utterance.

ausserwesentlich, nonessential, contingent.

aussetzen, to set out, put out, expose, display, suspend, put off, postpone, line, transplant, crop out, stop, pause, intermit, break.

aussetzend, intermittent, discontinuous.

Aussetzung, *f.* setting out, transplantation, exposure, intermission.

Aussicht, *f.*-**en,** outlook, view, perspective, prospect, chance; **in** ∼ **nehmen,** to contemplate.

aussichts-los, hopeless; **-reich,** promising.

aussickern, to trickle, ooze out, cease trickling.

aussieden, to boil out.

aussinnen, to contrive, devise.

aussintern, to ooze out, trickle out, percolate.

aussöhnen, to reconcile.

aussondern, to separate, secrete, excrete, eliminate, sort, reject.

Aussonderung, *f.* excretion, elimination.

aussortieren, to sort out, separate.

ausspannen, to stretch, spread, extend, unharness; **sich** ∼, rest, relax.

Ausspannung, *f.* relaxation.

Aussparung, *f.* saving (up), recess.

aussperren, to lock out.

Aussprache, *f.* pronunciation.

aussprechen, to pronounce, express, declare, state, say, speak out, finish speaking; **ausgesprochen,** pronounced, decided, outspoken.

aussprengen, to blast, sprinkle (water).

ausspringen, to dislocate, spring out, cease jumping.

ausspringend, salient.

ausspritzen, to spurt out, squirt out, wash by syringing, inject.

Ausspritzungsgang, *m.* ejaculatory duct.

Ausspruch, *m.* saying, utterance, decision.

aussprühen, to throw up, eject, belch, fly up (flame, sparks).

Aussprungswinkel, *m.* angle of reflection.

ausspülen, to wash (out), rinse, flush.

ausstaffieren, to equip.

Ausstand, *m.*-̈e, strike, arrears, debts.

ausständig, outstanding, in arrears.

ausstatten, to equip, fit out, furnish, supply, endow.

Ausstattung, *f.* equipment, fittings, outfit, dowry.

ausstäuben, to dust.

ausstechen, to dig out, cut out, carve, engrave.

ausstehen, to stand (out), be owing, strike, endure.

aussteifen, to stiffen, prop, stay, timber, reinforce.

aussteigen, to get out (of vehicle).

ausstellen, to put out, lay out, display, exhibit, draw up, expose, set out.

Aussteller, *m.* exhibitor.

Ausstellung, *f.* exhibition, show, display, censure.

aussterben, to become extinct, die out.

Ausstich, *m.* choicest wine; **-ware,** *f.* prime quality, finest brand.

ausstopfen, to stuff.

Ausstoss, *m.*-̈e, expulsion.

ausstossen, to throw out, thrust out, expel, evacuate, excrete, eliminate, discharge, emit, utter, burst forth.

Ausstoss-ladung, *f.* bursting charge; **-produkt,** *n.* waste products; **-system,** *n.* cleansing system.

Ausstossung, *f.* expulsion, evacuation, elimination.

Ausstossystem, *n.* cleansing system.

ausstrahlen, to radiate, emit, extend.

Ausstrahlung, *f.* radiation, emanation.

Austrahlungs-fläche, *f.* radiating surface; **-vermögen,** *n.* radiating capacity, emissivity; **-winkel,** *m.* angle of radiation.

ausstrecken, to stretch, extend, distend.

Ausstrecker, *m.* tensor, extensor muscle.

ausstreichen, to strike out, erase, smooth out, level, spread.

ausstreuen, to scatter, diffuse.

Ausstreuung, *f.* diffusion.

Ausstreuvorrichtung, *f.* dispersal mechanism.

Ausstrich, *m.*-e, smear, outcrop; **-präparate,** *n.pl.* smear preparations.

ausströmen, to stream out, flow out, emanate, escape, radiate.

Ausströmung, *f.* outflow, emanation, effusion, escape, effluence, flow, extruding.

Ausströmungs-öffnung, *f.* exhalant siphon, excretory, secretory opening; **-rohr,** *n.* delivery pipe.

ausstülpen, to evaginate, bulge, protrude.

Ausstülpung, *f.* protrusion, extroversion.

aussuchen, to choose, search out, select, sort; **ausgesucht,** exquisite, choice.

aussüssen, to wash (a precipitate), edulcorate, sweeten.

Aussüss-pumpe, *f.* leaching pump; **-rohr,** *n.* **-röhre,** *f.* washing tube.

austapezieren, to paper, line (as with linoleum, rubber, rugs, rags, etc.).

Austausch, *m.*-e, exchange, barter, interchange; **-adsorption,** *f.* adsorption exchange.

austauschbar, exchangeable, interchangeable.

austauschen, to exchange, interchange.

austauschfähig, exchangeable, interchangeable.

Austausch-klasse, *f.* crossover class or group; **-kombination,** *f.* recombination, crossover; **prozent,** *m.* crossover percent-age; **-unterdrücker,** *m.* crossover inhibitor, suppressor; **-wert,** *m.* crossover linkage, value; **-zahlen,** *f.pl.* crossover numbers, percentage.

austeilen, to distribute.

Auster, *f.*-n, oyster.

austilgen, to efface, destroy, obliterate, extirpate.

Austrag, *m.*-e, decision, issue, product.

austragen, to deliver, carry out, wear out, decide, cease bearing (tree).

austreibbar, *m.* expellable.

austreiben, to expel, drive out, shoot forth, eject.

Austreibung, *f.* expulsion.

austreten, to step out, go out, leave, retire, extravasate, dislocate, issue, come out.

Austritt, *m.*-e, leaving, emergence, extravasation, outlet, exit.

Austritts-kante, *f.* trailing edge of wing; **-pupille,** *f.* pupil of emergence; **-winkel,** *m.* angle of emersion or reflection.

austrocknen, to dry (up), parch, desiccate, drain.

Austrocknung, *f.* drying, desiccation, exsiccation.

Austrocknungs-fähigkeit, *f.* ability to withstand desiccation; **-rinde,** *f.* dried-out layer.

auströpfeln, austropfen, to drip out, drop out, cease trickling.

ausüben, to practice, exert, exercise, carry out.

auswachsen, to grow out, vegetate, sprout, heal up, grow up, grow deformed; **ausgewachsen,** grown out, full-grown.

auswägen, to weigh, tare.

Auswahl, *f.* choice, selection.

auswählen, to choose, select.

Auswahlvermögen, *n.* ability to select.

auswalzen, to roll out.

auswandern, to emigrate.

auswärmen, to warm, anneal.

auswärtig, outward, foreign.

auswärts, outward, without, abroad; **von ~,** from abroad.

Auswärts-dreher, *m.* supinator muscle; **-drehung,** *f.* supination; **-roller,** *m.* rotator muscle.

auswaschbar, capable of being washed out.

auswaschen, to wash (out), cleanse, rinse, edulcorate. bathe.

Auswaschung, *f.* washing out, erosion.

Auswäschung, *f.* elutriation.

Auswaschungsverlust, *m.* loss from washing, leaching.

auswässern, to soak, water.

auswechselbar, exchangeable, interchangeable, renewable, replaceable.

auswechseln, to exchange, interchange, doff.

Auswechslung, *f.* exchange, replacement, renewal.

Ausweg, *m.*-e, way out, outlet, vent, expedient, refuge.

ausweichen, to avoid, step aside, elude, evade, soften, soak.

ausweichend, evasive, elusive.

Ausweichung, *f.* deviation, displacement, deflection, evasion, soaking, flow.

ausweiden, to eviscerate, draw (poultry), graze off.

Ausweis, *m.*-e, proof, statement, credential.

ausweisen, to turn out, expel, banish, show, prove, make evident.

ausweitbar, extensible.

ausweiten, to widen, stretch.

auswendig, outside, exterior, extrorse, by heart.

auswerfen, to throw out, discharge, reject, expectorate.

auswertbar, evaluable.

Auswertung, *f.* evaluation, utilization.

auswettern, to weather; **er hat ausgewettert,** he has ceased storming.

auswickeln, to unwrap.

auswiegen, to weigh out.

auswinden, to wring out, wrench out, unscrew.

auswintern, to expose to the rigor of winter.

Auswinterung, *f.* winter killing (plants).

auswirken, to obtain, accomplish, workout.

auswischen, to wipe out.

auswittern, to effloresce, season (wood), get scent of, weather.

Auswitterung, *f.* efflorescence, weathering, seasoning (of wood).

Auswuchs, *m.*-e, outgrowth, enation, excrescence, tumor.

auswuchten, to balance, compensate.

Auswurf, *m.*-e, throwing out, discharge, sputum, expectoration, excretion, refuse, shake(s), trash, excrement; **-stoffe,** *m.pl.* excretions, excrement.

auszacken, to indent, notch; **ausgezackt,** denticulate(d), dentate.

auszehren, to consume, waste away.

Auszehrung, *f.* consumption.

auszeichnen, to mark out, distinguish; **ausgezeichnet,** excellent, distinguished.

Auszeichnung, *f.* distinction, labeling, mark.

ausziehbar, capable of being extracted, ductile.

ausziehen, to extract, draw (out), pull out, fade (colors), abstract, pull off, undress, stretch, extend move (out).

Auszieh-fallschirm, *m.* auxiliary parachute; **-tisch,** *m.*-e, extension table; **-tubus,** *m.* draw tube (of microscope).

Ausziehung, *f.* extraction.

Auszug, *m.*-e, extract, essence, tincture, infusion, decoction, removal, exodus, drawer, abstract; **-hauung,** *f.* cutting away (trees); **-mehl,** *n.* superfine flour.

auszugsweise, as an extract, or abstract from.

auszupfen, to pluck out.

Auszweigung, *f.* pruning, lopping, branching.

autark, self-sufficient economically.

authentisch, authentic.

autogen, autogenous.

Autoinfektion, *f.* autoinfection.

Autokatalyse, *f.* autocatalysis.

Autoklav, *m.* autoclave.

Autolack, *m.* motorcar enamel.

Automatenstahl, *m.* free-cutting (working, machining) steel, automatic screw steel.

automatisch, automatic.

autonom, autonomous.

Autopsie, *f.* autopsy.

Autor, *m.* author.

Autorenregister, *n.* author index.

autorisieren, to authorize.

Autorität, *f.* authority.

Auto-typiepapier, *n.* halftone paper; **-vakzinationsbehandlung,** *f.* treatment with autogenous vaccines.

autoxydabel, autoxidizable.

Auwald, *m.* lowland forest.

Avidität, *f.* avidity.

avisieren, to advise, inform.

Avivage, *f.* reviving (of color), preparation.

avivierecht, unaffected by reviving.

avivieren, to revive, restore (color).

avunkular, avuncular.

Axe, *f.* axis.

Axillarblüte, *f.* axillary flower.

axillarer Strang, *m.* dorsal cord, notochord.

Axt, *f.* ̈e, ax, hatchet.

Azalee, Azalie, *f.* azalea.

Azelainsäure, *f.* azelaic acid.

Azetat, *n.* acetate.

Azeton, *n.* acetone.

Azetyl, *n.* acetyl.

Azetylen, *n.* acetylene.

Aziäthan, *n.* aziethane.

Azid, *n.* trinitride azide, hydrazoate.

Aziditätsgrad, *m.* degree of acidity.

Azidoameisensäure, *f.* azido-formic acid.

azidolitischer Abbau, *m.* acidolytic (hydro-lytic) degradation (by means of acids).

Azobenzol, *n.* azobenzene.

Azot, *n.* nitrogen.

Azoxybenzol, *n.* azoxybenzene.

azozyklisch, azocyclic.

Azulminsäure, *f.* azulmic acid.

azurblau, azure.

azurn, azure.

Azurstein, *m.* lapis lazuli.

azyklisch, acyclic.

B

Babuin, *m.* baboon.

Bach, *m.* ̈e, brook, creek; **-amsel,** *f.* water ouzel (*Cinclus aquaticus*); **-binse,** *f.* water bulrush (*Juncus conglomeratus*); **-bunge,** *f.* brooklime (*Veronica beccabunga*).

Bache, *f.* wild sow.

Bach-forelle, *f.* brook trout (*Salmo fario*); **-hol(un)der,** *m.* water elder (*Viburnum opulus*); **-krebs,** *m.* crawfish (Astacus); **-kresse,** *f.* water cress (*Nasturtium officinale*).

bachliebend, brookloving, rivalis, growing by a brookside.

Bach-minze, *f.* round-leaved mint (*Mentha rotundifolia*); **-nelkenwurz,** *f.* water avens (*Geum rivale*); **-stelze,** *f.* wagtail (Motacilla); **-weide,** *f.* osier (*Salix helix*).

bac . . . , see also BAK . . . BAZ . . .

bacillär, bacillary.

Bacille, *f.* bacillus.

Bacillen-art, *f.* **-en,** kind of bacillus; **-färbung,** *f.* staining of bacilli; **-herd,** *m.* focus of bacilli; **-lehre,** *f.* bacteriology; **-vernichtend,** bacillicide.

Backapfel, *m.* ̈, baking apple, dried apple.

Backe, *f.*, cheek, jaw, gena.

backen, to bake, roast, fry, dry, adhere, stick, fire.

Backen, *m.* cheek, jaw, gena; **-arterie,** *f.* buccal artery; **-bart,** *m.* whiskers; **-bein,** *n.* jawbone, malar bone, maxillary bone; **bohrer,** *m.* master tap; **-brecher,** *m.* jaw crusher; **-drüse,** *f.* buccal gland; **-falte,** *f.* buccal fold; **-fistel,** *f.* buccal fistula; **-fläche,** *f.* buccal surface.

Backen-fortsatz, *m.* zygomatic process; **-haut,** *f.* skin of the cheek; **-höcker,** *m.* buccal eminence; **-höhle,** *f.* buccal cavity; **-hörnchen,** *n.* chipmunk; **-knochen,** *m.* malar bone; **-leisten,** *f.pl.* lateral plates, lateralia; **-schleimhaut,** *f.* buccal mucous membrane; **-tasche,** *f.* cheek (buccal) pouch; **-zahn,** *m.* molar tooth.

Bäcker, *m.* baker; **-beine,** *n.pl.* knock-knees.

Bäckerei, *f.* bakery.

Back-kohle, *f.* caking coal, binding coal; **-obst,** *n.* dried fruit; **-ofen,** *m.* oven; **-pflaume,** *f.* prune; **-pulver,** *n.* baking powder; **-stein,** *m.* brick; **-steinartig,** brick-shaped; **-werk,** *n.* pastry; **-zahn,** *m.* molar tooth.

Bad, *n.* ̈er, bath, dip, watering place.

baden, to bathe.

Bäderanordnung, *f.* cell-group arrangement.

Bade-schwamm, *m.* ̈e, sponge; **-wanne,** *f.* bathtub.

Badflüssigkeit, *f.* bath liquid, bath solution.

Badian, *m.* badian, star anise (*Illicium verum*).

Bad-kasten, *m.* cell; **-spannung,** *f.* bath tension, cell voltage; **-strecke,** *f.* (des Fadens), bath travel (of thread).

bäen, to bleat.

Bagage, *f.* luggage.

Bagasse, *f.* bagasse.

Bagger, *m.* dredger, excavator.

baggern, to dredge.

Baggertorf, *m.* drag (dredged) peat.

bähen, to foment, bathe, stupe, warm, heat, toast, force (plants).

Bahn, *f.*-en, track, road, way, path, orbit, channel, railway; **-brechend,** opening the way, pioneer; **-brecher,** *m.* pioneer; **-damm,** *m.* railway embankment; **-ebene,** *f.* plane of motion, orbital plane.

bahnen, to prepare, smooth, clear the way, facilitate.

Bahn-hof, *m.*⸚e, (railway) station; **-übergang,** *m.* orbital transition, railway crossing.

Bahre, *f.* barrow, stretcher, bier.

Bähung, *f.* fomenting.

Bähungsmittel, *n.* fomentation agent.

Bai, *f.* bay; **-salz,** *n.* sea salt.

Bajonettrohr, *n.* bayonet tube, closed tube.

Bakteriämie, *f.* bacteremia.

Bakterie, *f.* bacterium.

bakteriell, bacterial.

Bakterien, *f.pl.* bacteria; **-art,** *f.* kind or variety of bacteria; **-artig,** bacterioid; **-befund,** *m.* state in which bacteria are found; **-fäden,** *f.pl.* bacterial threads, bacterial chains; **-farben,** *f.pl.* stains for bacteria; **-färbung,** *f.* staining of bacteria; **-fäule,** *f.* soft rot; **-feindlich,** bactericidal; **-forscher,** *m.* bacteriologist; **-forschung,** *f.* bacteriological research.

Bakterien-gattung, *f.* genus of bacteria; **-gehalt,** *m.* bacterial content; **-geisseln,** *f.pl.* flagella; **-gift,** *n.* bacterial toxin, bactericide, ptomaine; **-haltig,** containing bacteria; **-hauf,** *f.* pellicle (film) of bacteria; **-impfung,** *f.* inoculation with bacteria; **-knoten,** *m.pl.* nodular bacterial swellings; **-krebs,** *m.* (der Kartoffeln), crown gall (of potatoes); **-kultur,** *f.* culture of bacteria; **-kunde,** *f.* bacteriology.

Bakterien-lampe, *f.* luminescence due to bacteria; **-lehre,** *f.* bacteriology; **-nährlösung,** *f.* solution for bacterial cultures; **-schädigung,** *f.* bacterial injury, inhibition; **-stamm,** *m.* strain of bacteria; **-tinktion,** *f.* staining of bacteria; **-tötend,** bactericidal; **-vernichtend,** bactericidal; **-wachstum,** *n.* bacterial growth; **-zählungen,** *f.pl.* counts of bacteria; **-züchtung,** *f.* culture of bacteria.

Bakterioden, *f.pl.* bacterial nodules.

Bakterio-loge, *m.* bacteriologist; **-logie,** *f.* bacteriology; **-logisch,** bacteriological; **-skopie,** *f.* bacterioscopy, bacteriological research.

Bakteriurie, *f.* bacteriuria.

bakterizid, bactericidal.

Bakterizidie, *f.* bactericidal action.

Balance, *f.* balance, equilibrium.

Balancier, *m.* beam (of balance).

balancieren, to balance.

Balane, *f.* balanid, Balanus, acorn barnacle.

Balata-gummi, *m.* balata gum; **-riemen,** *m.* balata belt.

bald, soon, presently, easily, readily, nearly ~ . . . ~, at one time . . . at another time . . . , now . . . now . . . , now . . . then . . . ; so ~ als . . . , as soon as . . . .

Baldachin, *m.* canopy.

Bälde, *f.* near future; **in** ~, soon.

baldig, speedy.

baldigst, very soon.

baldmöglichst, as soon as possible.

Baldrian, *m.* valerian; **-gewächse,** *n.pl.* Valerianaceae; **-säure,** *f.* valeric acid; **-wurzel,** *f.* valerian root.

baldtunlichst, as soon as possible.

Balg, *m.*⸚e, husk, pod, follicle, glume, cyst, shell, skin, bellows, slough; **-artig,** follicular, glumaceous, cystlike; **-auszug,** *m.* bellows extension; **-blumen,** *f.pl.* glumose flowers (Glumaceae); **-drüse,** *f.* follicular gland; **-gebläse,** *n.* bellows.

balgen sich, to fight, scuffle.

Balg-frucht, *f.* dehiscent fruit, follicle, caryopsis, utricle; **-geschwulst,** *n.* encysted tumor; **-höhle,** *f.* follicular cavity; **-kapsel,** *f.* follicle, cyamium, air bag, capsule; **-pilz,** *m.* Lycopodium; **-scheide,** *f.* follicular sheath; **-wand,** *f.* cyst wall; **-wasserbruch,** *m.* encysted hydrocele.

Bälkchen, *n.* little beam, trabecula.

Balken, *n.* beam, rafter, joist, girder, trabecula, corpus callosum; **-fasern,** *f.pl.* fibers of the pons; **-furche,** *f.* median groove of corpus callosum; **-gerüst,** *n.* trabecular framework; **-gewebe,** *n.* trabecular tissue; **-netz,** *n.* trabecular (network) stroma; **-polster,** *n.* pulvinus, splenium of corpus callosum.

Balken-schlagader, *f.* (anterior cerebral) artery of corpus callosum; **-schnabel,** *n.* rostrum of corpus callosum; **-stich,** *m.* puncture; **-waage,** *f.* beam balance; **-werk,** *n.* framework, beams; **-windung,** *f.* convolution of corpus callosum; **-zange,** *f.* fenestrated forceps.

Balkon, *m.* balcony.

Ball, *m.*⸚e, ball, globe, dance.

Ballast, *m.* ballast; **-stoff,** *m.* nonparticipating substance.

ballen, to form into a ball, conglomerate, cluster, clench.

Ballen, *m.* ball, eminence, pad, sole, bale, pack, bunion, 10 reams (of paper); **-artig,** in packet formation; **-fesselbeinband,** *n.* periople; **-pflanze,** *f.* ball plant; **-pflanzung,** *f.* ball planting, planting with a ball of roots and earth covered with burlap; **-polster,** *n.* pads of the plantar cushion.

ballförmig, spherical, globular.

ballig, slightly convex.

Ballisten, *pl.* ballistic (catapult) fruits.

ballistisch, ballistic.

Ballofen, *m.* balling (reheating) furnace.

Ballon, *m.* balloon, carboy, balloon flask; **-filter,** *n.* filtering flask.

ballotieren, to ballot.

Ballung, *f.* agglomeration.

Balsam, *m.* balsam, balm, salve, ointment; **-apfel,** *m.* balsam apple (*Momordica balsamina*); **-duft,** *m.* balsam(ic) scent; **-erzeugend,** balsamiferous; **-feige,** *f.* balsam fig (*Clusia rosea*); **-flasche,** *f.* balsam bottle; **-harz,** *n.* balsamic resin; **-holz,** *n.* xylobalsamum (*Amyris opobalsamum*).

balsamieren, to embalm, perfume.

Balsamine, *f.* garden balsam (*Impatiens balsamina*).

balsamisch, balsamic, balmy, soothing.

Balsam-kraut, *n.* moschatel (*Adoxa moschatellina*), balsam herb (*Dianthera repens*); **-pappel,** *f.* balsam poplar, tacamahac (*Populus balsamifera*); **-staude,** *f.* balsam shrub, balsam bush (Balsamodendron or Commiphora); **-strauch,** *m.* bdellium; **-tanne,** *f.* balsam fir, spruce.

balzen, to copulate, pair.

Balzjagd, *f.* stalking the cock.

Bambus, *m.* bamboo; **-rohr,** *n.* bamboo; **-zucker,** *m.* tabasheer.

banal, commonplace, banal.

Banane, *f.* banana.

Bananen-pisang, *m.* banana tree; **-wachs,** *n.* pisang wax.

band (binden), bound, tied.

Band, *m.*ː-e, binding, volume.

Band, *n.*ː-er, bond, band, ribbon, string, thread, belt, web, ligature, ligament, commissure, tie, strap, tape, graph, isopleth; **-achat,** *m.* banded (ribbon) agate.

Bandage, *f.* bandage, truss, tire.

band-ähnlich, ribbonlike, streaked, ligamentous; **-arbeit,** *f.* moving-belt production; **-artig,** ribbonlike, streaked, ligamentous; **-beinfügung,** *f.* joining of bones by ligaments, synneurosis; **-blatt,** *n.* ribbonlike leaf.

Bändchen, *n.* small ligament, small ribbon, small volume.

Bande, *f.* border, band, gang, troop.

Bandeisen, *n.* band (strap) iron; *pl.* hoops.

Bandenspektrum, *n.* band spectrum.

bändereich, voluminous.

Bänder-erschlaffung, *f.* relaxation of ligaments; **-lehre,** *f.* syndesmology; **-schneiden,** *n.* cutting serial sections in ribbon; **-ton,** *m.* varved clay.

Band-förderer, *m.* belt conveyor; **-förmig,** ligamentous; **-geissel,** *f.* tentacle; **-gelenk,** *n.* ligamentous (joint) symphysis; **-gras,** *n.* ribbon grass.

bandiert, fasciate.

bändigen, to tame, break in (of horses).

Band-kupplung, *f.* rim clutch; **-mass,** *n.*-e, tape measure; **-nelke,** *f.* carnation (*Dianthus caryophyllus*); **-scheibe,** *f.* interarticular disk, meniscus; **-seiltrommel,** *f.* bobbin; **-streifig,** streaked, banded; **-verbindung,** *f.* union by ligament.

Bandwurm, *m.*ː-er, tapeworm, cestoid; **-glied,** *n.* proglottis, segment of tapeworm; **-träger,** *m.* host of tapeworm.

bange, anxious

bangen, to be afraid.

Bangigkeit, *f.* anxiety, fear.

Baniane, *f.* banyan, banyan tree (*Ficus benjamina*).

Bank, *f.* bench, bank, shoal, bed, layer, plank, stratum; **durch die ~,** on the average, without exception; **-anweisung,** *f.* check, bank note.

bankerott, bankrupt, insolvent.

Bankett, *n.* banquet, feast, berm, shoulder.

Bankulnuss, *f.* candlenut (*Aleurites moluccana*).

Bankwesen, *n.* banking.

Bann, *m.* ban, constraint, spell.

bannen, to captivate, enchant, banish, confine.

Bannforst, *m.* forest preserve.

bansen, to pile up the sheaves.

Bär, *m.* bear, boar, rammer, pile driver.

-bar, -able, -ible.

bar, bare, naked, pure, cash, destitute (of); für ~, for cash.

Baratte, *f.* drum, baratte.

Barbar. *m.* barbarian.

Barbarakraut, *n.* winter cress (*Barbarea vulgaris*).

Barbe, *f.* barbel (*Barbus vulgaris*).

Barbenkraut, *n.* winter cress (*Barbarea vulgaris*).

Barbier, *m.* barber.

barbieren, shave, fleece, cheat.

Barchent, *m.* fustian.

bären-artig, bearish, ursine; **-fenchel,** *m.* spicknel (*Meum athamanticum*); **-klau,** *f.* bear's breech (Acanthus), cow parsnip (Heracleum); **-lauch,** *m.* wild garlic (*Allium ursinum*); **-spinner,** *m.* tiger moth; **-traube,** *f.* bearberry (*Arctostaphylos uva-ursi*); **-wurz,** *f.* spicknel (*Meum athamanticum*); **-zwinger,** *m.* bear garden.

Bar-frost, *m.* black (soil lifting) frost; **-fuss,** barefooted; **-häuptig,** bareheaded.

barg (bergen), saved, concealed, salvaged.

Barium, *n.* barium; **-hydrat,** *n.* barium hydroxide; **-nitrat,** *n.* nitrate of barium; **-superoxyd,** *n.* peroxide of barium.

Barke, *f.* bark, barge, shallow vat, tank.

Bärlapp, *m.* club moss, lycopod; **-gewächse,** *n.pl.* Lycopodiaceae; **-kraut,** *n.* lycopodium, club moss; **-mehl,** *n.* **-samen,** *m.* **-staub,** *m.* lycopodium (powder).

Bärlauchöl, *n.* broad-leaved garlic oil.

Bärme, *f.* leaven, yeast, barm.

barmherzig, merciful.

Bärmutter, *f.* womb, uterus.

Barnstein, *m.* brick, tile.

Barometer, *n.&m.* barometer; **-stand,** *m.* height or reading of the barometer.

Barre, *f.* **Barren,** *m.* bar, ingot, bullion.

Barsch, *m.* perch (fish).

barsch, rough, rude.

Barschaft, *f.* ready money, cash.

Barschheit, *f.* harshness, rudeness.

barst (bersten), burst, ruptured.

Bart, *m.* beard, barb, wattle, burr, fin, fash.

Barte, *f.* whalebone.

Bartenwale, *m.pl.* whalebone whales.

Bart-faden, *m.* barb, beard, antenna; **-flechte,** *f.* beard moss (*Usnea barbata*), barber's itch, sycosis; **-gras,** *n.* beard grass (Andropogon).

Bärtierchen, *n.pl.* bear animalcules, tardigrades.

bärtig, bearded, barbellate, glochidiate.

bart-los, beardless; **-moos,** *n.* beard moss (Phascum); **-nelke,** *f.* sweet William (*Dianthus barbatus*); **-seife,** *f.* shaving soap.

Bartstreif, *m.* malar stripe.

Bär-winde, *f.* bindweed (Calystegia); **-wurz,** *f.* spicknel (*Meum athamanticum*).

Baryt, *m.* baryta; **-artig,** barytic; **-erde,** *f.* barium oxide; **-flusspat,** *m.* fluorite with barium content; **-führend,** barytic, containing barium; **-gang,** *m.* barite vein; **-haltig,** barytic, containing barium; **-hydrat,** *n.* barium hydroxide; **-lauge,** *f.* barium hydroxide solution; **-salpeter,** *m.* barium nitrate, nitrobarite.

Baryt-spat, *m.* **-stein,** *m.* barite; **-weiss,** *n.* permanent white.

Baryum, *n.* barium; **-hydrat,** *n.* barium hydroxide; **-jodid,** *n.* barium iodide.

Barzahlung, *f.* cash payment.

Basal-blatt, *n.* basal leaf; **-glied,** *n.* terminal joint; **-knoten,** *m.* basal node; **-membran,** *f.* basal membrane; **-platte,** *f.* basal plate, sclerobase; **-scheibe,** *f.* basal disk; **-stumpf,** *m.* apophysis.

Basalt, *m.* basalt; **-ähnlich,** basaltic, basaltoid; **-felsen,** *m.* basaltic rock; **-förmig,** basaltiform; **-haltig,** containing basalt.

basaltieren, convert (slag) into a material resembling basalt.

Basal-windung, *f.* basal turn (of cochlea), convolution; **-winkel,** *m.* basal angle.

Base, *f.* base, alkali, basis, aunt, cousin.

Baseler Grün, *n.* Basle green, paris green, cupric acetoarsenite.

Basen-austausch, *m.* base exchange; **-bildner,** *m.* base former, basifier; **-wert,** *m.* base value.

Basicität, *f.* basicity.

Basidien, *pl.* conidiophores.

Basidienpilze, *m.pl.* Basidiomycetes.

basieren, to base, be based.

Basilarmembran, *f.* basilar(y) membrane.

Basilie, *f.* **Basilikum,** *n.* **Basilikumkraut,** *n.* (sweet) basil.

Basis, *f.* base, basis.

basisch, basic; **-essigsauer,** basic acetate of, subacetate of.

Basisfläche, *f.* basal surface, face.

Basität, Basizität, *f.* basicity.

Bass, *m.* bass (voice).

Bassin, *n.* reservoir, tank, basin.

Bast, *m.&n.* bast, inner bark, fiber, harl.

Bastard, *m.***-e,** hybrid, cross (breed); **-art,** *f.* crossbreed, hybrid species; **-begriff,** *m.* conception of a hybrid; **-bestäubung,** *f.* cross-pollination; **-erzeugung,** *f.* hybridization.

Bastardierung, *f.* hybridization.

Bastard-klee, *m.* alsike clover (*Trifolium hybridum*); **-kräftigkeit,** *f.* hybrid vigor; **-pflanze,** *f.* hybrid plant; **-schwächlichkeit,** *f.* hybrid weakness; **-tier,** *n.* hybrid (animal); **-zeugung,** *f.* hybridization; **-zucker,** *m.* raw sugar.

Bastern, *m.* raw sugar.

Bast-faser, *f.* bast (phloem) fiber; **-faserähnlich,** libriform; **-käfer,** *m.* bast beetle (Hylesinus); **-keil,** *m.* wedge of bast; **-körper,** *m.* phloem; **-papier,** *n.* manila paper; **-parenchym,** *n.* phloem parenchyma; **-ring,** *m.* libriform ring; **-seide,** *f.* raw silk, Persian sarcenet; **-strang,** *m.* bast fiber, strand.

bat (bitten), begged, asked for.

Batate, *f.* sweet potato.

Batist, *m.* cambric, batiste.

batschen, to ret (flax), batch (jute).

Batterie, *f.* battery; **-entladung,** *f.* discharging of a battery.

Batzen, *m.* caked mass, heavy lump; farthing.

Bau, *m.***-e,-ten,** structure, frame, form, building, cultivation; **-art,** *f.***-en,** type of construction, style, design; **-blech,** *n.* structural plate; **-breite,** *f.* over-all width.

Bauch, *m.* abdomen, belly, bowels, venter, stomach, swelling, bulging; **sich den ~ halten,** to hold one's side (with laughter).

Bauch-adergeflecht, *n.* coeliac plexus, solar plexus; **-atmen,** *n.* abdominal breathing, respiration; **-bedeckung,** *f.* abdominal wall; **-binde,** *f.* bellyband, abdominal fascia; **-blasenspalte,** *f.* exstrophy of the bladder; **-blatt,** *n.* abdominal plate; **-bruch,** *m.* abdominal hernia.

Bauch-cirrus, *m.* ventral cirrus; **-decke,** *f.* abdominal wall; **-deckenblutader,** *f.* epigastric vein; **-deckennaht,** *f.* abdominal

suture; **-drüse,** *f.* abdominal gland; **-eingeweide,** *n.* abdominal viscera; **-falte,** *f.* abdominal fold; **-feder,** *f.* abdominal feather.

Bauchfell, *n.* peritoneum; **-band,** *n.* peritoneal ligament; **-blatt,** *n.* peritoneal layer; **-bucht,** *f.* pouch of peritoneum; **-entzündung,** *f.* peritonitis; **-fläche,** *f.* peritoneal surface; **-fortsatz,** *m.* process of peritoneum; **-höhle,** *f.* peritoneal cavity; **-raum,** *m.* peritoneal cavity, space; **-überzug,** *m.* peritoneal covering.

Bauch-finne, *f.* ventral fin; **-fläche,** *f.* abdominal surface; **-flosse,** *f.* ventral fin; **-flosser,** *m.pl.* abdominal fish, subbrachiate; **-förmig,** ventricose, bulged; **-füsse,** *m.pl.* abdominal feet; **-füssler,** *m.pl.* Gastropoda.

Bauch-ganglienkette, *f.* ventral chain of ganglia; **-geflecht,** *n.* abdominal plexus; **-gegend,** *f.* abdominal region; **-grimmen,** *n.* abdominal colic; **-gurt,** *m.* girth; **-haut,** *f.* peritoneum; **-höhle,** *f.* abdominal cavity.

bauchig, bellied, convex, ventricose, swollen, inflated.

Bauch-kanalkern, *m.* ventral-canal nucleus; **-kanalzelle,** *f.* ventral-canal cell; **-kieme,** *f.* ventral gill; **-kiemer,** *m.pl.* Gasterobranchia; **-krampf,** *m.* colic; **-linie,** *f.* ventral line, linea alba; **-mark,** *n.* abdominal nervous cord; **-nabel,** *m.* umbilicus; **-naht,** *f.* abdominal suture; **-nervenkrank,** hypochondriacal.

Bauch-oberfläche, *f.* abdominal surface; **-pilze,** *m.pl.* Gasteromycetes; **-platte,** *f.* abdominal plate, sternum; **-presse,** *f.* ventral press; **-raum,** *m.* abdominal cavity; **-reden,** to ventriloquize; **-ring,** *m.* inguinal (abdominal) ring, somite; **-rinne,** *f.* ventral groove, endostyle.

Bauch-saugnapf, *m.* ventral sucker, suctorial pore; **-schiene,** *f.* fish-belly rail; **-schild,** *m.* plastron; **-schmerzen,** *m.pl.* abdominal pain; **-schnitt,** *m.* abdominal incision; **-seite,** *f.* ventral side; **-spalte,** *f.* ventral fissure, dehiscence.

Bauchspeichel, *m.* pancreatic juice; **-ausführungsgang,** *m.* pancreatic duct; **-drüse,** *f.* pancreas; **-drüsensaft,** *m.* secretion of the pancreas.

bauch-ständig, ventral; **-sternum,** *m.* ventral sternum, parasternum; **-stich,** *m.* tapping of the abdomen; **-stiel,** *m.* pedicle of allantois; **-strang,** *m.* umbilical cord; **-teil,** *m.* abdominal portion; **-tiere,** *n.pl.* Mollusca.

Bauch-wand, *f.* abdominal wall; **-wasser-sucht,** *f.* ascites; **-weh,** *n.* colic, abdominal pain; **-wirbel,** *m.* lumbar vertebra; **-wirbelsäule,** *f.* lumbar vertebral column; **-würmer,** *m.pl.* intestinal worms, ascarides.

bauen, to build, construct, erect, cultivate, raise, till, grow; ∼ **auf,** to base or rest on.

Bauer, *m.-,* builder, cultivator, farmer, peasant.

Bauer, *m.(n.).* cage.

Bauerde, *f.* arable soil.

Bäuerin, *f.* farmer's wife.

bäu(e)risch, rustic.

Bauern-betrieb, *m.* farming, agriculture; **-gut,** *n.* **-hof,** *m.* farm; **-sand,** *m.* builders' sand; **-stand,** *m.* peasantry; **-wetzel,** *m.* mumps.

Bau-fach, *n.∵er,* architecture; **-fähig,** arable, workable; **-fällig,** out of repair, dilapidated; **-fest,** solid; **-gewerbe,** *n.* building trade; **-grube,** *f.* excavation; **-holz,** *n.* timber; **-kunst,** *f.* architecture; **-länge,** *f.* over-all length.

baulich, architectural.

Baum, *m.∵e,* tree, arbor, beam, boom; **-achat,** *m.* dendritic agate, moss agate; **-ähnlich, -artig,** treelike, dendroid, arborescent.

Baumaterial, *n.* building material.

baumbewohnend, epiphytic, growing on trees.

Baumbrand, *m.* blight, necrosis.

Baumeister, *m.* architect, builder.

baumeln, to dangle.

bäumen, sich, to rear, prance.

Baum-falke, *m.* hobby (*Falco subbuteo*); **-farn,** *m.* tree fern; **-flechte,** *f.* tree lichen; **-form,** *f.* shape; **-förmig,** dendritic, arborescent; **-frass,** *m.* canker, (dry) rot; **-frevel,** *m.* damaging of trees; **-fuss,** *m.* climbing foot, pes arboreus; **-gang,** *m.* avenue of trees; **-garten,** *m.* orchard, nursery.

Baum-geländer, *n.* espalier; **-genossenschaft,** *f.* tree association; **-grassteppe,** *f.* savanna; **-grenze,** *f.* timber line, tree limit; **-grind,** *m.* scurf; **-gruppe,** *f.* cluster of trees grove; **-hacker,** *m.* woodpecker, nuthatch; **-harz,** *n.* resinous exudate; **-heide,** *f.* brier (*Erica arborea*); **-hoch,** tall as a tree.

Baum-höhenmesser, *m.* hypsometer; **-kieme,** *f.* proctal (dendritic) gill; **-läufer,** *m.* tree creeper; **-läuse,** *f.pl.* tree aphids; **-los,** treeless; **-messer,** *n.* pruning knife;

-messer, *m.* dendrometer; **-öl,** *n.* olive oil, sweet oil; **-reife,** *f.* ripeness of fruit; **-rinde,** *f.* bark, rind.

Baum-roden, *m.* uprooting of trees; **-rose,** *f.* hollyhock; **-schere,** *f.* pruning shears; **-schicht,** *f.* tree zone; **-schlag,** *m.* foliage; **-schmarotzer,** *m.* tree parasite; **-schröter,** *m.* stag beetle; **-schule,** *f.* nursery; **-schwamm,** *m.* agaric; **-senf,** *m.* candytuft; **-stamm,** *m.* tree trunk.

Baum-stark, stout as a tree, robust; **-stein,** *m.* dendrite agate; **-stumpf,** *m.* stump; **-stütze,** *f.* tree prop, tree support; **-vogel,** *m.* tree bird, arboreal bird; **-wachs,** *n·* grafting wax; **-wanze,** *f.* forest bug; **-wolle,** *f.* cotton.

baumwollen, (made of) cotton.

Baumwoll(en)-abfall, *m.∵e,* cotton waste; **-faden,** *m.* cotton thread; **-garn,** *n.* cotton yarn; **-gewebe,** *n.* cotton fabric, texture; **-kapsel,** *f.* cotton boll; **-kernöl,** *n.* cottonseed oil; **-kratze,** *f.* cotton cord; **-pflanze,** *f.* cotton (tree); **-saat,** *f.* cottonseed; **-samen,** *m.* cottonseed; **-samenöl,** *n.* cottonseed oil.

Baumwoll(en),-staude, *f.* cotton plant; **-stoff,** *m.* cotton material; **-waren,** *f.pl.* cotton goods; **-watte,** *f.* cotton wadding; **-weberei,** *f.* cotton mill; **-zellstoff,** *m.* cotton linters pulp; **-zeug,** *n.* cotton fabric; **-zwirn,** *m.* cotton thread.

Baum-wucherer, *m.* Dendrobium; **-wuchs,** *m.* growth; **-würger,** *m.* climbing bittersweet (*Celastrus*); **-wurzler,** *m.* Epidendrum, **-zucht,** *f.* arboriculture; **-züchter,** *m.* nursery man.

Bau-plan, -riss, *m.* ground plan, architect's sketch or plan.

Bausch, *m.* pad, compress, plug, bundle, lump; **in** ∼ **und Boden,** on the average, altogether.

Bäuschchen, *n.* little pad, plug.

Bausche, *f.* compress.

Bauschelastizität, *f.* resistance to creasing, wrinkleproofness.

bauschen, to swell out, bag, puff up, inflate.

bauschig, puffy, swelled.

Bauschung, *f.* swelling crease.

Bau-stein, *m.-e,* building stone, brick; **-stoff,** *m.* building material, nutrient; **-stoffwechsel,** *m.* constructive metabolism, anabolism.

Bauten, *pl.* buildings.

Bau-werk, *n.* building, edifice, structure; **-werksohle,** *f.* base of structure, foundation level.

Bau-wesen, *n.* architecture, building matters; **-würdig,** workable, payable; **-würdigkeitsgrenze,** *f.* limit of profitable working.

Baybeerenbaum, *m.* bebeeru, greenheart tree (*Nectandra rodioei*).

Bayöl, *n.* oil of bay.

bayrisch, Bavarian.

bazillär, bacillary.

Bazille, *f.* bacillus.

Bazillen-herd, *m.* focus of bacilli; **-träger,** *m.* bacillus carrier.

Bazillus, *m.* bacillus; **-stamm,** *m.* strain of bacillus.

Bdellium, *n.* bdellium.

beabsichtigen, to intend, have in view, aim at.

beabsichtigt, intended, intentional.

beachten, to heed, consider, notice, observe.

beachtenswert, worthy of consideration, noteworthy, remarkable.

beachtlich, considerable, noteworthy.

Beachtung, consideration, attention.

beackern, to till, cultivate, fallow.

Beamte, Beamter, *m.* official.

beängstigen, to alarm, fill with anxiety.

beanspruchen, to demand, require, claim.

Beanspruchung, *f.* requirement, claim, strain, stress, shear.

beanstanden, to object to.

beantragen, to propose.

beantworten, to answer, reply to.

Bearbeitbarkeit, *f.* workability, machinability.

bearbeiten, to work at, make, manipulate, elaborate, cultivate, till, treat, re-edit, compile, influence, arrange, adapt, revise, machine, finish.

Bearbeitung, *f.* cultivation, manufacture, working, machining.

Bearbeitungsgare, *f.* ready for use, friability (of soil).

beastet, branchy.

Beastung, *f.* amount of branches.

beaufsichtigen, to watch over, superintend, inspect.

beauftragen, to charge, authorize, commission, entrust with.

bebauen, to cultivate, work.

bebaute Fläche, ground area.

beben, to quiver, quake, tremble, oscillate.

Bebenmesser, *m.* seismograph.

beblättert, leafy, foliate.

bebrillt, spectacled.

bebrüten, to incubate, hatch, brood.

bebuscht, tufted, bushy.

Becher, *m.*-, cup, beaker, ascidium, cupule, bucket, calyx, ascus.

Becherchen, *n.* little cup.

Becher-cotyl, *m.* amphicotyledon; **-drüse,** *f.* crateriform gland; **-farn,** *m.* Cyathea; **-flechte,** *f.* cup lichen, cup moss (*Lichen pyxidatus*); **-förmig,** cup-shaped, crateriform, cupuliferous, cyathiform; **-frucht,** *f.* discocarpium, cynarrhodion, cupule, cupula, cup; **-früchtler,** *m.pl.* Cupuliferae; **-glas,** *n.* glass beaker; **-glaskolben,** *m.* Erlenmeyer flask.

Becher-hülle, *f.* cupule; **-keim,** *m.* gastrula; **-larve,** *f.* gastrula; **-mensur,** *f.* measuring cup; **-moos,** *n.* Cladonia (*Cladonia pyxidata*); **-pilz,** *m.* cup mushroom (Peziza); **-quallen,** *f.pl.* Calycozoa (Staurome-dusae); **-schwamm,** *m.* cup fungus; **-strauch,** *m.* Poterium; **-träger,** *m.* cupuliferous plant; **-werk,** *n.* bucket conveyer; **-zellen,** *f.pl.* mucous (goblet) cells.

Becken, *n.* pelvis, basin; **-achse,** *f.* pelvic axis; **-band,** *n.* pelvic ligament; **-bein,** *n.* pelvic bone, iliac; **-blastem,** *n.* pelvic blastema; **-boden,** *m.* pelvic floor, **-dach,** *n.* pelvic roof; **-darmhöhle,** *f.* pelvic intestinal cavity; **-drüse,** *f.* pelvic gland.

Becken-eingang, *m.* pelvic inlet, superior aperture of pelvis; **-eingeweide,** *n.* pelvic viscera; **-ende,** *n.* pelvic extremity; **-enge,** *f.* pelvic contraction; **-fehler,** *m.* deformity; **-gebiet,** *n.* pelvic region; **-geflecht,** *n.* pelvic plexus; **-gelenk,** *n.* pelvic articulation.

Becken-grube, *f.* iliac fossa; **-gürtel,** *m.* pelvic arch, girdle; **-kamm,** *m.* crest of ilium; **-knochen,** *m.* ilium, pelvic bone; **-krümmung,** *f.* pelvic curvature; **-raum,** *m.* pelvic cavity; **-verkrümmung,** *f.* pelvic distortion.

bedachen, to roof.

Bedacht, *m.* reflection, consideration, caution; ~ **auf,** intent on, mindful of.

bedächtig, deliberate, circumspect, cautious.

bedachtlos, inconsiderate.

bedachtsam, deliberate, circumspect.

bedanken, sich, to thank, decline (with thanks).

bedarf (bedürfen), requires, needs.

Bedarf, *m.* want, need, demand, requirement; **nach ~,** as occasion demands.

Bedarfs-deckung, *f.* supply, covering the need; **-fall,** *m.* **im ~,** in case of need; **-gegenstand,** *m.* requirement, requisite, object of need.

bedauerlich, regrettable, sad.

bedauern, to sympathize, regret, pity.

bedauernswert, deplorable, pitiable.

bedecken, to cover.

Bedecktkiemer, *m.pl.* Tectibranchia.

bedecktsamig, angiospermous.

Bedeckung, *f.* covering.

bedenken, to reflect, consider, provide for; **sich ~,** to hesitate, think of oneself.

Bedenken, *n.* consideration, hesitation, doubt, scruple; **-los,** unscrupulous.

bedenklich, doubtful, serious, critical, questionable.

Bedenklichkeit, *f.* critical state, seriousness.

bedeuten, to signify, mean, point out, intimate, state.

bedeutend, significant, considerable, important.

bedeutsam, significant.

Bedeutung, *f.* signification, importance, meaning.

bedeutungslos, insignificant, meaningless.

bedeutungsvoll, very significant.

bedienen, to serve, wait on, attend; **sich ~,** (*gen.*) to make use of, avail oneself of.

Bedienung, *f.* service, attendance, servants.

bedingen, to cause, settle, stipulate, depend on, limit, restrict, be caused, occasion.

bedingt, limited, conditional hypothetical, qualified, conditioned, metastable.

Bedingtheit, *f.* limitation, relationship, dependence, conditionality, restrictedness.

Bedingung, *f.* agreement, condition, stipulation, term(s), restriction, circumstance.

bedingungs-los, unconditional; **-weise,** conditionally.

bedrängen, to press hard, oppress, afflict.

Bedrängnis, *f.-se,* embarrassment, affliction.

bedrohen, to threaten.

bedrohlich, threatening.

bedrucken, to print over, print upon.

bedrücken, to oppress.

Bedrückung, *f.* oppression.

bedünken, to seem, appear.

bedürfen, to be in need, need, require.

Bedürfnis, *n.-se,* lack, want, need, requirement, necessity; **-los,** frugal.

bedürftig, (*gen.*) needy.

beehren, to honor, favor, have the honor.

beeidigen, to confirm by oath.

beeifern, to make (great) efforts to, strive, endeavor.

beeilen, to hasten, hurry.

Beeinflussbarkeit, *f.* susceptibility, modifiability, adaptability.

beeinflussen, to influence.

Beeinflussung, *f.* influence.

Beeinflussungsbereich, *n.* affected region.

beeinträchtigen, to injure, wrong, encroach upon.

beeinträchtigend, injurious, detrimental.

beeisen, to cover with ice, cover with iron.

beenden, to finish, end, terminate.

beendigen, to finish, end, terminate.

Beendigung, *f.* end, termination, finish.

beengen, to narrow, constrain, oppress, cramp.

beerben, to inherit, be heir to.

beerdigen, to bury, inter.

Beere, *f.* berry.

Beeren-apfel, *n.* Siberian crab (*Pirus baccata);* **-esche,** *f.* mountain ash (*Pirus aucuparia);* **-förmig,** berry-shaped, bacciform; **-fressend,** baccivorous; **-frucht,** *f.* berry; **-grün,** *n.* sap green; **-haufen,** *m.* syncarp; **-malve,** *f.* Malvaviscus; **-melde,** *f.* strawberry blight; **-tang,** *m.* gulfweed (*Sargossum bacciferum).*

Beeren-tragend, bacciferous; **-zapfen,** *m.* galbulus, arcesthide.

Beer-gelb, *n.* yellow buckthorn (*Rhamnus caroliniana);* **-kraut,** *n.* bilberry (*Vaccinium myrtillus);* **-melde,** *f.* strawberry blight; **-schwamm,** *m.* yaws, frambesia.

Beet, *n.-e,* (garden) bed, narrow bed, border.

Beete, *f.* (Bete), beet (root).

beetweise, in small lots.

befähigen, to enable, qualify.

befähigt, able, capable, adapted, fit.

Befähigung, *f.* qualification, authorization, capacity.

befahl, commanded, was commanding.

befahrbar, passable, accessible.

Befall, *m.ːe,* attack, infection.

befallen, to attack, be seized.

Befallstärke, *f.* severity of attack or infection.

befangen, embarrassed, confused, prejudiced.

befassen, sich to concern, deal with, be engaged.

Befehl, *m.*-e, command, order.

befehlen, (*dat.*) to command, order.

befehlend, imperative, dictatorial.

befehligen, (*dat.*) to command, order.

befestigen, to fasten, fix, attach, fortify, establish.

Befestigung, *f.* fastening, attachment, fixing, clamping.

Befestigungs-mittel, *n.* fixing agent; -ring, *m.* ring fastener; -schraube, *f.* setscrew.

befeuchten, to moisten, dampen, wet, irrigate.

Befeuchtung, *f.* moistening, dampening.

befiedern, sich to get feathers.

befiedert, pennate, fledged.

Befiederung, *f.* feathering feathers.

befiehlt (befehlen), commands.

befinden, to find, think proper; sich ∼, to be, feel, find oneself.

Befinden, *n.* opinion, state, condition.

befindlich, situated, existing, present.

beflecken, to soil, spot, stain, contaminate.

befleissen, befleissigen, sich ∼, (*gen.*) to apply oneself, study.

beflissen, (*gen.*) studious, engaged in.

beflügeln, to accelerate, lend wings to.

beflügelt, winged.

befohlen (befehlen), commanded, ordered.

befolgen, to follow (advice), obey.

befördern, to forward, accelerate, further, promote, transport.

Beförderung, *f.* forwarding, conveyance, dispatch, promotion, advancement.

Beförderungsmittel, *n.* means of forwarding or conveyance, promoter, adjuvant, opiate.

befrachten, to load.

befragen, to question; sich ∼ bei, to consult with.

befranzt, fringed, fimbriated.

befreien, to free, set free, release, rescue.

Befreiung, *f.* liberation, deliverance.

befremden, to surprise, astonish.

befremdlich, surprising, strange.

befreundet, intimate.

befriedigen, to satisfy, please.

befriedigend, satisfactory.

befruchten, to fertilize, fecundate, impregnate.

Befruchtung, *f.* fertilization, fructification; verborgene ∼, cryptogamy.

Befruchtungs-anthere, *f.* pollinating anther; -art, *f.* manner of fecundation; -fähig, capable of fecundation; -kelch, *m.* perianth of fructification; -schlauch, *m.* pollen tube; -staub, *m.* pollen; -teil, *m.* organ of fecundation; -träger, *m.* gonophore, receptacle (bearing stamens and carpels).

Befugnis, *f.*-se, right, authority, warrant.

befugt, authorized, competent.

befühlen, to feel, touch.

Befund, *m.*-e, finding, state, condition, result, circumstances, report.

befürchten, to fear, be apprehensive of, suspect.

befürworten, to support, recommend, advocate.

begaben, to bestow, endow.

begabt, gifted, talented, clever.

Begabung, *f.* talent.

begangen (begehen), used, committed.

begasen, to fumigate.

begatten, sich to copulate, mate, breed.

Begattung, *f.* copulation, coition, mating.

Begattungs-drüse, *f.* clasper gland; -fähigkeit, *f.* copulatory ability; -glieder, *n.pl.* claspers; -glocke, *f. bursa copulatoria;* -organ, *n.* copulative (generative) organ, intromittent organ; -stachel, *m.* copulatory clasper, spicule; -stadium, *n.* copulation stage; -tasche, *f. bursa copulatrix;* -werkzeug, *n.* genital apparatus; -zeit, *f.* time of pairing or of fecundation.

begeben, sich, to betake oneself, go, happen, occur; (*gen.*) to renounce.

Begebenheit, *f.* adventure, event, occurrence.

begegnen, sich, to behave toward, happen, meet, encounter, come upon.

begehen, to celebrate, commit, perform, make, walk through.

Begehr, *n.* desire, inquiry, demand.

begehren, to crave, demand, desire, want.

begehrenswert, desirable.

begehrlich, covetous, exacting.

begeistern, to animate, enthuse, enliven, inspire; sich für etwas ∼, to be enthusiastic about something.

Begeisterung, *f.* enthusiasm, inspiration.

begichten, charge (a blast furnace).

Begichtungsanlage, *f.* charging installation.

Begier, Begierde, *f.* avidity, desire, greed.

begierig, (*gen.*) eager, desirous, greedy.

begiessen, to moisten, sprinkle, water, wet.

Beginn, *m.* beginning, inception.

beginnen, to begin, start.

beginnend, initiative, incipient.

begipsen, to plaster.

beglaubigen, to attest, certify, confirm.

Beglaubigungsschreiben, *n.*-, credentials.

begleichen, to balance, settle.

Begleitbewusstsein, *n.* accompanying consciousness.

begleiten, to accompany, attend, enclose.

Begleiter, *m.*-, associate, companion, attendant, guide.

Begleit-erscheinung, *f.* attendant phenomenon, symptom; -farbe, *f.* fitting color; -gewebe, *n.* connective tissue; -parenchym, *n.* border parenchyma, leptome sheath; -pflanze, *f.* attending or accompanying plant; -reiz, *m.* accompanying stimulus; -stoff, *m.* accompanying substance, impurity; -wort, *m.* explanatory remark.

beglücken, to bless, favor, make happy.

beglückwünschen, to congratulate.

begnadigen, to pardon.

begnügen, sich, to be content.

begonnen (beginnen), begun.

begraben, to bury, conceal.

Begräbnis, *n.*-se, burial, funeral.

begrannt, aristate, bearded.

begreifen, to understand, comprise, conceive, include.

begreiflich, conceivable, intelligible; -erweise, as may be easily understood.

begrenzen, to limit, define, terminate, bound, confine, circumscribe.

begrenzt, limited, defined, local.

Begrenztheit, *f.* limitation, narrowness.

Begrenzung, *f.* limit, boundary, delimitation, localization.

Begrenzungs-falte, *f.* limiting fold; -linien, *f.pl.* lines of demarcation; -ring, *m.* balloon catch; -schicht, *f.* limiting layer.

Begriff, *m.*-e, conception, idea, notion, view; im Begriffe sein, to be on the point of.

begriffen (begreifen), im Entstehen ∼, forming, nascent; im . . . ∼, in the process of . . .

begrifflich, conceivable, conceptual; rein ∼, abstractly; ∼ bestimmen, to define.

Begriffs-bestimmung, *f.* definition; -bildung, *f.* formation of a concept, abstraction; -fach, *n.* category; -fassung, *f.* formulation of a concept; -gesellung, *f.* association of ideas; -vermögen, *n.* apprehension.

begründen, to found, establish, base, prove, confirm, substantiate.

Begründer, *m.*-, founder.

Begründung, *f.* establishment, foundation, founding, initiation, motivation; zur ∼ des, in support of.

Beguss, *m.* slip, engobe, icing (of a cake).

begrüssen, to salute, greet, welcome.

begünstigen, to favor, promote, support, patronize.

begutachten, to pass judgment on, to express an opinion on.

Begutachtung, *f.* judgment, arbitration, appraisal, expert opinion.

begütert, wealthy.

begütigen, to appease, calm, pacify.

behaart, hairy, hirsute, pilose, crinite, villous; -blättrig, dasyphyllous, woolly leaved, -stachelig, with prickly hairs.

behaftet, affected, afflicted, infected.

behagen, (*dat.*), to please.

Behagen, *n.*-, pleasure, comfort.

behaglich, agreeable, comfortable.

behalmt, bladed, stalked.

behalten, to keep, retain, carry, remember; recht ∼, to be right in the end; übrig ∼, to have left over; im Auge ∼, to keep in mind; wohl ∼, well-preserved.

Behälter, *m.*-, container, receiver, receptacle, reservoir, tank.

Behältnis, *n.*-se, receptacle, container, tank.

behandeln, to handle, manipulate, treat, work, use.

Behandlung, *f.* treatment.

Behandlungs-art, *f.*-en, method of treatment; -mittel, *m.* agent, reagent; -weise, *f.* method of treatment.

behängen, to hang.

beharren, to continue, persist, persevere.

beharrlich, persistent, constant, stubborn.

Beharrlichkeit, *f.* perseverance.

Beharrung, *f.* continuance, perseverance, obstinacy.

Beharrungs-vermögen, *n.* inertia, law of continuity; **-zustand,** *m.* permanence, resistance.

behaubt, cassideous, crested, helmet-shaped.

behauchen, to breathe on.

behauen, to hew, lop, prune, cut.

behaupten, to maintain, assert, contend; **sich ∼,** to hold one's own; **es wird behauptet,** it is asserted, claimed, reported; **zu Unrecht ∼,** to pretend.

Behauptung, *f.* assertion, proposition, maintaining contention; **blosse ∼,** mere conjecture.

Behausung, *f.* lodging, abode.

beheben, to remove, eliminate.

beheizen, to heat.

Behelf, *m.* shift, device, help.

behelfen, sich ∼, to manage.

behelmt, galeate.

behend(e), agile, nimble.

Behen-nuss, *f.* ben nut; **-nussbaum,** *m.* ben-nut tree (Moringa); **-öl,** *n.* oil of ben; **-säure,** *f.* behenic acid.

beherbergen, to harbor, shelter.

beherrschen, to rule, control, command, to be fully conversant with; **sich ∼,** to restrain oneself.

beherrscht, dominated, overtopped, oppressed.

beherzigen, to take to heart, consider, weigh in one's mind.

beherzigenswert, worthy of consideration.

beherzt, courageous.

behexen, to bewitch.

behilflich, helpful, serviceable, useful.

behindern, to hinder, delay.

behorchen, to listen to, spy out.

Behörde, *f.* authority, magistrate.

behördlich, official.

Behuf, *m.* purpose, object, behalf, use.

behufs, in behalf of, in order to, for the purpose of.

behuft, hoofed, shod.

behüten, to guard, preserve.

behutsam, cautious, careful.

bei, in the case of, at, near, by, on, about, with, near, close by, in, on, upon; **dicht ∼,** close to; **∼weitem,** by far; **beim Beginn,** when starting.

beibehalten, to retain, keep, continue.

Beiblatt, *n.*￫er, supplement, supplementary sheet.

beibringen, to administer, produce, teach, impart.

Beibringungsmittel, *n.* vehicle for drugs.

beidäugig, binocular.

beide, both, either; **-mal,** both times.

beidendig, at both ends.

beiderlei, of both sorts, of either sort.

beiderseitig, beiderseits, on both sides, mutually.

beidhändig, ambidextrous.

beidlebig, amphibious.

beieinander, together.

Beifall, *m.* approval, applause; **∼ finden,** to meet with approval.

beifällig, approving, favorable.

beifolgend, enclosed, annexed.

beifügen, to add, annex, attach.

Beifuss, *m.* mugwort (Artemisia).

Beigabe, *f.* addition, supplement.

beigeben, to add.

Beigeschmack, *m.* aftertaste, flavor.

Beiheft, *n.*-e, supplemental part or number, supplement.

Beihilfe, *f.* help, assistance, subsidy.

beikommen, to get at, reach.

Beil, *n.*-e, hatchet.

Beilage, *f.* addition, supplement, enclosure.

beiläufig, incidental, by the way.

beilegen, to add, enclose, attribute, settle.

Beilegung, *f.* settlement, adjustment, attribution.

Beileid, *n.* condolence, sympathy.

beiliegend, enclosed.

Beilstein, *m.* nephrite.

Beiluft, *f.* admixed air.

beim (bei dem), at or with the.

beimengen, to admix, add.

Beimengung, *f.* admixture, impurity.

beimessen, to attribute.

beimischen, to add, admix, mix with.

Beimischung, *f.* admixture, impurity.

beimpfen, to inoculate.

Bein, *n.*-e, leg, bone.

beinah(e), almost, nearly, all but.

Beiname, *m.* surname, nickname.

bein-artig, bony; **-asche,** *f.* bone ash; **-brech,** *m.* bog asphodel (*Narthecium ossifragum*); **-bruch,** *m.* leg fracture.

beinern, made of bone.

Beinerv, *m.* accessory vein or nerve.

Bein-fäule, *f.* caries; **-frass,** *m.* caries; **-fügung,** *f.* articulation; **-gerüst,** *n.* skeleton; **-haus,** *n.* charnel house; **-haut,** *f.* periosteum; **-höhle,** *f.* bone socket.

beinicht, bony, osseous.

beinig, bony, osseous.

Bein-kehle, *f.* hollow of the knee; **-kleid(er),** *n.* trousers; **-knopf,** *m.* condyle; **-knospe,** *f.* leg bud; **-los,** legless, boneless; **-mark,** *n.* bone marrow; **-mehl,** *n.* bone meal; **-paar,** *n.* pair of legs; **-röhre,** *f.* tibia; **-schiene,** *f.* cradle, splint.

Bein-schwarz, *n.* bone black, animal charcoal; **türkis,** *m.* bone turquoise, odontolite; **-well,** *m.* comfrey (Symphytum); **-wurz,** *f.* comfrey (Symphytum).

beiordnen, to adjoin, coordinate.

beipflichten, to assent, agree.

beirren, to confuse.

beisammen, together.

Beisatz, *m.* addition, alloy, admixture.

Beischlaf, *m.* cohabitation, coitus.

beischlafen, to copulate.

Beisein, *n.* presence.

beiseite, aside, apart.

beisetzen, to bury, inter, add, alloy, admix.

Beispiel, *n.*-e, example; **zum** ∼ (z.B.), for example.

beispiellos, unexampled, unparalleled.

Beispiellosigkeit, *f.* matchlessness.

beispielsweise, for example.

beispringen, to assist.

Beispross, *m.* secondary shoot.

Beissbeere, *f.* cayenne pepper.

beissen, to bite, burn, smart.

beissend, biting, sharp, pungent, sarcastic.

Beiss-kohl, *m.* beet (root) (*Beta vulgaris*); **-probe,** *f.* biting test; **-zahn,** *m.* incisor; **-zange,** *f.* nippers, pincers.

Beistand, *m.* assistance, supporter.

beistehen, to stand by, assist.

beisteuern, to contribute.

beistimmen, to agree, concur; **der Ansicht** ∼, to agree with that point of view.

Beitel, *m.* chisel.

Beitrag, *m.*-̈e, contribution, share, dues.

beitragen, to contribute, be conducive to.

beitreiben, to collect, drive in, recover.

Beitreibung, *f.* collection, foraging.

beitreten, to accede, join.

Beitritt, *m.* accession, joining.

Beiwagen, *m.* side car.

Beiwerk, *n.* accessories.

Beiwert, *m.* coefficient, factor.

beiwohnen, to be (present) at, attend, cohabit, be inherent.

Beiwort, *n.*-̈er, adjective, epithet, title.

Beiwurzel, *f.* adventitious root.

Beizahl, *f.* numerical coefficient.

beizählen, to count amongst.

Beiz-artikel, *m.* mordant style; **-brühe,** *f.* pickling liquor; **-bütte,** *f.* drench pit.

Beize, *f.* disinfectant, caustic, mordant, cauterization, corrosion, pickling.

beizeiten, early, betimes.

Beizempfindlichkeit, *f.* susceptibility of injury (from seed treatment).

beizen, to corrode, mordant, cauterize, stain, sauce (tobacco), pickle.

beizend, corroding, corrosive, caustic.

Beizendruck, *m.* mordant printing.

Beiz-farbe, *f.* mordant color; **-farbstoff,** *m.* mordant dye; **-flüssigkeit,** *f.* corrosive liquid; **-gelb,** *n.* mordant yellow; **-gerät,** *n.* apparatus for steeping; **-kraft,** *f.* corrosive or caustic power; **-maschine,** *f.* seed-treating machine; **-mittel,** *n.* corrosive, mordant, seed-treatment solution, pickler; **-ofen,** *m.* scaling furnace.

bejahen, to affirm, give consent.

bejahrt, aged.

bejammern, to deplore, lament.

bejammerns-wert, -würdig, deplorable.

bekalken, to lime.

bekämpfen, to combat, resist, oppose, control.

Bekämpfung, *f.* control (of diseases).

Bekämpfungsmassnahme, *f.* control measure.

bekannt, (*dat.*) renowned, noted, (well) known; **dürfte Ihnen wohl** ∼ **sein,** you are probably aware of; **als** ∼ **voraussetzen,** to take for granted; **mit etwas** ∼ **sein,** to be familiar with; **sich ~ machen mit,** to familiarize oneself with.

Bekannte, *m.&f.* acquaintance, friend.

bekanntermassen, bekanntlich, as is known, recognized.

Bekanntmachung, *f.* publication, announcement, notice, bulletin.

Bekanntschaft, *f.* acquaintance, knowledge.

bekappen, to lop (trees).

bekappt, hooded, cucullated

bekehren, to convert.

bekelcht, calyculate.

bekennen, to confess, acknowledge.

Bekenntnis, *n.*-se, confession, acknowledgment.

beklagen, to deplore, pity, complain; **sich ~,** to make a complaint.

beklagenswert, deplorable, pitiable.

bekleben, to placard, label, cover.

beklecke(r)n, to blot, blotch, daub.

beklecksen, to blot, blotch, daub.

bekleiden, to clothe, dress, attire, array; **sich ~,** to dress, cover over, encase, veneer, line; **ein Amt ~,** to hold a position.

Bekleidung, *f.* clothing, coating, casing, lining.

beklemmen, to oppress.

beklommen, oppressed, uneasy, anxious.

beklopfen, to tap, knock, percuss.

bekommen, (*dat.*) to get, receive, agree (with); **jemandem schlecht ~,** to agree badly with.

bekömmlich, beneficial.

beköstigen, to board, feed.

Beköstigungsanthere, *f.* the anther furnishing the food.

bekräftigen, to confirm, assert.

bekränzen, to wreathe, encircle.

bekritteln, to censure, criticize.

bekrusten, to incrust, crust.

Bekrustung, *f.* incrustation.

bekümmern, to afflict, trouble; **das bekümmert mich nicht,** that does not concern me; **sich über etwas ~,** to be grieved or troubled at; **sich um etwas ~,** to trouble oneself about something.

Bekümmernis, *f.* grief, affliction, trouble.

bekunden, to declare, depose, prove.

Bela, *f.* bel (*Aegle marmelos*).

beladen, to load, charge, burden, covered.

Belag, *m.* covering, coating, paving, fur.

belagern, to besiege.

Belagerung, *f.* siege.

Belagzelle, *f.* peptic cell, parietal cell.

Belang, *m.* importance; **nicht von ~,** of no consequence.

belangen, to concern, bring action against; **was mich belangt,** as for me.

belanglos, unimportant.

Belanussbaum, *m.* bel (*Aegle marmelos*).

belassen, to leave.

belasten, to load, weight, burden, charge, taint; **erblich belastet,** with hereditary disposition.

belästigen, to trouble, bother.

Belästigung, *f.* annoyance.

Belastung, *f.* load, burden, charge, hereditary taint.

Belastungs-fähigkeit, *f.* carrying capacity. **-wechsel,** *m.* load fluctuation; **-widerstand,** *m.* loading resistance.

belauben, to cover with leaves.

belaubt, leafy, frondous.

Belaubung, *f.* foliation, foliage.

Belaubungsdauer, *f.* duration of foliage.

belauern, to lie in wait for.

belaufen, to traverse, inspect; **sich ~,** to amount to.

belauschen, to overhear, spy out.

beleben, to animate, vivify, quicken, enliven, revive, resuscitate, brighten.

belebt, alive, lively.

Belebtschlammprozess, *m.* activated-sludge process.

Belebung, *f.* enlivenment, animation, improvement.

Belebungs-mittel, *n.* restorative; **-versuch,** *m.* attempt to restore life.

belecken, to lick.

Beleg, *m.*-e, proof, evidence, covering, coating, lining, fur.

belegen, to cover, line, face, prove, check, illustrate, mark, engage.

Beleg-knochen, *m.* covering (secondary) bone, membrane bone; **-knorpel,** *m.* overlying cartilage; **-körper,** *m.* covering body, investing body; **-schaft,** *f.* staff, gang of men, crew, personnel; **-schicht,** *f.* covering layer; **-stelle,** *f.* quotation.

belegtes Brot, sandwich.

Belegung, *f.* covering, coating, infliction.

Belegzelle, *f.* investing (parietal) cell, oxyntic cell, peptic cell.

belehnen, to invest.

belehren, to instruct, advise.

belehrend, instructive.

Belehrung, *f.* instruction, advice, correction.

beleibt, stout, corpulent.

beleidigen, to offend, wrong, insult.

beleimen, to glue, cover with glue.

belesen, well-read.

beleuchten, to light, illuminate, clear up; näher ∽, to examine closely.

Beleuchtung, *f.* illumination, lighting, elucidation, examination.

Beleuchtungs-abstand, *m.* lighting range, observation distance; **-apparat,** *m.* apparatus for illumination; **-bogen,** *m.* illuminating curve(d line); **-dauer,** *f.* duration of exposure to light; **-einrichtung,** *f.* illuminating device, installation; **-einstellung,** *f.* adjustment for illumination.

Beleuchtungs-kegel, *m.* illuminating cone; **-körper,** *m.* light (fitting); **-linse,** *f.* illuminating lens; **-mittel,** *n.* illuminant; **-schirm,** *m.* reflector; **-schwankung,** *f.* variation in illumination; **-spiegel,** *m.* reflecting mirror; **-vorrichtung,** *f.* illuminating device or attachment.

belfern, to yelp, scold.

Belgien, *n.* Belgium.

belichten, to expose (to light); zu lange ∽, to solarize, overexpose.

Belichtung, *f.* exposure (to light); übermässige ∽, solarization, overexposure.

Belichtungs-messer, *m.* exposure meter; **-stärke,** *f.* intensity of light; **-zeit,** *f.* exposure time.

belieben, to like, choose, be pleasing.

Belieben, *n.* inclination, pleasure.

beliebig, any, whatever, optional, arbitrary. at pleasure.

beliebt, popular, favorite; wenn's ∽, if you please; wie's Ihnen ∽, as you please.

Beliebtheit, *f.* popularity.

beliefern, to supply.

bellen, to bark.

belohnen, to reward, remunerate; es belohnt sich der Mühe, it is worth the trouble.

belüften, to ventilate, expose to the air.

belustigen, to amuse, divert; sich über etwas ∽, to make sport of.

bemächtigen, sich, *(gen.)* to seize upon, take possession of, master.

bemäkeln, to find fault with.

bemalen, to paint, color, stain, daub.

bemängeln, to find fault with.

bemannen, to man.

bemänteln, to cover, palliate, varnish.

bemeistern, to master; sich ∽, *(gen.)* to get possession.

bemerkbar, perceptible, noticeable.

bemerken, to note, mark, remark, notice.

bemerkenswert, worthy of note, remarkable.

bemerklich, sich ∽ machen, to attract attention.

Bemerkung, *f.* observation, remark, note, comment.

bemessen, to measure, proportion, exact, be measured, adjust.

bemitleiden, to pity.

bemittelt, well-to-do, well off.

bemodert, moldy.

bemoost, mossy.

bemühen, to trouble; sich ∽ zu, to endeavor to; sich ∽ um, to strive for.

Bemühung, *f.* trouble, pains, effort.

bemustern, to sample, ornament, figure.

bemuttern, to nurse.

benachbart, *(dat.)* neighboring, adjacent, vicinal.

benachrichtigen, to inform, notify.

benachteiligen, to prejudice, hurt, wrong be of disadvantage to.

benadelt, foliaged (with conifers).

Benadelung, *f.* foliage of conifers.

benagen, to gnaw at, nibble at.

benahm (benehmen), behaved.

benannt (benennen), named, called.

benarbt, scarred, cicatrized, covered with (mold) grass.

benebeln, to fog, dim, cloud, treat with gas.

Benediktenkraut, *n.* blessed thistle (*Cnicus benedictus*).

benehmen, sich to behave.

Benehmen, *n.* behavior, conduct

beneiden, to envy.

benennen, to name, call.

Benennung, *f.* nomenclature, naming, title, denomination.

benetzbar, wettable.

benetzen, to wet, moisten, sprinkle.

Benetzungs-fähigkeit, *f.* moistening capacity, **-verfahren,** *n.* sprinkling method; **-wärme,** *f.* heat of moistening.

Bengel, *m.* club, clapper, boor, rascal.

Benit(zucker), *m.* barley sugar.

Benöl, *n.* oil of ben.

benommen, benumbed, stupefied, confused.

benötigen, to want, need.

benötigt, necessary.

benutzbar, available, useful.

benutzen, to use, employ; **mit Vorteil** ∼, to profit by.

Benutzer, *m.* user.

Benutzung, *f.* use, employment, application.

Benzaldehyd, *m.* benzaldehyde.

benzarsinig, benzarsinous.

Benzin, *n.* benzine, gasoline, petrol; **-ersatz,** *m.* benzine substitute.

Benzochinon, *n.* benzoquinone.

Benzoe, *f.* benzoin (gum); **-harz,** *n.* benzoin (resin); **-lorbeer,** *m.* spicebush; **-salz,** *n.* benzoate; **-säure,** *f.* benzoic acid.

Benzol, *m.* benzene, benzol; **-bindung,** *f.* benzene linkage; **-flüssigkeit,** *f.* benzene liquid; **-kern,** *m.* benzene nucleus; **-kohlenwasserstoff,** *m.* benzol hydrocarbon; **-lack,** *m.* benzol varnish; **-reihe,** *f.* benzene series; **-rest,** *m.* benzene group or residue; **-ring,** *m.* benzene ring; **-wasserstoff,** *m.* hydrobenzol.

benzoylieren, to benzoylate.

Benzylchlorid, *n.* benzyl chloride.

beobachten, to observe, examine, obey, follow.

Beobachter, *m.*-, observer.

Beobachtung, *f.* observation, observance.

Beobachtungs-einstellung, *f.* adjustment for observation; **-fehler,** *m.* error in observation; **-gabe,** *f.* faculty for observation.

beohrt, auriculate.

bepacken, to pack, load.

bepflanzen, to plant.

bepflastern, to plaster over.

bepudern, to powder.

bequem, (*dat.*) convenient, easy, comfortable.

bequemen, sich, to conform, comply, submit.

Bequemlichkeit, *f.* convenience, comfort.

berandet, marginate.

Berapp, *m.* rough plaster, brown coat.

berappen, to remove bark, pay.

berasen, to cover with turf.

Beraser, *m.* turf-producing grass.

berast, grass-covered.

Berasung, *f.* sodding.

beraten, to advise, consult.

Berater, *m.* consultant.

beratschlagen, to consult, deliberate.

Beratung, *f.* advice, consultation, deliberation.

berauben, to rob, deprive.

beräuchern, to fumigate.

berauschen, to intoxicate.

Berauschungsmittel, *n.* intoxicant.

Berberin, *n.* berberine.

Berberisrinde, *f.* barberry bark.

Berberitze, *f.* barberry.

berechenbar, calculable, appreciable.

berechnen, to calculate, compute, charge.

Berechnung, *f.* calculation, account, computation, proportioning.

Berechnungs-art, *f.* mode of calculation; **-einheit,** *f.* unit of calculation; **-formel,** *f.* formula; **-weise,** *f.* method of calculation.

berechtigen, to entitle, authorize, qualify, justify.

berechtigt, justified, legitimate.

Berechtigung, *f.* authorization, right, privilege.

bereden, to persuade, talk over, confer.

Beredsamkeit, *f.* eloquence.

Beregnungsanlage, *f.* sprinkling system.

Bereich, *m.*-e, reach, range, region, domain, field.

bereichern, to enrich.

Bereicherung, *f.* enrichment.

Bereicherungsspross, *m.* enriching (accessory) leafy shoot.

bereifen, to cover with hoarfrost, hoop, put on a tire.

bereift, hoary, pruinous.

Bereifung, *f.* tire equipment, tires, hoarfrost.

bereisen, to travel over, visit.

bereit, ready, prepared.

bereiten, to prepare, make ready, make, cause, dress, ride over.

bereits, already, previously.

Bereitschaft, *f.* readiness.

bereitstellen, to prepare, furnish.

Bereitung, *f.* preparation, manufacture.

bereitwillig, ready, willing, eager, prompt.

bereuen, to repent, regret.

Berg, *m.*-e, mountain, hill, rock; **-ab,** downhill; **-abhang,** *m.* mountain slope; **-ader,** *f.* lode, vein; **-akademie,** *f.* school of mines; **-an,** uphill; **-arbeiter,** *m.* miner; **-art,** *f.* gang, matrix, vein material; **-asche,** *f.* an inferior kind of mineral blue; **-auf,** uphill.

Berg-bau, *m.* mining; **-blau,** *n.* mineral blue; **-braun,** *n.* umber; **-butter,** *f.* impure iron alum, rock butter; **-ebene,** *f.* tableland plateau.

bergen, to save, shelter, conceal, salvage.

Berg-erz, *n.* raw ore; **-fall,** *m.* landslide; **-farbe,** *f.* ocher; **-fluss,** *m.* colored quartz, fluorite, mountain stream; **-gang,** *m.* vein, lode; **-gegend,** *f.* mountainous region; **-glas,** *n.* rock crystal; **-grün,** *n.* mineral green, malachite; **-gut,** *n.* minerals, fossils; **-haar,** *n.* aminthus, fibrous asbestos.

Berg-halde, *f.* slag bank, dump, hillside; **-hang,** *m.* hillslide, slope; **-harz,** *n.* mineral pitch, asphalt; **-holz,** *n.* rockwood, ligniform asbestos.

bergig, mountainous, hilly.

berginisieren ("Bergius"), to hydrogenate.

Berg-kalk, *m.* mountain limestone; **-kessel,** *m.* gorge; **-kette,** *f.* chain of mountains; **-kiesel,** *m.* rock flint; **-kreide,** *f.* rock lime; **-kristall,** *m.* rock crystal; **-kunde,** *f.* orology; **-land,** *n.* hilly country; **-lehne,** *f.* slope, mountainside; **-mann,** *m.* miner.

Berg-männisch, mining, pertaining to miners; **-mehl,** *n.* mountain flour, rock farina; **-melisse,** *f.* calamint; **-milch,** *m.* mountain milk, agaric mineral; **-rot,** *n.* realgar, Indian red, cinnabar; **-rücken,** *m.* mountain ridge; **-rutsch,** *m.* landslide; **-salz,** *n.* rock salt; **-schwaden,** *m.* firedamp, chokedamp; **-seife,** *f.* mountain soap, alluvial ore, rock butter.

Berg-seite, *f.* hillside; **-strom,** *m.* torrent; **-sturz,** *m.* landslide; **-sturzschutt,** *m.* rockslide debris; **-sumpf,** *m.* bog (on mountain top); **-teegeist,** *m.* spirit of wintergreen.

Bergung, *f.* sheltering, saving, salvage.

Berg-wand, *f.* side of a mountain; **-werk,** *n.* mine; **-wesen,** *n.* mining; **-wetter,** *n.* firedamp, chokedamp; **-wolle,** *f.* mineral wool, asbestos; **-wiese,** *f.* mountain

meadow; **-zunder,** *m.* mountain tinder, asbestos.

Bericht, *m.* report, notice, information.

berichten, to inform, advise, notify, report (on).

Berichterstatter, *m.* reporter, correspondent.

berichtigen, to adjust, set right, correct, settle.

Berichtigung, *f.* correction.

Berichtigungs-grösse, *f.* amount of correction; **-wert,** *m.* correction value.

beriechen, to smell at.

berieseln, to cause to flow (trickle) over, spray, irrigate.

Berieselungs-bütte, *f.* washtub; **-kühler,** *m.* trickle cooler, spray cooler; **-turm,** *m.* wash tower, scrubber; **-verflüssiger,** *m.* trickling-type condenser.

berindet, barky, barked.

berippt, nerved.

Berippung, *f.* nervation.

beritten, mounted.

Berlinerblau, *n.* Prussian blue.

Bernstein, *m.* amber; **schwarzer** ∼, jet.

Berstein-alaun, *m.* aluminous amber; **-aldehyd,** *n.* succinicaldehyde; **-artig,** amberlike; **-erde,** *f.* mineral amber; **-fett,** *n.* ambrain; **-lager,** *n.* stratum of amber; **-salz,** *n.* succinate; **-säure,** *f.* succinic acid.

berosten, to become rusty.

Berst-druck, *m.* bursting strength; **-festigkeit,** *f.* bursting strength.

bersten, to burst, explode, rupture.

Bertram, *m.* pellitory (Anacyclus); **-garbe,** *f.* goosetongue (*Achillea ptarmica*); **-wurz,** *f.* Anacyclus.

berüchtigt, notorious, ill-famed.

berücken, to (en)snare.

berücksichtigen, to bear in mind, consider.

Berücksichtigung, *f.* regard, consideration.

Beruf, *m.*-e, calling, occupation, profession.

berufen, to call, appoint, appeal; **sich auf etwas** ∼, to refer to something.

beruflich, professional.

Berufs-kraut, *n.* horseweed, fleabane (*Erigeron canadensis*); **-mässig,** professional.

Berufung, *f.* summons, convocation, nomination, appointment.

beruhen, to rest, depend, be based on; **auf sich** ∼ **lassen,** to leave a thing alone.

beruhigen, to quiet, reassure, comfort, abate.

beruhigend, soothing, sedative.

Beruhigungsmittel, n. sedative, anodyne.

berühmt, famous, celebrated.

Berühmtheit, f. celebrity.

berühren, to touch, border on.

berührend, touching, tangent.

Berührung, f. contact, contiguity, connection, touching.

Berührungs-brücke, f. clamp connection; **-ebene,** f. tangential plane; **-elektrizität,** f. galvanism, contact electricity; **-empfindung,** f. perception (sensation) of contact; **-fläche,** f. contact surface; **-linie,** f. tangent; **-punkt,** m. point of contact; **-reiz,** m. contact stimulus; **-spannung,** f. contact potential; **-stelle,** f. place of contact; **-streifen,** m. contact strip, margin of contact.

berussen, to soot, smut.

Beryllerde, f. beryllia.

besäen, to sow, seed down, inoculate (media).

Besäen, n. seeding, inoculation.

besagen, to mean, signify, mention.

besagt, aforesaid.

Besamung, f. seeding, insemination.

Besamungshieb, m. seed cutting, thinning.

Besandung, f. sanding; **Prüfung durch ~,** sand test.

besänftigen, to appease, calm, soothe

Besänftigungsmittel, n. sedative

besass (besitzen), possessed.

Besatz, m. border, edging, trimming, stemming, tamping.

Besatzung, f. garrison, crew.

beschädigen, to damage.

beschaffen, to procure, supply, make, execute, constitute, condition.

Beschaffenheit, f. condition, nature, character, state, quality, disposition.

Beschaffung, f. providing, supply.

beschäftigen, to employ, occupy, concern.

Beschäftigung, f. occupation, business.

beschälen, to cover, bark, peel.

Beschäler, m. stallion.

Beschälseuche, f. *maladie de coït,* dourine.

beschalt, shelled.

beschämen, to make ashamed.

beschatten, to shade, shadow.

Beschattung, f. shading, protection.

Beschattungsgare, f. friability of soil through shadowing.

Beschau, f. examination, inspection.

beschauen, to behold, examine, inspect.

beschaulich, contemplative.

beschäumen, to cover with foam.

Bescheid, m. decision, answer, instruction, judgment; **-wissen,** to know, be acquainted with; **jemandem ~ geben,** to give information to someone.

bescheiden, to assign, inform, order; **~ sein,** to be modest, content.

Bescheidenheit, f. modesty.

bescheinen, to shine upon, illuminate.

bescheinigen, to certify, vouch for.

beschenken, to present with, confer.

bescheren, to give, bestow, shear, clip.

Bescherung, f. distribution of presents; **eine schöne ~!,** a pretty business!

beschicken, to load, charge, alloy, feed, prepare, mix, manage, attend to, convey, handle.

beschiessen, to fire on, bombard.

Beschiessung, f. bombardment.

beschimmeln, to grow moldy.

beschimpfen, to insult.

beschirmen, to shelter, cover, protect.

Beschlag, m. ̈e, seizure, efflorescence, moldiness, armature, fitting, coating; **in ~ nehmen,** to attach.

beschlagen, to cover, become coated, mold, effloresce, tarnish, versed, skilled.

Beschlag-nahme, f. occupation, confiscation; **-nehmen,** to seize, attach.

beschleichen, to surprise, steal upon, stalk.

beschleunigen, to accelerate, hasten, expedite, quicken, speed, force.

Beschleuniger, m. accelerator.

Beschleunigung, f. acceleration.

Beschleunigungs-faser, f. accelerator fiber; **mittel,** n. accelerator; **-reiz,** m. accelerative stimulus.

beschliessen, to finish, resolve, conclude, decide, close, determine.

Beschluss, m. ̈e, conclusion, determination, decision; **einen ~ fassen,** pass a resolution, decide.

Beschlussfassung, f. conclusion, decision.

beschmieren, to coat, smear, grease.

beschmutzen, to soil, stain.

beschneiden, to cut, trim, pare, dress, curtail, clip, circumcise.

beschneit, snow-covered.

beschnüffeln, to sniff at.

beschönigen, to gloss, varnish, palliate.

beschopft, tufted, comate.

beschränken, to limit, confine; sich auf etwas ∼, to restrict oneself to something.

beschränkt, limited, narrow, narrow-minded.

Beschränktheit, f. limitedness, confinement, shortness; narrow-mindedness.

Beschränkung, f. restriction.

beschreiben, to describe, write on, construct.

Beschreibung, f. description.

beschreiten, to walk on.

Beschriftung, f. labeling, lettering.

beschuhen, to shoe.

beschuldigen, to accuse.

beschuppt, covered with scales, loricate; -blättrig, lepidophyllous.

beschütten, to pour on, cover with.

beschützen, to protect.

beschwängert, conceived.

beschweift, tailed.

beschweissen, to stain with sweat.

Beschwerde, f. trouble, pain, annoyance, complaint, affection.

beschweren, to weigh, load, weight, charge, burden; sich ∼, to complain.

beschwerlich, burdensome, troublesome, difficult, complicated.

Beschwerung, f. loading, annoyance, weighting (of silk).

Beschwerungsmittel, n. loading material, weighting matter.

beschwichtigen, to allay, appease, soothe.

beschwindeln, to cheat.

beschwingt, winged.

beschwören, to confirm by oath, conjure.

beseelen, to animate, inspire.

besehen, to look at, inspect, examine.

beseitigen, to remove, do away with.

Beseitigung, f. removal, eliminating.

Besen, m.-, broom; -borsten, f.pl. broom setae; -ginster, m. broom (Cytisus scoparius) -kraut, n. broom (Cytisus sco-

parius); -reis, n. birch twig; -stiel, m. broomstick; -winde, f. broom bindweed (Convolvulus scoparius).

besessen (besitzen), possessed.

besetzen, to set, trim, border, stock, fill, engage, fit; besetzt sein, to be engaged, taken, filled up, occupied.

Besetzung, f. charge (of a furnace), filling, occupation.

besichtigen, to inspect, view, survey.

besiedeln, to settle, colonize.

Besiedelung, f. colonization.

Besiedelungs-dichtigkeit, f. density of population; -tüchtigkeit, f. capacity, fitness for colonization.

besiegeln, to seal.

besiegen, to defeat, conquer, overcome.

besinnen, sich, to consider, recollect; sich über etwas ∼, to reflect on something; ohne sich lange zu ∼, without a moment's reflection; sich hin und her ∼, to rack one's brain.

Besinnung, f. consideration, recollection, consciousness; zur ∼ bringen, to restore to life.

besinnungslos, unconscious.

Besitz, m. possession, property, landed estate; in ∼ nehmen, to occupy.

besitzen, to possess, occupy, hold, own, to be endowed with, to enjoy (health).

Besitzer, m. possessor, owner, occupant.

Besitztum, n. possession, property.

Besitzung, f. possession, property.

besonder, particular, special, specific. separate, singular, odd.

Besonderheit, f. peculiarity, individuality.

besonders, especially, separately, singularly, odd.

besonnen (besinnen), prudent, considerate. thoughtful, discreet.

besorgen, to care for, attend to, do, effect, fear, perform; einem etwas ∼, to get something for someone.

Besorgnis, f.-se, apprehension, fear, concern.

besorgt, anxious, careful.

bespannen, to cover with, harness horses.

Bespannung, f. covering, team of horses.

bespinnen, to cover, spin over.

besponnen, covered.

bespornt, spurred.

besprechen, to discuss, arrange, conjure, review, criticize; **sich ~,** to confer with someone.

Besprechung, *f.* discussion, conference, criticism, review; **sich auf eine ~ einlassen,** to enter into negotiations.

besprengen, to sprinkle.

besprengt, aspersed, besprinkled, spersed.

bespritzen, to sprinkle, spray.

besprochen (besprechen), discussed.

bespülen, to wash, rinse.

Bessemerbirne, *f.* Bessemer converter.

besser, better; **es geht ihm ~, es steht ~ mit ihm,** he is getting along better; **um so ~,** all the better.

bessern, to better, correct; **sich ~,** to grow (change for the) better.

Besserung, *f.* improvement, recovery.

best, best; **am besten,** best.

bestand (bestehen), consisted.

Bestand, *m.*-̈e, existence, duration, stability, amount, stock, stand, plantation.

bestandbildend, social, gregarious.

bestanden, stocked.

beständig, stable, constant, durable, permanent, steady, continuous.

Beständigkeit, *f.* stability, durability, permanency, persistency, perseverance, continuousness.

Beständigmachen, *n.* stabilizing, stabilization.

Bestands-aufnahme, *f.* inventory of stand, timber survey; **-begründung,** *f.* stand establishment; **-dichte,** *f.* density of crop; **-güte,** *f.* quality of crop; **-höhe,** *f.* height of crop; **-lockerung,** *f.* thinning; **-nachwert,** *m.* future value of a stand; **-schätzung,** *f.* estimate of stands; **-typus,** *m.* type of stand, association; **-wirtschaft,** *f.* method of management.

Bestandteil, *m.* constituent, ingredient.

bestärken, to confirm, strengthen.

bestätigen, to confirm, ratify, hold true, acknowledge; **sich ~,** to be confirmed.

Bestätigung, *f.* confirmation, verification, corroboration.

bestatten, to bury, inter.

bestäuben, to cover with dust or powder, pollinate.

bestäubt, dusty, pulverulent, pollinized, pruinose.

Bestäubung, *f.* pollination, dusting.

Bestäubungsvorrichtung, *f.* arrangements for pollination.

bestaunen, to look astonished at.

bestechen, to stitch, bribe.

bestechlich, corruptible.

Besteck, *n.*-e, case or set of instruments, knives, forks, etc.

bestecken (mit), to plant with, stick with pins.

bestehen, to consist, exist, persist, pass, be; **~ aus,** to consist of; **~ bleiben,** to stop, remain in existence; **auf einer Sache ~,** to insist upon a thing.

Bestehen, *n.* composition, existence, persistence.

besteigen, to ascend, mount.

bestellen, to order, appoint, engage, till, cultivate, plant; **schlecht (übel) bestellt sein,** to be in bad condition.

Bestellschein, *m.*-e, order blank, requisition.

Bestellung, *f.* arrangement, order, commission, cultivation, tillage.

Bestellungsart, *f.* type of cultivation.

bestenfalls, at best.

bestens, at best.

besteuern, to tax, assess.

bestgeeignet, most suitable.

bestialisch, bestial, brutal.

Bestie, *f.* beast, brute.

bestielt, petiolate, pedunculate.

bestimmbar, determinable, appreciable, definable.

bestimmen, to determine, fix, design, qualify, define, decide.

bestimmt, determined, definite, fixed, specific, certain; **zu etwas ~ sein,** to be destined; **bestimmte Gleichung,** determinate equation.

Bestimmtheit, *f.* definiteness, determination, certainty, firmness, exactness, precision; **mit ~ wissen,** to know positively.

Bestimmung, *f.* determination, appointment, definition, provision, destiny, decision, stipulation, estimation; **~ über etwas treffen,** to come to a decision; **nähere ~,** full instructions.

Bestimmungs-nährboden, *m.* determining nutrient medium; **-schlüssel,** *m.* key to the determination; **-tabelle,** *f.* table, key.

bestmöglich, best possible.

bestocken, to plant with.

bestockt, stocked.

Bestockung, *f.* formation of fresh shoots, tillering, stooling.

Bestockungsfähigkeit, *f.* ability for tillering or stooling.

bestossen, to trim, rough-plane, smooth, knock against.

bestrafen, to punish, correct.

bestrahlen, to irradiate.

Bestrahlung, *f.* irradiation.

Bestrahlungszeit, *f.* time of exposure to radiation.

bestreben, sich, to strive, endeavor.

bestrebt sein, to endeavor, strive for.

Bestrebung, *f.* striving, effort, exertion, endeavor, tendency.

bestreichen, to smear, spread, grease, brush, paint.

bestreitbar, contestable, disputable.

bestreiten, to dispute, defray.

bestreuen, to strew, sprinkle, powder.

bestricken, to ensnare.

bestritt (bestreiten), disputed.

bestritten (bestreiten), argued, discussed.

bestürmen, to assail, assault, solicit.

bestürzen, to feed, cover; **bestürzt machen,** to perplex, dismay; **bestürzt sein,** to be perplexed, amazed, confounded.

Bestürzung, *f.* consternation.

Bestwert, *m.* optimum.

Besuch, *m.*-e, visit, company.

besuchen, to visit, attend.

besudeln, to soil, pollute, contaminate.

betagt, aged, due.

Betain, *n.* betain(e).

betalgen, to tallow.

betasten, to touch, feel, handle, palpate.

betätigen, to prove, exemplify, participate; **sich ~,** put to work, get busy, be active in.

Betätigung, *f.* activity, operation, starting, proving, actuation.

betäuben, to stun, deafen, stupefy.

betäubend, narcotic, stupefying, temulentous.

betäubt, dizzy, stupefied, torpid.

Betäubung, *f.* stupefying, senselessness, stunning, stupor, narcosis.

Betäubungsmittel, *n.* narcotic.

betauen, to cover with dew.

Bete, *f.* beet, beetroot.

beteiligen, sich ~, to participate, be interested, be concerned.

beteiligt sein, to be concerned, interested.

Beteiligung, *f.* participation.

beteuern, to protest, swear to, assert solemnly.

betiteln, to give a title, name.

Beton, *m.* concrete; **-bruch,** *m.* concrete fracture, broken concrete; **-eisen,** *n.* reinforcing iron.

betonen, to accentuate, emphasize.

Betonie, *f.* betony (*Betonica officinalis*).

betonieren, to concrete, build with concrete.

Betonschicht, *f.*-en, layer of concrete.

Betonung, *f.* emphasis.

betören, to infatuate.

Betracht, *m.* consideration, regard, account; **ausser ~ lassen,** to leave out of consideration; **in ~ kommen,** to be taken into consideration, be of importance.

betrachten, to consider, regard, examine.

beträchtlich, considerable, important.

Betrachtung, *f.* consideration, observation, reflection, inspection, way of thinking.

Betrag, *m.*-̈e, amount, sum.

betragen, to amount to; **sich ~,** to behave.

Betragen, *n.* behavior, conduct.

betrauen, to entrust.

Betreff, *m.* reference, regard (to); **in ~ dessen,** as regards that; **in dem ~,** in that respect, as for that.

betreffen, to concern, befall, catch.

betreffend, concerning, concerned, in question.

betreffs, as regards; **~ einer Sache,** with regard to.

betreiben, to drive, carry on, manage, pursue.

betreten, to tread upon, enter upon.

betreuen, to take care of, attend to.

Betrieb, *m.* management, trade, industry, plant, works, factory, working, operation; **in ~ setzen, nehmen,** to set in operation, start: **ausser ~ setzen,** to put out of action.

betriebsam, active, industrious.

Betriebs-anlage, *f.* plant; **-art,** *f.* method of treatment; **-chemiker,** *m.* industrial chemist; **-druck,** *m.* operating pressure; **-einrichtung,** *f.* preparation of working plans; **-energie,** *f.* working energy; **-fähig,** in working condition; **-fertig,** ready for service; **-führung,** *f.* management; **-gas,** *n.* motor gas.

Betriebs-kapital, *n.* working capital; **-kosten,** *pl.* expenses; **-kraft,** *f.* motive power; **-leiter,** *m.* manager; **-regel,** *f.* standard of operation; **-spannung,** *f.* working voltage; **-stockung,** *f.* interruption; **-stoff,** *m.* fuel; **-stoffwechsel,** *m.* basal metabolism; **-störung,** *f.* breakdown.

Betriebs-wirtschaftslehre, *f.* theory of economic management; **-wissenschaftlich,** efficient, pertaining to industrial engineering; **-zeit,** *f.* working hours, shift, period of processing; **-zustand,** *m.* operating condition.

betrifft (betreffen), was das ∼, as for that.

betroffen, disconcerted, perplexed, dazed.

betrüben, to grieve.

betrübt, sad, grieved.

Betrug, *m.* deception, fraud.

betrüge (betragen), amounted to, would amount to.

betrügen, to deceive, cheat, defraud, dupe.

Bett, *n.*-**en,** bed, thalamus.

betteln, to beg.

betten, to embed, bed, put to bed.

Bett-stelle, *f.* bedstead; **-tuch,** *n.* sheet.

Bettung, *f.* bedding, bed.

Bettungs-ziffer, *f.* ratio of soil pressure to settlement.

Bettwanze, *f.* bedbug.

betüpfeln, betupfen, to dab, spot, dot.

Beuche, *f.* bucking, bucking lye.

beuchen, to buck, soak in lye.

Beuch-lange, *f.* bucking lye; **-wasser,** *n.* buck.

Beuge, *f.* bending, flexure; **-bewegung,** *f.* flexion; **-muskel,** *m.* flexor (muscle).

beugen, to bend, flex, deflect, curve, diffract, inflect, bow, humble.

Beuge-sehne, *f.* flexor (tendon); **-sehnenscheide,** *f.* sheath of flexor (tendon); **-seite,** *f.* flexor side; **-stellung,** *f.* position of flexion.

beugsam, flexible, pliant.

Beugung, *f.* bending, diffraction, flexure, flexion, curvature.

Beugungs-erscheinung, *f.* phenomenon of diffraction; **-falte,** *f.* flexure, movement fold; **-gitter,** *n.* diffraction grating.

Beule, *f.* boil, bruise, bump, swelling, ulcer.

Beulen-brand, *m.* boil smut; **-pest,** *f.* bubonic plague.

beunruhigen, to disquiet, trouble, alarm, worry, excite; **sich über etwas** ∼, to be alarmed about something.

beurkunden, to authenticate, verify.

beurlauben, to give leave of absence.

beurteilen, to judge, estimate, criticize, interpret, understand, review, form an opinion.

Beurteilung, *f.* judgment, valuation, estimation, criticism.

Beute, *f.* booty, spoil, prize, trough, beehive.

Beutel, *m.* bag, pouch, purse, bursa, sac, cyst; **-bär,** *m.* koala; **-knochen,** *m.* marsupial bone; **-marder,** *m.* dasyure.

beuteln, to crease, bag, bunch, swell out, pucker, beat flax.

Beutel-ratte, *f.* opossum, marsupian rat; **-sieb,** *n.* bolting sieve, bolter; **-star,** *m.* oriole; **-strahler,** *m.pl.* Cystoidea; **-tiere,** *n. pl.* Marsupialia; **-zeug,** *n.* bolting apparatus (for cloth).

bevölkern, to populate.

Bevölkerung, *f.* population.

Bevölkerungsbewegung, *f.* migration.

bevollmächtigen, to authorize, empower.

bevor, before.

bevorstehen, to be imminent, approach, impend.

bevorstehend, imminent, next, ensuing.

bevorzugen, to prefer, favor.

bewachsen, covered with, stocked, grown over.

bewaffnen, to arm, equip, fortify.

Bewaffnung, *f.* armament, equipment, armature.

bewahren, to keep, preserve, protect; **sich vor etwas** ∼, to guard against something.

bewähren, to verify, approve, confirm; **sich** ∼, to prove true, prove good, stand the test; **sich nicht** ∼, to prove a failure.

bewährt, tried, approved.

Bewahrung, *f.* preservation, keeping, conservation.

Bewährung, *f.* confirmation, trial.

Bewahrungsmittel, *n.* preservative, prophylactic.

bewaldet, wooded, woody.

Bewaldung, *f.* afforestation.

bewältigen, to overcome, master, accomplish.

bewandert, versed in, skilled in.

bewandt (bewenden), situated, qualified.

Bewandtnis, *f.* state of affairs; **eine ganz andere** ∼, things are quite different; **es hat damit eine ganz eigene** ∼, the situation is as follows.

bewässern, to water, moisten, irrigate.

Bewässerung, *f.* irrigation.

Bewässerungs-anlage, *f.* irrigation works; **-graben,** *m.* feeder; **-kanal,** *m.* irrigation canal.

bewegbar, movable, mobile.

bewegen, to agitate, excite, put in motion.

bewegen, sich, to move, induce; **sich** ∼ **lassen,** to be moved; **bewegende Kraft,** motive power.

Beweger, *m.* motor, mover.

Beweg-grund, *m.*￪e, motive; **-kraft,** *f.* motive power.

beweglich, movable, motile, versatile.

Beweglichkeit, *f.* mobility, flexibility.

Beweglichkeitsart, *f.* kind (degree) of mobility.

bewegt, agitated, moved, troubled.

Bewegung, *f.* motion, movement, stir, commotion.

Bewegungs-ebene, *f.* plane of motion; **-erscheinung,** *f.* appearance or effect of motion, motion, movement; **-fähig,** capable of movement; **-faser,** *f.* motor fiber; **-form,** *f.* form of motion; **-geschwindigkeit,** *f.* rate (speed) of locomotion; **-gewebe,** *n.* motor system; **-grösse,** *f.* momentum; **-kraft,** *f.* motive (power) force; **-lehre,** *f.* theory of motion.

Bewegungs-los, motionless; **-muskel,** *m.* motor muscle; **-organ,** *n.* organ of motion; **-reiz,** *m.* motor stimulus; **-richtung,** *f.* direction of movement; **-störung,** *f.* motor disturbance; **-trieb,** *m.* momentum; **-ursache,** *f.* cause of movement; **-vermögen,** *n.* power of movement; **-wahrnehmung,** *f.* perception of movement.

Bewegungs-welle, *f.* wave of motion; **-zustand,** *m.* state of motion.

bewehren, to arm.

Bewehrung, *f.* wrapping, (concrete) reinforcement.

Beweis, *m.*-e, proof, evidence, argument.

beweisbar, demonstrable.

beweisen, to prove, demonstrate, show; **sich als etwas** ∼, to prove oneself.

Beweis-führung, *f.* demonstration, reasoning; **-grund,** *m.* argument; **-kraft,** *f.* demonstrative power; **-mittel,** *n.* evidence, means of proving.

bewenden, to rest, drop; **es bei** (mit) **etwas** ∼ **lassen,** to acquiesce in a thing.

Bewerber, *m.* candidate, applicant, aspirant.

Bewerbungskampf, *m.* competition.

bewerfen, to pelt, plaster.

bewerkstelligen, to achieve, accomplish, perform.

bewerten, to rate, estimate, evaluate.

Bewertung, *f.* estimation, valuation, rating.

Bewertungsausgleich, *m.* valuation, adjustment.

Bewetterung, *f.* air conditioning.

bewickeln, to wrap round, envelop.

bewies (beweisen), proved, verified.

bewilligen, to grant, allow, permit.

Bewilligung, *f.* consent, permission, license.

bewimpert, ciliate(d).

bewirken, to effect, cause, produce, make.

bewirten, to entertain, treat.

bewirtschaften, to manage, carry on, work cultivate.

Bewirtschaftung, *f.* management, cultivation, farming.

Bewitterung, *f.* weathering.

bewog (bewegen), moved, stirred.

bewohnbar, habitable.

bewohnen, to inhabit, reside in, occupy.

Bewohner, *m.* inhabitant, resident, occupant, tenant.

bewölken, sich, to cloud over.

bewundern, to admire.

bewunderns-wert, -würdig, admirable, wonderful.

Bewunderung, *f.* admiration.

Bewurf, *m.* plaster.

bewurzeln, to take root.

bewurzelt, rooted.

Bewurzelung, *f.* root system, rooting.

bewusst, (*gen.*) conscious, aware, cognizant; **-los,** unconscious, instinctive, senseless; **-losigkeit,** *f.* unconsciousness.

Bewusstein, *n.* consciousness, knowledge; **inhalt,** *m.* content of consciousness.

bezackt, indented.

bezahlen, to pay.

Bezahlung, *f.* payment, settlement.

bezähmen, to tame, restrain.

bezahnt, indented, toothed.

Bezahnung, *f.* dentition.

bezaubern, to bewitch, enchant, charm.

bezeichnen, to mark, label, signify, denote.

bezeichnend, characteristic, significant.

Bezeichnung, *f.* marking, notation, mark, brand, symbol, designation.

Bezeichnungsweise, *f.* method of notation.

bezeigen, to show, express, manifest.

bezetteln, to label.

bezeugen, to testify, certify.

beziehen, to draw, order, buy, obtain, relate, refer, cover; sich auf etwas ~, to relate to something, base on.

Beziehung, *f.* relation, connection, reference, respect.

beziehungs-los, not connected, independent; -weise, respectively.

beziffern, to mark with figures or numbers.

Bezirk, *m.*-e, district, circuit, region, area.

Bezoar-stein, *m.* bezoar stone; -wurzel, *f.* contrayerva.

bezogen (beziehen), drawn, bought, referred; ~ auf, corresponding to, referred to, as compared with.

Bezug, *m.* covering, reference, relation.

bezüglich, relative to, with reference to.

Bezugnahme, *f.* reference.

Bezugs-bedingungen, *f.pl.* terms of delivery; -grösse, *f.* reference quantity; -quelle, *f.* source, market; -wert, *m.* relative value.

bezwecken, to aim at, intend.

bezweifeln, to doubt, question.

bezwingen, to master, overcome, subdue; sich ~, to restrain oneself.

Biber, *m.* beaver; -baum, *m.* magnolia; -fell, *n.* beaver skin; -geil, *n.* castoreum; -geilkampher, *m.* castorin; -geildrüse, *f.* castor gland; -geilsack, *m.* castoreum sac.

Bibernell(e), *f.* burnet saxifrage (Pimpinella).

Biber-pelz, *m.* beaver fur; -schwanz, *m.* flat roofing tile, beaver's tail.

Bibirin, *n.* bebeerine; -säure, *f.* bebeeric acid.

Bibliothek, *f.* library.

Bibliothekar, *m.*-e, librarian.

Bichromat, *n.* dichromate.

Bickberre, *f.* whortleberry, bilberry (*Vaccinium myrtillus*).

Biderivat, *n.*-e, bisubstituted derivative.

bieder, honest.

biegbar, flexible, pliable, bendable.

Biege, *f.* bend, curvature; -festigkeit, *f.* flexure, transverse strength, bending strength; -gleitung, *f.* flexural gliding; -muskel, *m.* flexor muscle.

biegen, to bend, curve, diffract, refract.

Biege-röhre, *f.* tube for bending; -spannung, *f.* bending stress, modulus of rupture; -zugspannung, *f.* flexural tensile stress.

biegsam, pliable, flexible, dilatable, bendable, ductile.

Biegsamkeit, *f.* flexibility, pliability, ductility.

Biegung, *f.* bending, deflection, flexure, curvature, windings.

Biegungs-beanspruchung, *f.* bending or flexural stress; -elastizität, *f.* flexibility; -festigkeit, *f.* bending strength; -vermögen, *n.* pliability.

Biene, *f.* bee.

Bienen-ausbeute, *f.* output, yield from bees; -blumen, *f.pl.* flowers pollinated by bees; -brut, *f.* larvae of bees; -harz, *n.* bee glue, propolis; -haube, *f.* bee veil; -haus, *n.* beehouse, apiary; -königin, *f.* queen bee; -korb, *m.* beehive; -kraut, *n.* thyme.

Bienen-nährpflanze, *f.* honey-producing plant; -orchis, *f.* beeflower (*Ophrys apifera*); -saug, *m.* dead nettle (Lamium); -schwarm, *m.* swarm of bees; -stand, *m.* apiary; -stock, *m.* beehive.

Bienen-wachs, *n.* beeswax; -weide, *f.* honey-yielding flora; -weisel, *m.* queen bee; -zucht, *f.* apiculture; -züchter, *m.* beekeeper.

Bier, *n.* beer, ale; -blume, *f.* froth of beer; -brauen, *n.* beer brewing; -brauerei, *f.* brewery; -fass, *n.* beer cask; -grand, *m.* underback; -hefe, *f.* brewer's yeast; -hefepilz, *m.* yeast plant; -schöne, *f.* fining for beer; -stein, *m.* beer scale; -wurze, *f.* (beer)wort.

Biesfliege, *f.* gadfly, botfly.

Biest, *n.*-er, beast; -milch, *f.* colostrum, beestings.

bieten, to offer, bid, show.

bigener Bastard, *m.* genus hybrid.

bigott, bigoted.

Bijou, *m.* jewel.

Bilanz, *f.* balance.

Bild, *n.* picture, image, figure, idea, illustration; **-aufrichtung,** *f.* erection of the image.

bilden, to form, shape, fashion, educate, cultivate, civilize.

bildend, forming, component, constituent, instructive.

Bilderachat, *m.* figured agate.

Bild-erzeugung, *f.* formation of the image; **-fänger,** *m.* motion-picture camera; **-feld,** *n.* image field; **-feldebenung,** *f.* flattening of the image; **-fenster,** *n.* picture gate, aperture; **-fläche,** *f.* perspective plane; **-grösse,** *f.* size of the image;- **hauer,** *m.* sculptor.

bildlich, pictorial, figurative, typical, graphic.

bildlos, without image, amorphous.

Bild-marmor, *m.* figured marble; **-mätsig,** pictorial.

Bildner, *m.* former, component.

Bildnis, *n.***-se,** portrait, image, picture, likeness.

Bild-punkt, *m.***-e,** image point, distance of distinct vision; **-raum,** *m.* field of vision.

bildsam, plastic, flexible, easy to shape.

Bildsamkeit, *f.* plasticity, flexibility.

Bild-säule, *f.* statue; **-schärfe,** *f.* precision (definition) of the image; **-schön,** very beautiful; **-seite,** *f.* face of coin, obverse, head; **-seitig,** on the image side; **-stecher,** *m.* engraver; **-stock,** *m.* cliché, cut, bracket, pedestal.

Bildung, *f.* formation, development, growth, structure, shape, training, organization, education, culture.

Bildungs-abweichung, *f.* deviation from normal development; **-bläschen,** *n.* formative or embryonic vesicle; **-dotter,** *m.* formative yolk; **-energie,** *f.* energy of formation; **-fähig,** capable of development; **-falte,** *f.* formative or growth fold; **-fehler,** *m.* malformation; **-gewebe,** *n.* formative tissue, meristem, cambium; **-hemmung,** *f.* arrest of development; **-kraft,** *f.* power of development.

Bildungs-punkt, *m.* center of development; **-schicht,** *f.* cambium; **-trieb,** *m.* formative (creative) force; **-vermögen,** *n.* capacity of development; **-wärme,** *f.* heat of formation; **-weise,** *f.* mode of formation; **-zelle,** *f.* formative or embryonic cell.

Bild-weite, *f.* focal length, image distance; **-werfen,** *m.* epidiascope, projector;

-werk, *n.* sculpture, imagery; **-wirkung,** *f.* photographic effect; **-wölbung,** *f,* curvature of the image or field; **-zeichen,** *n.* symbol.

Billard, *n.* billiards, billiard table.

Billett, *n.* ticket, note; **-schalter,** *m.* ticket office.

billig, just, fair, right, reasonable, cheap.

billigen, to approve of, consent to.

Billigkeit, *f.* fairness, equity, reasonableness, cheapness.

Billion, *f.* 1,000,000,000,000 (**Milliarde,** *f.* 1000 million).

Bilse, *f.* **Bilsenkraut,** *n.* henbane (*Hyoscyamus niger*).

bimmeln, to tinkle.

Bims, *m.* pumice stone.

bimsen, to rub with pumice stone.

Bimsstein, *m.* pumice stone; **-ähnlich,** **-artig,** pumiceous; **-seife,** *f.* pumice soap.

binär, binary.

Binarkies, *m.* marcasite.

Binde, *f.* band, bandage, ligature, sling, necktie; **-elektron,** *n.* binding (valence) electron; **-gewebe,** *n.* connective tissue.

bindegewebig, like connective tissue, fibrous.

Bindegewebs-balken, *m.* connective-tissue trabecula; **-brücke,** *f.* bridge (band) of connective tissue; **-erweichung,** *f.* softening; **-faden,** *m.* fiber of connective tissue; **-faser,** *f.* fiber of connective tissue; **-geschwulst,** *f.* tumor; **-haut,** *f.* connective-tissue membrane; **-hülle,** *f.* connective-tissue (fibrous) envelope.

Bindegewebs-leiste, *f.* ridge of connective tissue; **-netz,** *n.* reticulum; **-scheide,** *f.* connective-tissue sheath; **-schwarte,** *f.* thickening of connective tissue; **-spalte,** *f.* cleft in connective tissue; **-strang,** *m.* cord of connective tissue; **-umhüllung,** *f.* connective-tissue envelope; **-zerfall,** *m.* disintegration; **-zug,** *m.* band of connective tissue.

Bindeglied, *n.* connecting link.

Bindehaut, *f.* conjunctiva, membrane of connective tissue; **-gefäss,** *n.* vessel of conjunctiva; **-ring,** *m.* limbus (vascular region) of the conjunctiva; **-saum,** *m.* margin of conjunctiva.

Binde-kraft, *f.* binding power; **-mittel,** *n.* cement, binder, agglutinant.

binden, to bind, fix, combine, consolidate, unite, tie; **gebunden,** bound, combined, latent.

bindend, binding, obligatory.

Binde-strich, *m.* hyphen; **-substanz,** *f.* connective substance; **-ton,** *m.* ball clay; **-zeit,** *f.* setting time.

Bindfaden, *m.* string, twine.

bindig, binding, cohesive.

Bindigkeit, *f.* consistency, cohesiveness, binding power.

Bindung, *f.* binding, bond, combination, union, linkage, construction (of fabric).

bindungs-fähig, capable of binding; **-fähigkeit,** *f.* capacity to unite or combine with; **-isomerie,** *f.* isomerism of the union of atoms; **-kraft,** *f.* cohesive force; **-mittel,** *n.* agglutinant, cement; **-vermögen,** *n.* combining power; **-weise,** *f.* mode of combination.

Bingelkraut, *n.* mercury (Mercurialis).

binnen, within, inner, internal, interior; **-apparat,** *m.* Golgi (reticular) apparatus; **-blase,** *f.* internal vesicle; **-druck,** *m.* internal pressure; **-epithel,** *n.* endothelium; **-fach,** *n.* intraseptal chamber; **-gewässer,** *n.* inland water; **-handel,** *m.* domestic trade; **-meer,** *n.* inland sea; **-parasit,** *m.* endoparasite.

Binnen-raum, *m.* inner (interior) space; **-schmarotzer,** *m.* endoparasite; **-verkehr,** *m.* inland traffic; **-wald,** *m.* interior forest.

Binom, *n.* binomial.

Binomialkoeffizient, *m.* binomial coefficient.

binomisch, binomial.

Binse, *f.* rush (Juncus).

binsen-ähnlich, rushlike; **-artig,** rushlike; **-gewächse,** *n.pl.* Juncaceae.

Biochemie, *f.* biochemistry.

biogen, biogenic.

Biograph, *m.*-**en,** biographer.

Biolog(e), *m.*-**en,** biologist.

biologisch, biological.

Biophysik, *f.* biophysics.

Biquadrat, *n.* biquadrate, fourth power.

birgt (bergen) conceals, shelters, salvages.

Birke, *f.* birch (Betula).

Birken-gewächse, *n.* Betulaceae; **-kampher,** *m.* birch camphor, betulin; **-rindenöl,** *n.* oil of betula.

Birk-hahn, *m.* heath cock; **-huhn,** *n.* wild black grouse.

Birkling, *m.* rough boletus (Boletus scaber).

Birnbaum, *m.* pear tree (Pirus communis).

Birne, *f.* pear, pear-shaped object, (electric), bulb.

Birnenäther, *m.* pear ether.

birn(en)förmig, pear-shaped, pyriform.

Birn-essig, *m.* pear vinegar; **-most,** *m.* pear juice, perry; **-wein,** *m.* perry.

birst (bersten), bursts, explodes.

Birzstrauch, *m.* German tamarisk (Myricaria germanica).

bis, till, until, up to; ~ **auf,** until, even to, except; ~ **wann,** how long; ~ **zu,** up to.

Bisam, *m.* musk; **-artig,** musky; **-korn,** *n.* abelmosk seed, musk seed; **-kraut,** *n.* muskroot (Adoxa moschatellina); **-ratte,** *f.* muskrat.

Bischofs-hut, *m.* barrenwort; **-stab,** *m.* crozier.

bisher, hitherto, as yet, till now.

bisherig, hitherto, prevailing, till now, existing.

Biskuit, *n.* biscuit.

bislang, as yet, thus far.

biss (beissen), bit.

Biss, *m.* bite, sting.

Bisschen, *n.* bit, little bit.

bisschen, a little, wee bit.

Bissen, *m.* morsel, bit, bolus; **-weise,** by bits.

bissig, biting, snappish.

Biss-waffe, *f.* biting mouth parts; **-wunde,** *f.* wound caused by bite.

bisweilen, sometimes, occasionally.

Bitte, *f.* prayer, request.

bitte, please, pray.

bitten, to beg, ask, invite.

bitter, bitter, severe; **-erde,** *f.* magnesia; **-holz,** *n.* bitterwood, quassia; **-holzgewächse,** *n.pl.* Simarubaceae.

Bitterich, *m.* yellow succory (Picris hieracioides).

Bitter-kalk, -kalkspat, *m.* magnesium limestone, dolomite.

Bitterkeit, *f.* bitterness.

Bitter-klee, *m.* marsh trefoil, buck (bog) bean (Menyanthes trifoliata); **-kleesalz,** *n.* oxalic acid.

bitterlich, bitterish, bitterly.

Bitterling, *m.* yellowwort (Chlora perfoliata).

bitter-mandelartig, resembling bitter almond; **-mandelgeist,** *m.* spirit of bitter almond; **-mandelöl,** *n.* oil of bitter almond, benzaldehyde; **-mittel,** *n.* bitter, bitters;

-rinde, *f.* bitter (amargoso) bark; **-salz,** *n.* Epsom salts, magnesium sulphate; **-salzboden,** *m.* soil rich in magnesium sulphate; **-säure,** *f.* picric acid; **-spat,** *m.* magnesite; **-stein,** *n.* nephrite, saussurite, picrolite.

Bitter-stoff, *m.* bitter principle; **-süss,** bittersweet; **-süss,** *n.* bittersweet (*Solanum dulcamara*); **-süssigkeit,** *f.* bittersweetness; **-wasser,** *n.* bitter (almond) water (containing magnesium sulphate); **-wurzel,** *f.* gentian root.

Bituminisierung, *f.* bituminization.

bituminös, bituminous.

biversal, in two directions.

Blachfeld, *n.* open country.

Blachmal, *n.* dross, slag.

blähen, to inflate, cause flatulence, swell, distend.

Bläh-frucht, *f.* inflated fruit; **-sucht,** *f.* flatulence.

Blähung, *f.* flatulence, wind.

Blähungs-kolik, *f.* wind colic; **-mittel,** *n.* carminative; **-treibend,** carminative.

blaken, to smoke.

Blamage, *f.* disgrace, shame.

blamieren, to expose to ridicule.

blanchieren, to blanch, whiten.

Blanchissure, *f.* light spot (in dyeing).

blank, shining, bright, clear, clean, polished, smooth; **-beizen,** to pickle, dip; **-holz,** *n.* logwood; **-kochen,** to boil down (sugar) without graining; **-putzen,** to scour, polish; **-reiben,** *n.* polishing (by rubbing); **-tran,** *m.* clear, light-yellow cod-liver oil.

Blasapparat, *m.* blast apparatus.

Bläschen, *n.* vesicle, small blister, bladder, pustule, utricle, bubble; **-flechte,** *f.* shingles; herpes; **-förmig,** vesicular; **-hals,** *m.* neck of bladder, stalk of vesicle.

Blase, *f.* bubble, blister, vesicle, pustule, bladder, still; **-balg,** *m.* bellows; **-balgartig,** bellowslike.

blasen, to blow; **-ähnlich,** bladderlike, vesicular, folliculous; **-artig,** bladderlike, vesicular, folliculous; **-bildung,** *f.* bubble formation, blistering; **-bruch,** *m.* rupture; **-farn,** *m.* bladder fern (Cystopteris); **-fuss,** *m.* thrips; **-füsser,** *m.pl.* physopoda; **-galle,** *f.* cystic bile; **-gang,** *m.* vesicular duct.

Blasen-gärung, *f.* bubbling fermentation; **-gries,** *m.* urinary gravel; **-grün,** *n;* sapgreen; **-grund,** *m.* floor of vesicle;

-haar, *n.* bladderlike hair; **-hals,** *m.* neck of the bladder; **-höhle,** *f.* vesicular cavity; **-käfer,** *m.pl.* blister beetles, Spanish flies (Meloidae); **-keim,** *m.* blastula; **-kirsche,** *f.* bladder cherry, alkekengi.

Blasen-larve, *f.* blastula; **-lebergang,** *m.* cystic duct; **-niere,** *f.* cystic kidney; **-räumer,** *m.* scoop, curette; **-säure,** *f.* uric acid; **-schädel,** *m.* desmocranium; **-sonde,** *f.* catheter; **-pflaster,** *n.* blister plaster; **-spiere,** *f.* Physocarpus; **-stein,** *m.* vesical calculus.

Blasen-strauch, *m.* bladder senna (Colutea); **-tang,** *m.* sea tangle, seaweed (*Fucus vesiculosus*); **-weise,** in bubbles, bubble by bubble; **-wurm,** *m.* bladderworm; **-zählmethode,** *f.* bubble-counting method; **-ziehend,** blistering, vesicatory.

Blas(e)-ofen, *m.* blowing furnace, blast furnace; **-probe,** *f.* bubble test.

Bläser, *m.* blower.

Bläserei, *f.* blowing.

Blas(e)-rohr, *n.* blowpipe, blast pipe; **-tisch,** *m.* blowpipe table.

Blasformquerschnitt, *m.* cross section for the blast.

blasig (aufgetrieben), blistered, vesicular.

Blasigkeit, *f.* blistered state.

blass, pale, pallid.

Blässe, *f.* paleness.

blassfleischfarbig, incarnate, flesh-colored.

blassrot, pale red, reddish, pink.

Blastoplatte, *f.* blastoplate, germinal leaf.

Blatt, *n.* ̈er, leaf, lamina, membrane, plate, flake, fold, layer, sheet, blade, journal, newspaper; **-abfall,** *m.* defoliation; **-abschnitt,** *m.* leaf segment; **-achsel,** *f.* leaf axil; **-achselständig,** axillary; **-aderung,** *f.* leaf venation; **-ähnlich,** foliaceous; **-anlage,** *f.* leaf primordium, leaf rudiment; **-anordnung,** *f.* phyllotaxy.

Blatt-ansatz, *m.* stipule; **-artig,** leaflike; **-astständig,** cladodial; **-auge,** *n.* leaf bud; **-basis,** *f.* leaf base; **-beine,** *n.pl.* foliaceous legs; **-bildung,** *f.* scaling, foliation; **-blau,** *n.* phyllocyanin; **-bleiche,** *f.* chlorosis; **-brand,** *m.* leaf blight.

Blatt-bräune, *f.* leaf scorch; **-bürtig,** arising from a leaf.

Blättchen, *n.* leaflet, small leaf, lamina, lamella, membrane, flake, foliole; **-artig,** lamelliform, laminiform; **-pulver,** *n.* flake (leaf) powder.

Blatt-dorn, *m.-en,* leaf thorn; **-entleerung,** *f.* translocation; **-entwicklung,** *f.* foliation.

Blatter, *f.* pimple, blister, pustule.

Blätter-abfall, *m.* defoliation; **-brand,** *m.* leaf smut; **-bruch,** *m.* lamellar cleavage; **-busch,** *m.* fascicle; **-dach,** *n.* leaf canopy.

Blatterde, *f.* leaf mold.

Blätter-erz, *n.* foliated tellurium, nagyagite; **-förmig,** laminated, leaf-shaped; **-fressend,** leaf eating, phyllophagous; **-fresser,** *m.* phyllophagist.

Blattergift, *n.* toxin of smallpox, vaccine virus.

blätterig, leafy, foliated, laminated, foliaceous.

Blätter-kiemer, *m.pl.* Lamellibranchiata; **-kies,** *m.* lamellar pyrites; **-kohle,** *f.* foliated coal, slate coal; **-magen,** *m.* psalterium, omasum.

Blattern, *f.pl.* smallpox.

blättern, to turn over pages, pockmark.

Blatternarbe, *f.* pockmark.

Blatternimpfung, *f.* vaccination.

Blätter-pilz, *m.,* mushroom (Agaricus); **-schwamm,** mushroom (Agaricus); **-spat,** *m.* foliaceous spar; **-stein,** *m.* variolite; **-ton,** *m.* foliated clay.

Blatt-fadenranker, *m.* leaf tendril climber; **-farbstoff,** *m.* leaf pigment; **-feder,** *f.* leaf spring; **-federchen,** *n.* plumule; **-fläche,** *f.* lamina; **-flächenmessung,** *f.* measurement of leaf area; **-flechte,** *f.* foliose lichen; **-fleckenkrankheit,** *f.* leaf-spot disease, leaf-mold disease (tomato); **-fleisch,** *n.* parenchyma; **-flöhe,** *m.pl.* Psyllidae.

Blatt-flügelzelle, *f.* alar cell; **-flüssigkeit,** *f.* liquid in a leaf; **-folge,** *f.* leaf succession; **-förmig,** lamelliform; **-fuss,** *m.* foliaceous foot, phyllopodium; **-füsser,** *m.pl.* Phyllopoda; **-gelb,** *n.* xanthophyll; **-gewächs,** *n.* foliage plant; **-gewebe,** *n.* leaf tissue, mesophyll; **-gold,** *n.* gold leaf.

Blatt-goldgrundöl, *n.* oil base for varnish on which to apply gold leaf; **-grün,** *n.* chlorophyll; **-grund,** *m.* leaf base; **-grüntod,** *m.* chlorosis; **-häutchen,** *n.* sheath scale, cuticle, ligule; **-heuschrecke,** *f.* walking leaf (*Phyllum siccifolium*); **-hornkäfer,** *m.pl.* Lamellicornia; **-käfer,** *m.pl.* leaf beetles (Chrysomelidae); **-kaktus,** *m.* Epiphyllum; **-kanne,** *f.* cup, pitcher leaf.

Blatt-keim, *m.* plumule; **-keimer,** *m.* dicotyledon; **-kieme,** *f.* lamellar gill; **-kissen,** *n.* pulvinus; **-kleid,** *n.* foliage; **-kletterer,** *m.* leaf climber; **-knospe,** *f.* leaf bud; **-knospendeckung,** *f.* prefoliation,

estivation; **-knospenstand,** *m.* prefoliation, vernation; **-knoten,** *m.* leaf node.

Blatt-lack, *m.* shellac; **-laus,** *f.* plant louse, aphid, green fly, vine grub; **-lauskäfer,** *m.* ladybug; **-los,** aphyllous; **-lücke,** *f.* leaf gap; **-mark,** *n.* mesophyll; **-masse,** *f.* leaf material; **-metall,** *n.* sheet (leaf) metal, foil; **-narbe,** *f.* leaf scar; **-nervatur,** *f.* leaf venation.

Blatt-oberfläche, *f.* surface of leaf, epidermis; **-pflanze,** *f.* foliage plant; **-polster,** *n.* pulvinus; **-rand,** *m.* leaf margin; **-ranke,** *f.* leaf tendril; **-rankenträger,** *m.* plant bearing leaf tendrils; **-reich,** leafy, foliose.

blättrig, foliated.

Blatt-rippe, *f.* vein of leaf, nerve; **-roller,** *m.pl.* leaf roller (Tortricidae); **-rollkrankheit,** *f.* leaf-curl disease; **-rudiment,** *n.* leaf primordium; **-scheide,** *f.* leaf sheath; **-schicht,** *f.* horny lamina (hoof); **-schlauch,** *m.* pitcher (Ascidium); **-schneiderameise,** *f.* leaf-cutting ant; **-schuppe,** *f.* leaf scale.

Blatt-silber, *n.* silver leaf; **-skelett,** *n.* leaf skeleton; **-spindel,** *f.* (leaf) rachis; **-spitzenkletterer,** *m.* climber (by tip of leaf); **-spreite,** *f.* leaf blade, lamina; **-spur,** *f.* leaf trace; **-spurstränge,** *m.pl.* leaf-trace bundle; **-steckling,** *m.* leaf cutting, shoot, slip; **-stellung,** *f.* phyllotaxis, leaf arrangement.

Blattstiel, *m.* petiole; **-blatt,** *n.* phyllode; **-drüse,** *f.* petiolar gland; **-grübchen,** *n.* lenticel on petiole; **-kletterer,** *m.* petiole climber; **-narbe,** *f.* leaf scar; **-ranke,** *f.* petiolar tendril; **-ranker,** *m.* petiole climber.

Blatt-succulent, *m.* plant with succulent leaves; **-verfestigung,** *f.* strengthening of the leaf; **-wespen,** *f.pl.* sawflies (Tenthredinoidae); **-wickler,** *m.* leaf roller (Tortricidae); **-winkel,** *m.* axil; **-winkelständig,** axillary.

Blatt-zahn, *m.* leaf tooth; **-zinn,** *n.* tinfoil; zipfel, *m.* leaf lobe; **-zipfelförmig,** acutilobate; **-zunge,** *f.* ligule; **-zwischenständig,** interfoliaceous.

blau, blue; **-äugig,** blue-eyed; **-beere,** *f.* whortleberry, bilberry (*Vaccinium myrtillus*).

blaubrüchig, blue-brittle, blue-short.

Bläue, *f.* blue; blueness.

bläuen, to dye blue, turn blue, beetle.

Blau-eisenerde, *f.* earthy vivianite; **-erz,** *n.* vivianite; **-fäule,** *f.* blue rot, sap rot;

-fuss, *m.* lanner; **-gras,** *n.* bluegrass; **-grau,** bluish gray, livid; **-holz,** *n.* logwood, campeachy wood; **-kohl,** *m.* red cabbage.

bläulich, bluish; **-grün,** glaucous; **-weiss,** bluish white.

Blau-mühle, *f.* smalt mill; **-ofen,** *m.* flowing furnace; **-papier,** *n.* blueprint paper; **-pause,** *f.* blueprint (tracing); **-salz,** *n.* potassium ferrocyanide; **-säure,** *f.* hydrocyanic acid; **-säurehaltig,** containing hydrocyanic acid; **-schimmel,** *m.* bluishgray horse; **-schörl,** *m.* cyanite; **-spat,** *m.* lazulite.

Blau-stern, *m.* bluebell (Scilla); **-stich,** *m.* bluish tinge; **-stoff,** *m.* hydrocyanic acid, cyanogen; **-sucht,** *f.* cyanosis.

Bläuung, *f.* bluing.

Blech, *n.* sheet metal, sheet iron; **-büchse,** *f.* tin can; **-dose,** *f.* tin box, tin can; **-eisen,** *n.* sheet iron; **-schmied,** *m.* sheetmetal worker; **-tafel,** *f.* sheet iron, iron plate.

bleche(r)n, of tin (plate).

Blei, *n.* lead; **-abgang,** *m.* lead scum, dross; **-ablagerung,** *f.* deposit of lead; **-acetat,** *n.* lead acetate; **-arbeit,** *f.* plumbing, lead smelting; **-arsenat,** *n.* lead arsenate; **-arsenglanz,** *m.* sartorite; **-arsenik,** *m.* lead arsenate or arsenide; **-artig,** leadlike, plumbeous; **-asche,** *f.* lead dross; **-baum,** *m.* lead tree (*Arbor saturni*).

bleiben, to remain, stay; **stehen** ~, remain standing, stop; ~ **lassen,** leave undone; **stecken** ~, to get stuck; **übrig** ~, to be left over; **aus** ~, to stay away.

bleibend, lasting, permanent, unchanging, durable, fast, persistent.

Blei-blech, *n.* sheet lead, lead foil; **-block,** *m.* Trauzl block; **-blüte,** *f.* mimetite.

bleich, pale, pallid, white.

Bleiche, *f.* paleness, pallor, bleachery.

bleichen, to bleach, blanch, whiten, lose color, fade, turn white.

Bleicher, *m.* bleacher.

Bleich-erde, *f.* bleached horizon, fuller's earth; **-flotte,** *f.* bleaching liquor; **-flüssigkeit,** *f.* chlorine water; **-holländer,** *m.* bleaching (poaching) engine; **-kalk,** *n.* bleaching powder; **-lauge,** *f.* bleaching lye.

Bleichlorid, *n.* lead chloride.

Bleich-mittel, *n.* bleaching agent, decolorant; **-salz,** *n.* bleaching salt; **-sucht,** *f.* greensickness, chlorosis, etiolation; **-süchtig,** chlorotic, anemic.

Blei-chromat, *n.* lead chromate; **-dampf,** *m.* lead vapor, lead fume; **-erde,** *f.* earthy cerussite.

bleiern, leaden, dull, heavy.

Blei-essig, *m.* lead acetate; **-fählerz,** *n.* bournonite; **-farbig,** lead-colored, livid; **-feder,** *f.* lead pencil; **-folie,** *f.* lead foil; **-führend,** lead-bearing, plumbiferous; **-gang,** *m.* lead vein; **-gelb,** *m.* lead chromate, massicot; **-giesser,** *m.* plumber; **-glanz,** *m.* lead glance, galena.

Blei-glas, *n.* lead glass; **-glätte,** *m.* litharge; **-glimmer,** *m.* micaceous, cerussite, plumbogummite; **-gummi,** *m.* lead-pencil eraser, plumboresinite; **-haltig,** containing lead; **-holz,** *n.* leatherwood (*Dirca palustris*); **-hornerz,** *n.* **-hornspat,** *m.* phosgenite; **-hütte,** *f.* lead works; **-könig,** *m.* lead regulus.

Blei-kugel, *f.* lead bullet; **-lasur,** *f.* linarite; **-lot,** *n.* plumb line; **-lötung,** *f.* lead soldering; **-mennige,** *f.* minium, red lead; **-niere,** *f.* bindheimite; **-öl,** *n.* lead acetate in oil of turpentine; **-oxyduloxyd,** *n.* minium; **-peroxyd,** *n.* lead dioxide; **-rohr,** *n.* lead pipe.

Blei-safran, *m.* orange lead; **-salbe,** *f.* lead ointment; **-salpeter,** *m.* lead nitrate; **-sand,** *m.* white (bleached) sand; **-sauer,** plumbate of; **-säure,** *f.* plumbic acid; **-schlich,** *m.* lead slime; **-schrot,** *n.* lead shot; **-schwamm,** *m.* spongy lead; **-sicherung,** *f.* lead fuse.

Blei-spat, *n.* cerussite; **-speise,** *f.* lead speiss; **-spiegel,** *m.* specular galena; **-stein,** *n.* lead matte; **-stift,** *m.* lead pencil; **-superoxyd,** *n.* peroxide of lead; **-vergiftung,** *f.* lead poisoning; **-verhüttung,** *f.* lead smelting; **-vitriol,** *m.* lead vitriol, anglesite; **-wasser,** *n.* Goulard extract.

Blei-weiss, *n.* white lead; **-weissalbe,** *f.* lead carbonate ointment; **-wurz,** *f.* leadwort (Plumbago); **-wurzgewächse,** *n.pl.* Plumbaginaceae; **-zinnober,** *m.* red lead, minium; **-zucker,** *n.* lead acetate.

Blendart, *f.* hybrid species.

Blende, *f.* diaphragm, stop, screen, blende.

blenden, to blind, dazzle, shade, screen.

Blenden-ebene, *f.* plane of the diaphragm; **-öffnung,** *f.* diaphragm aperture; **-rohr,** *n.* screening tube; **-träger,** *m.* diaphragm carrier; **-vorrichtung,** *f.* diaphragm attachment.

Blendglas, *n.*⁀er, moderating (darkening) glass; ~ **laterne,** *f.* dark lantern.

Blendling, *m.* hybrid.

Blendlingsbestäubung, *f.* nothogamy.

Blend-scheibe, *f.* disk diaphragm; **-werk,** *n.* delusion.

Blesse, *f.* blaze, star, white spot.

blessieren, to wound.

Blick, *m.* look, flash, glance, view.

blicken, to glance, shine, look; **sich** ∼ **lassen,** to show oneself, appear.

Blicken, *n.* appearance of the "blick."

Blick-feld, *n.* field of vision; **-feldblende,** *f.* field stop; **-gold,** *n.* refined gold still containing silver; **-punkt,** *m.* visual (focus) point; **-richtung,** *f.* line of sight; **-silber,** *n.* refined silver; **-zielpunkt,** *m.* visual fixation end point.

blieb (bleiben), remained.

blies (blasen), blew.

blind, blind, dull, dim, tarnished.

Blinddarm, *m.* caecum; **-anhang,** *m.* vermiform appendix; **-entzündung,** *f.* appendicitis; **-gekröse,** *n.* mesocaecum; **-klappe,** *f.* ileocaecal valve; **-sack,** *m.* saccus caecus; **-tasche,** *f.* subcaecal fossa.

Blind-feuer, *n.* blank fire; **-gänger,** *m.* dud.

Blindheit, *f.* blindness.

Blindleitwert, *m.* susceptance.

Blindlicht, *n.* flashlight.

blindlings, blindly.

Blind-maus, *f.* mole rat; **-sack,** *m.* caecum; **-schlauch,** *m.* blind duct, hepatic duct; **-schleiche,** *f.* slowworm, blindworm; **-versuch,** *m.* blank test.

Blindwert, *m.* numerical result of blank test; ∼ **elektrischer Grössen,** wattless or imaginary component of electric values.

Blindwiderstand, *m.* reactance.

blinke(r)n, to glitter, sparkle, gleam.

Blinkfeuer, *n.* intermittent light.

blinzeln, to blink, wink, nictitate.

Blinzhaut, *f.* nictitating membrane.

Blitz, *m.* lightning, flash; **-ableiter,** *m.* lightning rod.

blitzen, to flash, lightning.

Blitz-licht, *n.* flashlight; **-pulver,** *n.* lycopodium; **-röhre,** *f.* fulgurite; **-schnell,** quick as a flash; **-strahl,** *m.* flash of lightning.

Block, *m.* block, boulder; **-blei,** *n.* pig lead; **-färbung,** *f.* staining in bulk; **-form,** *f.* ingot mold; **-hahn,** *m.* stopcock; **-halde,** *f.* boulder slope; **-haus,** *n.* log house; **-lehm,** *m.* boulder clay.

blöde, weak, timid, bashful, shy.

Blödsinn, *m.* imbecility, idiocy, nonsense.

blöken, to bleat.

blond, blond, fair.

bloss, mere, bare, nude, naked, deprived, sole, simply, only.

Blösse, *f.* nakedness, bareness, blank, clearing, gap, opening.

bloss-legen, to lay bare, expose; **-stellen,** to expose.

blühen, to bloom, blossom, flower, flourish, effloresce.

Blume, *f.* flower, aroma, bouquet.

blümen, to flower, adorn with figures.

Blumen-balg, *m.* glume; **-beet,** *n.* flower bed; **-binse,** *f.* flowering rush (*Butomus umbellatus*); **-binsengewächse,** *n.pl.* Juncaginaceae; **-blatt,** *n.* petal; **-blattarig,** petaloid; **-blattlos,** apetalous.

Blumen-deckblatt, *n.* involucral leaf (bractea), sepal; **-decke,** *f.* perianth; **-duft,** *m.* flower essence, perfume, fragrance; **-erde,** *f.* garden mold; **-fliegen,** *f.pl.* Anthomyidae; **-gärtner,** *m.* floriculturist; **-gehänge,** *n.* garland, festoon; **-gelb,** *n.* anthoxanthin; **-griffel,** *m.* style, pistil.

Blumen-honig, *m.* nectar; **-hülle,** *f.* perianth, perigone; **-käfer,** *m.pl.* Anthicidae; **-kelch,** *m.* calyx; **-knospe,** *f.* flower bud; **-knospenstand,** *m.* vernation.

Blumen-kohl, *m.* cauliflower; **-köpfchen,** *n.* glomerule; **-korso,** *m.* battle of flowers; **-kronblatt,** *n.* petal; **-krone,** *f.* corolla; **-pflanze,** *f.* phanerogamous plant; **-polyp,** *m.* anthozoon.

Blumen-rohr, *n.* arrowroot (*Canna edulis*); **-same,** *m.* seed; **-sauger,** *m.* hummingbird; **-scheide,** *f.* sheath; **-schirm,** *m.* umbel; **-seite,** *f.* hair side (leather); **-staub,** *m.* pollen; **-stengel,** *m.* flower stalk; **-stetigkeit,** *f.* preference for one flower.

Blumen-stiel, *m.* peduncle; **-stielchen,** *n.* pedicle; **-stock,** *m.* plant in a pot; **-strauss,** *m.* bunch of flowers; **-topf,** *m.* flowerpot; **-zucht,** *f.* floriculture; **-züchter,** *m.* florist; **-zweibel,** *f.* flower bulb.

blumig, flowery, bloomy.

Bluse, *f.* blouse.

Blut, *n.* blood; **-abgang,** *m.* loss of blood; **-arder,** *f.* blood vein, vessel; **-andrang,** *m.* congestion; **-arm,** bloodless, anemic, very poor; **-armut,** *f.* lack of blood, anemia; **-auge,** *n.* bloodshot eye, finger fern (*Comarum palustre*); **-ausleerend,** depletive; **-auswurf,** *m.* sputum containing blood.

Blut-bad, *n.* carnage, massacre; **-bahn,** *f.* blood vessel; **-bewegung,** *f.* blood circulation; **-bildend,** blood forming; **-bildner,** *m.* albuminoid; **-bildungsorgan,** *n.* organ to form blood.

Blut-blase, *f.* blood blister; **-blume,** *f.* arnica, bloodflower (Haemanthus); **-buche,** *f.* copper or purple beech (Fagus); **-druck,** *m.* blood pressure; **-drucksenkung,** *f.* lowering of blood pressure; **-dürstig,** bloodthirsty.

Blüte, *f.* blossom, flower, bloom.

Blutegel, *m.* leech.

bluten, to bleed, suffer.

Blüten-achse, *f.* floral axis; **-anschluss,** *m.* position (joining) of perianth parts; **-art,** *f.* kind of species of flower; **-auge,** *n.* flower bud; **-bau,** *m.* construction of flowers; **-becher,** *m.* cupula, hypanthium; **-befruchter,** *m.* pollinator.

blüten-bildend, floral forming; **-bildung,** *f.* formation of flowers; **-blatt,** *n.* petal; **-boden,** *m.* receptacle, torus; **-büschel,** *m.* tuft, fascicle (of flowers); **-decke,** *f.* perianth, involucre; **-dolde,** *f.* umbel.

Blüten-einsatz, *m.* the position (insertion) of the perianth parts; **-formel,** *f.* flower formula; **-füllung,** *f.* doubling (of flower); **-hülle,** *f.* perianth, perigone; **-hüllenblatt,** *n.* sepal; **-kätzchen,** *n.* catkin; **-kelch,** *m.* calyx.

Blüten-knäuel, *m.* glomerule, flower cluster; **-knospe,** *f.* flower bud; **-knospenanlage,** *f.* prefloration; **-kolben,** *m.* spadix; **-korb,** *m.* calathidium, capitulum; **-krone,** *f.* corolla; **-kuchen,** *m.* the edible receptacle of fruits, disk florets.

blüten-los, without flowers; **-pflanzen,** *f.pl.* flowering plants, phanerogams; **-reichtum,** *m.* abundance of flowers; **-schaden,** *m.* damage to flowers; **-schaft,** *m.* flower stalk, floral shoot; **-scheide,** *f.* spathe; **-schweif,** *m.* anthurus (a cluster of flowers at the end of a long stalk); **-spelze,** *f.* glume.

Blüten-stand, *m.* inflorescence; **-standboden,** *m.* receptacle of inflorescence; **-ständig,** floral; **-standstiel,** *m.* peduncle; **-staub,** *m.* pollen; **-stecher,** *m.* anthonomus; **-stengel,** *m.* peduncle; **-stiel,** *m.* pedicle; **-stielranke,** *f.* tendril formed by pedicle; **-stielständig,** pedunculate.

Blutentnahme, *f.* bloodletting.

Blüten-tragend, floriferous; **-traube,** *f.* raceme.

Blutentziehungsmittel, *n.* hemagogue.

Blüten-wachs, *n.* flower wax; **-zeichnung,** *f.* floral characteristics or markings.

Bluterguss, *m.* effusion of blood.

Blütezeit, *f.* time of flowering.

Blut-farbe, *f.* blood pigment; **-farbstoff,** *m.* blood pigment, hemoglobin; **-faserstoff,** *m.* fibrin; **-flecken,** *m.* blood stain; **-fleckenkrankheit,** *f.* morbus maculosus, purpura haemorrhagica; **-fluss,** *n.* hemorrhage; **-flüssig,** hemorrhagic; **-flüssigkeit,** *f.* blood plasma.

Blutgefäss, *n.***-e,** blood vessel; **-bahn,** *f.* blood-vessel tract; **-drüse,** *f.* endocrine gland; **-knäuel,** *m.* tuft of blood vessels; **-stamm,** *m.* trunk of blood vessel; **-system'** *m.* vascular (circulatory) system; **-zweig,** *m.* branch of blood vessel.

Blut-gerinnung, *f.* blood coagulation; **-gerinsel,** *n.* thrombus; **-gerüst,** *n.* scaffold; **-geschwulst,** *f.* hemotoma; **-geschwür,** *n.* furuncle, phlegmon; **-gierig,** bloodthirsty; **-gifte,** *n.pl.* blood toxins; **haargefäss,** *n.* capillary vessel; **-hund,** *m.* bloodhound.

blutig, bloody.

Blut-igel, *m.* leech; **-insel,** *f.* blood island; **-jung,** very young; **-klumpen,** *m.* blood clot; **-kohle,** *f.* blood charcoal.

Blutkörperchen, *n.* blood corpuscle; **-senkung,** *f.* sedimentation of red blood corpuscles.

Blut-kraut, *n.* bloodroot (*Sanguinaria canadensis*); **-kreislauf,** *m.* blood circulation; **-kuchen,** *m.* blood clot, placenta; **-lassen,** *n.* bloodletting; **-lauf,** *m.* circulation; **-laugensalz,** *n.* potassium ferrocyanide; **-laus,** *f.* American blight, woolly louse.

blutleer, anemic; ∼ **machen,** to restrict the flow of blood.

Blut-linie, *f.* blood (pure) line; **-los,** bloodless; **-mangel,** *f.* want of blood; **-masse,** *f.* mass of blood; **-mehl,** *n.* dry blood, blood meal; **-mittel,** *n.* blood tonic; **-plättchen,** *n.* blood platelet, *pl.* blood plates; **-reich,** rich in blood, full-blooded, plethoric; **-rot,** *n.* hematin, hemoglobin; **-ruhr,** *f.* dysentery.

blut-saugend, bloodsucking; **-sauger,** *m.* bloodsucker; **-schande,** *f.* incest; **-scheibe,** *f.* blood (cell) corpuscle; **-schlag,** *m.* apoplexy; **-stein,** *m.* bloodstone, hematite; **-stillend,** blood stanching, hemostatic, styptic; **-sturz,** *m.* bursting of a blood vessel, hemorrhage; **-sucht,** *f.* hemophilia.

Blutsverwandschaft, *f.* blood relationship.

blut-triefend, dripping with blood; **-trok-kenpräparat,** *n.* blood film, smear; **-tropfen,** *m.* drop of blood; **-umlauf,** *m.* blood circulation.

Blutung, *f.* bleeding.

Blutungs-druck, *m.* root pressure; **-wasser,** *n.* exudation water.

blut-unterlaufen, bloodshot; **-unterlaufung,** *f.* effusion; **-vergiessen,** *n.* bloodshed; **-vergiftung,** *f.* blood poisoning; **-verteilung,** *f.* blood distribution; **-verwandte,** *m.* blood relation; **-wärme,** *f.* blood heat; **-wasser,** *n.* lymph, serum; **-wassergefäss,** *n.* lymphatic vessel; **-wurz,** *f.* bloodwort (rootwort).

Bö, *f.* squall, gust (of wind).

Boa, *f.* boa.

Bock, *m.* he-goat, buck, ram, trestle, blunder, jack; **asche,** *f.* coal ashes; **-beinig,** bow-legged, stubborn.

Böckchen, *n.* kid.

bockig, obstinate, resistant, stubborn, refractory.

Bock-käfer, *m.pl.* long-horned beetles (Cerambycidae); **-leder,** *n.* buckskin; **-nuss,** *f.* souari nut (fruit of Caryocar); **-säure,** *f.* hircic acid.

bocks-ähnlich, hircinous; **-bart,** *m.* goats-beard (Tragopogon); **-dorn,** *m.* *Lycium barbarum.*

Bockseife, *f.* mountain soap.

Bocks-horn, *n.* fenugreek (*Trigonella purescens*); **-hornklee,** *m.* Trigonella; **-hörnlein,** *n.* carob bean.

Boden, *m.* ᵃ soil, ground, bottom, earth, basis, plate floor, attic; **festen ~ fassen,** to get a firm footing; **Grund und ~,** landed property; **zu ~ drücken,** to overwhelm.

Boden-ansprüche, *m.pl.* soil requirements; **-art,** *f.* soil type; **-aufschwemmung,** *f.* soil suspension; **-bearbeitung,** *f.* cultivation of the soil; **-beschaffenheit,** *f.* nature of the soil; **-besitz,** *m.* landed property; **-bessernd,** soil improving; **-bestandteile,** *m.pl.* components of the soil; **-bildung,** *f.* soil formation; **-blütige** (Pflanzen), thalami-florous (plants).

Bodendecke, *f.* ground cover; **lebende ~,** herbaceous soil covering.

Boden-druck, *m.* ground pressure; **-einfluss,** *m.* edaphic influence; **-entseuchung,** *f.* disinfection of the soil; **-erhebung,** *f.* rising ground; **-erhitzung,** *f.* heating of the soil; **-erschöpfung,** *f.* soil exhaustion; **-fauna,** *f.* bottom fauna; **-fluss,** *m.* soil movement;

-fräse, *f.* rotary cultivator; **-fruchtbarkeit,** *f.* soil fertility.

Boden-gare, *f.* bacteriological ripeness of the soil; **-gekriech,** *n.* soil movement; **-grenze,** *f.* edaphic limit; **-güte,** *f.* quality of soil, productive capacity; **-hefe,** *f.* grounds, dregs; **-hold,** adapted to (preferring) a certain soil; **-impfstoff,** *m.* soil inoculant; **-impfung,** *f.* inoculation of the soil; **-kolonne,** *f.* plate-type column; **-körper,** *m.pl.* precipitates (crystal phases).

Boden-kraft, *f.* fertility; **-kräuter,** *n.pl.* terrestrial (land) plants; **-krume,** *f.* surface soil; **-kunde,** *f.* soil science; **-kupfer,** *n.* copper bottoms; **-lockerung,** *f.* loosening of soil; **-los,** bottomless, enormous; **-luft,** *f.* entrapped air, air in soil pores; **-mehl,** *n.* fecula, starch; **-müdigkeit,** *f.* soil exhaustion.

Boden-nährstoff, *m.* soil nutrient; **-oberfläche,** *f.* surface; **-pappe,** *f.* mulch paper; **-pflege,** *f.* preservation; **-platte,** *f.* floor plate; **-probe,** *f.* soil sample; **-profil,** *n.* profile of the soil; **-punktmethode,** *f.* soil-point method; **-reinertrag,** *m.* net proceeds; **-satz,** *m.* sediment, deposit, dregs.

Boden-säurekrankheit, *f.* soil-acidity disease; **-schicht,** *f.* bottom layer, lowest stratum; **-see,** *m.* Lake Constance; **-senkung,** *f.* subsidence of the ground; **-skelett,** *n.* foundation of the soil, core; **-ständig,** hypogynous, receptacular, permanent; **-ständigen,** *m.pl.* permanent plant (population) community; **-stein,** *m.* bottom stone, bed stone, bittern; **-stet,** peculiar to (occurring on) certain soils; **-streu,** *f.* ground litter.

Boden-teig, *m.* underdough; **-übersichtskarte,** *f.* soil-survey chart; **-vag,** occurring on (adaptable to) any soil; **-verbesserung,** *f.* soil improvement; **-verfestigung,** *f.* soil stabilization; **-vergiftung,** *f.* soil poisoning; **-verhagerung,** *f.* impoverishment; **-verhältnisse,** *n.* soil conditions; **-verhartung,** *f.* hardening of soil; **-verschiedenartigkeit,** *f.* soil heterogeneity.

Boden-verschluss, *m.* compactness of the soil; **-verwilderung,** *f.* wild (untilled) state of the soil; **-wasser,** *n.* ground water; **-wuchs,** *m.* undergrowth; **-wurzel,** *f.* ordinary (ground) root; **-zahl,** *f.* number of plates; **-zustand,** *m.* condition of the soil.

bog (biegen), bent, curved.

Bogen, *m.* bow, bend, arc, curvature, sheet; **-artig,** arched, bowlike; **-blatt,** *n.* convex leaf; **-faser,** *f.* proximal barbule, arcuate fiber; **-flamme,** *f.* arc flame; **-förmig,** bow shaped, curved, arched, arcuate; **-furche,** *f.* arcuate fissure.

Bogen-gang, *m.* semicircular canal, arcade; **-gangsmündung,** *f.* aperture of semicircular canal; **-lampe,** *f.* arc lamp; **-läufig,** camptodromous; **-säge,** *f.* bow saw; **-sehne,** *f.* bowstring; **-strahl,** *m.* proximal barbule; **stück,** *n.* curved piece, return bend; **-wulst,** *m.* corpus callosum.

Bohle, *f.* thick plank.

bohlen, to plank.

Bohne, *f.* bean.

bohnen, to wax, polish.

Bohnen-baum, *m.* Laburnum; **-hülse,** *f.* pod; **-käfer,** *m.* weevil; **-kraut,** *n.* savory (*Satureia hortensis*); **-ranke,** *f.* beanstalk; **-stange,** *f.* bean pole; **-stecken,** *m.* bean stick, bean pole; **-strauch,** *m.* Cystissus laburnum.

Bohner, *m.* polisher; **-wachs,** *n.* polishing wax.

Bohnerz, *n.* pea ore (oölitic limonite), bean ore (pisolitic iron).

Bohr-anlage, *f.* drilling apparatus.

bohren, to bore, drill.

Bohrer, *m.*-, borer, drill, gimlet, perforator, auger, bit.

Bohr-fett, *n.* cutting oil; **-guss,** *m.* drillable casting; **-käfer,** *m.pl.* Ptinidae; **-klette,** *f.* burr fruit boring into the ground; **-krone,** *f.* tip of an auger; **-lochpfeife,** *f.* blown-out hole;**-mehl,** *n.* bore dust; **-öl,** *n.* soluble oil; **-probe,** *f.* core sample, boring test; **-schmant,** *m.* drilling mud.

Bohrung, *f.* boring, borehole.

Bolle, *f.* bulb, onion (*Allium cepa*).

Bollengewächs, *n.* bulbaceous plant.

Bologneser Flasche, *f.* Bologna flask.

Bolometer, *n.&m.* bolometer.

Bolus, *m.*, **-erde,** *f.* bole.

Bolzen, *m.*-, pin, bolt; **-mutter,** *f.* nut; **-scheibe,** *f.* washer.

Bombage, *f.* (on rolls) knob.

Bombe, *f.* bomb, shell.

Bonbon, *m.* candy.

Bonität, *f.* quality.

bonitieren, to value the soil.

Bonitierung, *f.* appraisement of the productivity.

Boot, *n.*-e, boat.

Bor, *n.* boron; **-ameisensäure,** *f.* boroformic acid.

Borax-kalk, *m.* calcium borate; **-perle,** *f.* borax bead; **-säure,** *f.* boric acid; **-weinstein,** *m.* boryl potassium tartrate.

Borchlorid, *n.* boron chloride.

Bord, *m.* border, edge, rim.

Börde, *f.* fertile plain.

Bordelaiser Brühe, *f.* Bordeaux mixture.

bördeln, to border, flange, turn over.

Bord-schwelle, *f.* **-stein,** *m.* curb(stone).

Borfluorwasserstoff, *m.* hydrofluoboric acid.

Bor(r)etschgewächse, *n.pl.* Boraginaceae.

Borg, *m.* credit, loan, borrowing.

Borgehalt, *m.* boron content.

borgen, to borrow.

Borium, *n.* boron.

Borkalk, *m.* calcium borate.

Borke, *f.* bark, rind, crust, scab, cortex, phloem.

Borken-käfer, *m.pl.* bark beetles; **-schuppe,** *f.* bark scales.

Born, *m.* well, spring.

borniert, narrow-minded.

Borretsch, *m.* borage.

Bor-salbe, *f.* boric (acid) ointment; **-säure,** *f.* boric acid.

Börse, *f.* purse, stock exchange.

Borste, *f.* bristle, seta, chaeta, fissure, crack.

Borsten-anordnung, *f.* arrangement of setae; **-artig,** setaceous; **-besen,** *m.* hair broom; **-bündel,** *n.* tuft of setae; **-fäule,** *f.* swine scurvy; **-förmig,** setaceous; **-füsse,** *m.pl.* parapodia; **-gras,** *n.* matweed (*Nardus stricta*); **-haar,** *n.* seta; **-hirse,** *f.* bristle grass (Setaria).

Borsten-kiefer, *m.pl.* Chaetognatha; **-kranz,** *m.* circle of setae; **-reihe,** *f.* row of setae; **-sack,** *m.* setigerous sac; **-tragend,** bearing, setiferous; **-wülste,** *f.pl.* parapodia covered with setae; **-würmer,** *m.pl.* bristle worms, chaetopoda; **-zelle,** *f.* bristle cell.

Borstickstoff, *m.* boron nitride.

borstig, bristly, setaceous, setiform, setose, strigose, surly.

Borte, *f.* border, edging, lace.

Bortelantrieb, *m.* bead (rim) drive.

Bor-wasserstoff, *m.* boron hydride; **-wolframsäure,** *f.* borotungstic acid.

bösartig, malignant, virulent.

Bösartigkeit, *f.* malignancy.

Böschung, *f.* slope, scarp.

Böschungswinkel, *m.* angle of (slope) elevation.

böse, (*dat.*) bad, evil, ill, noxious, sore, virulent; böser Vorsatz, evil intention, malice.

Bösewicht, *m.*-er, villain.

boshaft, malicious.

bossieren, to emboss, mold.

Bossierwachs, *n.* molding wax.

böswillig, malevolent.

bot (bieten), offered.

Botanik, *f.* botany.

Botaniker, *m.*-, botanist.

botanisch, botanical.

botanisieren, to go botanizing.

Botanisiertrommel, *f.* specimen box.

Bote, *m.* messenger.

Botschaft, *f.* message, embassy, news.

Böttcher, *m.* cooper.

Bottich, *m.*-e, vat, tub.

Botulismus, *m.* botulism.

Bouillon, *f.* broth, beef tea; -kultur, *f.* broth culture.

Bowle, *f.* bowl.

brach (brechen), broke.

brach, fallow, uncultivated; -acker, *m.* fallow land; -bearbeitung, *f.* working the uncultivated soil; -behandlung, *f.* fallow treatment.

Brache, *f.* fallowness.

brachen, to break up fallow land.

brachlegen, to lay fallow, devastate.

Brach-feld, *n.* fallow soil; -käfer, *m.* fern beetle (Scarabaeus); -schnepfe, *f.* curlew.

Brachsenkraut, *n.* quillwort (*Isoetes lacustris*).

Brach-weide, -wiese, *f.* fallow pasture.

brachte (bringen), brought.

Brack, *m.* refuse.

brackig, brackish, briny.

Brack-vieh, *n.* cast-off cattle; -wasser, *n.* brackish water; -wespen, *f.pl.* Braconidae.

Brachiodenfuss, *m.* podobranchia.

Bracteen, *pl.* bracts.

Bramme, *f.* slab of iron, bloom, ingot.

Brand, *m.*-e, burning, fire, combustion, blight, gangrene, wounds, smut, disease; -anfälligkeit, *f.* susceptiblity to smut; balsam, *m.* ointment for burns; -befall, *m.*

smut attack; -beule, *f.* smut boil; -blase, *f.* blister.

branden, to surge, break.

Brand-erde, *f.* hardpan; -erz, *n.* bituminous shale, idrialite; -fäule, *f.* brown rot; -fest, fireproof; -fläche, *f.* burn; -flecken, *m.* burn, gangrenous spot; -fleckenkrankheit, *f.* smut disease; -gold, *n.* refined gold; -harz, *n.* empyreumatic resin.

brandig, burnt, blighted, rusty, gangrenous.

Brand-kraut, *n. Phlomis herbaventi;* -loch, *n.* venthole; -marken, to brand; -mauer, *f.* partition wall; -messer, *m.* pyrometer; -mittel, *n.* remedy for burns or gangrene; -öl, *n.* empyreumatic oil; -pilz, *m.* smut fungus (Ustilago); -salbe, *f.* salve for burns; -schiefer, *m.* bituminous shale.

Brand-schott, *m.* fireproof bulkhead; -silber, *n.* refined silver; -stein, *m.* brick; -stiftend, incendiary.

Brandung, *f.* surf.

Brandungs-welle, *f.* breaker, surging billow; -zone, *f.* surf zone.

Brandwirtschaft, *f.* burning practice.

Brand-wunde, *f.* burn.

brannte (brennen), burnt.

Branntwein, *m.* spirits, brandy, whisky; -blase, *f.* still, kettle (for spirits); -brennerei, *f.* distillation, brandy or whisky distillery; -geist, *m.* rectified spirit; -hefe, *f.* alcohol ferment; -prober, *m.* alcoholometer.

branstig, having a burnt smell or taste.

Brasilholz, *n.* brazilwood.

Brassidinsäure, *f.* brassidic acid.

Brassinsäure, *f.* brassic acid.

Bratapfel, *m.*-, baked apple.

braten, to roast, bake, fry.

Braten, *m.* roast meat.

Bratfrischarbeit, *f.* roasting and refining.

Brau, Bräu, *m.* brew, malt liquor; -bottich, *m.* brewing vat.

Brauch, *m.* usage, custom.

brauchbar, serviceable, useful.

brauchen, to use, employ, want, need, consume, expend.

Braue, *f.* eyebrow.

brauen, to brew.

Brauer, *m.* brewer.

Brauerei, *f.* brewing, brewery; -hefe, *f.* brewer's yeast; -zwecke, *m.pl.* brewery purposes.

Braugerste, *f.* brewing barley.

braun, brown; **-algen,** *f.pl.* brown algae (Phaeophyceae); **-bleierz,** *n.* pyromorphite.

Bräune, *f.* brown color, quinsy.

Brauneisen-erz, *n.* **-stein,** *m.* brown iron ore, limonite.

bräunen, to brown, tan.

Braun-erde, *f.* intertextic fabric in brown earth; **-erz,** *n.* limonite; vivianite; **-heil,** *n.* selfheal (*Prunella vulgaris*); **-kalk,** *m.* dolomite; **-kette,** *f.* medullary spot, pith fleck, **-kohl,** *m.* broccoli (*Brassica oleracea*); **-kohle,** *f.* brown coal, lignite, peat coal; **-kohlenhaltig,** lignitiferous, lignitic; **-kräusen,** *f.pl.* fuzzy heads (in brewing); **-lauge,** *f.* brown liquor.

bräunlich, brownish.

Braun-manganerz, *n.* manganite; **-rost,** *m.* brown rust; **-rot,** *n.* colcothar; **-schliff,** *m.* steamed mechanical wood pulp; **-schuppenkraut,** *n.* cancerroot, strangleweed (Orobanche); **-späne,** *m.pl.* logwood shavings; **-spat,** *m.* dolomite; **-wurzgewächse,** *n.pl.* Scrophulariaceae.

Braunstein, *m.* manganese dioxide, pyrolusite; **-blende,** *f.* alabandite; **-kiesel,** *m.* rhodonite; **-rahm,** *m.* earthy manganite, bog manganese; **roter** ∼, rhodochrosite; **schwarzer** ∼, hausmannite.

Braun-tran, *m.* blubber, thick cod oil.

Bräunung, *f.* browning; dyeing brown.

Braunwurzgewächse, *n.pl.* Scrophulariaceae,

Braus, *m.* tumult, uproar.

Brause, *f.* effervescence; **-bad,** *n.* shower bath.

brausen, to fluster, tingle, hum, buzz, ferment, effervesce, douche.

Brause-pulver, *n.* effervescent powder; **ton,** *m.* bituminous clay; **-wasser,** *n.* soda water.

Braut, *f.* betrothed, bride.

Bräutigam, *m.* bridegroom, betrothed.

Brau-wasser, *n.* water for brewing, liquor; **-wesen,** *n.* brewing trade.

brav, honest, good, brave.

Brecharznei, *f.* emetic.

Brechbacken, *f.pl.* crusher jaws.

brechbar, breakable, brittle, fragile, refrangible.

Brech-bohne, *f.* kidney bean (*Phaseolus vulgaris*); **-durchfall,** *m.* diarrhea with vomiting; **-eisen,** *n.* crowbar, pinch bar.

brechen, to break, fracture, refract, crush, pulverize, destroy, vomit, gather, pluck,

decompose, mine, quarry, fold, blend, boil off, sprout, crease, crinkle, change.

brechend, refractive.

brechenerregend, emetic.

Brech-körner, *n.pl.* castor beans; **-krafteinheit,** *f.* diopter (optics); **-mittel,** *n.* emetic; **-nuss,** *f.* nux vomica; **-punkt,** *m.* point of refraction; **-reiz,** *m.* nausea; **-ruhr,** *f.* cholera; **-stange,** *f.* crowbar, pinch bar; **-stoff,** *m.* vomiting substance, emetine.

Brechung, *f.* refraction, aberration.

Brechungs-ebene, *f.* plane of refraction; **-exponent,** *m.* refractive index; **-gesetz,** *n.* law of refraction; **-indizes,** *pl.* refractive indices; **-kraft,** *f.* refractive power; **-verhältnis,** *n.* refractive index; **-vermögen,** *n.* refractive power; **-weinstein,** *m.* tartar emetic; **-winkel,** *m.* angle of refraction; **-wurzel,** *f.* ipecac.

Brechungs-azhl, *f.* refractive index; **-zustand,** *m.* condition of refraction.

Brech-wein, *m.* emetic wine, wine of antimony; **weinstein,** *m.* tartar emetic; **-werk,** *n.* crusher; **-wurzel,** *f.* ipecacuanha root.

Brei, *m.* pulp, mash, paste, porridge; **-artig,** pulpy, pasty, thickly fluid.

breiig, pulpy, pappy, viscous.

breit, broad, wide, flat; **-blättrig,** broad-leaved latifoliate.

Breite, *f.* width, breadth, latitude.

breiten, to spread, extend, expand, flatten; **-grad,** *m.* degree of latitude; **-wahrnehmung,** *f.* space (breadth, depth) perception.

breit-füssig, flat-footed; **-köpfig,** branchycephalic, platycephalous; **-randig,** broad brimmed; **-ringig,** broad ringed, broad zoned; **-rüssler,** *m.pl.* Anthribidae; **-würfig,** broadcast; **-zehig,** platydactylous.

Breiumschlag, *m.* poultice.

Brekzie, *f.* breccia.

Bremsbacke, *f.* brake shoe.

Bremse, *f.* horsefly, gadfly (Tabanus), barnacle, brake.

bremsen, to apply the brake(s).

Brems-flüssigkeit, *f.* (hydraulic) brake fluid; **-gitterröhre,** *n.* pentode; **-klotz,** *m.* brake (shoe) block; **-leiste,** *f.* retarding rail; **-stange,** *f.* brake rod; **-strahlen,** *m.pl.* radiative stopping; **-strahlung,** *f.* impulse "white" radiation, radiation due to retarding (of particles); **-tritt,** *m.* pedal.

Brenkas, *n.* fine East Indian tin.

Brenke, *f.* yeast tub.

Brenn-apparat, *m.* distilling apparatus, still, branding machine; **-arbeit,** *f.* fire assaying, burning; **-ätzverfahren,** *n.* pyrography.

brennbar, combustible, burnable.

Brennbarkeit, *f.* combustibility, inflammability.

Brenn-blase, *f.* alembic; **-blatt,** *n.* leaf with stinging hairs; **-borste,** *f.* stinging bristle; **-cylinder,** *m.* moxa; **-ebene,** *f.* focal plane; **-eisen,** *n.* branding (curling) iron.

brennen, to burn, calcine, cauterize, distill, smart, sting.

brennend, pungent, smarting, caustic.

Brenner, *m.* burner, distiller.

Brennerei, *f.* distillery, kiln; **-hefe,** *f.* distillery yeast.

Brennessel, *f.* stinging nettle (Urtica).

Brenn-fleckenkrankheit, *f.* anthracnose; **-gas,** *n.* fuel gas; **-geschwindigkeit,** *f.* rate of combustion; **-glas,** *n.* burning glass (lens); **-haar,** *n.* stinging hair; **-holz,** *n.* firewood; **-hülse,** *f.* cowhage (*Mucuna pruriens*); **-kapsel,** *f.* sagger; **-kegel,** *m.* pyrometric cone; **-kraut,** *n.* crowfoot, clematis (Ranunculaceae).

Brenn-linie, *f.* focal line, caustic curve; **-material,** *n.* fuel; **-materialverbrauch,** *m.* fuel consumption; **-mittel,** *n.* caustic; **-nessel,** *f.* stinging nettle (Urtica); **-ofen,** *m.* baking oven, kiln, furnace; **-öl,** *n.* lamp oil; **-palme,** *f.* jaggery palm (*Caryota urens*); **-punkt,** *m.* focal point; **-silber,** *n.* amalgam for silvering.

Brenn-spiegel, *m.* burning reflector, concave mirror; **-spiritus,** *m.* fuel alcohol; **-stahl,** *m.* blister steel; **-staub,** *m.* combustible powder, powdered fuel; **-stoff,** *m.* fuel; **-strahl,** *m.* focal ray; **-stunde,** *f.* burning hour, lamp hour; **-weite,** *f.* focal distance; **-wert,** *m.* calorific value; **-winde,** *f.* loasa (Cajophora); **-zylinder,** *m.* moxa; **zünder,** *m.* fuse, fuse train.

Brenz, *n.* empyreuma, combustible; **-apfelsäure,** *f.* maleic acid; **-cain,** *n.* pyrocain; **-essigäther,** *m.* **-essiggeist,** *m.* acetone; **-holzsäure,** *f.* pyroligneous acid; **-katechin,** *n.* pyrocatechol.

brenzlich, brenzlig, empyreumatic, tarry, burnt, smelling or tasting of burning; **brenzlige Säure,** *f.* pyroacid.

Brenz-öl, *n.* empyreumatic oil; **-säure,** *f.* pyroacid; **-traubenalkohol,** *m.* pyroracemic alcohol; **-traubensäure,** *f.* pyroracemic acid; **-weinsäure,** *f.* pyrotartaric acid.

Brett, *n.* board, plank, shelf; **-kohle,** *f.* bag coal; **-mühle,** *f.* sawmill, board mill.

Bretterwurzel, *f.* buttress root.

Brezel, *f.* pretzel.

bricht (brechen), breaks.

Brief, *m.* **-e,** letter; **-aufschrift,** *f.* address.

brieflich, by letter, in writing.

Brief-marke, *f.* postage stamp; **-papier,** *n.* writing paper; **-porto,** *n.* postage; **-schaften,** *f.pl.* letters, correspondence, writings, papers; **-stempel,** *m.* postmark; **-tasche,** *f.* portfolio; **-taube,** *f.* carrier pigeon; **-umschlag,** *m.* envelope, wrapper; **-wechsel,** *m.* correspondence.

Bries, *n.* thymus.

Brieseldrüse, *f.* thymus gland.

briet (braten), roasted, baked.

Brikett, *n.* briquette.

Brilliant, *m.* jewel; **-gelb,** *n.* brilliant yellow.

Brille, *f.* spectacles, eyeglasses.

Brillen-glaskondensor, *m.* spectacle-lens condenser; **-lupe,** *f.* spectacle magnifier; **-schlange,** *f.* cobra.

bringen, to bring, carry, take, put, yield, offer, produce; **zuwege** ∼, to accomplish; ∼ **auf,** to reduce to.

brisanter Sprengstoff, *m.* brisant explosive.

Brisanz, *f.* explosive power.

Brise, *f.* breeze.

Bröckchen, *n.* small piece, crumb.

bröck(e)lig, brittle, friable.

Bröck(e)ligkeit, *f.* brittleness.

brökeln, brocken, to crumble.

Bröckelstärke, *f.* lump starch.

Brocken, *m.* crumb, fragment, morsel; **-gestein,** *n.* breccia; **-stärke,** *f.* lump starch; **-weise,** piecemeal.

brodeln, to bubble.

Brodem, *m.* steam, exhalation.

Brokat, *n.* brocade.

Brom, *n.* bromine; **-äther,** *m.* ethyl bromide; **-beere,** *f.* blackberry (Rubus).

Brombeerstrauch, *m.* bramble.

bromhaltig, containing bromine.

Bromid, *n.* bromide.

bromieren, brominate.

Brom-kalium, *n.* potassium bromide; **-lack,** *m.* lacquer for bronze; **-natron,** *n.* sodium bromide, sodium hypobromite; **-salz,** *n.* bromate, bromide; **-spat,** *n.* bromyrite; **-verbindung,** *f.* bromine compound.

Bronchial-katarrh, m. bronchial catarrh; -schleim, m. bronchial mucus.

Bronze, f. bronze; -pulver, n. bronze powder; -mischlack, m. -tinktur, f. a bronze-pigmented lacquer or varnish.

bronzieren, to bronze, braze.

Brosam, m. Brosame, f. crumb, scrap.

Bröschen, n. sweetbread.

broschieren, to stitch, sew.

broschiert, in paper cover.

Broschüre, f. stitched book, pamphlet.

Brot, n.-e, bread, loaf; -baum, m. bread tree; -brei, m. bread paste, pap.

Brötchen, n. roll.

Brot-gärung, f. leavening of bread; -geschmack, n. steam taste; -getreide, n. bread cereals; -käfer, m. biscuit weevil, bread mite; -krankheit, f. disease in bread; -herr, m. employer.

Brotkorb, m. bread basket; den ~ zu hoch hängen, to take unfair advantage of, underpay.

Brot-korn, n. breadstuff; -los, unemployed; -raffinade, f. loaf sugar; -rinde, f. crust of bread; -schimmel, m. bread mold; -schnitte, f. slice of bread; -wurzel, f. cassava, yam.

Bruch, m.-̈e, break, scrap, quarry, fracture, swamp, breach, failure, rupture, hernia, crease; -ast, m. brittle branch; -band, n, truss; -beanspruchung, f. breaking stress, break strain; -belastung, f. breaking load; -blei, n. scrap lead; -dehnung, f. rupturing elongation, stretch, breaking tension; -boden, m. baggy soil; -fällig, dilapidated; -fest, resisting (pressure) breakage, tenacious.

Bruch-festigkeit, f. modulus of rupture, resistance to fracture, tensile strength; -fläche, f. surface of fracture; -frucht, f. loculicidal fruit; -fuge, f. joint of rupture; -gewicht, n. fractional weight; -gramm, n. fraction of a gram.

brüchig, brittle, friable, fragile; ~ werden, to become brittle, tender.

Bruch-knospe, f. accessory bud; -kraut, n. rupturewort (Herniaria); -kupfer, n. scrap copper; -last, f. breaking load; -modul, m. modulus of rupture; -pforte, f. aperture; -probe, f. breaking test; -rechnung, f. fractions; -sack, m. hernial sac; -spross, m. brittle branch, shoot.

bruch-sicher, unbreakable; -spannung, f. breaking stress; -stämmchen, n. brittle stem; -stein, m. quarrystone; -strich. m.

line between two parts of a fraction; -stück, n. fractional part; -stückweise, in fragments; -teil, m. fraction, portion; -waldtorf, m. forest peat; -weide, f. crack willow (Salix fragilis); -zahl, f. fractional number.

Brücke, f. bridge, pons.

Brücken-arm, m. median peduncle of cerebellum; -beuge, f. pontal flexure, Varolian bend; -echsen, f.pl. Rhynchocephalia; -glühzünder, m. bridge wire cap; -schenkel, m. median cerebellar peduncle; -wage, f. platform balance.

Brüden, m. liquor (milk, lye, etc.) vapor; -verdichtung, f. vapor recompression.

Bruder, m. brother, friar.

brüderig, adelphous.

Brühe, f. broth, soup, juice, liquor.

brühen, to scald, soak.

brühheiss, scalding hot.

Brühmesser, m. barkometer.

brüllen, to bellow, roar, howl.

Brüllfrosch, m. bullfrog.

brummen, to growl, grumble, hum, buzz.

Brummer, m. Brummfliege, f. bluebottle, meat fly (Musca comitoria).

brummig, grumbling.

Brunelle, f. selfheal (Prunella vulgaris).

Brunft, f. heat, rut, sexual desire.

Brunftzeit, f. rutting season.

Brünierbeize, f. bluing pickle.

brünieren, to brown, burnish, polish.

Brünierstein, m. burnishing stone, bloodstone.

Brunnen, m. well, spring, fountain; -faden, m. Crenothrix; -kresse, f. water cress (Nasturtium officinale); -pest, f. Crenothrix polyspora; -wasser, n. well water, spring water.

Brunst, f. condition of being in heat.

brünstig, ardent, in heat.

brunst-frei, anoestrous; -hemmend, oestrous-restraining; -hormon, m. oestrual hormone; -zyklus, m. oestrous cycle.

Brust, f.-̈e, thorax, breast, chest; -ader, f. mammary or thoracic gland (vein); -beere, f. jujube.

Brustbein, n. sternum, thoracic leg; -ansatz, m. sternal insertion; -ausschnitt, m. sternal notch; -drüse, f. thymus gland; -handgriff, m. manubrium of sternum; -kamm, m. sternal crest; -knochen, m. sternum; -knorpel, m. ensiform cartilage.

Brustbein-rand, *m.* margin of sternum; **-rippengelenk,** *n.* sternocostal articulation; **-schildmuskel,** *m.* sternothyroid muscle; **-schlüsseigeienk,** *n.* sternoclavicular articulation; **-spalte,** *f.* sternal cleft; **-zungenmuskel,** *m.* sternoglossus muscle.

Brust-beschwerde, *f.* chest complaint; **-blatt,** *n.* sternum, marsupial plate; **-drüse,** *f.* mammary, thoracic gland; **-eingeweide,** *n.* thoracic (viscera) organs; **-feder,** *f.* breast feather.

Brustfell, *n.* pleura; **-entzündung,** *f.* pleurisy; **-fieber,** *n.* bronchitis.

Brust-flosse, *f.* pectoral fin; **flosser,** *pl.* Thoracici; **-fuss,** *m.* thoracic leg; **-gang,** *m.* thoracic duct; **-gefäss,** *n.* mammary vessel; **-gegend,** *f.* thoracic region; **gürtel,** *m.* pectoral girdle.

Brust-haut, *f.* pleura; **-höhle,** *f.* thoracic cavity; **-kasten,** *m.* thorax; **-knochen,** *m.* sternum; **-knorpel,** *m.* costal cartilage; **-knoten,** *m.* thoracic ganglion; **-korb,** *m.* thorax; **-kreuz,** *n.* pectoral cross.

Brust-mark, *n.* dorsal part of spinal cord; **-muskel,** *m.* pectoral muscle; **-pulver,** *n.* pectoral powder; **-raum,** *m.* thoracic cavity; **-reinigend,** expectorant; **-ring,** *m.* segment of thorax; **-röhre,** *f.* thoracic duct.

Brust-scheidewand, *f.* mediastinum; **-schild,** *n.* breastplate, episternum; **-schildmuskel,** *m.* sternothyroid muscle; **-schlüsselbeingelenk,** *n.* sternoclavicular articulation; **-segment,** *n.* thoracic segment; **-seuche,** *f.* pleuropneumonia; **-ständig,** thoracic; **-stück,** *n.* thorax; **-umfang,** *m.* circumference of chest.

Brüstung, *f.* parapet, breast wall.

Brust-wand, *f.* thoracic wall; **-warze,** *f.* nipple; **-wirbel,** *m.* dorsal vertebra; **-wirbelsäule,** *f.* dorsal part of spine; **-wurz,** *f.* *Angelica silvestris;* **-zweig,** *m.* thoracic branch.

Brut, *f.* brood(ing), hatch(ing), fry, spawn, bulbil.

brutal, brutal.

Brut-amme, *f.* bee nurse; **-anstalt,** *f.* hatchery; **-apparat,** *m.* incubator; **-becher,** *m.* brood (gemma) cup; **-becherchen,** *n.* cyphella; **-beutel,** *m.* marsupium; **-blase,** *f.* brood vesicle; **-blatt,** *n.* leaf abscissed for vegetative propagation (Bryophyllum); **-ei,** *n.* egg for hatching.

brüten, to brood, incubate, hatch.

Brut-fleck, *m.* brood spot on brooding birds; **-gang,** *m.* breeding gallery; **-häufchen,** *n,* soredium; **-henne,** *f.* setting hen; **-kasten,**

m. incubator; **-kelch,** *m.* sterile calyx; **-keule,** *f.* appendix, process; **-knolle,** *f.* tuberlike prothallium; **-knospe,** *f.* brood bud.

Brut-korn, *n.* gemma, germ; **-körper,** *m.* brood body; **-nest,** *n.* brood nest; **-ofen,** *m.* incubator; **-pest,** *f.* foul brood; **-pflege,** *f.* brood care; **-platz,** *m.* breeding place; **-rahmen,** *m.* comb of brood.

Brut-sack, *m.* marsupial pouch; **-scheibe,** *f.* brood comb; **-schrank,** *m.* incubator; **-schüppchen,** *n.* brood scale; **-spross,** *m.* brood shoot; **-stätte,** *f.* breeding place; **-tasche,** *f.* brood pouch; **-teich,** *m.* spawning pond; **-temperatur,** *f.* incubation (blood) heat.

brutto, gross, in gross; **-formel,** *f.* empirical formula.

Brut-vorkeim, *m.* protonema (moss); **-wabe,** *f.* brood comb; **-wärme,** *f.* heat necessary for incubation; **-wurzelknöllchen,** *n.* tuber for vegetative reproduction; **-zelle,** *f.* blood cell; **-zwiebel,** *f.* brood bulb.

Bubon(en)pest, *f.* bubonic plague.

Buccoblätter, *n.pl.* buchu (leaves).

Buch, *n.* book, psalterium; **-drucker,** *m.* printer.

Buche, *f.* beech (Fagus).

Buchecker, *f.* beechnut.

Buchel, *f.* beechnut.

buchen, to book, enter; **-asche,** *f.* beech ashes; **-einbau,** *m.* underplanting beech; **-farn,** *m.* beech fern; **-hochwald,** *m.* beech forest; **-holzteer,** *n.* beech tar.

Bücherei, *f.* library.

Bücher-mappe, *f.* brief case; **-schrank,** *m.* bookcase; **-verzeichnis,** *n.* book list, book catalogue.

Buchfink, *m.* chaffinch.

Buch-führen, *n.* bookkeeping; **-halter,** *m.* bookkeeper, accountant; **-handel,** *m.* book trade; **-handlung,** *f.* book store.

Buchnuss, *f.* beechnut.

Buchsbaum, *m.* box tree (*Buxus sempervirens*).

Büchse, *f.* (cylindrical) box, case, bushing, pyxidium.

büchsen-artig, pyxidate; **-fleisch,** canned beef; **-förmig,** box-shaped; **-frucht,** *f.* preserved fruit; **-gemüse,** *n.* canned vegetables; **-macher,** *m.* gunsmith; **-metal,** *n.* bush (bearing) metal; **-stein,** *m.* iron pyrites.

Buchstabe, *m.* letter, type.

buchstabieren, to spell.

buchstäblich, literal.

Bucht, *f.* bay, sinus, fossa.

buchtig, sinuous, sinuate.

Buchublätter, *n.pl.* buchu leaves.

Buchung, *f.* entry.

Buchweizen, *m.* buckwheat.

Buckel, *m.* eminence, hump, knot, outgrowth.

buck(e)lig, humpbacked.

Buckelschorf, *m.* umbonate scab.

bücken, to bend, stoop.

Bückling, *m.* red herring, bloater.

Bude, *f.* booth, stall, shop.

Büffel, *m.* buffalo.

Bug, *n.* bend, bow, joint, articulation.

Bügel, *m.* bow, stirrup.

bügelecht, fast to ironing.

Bügeleisen, *n.* flatiron.

bügeln, to iron, smooth.

Buggelenk, *n.* shoulder bone, joint.

Buhne, *f.* spur dike, breakwater, groin.

Bühne, *f.* stage, scaffold.

Bukett, *f.* bouquet.

Bulben, *pl.* tubers.

Bulbillen, *pl.* brood buds.

Bulbus-schenkel, *m.* bulbar limb; **-wulst,** *f.* bulbar swelling.

Bulle, *m.* bull.

Bülte, *f.* hillock, solid part of bog.

bummeln, to saunter, loaf.

Bund, *m.*⁀e, band, tie, alliance.

Bund, *n.*-e, bundle, bunch.

Bündel, *n.* bundle, packet, parcel.

Bundes-rat, *m.* federal council; **-tag,** *m.* federal diet.

bündig, binding, convincing, valid, flush, level; **kurz und ~,** plain and concise.

Bündnis, *n.* alliance.

Bunsen-brenner, *m.* Bunsen burner.

bunt, variegated, many-colored, gay, bright; **-blätterig,** of variegated foliage.

Bunt-bleiche, *f.* branning; **-druck,** *m.* color print(ing); **-färben,** to stain; **-farbig,** variegated; **-fleckig,** spotted, motley; **-gewebe,** *n.* colored fabric.

Bunt-käfer, *m.pl.* Cleridae; **-kupfererz,** *n.*, **-kupferkies,** *m.* variegated copper ore, bornite; **-papier,** *n.* colored paper; **-sand-**stein, *m.* variegated (New Red) Sandstone; **-scheckigkeit,** *f.* variegation; **-schillernd,** iridescent, opalescent; **-specht,** *m.* woodpecker; **-stift,** *m.* colored pencil.

Bunzenarbeit, *f.* chased work.

Bürde, *f.* burden, load.

Burdonen, *pl.* graft hybrid.

Bürette, *f.* burette.

Burg, *f.* castle, stronghold.

Bürge, *m.* bail, surety, witness.

bürgen, to give bail, vouch (for), guarantee

Bürger, *m.*-, inhabitant, citizen.

bürgerlich, civil, common.

Bürgschaft, *f.* security, bail.

Burgunder, *m.* Burgundy (wine).

Büro, *n.* office.

Bursamundstück, *n.* entrance of bursa.

Bursche, *m.* youth, lad, student.

Bürste, *f.* brush.

bürsten, to brush; **-feuer,** *n.* brush sparking; **-förmig,** brush (whisk) shaped; **-gras,** *n.* beard grass (Polypogon); **-saum,** *m.* striated (brushlike) border; **-trieb,** *m.* brushlike (coniferous) shoot; **-zähne,** *m.pl.* brushlike teeth.

Bürzel, *m.* rump, uropygium; **-drüse,** *f.* coccygeal gland; **-krautgewächse,** *n.pl.* Portulacaceae.

Busch, *m.*⁀e, bush, shrub, copse, thicket, tuft, plume.

Büschel, *m.&n.* tuft, cluster, fascicle, panicle, corymb; **-artig,** tufted; **-atmer,** *m.pl.* Brachiopoda; **-entladung,** *f.* brush discharge; **-förmig,** tufted, clustered, fascicular, tasseled; **-kiemer,** *m.pl.* Lophobranchia; **-kuchen,** *m.* placenta; **-pflanzung,** *f.* bunch (multiple) planting; **-tragend,** corymbiferous; **-wuchs,** *m.* tufted, bushy growth.

Buschholz, *n.* underwood.

buschig, shrubby, dendroid, tufted, shaggy.

Busch-wald, *m.* bushwood, undergrowth; **-werk,** *n.* shrubbery; **-windröschen,** *n.* wood anemone (*Anemone nemorosa*).

Busen, *m.* bosom, breast, bay.

Bussard, *m.* buzzard.

büssen, to atone for, make good.

Büste, *f.* bust.

Butan, *n.* butane.

Butt, *m.* **Butte,** *f.* flounder.

Bütte, *f.* tub.

büttengefärbt, vat-colored, unbleached (paper).

Butter, *f.* butter; **-äther,** *m.* butyric ether, ethyl butyrate; **-blume,** *f.* buttercup; **-brot,** *n.* bread and butter; **-fass,** *n.* churn; **-fett,** *n.* butterfat, butyrin; **-form,** *f.* butter mold; **-klümpchen,** *n.pl.* butter granules.

buttern, to churn.

Butterpersäure, *f.* perbutyric acid.

Buttersäure, *f.* butyric acid; **-gärung,** *f.* butyric fermentation; **-pilze,** *m.pl.* butyric-acid bacteria; **-pilzinfektion,** *f.* butyric infection.

Butterwecken, *m.* bun, butter roll.

Butylalkohol, *m.* butyl alcohol, butanol.

Byssus, *m.* byssus, filament; **-drüse,** *f.* byssal gland; **-faden,** *m.* byssal thread.

C

Ca . . . , see also **Ka . . .**

Cachou, *n.* catechu.

cachoutieren, to dye with catechu.

Cade-, Cadi-, Cadin-öl, *n.* cade oil.

Cadmium, *n.* cadmium; **-haltig,** cadmiferous.

Caesium, *n.* cesium.

Caincawurzel, *f.* cahinca root.

Cajeput, *n.* cajuput.

calcifizieren, to calcify.

calcinierbar, calcinable.

calcinieren, to calcine.

Calcium, *n.* calcium; **-carbonat,** *n.* chalk, limestone, calcium carbonate; **-legierung,** *f.* calcium alloy; **-spiegel,** *m.* calcium level.

Caliber, *m.* gauge.

calibrieren, to calibrate.

Calomel, *n.* calomel, mercurous chloride.

Calorienwert, *m.* caloric value.

calorimetrieren, to measure with the calorimeter.

calorimetrisch, calorimetric.

calorisch, caloric, thermal.

Cambaholz, *n.* camwood.

Cambiformzelle, *f.* cambiform cell.

Cambium, *n.* cambium.

Camille, *f.* camomile.

camouflieren, to camouflage.

Campagne, *f.* campaign, working season.

Campane, *f.* bell jar.

Campeche-hanf, *m.* campeachy hemp; **-holz,** *n.* logwood.

Camphansäure, *f.* camphanic acid.

Campher (Kampfer), *m.* camphor.

Canarienfarbe, *f.* canary color, canarin.

Cannelkohle, *f.* cannel coal.

Canellarinde, *f.* canella bark.

Canthariden, *pl.* cantharides, Spanish fly.

Cantharinsäure, *f.* cantharidic acid.

capillar, kapillar, capillary; **-spannung,** *f.* capillary tension.

Caprinsäure, *f.* capric acid.

Capron-fett, *n.* caproin; **-säure,** *f.* capronic acid.

Caprylsäure, *f.* caprylic acid.

Carapa-fett, *n.* **-öl,** *n.* carapa oil.

Carbamid, *n.* carbamide.

Carbaminsäure, *f.* carbamic acid.

Carbanilsäure, *f.* carbanilic acid.

Carbidkohle, *f.* carbide carbon.

Carbol-kalk, *n.* carbolated lime; **-salbe,** *f.* ointment of phenol; **-säure,** *f.* carbolic acid; **-schwefelsäure,** *f.* sulphocarbolic acid, sulphophenic acid.

Carbonat, *n.* carbonate.

carbonieren, to carbonate.

carbonisieren, to carbonize, carbonate.

Carbonsäure, *f.* carboxylic (carbonic) acid.

carburieren, to carburet, carburize.

Carenz, *f.* omission, abstinence.

Carinalhöhle, *f.* carinal canal.

Carmin, *m.* carmine.

Carnauba-säure, *f.* carnaubic acid; **-wachs,** *n.* carnauba wax.

Carotin, *n.* carotin.

Carotte, *f.* carrot.

carpel-bürtig, of foliar origin; **-träger,** *m.* carpophore.

carposporangisch, carposporangial.

Carpospore, *f.* spore of fungus or alga.

Carposporium, *n.* envelope containing carpospores.

Carraghenmoos, *n.* carrageen moss, Irish moss.

Carreau, *n.* check, square.

Carub, *m.* carob.

Caryopse, *f.* caryopsis.

Cascarilla-rinde, *f.* cascarilla bark.

Casein, *m.* casein.

caseinartig, like casein, caseous.

Cäsium, *n.* cesium.

Casparischer (dunkler **Punkt**), Casparian (radial) dot.

Cassawastärke, *f.* tapioca.

Cassiarinde, *f.* cassia bark.

Cassie, *f.* cassia.

Castillianer (Seife), *f.* castile (soap).

Castor-körner, *n.pl.* castor beans; -nuss, *f.* castor bean; -öl, castor oil.

Catechu, *n.* catechu.

Cathartinsäure, *f.* cathartic acid.

Ce . . . , see also Ze . . . and Ke . . .

Ceder, *f.* cedar.

Cedern-harz, *n.* cedar resin; -(holz)öl, *n.* oil of cedar (wood).

Cedratöl, *n.* Cedroöl, *n.* citron oil.

Celasteröl, *n.* celastrus oil.

Cellit, *n.* secondary cellulose acetate.

Cellonlack, *m.* cellulose-acetate lacquer.

Cellulose-balken, *m.* bar of cellulose; -lösung, *f.* cellulose solution; -schlauch, *m.* cellulose envelope.

Celsiusgrad, *m.* Celsius (centigrade) degree.

Cement, *m.* cement.

censieren, to censure, criticize.

Censur, *f.* censorship.

Cent . . . , see also Zent . . .

Central-höhle, *f.* central cavity; -kern, *m.* central kernel, nucleus, granule; -körper, *m.* pseudonucleus (centrosome); -placenta, *f.* free central placenta; -spalte, *f.* central cleft; -strang, *m.* axial strand; -winkelständig, axial.

centrifugal, centrifugal (cymose).

centripetal, centripetal (cymose).

Cer, *m.* cerium.

Cerat, *n.* cerate.

Cerealien, *f.pl.* cereals.

Cerichlorid, *n.* ceric chloride.

Cerinstein, *m.* cerite.

Cerioxyd, *n.* ceric oxide.

Ceriterde, *f.* ceria earth.

Cerotinsäure, *f.* cerotic acid.

Ceroverbindung, *f.* cerous compound.

Ceroxyd, *n.* cerium oxide.

Chamäleon, *n.* chameleon; -lösung, *f.* potassium permanganate solution.

Champagner, *m.* champagne.

Champignon, *m.* mushroom (edible).

changierend, changeable, shot (variegated).

Changierung, *f.* traverse motion.

Chappeseide, *f.* spun silk.

Charakter, *m.* character; -fest, of firm character; -los, unprincipled.

charakterisieren, to characterize, distinguish.

Charakterzug, *m.* distinguishing trait.

Charge, *f.* batch, charge, heat.

chargieren, to charge.

Charlotte, *f.* shallot (*Allium ascalonicum*).

Charpie, *f.* lint.

Chätopoden, *n.pl.* chaetopods.

Chaussee, *f.* highway.

Chef, *m.* chief, head, principal.

chem., *abbr.* (chemisch), chemical.

Chemie, *f.* chemistry.

Chemilkalien, *n.pl.* chemicals.

Chemiker, *m.* chemist.

chemisch, chemical; -blau, *n.* chemic blue (indigo extract); -gelb, *n.* Cassel yellow; -grün, *n.* sap green; -rot, *n.* Venetian red.

Chemismus, *m.* chemism.

Chemolumineszenz, *f.* chemi(co)luminescence.

Chibouharz, *n.* cachibou.

Chiffer, Chiffre, *f.* cipher.

chiffrieren, to cipher, code.

Chilesalpeter, *m.* sodium nitrate.

China, *f.* China, Cinchona; -baum, *m.* cinchona tree; -baumartig, cinchonaceous.

Chinacetophenon, *n.* quinacetophenone.

China-eisenwein, *m.* bitter wine of iron; -gerbsäure, *f.* quinotannic acid; -gras, *n.* Boehmeria or *Urtica nivea*.

Chinaldin, *n.* quinaldine.

China-rinde, *f.* Peruvian bark, cinchona bark; -sauer, quinate of, combined with quinic acid.

Chinäthylin, *n.* quinethyline.

China-tinktur, *f.* tincture of cinchona; -wein, *m.* quinine wine; -wurzel, *f.* chinaroot.

Chinen, *n.* quinine.

Chinesisch-grün, *n.* Chinese green, lokao: -rot, *n.* Chinese red, red mercuric sulphide.

Chinid, *n.* quinide.

Chinidin, *n.* quinidine.

chinieren, to weave, cloud.

Chinin, *n.* quinine; **-eisen,** *n.* citrate of iron and quinine; **-eisencitrat,** *n.* citrate of iron and quinine; **-säure,** *f.* quininic acid.

Chinoidin, *n.* quinoidine.

Chinolin, *n.* quinoline.

Chinon, *n.* quinone.

Chinova-bitter, *n.* quinovin (quinova bitter).

Chinovin, *n.* quinovin.

Chirurg, *m.* surgeon.

chirurgisch, surgical.

Chitin-röhrchen, *n.* small chitin tube; **-schicht,** *f.* chitin layer.

Chlor, *n.* chlorine; **-ähnlich,** chlorinous; **-alaun,** *m.* chloralum; **-amyl,** *n.* amyl chloride; **-arseniklösung,** *f.* chloride of arsenic; **-artig,** chlorinous.

Chlorat, *n.* chlorate.

Chloräther, *m.* chloric ether.

Chloration, *f.* chlorination; *n.* chlorate iron.

Chlor-benzol, *n.* chlorobenzene; **-bleiche,** *f.* chlorine bleaching; **-bleispat,** *m.* phosgenite; **-cyan,** *n.* cyanogen chloride; **-echt,** fast to chlorine.

chloren, to chlorinate, gas.

Chlor-entwickler, *m.* chlorine generator; **-essigsäure,** *f.* chloroacetic acid; **-haltig,** containing chlorine; **-hydrat,** *n.* hydrochloride.

Chlorid, *n.* chloride.

chlorieren, to chlorinate.

Chlorierung, *f.* chlorination, chloridization.

Chlorigsäure, *f.* chlorous acid.

Chlorion, *n.* chlorine ion.

Chlorit, *m.* chlorite; **-spat,** *m.* spathic chlorite, foliated chlorite.

Chlor-kali, *n.* chloride of potassium, potassium hypochlorite; **-kalium,** *n.* potassium chloride; **-kalk,** *m.* chloride of lime; **-kalzium,** *n.* calcium chloride; **-knallgas,** *n.* chlorine detonating gas; **-kohlenoxyd,** *n.* carbonyl chloride; **-kohlensäureamid,** *n.* carbamyl chloride; **-kupfer,** *n.* copper chloride; **-lauge,** *f.* chloride of soda; **-magnesium,** *n.* magnesium chloride.

Chlor-messer, *m.* chlorometer; **-natronlösung,** *f.* solution of chlorinated soda; **-natrium,** *n.* sodium chloride.

Chloro-benzil, *n.* dichlorobenzil; **-form,** *n.* chloroform.

chloroformieren, to chloroform.

Chlorophyll, *n.* chlorophyll; **-los,** without chlorophyll.

Chlorose, *f.* chlorosis.

Chlor-oxyd, *n.* chlorine oxide; **-räucherung,** *f.* chlorine fumigation; **-säure,** *f.* chloric acid; **-säureanhydrid,** *n.* chloric anhydride; **-sulfonsäure,** *f.* chlorosulphonic acid; **-überträger,** *m.* chlorine carrier.

Chlorür, *n.* chloride.

Chlor-verbindung, *f.* chlorine compound; **-wasser,** *n.* chlorine water; **-wasserstoff,** *m.* hydrogen chloride; **-wasserstoffäther,** *m.* ethyl chloride; **-wasserstoffsäure,** *f.* hydrochloric acid; **-zink,** *n.* zinc chloride.

Chol(al)säure, *f.* cholalic (cholic) acid.

Cholera, *f.* cholera; **-bacterien,** *f.pl.* cholera vibrio; **-erreger,** *m.* cholera bacillus; **-spirillen,** *n.pl.* cholera vibrio.

Cholesterin, *n.* cholesterin, cholesterol.

Cholin, *n.* choline.

Cholsäure, *f.* cholic acid.

Chondroninsäure, *f.* chondron(in)ic acid.

Chor, *m.* chorus, choir.

Chordalfortsatz, *m.* chordal process.

Chorde, *f.* chord.

Chorionkreislauf, *m.* chorionic (umbilical) circulation.

Chrestomathie, *f.* anthology.

Christdorn, *m.* holly (*Ilex aquifolium*).

Christophs-kraut, *n.,f.* **-wurz,** *f.* baneberry (*Actaea spicata*).

Christ-palmöl, *n.* castor oil; **-rose,** *f.* *Helleborus*; **-wurz,** *f.* black hellebore.

Chrom, *n.* chromium, chrome.

Chromat, *n.* chromate.

Chromatinkern, *m.* chromatin, simple nucleus.

chromatisch, chromatic.

Chrom-blei, *n.* lead chromate; **-bleispat,** *m.* crocoite; **-chlorid,** *n.* chromic chloride; **-chlorür,** *n.* chromous chloride; **-echt,** fast to (chrome) potassium dichromate; **-gar,** chrome-tanned; **-gerbung,** *f.* chrome tanning; **-haltig,** containing chromium; **-hydroxyd,** *n.* chromic hydroxide; **-hydroxydul,** *n.* chromous hydroxide.

Chromichlorid, *n.* chromic chloride.

Chromierartikel, *m.* chrome style.

chromieren, to chrome.

Chromiverbindung, *f.* chromic compound.

Chromochlorid, *n.* chromous chloride.

Chromolyse, *f.* chromatolysis, chromolysis.

Chromomerenaustausch, *m.* exchange of chromomeres or chromosomes.

Chromosomen-anordnung, *f.* arrangement of chromosomes; -bestand, *m.* chromosome constitution; -gestalt, *f.* shape of chromosomes; -grösse, *f.* size of chromosomes; -paarung, *f.* pairing of chromosomes; -verkleinerung, *f.* chromosome diminution; -verklumpung, *f.* clumping of chromosomes; -verschmelzung, *f.* fusion of chromosomes; -vervielfachung, *f.* multiplying of chromosomes.

Chromoverbindung, *f.* chromous compound.

Chromo-oxychlorid, *n.* chromium oxychloride.

Chromoxyd, *n.* chromium oxide; -hydrat, *n.* chromium hydroxide; -natron, *n.* sodium chromite; -salz, *n.* chromic salt.

Chromoxydul, *n.* chromous oxide.

Chrom-rot, *n.* chrome red; -salpetersäure, *f.* chromonitric acid; -salz, *n.* chromium salt, chromate.

Chromsäure, *f.* chromic acid; -anhydrid, *n.* chromic anhydride.

chromsaures Kali, *n.* potassium chromate.

Chrom-schwefelsäure, *f.* chromolsulphuric acid; -silber, *n.* silver chromate; -sulfur, *n.* chromous sulphide; -verbindung, *f.* chromium compound.

chronisch, chronic.

Chrysalide, *f.* chrysalis.

Chrysanthemum, *n.* chrysanthemum.

Chrysatropasäure, *f.* chrysatropic acid.

Chylus, *m.* chyle.

Ci . . . , see also ZI . . . and KI . . .

Cibebe, *f.* large raisin.

Cichorie, *f.* chicory.

Cider-branntwein, *m.* cider brandy; -essig, *m.* cider vinegar; -trester, *m.pl.* cider (dressings), marc.

Cinchoninsäure, *f.* cinchoninic acid.

Cinnabarit, *n.* cinnabar, mercury ore.

circa, about.

cirkulieren, to circulate.

Cirrus-beutel, *m.* cirrus pouch; -wolke, *f.* cirrus cloud.

Cisstellung, *f.* cis position.

Ciströschengewächse, *n.pl.* Cistaceae.

Citat, *n.* quotation.

citieren, to cite, quote, summon.

Citrat, *n.* Citrone, *f.* citrate, lemon.

Citronensäure, *f.* citric acid.

civil, civil, moderate.

Cloake, *f.* cloaca, sewer.

Cloaken-höhle, *f.* atrial cavity; -raum, *m.* peribranchial cavity.

Cocablätter, *n.pl.* coca leaves.

Coccidiosis, *f.* coccidial disease.

Coccinsäure, *f.* coccinic acid.

Cochenille, *f.* cochineal.

Cochenillenbaum, *m.* cochineal tree.

Cochenille-säure, *f.* cochenillic acid.

Cocos-baum, *m.* coconut tree; -faser, *f.* coco fiber; -talg, *m.* coconut oil.

Codöl, *n.* cod-liver oil.

Coferment, *n.* coenzyme.

Coffein, *n.* caffeine.

cohobieren, to cohobate.

Colanuss, *f.* kola nut.

Colatur, *f.* filtrate.

Cölestin, *m.* celestite.

colieren, to filter.

Colloresin, *n.* methyl cellulose.

Colombowurzel, *f.* calumba (root).

Cölomsack, *m.* coelomic pouch.

Colonne, *f.* column.

colorimetrisch, colorimetric.

Columbasäure, *f.* acid from calumba root.

Columbeisen, *n.* columbite.

combinieren, to combine.

Commis, *m.* clerk.

Commissuralfurche, *f.* commissural groove.

Compensationserscheinung, *f.* compensation phenomenon.

comprimieren, to compress, condense.

Conchidien, *pl.* appressed, basal leaves.

Concrement, *n.* concretion.

conditionieren, to condition.

Conehülse, *f.* cone care.

conglobieren, to heap up.

Conidien, *f.pl.* conidia; -abschnürung, *f.* abjection of conidia; -kette, *f.* conidial chain; -köpfchen, *n.* conidial head; -lager, *n.* conidial sorus; -sprossung, *f.* conidial budding; -stand, *m.* conidial field; -träger, *m.* conidiophore.

Coniin, *n.* conine, coniine.

consociiert, congenital, gamophyllous.

constatieren, to state, ascertain, verify.

Constitualkampf, *m.* struggle with environment.

continuierlich, continuous.

Conto, *n.* account.

contrahierend, reduced.

Contraktionswurzel, *f.* contracting root.

Conus, *m.* cone.

Copulations-fortsatz, *m.* conjugation papilla; **-schlauch,** *m.* fertilization tube.

Copulieren, *n.* conjugation.

corollinisch, petaloid, corollaceous.

corrigieren, to correct.

corrodieren, to corrode.

Cosekante, *f.* cosecant.

Cosinus, *m.* cosine.

Cotangente, *f.* cotangent.

Cotorinde, *f.* coto bark.

Cotton-öl, *n.* cottonseed oil; **-strumpfware,** *f.* full-fashioned hosiery.

Cotyledonarknospe, *f.* cotyledonary bud.

Couleur, *f.* color.

Coupe, *n.* compartment.

coupieren, to cut.

Courant, *n.* currency.

Couvert, *n.* envelope, cover.

cracken, to crack.

Creme, *f.* cream.

Cribal-parenchym, *n.* phloem parenchyma; **priman,** *m.* element of protophloem; **-strang,** *m.* cribral cord; **-teil,** *m.* phloem.

Cribrovasal-bündel, *n.* **-strang,** *m.* (fibro) vascular bundle.

Cubeben, *n.pl.* cubebs; **-öl,** *n.* cubeb oil.

Cuiteseide, *f.* boiled-off silk.

Cuminsäure, *f.* cuminic acid.

Cupri-oxalat, *n.* cupric oxalate; **-oxyd,** *n.* cupric oxide.

Cuprocyanür, *n.* cuprous cyanide.

Cuproxam, *n.* cuprammonium.

Cuticular-krönchen, *n.* cuticular crown; **-leiste,** *f.* cuticular ridge; **-naht,** *f.* cuticular suture; **-perle,** *f.* cuticular bead; **-saum,** *m.* cuticular border; **-schicht,** *f.* cuticular layer; **-verdunstung,** *f.* cuticular transpiration; **-wall,** *m.* cuticular rampart; **-zapfen,** *m.* cuticular peg.

Cutininsäure, *f.* cutinic acid.

Cutinsäure, *f.* cutic acid.

Cuvette, *f.* bulb, trough, narrow test flume.

Cyan, *n.* cyanogen; **-äthyl,** *n.* ethyl cyanide; **-chlorid,** *n.* cyanogen chloride; **-eisen,** *n.* iron cyanide; **-essigsäure,** *f.* cyanoacetic acid; **-haltig,** containing cyanogen; **-kaiium,** *n.* potassium cyanide.

Cyanür, *n.* cyanide; **-säure,** *f.* cyanuric acid.

Cyan-verbindung, *f.* cyanogen compound; **-wasserstoffsäure,** *f.* hydrocyanic acid.

cyclisch, cyclic.

Cyclogeraniumsäure, *f.* cyclogeranic acid.

Cycloidschuppe, *f.* cycloid scale.

Cylinder-blende, *f.* substage diaphragm; **-epithel,** *n.* palisade layer of scutellum.

cymas, cymous.

Cymol, *n.* cymene.

Cypern, *n.* Cyprus.

Cypervitriol, *m.* **cyprischer Vitriol,** *m.* blue vitriol, copper sulphate.

Cypressen-nuss, *f.* cypress cone.

cystenartig, cystlike.

Cystenflüssigkeit, *f.* cystic fluid.

D

da, there, present, then, when, as, since.

dabei, thereby, near, there, moreover, in this case, in connection therewith, thereat, besides, therein; **nahe ~ sein,** to be on the point of; **~ bleiben,** to persist in a thing; **es bleibt ~,** it is settled.

Dach, *n.* roof; **-binder,** *m.* roof truss, roof bent; **-blech,** *n.* sheet metal for roofing; **-boden,** *m.* loft.

Dachel, Dächel, *m.* lump, bloom.

Dach-first, *m.* ridge; **-haut,** *f.* roofing, roof sheathing; **-kammer,** *f.* attic, garret;

-kehle, *f.* roof valley; **-kohle,** *f.* upper coal; **-pappe,** *f.* roofing paper; **-pfanne,** *f.* pantile.

dachig, imbricate.

Dachs, *m.* badger, dachshund.

Dachschiefer, *m.* roofing slate.

Dachs-fett, *n.* badger fat, grease; **-hund,** *m.* badger dog.

Dachstein, *m.* tile, slate, bituminous shale, roof rock.

Dachstuhl, *m.* ̈e, truss, framework (roof).

dachte (denken), thought.

Dachtrespe, *f.* roof brome grass (*Bromus tectorum*).

Dachung, *f.* roofing, slope.

Dachwurz, *f.* common houseleek.

dachziegelartig, imbricate.

dadurch, thereby, thus, by this, by that, in this way; ∼ **dass er es tat,** by doing so.

dafür, for this, for it, instead of it, therefore; ∼ **sprechen,** to support (a theory), speak in favor of; ∼, **dass,** for the fact that . . .

dagegen, against it, in comparison, in return, on the other hand.

daheim, at home.

daher, hence, thence, therefore, accordingly, consequently, from this.

dahin, thither, there, thereto, away, gone; **bis** ∼, until then.

dahin-gegen, on the other hand; **-gehen,** to tend to, perish, go there; **-gestellt** (sein lassen), (to leave) undecided, uncertain; **-gleiten,** to glide along; **-sausen,** to speed along; **-stehen,** to remain uncertain; **-tragen,** to carry away or there; **-welken,** to wither away.

dahinter, behind it, after that; ∼ **kommen,** to get at the bottom of a thing; **sich** ∼ **machen,** to set to work; ∼ **her sein,** to be after a thing; **es steckt etwas** ∼, there is something behind that.

Dahlie, *f.* dahlia.

damalig, at, or of, that time.

damals, at that time, then.

Damast, *m.* damask.

Damaszener, Damascene, damask; ∼ **Pflaume,** *f.* damson; ∼ **Rose,** *f.* damask rose.

damaszieren, to damascene, damask.

Dame, *f.* lady, queen (cards).

Damen-brett, *n.* checkerboard; **-spiel,** *n.* checkers, draughts.

Damhirsch, *m.* fallow buck; **-fell,** *n.* buckskin.

damit, therewith, with, by it, in order that.

Damm, *m.*∸e, dam, dike, bank, perineum; **-balken,** *m.* stop log (groove).

Dammara-fichte, *f.* dammara pine; **-firnis,** *m.* dammar varnish; **-harz,** *n.* dammar resin, dammarin.

dämmen, to dike, dam (up), stop (up), curb.

Dammerde, *f.* mold, humus, vegetable (black) earth, pit sand.

Dämmerung, *f.* twilight, dawn, dusk.

Dämmerungs-falter, *m.* hawk moth; **-schmetterling,** *m.* hawk moth; **-sehen,** *n.* seeing in the twilight; **-vogel,** *m.* hawk moth.

Damm-gegend, *f.* perineal region; **-grube,** *f.* foundry pit.

Dämmung, *f.* insulation, damming.

Dampf, *m.*∸e, steam, vapor, fume; **-abflussrohr,** *n.* vapor-discharge tube; **-abzugsspalte,** *f.* vapor fissure; **-artig,** vaporous; **-bad,** *n.* steam (vapor) bath; **-betrieb,** *m.* steam drive, working by steam; **-blase,** *f.* steam bubble, still heated by steam; **-blasenbildung,** *f.* vapor lock.

Dampf-darre, *f.* steam kiln; **-dicht,** steamtight; **-dichte,** *f.* vapor density; **-druck,** *m.* vapor pressure; **-druckerei,** *f.* steam color printing; **-druckmesser,** *m.* manometer, pressure gauge; **-echt,** fast to steaming.

dampfen, to give off vapor or steam, smoke, fume.

dämpfen, to suppress, check, damp, smother, put out, soften (color), steam, stew.

Dampf-entwässerungsapparat, *m.* steam-drying apparatus; **-entwickler,** *m.* **-erzeuger,** *m.* steam generator.

Dampfer, *m.*-, steamer, steamship.

Dämpfer, *m.*-, damper, steam cooker, autoclave.

dampf-förmig, in vapor form; **-gebläse,** *n.* steam blast, steam blower; **-gummi,** *n.* dextrin; **-heizung,** *f.* steam heating; **-hülle,** *f.* vaporous envelope.

dampfig, vaporous, steamy.

Dampfkessel, *m.*-, steam boiler; **-anlage,** *f.* steam (boiler) plant.

Dampf-kochtopf, *m.* steam cooker, sterilizer; **-kochung,** *f.* steam cooking; **-leitungsrohr,** *n.* steam pipe; **-messer,** *m.* manometer, steam gauge.

Dämpfmittel, *n.* neutralizer, sweetener.

Dampf-schwelung, *f.* destructive distillation with steam; **-spannung,** *f.* vapor pressure, steam tension; **-strahl,** *m.* steam jet, steam blast; **-strecke,** *f.* radius of action; **-topf,** *m.* digester, autoclave, pressure cooker; **-trockenschrank,** *m.* steam drying oven.

Dämpfung, *f.* steaming, suppressing, subduing, extinction.

Dämpfungsvorrichtung, *f.* damping device.

Dampf-wagen, *m.* steam car; **-wärme,** *f.* heat of vaporization; **-wäscherei,** *f.* steam laundry; **-wassertopf,** *m.* steam trap;

-zuführung, -zuleitung, *f.* steam supply (line).

danach, after that, thereupon, accordingly.

daneben, near it, beside it, besides.

Dank, *m.* thanks, reward.

dank, owing to, thanks to.

dankbar, (*dat.*) thankful, profitable.

danken (*dat.*) to thank.

dann, then; erst ∼, only then.

daran, thereon, thereat, about it, of it; ∼ ist nicht zu denken, that cannot be considered at all.

daran-geben, to give up; -glauben, to believe in it; -liegend, adjacent; -machen, to set to work, set about; -müssen, to submit to; -setzen, to venture, stake all; -wachsend, adnascent.

darauf, thereupon, thereon, afterward, upon it, to it; ∼ ausgehen, to aim at; ∼ bestehen, to insist on it; ∼ gefasst sein, to be prepared for it; ∼ halten, to lay stress on it; ∼ hinaus wollen, that is what I was aiming at; ∼ kommen, to hit upon (an idea); ∼ losziehen, to pull away at it; sich ∼ besinnen, to recall; sich ∼ einlassen, to venture upon it; sich ∼ verlassen, to depend on it.

darauf-folgend, following, ensuing, subsequent; -hin, thereupon; -lassen, *n.* doubling.

daraus, therefrom, thence, of it.

darben, to starve.

darbieten, to offer, present.

dar(e)in, therein, into it, to it.

darf (dürfen), is permitted, allowed to; es ∼ nicht, it must not.

Darg, *m.* peat.

Dargelegte, *n.* thing(s) displayed.

darin, therein, in it.

darlegen, to exhibit, show, display, explain.

Darlegung, *f.* explanation, statement.

Darlehen, *n.* loan.

Darm, *m.*∵e, gut, intestine; blinder ∼, caecum; dicker ∼, colon; dünner ∼, small intestine; gerader ∼, rectum; langer ∼. ileum; leerer ∼, jejunum.

Darm-abschnitt, *m.* portion of intestine; -amöbe, *f.* intestinal amoeba; -anhang, *m.* intestinal appendage; -ast, *m.* branch of intestine; -atmung, *f.* rectal respiration; -aufblähung, *f.* inflation of intestine; -bakterien, *n.pl.* intestinal bacteria; -bandwurm, *m.* tapeworm.

Darmbein, *n.* ilium; -aushöhlung, *f.* iliac fossa; -fläche, *f.* surface of the ilium; -flügel, *m.* wing of the ilium; -grube, *f.* iliac fossa; -höcker, *m.* iliac crest; -kamm, *m.* iliac crest.

Darmbein-muskel, *m.* iliacus; -rücken, *m.* dorsum of ilium; -schaufel, *f.* ventral surface of ilium; -schenkelmuskel, *m.* sartorius muscle; -stachel, *m.* spine of the ilium; -winkel, *m.* angle of the ilium.

Darm-bewegung, *f.* peristaltic movement; -blatt, *n.* entoderm; -blindsack, *m.* alimentary canal; -blutader, *f.* intestinal vein; -deckengewebe, *n.* gastral epithelium; -dottersackhöhle, *f.* intestinal cavity of yolk sac; -drüse, *f.* intestinal gland; -eingang, *m.* intestinal entrance; -entleerung, *f.* evacuation of intestine; -entzündung, *f.* enteritis.

Darm-erkrankung, *f.* intestinal affection; -faserblatt, *n.* visceral mesoblast, splanchnopleure; -fäule, *f.* dysentery; -fell, *n.* peritoneum; -gang, *m.* intestinal tract; -gas, *n.* intestinal gas; -gebiet, *n.* intestinal region; -gicht, *f.* ileus; -gift, *n.* enterotoxin; haut, *f.* intestinal coat.

Darm-höhle, *f.* intestinal cavity; -inhalt, *m.* intestinal contents.

Darm-kanal, *m.* intestinal canal; -klappe, *f.* intestinal valve; -knochen, *m.* ilium; -kot, *m.* feces; -lage, *f.* position of intestine; -larve, *f.* gastrula, intestinal larva; -leibeshöhle, *f.* coelenteron; -lose, *m.pl.* Agastraea.

Darm-nabel, *m.* intestinal navel; -netz, *n.* omentum; -oberfläche, *f.* surface of intestine; -parasit, *m.* intestinal parasite; -pforte, *f.* intestinal aperture; -rinne, *f.* intestinal groove, furrow, splanchnic gutter; -rohr, *n.* intestinal tube, alimentary canal; -saft, *m.* intestinal secretion; -saite, *f.* catgut; -saugader, *f.* intestinal lymphatic vessel.

Darm-schlauch, *m.* digestive pouch, gut; -schleim, *m.* intestinal mucus; -schleimhaut, *f.* intestinal mucous membrane; -schlinge, *f.* intestinal loop; -stein, *m.* enterolith; -stiel, *m.* vitelline duct; -system, *n.* digestive tract; -tiere, *n.pl.* metazoa; -traktus, *m.* intestinal tract; -überzug, *m.* intestinal coating.

Darm-verdauung, *f.* intestinal digestion; -wand, *f.* intestinal wall; -windung, *f.* looping of the intestine, intestinal convolution; -zotte, *f.* intestinal villus.

darnach, after that, thereupon, subsequently.

Darr-arbeit, *f.* liquation; **-boden,** *m.* drying floor, kiln, floor.

Darre, *f.* kiln (drying), pip, roup, withering, seed drying.

darreichen, to present, offer, administer.

darren, to kiln, liquate, dry.

Darr-gekrätz, *n.* slag, dross of copper; **-kupfer,** *n.* liquated copper; **-malz,** *n.* cured malt, kiln-dried malt.

darstellbar, capable of being prepared.

darstellen, to prepare, produce, manufacture, make, exhibit, present, describe.

Darstellung, *f.* presentation, preparation, production, exhibition, description, representation, construction, manufacture.

Darstellungs-verfahren, *n.* process of preparation; **-weise,** *f.* method of preparation, manner of representation.

dartun, to prove, verify.

darüber, over it, across it, about it, more, in the meantime; ∼**hinaus** (hinweg), beyond, above that.

darübergelagert, superimposed.

darum, around it, about it, therefore.

darunter, thereunder, under it, among them.

daruntergelagert, situated beneath.

Dasein, *n.* existence, presence, being.

Daseinsbedingung, *f.* conditions(s) of existence.

daselbst, there, in that place.

dasjenige, that one, that.

dass, that; **so dass,** in order that; **dass** . . . , the fact that . . .

Dasselfliegen, *f.pl.* botflies (Oestridae).

dastehen, to be there, stand there.

Daten, *n.pl.* dates, data, facts.

datieren, to date.

Dattel, *f.* date; **-baum,** *m.* date tree; **-palme,** *f.* date palm; **-pflaume,** *f.* persimmon.

Datum, *n.* date.

Datura, *f.* thorn apple, stramony.

Daube, *f.* stave.

Daubenholz, *n.* stavewood.

Dauer, *f.* duration, durability, permanence; **auf die** ∼**,** in the long run, permanently.

Dauer-apfel, *m.* winter apple; **-ausscheider,** *m.* chronic carrier; **-belastung,** *f.* steady or permanent load; **-beobachtung,** *f.* continuous observation; **-biegversuch,** *m.* endurance bending test; **-birne,** *f.* winter pear; **-bruch,** *m.* lasting rupture, fatigue fracture; **-bruchgrenze,** *f.* endurance limit; **-butter,** *f.* canned butter; **-cyst,** *m.* resting cyst.

Dauer-darm, *m.* metagaster, permanent intestine; **-ei,** *n.* winter egg, resting zygote; **-festigkeit,** *f.* durability, endurance; **-form,** *f.* permanent form; **-gewächs,** *n.* perennial; **-gewebe,** *n.* permanent tissue; **-haft,** durable, lasting, fast; **-haftigkeit,** *f.* durability, permanence; **-hefe,** *f.* permanent yeast; **-konidie,** *f.* resting conidium.

Dauer-leib, *m.* menosoma; **-lolch,** *m.* perennial rye grass; **-milch,** *f.* sterilized milk; **-mund,** *m.* metastoma; **-mycel,** *n.* rhizomorph.

dauern, to last, continue, keep.

dauernd, lasting, permanent, perennial.

Dauer-niere, *f.* metanephros; **-pflanze,** *f.* perennial; **-präparat,** *n.* permanent preparation; **-schlagfestigkeit,** *f.* resistance to repeated impact; **-schwärmer,** *m.* quiescent swarm spore; **-spore,** *f.* permanent spore; **-spross,** *m.* resting shoot; **-staude,** *f.* perennial herb; **-strang,** *m.* rhizomorph; **-strom,** *m.* continuous current.

Dauer-träger, *m.* chronic carrier; **-veränderung,** *f.* permanent change; **-verdrehungsversuch,** *m.* endurance torsion test; **-versuch,** *m.* endurance test, fatigue test; **-wald,** *m.* continuous forest; **-waren,** *f.pl.* preserves; **-weide,** *f.* permanent pasture, meadow; **-wiese,** *f.* permanent pasture, meadow; **-zeichen,** *n.* symbol; **-zelle,** *f.* resting (permanent) cell; **-zustand,** *m.* permanence.

Daumen, *m.* thumb, inch, cam, finger; **-abzieher,** *m.* abductor pollicis; **-anzieher,** *m.* adductor pollicis; **-ballen,** *m.* thenar eminence, ball of thumb; **-beuger,** *m.* flexor of thumb; **-gegend,** *f.* region of thumb; **-glied,** *n.* phalanx of thumb; **-klopfer,** *m.* abductor; **-kuppe,** *f.* tip of thumb; **-nagel,** *m.* thumbnail.

Daumen-rad, *n.* cam wheel; **-regel,** *f.* thumb rule; **-steuerung,** *f.* cam gear; **-strecker,** *m.* extensor of thumb; **-welle,** *f.* camshaft.

Däumling, *m.* ̈e, little thumb, cam, knob.

Daun, *m.* hemp nettle.

Daune, *f.* down, plumule.

davon, thereof, therefrom, of it, away; **-kommen,** to get off; **-machen,** to take to one's heels; **-tragen,** to carry away, obtain; **-ziehen,** to set out.

davor, before it, from it, for it.

dawider, against it.

dazu, to this, for this, thereto, besides, therefore, for this purpose, in addition; noch ∼, moreover.

dazumal, then, at that time.

dazwischen, between (them); -liegend, lying between, interjacent, intermediate; -schalten, to put between, interpose; -schieben, to put between, interpose; -stellen, to put between, interpose, interpolate; -treten, n. intercession, intervention.

Debet, n. debit.

Debüt, n. first appearance.

Decennien, n.pl. decades.

dechiffrieren, to decipher.

deckbar, coverable, superposable.

Deck-blatt, n.-er, bract, wrapper (of a cigar); -blattartig, bracteal; -blättchen, n. bracteole; -blätterhülle, f. involucre; -blattlos, abracteate.

Decke, f. cover, covering, envelope, integument, coat, roof, slab, ceiling, elytra.

Deckel, m. operculum, cover, lid; -abfall, m. carding waste; -kapsel, f. pyxidium.

deckeln, to cover with a lid.

Deckel-schnecke, f. operculate snail; -spinne, f. trap-door spider; -zelle, f. lid cell.

decken, to cover, defray, supply, serve, leap, cleanse, superpose, coincide; sich ∼, to be identical, cover oneself.

Decken, n. covering, cleansing, superposition; -bau, m. tectonic structure; -gewebe, n. epithelial tissue; -strich, m. covering coat, daub.

Decker, m. coverer, wrapper.

deck-fähig, of good covering power, opaque; -fähigkeit, f. hiding (covering) power; -farbe, f. body color, opaque color; -farbig, of good body, opaque (color); -feder, f. tectrice; -flügel, m. elytra; -flügler, m.pl. Coleoptera; -frucht, f. cover crop.

Deckglas, n. cover glass, cover slip; -kitt, m. cements (varnishes) for preparations; -kultur, f. culture under glass; -taster, m. cover-glass gauge; -tinktion, f. staining of cover-glass preparation.

Deck-haar, n. appressed silky hair; -haut, f. tegument, covering membrane; -hülle, f. covering; -hütchen, n. capsule (of explosives).

deckig, imbricate.

Deck-kiemer, m.pl. Tectibranchia; -kläre. f. -klärsel, n. fine liquor; -knochen, m, covering bone; -knorpel, m. covering cartilage; -kraft, f. covering power; -mantel, m. cloak, cover; -mittel, n. covering material; -moos, n. cushion-forming moss; -name, m. trade name.

Deck-pappe, f. resist, resist pasteboard; -platte, f. membrane tectoria, cover, roof plate; -rand, m. false indusium; -schicht. f. coat, cover, protective layer; -schichtenbildung, f. formation of a film; -schild, m. elytra; -schuppe, f. scale, elytra; -spelze, f. flowering glume, lemma, (upper) scale; -stopfen, n. flanged stopper; -stück, n. covering scale, hydrophilium (in a siphonophore).

Deckung, f. cover, remittance, dominance, security, congruence, supply (of needs), covering, mount, tupping.

Deckungs-erscheinung, f. epinasty, hyponasty; -grad, m. degree of dominance.

Deck-zellen, f.pl. stigmata; -zotto, f. shaggy hair.

decolorieren, to decolorize.

Decreusage, f. determination of gum.

Decylsäure, f. decylic (decoic) acid.

deduzieren, to deduce, infer.

defekt, defective.

defibriniert, defibrinated.

definieren, to define.

definiert, definite, defined.

Definierlinien, f.pl. define lines

definitiv, definite, permanent.

deflagrieren, to deflagrate.

deformieren, to deform.

Degebo, f. (Deutsche Gesellschaft für Boden Mechanik), German Society for Soil Mechanics.

Degen, m. sword.

Degeneration, f. degeneration.

Degenerations-form, f. degeneration (involution) form; -herd, m. center or focus of degeneration.

deglutieren, to swallow.

degorgieren, to wash out, cleanse.

degradieren, to degrade.

degraissieren, to remove fat, reduce in fat.

dehnbar, capable of being stretched, extensible, ductile, elastic, dilatable.

Dehnbarkeit, f. extensibility, flexibility, ductility, malleability.

Dehnbarkeitsmesser, *m.* ductilimeter.

dehnen, to extend, stretch, expand, dilate, widen.

Dehn-fuge, *f.* expansion joint; **-mass,** *n.* strain magnitude, modulus of elasticity.

Dehnspross, *m.* etiolated shoot.

Dehnung, *f.* extension, stretching, traction, elongation, expansion, dilation, widening, plastic flow.

Dehnungs-linie, *f.* (stress-) strain curve; **-messer,** *m.* extensometer; **-wärme,** *f.* heat of extension; **-zahl,** *f.* coefficient of extension, strain coefficient.

Dehydration, *f.* dehydration.

dehydrieren, to dehydrate, dehydrogenate.

Dehydroschleimsäure, *f.* dehydromucic acid.

Deich, *m.***-e,** dam, embankment.

Deil, *m.* bloom, lump, cake.

dein, your, yours.

dekadisch, decadic.

Dekaeder, *m.* decahedron.

Dekalin, *n.* decahydronaphthalene.

dekantieren, to decant.

dekapieren, to clear of rust, scour, pickle.

dekarbonisieren, to decarbonize.

dekatieren, to hot-press, steam, sponge.

Deklination, *f.* declination.

deklinieren, to decline, deviate.

Dekokt, *n.* decoction, infusion.

dekorieren, to decorate.

dekrepitieren, to decrepitate.

dekussiert, decussate, crossed, intersected.

deliquescieren, to deliquesce.

Delle, *f.* dent, depression.

Delphin, *m.* dolphin.

Deltamuskel, *m.* deltoid muscle.

Demant, *m.* diamond, adamant; **-blende,** *f.* eulytite; **-spat,** *m.* adamantine spar, corundum.

dementieren, to contradict, deny.

dementsprechend, accordingly, correspondingly.

demgegenüber, on the other hand, as opposed to that, compared with this.

demgemäss, accordingly.

demnach, according to that, therefore.

demnächst, shortly, soon after, early.

demontierbar, dismountable.

demontieren, to dismount, dismantle, take apart.

demulzieren, to soften, become demulcent.

demungeachtet, nevertheless, notwithstanding.

Demut, *f.* humility.

demzufolge, accordingly.

denaturalisieren, to denaturalize, mix with methyl.

denaturieren, to denature, denaturize.

Denaturier(ungs)mittel, *n.* denaturant.

Dendrachat, *m.* **Dendritenachat,** *m.* dendritic agate.

dendritisch, dendritic, treelike.

denen, to them, to whom, to which.

denitrieren, to denitrate.

Denitriermittel, *n.* denitrating agent.

denitrifizieren, to denitrify.

Denkart, *f.* way of thinking.

denkbar, conceivable, thinkable.

denken, to think, imagine, reflect; **an etwas** ∼, to remember, think about; **sich etwas** ∼, to imagine something; **es lässt sich** ∼ **dass,** it can be imagined that; **auf etwas** ∼, to plan something.

Denk-mal, *n.*-**er,** monument, memorial; **-schrift,** *f.* memoir, memorial; **-vermögen,** *n.* reasoning, capacity to think; **-würdig,** memorable, notable.

denn, for, because, then; **es sei** ∼, unless.

dennoch, yet, however.

Depesche, *f.* dispatch, telegram.

dephlegmieren, to dephlegmate.

deplacieren, to displace.

depolarisieren, to depolarize.

depolymerisieren, to depolymerize.

Depot, *n.* storehouse, depot.

Depressionszustand, *m.* depressed condition.

deprimieren, to depress, deject, discourage.

derart, in such a way, so much.

derartig, such, of that kind.

derb, solid, compact, firm, hardy, stout, rough, rude; **-erz,** *n.* massive ore; **-gehalt,** *m.* solid (cubic) contents.

Derbheit, *f.* solidity, compactness.

Derb-stückig, lumpy, large-sized; **-wandig,** solid-walled, thick-walled.

dereinst, some (future) day.

deren, whose.

derentwillen, um, on whose account.

derer, of these, of those, of them, their.

dergestalt, such, so, in such a way.

dergleichen, such, the like.

Derivat, *n.* derivative.

Derivierte, *f.* derived line, point, result.

derjenige, diejenige, dasjenige, that one, the one, he who, she who, he (she, it).

derlei, of that sort, such, that sort of thing.

dermassen, so much, so, in such a way.

dermatisch, cutaneous.

derselbe, the same, the latter, this, they.

derzeit(ig), at this (that) time, actually, present.

Desaggregation, *f.* disintegration.

desamidieren, to deaminate, deamidate.

desensibilieren, to desensitize.

desfalls, in that case.

desgleichen, such as, likewise, ditto.

deshalb, therefore, for that reason.

Desinfektion, *f.* disinfection.

Desinfektions-kraft, *f.* disinfecting, germicidal value; **-massnahme,** *f.* disinfecting measure; **-mittel,** *n.* disinfectant; **-wasser,** *n.* disinfecting liquid; **-wirkung,** *f.* disinfecting action.

Desinfektor, *m.* disinfectant.

desinfizieren, to disinfect.

Desintegrator, *m.* cage mill.

desintegrieren, to disintegrate.

Desmotropie, *f.* desmotropism, tautomerism.

Desodorationsmittel, *n.* deodorizer.

desodor(is)ieren, to deodorize.

Desodorisierungsmittel, *n.* deodorant.

Desoxydation, *f.* deoxidation.

desoxydieren, deoxidize.

dessen, whose, of him, of it.

dessenungeachtet, nevertheless.

Dessin, *n.* design, pattern.

Destillat, *n.*-e, distillate.

Destillation, *f.* distillation.

Destillations-apparat, *m.* distilling apparatus; **-aufsatz,** *m.* distillation head, fractionating column; **-gefäss,** *n.* distilling vessel; **-kolben,** *m.* distilling flask.

Destillier-apparat, *m.* distilling apparatus, still; **-aufsatz,** *m.* fractionating column; **-betrieb,** *m.* refinery.

destillierbar, distillable.

Destillier-blase, *f.* retort, distilling vessel, shell still; **-kolben,** *m.* distilling flask, retort.

destillieren, to distill.

desto, so much, so much the . . . ; **je** . . . ~ . . . , the . . . the . . . ; ~ **besser,** all the better; **nichts ~ weniger,** nevertheless.

destomehr, so much the more.

deswegen, for the reason, therefore.

Deszendenz-prinzip, *n.* principle of evolution; **-theorie,** *f.* theory of heredity.

Detacheur, *m.* spot cleaner.

Detachiermittel *n.* detergent, spot cleaner.

Determinations-problem, *n.* problem of determination; **-quelle,** *f.* source of determination; **-vorgang,** *m.* determination process.

detonieren, to detonate.

deuchte (dünken), thought, seemed.

Deul, *m.* bloom, lump, cake.

deutbar, explainable, explicable.

deuten, to point at, indicate, interpret.

deutlich, distinct, clear, plain, evident.

deutsch, German.

deutsches Geschirr, stamper, mill stamping.

Deutsches Reich, German Empire.

Deutung, *f.* interpretation, explanation.

Deutungsversuch, *m.* attempt to interpret.

Deviationsmoment, *n.* momentum of deviation, product of inertia.

Devise, *f.* device, motto, foreign bill (of exchange).

Dextrinvergärung, *f.* fermentation of dextrin.

Dextronsäure, *f.* dextronic (dextrogluconic) acid.

Dezennium, *n.* decade.

Dezigramm, *n.* decigram.

dezimal, decimal; **-bruch,** *m.* decimal fraction; **-bruchstelle,** *f.* decimal place; **-stelle,** *f.* place of decimals; **-waage,** *f.* decimal balance.

Diachylonsalbe, *f.* diachylon ointment.

Diagnose, *f.* diagnosis.

Diagonale, *f.* diagonal.

Dialysator, *m.* dialyzer.

Dialyse, *f.* dialysis.

dialysierbar, dialyzable.

dialysieren, to dialyze.

Dialysierpapier, *n.* dialyzing paper.

dialysisch, dialystic.

dialytisch, dialytic.

diamagnetisch, diamagnetic.

Diamant, *m.*-en, diamond; -artig, adamantine, diamondlike; -glanz, *m.* adamantine luster; -spat, *m.* adamantine spar, corundum; -stahl, *m.* very hard steel, tool steel.

Diametralebene, *f.* diametric plane.

diametral, diametric(al).

Diamidobenzol, *n.* diaminobenzene.

Diaminblau, *n.* diamine blue.

Diaminosäure, *f.* diamino acid.

diandrisch, diandrian.

Dianenbaum, *m.* silver tree (*Arbor dianae*).

diaphan, diaphanous, transparent.

diaphoretisch, diaphoretic.

Diaphragma, *n.* diaphragm.

Diapositiv, *n.* transparency, lantern slide.

Diastase, *f.* diastase; -bildung, *f.* formation of diastase; -wirkung, *f.* diastatic action.

diastatisch, diastatic.

Diät, *f.* diet.

Diätetik, *f.* dietetics.

diätetisch, dietetic.

diatherm, diathermic.

diatherm (an), diathermal, diathermanous, permeable to heat.

diatomisch, diatomic.

Diazobenzol, *n.* diazobenzene.

diazotieren, to diazotize.

Diazoverbindung, *f.* diazo compound.

dibenzoylieren, to have two benzoyl groups added, forming dibenzoyl.

Dicabonsäure, *f.* dicarboxylic acid.

Dichinol, *n.* diquinol.

Dichinolin, *n.* diquinoline.

Dichlormethan, *n.* dichloromethane.

dichopodiale Sprossverkettung, *f.* dichotomy (condition of forking in pairs).

dichotrophe, heterotropic.

Dichroismus, *m.* dichroism.

Dichromsäure, *f.* dichromic acid.

Dichrosalz, *n.* dichroic salt.

dicht, tight, dense, impervious, leakproof, compact, close, firm, thick, near; -belaubt, with thick foliage; -blätterig, thick-leaved, confertifolious; -blumig, confertiflorous; -brennen, to vitrify; -druck, *m.* leakage pressure.

Dichte, *f.* density, tightness, thickness, firmness; -flasche, *f.* specific-gravity bottle; -messer, *m.* densimeter, areometer.

dichten, to make tight, condense, compact.

Dichter, *m.* poet.

Dichteverhältniss, *n.* relative density.

dichtgedrängt, compact.

Dichtheit, *f.* tightness, imperviousness, closeness, density, firmness.

Dichtigkeit, *f.* density.

Dichtigkeitsgrad, *m.* consistency, degree of denseness.

dicht-schliessend, closing tightly, tight; -seidenhaarig, holosericeous, covered with fine silky pubescence.

Dichtung, *f.* making tight, packing, density, compaction, consolidation, rendering impermeable, poetry.

Dichtungs-material, *n.* -mittel, *n.* packing (calking) material, packing.

dick, thick, dense, big, stout, bulky, fat, inflated, swollen.

Dickauszug, *m.* inspissated extract.

Dickblatt, *n.* houseleek (Crassula), succulent leaf; -gewächse, *n.pl.* Crassulaceae.

Dickdarm, *m.* large intestine, colon, great gut; -ausgang, *m.* anus; -drüse, *f.* gland of large intestine; -gekröse, *n.* colic mesentery; -klappe, *f.* ileocaecal valve; -schleimhaut, *f.* mucous membrane of colon.

Dicke, *f.* thickness, diameter, width, consistency; -milch, *f.* curdled milk.

Dicken-messer, *m.* caliper, thickness gauge; -wachstum, *n.* growth in thickness.

Dick-farbe, *f.* thick color; -fellig, thickskinned, pachydermous, callous; -flüssig, viscous, viscid; -flüssigkeit, *f.* thick liquid, viscidity; -früchtig, pachycarpous; -fuss, *m.* stone curlew or stone plover, (*Pontederia crassipes*); -füssig, pachypod; -häuter, *m.* pachyderm.

Dickicht, *n.* thicket, covert.

Dick-kopf, *m.* blockhead, chub; -kopffalter, *m.pl.* skippers; -maische, *f.* thick mash, decoction; -milch, *f.* curdled milk; -pfanne, *f.* concentration pan; -saft, *m.* thick liquor, sirup; -schalig, thick-shelled; -schnäb(e)lig, thick-billed; -wandig, thickwalled.

Dicyan, *n.* dicyanogen, cyanogen gas.

Didym, *n.* didymium.

die, the, who, which, this, that.

Dieb, *m.* thief; -stahl, *m.* theft, larceny.

diejenige, that, that one.

Diele, *f.* board, plank, deal, vestibule ceiling, flooring.

Dielektrikum, *n.* dielectric.

dielektrisch, dielectric.

Dielenbalken, *m.* joist.

Dieme, *f.* rick.

dienen, (*dat.*) to serve.

Diener, *m.*-, servant.

dienlich, serviceable, useful, expedient.

Dienst, *m.*-e, service, duty, employment.

dienstbar, serviceable.

Dienstbarkeit, *f.* servitude.

dienst-bereit, ready to serve, obliging; **-gradbezeichnung,** *f.* rating; **-herr,** *m.* employer, master; **-leistung,** *f.* service (rendered), function; **-lohn,** *m.* wages; **-los,** out of employment.

diesbezüglich, relating thereto, concerning this.

dieselbe, the same.

Dieselöl, *n.* Diesel oil.

dieser, diese, dieses, this, this one, the latter.

diesmal, this time, now, for once.

diesseit(s), (*gen.*) on this side of.

Dietrich, *m.* picklock, skeleton key.

Differdinger Träger, *m.* wide T-flanged steel I-beam.

Differential-gleichung, *f.* differential equation; **-rechnung,** *f.* differential calculus.

differentiell, differential.

Differenz, *f.* difference.

differenzieren, to differentiate.

Differenzierung, *f.* differentiation.

Differenzierungsvorgang, *m.* process of differentiation.

differieren, to differ.

diffundieren, to diffuse.

diffus, diffuse, diffused.

diffusions-fähig, diffusible; **-fähigkeit,** *f.* diffusibility; **-geschwindigkeit,** *f.* rapidity of diffusion; **-gleichgewicht,** *n.* diffusion equilibrium; **-kraft,** *f.* power of diffusion; **-strom,** *m.* diffusion current; **-vermögen,** *n.* diffusibility.

Digallussäure, *f.* digallic or tannic acid.

digerieren, to digest.

Digerierung, *f.* digestion.

Digestionsdrüse, *f.* digestive gland.

Digestiv-mittel, *n.* digestive; **-salz,** *n.* digestive salt, potassium chloride.

Digestorium, *n.* hood, fume cupboard.

Dignität, *f.* dignity, importance.

digonal, twofold, two-sided.

Diharnstoff, *m.* diurea.

dihydratisch, dihydric, divalent.

diklinisch, diclinous, dioecious, unisexual, imperfect.

Dikotyl, *n.* dicotyledon.

Dikotyledonen, *pl.* dicotyledons.

Dikotylenholz, *n.* wood of dicotyledon.

Diktam, *m.* dittany.

Dilation, *f.* dilation, dilatation.

Dilettant, *m.* amateur.

Dille, *f.* socket, nozzle.

Dillenkante, *f.* gonys.

Dill-kraut, *n.* dill (*Anethum graveolens*); **-öl,** *n.* dill oil, anethol; **-samen,** *m.* dillseed.

diluvisch, diluvian, diluvial.

Diluvium, *n.* diluvium.

dimensionieren, to dimension.

dimer, dimeric.

Dimethyläther, *m.* dimethyl ether.

dimethyliert, dimethylated.

Dimilchsäure, *f.* dilactic acid.

dimorph, dimorphous.

Dimorphie, *f.* **Dimorphismus,** *m.* dimorphism.

dimorphisch, dimorphous.

Dinaphtylin, dinaphthyline.

Ding, *n.*-e, thing, object, being; **das ~ an sich,** the thing in itself; **vor allen ~,** primarily, chiefly, above all else.

Dingbezug, *m.* relation to things, cause and effect.

dingen, to hire.

Dingglas, *n.* objective (of a lens).

Dinicotinsäure, *f.* dinicotinic acid.

dinitrieren, to introduce two nitro groups.

Dinkel, *m.* spelt, bearded or German wheat.

Dinorm, *f.* (D. I. N., Deutsche Industrie normen), German industrial standards.

Diopter, *n.* diopter, sight, sightvane.

Diorit, *m.* diorite, greenstone.

Dioxychinon, *n.* dihydroxyquinone.

Dioxyd, *n.* dioxide.

diözisch, dioecious (separate sexes).

diphasisch, diphase, diphasic.

Diphensäure, *f.* diphenic acid.

Diphenylborchlorid, *n.* diphenylboron chloride.

Diphosphorsäure, *f.* diphosphoric acid.

Diphtherie-gift, *n.* diphtheria toxin; **-heil-serum,** *n.* diphtheria antitoxin, diphtheria serum; **-nährboden,** *m.* culture medium for diphtheria bacillus.

Diphtheritis, *f.* diphtheria.

dipleurisch, two-layered.

Dipnoër, *pl.* Dipnoi, Batrachia.

dipol, dipolar.

Dippelhafer, *m.* bearded darnel.

Dippelsöl, *n.* Dippel's oil.

Diptam, *m.* dittany.

Dipterenblume, *f.* dipterous flower.

direkt, direct.

Direktive, *f.* general instructions.

Dirigent, *m.* director, manager, leader.

dirigieren, to direct, manage, conduct.

Disäure, *f.* diacid, dibasic (pyro) acid.

dischweflig, disulphurous.

diskontieren, to discount.

diskontinuierlich, discontinuous.

Diskontinuität, *f.* discontinuity.

Diskus-drüse, *f.* receptacle gland; **-lappen,** *m.* lobe (glandular) of receptacle; **-schuppe,** *f.* scale on receptacle.

diskutieren, to discuss.

Dislokationsmetamorphose, *f.* metamorphosis by dislocation.

dispensieren, to dispense, exempt, distribute.

dispergieren, to disperse.

dispergierend, dispersing, dispersive.

dispers, disperse, dispersed.

Dispersion, *f.* standard deviation.

Dispersions-mittel, *n.* dispersion medium; **-vermögen,** *n.* dispersive power.

Dispersitätsgrad, *m.* degree of dispersion.

Disponent, *m.* manager.

disponibel, disposable, available.

disponieren, to dispose, arrange.

Disproportionierung, *f.* rearrangement, disproportionation.

Dissertation, *f.* dissertation, thesis.

disserzieren, to dissect.

dissimilieren, to decompose, simulate.

Dissonanz, *f.* dissonance.

Dissoziations-spannung, *f.* dissociation tension; **-vermögen,** *n.* dissociating power.

dissoziierbar, dissociable.

dissoziieren, to dissociate.

distal, distal.

Distel, *f.* thistle; **-blatt,** *n.* prickly leaf; **-blätterig,** armed with prickles; **-falter,** *m.* thistle butterfly; **-fink,** *m.* goldfinch.

Disulfaminsäure, *f.* disulphamic acid.

Disulfosäure, *f.* disulphonic acid.

Disziplin, *f.* discipline, theory, doctrine.

Ditarinde, *f.* dita bark.

dithionig, hyposulphurous.

Dithionsäure, *f.* dithionic acid.

diuretisch, diuretic.

Divergenz, *f.* divergence.

divergieren, to diverge.

divergierend, divergent, diverging.

dividieren, to divide.

Diweinsäure, *f.* ditartaric acid.

Diwolframsäure, *f.* ditungstic acid.

Döbel, *m.* pin, peg, dowel, dobule, chub.

doch, however, yet, still, surely, indeed; ~ **noch,** still; ~ **noch immer,** still undoubtedly.

Docht, *m.* wick; **-kohle,** *f.* cored carbon.

Docke, *f.* bundle, skein, stook, shock, doll, dock.

docken, to wind in skeins, bind.

Dodekaeder, *n.* dodecahedron.

dodekaedrisch, dodecahedral.

Dogge, *m.* bulldog.

Dögling, *m.* bottle-nosed whale.

Döglingstran, *m.,* arctic sperm oil, doegling oil.

Dohle, *f.* jackdaw, chough.

Dolch, *m.* dagger; **-zahn,** *m.* laniary (canine) tooth.

Döldchen, *n.* umbellet.

Dolde, *f.* umbel, cone, strobile.

dolden-blütig, **-blumig,** umbelliferous, umbellate(d); **-blütler,** *m.pl.* Umbelliferae; **-bräune,** *f.* browning (of hop cones); **-erbse,** *f.* crown pea; **-förmig,** umbelliform; **-gewächse,** *n.pl.* Umbelliferae.

Dolden-rebe, *f.* Virginia creeper (*Ampelopsis quinquefolia*); **-rispe,** *f.* umbellike panicle; **-schraubel,** *f.* umbellike bostryx, cymose inflorescence; **-träger,** *m.pl.* umbellifers; **-traube,** *f.* corymb, umbellike raceme; **-wickel,** *m.* umbellike cincinnus, a scorpioid cyme.

doldig, umbellate; **-rispig,** paniculate(d).

dolieren, to pare, shave.

Dolmetscher, *m.* interpreter.

Dolomit, *n.* dolomite.

dolomitisieren, to dolomitize.

Dom, *m.* dome, cupola, canopy, cathedral.

Doma, *n.* dome.

Domänwald, *m.* state forest.

Dominanz, *f.* dominance.

dominieren, to dominate.

Dompfaff, *m.* bullfinch.

Donner, *m.* thunder; **-bart,** *m.* houseleek (*Sempervivum tectorum*); **-keil,** *m.* thunderbolt.

donnern, to thunder.

Donnerstrahl, *m.* lightning flash.

Doppel, *n.* duplicate; **-atomig,** diatomic; **-austausch,** *m.* double crossing over; **-balg,** *m.* bifollicle; **-beere,** *f.* double berry; **-befruchtung,** *f.* double fertilization; **-bestäubung,** *f.* simultaneous pollination with two kinds of pollen; **-biegung,** *f.* double bend, bending in two directions; **-bild,** *n.* double image; **-bindung,** *f.* double bond, linkage.

Doppel-boden, *m.* double or false bottom; **-brechend,** double refractive; **-brechung,** *f.* double refraction, birefringence; **-chlorid,** *n.* bichloride, dichloride; **-chromsauer,** bichromate of; **-draht-Zwirnmaschine,** *f.* double twisting machine (DD twister); **-dreizack,** *m.* sea arrow grass (*Triglochin maritima*); **-fädig,** bifilar; **-falznummer,** *f.* twofold number; **-falzzahl,** *f.* double folds (of film).

doppel-farbig, dichromatic; **-farbigkeit,** *f.* dichroism; **-färbung,** *f.* double staining, counterstaining; **-fernrohrlupe,** *f.* binocular telescopic magnifier; **-früchtig,** amphicarpous; **-füsser,** *m.pl.* Diplopoda; **-gänger,** *m.* double; **-gängig,** bifilar; **-gestaltung,** *f.* dimorphism; **-gitter,** *n.* double grid.

doppel-häuptig, dicephalous; **-hub,** *m.* up and down stroke; **-kappe,** *f.* Allegheny vine (*Adlumia cirrhosa*); **-keulig,** biclavate; **-kohlensauer,** bicarbonate of; **-lebig,** amphibious; **-masstab,** *m.* two-scale rule; **-oxalsauer,** bioxalate of; **-polig,** bipolar; **-punkt,** *m.* colon.

Doppel-punktstäbchen, *n.* polar-staining bacillus; **-reihe,** *f.* double row; **-salz,** *n.* double salt; **-schale,** *f.* double dish (with cover), Petri dish; **-schichtig,** two-layered; **-schnittig,** with double cross section (as a U-stirrup); **-schwefeleisen,** *n.* iron disulphide; **-schwefelsäure,** *f.* disulphuric acid; **-schwefligsauer,** bisulphite of; **-schwiele,** *f.* double callus.

doppel-seitig, bilateral; **-sinnig,** ambiguous; **-spat,** *m.* Iceland spar; **-spitzig,** biacuminate; **-spul-Spinnmachine,** *f.* nonidle spinning machine; **-stark,** double strength; **-stück,** *n.* duplicate.

doppelt, double, twofold, twice; **-borsauer,** biborate of; **-chlorzinn,** *n.* stannic chloride; **-chromsauer,** bichromate of; **-dreizählig,** biternate; **-fiederspaltig,** bipinnate; **-gefiedert,** bipinnate; **-gepaart,** bigeminate; **-gesägt,** biserrate; **-gummiert,** doubly impregnated with rubber.

doppelt-hochrund, convexo-concave, biconvex; **-kleesauer,** binoxalate of; **-kohlensauer,** bicarbonate of; **-schwefeleisen,** *n.* iron disulphide; **-spitzig,** two pointed.

Doppel-tubus, *m.* binocular tube; **-umsetzung,** *f.* double decomposition.

Doppelung, *f.* doubling.

Doppel-verbindung, *f.* double compound; **-wägung,** *f.* double weighing; **-wandig,** double-walled; **-weghahn,** *m.* two-way cock; **-wickel,** *m.* double cyme; **-wirkend,** double-acting; **-wurzel,** *f.* double root; **-zentner,** *m.* double centner, 100 kilograms; **-zersetzung,** *f.* double decomposition; **-züngig,** double-dealing, double-faced, deceitful.

Dorf, *n.* village.

Dorn, *m.* thorn, prong, spine, mandrel, core bar, pin, bolt; **-apfel,** *m.* datura, stramony; **-artig,** acanthaceous, spinous; **-blättrig,** spinulifolious; **-butte,** *f.* turbot.

Dörnchen, *n.* spinule.

Dorn-dreher, *m.* red-backed shrike; **-eidechse,** *f.* stellion.

dornen, to expand by mandrel.

Dornenwand, *f.* thorn (graduation) wall.

Dörnerschlacke, *f.* puddling slag, bulldog.

Dorn-fortsatz, *m.* spinal process, acantha; **-gebüsch,** *n.* thornbush; **-hai,** *m.* pricked dogfish.

dornig, thorny, spiny.

Dornstein, *m.* thornstone.

Dornstrauch, *m.* ̈-er, brier.

dorren, to (become) dry, parch, wither.

dörren, to dry, desiccate, bake, calcine.

Dörr-fleckenkrankheit, *f.* dry-spot disease, blight; **-gemüse,** *n.* dried vegetables; **-obst,** *n.* dried fruit.

Dorsal-kapsel, *f.* dorsal cup; **-schale,** *f.* dorsal valve; **-strang,** *m.* dorsal or marginal cord; **-wärts,** toward the dorsum.

D ›rsch, *m.* cod fish; -lebertran, *m* cod-
l.ver oil.

dorsiventral, dorsoventral.

dort, there, yonder; ~ selbst, right there.

dorthin, thither, there.

dortig, of that place.

Dose, *f.* box, can, dose, (pressure) cell.

Dosen-barometer, *n.* aneroid barometer;
-deckel, *m.* cheesebox still; -entwicklung,
f. tank development; milch, *f.* (evaporated) milk.

dosieren, to determine, dose, measure out.

Dosierung, *f.* determination, dosage, dosing.

Dosis, *f.* dose.

Dossierung, *f.* slope.

Dost(en), *m.* origan (Origanum).

Dostenöl, *n.* origanum oil.

Dostkraut, *n.* origan, marjoram, thyme.

Dotter, *m.* yolk, vitellus, gold-of-pleasure
(Camelina); -ball, *m.* vitelline sphere;
-blase, *f.* vitelline sac; -blume, *f.* marsh
marigold (*Caltha palustris*); -furchung, *f.*
yolk segmentation; -gang, *m.* yolk duct;
-gefäss, *n.* vitelline vessel; -gelb, *n.* yolk
(of the egg).

Dotter-haut, *f.* vitelline membrane; -häut-
chen, *n.* vitelline membrane; -hof, *m.*
vitelline area; -höhle, *f.* vitelline cavity;
kern-, *m.* yolk nucleus; -klüftung, *f.* yolk
segmentation; -korn, *n.* yolk granule;
körperchen, *n.* vitelline corpuscle; -kreis-
lauf, *m.* vitelline circulation; -kugel, *f.*
vitelline sphere.

Dotter-loch, *n.* blastopore, opening into
yolk; -pforte, *f.* micropyle; -plättchen, *n.*
vitelline or proligerous disk; -reich, rich
in deutoplasm; -rinne, *f.* yolk groove;
-sack, *m.* vitelline sac; -sackgefäss, *n.*
vitelline vessel; -sackhohlraum, *m.* yolk-
sac (vitelline) cavity.

Dotter-scheibe, *f.* vitelline disk; -scholle, *f.*
mass of yolk; -stiel, *m.* yolk stalk; -stöcke,
m.pl. vitellaria; -strang, *m.* vitelline cord;
-wegnahme, *f.* yolk removal; -weide, *f.*
golden willow (*Salix vitellina*); -zelle, *f.*
vitelline cell.

doublieren, to double, concentrate.

Dozent, *m.* teacher, lecturer.

Drache(n), *m.* dragon, kite, flying lizard.

Drachen-baum, *m.* dragon tree (*Dracaena
draco*); -blat, *n.* dragon's leaf (Draco-
phyllum); -blut, *n.* dragon's blood; -blut-
baum, *m.* dragon tree; -fisch, *m.* dragonet;
-kopf, *m.* dragonhead (*Dracocephalum*

canescens), scorpaenoid; -kraut, *n.* dragon-
wort (Dracontium); -maul, *n. Horminium
pyrenaicum.*

dragieren, to coat (pills).

Dragonne, *f.* dragonet.

Dragun, *m.* tarragon; -trat, *n.* -wermut-
kraut, *n.* tarragon.

Draht, *m.* ̈e, wire, thread, twist, grain
(of wood); -bund, *m.* coil of wire; -bürste,
f. wire brush.

drahten, to wire.

Draht-einstich, *m.* stab of stab culture;
-faser, *f.* wire mold; -gaze, *f.* wire netting;
-geflecht, *n.* wire netting; -gewebe, *n.*
wire cloth, wire gauze; -lager, *n.* groove;
-lehre, *f.* wire gauge; -leitung, *f.* conducting wire; -los, wireless; -netz, *n.* wire
netting, wire gauze.

Draht-schenkel, *m.* wire shank; -schotter,
m. crushed rock wrapped in wire mesh;
-segge, *f.* smaller-panicled sedge; -seil-
bahn, *f.* (wire) cableway; -speichenrad, *n.*
wire spoke wheel; -stift, *m.* wire nail,
wire tack.

Draht-verhau, *m.* (barbed) wire barrier;
-wurm, *m.* wire worm; -zange, *f.* pliers,
nippers; -zaun, *m.* wire fence; -ziehen, *n.*
wire drawing; -zug, *m.* wire mill, wire
drawing.

drainieren, to drain.

Drainröhre, *f.* draining tile.

Drall, *m.* twist, rifling, angular momentum.

drall, tight, buxom, robust.

Dränage, *f.* drainage.

Drang, *m.* throng, distress, pressure, impulse, craving.

drang (dringen), urged, pressed.

drängen, to press, crowd, urge; sich ~. to
push.

Drass, *m.* dregs.

drauf (darauf), thereupon, thereon, afterward; -sicht, *f.* plan, top view.

draussen, outside, without, abroad.

drechseln, to turn (on a lathe), elaborate.

Drechsler, *m.* turner; -ware, *f.* turnery
ware.

Dreck, *m.* dirt, filth, dung.

Dreh-achse, *f.* axis of rotation; -bank, *f.*
lathe.

drehbar, capable of being turned, rotatory;
-eingesetzt, pivoted.

Dreh-bewegung, *f.* rotary movement or
motion; -buch, *n.* scenario; -ebene, *f.*
plane of rotation.

drehen, to turn, rotate, roll, spin, wind, revolve.

drehend, turning, rotatory.

Dreher, *m.* turner, rotator, lathe hand.

Dreh-feld, *n.* rotary field, three-phase field; **-gelenk,** *n.* pivot joint; **-kondensator,** *m.* variable condensor; **-kraft,** *f.* torsional force; **-kreuz,** *n.* turnstile, sparger; **-moment,** *n.* twisting or torsional moment, torque; **-pol,** *m.* center of rotation; **-punkt,** *m.* point of rotation, pivot, fulcrum; **-schaufel,** *f.* turbine vane or bucket; **-scheibe,** *f.* turntable, potter's wheel; **-sinn,** *m.* direction of rotation.

Dreh-späne, *m.pl.* turnings; **-spannung,** *f.* torsional stress; **-spiegelung,** *f.* rotatory reflection; **-spule,** *f.* moving coil; **-spulgalvanometer,** *m.&n.* moving coil galvanometer; **-stahl,** *m.* turning tool; **-strom,** *m.* rotary current, three-phase current; **-stromgenerator,** *m.* rotatory current generator, three-phased generator.

Drehung, *f.* rotation, torsion, torque, twist.

Drehungs-achse, *f.* axis of rotation; **-festigkeit,** *f.* resistance to torsion; **-streuung,** *f.* rotatory dispersion; **-winkel,** *m.* angle of rotation.

Dreh-vektor, *m.* rotation vector; **-vermögen,** *n.* rotatory power; **-versuch,** *m.* torsion (turning) test; **-waage,** *f.* torsion balance; **-wirbel,** *m.* rotatory vertebra; **-wuchs,** *m.* tortuous growth, torsion of fibers, spiral grain; **-wüchsig,** spiral grained, twisted fibered; **-zahl,** *f.* speed of rotation.

drei, three; **-achsig,** triaxial; **-ährig,** three spiked; **-atomig,** triatomic; **-basisch,** tribasic; **-bein,** *n.* tripod; **-biss,** *m.* Tridax; **-blatt,** *n.* trefoil (Trillium); **-blätterig,** three-leaved, trifoliate.

drei-blumenblättrig, three-petaled; **-borstengras,** *n.* Trisetum; **-borstig,** trisetose; **-brachen,** to trifallow; **-brenner,** *m.* triple burner; **-brüderig,** triadelphous; **-doppelt,** triple, treble.

Dreieck, *n.* triangle; **-darstellung,** *f.* presentation by the triangle method.

dreieckig, triangular, three-cornered, deltoid.

Dreiecks-bein, *n.* triangular bone; **-krabbe,** *f.* (inachus crab); **-lehre** *f.* trigonometry; **-pflanzung,** *f.* triangle planting; **-verband,** *m.* triangle planting; **-winkel,** *m.* angle of a triangle.

Dreiergruppe, *f.* group of three.

dreierlei, of three kinds.

drei-fach, triple, threefold, treble; **-fächerig,** trilocular, three-celled; **-faltigkeitsblümchen,** *n.* chickweed (*Trientalis europaea*); **-farben,** three-color, trichrome; **-farbigkeit,** *f.* trichroism; **-fiederspaltig,** tripennate.

drei-flächig, three-faced, trihedral; **-flächner,** *m.* trihedron; **-fuss,** *m.* tripod; **-füssig,** three-footed, tripedal; **-gabelig,** trifid, trifurcated; **-gelenkbogen,** *m.* three-hinged arch; **-gliedrig,** three-membered, in three sections, trinomial; **-halskolben,** *m.* three-necked flask.

Dreiheit, *f.* triad.

drei-kantig, three-cornered, three-edged, triangular; **-kernig,** trinuclear; **-klappig,** three-valved, trivalvular; **-knotig,** trinodal; **-köpfig,** triceps; **-lappig,** trilobate; **-leiter** system, *n.* three-wire system; **-mal,** threefold, three times; **-malig,** occurring three times, triple; **-männ(er)ig,** triandrian.

drei-paarig, tergeminal; **-phasenstrom,** *m.* triphase current; **-reihig,** trifarious; **-ring,** *m.* three-membered ring; **-salz,** *n.* trisalt; **-säurig,** triacid, **-schenkelig,** three-legged; **-schenkelrohr,** *n.* three-way tube; **-schichtig,** three-layered; **-schneidig,** three-edged, triquetrous.

drei-seitig, three-sided, trilateral, triangular; **-spaltig,** trifid; **-spitzig,** tricuspidate.

dreissig, thirty.

dreissigste, thirtieth.

dreist, bold, daring, confident.

Drei-steinwurzel, *f.* feverroot (*Triosteum perfoliatum*); **-stellig,** three-place(d).

Dreistoff-kristallart, *f.* ternary crystal type; **-legierung,** *f.* three-component (ternary) alloy; **-system,** *m.* three-component system.

drei-stufig, tricaulate; **-teilig,** three-part, tripartite; **-undeinachsig,** monotrimetric.

Dreiweg-hahn, *m.* three-way cock; **-schalter,** *m.* three-way switch; **-stück,** *n.* three-way piece, three-way tube.

drei-weibig, trigynian, with three pistils; **-wertig,** trivalent; **-winkelig,** triangular.

Drei-zack, *m.* trident, arrow grass (Triglochin); **-zählig,** threefold, triple, ternate; **-zahn,** *m.* health grass; **-zähnig,** three-toothed, three-pronged; **-zehn,** thirteen; **-zeilig,** triseriate, tristichous; **-zipfelig,** tricuspidate.

Drell, *m.* tickling.

Drempel, *m.* sill for sealing base of gates.

dreschen, to thrash, thresh.

Dreschflegel, *m.* flail.

dressieren, to train.

Drillbohrer, *m.* drill, borer.

drillen, to drill, turn.

Drillich, *m.* ticking.

Drilling, *m.* triplet; **-salz,** *n.* triple salt.

Drill-kraft, *f.* twisting force, torsion; **-maschine,** *f.* ridge drill.

Drillung, *f.* torsion, twist.

drin (darin), therein.

dringen, to press, rush, penetrate; **auf etwas ∼,** to insist on a thing.

dringend, pressing, urgent.

dringlich, pressing, urgent.

Dringlichkeit, *f.* urgency.

drinnen, within, in, indoors.

drischt (dréschen), thrashes.

dritt, third.

Drittel, *n.* third; **-sauer,** tribasic; **-silber,** *n.* tiers argent, aluminical silver.

drittens, thirdly, in the third place.

dritthalb, two and a half.

droben, above, up there.

Droge, *f.* drug.

Drogen-händler, *m.* druggist; **-handlung,** *f.* drug business, drugstore; **-kunde,** *f.* pharmacology; **-lehre,** *f.* pharmacology; **-waren,** *f.pl.* drugs.

Drogerie, *f.* drugstore; **-geschäft,** *n.,* drug trade.

Droget(t), *m.* drugget.

Drogist, *m.* druggist.

Drohne, *f.* drone.

drohen, (*dat.*) to threaten, menace.

dröhnen, to rumble, roar, boom.

drohnen-brütig, laying only drone eggs; **-schlacht,** *f.* slaughter of the drones; **zelle,** *f.* drone cell.

drollig, droll, funny, comical.

Dromedar, *n.* dromedary.

drosch (dreschen), thrashed.

Drossel, *f.* thrush, throttle, throat; **-ader,** *f.* jugular vein; **-adergrube,** *f.* jugular fossa; **-aderloch,** *n.* jugular foramen; **-bein,** *n.* clavicle; **-fortsatz,** *m.* jugular or styloid process; **-geflecht,** *n.* jugular plexus; **-grube,** *f.* jugular fossa; **-kiefermuskel,** *m.* jugulomandibular muscle; **-klappe,** *f.* choke (check) valve, damper.

drosseln, to throttle.

Drossel-rinne, *f.* cervical groove; **-ventil,** *n.* throttle valve; **-zelle,** *f.* valve cell; **-zungenbeinmuskel,** *m.* jugulohyoid muscle.

drüben, over there, yonder.

drüber (darüber), over that, over it.

Druck, *m.-e,* pressure, compression, printing; **-abnahme,** *f.* reduction of pressure; **-änderung,** *f.* change of pressure; **-anstieg,** *m.* increase of pressure; **-beanspruchung,** *f.* compressive stress; **-behälter,** *m.* pressure vessel; **-birne,** *f.* monte-jus, acid egg; **-blau,** *n.* printing blue; **-dicht,** tight; **-elektrizität,** *f.* piezoelectricity.

drucken, to print; **drücken,** to press.

Druckentwickelung, *f.* development of pressure.

Drucker, *m.-,* printer.

Drücker, *m.* trigger, latch, handle.

Druckerei, *f.* printing works, printing.

Druckerfarbe, *f.* printer's ink.

Druck-erhitzung, *f.* heating under pressure; **-erhöhung,** *f.* increase of pressure; **-erniedrigung,** *f.* lowering of pressure.

Druckerschwärze, *f.* printer's ink, black.

Druckfehler, *m.* misprint, typographical error; **-festigkeit,** *f.* resistance to pressure, compressive strength; **-gang,** *m.* progress of pressure; **-gefälle,** *n.* pressure gradient; **-höhe,** *f.* head, height (of water); **-kasten,** *m.* pneumatic caisson; **-kattun,** *m.* printed calico; **-knopf,** *m.* push button, bell push, snap; **-kolben,** *m.* pressure flask, piston; **-legung,** *f.* publishing, printing, setting up.

Druck-leitung, *f.* pressure piping; **-linie,** *f.* axis of pressure; **-luft,** *f.* compressed air; **-luftpumpe,** *f.* air compressor; **-messer,** *m.* pressure gauge, manometer; **-papier,** *n.* printing paper; **-platte,** *f.* printing plate, engraving; **-probe,** *f.* pressure test, squeezing test, proof; **-rohr,** *n.,* **-röhre,** *f.* pressure tube, force pipe.

Druck-sache, *f.* printed matter; **-schraube,** *f.* pressing screw, thumbscrew, attachment screw; **-schrift,** *f.* publication, print, type; **seite,** *f.* page; **-spannung,** *f.* compressive stress, turgor; **-steigerung,** *f.* increase of pressure; **-stempel,** *m.* piston; ram; **-stoss,** *m.* water hammer; **-stutzen,** *m.* pressure connection; **-veränderung,** *f.* change in pressure.

Druck-verband, *m.* compressive bandage; **-verfahren,** *n.* printing process; **-verlauf,** *m.* pressure or stress distribution; **-walze,** *f.* pressure cylinder, printing roller; **-wasser,** *n.* pressure water, water for hydraulic work; **-welle,** *f.* pressure wave; **-wirkung,** *f.* pressure, action of pressure; **-zeug,** *n.* printing cloth; **-zunahme,** *f.* increase of pressure; **-zwiebel,** *f.* pressure bulb.

Drudenfuss, *m.* club moss (*Lycopodium clavatum*).

drum (darum), around it, for that reason, therefore.

drunter (darunter), under it, below; ~ **und drüber,** upside down.

Drüschen, *n.* small gland, glandule.

Druse, *f.* druse, strangles, nodule, granule.

Drüse, *f.* gland.

drusen, to become dreggy or feculent.

Drusen, *f.pl.* dregs, sediment, lees, granules; **-asche,** *f.* calcined (wine) lees.

Drüsen-anlage, *f.* gland primordium, rudiment; **-arm,** poor or wanting in glands; **-artig,** glandular; **-ausführungsgang,** *m.* excretory glandular duct; **-bau,** *m.* structure of gland; **-beutel,** *m.* glandular pouch; **-bläschen,** *n.* glandular vesicle; **-blatt,** *n.* entoderm, glandular leaf; **-blattartig,** andenophyllous.

Drüsen-deckel, *m.* cells closing or surrounding a gland; **-epithel,** *n.* glandular epithelium; **-feld,** *n.* gland area; **-fläche,** *f.* glandular surface; **-fleck,** *m.* glandular spot; **-förmig,** glandular; **-führend,** glandular; **-gang,** *m.* glandular duct; **-gewebe,** *n.* glandular tissue.

Drüsen-haar, *n.* glandular hair, excretory hair; **-haufen,** *m.* collection of glands; **-haut,** *f.* gland membrane; **-höle,** *f.* gland cavity; **-hohlraum,** *m.* glandular cavity; **-inhalt,** *m.* content of gland.

Drüsen-kapsel, *f.* gland capsule; **-klee,** *m.* Psoralea; **-knäuel,** *m.* coil of gland; **-korn,** *m.* acinus of a gland; **-körper,** *m.* body of a gland; **-krankheit,** *f.* gland disease, scrofula; **-kropf,** *m.* goiter; **-kunde,** *f.* adenology; **-lehre,** *f.* adenology; **-leiste,** *f.* gland ridge; **-lichtung,** *f.* gland lumen.

Drüsen-magen, *m.* proventriculus, glandular stomach; **-mündung,** *f.* gland orifice; **-paket,** *n.* collection of glands, glandular packet; **-raum,** *m.* glandular cavity; **-saft,** *m.* glandular secretion; **-scheibe,** *f.* glandular disk; **-schicht,** *f.* glandular layer; **-schlauch,** *m.* gland tube, duct; **-schuppe,** *f.* glandular scale.

Drüsen-sekret, *n.* glandular secretion; **-stengelig,** glandular stemmed or stalked; **-tätigkeit,** *f.* gland activity; **-träger,** *m.* Adenophora; **-träubchen,** *n.* racemous

gland of pancreas; **-traube,** *f.* acinus of a gland; **-zotte,** *f.* glandular shaggy hair.

drusig, drusy, drused.

drüsig, glandular.

dualistisch, dualistic.

Dübel, *m.* dowel pin, peg, plug.

Dublett, *f.* duplicate, double.

dublieren, to double, concentrate.

Dublierstein, *m.* concentrated metal, regulus.

ducken, to humble, submit.

Ducker, *m.* siphon, one that ducks, duikerbok, impoon.

Dücker, *m.* sea duck, culvert.

Duckstein, *m.* calcareous tufa.

duff, dull.

Duft, *m.* odor, scent, fragrance, bloom. exhalation, vapor, perfume, aroma.

duften, to be fragrant, smell, sweat.

Duftessig, *m.* aromatic vinegar.

duftig, fragrant, odorous.

Duftigkeit, *f.* haziness.

duft-los, odorless, inodorous; **-losigkeit,** *f.* lack of odor; **-organ,** *n.* organ of scent; **-reich,** fragrant, perfumed; **-stoff,** *m.* odorous substance, perfume.

Dugong, *m.* dugong, sea cow.

Duktilität, *f.* ductility.

Dulcit, *n.* dulcitol, dulcite.

dulden, to suffer, endure, bear, tolerate.

dumm, stupid, dull, slow, foolish.

Dummkoller, *m.* (blind) staggers.

dumpf, close, damp, hollow, dull.

dumpfig, musty, moldy.

Dune, *f.* down (of birds).

Düne, *f.* dune, sandy beach.

Dünenaufforstung, *f.* afforestation of dunes.

Dunen-feder, *f.* down; **-fleck,** *m.* down spot, macula plumosa.

Dünen-gräser, *n.pl.* grasses growing on sand dunes; **-hafer,** *m.* beach grass (*Ammophila arundinacea*); **-pflanze,** *f.* dune plant; **-rose,** *f.* Scotch rose (*Rosa spinosissima*).

Dunen-spule, *f.* quill of the down; **-strahl,** *m.* barbule.

Dünental, *n.* dune valley.

Dung, *m.* manure, fertilizer, dung; **-artig,** dunglike, stercoraceous.

Dünge-bedürfnis, *n.* fertilizer need or requirement; **-gips,** *m.* gypsum for manuring;

-jauche, *f.* dung water, liquid manure; -kalk, *m.* manuring lime; -mittel, *n.* manure, fertilizer.

düngen, to fertilize, manure.

Düngepulver, *n.* powdered manure.

Dünger, *m.* manure, fertilizer, dung; -bedarf, *m.* fertilizer requirement.

Dungerde, *f.* vegetable earth, mold, humus, compost.

Dünger-fabrik, *f.* fertilizer factory; -fordernd, requiring fertilizer; -gabe, *f.* yield, amount of manure; -haufen, *m.* manure heap; -liebend, reacting favorably to fertilization; -versuch, *m.* fertilizer experiment; -wert, *m.* manurial value.

Düngesalz, *n.* saline manure, fertilizer salt.

Dunghaufen, *m.* dungheap, dunghill, manure heap.

Düngung, *f.* manuring fertilizing.

Düngungsfrage, *f.* fertilizer question.

dunig, downy.

Dunkel, *n.* dark, darkness, obscurity.

dunkel, dark, dim; -blau, dark-blue, cyanaeus, cornflower-colored; -braun, dark-brown; -farbig, dark-colored; -färbung, *f.* darkening.

Dunkelfeld, *n.* dark field; -beleuchtung, *f.* dark-field illumination; -beobachtung, *f.* dark-field observation; -blende, *f.* dark-field stop.

dunkel-gelb, dark-yellow; -grau, dark-gray; -grün, dark-green.

Dunkelheit, *f.* darkness, obscurity.

Dunkel-käfer, *m.pl.* Tenebrionidae; -kammer, *f.* darkroom, camera obscura.

dunkeln, to grow dark, darken, dim.

dunkel-rot, dark-red; -rotglut, *f.* dull-red heat; -rotgültigerz, *n.* dark-red silver ore; -starre, *f.* rigor due to darkness (dark rigor); -violett, deep violet or purple.

dünken, to seem, appear.

dünn, thin, dilute, slender, rare; -bewaldet, sparsely wooded; -blättig, leptophyllous, tenuifolious.

Dünndarm, *m.* small intestine; -gekröse, *n.* mesentery of ileum.

Dünne, *f.* thinness, diluteness.

dünnen, to thin.

dünn-flüssig, thinly liquid, watery; -flüssigkeit, *f.* fluidity, thinly liquid state; -geschichtet, thinly stratified; -saft, *m.* thin juice; -schalig, thin-skinned, thin-shelled; -schlagen, to beat out thin;

-schleifen, to grind (cut) thin; -schliff, *m.* thin section; -schuppig, in thin scales; -wandig, thin-walled; -wurzlig, leptorrhizal.

Dunst, *m.ˉe*, vapor, steam, fume, smoke; -abzug, *m.* hood; -artig, gaseous, vaporlike; -bildung, *f.* haze (vapor) formation.

Dünnstein, *m.* thin matte, table diamond.

dunsten, dünsten, to evaporate, steam, smoke.

Dunst-essig, *m.* aromatic vinegar; -förmig, gaseous, vaporous; -hülle, *f.* atmosphere, vaporous envelope.

dunstig, vaporous, steamy, misty, moist

Dunstigkeit, *f.* vaporousness.

Dunst-kreis, *m.* atmosphere; -loch, *n.* vent, air hole; -los, vaporless, fumeless; obst, *n.* stewed fruit.

duplikativ, conduplicate.

duplizieren, to duplicate, double.

Duralsack, *m.* dural sac.

durch, through, by, owing to, by means of; -aus nicht, by no means; -aus, throughout, completely, absolutely, by all means; ∼ und durch, throughout.

durch-arbeiten, to finish, complete, work through, elaborate; -ätzen, to eat through, corrode; -backen, to bake thoroughly; -beissen, to bite through; -beizen, to corrode; -beuteln, to bolt (flour); -biegen, to sag, bend through; -biegung, *f.* sagging, deflection, (co)flexure; -bilden, to perfect, improve; -bittern, to make thoroughly bitter.

durch-blasen, to blow through; -blättern, to turn the pages of, glance at, split into lamellae; -blicken, to become visible, look through, penetrate; -bohren, to perforate, bore through, pierce; -bohrung, *f.* perforation; -brechen, to break (through), cut, pierce, punch, perforate, appear; -brennen, to burn through, elope.

durch-bringen, to see a thing (person) safely through, get through a difficulty, conclude a thing, waste, spend; -brochen, pierced, perforated.

Durchbruch, *m.* breaking out, escape, eruption, opening, aperture, breach, triumph; zum ∼ kommen, to burst forth.

Durch-bruchsöffnung, *f.* eruption, opening, vacuity; -dampfen, to fill with vapor or steam; -dämpfen, to steam; -dringbar, penetrable, permeable; -dringbarkeit, *f.* permeability; -dringen, to penetrate, permeate, pervade; -dringend, penetrating; -dringlich, permeable.

Durch-dringlichkeit, *f.* penetrability; **-dringung,** *f.* penetration, permeation; **-dringungsvermögen,** *n.* penetrating power; **-drücken,** to press through; **-drüngenheit,** *f.* permeation; **-duften,** to scent, perfume; **-dünsten,** to fill with vapor; **-einander,** confusedly; **-fahrt,** *f.* thoroughfare, passage; **-fall,** *m.* diarrhea, failure; **-fallast,** *m.* loose knot.

durch **-fallen,** to fall through, be transmitted (of light), fail; **-färbbar,** penetrable with color; **-färben,** to dye thoroughly; **-faulen,** to rot through; **-femeln,** to select, cull out, prick out; **-feuchten,** to soak, moisten; **-feuern,** to heat thoroughly; **-filtrieren,** to filter (through); **-fliessen,** to flow through.

Durchfluss, *m.* flowing through, discharge; **-fehler,** *m.* drainage error; **-zeit,** *f.* time or rate of flow.

durch **-forschen,** to investigate (thoroughly); **-forschung,** *f.* examination, investigation, analysis; **-forsten,** to thin; **-forstung,** *f.* thinning, afforestation.

Durchforstungs-ertrag, *m.* returns from thinning; **-versuch,** *m.* thinning experiment.

durch-fressen, to eat through, corrode; **-frieren,** to freeze through, chill; **-fuhr,** *f.* transport; **-führbar,** practicable, feasible; **-führbarkeit,** *f.* practicability, feasibility; **-führen,** to lead through, convey through, carry out, accomplish; **-führung,** *f.* leading through, accomplishment, execution.

Durch-gang, *m.* ̈e, passage, duct, transit; **-gängig,** penetrable, permeable, general(ly), usual(ly); **-gangshahn,** *m.* two-way (straightway) cock; **-gangsprofil,** *n.* clearance; **-gangspunkt,** *m.* point of passage; **-gären,** to ferment sufficiently; **-geben,** to filter, strain, transmit.

durchgehen, to go through, run away, be transmitted, examine; ∼ **lassen,** to let through, pass through.

durch-gehend, piercing, passing through, continuous, transmitted; **-gehends,** throughout, generally; **-gerben,** to tan thoroughly; **-geseihtes,** *n.* filtrate; **-giessen,** to pour through, strain, percolate; **-glühen,** to anneal thoroughly; **-greifend,** decisive; **-guss,** *m.* filter, strainer, pouring through, filtration, percolation, sink; **-halten,** to hold out (to the end), to carry right through; **-hauen,** to cut through.

durch-heizen, to heat thoroughly; **-hieb,** *m.* improvement cutting or trimming; **-hitzen,** to heat thoroughly; **-kälten,** to chill thoroughly; **-klären,** to clear or clarify

thoroughly; **-kochen,** to boil thoroughly; **-kommen,** to come through, get along or through, recover; **-können,** to be able to pass through; **kreuzen,** to cross, traverse, intersect; **-kreuzt,** decussate.

Durch-kreuzung, *f.* crossing, decussation; **-kriechen,** to crawl through; **-kühlen,** to cool or chill thoroughly; **-lass,** *m.* filter, opening, outlet, culvert, passage; **-lassen,** to filter, strain, transmit, let through; **-lässig,** permeable, pervious, penetrable; **-lässigkeit,** *f.* permeability, porosity, perviousness; **-lässigkeitsverminderung,** *f.* decrease in permeability; **-lasstelle,** *f.* transfusion area (tissue); **-lassung,** *f.* filtering, transmission.

Durch-lauf, *m.* ̈e, sieve, passage, colander, diarrhea; **-laufbalken,** *m.* continuous beam; **-laufen,** to filter, run through, pass through, traverse; **-laufend,** continuous; **-laugen,** to steep in lye, lixiviate thoroughly; **-läutern,** to purify, clean; **-leiten,** to pass through, conduct; **-lesen,** to peruse, read through; **-leuchten,** to shine through, illuminate, irradiate. test (eggs); **-leuchtung,** *f.* illumination, fluoroscopy.

durch-lochen, to perforate, punch, core; **-löchern,** to perforate, pierce, punch; **-löcherung,** *f.* perforation; **-lüften,** to ventilate, air; **-lüftung,** *f.* aeration, ventilation; **-lüftungsfähig,** capable of ventilation; **-machen,** to go through, pass through, traverse; **-messen,** to measure, pass through, traverse.

Durchmesser, *m.* -, diameter; **-schwindung,** *f.* skrinkage in diameter.

durch-mischen, to mix thoroughly, intermix; **-mustern,** to examine closely, scrutinize, inspect, review; **-nässen,** to wet thoroughly, saturate, soak; **-nehmen,** to go through, discuss; **-netzen,** to wet through; **-pressen,** to pass through, squeeze through, strain; **-probieren,** to test (thoroughly); **-queren,** to traverse, cross; **-räuchern,** to fumigate, smoke thoroughly; **-rechnen,** to calculate, check.

durch-reiben, to rub through, chafe, gall, strain; **-reissen** to tear asunder, break; **-rosten,** to rust through; **-rösten,** to roast thoroughly; **-rühren,** to stir thoroughly; **-sättigen,** to saturate; **-satz,** *m.* drive, throughput (of a unit); **-satzzeit,** *f.* time per charge, rate of charging; **-säuern,** to acidify, make sour, leaven; **-saugen,** to suck through.

durch-scheinend, translucent, transparent; **-schiessen,** to shoot through, traverse, interleave; **-schimmern,** to shine through;

-schlag, *m.*ˑˑe, strainer, punch, piercer, carbon copy, opening, puncture.

durchschlagen, to strain, punch, perforate, beat through, traverse, to prove efficacious get through, penetrate; **sich** ~, to fight one's way through.

durchschlagend, complete, thorough, efficacious, telling, marked, decisive.

Durchschlag-festigkeit, *f.* disruptive strength; **-papier,** *n.* carbon paper.

Durchschlagskraft, *f.* piercing effect, puncture resistance, breakdown (in electricity).

Durchschlag-spannung, *f.* breakdown pressure, disruptive voltage.

durchschneiden, to intersect, cross, cut through, pierce.

Durchschneidung, *f.* bisection, intersection.

Durchschnitt, *m.*-e, cut, section, average, mean, intersection; **im** ~, on the average.

durchschnittlich, average, on an average.

Durchschnitts-alter, *n.* average age, **-bestimmung,** *f.* average determination; **-ertrag,** *m.* average yield; **-eigenschaften,** *f.pl.* average properties; **-geschwindigkeit,** *f.* average speed or celerity; **-kreis,** *m.* circle formed by a section; **-probe,** *f.* average sample; **-punkt,** *m.* point of intersection; **-wert,** *m.* mean value; **-zahl,** *f.* mean; **-zuwachs,** *m.* mean increment, average accretion.

Durchschuss, *m.* woof, weft, interlinear space.

durch-schütteln, to shake thoroughly, agitate; **-schwängern,** to impregnate thoroughly, saturate; **-schwefeln,** to sulphur(ize) thoroughly; **-schwelen,** to smolder; **-schwitzen,** to sweat, ooze through; **-seihen,** strain, filter, percolate; **-seiher,** *m.* strainer, filter; **-seihung,** *f.* straining, filtration.

durchsetzen, to permeate, penetrate, infiltrate, sieve, sift, intersect, carry (put) through.

durchsetzt mit, interspersed with.

Durchsetzung, *f.* putting through.

Durchsicht, *f.* view, inspection.

durchsichtig, transparent, clear.

Durchsichtigkeit, *f.* transparency, clearness.

Durchsichtigkeitsgrad, *m.* degree of transparency.

Durchsichtsfarbe, *f.* transparent color.

durch-sickern, to trickle through, filter (seep) through, percolate; **-sieben,** to sift, sieve, screen, bolt; **-sieden,** to boil tho

oughly; **-sintern,** to trickle through, percolate; **-sprechen,** to discuss; **-sprengt,** mixed; **-spülen,** to rinse well, wash well; **-stechen,** to pierce, stab, cut, prick; **-stellt,** mixed; **-stich,** *m.* piercing, cutoff, intercepting cut, cutting.

durch-stossen, to push through; **-stosspunkt,** *m.* perforation point; **-strahlen,** to radiate through, shine through, penetrate with rays; **-strahlung,** *f.* irradiation, passing through (of rays); **-streichen,** to cross out, run through, go through, sift, screen; **-streifen,** to travel, roam through; **-strömen,** to stream through, flow through; **-strömung,** *f.* streaming through, perfusion.

Durchströmungs-apparat, *m.* perfusion apparatus; **-flüssigkeit,** *f.* perfusion fluid; **-linie,** *f.* line of seepage.

durch-suchen, to examine, search through; **-suchung,** *f.* examination; **-süssen,** to sweeten thoroughly, edulcorate; **-tränken,** to saturate, impregnate, infiltrate; **-tränkung,** *f.* infiltration, impregnation, imbibition, saturation; **-treiben,** to drive or force through; **-trieben,** cunning, crafty; **-tritt,** *m.* passage, entrance.

Durchtritts-grad, *m.* degree of passing or passage; **-stelle,** *f.* exit, point of passage.

durch-trocknen, to dry thoroughly; **-wachsen,** to grow through, intermingle, interpenetrate, perfoliate(d); **-wachsung,** *f* penetration, proliferation; **-wanderung,** *f.* passing through, diffusion; **-wärmen,** to warm thoroughly; **-wärmig,** diathermic; **-waschen,** to wash thoroughly; **-wässern,** to soak; **-weg,** throughout.

durch-weichen, to soften, soak; **-werfen,** to sift, screen, bolt; **-wühlen,** to turn over; **-wurf,** *m.* screen, sieve, riddle; **-zeichnen,** to trace; **-ziehen,** to draw through, traverse, penetrate, pass through; **-ziehglas,** *n.* slide; **-zug,** *m.* passage, circulation, through draft.

dürfen, to be permitted, may, can, need, dare, be likely, ~ (with neg.), must not.

dürftig, needy, scanty, poor, insufficient.

Durochinon, *n.* duroquinone.

Durol, *n.* durene.

dürr, dry, arid, dried, withered, dead, sterile, lean, thin.

Dürre, *f.* dryness, drought.

Dürr-futter, *n.* dry food, hay; **-grenze,** *f.* arid boundary, arid transition zone; **-holz,** *n.* dry wood; **-ständer,** *m.* standing dead tree.

Durst, *m.* thirst.

dürsten, to be thirsty.

durstig, thirsty, eager.

Düse, *f.* nozzle, mouthpiece, blast pipe, tuyère.

Düsenrohr, *n.* jet tube, sparger, steam pretzel.

düster, dark, gloomy, dusky.

Düte, *f.* paper bag.

Dutzend, *n.*-e, dozen.

Dynamik, *f.* dynamics.

dynamisch, dynamic.

Dynamomaschine, *f.* dynamo.

dysenterisch, dysenteric.

E

Ebbe, *f.* ebb (tide).

eben, even, plane, two-dimensional, level, smooth, exactly, just, precisely, really; ~ **deshalb,** for that very reason; ~ **jener,** just that one.

Ebenbaum, *m.* ebony tree.

Eben-bild, *n.* image, likeness; **-bürtig,** of equal birth, equal.

eben-da (selbst), at the very (same) place; **-dort,** just there, at that place.

Ebene, *f.* plain, plane.

eb(e)nen, to level, flatten, smooth.

ebenerwähnt, just mentioned.

ebenfalls, likewise, also, equally.

ebenflächig, plane.

ebengenannt, just mentioned.

Eben-holz, *n.* ebony; **-holzgewächse,** *n.pl.* Ebenaceae.

ebenieren, to ebonize.

Ebenmass, *n.*-e. symmetry, proportion, harmony.

eben-mässig, symmetrical, proportionate; **-so,** just so, just as, as well as, likewise; **-sogut,** just as well; **-solch,** similar, like; **-sosehr, -soviel,** just as much, as many; **-sowenig,** just as little; **-strauss,** *m.* corymb(us).

Eber, *m.* boar; **-esche,** *f.* mountain ash (*Sorbus aucuparia*); **-raute,** *f.* southernwood (*Artemisia abrotanum*); **-wurz(el),** *f.* carline thistle (*Carlina vulgaris*).

ebnen, to level, flatten, smooth, plane.

ebullieren, to boil up, break out, bubble.

Echolot, *n.* echosonic fathometer, sonic depth finder.

echt, genuine, true, unadulterated, pure, real, fast, essential; **-blau,** *n.* fast blue, induline; **-gelb,** *n.* fast yellow.

Echtheit, *f.* genuineness, authenticity, fastness, purity.

Eck, *n.*-en, angle.

Ecke, *f.* angle, edge, corner, summit.

Eckeisen, *n.* gusset plate.

Eckencollenchym, *n.* corner collenchyma.

Ecker, *f.* acorn, mast, beechnut; **-doppen,** *f.pl.* acorn galls.

Eckerich, *n.* mast proper, crop of acorns

Eck-fittich, *m.* lesser coverts (of the carpus); **-flügel,** *m.* allula, false wing; **-flügler,** *m.* vanessa; **-holz,** *n.* squared timber.

eckig, angular, cornered, awkward.

Eck-schiene, *f.* corner bar; **-strebe,** *f.* bar (hoof of horse); **-zahn,** *m.* canine tooth.

Ectodermverdickung, *f.* ectodermal thickening.

Edaphon, *n.* edaphon, microscopic life of the soil.

edel, noble, inert, rare, precious, rich, vital; **-auge,** *n.* bud (used for grafting); **-erde,** *f.* rare earth; **-falke,** *m.* (trained) falcon; **-galmei,** *m.* smithsonite; **-gamander,** *m.* germander; **-hirsch,** *m.* stag, red deer; **-kamille,** *f.* large camomile; **-kastanie,** *f.* chestnut (*Castanea sativa*); **-metall,** *n.* precious metal.

edel-mütig, noble, generous; **-reis,** *n.* scion, graft; **-rost,** *m.* patina; **-salbei,** *m.* common sage; **-schule,** *f.* nursery garden (for grafting trees); **-schwein,** *n.* domesticated pig, swine; **-sorten,** *f.pl.* domesticated species; **-spat,** *m.* adularia; **-stahl,** *n.* refined steel; **-stein,** *m.* precious stone, jewel.

Edel-tanne, *f.* silver fir (*Abies picea*); **-weiss,** *n.* lion's-foot (*Gnaphalium leontopodium*); **-wild,** *n.* red deer, large game.

edieren, to edit, publish.

edulkorieren, to edulcorate, wash.

Efeu, *m.* ivy (*Hedera helix*).

Effekt, *m.*-en, effect, power.

Effekten, *n.pl.* securities, stocks, bonds.

efferveszieren, to effervesce.

effloreszieren, to effloresce.

egal, equal, even.

egalisieren, to equalize, level, flatten.

Egalität, *f.* equality.

Egel, *m.* leech; **-würmer,** *m.pl.* Hirudinea.

Egestionsöffnung, *f.* atrial or evacuation opening.

Egge, *f.* harrow, selvage.

eggen, to harrow.

Egoutteur, *m.* dandy roll, pulp roller.

egrenieren, to clean (gin) cotton.

Egreniermaschine, *f.* (cotton) gin.

Ehe, *f.* matrimony, marriage.

ehe, before, ere.

ehedem, formerly.

ehemalig, former, past, late.

ehemals, formerly.

eher, earlier, sooner, rather, formerly; **noch ∼,** still more.

ehern, brazen, bronze.

eheste, soonest, next; **am ehesten,** most nearly, first.

ehrbar, honorable, respectable, modest.

Ehrbegierde, *f.* ambition.

Ehre, *f.* honor, character, reputation.

ehren, to honor, esteem; **-haft,** honorable; **-mitglied,** *n.* honorary member; **-preis,** *m.* prize, speedwell, Veronica; **-rettung,** *f.* vindicaticn; **-stelle,** *f.* position of honor; **-voll,** honorable; **-wert,** honorable, respectable.

Ehrgeiz, *m.* ambition.

ehrlich, honest, fair, reliable, true, honorable.

Ei, *n.***-er,** egg, ovum; **-ablage,** *f.* oviposition, egg laying; **-achse,** *f.* axis of the ovum; **-albumin,** *n.* egg albumen; **-apparat,** *m.* egg apparatus; **-ausstossung,** f. expulsion of the ovum; **-ballung,** *f.* oösphere formation; **-bau,** *m.* egg structure.

Eibe, *f.* yew.

Eibengewächse, *n.pl.* Taxaceae.

Ei-bereich, *m.&n.* part of the egg; **-bildung,** *f.* ovulation, oögenesis.

Eibisch, *m.* marsh mallow (*Althaea officinalis);* **-wurzel,** *f.* marsh-mallow root.

Eich-amt, *n.* bureau of standards, testing (gauging) office; **-apfel,** *m.* oak gall, gallnut; **-baum,** *m.* oak tree.

Eiche, *f.* oak, gauge, standard.

Eichel, *f.* acorn, glans penis; **-doppe,** *f.* acorn cup; **-förmig,** acorn-shaped, glandiform; **-frucht,** *f.* acorn; **-häher,** *m.* jay (*Garrulus glandarius);* **-kelch,** *m.* acorn cup; **-krone,** *f.* crown of glans; **-mast,** *f.*

acorn (oak) mast; **-zucker,** *m.* acorn sugar, quercitol.

eichen, to gauge, measure, standardize, test, calibrate.

Eichen, *n.* calibration, little egg, ovule.

eichen, oaken, made of oak; **-bestand,** *m.* stand of oak trees, oakwood; **-blättrig,** quercifolious; **-galle,** *f.* oak gall, oak apple; **-gerbsäure,** *f.* quercitannic acid, oak tannin; **-gerbstoff,** *m.* quercitannic acid, oak tannin; **-holz,** *n.* oakwood, oak; **-kern,** *m.* acorn; **-lohe,** *f.* tanbark; **-mehl,** *n.* powdered oak bark.

Eichen-mischwald, *m.* forest chiefly of oak trees; **-reichtum,** *m.* wealth of oak trees; **-rinde,** *f.* oak bark; **-samen,** *m.* acorn; **-schälwald,** *m.* oak-coppice wood, oak forest (for tanbark); **-wickler,** *m.* oak leaf roller.

Eicher, *m.* gauger.

eich-fähig, capable of adjustment; **-gas,** *n.* standard gas; **-holz,** *n.* oakwood, oak; **-horn,** *n.* squirrel; **-hörnchen,** *n.* **kätzchen,** *n.* squirrel; **-kurve,** *f.* calibration curve; **-mass,** *n.* gauge, standard measure; **-meister,** *m.* gauger, adjuster, calibrator; **-nagel,** *m.* gauge mark; **-pfahl,** *m.* calibration post.

Eichung, *f.* gauging standardization, calibration.

Eichwert, *m.* standard value.

Eid, *m.* oath.

Eidechse, *f.* lizard.

Eidechsenwurz, *f.* Sauromatum.

Eiderd(a)unen, *f.pl.* eiderdown.

eidesstattliche Versicherung, *f.* affirmation.

Eidgenoss, *m.* confederate.

Eidotter, *m.* egg yolk; **-fett,** *n.* lecithin.

Eier, *n.pl.* eggs.

Eierchen, *n.* ovule.

Eier-dotter, *m.* yolk, vitellus; **-drüse,** *f.* corpus luteum; **-frucht,** *f.* eggplant; **-gang,** *m.* oviduct; **-kelch,** *m.* egg calyx; **-kuchen,** *m.* omelet, pancake; **-legen,** *n.* laying of eggs, ovipositing (of insects); **-legend,** oviparous; **-nährboden,** *m.* egg (nutrient) medium; **-sack,** *m.* ovarian follicle.

Eier-schale, *f.* **eggshell;** **-schlauch,** *m.* ovarian follicle; **-schwamm,** *m.* chantarelle, mushroom; **-stein,** *m.* oölite, egg stone; **-stock,** *m.* ovary.

Eierstocks-anlage, *f.* rudiment of ovary; **-ei,** *n.* ovarian egg; **-gekröse,** *n.* mesovarium; **-geschwulst,** *f.* tumor on the ovary.

Eifer, *m.* zeal, eagerness, desire, passion; **-sucht,** *f.* jealousy, rivalry.

eiförmig, egg-shaped, oval, ovoid.

eifrig, zealous, eager, ardent, earnest.

Ei-furche, *f.* primitive groove; **-furchung,** *f.* segmentation of the egg.

Ei-gang, *m.* oviduct; **-gelb,** *n.* yolk.

eigen, (*dat.*) own, individual, proper, locally owned, spontaneous, characteristic, specific, special; **das ist ihm** ~, that is peculiar to him; ~ **sein,** to belong to, own, be native (to).

Eigen-art, *f.*-en, peculiarity, individuality; **-artig,** peculiar, singular, original; **-artigerweise,** strange to say, oddly; **-artigkeit,** *f.* peculiarity; **-befruchtung,** *f.* autogamy; **-bewegung,** *f.* spontaneous, individual, or active movement; **-doppelbrechung,** *f.* double refraction; **-drehung,** *f.* spontaneous torsion, proper rotation; **-energie,** *f.* characteristic energy; **-farbe,** *f.* intrinsic (proper) color.

eigen-farbig, self-colored; **-frequenz,** *f.* fundamental (natural) frequency; **-funktion,** *f.* characteristic function; **-gestaltung,** *f.* automorphosis; **-gewicht,** *n.* specific (own) weight; **-händig,** with one's own hand.

Eigenheit, *f.* peculiarity, idiosyncrasy.

Eigen-licht, *n.* own light; **-mächtig,** arbitrar(il)y; **-mittel,** *n.* private funds, specific remedy; **-name,** *m.* proper name; **-nützig,** selfish; **-potential,** *n.* natural potential; **-richtung,** *f.* autotropism; **-wert,** *m.* characteristic number (value).

eigens, expressly.

Eigenschaft, *f.* quality, property, attribute, character, nature, condition; *pl.* good points.

Eigenschafts-verkettung, *f.* correlation; **-wort,** *n.* adjective.

Eigen-schutz, *m.* self-protection; **-schwingung,** *f.* characteristic vibration; **-sinn,** *m.* stubbornness; **-strahlung,** *f.* proper radiation, characteristic radiation; **-süchtig,** selfish, self-seeking.

eigentlich, true, real, proper, essential, actual, properly speaking.

Eigentum, *n.*-er, property.

Eigentümer, *m.* owner.

eigentümlich, (*dat.*) own, characteristic, peculiar.

Eigentümlichkeit, *f.* characteristic, peculiarity.

Eigen-vergiftung, *f.* autointoxication; **-vergrösserung,** *f.* natural size, primary magnification; **-viskosität,** *f.* specific viscosity; **-wärme,** *f.* specific heat, body heat; **-wert,** *m.* proper value; **-zustand,** *m.* characteristic state.

eignen, to suit, qualify, be qualified, be suited; **sich zu etwas** ~, **sich** ~ **für,** to be adapted, be suitable; **geeignet,** suitable, fit, well adapted or qualified.

Eignung, *f.* adaptation, suitability.

Ei-haut, *f.* egg membrane, amniotic membrane, chorion; **-hülle,** *f.* egg membrane, sheath; **-hüllen,** *f.pl.* (sekundäre) embryonic membranes; **-kapsel,** *f.* Graafian follicle; **-kelch,** *m.* egg calyx; **-kern,** *m.* egg nucleus, germinal vesicle; **-knospe,** *f.* oögonium (Chara); **-körper,** *m.* body of ovum; **-kugel,** *f.* oösphere.

Eiland, *n.* island, isle.

Eile, *f.* haste, speed.

Eileiter, *m.* oviduct, Fallopian tube.

eilen, to hasten, hurry.

eilends, quickly.

eilfertig, hasty.

Eilgut, *n.*-er, express goods.

eilig, hasty, speedy.

Eilzug, *m.*-e, fast train.

Eimembran, *n.* egg membrane.

Eimer, *m.*-, bucket, pail.

Eimund, *m.* micropyle.

ein, one; **einer,** some one; **eins,** (numeral) one; **ein für allemal,** once for all; **ein oder ander,** one or another.

ein-achsig, uniaxial, haplocaulic; **-ander,** one another, each other; **-ankerumformer,** *m.* converter; **-armig,** one-armed; **-artig,** of one kind of species, xenogamous.

einarbeiten, to train, break in.

einäschern, to burn to ashes, incinerate, calcine.

Einäscherung, *f.* incineration, calcination.

einatembar, respirable.

einatmen, to inhale.

Einatmung, *f.* inspiration, inhalation.

einatomig, monatomic.

einätzen, to etch in.

einäugig, monocular, one-eyed.

einbadig, single-bath.

Einbalgung, *f.* encystment.

einbalsamieren, to embalm.

Einbalsamierung, *f.* embalming.

Einband, *m.* ̈-e, binding, cover.

einbasig, monobasic.

einbasisch, monobasic.

Einbau, *m.*-ten, building in, installation, mixing in, underplanting.

einbauen, to build in.

Einbeere, *f.* herb Paris, truelove, oneberry (*Paris quadrifolia*).

einbegreifen, to comprise, include, imply.

einbehalten, to keep back, retain.

einbeizen, to etch into.

einbetten, to imbed, heel in.

Einbettung, *f.* imbedding, imbedment.

einbeulen, to bulge.

einbeziehen, to draw in, include, implicate.

einbiegen, to bend in, turn down, inflect.

Einbiegung, *f.* curvature, inflection.

einbilden, to imagine, think, pride oneself.

Einbildung, *f.* imagination, fancy.

Einbildungskraft, *f.* power of imagination.

einbinden, to bind, tie up.

einblasen, to blow in(to), insufflate, inject.

einblättrig, monophyllous, monopetalous.

einbläuen, to blue.

Einblendung, *f.* adjustment, focusing, concentration (of rays).

Einblick, *m.* insight.

einblumig, uniflorous.

einbohren, to bore into.

Einbohrung, *f.* burrowing.

Einbrandtiefe, *f.* penetration of burning or fusion.

einbrechen, to break (in), begin.

einbrennen, to burn in, anneal, cauterize, sulphur, mark.

Einbrennfirnis, *m.* stoving varnish, baking lacquer.

einbringen, to bring in, yield, realize, insert, introduce.

Einbringung, *f.* introduction.

Einbruch, *m.* breaking in, burglary.

einbrüderig, monadelphous.

einbrühen, to scald.

einbuchten, to groove, indent.

Einbuchtung, *f.* indentation, inlet, indenture, rounding, inflection.

einbürgern, to adopt, naturalize; sich ~, to become naturalized, become acclimated, come into use, gain vogue.

Einbusse, *f.* loss, damage.

einbüssen, to lose.

Eindampfapparat, *m.*-e, evaporating apparatus.

eindampfen, to evaporate, concentrate, boil down, inspissate, steam.

Ein-dampfen, *n.* -dampfung, *n.* evaporation.

eindauern, to preserve.

eindecken, to cover, surface.

Eindeckung, *f.* covering, roofing, surfacing.

eindellen, to dent.

Eindellung, *f.* sinking in.

eindeutig, plain, clear, unequivocal, specific.

eindichten, to condense.

Eindicke, *f.* thickening, concentration.

eindicken, to thicken, condense, inspissate, concentrate.

Eindicken, *n.* **Eindickung,** *f.* livering (of paints), bodying (of oils), thickening (of sludges, etc.).

Eindickung, *f.* inspissation, thickening, concentration.

Eindickungsmittel, *n.* thickening agent.

eindimensional, unidimensional.

eindorren, to shrink, dry up.

eindrängen, to force in, intrude.

Eindrehschnecke, *f.* feed screw.

eindringen, to press in, penetrate, infiltrate.

Eindringen, *n.* penetration, entrance, invasion.

eindringlich, impressive, forcible, penetrative.

Eindringling, *m.* invader, intruder.

Eindringungsfähigkeit, *f.* penetrativity, ability to infiltrate.

Eindruck, *m.* ̈-e, impression, sensation; **eindrucken,** to ground in, block in.

eindrücken, to imprint, impress, insert, indent, crush in, flatten (down), compress.

Eindruckfarbe, *f.* grounding in.

eindrucksvoll, impressive.

ein-dunsten, -dünsten, to impregnate with vapor.

Eindunstung, *f.* evaporation.

einebnen, to level, even up, plane, demolish.

eineggen, to harrow in.

eineiig, produced from a single ovum, identical, one-egged.

einen, to unite, form into one.

einengen, to compress, confine, concentrate, narrow down, contract.

Einer, *m.* unit, digit.

einer, one.

einerlei, of one kind, all the same; ~ **ob,** regardless of whether; **es ist mir ~,** it is all the same to me.

einernten, to gather, harvest.

einerseits, einesteils, on the one hand.

einfach, simple, single, incomposite, elementary, primitive, plain, mono-, proto-; **-basisch,** monobasic; **-blättrig,** simple leaved; **-brechend,** singly refracting; **-brechung,** *f.* simple refraction; **-bromjod,** *m.* iodine monobromide; **-chlorschwefel,** *m.* protochloride of sulphur; **-chlorzinn,** *n.* protochloride of tin, stannous chloride.

einfacher Körper, *n.* element, simple substance.

einfächerig, simple one-celled, single, unilocular, monolocular.

einfachfrei, univariant, having one degree of freedom.

Einfachheit, *f.* simplicity, singleness.

einfach-kammig, single-combed; **-kohlensauer,** neutral carbonate of; **-typus,** *m.* simple type; **-wirkend,** single-acting.

einfädeln, to thread, contrive.

einfahren, to drive in, carry in, get in, break in.

Einfahrt, *f.***-en,** entrance, drive, entering.

Einfall, *m.*̈**e,** falling in, fall, inroad, idea, incidence.

einfallen, to fall upon, fall in, interrupt, dip, be incident; **es fällt mir gerade ein,** it just comes to my mind, it just occurs to me.

einfallend, incident.

Einfalls-lot, *n.* perpendicular; **-richtung,** *f.* direction of incidence; **-stelle,** *f.* point of incidence; **-schacht,** *m.* drop shaft; **-strahl,** *m.* incident ray; **-winkel,** *m.* angle of incidence.

Einfalt, *f.* simplicity, simpleness.

einfangen, to capture, catch, seize.

Einfangung, *f.* capture.

einfärben, to color.

einfarbig, one-colored, monochromatic.

Einfärbung, *f.* inking, steeping in dye, imbibition (of paints).

einfassen, to enclose, barrel, bind, set, border, surround.

Einfehmung, *f.* pannage.

einfetten, to grease, oil, lubricate.

Einfettung, *f.* greasing, oiling, lubrication.

einfeuchten, to moisten, dampen, wet.

einfinden, to appear.

einflechten, to weave in, interlace, insert.

einfliessen, to flow in, come in.

einflössen, to instill, infuse.

Einfluss, *m.* influence, influx, bearing effect.

einflussreich, influential.

Einfluss-rohr, *n.* **-röhre,** *f.* inlet pipe.

einformen, to mold.

einförmig, uniform, monotonous.

einfressen, to corrode, devour.

einfriedigen, to fence, enclose.

Einfriedigung, *f.* fencing, enclosure.

einfrieren, to freeze up.

einfügen, to insert, inosculate, fit in, inoculate, rabbet, secure.

Einfügung, *f.* insertion, fitting.

Einfügungsstelle, *f.* point of insertion.

Einfuhr, *f.* import(ation), supply.

einführen, to introduce, import, inaugurate, insert, feed into.

Einfuhröffnung, *f.* orifice for intake.

Einführung, *f.* introduction, importation, installation.

Einfuhrwaren, *f.pl.* imports.

einfüllen, to fill (in), pour in.

Einfüll-stoff, *m.* filling, packing; **-trichter,** *m.* funnel tube.

Eingabe, *f.* presentation, petition, application.

eingablig, single-forked, single-pronged.

Eingang, *m.*̈**e,** entrance, importation, shrinkage (of fabric), orifice, mouth, receipt; ~ **finden,** to find acceptance.

Ein-gänger, *m.* **-siedler,** *m.* solitary boar.

eingängig, single-thread.

eingangs, at the beginning, outset; **-öffnung,** *f.* opening of entrance; **-pforte,** *f.* opening porta.

ein-geben, to give, administer; **-gebettet,** imbedded; **-gebildet** (-bilden), imaginary, conceited, presumptuous; **-gebogen** (-biegen), inflexed, infected, sinuous, crenated; **-geboren,** inborn, innate, native, indigenous; -gebuchtet, sinuous; -gebürgert, established, adopted; -gedenk, mindful; -gedickt, thickened; -geengt, local.

ein-gefaltet, plicate; -gefügt, inserted; -gegangen (-gehen), entered, perished.

eingehen, to go in, come in, enter, arrive, shrink, contract, cease, aggress, perish; auf etwas ∼, to agree to something, deal with, mention.

ein-gehend, going in, thorough(ly); exhaustive(ly), in detail; -gehüllt, involucrate; -gekerbt, grooved; -geklemmt, squeezed in, grasped, clamped; -gekrümmt, incurved; -gelagert, embedded, enclosed; -gelassen, countersunk (of screws); -gemacht, preserved; -gemachtes, n. preserves; -genommen (-nehmen), prejudiced, heavy, dizzy.

ein-gerichtet, arranged; -gerollt, involuted; -gesalzen, salted, corned; -geschichtet (einschichten), embedded; -geschlagen, induplicated; -geschlechtig, unisexual, diclinous; -geschliffen, ground-in (glass stopper); -geschlossen (-schliessen), enclosed, included; -geschmolzen (einschmelzen), fused; -geschnitten, incised.

ein-geschoben (-schieben), inserted, interpolated; -geschränkt, cramped, limited; -geschrieben, imprinted, inscribed, enclosed; -gespannt, with fixed ends; -gesprengt, scattered, interspersed; -gestehen, to confess, admit, own (up); -gestellt sein, to be focused; -gestülpt, incurved, invaginated; -gewachsen, grown in.

Eingeweide, n. bowels, viscera, intestine, entrails; -arterie, f. cardiac artery, coeliac axis; -ganglion, n. visceral ganglion; geflecht, n. visceral or solar plexus; -höhle, f. visceral cavity; -knäuel, m. intestinal coil, knotting.

Eingeweide-lehre, f. splanchnology, enterology; -muskel, f. intestinal muscle; -nervensystem, n. visceral nervous system; -sack, m. visceral or intestinal sac; -schlagader, f. coeliac artery; -wurm, m. intestinal parasite, entozoon.

ein-gewickelt, involute, convolute; -gewühlt, dug in, buried in the ground; -gewurzelt, deep rooted; -gezogen, retracted, secluded.

eingiessen, to pour in, infuse.

Eingiessung, f. pouring in, infusion, transfusion.

Eingitterröhre, f. Triode.

eingleisig, single-track, single line.

eingliederige Zahlengrösse, f. monomial.

eingliedern, sich, to fit in, make oneself a part of.

Eingliederung, f. classification, division, insertion.

eingraben, to dig in, bury, engrave, furrow.

eingreifen, to catch, lock, intervene, interlock, act, invade, infringe.

Eingreifen, n. intervention, interference, action, infringement.

eingreifend, effective, radical.

eingrenzen, to enclose, limit, localize.

Eingriff, m.-e, interference, action, treatment, method of attack, connection; im ∼, in gear.

Einguss, m. pouring in, infusion, mold.

einhägen, to fence in.

einhaken, to hook in, fasten.

Einhalt, m. check, interruption, restraint.

einhalten, to check, stop, keep (in), cease, prohibit, adhere to (directions).

einhändig, singlehanded.

einhändigen, to hand over, deliver.

Einhängeblende, f. interchangeable diaphragm.

einhängen, to suspend into.

einharken, to rake in.

einhauen, to cut in, cut open, break in.

einhäusig, monoecious.

Einhäusigkeit, f. monoecia.

einhegen, to fence in.

einheimisch, indigenous, native, domestic, endemic.

Einheit, f. unit, unity, uniformity.

einheitlich, undivided, united, uniform, homogeneous.

Einheitlichkeit, f. uniformity, homogeneity, centralization.

Einheits-eigenschaften, f.pl. uniform properties; -masse, f. unit mass; -quantität, f. single quantity.

einhellig, unanimous.

einhelmig, monandrous.

einher, along; ∼ gehen, to proceed, activate, go along, accompany; ∼ schreiten, to walk along.

einholen, to overtake, make up, obtain, haul in.

einhüllen, to wrap up, imbed, cover, envelop; einhüllende Kurve, f. envelope.

einig, (gen.) united, in accord, one, one only.

einige, some, several, a few; **nach einiger Zeit,** after a time; **in einigen Fällen,** in some cases.

einigen, to unite, unify; **sich ~,** to come to an agreement.

einigen, *dat. pl.* to or for some.

einigermassen, in some degree, to some extent, somewhat.

einiges, something, some things.

Einigkeit, *f.* unity, agreement, harmony.

Einigungskitt, *m.* cement, putty.

einimpfen, to inoculate.

Einimpfung, inoculation, vaccination.

einjährig, of one year, annual.

einkalken, to lime, treat in lime water.

einkammerig, monothalamous, monocystic, unilocular, single-chambered.

Einkapselung, *f.* encystment, encapsulation.

Einkauf, *m.¨e,* buying, purchase.

einkehren, to enter, turn in.

einkeilen, to wedge in.

einkellern, to store in a cellar, lay in or up.

einkerben, to notch, indent.

Einkerbung, *f.* notching, incisure, indentation.

einkernig, uninucleate, mononuclear.

einklammern, to enclose in brackets or parentheses, cramp.

Einklang, *m.¨e,* harmony, unison, accord; **im ~ stehen mit,** to be in harmony with, agree with.

einklappig, univalvular.

einkleiden, to clothe, dress.

Einknickung, *f.* flexure, folding, bending.

einkochen, to boil down, evaporate, condense.

Einkochung, *f.* boiling down, evaporation.

Einkommen, *n.* income, revenue, proceeds.

Einkristall, *m.* single crystal.

Einkünfte, *f.pl.* income, revenue.

einkürzen, to curtail, shorten, cut back, reduce.

einlaben, to coagulate.

einladen, to load in, invite.

Einlage, *f.* laying in, insertion, enclosure, filler, deposit, investment.

einlagern, to infiltrate, embed, deposit, intercalate, store.

Einlagerung, *f.* infiltration. deposition, deposit, stratification.

Einlagerungsverbindung, *f.* intercalation compound.

Einlass, *m.¨e,* inlet, letting in, admission.

einlassen, to let in, admit, insert, introduce. countersink (a screw); **sich auf etwas ~,** to engage in something, have to do with something.

Einlass-pore, *f.* incurrent canal (of a sponge); **-rohr,** *n.* inlet tube or pipe; **-stück,** *n.* insert; **-ventil,** *n.* inlet valve.

Einlauf, *m.¨e,* cylsma, inlet; **-bauwerk,** *n.* intake structure.

einlaufecht, unshrinkable.

einlaufen, to enter, arrive, contract, shrink, receive; come to hand.

Einlaufgitter, *n.* trash rack.

einlaugen, to soak in lye.

einleben, to become familiar.

einlegen, to put, place, lay (in), embed, soak, steep, pickle, preserve, put up, insert; **sich für jemand ~,** to intercede for someone.

einleiten, to introduce, conduct, inject, preface, initiate, start, feed into, pass in.

Einleitung, *f.* introduction, preface, preparation.

Einleitungsrohr, *n.* delivery tube.

einlenken, to articulate.

Einlenkung, *f.* articulation.

einleuchten, to be clear.

einleuchtend, evident, obvious.

einliefern, to deliver.

einlippig, unilabiate.

einlöten, to solder in.

einmachen, to preserve, can, conserve, pickle, knead.

Einmach-essig, *m.* pickling vinegar; **-salz,** *n.* preserving salt.

einmaischen, to dough in (malt), mash in, mix in, blend.

einmal, once, first, ever; **auf ~,** all at once, suddenly; **nicht ~,** not even; **noch ~,** once more; **~ . . . , zum andern,** at one time . . . at another time.

Einmaleins, *n.* multiplication table.

einmalig, single, solitary, occurring but once.

einmarinieren, to pickle (herring).

einmauern, to wall in, enclose, embed.

einmengen, to intermix, interfere with.

einmieten, to store (potatoes), put away.

Einmieter, *m.* tenant, inquiline.

einmischen, to mix in, intermix, blend, interfere.

Einmischung, *f.* introduction, mixture.

einmitten, to center, adjust (a lens).

einmünden, to empty, discharge, inosculate, enter, fit (in).

einmütig, of one mind, united, unanimous.

Einnahme, *f.* taking in, receipt(s), income.

einnehmen, to occupy, take (in), receive, collect, captivate, overcome.

Einöde, *f.* desert, wild.

einölen, to oil, lubricate.

einordnen, to arrange, classify.

Einordnung, *f.* arrangement, classification.

einpacken, to pack, embed.

einpassen, to fit (in), adjust.

einpflanzen, to inoculate, graft, implant.

Einpflanzung, *f.* implantation.

Einphasen-anker, *m.* single-phase armature; **-leitung,** *f.* single-phase wiring.

einphasig, one-phase, single-phase.

einpökeln, to pickle, cure, corn.

einpolig, unipolar.

einprägen, to impress, imprint.

einprägsam, impressive.

einpressen, to press, compress, force in.

einprozentig, one per cent.

einpudern, to powder.

einpumpen, to pump in.

einquantig, single, of one quantum.

einquellen, to steep, soak.

einrahmen, to frame.

Einrahmung, *f.* framing.

einrammen, to drive (piles).

einräuchern, to fumigate, smoke.

Einräucherung, *f.* fumigation.

einräumen, to furnish, stow away, yield, concede, admit.

einrechnen, to include.

Einrede, *f.* objection, protest.

einreden, to talk into. interrupt, object, suggest.

einreiben, to rub in, smear, grease.

Einreibesalbe, *f.* rubbing ointment, liniment.

Einreibung, *f.* rubbing in, liniment, embrocation.

Einreibungsmittel, *n.* liniment. embrocation.

einreichen, to deliver, hand in, present.

einreihen, to (ar)range, insert, enroll.

einreihig, single series, unilateral.

einreissen, to rend, tear, demolish, spread.

Einreissfestigkeit, *f.* tearing strength.

einrennen, to melt or run down.

einrichten, to arrange, adjust, install, manage, organize; **sich ~,** to establish oneself.

Einrichtung, *f.* arrangement, contrivance, establishment, equipment, furniture, setting, organization, adaptation.

Einrichtungs-erneuerung, *f.* renewal of working plans; **-werk,** *n.* working plan.

Einriss, *m.* rent, fissure, crack.

einrollen, to roll in, curl (paper).

Einrollung, *f.* involution.

einrosten, to rust in, become rusty.

einrücken, to insert, throw in, engage.

einrühren, to mix, stir (up or in), beat (eggs).

einrussen, to cover with soot.

Eins, *f.,* **eins,** one; **~ sein,** *n.* union, unity; **~ werden,** *n.* unification, agreement.

Einsaat, *f.* seeding, seed (for sowing).

Einsackung, *f.* encystment, invagination.

einsäen, to sow (in).

einsalben, to grease, anoint, embalm.

einsalzen, to salt (down), corn, pickle.

Einsalzung, *f.* salting.

einsam, lonely, solitary, retired.

einsamenlappig, monocotyledonous.

einsamig, monospermous, with one seed.

einsammeln, to gather, collect, pick.

Einsatz, *m.* ̈-e, insertion, putting in, deposit, batch, charge, extension, segment; **-blende,** *f.* interchangeable diaphragm; **-gewichte,** *n.pl.* set of weights; **-härtung,** *f.* casehardening; **-korb,** *m.* test-tube cage; **öffnung,** *f.* charging opening; **-pulver,** *n.* cementing powder; **-schicht,** *f.* case; **-stück,** *n.* inserted piece.

einsäuern, to acidify, sour, ensilage, pickle (in vinegar), leaven.

Einsäuerung, *f.* acidification, souring, pickling, leavening, ensilage formation.

Einsaugader, *f.* absorbent vessel.

Einsaugemittel, *n.* absorbent.

einsaugen, to absorb, suck (up or in), soak in.

einsaugend, absorbent, absorptive.

Einsaugung, *f.* absorption, imbibition, suction.

Einsaugungsfähigkeit, *f.* absorptivity.

einsäurig, monoacid.

einschalig, univalvate, univalve.

einschalten, to put in, insert, intercalate, introduce, connect, interpolate, switch in or on.

Einschalter, *m.*-, circuit closer, switch.

einschärfen, to inculcate, enjoin, impress.

einschätzen, to estimate, evaluate.

Einschätzung, *f.* assessment.

einschenken, to pour in or out into.

einschichten, to embed, stratify, arrange in layers.

einschichtig, one-layered, single.

einschieben, to shove in, put in, insert.

Einschiebung, *f.* interpolation, shoving in.

Einschiessen, *n.* ranging.

einschiffig, one-aisled (of a building).

einschlafen, to fall asleep.

einschläfern, to narcotize, lull, make drowsy.

einschläfernd, narcotic, soporific, hypnotic.

Einschläferungsmittel, *n.* sporofic, narcotic, opiate.

Einschlag, *m.*-̈e, wrapper, envelope, plait, fold, handshake, nursery (for young trees), felling, return.

einschlagen, to wrap up, strike in, drive in, break, punch, cover, follow, adopt, sink in, succeed, shake hands, bandage, heel in, embed in earth.

Einschlagen, *n.* heeling in (nursery stock).

einschlägig, belonging, appertaining, relating to, respective, appropriate.

Einschlag-lupe, *f.* folding magnifier, pocket lens; **-papier,** *n.* wrapping paper.

einschlämmen, to fill up (with silt).

einschleichen, to creep, crawl in.

einschleifen, to grind in, engrave, cut in.

Einschleppung, *f.* introduction, importation.

einschliessen, to include, enclose, surround, seal in, embed, confine, form (an angle).

einschliesslich, inclusive(ly), including.

Einschliessung, *f.* inclusion.

einschlucken, to gulp down, absorb.

einschlüpfen, to slip in.

einschlürfen, to sip in.

Einschluss, *m.*-̈e, inclusion; **-mittel,** *n.* embedding, medium, mounting medium;

-rohr, *n.* sealed tube; **-thermometer,** *n.* enclosed-scale thermometer.

einschmalzen, to grease, oil.

einschmauchen, to smoke, fumigate.

einschmelzen, to melt down, fuse.

Einschmelz-glas, *n.* fusible glass; **-rohr,** *n.* sealing tube; **-röhre,** *f.* sealing tube.

einschmieren, to smear, grease, lubricate.

Einschmierung, *f.* greasing, lubrication, inunction.

einschneiden, to cut (in), cut up, cut out, notch, indent, triangulate.

einschneidend, incisive.

Einschnitt, *m.*-̈e, incision, cut, notch, indentation, excavation.

einschnittig, (in) single shear.

einschnüren, to constrict, strangulate, lace up, contract.

einschnürig, irregular (bole), curved.

Einschnürung, *f.* constriction, binding up stricture, choking, contraction, necking, reduction in area.

einschränken, to restrict, confine, limit, restrain, retard.

Einschränkung, *f.* limitation, restriction, reservation.

einschreiben, to enter, inscribe, note, register, record.

einschrumpfen, to shrink, shrivel, dry up, desiccate.

einschütten, to pour in, put in.

einschwärzen, to blacken, ink.

einschwefeln, to sulphur, sulphurize.

einschwöden, to daub with ashes and lime.

einsehen, to look into, understand, comprehend, perceive.

Einsehen, *n.* insight, investigation, judgment, consideration.

einseifen, to soap.

ein-seigen, -seihen, to infiltrate.

einseitig, unilateral, one-sided, unbalanced, partial, biased; **-blühend,** secundiflorus.

einseitiger Bastard, *m.* a hybrid resembling only one parent.

einseitiger Hoftüpfel, *m.* half-bordered pit.

Einseitkiemer, *m.pl.* Monopleurobranchia (conch).

einseitwendig, unilateral, homomallous, turning on one side.

einsenden, to send in.

einsenken, to sink, immerse, dip, plant, cove, depression.

Einsenkung, *f.* indentation, sinking in.

einsetzen, to set in, put in, insert, plant, preserve, establish, stake; **sich ~ für,** to go in for, support, intervene.

Einsetzen, *n.* setting in, putting in, insertion, installation, establishment, casehardening.

Einsetz-gewichte, *n.pl.* set of weights; **-tür,** *f.* charging door.

Einsicht, *f.* examination, understanding, insight, intelligence, opinion.

einsichtig, intelligent, judicious, sensible.

einsickern, to trickle in, sink in, infiltrate.

einsieden, to boil down.

Einsiedler, *m.* hermit.

einsondern, to secrete internally.

Einsonderungsdrüse, *f.* endocrine gland.

einspannen, to frame, fasten in, insert, stretch, clamp, attach, restrain, fix.

Einspannungsmoment, *n.* (fixed) end moment.

einspeicheln, to salivate, be salivated.

einspielen, to practice, balance.

Einsprache, *f.* objection, protest, exception.

einsprengen, to sprinkle, intersperse, mix, burst (open), intermingle, admix, disseminate, interstratify.

einspringen, to leap or spring at, re-enter, catch in, shrink, contract.

einspritzen, to insert, inject, squirt in, syringe, grout.

Einspritz-hahn, *m.⁻e,* injection cock or tube; **-karburetter,** *m.* spray carburetor; **-röhre,** *f.* injection cock or tube.

Einspritzung, *f.* injection.

Einspruch, *m.⁻e,* objection, exception.

Einsprung, *m.* shrinkage (of fabric).

einst, some day, once.

einstampfen, to ram down, stamp, reduce, pulverize, rod.

Einstandspreis, *m.-e,* cost price.

einstäuben, to dust, powder.

einstechen, to perforate, stick in, pierce.

einstehen, to answer, guarantee.

einsteigen, to step into, enter.

Einsteigschacht, *m.* manhole.

einstellbar, adjustable.

einstellen, to put in, set in, standardize, discontinue, stop, suspend, regulate, lay up, focus, adjust, engage, make up (to).

Einsteller, *m.* regulator, thermostat.

Einstellfläche, *f.* surface of reference.

einstellig, one place, unit; **einstellige Zahl,** unit, one digit number.

Einstell-lupe, *f.* focusing lens; **-marke,** *f.* reference mark; **-raum,** *m.* garage; **-scheibe,** *f.* focusing screen.

Einstellung, *f.* adjustment, attitude, presentation, reference, suspension, strike, discontinuance.

Einstellungs-bewegung, *f.* focusing movement; **-ebene,** *f.* focusing plane, plane of reference; **-fläche,** *f.* surface of reference; **-vermögen,** *n.* provision for adjustment.

Einstich, *m.-e,* puncture, injection, incision; **-injektion,** *f.* interstitial injection; **-linie,** *f.* line of stab (in stab culture).

einstig, former, previous, future.

einstimmen, to agree, accord, harmonize.

einstimmig, unanimous.

einstossen, to thrust in, ram down, break.

einstrahlen, to radiate upon.

Einstrahler, *m.* uniaxial spicule.

Einstrahlung, *f.* irradiation.

einstreichen, to rub, nick, slit, fill up, take in.

einstreuen, to strew, sprinkle, intersperse.

Einstreumaterial, *n.* bedding material.

einströmen, to stream in, flow in.

Einströmungs-öffnung, *f.* inhalant opening or siphon; **-rohr,** *n.* **-röhre,** *f.* inlet tube or pipe, steam pipe.

Einströmventil, *n.* inlet valve.

einstufig, haplocaulic, single-stage.

einstülpen, to turn inward, invaginate.

Einstülpung, *f.* invagination, inversion.

Einstülpungsöffnung, *f.* aperture of invagination.

einstündig, of an hour's duration.

einstürzen, to fall in, collapse.

einstutzen, to cut back.

einstweilen, meanwhile.

einsumpfen, to wet, soak.

einsüssen, to sweeten (ensilage).

eintägig, ephemeral, lasting one day.

Eintags-blüte, *f.* ephemeral flower; **-fliege,** *f.* May fly, dayfly, ephemeral fly.

eintauchen, to dip, plunge, immerse, steep.

Eintauchfläche, *f.* immersed area.

Eintauchung, *f.* immersion.

Eintausch, *m.* exchange, bartering.

eintauschen, to exchange.

einteigen, to make into paste or dough.

einteilen, to divide, distribute, classify, separate; in Grade ∼, to graduate.

einteilig, one-part, single.

Einteilung, *f.* division, graduation, separation, distribution, classification.

eintönig, monotonous, pure (of a stand).

Eintopfgericht, *n.*-e, one-course dinner, stew.

Eintracht, *f.* harmony, unity.

Eintrag, *m.*^{:-}e, entry, registration, damage, prejudice, furnish (paper manufacturing).

eintragen, to carry in, introduce, enter, record, register, yield, produce.

einträglich, profitable.

Eintragung, *f.* carrying in, entry, inoculation, registration, detriment.

eintränken, to soak, steep, impregnate.

einträufeln, to drop in, instill.

eintreffen, to arrive, happen, come true.

eintreiben, to drive in, rub in, collect.

eintreten, to enter, set in, commence, occur, happen, tread in or down, intercede; für etwas ∼, to champion something.

Eintreten, *n.* beginning, occurrence.

eintrichtern, to pour in with a funnel.

Eintrieb *m.* pannage.

entriebig, one-stemmed.

Eintritt, *m.* entrance, beginning, entry, accession, admission, appearance, incidence.

Eintritts-stelle, *f.* inlet, place of entry; -temperatur, *f.* inlet temperature.

eintrocknen, to dry (up), desiccate, shrink (in drying).

ein-tropfen, -tröpfeln, to drop in, instill.

einüben, to practice.

ein-und-einachsig, orthorhombic.

einverleiben, to embody, incorporate.

Einverleibung, *f.* incorporation.

Einvernehmung, *f.* understanding, agreement.

einverstanden, agreed.

Einverständnis, *n.* agreement, understanding, intelligence.

Einwaage, *f.* Einwägung, *f.* amount weighed, sample.

einwachsen, to grow into.

einwägen, to weigh in, level.

einwalzen, to roll (into or down).

Einwand, *m.*^{:-}e, objection, exception.

einwandern, to immigrate.

einwandfrei, unobjectionable, incontestable, satisfactory, perfect.

einwärts, inward; -beugung, *f.* pronation; -dreher, *m.* pronator muscle; -gebogen, inflexed; -wender, *m.* pronator muscle; -zieher, *m.* adductor muscle.

einwässerig, one-bath.

einwässern, to lay, steep or soak (in water).

Einwässerung, *f.* steeping, soaking.

einweben, to weave in.

einweibig, monogynous, asexual.

einweichen, to steep, soak, soften, macerate infuse.

Einweichung, *f.* steeping.

Einweihung, *f.* dedication.

einwenden, to object, oppose.

einwerfen, to throw in.

einwertig, monovalent, univalent.

einwickeln, to wrap up, envelop, enclose.

einwilligen, to consent, approve.

einwirken, to act, influence, work in.

Einwirkung, *f.* action, influence, impression, effect.

Einwirkungsdauer, *f.* duration of action.

Einwohner, *m.* inhabitant.

Einwucherungsstelle, *f.* point of inward proliferation.

Einwurf, *m.* objection, reply, insertion, slot.

einwurzeln, to root; fest eingewurzelt, firmly rooted.

Einzahl, *f.* single number.

Einzahlung, *f.* payment.

einzäunen, to fence.

Einzäunung, *f.* fencing, enclosure.

einzehren, to suffer loss (consume) by evaporation.

Einzehrung, *f.* loss by evaporation.

einzeichnen, to mark in, note, subscribe.

einzel, individual, single, particular, sole, simple, separate; -anführung, *f.* specification; -aufsatz, *m.* individual article, single attachment; -auge, *n.* cyclops· -baum, *m.* single tree; -beobachtung, *f.*

single observation; **-bestand,** *m.* a single stand, an individual association; **-bestim-mung,** *f.* single determination; **-bewegung,** *f.* single movement; **-bild,** *n.* individual image.

Einzel-blatt, *n.* single leaf; **-darstellung,** *f.* single presentation, separate treatment; **-entdeckung,** *f.* individual discovery; **-erscheinung,** *f.* isolated phenomenon; **-fall,** *m.* particular case; **-frucht,** *f.* simple fruit; **-gabe,** *f.* single dose; **-gebiet,** *n.* separate department; **-gebrauch,** *m.* individual use; **-gefühl,** *n.* solitary feeling; **-grenze,** *f.* individual limit.

Einzelheit, *f.*-en, detail, particular, singleness.

Einzel-induktionsschlag, single-induction shock; **-kokken,** *m.pl.* discrete cocci; **-koralle,** *f.* individual polyp; **-kornstruktur,** *f.* single-grain structure; **-last,** *f.* concentrated load.

Einzellenstadium, *n.* unicellular stage.

einzellig, single-celled, unicellular.

Einzel-meinung, *f.*-en, individual opinion; **-mischung,** *f.* mixture by single trees or isolated plants.

einzeln, individual, single, separate, one by one, singly.

Einzelne, *n.* detail; **im einzelnen,** individually, separately, in detail; **ins einzelne gehend,** down to the minutest details.

Einzel-nuss, *f.* achene, individual nutlet; **-pflanzung,** *f.* planting by single trees; **-potential,** *n.* single potential; **-stand,** *m.* scattering stand of single trees; **-stehend,** scattering, isolated; **-teil,** *m.* single (separate) part; **-teilchen,** *n.* single particle; **-titer,** *m.* filament denier; **-vergrösserung,** *f.* primary magnification.

Einzel-verkauf, *m.* retail; **-zelle,** *f.* individual cell; **-zucht,** *f.* individual selection.

einziehbar, retractible, recoverable.

einziehen, to draw in, pull in, absorb, inhale, inspire, reduce, level, fill up, lessen, collect, confiscate, infiltrate, enter, shrink, contract, retire, soak in.

Einziehungsmittel, *n.* absorbent.

einzig, only single, alone, unique, sole; ~ **und allein,** solely, purely, entirely.

einzigartig, unique.

einzuckern, to sugar, preserve.

Einzug, *m.*-e, entry, entrance.

Einzugsgebiet, *n.*-e, catchment area, watershed, drainage area.

Ei-oberfläche, *f.* surface of ovum; **-querschnitt,** *m.* egg-shaped section; **-reifung,** *f.* maturation of the ovum; **-röhre,** *f.* ovariole, ovarian duct; **-rund,** oval.

Eis, *n.* ice; **-abkühlung,** *f.* cooling or refrigeration (with ice).

Eisack, *m.* yolk sac.

eis-ähnlich, icelike, glacial; **-alaun,** *m.* rock alum; **-ansatz,** *m.* layer of ice; **-artig,** icelike, glacial; **-bär,** *m.* polar bear; **-beere,** *f.* snowberry (*Chiococca racemosa*); **-bruch,** *m.* breaking up of ice.

Eischale, *f.* eggshell.

Eischalenhaut, *f.*-e, envelope of ovum.

Eisdecke, *f.* sheet of ice.

Eisen, *n.* iron, iron instrument, horseshoe; **-abbrand,** *m.* iron waste; **-abfälle,** *m.pl.* scrap iron; **-ablagerung,** *f.* deposit of iron; **-ähnlich,** ironlike, ferruginous, chalybeate; **-alaun,** *m.* iron alum; **-ammonalaun,** *m.* ammonium ferric alum; **-antimonerz,** *n.* **-antimonglanz,** *m.* berthierite; **-arm,** poor in iron; **-arsenik,** *n.* iron arsenide.

Eisen-artig, ironlike, ferruginous, chalybeate; **-arznei,** *f.* ferruginous remedy; **-asbest,** *m.* fibrous silica; **-aufnahme,** *f.* absorption of iron; **-bad,** *m.*-er, iron bath (containing salts); **-bahn,** *f.* railroad, railway; **-bahnschwelle,** *f.* railroad sleeper, tie; **-bahnzug,** *m.* railroad train; **-bakterien,** *n.pl.* iron bacteria; **-bedarf,** *m.* iron requirement; **-beizung,** *f.* use of iron mordant, pickling.

Eisen-beton, *m.* reinforced concrete; **-blauerde,** *f.* earthy vivianite; **-blausäure,** *f.* ferrocyanic acid; **-blech,** *n.* sheet iron, iron plate; **-blende,** *f.* pitchblende; **-blumen,** *f.pl.* iron flowers, ferric chloride; **-blüte,** *f.* flos ferri aragonite; **-bromürbromid,** *n.* ferrosoferric bromide; **-brühe,** *f.* iron mordant; **-carbid,** *n.* carbide of iron.

Eisen-chlorid, *n.* iron chloride, ferric chloride; **-chlorür,** *n.* ferrous chloride; **-chrysolith,** *m.* hyalosiderite, fayalite; **-cyanfarbe,** *f.* iron-cyanogen pigment; **-cyanür,** *n.* ferrous cyanide; **-draht,** *m.* steel wire; **-drahtnetz,** *n.* steel; **-einlage,** *f.* steel (reinforcement) insert, netting; **-erde,** *f.* ferruginous earth, iron earth; **-erz,** *n.* iron ore.

Eisen-farbe, *f.* iron gray; **-feinschlacke,** *f.* iron-refinery slag; **-fleckigkeit,** *f.* stain, internal rust spot; **-flüssigkeit,** *f.* iron liquid or liquor; **-frischflammofen,** *m.* puddling furnace; **-führend,** iron-bearing, ferriferous; **-gang,** *m.* iron lode, iron-ore vein; **-gans,** *f.* iron pig; **-gehalt,** *m.* iron content; **-glanz,** *m.* iron glance, specular iron.

Eisen-glas, *n.* fayalite; **-glimmer,** *m.* micaceous iron ore; **-graupen,** *f.pl.* granular bog iron ore; **-grund,** *m.* iron liquor; **-guss,** *m.* iron casting, cast iron; **-haltig,** containing iron; **-hart,** *m.* ferriferous gold sand; **-hochbau,** *m.* steel (iron) skeleton construction.

Eisenhut, *m.* aconite monk's hood, (*Aconitum napellus*); **-blätterig,** aconitifolious.

Eisen-hydroxydul, *n.* ferrous hydroxyde; **-jodid,** *n.* iron (ferric) iodide; **-jodür,** *n.* ferrous iodide; **-jodürjodid,** *n.* ferrosoferric iodide; **-kalium,** *n.* potassium ferrate; **-kies,** *m.* pyrite; **-kiesel,** *m.* ferruginous flint; **-kitt,** *m.* iron-rust cement; **-kobalterz,** *n.* **-kobaltkies,** *m.* cobaltite; **-kohlenoxyd,** *n.* iron carboxide.

Eisen-kohlenstoff, *m.* iron carbide; **-kraut,** *n.* vervain; **-krautgewächse,** *n.pl.* Verbenaceae; **-lebererz,** *n.* hepatic iron ore; **-lichtfunken,** *m.* iron arc spark; **-magnetisch,** ferromagnetic; **-manganerz,** *n.* manganiferous iron ore; **-mann,** *m.* scaly red hematite; **-mennige,** *f.* red ocher; **-mittel,** *n.* iron tonic, ferruginous remedy.

Eisen-mohr, *m.* ethiops martial, earthy magnetite, **-mulm,** *m.* earthy iron ore; **-nickelkies,** *m.* pentlandite; **-niere,** *f.* eaglestone; **-ocker,** *m.* (iron) ocher; **-oxychlorid,** *n.* ferric oxychloride.

Eisenoxyd, *n.* iron oxide, ferric oxide; **-hydrat,** *n.* ferric hydroxide.

Eisen-oxydul, *n.* ferrosoferric oxide; **-salz,** *n.* ferric salt.

Eisenoxydul, *n.* protoxide of iron, ferrous oxide; **-hydrat,** *n.* ferrous hydroxide; **-oxyd,** *n.* ferrosoferric oxide, magnetic iron oxide; **-salz,** *n.* ferrous salt.

Eisen-oxydverbindung, *f.* ferric compound; **-pastille,** *f.* iron lozenge; **-pecherz,** *n.* limonite; **-pulver,** *n.* iron dust; **-rahm,** *m.* a porous form of hematite; **-resin,** *m.* humboldtine; **-rhodanid,** *n.* ferric (thiocyanate) sulphocyanate; **-rhodanür,** *n.* ferrous (thiocyanate) sulphocyanate; **-rogenstein,** *m.* oölitic iron ore; **-rost,** *m.* iron rust; **-rot,** *n.* clocothar.

Eisen-salmiak, *m.* ammoniated iron; **-säuerling,** *m.* chalybeate water; **-säure,** *f.* ferric acid; **-schaum,** *m.* kish; **-schiene,** *f.* iron rail; **-schüssig,** containing iron, ferruginous; **-schwarz,** *n.* iron black graphite; lampblack; copperas black; **-schwärze,** *f.* graphite, earthy magnetite, currier's ink; **-selenür,** *n.* ferrous selenide; **-silberglanz,** *m.* sternbergite.

Eisen-sinter, *m.* pitticite, iron dross; **-spat,** *m.* siderite, spathic iron; **-spiegel,** *m.* specular iron; **-stange,** *f.* iron bar; **-stein,** *m.* ironstone, iron ore; **-steinmark,** *n.* lithomarge containing iron; **-stückchen,** *n.* scrap of iron; **-sumpferz,** *n.* bog iron ore; **-titan,** *n.* ferrotitanium; ilmenite; **-ton,** *m.* clay ironstone, iron clay.

Eisen-tongranat, *m.* almandite; **-vitriol,** *n.* iron vitriol, hydrous ferrous, sulphate; **-wasser,** *n.* chalybeate (iron) water; **weinstein,** *m.* iron and potassium tartrate, tartrated iron; **-werk,** *m.* iron works; **-zinkblende,** *f.* marmatite; **-zinkspat,** *m* ferruginous calamine; **-zinnerz,** *n.* ferriferous cassiterite; **-zucker,** *m.* saccharated ferric oxide.

eisern, made of iron.

Eis-essig, *m.* glacial acetic acid; **-gekühlt,** cooled with ice; **-glas,** *n.* frosted glass; **-hülle,** *f.* glacial covering.

eisig, icy.

Eisigkeit, *f.* iciness.

eis-kalt, ice cold; **-kasten,** *m.* icebox; **-kluft,** *f.* frost crack; **-kraut,** *n.* ice plant (*Mesembryanthemum crystallinum*); **-kruste,** *f.* crust of ice; **-kühlen,** to cool with ice; **-meer,** *n.* polar sea.

Eisodial-leiste, *f.* anterior ridge of stomate; **-öffnung,** *f.* anterior opening of stomate.

Eis-phosphorsäure, *f.* glacial phosphoric acid; **-punkt,** *m.* freezing point; **-spat,** *m.* glassy feldspar.

Eistadium, *n.* egg stage.

Eis-stein, *m.* cryolite; **-trieb,** *m.* ice flow; **-vogel,** *m.* kingfisher; **-zacken,** *m.* **-zapfen,** *m.* icicle; **-zeit,** *f.* glacial period.

Eiteilung, *f.* segmentation of ovum.

eitel, idle, vain, pure, futile.

Eitelkeit, *f.* vanity.

Eiter, *m.* pus; **-ähnlich,** purulent; **-ansammlung,** *f.* accumulation of pus; **-artig,** purulent; **-bakterien,** *n.pl.* pus-forming (pyogenic) bacteria; **-befördernd,** suppurative, pyogenic.

eiter-bildend, pyogenic; **-bildung,** *f.* pus formation, suppuration; **-erreger,** *m.* exciting cause of suppuration; **-erzeugend,** suppurative, pyogenic; **-gang,** *m.* fistula; **-herd,** *m.* suppurative focus.

eiterig, purulent, puriform.

Eiterkokken, *m.pl.* pyogenic cocci.

eitern, to suppurate.

Eiter-pilz, *m.* pyogenic organism; **-stoff,** *m.* purulent matter.

Eiterung, *f.* suppuration.

Eiterungserreger, *m.* suppurative agent or organism.

Eiter-vergiftung, *f.* pyemia; **-verhaltung,** *f.* retention of pus; **-zelle,** *f.* pus corpuscle.

eiterziehend, suppurative, pyogenic.

Eiumfang, *m.* circumference of egg.

Eiweiss, *n.* protein, albumin, white of egg; **-abbau,** *m.* proteolysis; **-ähnlich,** albuminoid; **-ähnlichkeit,** *f.* similarity to albumin; **-arm,** poor in albumin; **-art,** *f.* variety of albumin or protein; **-artig,** albuminous, albuminoid; **-bedarf,** *m.* albumin requirement; **-drüse,** *f.* albuminous (salivary) gland; **-erzeugung,** *f.* generation or formation of albumin.

eiweiss-förmig, albuminous; **-haltig,** containing albumin or protein; **-harnen,** *n.* albuminuria; **-haushalt,** *m.* use of (economy of) albumin; **-körper,** *m.* albuminous body, protein; **-leim,** *m.* albumin glue, gluten protein; **-lösung,** *f.* albumin solution; **-organismus,** *m.* protein organism; **-reaktion,** *f.* test for presence of albumin; **-schlauch,** *m.* myrosin container.

Eiweiss-spaltend, proteolytic; **-spaltung,** *f.* decomposition of albumin; **-stoff,** *m.* protein; **-verdauung,** *f.* assimilation of albumin; **-zelle,** *f.* albumin cell.

Eizelle, *f.* egg, ovum, oösphere, oöcyte.

Eka-Bor, *n.* ekaboron.

Ekel, *m.* nausea, disgust; **-erregend,** nauseating, disgusting; **-haft,** disgusting, offensive.

eklatant, brilliant.

Ekrüseide, *f.* ecru silk.

Ektoparasit, *m.* ectoparasite.

Ektropium, *n.* eversion of the edge, ectropion.

Ekzem, *n.* eczema.

Elainsäure, *f.* oleic acid.

elastisch, elastic.

Elastizität, *f.* elasticity.

Elastizitäts-modul, *m.* modulus of elasticity; **-welle,** *f.* elastic wave; **-zahl,** *f.* modulus of elasticity.

Elaterenträger, *m.* elaterophore.

Elatsäure, *f.* elatic acid.

Elchrüssel, *m.* elk proboscis.

Elefant, *m.* elephant.

Elefanten-laus, *f.* cashew nut; **-nuss,** *f.* ivory nut.

Elektawolle, *f.* first-class wool.

elektiv, selective, favored; **-nährboden,** *m.* selective medium.

Elektriker, *m.* electrician.

elektrisch, electric.

elektrisierbar, electrifiable.

elektrisieren, to electrify.

Elektrisiermaschine, electrical machine.

Elektrisierung, *f.* electrification.

Elektrizität, *f.* electricity.

Elektrizitäts-bewegung, *f.* electric motion; **-entladung,** *f.* electric discharge; **-fluss,** *m.* flow of electricity; **-ladung,** *f.* electric charge; **-leiter,** *m.* electric conductor; **-leitung,** *f.* conduction of electricity; **-menge,** *f.* quantity of electricity; **-messer,** *m.* **-waage,** *f.* electrometer; **-zeiger,** *m.* electroscope.

Elektrode, *f.* electrode.

Elektroden-abstand, *m.* distance between electrodes; **-fläche,** *f.* surface of the electrode; **-spannung,** *f.* electrode potential.

Ekektrolyse, *f.* electrolysis.

elektrolysieren, to electrolyze.

Elektrolyt, *m.* electrolyte.

elektrolytisch, electrolytic.

Elektromagnetismus, *m.* electromagnetism.

Elektron, *n.* electron.

Elektronen-aussendung, *f.* emission of electrons; **-drall,** *m.* electron spin; **-hülle,** *f.* shell of electrons; **-röhren-verstärker,** *m.* vacuum-tube amplifier; **-stoss,** *m.* electronic collision or impact; **-wolke,** *f.* cloud of electrons.

Elektronoskopie, *f.* electron spectroscopy.

Elektrophor, *m.* electrophorus.

elektropositiv, electropositive.

Elektropositivität, *f.* electropositive state.

elektrostatisch, electrostatic.

Element, *n.*-e, element, cell battery.

elementar, elementary; **-atom,** *n.* fundamental (basic) atom; **-stoff,** *m.* elementary matter, element; **-teil,** *m.* elementary part.

Elementart, *f.* kind of element, type of cell.

Elementen-begriff, *m.* concept of the element; **-messung,** *f.* stoichiometry; **-verwandlung,** *f.* transformation of an element.

Element-gefäss, *n.* **-glas,** *n.* battery jar; **-grösse,** *f.* size of cell; **-kohle,** *f.* cell carbon; **-schlamm,** *m.* battery mud.

Elemi-harz, *n.* elemi, gum elemi, **-öl,** *n.* elemi oil.

Elen, *m.&n.* elk.

Elend, *n.* misery, distress.

elend, miserable, needy, pitiful, ill.

elf, eleven.

Elfenbein, *n.* ivory; **-ähnlich,** ivorylike; **-artig,** ivorylike; **-farbig,** ivory-colored; **-rasse,** *f.* ivory strain; **-substanz,** *f.* dentine; **-weiss,** eburneous, ivory white.

elfte, eleventh.

eliminieren, to eliminate.

Eliminierung, *f.* elimination.

Ellagen-gerbsäure, *f.* **-säure,** *f.* ellagic acid.

Ellbogen, *m.* elbow; **-bein,** *n.* ulna; **-beuger,** *m.* flexor of the elbow; **-fortsatz,** *m.* olecranon process; **-gelenk,** *n.* elbow joint, cubital articulation; **-grube,** *f.* olecranon fossa.

Ellbogen-höcker, *m.* olecranon; **-knochen,** *m.* ulna; **-rand,** *m.* rim of elbow joint; **-röhre,** *f.* radius; **-strecker,** *m.* extensor of elbow; **-wirbel,** *m.* elbow whorl.

Elle, *f.* ell, yard, ulna.

Ellen-ader, *f.* cubitus; **-beuge,** *f.* bend of elbow; **-bogen,** *m.* elbow; **-köpfchen,** *n.* head of ulna; **-kronenfortsatz,** *m.* coronoid process of ulna; **-querader,** *f.* cubital cross vein; **-seite,** *f.* ulnar side; **-waren,** *f.pl.* dry goods, drapery goods; **-zelle,** *f.* cubital cell.

Eller, *f.* alder (*Alnus glutinosa*).

Ellipsenbahn, *f.* elliptic orbit.

ellipsoidförmig, ellipsoidal.

elliptisch, elliptic, elliptical.

Elmsfeuer, *n.* St. Elmo's fire.

Elritze, *f.* minnow (*Phoxinus laevis*).

Elsbeerbaum, *m.* service tree (*Sorbus torminalis*).

Else, *f.* alder, shad; **-beere,** *f.* serviceberry. (*Pyrus* or *Sorbus torminalis*).

Elster, *f.* magpie (Pica).

elterlich, parental.

Eltern, *pl.* parents; **-fürsorge,** *f.* parental care; **-zeugung,** *f.* tocogony, parental generation.

eluieren, to elute, wash out, extract.

elutrieren, to elutriate, wash.

Eluvialboden, *m.* residual soil.

Email, *n.* **Emaille,** *f.* enamel.

email(le)artig, enamellike.

emaillieren, to enamel.

Emailschicht, *f.* coat of enamel.

Emanzipation, *f.* emancipation.

Embryo, *m.* embryo; **-anlage,** *f.* embryo primordium, embryonic rudiment; **-blut,** *n.* blood of the embryo; **-ernährung,** *f.* fetal nutrition; **-körper,** *m.* fetal body; **-kügelchen,** *n.* globular proembryo.

Embryonal-entwicklung, *f.* fetal development; **-feld,** *n.* embryonic area; **-fleck,** *m.* embryonic spot; **-gehirn,** *n.* embryonic brain; **-haut,** *f.* fetal appendage; **-hülle,** *f.* embryonic sheath; **-kammer,** *f.* embryonic shell, protoconch; **-schild,** *m.* embryonic shield, area; **-zelle,** *f.* embryonic cell.

Embryo-sackmutterzelle, *f.* embryo sac, mother cell; **-träger,** *m.* suspensor, corda embryonalis.

emetisch, emetic.

eminent, distinguished.

Emissions-lehre, *f.* theory of emission; **-vermögen,** *n.* emissive power.

emittieren, to emit.

emollieren, to soften.

empfahl (empfehlen), recommended; **er ∼ sich,** he took leave.

Empfang, *m.* reception, receipt.

empfangen, to receive, conceive.

Empfänger, *m.* receiver.

empfänglich, receptive, susceptible, predisposed.

Empfänglichkeit, *f.* susceptibility, receptiveness.

Empfängnis, *f.* **-se,** conception; **-faden,** *m.* trichogyne; **-fähig,** receptive; **-fleck,** *m.* receptive spot; **-hügel,** *m.* elevation in egg. cell surface, fertilization cone.

empfehlen, to recommend; **sich ∼,** to take leave, bid farewell.

empfehlenswert, (re)commendable, advisable, eligible.

empfiehlt (empfehlen), **er ∼ sich,** he says farewell.

empfindbar, sensible, perceptible.

Empfindbarkeit, *f.* perceptibility, sensitiveness.

empfinden, to feel, perceive, experience.

empfindlich, sensitive, sensible, irritable severe, susceptible.

Empfindlichkeit, *f.* susceptibility, sensitiveness.

empfindlichmachen, to sensitize, render sensitive.

Empfindung, *f.* sensation, feeling, perception, sentiment.

Empfindungs-änderung, *ı.* change of sensation, alternation of feeling; **-apparat,** *m.* apparatus of perception; **-faser,** *f.* sensory-nerve fiber; **-inhalt,** *m.* sensory content; **-los,** senseless, devoid of feeling or sensation, unfeeling, numb; **-reflex,** *m.* sensory reflex; **-vermögen,** *n.* capacity for feeling, sensitive faculty, receptivity; **-zelle,** *f.* sensory cell.

empföhle (empfehlen), would recommend.

empfohlen (empfehlen), ∼ **haben,** to have recommended; **sich** ∼ **haben,** to have taken leave.

empfunden (empfinden), felt, noticed.

Emphysemknistern, *n.* emphysema crackling.

empirisch, empiric(al).

empor, up, upward; **-blühen,** to grow, rise, prosper; **-dringen,** to stand out, rise, project.

empören, to stir up, excite.

empor-gerichtet, vertical, raised (up), upright; **-heben,** to lift up, raise; **-klettern,** *°*o climb up; **-kommen,** to rise, ascend, prosper, come up to; **-ragen,** to stand out, project; **-recken,** to stretch or creep up; **-richten, sich,** to rise; **-saugen,** to suck up; **-schicken,** to send up; **-schiessen,** to shoot up, spring up; **-schnellen,** *n.* sudden rise, jumping; **-steigen,** to ascend, rise.

Empörung, *f.* indignation, rising, revolt, rebellion.

empor-wachsen, to grow up; **-wölben,** to arch up; **-ziehen,** to raise, draw up; **-züchten,** to breed (upward).

empyreumatisch, empyreumatic.

emsig, diligent, industrious.

emulgieren, to emulsify.

emulsieren, to emulsify.

Emulsierungsmittel, *n.* emulsifying agent.

Emulsin, *n.* emulsin.

emulsionieren, to emulsionize.

Emulsions-bildung, *f.* formation of an emulsion; **-fähig,** emulsifiable; **-verfahren,** *n* emulsion process.

Enantiotropie, *f.* enantiotropy.

End-abschnitt, *m.* terminal portion; **-anhang,** *m.* terminal appendage; **-apparat,** *m.* final apparatus; **-arterie,** *f.* terminal artery; **-ausstülpung,** *f.* terminal evagination.

End-bäumchen, *n.* telodendron; **-blase,** *f.* terminal vesicle; **-blättchen,** *n.* small terminal leaf; **-blüte,** *f.* terminal flower;

-borste, *f.* terminal seta or bristle; **-bukett,** *n.* telodendron; **-büschel,** *n.* terminal fascicle; **-darm,** *m.* hind-gut, rectum, proctodaeum, terminal intestine.

Ende, *n.*-n, end, limit, termination, purpose, point, tine, extremity, result; ∼ **und kein** ∼, without end; **zu dem** ∼, **dass,** in order that; **letzten Endes,** in the final analysis, finally; **zu** ∼ **führen,** to complete.

End-ecke, *f.* -eck, *n.* summit, terminal angle.

endemisch, endemic.

enden, to end, terminate, conclude, cease, die.

Enden, *n.pl.* points.

End-ergebnis, *n.*-se, final result; **-ertrag,** *m.* final yield; **-faden,** *m.* terminal filament or flagellum; **-feld,** *n.* end span; **-fingerknochen,** *m.* terminal phalanx; **-fläche,** *f.* terminal face; **-form,** *f.* final form.

End-geflecht, *n.*-e, terminal plexus; **-geschwindigkeit,** *f.* final velocity; **-glied,** *n.* final segment, phalanx, terminal member; **-gültig,** final, ultimate, conclusive definitive; **-hieb,** *m.* final cutting, removal.

endigen, to end, terminate.

Endigung, *f.* ending.

Endivie, *f.* endive, (wild) chicory.

End-klotz, *m.* top log; **-knick,** *m.* final bend; **-knospe,** *f.* terminal bud; **-knoten,** *m.* terminal node; **-kohlenstoff,** *n.* last carbon atom; **-kralle,** *f.* terminal claw, pretarsus.

endlich, finite, final, ultimate, late, after all.

Endlichkeit, *f.* finiteness.

endlos, endless, infinite.

End-lösung, *f.* final solution; **-moräne,** *f.* terminal moraine; **-nüance,** *f.* final shade; **-nutzung,** *f.* final yield.

Endokarditis, *f.* endocarditis.

Endokard-kissen, -polster, *n.* endocardial cushion.

Endo-plasma, *n.* endoplasm; **-plasmaeinheit,** *f.* endoplasmic unit.

Endosches Fuchsinagar, *n.* Endo's fuchsin agar.

endosmotisch, endosmotic.

Endosmose, *f.* endosmosis.

Endo-sperm, *m.* endosperm; **-sporen,** *f.pl.* endospores.

Endothel, *n.* endothelium.

endotherm(isch), endothermic.

Endotoxin, *n.* endotoxin.

End-polklemme, *f.* end terminal; **-produkt,** *n.* final product, end prodúct; **-punkt,** *m.* end point, final (extreme) point, terminus, destination; **-raife,** *f.* cercus; **-resultat,** *n.* final result; **-schlinge,** *f.* terminal loop; **-spannung,** *f.* final strain, final voltage; **-stadium,** *n.* final stage; **-ständig,** standing at the end, end, terminal, apical, acrocarpous; **-stück,** *n.* final or terminal piece.

End-tasche, *f.* terminal pouch, alveolus; **-teil,** *m.* tip of proximal barbule; **-trieb,** *m.* terminal shoot.

Endung, *f.* ending.

End-ursache, *f.* final cause; **-verzweigung,** *f.* terminal ramification; **-wert,** *m.* final value; **-zapfen,** *m.* terminal cone; **-zehenknochen,** *m.* terminal phalanx (of toe); **-zelle,** *f.* terminal (apical) cell; **-ziel,** *n.* ultimate objective; **-zustand,** *m.* terminal state; **-zweck,** *m.* aim, purpose.

Energetik, *f.* energetics.

Energie-abgabe, *f.* release of energy; **-abnahme,** *f.* decrease in energy; **-änderung,** *f.* energy change; **-art,** *f.* form of energy; **-aufspeicherung,** *f.* storage of energy; **-aufwand,** *f.* expenditure of energy; **-bedarf,** *m.* demand for energy; **-betrag,** *m.* amount of energy; **-einheit,** *f.* unit of energy; **-gleichung,** *f.* energy equation.

Energie-inhalt, *m.* amount of energy contained; **-liefernd,** energy producing; **-niveau,** *n.* energy level; **-quelle,** *f.* source of energy; **-umsatz,** *m.* energy transformation; **-umwandlung,** *f.* transformation of energy; **-verbrauch,** *m.* consumption of energy; **-vergeudung,** *f.* waste of energy; **-verlust,** *m.* loss of energy; **-verteilung,** *f.* distribution of energy; **-zufuhr,** *f.* addition of energy.

energisch, energetic.

eng, narrow, close, tight; **-benachbart,** closely adjacent; **-begrenzt,** limited, small; **-brüstigkeit,** *f.* broken wind, difficult breathing, heaves.

Enge, *f.* narrowness, closeness, tightness, constriction, isthmus.

Engel, *m.* angel; **-rot,** *n.* colcothar; **-süss,** *n.* polypody root (*Polypodium vulgaris*); **-wurz,** *f.* angelica (*Angelica archangelica*).

Engerling, *m.* larva (of cockchafer).

Enghalsflasche, *f.* narrow-necked bottle.

englische, English.

englische Erde, *f.* rottenstone.

englisches Gewürz, pimento, allspice; ∼ **Kollodium,** flexible collodion; ∼ **Pflaster,** court plaster; ∼ **Pulver,** powder of Algaroth; ∼ **Rot,** colcotahr; ∼ **Salz,** Epsom salt, magnesium sulphate.

Englisch-gelb, *n.* patent yellow, lead oxychloride.

eng-lochig, with small holes, fine-pored; **-lumig,** narrow-celled; **-maschig,** close-meshed; **-mündig,** with a narrow opening; **-porig,** with narrow pores; **-ringig,** narrow-ringed, narrow-zoned.

Engobe, *m.* engobe, slip.

engobieren, to coat with engobe.

en gros, wholesale.

enkaustisch, encaustic.

Enkel, *m.* ankle, grandchild, grandson; **-kern,** *m.* granddaughter nucleus.

Enlevage, *f.* discharge.

enneandrisch, enneandrous.

enorm, enormous.

Ensilage, *f.* ensilage.

entaktivieren, to render inactive.

entalkoholisieren, to dealcoholize.

entamidieren, to deanimize, deamidize.

entarten, to degenerate, deteriorate.

entartet, degenerate, debased, abnormal.

Entartung, *f.* degeneration.

Entaschung, *f.* ash removal.

entästen, to lop, trim, prune.

Entästung, *f.* lopping off.

entäussern, to divest, deprive of.

entbasten, to degum (silk).

entbehren, to miss, be without, be deprived, lack, do without, dispense with.

entbehrlich, dispensable, unnecessary.

entbinden, to disengage, set free, liberate evolve, deliver.

Entbindung, *f.* disengagement, setting free release, evolution, delivery, parturition.

Entbindungs-flasche, *f.* generating flask **-rohr,** *n.* delivery tube.

entbittern, to deprive of bitterness.

entblättern, to defoliate.

entbleien, to deprive of lead.

entblössen, to uncover, divest, strip, deprive, bare.

entblösst, denuded.

entbrennen, to be inflamed, be kindled.

entbunden (entbinden), liberated, evolved.

entdecken, to discover, disclose.

Entdecker, *m.-,* discoverer.

Entdeckung, *f.* discovery, disclosure.

entdenaturieren, to free from denaturants.

Ente, *f.* duck, duck-shaped vessel.

entehren, to disgrace, dishonor.

enteignen, to expropriate.

Enteignungsrecht, *n.* right of expropriation.

enteisen, to de-ice.

enteisenen, to deprive of iron, remove iron.

Enteisenung, *f.* removal of iron.

Enteiser, *m.* ice guard.

Entenfang, *m.* duck decoy.

Entenfuss, *m.* podophyllum, May apple.

Entengrütze, *f.* duckweed (*Lemna minor*).

Enteritis, *f.* enteritis.

entfachen, to kindle, fan, light.

entfallen, to fall, drop, slip; ~ auf, to fall to the share of.

Entfall, *m.* soap, waste, loss.

entfalten, to unfold, develop, display, evolve.

Entfaltung, *f.* development, unfolding expansion, display.

Entfaltungsfähigkeit, *f.* capacity for opening or unfolding.

entfärbbar, capable of being decolorized.

entfärben, to decolorize, bleach, fade, grow pale.

Entfärbung, *f.* decolorization, destaining, bleaching, growing pale.

Entfärbungsmittel, *n.* decoloring agent, decolorant.

entfasern, to divert of fibers, string (beans).

entfernen, to remove, withdraw, depart, retire, deviate, cull out.

entfernt, distant, removed.

Entfernung, *f.* removal, absence, distance, retirement.

Entfernungs-kraft, *f.* centrifugal force; **-punkt,** *m.* apsis.

entfetten, to remove fat, ungrease, scour, reduce obesity.

Entfettung, *f.* removal of fat.

Entfettungsmittel, *n.* scouring (degreasing) agent, detergent, remedy for obesity.

Entfeuchter, *m.* desiccator.

entflammbar, inflammable.

Entflammbarkeit, *f.* inflammability.

entflammen, to inflame, kindle, flash.

Entflammungspunkt, *m.* flash point.

entfleischen, to strip of flesh.

entfliehen, to escape.

entfliessen, to flow, emanate.

entflocken, to deflocculate.

Entflockung, *f.* deflocculation.

entflügeln, to sever wings (from seed).

entfremden, to estrange, abandon, conceal.

entführen, to carry off.

entfuseln, to rectify, remove fusel oil from.

entgasen, to extract gas from.

Entgasung, *f.* degassing, dry distillation.

entgegen, against, opposite, toward, counter, contrary to; **-bringen,** to offer; **-eilen,** to hasten toward; **-gehen,** to go to meet, face, encounter; **-gesetzt,** opposite, opposed, contrary; **-halten,** to contrast, object; **-haltung,** *f.* prior art (reference), checking against prior art; **-kommen,** to come to meet; **-kommen,** *n.* cooperation, obligingness, friendly advance; **-nehmen,** to accept, receive.

entgegen-setzen, to oppose, place in opposition; **-stehen,** to oppose, be opposed; **-stellen,** to set off for comparison, contrast; **-treten,** to move toward, come to meet, oppose, face, stand up to, confront **-wenden,** to turn toward; **-wirken,** to counteract, check; **-ziehen,** to advance.

entgegnen, (*dat.*) to reply, meet.

entgehen, to escape, avoid; ~ lassen, to let slip.

entgeisten, to deprive of life or spirit, dealcoholize.

Entgeistung, *f.* stripping of alcohol.

entgelten, to suffer, pay for.

entgerben, to detan.

entgerbern, to wash (wool).

entgiften, to remove poison, detoxicate

Entgiftung, *f.* detoxification.

Entgiftungsmittel, *n.* detoxicating agent.

entglasen, to devitrify.

Entgleisung, *f.* derailment, boner (*faux pas*).

entgrannen, to awn, hummel (barley).

entgummieren, to degum.

enthaaren, to unhair, depilate.

enthaarend, depilatory.

Enthaarung, *f.* unhairing, depilation.

enthalogenisieren, to dehalogenate, dehalinate.

enthalten, to contain, hold, include; sich ~, (*gen.*) to abstain or refrain (from).

enthaltsam, abstemious, temperate, sober

enthärten, to soften.

entharzen, to deprive of resin.

enthäuten, to remove skin, flay.

entheben, to exonerate, remove, exempt, dismiss.

Entholzung, *f.* delignification.

enthüllen, to uncover, unfold, unveil, disclose.

enthülsen, to husk, hull, shell, peel.

enthydratisieren, to dehydrate.

entkalken, to decalcify, free from lime.

Entkalkung, *f.* decalcification, deliming.

entkampfern, to deprive of camphor.

entkarboxylieren, to decarboxylate.

entkeimen, to degerminate, germinate, sprout, spring up, destroy bacteria, disinfect, remove sprouts, sterilize.

Entkeimung, *f.* germination, removal of germs (bacteria).

entkernen, to stone, core (fruit).

entkieseln, to desilicify.

entkleiden, to undress, strip.

entknospen, to unfold, (break) open.

entkohlen, to decarbonize.

entkörnen, to shell, clean, gin.

entkräften, to weaken, exhaust, debilitate, enervate, impoverish.

Entkräftigung, *f.* weakening.

Entkräftung, *f.* debilitation, exhaustion, inanition.

entkuppeln, to uncouple, disconnect.

entladen, to discharge, unload, explode, go off.

Entlade-spannung, *f.* discharge voltage; -strom, *m.* discharge current.

Entladung, *f.* discharge.

Entladungs-ercheinung, *f.* appearance or effect of discharging; -gefäss, *n.* discharge tube; -geschwindigkeit, *f.* velocity of discharge; -kreis, *m.* region of discharge; -spannung, *f.* tension (voltage); -vorgang, *m.* process of discharge.

entlang, along; -streifen, to brush along, graze along.

entlarven, to unmask.

entlassen, to dismiss, discharge.

entlasten, to unload, discharge, release, exonerate, relieve of a load.

Entlastungswehr, *n.* spillway weir.

entlauben, to defoliate, strip.

entlaubt, defoliated, leafless.

entledigen, sich, to rid itself (oneself) of.

entleeren, to empty, discharge, evacuate.

Entleerung, *f.* emptying, evacuation, discharge.

Entleerungs-apparat, *m.*-e, discharging apparatus, gland; -kammer, *f.* discharging chamber.

entlegen, distant, remote.

entlehnen, to borrow, take, derive.

entleimen, to degum.

entleuchten, to deprive of light, shine.

entlüften, to deprive of air, deaerate. ventilate.

entmagnetisieren, to demagnetize.

entmannen, to emasculate, castrate.

Entmilzung, *f.* splenectomy.

entmischen, to separate into component parts, disintegrate, decompose.

Entmischung, *f.* disintegration, dissociation.

entmutigen, to discourage.

Entnahme, *f.* taking.

entnässen, to deprive of moisture, dry.

entnebeln, to free from mist or fog.

Entnebelungsanlage, *f.* fume-dispersion installation.

entnehmen, to take (from or out), withdraw, infer, conclude.

entnimmt (entnehmen), takes (from).

entnommen (entnehmen), removed, withdrawn.

Entoderm-rohr, *m.* entodermal tract; -säckchen, *n.* entoderm rudiment, archenteron; -tasche, *f.* entodermal pouch.

Entöken, *n.* a commensal living in another organism.

entölen, to free from oil.

Entomologe, *m.* entomologist.

Entoplasma, *n.* endoplasm.

Entozoen, *n.pl.* entozoa, intestinal worms.

entpesten, to disinfect.

entphosphoren, to dephosphorize.

Entpolymerisierung, *f.* depolymerization.

entpressen, to press out, squeeze out, extort.

entpuppen, to break the cocoon.

Entquellung, *f.* shrinkage of gels, syneresis.

entrahmen, to remove cream, skim.

entraten, to dispense (with).

enträtseln, to unravel, decipher, explain.

entreissen, to snatch, tear away, rescue.

entrichten, to pay, discharge (debt).

entrinden, to decorticate, remove bark, peel.

Entrindung, *f.* barking.

Entropie, *f.* entropy.

entrosten, to free from rust.

entsagen, to renounce, abandon, give up.

entsalzen, to free from salt.

entsamen, to dehusk, shell, remove seed.

entsanden, to desilt, remove sand.

Entsatz, *m.*∸e, relief, rescue.

entsäuchen, disinfect.

entsäuern, to free from acid, decarbonate, deoxidize, deacidify.

entschädigen, to indemnify, compensate for.

entschälen, to shell, peel.

entschäumen, to skim, scum, foam off, despumate.

entscheiden, to decide.

entscheidend, decisive, final.

Entscheidung, *f.* decision, crisis.

Entscheinungsmittel, *n.* deblooming agent.

entschieden, decided, determined.

entschlacken, to remove slag.

entschlagen, sich, (*gen.*) to get rid of, dismiss.

entschlammen, to free from mud or slime.

entschleimen, to remove slime.

Entschleimung, *f.* removal of mucilage or slime.

entschlichten, to desize, free from size, undress.

entschliessen, to decide, resolve.

entschlossen, decided, determined.

Entschlossenheit, *f.* resolution, decision.

entschlüpfen, to escape.

Entschluss, *m.*∸e, resolution, decision.

entschuldigen, to excuse.

entschwefeln, to desulphurize.

Entschwefelung, *f.* desulphurization.

entschweissen, to scour, degrease.

entschwinden, to disappear, vanish.

entseifen, to remove soap, rinse.

entsenden, to dispatch.

entsetzen, to displace, dismiss, remove, relieve, frighten, be horrified.

entsetzlich, terrible, atrocious, enormous, awful.

entseuchen, to disinfect, sterilize.

entsinnen, sich, (*gen.*) to remember.

entspannen, to relax, relieve tension.

Entspannung, *f.* relaxation, decrease in pressure, release from tension.

Entspannungs-naht, *f.* interrupted suture (to relieve tension); **-verdampfer,** *m.* flash chamber.

entspinnen, sich, to arise, begin.

entsprechen, (*dat.*) to correspond, answer, comply with.

entsprechend, corresponding, suitable, adequate, according.

entspringen, to arise, spring, originate.

entstammen, to originate from, be descended from.

entstand (entstehen), resulted.

entstänkern, to deodorize.

entstauben, to remove dust, dust (off).

entstehen, to arise, originate, be formed, result, occur.

entstehend, arising, resulting; **eben** ∼, nascent, incipient.

Entstehung, *f.* origin, beginning, formation.

Entstehungs-art, *f.* mode of origin; **-bedingung,** *f.* condition of formation; **-weise,** *f.* manner of origin; **-zustand,** *m.* nascent state, embryonic condition, incomplete state.

entsteigen, to rise from, spring from.

entstellen, to disfigure, distort, mutilate.

entströmen, to flow, escape (from).

enttäuschen, to disappoint, undeceive, disillusion.

entvölkern, to depopulate.

entwachsen, to outgrow, grow from.

entwaldet, deforested, cleared.

Entwaldung, *f.* deforestation.

entwässerbar, capable of being dehydrated.

entwässern, to remove water, drain, discharge, dehydrate, desiccate, concentrate, rectify.

entwässert, dehydrated, anhydrous, concentrated, rectified, drained.

Entwässerung, *f.* dehydration, desiccation, concentration, drainage.

Entwässerungs-graben, *m.* drain, draining ditch; **-mittel,** *n.* dehydrating agent; **-rohr,** *n.* tile, drain pipe; **-schleuse,** *f.* sluice.

entweder, either.

entweichen, to escape, leak, disappear.

Entweichung, *f.* escape.

Entweichungsventil, *n.* escape valve.

entwerfen, to trace out, sketch, plan.

entwerten, to depreciate, reduce, decrease (in value), cancel (stamps).

entwesen, to disinfect, sterilize.

entwickeln, to develop, evolve, disengage, generate, unfold, display, deliver.

Entwickler, *m.* generator, developer.

Entwicklung, *f.* development, evolution, disengagement, generating, unfolding, explanation, formation.

Entwicklungs-ablauf, *m.* course of development; **-änderung,** *f.* change in development; **-art,** *f.* kind of development; **-bad,** *n.* developing bath; **-bedingung,** *f.* condition of development; **-bestimmung,** *f.* determination of fate in development; **-erregung,** *f.* forcing, activation; **-erscheinung,** *f.* phenomenon of development; **-fähig,** capable of development; **-fähigkeit,** *f.* viability.

Entwicklungs-farbstoff, *m.* mordant; **-fehler,** *m.* defect in development; **-folge,** *f.* successive stages in development; **-forschung,** *f.* study of development; **-gang,** *m.* evolution, course of development, ontogeny, phylogeny; **-gefäss,** *n.* generating vessel, generator; **-geschehen,** *n.* process of development; **-geschichte,** *f.* history of development; **-geschichtlich,** ontogenetic, embryological; **-gesetz,** *n.* law of development; **-hemmung,** *f.* inhibition in development.

Entwicklungs-höhe, *f.* degree of differentiation; **-lehre,** *f.* theory of development, embryology; **-mittel,** *n.* developer; **-möglichkeit,** *f.* developmental possibility or potency; **-periode,** *f.* growing period, puberty; **-potenz,** *f.* developmental potency; **-reihe,** *f.* order of development; **-richtung,** *f.* direction of development; **-röhre,** *f.* delivery tube, delivery pipe; **-schicksal.** *n.* fate in development.

Entwicklungs-störung, *f.* disturbance in development; **-stufe,** *f.* stage of development, phase; **-unterbrechung,** *f.* interruption in development; **-ursache,** *f.* cause of development; **-verlauf,** *m.* course of development; **-vorgang,** *m.* course of development, process; **-wiederholung,** *f.* repetition of development; **-zone,** *f.* zone of development.

entwinden, to wring, wrest from.

entwipfeln, to top off, pollard.

entwirft (entwerfen), projects, designs.

entwirren, to unravel, disentangle.

entwöhnen, to wean, disaccustom.

entworfen (entwerfen), projected, planned.

Entwurf, *m.* ̈e, sketch, outline, design, model.

entwurzeln, to uproot, eradicate.

Entzerrungsgerät, *n.* rectifier.

entziehen, to take away, withdraw, extract, deprive, entrain.

Entziehung, *f.* abstraction, withdrawing, deprivation.

entziffern, to decipher.

entzücken, to charm, enchant.

entzuckern, to extract sugar from.

entzündbar, inflammable.

Entzündbarkeit, *f.* inflammability.

entzünden, to ignite, kindle, light, inflame, take fire.

entzundern, to free from scale, scale.

entzündlich, inflammable, inflammatory.

Entzündlichkeit, *f.* inflammability.

Entzündung, *f.* ignition, inflammation.

Entzündungs-erscheinung, *f.* symptoms of inflammation; **-herd,** *m.* focus of inflammation; **-probe,** *f.* ignition test; **-prozess,** *m.* inflammatory process; **-punkt,** *m.* ignition point.

entzwei, in two, asunder.

entzweien, to estrange, disunite.

entzweispringen, to crack, burst or break in two.

entzweit, at variance, divided.

Enzian, *m.* gentian; **-gewächse,** *n.pl.* Gentianaceae; **-wurzel,** *f.* gentian root

Enzyklopädie, *f.* encyclopedia.

Enzym, *n.* enzyme.

enzymatisch, enzymatic, enzymic.

Enzymbestand, *m.* ̈e, amount of enzyme.

enzymisch, enzymic.

Enzymwirkung, *f.* enzyme action.

Eocän, *n.* eocene.

Eosin, *n.* eosin.

Epheu, *m.* ivy (*Hedera helix*).

Epidemie, *f.* epidemic.

epidemiologisch, epidemiological.

epidemisch, epidemic.

Epidermis, *f.* epidermis; **-zelle,** *f.* epidermic cell.

Epihydrinsäure, *f.* epihydrinic acid.

epileptiform, epileptoid.

Epithel, *n.* epithelium; **-gewebe,** *n.* epithelial tissue.

Epithelialbekleidung, *f.* epithelial covering.

Epithel-körperchen, *n.pl.* parathyroid glands; **-lage,** *f.* epithelial layer; **-perlen,** *f.pl.* epithelial pearls; **-scheide,** *f.* epithelial sheath; **-zelle,** *f.* epithelial cell.

Epizootie, *f.* epizootic.

Epoche, *f.* epoch; **-machend,** epoch-making.

Epöken, *n.* commensal living on another organism.

Eppich, *m.* celery (*Apium graveolens*).

Eprouvette, *f.* cylinder, reagent glass, test tube.

Equisetsäure, *f.* equisetic (aconitic) acid.

er, he, it.

erachten, to consider, deem.

Erachten, *n.* opinion, judgment; **meines Erachtens,** in my opinion.

erarbeiten, to achieve by work.

Erbanlage, *f.* hereditary factor.

erbarmen, sich, (*gen.*) to pity, have mercy.

erbauen, to build, construct, erect.

Erbauer, *m.* builder, founder.

Erbauung, *f.* building, construction. foundation, edification.

Erbe, *m.*-n, heir.

Erbe, *n.* inheritance.

erbeben, to shake, tremble

Erbeinheit, *f.* gene.

erben, to inherit.

Erberfahrungen, *f.pl.* genetical data.

erbeuten, to capture, get as booty.

Erbfaktor, *m.*-en, hereditary factor.

Erbfaktoren-analyse, *f.* factor analysis; **-paar,** *n.* factor pair, allelomorph.

Erb-folge, *f.* succession; **-gang,** *m.* mode of inheritance; **-gruppe,** *f.* hereditary group or complex.

erbieten, to offer.

Erbinerde, *f.* erbia, erbium oxide.

erbitten, to ask, request.

erbittern, to embitter, exasperate.

erbittert, bitter.

erblasen, to produce in blast furnace.

erblassen, to fade, grow pale, die.

erblich, hereditary.

Erblichkeit, *f.* heritability, heredity.

Erblichkeits-träger, *m.* carrier of heredity; **-verhältnisse,** *n.pl.* genetic relations (basis).

erblicken, to behold, discover.

erblinden, to go blind.

erbohren, to bore; öl ∼, to strike oil.

erbötig, willing, ready.

erbrechen, to break open, vomit.

erbringen, to produce (proof).

Erbschaft, *f.* inheritance.

Erbse, *f.* pea.

Erbsen-baum, *m.* Siberian acacia; **-bein,** *n.* pisiform bone; **-blattrandkäfer,** *m.* pea weevil; **-blüte,** *f.* pea blossom; **-erz,** *n.* pea ore; **-förmig,** pealike, pisiform; **-früchtig,** pisocarpous, pealike fruit; **-gross,** of the size of a pea; **-grün,** pea-green; **-käfer,** *m.* pea weevil.

Erbsen-mehl, *n.* pea flour, pea meal; **-reisig,** *n.* peasticks; **-stein,** *m.* peastone, pisolite; **-strauch,** *m.* Caragana; **-wicke,** *f.* pea-shaped vetch (*Ervum pisiforme*).

Erb-stück, *n.* heirloom; **-substanz,** *f.* idiochromatin, germ plasm; **-zahl,** *f.* number of parental types.

Erd-ableitung, *f.* earth connection, ground; **-achse,** *f.* axis of the earth.

erdacht (erdenken), imagined, invented.

Erd-algen, *f.* terrestrial algae; **-alkalien,** *f.pl.* alkaline earths.

Erdalkali-metall, *n.* metal of the alkaline earths; **-oxyd,** *n.* oxide of an alkaline earth metal.

erd-alkalisch, alkaline-earth; **-apfel,** *m.*, potato, truffle, mandrake, cyclamen; **-arbeit,** *f.* earthwork; **-artig,** earthy; **-assel,** *f.* millepede; **-balken,** *m.* sod; **-ball,** *m.* terrestrial globe; **-ballen,** *m.* rootball, ball of earth; **-bau,** *m.* earthwork; **-bearbeitung,** *f.* cultivation of the soil.

Erd-beben, *n.* earthquake; **-beerbaum,** *m.* strawberry tree (*Arbutus unedo*); **-beere,** *f.* strawberry; **-beschreibung,** *f.* geography; **-birne,** *f.* Jerusalem artichoke; **-boden,** *m.* ground, soil; **-brot,** *n.* sowbread (*Cyclamen europaeum*).

Erde, *f.* earth, soil, ground.

Erdeichel, *f.* earthnut, peanut (*Arachis hypogaea*), heath nut (*Lathyrus tuberosus*).

erden, to ground, earth.

Erdenge, *f.* isthmus.

erdenken, to devise, invent, conceive.

erdenklich, conceivable.

Erd-falle, *f.* soil trap; **-farbe,** *f.* earthy color; mineral color; **-farben, -farbig,** earth-colored; **-ferkel,** *n.* ground hog; **-feucht,** damp, moist; **-feuer,** *n.* ground fire, subterranean fires; **-flachs,** *m.* amianthus; **-forscher,** *m.* geologist; **-gang,** *m.* vein, tunnel, adit.

Erd-gas, *n.* natural gas; **-gelb,** *n.* yellow ocher; **-geruch,** *m.* earthy odor; **-geschichte,** *f.* geology; **-geschmack,** *m.* earthy taste; **-geschoss,** *n.* ground floor.

Erd-glas, *n.* selenite; **-gürtel,** *m.* zone; **-haltig,** containing earth; **-harz,** *n.* asphalt; **-höhle,** *f.* cave in the earth; **-holz,** *n.* semishrub.

erdichten, to invent, devise.

erdig, earthy, terrestrial.

Erd-innere, *n.* interior of the earth; **-kalk,** *m.* limestone; **-keil,** *m.* soil wedge; **-klumpen,** *m.* clod.

Erdkobalt, *m.* earthy cobalt, asbolite; grüner ~, annabergite, nickel ocher; roter ~, earthy erythrite, cobalt crust; schwarzer ~, asbolane, asbolite.

Erd-kohle, *f.* lignitic earth, brown coal, peat; **-körper,** *m.* terrestrial body; **-krümchen,** *n.* bit of earth, earth crumb; **-krume,** *f.* vegetable mold, black earth, surface soil; **-kruste,** *f.* earth's crust; **-kugel,** *f.* terrestrial globe; **-kunde,** *f.* geography, geology; **-mandel,** *f.* chufa (*Cyperus esculentus*); **-masse,** *f.* quantity of earth.

Erdmassen-ausgleichung, *f.* leveling, equalization of earthwork; **-berechnung,** *f.* calculation of cutting.

Erd-mast, *f.* ground mast; **-maus,** *f.* field mouse or vole; **-mehl,** *n.* siliceous (infusorial) earth; **-messkunst,** *f.* geodesy; **-metall,** *n.* earth metal; **-mischung,** *f.* soil mixture; **-moos,** *n.* club moss; **-nuss,** *f.* peanut (*Arachis hypogaea*); **-nussöl,** *n.* arachis oil; **-oberfläche,** *f.* earth's surface.

Erd-öl, *n.* petroleum; **-orchidee,** *f.* terrestrial orchid; **-pech,** *n.* mineral pitch, asphalt, bitumen; **-haltig,** asphaltic; **-periode,** *f.* geologic period; **-probe,** *f.* soil (test) sample; **-quadrant,** *m.* the earth's quadrant; **-rauch,** *m.* fumitory (*Fumaria officinalis*); **-reich,** *n.* ground, earth, land; **-riese,** *f.* land slide; **-rinde,** *f.* earth's crust.

erdrosseln, to strangle, throttle.

erdrücken, to smother; stifle.

Erd-rutsch, *m.* landslide; **-salz,** *n.* rock salt, saline efflorescence on soil; **-scheibe,** *f.* sowbread, cyclamen; **-schellack,** *m.* acaroid resin; **-schicht,** *f.* layer of earth, stratum, subsoil; **-schierling,** *m.* hemlock (*Conium maculatum*); **-schlacke,** *f.* earthy slag; **-schluss,** *m.* earth connection, ground; **-schlüsselblume,** *f.* primrose; **-schuss,** *m.* ground shot; **-schwamm,** *m.* mushroom.

Erd-schwefel, *n.* lycopodium; **-seife,** *f.* mountain soap, a kind of clay; **-stamm,** *m.* stump of tree, prostrate stem; **-staude,** *f.* herbaceous perennial plant; **-stein,** *m.* eaglestone, aetites; **-stern,** *m.* Geaster; **-strauch,** *m.* undershrub; **-talg,** *m.* mineral tallow, hatchettite, ozocerite; **-talk,** *m.* earthy talc; **-teer,** *m.* mineral tar, maltha, pissasphalt, bitumen; **-teil,** *m.* continent, part of the world.

erdulden, to suffer, endure.

Erdung, *f.* ground(ing).

Erd-untersuchung, *f.* soil investigation; **-verbindung,** *f.* ground connection.

erdverlegte Rohre, *n.pl.* underground pipes.

Erd-wachs, *n.* ozocerite, mineral wax; **-weg,** *m.* dirt road, mud road; **-widerstand,** *m.* passive earth pressure; **-wurzel,** *f.* common root.

ereignen, to happen, occur.

Ereignis, *n.*-se, event, occurrence.

ereilen, to overtake.

ererben, to inherit.

erfahren, to hear, learn, discover, understand, experience, undergo; experienced, expert, practical.

Erfahrung, *f.* experience, knowledge, practice, result.

Erfahrungs-anhalt, *m.* point supported by experience; **-assoziation,** *f.* association by experience; **-gemäss, -mässig,** empirical, according to experience; **-satz,** *m.* empirical theorem; **-tafel,** *f.* experimental table; **-zahl,** *f.* empirical coefficient.

erfassen, to grasp, seize, comprehend, bite.

Erfassungsreiz, *m.*-e, stimulus of apprehension.

erfinden, to invent, find out.

Erfinder, *m.* inventor, designer, author.

erfind-erisch, -sam, inventive, ingenious.

Erfindung, *f.* invention, discovery, device.

Erfindungsbeschreibung, *f.* inventor's consent form.

Erfolg, *m.*-e, result, success, effect.

erfolgen, to follow, ensue, result, take place.

erfolg-los, unsuccessful; **-reich,** successful.

erfolgt, successful, taken place, actual.

erforderlich, requisite, necessary.

erfordern, to require, necessitate, demand.

Erfordernis, *n.***-se,** exigency, necessity, demand, requisite.

erforschen, to explore, investigate, discover.

Erforscher, *m.***-,** investigator, discoverer.

Erforschung, *f.* investigation, research, discovery.

erfragen, to ascertain, inquire.

erfreuen, sich, (*gen.*) to delight, be glad, enjoy.

erfreulich, delightful, gratifying.

erfreulicherweise, happily, fortunately.

erfrieren, to freeze to death, chill, be killed by frost.

erfrischen, to refrigerate, freshen, refresh, cool.

Erfrischung, *f.* refrigeration, refreshing, refreshment.

erfroren (erfrieren), frozen, frostbitten.

erfuhr (erfahren), experienced.

erfüllbar, fulfillable, reasonable.

erfüllen, to impregnate, fill (up), fulfill; **sich ～,** to come true, take place.

Erfüllung, *f.* accomplishment, realization; **in ～ gehen,** to materialize.

Erg, *n.* erg, ergon.

ergab (ergeben), resulted.

ergänzen, to complete, supply, supplement, make up, restore, replenish, support.

ergänzend, complementary, supplementary.

Ergänzung, *f.* completion, restoration, supplement, complement, supplying.

Ergänzungs-band, *m.* **-buch,** *n.* supplement(ary volume); **-farbe,** *f.* complementary color; **-kanälchen,** *n.* supplemental tubule; **-nährstoff,** *m.* accessory food factor, vitamin; **-platte,** *f.* completing plate; **-werk,** *n.* supplement.

ergeben, sich, to yield, show, obtain, result, appear, submit, produce, devote; **sich einer Sache ～,** to devote oneself to a thing; **sich in etwas ～,** to acquiesce in something; **sich aus etwas ～,** to result from something; **～ sein,** to be devoted; **hieraus ergibt sich,** it follows from this; **es ergibt sich, dass,** it happens (follows) that.

ergebend, resulting.

ergebenst, most humble, yours truly.

Ergebnis, *n.* result, product, yield, conclusion; **zu keinem ～ führen,** to lead (yield, give) no result, prove a failure.

ergebnislos, resultless, futile.

ergehen, sich, to walk about, be published, issued, happen, fare; **sich in etwas ～,** to indulge in hopes; **etwas über sich ～ lassen,** to submit to something.

ergibt sich (ergeben), surrenders, results, produces, shows.

ergiebig, productive, yielding, abounding, rich.

Ergiebigkeit, *f.* richness, productiveness, abundance, yield, depth, fertility.

ergiessen, to pour forth, discharge.

erglühen, to (begin to) glow, kindle.

ergrauen, to turn gray.

ergreifen, to seize, catch, grasp, apprehend, stir, take up, affect, attack; **die Feder ～,** to take up the pen; **das Wort ～,** to begin to speak.

ergreifend, moving, touching.

ergründen, to investigate, ascertain, discover, fathom.

ergrünen, to become green (verdant).

Erguss, *m.* ̈e, effusion, outpouring, discharge, overflow(ing); **-gestein,** *n.* igneous rock.

erhaben, raised, lofty, elevated, elated, embossed, relief, convex, tall, sublime, illustrious, plastic.

Erhabenheit, *f.* elevation, eminence, convexity, protuberance, prominence, relief.

Erhalt, *m.* saving.

erhaltbar, preservable, obtainable.

erhalten, to keep (up), preserve, maintain, retain, remain, support, receive, obtain, get, secure, remain firm, keep steady; **sich ～,** to keep alive, last; **～ bleiben,** to be preserved.

erhältlich, obtainable, to be had.

Erhaltung, *f.* preservation, maintenance, support, conservation, reception, procuring, obtaining.

Erhaltungs-mittel, *n.* preservative, support, antiseptic; **-spross,** *m.* essential (nourishing) shoot; **-umsatz,** *m.* basal metabolism.

erhängen, to hang.

erhärten, to harden, set, corroborate, confirm, prove, verify.

Erhärtung, *f.* hardening, confirmation, proof.

erhaschen, to snatch, seize, catch up.

erheben, to raise, lift, rise.

erheblich, considerable, important.

Erhebung, *f.* raising, elevation, promotion, census, survey, rising, collection, levying, inquiry, canvassing.

erheischen, to demand, require.

erheitern, to brighten, cheer (up).

erhellen, to light up, illuminate, brighten, expose, become clear or apparent.

Erhellung, *f.* illumination, exposure.

erhielt (erhalten), obtained.

erhitzen, to heat, make hot, pasteurize, inflame, become angry.

erhitzend, heating, stimulating.

erhitzt, preheated.

Erhitzung, *f.* heating, growing hot, excitement.

erhoben (erheben), raised.

erhöhen, to raise, increase, erect, elevate, accelerate, improve.

Erhöhung, *f.* raising, elevation, improvement, exaltation.

Erhöhungsklotz, *m.* raising block.

erholen, sich, to recover, get well, come to.

Erholung, *f.* recovery, recreation, relaxation.

Erholungs-bedürfnis, *n.* need of recovery; -fähigkeit, *f.* recuperative ability.

erhören, to listen to, hear, grant.

Erika, *f.* heather (Erica).

erinnern, to remind, state, draw attention to, mention, call to mind, suggest, admonish; sich ~, (*gen.*) to remember; sich einer Sache ~, to remember a thing; es sei daran erinnert, let me remind you of.

Erinnerung, *f.* remembrance, memory, recollection, admonition, reminder.

Erinnerungs-bild, *n.* recollected image, memory picture; -vorstellung, *f.* memory image.

erkalten, to cool, grow cold.

erkälten, to cool, chill, catch cold.

Erkaltung, *f.* cooling down.

Erkältung, *f.* cold, catarrh, cooling, refrigeration.

erkannt (erkennen), recognized, detected.

erkaufen, to purchase, bribe, corrupt.

erkennbar, recognizable, discernible, perceptible.

erkennen, to detect, diagnose, perceive, recognize, discern, distinguish, take cognizance of, decide, pass sentence; an

etwas ~, to recognize by something; es lässt sich nicht ~ ob, it is impossible to know whether; sich zu ~ geben, to make oneself known; ~ lassen, to exhibit, reveal.

erkenntlich, grateful.

Erkenntnis, *f.* perception, knowledge, cognizance, recognized fact; -theorie, *f.* perception theory.

Erkennung, *f.* recognition, diagnosis, detection.

Erkennungs-merkmal, *n.*-e, sign of recognition; -schwelle, *f.* limen, threshold; -zahlen, *f.pl.* index numbers; -zeichen, *n.* characteristic, diagnostic symptom, distinctive mark.

erklärbar, explainable, explicable.

erklären, to explain, illustrate, clear up, declare, interpret.

erklärlich, apparent, evident, explainable, obvious.

Erklärung, *f.* explanation, illustration, interpretation, declaration.

erklimmen, to climb up, ascend, reach.

erkranken, to fall ill, sicken.

erkrankt, diseased.

Erkrankung, *f.* illness, falling sick.

erkundigen, to inquire.

Erkundigung, *f.* inquiry.

erlahmen, to tire, become paralyzed.

erlangen, to reach, procure, acquire.

Erlass, *m.*-̈e, remission, order, edict, reduction, exemption, decree.

erlassen, to issue, publish, remit, release.

erlauben, to allow, permit.

Erlaubnis, *f.* permission, grant, leave, license.

erlaucht, illustrious, noble.

erläutern, to explain, interpret, illustrate.

Erle, *f.* alder (*Alnus glutinosa*).

erleben, to experience, pass through.

Erlebnis, *n.*-se, experience, event, occurrence.

erledigen, to dispose of, discharge, settle, remove, vacate.

Erledigung, *f.* settlement, carrying out, solution, arrangement.

erlegen, to lay down, pay, kill.

erleichtern, to make easy, lighten, facilitate.

Erleichterung, *f.* easing, relief, alleviation.

erleiden, to suffer, undergo, bear, endure.

Erlen-baum, *m.* alder (tree); -bruch, *m.* alder swamp, grove of alder trees; -holz, *n.* alder wood; -kohle, *f.* charcoal of alder.

Erlenmeyerkolben, *m.* Erlenmeyer flask.

Erlenzeisig, *m.* siskin (*Carduelis spinus*).

erlesen, to select, choose.

erleuchten, to illuminate.

erliegen, to succumb, sink.

erlitten (erleiden), suffered, submitted to.

erlogen (erlügen), fabricated, false.

Erlös, *m.* proceeds, income.

erloschen, dull, dim, obscure, dead, expired.

erlöschen, to go out, be extinguished, grow dull or dim, expire, be effaced.

erlösen, to save, redeem, release, free.

ermächtigen, to empower, authorize.

ermahnen, to exhort, remind.

ermangeln, to be in want of; **an nichts $\sim$ lassen,** to spare nothing.

Ermang(e)lung, *f.* want, deficiency, failure.

ermässigen, to moderate, reduce.

ermatten, to weary, tire.

ermessen, to measure, estimate, judge, consider.

Ermessen, *n.* judgment, estimate; **meines Ermessens,** in my judgment.

ermitteln, to ascertain, find out.

Ermittlung, *f.* ascertainment, discovery, determination, regulation.

ermöglichen, to make possible, bring about.

ermüden, to tire, fatigue, exhaust.

Ermüdung, *f.* fatigue, weariness.

Ermüdungs-erscheinung, *f.* appearance of fatigue; -festigkeit, *f.* resistance to fatigue; -gift, *n.* toxin of fatigue; -grenze, *f.* endurance limit; -messung, *f.* measuring fatigue; -stoff, *m.* product of fatigue.

ermuntern, to rouse, urge, encourage.

ernähren, to nourish, feed, support.

ernährend, nourishing, nutritive.

Ernährung, *f.* nutrition, food, alimentation, feeding, support, maintenance.

Ernährungs-bahn, *f.* nutritive tract; -bedingung, *f.* food requirement, condition of nutrition; -bedürfnis, *n.* food requirement; -boden. *m.* nutritive medium; -faktor, *m.* nutritive or dietary factor; -flüssigkeit, *f.* nutritive liquid, -frassgang, *m.* feeding mine or chamber (of bark beetles); -genossenschaft, *f.* symbiosis, partnership to secure food; -geschäft. *n.* nutrition.

Ernährungs-kanal, *m.* alimentary tract; -kunde, *f.* dietetics; -loch, *n.* nutritive foramen; -physiologie, *f.* physiology of nutrition; -reaktion, *f.* food reaction; -spross, *m.* innovation (nourishing) shoot; -stoff, *m.* -substanz, *f.* nutritive material, trophoplasm.

Ernährungs-vergiftung, *f.* alimentary intoxication; -versuch, *m.* experiment on nutrition; -weise, *f.* manner of nutrition, feeding habit; -werkzeug, *n.* organ of nutrition; -wert, *m.* nutritive value; -zelle, *f.* nutritive cell; -zustand, *m.* nutritional condition.

ernennen, to appoint, nominate.

erneue(r)n, to renew, renovate, refresh, revive, repair; erneut, again, anew.

Erneuerung, *f.* renewal.

erniedrigen, to lower, humble.

Erniedrigung, *f.* lowering, reduction, depression, humiliation.

Ernst, *m.* seriousness, severity, (in) earnest.

ernst, serious, earnest, solemn, severe.

ernsthaft, serious.

ernstlich, earnest, eager, serious.

Ernte, *f.* harvest, crop, produce, yield, gathering; -ameise, *f.* harvester ant; -ertrag, *m.* crop yield; -maschine, *f* harvesting machine.

ernten, to harvest, reap, gather.

Erntevorhersage, *f.* (estimated) crop prediction.

erobern, to conquer, take.

Eroberung, *f.* conquest.

erodieren, to erode.

eröffnen, to open, inaugurate, discover, disclose, start.

eröffnend, opening, disclosing, aperient.

Eröffnung, *f.* opening beginning, notification, communication.

erörtern, to discuss, debate.

Erörterung, *f.* discussion, debate.

Erosion, *f.* erosion.

erproben, to try, test.

erquicken, to refresh, revive.

erraten, to guess, solve.

erratisch, erratic.

errechnen, to compute, calculate.

erregbar, excitable, irritable, sensitive.

Erregbarkeit, *f.* excitability.

erregen, to excite, stimulate, agitate, irritate.

erregend, exciting, stimulating; **erregendes Mittel,** stimulant.

Erreger, *m.*-, exciter, exciting cause, agitator, instigator, producer; **-flüssigkeit,** *f.* exciting fluid; **-gleichrichter,** *m.* exciting rectifier; **-salz,** *n.* exciting salt; **-spannung,** *f.* exciting voltage; **-strom,** *m.* exciting current.

erregt, excited.

Erregung, *f.* stimulation, excitation.

Erregungs-flüssigkeit, *f.* exciting fluid; **-formel,** *f.* excitation formula; **-gleichgewicht,** *n.* state in which stimuli balance each other; **-leitung,** *f.* conduction of stimulus; **-periode,** *f.* period of excitation; **-plus,** *n.* surplus stimulation; **-punkt,** *m.* point of excitation; **-spannung,** *f.* exciting voltage; **-stadium,** *m.* stage of excitation; **-vorgang,** *m.* stimulation process.

erreichbar, attainable.

erreichen, to reach, attain, come up to, get.

erretten, to save. rescue.

errichten, to erect, establish, raise.

erringen, to obtain, achieve, win.

errungen (erringen), won, obtained.

Errungenschaft, *f.* acquisition, achievement, progress.

Ersatz, *m.*-e, substitute, replacement, equivalent, compensation; **-deckel,** *m.* extra cover, spare lid; **-fähigkeit,** *f.* ability to replace, equivalency; **-faser,** *f.* substitute fiber, intermediate fiber; **-faserzelle,** *f.* substitute fiber (cell); **-gewicht,** *n.* equivalent weight; **-gipfel,** *m.* substitute treetop; **-knochen,** *m.* substitute bone, membrane bone, permanent bone.

Ersatz-menge, *f.* equivalent amount; **-mittel,** *n.* substitute; **-präparat,** *n.* substitute preparation; **-spross,** *m.* replacing shoot; **-stoff,** *m.* substitute; **-stück,** *n.* extra part, spare part; **-teil,** *m.* reserve (spare) part, fittings; **-zahn,** *m.* permanent tooth.

ersaufen, to be drowned.

ersäufen, to drown, flood.

erschaffen, to create, produce.

erschallen, to sound, resound.

erscheinen, to appear, be published, show, reveal; ~ **lassen,** to bring out, publish.

Erscheinung, *f.* phenomenon, manifestation, appearance, vision; **in** ~ **treten,** appear.

Erscheinungs-form, *f.* shape, phase, state, manifestation, phenotype, genotype, embodiment; **-komplex,** *m.* nature of the phenomenon; **-typus,** *m.* phenotype.

erschiessen, to shoot, kill.

erschlaffen, to relax, slacken.

Erschlaffung, *f.* debility, relaxing.

erschliessen, to open, disclose, infer, conclude.

erschöpfen, to exhaust.

erschöpfend, exhaustive, thorough.

Erschöpfung, *f.* exhaustion, faintness, weariness.

erschrecken, to frighten, startle, be terrified.

erschüttern, to shake, stir, impress, tremble, vibrate, shock.

erschütternd, concussive, touching.

Erschütterung, *f.* concussion, shaking, vibration, shock; ~ **des Bodens,** subsoiling.

Erschütterungs-ladung, *f.* cracking charge; **reiz,** *m.* contact stimulus, thigmotropism; **-sinn,** *m.* vibration sense; **-welle,** *f.* earth(quake) wave; **-zeiger,** *m.* seismograph.

erschweren, to make heavy, render difficult. aggravate, impede.

Erschwerung, *f.* weighting, aggravation, impediment.

erschwing-en, to afford, supply with difficulty; **-lich,** reasonable.

ersehen, to learn, see, infer, note, distinguish.

ersetzbar, replaceable.

ersetzen, to replace, substitute, displace, compensate, recover.

Ersetzung, *f.* replacement, substitution, conpensation.

ersichtlich, visible, evident, manifest.

ersinnen, to conceive, devise.

ersoffen (ersaufen), drowned.

erspähen, to detect, spy out.

ersparen, to save. spare, economize.

Ersparnis, *f.* saving(s), economy.

erspriesslich, useful, profitable.

erst, first, only, yet, not until, previously; ~ **recht,** all the more, only; ~ **jetzt,** not until now.

erstanden (erstehen), arisen.

Erstanlage, *f.* prime rudiment.

Erstärkung, *f.* primary growth in thickness, primary thickening.

erstarren, to solidify, congeal, harden, coagulate, become stiff, numb, or torpid.

Erstarren, *n.* solidification; **zum** ~ **bringen,** to solidify.

Erstarrung, *f.* solidification, congelation, stiffness.

Erstarrungs-punkt, *m.* coagulation point; **-wärme,** *f.* heat of fusion.

erstatten, to restore, render, return, give.

erstaunen, to be surprised or astonished (at).

Erstaunen, *n.* surprise, astonishment.

erstaunlich, remarkable, amazing.

erste, first; **der erstere,** the former; **in erster Linie,** in the first place, first of all.

erstehen, to arise, originate, buy at auction.

ersteigen, to climb.

erstellen, to set up, erect, complete.

erstens, in the first place, to begin with.

erstere, former.

erstgenannt, afore-mentioned, first named, former.

ersticken, to suffocate, choke, smother.

Erstickung, *f.* asphyxia(tion), suffocation, choking.

Erstickungs-gefahr, *f.* danger of suffocation; **-tod,** *m.* asphyxiation.

erstlich, first.

Erstlings-aufgabe, *f.* initial assignment; **-blatt,** *u.* primary leaf; **-dune,** *f.* nestling feather; **-früchte,** *f.pl.* first fruit (of season); **-gefieder,** *n.* nestling plumage.

erstmalig, for the first time.

Erstmilch, *f.* colostrum.

erstrahlen, to radiate, shine, gleam.

erstreben, to strive for, aspire, attain.

erstrebenswert, worthy of effort.

erstrecken, to extend, reach, stretch.

ersuchen, to request, desire, beseech.

ertappen, to catch, surprise.

erteilen, to bestow, allot, give, apportion, impart, grant.

Erteilungsakten, *f.pl.* documentary record.

ertönen, to sound, resound.

Ertrag, *m.* ᵉe, yield, returns, proceeds, profit, crops, produce, income.

ertragen, to bear, endure, tolerate.

erträglich, tolerate, passable, bearable, endurable, profitable.

ertragreich, fruitful, productive.

Ertrags-ausfall, *m.* loss of yield; **-ermittlung,** *f.* calculation (computation) of the yield; **-fähig,** productive; **-fähigkeit,** *f.* productivity; **-feststellung,** *f.* determination of yield.

Ertrags-höhe, *f.* yield; **-regelung,** *f.* regulating returns; **-steigerung,** *f.* increasing the yield; **-tafel,** *f.* yield table; **-verlauf,** *m.* course of returns; **-vermögen,** *n.* yielding power; **-wert,** *m.* expectation value.

ertränken, to drown.

erträumen, to imagine, dream of.

ertrinken, to be drowned.

ertrüben, to become turbid.

erübrigen, to save, spare, remain (to add or say); **es erübrigt nur noch hinzuzufügen, dass . . . ,** there remains nothing to add but that . . .

Erucasäure, *f.* erucic acid.

Eruptivgesteine, *n.pl.* volcanic rocks.

erwachen, to (a)wake.

erwachsen, grown, adult; resulted, proceeded.

erwägen, to weigh, consider.

erwählen, to choose, elect.

erwähnen, to mention.

Erwähnung, *f.* mention; ∼ **tun** to mention.

erwärmen, to warm, heat.

Erwärmung, *f.* warming, heating.

Erwärmungskraft, *f.* calorific ᵉ heating power.

erwarten, to expect, await.

Erwartungswert, *m.* expectation (prospective) value.

erwecken, to waken, rouse, inspire, animate

erwehren, sich, (*gen.*) to keep off, restrain.

erweichen, to soften, soak, mollify, mellow.

erweichend, softening, emollient, demulcent.

Erweichung, *f.* softening, mollification.

Erweichungsmittel, *n.* softening agent, emollient.

Erweis, *m.* proof, demonstration.

erweisen, to prove, show, demonstrate, he found; **sich** ∼, to be found as.

erweitern, to enlarge, widen, expand, extend, distend, dilate.

Erweiterung, *f.* widening, dila(ta)tion, enlargement.

erweiterungsfähig, dilatable.

Erwerb, *m.* acquisition, gain, profit, returns.

erwerben, to acquire, earn, gain.

Erwerbgartenbau, *m.* commercial horticulture.

erwidern, to return, reciprocate, reply

erwies (erweisen), showed, proved

erwirken, to effect, achieve.

erwischen, to catch, capture.

erwischt, caught, found.

erworben (erwerben), acquired.

erwünscht, wished for, desired.

Erysipel, *n.* erysipelas.

Erythem, *n.* erythema.

Erythrozyten, *n.pl.* erythrocytes.

Erz, *n.* ore, metal, bronze; **-abfälle,** *m.pl.* tailings; **-ader,** *f.* mineral vein, lode.

erzählen, to tell, relate, report.

Erz-arbeiter, *m.* metalworker, bronzeworker; **-arm,** yielding poor ore; **-aufbereitung,** *f.* ore dressing; **-brechmaschine,** *f.* ore crusher, **-dumm,** extremely stupid.

erzeugen, to produce, grow, generate, engender, beget.

Erzeuger, *m.-,* producer, generator, procreator, parent.

Erzeugnis, *n.-se,* production, product, yield.

Erzeugung, *f.* production, procreation, generation.

Erzeugungs-kreis, *m.* generative circle; **-linie,** *f.* generatrix; **-ort,** *m.* place of production.

erz-farbig, bronze-colored; **-führend,** ore-bearing; **-gang,** *m.* mineral vein; **-gestein,** *n.* ore-bearing rock; **-gicht,** *f.* ore charge; **-giesserei,** *f.* bronze (brass) foundry; **-glühfrischen,** *n.* refining with iron ore; **-graupe,** *f.* coarse grain of ore; **-grube,** *f.* mine; **-haltig,** containing ore; **-hütte,** *f.* smelting works.

erziehen, to educate, bring up, rear, grow, tend, raise.

Erzieher, *m.* educator, tutor, trainer.

erzieherisch, erziehlich, educational.

Erziehung, *f.* education, rearing, raising.

Erziehungshieb, *m.* improvement cutting.

erzielen, to obtain, attain, produce, aim, strive, realize.

Erz-kies, *m.* metalliferous pyrites; **-kunde,** *f.* metallurgy; **-lager,** *n.* **-lagerstätte,** *f.* ore deposit; **-metalle,** *n.pl.* heavy metals; **-mittel,** *n.* lode ore.

Erz-mutter, *f.* matrix; **-niere,** *f.* kidney-shaped ore; **-ofen,** *m.* smelting furnace; **-probe,** *f.* ore assay(ing), ore sample; **-scheider,** *m.* ore separator; **-stahl,** *m.* ore steel, mine steel.

erzürnen, to anger, provoke, irritate.

erzwingen, to force, enforce, extort.

erzwungen, induced, forced, affected, simulated, artificial.

Erzzerkleinerung, *f.* ore crushing.

es, it; ~ **gibt,** there is, there are; ~ **ist,** there is; ~ **sind,** there are.

Esche, *f.* ash (*Fraxinus excelsior*).

Eschel, *m.* zaffer.

Eschen,-ahorn, *m.* box elder (*Acer negundo*); **-blätterig,** ash-leaved; **-holz,** *n.* ash wood, ash; **-wurz,** *f.* fraxinella, dittany.

Esdragon, *m.* tarragon (*Artemisia dracunculus*).

Esdragol, *n.* estragole.

Esel, *m.* ass, donkey, drainage horn.

Eselsohr, *n.* (dog-eared) corner.

Eseresamen, *m.* Calabar bean.

Esparsette, *f.* sainfoin (*Onobrychis sativa*).

Espe, *f.* aspen poplar (*Populus tremula*).

essbar, edible.

Esse, *f.* chimney, forge, hearth.

Esseisen, *n.* tuyère.

essen, to eat.

Essen, *n.* eating, feeding, meal, food, dish; **-klappe,** *f.* damper.

essentiell, essential.

Essenz, *f.* essence.

Essig, *m.* vinegar; **-älchen,** *n.* vinegar eel; **-artig,** acetous, acetic, vinegarlike; **-äther,** *m.* acetic ether, ethyl acetate; **-baum,** *m.* elm-leaved sumach, tanner's sumach (*Rhus coriaria*); **-bereitung,** *f.* vinegar making; **-bildung,** *f.* acetification.

Essig-essenz, *f.* vinegar essence; **-ester,** *m.* acetic ester, ethyl acetate; **-fabrik,** *f.* vinegar factory; **-gärung,** *f.* acetic fermentation; **-geist,** *m.* acetone; **-haltig,** containing vinegar; **-honig,** *m.* oxymel.

Essig-messer, *m.-,* acetometer; **-mutter,** *f.* mother of vinegar; **-naphtha,** *f.* ethyl acetate; **-pilz,** *m.* vinegar plant (*Mycoderma aceti*); **-rose,** *f.* French rose; **-salz,** *n.* acetate; **-sauer,** acetic, sour as vinegar.

Essigsäure, *f.* acetic acid; **-anhydrid,** *n.* acetic anhydride; **-äther,** *m.* acetic ether; **-bakterien,** *f.pl.* acetic acid bacteria; **-gärung,** *f.* acetic fermentation; **-haltig,** containing acetic acid; **-messer,** *m.* acetometer; **-salz,** *n.* acetate.

Essig-schaum, *m.* flower of vinegar; **-sirup,** *m.* oxymel; **-sprit,** *m.* triple vinegar; vinegar essence; **-ständer,** *m.* vinegar tun;

graduator; -stube, *f.* vinegar (warm) room; -zucker, *m.* oxysaccarum.

Ess-lust, *f.* appetite; -waren, *f.pl.* provisions, eatables.

Ester, *m.* ester; -ähnlich, resembling an ester; -artig, esterlike; -bildung, *f.* ester formation, esterification.

esterifizieren, to esterify.

Ester-säure, *f.* ester acid; -zahl, *f.* ester number.

Estragon, *m.* tarragon (*Artemisia dracunculus*).

Estrich, *m.* plaster floor, pavement, flagstone, finish.

estrifizieren, to esterify.

etablieren, sich, to establish oneself.

Etablissement, *n.* establishment.

Etage, *f.* floor, story, deck (machine), tier.

Etagen-cambium, *n.* initial layer of cambium; -ofen, *m.* shelved oven or kiln; -presse, *f.* multilayer press, multiplex; -wuchs, *m.* growth in tiers.

Etagere, *f.* shelf, stand, bracket, rack.

Etappe, *f.* stage.

Etat, *m.* statement, budget, annual yield.

Etats-bestimmung, *f.* determination of capability; -jahr, *n.* fiscal year.

Etikette, *f.* etiquette, label, tag.

etikettieren, to label, tag.

Etiolinkorn, *n.* chloroplast that has not acquired its green color.

etliche, some, several, few.

Etui, *n.* case, box.

etwa, perhaps, about, nearly, perchance.

etwaig, eventually, likely to be, contingent.

etwas, some, something, somewhat, rather.

Eucalyptusöl, *n.* eucalyptus oil.

euch, you, to you, yourselves.

Euchinin, *n.* euquinine.

Euchlor, *n.* euchlorine.

eudiometrisch, eudiometric.

euer, of you, your, yours.

Eugensäure, *f.* eugenic acid, eugenol.

Euklas, *m.* euclase.

Eule, *f.* owl, night moth (Noctua).

eurig, yours.

eustachisch, Eustachian.

eutektisch, eutectic.

Euter, *n.* udder; -entzündung, mastitis of cows; -tuberkulose, *f.* tuberculosis of udder.

evakuieren, to evacuate, empty, exhaust.

Evakuierungskessel, *m.* vacuum boiler.

evaporieren, to evaporate.

eventuell, eventual(ly), if necessary, possible, if so, perhaps.

Everinsäure, *f.* everninic acid.

Evolvente, *f.* involute.

evolvieren, to evolve.

evomieren, to vomit.

ewig, eternal, perpetual, endless, ever, unceasingly, forever.

Ewigkeit, *f.* eternity, perpetuity.

exakt, accurate, exact.

Exaktheit, *f.* exactness.

Examen, *n.* examination.

Excenter, *m.* eccentric.

Excentricität, *f.* eccentricity.

excentrisch, eccentric.

Excretbehälter, *m.* excretion container.

Exemplar, *n.*-e, sample, specimen, copy. example.

Existenz, *f.*-en, existence; -bedingungen, *f.pl.* conditions of life; -fähig, capable of existence.

existieren, to exist.

Exitus, *m.* death.

exklusiv, exclusive.

Ekretionsbehälter, *m.* excretion container.

Exkurs, *m.* digression.

Exlibris, *n.* bookplate.

exothermisch, exothermic.

expandieren, to expand, dilate.

expedieren, to dispatch, forward.

Expedition, *f.* expedition, enterprise, office.

Experiment, *n.* experiment.

Experimentator, *m.* experimenter.

experimentell, experimental.

experimentieren, to experiment.

Expirationsluft, *f.* exhaled air.

Explantat, *n.* explant.

explodierbar, explosive.

explodieren, to explode.

explosibel, explosive.

explosions-artig, explosive; -druck, *m.* explosion pressure; -fähig, explosive; -sicher, explosion-proof; stoss, *m.* explosive (impact) impulse; -welle, *f.* wave of explosion.

Explosiv-geschoss, *n.* -̈e, explosive missile; -**kraft,** *f.* explosive force; -**maschine,** *f.* combustion engine; -**stoff,** *m.* explosive substance, explosive.

exponieren, to expose.

Exposition, *f.* exposure, exposition, aspect.

Expositions-dauer, *f.* duration of exposure; -**zeit,** *f.* time of exposure.

Exsikkator, *m.* exsiccator, desiccator, drier.

Exsudat, *n.* exudate, exudation; -**bildung,** *f.* development of exudation.

extensiv, extensive.

extirpieren, to extirpate.

extrahierbar, extractable.

extrahieren, to extract.

Extrahierung, *f.* extraction.

Extrakt, *m.&n.*-e, extract; -**brühe,** *f.* extract liquor; -**gehalt,** *m.* extract content.

Extraktions-apparat, *m.*-e, extraction apparatus; -**hülse,** *f.* extraction shell, thimble.

Extraktstoff, *m.* extract.

Extraovat, *n.* egg extrusion.

extrapolieren, to extrapolate.

Extremität, *f.* extremity, appendage.

Extremitäten-bildung, *f.* limb formation; -**knospe,** *f.* limb bud.

Extremwert, *m.* extreme value.

Exzenterrolle, *f.* follower of eccentric.

exzentrisch, eccentric.

exzidieren, to excise.

F

Fabel, *f.* fable, fiction; -**lehre,** *f.* fabulous; -**lehre,** *f.* mythology.

Fabrik, *f.*-en, factory, works, mill, plant, establishment; -**anlage,** *f.* manufacturing plant.

Fabrikant, *m.*-en, manufacturer, maker.

Fabrikarbeit, *f.* factory labor, manufactured article.

Fabrikat, *n.*-e, manufacture, product, make, (textile) fabric.

Fabrikation, *f.* manufacturing, production.

Fabrik-betrieb, *m.* factory operation; -**gold,** *n.* gold leaf; -**marke,** *f.* trade-mark; -**mässig,** industrial, by machinery; -**öl,** *n.* oil for factory use; -**ware,** *f.* manufactured article; -**wesen,** *n.* manufacturing industry; -**zeichen,** *n.* trade-mark.

fabrizieren, to make, manufacture.

fäcal, fecal.

Fäcalien, *pl.* feces.

Fäces, *pl.* feces.

facettiert, faceted.

Fach, *n.*-̈er, compartment, division, cell, loculus, partition, drawer, shelf, branch, department, profession, subject, specialty, lot; **gefächert,** chambered.

-**fach,** -fold; **zehn** ⌢, tenfold.

Fach-arbeiter, *m.*-, expert or skilled worker; -**artig,** cellular; -**arzt,** *m.* specialist; -**ausdruck,** *m.* technical expression; -**ausschuss,** *m.* professional committee; -**bildung,** *f.* professional (technical) education.

Fächel, *m.* rhipidium, a fan-shaped cyme.

fächeln, to fan, ventilate.

fachen, to ply (yarn).

Fächer, *m.*-, fan; -**ahorn,** *m.* fan maple (*Acer palmatum*); -**artig,** fan-shaped, flabellate; -**auge,** *n.* faceted eye; -**blätterig,** flabellate; -**brenner,** *m.* fantail burner; -**förmig,** fan-shaped, flabelliform; -**gerste,** *f.* bearded barley.

fächerig, divided into compartments, locular, loculate.

Fächer-strahl, *m.* segment of labelliform leaf (palms); -**tracheen,** *f.pl.* book or tracheary lungs.

Fächerung, *f.* locule formation, formation of compartments by diaphragms.

Fächerzüngler, *m.pl.* Rhipidoglossa.

Fach-genosse, *m.*-n, professional colleague; -**kenntnis,** *f.* technical knowledge; -**kundlich,** expert; -**mann,** *m.* expert, specialist; -**männisch,** professional expert; -**mässig,** professional; -**ordung,** *f.* classification; -**schule,** *f.* technical school; -**spaltig,** loculicidal; -**sprache,** *f.* technical language.

Fach-werk, *n.* framework, truss, allotment, compartment; -**werkträger,** *m.* truss; -**wissenschaft,** *f.* special branch, specialty; -**wörterbuch,** *n.* technical dictionary; -**zeitschrift,** *f.* technical journal.

Facit, *n.* sum, result, answer.

Fackel, *f.*-n, torch; -**baum,** *m.* marsh elder; -**diestel,** *f.* torch thistle; -**fliege,** *f.* lantern fly; -**föhre,** *f.* Scotch pine; -**kohle,** *f.* cannel coal; -**palme,** *f.* sage palm.

Façon, *f.* fashion, cut, style.

façonnieren, to fashion, figure, convert.

Façonnierung, *f.* conversion.

Fädchen, n.-, small thread, filament; -substanz f. filar substance.

fade, insipid, flat, stale.

Faden, m.∺, thread, filament, linen, fiber, twine, fathom, grain, string; -abschnitt, m. thread segment; -ähnlich, threadlike, filamentous, filiform; -alge, f. filamentous alga; -artig, threadlike, filamentous, filiform; -bakterien, n.pl. thread-forming bacteria; -elektrometer, n. fiber electrometer; -feder, f.-n, filoplume; -flechte, f. filamentous lichen; -förmig, filiform, filamentous.

Faden-führer, m. thread guide; -gerüsttheorie, f. filar theory of protoplasmic structure; -holz, n. cordwood; -keimung, f. germination by a germ tube; -kieme, f. filiform gill; -klee, m. slender clover (*Trifolium filiforme*); -kreuz, n. crossed threads, spider lines, reticule, crosshairs; -molekül, n. filamentary molecule; -netz, n. cross hairs; -pilz, m.-e, filamentous fungus, mold, Hyphomycetes.

Faden-plasma, n. filar substance; -plasmodium, n. filamentous plasmodium; -ranke, f. axial branch tendril; -scheide, f. sheath enclosing swarm spores; -scheinig, sleazy, threadbare; -wurm, m. nematode; -ziehend, ropy, stringy.

fädig, thready, filaceous.

Faekalien, f.pl. night soil, human dung.

Fahamblärter, n.pl. faham leaves (*Angraecum fragans*).

fähig, (*gen.*) capable, able, apt.

Fähigkeit, f. capability, ability, capacity.

fahl, fallow, pale, fawn, dun, earth-colored, ashy, sallow, faded, livid, drab; -erz, n. fahlore, tetrahedrite; -gelb, fallow, yellowish; -grau, grayish, livid, ashy gray; -rot, fawn; -stein, m. pale gray slate.

fahnden (nach), to search (for).

Fahne, f. flag, standard, "policeman," vane, beard (of quill), trail (of smoke).

Fahnengrund, m. base of vane.

Fahrbahn, f. (wagon) road, track.

fahrbar, passable, transportable, practicable, movable.

Fahrbereich, n. radius (range) of action.

fahren, to ride, drive, to, travel; ∼ lassen, to let go, abandon, give up.

Fahrer, m. chauffeur.

Fahr-geld, n.-er, fare; -geleise, n. wheel rut; -gestell, n. chassis (of auto).

fährig, open.

Fahrkarte, f. ticket.

fahrlässig, careless, negligent.

Fährlichkeit, f. peril.

Fahr-rad, n.∺er, bicycle; -strecke, f. range of action; -stuhl, m. elevator, hoist, wheel chair.

Fahrt, f.-en, journey, trip, passage, drive.

Fährte, f. trail, track, (foot)print.

Fahr-weg, m. wagon road, driveway; -zeug, n. vehicle, vessel; -zeugmotor, m. automotive engine.

fäkal, fecal; -bakterien, n.pl. fecal bacteria.

Fäkalien, n.pl. feces.

Fäkalstoff, m. fecal substance.

Faktis, n. factice, rubber admixture.

faktisch, real, actual.

Faktor, m. factor, gene, manager, agent.

Faktoren-abstossung, f. spurious allelomorphism; -austausch, m. crossing over; -kette, f. factor chain; -koppelung, f. gametic coupling, linkage; -tabelle, f. table of factors.

Faktur(a), f. invoice.

Fäkulenz, f. sediment, yeast, dregs, feculence.

fakultativ, facultative, potential.

falb, pale-yellow, pale, fallow.

Falke, m. falcon, hawk.

falkenartig, falconine, accipitrine.

Fall, m.∺e, fall, decline, descent, case, event, yield, accident, failure; **auf jeden ∼, auf alle Fälle**, in any case, at all events; **auf keinen ∼**, in no case, by no means; **im Falle (auf den Fall), dass**, in case that.

Fallbad, n. setting (coagulating) bath.

Fäll-apparat, m.∺e, precipitation apparatus; -axt, f. felling ax.

fällbar, precipitable, ready to fell.

Fällbarkeit, f. precipitability.

Fällbottich, m. precipitating vat.

Falle, f. trap, valve, bolt, leaf, sluice gate.

fallen, to fall, drop, separate, be deposited, sink, abate; **an einen ∼, to inherit; ins Gewicht ∼**, to be of great weight; **in die Augen ∼**, to strike the eye; **die Arbeit fällt ihm schwer**, the work is hard (difficult) for him; **∼ lassen**, to drop, discard.

fällen, to precipitate, drop, cut, fell, pass; **ein Urteil ∼**, to pass judgment.

Fallenbau, m. construction of traps.

Fäller, m. precipitator.

Fällflüssigkeit, *f.* precipitating liquid.

Fall-frucht, *f.* deciduous fruit: **-gesetz,** *n.* law of gravity; **-hammer,** *m.* drop hammer, pile driver, falling weight; **-häutchen,** *n.* valve; **-höhe,** *f.* sedimentation depth, height of fall, stroke.

fallieren, to fail.

fällig due, payable.

Fälligkeit, *f.* settling (precipitation) .elocity.

Fällkessel, *m.* precipitation vessel.

Fallkraut, *n.* arnica.

Fäll-methode, *f.* precipitation method; **-mittel,** *n.* precipitating agent, precipitant.

Fall-nest, *n.* trap nest; **-obst,** *n.* windfalls; **-pendel,** *n.* friction pendulum; **-rohr,** *n.* down pipe, waste pipe.

falls, in case, provided.

Fall-schirm, *m.*-e, parachute; **-strecke,** *f.* distance of falling; **-sucht,** *f.* epilepsy; **-tür,** *f.* trap door.

Fällung, *f.* precipitation, felling, cutting.

Fällungs-kraft, *f.* precipitating power; **-mittel,** *n.* precipitant; **-reaktion,** *f.* precipitation reaction; **-vermögen,** *n.* precipitating power; **-wärme,** *f.* heat of precipitation; **-zeit,** *f.* felling season, cutting time.

Fall-werk, *n.*-e, stamp, pile driver; **-winkel,** *m.* angle of inclination.

falsch, false, counterfeit, pseudo-, artificial, adulterated, wrong, deceitful.

fälschen, to falsify, adulterate, counterfeit, forge.

Fälscher, *m.*-, adulterator, falsifier, forger.

fälschlich, false, erroneous; **-erweise,** falsely, erroneously, by mistake.

Fälschung, *f.* falsification, fraud.

Fälschung(s)mittel, *n.* adulterant.

Falte, *f.* fold, plait, wrinkle, flexure, bend.

falten, to fold, plait, wrinkle; **-blatt,** *n.* visceral lamina or layer; **-filter,** *n.* folded (plaited) filter; **-frei,** without folds; **-hülle,** *f.* covering fold; **-los,** without folds.

Falten-magen, *m.* third stomach of ruminants; **-paar,** *n.* pair of folds; **-rohrbogen,** *m.* creased bend; **-schwamm,** *m. Helvella crispa;* **-werfen,** *n.* creasing, puckering, draping; **-wespen,** *f.pl.* Vespidae.

Falter, *m.*-, folder, creaser, moth, butterfly, lepidopter, third stomach of ruminants; **-blumen,** *f.pl.* plants pollinated by Lepidoptera.

faltig, wrinkled, having folds, in plaits or creases, puckered.

-fältig, -fold; zehn- tenfold; **mehr-** multiple.

Faltung, *f.* folding, plaiting, wrinkling ~ **(der Blätter),** vernation.

Faltungspunkt, *m.* plait fold, point of folding.

Falz, *m.*-e, fold, notch, groove, flute, furrow, edge.

falzen, to fold, groove, flute, rabbet.

Falzfestigkeit, *f.* folding endurance.

Falzziegel, *m.* grooved tile.

Familie, *f.* family, generation, lineage.

Familien-auslese, *f.* family selection; **-forschung,** *f.* genealogical investigation.

fand (finden), found.

Fang, *m.*-e, catch, capture, trap, stab, fang, tusk, claw, talon; **-arm,** *m.* tentacle, arm (for grasping); **-baum,** *m.* trap tree, lime tree; **-bein,** *n.* prehensile paw, or claw; **-borste,** *f.* prehensile bristle; **-eisen,** *n.* spring trap.

fangen, to catch, capture, hook, trap, secure, snare.

Fänger, *m.* catcher.

Fang-faden, *m.* tentacle; **-fuss,** *m.* claw (for grasping); **-graben,** *m.* ditch for trapping insects; **-haar,** *n.* glandular hair; **-knospe,** *f.* bud of tentacle; **-kralle,** *f.* claw for grasping; **-pflanze,** *f.* trap plant, insectivorous plant; **-rechen,** *m.* terminal boom; **-stoff,** *m.* stuff, pulp (paper).

Farb-abänderung, *f.* change in color; **-absatz,** *m.* dyeing difference; **-auszüge,** *m.pl.* color component (images); **-bad,** *n.* dye bath; **-band,** *n.* typewriter ribbon; **-brühe,** *f.* dye liquor; **-druck,** *m.* color (printing) print

färbbar, colorable, stainable.

Färbbarkeit, *f.* colorability, stainability.

Farbe, *f.* color dye, pigment, complexion, stain, paint, hue, tint; **-band,** *n.* dye band.

Färbe, *f.* staining, dyeing; **-artikel,** *m.* dyed style; **-bad,** *n.* dye bath; **-brühe,** *f.* dyeing liquor

farbecht, of fast color.

färbe-fähig, capable of being colored or stained; **-fass,** *n.* dye (beck) tub; **-flechte,** *f.* dyer's moss; **-dotte,** *f.* dye bath; **-flüssigkeit,** *f.* dyeing liquid, staining fluid.

Farbe-gewinnung, *f.* obtaining of dyes; **-haltend,** holding color, fast.

Färbe-holz, *n.* dyewood; **-kraft,** *f.* tinting strength.

farb(e)los, colorless, achromatic.

Färbe-methode, f. method of staining or dyeing; -mittel, n. coloring agent, pigment, dye.

färben, to color, stain, dye; sich ∼, to molt.

Farben-abbeizmittel, n. paint remover; -abstreichmesser, n. knife for removing excess dye; -abweichung, f. chromatic aberration; -änderung, f. alteration of color; -band, n. spectrum; -bild, n. colored image, colored spectrum; -blind, color-blind; -blindheit, f. color blindness; -bogen, m. iris; -brechung, f. color (blending) refraction.

färbend, coloring, staining.

Farben-distel, f. safflower (Carthamus tinctorius); -druck, m. color printing; -empfindung, f. sense (perception) of color, chromatic sensation; -erde, f. colored earth; -erscheinung, f. chromatic phenomenon; -erzeugend, chromogenic, color producing; -erzeuger, m. chromogen; -fehler, m. chromatic defect; -gebung, f. coloration; -gewerbe, n. dyeing trade, color industry.

Farben-grund, m. ground color; -holz, n. dyewood; -körper, m. coloring matter, pigment; -korrektion, f. color correction (achromatism); -kreis, m. color disk; -lehre, f. science of color, chromatics; -leiter, m. color scale; -los, colorless, achromatic; -mass, n. colorimeter; -messer, m. chromatometer.

Farben-messung, f. chromatometry, colorimetry; -ofen, m. enameling furnace; -rand, m. iris; -reiben, n. color grinding; -reich, richly colored; -rein, colorless; -reinheit, f. chromatic purity; -säume, m.pl. color fringes; -schattierung, f. hue, shading; -schiller, m. color play, iridescence.

farben-schillernd, iridescent; -sehen, n. color vision; -sinn, m. sense of color; -spektrum, n. chromatic spectrum; -steindruck, m. chromolithography; -stufe, f. color gradation, shade, tint; -ton, m. color tone, hue; -umschlag, m. color change; -verändernd, altering colors; -veränderung, f. change in color, discoloration.

Farben-verdünner, m. thinner; -verdünnungsfaktor, m. color diluting factor; -verteilung, f. color (pattern) distribution; -wechsel, m. change in color; -wurzel, f. madder; -zerstreuung, f. color dispersion.

Färbe-pflanzen, f.pl. dye crops; -prozess, m dyeing (coloring) process.

Färber, m.-, dyer; -baum, m. Venetian sumac (Cotinus); -blume, f. woodwax(en); -distel, f. safflower (Carthamus tinctorius).

Färberei, f. dyeing, dyeworks.

Färber-eiche, f. dyer's oak, quercitron (Quercus tinctoria); -erde, f. Armenian bole; -flechte, f. archil, dyer's moss (Roccella tinctoria); -ginster, m. dyer's broom (Genista tinctoria); -kraut, n. dyer's weed; -kreuzdorn, m. dyer's buckthorn (Rhamnus infectoria); -maulbeerbaum, m. dyer's mulberry (Morus tinctoria); -moos, n. dyer's moss, archil; -ochsenzunge, f. dyer's alkanet (Alkanna tinctoria).

Färber-rinde, f. quercitron bark; -rot, n. alizarin; -röte, f. madder; -saflor, m. safflower; -waid, m. dyer's woad; -wau, m. dyer's weed, yellowweed; -wurzel, f. madder.

Färbe-stoff, m.-e, coloring matter, pigment; -vermögen, n. coloring power, tinctorial power; -zeit, f. molting time.

Farb-fehler, m. color defect; -fertig, ready for coloring; -flüssigkeit, f. staining solution; -gut, n. goods to be dyed; -holz, n. dyewood.

farbig (farbicht), colored, stained, chromatic.

Färbkraft, f.-e, strength of stain, coloring power.

Farb-kreiselmethode, f. color-disk method: -los, colorless, hyaline, achromatic; -lösung, f. staining solution; -markierung, f. color marking; -messend, colorimetric; -mine, f. colored lead (for pencils); -muster, n. color pattern; -nuance, f. color shade, tint; -reaktion, f. color reaction; -saum, m. color fringe; -stein, m. dyestone; -stift, m. colored pencil.

Farbstoff, m.-e, coloring matter, pigment, stain, dye; -aufnahme, f. dye absorption; -bildung, f. chromogenesis, formation of pigment; -brühe, f. dye liquor; -character, m. coloring property; -erzeugend, chromogenic; -haltig, containing coloring matter or pigment; -lösung, f. dye solution, staining solution; -niederschlag, m. precipitation of dye or color.

Farb-stufe, f. color gradation, tint, shade.

Farbton, m.-e, color, hue, tint or tone.

Färbung, f. dyeing, coloring, staining, pigmentation, hue, tinge.

färbungs-fähig, capable of being colored, or stained; -methode, f. staining method;

-unterschied, *m.* differentiation by staining; **-vermögen,** *n.* tinctorial power, coloring power.

Farb-unruhe, *f.* uneven dyeing; **-wechsel,** *m.-,* change of color; **-zelle,** *f.* pigment cell.

Farin, *m.* **-zucker,** *m.* brown sugar, moist sugar.

Farn, *m.* fern; **-blattaderung,** *f.* fern-frond venation; **-kraut,** *n.* fern; **-pflanzen,** *f.pl.* Pteridophyta; **-vorkeim,** *m.* fern spore.

Farre, *m.* young bull, steer.

Färse, *f.* heifer.

Fasan, *m.* pheasant.

Faschine, *f.* fascine, bundle of fagots.

Fasciation, *f.* fasciation.

Fasel, *f.* kidney bean (*Phaseolus vulgaris*).

Fasel, *m.&f.* propagation, brood, embryo, fetus.

faseln, fasern, to unravel, drivel.

Faser, *f.-,* fiber, thread, filament, string, grain; **-ähnlich,** fibroid; **-alaun,** *m.* halotrichite; **-anhäufung,** *f.* accumulation of fibers or filaments; **-artig,** fibrous, filamentary, grained; **-band,** *n.* accessory ligament; **-blatt,** *n.* mesoderm; **-blend,** *f.* fibrous sphalerite; **-borke,** *f.* bark consisting largely of fibers; **-büschel,** *n.* bundle of fibers.

Fäserchen, *n.-,* little fiber, fibril, filament.

Faser-durchkreuzung, *f.* optic commissure, chiasma; **-gärbung,** *f.* coloration of the fiber; **-förmig,** fibrous, filiform, filamentous; **-franse,** *f.* fringe of fibers; **-gehalt,** *m.* fiber content; **-gewebe,** *n.* fibrous tissue; **-grübchen,** *n.* sterile conceptacle, scaphidium, cryptostomate; **-haut,** *f.* fibrous membrane; **-hülle,** *f.* fibrous capsule, covering or sheath.

faserig, fibrous, filamentous, stringy, fuzzy.

Faser-kalk, *m.* fibrous calcite, aragonite; **-kiesel,** *m.* fibrolite; **-knorpel,** *m.-,* fibrous cartilage; **-kreuzung,** *f.* optic commissure, chiasma; **-los,** fiberless; **-lücke,** *f.* fibrous interstice or space, interfibrillar space.

fasern, to feaze, fuzz, ravel (out), unweave.

Faser-richtung, *f.* direction or course of fiber; **-schicht,** *f.* fibrous layer; **-spannung,** *f.* fiber stress.

Faserstoff, *m.-e,* fibrin, fibrous material; **-artig,** fibrinous.

Faser-strang, *m.-̈e,* cord of fibers; **-torf,** *m.* fibrous (peat) root; **-tracheide,** *f.* fiber tracheid.

Faserung, *f.* fibrillation, texture.

Faser-verlauf, *m.* course of fibers; **-wirbel,** *m.* gnarl of fibers; **-wurzel,** *f.* fibrous root; **-zeolith,** *m.* natrolite; **-züge,** *m.pl.* fiber tracts, fasciculus of fibers.

fasrig, fibrous, filamentous.

Fass, *n.-̈er,* cask, barrel, keg, vat, tank, tub.

fassbar, comprehensible.

Fassbare, *n.* something tangible.

Fassbier, *n.* draft beer.

Fässchen, *n.-,* small barrel, keg.

Fassdaube, *f.* stave.

fassen, to seize, grasp, take, put, mount, set, hold, contain, include; **sich ~,** to compose oneself; **ins Auge ~,** to keep in mind; **gefasst,** seized, resigned, composed, calm, prepared; **sich kurz ~,** to be brief.

Fass-gärung, *f.* cask fermentation; **-gä-rungssystem,** *n.* cleansing system; **-geläger,** *n.* cask deposit, bottoms.

fasslich, comprehensible, conceivable.

Fassoneisen, *n.* rolled steel (member) shape.

Fasspech, *n.* cooper's pitch, pitch in casks.

Fassung, *f.* seizing, capture, frame, wording, style, form, edition, capacity, holder, socket, composure; **ganz ausser ~ sein,** to be completely beside oneself; **aus der ~ bringen,** to disconcert, upset; **aus der ~ kommen,** to lose one's self-control.

Fassungs-raum, *m.-̈e,* capacity; **-vermögen,** *n.* power of comprehension.

Fasszwickel, *m.* try cock.

fast, almost, nearly.

Fastage, *f.* casks, cooperage, barrels and casks.

fasten, to fast.

Faszie, *f.* fascia; **-streifen,** *m.* fascia strip.

fauchen, to hiss, puff.

faul, rotten, putrid, carious, foul, decaying, lazy, slow, brittle, worthless.

faulbar, putrescible, corruptible.

Faul-baum, *m.* alder buckthorn (*Rhamnus frangula*), bird cherry (*Prunus padus*); **-brand,** *m.* smut (wheat); **-bruch,** *m.* shortness, brittleness; **-brut,** *f.* foul brood; **-butte,** *f.,* **-bütte,** *f.* fermenting trough.

Fäule, *f.* rottenness, dry rot, blight.

faulen, to rot, putrefy, decompose.

fäulen, to cause to putrefy.

faulend, rotting, putrescent, septic, putrid.

Faulenzer, *m.* idler, reckoner.

Faulgas, *n.* sewer gas.

faulig, rotten, putrid, moldy.

Faulkern, *m.*ᵉe, heart rot.

Fäulnis, *f.*-se, putrefaction; **-alkaloid,** *n.* ptomaine; **-bakterium,** *n.* putrefactive bacterium; **-base,** *f.* ptomaine; **-befördernd,** septic, putrefactive; **-beständigkeit,** *f.* resistance to rotting; **-bewirkend,** septic putrefactive; **-bewohner,** *m.* saprophyte; **-blasen,** *f.pl.* blisters of putrefaction; **-erregend,** septic, putrefactive.

Fäulnis-erreger, *m.* putrefactive agent; **-fähig,** putrefiable, decomposable; **-gift,** *n.* septic poison; **-hemmend,** antiseptic; **-hindernd,** antiseptic; **-unfähig,** unputrefiable, imputrescible; **-verhindernd,** antiseptic; **-vorgang,** *m.*process of putrefaction; **-widrig,** antiseptic.

Faulschlamm, *m.* sapropel activated sludge.

Faultier, *n.* sloth (Bradypus).

Faulung, *f.* rotting, putrefaction, decay.

Faul-weizen, *m.* smut fungus; **-werden,** *n.* putrefaction.

Faum, *f.* foam, froth.

Faust, *f.*ᵉe, fist, grasp, grip; **-gelenk,** *n.* wrist joint; **-gross,** the size of a fist; **-regel,** *f.* rule of thumb.

Favus (krankheit), *f.* favus.

Fäzes, *f.pl.* feces.

Fazialis, *m.* facial nerve; **-verzweigungen,** *f.* ramifications of facial nerve.

Fazies, *f.* facies, face, aspect; **-wechsel,** *m.* change of surface.

Fechser, *m.* set of vine.

fechten, to fight, fence.

Feder, *f.*-n, feather, plume, pen, down, spring, spline; **-ähnlich,** featherlike, plumaceous, springlike; **-alaun,** *m.* feather alum, halotrichite, alungoen, amianthus; **-artig,** featherlike, plumaceous; springlike; **-ast,** *m.* ramus; **-balg,** *m.* papilla of feather; **barometer,** *m.&n.* aneroid barometer; **-bart,** *m.* vexillum; **-borstengras,** *n.* Pennisetum; **-busch,** *m.* tuft of feathers, crest.

Federchen, *n.* plumule.

Feder-erz, *n.* jamesonite; **-fahne,** *f.* vane, vexillum, trimmed feather; **-feld,** *n.* pteryla; **-fluren,** *f.pl.* pterylae; **-förmig,** feathery, plumiform; **-gips,** *m.* fibrous gypsum; **-gras,** *n.* feather grass (*Stipa pennata);* **-haar,** *n.* filamentous hair; **-hart,** springy, elastic; **-harz,** *n.* India rubber, caoutchouc.

federich, federig, feathered, feathery, plumose.

Feder-kelch, *m.* pappus; **-kiel,** *m.* quill, keel; **-kleid,** *n.* plumage; **-konstante,** *f.* elasticity constant; **-kraft,** *f.* elasticity; **-kräftig,** elastic, springy; **-krone,**/. pappus, aigret; **-motte,** *f.* plume moth.

federn, to lose feathers, molt, be elastic, spring.

federnd, molting, elastic; **federnder Fadenführer,** *m.* spring thread guide.

Feder-nelke, *f.* feathered pink; **-ring,** *m.* split lock washer; **-seele,** *f.* the pith of a feather quill; **-stahl,** *m.* pen or spring steel; **-strahl,** *m.* radius of a feather, feather barbule; **-ventil,** *n.* spring valve; **-vieh,** *n.* poultry; **-wachstum,** *n.* growth of the feathers; **-waage,** *f.* spring balance; **-wechsel,** *m.* molting.

Feder-weiss, *n.* amianthus, fibrous gypsum, French chalk; **-wild(bret),** *n.* wild fowl, winged game; **-zahnegge,** *f.* springtime harrow; **-zahngrubber,** *m.* springtime cultivator; **-zange,** *f.* spring pincers; **-zeichnung,** *f.* pen drawing, feather markings; **-zinken,** *m.* tooth of a spring-tooth harrow.

Fege, *f.* sieve, screen, riddle; **-apparat,** *m.* stylar brush; **-haar,** *n.* stylar hair.

fegen, to sweep, clean, winnow, wipe, rub.

Fege-salpeter, *m.* saltpeter sweepings; **-sand,** *m.* scouring sand; **-schober,** *m.* scum pan.

Fegsel, *n.* sweepings.

fehlbar, fallible.

Fehlbetrag, *m.*ᵉe, deficit, deficiency.

fehlen, (*dat.*) to fail, miss, err, be missing, be absent, lack; **es fehlt uns an Geld,** we are in need of money; **an mir soll es nicht ∼, dass,** it shall not be my fault if; **es an nichts ∼ lassen,** to spare no pains or expense.

Fehlen, *n.* absence.

Fehler, *m.*-, error, mistake, blunder, fault, defect, flaw; **-ausgleichung,** *f.* equalization of errors; **-fortpflanzungsgesetz,** *n.* law of probability, propagation of error; **-frei,** faultless, correct, sound, clear; **-grenze,** *f.* limit of error, tolerance.

Fehlergrösse, *f.* size of error; **prozentuale ∼,** percentage of error.

fehler-haft, faulty, defective, deficient; **-möglichkeit,**/. possibility of error; **-quelle,** *f.* source of error; **-verteilungsgesetz,** *n.* error-distribution law; **-wahrscheinlichkeitsrechnung,** *f.* calculation of probable error.

Fehl-geburt, *f.* abortion, miscarriage; **-gehen,** to go wrong; **-gewächs,** *n.* crop failure; **-griff,** *m.* mistake, blunder.

Fehlingsche Lösung, Fehling's solution.

Fehl-jahr, *n.*-e, bad (fail) year, off year; **-prognose,** *f.* false prognosis; **-rippe,** *f.* false rib; **-schlag,** *m.* disappointment, failure; **-schluss,** *m.* false inference, fallacy, paralogism; **-stelle,** *f.* flow; **-schuss,** *m.* misfire; **-tritt,** *m.* mistake.

Fehn, *m.&n.* fen, bog; **-kultur,** *f.* peat culture or cutting.

feien, to make proof against, charm.

Feier, *f.* celebration, festival, holiday, rest.

feierlich, festive, solemn, ceremonious.

Feierlichkeit, *f.* festivity, ceremony.

feiern, to celebrate, honor, rest (from work), strike.

Feier-stunde, *f.* leisure hour, recreation; **-tag,** *m.* holiday.

feig(e), cowardly, timid.

Feigbohne, *f.* lupine.

Feige, *f.* fig.

Feigen-baum, *m.*-̈e, fig tree; **-frucht,** *f.* fig fruit, syconium; **-kaktus,** *m.* prickly pear, Indian fig tree (*Opuntia vulgaris*); **-mücke,** *f.* fig gnat.

Feigwurz, *f.* figwort (*Ranunculus ficaria*).

feil, for sale, mercenary.

Feile, *f.* file.

feilen, to file, polish.

Feilicht, *n.* filings.

Feilmaschine, *f.* shaper.

feilschen, to bargain.

Feil-sel, *n.*, **-späne,** *m.pl.* **-staub,** *m.* filings.

Feim(en), *m.* 104 bundles (straw), corn stack, rick.

fein, fine(ly), thin, delicate, small, soft, acute, refined, nice; **feiner Titer,** *m.* fine denier.

Fein-arbeit, *f.* delicate (precision) work; **-bau,** *m.* fine or detailed structure; **-bewegung,** *f.* slow motion, fine adjustment,; **-bewimpert,** fringed with fine hairs; **-blasig,** having small bubbles; **-blech,** *n.* thin metal plate; **-brennen,** to refine.

Feind, *m.*-e, enemy, foe.

feindlich, (*dat.*) hostile, opposed.

Feindschaft, *f.* hostility, enmity.

Feindseligkeit, *f.* hostility, enmity.

Feine, *f.* fineness.

feine(r)n, to refine.

Fein-erde, *f.* garden soil, fine earth; **-faserig,** fine-fibered, fine-grained; **-fein,** very fine, superfine; **-feuer,** *n.* refinery; **-führungs-schlitten,** *m.* slow-motion slide carriage; **-gehalt,** *m.* fineness; **-gekerbt,** crenulate; **-gelpulvert,** finely powdered; **-gespitzt,** sharp, pointed, cuspidate; **-haarig,** pubescent.

Feinheit, *f.* fineness, gracefulness, fine detail, refinement, delicacy, closeness (of grain in wood).

Feinheitsgrad, *m.* degree of fineness.

Fein-kies, *m.* fine ore, fines; **-körnig,** fine-grained; **-kristallinisch,** finely crystalline; **-lochig,** fine-holed, fine-pored; **-mahlen,** to grind fine, triturate; **-maschig,** fine-meshed; **-messer,** *m.* micrometer; **-porig,** finely porous; **-prozess,** *m.* refining process; **ringig,** fine-ringed.

Fein-sand, *m.* fine-grained sand; **-schlacke,** *f.* refinery slag; **-schmeckend,** delicate (in taste), savory, epicurean; **-schrot,** *m.&n.* fine groats, finely crushed malt; **-schutt,** *m.* fine rock debris; **-verteilt,** finely divided; **-waage,** *f.* precision balance; **-wollig,** lanugin(ous); **-zellig,** fine-celled, finely cellular; **-zerkleinert,** finely divided, finely ground; **-zerteilt,** finely divided.

Feinzeug, *n.* pulp; **-holländer,** *m.* beater, beating engine.

Fein-zinn, *n.* grain tin; **-zucker,** *m.* refined sugar.

feist, fat, stout, plump.

Feist, *n.* fat, suet (of deer); **-zeit,** *f.* season for venison.

Felbel, *m.&f.* feather shag, velveteen.

Felber, *m.* white willow (*Salix alba*).

Feld, *n.*-er, field, land, soil, panel, department; **-ahorn,** *m.* common maple (*Acer campestre*); **-anbauversuch,** *m.* field trial; **-bau,** *m.* agriculture, farming; **-beifuss,** *m.* wormwood (*Artemisia campestris*); **-biene,** *f.* wild bee; **-brand,** *m.* clamp burning.

Feldchen, *n.* areole.

Feld-dichte, *f.* strength of field; **-dienst,** *m.* active (military) service; **-flasche,** *f.* water bottle.

Felderung, *f.* division into areas, tesselation.

Feld-frucht, *f.*-̈e, farm product; **-gerät,** *n.* agricultural implements, field equipment; **-grasswirtschaft,** *f.* grazing culture; **-grau,** military gray; **-heuschrecken,** *f.pl.* Acrididae; **-kamille,** *f.* camomile (*Matricaria chamomilla*); **-klee,** *m.* white clover.

rabbit-foot clover; **-kümmel**, *m.* wild caraway, wild thyme; **-mässig**, in fields, for the field; **-maus**, *f.* field mouse.

Feld-messen, *n.* land surveying; **-messer**, *m.* land surveyor; **-mitte**, *f.* center of span; **-ofen**, *m.* camp kiln, field oven; **-rauch**, *m.* fumitory (*Fumaria officinalis*); **-raute**, *f.* fumitory (*Fumaria officinalis*); **-rüster**, *m.* common elm (*Ulmus campestris*); **-salat**, *m.* lamb's-lettuce (*Valerianella olitoria*); **-spannung**, *f.* field voltage.

Feldspat, *m.* feldspar; **-ähnlich**, feldspathic; **-artig**, feldspathic.

Feld-sperling, *m.* tree sparrow; **-stärke**, *f.* field intensity; **-stecher**, *m.* field glass; **-stein**, *m.* boulder, landmark; **-thymian**, *m.* wild thyme; **-ulme**, *f.* common elm (*Ulmus campestris*); **-verzerrung**, *f.* field distortion; **-weite**, *f.* span (dimension); **-wirtschaft**, *f.* agriculture; **-ziegel**, *m.* clamp brick; **-zug**, *m.* campaign.

Felge, *f.* fallow. rim, felly, felloe.

Fell, *n.*-e, skin, hide, pelt, fur, coat; **-eisen**, *n.* knapsack; **-leim**, *m.* hide glue; **-schmitzer**, *m.* dyer of skins; **-späne**, *m.pl.* hide parings; **-zeichnung**, *f.* coat pattern.

Fels(en), *m.* rock, cliff; **-art**, *f.* kind of rock; **-bewohner**, *m.* cragsman, rock-inhabiting plant; **-block**, *m.* boulder; **-boden**, *m.* rock soil.

Felsen, *m.* cliff, rock; **-ader**, *f.* dike, rock (vein) seam; **-alaun**, *m.* rock alum; **-bein**, *n.* petrosal bone, petrous portion of temporal bone; **-beinpyramide**, *f.* petrous portion of temporal bone; **-birne**, *f.* rock pear (*Amelanchier vulgaris*); **-blutader**, *f.* petrosal sinus; **-flora**, *f.* rock flora; **-flur**, *f.* fell field; **-fortsatz**, *m.* petrous portion of temporal bone.

Felsen-gebirge, *n.* Rocky Mountains; **-glimmer**, *m.* mica; **-hinterkopfnaht**, *f.* petro-occipital suture; **-huhn**, *n.* stone grouse; **-kirsche**, *f.* *Prunus mahaleb;* **-kresse**, *f.* rock pepperwort (*Lepidium petraeum*); **-mispel**, *f.* *Amelanchier vulgaris;* **-öl**, *n.* rock oil (petroleum); **-salz**, *n.* saltpeter; **-schlundmuskel**, *m.* stylopharyngeal muscle.

Felsen-trompetenmuskel, *m.* salpingopharyngeal muscle; **-tundra**, *f.* rock tundra; **-wand**, *f.* wall of rock.

Fels-formation, *f.* rock formation; **-gebilde**, *n.* formation of rock; **-geröll**, *n.* rock debris; **-glimmer**, *m.* mica; **-grat**, *m.* high rocky ridge; **-hafter**, *m.* epilithophyte.

felsig, rocky, rocklike.

Fels-inwohner, *m.* endolithophyte; **-kopfflur**, *f.* vegetation of mountain top; **-löser**, *m.* rock loosener, plant with underground root stems; **-öl**, *n.* petroleum; **-schlipf**, *m.* rockslide; **-spaltengesellschaften**, *f.pl.* associations of rock-inhabiting plants.

Fels-strand, *m.* rocky shore; **-trümmer**, *m.* fragment of rock, debris; **-understand**, *m.* shelter beneath a rock, rock cave; **-wandbewohner**, *m.pl.* plants growing on rock walls; **-wurzler**, *m.* rhizolithophyte.

Femelschlagbetrieb, *m.* shelterwood-selection system.

Fench, *m.* bristle grass (Setaria).

Fenchel, *m.* fennel (*Foeniculum vulgare*); **-holz**, *n.* sassafras wood.

Fenn, *m.* marshy ground, fen.

Fennich, *m.* Setaria.

Fenster, *n.*-, window, gate; **-glas**, *n.* window glass; **-kitt**, *m.* glazier's putty; **-leder**, *n.* chamois leather; **-scheibe**, *f.* windowpane: **-sturz**, *m.* **-träger**, *m.* **-überlage**, *f.* lintel, beam over window.

Ferien, *f.pl.* holidays, vacation.

Ferkel, *n.* piglet, suckling pig; **-kaninchen**, *n.* agouti; **-kraut**, *n.* cat's-ear (*Hypochoeria radicata*); **-maus**, *f.* guinea pig (*Cavia cobaya*).

ferkeln, to farrow.

Ferment, *n.* ferment, enzyme; **-ausscheidung**, *f.* secretion of enzyme.

fermentieren, to ferment.

Fermentierungsvorgang, *m.*-e, fermentation process.

Fermentwirkung, *f.* ferment action, fermentation.

fern, (*dat.*) far, distant.

Fernambukholz, *n.* brazilwood.

Fern-aufnahme, *f.* long-range photograph; **-auslösung**, *f.* release from a distance.

Ferne, *f.* distance, remoteness.

ferner, further, farther, besides, additional; **-hin**, further along, furthermore.

Fern-glas, *n.*-er, telescope, field glass; **-halten**, to keep away; **-haltung**, *f.* prevention, keeping off; **-hörer**, *m.* telephone receiver; **-korrektion**, *f.* correction for distance; **-messung**, *f.* remote measurement; **-mündlich**, by telephone; **-photographie**, *f.* telephotography; **-punkt**, *m.* far point; **-rohr**, *n.* telescope.

Fern-rohrlupe, *f.* telescopic magnifier; **-sagen**, to telephone; **-schreiber**, *m.* telegraph, distant recorder; **-schuss**, *m.* shot at long range; **-sehen,** *n.* television: **-sehpunkt,** *m.* greatest distance; **-sicht,** *f.* perspective, distant view; **-sprecher,** *m.* telephone; **-steuerung,** *f.* remote control; **-tastsinn,** *m.* perceptibility of distance.

Fern-wahrnehmungsapparat, *m.* distance recording apparatus; **-wirkung,** *f.* distant action, telepathy; **-zeichnung,** *f.* perspective drawing.

Ferri-acetat, *n.* ferric acetate; **-ammonsulfat,** *n.* ammonium ferric sulphate; **-chlorid,** *n.* ferric chloride; **-chlorwasserstoff,** *m.* ferrichloric acid.

Ferricyan-kalium, *n.* potassium ferricyanide; **-natrium,** *n.* sodium ferricyanide; **-verbindung,** *f.* ferricyanide; **-wasserstoff,** *m.* ferricyanic acid.

Ferri-hydroxyd, *n.* ferric hydroxide; **-kaliumsulfat,** *n.* ferric potassium sulphate; **-nitrat,** *n.* ferric nitrate; **-oxyd,** *n.* ferric oxide; **-phosphat,** *n.* ferric phosphate; **-rhodanid,** *n.* ferric thiocyanate, ferric sulphocyanate; **-salz,** *n.* ferric salt; **-sulfat,** *n.* ferric sulphate; **-sulfid,** *n.* ferric sulphide; **verbundung,** *f.* ferric compound.

Ferrit, *n.* ferrite (soft pure iron).

Ferro-acetat, *n.* ferrous acetate; **-bor,** *n.* ferroboron; **-carbonyl,** *n.* iron carbide; **-cyan,** *n.* ferrocyanogen; **-cyanid,** *n.* ferrous cyanide, ferrocyanide; **-cyankalium,** *n.* potassium ferrocyanide; **-ferricyanid,** *n.* ferrous ferricyanide; **-ferrioxyd,** *n.* ferrosoferric oxide; **-nitrat,** *n.* ferrous nitrate; **-oxalate,** *n.* ferrous oxalate.

Ferro-oxyd, *n.* ferrous oxide; **-phosphate,** *n.* ferrous phosphate; **-phosphor,** *n.* ferrophosphorus; **-salz,** *n.* ferrous salt; **-sulfat,** *n.* ferrous sulphate; **-sulfid,** *n.* ferrous sulphide; **-verbindung,** *f.* ferrous compound.

Ferse, *f.* heel, metatarsus.

Fersen-ballen, *m.* ball of the heel; **-bein,** *n.* heel bone, calcaneum, os calcis; **-flechse,** *f.* tendon of Achilles; **-fuss,** *m.* calcaneum; **-knochen,** *m.* os calcis; **-sprungbeingelenk,** *n.* astragalocalcanear ligament; **-würfelbeinband,** *n.* calcaneocuboid ligament.

fertig, ready, done, finished, accomplished, finished, ready-made, complete, insolvent, skilled, ruined; **mit etwas** (jemandem) ∼ **werden,** to get along with something (someone).

fertigen, to prepare, make (ready), manufacture, do.

Fertig-erzeugnis, *f.***-se,** finished product; **-gebildet, -gemacht,** finished, completed.

Fertigkeit, *f.* readiness, practice, skill, dexterity.

Fertig-machen, *n.* finishing; **-stellen,** to complete, run, finish; **-stellung,** *f.* finishing, completion.

Fertigung, *f.* making (ready), manufacture.

Fertilität, *f.* fertility.

Ferulasäure, *f.* ferulic acid.

Fessel, *f.* fetters, shackles, pastern, fetlock.

Fesselbein, *n.* large pastern bone; **-band,** *n.* ligament of pastern bone; **-gelenk,** *n.* pastern joint.

Fessel-blutader, *f.* tibial vein; **-gelenk,** *n.* fetlock joint.

fesseln, to fetter, bind, captivate, fasten.

Fest, *n.* feast, festival, holiday.

fest, compact, solid, firm, strong, fast, substantial, fixed, tight, stable, permanent proof, steady, closely, stiff, stout, enduring; **-backen,** to cake together; **-binden,** to tie fast, to fasten.

Feste, *f.* hard rock, fortress, firmament, density, hawk's-beard (Crepis).

fest-frieren, to freeze solid; **-gebunden,** fastened; **-gehalt,** *m.* solid contents; **-geklemmt,** clamped in; **-gelagert,** compact, firmly consolidated; **-gewachsen,** attached, grown fast.

fest-geworden, solidified; **-haften,** to cling tight, adhere strongly; **-halten,** to hold (fast), retain, fix, stop, adhere (strongly), clasp, arrest, cling, detain; **-haltend,** tenacious; **-haltungsvermögen,** *n.* holding capacity; **-heften,** to attach firmly.

festigen, to make firm, consolidate, secure, establish, condense.

Festigkeit, *f.* solidity, firmness, steadiness, stability (density), tenacity, strength, resistance, durability, consistence, tensile strength.

Festigkeits-eigenschaft, *f.* stress (tensile) property, solidity; **-grenze,** *f.* limit of stability or density; **-lehre,** *f.* science of strength of materials; **-zahl,** *f.* stability ratio, strength coefficient.

Festigungsgewebe, *n.* mechanical tissue.

fest-kitten, to cement; **-kleben,** to stick fast; **-land,** *n.* continent, mainland; **-legen,** to fix, place, determine, define, bed, moor; **-legung,** *f.* fixation.

festlich, festive, solemn, magnificent.

fest-liegend, (firmly) fixed; **-machen,** to solidify, to make fast, fasten, fix, attach, settle; **-meter,** *m.&n.* cubic meter; **-nor-**

-miert, fixed, permanent; -punkt, *m.* fixed point, anchorage; -schiebe *f.* fixed pulley.

Fest-schrift, *f.* festival or anniversary publication; -setzen, to establish, settle, arrange, fix; -setzung, *f.* establishment, settlement, stipulation, arrangement, appointment; -sitzen, to sit fast, remain permanently, settle down; -sitzend, attached, (firmly) fixed; -stecken, to attach firmly.

feststehen, to stand fast, be fixed; es steht fest, it is quite certain.

fest-stehend, fixed, stationary, constant, stable, established; -stellbar, ascertainable, capable of proof; -stellen, to establish, fix, determine, ascertain; -stellung, *f.* establishment; -stoffgehalt, *m.* solids content.

Festung, *f.* fortification.

fest-wachsen, to grow fast, become attached; -weich, semisolid; -werden, *n.* solidification, coagulation; -werden, to set; -wert, *m.* fixed value, constant.

fett, fatty, oily, aliphatic, fat, rich, fertile, adipose, obese, lucrative.

Fett, *n.* fat, grease, adipose tissue; -abfall, *m.* fatty refuse; -abfälle, *m.pl.* fatty refuse; -abscheider, *m.* grease separator; -ähnlich, fatlike, fatty; -ansatz, *m.* corpulence; -arm, poor in fat; -aromatisch, aliphatic aromatic; -artig, fatlike, fatty.

Fett-bedarf, *m.* fat requirement; -bestandteil, *m.* fatty constituent; -bestimmung, *f.* fat determination; -bildner, *m.* fat former, elaioplast; -bildung, *f.* fat formation; -dicht, fat-tight; -druck, *m.* bold-faced type; -drucken, to print in boldface; -drüse, *f.* sebaceous (fat) gland.

Fette, *f.* fatness, greasiness.

fetten, to fatten, oil, lubricate, grease.

Fett-entziehung, *f.* fat extraction; -fang, *m.* grease trap; -farbstoff, *m.* color for fats, fat stain, lipochrome; -fleck(en), *m.* grease spot; -flosse, *f.* adipose fin; -gar, oil-tanned (leather).

Fett-gas, *n.* oil gas; -gedruckt, boldface, heavily printed; -gehalt, *m.* fat content; -gewebe, *n.* fatty tissue, adipose tissue; -glänzend, having a greasy luster; -grieben, *f.pl.* cracklings.

fett-haltig, containing fat, fatty; -härtung, *f.* hardening of fat(s); -harz, *n.* oleoresin; -haut, *f.* adipose membrane, subcutaneous fatty layer; -hefe, *f.* fatty yeast (*Endomyces vernalis*); -heit, *f.* fatness; -henne, *f.* stonecrop (Sedum).

fettig, fat(ty), greasy, unctuous, adipose.

Fettigkeit, *f.* fatness, greasiness.

Fett-kohle, *f.* bituminous coal; -körper, *m.* fat body, fatty compound; -kraut, *n.* butterwort (*Pinguicula vulgaris*); -kügelchen, *n.* fat globule; -lösend, fat-dissolving; -löslich, soluble in fat; -magen, *m.* fourth stomach of ruminants; -matte, *f.* lush (Alpine) mountain meadow; -noppe,*f.* grease spot; -pflanze, *f.* Crassula, succulent plant.

Fett-platte, *f.* fatty plastid (of Peridineae); -polster, *n.* cushion of fat, subcutaneous fatty tissue; -ponceau, *n.* fat ponceau, scarlet red; -puddeln, *n.* pig boiling (iron); -quarz, *m.* greasy quartz; -reich, rich in fat; -reihe,*f.* fatty compounds, aliphatic series; -reservemittel, *n.* fat (wax) resist; -sauer, combined with fatty acid; -säure, *f.* fatty acid.

Fett-schlicht, *f.* layer of fat; -schmiere, *f.* fat liquor, lubricant; -schweiss, *m.* fatty sweat, yolk (of wool); -seife, *f.* soap from fats; -sein, *n.* fatness, greasiness, ropiness (of wine); -spaltend, fat-cleaving, lipolytic; -spaltung, *f.* fat-splitting; -spritze, *f.* grease gun; -stein, *m.* eleolite; -stift, *m.* wax (pencil), crayon.

Fett-stoffwechsel, *m.* fat metabolism; -sucht, *f.* fatty degeneration, obesity, adiposity; -ton, *m.* fuller's earth; -überzug, *m.* covering of fat.

Fettung, *f.* oiling.

Fett-verbindung, *f.* fatty (aliphatic) compound; -verseifung, *f.* saponification of fat; -wachs, *n.* adipocere; -wolle, *f.* grease wool, yolk wool; -zersetzung, *f.* fat decomposition.

Fetzen, *m.* shred, tatter, particle, scrap, trifle.

feucht, moist, humid, damp, wet; auf feuchtem Wege, by wet process.

Feuchte, *f.* moistness, dampness; -messer, *m.* hygrometer; -schreiber, *m.* humidity recorder.

feuchten, to moisten, dampen, wet.

Feuchtheit, *f.* moistness, dampness.

Feuchtigkeit, *f.* moisture (content), moistness, dampness, humidity, humor, phlegm.

Feuchtigkeits-gehalt, *m.* moisture content; -grad, *m.* degree of moisture, humidity, or saturation; -messer, *m.* hygrometer; -niederschlag, *m.* deposit of moisture; -zeiger, *m.* hygroscope.

feuchtwarm, moist and warm.

Feuer, *n.* fire, furnace, ardor, spirit, forge, hearth, vigor, light; -beständig, fireproof, resistant to fire or heat, refractory; -beständigkeit, *f.* fire-resistive quality; -bestattung, *f.* cremation; -blende, *f.* fireblende, pyrostilpnite; -fangend, inflammable; -farbig, flame-colored.

feuerfest, fireproof; **feuerfester Ton,** *m.* fireclay; **feuerfester Ziegel,** *m.* firebrick.

Feuer-festigkeit, *f.* fireproofness, refractoriness; -flüssig, molten, liquid to melting temperature; -führung, *f.* firing, method of firing; -funke, *m.* spark of fire; -gefährlich, liable to catch fire, inflammable, combustible; -hahn, *m.* fireplug, hydrant.

Feuer-kitt, *n.* fireproof cement; -krücke, *f.* furnace rake; -leitung, *f.* range finding, range keeping, priming, fuse; -los, fireless, lusterless; -löschapparat, *m.* fire extinguisher; -löschmittel, *n.* fire-extinguishing substance; -material, *n.* fuel.

feuern, to fire, heat, animate, burn, spark, glow.

Feuernelke, *f.* scarlet lychnis (*Lychnis chalcedonica*).

Feuer-punkt, *m.* focus, hearth; -raum, *m.* combustion chamber, firebox, furnace, hearth, fireplace; -raumbelastung, *f.* furnace heat release; -saft, *m.* slag bath; -schein, *m.* gleam of fire, lurid glow; -schwamm, *m.* tinder, punk.

Feuersgefahr, *f.* danger of fire, fire hazard.

feuersicher, fireproof, fire-resistant.

Feuer-stätte, *f.* -stelle, *f.* hearth, fireplace.

Feuerstein, *m.* flint; -knolle, *f.* flinty concretion.

Feuerung, *f.* firing, fire, heating, furnace, fuel, hearth, fireplace.

Feuerungs-anlage, *f.* furnace, hearth, fireplace; -bedarf, *m.* -bedürfnis, *n.* fuel need; -material, *n.* fuel; -verzinnung, *f.* hot tin plating; -wache, *f.* fire patrol; -werk, *n.* fireworks; -wehr, *f.* fire department; -widerstandsfähig, resistant to fire; -zeug, *n.* tinderbox, matchbox; -ziegel, *m.* firebrick; -zug, *m.* heating flue, fire tube.

feurig, fiery, igneous, burning, hot, ardent, spirited, bright, loud.

Fibel, *f.* primer.

Fibereis, *n.* fibrocrystalline ice.

Fibrille, *f.* fibril.

Fibrillen-bündel, *n.* fibrillary bundle; -hypothese, *f.* fibrillar theory.

Fibrin, *n.* fibrin; -haltig, containing fibrin, fibrinous.

Fibrinogen, *n.* fibrinogen.

fibrös, *f.* fibrous.

Fibrovasal-bündel, *n.* fibrovascular bundle; -strang, *m.* fibrovascular strand.

Fichte, *f.* spruce, pine.

Fichten-bestand, *m.* spruce stand; -blattwespe, *f.* spruce sawfly; -borkenkäfer, *m.* spruce beetle; -harz, *n.* spruce resin, rosin; -hiebzug, *m.* thinning of spruce stand; -holz, *n.* spruce wood.

Fichten-nadelöl, *n.* pine-needle oil; -nadelrost, *m.* spruce-needle rust; -säure, *f.* pinic acid; -spargel, *m.* pinesap, birdsnest (*Monotropa hypopitys*); -spinner, *m.* black-arches (*Ocneria monacha*); -triebgallenlaus, *f.* spruce gall aphis; -wirtschaft, *f.* spruce management.

Fieber, *n.* fever; **aussetzendes** ∼, intermittent fever.

fieber-artig, feverish, febrile; -arznei, *f.* febrifuge; -fest, immune to fever; -haft, feverish; -heilbaum, *m.* Eucalyptus; -klee, *m.* marsh trefoil, buck bean (*Menyanthes trifoliata*); -kraut, *n.* feverfew (*Matricaria parthenium*); -los, free from fever; -mittel, *n.* febrifuge; -mücke, *f.* gnat, mosquito (causing malaria).

fiebern, to have fever, be feverish.

Fieber-pulver, *n.* ague powder; -rinde, *f.* cinchona bark; -vertreibend, febrifuge; -widrig, febrifuge.

Fieder, *f.* leaflet, pinnule, bar, pinna; -artig, pinnate(d); -blatt, *n.* pinna; -blättchen, *n.* pinnule; -blättergewächse, *n.pl.* plants possessing pinnate leaves; -förmig, pinnate; -lamelle, *f.* barb (secondary) quill; -lappig, having pinnate lobes.

fiedern, to feather.

Fieder-palme, *f.* palm with pinnate leaves; -spaltig, pinnate, pinnatifid; -streifung, *f.* orientation of striae; -teilig, having pinnate parts.

fiel (fallen), fell.

Figur, *f.* figure, illustration, diagram.

Figurendruck, *m.* topical printing; -artikel, *m.* topical style.

figurieren, to figure.

figürlich, figurative.

fiktiv, imaginary, fictitious, fictive.

Filarmasse, *f.* filar protoplasm.

Filiale, *f.* branch (establishment).

Filiasäure, *f.* filicic acid.

Filigran, *n.* filigree.

Filixsäure, *f.* filicic acid.

Film, *m.* film, skin.

Filter, *m.* filter; **-anlage,** *f.* filtration plant; **-bewegung,** *f.* seepage flow; **-brücke,** *f.* filter bracket; **-dicke,** *f.* thickness of the filter; **-element,** *n.* filter cell. **-fläche,** *f.* area; **-flächenausnutzung,** *f.* utilization; **-fortsätze,** *m.pl.* gill rakers; **-gerät,** *n.* filter; **-kerze,** *f.* filter candle; **-körper,** *m.* main part.

Filterkuchen, *m.* solid residue, sludge, residual layer; **-leistung,** *f.* residue per unit time per unit area.

Filtermittel, *n.* filter(ing) material, filter leaf; **-träger,** *m.* container for filter material or leaf; **-unterlage,** *f.* intermediate screen or layer.

filtern, to filter.

Filtern, *n.* filtering.

Filter-papier, *n.* filter paper; **-plättchen,** *n.* (small) filter plate; **-rest,** *m.* residue on the filter; **-rohr,** *n.* perforated (well) pipe; **-rückstand,** residue on the filter; **-schicht,** *f.* filter layer; **-träger,** *m.* filter (holder) ring; **-turm,** *m.* filter tower.

Filterungs-dauer, *f.* time of filtering; **-hilfsmittel,** *n.* agent for promoting filtering process.

Filter-versuch, *m.* seepage test; **-watte,** *f.* filter wadding; **-zelle,** *f.* unit.

Filtrat, *n.* filtrate; **-leistung,** *f.* filtrate capacity.

filtrations-fähig, capable of filtration; **-kraft,** *f.* filtration efficiency.

Filtrier-apparat, *m.* filtering apparatus; **-aufsatz,** *m.* filtering attachment.

filtrierbar, filterable.

filtrieren, to filter, strain.

Filtrier-erde, *f.* filtering earth; **-fläche,** *f.* filtering surface; **-flasche,** *f.* filtering flask; **-gestell,** *n.* filter stand; **-hut,** *m.* filtering funnel; **-nutsche,** *f.* suction filter; **-papier,** *n.* filter paper; **-sack,** *m.* filter bag, percolator; **-stutzen,** *m.* filtering jar; **-trichter,** *m.* filtering funnel; **-tuch,** *n.* filtering cloth.

Filtrierung, *f.* filtering, filtration.

Filz, *m.* felt, tomentum, felt hat, blanket, miser; **-alge,** *f.* felted alga; **-artig,** feltlike.

Filzbarkeit, *f.* felting property.

filzen, to felt.

filz-fähig, capable of felting; **-fähigkeit,** *f.* felting property; **-falte,** *f.* crease in the felt; **-gewebe,** *n.* felted tissue; fungus tissue, **-haar,** *n.* felted hair.

filzig, feltlike, of felt, tomentous, downy.

Filz-krankheit, *f.* rhizoctonia disease (of potato); **-moose,** *n.pl.* felt-forming mosses; **-tuch,** *n.* felted cloth, felt.

filzwollig, like felted wool.

Fimmel, *m.* fimble hemp, female hemp.

finden, to find, discover, understand, think, be found, exist, be; **sich** ~, to find oneself; **das wird sich schon** ~, that will, no doubt, come out all right; **es** ~ **sich,** there are, there is; **es wird sich** ~, **dass,** it will be found that; **sich in etwas** ~, to put up with something; **sich zurecht** ~, to find one's way about.

Findigkeit, *f.* ingenuity.

Findling, Findlingsblock, *m.* foundling, erratic block, drift boulder.

fing (fangen), caught; **fing an,** began.

Finger, *m.*-, finger, digit, toe; **-band,** *n.* digital ligament; **-bein,** *n.* digital phalanx; **-beuger,** *m.* flexor of the finger; **-dick,** as thick as a finger; **-druck,** *m.* pressure of the finger; **-förmig,** digitate, digital; **-futter,** *n.* finger stall; **-gelenk,** *n.* finger joint, articulation between the digits; **-glied,** *n.* phalanx of a finger.

Finger-grube, *f.* digital fossa; **-hirse,** *f.* finger grass (Eleusine); **-hut,** *m.* thimble, foxglove (Digitalis); **-knochen,** *m.* digital phalanx; **-kraut,** *n.* cinquefoil (Potentilla); **-kuppe,** *f.* fingertip; **-ling,** *m.* finger stall; **-nagel,** *m.* fingernail; **-probe,** *f.* rule of thumb; **-sehne,** *f.* digital tendon.

Finger-spitze, *f.* fingertip; **-spitzengefühl,** *n.* instinct, intuition; **-strecker,** *m.* extensor (muscle) of finger; **-verwachsung,** *f.* adhesion of fingers, syndactylia; **-zeig,** *m.* pointing with the finger, indication, cue, hint.

fingieren, to simulate, pretend, invent.

fingiert, fictitious, imaginary.

Fink, *m.* finch.

Finne, *f.* pimple, pustule, fin, cysticercus.

Finnen-anlage, *f.* cysticercus, blastema stage; **-krankheit,** *f.* bladder-worm disease.

finnig, measly.

finster, dark, obscure, gloomy.

Finsternis, *f.* darkness, obscurity, eclipse.

Fioringras, *n.* bent grass, redtop grass, (*Agrostis alba*).

Firma, *f.*-en, firm.

firn, of last year.

Firn, *m.* glacier (last year's) snow, firn; **-gürtel,** *m.* region of perpetual snow.

Firnis, *m.* varnish, primer; **-artig,** varnish-like; **-papier,** *n.* glazed paper.

firnissen, to varnish, lacquer.

Firnmasse, *f.* glacier ice, lacquer.

First, *m.* ridge, peak (mountain), (mining) roof; **-balken,** *m.* ridge purlin.

Fisch, *m.* fish; **-augenstein,** *m.* apophyllite; **-behälter,** *m.* tank, reservoir; **-bein,** *n.* whalebone; **-bestand,** *m.* crop of fish; **-blase,** *f.* fish bladder, sounds, isinglass; **-brut,** *f.* fry; **-dünger,** *m.* fish manure.

fischen, to fish.

Fischerei, *f.* fishing, fishery.

Fisch-fang, *m.* catch of fish, fishing; **-fleischvergiftung,** *f.* fish-flesh poisoning; **-gesetz,** *n.* fishery law; **-gräte,** *f.* fishbone; **-köder,** *m.* bait; **-körner,** *n.pl.* Indian berries (*Cocculus indicus*); **-laich,** *m.* hard roe, spawn.

Fischleim, *m.* fish glue, isinglass, ichthyocolla; **-gummi,** *n.* sarcocolla.

Fisch-mehl, *n.* fish meal; **-milch,** *f.* soft roe; milt; **-öl,** *n.* fish oil, ichthyol; **-ölseife,** *f,* fish-oil soap; **-ordnung,** *f.* fishing regula, tion; **-otter,** *f.* otter; **-pass,** *m.* fish ladder. **-satz,** *m.* fish for brood, spawn; **-säugetiere-** *n.pl.* Natantia, Cetacea; **-schwanz,** *m.* fish tail.

Fisch-speck, *m.* fish blubber; **-tran,** *m.* fish oil; **-zeug,** *n.* fishing tackle; **-zucht,** *f.* fish culture, pisciculture.

Fisettholz, *n.* young fustic (*Rhus cotinus*).

Fissur, *f.* fissure.

Fistel, *f.* fistula, falsetto; **-holz,** *n.* young fustic; **-kassie,** *f.* purging (tuberous) cassia (*Cassia fistula*).

fistulös, fistular, fistulous.

Fittich, *m.* wing, pinion.

fitzen, to lace.

fix, fixed, fast, smart, alert.

Fixage, *f.* fixing.

Fix-bleiche, *f.* chloride of lime bleaching; **-färberei,** *f.* fast dyeing, dyeing by staining.

Fixierbad, *n.* "er, fixing bath.

fixieren, to fix, harden, stare at.

Fixier-flüssigkeit, *f.* fixing liquid; **-mittel,** *n.* fixing agent, fixative; **-natron,** *n.* sodium thiosulphate; **-salz,** *n.* fixing salt.

Fixierung, *f.* fixation, hardening.

flach, flat, level, even, plain, shallow, smooth, superficial; **-blatt,** *n.* flat leaf; **-brenner,** *m.* flat-flame burner.

Fläche, *f.* surface, face, flatness, plain, expanse, level, sheet, area, plane, facet.

Flacheisen, *n.* square (steel) bars, flats.

Flächen-anziehung, *f.* surface (adhesion) attraction; **-bearbeitung,** *f.* finish; **-dichte,** *f.* density of surface; **-dimension,** *f.* area, areal dimension; **-einheit,** *f.* superficial unit, unit of surface; **-form,** *f.* form of a plane; **-förmig,** flattened, flat; **-geschwindigkeit,** *f.* superficial velocity; **-grösse,** *f.* area; **-helle,** *f.* brightness of a surface.

Flächen-inhalt, *m.* area; **-läufig,** fan-shaped, venationlike (diadromous); **-mass,** *n.*-e, surface (square) measure; **-messer,** *m.* planimeter; **-messung,** *f.* surface measurement; **-raum,** *m.* area; **-reich,** having many faces; **-ständig,** parietal; **-stellung,** *f.* epistrophy (of plastids); **-umriss,** *m.* perimeter, surface outline.

Flächen-wachstum, *n.* growth in area; **-wert,** *m.* surface value; **-winkel,** *m.* plane angle; **-zahl,** *f.* square number, number of faces.

flach-gewunden, planispiral; **-gründig,** shallow.

Flachheit, *f.* flatness.

-flächig, faced, -hedral; **fünf-,** pentahedral.

Flach-keil, *m.* flat key; **-land,** *n.* plain, lowland, level country; **-moor,** *n.* shallow moor, marsh, swamp; **-moorwiese,** *f.* low-moor meadow.

Flächner, *m.* polyhedron.

flachrund, round and flat-bottomed.

Flachs, *m.* flax.

Flach-schnitt, *m.*-e, horizontal section; **-schorf,** *m.* shallow scab.

flächse(r)n, flaxen, of flax.

flachs-farben, flaxen (colored); **-lilie,** *f.* New Zealand flax (*Phormium tenax*); **-müdigkeit,** *f.* flax-sick soil.

Flachspross, *m.* cladode, phylloclad.

Flachs-samen, *m.*-, flaxseed, linseed; **-samenöl,** *n.* flaxseed oil; **-seide,** *f.* flax dodder; **-stein,** *m.* amianthus, asbestos.

Flach-wasser, *n.* shallow water; **-wasserwelle,** *f.* shallow-water wave; **-wunde,** *f.* surface wound; **-wurzelig,** shallow-rooted; **-wurzeligkeit,** *f.* shallow-rootedness; **-zange,** *f.* pliers, tongs with flat jaws.

flackerig, flickering, uncertain.

flackern, to flicker, flare.

Flacon, *m.&n.* small bottle.

Flader, *f.* curl, streak, **flaw**, speckle, vein, knot.

fladerig, curled, veined, streaked.

Flagellaten, *pl.* flagellata.

Flagge, *f.* flag, colors; hook (spinning defect).

Flak (Fliegerabwehrkanone), *f.* -geschütz, *n.* antiaircraft gun.

Flakon, *m.&n.* small bottle.

flambieren, to flame, singe.

flammbar, inflammable, flammable.

Flamme, *f.* flame, light, flash.

flammen, to flame, blaze, burn, glow, singe, flare; **-bogen,** *m.* electric arc; **-frischarbeit,** *f.* fining in a reverberatory furnace; **-gas,** *n.* gas feeding a flame; **-los,** flameless; **-sicher,** flameproof; **-werfer,** *m.* flame thrower.

flammfarbig, flame (rainbow) colored.

Flammfärbung, *f.* flame coloration.

flammieren, to flame, burn, glow.

flammig, watered (of fabrics), veined, spotted, flecked, grained (of wood), flamelike, blazing.

Flamm-kohle, *f.* steam coal; **-ofen,** *m.* reverberatory furnace; **-punkt,** *m.* flash point; **-rohr,** *n.*, fire tube, flue; **-rohrkessel,** *m.* internal furnace boiler.

Flanell, *m.* flannel.

Flanke, *f.* flank, side.

Flanken-chimäre, *f.* sectorial chimera; **-lage,** *f.* parastrophy (of plastids); **-naht,** *f.* side seam.

flankieren, to flank.

Flansch, *m.* flange.

Fläschchen, *n.* small bottle or flask.

Flasche, *f.* bottle, flask, jar, cylinder.

Flaschen-baum, *m.* custard apple (*Anona squamosa*); **-förmig,** lageniform, ampullaceous, bottle-shaped; **-hals,** *m.* neck of a bottle; **-inhalt,** *m.* contents of a flask or cylinder; **-kappe,** *f.* bottle cap; **-kürbis,** *m.* bottle gourd; **-schild,** *n.* bottle label; **-verschluss,** *m.* stopper; **-zug,** *m.* pulley.

Flaser, *f.* vein, streak.

flaserig, curled, speckled, streaked.

Flatter-binse, *f.* soft rush; **-gras,** *n.* millet (*Milium effusum*).

flattern, to flutter, float, flicker, fly, wave, be flighty.

Flatter-russ, *m.* lampblack; **-tiere,** *n.pl.* alipeds (Chiroptera).

flau, feeble, faint, weak, dull, slack.

flauen, to buddle, become weak or dull.

Flaum, *m.* down, tomentum, fluff, fat, lard; **-feder,** *f.* down, plumule; **-haar,** *n.* down, pubescence, lanugo hair; **-haarig,** pubescent.

flaumig, downy, fluffy, pubescent.

Flaus, Flausch, *m.* tuft (of hair).

Flechse, *f.* tendon, sinew.

Flechsen-bein, *n.* tibia; **-haube,** *f.* calotte, coif, caul, epicranium.

Flechte, *f.* lichen, plait, twist, herpetic eruption.

flechten, to plait, braid, twist, interweave; **-farbstoff,** *m.* lichen coloring matter; **-heide,** *f.* lichen heath; **-matte,** *f.* carpet of lichens; **-pilz,** *m.* lichen fungus; **-rot,** *n.* orcein; **-säure,** *f.* lichenic (fumaric) acid; **-stärkemehl,** *n.* lichenin, moss starch.

Flecht-werk, *n.* wickerwork, wattlework; **-zaun,** *m.* wattle fence.

Fleck, *m.* spot, speck, stain, blot, flaw, patch.

flecken, to stain, spot, speckle, soil.

Flecken, *m.pl.* measles; **-bildung,** *f.* spotting, formation of macules; **-frei,** stainless; **-los,** stainless; **-krankheit,** *f.* spot, blight.

Fleckfieber, *n.* spotted fever, typhus.

fleckig, spotted, speckled, stained, mottled, brindle, flawy; ~ **werden,** to spot, stain.

Fleck-stein, *m.* scouring stone; **-typhus,** *m.* typhus, spotted fever.

Fleckung, *f.* patching, marking.

Fleck-wasser, *n.* scouring water; **-vieh,** *n.* spotted cattle.

Fleder-mausblütler, *m.pl.* flowers pollinated by bats; **-mausbrenner,** *m.* batswing burner; **-mäuse,** *f.pl.* bats (*Chiroptera*); **-tier,** *n.* chiropter.

flehen, to implore, entreat.

Fleisch, *n.* flesh, meat, pulp; **-beschau,** *f.* meat inspection; **-brühe,** *f.* meat broth; **-dekokt,** *n.* meat decoction, juice of meat.

fleischen, to flesh.

Fleischer, *m.* butcher.

Fleisch-extrakt, *m.&n.* meat extract; **-farbe,** *f.* flesh color; **-faser,** *f.* muscle fiber; **-fäulnis,** *f.* spoiling or putrefaction of meat; **-fliegen,** *f.pl.* Sarcophagidae; **-fressend,** carnivorous; **-fresser,** *m.* carnivore; **-gift,** *n.* meat toxin, ptomaine; **-gummi,** *n.* sarcocolla; **-haut,** *f.* sarcocarp, sarcoderm, muscular coating or membrane.

fleischig, fleshy, carnose, pulpy.

Fleisch-kohle, *f.* animal charcoal; **-leim,** *m.* sarcocolla; **-kost,** *f.* meat diet; **-krone,** *f.* cornet (hoof); **-kühlanlange,** *f.* cold storage of meat; **-los,** meatless, vegetarian; **-magen,** *m.* gizzard; **-milchsäure,** *f.* sarcolactic acid; **-nadel,** *f.* flesh spicule; **-peptonagar,** *m.* nutrient agar.

Fleisch-rippe, *f.* false rib; **-rot,** flesh-colored; **vergiftung,** *f.* meat poisoning; **-warze,** *f.* caruncle; **-warzig,** papillose, caruncular; **-wasser,** *n.* meat broth; **-zahn,** *m.* canine tooth; **-zucker,** *m.* inositol, inosite, muscle sugar.

Fleiss, *m.* diligence, industry, purpose, application; **mit** ~, purposely, intentionally.

fleissig, diligent, industrious.

flicht (flechten), plaits, braids.

flicken, to patch.

Flickgewebe, *n.* scar tissue (cicatricial tissue).

Flieder, *m.* elder, lilac.

Fliege, *f.* fly.

fliegen, to fly, shift; **-blume,** *f.* flower pollinated by flies; **-gift,** *n.* fly poison; **-holz,** *n.* quassia wood; **-papier,** *n.* fly-paper; **-pilz,** *m.* fly agaric (*Amanita muscaria); -pulver,* *n.* fly powder; **-schwamm,** *m.* toadstool, fly agaric, fly fungus (*Amanita muscaria); -stein,* *m.* native arsenic or cobalt.

Flieger, *m.* flier, aviator; **-aufnahme,** *f.* aerial photography; **-film,** *m.* aero film.

fliehen, to flee, escape.

Fliehkraft, *f.* ̈e, centrifugal force.

Fliese, *f.* flag, floor or wall tile, paving brick.

Fliess, *n.* fleece; **-arbeit,** *f.* continuous production; **-betrieb,** *m.* continuous operation.

Fliessboden, *m.* moving soil.

fliessen, to flow, run, melt, blot, bleed.

Fliessen, *n.* flow, flowing.

fliessend, flowing, running, liquid, melting.

Fliess-erdewulst, *f.* soil-ridge formation from erosion; **-fähigkeit,** *f.* fusibility; **-geschwindigkeit,** *f.* velocity of flow; **-glätte,** *f.* wet litharge; **-grenze,** *f.* flow limit; yield value, liquid limit; **-harz,** *n.* oleoresin, turpentine; **-kohle,** *f.* colloidal fuel; **-kunde,** *f.* rheology; **-ofen,** *m.* pyrites kiln; **-papier,** *n.* blotting paper.

Fliess-papierscheibe, *f.* disk of blotting paper; **-probe,** *f.* flow (test) sample; **-sand,** *m.* quicksand; **-wasser,** *n.* running water, lymph.

Flimmer, *m.* glitter, glimmer, tinsel, spangle, mica; **-bewegung,** *f.* ciliary or vibratile movement; **-bogen,** *m.* ciliated arch; **-epithel,** *n.* ciliated epithelium, external ciliation; **-geissel,** *f.* fimbricate cilium, ciliary flagella; **-grube,** *f.* ciliated pit or groove; **-haar,** *n.* cilium; **-haut,** *f.* ciliated membrane; **-läppchen,** *n.* vibratile cilium, flame, ciliated lobe or lobule; **-larve,** *f.* ciliated larva.

flimmern, glitter, glisten, sparkle, scintillate.

flimmernd, glittering.

Flimmer-rinne, *f.* ciliated groove; **-schein,** *m.* sparkling luster; **-schlag,** *m.* ciliary movement; **-schlagumkehr,** *f.* ciliary reversal; **-strom,** *m.* ciliary current; **-trichter,** *m.* ciliated funnel; **-zelle,** *f.* ciliated cell.

flink, agile, quick, alert, brisk.

Flinte, *f.* gun, rifle.

Flinten-lauf, *m.* gun barrel; **-schrot,** *n.* small (gun) shot.

Flintstein, *m.* flint (stone).

Flinz, *m.* siderite.

Flitter, *m.* spangle, tinsel; **-erz,** *n.* ore in glittering laminas; **-glas,** *n.* pounded glass for frosting; **-gold,** *n.* Dutch metal, tombac.

flittern, to glitter, glisten, sparkle.

Flitter-sand, *m.* micaceous sand.

flocht (flechten), plaited, braided.

Flocke, *f.* flake, flock (of wool).

flocken, to form flakes or flocks, flake, flocculate; **-artig,** flakelike, flocculent; **-bildung,** *f.* flocculation, coagulation; **-blume,** *f.* centaury; **-erz,** *n.* mimetite; **papier,** *n.* flock paper; **-reaktion,** *f.* flocculation test; **-salpeter,** *m.* efflorescent saltpeter; **-struktur,** *f.* crumb structure (in loess).

flockig, flocculent, flaky; **-käsig,** curdy.

Flockseide, *f.* floss silk.

Flockung, *f.* flocculation.

Flockungsreaktion, flocculation test.

Flockwolle, *f.* flock wool, short wool.

flog (fliegen), flew.

floh (fliehen), fled.

Floh, *m.* flea; **-farbe,** *f.* puce color; **-knöterich,** *m.* willowweed, spotted knotgrass (*Polygonum persicaria); -kraut, n.* fleabane; **-krebs,** *m.* water flea (Amphipoda); **-samen,** *m.* fleawort seed, psyllium seed; **-stich,** *m.* fleabite.

Flor, *m.* bloom, blossom, blooming, gauze, nap, pile.

Florettseide, *f.* floss silk.

Florideen, *pl.* Florideae.

Floss, *n.* raft, pig iron, float.

flössbar, floatable.

Floss-bett, *n.* pig mold.

Flosse, *f.* fin, float, pig iron, blade.

flössen, to float, raft.

Flossen-anlage, *f.* rudiment of fin; **-besatz,** *m.* border, vesture of fin; **-förmig,** finlike; **-füsser,** *m.pl.* fin-footed animals (Pteropoda); **-saum,** *m.* fin (edge); **-stachel,** *m.* fin ray.

Floss-gasse, *f.* raft channel; **-holz,** *n.* raft wood; **-ofen,** *m.* flowing furnace.

flott, afloat, brisk, smooth, gay.

Flotte, *f.* fleet, navy, dye liquor; **lange** $\sim$, dilute dye liquor.

Flotten-gefäss, *n.* color reservoir; **-verhältnis,** *n.* bath ratio, consistency.

flottieren, to float, swim, treat by flotation.

Flott-seide, *f.* untwisted silk; **-stahl,** *m.* ingot steel.

Flotzmaul, *n.* muzzle (of cattle).

Flöz, *n.* layer, stratum, seam, bed.

fluatieren, to form fluosilicate (on concrete, etc.), impermeabilize.

Fluch, *m.* curse.

Flucht, *f.***-en,** flight, line, row, play, swing, escape, disappearance; **-bewegung,** *f.* motion of flight; **-ebene,** *f.* vanishing plane.

flüchten, to flee, escape.

Fluchtholz, *n.* rule, level.

flüchtig, volatile, moving, shifting, fugitive, fleeting, fragile, superficial, fleet, fickle, hasty.

flüchtigen, to volatilize.

Flüchtigkeit, *f.* volatility, fleetness.

Flucht-linie, *f.* building line; **-linientafel,** *f.* nomograph; **-punkt,** *m.* vanishing point; **-reaktion,** *f.* flight reaction.

fluchtrecht, flush.

Flug, *m.*¨**e,** flight, covey, flying, flock, swarm; **-asche,** *f.* light (flying) ashes; **-bahn,** *f.* line of flight; **-blatt,** *n.* fly sheet, handbill, pamphlet; **-brand,** *m.* loose smut.

Flügel, *m.* wing, ala, lobe, vane, branch, flap, scoop, casement, blade, grand piano; **-bein,** *n.* pterygoid bone, sphenoid bone; **-bug,** *n.* bend of wing; **-decke,** *f.* elytra, wing coverts; **-decken,** *f.pl.* (kleine) lesser coverts; **-deckenabsturz,** *m.* elytral declivity; **-deckennaht,** *f.* suture of elytra;

-dreieck, *n.* trigonulum; **-feder,** *f.* wing feather, pinion; **-flur,** *f.* pteryla, feather tracts of a bird's body.

Flügel-förmig, wing-shaped; **-fortsatz,** *m.* pterygoid process; **-frucht,** *f.* samara, a winged fruit; **-gaumengrube,** *f.* pterygomaxillary (palatine) fossa; **-gaumenmuskel,** *m.* pterygopalatine muscle; **-geäder,** *n.* network of small veins; **-gebläse,** *n.* fan blower; **-grube,** *f.* pterygoid fossa; **-häutchen,** *n.* membranule, the small opaque space of wing (Odonata); **-kiefermuskel,** *m.* pterygomaxillary muscle; **-knorpel,** *m.* alar cartilage.

Flügel-knoten, *m.* nodus (in wing of Odonata); **-kühler,** *m.* fan cooler; **-lappen,** *m.* alar lobe; **-loch,** *n.* alar foramen; **-los,** without wings; **-mal,** *n.* pterostigma; **-muskel,** *m.* pterygoid muscle, alar muscle; **-mutter,** *f.* wing nut.

flügeln, to wing.

Flügel-platte, *f.* alar plate; **-pumpe,** *f.* semirotary (wing) pump, oscillating pump; **-rad,** *n.* screw wheel, propeller; **-raine,** *m.pl.* apteria ali; **-rand,** *m.* margin of the wing, edge of vagina; **-rinne,** *f.* pterygoid fossa; **-scheide,** *f.* pterotheca.

Flügel-schlundkopfmuskel, *m.* pterygopharyngeal muscle; **-schnecken,** *f.pl.* Pteropoda; **-schraube,** *f.* wing screw, wing nut; **-schüppchen,** *n.* tegula, squama, small lobes at wing base; **-ulme,** *f.* wing(ed) elm; **-zungenbeinmuskel,** *m.* pterygohyoid muscle.

Flugfrüchtler, *m.pl.* plants producing winged seed.

flügge, fledged.

Flug-gewebe, *n.* structures for aiding in wind dissemination; **-hafen,** *m.* airport; **-hafer,** *m.* wild oat (*Avena fatua*); **-haut,** *f.* flying membrane, patagium; **-hörnchen,** *n.* flying squirrel; **-huhn,** *n.* sand grouse.

Flug-jahr, *n.* swarm year; **-kraft,** *f.* power of flight; **-linie,** *f.* line of flight; **-loch,** *n.* flight hole; **-mehl,** *n.* mill dust; **-organ,** *n.* flying organ (aiding in wind dissemination).

flugs, quickly, at once, instantly.

Flugsand, *m.* shifting sand, drift (blown) sand, quicksand; **-bindung,** *f.* fixation of shifting sands; **-düne,** *f.* shifting sand dune.

Flug-schrift, *f.* handbill, pamphlet; **-staub,** *m.* flue dust, smoke, fume, chimney soot; **-staubkammer,** *f.* condensing chamber; **-tätigkeit,** *f.* flying activity; **-vermögen,** *n.* power of flight; **-werkzeug,** *n.* organ of flight; **-wesen,** *n.* aviation; **-zeit,** *f.* flight;

(season) period, -zeug, *n.* airplane, flying machine.

Fluh, *f.* (Beton), concrete, soil stratum, mass of rock.

Fluid (um), *n.* fluid.

Fluidität, *f.* fluidity.

Flukkan, *n.* flucan, gauge (watery material).

fluktuieren, to fluctuate.

fluktuös, fluctuating.

Flunder, *m.* flounder.

Fluor, *n.* fluorine; -ammonium, *n.* ammonium fluoride; -benzol, *n.* fluorobenzene; -bor, *n.* boron fluoride; -borsäure, *f.* fluoboric acid.

Fluorescin, *n.* fluorescein.

Fluoreszenz, *f.* fluorescence.

fluoreszieren, to fluoresce.

Fluorgehalt, *m.* fluorine content.

Fluorid, *n.* fluoride.

Fluor-jod, *n.* iodine fluoride; -kieselsäure, *f.* fluosilicic acid; -salz, *n.* fluoride; -säure, *f.* fluoric acid; -silikat, *n.* -siliziumverbindung, *f.* fluorsilicate; -verbindung, *f.* fluorine compound; -wasserstoff, *m.* hydrogen fluoride, hydrofluoric acid; -wasserstoffsauer, fluoride of; -wasserstoffsäure, *f.* hydrofluoric acid.

Fluorür, *n.* fluoride.

Flur, *f.* field, plain, pasture; -bereinigung, *f.* field clearing.

Flur, *m.* vestibule, floor, hall, corridor.

Fluse, *f.* slub.

flusig, slubby.

Fluss, *m.* river, stream, flux, fluor spar, fusion, flow, flowing, discharge, catarrh; -ampfer, *m.* water dock or water sorrel; -bett, *n.* river bed; -eisen, *n.* ingot iron, soft steel; -erde, *f.* earthy fluorite; -formation, *f.* river formation; -gebiet, *n.* river basin; -geschwelle, *n.* estuary (of a tidal river); -harz, *n.* resin, gum animé.

flüssig, liquid, fluid.

Flüssigkeit, *f.* liquid, fluid, liquor, humor.

Flüssigkeits-austausch, *m.* fluid balance, exchange of liquid; -blase, *f.* fluid vesicle; -druck, *m.* pressure of a liquid; -mass, *n.* liquid measure; -menge, *f.* amount of liquid; -oberfläche, *f.* liquid surface; -säule, *f.* column of liquid; -schicht, *f.* fluid stratum; -spiegel, *m.* surface of a liquid; -spindel, *f.* hydrometer, float; -wärme, *f.* latent heat of liquid.

flüssig-machen, to liquefy; -werden, to become liquescent.

Flüssig-machen, *n.* -machung, *f.* liquefaction; -werden, *n.* to liquefy, melt.

Fluss-kies, *m.* river gravel; -kieselsäure, *f.* fluosilicic acid; -krebs, *m.* river crayfish; -mittel, *n.* fluxing material, flux, antirheumatic remedy; -ofen, *m.* flowing furnace; -pferd, *n.* hippopotamus.

Fluss-pulver, *n.* flux powder; -punkt, *m.* melting point; -sand, *m.* river sand; -säure, *f.* hydrofluoric acid; -schlamm, *m.* river silt or mud; -schmiedeeisen, *n.* malleable ingot iron.

Flusspat, *m.* fluorspar, fluorite; -linse, *f.* fluorite lens; -säure, *f.* hydrofluoric acid.

Fluss-stahl, *m.* ingot steel, soft steel; -stein, *m.* compact fluorite; -trübe, *f.* muddy condition of river water; -ufer, *n.* bank of a stream; -verlagerung, *f.* change in the course of a river; -wasser, *n.* river water.

flüstern, to whisper.

Flut, *f.* flood, (high) tide, crowd; -bewegung, *f.* tide, movement of the tide.

fluten, to swell, rise, surge.

flutend, streaming, submerged (mass).

Flut-gehölz, *n.* tidal woodland; -linie, *f.* high-tide mark.

focht (fechten), fought.

Fohlen, *m.* foal, colt.

Föhre, *f.* Scotch pine or fir.

Föhrenreisermoor, *n.* coniferous moor.

Fokustiefe, *f.* focal depth.

Folge, *f.* sequence, series, succession, set, future, consequence, result, conclusion, effect, compliance; die ~ sein von, to be due to; zur ~ haben, to result in, bring about; ~ leisten, to respond, obey; in der ~, subsequently, afterwards, in the future.

Folge-blatt, *n.* mature type of leaf (metaphyll); -erscheinung, *f.* effect, result, consequent phenomenon; -meristem, *n.* secondary meristem.

folgen, (dat.) to follow, succeed, ensue; im (aus) folgenden, in (from) the following discussion.

folgender-massen, -weise, as follows, in the following manner.

folgen-los, without results; -reich, having important consequences; -schwer, momentous, portentous, important, grave.

Folge-punkte, *m.pl.* consequent (poles) points, points of conclusion; -reaktion, *f.* consecutive reaction; -recht, -richtig, consistent, conclusive, logical; -richtigkeit, *f.* consistency, logical accuracy.

folgern, to conclude, infer, deduce.

Folgerung, *f.* conclusion, inference, induction.

Folge-satz, *m.* deduction, conclusion; **-wirkung,** *f.* resultant, consequence; **-zeit,** *f.* following period, future, time to come (afterward).

folglich, consequently.

folgsam, (*dat.*) obedient.

Folie, *f.* foil, film.

foliieren, to cover with foil, silver, page (a book).

Folio, *n.* page, folio.

Follikel, *m.* follicle; **-hormon,** *n.* follicle hormone; **-trichter,** *m.* funnel of the follicle.

Fond, *m.* foundation, base, basis, capital, bottom.

forcieren, to force; overtax.

Forcierkrankheit, *f.* strain disease.

forciert, severe, forced.

Förderanlage, *f.* conveying (equipment) system.

Förderer, *m.* promoter, accelerator, conveyer.

Förder-erz, *n.* pit ore; **-gerüst,** *n.* head frame (of a coal mine); **-gut,** *n.* output, material delivered; **-höhe,** *f.* height, level; **-kohle,** *f.* run-of-the-mine coal.

förderlich, serviceable, effective, speedy.

Förder-menge, *f.* **-quantum,** *n.* output.

fordern, to demand, request, ask, require, summon, challenge.

fördern, to further, promote, advance, help, expedite, hasten, encourage, accelerate, raise, convey, transport; **zutage** ~, to extract, bring to light.

Förder-schnecke, *f.* screw conveyer; **-technik,** *f.* handling of materials.

Forderung, *f.* demand, requisition.

Förderung, *f.* furthering, promotion.

Förderungsmittel, *n.* adjuvant.

Forelle, *f.* trout.

Forelleneisen, *n.* mottled white pig iron.

forensisch, forensic.

Forke, *f.* fork.

Form, *f.* form, shape, cut, size, usage, mold, frame.

Formänderung, *f.* change of form, deformation.

formänderungs-fähig, capable of deformation; **-fähigkeit,** *f.* plasticity, ductility; **-wirkungsgrad,** *m.* efficiency.

Formart, *f.* form species, change of species.

Format, *n.* form, shape, size, format.

Formations-bildner, *n.* pioneer plants, plants initiating a new formation; **-folge,** *f.* succession; **-glied,** *n.* subtype, association member; **-gruppe,** *f.* formation (association); **-klasse,** *f.* vegetation (formation) type.

formativ, formative, molding, shaping; **formativer Stoff,** *m.* building material; **formatives Cytoplasma,** *n.* kinoplasm; **formatives Wachstum,** *n.* morphogenic growth.

Formausgestaltung, *f.* development of the external form.

formbar, plastic, capable of being shaped.

Formbarkeit, *f.* plasticity.

Form-bestandteil, *m.* constituent; **-bildung,** *f.* structure; **-bildungsvorgang,** *m.* morphogenic process **-eisen,** *n.* special steel (iron) bar.

Formel, *f.* formula; **-bild,** *n.* structural formula.

Formelement, *n.* structural element, morphologic unit.

formen, to form, shape, fashion, mold, cast; **-kreis,** *m.* group (association); **-mannigfaltigkeit,** *f.* diversity of form; **-reihe,** *f.* series of forms; **-sinn,** *m.* sense of form.

Formerde, *f.* molding clay.

Formerei, *f.* molding shop, molding operation.

Form-gattung, *f.* form genus; **-gebung,** *f.* profiling, shaping; **-gestaltung,** *f.* form, shape; **-haltend,** retaining form or shape; **-höhe,** *f.* form height.

Formiat, *n.* formate.

formieren, to form.

Form-körper, *m.* molded body; **-lehre,** *f.* profile gauge.

förmlich, formal, proper, plain, express(ly), downright.

Formling, *m.* briquette.

formlos, formless, amorphous, amorphic.

Formopersäure, *f.* performic acid.

Form-spaltung, *f.* polymorphism; **-stein,** *m.* shaped brick; **-stück,** *n.* fitting, special shape; **-veränderung,** *f.* modification (of form); **-wechsel,** *m.* form change.

Formular, *n.* form, blank, schedule.

formulieren, to formulate.

Formulierung, *f.* formulation, definition.

Formung, *f.* formation.

Formylsäure, *f.* formic acid.

Formzahl, *f.* form factor, form number

forsch, vigorous, strong.

forschen, to investigate, search.

Forscher, *m.*-, investigator, inquirer.

Forschung, *f.* investigation, research, inquiry; der ∼ war geholfen, research was furthered.

Forschungs-anstalt, *f.* research station or institute, laboratory; **-arbeit,** *f.* research work; **-gebiet,** *n.* field of research; **-geist,** *m.* spirit of research; **-mikroskop,** *n.* research microscope.

Forst, *m.* forest; **-amt,** *n.* office of the local forest superintendent; **-beamte,** *m.* forest officer; **-beflissener,** *m.* forest student; **-benutzung,** *f.* forest utilization; **-berechtigung,** *f.* forest right.

Forst-betrieb, *m.* forest management; **-bezirk,** *m.* forest range; **-botanik,** *f.* dendrology, tree botany; **-diebstahl,** *m.* theft of forest produce; **-diensteinrichtung,** *f.* organization of forest service; **-einrichter,** *m.* organizer; **-einrichtung,** *f.* forest (regulation) management.

Förster, *m.* forester, forest ranger.

Forst-etat, *m.* forest budget; **-fach,** *n.* science of forestry; **-frevel,** *m.* forest offense; **-garten,** *m.* arboretum, nursery; **-gerät,** *n.* implement, tool; **-gesetz,** *n.* forest law; **-haushalt,** *m.* forest economy or management; **-insekt,** *n.* forest insect; **-kunde,** *f.* forestry.

forstlich, forestral, relating to forests.

Forst-ordnung, *f.* forest regulation; **-personal,** *n.* forest staff; **-politik,** *f.* forest policy; **-revier,** *n.* forest range; **-schutz,** *m.* forest protection; **-schutzbeamte,** *m.* forest guard; **-statistik,** *f.* forest statistics; **unkraut,** *n.* forest weed.

Forst-vermessung, *f.* forest survey; **-verwaltung,** *f.* forest administration; **-wart,** *m.* forest warden; **-wegweiser,** *m.* forest directory; **-wesen,** *n.* forestry; **-wirt,** *m.* silviculturist; **-wirtschaft,** *f.* forestry; **-wirtschaftslehre,** *f.* forest economy; **-wissenschaft,** *f.* science of forestry.

fort, forward, on, forth, away; ∼ **und** ∼, on and on, forever; **und so** ∼ and so on.

fortan, henceforth.

Fort-bestand, *n.* continuance; **-bestehen,** to continue; **-bewegen,** to move away

or along, progress, propel; **-bewegung,** *f.* locomotion, progression.

Fortbewegungs-organ, *n.* organ of locomotion; **-weise,** *f.* manner of locomotion.

Fortbildung, *f.* construction, finishing of one's education.

Fortbildungsgewebe, *n.* cambium.

fortbringen, to carry away, remove, convey, rear, bring forward, support, maintain.

Fort-dauer, *f.* permanence, duration; **-dauern,** to continue, last; **-entwickeln,** to continue developing; **-fahren,** to continue, set off, depart, go on; **-fallen,** to be wanting, cease; **-fliessen,** to flow away, run off; **-führen,** to continue, carry on or away, convey, prosecute.

Fortgang, *m.* going away, progress, advance.

fortgehen, to continue, go on, go away, depart, proceed.

fort-geschritten, progressed; **-gesetzt,** continued; **-glimmen,** continue to smolder; **-kochen,** to boil away or off; **-kommen,** to get away, prosper, thrive, progress; **-kommen,** *n.* escape, getting on, success.

fort-lassen, to let go, leave out, omit; **-laufen,** to run away; **-laufend,** continuous, successive, continual; **-leiten,** to remove, transmit, conduct, propagate; **-leitung,** *f.* propagation, transmission, carrying off; **-nehmen,** to take away, remove; **-pflanzen,** to propagate, transmit, spread, communicate, reproduce, regenerate; **-pflanzung,** *f.* propagation, reproduction, transmission, spreading, communication, convection.

Fortpflanzungs-apparat, *m.* reproductive organ, propagatorium; **-bläschen,** *n.* vesicle of evolution, embryonic vesicle; **-geschwindigkeit,** *f.* velocity of propagation; **-organe,** *n.pl.* reproductive organs; **-periode,** *f.* breeding or propagation season; **-polyp,** *m.* reproductive polyp.

Fortpflanzungs-richtung, *f.* direction of propagation; **-schicht,** *f.* reproducing layer; **-trieb,** *m.* sexual or generative instinct; **-vermögen,** *n.* reproductive power; **-zelle,** *f.* spore, sexual cell, propagative cell; **-züchtung,** *f.* subsequent cultivation.

fort-rieseln, to ripple (over pebbles); **-rücken,** to move away or on, advance, progress; **-satz,** *m.* continuation, appendix, process; **-schaffen,** to take away, remove, get rid of, discharge; **-schieben,** to move on, move; **-schleudern,** to cast or fling away; **-schreiten,** to step forward, progress, **-schreitend,** progressive.

Fort-schritt, *m.*-e, advance(ment), progress, improvement; -schrittlich, progressive, liberal; -senden, to send away, dispatch; -setzen, to continue, carry on, resume, transplant, set away; -setzung, *f.* continuation, prosecution; -tragen, to carry away, transport; -treiben, to drive forward; -wachsen, to continue to grow.

fortwährend, continual, permanent, constant.

fossil, fossil.

fötal, fetal; -organ, *n.* fetal organ.

foto-chemisch, photochemical; -graphisch, photographic.

Fötus, *m.* fetus.

Fournier, *n.* veneer.

fournieren, to veneer.

Fracht, *f.* freight, cargo, load, portage; -brief, *m.* waybill, bill of lading; -geld, *n.* freight, cartage; -raum, *m.* tonnage.

Frage, *f.* question, problem, demand, inquiry; in ∼ kommen, to come into question, be concerned; der in ∼ stehende Punkt, the point in question; in ∼ stellen, to question, doubt; die ∼ nahe legen, to raise the question.

Fragebogen, *m.* questionnaire.

fragen, to ask, question; es fragt sich, ob, it is a question whether, it is doubtful whether; ∼ nach, to ask for.

Frage-stellung, *f.* question(ing); -zeichen, *n.* interrogation point.

fraglich, questionable, doubtful, in question.

Fragment, *n.* fragment.

fragwürdig, doubtful questionable.

fraktionär, fractional.

Fraktionieraufsatz, *m.* fractionating top section.

fraktionieren, to fractionate.

Fraktionier-kolben, *m.* fractionating flask; -turm, *m.* fractionating tower.

Fraktur, *f.* fracture.

Frambösie, *f.* frambesia, yaws.

franko, postpaid, prepaid.

Franse, *f.* fringe.

Fransen, *f.pl.* fimbriae.

Franz-band, *m.* calf binding (of a book); -branntwein, *m.* brandy, cognac; -gold, *n.* French leaf gold.

Franzosen-harz, *n.* guaiacum; -holz, *n.* pulley wood, guaiacum wood.

französische Beeren, buckthorn berries, Avignon berries.

fräsen, to mill, fraise.

Fräser, *m.* milling cutter.

Fräs-kultur, *f.* tilling by a pulverizer ("fras" machine); -maschine, *f.* milling machine.

frass (fressen), ate, corroded.

Frass, *m.* food, feed, corrosion, damage done by insects, devastation; -bild, *n.* gallery design (bark beetles); -gang, *m.* larval gallery; -mehl, *n.* frass (larval excrement); -spur, *f.* feeding evidence; -zeit, *f.* feeding time.

Frau, *f.* woman, wife, lady, Mrs.

Frauen-distel, *f.* Scotch thistle; -eis, *n.* selenite; -flachs, *m.* toadflax (*Linaria vulgaris*); -glas, *n.* selenite; -haar, *n.* maidenhair (*Adiantum capillus-veneris*); -haft, womanlike; -milch, *f.* human milk; -schuh, *m.* lady's-slipper (*Cypripedium calceolus*); -spat, *m.* selenite; -spiegel, *m.* Venus's looking glass.

Fräulein, *n.* young lady, Miss.

Fraunhoferlinien, *f.pl.* absorption lines.

frech, bold, daring, audacious.

frei, free, uncombined, liberal, loose, bold, independent, unrestrained, open, postpaid, exempt, vacant; ∼ bleiben, to remain exposed; ∼ halten, to keep free, unoccupied; ∼ liegen, to be open; ∼ stehen, to be unsupported.

frei-beweglich, motile; -blätterig, polysepalous; -bleibend, not binding; -brief, *m.* charter, license, permit; -drehen, to throw (ceramics).

Freie, *n.* open air.

Frei-gabe, *f.* release; -geben, to release; -gebig, generous, liberal; -halten, to pay for (someone), treat.

Freiheit, *f.* freedom, liberty, franchise; in ∼ setzen, to set free, liberate.

Freiheitsgrad, *m.* degree of freedom.

Frei-lage, *f.* exposed site, unsheltered situation; -landüberwinterung, *f.* hibernating in the open; -landzucht, *f.* rearing (growth) in the open; -länge, *f.* span, unsupported length; -lassen, to set free, liberate; -lebend, free living; -legen, to expose, lay open; -leitung, *f.* open wire, circuits, overhead line, open-air piping.

freilich, to be sure, indeed, of course.

frei-liegend, to be open; -liegend, exposed; -machen, to set free, liberate; -machung, *f.* liberation; -marke, *f.* postage stamp; -mut, *m.* frankness, sincerity; -schwebend, free floating; -sinnig, liberal minded;

-spiegelstollen, *m.* nonpressure tunnel; **-sprechen,** to acquit, absolve.

Frei-staat, *m.* republic; **-stand,** *m.* isolation, open position; **-stehen,** to be at liberty; be permitted; **-stehend,** isolated; **-stellen,** to set free, isolate; **-stellung,** *f.* isolation; **-strahl,** *m.* free jet, impulse; **-träger,** *m.* simple beam; **-wandlage,** *f.* epistrophe (of plastids); **-wasser,** *n.* clear water.

Frei-werden, *n.* becoming free, liberation; **-werdend,** (being) set free, nascent; **-willig,** spontaneous, voluntary, free; **-willige(r),** *m.* volunteer; **-zügig,** free to move, privileged.

fremd, (*dat.*) foreign, strange, exotic, heterogeneous, peculiar; **-artig,** heterogeneous, odd, strange, unfamiliar, foreign; **-befruchtung,** *f.* cross-fertilization; **-bestäubung,** *f.* allogamy, cross-pollination.

Fremde, *m.&f.* stranger, foreigner, visitor.

Fremde, *f.* foreign country.

Fremd-gehäuse, *n.* shell of a hermit crab; **-geschlechtlich,** of the opposite sex; **-körper,** *m.* foreign substance, body or matter, **-sprachig,** foreign language, speaking a foreign language; **-stoff,** *m.* foreign substance, impurity; **-wort,** *n.* foreign word.

Frequenz, *f.* frequency, crowd, attendance, traffic.

fressen, to corrode, eat, seize, gall.

Fressen, *n.* food.

fressend, corrosive.

fress-gierig, voracious, greedy; **-knospe,** *f.* hydranth, nutritive polyp; **-polyp,** *m.* nutritive polyp; **-werkzeuge,** *n.pl.* masticating apparatus; **-zelle,** *f.* phagocyte.

Frettchen, *n.* ferret; **-seuche,** *f.* ferret disease.

frettieren, to ferret.

Freude, *f.* joy, comfort, gladness, enjoyment.

freudig, joyful, glad.

freuen, to make glad; **sich ~,** to rejoice, be glad.

Freund, *m.* friend, acquaintance.

freundlich, (*dat.*) friendly, kind, amiable, pleasant.

Freundschaft, *f.* friendship, acquaintance, friends.

Frevel, *m.* violation, misappropriation.

freveln, to misappropriate, transgress, steal, trespass.

Frevler, *m.* offender.

Friede, *f.* peace.

friedfertig, peaceable.

friedlich, peaceful.

frieren, to freeze, congeal, feel cold.

Frieren, *n.* chill, freezing, shivering, ague.

Frierpunkt, *m.* freezing point.

Friesel, *m.* military fever.

Friktionsmesser, *m.* friction meter.

frisch, fresh, green, cool, vigorous, brisk, gay, new, bright, cheerful; **-arbeit,** *f.* (re)fining process, fining; **-blei,** *n.* refined lead; **-dampf,** *m.* live steam.

frischen, to (re)fine, revive, farrow.

Frischerei, *f.* finery.

Frisch-esse, *f.* refining furnace, refinery; **-gebrannt,** freshly burned; **-gefällt,** freshly precipitated; **-gewicht,** *n.* fresh weight, green weight; **-glätte,** *f.* hard litharge; **-schlacke,** *f.* refinery cinders, oxidizing slag; **-stück,** *n.* liquation cake; **-wasserkläranlage,** *f.* water-filtering plant.

Frischung, *f.* refining, reviving, refreshing, purification, oxidation.

frisst (**fressen**), eats, corrodes.

Frist, *f.* time, space of time, interval, respite.

fristen, to delay, put off.

fritten, to frit, sinter.

Fritter, *m.* coherer.

Frittofen, *m.* frit kiln, calcar.

froh, (*gen.*) glad, joyful, cheerful, happy.

fröhlich, joyful, glad, merry.

Froh-sinn, *m.* cheerfulness; **-wüchsig,** fast-growing, thrifty.

fromm, pious, gentle, devout.

frommen, (*dat.*) to avail, benefit.

Fron, *f.* compulsory service, dues.

Frontal-ebene, *f.* **-scheibe,** *f.* frontal plane.

fror (**frieren**), froze.

Frosch, *m.* ⸚e, frog, cam, arm, carney, ranula; **-ader,** *f.* ranine artery; **-arten,** *f.pl.* batrachians; **-biss,** *m.* frogbit; **-bissgewächse,** *n.pl.* Hydrocharitaceae; **-ei,** *n.* frog's egg; **-geschwulst,** *n.* lampas, ranula; **-klappe,** *f.* type of flap valve; **-laich,** *m.* frog spawn; **-laichpflaster,** *n.* lead plaster.

Frosch-löffel, *m.* water plantain (*Alisma plantago*); **-löffelgewächse,** *n.pl.* Alismaceae; **-lurche,** *f.* Anura; **-schenkel,** *m.* frog's leg; **-schwimmhaut,** *f.* frog web.

Frost, *m.* frost, cold, chill; **-beständigkeit,** *f.* resistance to frost; **-beule,** *f.* chilblain; **-blase,** *f.* frost blister.

frösteln, to chill, to feel chilly.

frost-empfindlich, frost tender, sensitive to frost; **-gefährlich,** frost sensitive; **-grad,** *m.* degree of frost; **-hart,** frost hardy; **-härte,** *f.* cold resistance; **-hebung,** *f.* frost heave; **-lage,** *f.* frost locality; **-leiste,** *f.* frost rib; **-mischung,** *f.* freezing mixture; **-punkt,** *m.* freezing point.

Frost-riss, *m.* frost crack; **-rissig,** frost-cracked; **-schaden,** *m.* injury or damage by frost; **-schnitt,** *m.* frozen section; **-schutz-mittel,** *n.* antifreezing agent; **-spalte,** *f.* frost fissure; **-spanner,** *m.* winter moth (*Cheimatobia brumata*); **-zone,** *f* frosty zone.

frottieren, to rub, brush.

Frucht, *f.* ≞e, fruit, embryo, fetus, profit, produce, product, grain, crop; **-abtreibungs-mittel,** *n.* abortifacient; **-achse,** *f.* axis of the embryo; **-anfang,** *m.* beginning of fructification; **-anhang,** *m.* embryonic appendage; **-ansatz,** *m.* setting of fruit; **-artig,** fruitlike; **-äther,** *m.* fruit (ether) essence.

fruchtbar, fruitful, fertile, prolific, plentiful, productive.

Fruchtbarkeit, *f.* fertility, fecundity.

Frucht-becher, *m.* receptacle, cupule; **-behälter,** *m.* conceptacle, uterus, pericarp; **-bildung,** *f.* fruit formation, fructification; **-blatt,** *n.* carpophyll, carpel, macrosporophyll; **-boden,** *m.* receptacle, placenta, thalamus; **-brand,** *m.* ergot, blight, head smut; **-branntwein,** *m.* fruit brandy.

fruchten, to bear fruit, have effect, be of use.

Frucht-essig, *m.* fruit vinegar; **-fach,** *n.* locule; **-faden,** *m.* filamentous sporophore, hypha; **-fleisch,** *n.* fruit pulp; **-folge,** *f.* crop rotation; **-halter,** *m.* uterus; **-häuf-chen,** *n.* sorus; **-haufen,** *m.* sorose (pineapple).

Frucht-haut, *f.* amnion, chorion, fetal membrane, pericarp; **-hautzotte,** *f.* villus of the chorion; **-hof,** *m.* embryonic area, area of germination; **-hülle,** *f.* fetal envelope, envelope of the egg, receptacle, spermotheca, hull, husk; **-hypha,** *f.* paraphysis, fruiting hypha; **-kapsel,** *f.* sporocarp; **-kätzchen,** *n.* catkin.

Frucht-keim, *m.* embryo; **-kelch,** *m.* calyx; **-klappe,** *f.* valve; **-knöllchen,** *n.* archegoniophore; **-knopf,** *m.* venter of archegonium; **-knospe,** *f.* fruit bud, embryo.

Fruchtknoten, *m.* ovary; **gefächerter** ∿, chambered ovary.

Fruchtknoten-wandung, *f.* ovary wall; **-wulst,** *f.* gynobase, enlargement of the torus.

Frucht-kopf, *m.* head of fetus; **-köpfchen,** *n.* fruiting head; **-körper,** *m.* fruit body, sporophore; **-körperanlage,** *f.* primordium of fruit body, receptacle, anlage; **-kuchen,** *m.* fetal placenta; **-lager,** *n.* hymenium, thalamus, sporangium; **-los,** fruitless, barren, sterile.

Frucht-röhre, *f.* pistil; **-saft,** *m.* fruit juice; **-säulchen,** *n.* columella; **-schale,** *f.* peel, pericarp; **-schicht,** *f.* sporogenous layer; **-schnabel,** *m.* beak; **-schuppe,** *f.* cone scale.

Frucht-schwanz, *m.* cauda, taillike appendage of fruit; **-stand,** *m.* fructification, fruiting condition, syncarpy; **-stiel,** *m.* pedicel, seta, peduncle; **-tragend,** fruit bearing; **-träger,** *m.* sporophore, conidiophore, germinal hypha.

Fruchtungs-kern, *m.* fertilized egg, fusion nucleus; **-vermögen,** *n.* fertility.

Frucht-wand, *f.* pericarp; **-wasser,** *n.* fetal fluid, amnion fluid; **-wasserhaut,** *f.* amnion; **-wasserhöhle,** *f.* amnion cavity; **-wechsel,** *m.* crop rotation; **-zucker,** *m.* levulose; **-zweig,** *m.* fertile branch.

frug (fragen), asked.

früh, early, premature, speedy, soon; **heute** ∿, early this morning.

Frühbeet, *n.* hotbed; **-kasten,** *m.* hotbed (for forcing).

Frühe, *f.* (early) morning.

früher, earlier, former(ly).

Früh-frost, *m.* early frost; **-hochfest,** of high early strength; **-holz,** *n.* springwood.

Frühjahr, *n.* spring; **-blühend,** vernal, blooming in spring.

Frühjahrs-holz, *n.* springwood; **-mauser,** *f.* spring molt; **-pflanzung,** *f.* spring planting.

Frühling, *m.* spring.

Früh-reife, *f.* precociousness, earliness (of ripening), prematurity; **-saat,** *f.* first sowing; **-stadium,** *n.* early stage; **-stück,** *n.* breakfast; **-treiberei,** *f.* forcing; **-zeit,** *f.* early epoch; **-zeitig,** early, premature, precocious, untimely; **-zündung,** *f.* premature shot, preignition.

Fruktose, *f.* fructose, levulose.

Fuchs, *m.* ≞e, fox, sorrel horse, freshman, fluke, trestle, jack, flue, tortoise-shell Vanessa; **-brücke,** *f.* flue bridge, back bridge wall.

Fuchsaffe, *m.* lemur.

Fuchsia, *f.* fuchsia.

fuchsig, foxy.

Fuchsin, *n.* fuchsin.

Füchsin, *f.* vixen, she-fox.

Fuchsin-agar, *m.* fuchsin agar; **-tinktion,** *f.* staining with fuchsin.

Fuchs-jagd, *f.* fox hunting; **-rot,** foxy, reddish brown.

Fuchsschwanz, *m.* foxtail (*Amarantus caudatus*); **-gewüchse,** *n.pl.* Amarantaceae; **-gräser,** *n.pl.* Alopecuroidae.

Fuchtel, *f.* blade, sword, rod.

Fuder, *n.* cartload, wine measure.

Fug, *m.* right, authority, permission.

Fuge, *f.* joint, slit, suture, groove, commissure, seam.

fügen, to join, unite, add, yield.

Fugen-dichtung, *f.* impermeabilizing of (highway) joints; **-fläche,** *f.* surface of commissure; **-gelenk,** *n.* articulation, synarthrosis; **-verbindung,** *f.* symphysis; **-wandlage,** *f.* apostrophe.

füglich, conveniently, reasonably, easily, suitable, right(ly).

fügsam, tractable, yielding, pliant.

Fügung, *f.* joining, fitting, resignation, articulation.

fühlbar, sensible, tangible, palpable, perceptible, tactile.

Fühlborste, *f.* tactile bristle.

fühlen, to feel.

Fühlen, *n.* feeling, perception, sensation.

Fühler, *m.* antenna, tentacle, palp(us); **-artig,** feelerlike; **-borste,** *f.* seta (of antenna), arista; **-furche,** *f.* antennal scrobe; **-geissel,** *f.* funiculus or flagellum of antenna; **-gelenk,** *n.* antenna joint.

Fühler-glied, *n.* antennal segment; **-griffel;** *m.* stylus; **-keule,** *f.* antennal club, clava; **-lappen,** *m.* olfactory lobe; **-naht,** *f.* antennal suture; **-schaft,** *m.* scape of antenna.

Fühl-glied, *n.* sensitive element; **-haar,** *n.* tactile hair; **-horn,** *n.* antenna; **-papilla,** *f.* tactile papilla; **-spitze,** *f.* palp; **-tüpfel,** *m.* tactile pit.

Fühlung, *f.* feeling, sensation, contact, touch.

fuhr (fahren), drove; ∼ **fort,** continued.

Fuhre, *f.* carrying, conveyance, carriage, cart, load.

führen, to lead, guide, conduct, carry, convey, direct, bear, wear, carry on, cause, handle; **zum Tode** ∼, to prove fatal.

Führer, *m.*, leader, conductor, guide; **-schein,** *m.* driver's license.

Fuhrmann, *m.* driver, carter.

Führung, *f.* leading, conduct, guidance, behavior.

Führungs-stange, *f.* guide rod; **-stück,** *n.* gubernaculum, accessory male organ.

Fuhrwerk, *n.* vehicle.

Füllapparat, *m.* filling apparatus, bottling apparatus.

Fülle, *f.* filling, fulness, abundance.

füllen, to fill (up), pour, put (in), load, stuff.

Füllen, *n.* filling, foal, colt.

Füller, *m.* filler.

Fullererde, *f.* fuller's earth.

Füll-flüssigkeit, *f.* immersion liquid; **-gewebe,** *n.* plerome, parenchyma, complementary tissue (of lenticels); **-haus,** *n.* filling (room) house; **-holz,** *n.* gap cover; **-horn,** *n.* cornucopia; **-körpersäule,** *f.* packed tower; **-masse,** *f.* filling material; **-säure,** *f.* electrolyte, accumulator acid; **-schwall,** *m.* water bore.

Füll-sel, *n.* stuffing; **-stab,** *m.* web member (of truss); **-strich,** *m.* filling level; **-trichter,** *m.* filling funnel, hopper.

Füllung, *f.* filling, stuffing, charge, packing, cutoff, panel; ∼ **der Blüte,** *f.* doubling in flowers.

Füllungsstab, *m.* web member.

Füllzelle, *f.* complementary cell.

fulminieren, to fulminate.

Fumarsäure, *f.* fumaric acid.

Functionieren, *n.* action.

Fund, *m.*-e, discovery, finding, find, invention.

Fundament, *n.* foundation, base, basis.

fundamental, fundamental; **-satz,** *m.* fundamental principle.

fundieren, to found, fund, establish.

Fundierung, *f.* foundation.

fündig, ore-bearing.

Fundort, *m.*-e, habitat, locality.

Fundstätte, *f.* place of discovery.

Fundusdrüse, *f.* gastric gland, rennet, labgland of stomach.

Fundzettel, *m.*-, locality label.

fünf, five; **-atomig,** pentatomic; **-basisch,** pentabasic; **-blätterig,** quinquefoliate, pentaphyllous; **-eck,** n. pentagon; **-fach,** fivefold, quintuple; **-fächerig,** five-celled, quinquelocular; **-gliedrig,** five-membered; **-mal,** five times; **-ring,** m. five-membered ring; **-seitig,** five-sided, pentahedral.

fünfte, fifth.

Fünftel, n. fifth, fifth part.

Fünfverband, m. quincunx planting.

fünfwertig, quinquevalent, pentavalent.

Fünfwertigkeit, f. quinquevalence, pentavalence.

fünf-zählig, quinate, quinary, quintuple; **-zehig,** pentadactylous, quinquedigitate.

fünfzig, fifty.

fungieren, to function, act, officiate.

fungizid, fungicidal.

fungös, fungous.

Funiculusabbruchstelle, f. hilum (of seed).

Funke(n), m. spark, flash, sparkle, gleam.

funkelig, sparkling, glittering.

funkeln, to sparkle, flash, scintillate, shine.

funken-ähnlich, sparklike; **-bildung,** f. spark formation; **-entladung,** f. spark discharge; **-frei,** free from sparks; **-garbe,** f. shower of sparks; **-geber,** m. sparking (coil) device, spark transmitter; **-holz,** n. touchwood; **-induktor,** m. induction coil; **-los,** sparkless; **-sammler,** m. spark condenser.

Funken-schlagweite, f. spark distance; **-spannung,** f. spark voltage; **-spektrum,** n. spark spectrum; **-spiel,** n. play of sparks; **-sprühen,** n. emission of sparks, scintillation; **-strecke,** f. spark gap; **-zünder,** m. jump spark cap; **-zündung,** f. spark ignition.

Funktion, f. function; **sich in** ∼ **befinden,** to exercise a function; **in** ∼ **treten,** to serve, act, officiate, function.

funktionieren, to function.

Funktions-bedingung, f. conditions of activity; **-stärke,** f. functional capacity. **-wechsel,** m. change in function; **-wert,** m. functional value.

für, for, in favor of, in lieu of; ∼ **sich,** apart, separate, of (by) itself; **was** ∼ **ein,** what kind of; **fürs erste,** for the present, first(ly); **ein** ∼ **allemal,** once (and) for all; ∼ **und wider,** pro and con; **an und** ∼ **sich,** in itself, apart from; ∼ **und** ∼, forever and ever.

Fürbitte, f. intercession.

Furche, f. furrow, ridge, groove, sulcus, channel, wrinkle.

furchen, to furrow, crease, groove, sulcate; **-pleuren,** f.pl. furrowed pleura; **-saat,** f. sowing in furrows; **-spatel,** f. grooved spatula; **-zahn,** m. proteroglyphic or tubular (grooved) tooth.

Furcht, f. fear, fright, anxiety, horror, dread

furchtbar, fearful, terrible, dreadful.

fürchten, to fear, be afraid.

fürchterlich, frightful, dreadful, horrid.

furcht-erregend, frightening; **-losigkeit,** fearlessness.

furchtsam, timid, fainthearted.

Furchung, f. furrowing, segmentation. cleavage, sulcation.

Furchungs-abschnitt, m. cleavage sphere; **-blase,** f. blastula; **-furche,** f. segmental groove; **-höhle,** f. cleavage cavity; **-kern,** m. segmentation nucleus; **-kugel,** f. cleavage sphere, blastomere; **-prozess,** m. process of cleavage; **-spalte,** f. cleavage fissure; **-spindel,** f. cleavage spindle; **-zelle,** f. blastomere.

fürliebnehmen, to be satisfied (with), put up (with).

Furnier, n. veneer.

furnieren, to veneer, inlay.

Fürsorge, f. care, solicitude.

Fürst, m. prince.

fürstlich, princely.

Furt, f. ford, passage, crossing.

Furunkel, m. furuncle.

fürwahr, in truth, indeed.

Fusel, m. fusel oil, bad spirits or liquor; **-frei,** free from fusel oil; **-haltig,** containing fusel oil; **-öl,** n. fusel oil.

fuselig, containing fusel oil.

Fusionspunkt, m. fusing point, melting point.

Fuss, m.∵e, foot, tarsus, base, pedal, leg; **zu** ∼, on foot.

Fuss-ballen, m. ball of the foot; **-band,** n. ligament of the foot; **-bank,** f. shoulder (of earth), footstool; **-beuge,** f. instep; **-blatt,** n. May apple (*Podophyllum peltatum*), sole of foot, plantar surface, sclerobase; **-boden,** m. floor, flooring, ground; **-brett,** n. pedal; **-drüse,** f. pedal gland.

fussen, to stand, rely, depend, base.

fussend, founded, based.

fuss-fällig, prostrate; **-förmig,** pedate; **-gänger,** *m.* pedestrian.

Fussgelenk, *n.* articulation of the foot, ankle joint, fetlock joint; **-gegend,** *f.* region of the instep.

Fuss-gestell, *n.* pedestal, base, foot; **-gewölbe,** *n.* arch of the foot, plantar arch; **-glätte,** *f.* black, impure litharge; **-glied,** *n.* tarsal joint; **-kiefer,** *m.* maxilliped, maxilla; **-klaue,** *f.* claw.

Fussknöchel, *m.* ankle, malleolus; **-gelenk,** *n.* ankle joint.

Fuss-krankheit, *f.* foot rot, whiteheads; **-los,** apodous; **-mehl,** *n.* the lowest grade of flour; **-nervig,** pedately veined; **-note,** *f.* footnote; **-pfad,** *m.* footpath; **-platte,** *f.* basal plate; **-punkt,** *m.* nadir, foot; **-reihe,** *f.* row of feet, ambulacrum; **-rollenentzündung,** *f.* navicular disease, podo trochilitis.

Fuss-rücken, *m.* dorsum of the foot; **-scheibe,** *f.* pedal disk; **-sohle,** *f.* sole of the foot; **-sohlenfläche,** *f.* plantar surface; **-spann,** *m.* instep; **-spur,** *f.* footprint, track; **-stock,** *m.* basal part of hair.

Fusstummel, *m.* parapodium; **-ast,** *m.* (oberer ∼) notopodium; (unterer ∼) neuropodium.

Fusswulst, *f.* foot or region of the foot.

Fusswurzel, *f.* tarsus; **-bein,** *n.* tarsal bone; **-gelenk,** *n.* tarsal articulation; **-knochen,** *m.* tarsal bone; **-mittelfussgelenk,** *n.* tarsometatarsal joint or ligament.

Fusszehe, *f.* toe of the foot.

Fustage, *f.* barrels, casks.

Fustik (holz), *n.* fustic (wood).

Futter, *n.* food, feed, fodder, nutriment, forage, lining, casing, coating, covering.

Futteral, *n.* case, casing box.

Futter-aufwand, *m.* food requirement; **-bau,** *m.* culture of forage; **-behälter,** *m.* manger; **-biene,** *f.* worker bee; **-blech,** *n.* fill plate; **-bohne,** *f.* horse bean; **-brei,** *m.* fodder made into paste; **-erbse,** *f.* field pea (*Pisum arvense*); **-gerste,** *f.* barley for cattle; **-getreide,** *n.* grain for feeding.

Futter-gewächs, *n.* forage plant; **-haar,** *n.* feeding hair (in orchids); **-kalk,** *m.* a calcium compound, feed lime; **-klee,** *m.* red clover; **-korn,** *n.* grain for feeding; **-kräuter,** *n.pl.* forage plants; **-laub,** *n.* leaf fodder; **-mauer,** *f.* retaining wall; **-mittel,** *n.* fodder; **-mittelanalyse,** *f.* analysis of food or food products.

füttern, to feed, provide, line, case, coat.

Futter-pflanze, *f.* forage plant; **-ration,** *f.* diet, ration; **-ring,** *m.* collet; **-rohr,** *n.* casing pipe; **-rübe,** *g.* common turnip (*Brassica rapa*); **-saft,** *m.* brood food, royal jelly; **-stein,** *m.* lining brick.

Futterstoff, *m.* lining; glänzender ∼, sateen.

Futterstroh, *n.* forage (feed) straw.

Fütterung, *f.* feeding, fodder.

Fütterungs-infektion, *f.* infection by feeding; **-lehre,** *f.* theory of feeding; **-tuberkulose,** *f.* alimentary tuberculosis; **-versuch,** *m.* feeding experiment.

Futter-verbrauch, *m.* food consumption; **-wert,** *m.* fodder value; **-wicke,** *f.* common vetch (*Vicia sativa*); **-wiese,** *f.* meadow for fodder; **-wurzel,** *f.* forage root; **-zumessung,** *f.* mixing or apportioning of fodder.

G

gab (geben), gave; es ∼, there was (were).

Gabanholz, *n.* camwood.

Gabe, *f.* gift, dose, alms, talent.

Gabel, *f.*-**n,** (pitch)fork, crotch, tendril; **-ader,** *f.* dichotomous vein; **-anker,** *m.* grapnel; **-artig,** forked, furcate, bifurcated, dichotomous; **-basidium,** *n.* forked basidium; **-bein,** *n.* forked (wish) bone; **-darm,** *m.* (forked alimentary tract); **-förmig,** forked, furcati, bifurcated, dichotomous; **-gang,** *m.* forked gallery; **-haar,** *n.* branched hair, dichotomous hair.

gabelig, furcate, bifurcate, forked, branched.

Gabel-klammer, *f.* forked clamp; **-knochen,** *m.* furcula, wishbone; **-mass,** *n.* caliper, diameter gauge; **-mehl,** *n.* superfine flour.

gabeln, to fork, bifurcate, branch off, ramify.

Gabel-rohr, *n.* forked tube or pipe; **-röhre,** *f.* forked tube or pipe; **-schlüssel,** *m.* fork wrench; **-schwanz,** *m.* puss moth; **-schwanzig,** with a forked tail; **-spaltig,** forked; **-teilung,** *f.* bifurcation; **-trieb,** *m.* forked branch.

Gabelung, *f.* bifurcation, dichotomy.

Gabel-wender, *m.* forked branch, hay tedder; **-wuchs,** *m.* forked branch; **-zotte** *f.* forked shaggy hair.

gackeln, to cackle, cluck.

gackern, to cackle, cluck.

Gadolinerde, *f.* gadolinia, gadolinium oxide.

gaffen, to gape, stare.

Gagat, *m.* -kohle, *f.* jet.

Gagel, *m.* sweet gale, bog myrtle (*Myrica gale*); **-gewächse,** *n.pl.* Myricaceae; **-sträucher,** *m.pl.* Myricaceae.

gähnen, to yawn.

Gais, *f.* goat, doe.

Gaisblatt, *n.* (Geissblatt) woodbine, honeysuckle (*Lonicera periclymenum*).

Galaktose, *f.* galactose.

Galangawurzel, *f.* galingale (*Alpinia officinarum*).

Galanterie-arbeit, *f.*-en, fancy goods, (imitation) jewelry; **-waren,** *f.pl.* fancy goods, (imitation) jewelry.

Galban, *n.* -harz, *n.* galbanum.

Galeriewälder, *m.pl.* fringing forests.

Galette, *f.* godet, godet wheel.

Galgant, *m.* galingale; **-wurzel,** *f.* galingale (root).

Galgen, *m.* gallows; **-holz,** *n.* touchwood.

Galitzenstein, *m.* white vitriol, zinc sulphate.

gallabtreibend, cholagogue, bile removing.

Gallapfel, *m.* -̈, (nut) gall, gallnut, oak apple; **-aufguss,** *m.* infusion of nutgalls; **-beize,** *f.* gall steep; **-(gerb)säure,** *f.* gallotannic acid.

Gallat, *n.* gallate.

Gallbeize, *f.* gall steep.

Galle, *f.* gall, bile, gallnut, protuberance.

Galleiche, *f.* gall oak (*Quercus infectoria*).

gallen, to gall, treat with gallnuts, remove the gall from; **-abführend,** cholagogue, bile removing; **-absonderung,** *f.* secretion of bile; **-ader,** *f.* cystic vein; **-artig,** biliary; **-ausführungsgang,** *m.* excretory bile duct; **-behälter,** *m.* gall bladder; **-bitter,** bitter as gall; **-bitter,** *n.* picromel; **-blase,** *f.* gall bladder.

Gallen-blasengang, *m.* cystic canal or duct; **-blasenstein,** *m.* cystic calculus, gallstone; **-braun,** *n.* bilirubin; **-darm,** *m.* duodenum; **-farbstoff,** *m.* bile pigment; **-fett,** *n.* cholesterin; **-fettsäure,** *f.* bile acid; **-gang,** *m.* bile duct; **-gangplatte,** *f.* bile-duct rudiment; **-gangsystem,** *n.* biliary tract.

Gallen-gelb, *n.* bilirubin; **-grün,** *n.* biliverdin; **-kanal,** *m.* bile duct;- **rinde,** *f.* epidermis of a gall.

Gallensalz, *n.* bile salt; **-Agaragar,** bile-salt agar.

Gallen-säure, *f.* bile acid; **-stein,** *m.* gallstone, biliary calculus; **-steinfett,** *n.* cholesterol; **-süss,** *n.* picromel; **-talg,** *m.* cholesterin; **-treibend,** cholagogic; **-wachs.** *n.* cholesterin; **-weg,** *m.* bile duct; **-zucker,** *m.* picromel.

Gallert, *n.* gelatin, jelly, glue; **-ähnlich,** jellylike, gelatinous, colloid(al); **-anhängsel,** *n.* gelatinous appendage; **-artig,** jellylike, gelatinous, colloid(al); **-bildung,** *f.* formation of gelatinous substance.

Gallerte, *f.* jelly, gelatin, glue, colloid matter.

Gallert-filz, *m.* gelatinous felt; **-flechte,** *f.* gelatinous lichen; **-gewebe,** *b.* gelatinous tissue; **-glocke,** *f.* (gelatinous) bell or umbrella; **-hülle,** *f.* gelatinous envelope, periblast.

gallertig, jellylike, gelatinous.

Gallert-kapsel, *f.* gelatinous capsule; **-körper,** *m.* vitreous body; **-moos,** *n.* Irish moss, carrageen; **-säure,** *f.* pectic acid; **-schicht,** *f.* gelatinous layer; **-schwamm,** *m.* slimesponge (Myxospongia); **-spore,** *f.* gelatinous spore; **-stiel,** *m.* gelatinous stalk; **-substanz,** *f.* colloid substance.

Galletseide, *f.* silk waste.

Gallgersäure, *f.* gallic (gallotannic) acid, tannin.

Gallichlorid, *n.* gallic chloride.

gallieren, to gall, treat with gallnut extract.

gallig, biliary, bilious.

Galli-hydroxyd, *n.* gallic hydroxide; **-oxyd,** *n.* gallic oxide; **-salz,** *n.* gallic salt.

gallisieren, to gallize.

Gallium-chlorid, *n.* gallic chloride; **-chlorür,** *n.* gallous chloride.

Gall-milbe, *f.* gall mite (Phytoptus); **-mücke,** *f.* gall gnat (Cecidomyia).

Gallo-chlorid, *n.* gallous chloride.

Gall-seife, *f.* gall soap; **-stoff,** *m.* bile substance; **-sucht,** *f.* jaundice.

Gallus, *m.* gallnuts; **-gerbsäure,** *f.* gallotannic acid, tannic acid; **-sauer,** gallate of; **-säure,** *f.* gallic acid; **-säuregärung,** *f.* gallic fermentation; **-tinte,** *f.* gallnut ink.

Gallwespen, *f.pl.* gallflies (Cynipidae).

Galmei, *m.* galmey, calamine.

galt, see GELTEN for idioms.

galvanisch, galvanic.

galvanisieren, to galvanize, electroplate.

Galvanisierung, *f.* galvanization.

Galvanismus, *m.* galvanism.

Galvano-stegie, *f.* electroplating, electro-deposition; **-plastic,** *f.* electrotyping.

Gamander, *m.* germander (Teucrium)

Gambe, *f.* jamb (in ceramics).

Gamete, *f.* gamete.

Gammaeule, *f.* *Plusia gamma.*

Gammastrahlen, *m.pl.* gamma rays.

Ganaschdrüse, *f.* submaxillary gland (of horse).

Ganasche, *f.* inferior maxilla, lower jaw (of horse).

Ganaschgegend, *f.* submaxillary (buccal) region (of horse).

Gang, *m.*⸚e, motion, action, working, condition or state; course, path, passage, burrow, gallery, duct, canal, going, gait, pace, walk, round, shift, progress, process, procedure, pitch (of thread), variation (of a curve), way, corridor; **im ~ bleiben,** to keep in motion; **in ~ bringen,** to set in motion, introduce; **in ~ erhalten,** to keep going; **in ~ kommen,** to get into action; **in ~ bringen** or **setzen,** to start, set in motion; **gang (gäng) und gäbe,** the usual thing; **toter ~,** lost motion; **Anzahl der Gänge auf dem Zoll,** threads per inch (of screws, etc.).

Gangart, *f.* gangue, matrix, gait, pace.

gangbar, pervious, passable, current, marketable, prevalent.

Gang-bein, *n.* walking leg, ambulatory limb; **-erz,** *n.* vein ore; **-gesteine,** *n.pl.* gangue, dredges, loadstones; **-höhe,** *f.* pitch (of a screw), threading incline.

Ganglien, *n.pl.* ganglia; **-knoten,** *m.* ganglion; **-lage,** *f.* ganglionic layer; **-leiste,** *f.* neural crest; **-schicht,** *f.* ganglionic layer.

Gangmasse, *f.* gangue, vein material.

Gangrän, *f.* gangrene; **-herd,** *m.* gangrene focus.

Gang-unterschied, *m.* phase difference.

Ganoidschuppe, *f.* ganoid scale.

Gans, *f.*⸚e, goose.

Gänse-blümchen, *n.* daisy; **-blume,** *f.* daisy; **-distel,** *f.* sow thistle (*Sonchus*); **-feder,** *f.* goose quill; **-füsschen,** *n.pl.* quotation marks; **-fussgewächse,** *n.pl.* Chenopodiaceae; **-haut,** *f.* goose flesh, creeps.

Gänserich, *m.* gander.

Ganter, *m.* support, gantry.

Ganz, *f.* pig (of iron).

ganz, whole, complete, all, total, perfect, wholly, entirely, quite, very; **~ -ander,** entirely different; **~ besonders,** more, especially; **~ und gar,** wholly, totally, absolutely; **~ gewiss,** most certainly; **~ und gar nicht,** not at all, by no means; **im ganzen,** on the whole, taken altogether; **~ gleich,** quite immaterial, identical; **im ganzen genommen,** taking everything into consideration; **im grossen und ganzen,** on the whole.

ganzblätterig, intergrifolious.

Ganze, Ganzes, *n.* whole, whole number, totality.

Ganz-explantat, *n.* explant of whole organism; **-holländer,** *m.* beater, beating engine (for paper); **-holz,** *n.* round timber, logwood.

gänzlich, whole, full, complete(ly), absolute(ly).

Ganz-mahlen, *n.* beating; **-randig,** entire margined; **-varianten,** *m.pl.* integrated variates; **-zahlig,** integral.

Ganzzeug, *n.* whole stuff, pulp; **-holländer,** *m.* beating engine, beater; **-kasten,** *m.* stuff chest.

gar, ready, done, cooked, purified, refined, tanned, dressed, entirely, fully, quite, very, at all, even; **~ bald,** very soon; **~ kein,** none at all; **~ machen,** to finish, refine; **~ nicht,** not at all; **~ nichts,** nothing at all; **~ zu viel,** far too much.

Gäranstieg, *m.* time required for the maximum enzyme action.

garantieren, to guarantee, warrant.

Gararbeit, *f.* (re)fining.

Garaus, *m.* finishing stroke, ruin.

gärbar, fermentable.

Garbe, *f.* sheaf, pile, yarrow, milfoil (Achillea).

garben, to sheave, bundle, weld.

Gärbottich, *m.* fermenting vat.

gar-brennen, to fire (burn) thoroughly; **-brühe,** *f.* finishing (dressing) liquor.

Gärbstahl, *m.* shear (wrought) steel.

Gär-dauer, *f.* duration of fermentation.

Gardine, *f.* curtain.

Gär-druck, *m.* fermentation pressure; **-dünger,** *m.* fermented manure.

Gare, *f.* mellowness, friable condition of soil.

Gäre, *f.* fermentation, yeast, (wine) bouquet.

Gareisen, n. refined iron, trial rod.

garen, to dress, refine.

gären, to ferment.

Garerz, n. roasted ore.

gär-fähig, fermentable; **-fass,** n. fermenting cask; **-flüssigkeit,** f. fermentable liquid.

garfrischen, to refine thoroughly.

Gär-führung, f. method of fermentation; **gefäss,** n. fermenting vessel.

gar-gang, m. normal working, thorough refining; **-gekrätz,** n. refinery slag; **-herd,** m. refining hearth.

Gär-kammer, f. fermenting room; **-kölbchen,** n. fermentation saccharimeter; **-kraft,** f. fermenting power.

Gar-krätze, f. refinery slag; **-machen,** to refine.

Gärmittel, n. ferment.

Garn, n. yarn, thread, twine, net.

Garnele, f. shrimp, prawn.

Garnfärberei, f. yarn dyeing.

garnieren, to trim, garnish.

Garnitur, f. trimming, fittings, mountings.

Garnschlichtung, f. yarn sizing.

Gar-ofen, m. refining furnace; **-probe,** f. refining assay.

Gär-probe, f. fermentation test; **-produkt,** n. fermentation product; **-raum,** m. fermenting room.

Gar-schaum, m. kish; **-scheibe,** f. disk of refined copper; **-span,** m. coating of metal on the trial rod.

Gärstoff, m. ferment.

Garstück, n. lump of purified salt.

Gärtätigkeit, f. fermenting activity.

Garten, m. garden; **-bau,** m. horticulture; **-bohne,** f. kidney bean; **-distel,** f. globe articl oke (*Cyanara scolymus*); **-kerbel,** m. garden chervil (*Scandix cerefolium*); **-kresse,** f. garden peppergrass or garden cress (*Lepidium sativum*); **-lattich,** m. lettuce (*Lactuca sativa*); **-melde,** f. orach, mountain spinach (*Atriplex hortensis*); **-raute,** f. common rue (*Ruta graveolens*); **-schere,** f. pruning shears.

Gärtner, m.-, gardener.

Gärtnerei, f. gardening, horticulture.

gärtuchtig, vital.

Gärung, f. fermentation.

Gärungs-alkokol, m. alcohol, grain; **-bakterien,** n.pl. fermentation bacteria; **-buttersäure,** f. butyric acid; **-erregend,** fermentative, zymogenic; **-erreger,** m. fermentative agent; **-erzeugend,** fermentable; **-fähig,** fermentable; **-fähigkeit,** f. fermentability; **-gewerbe,** fermentation industry; **-hemmend,** arresting fermentation.

Gärungs-kohlensäure, f. carbon dioxide of fermentation; **-kölbchen,** n. fermentation tube; **-lehre,** zymology; **-mikroben,** organisms of fermentation; **-mittel,** n. ferment; **-pilz,** m. fermentation fungus; **-probe,** f. fermentation test; **-säure,** f. acid from fermentation; **-stoff,** m. ferment; **-verfahren,** n. method of fermentation.

Gärungs-verhindernd, antifermentative; **-vermögen,** n. fermentative power; **-vorgang,** m. fermentation process; **-widrig,** antizymotic, antifermentative; **-zeit,** f. time of fermentation.

Gär-verfahren, n. fermentation method; **-vermögen,** n. fermenting capacity; **-vorgang,** m. fermentation process.

Garwaage, f. brine gauge (salt).

Gärwärme, f. heat of fermentation.

Gas, n.-e, gas; **-abgabe,** f. escape of gas; **-ableitungsrohr,** n. gas delivery tube; **-ähnlich,** resembling gas, gaseous; **-angriff,** m. gas attack; **-anlage,** f. **-anstalt,** f. gas plant, gas works; **-anzünder,** m. gas lighter; **-arm,** poor in gas; **-art,** f. kind of gas.

gas-artig, gaseous; **-aufnahme,** f. gas absorption; **-bazillus,** m. gas-producing bacillus; **-bedarf,** m. gas consumption; **-behälter,** m. gas holder, gasometer; **-beleuchtung,** f. gas lighting.

Gas-bereitung, f. gas-making; **-bildend,** gas-forming; **-bildner,** m. gas former, gas producer; **-bildung,** f. gas production; **-blase,** f. gas bubble; **-brenner,** m. gas burner.

gäschen, to foam.

gas-dicht, gastight; **-dichte,** f. gas density; **-druck,** m. gas pressure; **-durchlässigkeit,** f. permeability for gas; **-einsteller,** m. gas regulator.

gasen, to gas, develop gas.

Gas-entbindung, f. generation of gas; **-entladung,** f. discharge; **-entweichung,** f. escape of gas; **-entwickler,** m. gas generator; **-entwicklung,** f. gas production, gas evolution; **-erzeugend,** gas-producing; **-erzeugung,** f. production of gas; **-fabrik,** f. gas works; **-fang,** m. gas take, gas collector; **-feuerung,** f. gas heating.

Gas-flasche, *f.* gas cylinder; **-form,** *f.* gaseous state; **-förmig,** gaseous; **-frischen,** *n.* gas pudding; **-gebläse,** *n.* gas (blast) compression; **gehalt,** *m.* gas content; **-gemenge,** *n.* gas(eous) mixture; **-gemisch,** *n.* gas(eous) mixture; **-geruch,** *m.* odor of gas; **-gestalt,** *f.* gaseous form.

Gas-gewinnung, *f.* gas production; **-glüh-licht,** *n.* incandescent gas light; **-haltig,** containing gas; **-heizung,** *f.* gas heating; **-hohlraum,** *m.* gas pocket, air pocket.

gasieren, to gas.

gasig, gaseous.

Gas-kette, *f.* gas cell; **-kocher,** *m.* gas burner, gas stove; **-kraftmaschine,** *f.* gas engine; **-krieg,** *m.* gas warfare; **-leitung,** *f.* gas conduction, gas pipe; **-leitungsröhre,** *f.* gas-conducting tube, gas pipe; **-licht,** *n.* gas light; **-maskenfilter,** *m.* respirator; **-menge,** *f.* amount of gas; **-messung,** *f.* gas measurement.

Gas-mine, *f.* gas shell; **-mischung,** *f.* gas mixture; **-motor,** *m.* gas engine, gas motor; **-ofen,** *m.* gas furnace, gas stove.

gasös, gaseous.

Gas-pfeife, *f.* gas pipe; **-probe,** *f.* gas test-(ing); **-prüfer,** *m.* gas tester; **-quelle,** *f.* gas well; **-raum,** *m.* gas volume; **-reich,** rich in gas; **-reiniger,** *m.* gas purifier; **-rest,** *m.* gas residue; **-rohr,** *n.* gas tube; **-russ,** *m.* gas soot.

Gas-sack, *m.* gas bag; **-sammler,** *m.* gas tank; **-sauger,** *m.* gas exhauster, suction fan; **-schlauch,** *m.* gas tube; **-schutz,** *m.* gas defense; **-schutzgerät,** *n.* gas mask; **-schwade,** *f.* gas fumes.

Gasse, *f.* street, lane, alley.

Gas-spannung, *f.* gas pressure; **-spürer,** *m.* gas detector; **-stoffwechsel,** *m.* gaseous metabolism, gas exchange; **-strahl,** *m.* gas jet; **-strom,** *m.* current of gas; **-ström-ung,** *f.* gas current; **-sumpf,** *m.* low-lying gas cloud.

Gast, *m.* guest, stranger, visitor, customer.

Gäst, *f.* yeast.

gastechnisch, relating to gas engineering.

Gasteer, *m.* gas tar.

Gast-haus, *n.* **-hof,** *m.* inn, hotel; **-mahl,** *n.* banquet, feast.

Gas-toter, *m.* gas victim.

Gasträa, *n.* primeval larval form.

Gastraltasche, *f.* gastric diverticulum.

Gas-trennung, *f.* separation of gas(es); **-trockner,** *m.* gas drier.

Gastrolle, *f.* star role.

Gastrula, *f.* gastrula.

Gas-uhr, *f.* gas meter; **-ventil,** *n.* gas valve; **-verbrauch,** *m.* gas consumption; **-verdich-ter,** *m.* gas compressor; **-verflüssigung,** *f.* liquefaction of gas(es); **-vergiftung,** *f.* gas poisoning; **-volumen,** *n.* gas volume; **-volumetrisch,** gasometric; **-wage,** *f.* gas balance; **-wanne,** *f.* gas trough.

Gas-waschflasche, *f.* gas-washing bottle; **-waschturm,** *m.* gas-washing tower, gas scrubber; **-wasser,** *n.* gas liquor; **-wechsel,** *m.* gas exchange, gaseous metabolism; **-werfer,** *m.* gas projector; **-werk,** *n.* gasworks; **-wolke,** *f.* gas wave, gas cloud; **-wolkenangriff,** *m.* cloud gas attack; **-zähler,** *m.* gas meter; **-zufuhr,** *f.* gas supply.

Gas-zuleitungsrohr, *n.* gas inlet tube; **zünder,** *m.* gas lighter; **-zustand,** *m.* gaseous condition.

Gatte, *m.* husband.

Gattenwahl, *f.* assortative mating.

Gatter, *n.* grate, lattice, railing, saw, trellis.

gattern, to refine (tin).

gattieren, to mix, sort, classify.

Gattin, *f.*-nen, wife.

Gattung, *f.*-en, genus, type, species, family, race.

Gattungs-bastard, *m.* genus hybrid; **-kreu-zungen,** *f.pl.* genus crosses; **-name,** *m.* generic name; **-verwandte,** *m.pl.* congeners, allied species.

Gauchheil, *n.* scarlet pimpernel (*Anagallis arvensis*), selfheal (*Prunella vulgaris*).

Gaufre, *f.* pebble.

gaufrieren, to goffer, emboss, print.

gaukelhaft, juggling, deceptive.

gaukeln, to juggle, flit about.

Gauklerblume, *f.* monkey flower (*Mimulus luteus*).

Gaumen, *m.* palate, gum; **-bein,** *n.* palatine bone; **-bogen,** *m.* palatine arch; **-drüse,** *f.* palatine gland; **-falte,** *f.* palatine ridge; **-flügel,** *m.* pterygoid apophysis or process; **-fortsatz,** *m.* palatine process; **-geschwür,** *n.* palatine ulcer; **-gewölbe,** *n.* palatine arch; **-heber,** *m.* levator palati.

Gaumenkeilbein-höhle, *f.* sphenopalatine sinus; **-knoten.** *m.* sphenopalatine gan-glion.

Gaumen-knochen, *m.* palatine bone; **-leiste,** *f.* ridge of the palate; **-loch,** *n.* palatine foramen; **-lücke,** *f.* cleft; **-mandel,** *f.*

palatine (pharyngeal) tonsil; **-naht,** *f.* palatine suture; **-öffnung,** *f.* palatine vacuity or opening; **-reihe,** *f.* palatine series; **-rinne,** *f.* palatine sulcus.

Gaumen-schlundkopfmuskel, *m.* palato-pharyngeus muscle; **-segel,** *n.* soft palate, velum; **-segeldrüse,** *f.* gland of the soft palate; **-spalte,** *f.* palatine cleft; **-stachel,** *m.* posterior nasal spine; **-staffeln,** *f.pl.* rugae palati (horse); **-vorhang,** *m.* soft palate; **-wurzel,** *f.* root of the palate; **-zungenbogen,** *m.* anterior pillar of fauces.

gautschen, to couch (paper).

Gayerde, *f.* **Gaysalpeter,** *m.* native saltpeter (earth).

Gaze, *f.* gauze, cheesecloth, canvas, net; **-docht,** *m.* wick of gauze; **-schleier,** *m.* gauze veil.

Geäder, *n.* (group of) veins, veined structure, blood vessels.

geädert, veined, nerved.

geartet, composed, constituted.

Geäse, *n.* pasture, deer fodder.

Geäst, *n.* branches.

geäussert, uttered, enunciated, expressed.

Gebäck, *n.* baker's wares, pastry, baking, batch.

Gebalk, *n.* timberwork, framework.

gebar (gebären), bore, brought forth.

Gebärde, *f.* gesture, appearance, demeanor, mien, air.

Gebaren, *n.* behavior, appearance.

gebären, to bear, bring forth.

Gebären, *n.* parturition, childbirth.

Gebärmutter, *f.* uterus, womb; **-drehung,** *f.* torsion of the womb; **-höhle,** *f.* cavity of the uterus; **-schleimhaut,** *f.* endometrium; **-wand,** *f.* uterine wall.

Gebär-organ, *n.* uterus; **-parese,** *f.* milk fever.

Gebäude, *n.-,* building, structure.

Gebein, *n.* skeleton, bones, remains.

geben, to give, yield, render, emit, evolve, express; **sich ~,** to give, in, abate, yield, prove, stretch; **es gibt,** there is, there are; **er gibt nichts um das,** he cares nothing for that; **es muss ~,** there must be.

Geber, *m.* giver, donor, transmitter, sender.

Gebet, *n.* prayer; **ins ~ nehmen,** to question closely.

gebeten (bitten), begged, asked.

gebiert (gebären) bears, brings forth.

Gebiet, *n.-e,* territory, region, district, department, province, domain, sphere, field, branch.

gebieten, *(dat.)* to order, command, rule.

gebieterisch, imperious, imperative, commanding.

Gebietsformation, *f.* district formation.

Gebilde, *n.* structure, system, organization, product, form, image, formation.

gebildet, accomplished, cultured, shaped.

Gebinde, *n.* bundle, package, skein, sheaf, barrel.

Gebirge, *n.-,* mountains, mountain system, rock.

Gebirgs-art, *f.* kind of rock; **-bildung,** *f.* mountainous formation; **-kamm,** *m.* mountain ridge; **-kammähnlich,** serrate; **-zug,** *m.* mountain range.

Gebiss, *n.-e,* dentition, set of teeth.

gebissen (beissen), bitten.

Gebläse, *n.-,* blast, bellows, blower; **-ofen,** *m.* blast furnace; **-öffnung,** *f.* mouth of a torch; **-röhre,** *f.* blast pipe, tuyère.

geblättert, foliate(d), laminated.

gebleicht (bleichen), bleached.

geblichen (bleichen), bleached.

geblieben (bleiben), remained, stayed.

geblümt, mottled, wavy, flowered.

Geblüt, *b.* blood, race.

gebogen (biegen), bent, vaulted, refracted.

geboren (gebären), born, native.

geborgen (bergen), hidden.

geborsten (bersten), burst, cracked

Gebot, *n.-e,* bid(ding), command(ment), advance, offer; **zu ~ stehen,** to be at (one's) disposal.

geboten (bieten), offered, bid.

geboten (gebieten), ordered; **es wird ~ sein,** it seems advisable.

Gebräch, *n.* boar's snout.

gebracht (bringen), brought.

gebrannt (brennen), burnt

gebrannter Kalk, *m.* quicklime.

Gebräu, *n.* brew(ing), mixture.

Gebrauch, *m.* use, custom, habit, fashion.

gebrauchen, to use, employ, make use of.

gebräuchlich, common, usual, customary, current, ordinary.

Gebrauchs-anweisung, *f.* directions (for use); **-dosis,** *f.* usual strength of dosage;

-fähig, usable, serviceable; **-fertig,** ready for use; **-gegenstand,** *m.* commodity; **-gut,** *n.* commodity; **-hund,** *m.* all-round dog; **-muster,** *n.* patent, sample; **-vorschrift,** *f.* directions (for use); **-wasser,** *n.* tap water, fresh water; **-wert,** *m.* utilization value, intrinsic value.

gebraucht, used, second-hand, worn out.

gebrech, brittle, soft, fragile.

gebrechen, to be in need of.

Gebrechen, *n.* want, need, defect, infirmity.

gebrechlich, weak, feeble, fragile.

gebrochen (brechen), broken.

Gebrüder, *m.pl.* brothers.

Gebrüll, *n.* roaring.

Gebrumm, *n.* growling.

gebuchtet, sinuous, undulate.

gebuckelt, umbonate.

Gebühr, *f.* duty, obligation, due, decency, fee, tax, title.

gebühren, to be due, belong; **sich ∼,** to be proper, be fitting.

gebührend, due, be fitting, proper.

gebührendermassen, duly, properly.

Gebund, *n.* bunch, bundle, skein.

gebündelt, fasciculate, in fascicles.

gebunden (binden), bound.

gebüren, to be due to.

Geburt, *f.*-en, birth, parturition, labor, offspring, delivery, descent, race, origin.

Geburtenüberschuss, *m.* excess in birth rate.

gebürtig, native, born.

Geburts-achse, *f.* pelvic axis, axis of delivery; **-häutchen,** *n.* chorion; **-hilfe,** *f.* obstetrics; **-kunde,** science of obstetrics; **-lehre,** *f.* science of obstetrics; **-not,** *f.* labor; **-tag,** *m.* birthday; **-vorgang,** *m.* process of labor, parturition; **-weg,** *m.* genital passage.

Gebüsch, *n.* bushes, thicket, bushwood, shrubbery, undergrowth; **-niederwuchs,** *m.* chaparral, low shrub vegetation.

gedacht (denken), thought, aforesaid.

Gedächtnis, *n.* recollection, remembrance, memory, memorial; **-bein,** *n.* occipital bone; **-leistung,** *f.* ability to memorize.

Gedanke, *m.* thought, opinion, idea, notion; **sich Gedanken machen,** to think, meditate.

Gedanken-bein, *n.* parietal bone; **-folge,** *f.* train of thought; **-gang,** *m.* train of thought.

gedanklich, intellectual.

Gedärm, *n.*-e, intestines, entrails.

Gedeck, *n.* -e, covering, cover, table linen.

gedeihen, to prosper, thrive, grow, proceed, flourish, succeed.

Gedeihen, *n.* growth, vitality, vigor, success increase, prosperity.

gedeihlich, prosperous, beneficial, favorable wholesome, profitable.

gedenken, to think, be mindful, intend, remember.

Gedenken, *n.* memory.

gedeucht (dünken), seemed.

Gedicht, *n.*-e, poem.

gedichtet, made tight, packed, sealed.

gediegen, solid, compact, native, pure, genuine, superior.

Gediegenheit, *f.* native state, solidity, purity, intrinsic value.

gedieh, gediehen (gedeihen), thrived, prospered, grown.

gedornt, thorny.

Gedränge, *n.* thronging, crowd.

gedrängt, crowded, compact, dense.

gedrängte Rasenbildner, *m.pl.* plants growing in dense, nonspreading clumps.

gedreht, contorted, twisted.

gedreit, trifoliate.

gedroschen (dreschen), threshed.

gedrungen (dringen), sturdy, compact, crowded, solid, thickset.

Geduld, *f.* patience, endurance, forbearance.

gedunsen, bloated, puffed up.

gedurft (dürfen), **er hat ∼,** he was permitted.

geeignet, suited, appropriate, adapted, proper, fit, qualified.

Geest, *f.* sandy soil, high and dry soil.

gefächert, chambered.

Gefahr, *f.*-en, danger, hazard, risk.

gefährden, to endanger.

gefäLrlich, dangerous.

gefahrlos, without danger, safe.

Gefährte, *m.* companion, associate.

gefahrvoll, dangerous.

Gefäll(e), *n.* fall, gradient, grade, incline, slope, fallen timber, income.

gefallen, (*dat.*) to please; **sich ∼ lassen,** to agree with, consent to.

gefallen (fallen), fallen, degraded, separated.

gefallen (gefallen), pleased.

Gefallen, *n.* kindness, pleasure, favor.

gefällig, pleasing, agreeable, obliging, kind.

gefälligst, please.

gefällt (fällen), precipitated, felled cut.

gefaltet, plicate, folded.

Gefangene(r), *f. &m.* prisoner.

Gefangenschaft, *f.* captivity.

Gefängnis, *n.*-se, prison.

gefärbt, colored, dyed, stained, tinted.

Gefäss, *n.*-e, vessel, receptacle, blood vessel, canal, tube, hilt; **-ausbreitung,** *f.* distribution of vessels; **-balken,** *m.* vascular trabecula; **-bau,** *m.* vascular structure; **-berstung,** *f.* rupture of a vessel; **-bezirk,** *m.* vascular region; **-blatt,** *n.* vascular layer; **-bündel,** *n.* vascular bundle; **-drüse,** *f.* vascular gland.

Gefäss-einmündung, *f.* anastomosis; **-erweiterung,** *f.* dilation of vessel; **-geflecht,** *n.* plexus of vessels; **-geschwür,** *n.* ulcer of a vessel; **-glied,** *n.* individual segment of a vessel; **-haut,** *f.* vascular membrane, choroid; **-hof,** *m.* vascular area; **-höhle,** *f.* vascular cavity.

gefässig, vascular.

Gefäss-knäuel, *m.* glomerule; **-knoten,** *m.* vascular nodule; **-krampf,** *m.* vascular spasm; **-kryptogamen,** *m.pl.* vascular cryptograms; **-lehre,** angiology; **-lücke,** *f.* leaf gap, vascular space; **-ofen,** *m.* closed furnace; **-öffnung,** *f.* vascular aperture, orifice of vessel; **-pflanze,** *f.* potted plant; **-querschnitt,** *m.* cross section of a vessel; **-raum,** *m.* capacity of the container.

Gefäss-scheide, *f.* vascular sheath; **-schlinge,** *f.* vascular loop; **-spannung,** *f.* vascular tension; **-stamm,** *m.* vascular trunk; **-strang,** *m.* vascular cord.

gefasst, collected, prepared, calm.

Gefäss-teil, *m.* hadrome, xylem, vascular bundle; **-unterbindung,** *f.* vascular ligature; **-veränderung,** *f.* vascular change; **-verbindung,** *f.* vascular connection; **-verengerung,** *f.* vasoconstriction; **-verengung,** *f.* vascular innervation; **-versorgung,** *f.* supply of vessels; **-verstoptung,** *f.* plugging of vessels; **-versuch,** *m.* pot experiment; **-verzweigung,** *f.* ramification of vessels.

Gefäss-wand, *f.* side of a vessel; **-zerreissung,** *f.* vascular rupture; **-zweig,** *m.* branch of a vessel.

Gefecht, *n.* fight(ing), combat, action.

gefeit, charmed.

gefeldert, areolate.

gefertigt, made, prepared.

Gefieder, *n.* feathers, plumage.

gefiedert, pinnate, feathered; **zweijochig** ∽, having two pairs of pinnae.

gefiel (gefallen), pleased.

Gefilde, *n.* tract of land.

gefingert, digitate.

geflammt, mottled, wavy.

Geflecht, *n.* plexus, reticulum, pleated work, texture.

gefleckt, spotted, stained, freckled.

geflissentlich, assiduous, willful, intentional, on purpose.

geflochten (flechten), plaited, interwoven.

geflogen (fliegen), flown.

geflohen (fliehen), fled.

geflossen (fliessen), flowed, molten.

Geflügel, *n.* fowl, poultry; **-bestand,** *m.* stock of poultry; **-cholera,** *f.* chicken cholera; **-cholerabazillus,** bacillus of chicken cholera; **-pest,** *f.* chicken plague; **-pocken,** *f.pl.* chicken pox; **-septikämie,** *f.* chicken cholera.

geflügelt, pinnate(d) winged, alated.

Geflügel-tuberkulose, *f.* avian tuberculosis; **-zucht,** *f.* breeding of poultry, poultry husbandry.

gefochten (fechten), fought.

Gefolge, *n.* followers, train, attendants; **im** ∽ **haben,** to lead to, result in.

gefranst, fimbriate, fringed.

gefrässig, voracious, greedy.

gefressene, *n.* food consumed or devoured.

Gefrierapparat, *m.* freezing apparatus, freezer.

gefrierbar, congealable, freezable.

Gefrierdurchschnitt, *m.* frozen section.

gefrieren, to freeze, congeal.

Gefrierer, *m.* freezer, congealer.

Gefrier-fleisch, *n.* frozen meat; **-mikrotom,** *n.* freezing microtome; **-punkt,** *m.* freezing point; **-punktserniedrigung,** *f.* lowering of freezing point; **-schnitt,** *m.* frozen section; **-schrank,** *m.* refrigerator, freezing chamber; **-vorrichtung,** *f.* freezing apparatus.

gefroren (frieren), frozen, congealed.

Gefrorene(s), *n.* something frozen, ice (cream).

Gefüge, *n.* joint, articulation, structure, texture, stratification; **-aufbau,** *m.* structure synthesis; **-losigkeit,** *f.* lack of structure, texture, or grain.

gefügig, pliable, pliant, flexible.

Gefühl, *n.* (sense of) feeling, touch, sentiment, emotion, sensation, sensitiveness; **-los,** hardhearted, apathetic, insensible.

Gefühls-haar, *n.* tactile hair; **-nerv,** *m.* sensory nerve; **-sinn,** *m.* sense of touch; **-werkzeug,** *n.* sensory apparatus or organ.

gefüllt (Blüte), double (flower).

gefunden (finden), found.

gefurcht, grooved, sulcate.

gegabelt, furcate, forked, dichotomous.

gegangen (gehen), gone; **er ist ∼,** he went.

gegebenenfalls, in a given case, if necessary.

gegen, toward, against, about, compared with, opposite, counter; **-arznei,** *f.* antidote; **-bemerkung,** *f.* criticism, reply; **-bewegung,** *f.* countermovement; **-beweis,** *m.* counterevidence; **-beziehung,** *f.* correlacion; **-bezug,** *m.* correlation; **-bild,** *n.* counterpart, antitype.

Gegend, *f.* region, quarter, country.

Gegen-drehpunkt, *m.* opposing or rotating force, opposing torsion; **-druck,** *m.* counterpressure, reaction, resistance; **-einander,** toward (or against) one another, reciprocally, mutually; **-farbe,** *f.* complementary color; **-färbung,** *f.* contrast straining; **-feuer,** *n.* backfire; **-füssler,** *m.pl.* antipodes; **-gewicht,** *n.* counterweight; **-gift,** *n.* antidote, antivenin; **-grund,** *m.* contrary reason, objection.

Gegen-induktion, *f.* back induction; **-ion,** *m.* anion or ion of opposite charge; **-kraft,** *f.* opposing force, reaction; **-läufig,** anatropous; **-mittel,** *n.* antidote, remedy; **-mutter,** *f.* lock nut; **-reiz,** *m.* counterirritant or irritation; **-reizung,** *f.* counterirritation; **-satz,** *m.* contrast, opposition; **-schein,** *n.* reflection, counterglow.

Gegen-seite, *f.* opposite (reverse) side; **-seitig,** mutual, reciprocal, opposite, contrary; **-septum,** *n.* counterseptum; **-sonne,** *f.* parhelion, mock sun; **-stand,** *m.* object, matter, subject; **-ständig,** opposite; **-ständlich,** objective; **-standsglas,** *n.* object glass; **-standslos,** without object, meaningless; **-stoff,** *m.* antibody, antidote.

Gegen-strahl, *m.* reflected ray, reflection; **-strom,** *m.* countercurrent; **-stromkühler,** *m.* countercurrent condenser; **-stück,** *n.* counterpart, match, companion; **-taktaufzeichnung,** *f.* push-pull recording, backstroke on counterstroke recording; **-teil,** *n.*

contrary, opposite, converse, counterpart, reverse; **-teilig,** opposite, to the contrary.

gegenüber, over against, opposite, facing; **-blätterig,** oppositifolious; **-liegen,** to lie opposite, face; **-stehen,** to stand or be opposite to.

Gegen-versuch, *m.* control experiment; **-wart,** *f.* presence, present; **-wärtig,** present, at present; **-welle,** *f.* countershaft; **-wert,** *m.* equivalent; **-winkel,** *m.* alternate (opposite) angle; **-wirken,** to counteract, react; **-wirkend,** counteracting, reacting; **-wirkung,** *f.* countereffect, reaction; **-zug,** *m.* countermove.

gegessen (essen), eaten.

gegittert, cancellate, latticed, areolar.

geglättet, levigate, smooth (as if polished).

geglichen (gleichen), resembled, equaled.

gegliedert, articulate.

geglitten (gleiten), glided.

geglommen (glimmen), glimmered, glowed.

Gegner, *m.* opponent, enemy.

gegnerisch, adverse.

gegolten (gelten), **es hat ∼ für,** it was considered as.

gegoren (gären), fermented.

gegossen (giessen), poured, cast.

gegriffen (greifen), seized.

gegürtelt, zonate, girdled.

gehaben, sich, to behave, conduct, fare.

Gehalt, *n.* content(s), capacity, constituent(s), ingredients, yield, strength, nay, value, salary; **-reich,** rich (in content), substantial.

Gehaltsbestimmung, *f.* determination of content, analysis, assay.

Gehänge, *n.* slope, hanging, incline, declivity, festoon, schutt; **-schutt,** *m.* rock debris of slopes; **-ton,** *m.* residual clay.

Gehau, *n.* felled trees.

gehäuft, aggregate, accumulated; **-früchtig,** symphicarpous, with confluent fruits.

Gehäuse, *n.* receptacle, core, case, casing, box, shell, housing, capsule, perithecium; **-bau,** *m.* case building.

Gehbein, *n.* pes gradarius, plantigrade limb.

geheftet, fastened, stitched.

Gehege, *n.* fence, hedge.

geheim, secret, private, hidden, concealed. invisible (ink); **-mittel,** *n.* secret remedy, patent medicine, arcanum.

Geheimnis, *f.-se,* secret, mystery.

geheimnisvoll, mysterious, secretive.

Geheimrat, *m.* privy councilor.

Geheiss, *n.* order, command, bidding.

gehen, to go, walk, tramp, fare, work, act; **vor sich ~,** to go on, take place; **von statten ~,** to come about; **zu Ende ~,** to become exhausted; **zu Grunde ~,** to perish; **es geht um dies,** it is a question of this; **das geht nicht,** that cannot be done, that will not do; **das geht nicht an,** that is impossible; **es geht ihm gut,** he is doing well.

Geheul, *n.* howling.

Gehfuss, *m.* walking leg, ambulatory leg; **-ast,** *m.* endopodite (of schizopodal leg).

Gehilfe, *m.* helper, assistant.

Gehilfin, *f.* synergid, helper.

Gehirn, *n.* brain; **kleines ~,** cerebellum.

Gehirn-anhang, *m.* pituitary body; **-anhangsstiel,** *m.* peduncle of pituitary body; **-anlage,** *f.* rudiment of brain; **-balken,** *m.* corpus callosum; **-band,** *n.* commissure of the brain; **-behälter,** *m.* cranium skull; **-bezirk,** *m.* brain area; **-bläschen,** *n.* cerebral vesicle; **-blatt,** *n.* fontanel; **-brücke,** *f.* pons Varolli.

Gehirn-enge, *f.* isthmus encephali; **-erschütterung,** *f.* concussion of the brain; **-falte,** *f.* cerebral fold, convolution of the brain; **-fett,** *n.* cerebrin; **-ganglion,** *n.* cerebral or cephalic ganglion; **-gewölbe,** *n.* fornix of the brain; **-grund,** *m.* base of the brain; **-haut,** *f.* cerebral meninges; **-herd,** *m.* focus in the brain; **-höhle,** *f.* cerebral ventricle.

Gehirn-kammer, *f.* ventricle of the brain; **-kapsel,** *f.* cranium; **-krümmung,** *f.* cerebral convolution of gyrus; **-lappen,** *m.* lobe of the brain; **-mark,** *n.* white matter of the brain or medulla; **-narbe,** *f.* cerebral cicatrix; **-nerv,** *m.* cerebral nerve.

Gehirn-rinde, *f.* cerebral cortex; **-schale,** *f.* cranium, skull; **-scheidewand,** *f.* septum lucidum; **-schenkel,** *m.* cerebral peduncle; **-schlag,** *m.* cerebral apoplexy; **-schwiele,** *f.* corpus callosum; **-spalte,** *f.* cerebral fissure; **-wulst,** *f.* hippocampus major.

gehoben (heben), lifted, raised.

Gehöft, *n.* farm, countryseat.

gehöfter (Tüpfel), *m.* bordered (pit).

geholfen (helfen), helped.

Gehölz, *n.* wood, woodland, copse; **-formation,** *f.* woodland formation; **-klima,** *n.* woodland climate.

Gehör, *n.* hearing, ear; **-bläschen,** *n.* auditory vesicle, otocyst; **-blase,** *f.* auditory vesicle.

gehorchen, (*dat.*) to obey.

Gehörempfindung, *f.* auditory impression.

gehören, (*dat.*) to belong, appertain to; **es gehört sich,** it is proper, becoming.

Gehör-fehler, *m.* defect of hearing; **-gang,** *m.* auditory canal; **-haar,** *n.* auditory cilium; **-höhle,** *f.* auditory cavity.

gehörig, belonging, appertaining to, referring to, requisite, due, proper, well, thoroughly.

Gehör-kapsel, *f.* otic capsule; **-kapselknochen,** *n.pl.* bones of the ear region; **-knöchelchen,** *n.* auditory ossicle; **-knochen,** *m.* auditory ossicle; **-lehre,** *f.* acoustics; **-loch,** *n.* auditory foramen; **-los,** deaf; **-mangel,** *m.* defect of hearing.

Gehörn, *n.* antlers, horns; **-früchtig,** corniculate.

Gehör-organ, *n.* organ of hearing; **-rohr,** *n.* ear trumpet.

gehorsam, (*dat.*) obedient.

Gehör-sand, *m.* otolith; **-schnecke,** *f.* cochlea; **-sinn,** *m.* auditory sense; **-stäbchen,** *n.* auditory rod; **-steinchen,** *n.* otolith; **-täuschung,** *f.* auditory illusion; **-trichter,** *m.* ear trumpet.

Gehör-trommel, *f.* tympanum; **-trompete,** *f.* Eustachian tube; **-vorhof,** *m.* auditory vestibule; **-wasser,** *n.* fluid of the inner ear; **-weg,** *m.* auditory passage; **-werkzeug,** *n.* auditory apparatus.

Gehre, *f.* Gehrung, *f.* bevel, miter.

Gehrung, *f.* bevel, miter, wedge.

Gehweg, *m.* sidewalk, path.

Gehwerkzeug, *n.* locomotor organ.

Geier, *m.* vulture, hawk.

Geige, *f.* violin.

geigenförmig, panduriform, violin-shaped.

Geigenharz, *n.* rosin, colophony.

geil, luxuriant, rich, fertile, proud, lewd, in heat; **-heit,** *f.* luxuriance, lasciviousness; **-stelle,** *f.* area of rank growth.

Geiss, *f.* (she) goat, doe; **-bart,** *m.* meadowsweet, goatsbeard (*Spiraea aruncus*), (*Tragopogon pratensis*); **-bartskraut,** *n.* goatsbeard (*Spiraea aruncus*), (*Tragopogon pratensis*); **-blatt,** *n.* honeysuckle (*Caprifolium perfoliatum*); **-blattgewächse,** *n.pl.* Caprifoliaceae; **-bock,** *m.* he-goat.

Geissel, *f.* flagellum, cilium, whip, scourge, pest; **-anordnung,** *f.* arrangement of flagella; **-beize,** *f.* mordant used in staining; **-epithel,** *n.* ciliated epithelium; **-faden,** *m.* flagellum, cilium; **-färbung,** *f.* staining of flagella; **-fortsatz,** *m.* flagellumlike process.

Geissel-glied, *n.* segment of funiculus; **-infusorium,** *n.* flagellate; **-kammer** *f.* ciliated chamber; **-kern,** *m.* flagellated nucleus; **-kleid,** *n.* Peritricha; **-schwärmer,** *m.* flagellate spore, zoospore; **-skorpione,** *m.pl.* whip scorpion (Pedipalpi); **-spinnen,** *f.pl.* whip scorpion.

Geissel-tierchen, *n.* flagellate; **-tragend,** flagellated, bearing cilia; **-träger,** *m.pl.* mastigophora (Flagellatae); **-wimper,** *f.* large cilium.

Geiss-fuss, *m.* goatsfoot, goutweed, ashweed, (*Aegopodium podagraria*); **-klee,** *m.* laburnum (*Cytisus laburnum*), hogweed (*Cytisus scoparius*); **-raute,** *f.* goat's-rue (*Galega officinalis*).

Geist, *m.* spirit, mind, soul, ghost, intelligence, imagination.

geistesabwesend, absent-minded.

Geisteswissenschaft, *f.* mental science.

geistig, spirituous, alcoholic, intellectual, volatile, mental.

geistlich, spiritual, sacred.

geistlos, spiritless, lifeless, senseless.

geist-reich, -voll, ingenious, clever, witty.

Geiz, *m.* avarice, stinginess, shoot, sucker.

geizig, avaricious, stingy.

gekämmt, pectinate.

gekannt (kennen), known.

gekeimt, germinated.

gekerbt, crenate.

gekernt, nucleated, having a nucleus.

gekielt, carinated, keeled.

geklappter Querschnitt, *m.* collapsed ribbon-shaped cross section.

geklommen (klemmen), pinched.

geklommen (klimmen), climbed.

geklungen (klingen), sounded, rung.

geknäuelt, glomerate, coiled.

geknickt, geniculate.

gekniet, geniculate, bent, refracted.

gekniffen (kneifen), squeezed, pinched.

Geknirsche, *n.* gnashing (of teeth), crunching.

Geknister, *n.* (de)crepitation, crackling.

gekonnt (können), **er hat** ~, he was able.

geköpt, capitate.

gekoppelt, linked.

gekoren (küren), chosen.

gekörnelt, granular.

gekörnt, granulated.

Gekrätz, *n.* waste, refuse, slag, dross; **-ofen** *m.* almond furnace.

gekreuzt, crossed, decussate.

Gekriech, *n.* creep.

gekrischen (kreischen), screamed.

gekrochen (kriechen), crept, crawled.

Gekrös-arterie, *f.* mesenteric artery; **-drüse** *f.* mesenteric gland.

Gekröse, *n.* mesentery, giblets (goose).

Gekrös-gang, *m.* pancreatic duct; **-geflecht,** *n.* mesenteric plexus; **-haut,** *f.* mesenteric endothelium; **-wurzel,** *f.* root of the mesentery.

gekrümmt, curved, bent, campylotropous.

Gel, *n.-e,* gel.

geladen, charged, loaded.

Geläger, *n.* deposits, dregs, bottoms.

gelagert, beaten down, lodged, mounted on bearings, laid, stratified.

Gelände, *n.* (tract of) land, ground, territory, country, terrain.

Geländer, *n.* railing, balustrade.

Geländetiefe, *f.* lowland, depth of lot.

gelang (gelingen), **es** ~ **ihm,** he succeeded.

gelangen, to arrive, reach, attain, come; **dazu** ~, to reach the point; ~ **an,** to gain access to; ~ **in,** to get into, arrive at.

gelappt, lobed, lobate.

gelartig, gellike.

Gelass, *m.* space, room.

Gelatine, *f.* gelatin; **-artig,** gelatinous; **-folie,** *f.* sheet gelatin; **-leim,** *m.* gelatin glue; **-lösung,** *f.* gelatin solution; **-schicht,** *f.* gelatin layer, stratum; **-stichkultur,** *f.* gelatin stab culture; **-verflüssigung,** *f.* liquefaction of gelatin.

gelatin(is)ieren, to gelatinize.

gelatinös, gelatinous.

geläufig, fluent, ready, easy, familiar.

gelaunt, disposed; **gut (schlecht)** ~, in good (bad) humor.

Geläut(e), ringing, chimes.

geläutert, purified.

gelb, yellow; **-antimonerz,** *n.* cervantite; **-berre,** *f.* Avignon berry; **-beizen,** *n.* yellowing; **-blausauer,** ferrocyanic, ferrocyanide of . . . **-bleierz,** *n.* wulfenite, yellow lead ore; **-braun,** yellowish brown; **-brennen,** to dip, pickle; **-brennsäure,** *f.* pickling acid.

Gelbe, *n.* yellow, yolk.

Gelb-eisenerz, *n.* yellow ocher; **-eisenkies,** *m.* pyrite; **-eisenstein,** *m.* yellow ironstone, limonite; **-erde,** *f.* yellow ocher; **-erz,** *n.* yellow ore, limonite; **-färben,** to color, yellow; **-farbig,** yellow; **-fieber,** *n.* yellow fever; **-filzig,** yellow tomentose; **-gar,** tanned.

gelb-giessen, to cast in (brass) copper; **glut,** *f.* yellow heat; **-grau,** yellowish-gray; **-grün,** yellowish-green; **-guss,** *m.* brass.

Gelbheit, *f.* yellowness.

Gelb-holz, *n.* yellowwood (Cladrastis, Xanthoxylum).

Gelbildung, *f.* gel formation.

Gelb-kali, *n.* potassium ferrocyanide; **-kraut,** *n.* yellowweed (*Reseda luteola*); **-kupfer,** *n.* brass, yellow copper.

gelblich, yellowish.

Gelb-rost, *n.* stripe rust, yellow, rust, (*Puccinia glumarum*); **-schoten,** *f.pl.* wongshy (fruit of Gardenia); **-sprenkelung,** *f.* yellow mottling; **-stichig,** yellow tinged, yellowish; **-sucht,** *f.* jaundice; **-weiss,** cream-colored, ochroleucous; **-werdend,** yellowing, flavescent; **-wurz,** *f.* turmeric, yellowroot (Xanthorrhiza).

Geld, *n.* money; **-ertrag,** *m.* revenue; **-hilfe,** *f.* subsidy (resources); **-mittel,** *n.pl.* pecuniary means; **-münze,** *f.* coin; **-schein,** *m.* paper money; **-schrank,** *m.* safe; **-strafe,** *f.* fine; **-stück,** *n.* piece of money; **-währung,** *f.* standard, currency; **-wesen,** *n.* monetary matters.

Gelée, *n.* jelly.

gelegen (liegen), situated; (*dat.*) convenient, fit, proper, opportune, important; **mir ist daran ~,** I am anxious, I am concerned.

Gelegenheit, *f.* occasion, opportunity.

gelegentlich, accidental, occasional, incidental, now and then, by chance.

gelehrig, teachable, docile.

Gelehrsamkeit, *f.* learning, scholarship

gelehrt, learned.

Gelehrte(r), *m.* learned man, scholar.

Geleise, *n.* track, rut.

geleiten, to accompany, conduct, escort.

Geleitzelle, *f.* companion cell.

Gelenk, *n.* joint, wrist, articulation, hinge, link; **-band,** *n.* articular ligament; **-basalt,** *m.* flexible basalt; **-bau,** *m.* structure of a joint, articulation; **-bein,** *n.* articulate bone, sesamoid bone; **-beuge,** *f.* flexor of a

joint; **-bruch,** *m.* fracture; **-drüse,** *f.* synovial gland.

Gelenk-egge, *f.* jointed harrow; **-ende,** *n.* articular extremity; **-fett,** *n.* synovial fluid, fat; **-fläche,** *f.* articular surface; **-flächenrichtung,** *f.* direction of the joint surfaces; **-flüssigkeit,** *f.* synovial fluid; **-fortsatz,** *m.* articular or condyle process; **-fuge,** *f.* joint commissure.

Gelenk-gegend, *f.* region of a joint; **-grube,** *f.* articular fossa, glenoid cavity, acetabulum; **-haar,** *n.* hinged hair; **-haut,** *f.* synovial membrane; **-höcker,** *m.* articular eminence, (occipital) condyle; **-höhle,** *f.* articular cavity; **-hügel,** *m.* articular prominence.

gelenkig, articulate, flexible, pliant, pliable, supple, jointed, nimble.

Gelenk-kapsel, *f.* capsular ligament; **-kette,** *f.* flexible chain; **-knöchelchen,** *n.* sesamoid bone, bone-forming part of a joint; **-knopf,** *m.* condyle, head of bone; **-knorpel,** *m.* articular cartilage; **-knorren,** *m.* condyle; **-knoten,** *m.* movable part of articulation; **-kopf,** *m.* articular head, condyle, **-leim,** *m.* synovial fluid.

Gelenk-pfanne, *f.* articular cavity, acetabulum (of styloid cavity); **-polster,** *n.* pulvinus; **-quarz,** *m.* flexible sandstone; **-ranke,** *f.* jointed tendril; **-raum,** *m.* articular cavity; **-rheumatismus,** articular rheumatism, rheumatoid arthritis; **-rolle,** *f.* (trochlear) condyle; **-saft,** *m.* synovial fluid; **-schalig,** crustaceous; **-schmiere,** *f.* synovia; **-schwamm,** *m.* white swelling.

Gelenk-spalt, *m.* articular cleft; **-steifheit,** *f.* ankylosis; **-streifen,** *m.* hinge cell (in grass leaf); **-teil,** *m.* articular portion, condyle; **-verbindung,** *f.* articulation; **-vertiefung,** *f.* segment depression; **-verwachsung,** *f.* joint adhesions; **-wand,** *f.* joint boundary of capsule; **-wasser,** *n.* synovial fluid; **-winkel,** *m.* atricular angle; **-zelle,** *f.* hinge cell.

Gelf, *m.* silver-bearing pyrites; **-erz,** *n.* **-kupfer,** *n.* chalcopyrite.

geliehen (leihen), borrowed.

gelind, soft, gentle, mild, smooth.

gelingen, (*dat.*) to succeed; **es gelingt mir,** I succeed; **es gelingt,** it is possible.

gelitten (leiden), suffered.

geloben, to promise, pledge.

gelocht, pierced, perforated.

gelogen (lügen), lied, deceived.

gelöschter Kalk, *m.* hydrated (slaked) lime.

gelöst, dissolved, in solution.

Gelsemien, *n.* gelsemium; **-wurzel,** *f.* gelsemium root.

gelt, dry, barren.

Gelte, *f.* pail, tub.

gelten, to be of value, have weight, be true or valid, pass, be considered, apply, concern; **es gilt (galt),** it is (was) a question of; ∼ **für,** to pass for; **es gilt zu handeln,** there is need of action; **das gilt nicht,** it is not fair.

geltend, sich ∼ **machen,** to assert oneself, claim recognition, hold true, make itself felt.

Geltung, *f.* worth, value, importance, currency; **zur** ∼ **kommen gelangen,** to become important, come into play.

gelungen (gelingen), **es ist mir** ∼, I succeeded.

Gelüst, *n.* desire, longing.

gem., *abbr.* (gemischt), mixed.

Gemach, *n.* room, apartment.

gemach, slow(ly), gentle.

gemächlich, slow, gentle, easy, soft, comfortable.

Gemahl, *m.* consort, husband; **-in,** wife.

gemahnen, to remind.

Gemälde, *n.* painting, picture.

gemäss, (*dat.*) according to, conformable to, in consequence of.

gemässigt, moderate, temperate.

Gemäuer, *n.* masonry.

gemein, (*dat.*) common, ordinary, general, mean, base, vulgar; **-besitz,** *m.* communal property.

Gemeinde, *f.* community, municipality, congregation; **-wald,** *m.* communal forest.

Gemeinfliegen, *f.pl.* Muscidae.

Gemeinfrucht, *f.* carcerule.

Gemeinheit, *f.* meanness, baseness.

gemein-jährig, mean annual; **-nützig,** of public benefit, generally useful.

gemeinsam, (*dat.*) common, mutual, joint;

Gemein-schaft, *f.* community, society; **-schaftlich,** common, mutual, joint; **-schaftsarbeit,** *f.* co-operative work; **-verständlich,** popular; **-weide,** *f.* common pasture; **-wesen,** *n.* commonwealth, community at large.

Gemenganteil, *m.* constituent part or ingredient of a mixture.

Gemenge, *n.* mixture, conglomerate; **-asche,** *f.* test ashes.

Gemeng-stoff, constituents, ingredients; **-teil,** *m.* constituent.

gemieden (meiden), avoided.

gemindert, lessened, diminished, reduced.

Gemisch, *n.* mixing, (ad)mixture, medley.

gemischt, mixed, diffused; **-körnig,** of various grain sizes.

Gemme, *f.* gem, cameo.

gemocht (mögen), **er hat** ∼, he cared to.

gemolken (melken), milked.

Gemse, *f.* chamois.

Gemsleder, *n.* chamois (leather).

Gemüll, *n.* rubbish, bee waste.

Gemüse, *n.* vegetables; **-bau,** *m.* vegetable gardening; **-samenzucht,** *f.* vegetable-seed breeding.

gemusst (müssen), **er hat** ∼, he was obliged to.

gemustert, examined, (fancy) figured.

Gemüt, *n.* feeling, soul, mind, heart.

gemütlich, comfortable, cozy, good-natured, genial, pleasant.

Gemütsbewegung, *f.* emotion, excitement.

Gen, *n.* gene, factor.

genabelt, umbilicate.

genähte, *n.* what has been sewed.

genannt (nennen), named.

genas (genesen), he recovered.

genau, exact, accurate, true, punctual, close, precise, tight, economical.

Genaueres, *n.* more precise information.

Genauigkeit, *f.* accuracy, exactness.

Genauigkeits-grad, *m.* degree of accuracy; **-mass,** *n.* measure of exactness.

genehm, agreeable, suitable, acceptable.

genehmigen, to approve of, agree, accede, allow.

geneigt, (*dat.*) inclined, sloping, disposed to.

Geneigtheit, *f.* incline, slope, inclination, (kind) disposition.

Generalnenner, *m.* common denominator.

Generations-reihe, *f.* series of generations; **-wechsel,** *m.* alternation of generations, metagenesis.

Generator, *m.* producer, generator.

generell, general.

generisch, generic.

Genese, *f.* genesis, formation.

genesen, to recover, convalesce, get better, be delivered.

Genetik, *f.* genetics.

genetisch, genetic.

Genever, *m.* Holland gin.

genial, gifted, full of genius, ingenious.

Genick, *n.* nape, (back of the) neck; -beule, *f.* poll evil, boil on the back of the neck; -drüse, *f.* cervical gland; -grube, *f.* hollow of neck; -starre, *f.* cerebrospinal meningitis.

Genie, *n.* genius; -corps, *n.* corps of engineers.

genieren, to incommode, trouble; sich nicht ∼, not to mind.

geniessbar, relishable, palatable, edible.

geniessen, to enjoy, take, eat or drink.

Geniste, *n.* nest, waste, rubbish, broom.

Genital-anhang, *m.* genital appendage; -fuss, *m.* gonopod; -glocke, *f.* gonophore; -höcker, *m.* genital process, eminence; -kapsel, *f.* genital sac; -reizung, *f.* genital irritation; -schlauch, *m.* uterus and vagina; -spalte, *f.* genital cleft; -strang, *m.* genital cord; -tasche, *f.* genital pouch.

genommen (nehmen), taken.

genoss (geniessen), enjoyed.

Genoss(e), *m.* companion, associate.

Genossenschaft, *f.* company, society, association, fellowship, partnership, guild.

genossenschaftlich, cooperative.

Genre, *n.* kind, sort.

gentianaviolett, gentian violet.

Genträger, *m.* carrier of the gene.

genug, enough.

Genüge, *f.* sufficiency; zur ∼, enough; ∼ tun, to comply with.

genügen, (*dat.*) to suffice, be enough, satisfy.

genügend, sufficient, satisfactory.

genügsam, content, easily pleased, temperate, nonexacting, frugal.

Genugtuung, *f.* satisfaction, reparation.

Genuss, *m.* enjoyment, pleasure, taking (food or drink); -mittel, *n.* means of enjoyment, condiment; -reich, enjoyable; -reife, *f.* ripe for consumption; -süchtig, pleasure-seeking, sensual; -zweck, *m.* food purpose.

Genzian, *m.* gentian.

Geolog, *m.* geologist.

geologisch, geological.

Geometrie, *f.* geometry.

geometrisch, geometric(al); geometrische Reihe, *f.* geometrical progression.

Geophysik, *f.* geophysics.

Georgine, *f.* dahlia.

gepaart, paired.

Gepäck, *n.* baggage.

gepfiffen (pfeifen), whistled.

gepflogen (pflegen), cultivated, exercised; nach gepflogenem Rate, after due deliberation.

Gepflogenheit, *f.* custom, usage, habit.

Gepräge, *n.* impression, (im)print, stamp, coinage, feature, character.

gepriesen, (preisen), praised.

gepulvert, powdered, pulverized.

gequollen (quellen), swelled, soaked.

Gerade, *f.* straight line.

gerade, straight, direct, even, just, upright, plain; ∼ aus, straight ahead; ∼ deshalb, for this particular reason; ∼ Zahl, *f.* even number.

geradeswegs, straightway, directly.

geradezu, straight on, immediately, frankly.

Gerad-flügler, *m.* Orthoptera; -läufig, straight, orthotropous; -linig, straight, rectilinear; -schaftig, straight boled, cylindrical; -schaftigkeit, *f.* straightness of stem; -sichtig, direct-vision; -wertig, of even valence; -zahlig, even numbered.

gerandet, emarginate, bordered.

Geranium, *n.* geranium.

gerannt (rennen), run, extracted.

Gerät, *n.* tools, apparatus, utensils, instruments, plant, furniture, appliances.

geraten, to come, fall, get (into); gut ∼, to prosper, succeed; auf einen Gedanken ∼, to hit upon an idea; das ist ihm ∼, he succeeded.

geraten (raten), advised, advisable, guessed.

geraten, successful, prosperous.

Geratewohl, aufs ∼, at random, at all risks.

Gerätschaft, *f.* tools, outfit, utensils, apparatus.

geraum, ample, long.

geräumig, spacious, roomy, ample, large.

Geräusch, *n.* noise, murmur, clamor, mixture of tones, stir; -los, noiseless; -voll, noisy.

gerauht, napped ' fabrics).

Gerb-anlage, *f.* tannery; -auszug, *m.* tanning extract.

gerbbar, tannable.

Gerbe-brühe, -flüssigkeit, *f.* tan(ner's) liquor, ooze; -mittel, *n.* tanning medium, tan.

gerben, to tan, hull; **sämisch** ∼, to chamois weiss ∼, to taw.

Gerber, *m.* tanner, currier; **-baum,** *m.* tanner's sumac (*Rhus coriaria*).

Gerberei, *f.* tanning, tannery.

Gerber-fett, *n.* (leather) dégras, stuff; **-kalk,** *m.* slaked (gas) lime; **-lohe,** *f.* tanbark; **-strauch,** *m.* tanner's sumac (*Rhus coriaria*): **-strauchgewächse,** *n.pl.* Coriariaceae; **-träger,** *m.* cantilever structure; **-wolle,** *f.* skin wool.

Gerbe-vermögen, *n.* tanning power; **-versuch,** *m.* tanning experiment.

Gerb-leim, *m.* tannic acid glue; **-lohe,** *f.* tanbark; **-lösung,** *f.* tannic acid solution; **-pflanze,** *f.* tanniferous plant; **-rinde,** *f.* tanbark; **-säure,** *f.* tannic acid; **-stahl,** *m.* shear (tilted) steel, polishing steel, burnisher.

Gerbstoff, *m.* tanning matter, tannin; **-behälter,** *m.* tannin sac; **-extrakt,** *m.* tannin extract; **-gehalt,** *m.* tannin content; **-haltig,** tanniferous; **-rot,** *n.* phlobaphene; **-schlauch,** *m.* tannin sac; **-zelle,** *f.* tannin cell.

Gerbung, *f.* tanning.

gerecht, righteous, just, fair, right, equitable, legitimate, fit, lawful; ∼ **werden,** (*dat.*) to do justice to, satisfy.

Gerechtigkeit, *f.* justice, righteousness, fairness.

Gerede, *n.* talk(ing), rumor, report.

Gereibe, *n.* rubbing.

gereichen, to cause, turn out, prove, rebound, be.

gereiht, connected, joined.

gereuen, to repent, regret.

Gericht, *n.* court, judgment, tribunal, jurisdiction, dish.

gerichtet, directed.

gerichtlich, judicial, forensic, lawful, legal.

Gerichtsamt, *n.* court; **-mann,** *m.* judge.

Gerichtsbarkeit, *f.* jurisdiction.

Gerichts-hof, *m.* court, tribunal; **-rat,** *m.* judge, counselor.

gereiben, ground, grated.

gerieft, grooved, channeled.

Geriesel, *n.* ripple, drizzling.

geriet (geraten), got, came.

gering, small, slight, moderate, deficient, unimportant, limited, trifling, ordinary, common, bad; ∼ **achten,** to have little regard for; ∼ **schätzen,** to attach little value to.

geringelt, annulate, ringed

geringer, inferior, less.

gering-fügig, unimportant, insignificant, trivial, petty; **-haltig,** poor, low, base, lowgrade, lean; **-schätzung,** *f.* contempt, disregard.

geringst, least, slightest.

geringwertig, of small value.

gerinnbar, coagulable, congealable.

Gerinne, *n.* running, flowing, channel, conduit, gutter.

gerinnelt, canaliculate, channeled.

gerinnen, to coagulate, curdle, congeal, gel.

Gerinnsel, *n.* coagulated mass, curd, clot.

Gerinnstoff, *m.* coagulant, coagulator.

gerinnt, canaliculate.

Gerinnung, *f.* coagulation.

gerinnungs-fähig, coagulable; **-masse,** *f.* coagulum, gel; **-mittel,** *n.* coagulant, coagulator; **-zeit,** *f.* coagulation time.

Gerippe, *n.* skeleton, framework, carcass.

gerippt, ribbed, fluted, costate.

gerissen (reissen), torn, sly, cunning.

geritten (reiten), ridden.

Germanichlorid, *n.* germanic chloride.

Germanium-fluorwasserstoffsäure, *f.* fluogermanic acid; **-oxyd,** *n.* germanium oxide; **-oxydul,** *n.* germanous oxide; **-sulfid,** *n.* germanium (germanic) sulphide; **-sulfür,** *n.* germanous sulphide; **-wasserstoff,** *m.* germanium hydride.

Germanosulfide, *n.* germanous sulphide.

Germer, *m.* false (white) hellebore (*Veratrum album*).

gern, gladly, with pleasure, willingly; **ich möchte** ∼, I should like; ∼ **haben,** to be fond of, like to.

gerochen (riechen), smelled.

Geröll, *n.* pebbles, gravel, boulders, rubbish, rolling rock; **-halde,** *f.* hillside covered with rock debris; **-stein,** *m.* pebble, boulder; **-vegetation,** *f.* vegetation of gravel; **-wüste,** *f.* stony desert.

gerollt, lifted (of lacquer).

geronnen (gerinnen), coagulated, curdled, clotted.

Gerste, *f.* barley; **-entgranner,** *m.* barley awner.

Gersten-flugbrand, *m.* loose smut of barley; **-graupen,** *f.pl.* pearl barley; **-hartbrand,** *m.* covered smut of barley; **-korn,** *n.* barley corn, sty; **-mehl,** *n.* barley flour; **-schleim,**

m. barley water; **-stärke,** *f.* barley starch; **-stoff,** *m.* hordein.

Gerte, *f.* switch, rod, sapling, small pole.

Geruch, *n.* smell, odor, scent, fragrance, savor; **-frei,** free from odor, odorless; **-los,** odorless, savorless, scentless; **-losigkeit,** *f.* inodorosness; **-reich,** rich in odor, fragrant.

Geruchs-apparat, *m.* olfactory apparatus; **-empfindlichkeit,** *f.* olfactory sensitivity; **-gegend,** *f.* olfactory region; **-grube,** *f.* olfactory fossa; **-hügel,** *m.* olfactory tuber; **-kapsel,** *f.* nasal capsule; **-knochen,** *m.* ethmoid bone; **-knospe,** *f.* olfactory bud.

Geruchs-reiz, *m.* olfactory irritant; **-schleimhaut,** *f.* olfactory epithelium; **-sinn,** *m.* sense of smell; **-stoff,** *m.* odorous substance; **-werkzeug,** *n.* olfactory apparatus.

Gerücht, *n.* rumor, report.

Gerümpel, *n.* lumber, rubbish, trash.

gerungen (ringen), wrung, struggled.

gerunzelt, wrinkled.

Gerüst, *n.* frame(work), stroma, reticulum, scaffold(ing), crate, trestle, stage; **-eiweiss,** *n.* scleroprotein; **-faser,** *f.* framework fiber; **-stange,** *f.* scaffolding pole; **-theorie,** *f.* reticular theory; **-werk,** *n.* framework, stroma; **-zellulose,** *f.* pure cellulose.

gesägt, serrate.

Gesagte, *n.* what has been said.

gesalzen, salted.

gesamt, total, whole, entire, complete; **-alkali,** *n.* total alkali; **-alterszuwachs,** *m.* total increment; **-ansicht,** *f.* general view; **-bedarf,** *m.* total requirement; **-blütenstand,** *m.* entire inflorescence; **-blutmenge,** *f.* blood volume; **-brechung,** *f.* total refraction; **-energiebedarf,** *m.* total energy requirement; **-gebiet,** *n.* entire territory, whole field; **-gestaltung,** *f.* whole form.

Gesamtheit, *f.* totality, generality.

Gesamt-helligkeit, *f.* total intensity of light; **-konzentration,** *f.* final strength; **-leistungsfähigkeit,** *f.* total capacity or output; **-lösliches,** *n.* total soluble matter; **-menge,** *f.* total (quantity); **-rohfaser,** *f.* total crude fiber; **-rückstand,** *m.* total residue; **-säure,** *f.* total acid; **-schätzung,** *f.* total estimate; **-schwefel,** *m.* total sulphur.

Gesamt-schwerpunkt, *m.* common center of gravity; **-spannung,** *f.* total voltage; **-stoffwechsel,** *m.* total metabolism; **-vergrösserung,** *f.* total magnification; **-verhalten,** *n.* general behavior; **-wassergehalt,** *m.*

total water content; **-widerstand,** *n.* total resistance; **-wuchsleistung,** *f.* total growth; **-zahl,** *f.* total number.

gesandt (senden), sent.

Gesandte, *m.* messenger, ambassador.

Gesang, *m.* singing, song, hymn.

Gesäss, *n.* seat, buttock, posterior, anus, floor; **-bein,** *n.* ischium; **-bruch,** *m.* gluteal hernia; **-furche,** *f.* gluteal fold; **-gegend,** *f.* gluteal region; **-knochen,** *m.* ischium; **-knorren,** *m.* ischial tuberosity; **-muskel,** *m.* gluteal muscle; **-schlagader,** *f.* gluteal artery; **-schwiele,** *f.* gluteal callosity; **-wirbel,** *m.* sacral vertebra.

gesättigt, saturated.

gesäumt, square sawn, squared.

Geschabsel, *n.* scrapings.

Geschäft, *n.* business, affair, dealings, trade, occupation, firm.

geschäftig, busy, active, fussy, officious.

geschäftlich, commercial, businesslike; professional.

Geschäfts-betrieb, *m.* management; **-führung,** *f.* managing; **-lage,** *f.* market, business, trade, commercial status; **-leben,** *n.* business, trade; **-tüchtig,** enterprising.

geschah (geschehen), happened.

geschehen, (*dat.*) to happen, chance, come to pass, be done.

Geschehnis, *n.* occurrence.

Gescheide, *n.* numbles.

gescheit, intelligent, keen, sensible, clever.

gescheitert, frustrated, wrecked.

Geschenk, *n.* present, gift.

Geschichte, *f.* history, tale; **eine schöne ∼!** a nice thing!

geschichtet, stratified, laminated.

geschichtlich, historical.

Geschick, *n.* skill, ability, fate, destiny.

Geschicklichkeit, *f.* skill, cleverness, ingenuity.

geschickt, skilled, qualified, clever.

Geschiebe, *n.* boulder, detritus, bed load, shoving, pushing; **-führung,** *f.* bed-load transport, detritus carried by river water; **-lehm,** *m.* glacial loam; **-mergel,** *m.* boulder clay; **-trieb,** *m.* aggregate of detritus carried by a river.

geschieden, separated.

geschiefert, exfoliated.

geschieht (geschehen), happens.

geschiener (scheinen), shone, seemed.

geschindelt, imbricate.

Geschirr, *n.* vessel, ware, utensils, implements, tools, apparatus, hardness; **-guss,** *m.* pottery casting; **-holz,** *n.* wood for implements; **-leder,** *n.* harness leather.

geschlängelt, tortuous.

Geschlecht, *n.*-er, sex, genus, kind, species, race, stock, generation, gender.

Geschlechter-spaltung, *f.* male (female) sterility (dichogamy, heterostylism); **-um-schlag,** *m.* alternation in sex among unisexual plants.

geschlechtlich, sexual, generic.

geschlechtlos, asexual.

Geschlechts-apparat, *m.* sex apparatus; **-art,** *f.* generic character, genus, species; **-begrenzt,** sex-limited; **-bestimmung,** *f.* sex differentiation; **-chromosom,** *m.* sex chromosome; **-drüse,** *f.* genital gland, ovary, testicle, gonad; **-drüsengewebe,** *n.* sex-gland tissue; **-falte,** *f.* genital fold.

Geschlechts-gang, *m.* genital passage; **-gebunden,** sex-linked; **-gefühl,** *n.* sex impulse; **-gegensatz,** *m.* sex contrast; **-gen,** *n.* sex gene; **-glied,** *n.* sex organ; **-hormon,** *n.* sex hormone; **-kapsel,** *f.* gonad; **-kern,** *m.* gamete nucleus; **-los,** asexual, agamic; **-merkmal,** *n.* sex characteristic.

Geschlechts-namen, *m.* genus name; **-nei-gung,** *f.* sexual impulse; **-öffnung,** *f.* genital orifice; **-organe,** *n.pl.* sex organs, gonads, genitals; **-pflanze,** *f.* phanerogam, flowering plant; **-reife,** *f.* puberty; **-reizend,** aphrodisiac; **-strang,** *m.* spermatic cord; **-trieb,** *m.* sexual desire.

Geschlechts-umkehr, *f.* sex reversal; **-um-schlag,** *m.* alternation of sex (among unisexual plants); **-umwandlung,** *f.* sex reversal; **-verhältnis,** *n.* sex ratio; **-ver-wandlung,** *f.* sex modification; **-wechsel,** *m.* change of sex; **-weg,** *m.* sexual duct or passage; **-werkzeug,** *n.* sexual apparatus; **-wulst,** *m.* genital eminence.

geschlichen (schleichen), crept, crawled, sneaked.

geschliffen (schleifen), sharpened, polished.

geschlissen (schleissen), split, worn.

geschloffen (schliefen), glided, crept.

geschlossen (schliessen), closed, crowded, consistent, unbroken, dense, fully stocked, continuous.

Geschlossenheit, *f.* inclusiveness.

geschlungen (schlingen), slung, twisted, wound.

Geschmack, *m.* taste, flavor, relish, liking, fancy.

geschmacklich, regarding taste.

geschmack-los, tasteless, stale, insipid, flat; **-losigkeit,** *f.* tastelessness.

Geschmacks-becher, *m.* taste bud; **-ein-druck,** *m.* taste impression; **-knospe,** *f.* taste bud; **-organ,** *n.* organ of taste, gustatory organ; **-sinn,** *m.* sense of taste; **-warze,** *f.* gustatory or lingual papilla.

Geschmeide, *n.* jewelry.

geschmeidig, pliable, bendable, flexible, ductile, pliant, supple, soft, ductile, malleable, versatile, smooth, yielding.

geschmissen (schmeissen), thrown, hurled, blown.

geschmolzen (schmelzen), melted, molten, fused.

geschnäbelt, provided with a beak, rostrate(d).

geschnitten (schneiden), cut.

geschoben (schieben), pushed, shoved.

gescholten (schelten), scolded.

Geschöpf, *n.* creature.

geschoren (scheren), shorn, cropped.

Geschoss, *n.*-e, shoot (plant), projectile, missile, story, floor.

geschossen (schiessen), shot.

Geschoss-körper, *m.* projectile (body); **-treibend,** ballistic.

geschränkte Röllchen, *n.pl.* angle-axis rollers.

Geschrei, *n.* outcry, shriek, rumor, stir, disrepute.

geschrieben (schreiben), written.

geschrieen (schreien), shouted, cried out.

geschritten (schreiten), stridden, stepped.

geschroben (schrauben), screwed.

geschult, trained.

geschunden (schinden), skinned, scalped.

Geschür, *n.* dross, scoria.

Geschütz, *n.* gun, cannon; **-bronze,** *f.* gun metal.

geschützt, protected, patented.

geschwänzt, caudate, long-tailed.

geschweift, cranked, curved.

geschweigen, not mention, omit; **ge-schweige denn,** not to mention, not so much.

geschwiegen (schweigen), kept silent; (geschweigen), omitted.

geschwind, fast, quick, swift, prompt, immediate.

Geschwindigkeit, *f.* velocity, speed, dispatch, haste.

Geschwindigkeits-gleichung, *f.* velocity equation; **-messer,** *m.* speed indicator.

Geschwister, *pl.* brother and sister; **-kreuzung,** *f.* sib mating.

geschwisterlich, fraternal.

geschwollen (schwellen), swollen, bloated, swirled.

geschwommen (schwimmen), swum.

geschworen (schwären), ulcerated, festered.

geschworen (schwören), sworn.

Geschwulst, *f.* swelling, tumor, new growth.

geschwunden (schwinden), disappeared, vanished.

geschwungen (schwingen), swung, balanced.

Geschwür, *n.* ulcer, abscess, boil, festering.

Gesell(e), *m.* companion, comrade, mate, journeyman.

gesellen, to join, associate.

gesellig, companionable, sociable, gregarious (plant).

Geselligkeit, *f.* sociability.

Gesellschaft, *f.* association, society, company, partnership.

Gesellschaften, *f.pl.* populations.

Gesellschafts-bildung, *f.* association (formation of an); **-einheit,** *f.* association type; **-komplex,** *m.* association complex; **-merkmal,** *n.* distinguishing character of an association; **-treue,** *f.* fidelity; **-verbreitung,** *f.* synchorology, distribution of plant association; **-wissenschaft,** sociology.

Gesenk, *n.* hollow, slope, cavity, pit, sump, swage; **-schmieden,** *n.* drop forging.

gesessen (sitzen), sat, seated.

Gesetz, *n.* law, rule, precept, statute; ~ **der "Erstbelastung,"** *f.* "virgin curve."

Gesetz-entwurf, *m.* legislative bill; **-gebend,** legislative; **-gebung,** *f.* legislation.

gesetzlich, lawful, legal; **-geschützt,** protected by law, copyrighted, patented.

gesetz-mässig, lawful, regular, according to laws, in accordance with theoretical principles; **-mässigkeit,** *f.* legality, regularity.

gesetzt (setzen), set, placed, fixed, established, steady, serious, supposing, in case.

Gesetzvorschlag, *m.* bill, motion.

Gesicht, *m.***-er,** eyesight, face, physiognomy, countenance, vision; **zu** ~ **bekommen,** to get to see.

Gesichts-achse, *f.* visual axis; **-borste,** *f.* prefrontal bristle; **-falte,** *f.* facial wrinkle; **-feld,** *n.* field of vision; **-gegend,** *f.* facial region; **-hautmuskel,** *m.* facial muscle; **-höcker,** *m.* frontal tubercle; **-knochen,** *m.* facial bone; **-kreis,** *m.* field of vision, horizon; **-krem,** *m.* face cream.

Gesichts-lähmung, *f.* facial paralysis; **-linie,** *f.* visual (facial) line; **-muskel,** *m.* facial muscle; **-naht,** *f.* facial suture; **-punkt,** *m.* aspect, viewpoint; **-raum,** *m.* optical space; **-schlagader,** *f.* facial artery; **-sinn,** *m.* sense of vision; **-strahl,** *m.* visual ray; **-verletzung,** *f.* facial injury.

Gesichts-wahrnehmung, *f.* visual perception; **-winkel,** *m.* visual (optic or facial) angle; **-zug,** *m.* facial feature.

Gesims, *n.* ledge, ridge, molding, cornice, shelf; **-artig,** cornicelike.

Gesinnung, *f.* mind, disposition, feeling, opinion.

gesittet, mannered, behaved, bred, polite, civilized.

gesoffen (saufen), drunk.

gesogen (saugen), sucked.

gesondert, separate.

gesonnen (sinnen), meditated, inclined, disposed, willing.

gesotten (sieden), boiled.

gespalten, clefted, fissile.

Gespann, *n.* group, bottom plate, yoke, team, couple, pair.

gespannt (spannen), stretched, tight, intense.

Gespenst, *n.***-er,** phantom, ghost, specter, apparition.

gespieen (speien), spat.

Gespinst, *n.* cocoon, web, spinning package, spun (yarn) goods, textile fabric; **-faser,** *f.* textile fiber; **-gehäuse,** *n.* cocoon; **-hülle,** *f.* spun casing; **-motte,** *f.* web moth, ermine moth; **-pflanze,** *f.* textile plant, fiber plant.

gesplissen (spleissen), split.

gesponnen (spinnen), spun.

Gespräch, *n.***-e,** conversation, talk, dialogue.

gespreizt, stilted, affected; **-armig,** spreading.

gesprenkelt, adspersed, mottled, speckled.

gesprochen (sprechen), spoken.

gesprossen (spriessen), sprouted.

gesprungen (springen), jumped.

gestachelt, prickly, thorny.

Gestade, n. bank, shore, coast.

Gestalt, f.-en, form, figure, shape, aspect, frame, manner, stature; -änderung, f. change of form, metamorphosis.

gestalten, to form, shape, mold, fashion; sich ∿, to assume a form, proceed.

Gestalter, m. designer.

Gestalt-faktor, m. form inclosure, factor, form, completion factor; -los, amorphous, formless, shapeless; -losigkeit, f. shapelessness, amorphousness.

Gestaltswahrnehmung, f. perception of configuration.

Gestaltung, f. formation, configuration, shaping, state, condition, situation, design.

Gestaltungs-trieb, m. creative impulse; -vermögen, n. variability.

Gestaltveränderung, f. change of form or shape.

gestanden (gestehen), confessed, avowed.

gestanden (stehen), stood.

Geständnis, n.-se, confession, admission, acknowledgment.

Gestänge, n.pl. poles, rods, bars, rails.

Gestank, n. stench, bad smell, stink.

gestatten, to allow, permit, consent to.

gestaucht, m. short, compressed, dammed up.

Geste, f. gesture.

gesteckt, stuck.

gestehen, to confess, admit, coagulate, curdle, congeal, clot.

Gestehungs-kosten, f.pl. working costs; -preis, m. cost price.

Gestein, n. rock, mineral, stone, rock stratum; -bildend, rock-forming.

Gestein(s)-art, f. (kind of) rock; -aufschliessung, f. rock weathering; -flur, f. rock vegetation; -kunde, petrology, mineralogy, geology; -mantel, m. lithosphere; -pflanze, f. plant growing on rocks; -probe, f. mineral test; -rest, m. rock residue; -schutt, m. rock debris, talus; -unterlage, f. rocky subsoil.

Gestell, n. frame, stand, trestle, holder, hearth, crucible, support, framework, rack, opened line; -boden, m. crucible (hearth) bottom.

gestern, yesterday.

gestiegen (steigen), climbed.

gestielt, petiolate, pedunculate, stalked, stipitate.

Gestirn, n. star(s), constellation.

gestirnt, starry, covered with stars.

gestoben (stieben), dispersed, scattered.

Gestöber, n. snowstorm, dust storm.

gestochen (stechen), pricked, stung.

gestohlen (stehlen), stolen.

Gestör, n. raft section.

gestorben (sterben), deceased, dead, died.

gestört, disturbed (natural structure destroyed).

gestrahlt, radiated.

Gesträuch, n. bushes, shrubbery, shrubwood, thicket.

gestreckt, stretched, attenuate; -gliedrig, having elongated internodes.

gestreift, striate(d), striped.

gestrichelt, lineate(d), striose.

gestrichen (streichen), stroked, rubbed, stained, painted.

gestrig, of yesterday, yesterday's.

gestritten (streiten), disputed, contended.

Gestrüpp, n. bushes, thicket, underbrush, tangled growth, scrub.

Gestüb(b)e, n. charcoal, dust mixed with soil.

gestunken (stinken), stunk.

Gestüt, n. stud (horses).

gestutzt, trimmed.

Gesuch, n. request, demand, application.

gesucht, sought for, in demand.

gesund, sound, healthy; -brunnen, m. mineral spring.

gesunden, to recover.

Gesundheit, f. health.

gesundheitlich, sanitary, hygienic.

Gesundheits-amt, n. board of health; -pflege, f. sanitation, hygiene; -zeugnis, n. certificate of health.

gesungen (singen), sung.

gesunken (sinken), sunk.

Getäfel, n. wainscoting, paneling, inlaying.

getan (tun), done, made; gesagt ∿, no sooner said than done.

geteilt, parted, divided; -blättrig, with divided leaves.

getigert, striped.

getönt, tinted.

Getöse, *n.* turmoil.

Getränk, *n.* beverage, drink, potion, liquor.

getrauen, to dare, venture, trust.

Getreide, *n.* grain, cereals, crops; **-art,** *f.* kind of grain, cereal; **-bau,** *m.* corn growing; **-bestand,** *m.* cereal crop; **-blasenfüsse,** *m.pl.Limothrips cerealium;* **-brand,** *m.* cereal smut; **-branntwein,** *m.* whisky from grain; **-brennerei,** *f.* grain distillery; **-frucht,** *f.* cereal.

Getreide-hackkultur, *f.* cereals in row culture; **-halmwespe,** *f.* wheat-stem sawfly (*Cephus pygmaeus*); **-korn,** *n.* grain; **-krebs,** *m.* grain weevil; **-kümmel,** *m.* kümmel (a spirit); **-laufkäfer,** *m.* Zabrus; **-lupe,** *f.* seed microscope; **-rost,** *m.* cereal rust; **-schnaps,** *m.* whisky from grain; **-stroh,** *n.* (cereal) straw.

getrennt, separated, separate; **-blumig,** dioecious; **-geschlechtlich,** dioecious, separation of genital organs, having the sexes separate; **-geschlechtigkeit,** *f.* diclinism; **-läufig,** running separately.

getreu, faithful, true.

Getriebe, *n.* driving, motion, bustle, busy life, working gear, motive power, machinery, mechanism, pinion, linkage; **-lehre,** *f.* kinetics.

getrieben (treiben), driven, drifted.

getrocknet, dried, desiccated.

getroffen (treffen), hit, struck.

getroffen (triefen), dripped.

getrogen (trügen), deceived.

getropft, spotted, guttate.

getrost, confident, hopeful, courageous.

getrübt, turbid, cloudy, opaque, dull.

getüpfelt, spotted, pitted, punctuate, guttate.

getupft, dotted, spotted.

geübt, experienced, skilled.

Geviert(e), *n.* square(ness), quadrate; **ins** ~ **bringen,** to square.

geviert, square(d), quaternary; **-meter,** *m.&n.* square meter.

Gewächs, *n.* growth, plant, growing, tumor, vintage, breeding.

gewachsen, grown, undisturbed (of soil).

Gewächs-haus, *n.* greenhouse, hothouse; **-kunde,** *f.* botany.

gewahr, ~ **werden,** to perceive, become aware.

Gewähr, *f.* guarantee, surety, security, bail.

gewahren, to perceive, discover.

gewähren, to grant, accord, concede, give, furnish.

gewähr-leisten, to warrant, guarantee, vouch; **-leistung,** *f.* guarantee.

gewahrt, protected, preserved.

Gewalt, *f.* power, force, authority, violence, influence; **sich** ~ **antun,** to restrain oneself.

gewaltig, powerful, forcible, mighty, strong, huge, immense, vast, enormous.

gewaltsam, violent.

gewalttätig, violent, brutal.

gewalzt, milled, rolled.

Gewand, *n.* -er, garment, vestment.

gewandt (wenden), turned, agile, active, adroit, versatile.

Gewandtheit, *f.* versatility.

gewann (gewinnen), won, earned.

gewärtig, (*gen.*) awaiting, expectant.

gewärtigen, to expect, look forward to.

gewaschen, washed.

Gewässer, *n.* waters, stream, flood, body of water: **-kunde,** *f.* hydrology.

Gewebe, *n.* tissue, texture, web, textile fabric; **-atmung,** *f.* tissue respiration; **-bestandteil,** *m.* tissue constituent; **-blastem,** *n.* blastemal tissue; **-brei,** *m.* tissue pulp; **-draht,** *m.* gauze wire; **-farbstoff,** *m.* histohematin; **-feindlich,** tissue destroying; **-fetzen,** *m.* shred of tissue; **-flüssigkeit,** *f.* tissue fluid.

Gewebe-kitt, *m.* tissue cement; **-kultur,** *f.* tissue culture; **-lage(r),** layer of tissue; **-lehre,** *f.* histology; **-pfropfen,** *m.* tissue plug; **-schädigung,** *f.* injury to tissue; **-schicht,** *f.* stratum or layer; **-schrumpfung,** *f.* shrinking of the tissues; **-spalt,** *m.* fissure; **-verband,** *m.* tissue; **-waren,** *f.pl.* textile goods, textiles; **-züchtung,** *f.* tissue culture.

Gewebs-, see GEWEBE- in compounds.

gewedelt, flabellate.

Gewehr, *n.* arms, gun, rifle, tusk (boar).

Geweih, *n.* horns, antlers; **-ende,** *n.* prong of antler.

geweiht, consecrated.

Geweihzacken, *m.* antler process or prong.

gewellt, wavy, corrugated.

Gewerbe, *n.* trade, profession, industry, vocation; **-ausstellung,** *f.* industrial exposition; **-schule,** *f.* technical (industrial) school.

Gewerb-fleiss, *m.* industrial activity, industry; **-kunde,** *f.* technology; **-kundlich,** technological; **-lich, -tätig,** industrial; **-treibende(r),** *m.* artisan, tradesman.

Gewerk, *n.* trade, works, machinery, produce; **-schaft,** *f.* trade union; **-verein,** *m.* trade union.

gewesen (sein), been.

gewichen (weichen), yielded.

Gewicht, *n.*-er, weight, gravity, importance, stress; **schwer ins ∼ fallen,** to be of great importance; **spezifisches ∼,** specific gravity or weight (gravity, without units; weight, if with units; both the same in the metric system).

gewichtig, heavy, weighty, important.

Gewichts-abgang, *m.* loss in weight; **-abnahme,** *f.* decrease in weight; **-analyse,** *f.* gravimetric analysis; **-bestimmung,** *f.* determination of weight; **-einheit,** *f.* unit of weight; **-konstanz,** *n.* constancy of weight; **-menge,** *f.* (amount of) weight.

Gewichts-prozent, *n.* percentage by weight; **-satz,** *m.* set of weights; **-stück,** *n.* weight; **-teil,** *m.* part by weight; **-verhältnis,** *n.* proportion by weight; **-verlust,** *m.* loss in weight; **-zunahme,** *f.* increase in weight.

gewiesen (weisen), showed, pointed.

gewillt, willing, inclined, disposed.

Gewimmel, *n.* multitude, throng.

gewimpert, ciliate, fringed.

Gewinde, *n.* winding, coil, skein, (screw) thread, worm, spire; **-bahren,** *n.* tapping; **-glas,** *n.* glass tube with screw cap; **-schneiden,** *n.* threading; **-steigung,** *f.* screw pitch.

gewinkelt, angled, angular.

Gewinn, *m.* yield, proceeds, winning, gain, earnings, profit.

gewinnbar, obtainable.

gewinnen, to obtain, win, gain, earn, reclaim, get, extract, produce, prepare.

gewinnsüchtig, greedy.

Gewinnung, *f.* obtaining, production.

Gewinnungsweise, *f.* means of preparation or obtaining. extraction method.

Gewirr, *n.* confusion.

gewiss, (*gen.*) sure, fixed, certain, indeed.

Gewissen, *n.* conscience.

gewissenhaft. conscientious.

gewissermassen, to a certain degree, to some extent, as it were.

Gewissheit, *f.* certainty, assurance, proof.

Gewitter, *n.* (thunder) storm.

gewoben (weben), woven.

gewogen (wägen, wiegen), weighed.

gewogen, (*dat.*) kindly disposed.

gewöhnen, to accustom, habituate, familiarize, domesticate.

Gewohnheit, *f.* habit, custom, usage, fashion.

Gewohnheits-handlung, *f.* habitual act; **-rasse,** *f.* biologic species, established race.

gewöhnlich, usual, customary. common, general.

gewohnt, accustomed.

Gewöhnung, *f.* accustoming, habituation, acclimatization.

Gewölbe, *n.* vault, arch, cellar; **-bildung,** *f.* pellet formation.

gewonnen (gewinnen), won, earned, gained, obtained.

geworben (werben), aspired.

geworden (werden), become.

geworfen (werfen), thrown.

Gewühl, crowd, tumult.

gewunden (winden), wound, twisted, sinuous, contorted, spiral, tortuous.

gewürfelt, tessellate, chequered.

Gewürm, *n.* worms, creeping things, reptiles, vermin.

Gewürz, *n.* spice, seasoning, aromatics; **-artig,** spicy, aromatic; **-essig,** *m.* aromatic vinegar; **-haft,** spicy, aromatic; **-handel,** *m.* spice trade, grocery business; **-kräuter,** *n.pl.* spice plants; **-nelken,** *f.pl.* cloves; **-nelkenöl,** *n.* clove oil; **-pulver,** *n.* aromatic powder; **-strauch,** *m.* strawberry shrub, Carolina allspice (*Calycanthus floridus*); **-tinktur,** *f.* aromatic tincture.

gewürzt, spiced, seasoned.

Gewürzwaren, *f.pl.* spices, groceries.

gewusst (wissen), known.

gezackt, notched, jagged, pectinate, serrated.

Gezäh (e), *n.* tools.

gezahnt, denticulate, dentate, toothed, serrated.

gezehnt, denary, decimal.

Gezeit, *f.* tide.

Gezeiten-hub, *m.* difference in water level (low or high tide); **-strand,** *m.* tide beach.

Gezelt, *n.* sensorium, pavilion, tent.

Gezeug, *n.* (set of) tools.

geziehen (zeihen), accused, charged.

geziemen, (*dat.*) to become, befit, be proper or suitable.

Gezirpe, *n.* (much) chirping.

gezogen (ziehen), drawn, pulled, extracted, cultivated.

Gezweige, *n.* (aggregate of) branches.

gezweit, binary, in twos.

gezweiteilt, bipartite.

gezwieselt, forked.

gezwungen (zwingen), forced, compulsory.

gibt (geben), gives; **es ~,** there is, there are.

Gicht, *f.* gout, arthritis, mouth or throat of furnace or total charge; **-artig,** gouty, arthritic; **-brüchig,** paralytic, palsied; **-gas,** *n.* blast-furnace gas; **-mittel,** *n.* remedy for gout; **-rauch,** *m.* top smoke; **-rose,** *f.* rhododendron, peony (Paeonia); **-rübe,** *f.* bryony (Bryonia); **-staub,** *m.* blast-furnace dust.

Gichtung, *f.* charging (a furnace).

gichtwidrig, antiarthritic.

giebt (geben) gives; **es ~,** there is, there are.

Giemsa-Lösung, *f.* Giemsa stain.

Gier, *f.* greed(iness), avidity, eagerness.

gierig, greedy, covetous.

Giersch, *m.* goutweed, ashweed, goatsfoot (*Aegopodium podagraria*).

giessbar, capable of being poured.

giessbecken-förmig, arytenoid; **-knorpel,** *m.* arytenoid cartilage.

Giessbett, *n.* casting bed.

giessen, to pour, water, shed forth, found, mold, cast.

Giesser, *m.* founder, caster, molder, melter, smelter, pouring vessel.

Giesserei, *f.* foundry; **-fertigerzeugnis,** *m.* finished foundry product.

Giesserschwärze, *f.* molder's black.

giessfähig, capable of being poured.

Giess-kanne, *f.* sprinkling can; **-kasten,** *m.* casting mold; **-mutter,** *f.* matrix, mold; **-pfanne,** *f.* ladle.

Gift, *n.* poison, venom, toxin, virus, fury, malice; **-abtreibend,** antitoxic, antidotal; **-artig,** poisonous; **-arznei,** *f.* antidote; **-bereitend,** venenifluous; **-bildung,** *f.* formation of toxin; **-bindung,** *f.* binding of toxin; **-blase,** *f.* bladder containing the venom, venom sac; **-drüse,** *f.* poison gland; **-erz,** *n.* arsenic ore.

Gift-fang, *m.* venomous fang; **-fest,** immune to poison; **-frei,** free from poison; **-gas,** *n.* poison gas; **-gruppe,** *f.* toxin group; **-hahnenfuss,** *m.* cursed crowfoot, marsh crowfoot (*Ranunculus sceleratus*); **-haltig,** containing poison, poisonous, toxic; **-hütte,** *f.* arsenic works.

giftig, poisonous, venomous, virulent, toxic, malignant.

Giftigkeit, *f.* poisonousness, virulence.

Gift-immunität, *f.* immunity to toxin; **-jasmin,** *m.* Carolina jessamine (*Gelsemium sempervirens*); **-kiess,** *m.* arsenopyrite; **-köder,** *m.* poison bait; **-kraut,** *n.* wolfsbane (Aconitum); **-kunde,** *f.* toxicology; **-lattich,** *m.* strong-scented lettuce (*Lactuca virosa*); **-lehre,** *f.* toxicology; **-los,** nonpoisonous; **-mehl,** *n.* arsenic trioxide.

Gift-mittel, *n.* antidote; **-molekül,** *n.* toxin molecule; **-primel,** *f.* (*Primula abconia*); **-rauch,** *m.* sublimed arsenic trioxide; **-schlange,** *f.* poisonous snake; **-schutz,** *m.* protection against toxin; **-schwamm,** *m.* poisonous mushroom; **-sekret,** *n.* poison exudate or secretion; **-stachel,** *m.* poisonous sting; **-stein,** *m.* white arsenic.

Gift-stoff, *m.* poisonous matter, poison, virus; **-sumach,** *m.* poison ivy (*Rhus toxicodendron*); **-wende,** *f.* swallowwort (*Cynanchum vincetoxicum*); **-widrig,** antitoxic; **-wirkung,** *f.* poisonous action or effect; **-wurzel,** *f.* swallowwort (*Vincetoxicum officinale*); **-zahn,** *m.* poison fang.

Gilbe, *f.* yellow(ish) color, yellow (ocher), dyer's-weed (*Reseda luteola*).

gilben, to turn (color) yellow.

gilbig, ocherous.

Gilb-kraut, *n.* dyer's-weed (*Reseda luteola*); **-weiderich,** *m.* loosestrife (*Lysimachia vulgaris*); **-wurzel,** *f.* turmeric (*Curcuma longa*).

gilt (gelten), is worth, is true.

giltig, valid.

Gimpel, *m.* bullfinch.

ging (gehen), went.

Ginster, *m.* broom (Genista).

Gipfel, *m.* (tree)top, summit, climax, apex, pinnacle; **-ähre,** *f.* terminal spike(let); **-blüte,** *f.* terminal flower; **-dürre,** *f.* dying of treetops, stag-headedness; **-förmig,** fastigiate; **-holz,** *n.* top branches or twigs; **-knospe,** *f.* terminal bud, end bud.

gipfeln, to culminate, top.

Gipfel-rollen, *n.* leafroll of tip of shoot; **-ständig,** terminal, apical; **-trieb,** *m.* leader shoot.

Gips, *m.* gypsum, plaster of Paris, calcium sulphate; **-abdruck,** *m.* plaster cast; **-abguss,** *m.* plaster cast; **-arbeiter,** *m.* plasterer, stuccoworker; **-artig,** gypseous; **-brei,** *m.* paste of gypsum; **-brennen,** *n.* gypsum burning; **-brennerei,** *f.* calcination of gypsum; **-brennofen,** *m.* plaster kiln.

gipsen, to plaster, manure, fertilize (with gypsum); gypseous.

Gipser, *m.* plasterer.

Gips-erde, *f.* gypseous soil, earthy gypsum; **-geröll,** *n.* moving gypsum debris; **-gu(h)r,** *m.* earthy gypsum; **-guss,** *m.* plaster cast(ing); **-haltig,** calcareous, containing gypsum; **-kalk,** *m.* plaster lime.

Gips-lösung, *f.* calcium sulphate solution; **-mehl,** *n.* powdered (gypsum) plaster; **-mergel,** *m.* gypseous marl; **-mörtel,** *m.* plaster, stucco; **-spat,** *m.* sparry gypsum, selenite; **-stein,** *m.* gypseous stone.

Girland, *f.* garland.

gischen, to foam, froth, ferment, bubble, effervesce.

Gischt, *m.* foam, froth, yeast, fermentation, spray.

Gitter, *n.* grating lattice, screen, rack, fence, grid, bars; **-artig,** latticelike, grated; **-bremse,** *f.* washboard tension; **-brücke,** *f.* lattice bridge; **-faser,** *f.* lattice fiber, reticulated fibril; **-förmig,** retiform, trellised; **-tüpfel,** *m.pl.* (closely) crowded pits; **-werk,** *n.* lattice; **-zelle,** *f.* grated cell.

Glacé-leder, *n.* glacé leather; **-papier,** *n.* glazed paper.

glacieren, to freeze, gloss, glaze.

Gladiole, *f.* Gladiolus.

glandern, to calender.

Glanz, *m.* brightness, brilliancy, luster, glitter, polish, glance, glaze, splendor, gloss, shine; **-arsenikkies,** *m.* löllingite; **-blende,** *f.* alabandite; **-braunstein,** *m.* hausmannite; **-brenne,** *f.* burnishing bath.

Glänze, *f.* gloss, glaze, polishing material.

Glanz-effekt, *m.* gloss, luster; **-eisen,** *n.* silvery-gray iron; **-eisenerz,** *n.* **-eisenstein,** *m.* specular iron ore, hematite.

glänzen, to glaze, gleam, glisten, gloss, luster, shine.

glänzend, brilliant, shining, glossy.

glanz-erz, *n.* argentite.

glanzfein, brilliant.

Glanz-firnis, *m.* glazing varnish; **-gold,** *n.* brilliant gold, imitation gold foil; **-gras,** *n.* canary grass (*Phalaris arundinacea);* **-käfer,** *m.pl.* Nitidulidae; **-karton,** *m.* glazed pasteboard; **-kattun,** *m.* glazed calico; **-kobalt,** *m.* glance cobalt, cobaltite; **-kohle,** *f.* anthracite, glance coal, lustrous carbon; **-kopf,** *m.* hematite; **-lack,** *m.* brilliant varnish.

Glanz-leder, *n.* patent leather; **-leinwand,** *f.* glazed linen; **-leistung,** *f.* outstanding achievement; **-lohe,** *f.* silver bark; **-los,** lusterless, dull, dim, mat; **-manganerz,** *n.* manganite; **-messing,** *n.* polished brass; **-metall,** *n.* speculum metal; **-öl,** *n.* gloss oil; **-papier,** *n.* glazed paper.

Glanz-pappe, *f.* glazed (paper) board; **-rinde,** *f.* silver bark; **-rot,** *n.* colcothar; **-russ,** *m.* a lustrous form of soot, lampblack; **-schleifen,** to polish; **-schuss,** *m.* shiner.

Glanz-silber, *n.* silver glance, argentite; **-stärke,** *f.* gloss starch; **-stoff,** *m.* rayon, glazed fabric, artificial silk; **-voll,** brilliant, splendid; **-wichse,** *f.* polishing paste; **-zahl,** *f.* gloss value.

Glas, *n.* ~er, glass; **-achat,** *m.* obsidian; **-aderhaut,** *f.* vitreous membrane; **-ähnlich,** glasslike, glassy, vitreous; **-artig,** glasslike, glassy, vitreous; **-bildung,** *f.* formation of glass, vitrification.

Glas-birne, *f.* glass bulb, globe; **-blase,** *f.* bubble in glass; **-blasen,** *n.* glass blowing; **-bläser,** *m.* glassblower; **-brennen,** *n.* annealing of glass; **-brocken,** *m.pl.* glass waste, cullet.

Gläschen, *n.* small glass or vessel.

Glaser, *m.* glazier; **-kitt,** *m.* glazier's putty.

gläsern, glass, glassy, vitreous.

Glas-erz, *n.* argentite; **-fabrik,** *f.* glassworks, glass factory; **-faden,** *m.* glass thread (defect in glass); **-färben,** *n.* glass staining; **-farbig,** glassy, hyaline; **-feuchtigkeit,** *f.* vitreous humor; **-flasche,** *f.* glass bottle, flask; **-flügel,** *m.* transparent wing; **-flügler,** *m.* clearwings (Sesia); **-fluss,** *m.* glass flux, vitreous paste, enamel.

Glas-förmig, glasslike, vitriform; **-fritte,** *f.* glass frit; **-galle,** *f.* glass gall, sandiver; **-gefäss,** *n.* glass vessel; **-geräte,** *m.pl.* glass apparatus, **-gespinst,** *n.* spun glass, glass cloth; **-glanz,** *m.* vitreous luster, frost; **-glänzend,** glassy, lustrous; **-glocke,** *f.* glass bell, bell jar, glass cover; **-grün,** bottle-green.

Glas-hafen, *m.* glass pot; **-hahn,** *m.* glass stopcock; **-härte,** *f.* glass hardness:

härten, n. tempering of glass; **-haut,** f. vitreous layer, cellophane, hyaloid membrane; **-hautlamelle,** f. vitreous lamella; **-hell,** clear as glass, transparent; **-hütte,** f. glass factory.

glasieren, to glaze, gloss, varnish, enamel.

glasig, glassy, vitreous, hyaline.

Glasigkeit, f. kernel texture, glassiness.

Glas-isolator, m. glass insulator; **-kalk,** m. glass gall; **-kattun,** m. glass cloth; **-kitt,** m. glass cement, putty; **-kolben,** m. glass flask; **-kopf,** m. hematite, (brauner, gelber) limonite, (schwarzer) psilomelane.

Glaskörper, m. vitreous humor; **-raum,** m. cavity of the vitreous humor; **-schicht,** f. stratum of the vitreous humor.

Glas-kraut. n. wall pellitory (*Parietaria officinalis*,), glasswort (*Salicornia herbacea*); **-kugel,** f. glass bulb; **-kühlen,** n. annealing of glass; **-lava,** f. volcanic glass; **-löffel,** m. glass spoon; **-macherseife,** f. glassmaker's soap, manganese dioxide; **-malz,** n. brittle malt; **-masse,** f. glass metal, frit; **-opal,** m. hyalite.

Glas-pulver, n. glass powder; **-rohr,** n. glass tube; **-röhre,** f. glass tube; **-salz,** n. glass gall; **-satz,** m. glass composition; **-schale,** f. glass dish; **-schaum,** m. glass gall; **-scheibe,** f. pane of glass; **-scherben,** f.pl. broken glass; **-schlacke,** f. glass gall.

Glas-schliff, m. glass grinding; **-schmelz,** m. enamel, glasswort (*Salicornia herbacea*); **-schmutz,** m. glass gall; **-schneider,** m. glass cutter; **-schörl,** m. axinite; **-schwärmer,** m.pl. Sesiidae; **-schweiss,** m. glass gall; **-spritze,** f. glass syringe; **-stab,** m. glass rod; **-staub,** m. glass dust, powdered glass.

Glas-stein, m. axinite, paste (for imitation gems), glass brick; **-stopfen,** n. glass stopper; **-stöpselflasche,** f. glass-stoppered bottle; **-tiegel,** m. glass crucible; **-träne,** f. glass tear, Prince Rupert's drop; **-trichter,** m. glass funnel.

Glasur, f. glaze, varnish, icing, frosting, enamel, gloss; **-brand,** m. glaze baking.

glasuren, to glaze, enamel.

Glasur-erz, n. alquifou.

Glas-wanne, f. glass trough, crucible; **-waren,** f.pl. glassware; **-wolle.** f. glass wool.

glatt, smooth, even, flat, glossy, polished, flush, close to, hairless, glabrous, plain, straightforward, insinuating.

Glätt(an)frischen, n. reduction of litharge.

glattbrennen, to subject to glost burn.

Glätte, f. smoothness, polish, litharge.

Glatteis, n. glazed frost, rime, slippery ice.

glätten, to polish, finish, burnish, plane, glaze, smooth, calender.

Glatt-färberei, f. plain dyeing; **-feuer,** n. sharp fire; **-hafer,** m. Arrenatherum; **-ofen,** m. glost (fini..hing) kiln; **-randig,** entire or smooth-edged; **-rindig,** smoothrinded; **-scherbe,** f. potsherd; **-walze,** f. smooth roller; **-wasser,** n. last run of wort, lees.

Glättwalze, f. smooth roller.

Glatze, f. balk spot.

Glaube, m. belief, faith, trust, credit.

glauben, (dat.) to believe, think, have faith.

Glaubersalz, n. Glauber's salt, sodium sulphate.

gläubig, faithful, believing.

Gläubiger, m. creditor.

glaublich, credible, likely, probable.

glauch, glaucous, sea-green, poor, clear.

Glauch-erz, n. poor ore.

glaukonitisch, glauconitic.

Glazialschutt, m. glacial detritus.

glazieren, to glaze.

gleich, (dat.) equal, alike, same, similar, constant, level, straight, uniform, directly, at once; **es ist ∼ viel,** it is quite indifferent to me; **ganz ∼,** quite immaterial.

gleich-achsig, coaxial; **-altrig,** even-aged, of the same age; **-artig,** of the same kind, similar, analogous, homogeneous; **-bedeutend,** equivalent, synonymous, homologous, convertible; **-berechtigt,** of equal rights; **-blätterig,** isophyllous (leaves alike); **-bleiben,** to remain constant, unchanged; **-bleibend,** constant, invariable; **-deutig,** synonymous, equivalent.

gleichen, (dat.) to (make) equal, be like, adjust, make alike, equalize, smooth, level.

gleicherweise, in like manner.

gleich-falls, likewise, also, in the same way; **-farbig,** of the same color, concolor, isochromatic; **-feld,** n. constant magnetic field; **-flächig,** isohedral (like surface); **-flügler,** m.pl. Homoptera; **-förmig,** uniform, even, isomorphous, homogeneous, monotonous; **-gekörnt,** even-grained; **-gelappt,** equilobed; **-gerichtet,** rectified, similarly directed; **-gesinnt,** like-minded.

gleich-gespannt, of equal tension; **-gestaltet, -gestaltig,** isomorphic; **-gewicht,** n. equilibrium, balance.

Gleichgewichts-bedingung, *f.* equation (condition) of equilibrium; **-gesetz,** *n.* law of equilibrium; **-lehre,** *f.* statics; **-störung,** *f.* displacement (disturbance) of equilibrium; **-verhältnis,** *n.* equilibrium ratio; **-verrchiebung,** *f.* displacement of equilibrium; **-zustand,** *m.* state of equilibrium.

gleich-gross, equal (in size); **-gültig,** indifferent, unconcerned, apathetic; **-gültigkeit,** *f.* indifference.

Gleichheit, *f.* equality, parity, likeness, uniformity.

gleich-kiemig, homobranchial; **-klappig,** equivalvate; **-kommen,** to come up to, be equal to; **-laufend,** parallel, rotating clockwise; **-lautend,** corresponding; **-liegend,** in like position, similarly situated.

Gleich-mässig, proportionate, symmetrical, regular, even, homogeneous, uniform; **-gefiedert,** paripinnate.

gleich-mut, *m.* equanimity; **-namig,** of the same name, like, having the same denominator.

Gleichnis, *n.* simile, image, parable.

gleich-richten, to rectify; **-richter,** *m.* rectifier; **-richtung,** *f.* rectifying, rectification.

gleichsam, so to say, as it were, almost, to some extent.

gleich-schalig, equivalvate; **-schenkelig,** isosceles; **-schnell,** equally rapid; **-schwer,** of equal weight, equally difficult; **-seitig,** equilateral; **-sinnig,** accordant, congenial, compatible, synonymous; **-spannung,** *f.* direct- (continuous-) current voltage; **-stellen,** to put parallel, compare; **-stellig,** holding the same place.

Gleichstrom, *m.* direct current, parallel (current) flow; **-leitung,** *f.* direct-current line; **-widerstand,** *m.* resistance to direct current.

gleichteilig, homogeneous, of equal parts, isomerous.

Gleichung, *f.* equation.

gleich-verhaltend, of similar properties; **-viel,** just as much, equally, no matter; **-warm,** of uniform temperature; **-weit,** of uniform width, equidistant, parallel; **-wertig,** equivalent; **-wertigkeit,** *f.* equivalence, **-winklig,** equiangular; **-wohl,** yet, however; **-zeitig,** simultaneous, contemporary, synchronous; **-zu,** straightway.

Gleis, *n.* track, road, line.

Gleise, *f.* parallel (line).

Gleiss, *m.* **Gleisse,** *f.* fool's-parsley (*Aethusa cynapium*).

Gleit-bahn, *f.* slide, chute; **-bewegung,** *f.* sliding on transverse motion.

gleiten, to glide, slide, chute, slip.

Gleit-fläche, *f.* gliding plane, plane of failure, sliding surface; **-flügel,** *m.* gliding wing; **-lager,** *n.* slide bearing, plain bearing; **-muskel,** *m.* protractor, slider; **-mass,** *n.* **-modul,** *m.* transverse modulus of elasticity.

Gleit-schiene, *f.* slide bar, guide, skid-**-skala,** *f.* sliding scale; **-sicherheit,** *f.* resistance to sliding.

Gleitungszahl, *f.* shear modulus.

Gletscher, *m.* glacier; **-boden,** *m.* glacial soil; **-salz,** *n.* Epsom salt; **-schliff,** *m.* glacial erosion, rock polished by a moving glacier; **-schutt,** *m.* glacial drift, moraine.

glich (gleichen), equaled, resembled.

Glied, *n.* limb, internode, member, joint, part, term, link, degree, portion, rank, segment, metamere, phytomer.

Glieder-band, *n.* articular ligament; **-bau,** *m.* articulation, structure of limbs; **-borste,** *f.* articular bristle; **-brand,** *m.* gangrene of a limb; **-egge,** *f.* articulate harrow; **-flosse,** *f.* articulate fin.

Glieder-frucht, *f.* loment; **-fuge,** *f.* articulation; **-füssler,** *m.pl.* Arthropoda; **-gicht,** *f.* arthritic gout; **-haar,** *n.* articulate hair; **-hülse,** *f.* loment; **-knöchel,** *m.* phalanx.

gliedern, to arrange, organize, join, articulate, segment.

Glieder-schote, *f.* biloment; **-schwund,** *m.* atrophy of limbs; **-spore,** *f.* arthrospore; **-tiere,** *n.pl.* articulate animals (Arthropoda).

Gliederung, *f.* arrangement of parts, classification, organization, articulation, segmentation.

Glieder-würmer, *n.pl.* Annelida; **-zahl,** *f.* number of members; **-zelle,** *f.* articulate cell, zygospore; **-zucken,** *n.* convulsive movement of the limbs.

Gliedmassen, *n.pl.* limbs, articulated appendages; **-knospe,** *f.* limb bud; **-skelett,** *n.* appendicular skeleton, skeleton of the limbs.

Glied-nummer, *f.* number of a member; **-wasser,** *n.* synovial fluid; **-weise,** link by link.

glimmen, to burn faintly, glimmer, smolder

Glimmentladung, *f.* silent discharge.

Glimmer, *m.* glimmer, glow, mica; **-artig,** micaceous; **-blättchen,** *n.* sheet mica;

-gestein, *m.* micaceous rock; **-haltig,** micaceous.

glimmern, to glimmer, sparkle.

Glimmer-plättchen, *n.* mica plate, sheet mica; **-reich,** rich in mica; **-sand,** *m.* micaceous sand; **-schiefer,** *m.* mica schist; **-ton,** *m.* mica clay.

Glimmlicht, *n.* faint light; **-leuchtröhre,** *f.* neon lamp, cathode-ray tube.

Glimmstreckenspaunungsteiler, *m.* glow-tube voltage regulator, hot-wire voltmeter.

glimpflich, fair, moderate, gentle.

glitt (gleiten), slid, glided.

glitzern, to glitter, sparkle.

Globumin, *n.* globumin.

Glöckchen, *n.* bell jar, little bell.

Glocke, *f.* bell jar, bell, receiver, clock, bell-shaped calyx, arch formation in sand.

Glocken-blume, *f.* bellflower (Campanula); **-bronze,** *f.* bell metal; **-erz,** *n.* bell metal; **förmig,** bell-shaped; **-gastrula,** *f.* archigastrula; **-giesser,** *m.* bell founder.

Glocken-gut, *n.* **-metall,** *n.* bell metal; **-mündung,** *f.* opening of the bell; **-polyp,** bell polyp; **-tierchen,** *n.pl.* Campanularia (Vorticellae); **-speise,** *f.* bell metal; **-trichter,** *m.* bell funnel.

glockig, campanulate, bell-shaped.

glomm (glimmen), glimmered.

Glossinen, *pl.* Glossina (tsetse flies).

Glottis, *f.* glottis.

glotzen, to stare.

Glucinerde, *f.* glucina, beryllia.

Glück, *n.* fortune, good luck, happiness, success.

Glucke, *f.* setting hen.

glucken, to cluck, gurgle.

glücken, (*dat.*) to prosper, succeed.

glücklich, fortunate, lucky, successful, happy.

glücklicherweise, fortunately, happily.

Glücksspinne, *f.* money spider (*Epiblemum scenicum*).

Glüh-asche, *f.* embers, glowing ashes; **-behandlung,** *f.* annealing; **-beständig,** stable at red heat; **-birne,** *f.* incandescent bulb; **-draht,** *m.* incandescent filament; **-eisen,** *n.* glowing iron.

glühen, to glow, ignite, calcine, anneal, mull.

glühend, incandescent, glowing, ardent.

Glüh-faden, *m.* incandescent filament; **-farbe,** *f.* glowing-red color; **-frischen,** *n.* cementation process; **-hitze,** *f.* glowing (red) heat; **-kathode,** *f.* incandescent cathode; **-kolben,** *m.* retort; **-körper,** *m.* incandescent body or mantle; **-lampe,** *f.* incandescent lamp.

Glühlicht, *n.* incandescent light; **-brenner,** *m.* incandescent burner; **-körper,** *m.* incandescent mantle; **-strumpf,** *m.* incandescent mantle.

Glüh-ring, *m.* crucible triangle; **-rohr,** *n.* glow pipe, ignition tube; **-rückstand,** *m.* ignition residue, hot scale; **-sand,** *m.* refractory sand; **-schälchen,** *n.* igniting capsule; **-schale,** *f.* cupel; **-schiffchen,** *n.* combustion boat; **-span,** *m.* iron scale; **-stoff,** *m.* incandescent material; **-strumpf,** *m.* incandescent mantle.

Glühung, *f.* glowing, ignition, annealing, calcination.

Glüh-verlust, *m.* heat loss; **-wachs,** *n.* gilder's wax; **-wein,** *m.* mulled wine; **-wurm,** *m.* glowworm.

Glukonsäure, *f.* gluconic acid.

Glukose, *f.* glucose, grape sugar.

Glukosurie, *f.* glycosuria.

Glut, *f.* glow, incandescence, fire, ardor, passion.

Glutaminsäure, *f.* glutamic acid.

Glutarsäure, *f.* glutaric acid.

Glut-asche, *f.* embers, hot ashes; **-flüssig,** molten, fused; **-hitze,** *f.* glowing heat.

Glutin, *n.* gluten.

glutinös, glutinous.

glutrot, glowing red.

Gluzinsäure, *f.* glucic acid.

Glycerin-leim, *m.* glycerin jelly; **-phosphorsäure,** *f.* glycerophosphoric acid; **-säure,** *f.* glyceric acid.

Glycin, *n.* glycine; **-erde,** *f.* glucina, beryllia.

Glycium, *n.* glucinum, beryllium.

Glycosid, *n.* glucoside.

Glykocholsäure, *f.* glycocholic acid.

Glykogen, *n.* glycogen.

Glykol-säure, *f.* glycolic acid; **-ursäure,** *f.* glycoluric acid.

Glykolyse, *f.* glycolysis.

glykolytisch, glycolytic.

Glykose, *f.* glucose.

Glykosid, *n.* glucoside.

Glykoson, *n.* glucosone.

Glyoxalsäure, *f.* glyoxalic acid.

Glyzerin, *n.* glycerin, glycerol; **-agar,** *n.* glycerin agar; **-bouillon,** *f.* glycerin broth; **-galle,** *f.* glycerinated bile; **-leim,** *m.* glycerin jelly.

Glyzerol, *n.* glycerol.

Glyzid, *n.* glycide; **-säure,** *f.* glycidic acid.

Gnade, *f.* grace, mercy, favor, pardon.

Gnaden-geld, *n.* pension, allowance; **-kraut,** *n.* hedge hyssop (Gratiola); **-stoss,** *m.* finishing blow.

gnädig, gracious, merciful, kind, favorable.

Gneis, *m.* gneiss, crystalline rock.

Goapulver, *n.* Goa powder.

Gold, *n.* gold; **-after,** *m.* brown-tail moth; **-ammer,** *m.* yellowhammer (*Emberiza citrinella*); **-amsel,** *f.* golden oriole; **-anstrich,** *m.* gilding; **-artig,** goldlike, golden; **-ather,** *m.* gold chloride in ether; **-auflösung,** *f.* gold solution; **-belag,** *m.* gold coating; **-beleg,** *m.* gold coating.

Gold-beryll, *m.* chrysoberyl; **-blatt,** *n.* gold (leaf) foil; **-blick,** *m.* glance of gold; **-butt,** *m.* plaice; **-chlorid,** *n.* gold chloride; **-chlorür,** *n.* aurous chloride; **-chlorwasserstoff,** *m.* chlorauric acid; **-cyanür,** *n.* aurous cyanide; **-draht,** *m.* gold wire; **-erde,** *f.* auriferous earth.

Gold-erz, *n.* gold ore; **-farbe,** *f.* gold color; **-fasan,** *m.* golden pheasant; **-fink,** *m.* goldfinch; **-führend,** gold-bearing; **-gehalt,** *m.* gold content; **-gelb,** golden-yellow; **-gewicht,** *n.* gold (troy) weight; **-glanz,** *m.* golden luster; **-glänzend,** shining like gold.

Gold-glätte, *f.* gold litharge; **-glimmer,** *m.* yellow mica; **-grund,** *m.* gold size; **-hafer,** *m.* yellow oats; **-haltig,** auriferous; **-jodid,** *n.* gold (auric) iodide; **-jodür,** *n.* aurous iodide; **-käfer,** *m.* gold beetle; **-kaliumbromür,** *n.* potassium aurobromide; **-kalk,** *m.* gold oxide.

Gold-kies, *m.* auriferous pyrites, gravel; **-klee,** *m.* black medic, yellow trefoil; **-klumpen,** *m.* gold nugget; **-könig,** *m.* regulus of gold; **-kupfer,** *n.* Mannheim gold (brass); **-lack,** *m.* gold varnish, wallflower (*Cheiranthus cheiri*); **-legierung,** *g.* gold alloy; **-leim,** *m.* gold size; **-lösung,** *f.* gold solution; **-macherkunst,** *f.* alchemy; **-milz,** *f.* golden saxifrage (*Chrysosplenium alternifolium*).

Goldoxydul, *n.* aurous oxide; **-verbindung,** *f.* aurous compound.

Gold-oxydverbindung, *f.* auric compound; **-papier,** *n.* gilt (gold) paper; **-plattiert,** gold-plated; **-probe,** *f.* gold assay; **-regen,**

m. goldenrod (*Cytisus laburnum*); **-reich,** rich in gold; **-rute,** *f.* goldenrod (Solidago); **-salz,** *n.* gold salt; **-säure,** *f.* auric acid; **-schale,** *f.* gold dish, gold cup, cupel.

Gold-schaum, *m.* gold leaf, tinsel, imitation gold leaf, Dutch foil; **-scheiden,** *n.* gold refining; **-scheidewasser,** *n.* aqua regia; **-schlag,** *m.* gold (leaf) foil; **-schlägerhaut,** *f.* goldbeater's skin; **-schlich,** *m.* gold slimes; **-schmied,** *m.* goldsmith; **-schnitt,** *m.* gilt edge; **-siegellack,** *m.* gold sealing wax; **-stein,** *m.* auriferous stone, touchstone.

Gold-streichen, *n.* gold test; **-stück,** *n.* gold (piece) coin; **-sulfür,** *n.* aurous sulphide; **-tropfen,** *m.pl.* ethereal tincture of ferric chloride; **-verbindung,** *f.* gold compound; **-zyanür,** *n.* aurous cyanide.

Golf, *m.* gulf.

gölte, (gelten), would equal, would hold (true).

Gonidien, *pl.* conidia.

gönnen, to favor, wish, grant.

Gönner, *m.* well-wisher, patron.

Gonokokkus, *m.* (Gonokokken *pl.*), gono coccus.

Gonorrhöe, *f.* gonorrhea.

Goochtiegel, *m.* Gooch crucible.

gor (gären), fermented.

goss (giessen), poured.

Gosse, *f.* gutter, drain.

Gott, *m.* God.

Götter-baum, *m.* tree of heaven (*Ailanthus glandulosa*); **-speise,** *f.* ambrosia; **-trank,** *m.* nectar.

Gottes-gnadenkraut, *n.* hedge hyssop; **-käfer,** *m.* ladybird.

Göttin, *f.* goddess.

Goudron, *n.* asphalt, tar.

Grab, *n.* grave, tomb.

Grabbein, *n.* fossorial leg.

graben, to dig, spade, engrave, cut, stub, grub out.

Graben, *m.* ditch, dike, drain, trench; ~ **ziehen,** to dig ditches.

Graben-pflug, *m.* ditch plow; **-saat,** *f.* sowing in trenches.

Gräber, *m.* digger.

Grab-heuschrecken, *f.pl.* Grillidae; **-legung,** *f.* interment, burying; **-scheit,** *n.* spade, shovel; **-schrift,** *f.* epitaph; **-stichel,** *m.* graving tool, chisel; **-wespe,** *f.* fossorial or sand wasp (Sphex).

Grad, *m.* degree, grade, rank, stage; **-abteilung,** *f.* graduation, scale; **-bogen,** *m.* graduated arc; **-einteilung,** *f.* graduation, scale; **-faserig,** straight-grained; **-flügler,** *m.pl.* Orthoptera.

Gradiente, *f.* gradient.

gradieren, to graduate.

Gradierhaus, *n.* graduation house.

Gradierung, *f.* graduation.

Gradier-wage, *f.* brine gauge; **-werk,** *n.* graduation works, cooling arrangement.

Grädigkeit, *f.* (degree of) concentration, number of degrees.

gradlinig, in a straight line.

Grad-messer, *m.* graduator; **-teilung,** *f.* graduation, scale.

graduieren, to graduate.

Gradverwandtschaft, *f.* graduated affinity, degree of affinity.

Graf, *m.* count, earl.

grafisch, graphic.

Grafit, *n.* graphite.

Gram, *m.* grief, sorrow, affliction.

Gram-Färbung, *f.* Gram staining.

Gramm, *n.* gram; **-äquivalent,** *n.* gram equivalent; **-atom,** *m.* gram atom.

Gramsche Entfärbung, *f.* decolorization in Gram's method.

Gramsche Färbung, *f.* Gram staining.

Gran, *n.* (m.) grain.

Granadilholz, *n.* granadilla wood.

Granalien, *f.pl.* granulated metal.

Granat, *m.* garnet; **-apfel,** *m.* pomegranate; **-apfelgewächse,** *n.pl.* Punicaceae; **-artig,** garnetlike, granetlike; **-baum,** *m.* pomegranate tree (*Punica granatum*); **-dodekaeder,** *n.* rhombic dodecahedron.

Granate, *f.* shell, grenade, pomegranate.

Granatill-holz, *n.* granadilla wood; **-öl,** *n.* physic-nut oil; **-samen,** *n.* physic nut.

Granatoeder, *n.* rhombic dodecahedron.

Granat-rinde, *f.* pomegranate bark; **-rot,** garnet(red); **-trichter,** *m.* shell hole; **-wurzelrinde,** *f.* pomegranate root bark.

Grand, *m.* coarse sand, fine gravel.

granieren, to granulate, grain.

Granit, *m.* granite; **-ähnlich,** granitelike, granitic, granitoid; **-artig,** granitelike, granitic, granitoid; **-blockmoos,** *n.* moss of granite erratics.

graniten, of granite.

Granit-fels(en), *m.* granitic rock; **-förmig,** granitiform; **-geröllhalde,** *f.* granite boulder slope.

Granne, *f.* awn, beard, bristle, arista.

grannen-förmig, aristate; **-haar,** *n.* straight hair; **-los,** muticous, awnless.

Granulations-bildung, *f.* development of granulation; **-gewebe,** *n.* granulation tissue.

granulieren, to granulate, grain.

granulös, granular.

Grapen, *m.* iron mixing pot.

graphisch, graphic.

Graphit, *m.* graphite; **-ähnlich,** graphitelike, graphitoidal; **-artig,** graphitelike, graphitoidal.

graphitieren, to coat with graphite.

graphitisch, graphitic.

Graphit-schmelztiegel, *m.* graphite crucible; **-schmiere,** *f.* graphite lubricant; **-spitze,** *f.* carbon (of an arc lamp); **-stift,** *m.* lead pencil; **-tiegel,** *m.* graphite crucible.

Gras, *n.* grass; **-arten,** *n.pl.* gramineous plants; **-artig,** gramineous, herbaceous; **-baum,** *m.* Xanthorrhoea; **-bazillen,** *m.pl.* grass bacilli; **-blattpolster,** *n.* nodal swelling of grass stem; **-blättrig,** graminifolious; **-ebene,** *f.* grassy plain, prairie, savanna.

grasen, to graze, mow grass.

Gräser, *n.pl.* grasses (Gramineae, Poaceae), grass cutter.

Grasflur, *f.* grassland; **-formation,** *f.* grassland formation; **-gebiet,** *n.* grassland district; **-klima,** *n.* grassland climate.

gras-fressend, graminivorous, herbivorous; **-fresser,** *m.* graminivore, heribivore; **-frucht,** *f.* grain, caryopsis; **-grün,** grass green; **-halm,** *m.* grass blade; **-heide,** *f.* prairie, grass heath; **-hüpfer,** *m.* grasshopper.

grasig, grassy, grass-grown.

Gras-leinen, *n.* grass cloth; **-lilie,** *f.* lily spiderwort (*Anthericum liliago*); **-mähmaschine,** *f.* grass cutter; **-moor,** *n.* grass moor; **-mücke,** *f.* warbler; **-narbe,** *f.* grassy covering, turf; **-öl,** *n.* grass oil, citronella oil; **-pilz,** *m.* grass bacillus, toadstool.

grassieren, to rage, spread, prevail (disease).

Gras-steppe, *f.* prairie, savanna land; **-tetanie,** *f.* grass disease, staggers; **-wuchs,** *m.* growth of grass; **-wurzel,** *f.* grass root, quack grass (*Rhizoma graminis*); **-wüste,** *f.* grassy waste.

Grat, *m.* edge, ridge, burr, spine.

Gräte, *f.* fishbone, edge, ridge, spine, spinous process.

Grätenschlüsselbeinband, *n.* acromioclavicular ligament.

grau, gray.

Grau-braunstein, *m.* manganite; **-braunsteinerz,** *n.* pyrolusite; **-eisenerz,** *n.* mascasite.

grauen, (*dat.*) to turn gray, dawn, dread; **-haft, -voll,** dreaded, horrid.

Grau-erz, *n.* galena; **-farbig,** gray-colored; **-gelb,** grayish yellow; **-golderz,** *n.* nagyagite; **-gültigerz,** *n.* tetrahedrite; **-guss,** *m.* gray-iron casting; **-kalk,** *m.* lime containing magnesia salts, crude calcium acetate; **-kupfererz,** *n.* chalcocite, tennantite, tetrahedrite; **-leiter,** *f.* gray scale.

gräulich, grayish.

Graumanganerz, *n.* gray manganese ore, manganite.

Graumontsamen, *m.* pumpkin seed.

Graupe, *f.* peeled (barley) grain, knot, grain.

graupeln, to sleet, drizzle.

Graupen, *f.pl.* pearl barley, groats.

Graupen-erz, *n.* granular ore; **-kobalt,** *m.* smaltite; **-schleim,** *m.* barley water; **-schörl,** *m.* aphrizite.

graupig, granular.

Graus, *m.* rubble, small fragments, horror, dread.

grausam, cruel, horrible, inhuman.

Grau-schimmel, *m.* gray mold; **-spiegel,** *m.* gray spiegel iron; **-spiessglanz,** *m.* **-spiessglanzerz,** *n.* **-spiessglaserz,** *n.* gray antimony ore, antimonite, stibnite; **-wacke,** *f.* graywacke; **-weiss,** gray-white, argillaceous.

gravieren, to engrave, aggravate.

gravimetrisch, gravimetric.

Grazie, *f.* grace.

Greif-apparat, *m.* organ for grasping; **-bagger,** *m.* single-bucket excavator.

greifbar, seizable, graspable, tangible.

Greifben, *n.* cheliped.

greifen, to grasp, seize, touch, grip, snatch, catch, take root; **etwas aus der Luft** ∼, to fabricate, imagine; **ineinander** ∼, to interlace.

Greifer, *m.* grab, catcher, gripper, (pulldown) claw; **-stift,** *m.* positioning pin.

Greif-füsse, *m.pl.* legs for grasping, gnathopods; **-hand,** *f.* chela; **-waffe,** *f.* prehensile weapon; **-zange,** *f.* prehensile pincers; **-zirkel,** *m.* calipers.

greis, gray with age, old, aged, senile.

Greisenalter, *n.* old age.

grell, bright, dazzling, shrill, harsh, glaring, piercing.

Grenadillholz, *n.* granadilla wood.

Grenz-alkohol, *m.* limit (saturated) alcohol; **-abmarkung,** *f.* boundary settlement; **-belastung,** *f.* critical load; **-bestimmung,** *f.* boundary settlement; **-blatt,** *n.* limiting leaf or membrane, lamina, **-dichte,** *f.* density limit.

Grenze, *f.* limit, boundary, end, frontier, limitation, edge, border.

grenzen, to border on, touch on, adjoin, be next to.

grenzenlos, unlimited, infinite, enormous, immeasurable.

Grenz-fall, *m.* limiting case, extreme case; **-filament,** *n.* marginal filament; **-fläche,** *f.* interface, marginal surface, limiting surface; **-flächenerscheinung,** *f.* interfacial tension; **-furche,** *f.* boundary groove; **-gesetz,** *n.* limit law; **-gewebe,** *n.* limiting tissue, integument; **-häutchen,** *n.* tertiary lamella, inner layer of cell wall; **-kohlenwasserstoff,** *m.* saturated hydrocarbon; **-konzentration,** *f.* threshold concentration.

Grenz-kurve, *f.* limiting curve; **-lamelle,** *f.* marginal layer; **-linie,** *f.* boundary line; **-marke,** *f.* boundary mark; **-mauer,** *f.* boundary wall; **-membran,** *f.* limiting membrane; **-nutzen,** *m.* limit of use, utilization threshold; **-plasmolyse,** *f.* threshold of plasmolysis; **-potentialdifferenz,** *f.* difference in potential of terminals; **-regulierung,** *f.* demarcation.

Grenz-rinne, *f.* limiting furrow; **-scheide,** *f.* boundary; **-schicht,** *f.* limiting layer, marginal (inner) layer; **-spannung,** *f.* limiting (edge) stress; **-stein,** *m.* landmark, boundary stone; **-strang,** *m.* sympathetic nerve, gangliated cord; **-unterhaltung,** *f.* upkeep of boundaries; **-verbindung,** *f.* terminal (compound) member, saturated compound; **-wert,** *m.* limiting value, limit, threshold value; **-winkel,** *m.* critical angle.

Grenz-zahl, *f.* limit value, limit figure; **-zelle,** *f.* heterocyst, limiting or boundary cell; **-zustand,** *m.* limiting state.

greulich, horrible, abominable, detestable, atrocious.

Greze, *f.* raw silk.

Grieben, *f.pl.* greaves, cracklings.

griechisch, Greek; **griechisches Heu,** *n.* fenugreek.

Gries, *m.* gravel, grit, groats, grain sizes.

griesicht, gries(el)ig, gravelly, gritty, sabulous.

Griess, *m.* grit. gravel, coarse sand, grits, semolina, dusty coal, groats; **-holz,** *n.* nephritic wood; **-kohle,** *f.* dust coal, smalls; **-mittel,** *n.* remedy for gravel; **-stein,** *m.* urinary calculus, gravel, jade; **-wurzel,** *f.* pareira brava.

griff (greifen), seized.

Griff, *m.* handle, grip, manubrium, grasp, knob, claw, hook, touch. feel, adhesive disk.

Griffel, *m.* stylus, slate pencil, style, pistil; **-bein,** *n.* splint bone, styloid bone; **-bürste,** *f.* stylar brush; **-canal,** *m.* conducting tissue of style; **-förmig,** styloid; **-fortsatz,** *m.* styloid process; **-fuss,** *m.* pseudopodium.

Griffel-loch, *n.* stylomastoid foramen; **-los,** without pistils, acephalous; **-polster,** *n.* stylopod; **-säule,** *f.* column, style; **-schlundmuskel,** *m.* stylopharyngeus muscle; **-warzenloch,** *n.* stylomastoid foramen; **-zelle,** *f.* manubrium.

Griffstopfen, *m.* stopper with thumbpiece.

Griffzelle, *f.* manubrium, external tubular cell (of Chara).

Grille, *f.* cricket, whim, crotchet, fad, freak, anxious thoughts.

Grimmdarm, *m.* colon; **-anhang,** *m.* appendix; **-entzündung,** *f.* colitis; **-gekröse,** *n.* mesocolon; **-klappe,** *f.* ileocolic valve; **-zerreissung,** *f.* rupture of colon.

grimmen, to gripe, be in fury, rage.

Grimmen, *n.* colic.

Grind, *m.* scab, scurf, crust, mange.

Grinde, *f.* bog.

Grind-krankheit, *f.* rhizoctonia disease, black scurf; **-wurzel,** *f.* bitter dock root.

grinsen, to grin, stare, sneer, begin to melt.

Grippe, *f.* influenza.

grob, rude, coarse, thick, stout, heavy, approximate, rough; **grober Titer,** *m.* coarse denier.

Grob-blech, *n.* plate; **-fadig,** coarse-threaded; **-faserig,** coarse-fibered, coarse-grained; **-gepulvert,** coarsely powdered; **-geröll,** *n.* coarse moving rock debris; **-gewicht,** *n.* gross weight; **-gezackt,** coarsely serrated; **-jährig,** broadringed; **-keramik,** *f.* ordinary ceramic ware; **-kies,** *m.* coarse gravel.

Grob-korn, *n.* coarse grain; **-körnig,** large grained, coarsely granular; **-kristallinisch,** coarsely crystalline.

gröblich, rather gross or coarse.

Grob-mörtel, *m.* coarse mortar, concrete; **-rinde,** *f.* rhytidome, coarse bark; **-ringig,** broad ringed; **-runzelig,** coarsely wrinkled or puckered; **-sand,** *m.* coarse sand; **-schrot,** *n.&m.* coarse groats; **-schutt,** *m.* coarse rock debris; **-sieb,** *n.* coarse sieve; **-strahlig,** coarsely fibrous; **-zerkleinerung,** *f.* coarse crushing.

Gros, *n.* gross.

gross, great, big, tall, large, capital; **im grossen,** on a large scale, wholesale; **im grossen und ganzen,** on the whole, generally.

gross-artig, grand, imposing, sublime; **-betrieb,** *m.* wholesale trade, operation on a large scale; **-blättrig,** large-leaved, coarsely foliated, grandifoliate, megaphyllous; **-blattrosetten,** *f.pl.* large-leaved rosette plants.

Grösse, *f.* magnitude, quantity, size, amount.

Grössen-erblichkeit, *f.* size inheritance; **-faktor,** *m.* varialbe, size factor; **-lehre,** *f.* mathematics, geometry; **-ordnung,** *f.* order of magnitude, arrangement as to size, dimension, volume, quantity, value, magnitude.

grossenteils, to a great extent, in large part, mostly.

Grössenverteilungskurve, *f.* frequency curve.

Gross-fabrikation, *f.* large-scale manufacture; **-faserig,** large- (coarse-) fibered; **-füssig,** macropodous; **-gefieder,** *m.* the rectrices and remiges (of a bird's plumage); **-gewerbe,** *n.* manufacture on a large scale; **-gliederig,** coarse-limbed; **-grubig,** lacunate; **-handel,** *m.* wholesale business; **-herzig,** magnanimous, noble-minded.

Grosshirn, *m.* cerebrum; **-brückenbahn** (vordere) *f.* frontal tract of crusta; **-furche,** *f.* sulcus of cerebrum; **-hemispäre,** *f.* cerebral hemisphere; **-kammer,** *f.* cerebral ventricle; **-lappen,** *m.* cerebral lobe; **-mantel,** *m.* cortex of cerebrum; **-rinde,** *f.* cerebral cortex; **-schenkel,** *m.* cerebral peduncle; **-windung,** *f.* cerebral convolution.

gross-jährig, of (full) age; **-klima,** *n.* regional climate; **-köpfig,** large-headed, macrocephalous; **-kraftwerk,** *n.* super-power station; **-kronig,** large-crowned; **-lückig,** coarsely porous, coarse-grained;

-mütig, magnanimous, generous; **-schmet-terlinge,** *m.pl.* Macrolepidoptera; **-spore,** *f.* macrospore; **-technik,** *f.* large-scale engineering; **-technisch,** large-scale (of commercial production).

grösstenteils, for the most part, mainly, chiefly.

grösstmöglich, greatest possible, as large as possible.

Grösstwert, *m.* maximal value.

Gross-verkauf, *m.* wholesale; **-wild,** *n.* deer, big game.

Grosszahl-forschung, *f.* **-untersuchung,** *f.* statistics, statistical analysis.

Gross-zehe, *f.* large toe; **-ziehen,** to rear; **-zügig,** on a large scale, generous.

Grotte, *f.* grotto.

grub (graben), dug.

Grübchen, *n.* little hole, small pit, dimple, fossula, lacuna; **-bildung,** *f.* pitting.

Grube, *f.* mine, quarry, pit, hole, cavity, fossa, ditch, depression, fovea, excavation.

grübeln, to brood, ponder, meditate.

Gruben-ausbau, *m.* pit arch; **-bau,** *m.* underground working; **-betrieb,** *m.* mining; **-dampf,** *m.* choke damp; **-gas,** *n.* marsh gas, methane, firedamp; **-holz,** *n.* mine timber; **-klein,** *n.* smalls, slack; **-sand,** *m.* pit sand, dug sand; **-verkohlung,** *f.* pit charcoal burning; **-wetter,** *n.* mine damp.

Grude, *f.* carbonization coke; **-koks,** *m.* lignite coke.

Grummet, *n.* aftermath, second hay crop.

grün, green, live, verdant, shooting; **-ähre,** *f.* Chloranthus; **-algen,** *f.pl.* Chlorophyceae; **-ästung,** *f.* pruning of green (live) branches; **-blau,** greenish-blue; **-bleierz,** *n.* green lead ore; **-blumig,** viridiflorous, with green flowers; **-blütigkeit,** *f.* chloranthy.

Grund, *m.* ̈e, ground, motive, reason, estate, sediment, soil, bottom, foundation, base, fundus; **auf** ∼, on the basis of, on the strength of; **auf den** ∼ **gehen,** to find out, solve; **von** ∼ **aus,** from the very bottom, basically; ∼ **and Boden,** landed property; **aus welchem Grunde,** for what reason, from what cause; **im Grunde,** at bottom, after all, fundamentally; **im Grunde genommen,** actually; **zu Grunde (zugrunde) legen,** take as a basis or point of departure; **zu Grunde (zugrunde) liegen,** be at the bottom of, be the basis of.

Grund-achse, *f.* rhizome; **-ader,** *f.* basal vein; **-anschauung,** *f.* fundamental idea, basic conception; **-anstrich,** *m.* ground coat, priming coat; **-bahn,** *f.* ground orbit; **-bau,** *m.* foundation; **-bedingung,** *f.* fundamental condition; **-begriff,** *m.* fundamental conception, basic idea; **-bein,** *n.* basal bone, sphenoid; **-besitz,** *m.* real estate, landed property; **-bestandteil,** *m.* elementary constituent, element; **-blatt,** *n.* basal leaf.

Grund-bruchgefahr, *f.* danger of foundation failure or soil movement; **-düngung,** *f.* fertilization of the soil; **-eigenschaft,** *f.* fundamental character; **-einheit,** *f.* fundamental unit.

gründen, to found, establish, ground, promote, groove; **sich** ∼ **auf,** to be based on.

Gründer, *m.* founder, promoter.

Grund-falsch, absolutely false; **-farbe,** *f.* ground color, priming color; **-faser,** *f.* elementary fiber; **-feuchtigkeit,** *f.* soil moisture; **-firnis,** *m.* priming varnish; **-fläche,** *f.* basal surface, area; **-flüssigkeit,** *f.* suspending liquid; **-form,** *f.* primary form or type; **-formel,** *f.* fundamental formula; **-gebirge,** *n.* primitive rocks.

Grund-geilheit, *f.* luxuriance of the soil; **-gerechtigkeit,** *f.* territorial jurisdiction, right of landowner, servitude, easement; **-gesetz,** *n.* fundamental law; **-gestein,** *n.* underlying rock; **-gewebe,** *n.* fundamental tissue; **-gleichung,** *f.* basic equation; **-glied,** *n.* basal member, subcoxa, trochantin, basipodite, proximal phalanx; **-heil,** *n.* mountain parsley (*Pneucedanum oreoselinum*).

Grundierbad, *n.* bottoming bath.

grundieren, to ground, prime, size, stain, bottom, prepare.

Grundier-farbe, *f.* priming color; **-firnis,** *m.* **-lack,** *m.* filler; **-salz,** *n.* preparing salt, sodium stannate; **-schicht,** *f.* priming coat.

Grundierung, *f.* grounding, priming.

Grund-immunität, *f.* primary immunity; **-kapital,** *n.* original stock; **-knorpel,** *m.* primitive (cricoid) cartilage; **-konstante,** *f.* fundamental constant; **-körper,** *m.* fundamental substance; **-kraft,** *f.* primary (primitive) force; **-kreis,** *m.* circumference of the base.

gründl., *abbr.* (gründlich), thoroughly.

Grund-lage, *f.* groundwork, foundation, base, rudiments, matrix, basement; **-lamelle,** *f.* fundamental lamella; **-lawine,** *f.* rock or earth slide; **-legend,** fundamental; -lehre, *f.* foundamental doctrine, first principles.

gründlich, solid, profound, thorough.

Grund-linie, *f.* ground line, base line, basis, outline; -los, groundless, baseless, without foundation; -mass, *n.* (basic) standard; -masse, *f.* ground mass, stroma; -meristem, *n.* fundamental meristem; -moräne, *f.* ground moraine; -mörtel, *m.* concrete; -pegel, *m.* settlement gauge; -pfeiler, *m.* main support, principal axis; -platte, *f.* base plate, lobe plate.

Grund-problem, *n.* fundamental problem; -quadrat, *n.* endothecium; -regel, *f.* principle, axiom; -riss, *m.* outline, ground plan, cross section, sketch; -satz, *m.* principle, axiom; -sätzlich, systematic, based on principles; -schicht, *f.* fundamental (primary) layer; -schlamm, *m.* bottom mud; -schwelle, *f.* stream-bed barrier, railway tie, groundsel; -sorte, *f.* native variety.

Grund-spirale, *f.* genetic spiral; -ständig, basal, sessile; -stein, *m.* foundation stone, cornerstone, pyrite; -steuer, *f.* tax, ground rent; -stock, *m.* matrix; -stoff, *m.* element, raw material, base.

Grund-stoffwechsel, *m.* basal metabolism; -strich, *m.* down stroke, first coat; -stück, *n.* estate, landed (real) property; -substanz, *f.* element, ground substance, matrix; -teilchen, *n.* fundamental particle, atom; -ton, *m.* fundamental tone; -umsatz, *m.* basal metabolism.

Gründung, *f.* foundation, establishment, priming, first coat (paint).

Gründünger, *m.* green manure.

Grund-ursache, *f.* primary cause; -verschieden, fundamentally different; -versuch, *m.* fundamental experiment.

Grundwasser, *n.* (under)ground water, tellurian water; -geschwindigkeit, *f.* velocity of underground water movement; -speisung, *f.* source of underground water supply; -spiegel, *m.* ground-water level, water table.

grund-wesentlich, essential; -zahl, *f.* unit, base number, cardinal number; -zelle, *f.* basal cell; -zug, *m.* characteristic feature; -zungemuskel, *m.* hyoglossus muscle.

Grüne, *f.* greenness, green, green lawn.

Grüneisen-erde, *f.* -erz, *m.* -stein, *m.* green iron ore, dufrenite.

grünen, to become (grow) green, green.

Grün-erde, *f.* green earth; -fäule, *f.* green rot; -gelb, greenish-yellow; -holz, *n.* green

heartwood; -kalk, *m.* gas lime; -kohl, *m.* kale, colewort; -landsmoor, *n.* fen, wet meadow.

grünlich, greenish; -blau, greenish blue.

Grün-malz, *n.* green malt; -mist, *m.* green manure; -moor, *n.* low moor; -öl, *n.* anthracene oil; -rost, *m.* verdigris; -rostig, eruginous; -sand, *m.* -sandstein, *m.* greensand; -schwarz, greenish black.

Grünspan, *m.* verdigris; -blumen, *f.pl.* acetous salt, crystals of verdigris; -essig, *m.* -geist, *m.* -spiritus, *m.* spirit of verdigris.

Grün-spat, *m.* a variety of diopside; -star, *m.* glaucoma; -stein, *m.* greenstone, traprock, diabase; -sucht, *f.* chlorosis.

grunzen, to grunt.

Gruppe, *f.* group, cluster, clump, set.

Gruppen-mischung, *f.* mixture by groups; -weise, in groups; -wirtschaft, *f.* group system.

gruppieren, to group, classify.

Grus, *m. & n.* smalls, grit, small coal, slack, fine gravel, debris; -boden, *m.* soil formed from rock debris; -kakao, *m.* cacao husks; -kohle, *f.* small coal, slack.

Gruss, *m.* -̈e, greeting, salutation.

grüssen, to greet, salute.

Grütz-beutel, *m.* atheroma; -brei, *m.* porridge, mush, cereal pap.

Grütze, *f.* grits, groats, porridge.

Grützschleim, *m.* gruel.

Guajak, *m.* guaiacum (*Guaiacum officinale*); -harz, *n.* guaiacum resin; -probe, *f.* guaiacum reaction.

Guajol, *n.* guaiol.

Guäthol, *n.* guethol.

gucken, to look, peep, gaze.

Gucklock, *n.* peephole.

Gulden, *m.* gulden, guilder, florin.

Gülle, *f.* liquid manure.

gültig, valid, good, binding, current, authentic, applicable.

Gültigkeit, *f.* validity, legality, applicability, availability.

Gültigkeitsbereich, *m.* validity range.

Gummi, *n.* gum, India rubber; -abfälle, *m.pl.* scrap rubber; -arabicum, gum arabic; -art, *f.* variety of gum; -artig, gumlike, gummous, elastic; -band, *n.* rubber band, elastic; -baum, *m.* gum tree; -binde, *f.* rubber bandage; -blase, *f.* rubber bulb; -elastikum, *n.* rubber.

gummieren, to gum, size.

Gummi-ersatz, *m.* rubber substitute; **-erz,** *n.* gummite; **-fichte,** *f.* balsam fir; **-flasche,** *f.* rubber bottle; **-fluss,** *m.* gummosis.

gummig, gummy.

Gummi-gutt, *n.* gamboge; **-haltig,** containing gum, gummy; **-handschuh,** *m.* rubber glove; **-harz,** *n.* gum resin; **-hütchen,** *n.* rubber cap or teat; **-isolierung,** *f.* rubber insulation; **-käppchen,** *n.* (small) rubber cap; **-lösung,** *f.* gum solution, mucilage; **-packung,** *f.* rubber packing; **-pfropf,** rubber stopper.

Gummi-pfropfen, *m.* rubber stopper; **-sauger,** *m.* rubber suction bulb; **-säure,** *f.* gummic (arabic) acid; **-schlauch,** *m.* rubber tubing, hose, tubing; **-schleim,** *m.* mucilage; **-sirup,** *m.* syrup of acacia; **-stein,** *m.* hyalite; **-stempel,** *m.* rubber stamp; **-stoff,** *m.* gum substance; **-stopfen,** rubber stopper.

Gummi-stöpsel, *m.* rubber stopper; **-tragant,** *m.* gum tragacanth; **-verbindung,** *f.* rubber connection; **-waren,** *f.pl.* rubber goods; **-zucker,** *m.* arabinose.

gummös, gummy.

Gundelrebe, *f.* **Gundermann,** *m.* ground ivy (*Glechoma hederacea*).

Günsel, *m.* Ajuga, bugle (botany).

Gunst, *f.* favor, kindness; **zu Gunsten,** in favor (of), for the benefit (of).

günstig, favorable, propitious, convenient.

Gur, *f.* guhr, diatomaceous earth.

Guranuss, *f.* guru nut, cola nut.

Gurgel, *f.* pharynx, throat, gullet; **-ader,** *f.* jugular vein; **-bein,** *n.* clavicle; **-klappe,** *f.* uvula; **-mittel,** *n.* gargle.

gurgeln, to gargle, gurgle.

Gurgel-vene, *f.* jugular vein; **-wasser,** *n.* gargle.

Gurke, *f.* cucumber.

Gurkenkraut, *n.* borage.

Gurt, *m.* belt, girdle. girth, strap, chord.

Gürtel, *m.* belt, girdle, (waist)band, zone; **-bein,** *n.* sphenoethmoid bone; **-furche,** *f.* transverse groove; **-pflanzung,** *f.* planting in circles; **-schorf,** *m.* zonate scab; **-tiere,** *n.pl.* armadillos (Cingulatae).

gürten, to grid, girdle.

Gurtförderer, *m.* belt conveyer.

Guss, *m.* ̈e, casting, rounding, shower, gate, gutter, pouring, spout, font; **-barre,** *f.* cast bar; **-blase,** *f.* flaw in a casting, air bubble; **-blei,** *n.* cast lead, **-block,** *m.* ingot; **-bruch,** *m.* broken castings, cast-metal scrap; **-eisen,** *n.* cast iron, pig iron; **-fehler,** *m.* casting flaw; **-flasche,** *f.* molding flask; **-form,** *f.* (casting) mold.

Guss-kasten, *m.* molding box; **-messing,** *n* cast brass; **-mörtel,** *m.* concrete, cement; **-naht,** *f.* casting burr, fash, seam; **-schlicker,** *m.* casting slip; **-stahl,** *m.* cast steel; **-stein,** *m.* sink, drain; **-stück,** *n.* cast, casting; **-wachs,** *n.* casting wax; **-waren,** *f.pl.* castings.

gut, good, well, beneficial, advantageous; ~ **begründet,** well-founded; **etwas für** ~ **halten,** to approve of something; ~ **sein lassen,** to let pass, leave alone; **so** ~ **wie,** as well as; **so** ~ **wie kein,** practically no; **kurz und** ~, in short.

Gut, *n.* ̈er, goods, material, possession, property, estate, farm, product.

Gutachten, *n.* expert opinion, decision, verdict.

gutachtlich, authoritative.

gutartig, good-natured, mild, nonmalignant.

Güte, *f.* goodness, kindness, worth, quality, class, grade, virtue; **-abstufung,** *f.* gradation in quality; **-eigenschaft,** *f.* quality (of goods); **-grad,** *m.* (degree of) quality, efficiency.

Güter, *n.pl.* goods, wares, commodities; **-zug,** *m.* freight train.

Güte-stufe, *f.* grade of quality; **-verhältnis,** *n.* efficiency; **-zahl,** *f.* index of quality.

Gut-gewicht, *n.* good (fair) weight, allowance, tare; **-haben,** *n.* balance, credit.

gütig, good, kind, gracious.

gut-sagen, to be responsible (for); **-schliessend,** tight-fitting; **-schmecker,** *m.* gastronomist, epicure; **-schrift,** *f.* credit.

Gutti, *n.* gamboge.

gut-willig, willing, voluntary; **-ziehend,** drawing well, with a good draft.

Gymnasium, *n.* (German) gymnasium, a classical school.

Gymnospermen, *pl.* gymnosperms.

Gyps, *m.* gypsum; **-niederschlag,** *m.* precipitate of gypsum.

Gyroskop, *n.* gyroscope.

H

Haar, *n.*-e, hair, nap, pile, filament, wool, bristle; -ader, *f.* capillary vein; -alaun, *m.* capillary alum; -anlage, *f.* hair primordium or rudiment; -artig, hairlike, capillary, piliform.

Haarbalg, *m.* hair follicle; -drüse, *f.* sebaceous gland; -höhle, *f.* cavity of hair follicle; -mündung, *f.* orifice of hair follicle; -scheide, *f.* sheath of hair follicle; -trichter, *m.* funnel of hair follicle.

Haar-band, *n.* ²er, ciliary (band) process; -beize, *f.* depilatory; -bekleidung, *f.* hair formation; -besatz, *m.* hairy covering, hair; -bildung, *f.* hair formation; -blume, *f.* snake gourd (*Trichosanthes anguina*); -blutgefäss, *n.* capillary (blood vessel); -boden, *m.* hair bed; -bürstchen, *n.* pollen brush; -büschel, *m.* coma, tufted hair, tuft of setae.

Haar-dichte, *f.* density of hair; -drüse, *f.* gland of hair follicle; -dünn, hair-thin, capillary; -erz, *n.* capillary ore; -erzeugungsmittel, *n.* hair restorer; -farbe, *f.* hair dye, color of hair; -färbemittel, *n.* hair dye.

Haar-faser, *f.* capillary filament, hair fiber; -faserig, filamentous; -feder, *f.* filoplume, hair spring; -fein, fine as a hair; -flieger, *m.* seed or fruit with hairlike flying organs; -flügel, *m.* hairy wing; -form, *f.* kind of hair; -förmig, capillary, hair-shaped, piliform.

Haar-gefäss, *n.* capillary vessel or tube; -gefässnetz, *n.* capillary network; -geflecht, *n.* capillary plexus, capillitium; -gitter, *n.* nectar guide, barrier to pollen robbers; -gras, *n.* rye grass (*Elymus europaeus*); -grübchen, *n.* cryptostomate.

haarig, hairy, pilose.

Haar-kegel, *m.* hair cone; -keim, *m.* hair papilla, hair germ; -kelch, *m.* pappus; -kies, *m.* millerite, pyrites; -kleid, *n.* hair covering or coat; -knopf, *m.* bulb of hair; -kraft, *f.* capillarity; -krone, *f.* pappus, aigrette, crown of hair; -kupfer, *n.* capillary copper; -los, hairless, bald, napless; -losigkeit, *f.* hairlessness, baldness; -mark, *n.* medulla of hair; -mücken, *f.pl.* March flies, sand flies (Bibionidae).

Haar-nadel, *f.*-n, hairpin; -oberhäutchen, *n.* cuticle of hair; -papille, *f.*-n, hair papilla; -pelz, *m.* fur; -pinsel, *m.* camel's-hair brush; -reuse, *f.* nectar guide, barrier to pollen robbers; -rinde, *f.* cortex of hair; -riss, *m.* hair crack, craze; -rissig, crazed;

-rohr, *n.* capillary tube; -röhrchen, *n.* capillary tube; -röhrchenkraft, *f.* capillarity; -röhrchennetz, *n.* capillary network; -röhrenanziehung, *f.* capillary attraction.

Haar-sack, *m.* hair follicle; -säckchen, *n.* hair follicle, sheath; -salbe, *f.* pomade; -salz, *n.* hair salt, halotrichite; -schaft, *m.* hair shaft; -scharf, very sharp, extremely precise or accurate; -schärfe, *f.* extreme precision, great exactitude; -scheibe, *f.* hair disk; -scheide, *f.* hair sheath; -scheitel, *m.* vertex, parting of the hair.

Haar-schlinge, *f.* fine-drawn loop; -schwefel, *m.* capillary sulphur; -schweif, *m.* coma, tail (of a comet); -seite, *f.* hair side, grain side; -silber, *n.* capillary silver; -spalte, *f.* fine fissure, cleft; -spitze, *f.* tip or point of the hair; -sterne, *m.pl.* Crinoidea, sea lilies, comatulalid; -strang, *m.* hair cord, brimestonewort, sulphurwort (Peucedanum).

Haar-tasche, *f.* hairy follicle; -tragend, hairy, piliferous; -überzug, *m.* covering of hairs; -verlauf, *m.* hair lines; -vertilgungsmittel, *n.* depilatory; -vitriol, *m.* capillary epsomite; -vorkeim, *m.* primary hair germ.

Haar-warze, *f.* wart of hairs; -waschmittel, hair wash; -wasser, *n.* hair wash; -wechsel, *m.* molting; -wild, *n.* furred game, ground game; -wurzel, *f.* fibrous root, hair root, (*pl.*) root hairs; -wurzelscheide, *f.* sheath of the hair root; -zapfen, *m.* hair papilla; -zwiebel, *f.* hair bulb.

Haar- und Feder-wild, fur-and-feather game.

Habe, *f.* property, possessions, effects, goods.

haben, to have, hold, possess; im Auge ~, to have in view; im Gange ~, to have in full swing; nötig ~, to be necessary; das hat nichts zu sagen, that does not mean (signify) much; acht ~ auf, to pay attention to; lieb (gern) ~, to like; lieber ~, to prefer; am liebsten~, to prefer above all; ~ . . . zu, to have to, must; es hat sich, there is, it is; es zu tun ~ mit, to have to deal with, be concerned about.

Haben, *n.* credit.

habhaft werden, (*gen.*) to obtain, seize, catch.

Habicht, *m.* hawk.

Habichts-knorpel, *m.* cariniform cartilage (of sternum); -kraut, *n.* hawkweed (Hieracium); -schnabel, *m.* hawk beak.

Habilitationsschrift, *f.* inaugural dissertation.

habituell, habitual.

Habitus, *m.* habit.

Habsucht, *f.* avidity, avarice.

Hackbau, *m.* truck gardening.

Hacke, *f.* hoe, mattock, pick, claw, heel.

hacken, to hoe, hack, chop, mince.

Hacken, *m.* heel.

Hacker, *m.* chipper.

Hack-fleisch, *n.* chopped meat, minced meat; **-früchte,** *f.pl.* truck crops (potatoes, turnips, and cabbage); **-geräte,** *n.pl.* implements for hoeing; **-klotz,** *m.* butchers' block; **-kultur,** *f.* truck gardening; **-maschine,** *f.* chipper, rag cutter; **-messer,** *n.* chopper, cleaver; **-salz,** *n.* salt for minced meat; **-schnitzel,** *n.pl.* hogged chips; **-span,** *m.* chip.

Häcksel, *n.&m.* chopped straw; **-maschine,** *f.* straw cutter, chaff cutter; **-sieb,** *n.* box sieve.

Hader, *m.* rag, dispute, quarrel.

Haderer, *m.* tusk, fang.

had(e)rig, short (of iron).

Hadern-drescher, *m.* **-stäuber,** *m.* duster, willow.

Hadernlade, *f.* rag chest.

hadrozentrisch, amphicribral.

Hafen, *m.* harbor, port, haven, pot; **-ofen,** *m.* pot furnace.

Hafer, *m.* oats; **-brand,** *m.* oats smut; **-flocken,** *f.pl.* rolled oats, oatmeal; **-flugbrand,** *m.* loose smut of oats; **-gras,** *n.* wildoats, oat grass; **-kronenrost,** *m.* crown rust of oats; **-mehl,** *n.* oatmeal; **-schleim,** *m.* oat gruel; **-stärke,** *f.* oat starch; **-wurzel,** *f.* salsify (*Tragopogon porrifolius*).

Haff, *n.* a long, shallow body of water almost cut off from the sea by a narrow sandy strip or spit.

Hafner, *m.* potter; **-erz,** *n.* galena, alquifou, potter's ore.

Haft, *f.* custody, confinement.

Haft, *m.* clamp, tie, fastening, agglutinative property; **-ballen,** *m.* adhesive disk; **-band,** *n.* accessory ligament.

haftbar, liable, responsible.

Haft-bein, *n.* copulatorial leg; **-blase,** *f.* appressor(ium); **-borste,** *f.* frenulum; **-druck,** *m.* adhesive pressure, pressure of solution.

haften, to adhere, cling, be liable, answer for.

Haften, *n.* **-bleiben,** *n.* stick, adhering, adhesion.

Haft-faden, *m.* adhesive process; **-fähigkeit,** *f.* adhesion; **-faser,** *f.* rhizoid; **-festigkeit,** *f.* tenacity, adhesive resistance, firmness; **-fläche,** *f.* surface of adhesion; **-glied,** *n.* adhesive organ, stipes; **-intensität,** *f.* intensity of adhesion, solution pressure; **-kraft,** *f.* adhesion; **-läppchen,** *n.pl.* arolia, pads between the claws (of insects); **-lappen,** *m.* jugum, a forewing lobe (of moths with no frenulum).

Haft-mittel, *n.* adhesive; **-napf,** *m.* adhesive bowl; **-organ,** *n.* prehensile organ, appressor(ium), clasping organ; **-pflicht,** *f.* liability; **-röhrchen,** *n.* adhesive tubule; **-scheibe,** *f.* adhesive disk, suctorial disk, sucker, attachment disk; **-scheibenranke,** *f.* tendril terminating in an adhesive disk; **-spannung,** *f.* bond stress; **-stiel,** *m.* body stalk.

Haftung, *f.* adhesion, liability, security, adsorption.

Haft-vermögen, *n.* adhesive power; **-wurzel,** *f.* anchoring root, aerial root, rhizoid, holdfast; **-zotten,** *f.pl.* anchoring villi.

Hag, *m.* hedge, enclosure, pile, bush, grove, meadow, coppice.

Hage-buche, *f.* hornbeam (*Carpinus betulus*); **-butte,** *f.* hip, haw (fruit of roses); **-dorn,** *m.* hawthorn (Crataegus).

Hagel, *m.* hail, small shot, chalazion, tread.

hageln, to hail.

Hagel-schlag, *m.* hailstorm, damage done by hail; **-schnur,** *f.* chalaza.

Hager, *m.* forest humus soil.

hager, haggard, thin, lean, unproductive.

Hahn, *m.* ̈e, cock, stopcock, tap, faucet, rooster.

Hahnenfuss, *m.* cocksfoot, crowfoot, buttercup (Ranunculus); **-ähnlich,** ranunculoid.

Hahnenkamm, *m.* cockscomb (Celosia), (*Rhinanthus cristagalli*), frog-stay (hoof of horse); **-artig,** cockscomblike.

Hahnensporn, *m.* cockspur.

Hahnentritt, *m.* cicatricula (of egg), cock's tread(le), copulation.

Hahnstopfen, *n.* cock stopper.

Hai, *m.* shark.

Haidekraut, *n.* ling (*Calluna vulgaris*), heather (Erica).

Haifisch-embryo, *m.* embryo of the shark; **-leder,** *n.* shark leather; **-tran,** *m.* shark-liver oil.

Hain, *m.* grove, wood, woodlot, thicket; **-artig,** grovelike; **-blume,** Nemophila; **-buche,** *f.* hornbeam (*Carpinus betulus*); **-farn,** *m.* Alsophila; **-simse,** *f.* wood rush (Luzula).

Häkchen, *n.* hooklet, clasp, barbicel of proximal barbule, apostrophe.

Häkelgarn, *n.* crochet thread.

häkeln, to crochet, hook.

haken, to hook.

Haken, *m.* hook, clasp, tusk, catch, difficulty, rabble; **-band,** *n.* coracoid ligament; **-bein,** *n.* unciform bone; **-bewaffnet,** hooked; **-borste,** *f.* hooked bristle, uncinate seta; **-fadenführer,** *m.* hook thread guide; **-faser,** *f.* distal barbule; **-förmig,** hooklike, unciform; **-fortsatz,** *m.* coracoid process; **-haar,** *n.* hooked or barbed hair.

Haken-kletterer, *m.* plant climbing by metamorphosed thorns; **-klimmer,** *m.* hook climber; **-knochen,** *m.* unciform bone; **-kranz,** *m.* circle of hooklets; **-probe,** *f.* hook test (sugar); **-rüssel,** *m.* hookleted head; **-schlüsselbein,** *n.* coracoid bone; **-tragend,** provided with hooks; **-windung,** *f.* unciform convolution; **-wurm,** *m.* hookworm.

hakig, hooked; **-gekrümmt,** aduncate.

halb, half, hemi-, semi-; **-alaun,** *m.* impure alum; **-aldehyd,** *m.* (*n.*) semialdehyde; **-art,** *f.* subspecies; **-aufrecht,** suberect; **-beständig,** metastable; **-bleiche,** *f.* half bleach; **-blende,** *f.* half diaphragm; **-blut,** half-bred; **-bogen,** *m.* hemicycle, quadrant rail; **-bürger,** *m.* denizen, plant suspected of foreign origin.

Halb-chlorschwefel, *m.* sulphur subchloride (monochloride); **-cirkelförmig,** semicircular; **-cylindrisch,** semicylindrical; **-daune,** *f.* semiplume; **-deckel,** *m.* hemielytra; **-decker,** *m.pl.* Hemiptera; **-deckflügel,** *m.* hemielytra; **-deckflügler,** *m.pl.* Hemiptera; **-dornmuskel,** *m.* semispinal muscle; **-dune,** *f.* semiplume.

Halb-dunkel, *n.* twilight, semidarkness, dusk; **-durchlässig,** semipermeable; **-durchmesser,** *m.* radius, semidiameter; **-durchsichtig,** semitransparent; **-durchsichtigkeit,** *f.* semitransparency; **-edelstein,** *m.* semiprecious stone; **-eirund,** semioval; **-emporragend,** semierect.

halben, halber, (*gen.*) in behalf of, on account of; **vorsichts ∼,** for the sake of precaution.

Halb-ese., *m.* onager, kiang (*Equus hemionus*); **-fabrikat,** *n.* semimanufacture, intermediate product; **-fäulnisbewohner,** *m.* semisaprophyte; **-fest,** semisolid; **-fett,** (of coal) semibituminous; **-flächig,** hemihedral; **-flächner,** *m.* hemihedron; **-flechte,** *f.* semilichen; **-flügel,** *m.* hemielytra; **-flügler,** *m.pl.* Hemiptera, Staphylinidae.

halb-flüssig, semiliquid, semifluid; **-franzband,** *m.* half-calf binding; **-frucht,** *f.* semifruit, accessory fruit; **-gefiedert,** pinnatifid; **-gefüllt,** half full; **-gelenk,** *n.* amphiarthrosis; **-gesättigt,** half-saturated; **-glatt,** semiglabrous; **-gut,** *n.* tin containing much lead; **-harz,** *n.* crude resin.

Halbheit, *f.* imperfection, superficiality, indecision.

Halb-holländer, *m.* washing engine; **-hufer,** *m.pl.* Subungulatae.

halbieren, to halve, bisect.

Halbierung, *f.* halving.

Halbinsel, *f.* peninsula.

halbisch, metastable.

Halb-jahr, *n.* half year; **-jährlich,** semi-annual; **-kochen,** *n.* partial boiling, parboiling; **-koks,** *m.* semicoke; **-kolloid,** *n.* semicolloid.

Halbkreis, *m.* semicircle; **-artig,** semicircular; **-förmig,** semicircular.

Halb-kugel, *f.* hemisphere; **-kugelig,** hemispherical; **-kugellinse,** *f.* semicircular lens; **-lederband,** *m.* half-leather binding; **-leinen,** *n.* half linen (binding); **-leinwand,** *f.* half linen (binding); **-leiter,** *m.* semiconductor; **-literkolben,** *m.* half-liter flask; **-mahlen,** to half-crush; **-mattglasur,** *f.* semimat glaze.

Halb-messer, *m.* radius, **-metall,** *n.* semimetal; **-metallglanz,** *m.* submetallic luster; **-monatlich,** semimonthly; **-mond,** *m.* half-moon; **-mondförmig,** lunulate, crescent-shaped; **-nierenförmig,** shape of half a kidney; **-nitril,** *n.* seminitrile; **-normal,** half-normal, seminormal; **-pass,** *m.* broken amble.

Halb-porzellan, *n.* semiporcelain; **-racemisch,** semiracemic; **-raum,** *m.* semi-infinite body (space); **-reduktion,** *f.* semireduction, partial reduction; **-rund,** half-round, semicircular, semicylindrical; **-sauer,** semiacid; **-schatten,** *m.* half-shade, half-shadow, penumbra; **-schattenholzart,** *f.* semishade tolerant tree; **-schattenpolarisator,** *m.* polarizing prisms.

Halb-schmarotzer, *m.* semiparasite; **-schwefeleisen,** *n.* iron hemisulphide;

-**schwefelkupfer,** *n.* cuprous sulphide; -**sehnig,** semitendinous; -**seide,** *f.* half silk; -**seite,** *f.* half a page; -**seitenzwitter,** *m.* unilateral hermaphrodite; -**seitig,** relating to one side (or one half), semilateral, unilateral; -**spaltpfropfen,** *n.* cleft grafting; -**spezifisch,** semispecific.

Halb-stahl, *m.* semisteel; -**stammrose,** *f.* half-standard rose; -**stielrund,** semiterete.

Halbstoff, *m.* half stuff, first stuff; -**holländer,** *m.* breaker.

Halb-strauch, *m.* undershrub; -**strauchig,** somewhat shrubby; -**tief,** half the depth, shallow; -**trocken,** half-dry; -**vitriolblei,** *n.* lanarkite; -**walzig,** semicylindrical; -**wassergas,** *n.* semiwater gas; -**weich,** half-soft, partly soft; -**wertdruck,** *m.* half-value pressure; -**wertsbreite,** *f.* width at half of maximum intensity.

Halb-wertzeit, *f.* half-life period; -**wüste,** *f.* semidesert; -**zahlig,** half numberly; -**zeit,** *f.* half-life (time) period; -**zeitkonstante,** *f.* half-life (time) constant; -**zeug,** *n.* half stuff (paper), hemicellulose; -**zeug,** *n.* half stuff, first stuff, half-finished product; -**zirkel,** *m.* semicircle.

Halde, *f.* slope, hillside, heap, dump.

Halden-erz, *n.* waste-heap ore; -**schlacke,** *f.* discarded slag.

half (helfen), helped.

Halfa, *f.* esparto (grass).

Hälfte, *f.* half, moiety.

Halfter, *m.* halter, head collar.

Hälftflächner, *m.* hemihedron.

Hall, *m.* sound, peal, resonance, clang, acoustics.

Halle, *f.* hall, vestibule.

hallen, to (re)sound.

Halm, *m.*-**e,** stalk, culm, haulm, stem, blade, straw; -**festigkeit,** *f.* haulm strength; -**frucht,** *f.* cereal; -**knoten,** *m.* node (of grass); -**wespen,** *f.pl.* stem sawflies (cephae).

Halochemie, *f.* chemistry of salts.

Halogenalkyl, *n.* alkyl halide.

Halogenid, *n.* halide.

halogenieren, to halogenate, halinate.

Halogenierung, *f.* halogenation.

Halogen-kohlenstoff, *m.* carbon halide; -**metall,** *n.* metallic halide; -**quecksilber,** *n.* mercury halide; -**schwefel,** *m.* sulphury halide; -**substituiert,** halogen-substituted; -**überträger,** *m.* halogen carrier; -**ür,** *n.* halide; -**verbindung,** *f.* halogen compound.

Halogenwasserstoff, *m.* hydrogen halide; -**säure,** *f.* hydrohalic acid.

Haloid, *n.* halide, haloid salt; -**salz,** *n.* halide, haloid salt; -**wasserstoff,** *m.* hydrogen halide.

Hals, *m.*-̈e, neck, beak, throat, stem, collar; ~ **über Kopf,** headlong, head over heels.

Hals-ader, *f.* cervical or jugular vein; -**arterie,** *f.* carotid artery; -**band,** *n.* neck ribbon, necklace, collar; -**bein,** *n.* clavicle, hyoid bone; -**beugung,** *f.* neck arch (horse), cervical flexure; -**blutader,** *f.* jugular vein; -**bräune,** *f.* throat affection, diphtheria; -**bucht,** *f.* cervical sinus; -**drüse,** *f.* cervical gland; -**eingeweide,** *n.pl.* cervical viscera.

Hals-entzündung, *f.* inflammation of the throat; -**feder,** *f.* cervical feather; -**fistel,** *f.* cervicle fistula; -**flosse,** *f.* pectoral fin; -**gefieder,** *n.* cervical feathers; -**geflecht,** *n.* cervical plexus; -**gegend,** *f.* cervical region; -**gelenk,** *n.* cervical articulation; -**haut,** *f.* ̈e, skin of the neck; -**höhle,** *f.* cervical cavity.

Hals-kanalzelle, *f.* neck canal cell; -**knoten,** *m.* cervical ganglion; -**kopfpulsader,** *f.* carotid artery; -**kragen,** *m.* collar; -**mandel,** *f.* tonsil; -**mark,** *n.* cervical spinal cord; -**muskel,** *m.* cervical muscle, nuchal muscle, muscle of the neck; -**ring,** *m.* collar; -**röhre,** *f.* trachea, windpipe.

Halsschild, *m.* thoracic shield, prothorax; -**hinterecke,** *f.* posterior corner of thoracic shield; -**vorderrand,** *m.* anterior margin of thoracic shield.

Hals-schlagader, *f.* carotid artery; -**seitenflur,** *f.* pteryla colli lateralis; -**seitenraine,** *m.pl.* apteria colli lateralia; -**vene,** *f.* jugular vein; -**weh,** sore throat.

Halswirbel, *m.* cervical vertebra, cervical whorl; -**band,** *n.* cervical vertebral ligament; -**bein,** *n.* cervical vertebra; -**dorn,** *m.* spinous process of cervical vertebra; -**gelenk,** *n.* articulation of cervical vertebra; -**säule,** *f.* cervical segment of vertebral column.

Halszäpfchen, *n.* uvula.

Halt, *m.* hold, holding, halt, stop, firmness, support, yield; ~ **machen,** to stop, halt.

hält (halten), holds.

haltbar, stable, firm, lasting, durable, fast, tenable, permanent.

Haltbarkeit, *f.* stability, durability, keeping quality, endurance.

Haltbarmachen, *n.* making stable, stabilizing, preserving.

Halte-bändchen, *n.* (cheek) ligament; **-kraft,** *f.* cohesion.

halten, to hold (on), keep, deliver, consider, stop, take, give; **sich ~ an,** to keep to; **sich ~,** to maintain oneself; **viel auf etwas ~,** to think a lot of a thing; **für etwas ~,** to regard as; **sich das Gleichgewicht ~,** to balance; **~ für,** to consider; **~ zu jemandem,** to be faithful to; **konstant ~,** to maintain.

Haltepunkt, *m.* halting point, stopping place.

Halter, *m.* holder, support, receptacle, handle, keeper, clamp, tie.

Hälter, *m.* holder, reservoir.

Halterarm, *m.* supporting arm.

Halteren, *pl.* halteres (of Diptera); **-deckel,** *m.* squama of the halteres.

Halte-zahn, *m.* pilot pin, catch; **-zange,** *f.* claspers; **-zeit,** *f.* halt, pause.

haltig, containing, holding, bearing.

haltlos, unstable, unsteady, infirm, loose.

Haltung, *f.* holding, conduct, behavior, attitude, bearing, state, position, harmony.

Haltungs-reflex, *m.* postural reflex.

Haltwaren, *f.pl.* preserves.

Hämalaun, *m.* hemalum.

Hämatin, *n.* hematin.

Hämatit, *m.* hematite; **-eisen,** *n.* hematite iron.

Hämatokrit, *f.* hematocrit.

Hämatoxylin, *n.* hematoxylin.

Hämin, *n.* hemin.

hämisch, malicious.

Hammel, *m.* wether, mutton; **-fett,** *n.* mutton fat; **-fleisch,** *n.* mutton; **-fleischbrühe,** *f.* mutton broth; **-talg,** *m.* mutton tallow.

Hammer, *m.* hammer, malleus (of the ear).

hämmerbar, malleable; **-keit,** *f.* malleability.

Hammer-eisen, *n.* wrought iron; **-fortsatz,** *m.* process of the malleus; **-gar,** toughpitch, tough; **-gelenk,** *n.* articulation of the malleus; **-griff,** *m.* handle of the malleus; **-hals,** *m.* neck of the malleus; **-knorpel,** *m.* cartilage of the malleus; **-kopf,** *m.* head of the malleus.

hämmern, to hammer, forge.

Hammer-schlacke, *f.* hammer scale; **-schlag,** *m.* hammer scale, hammer blow, roll scale, iron oxide.

Hämo-chininsäure, *f.* hemoquinic acid; **-cytometer,** *m.* hemocytometer; **-globin,** *n.* hemoglobin; **-globinurie,** *f.* hemoglobinuria; **-lyse,** *f.* hemolysis; **-lysine,** *f.* hemolysins; **-lytisch,** hemolytic; **-pyrrol,** *n.* hemopyrrole.

hämorrhagisch, hemorrhagic.

Hämostasis, *f.* hemostasis.

Hamster, *m.* common hamster, marmot.

Hand, *f.:-e,* hand; **an die ~ gehen,** to aid; **das liegt auf der ~,** that is obvious; **auf eigene ~,** at one's own risk; **an ~ von,** with the aid of, on the basis of, by means of; **von der ~,** offhand.

Hand-arbeit, *f.:-en,* handwork, manual labor; **-arbeiter,** *m.* manual laborer; **-ausgabe,** *f.* pocket edition; **-ballen,** *m.* eminence of the hand; **-band,** *n.* ligament of the hand; **-bein,** *n.* bone of the hand.

Hand-betrieb, *m.* hand (driven) power, or operation; **-beuger,** *m.* flexor of the hand; **-blätterig,** palmate; **-buch,** *n.* manual, handbook, compendium; **-decken,** *f.pl.* the primary coverts; **-einstellung,** *f.* adjustment by hand.

Händedesinfektion, *f.* disinfection of hands.

Handel, *m.-,* commerce, trade, business, affair, action, traffic, quarrel; **im ~,** on the market; **in den ~ bringen,** to put on the market; **in den ~ gelangen,** to come (get) on the market; **in den ~ kommen,** to be put on the market;

handeln, to act, proceed, negotiate, handle, deal, trade; **~ um,** to treat, be about; **es handelt sich um . . . ,** it concerns, we are dealing with, it is a question of . . . ; **von etwas ~,** to treat of, deal with.

Handels-amt, *n.* board of trade; **-analyse,** *f.* commercial analysis; **-artikel,** *m.* article of commerce, commodity; **-benzol,** *f.* commercial benzene; **-betrieb,** *m.* traffic; **-chemiker,** *m.* analytical chemist; **-dünger,** *m.* commercial fertilizer; **-eigenschaft,** *f.* commercial value; **-gesellschaft,** *f.* (trading) company; **-gesetz,** *n.* commercial law.

Handels-harzleim, *m.* commercial rosin size; **-kammer,** *f.* chamber of commerce; **-kautschuk,** *m.* commercial rubber; **-laboratorium,** *n.* commercial laboratory; **-leute,** *pl.* tradesmen; **-mann,** *m.* tradesman, merchant; **-schiff,** *n.* trading vessel; **-scheiferei,** *f.* commercial grinding plant, pulp-mill; **-silber,** *n.* commercial silver; **-sorte,** *f.* commercial variety.

handels-üblich, customary in commerce, of commercial size; **-verein,** *m.* commercial association; **-waren,** *f.* commercial articles, merchandise; **-wert,** *m.* commercial value; **-zeichen,** *n.* trademark; **-zink,** *n.* commercial zinc; **-zweig,** *m.* branch of trade.

Hand-fertigkeit, *f.* manual skill, dexterity; **-fläche,** *f.* the (palmar) surface of the hand.

handförmig, palmate; **-gespalten,** palmatifid.

Hand-gebläse, *n.* hand blower; **-gebrauch,** *m.* daily use; **-gelenk,** *n.* wrist joint; **-gerüst,** *n.* skeleton of the hand; **-granate,** *f.* hand grenade; **-greiflich,** palpable, obvious, evident, downright; **-griff,** *m.* handle, grasp, handshake, knack, trick, method, manipulation, manubrium; **-habe,** *f.* handle, hold, grip, aid, ways or means, manubrium; **-haben,** to handle, maintain, manipulate, operate, manage, apply, deal with; **-habung,** *f.* handling, manipulation, application.

Hand-hautmuskel, *m.* cutaneous muscle of the hand; **-heiss,** lukewarm, of the temperature of the hand; **-knöchel,** *m.* knuckle; **-knochen,** *m.* bone of the hand.

Händler, *m.* dealer, retailer.

handlich, handy, manageable.

Handlichkeit, *f.* handiness.

Handlung, *f.* trade, commerce, shop, establishment, action, plot, act, deed, transaction, firm, business.

Handlungsweise, *f.* procedure.

hand-nervig, palmately veined; **-puddeln,** to puddle by hand; **-rand,** *m.* edge of wing; **-reibe,** *f.* hand grater.

Handrücken, *m.* back of the hand; **-band,** *n.* dorsal ligament of the hand; **-gegend,** *f.* dorsal region of the hand.

Hand-saat, *f.* sowing by hand; **-säge,** *f.* handsaw; **-scheidung,** *f.* separation, sorting by hand; **-schmierung,** *f.* hand lubrication; **-schrift,** *f.* handwriting, manuscript, signature; **-schriftlich,** in longhand; **-schuh,** *m.* glove; **-schwingen,** *f.pl.* primaries; **-sehne,** *f.* tendon of the hand; **-sehnespanner,** *m.* palmaris longus.

Hand-steuerung, *f.* hand gear; **-strich,** *m.* hand molding; **-stück,** *n.* specimen of handy size; **-teller,** *m.* palm of the hand; **-tuch,** *n.* towel.

Handumdrehen, im ∼, in a turn of the hand, in a jiffy.

Hand-verkauf, *m.* retail; **-voll,** *f.* handful; **-waage,** *f.* hand balance; **-wärme,** *f.* heat (or warmth) of the hand; **-werk,** *n.*-**er,** handicraft, trade, guild; **-werker,** *m.*

mechanic, workman; **-werksbursche,** *m.* craftsman, traveling artisan, journeyman; **-werksmässig,** workmanlike, mechanical; **-werkzeug,** *n.* tools, instruments; **-wörterbuch,** *n.* abridged dictionary.

Handwurzel, *f.* wrist, carpus, wrist joint; **-band,** *n.* carpal ligament; **-bein,** *n.* wrist bone, carpal bone; **-gegend,** *f.* carpal region; **-gelenk,** *n.* wrist joint; **-knochen,** *m.* wrist bone; **-kreuz,** *n.* carpal cross (meeting of hair lines); **-mittelhandgelenk,** *n.* carpometacarpal joint; **-ringband,** *n.* annular ligament of wrist.

Hanf, *m.* hemp (*Cannabis sativa*); **-artig,** hemplike, hempen; **-bau,** *m.* cultivation of hemp; **-faden,** *m.* hemp fiber, hemp twine; **-korn,** *n.* hempseed; **-korngross,** of the size of hempseed.

Hänfling, *m.* linnet.

Hanf-nessel, *f.* hemp nettle (*Galeopsis tetrahit*); **-öl,** *n.* hempseed oil; **-saat,** *f.* hemp; **-samen,** *m.* hempseed; **-säure,** *f.* linoleic acid; **-seil,** *n.* hemp rope, hemp cord; **-tod,** *m.* branchy broomrape (*Orobanche ramosa*); **-wurzel,** *f.* dodder, strangleweed.

Hang, *m.*ˑˑe, slope, incline, declivity, inclination, disposition, propensity, bent, dip.

Hänge, *f.* drying loft, ager, adhesion.

Hänge-birke, *f.* weeping birch (*Betula alba pendula*); **-blatt,** *n.* pendent leaf; **-blütige,** *f.pl.* Penduliflorae (wind fertilized), pendulous flowers; **-frucht,** *f.* cremocarp; **-muskel,** *m.* cremaster, suspensory muscle.

hangen, hängen, to hang, hang up, suspend, correlate, attach, hang (execute), adhere, cling, be suspended; **sich an etwas ∼,** to depend upon something; **∼ bleiben,** to be caught, adhere to; **∼ lassen,** to let drop, droop.

Hängenbleiben, *n.* retention, adherence (of leaves).

hangend, hängend, hanging, pendent, drooping, weeping, suspended, pendulous.

Hang(e)quelle, *f.* spring issuing from a slope.

Hänge-tropfen, *m.* hanging drop; **-weide,** *f.* weeping willow (*Salix babylonica*); **-werk,** *n.* truss frame; **-zweig,** *m.* pendant shoot.

Hangwald, *m.* forest covering a steep slope.

Hansel, *m.* return wort.

Hantel, *f.* dumbbell; **-förmig,** dumbbell-shaped.

hantieren, to work, manipulate, operate, manage, be occupied (busy).

Hantierung, *f.* handling, manipulation, occupation.

Haplosporidien, *n.pl.* haplosporidia.

Haptine, *n.pl.* haptines.

haptisch, tangible, by touch.

haptophor, haptophore.

Härchen, *n.* little hair, cilium; **-kranz,** *m.* ciliary corona.

Harfe, *f.* harp.

Häring, *m.* herring.

Harke, *f.* rake.

harken, to rake.

Harm, *m.* sorrow, harm.

harmlos, harmless.

harmonieren, to harmonize.

harmonisch, harmonious.

Harn, *m.* urine; **-absatz,** *m.* urinary sediment or deposit; **-absonderung,** *f.* urinary secretion; **-abtreibend,** diuretic; **-analyse,** *f.* urinalysis; **-apparat,** *m.* urinary apparatus; **-artig,** urinous, like urine; **-ausscheidung,** *f.* excretion of urine; **-benzoesäure,** *f.* hippuric acid; **-bildung,** *f.* formation of urine; **-blase,** *f.* urinary bladder.

Harnblasen-gang, *m.* urethra; **-hals,** *m.* neck of the bladder; **-höhle,** *f.* cavity of the bladder; **-wand,** *f.* wall of the bladder.

Harnblau, *n.* indican.

harnen, to urinate, micturate.

harn-fähig, capable of passage into urine; **-farbstoff,** *m.* urinary pigment; **-gang,** *m.* urinal passage; **-gärung,** *f.* fermentation of urine; **-gefässe,** *n.pl.* urinary vessels; **-haut,** *f.* allantois.

harnig, uric, urinous.

Harn-kanälchen, *n.pl.* urineferous tubules; **-kolloid,** *n.* urinary colloid; **-kraut,** *n.* a diuretic plant, base rocket, mignonette (*Reseda luteola*); **-lehre,** *f.* urinology: **-leiter,** *m.* ureter, urinal passage, catheter; **-messer,** *m.* urinometer.

Harn-niederschlag, *m.* urinary deposit; **-organ,** *n.* urinary organ; **-oxyd,** *n.* xanthic oxide; **-phosphor,** *m.* urinary phosphorus; **-probe,** *f.* test for urine, sample of urine; **-prüfung,** *f.* urinalysis; **-röhre,** *f.* urethra, renal tubule.

Harnröhren-mündung, *f.* orifice of urethra; **-scheidewand,** *f.* urethrovaginal septum; **-zwiebel,** *f.* bulb of urethra.

Harn-rosa, *f.* urorosein; **-ruhr,** *f.* diabetes; **-sack,** *m.* allantois; **-salz,** *n.* salt found in urine; **-sand,** *m.* urinary gravel; **-satz,** *m.* urinary deposit; **-sauer,** urate of; **-säure,** *f.* uric acid; **-säurestein,** *m.* uric acid calculus; **-schnur,** *f.* urachus; **-stein,** *m.* urinary calculus.

Harnstoff, *m.* urea; **-gärung,** fermentation of urea; **-stickstoff,** *m.* urea nitrogen.

Harn-strang, *m.* urachus; **-treibend,** diuretic; **-untersuchung,** *f.* examination of urine; **-waage,** *f.* urinometer; **-weg,** *m.* urinary passage; **-werkzeug,** *n.* urinary organ; **-zucker,** *m.* sugar in urine.

harren, to wait, stay, tarry.

hart, hard, firm, solid, hardy, difficult; ∼ **an,** close by; **es wird** ∼ **halten zu,** it will be no easy matter to; ∼ **bedrängt,** hard beset; **es kommt ihm** ∼ **an,** he finds it hard.

Hart-bast, *m.* hard bast; **-blei,** *n.* hard lead; **-borste,** *f.* crack formed during hardening, fissure; **-brand,** *m.* covered smut; **-brandstein,** *m.* hard-burned brick; **-braunstein,** *m.* braunite.

härtbar, capable of being hardened.

Härte, *f.* hardness, hardening, costiveness, tempering.

Härte-bestimmung, *f.* determination of hardness; **-flüssigkeit,** *f.* tempering liquid. **-gebilde,** *n.* hard formation; **-grad,** *m*; degree of hardness, temper; **-messer,** *m.* hardness gauge; **-mittel,** *n.* hardening agent.

härten, to harden, temper, grow hard, congeal, caseharden.

Härte-ofen, *m.* hardening furnace; **-prüfung,** *f.* hardness test; **-pulver,** *n.* tempering (cementing) powder; **-riss,** *m.* crack; **-skala,** *f.* scale of hardness; **-verfahren,** *n.* hardening process.

Hart-floss, *n.* specular iron, spiegel; **-flügler,** *m.pl.* Coleoptera; **-gelötet,** hard-soldered; **-gesotten,** hard-boiled; **-giessen,** to caseharden, chill-cast; **-glas,** *n.* hard glass; **-glasbecher,** *m.* hard-glass beaker; **-gummi,** *n.* hard rubber; **-gummitisch,** *m.* vulcanite stage (microscope); **-guss,** *m.* chill casting.

Hart-harz, *n.* hard (solid) resin; **-heu,** *n.* St.-John's-wort (Hypericum); **-holz,** *n.* hardwood.

Hartlaub-formation, *f.* sclerophyllous formation; **-gehölz,** *n.* sclerophyllous woodland; **-stufe,** *f.* zone of sclerophytes.

Hart-kies, *m.* **-kobalterz,** *n.* skutterudite; **-leibig,** costive; **-leibigkeit,** *f.* costiveness, constipation, confinedness; **-lot,** *n.* hard solder; **-löten,** to braze, hard-solder; **-machen,** *n.* hardening; **-manganerz,** *n.*

psilomelane, braunite; **-näckıg,** stubborn, obstinate; **-pech,** *n.* hard pitch, dry pitch; **-porzellan,** *n.* hard porcelain.

Hart-post, *f.* bank paper, typewriting paper; **-riegel,** *m.* privet (Ligustrum), cornel, red dogwood (*Cornus sanguinea*); **-riegelwächse,** *n.pl.* Cornaceae; **-schale,** *f.* hard shell; **-schalig,** hard-shelled; **-schicht,** *f.* hard or stony layer; **-spat,** *m.* andalusite; **-spiritus,** *m.* solid alcohol; **-stahl,** *m.* hard steel; **-steingut,** *n.* hard whiteware.

Härtung, *f.* hardening.

Härtungs-kohle, *f.* temper carbon, hardening carbon; **-mittel,** *n.* hardening agent.

Hart-waren, *f.pl.* hardware; **-weizen,** *m.* durum wheat; **-werden,** *n.* hardening; **-wiese,** *f.* sour meadow; **-zinn,** *n.* pewter.

Harz, *n.* resin, rosin; **-ähnlich,** resinlike, resinous; **-artig,** resinlike, resinous; **-baum,** *m.* pine (pitch) tree; **-behälter,** *m.* resin receptacle or canal; **-beule,** *f.* resin cavity, gall; **-cerat,** *n.* rosin cerate; **-drüse,** *f.* resin gland; **-elektrizität,** *f.* negative electricity.

harzen, to be resinous, to be sticky, to gather resin, tap for resin, rub with resin.

Harzen, *n.* bleeding, tapping, boxing.

Harz-essenz, *f.* rosin spirit, pinolin; **-ester,** *m.* ester gum, resin ester; **-fichte,** *f.* pitch pine; **-firnis,** *m.* resin varnish; **-fleck,** *m.* resin spot (paper); **-fluss,** *m.* exudation of resin; **-galle,** *f.* resin gall; **-gang,** *m.* resin duct; **-gebend,** yielding resin; **-glanz,** *m.* resinous luster; **-haltig,** containing resin.

harzig, resinous.

Harz-kitt, *m.* resinous cement; **-kohle,** *f.* resinous coal; **-kuchen,** *m.* cake or lump of rosin; **-lack,** *m.* resin varnish; **-leim,** *m.* rosin size; **-naphta,** *f.* resin oil; **-nutzung,** *f.* resin tapping; **-produkt,** *n.* resin product; **-reich,** rich in resin; **-röhre,** *f.* resin duct.

Harz-salbe, *f.* rosin cerate; **-salz,** *n.* resinate; **-sauer,** resinate of; **-säure,** *f.* resin(ic) acid; **-scharrer,** *m.* resin tapper; **-seife,** *f.* resin soap, resinate; **-spiritus,** *m.* resin spirit; **-stoff,** *m.* resinous substance; **-tanne,** *f.* pitch pine, pitch fir; **-teer,** *m.* resinous tar; **-zelle,** *f.* resin cell.

haschen, to catch, seize, snatch.

haschieren, to hash, mince, hatch.

Haschisch, *n.* hashish.

Hase, *m.*-**n,** common hare, coward.

Hasel, *f.* hazel, dace; **-busch,** *m.* hazel bush; **-gerte,** *f.* hazel switch; **-huhn,** *n.*

hazel grouse, hazel hen; **-maus,** *f.* common dormouse; **-nuss,** *f.* hazelnut; **-nussgrösse,** *f.* size of a hazel nut; **-strauch,** *m.* hazel tree; **-wurz,** *f.* hazelwort (*Asarum europaeum*); **-zeit,** *f.* era of the hazel bush.

Hasen-klee, *m.* trefoil (Trifolium); **-kohl,** *m.* wood sorrel; **-ohr,** *n.* hare's-ear (*Bupleurum rotundifolium*); **-scharte,** *f.* harelip; **-schwanz(gras),** *m.* (*n.*), Lagurus.

Häsin, *f.* doe hare.

Häslein, Häschen, *n.* leveret.

Haspe, *f.* hinge, hasp, staple, clamp.

Haspel, *m.* reel, windlass; **-holm,** *m.* slat of reel fly.

haspeln, to reel, wind.

Hass, *m.* hate, hatred.

hassen, to hate.

hässlich, ugly.

Hast, *f.* haste, hurry.

hastig, hasty.

Hau, *m.* felling, cut(ting), hewing.

haubar, mature, fellable, fit for cutting.

Haubarkeit, *f.* maturity, ripeness for felling.

Haubarkeits-alter, *n.* age for felling; **-ertrag,** *m.* yield from felling.

Haube, *f.* hood, cap, calyptra, dome, crest, tuft, tegmentum.

Haubenkeim, *m.* hooded nuclear germ, tegmentum of the embryo, protective bud scale.

Haubenlerche, *f.* crested lark (*Alauda cristata*).

Haubitze, *f.* howitzer.

Hauch, *m.* breath, exhalation, breathing, aspiration, tinge.

hauchen, to breathe, exhale.

Haue, *f.* hoe, mattock, pick(ax).

hauen, to hew, fell, chop, cut, whip, strike (out), lumber, mow.

Hauer, *m.* hewer, cutter, chopper.

Hauer, Hauzähne, *m.pl.* tusks, fangs.

Häufchen, *n.* little heap.

Haufe, Haufen, *m.* heap, pile, batch, agglomeration, cluster, crowd, mass, group, quantity.

Häufelkultur, *f.* hilling practice (in cultivation).

häufeln, to raise earth about plants, hill.

Häufelpflug, *m.* lister, ridge plow (used for hilling).

Haufen-führen, *n.* couching, flooring; -röstung, *f.* heap roasting; -verkohlung, *f.* charcoal burning (in piles).

häufen, to pile, accumulate, amass, pile (up), increase.

häufig, frequent, repeated, numerous, abundant, often.

Häufigkeit, *f.* frequency.

Häufigkeits-grad, *m.* percentage of frequency; -kurve, *f.* frequency curve; -stufe, *f.* degree of frequency; -verteilung, *f.* frequency distribution.

Häufung, *f.* heaping, accumulation, congestion.

Haufwerk, *n.* aggregate, mine run.

Hauhechel, *f.* restharrow (*Ononis repens*).

Haupt, *n.* head, chief, principal; -abschnitt, *m.* chief section (paragraph); -abteilung, *f.* principal division; -achse, *f.* main axis; -achselprodukt, *n.* leader (shoot), main axis product; -achsenknospe, *f.* leader bud; -ader, *f.* principal vein; -anteil, *m.* principal constituent; -ast, *m.* main branch; -aufgabe, *f.* main task.

Haupt-augenmerk, *n.* chief aim or attention; -bedeutung, *f.* chief importance; -bedingung, *f.* chief condition or requirement; -bedürfnis, *n.* chief requirement; -bestand, *m.* principal crop; -bestandteil, *m.* chief constituent; -bestäuber, *m.* principal pollinator; -beweis, *m.* main proof; -bildungsherd, *m.* principal seat of formation; -bindung, *f.* principal union or bond.

Haupt-blutader, *f.* cephalic vein; -brennpunkt, *m.* principal focus; -brennweite, *f.* principal focal distance; -buch, *n.* ledger; -darm, *m.* mesodaeum (Metazoa); -dotter, *m.* principal yolk; -ebene, *f.* principal plane; -erzeugnis, *n.* principal product; -farbe, *f.* primary color; -florenreich, *n.* principal floral division.

Haupt-form, *f.* chief form; -formation, *f.* formation; -fundort, *m.* principal locality, place of discovery; -gang, *m.* principal duct; -gärung, *f.* fermentation; -gegend, *f.* principal region; -geissel, *f.* principal flagellum; -gesetz, *n.* fundamental law; -gesichtsknochen, *m.* principal facial bone; -haar, *n.* hair of the head.

Haupt-hohlraum, *m.* principal lumen or cavity; -holzart, *f.* prevailing species; -keim, *m.* principal germ; -keimbahn, *f.* principal germ tract; -kenner, *m.* chief (outstanding) expert; -kette, *f.* principal chain; -kiel, *m.* the quill (of a feather); -klasse, *f.* principal class; -körperschlag-

ader, *f.* main body artery; -leitung, *f.* main.

haupt-los, headless, 'acephalous; ' -lymphstamm, *m.* ductus thoracicus; -mann, *m.* captain; -masse, *f.* principal mass, bulk; -menge, *f.* bulk, principal quantity; -merkmal, *n.* distinctive feature; -mittelfussknochen, *m.* large metacarpal (metatarsal) bone; -moment, *n.* main point; -nährstoff, *m.* chief nutritive substance; -nahrung, *f.* staple food, chief food.

Haupt-nenner, *m.* common denominator; -nerv, *m.* principal vein; -nervensystem, *n.* central nervous system; -nutzung, *f.* principal produce; -öffnung, *f.* principal aperture; -ölbad, *n.* white steeping; -pflaster, *n.* opium plaster; -postamt, *n.* general post office; -punkt, *m.* principal point; -quelle, *f.* chief source.

Haupt-reaktion, *f.* principal reaction; -redakteur, *m.* chief editor; -register, *n.* general index; -richtung, *f.* primary course; -rippe, *f.* primary vein, midrib of leaf; -rohr, *n.* main tube or pipe; -rolle, *f.* leading part.

Hauptsache, *f.* chief matter, main point or thing; in der ∼, mainly, chiefly; der ∼ nach, in substance.

hauptsächlich, main, principal, chiefly, especially, essentially, particularly.

Haupt-satz, *m.* ⁻e, fundamental principle, axiom; -schädlichkeit, *f.* principal noxious agent or influence; -schlagader, *f.* aorta; -schlüssel, *m.* master key; -schnitt, *m.* principal section; -schwingung, *f.* principal vibration; -septum, *n.* cardinal septum; -serie, *f.* principal series; -sicherung, *f.* main fuse; -sinnesorgan, *n.* special sense organ.

Haupt-spannungsverhältnis, *n.* principal stress ratio; -spirale, *f.* primary coil; -spitze, *f.* principal cusp or point; -spross, *m.* leading shoot; -spule, *f.* primary coil; -stadt, *f.* metropolis, capital; -stamm, *m.* chief trunk; -stirnbein, *n.* frontal bone; -strom, *m.* main current; -stück, *n.*-e, principal part.

Haupt-stütze, *f.* main support; -teil, *m.* principal part; -trieb, *m.* leading shoot; -typ(us), *m.* principal type; -ursache, *f.* chief cause; -valenz, *f.* principal valence; -verdienst, *m.* chief merit; -vertreter, *m.* main substituent, typical item, principal representative; -vorkommen, *n.* principal occurrence; -wert, *m.*-e, chief value.

Haupt-wimperkranz, *m.* prototroch; -wirbel, *m.* atlas; -wirkung, *f.* principal effect; -wurzel, *f.* taproot, main root; -zahl, *f.* cardinal number; -zellen, *f.pl.* central or chief cells; **-zug,** *m.* principal feature; **-zweig,** *m.* main branch.

Haus, *n.* ̈er, house, home, cottage, mansion, dwelling, family; **von ~ aus,** originally, natively, by nature; **zu Hause,** at home; **nach Hause,** (toward) home, homeward.

Haus-apotheke, *f.* family medicine chest; **-arznei,** *f.* domestic remedy; **-arzt,** *m.* family doctor; **-besitzer,** *m.* house owner, landlord; **-biene,** *f.* domestic bee; **-brand,** *m.* domestic fuel.

hausen, to dwell, live, reside, keep house, behave badly, ravage.

Hausen, *m.* sturgeon; **-blase,** *f.* isinglass.

Haus-ente, *f.* domestic duck; **-esel,** *m.* ass, donkey; **-gans,** *f.* domestic goose; **-gebrauch,** *m.* family custom, domestic use; **-gerät,** *n.* household utensils or furniture; **-halt,** *m.* household, budget, economy, housekeeping; **-hälter,** *m.* housekeeper, steward, economist; **-huhn,** *n.* domestic fowl; **-hund,** *m.* dog; **-haltungsführung,** *f.* household management.

Haus-katze, *f.* domestic cat; **-laub,** *n.* **-lauch,** *m.,* **-lauf,** *m.* houseleek (*Sempervivum tectorum*).

häuslich, domestic, economical, thrifty.

Haus-mittel, *n.* household remedy, medicine; **-müll,** *n.* household refuse; **-schaf,** *n.* sheep; **-schwalbe,** *f.* house swallow, house martin; **-schwamm,** *m.* house (dry rot) fungus (*Merulius lacrimans*); **-seife,** *f.* household (common) soap; **-spitzmaus,** *f.* shrew; **-taube,** *f.* pigeon, dove.

Haustein, *m.* ashlar, hewn stone.

Haus-tier, *n.* domesticated animal; **-wanze,** *f.* bedbug; **-wirtschaft,** *f.* housekeeping, economy; **-wurz,** *f.* houseleek (*Sempervivum tectorum*); **-ziege,** *f.* goat.

Haut, *f.* ̈e, skin, integument, membrane, epidermis, pellicle, tunic, coat, hide, film, crust; **äussere ~,** epidermis; **durchsichtige ~,** cornea; **harte ~,** sclerotic coat.

haut-artig, skinny, dermoid; **-atmung,** *f.* cutaneous respiration; **-ausdunstung,** *f.* evaporation from the skin; **-ausschlag,** *m.* rash; **-auswuchs,** *m.* cutaneous outgrowth; **-bezirk,** *m.* epidermis, region of the skin.

Haut-bildungsgewebe, *n.* dermatogen; **-bildungsvermögen,** *n.* power of film formation; **-blastomykose,** *f.* blastomycetic dermatitis; **-blatt,** *n.* ectoderm, epiblast; **-blutader,** *f.* cutaneous vein; **-bräune,** *f.* croup; **-brücke,** *f.* bridge of skin, dermal projection; **-carcinom,** *n.* skin carcinoma.

Häutchen, *n.* thin skin, film, cloud, nebula, pellicle, membrane.

Haut-decke, *f.* cutaneous covering, integument; **-drüse,** *f.* epidermal gland, sebaceous gland; **-einstülpung,** *f.* infolding or invagination of the skin.

häuten, to shed (cast) the skin, skin, molt.

Haut-falte, *f.* skin fold; **-farbe,** *f.* complexion; **-farbstoff,** *m.* pigment of the skin; **-farn,** *m.* goldilocks (Hymenophyllum); **-faserblatt,** *n.* somatopleura, hypoderm; **-fetzen,** *m.* scale; **-flache,** *f.* surface of the skin.

Haut-flügel, *m.* membranous wing; **-flügler,** *m.pl.* Hymenoptera; **-frucht,** *f.* diclesium (an achene in free covering of perianth); **-gebild,** *n.* skin formation; **-gelenk,** *n.* membranous joint; **-gewebe,** *n.* periderm, dermatogen, dermal tissue; **-hülle,** *f.* integument.

häutig, skinny, cutaneous, membranous, dermoid.

Haut-keim, *m.* (skin bud) dermoblast, blastoderm; **-knochen,** *m.* membrane bone, dermal bone; **-knochengerüst,** *n.* dermoskeleton; **-knorpel,** *m.* membranous cartilage; **-krankheit,** *f.* skin disease; **-krebs,** *m.* cancer of the skin, epithelioma; **-lappen,** *m.* flap of skin.

Haut-lehre, *f.* dermatology; **-leiste,** *f.* dermal ridge, cutaneous border; **-mikrophyten,** *pl.* bacterial flora of the skin; **-muskelschlauch,** *m.* dermal muscular tunic, cuticulomuscular tube; **-nabel,** *m.* navel, umbilicus; **-naht,** *f.* cutaneous suture; **-oberfläche,** *f.* surface of the skin.

Haut-pflege, *f.* care of the skin; **-reaktion,** *f.* cutaneous reaction; **-reinigend,** skin cleansing; **-reiz,** *m.* skin irritant; **-reizend,** irritating to the skin; **-rotz,** *m.* glanders, farcy; **-salbe,** *f.* sebaceous matter, ointment for skin; **-schicht,** *f.* dermal layer, periderm, plasma membrane; **-schild,** *m.* dermal plate.

Haut-schmiere, *f.* sebaceous humor; **-schuppe,** *f.* scale; **-schwiele,** *f.* callus; **-sinnesorgan,** *n.* tactile organ, setiferous sense organ; **-skelett,** *n.* dermal skeleton, exoskeleton; **-system,** *n.* dermal system; **-talg,** *m.* sebaceous matter (of the skin); **-übel,** *n.* skin disease.

Häutung, *f.* molting, shedding (of the skin), desquamation, exfoliation.

Häutungsvorgang, *m.* shedding of the skin.

Haut-verknöcherung, *f.* ossification of skin; **-wanzen,** *f.pl.* Acanthiidae; **-warze,** *f.*

cutaneous wart or papilla; **-wurzelig,** hymenorrhizal (membranous rootlike); **-zahn,** *m.* dermal (skin) tooth.

Hauungsplan, *m.* system of cutting.

Hauzähne, *m.pl.* tusks, fangs.

Hebamme, *f.* midwife.

hebärztlich, obstetric.

Hebe-arm, *m.* lever; **-baum,** *m.* lever, crowbar, pole; **-daumen,** *m.* cam, lifter; **-eisen,** *n.* crowbar.

Hebel, *m.-,* lever; **-arm,** *m.* lever arm; **-kraft,** *f.* leverage; **-waage,** *f.* beam (lever) -scale, ∼ **werk,** *n.* system of levers.

heben, to lift, raise, heave, elevate, further, favor, balance, praise, remove, reduce, cancel; **sich** ∼, to arise, go.

Hebe-pumpe, *f.* lift(ing) pump; **-punkt,** *m.* fulcrum.

Heber, *m.* levator muscle, siphon, elevator. lifter; **-haarrohr,** *n.* capillary siphon.

hebern, to siphon, pipette.

Heber-rohr, *n.* siphon (tube); **-säure-messer,** *m.* hydrometer syringe.

Hebe-vorrichtung, *f.* lifting apparatus, lever; **-werk,** *n.* lifting apparatus, gin, jack; **zeug,** *n.* lifting apparatus, gin, jack.

Hebung, *f.* lifting, heaving (of frost).

hecheln, to hatchel, hackle, comb, criticize.

Hechelzahn, *m.* tooth of a hatchel, prehensile tooth.

Hecht, *m.* pike (fish); **-kopf,** *m.* pike-head (of horses).

Hecke, *f.* hedge, hatch(ing), brood, copse.

Hecken-kirsche, *f.* fly honeysuckle (*Lonicera xylosteum*); **-pflanze,** *f.* hedge plant; **-rose,** *f.* dog rose (*Rosa canina*).

Hede, *f.* tow.

Hederich, *m.* hedge mustard (*Erysimum cheiranthoides*), ground ivy.

Heer, *n.* -e, army, host, troops; **-strasse,** *f.* highway, military road.

Hefe, *f.* yeast, barm, dregs, sediment; **-apparat,** *m.* yeast propagator; **-art,** *f.* variety of yeast; **-gabe,** *f.* quantity of yeast for a pitching; **-geben,** *n.* adding yeast to the wort, pitching.

hefen-ähnlich, yeastlike, yeasty; **-enzym,** *n.* enzyme of yeast; **-extract,** *m.* yeast extract; **-pflanze,** *f.* yeast plant; **-pilz,** *m.* yeast fungus; **-pulver,** *n.* baking powder; **-rüb,** yeasty, muddy.

Hefe-nukleinsäure, *f.* nucleic acid of yeast; **-pilz,** *m.* yeast fungus; **-reinzucht,** *f.*

pure culture of yeast; **-sprossung,** *f.* yeastlike budding; **-suspension,** *f.* suspension of yeast; **-wanne,** *f.* yeast trough; **-zelle,** *f.* yeast cell.

hefig, yeasty, yeastlike.

Heft, *n.*-e, part, number (of periodical), exercise book, stitched book, handle, hilt.

heften, to fasten, attach, hook, fix, stitch, sew; **geheftet,** in sheets (stitched, but not bound).

heftig, violent, severe, fierce, vigorous, intense, brisk, strong, rough.

Heftigkeit, *f.* violence, intensity, hastiness, ardor.

Heftniet, *n.* stitch rivet.

Heftpflaster, *n.* adhesive plaster.

heftweise, in numbers, serially.

hegen, to enclose, preserve, fence, cherish, fasten, entertain, feel, shelter, protect.

Hegenwisch, *m.* truss of straw, wisp.

Hegezeit, *f.* close time, closed season.

Hehl, *n.* secrecy.

hehlen, to conceal.

hehr, sublime, high, lofty.

Heide, *m.* heathen, pagan.

Heide, *f.* heath, heather; **-ähnlich,** ericaceous; **-blättrig,** ericaceous; **-erde,** *f.* heath soil; **-korn,** *n.* buckwheat (*Polygonum fagopyrum*); **-kraut,** *n.* heather, heath (Erica), ling (Calluna); **-krautgewächse,** *n.pl.* Ericaceae.

Heidelbeere, *f.* whortleberry, blueberry, bilberry (*Vaccinium myrtillus*).

Heide-moor, *n.* heath moor; **-plagge,** *f.* sod of heath; **-torf,** *m.* peat, heath, raw humus; **-wald,** *m.* thin forest on heath.

Heidschuncke, *f.* sheep kept on heaths.

heikel, delicate, particular, critical.

heil, whole, safe and sound, restored, cured.

Heil, *n.* welfare, happiness, safety, luck, hail! **-anstalt,** *f.* hospital, sanatorium.

heilbar, curable.

Heil-brunnen, *m.* mineral spring; **-butt,** *m.* halibut.

heilen, to heal, cure, be cured.

heil-fähig, curable; **-faktor,** *m.* healing factor; **-formel,** *f.* prescription.

heilig, holy, sacred; **-bein,** *n.* sacral bone.

heiligen, to hallow, sanctify; **-harz,** *n.* guaiacum resin; **-holz,** *n.* holy wood, lignum vitae, guaiacum wood; **-stein,** *m.* cuprum aluminatum.

Heil-kraft, *f.*-̈e, curative power; **-kräftig,** medicinal, curative, healing, therapeutic; **-kraut,** *n.* medicinal herb; **-kunde, kunst,** *f.* medical science; **-mittel,** *n.* remedy, medicament; **-mittellehre,** *f.* pharmacology; **-pflanze,** *f.* officinal or medicinal plant.

Heilpflaster, *n.* healing plaster; **englisches** ~, court plaster.

Heil-quelle, *f.* medicinal (mineral) spring; **-salbe,** *f.* healing (salve) ointment.

heilsam, (*dat.*) wholesome, healthy, beneficial.

Heilserum, *n.* curative serum, antitoxin.

Heilung, *f.* cure, recovery, healing.

Heilungsvorgang, *m.* healing process.

Heil-verfahren, *n.* healing process; **-wert,** *m.* therapeutic value; **-wesen,** *n.* medical affairs; **-wirkung,** *f.* curative effect; **-wissenschaft,** *f.* medical science.

Heim, *n.* home, dwelling.

Heimat, *f.* native place or country.

Heimchen, *n.* (house) cricket.

Heimfinden, *n.* homing instinct (of bees), finding the way home.

heimisch, native, indigenous, domestic.

Heimkehrfähigkeit, *f.* homing instinct, ability to find the way home.

heimlich, secret, concealed, private.

heimsuchen, to infest (haunt) or overrun a place.

heimtückisch, malicious, treacherous.

heimzahlen, to repay, refund, pay back.

Heirat, *f.* marriage, match.

heiraten, to marry, wed.

heischen, to demand, request, require.

heiser, hoarse, husky.

heiss, hot, torrid, ardent, burning, passionate; **-blütig,** warm-blooded, hot-tempered; **-brüchig,** hot-short; **-dampf,** *m.* superheated (hot) steam.

Heisse, *f.* charge of pig (in smelting).

heissen, to call, bid, order, be called, mean, be, signify; **das heisst,** that is; **es heisst,** it says, they say, it is said, it is reported; **ich heisse,** my name is.

heissgar, too hot, kishy.

Heiss-kühlung, *f.* cooling by evaporation; **-laufen,** to (over)heat.

Heissluft, *f.*-̈e, hot air; **-beize,** *f.* hot-air treatment; **-trichter,** *m.* hot-air funnel; **-trocknung,** *f.* hot-air drying.

Heisswasser-behälter, *m.* hot-water container; **-beize,** *f.* hot-water treatment; **-heizung,** *f.* hot-water heating; **-trichter,** *m.* hot-water funnel.

Heisswerden, *n.* becoming hot, heating.

Heister, *m.* sapling, young tree, young beech.

heiter, serene, clear, fair, cheerful, bright, merry.

Heiz-apparat, *m.*-e, heating apparatus; **-bar,** easily heated; **-draht,** *m.* heating wire (filament).

Heize, *f.* charge of pig (in smelting).

Heizeffekt, *m.* heating effect.

heizen, to heat, fire.

Heizer, *m.* fireman, stoker, heater.

Heiz-faden, *m.* heating filament; **-fähigkeit,** *f.* heating capacity; **-fläche,** *f.* heating surface; **-flächenbelastung,** *f.* heat transferred per unit surface; **-gas,** *n.* fuel gas; **-kessel,** *m.* kettle, boiler; **-körper,** *m.* heating element, heater, radiator; **-kraft,** *f.* fuel value, heating power; **-kranz,** *m.* ring burner; **-loch,** *n.* fire door, stokehole.

Heiz-mantel, *m.* heating jacket; **-material,** *n.* fuel; **-mittel,** *n.* heating medium; **-oberfläche,** *f.* heating surface; **-öl,** *n.* fuel oil; **-platte,** *f.* hot plate; **-raum,** *m.* heating chamber, fire place; **-rohr,** *n.* heating tube, fire tube; **-röhre,** *f.* heating tube, fire tube; **-röhrenkessel,** *m.* fire-tube boiler.

Heiz-schlange, *f.* heating coil; **-schrank,** *m.* oven, heating chamber; **-stoff,** *m.* fuel; **-tisch,** *m.* heating stage.

Heizung, *f.* heating, firing, fuel.

Heizungs-anlage, *f.* heating plant; **-vorrichtung,** *f.* heating (apparatus) contrivance.

Heiz-verlust, *m.* loss of heat; **-vorrichtung,** *f.* heating apparatus.

Heizwert, *m.*-e, heating (calorific) value; **-bestimmung,** *f.* determination of calorific value; **-untersuchung,** *f.* calorimetric investigation.

Heiz-wirkung, *f.* heating effect; **-zug,** *m.* heating flue; **-zweck,** *m.* heating purpose.

Hektar, *m.&n.* hectare (2.47 English acres).

Hektoliter, *m.* hectoliter (22 gallons).

Held, *m.* hero.

helfen, (*dat.*) to help or assist, aid, promote, be of use; **da ist nicht zu** ~, nothing can be done about that; **es hilft nichts,** it does no good.

Helfer, *m.* -, helper, assistant.

Helio-echtrot, *n.* sunfast red; **-farbstoff**, *m.* helio coloring matter.

Helium-entwicklung, *f.* production of helium; **-gehalt**, *m.* helium content; **-kanalstrahl**, *m.* helium-canal ray; **-kern**, *m.* helium nucleus.

hell, bright, clear, brilliant, light, pale, transparent, pellucid, loud, shrill.

hellblau, light blue; **-grün**, light bluish-green.

Helle, *f.* brightness, transparency, luminosity, clearness.

hellen, to (make) clear, clarify, elucidate.

Heller, *m.* heller, (half a) farthing, mite.

hell-farbig, light-colored; **-feldbeleuchtung**, *f.* bright-field illumination; **-gelb**, light yellow, straw-colored; **-grün**, light green.

Helligkeit, *f.* brightness, light intensity.

Helligkeits-sehen, *n.* brightness vision; **-unterschiede**, *m.pl.* variations in the light intensity; **-wert**, *m.* degree of brightness.

hellmatt, semidull, slightly dulled.

Hell-rotglut, *f.* bright red heat; **-tran**, *m.* a clear, light-yellow cod oil; **-weiss**, clear (bright) white.

Helm, *m.* helmet, casque; **-kolben**, *m.* distilling flask; **-rohr**, *n.* **-schnabel**, *m.* beak nose of a still.

Hemalbogen (oberer), *m.* neural spine; ∼ (unterer), *m.* hemal spine.

Hemd, *n.*-e, shirt, chemise, linen.

Hemieder, *n.* hemihedron, hemihedral form.

hemiedrisch, hemihedral.

Hemimellitsäure, *f.* hemimellitic acid.

Hemisphäre, *f.* hemisphere.

Hemisphärenwand, *f.* wall of the hemispheres.

hemitrop, hemitrope.

hemmen, to stop, check, arrest, obstruct, curb, clog, hinder, retard, lag, inhibit.

Hemmnis, *n.*-se, obstruction, check, impediment, obstacle.

Hemmung, *f.* stopping hindrance, retardation, restraint, inhibition, arrest, suppression, contraction.

Hemmungs-band, *n.* check ligament; **-bildung**, *f.* hypoplasia, arrested development, structural defect, malformation; **-körper**, *m.* retarding substance (body); **-umkehr**, *f.* reversal in inhibition.

Hengst, *m.* stallion, jack(ass).

Henkel, *m.* handle, lug, ear; **-schale**, *f.* casserole.

Henne, *f.* hen.

Hennenfiedrigkeit, *f.* hen-feathering.

hepatisch, hepatic.

Heptanaphten, *n.* heptanaphthene.

her, here, hither, since, ago; **hin und** ∼, to and fro; **von je** ∼, always; **von alters** ∼, of old.

herab, down, downward, down here; **-drücken**, to press down, depress; **-drücker**, *m.* depressor muscle; **-fliessen**, to flow down, run down; **-gehen**, to extend downward; **-hängend**, pendent, hanging down; **-lassen**, to let down; **-laufend**, decurrent, running down.

herab-mindern, to diminish, decrease, reduce; **-rieseln**, to trickle down; **-senken**, to lower; **-setzen**, to reduce, decrease, minimize, abate, degrade, disparage, lower; **-setzung**, *f.* lowering, decrease, reduction, degradation, undervaluation; **-sinken**, to drop, fall; **-steigen**, to descend; **-transformieren**, to step down.

heran, on, up, near, along(side); **-bilden**, to bring up, educate.

heranmachen, sich ∼ **an**, to undertake.

heran-nahen, to approach; **-treten**, to confront, approach; **-wachsen**, to grow up; **-ziehen**, to draw near or on, attract, call upon, refer to, use, bring up, bring into play, educate, consult; **-zieher**, *m.* adductor muscle.

Heranziehung, *f.* drawing in; **in** ∼ **von**, in cooperation with.

herauf, up here, up to(ward); **-ziehen**, to draw up.

heraus, out, out there, forth; **-arbeiten**, to form, modulate, work out; **-bekommen**, to find out, get back or out, elicit, solve, receive, arrive at; **-bilden**, to develop; **-bildung**, *f.* formation, evolution; **-bringen**, to get, or put out, turn out, drawn out, make out; **-drängen**, to drive out; **-fahren**, to pass out; **-finden**, to find out, discover; **-fordern**, to challenge, provoke, defy.

Heraus-gabe, *f.* editing, edition, bringing out, publication, issue, giving up; **-geben**, to edit, publish, give out, give back; **-geber**, *m.* publisher, editor; **-greifen**, to single (pick) out, choose; **-klopfen**, to beat out; **-kommen**, to come out, get out, be published, result, issue; **-lösen**, to dissolve out; **-nehmbar**, removable; **-nehmen, sich**, to presume, usurp; **-ragen**, to project.

heraus-rauschen, to rush out (suddenly); **-rücken,** to move out; **-schälen,** to sift, pick out, shell; **-schalten,** to sift; **-schlagen,** to beat out, strike from, obtain; **-schwemmen,** to wash out; **-stellen,** to come out, turn out, prove; **-treiben,** to drive out, expel; **-treten,** to protrude, emerge, retire, step out; **-wachsen,** to sprout (shoot) out, grow out; **-ziehen,** to draw out, extract.

herb, harsh, sharp, tart, acid, rough, scour, raw.

herbei, here, hither, near, on; **-führen,** to bring on or about, cause, produce, involve; **-rufen,** to call in; **-schaffen,** to bring up, find, collect, procure, furnish, raise.

Herberge, *f.* shelter, inn.

herblich, somewhat harsh or tart.

Herbst, *m.* autumn; **-färbung,** *f.* autumn colors, autumnal tints; **-furche,** *f.* fall plowing; **-holz,** *n.* late wood, summer wood; **-laubfall,** *m.* autumnal leaf fall; **-löwenzahn,** *n.* fall dandelion; **-mauser,** *f.* molt(ing); **-pflanzung,** *f.* fall planting; **-rose,** *f.* hollyhock; **-zeitlose,** *f.* meadow saffron (Colchicum).

Herd, *m.* heath, fireplace, home, center, focus, seat, smelting chamber, decay; **-asche,** *f.* hearth ashes.

Herdbuch, *n.* herdbook.

Herde, *f.* herd, flock, multitude, drove, crowd.

Herd-formerei, *f.* open-sand molding; **-frischeisen,** *n.* hearth-refined iron; **-frischen,** *n.* hearth refining; **-frischprozess,** *m.* refinery process; **-frischroheisen,** *n.* pig iron for refining; **-glas,** *n.* glass that has run down into the hearth; **-guss,** *m.* open-sand casting; **-mauer,** *f.* cutoff wall; **-ofen,** *m.* hearth furnace; **-raum,** *m.* heating chamber; **-stahl,** *m.* fined steel.

herein, in(to), come in; **-bringen,** to harvest, gather (in); **-treten,** to step in; **-ziehen,** to draw in.

herführen, to conduct here, lead on, usher in.

Hergang, *m.* course of events, affair, circumstances, proceedings.

hergeben, to deliver, yield, surrender.

hergebracht (herbringen), established, conventional, traditional.

herhalten, to hold out, suffer, submit to, pay, serve as a makeshift.

Hering, *m.* herring.

Herings-könig, *m.* John Dory; **-öl,** *n.*, **-tran,** *m.* herring oil.

herkommen, to come (here), come on, originate, descend from, be derived.

Herkommen, *n.* origin, descent, extraction, usage, custom.

herkömmlich, customary, usual, traditional.

Herkunft, *f.* ̈e, arrival, origin, source, derivation.

Herkunfts-kontrolle, *f.* checking the origin or source; **-ort,** *m.* place of origin.

herleiten, to derive, deduce, lead from, conduct; **sich ∼ von,** to be derived from.

Hermelin, *n.* ermine.

Hermesfinger, *m.* hermodactyl.

hermetisch, hermetic.

hernach, after(ward), thereafter, then.

Herr, *m.* master, lord, ruler, gentleman, Mr.

herrechnen, to enumerate.

Herrenpilz, *n.* eatable mushroom.

herrichten, to arrange, prepare.

herrlich, magnificent, delicious, grand, excellent, glorious.

Herrlichkeit, *f.* grandeur, magnificence, splendor, excellence.

Herrschaft, *f.* control, power, domain, employer, master.

herrschen, to rule, reign, prevail, dominate.

herrschend, dominant, prevailing, ruling.

Herrscher, *m.* ruler, governor, prince, monarch.

herrühren, to proceed, result from, be due (to), come (from), be derived from.

hersagen, to recite, repeat.

herschieben, to shove this way.

herstammen, to descend from, develop out of.

herstellbar, capable of being produced, feasible, mendable, curable.

herstellen, to produce, prepare, make, manufacture, restore, cure; **wieder ∼,** restore.

Hersteller, *m.* maker, producer, manufacturer.

Herstellung, *f.* production, manufacture, restoration, preparation.

Herstellungs-mittel, *n.* restorative; **-preis,** *m.* cost or price of production; **-verfahren,** *n.* method of production; **-vorschrift,** *f.* recipe, prescription.

herüber, this way, over (here); **-bringen,** to bring over or across.

herum, around, about; **-drehen,** to turn around, misconstrue; **-legen,** to place about; **-schweifen,** to wander about, rove; **-tasten,** to grope about; **-treiben,** to prowl about, drive around.

herunter, down (here), low, straight down, **-drücken,** to lower, depress; **-kommen,** to come down, fall off, decay; **-lassen,** to let down, drop, lower; **-schwemmen,** to wash down; **-setzen,** to reduce, undervalue, depreciate; **-trocknen,** to reduce by drying.

hervor, forth, forward, out, from under; **-brechen,** to break out, come forth, appear; **-bringen,** to bring forth, yield, produce, create, cause, effect; **-bringung,** *f.* production.

hervorgehen, to (a)rise, result, go forth, follow, come forth, issue, proceed; **es geht daraus hervor,** hence it follows.

hervor-heben, to bring into prominence, emphasize, display; **-kommen,** to come out of; **-ragen,** to project, stand out, be prominent; **-ragend,** protruding, outstanding, excellent, prominent; **-ragung,** *f.* protuberance, promontory; **-rufen,** to call forth, bring about, develop, occasion, produce, cause.

hervor-schiessen, to shoot up, come forth, appear suddenly; **-springen,** to project; **-stehend,** prominent, projecting, outstanding; **-strecken,** to extend, stretch forth; **-stürzen,** to rush forward; **-treten,** to step forward, be prominent, appear; **-tun, sich,** to distinguish oneself; **-wachsen,** to grow out; **-wölbung,** *f.* prominence, swelling.

Herz, *n.*-**en,** heart, core, kernel, bosom, center, heartwood; **-ader,** *f.* coronary vein; **-balken,** *m.* trabecula cordis, columna cornea; **-bein,** *n.* sternum, os cordis; **-beutel,** *m.* pericardium; **-beutelgegend,** *f.* pericardial region; **-beutelhöhle,** *f.* pericardial cavity.

Herz-blatt, *n.* young, unopened leaf bud, diaphragm, sternum (*Parnassia palustris*); **äusseres** ∼, parietal layer of pericardium; **inneres** ∼, visceral pericardium.

herz-blätterig, cordate; **-bräune,** *f.* angina pectoris; **-bündel,** *n.* pericardium.

Herzensgüte, *f.* kindness of heart.

Herz-excenter, *m.* heart cam; **-fäule,** *f.* heart rot; **-fehler,** *f.* heart disease; **-fell,** *n.* pericardium; **-förmig,** heart-shaped, cordate; **-geflecht,** *n.* cardiac plexus; **-gegend,** *f.* cardiac region; **-gekröse,** *n.* cardiac mesentery, mesocardium; **-ge-**

spann, *n.* motherwort (*Leonurus cardiaca*); **-gift,** *n.* cardiac poison; **-grube,** *f.* pit of the stomach, epigastrium.

herzhaft, hearty, brave, valiant, strong, bold, audacious.

Herz-hälfte, *f.* half or side of the heart; **-haut,** *f.* (äussere), pericardium, (innere), endocardium; **-höhle,** *f.* cavity of the heart.

herzig, hearty, dear, lovely, sweet.

Herz-kammer, *f.* ventricle of the heart; **-kammerscheidewand,** *f.* ventricular septum; **-kappe,** *f.* covering of the heart; **-klappe,** *f.* valve of the heart; **-klappenentzündung,** *f.* endocardite; **-klopfen,** *n.* palpitation of the heart; **-knorpel,** *m.* sternum, sternal cartilage; **-kurve,** *f.* cardioid; **-läppchen,** *n.* auricular appendage; **-leiden,** *n.* heart disease; **-leistung,** *f.* cardiac activity.

herzlich, cordial, heartfelt, sincere, true, loving, tender, heartily, extremely, very.

Herz-mittel, *n.* cardiac remedy; **-mündung,** *f.* caridac orifice; **-muschel,** *f.* cockle (*Cardium edule*); **-muskel,** *m.* cardiac muscle; **-muskelentzündung,** *f.* endocardite; **-nebenkammer,** *f.* cardiac auricle; **-nocken,** *m.* heart cam; **-oberfläche,** *f.* cardiac surface; **-ohr,** *n.* auricle of the heart; **-platte,** *f.* heart plate.

Herz-reiz, *m.* cardiac stimulant or irritant; **-sack,** *m.* pericardium; **-scheidewand,** *f.* cardiac septum; **-schlag,** *m.* heart beat, cardiac paralysis; **-schlagvolumen,** *n.* cardiac output; **-schleife,** *f.* cardiac loop, **-spitze,** *f.* apex of heart; **-stillstand,** *m.* heart failure, perisystole; **-stück,** *n.* center piece, crossing frog; **-tätigkeit,** *f.* action of the heart, heart beat.

herzu, here, hither, near.

Herz-ventil, *n.* heart valve; **-vorhof,** *m.* auricle; **-vorhofskammerklappe,** *f.* auriculoventricular valve; **-vorhofswand,** *f.* auricular wall; **-vorkammer,** *f.* auricle; **-wasser,** *n.* pericardial fluid; **-wulst,** *f.* heart swelling; **-wurzel,** *f.* taproot, main root, primary root; **-zentrum,** *n.* center of the heart.

Hessenfliege, *f.* Hessian fly.

hetero-atomig, heteratomic; **-cyclisch,** heterocyclic.

heterogametisch, digametic.

heterogen, heterogeneous.

heterogene, ∼ **Befruchtung,** *f.* cross-fertilization; ∼ **Bestäubung,** *f.* cross-pollination; ∼ **Zeugung,** *f.* heterogenesis.

Hetero-genesis, *f.* heterogenesis; **-genität,** *f.* heterogeneity; **-log,** heterologous; **-plastisch,** heteroplastic; **-spor,** heterospore; **-zygote,** *f.* heterozygote; **-zygotisch,** heterozygous; **-zyklus,** *m.* heterocycle.

Hetze, *f.* hurry, hunt (with dogs).

hetzen, to chase, egg on.

Heu, *n.* hay; **-bazillengruppe,** *f.* hay-bacillus group; **-bazillus,** *m.* hay bacillus.

heuen, to make hay.

heuer, this year, at this time, now.

heuern, to hire, rent, charter.

Heuerzeugung, *f.* production of hay.

Heuinfus, *m.* hay infusion.

heulen, to howl, yell, roar.

Heupferd, *n.* grasshopper.

heurig, current, this year's.

Heu-schrecke, *f.* locust, grasshopper; **-schreckenbaum,** *m.* locust (tree).

heute, today; ~ **morgen,** this morning; ~**nacht,** tonight.

heutig, of today, present, actual, modern.

heutigestags, nowadays, at the present time.

heutzutage, at present, nowadays.

Heuwender, *m.* hay tedder.

Heveabaum, *m.* hevea tree, rubber tree.

hexa-cyclisch, -zyklisch, hexacyclic.

Hexaeder, *n.* hexahedron.

hexagonal, hexagonal.

Hexahydro-benzol, *n.* hexahydrobenzene; **-pyridin,** *n.* piperidine, hexahydropyridine.

Hexe, *f.* witch, hag.

Hexen-besen, *m.* witch's broom; **-kraut,** *n.* enchanter's nightshade (*Circaea*); **-mehl,** *n.* lycopodium; **-meister,** *m.* sorcerer, wizard; **-pulver,** *n.* lycopodium; **-schuss,** *m.* lumbago.

Hexogen, *n.* trimethylenetrinitroamine (T₄).

Hexonsäure, *f.* hexonic acid.

Hexose, *f.* hexose.

Hibernakel, *m.* hibernacle, winterbud.

hieb (hauen), struck, chopped, cut.

Hieb, *m.***-e,** stroke, cut(ting), slash(ing), felling.

hiebei (hierbei), hereby, herewith.

Hiebs-ergebnis, *n.* result of felling; **-fläche,** *f.* cutting area; **-folge,** *f.* succession of cut-

tings; **-führung,** *f.* management (system) of cuttings; **-plan,** *m.* plan of cuttings, **-reif,** ripe for the ax; **-satz,** *m.* yield; annual cut; **-zug,** *m.* cutting series.

hielt (halten), held.

hier, here; **-an,** hereon, hereat, at this; **-auf,** hereupon, upon this; **-aus,** from this, hence; **-bei,** hereby, herewith, hereat, during (this process), in so doing; **-durch,** through here, by this means, due to this, hereby; **-ein,** in this, herein.

hier-für, for this, for it; **-her,** hither, here; **-hin,** hither, this way; **-in,** herein, in this, inside; **-mit,** herewith, with it; **-nach,** hereafter, after this, according to this.

Hiersein, *n.* presence, being here.

hier-über, about this, over here, regarding this, on this account; **-um,** around this, hereabout, concerning this; **-von,** from this; **-zu,** hereto, to this, moreover, in addition to this.

hiesig, in or of this place, local, native, indigenous.

hiess (heissen), was called, called.

Hilfe, *f.* help, assistance, aid, relief, support, remedy, accessory, auxiliary.

hilf-los, helpless; **-reich,** helpful.

Hilfs-ameise, *f.* worker ant, ant slave; **-apparate,** *m.pl.* accessories; **-arbeiter,** *m.* assistant, helper; **-band,** *n.* accessory ligament; **-beize,** *f.* auxiliary mordant; **-betrieb,** *m.* auxiliary department, sideline; **-dünger,** *m.* auxiliary fertilizer; **-einrichtung,** *f.* auxiliary arrangement; **-fortsatz,** *m.* accessory process; **-geld,** *n.* subsidy.

Hilfs-grösse, *f.* auxiliary or subsidy quantity; **-ladung,** *f.* auxiliary charge; **-leitung,** *f.* auxiliary line, conduit; **-loben,** *f.pl.* accessory lobes; **-massnahmen treffen,** to take first-aid measures, give first aid; **-mittel,** *n.* help, aid, expedient, adjuvant remedy, instrument; **-quelle,** *f.* resource, expedient; **-stativ,** *n.* auxiliary stand; **-stoff,** *m.* adjuvant substance, accessory material; **-teilung,** *f.* auxiliary graduation.

Hilfs-vorrichtung, *f.* auxiliary contrivance or device; **-werkzeug,** *n.* accessory organ; **-winkel,** *m.* auxiliary angle.

Himbeer-äther, *m.* **-essig,** *m.* raspberry (ether) essence; **-käfer,** *m. pl.* Byturidae; **-spat,** *m.* rhodochrosite; **-strauch,** *m.* raspberry bush.

Himbeere, *f.* raspberry.

Himmel, *m.* sky, heaven, canopy; **-blau,** sky-blue, azure, ultramarine blue; **-blau,** *n.* cerulean blue.

Himmels-bedeckung, *f.* cloudiness; **-brot,** *n.* manna; **-gegend,** *f.* quarter of the heavens; **-gerste,** *f.* naked barley; **-korn,** *n.* naked barley; **-körper,** *m.* celestial body; **-kunde,** *f.* astronomy; **-leitergewächse,** *n.pl.* Polemoniaceae; **-luft,** *f.* ether; **-mehl,** *n.* earthy gypsum; **-schlüssel,** *m.* primrose (*Primula vulgaris*); **-strich,** *m.* zone, latitude, climate, region.

himmlisch, heavenly, celestial.

hin, there, thither, away, hence, out, along, gone, lost, ruined, exhausted, toward; ∼ **und her,** hither and thither, to and fro, back and forth; ∼ **und zurück,** there and back, ∼ **und wieder,** now and again; **es ist noch lange,** ∼, it is a long time yet.

Hin-und-Herbewegung, *f.* back-and-forth movement.

hin und hergebogen, retroflexed, bent back and forth.

hin und hergehen, to reciprocate, go back and forth.

hinab, down there, downward(s); **-drücken,** to press down; **-steigen,** to descend; **-ziehen,** to extend down.

hinauf, up, up to; **bis** ∼, up to.

hinauf-heben, to lift up; **-setzen,** to set up, put up; **-transformieren,** to step up voltage.

hinaus, out, beyond.

hinausgehen, to go out; **darüber** ∼, to exceed, go beyond.

hinausgelangen, to reach, arrive; **über etwas** ∼, to get beyond.

hinauslaufen, to run (come) out; ∼ **auf,** to amount to.

hinaus-ragen, to project out; **-schieben,** to push out, to expel; **-schiessen,** to shoot beyond, exceed; **-waschen,** to wash out.

Hinblick, *m.* glance, look, view, regard, consideration; **in** ∼ **auf,** in regard to.

hinbringen, to bring, take, carry, pass or spend (time).

hinderlich, obstructive, troublesome.

hindern, to prevent, hinder, stop.

Hindernis, *n.*-se, hindrance, barrier, obstacle; **-methode,** *f.* obstruction method.

Hinderung, *f.* hindrance, prevention.

hindeuten, to point at or to.

Hindin, *f.* hind, doe.

hindurch, through(out); **lange Zeit** ∼, for a long time.

hindurch-dringen, to penetrate; **-fallen,** to pass (travel) through; **-leiten,** to lead through; **-saugen,** to suck through.

hinein, in, inside, into; **-beziehen,** to draw in, incorporate, include; **-bringen,** to bring in; **-dringen,** to penetrate; **-erstrecken** (sich), to extend into; **-gelangen,** to get in, enter; **-geraten,** to get in, enter; **-ragen,** to project into, extend into, stick into, be embedded in; **-verlegen,** to place into, project; **-ziehen,** to pull in, drag in, implicate, involve.

hinfahren, to go, drive along, pass away, depart.

hinfällig, decaying, declining, perishable, feeble, deciduous, weak.

hinfliessen, to flow toward.

hinfort, henceforth.

hing (hängen), hung.

Hingabe, *f.* devotion.

hingeben, to give up, surrender, abandon.

Hingebung, *f.* devotion, surrender.

hingegen, on the contrary, but, whereas.

hingehen, to go there, pass, proceed.

hingehören, to belong to.

hingewiesen, pointed to.

hingleiten, to glide along.

hinhalten, to hold out, put off, hold off, present.

hinhören, to listen, hark, attend.

hinken, to limp, go lame, be imperfect.

hinkommen, to come there, arrive; **wo sind . . . hingekommen,** what has become of . . . .

hinlangen, to arrive at, get to.

hinlänglich, sufficient, adequate.

hinleiten, hinlenken, to lead or conduct to.

hinnehmen, to accept, submit to.

hinreichen, to suffice, do, stretch out.

hinreichend, sufficient.

hinreissen, to tear away, be carried away.

hinreissend, enchanting, charming.

hinrichten, to turn, direct, execute, ruin, spoil.

hinschreiben, to write (down).

hinsehen, to look watch.

Hinsicht, *f.* respect, consideration, regard, reference, view.

hinsichtlich, with regard to.

hinstellen, to place or put, bring forward, set down, state, set forth.

hintan, behind, aside, after, back.

hinten, behind, after, in the rear, at the back; nach ~, backwards; von ~ her, from behind.

hinter, behind, after, back; -ader, *f.* anal vein; -afterpapillen, *f.pl.* postanal papillae; -ansicht, *f.* rear view; -antenne, *f.* second antenna; -backe, *f.* buttock; -backenzahn, *m.* hind molar, hind grinder; bein, *n.* hind leg; -bleiben, to remain behind, survive; -bliebene, *m.&f.* survivor.

hinter-bringen, to give information of, inform of, pack away; -burst, *f.* metathorax, metasternum; -bruststück, *n.* metasternum; bug, *n.* popliteal space; -damm, *m.* posterior perineum; -darm, *m.* rectum.

hintere Hauptader, *f.* cubitus.

hintereinander, one after another, in succession, running, in series; -schalten, to connect in series.

Hinter-ende, *n.* posterior end; -feld, *n.* anal field; -ferse, *f.* hind tarsus; -fläche, *f.* posterior surface; -flügel, *n.* hind wing, posterior wing; -fühler, *m.* antenna, antennules, second antenna; -fuss, *m.* hind leg, posterior part of foot.

Hinter-glied, *n.* posterior member; -gliedmasse, *f.* posterior limb; -grund, *m.* background; -halt, *m.* ambush, reserve; -hand, *f.* metacarpus; -handmuskulatur, *f.* muscles of the pelvic limb; -haupt, *m.* occiput.

Hinterhaupts-bein, *n.* occipital bone; -beinvorsprung, *m.* occipital protuberance; -blutleiter, *m.* occipital sinus; -bogen, *m.* curve of occipital bone; -dreieck, *n.* occipital triangle, cuneus, small triangular area of the vertex; -gegend, *f.* occipital region; -gelenk, *n.* atlo-occipital articulation; -kamm, *m.* occipital crest.

Hinterhaupts-lappen, *m.* occipital lobe; -loch, *n.* occipital foramen; -naht, *f.* occipital suture; -schild, *m.* occipital bone; -schläfengrube, *f.* occipitotemporal sulcus; -stachel, *m.* occipital spine; -windung, *f.* occipital convolution; -wirbel, *m.* occipital vertebra.

hinterher, behind, in the rear, after(ward).

Hinter-hirn, *n.* hind brain; -hof, *m.* inner cavity of stomate; -horn, *n.* posterior horn; -kiefer, *m.* labium, second maxilla; -kiemer, *m.pl.* Opisthobranchiata; -kinnbacken, *m.* posterior jaw; -kopf, *m.* occiput; -lappen, *m.* posterior lobe.

hinter-lassen, to leave (behind), bequeath; -legen, to deposit; -leib, *m.* abdomen, dorsum, back of body.

Hinterleibs-borste, *f.* abdominal bristle; -ring, *m.* abdominal segment; -schild, *m.* abdominal tergite.

Hinter-licht, *n.* light from behind; -metatarsus, *m.* metatarsus of hind leg; -rand, *m.* posterior margin; -rippe, *f.* cubitus; -rücken, *m.* metanotum, lower back; -schenkel, *m.* thigh.

Hinter-schildchen, *n.* postscutellum; -schuppe, *f.* supraoccipital bone; -schwinge, *f.* secondary remex; -schwingen, *f. pl.* secondary remiges; -seite, *f.* rear side; -spalte, *f.* posterior cleft.

hinterst, hindmost, last.

Hinter-stirnbein, *n.* postfrontal bone; -strang, *m.* hind trace, funiculus posterior; -stück, *n.* posterior segment; -teil, *m.* posterior part; -viertel, hindquarter; -wäldler, *m.* backwoodsman; -zelle, *f.* anal cell.

hintumläufig, opisthodomous.

hinüber, over, across, beyond; -blicken, to look across; -reissen, to carry over.

Hinundherbewegung, *f.* oscillating motion.

hinunter, down (there), below, downward(s); -schlucken, to swallow; -setzen, to put down, put below.

Hinweg, *m.* the way there or thither.

hinweg, away, off; -gehen, to pass over; -gleiten, to glide over; -laufen, to run along, extend; -setzen, to put aside, disregard, treat with indifference, ignore, jump over.

Hinweis, *m.*-e, hint, indication, reference.

hinweisen, to refer, indicate, direct, point (to), hint.

hin-welken, to fade away, waste away, wither; -welkend, marcescent.

hinwerfen, to throw (down), jot down or sketch.

hinziehen, to draw or pull toward, delay, draw out, attract.

hinzu, besides, to it, moreover, towards, in addition; -addieren, to add; -fügen, to add; -fügung, *f.* addition; -geben, to add; -giessen, to pour into, add; -kommen, to come up to, be added; -kommend, additional, accessory, adventitious; -nahme, *f.* combination, inclusion, addition; -schalten, to switch in, turn on.

hinzu-setzen, to add; -strömen, to flow in; -träufeln, to add by dropping; -treten, to join, be added, supervene; **-tritt,** *m.* approach, accession; **-tropfen,** to add by dropping; **-tun,** to add.

Hiobstränen, *f.pl.* Job's tears (*Colix lachryma*).

Hippursäure, *f.* hippuric acid.

Hirn, *n.* brain; **-abschnitt,** *m.* brain section.

Hirnanhang, *m.* pituitary body or gland; **-drüse,** *f.* hypophysis, pituitary gland; **-saft,** *m.* secretion of the hypophysis.

Hirn-balken, *m.* corpus callosum; **-blase,** *f.* cerebral vesicle; **-blutleiter,** *m.* cerebral sinus; **-brücke,** *f.* pons Varolii; **-deckel,** *m.* cranium; **-falte,** *f.* cephalic or cerebral lobe; **-felle,** *n.pl.* meninges; **-fett,** *n.* cerebrin; **-fläche,** *f.* surface of the brain, end grain, cross section; **-fuss,** *m.* base of the brain.

Hirn-ganglien, *n.pl.* cerebral ganglia; **gewölbe,** *n.* fornix; **-halbkugel,** *f.* cerebral hemisphere; **-haut,** *f.* dura mater, cerebral meninges; **-höhle,** *f.* ventricle of the brain; **-holz,** *n.* cross-cut timber; **-kammer,** *f.* cerebral ventricle; **-kapsel,** *f.* cranium; **-knoten,** *m.* cerebral ganglion, pons Varolii.

Hirn-lappen, *m.* cerebral lobe; **-mark,** *n.* medullary substance of the brain; **-nervenkern,** *m.* nucleus of the branial nerve; **-rautengrube,** *f.* fossa rhomboidalis, fourth ventricle; **-rinde,** *f.* cerebral cortex; **-rohr,** *n.* cerebral furrow, cephalic portion of medullary tube; **-rückenmark,** *n.* cerebrospinal medulla.

Hirnschädel, *m.* cranium; **-dach,** *n.* vertex of the skull; **-decke,** *f.* epicranium; **-gewölbe,** *n.* arch of the cranium; **-haut,** *f.* pericranium.

Hirn-säure, *f.* cerebric acid; **-schale,** *f.* cranium; **-schalenhaut,** *f.* pericranium; **-schenkel,** *m.* cerebral peduncle; **-schnitt,** *m.* cross section; **-schwiele,** *f.* corpus callosum; **-sichel,** *f.* falx cerebri; **-spalte,** *f.* cerebral fissure; **-stamm,** *m.* brain stem, cerebral axis; **-stiel,** *m.* cerebral peduncle.

Hirn-stock, *m.* brain stem, peduncle; **-teil,** *m.* brain portion; **-windung,** *f.* cerebral convolution.

Hirsch, *m.* stag, deer, hardwood; **-dorn,** *m.* buckthorn (*Rhamnus catharticus*); **-fänger,** *m.* hanger, cutlass, hunting knife; **-geweihartig,** antler-shaped; **-horn,** *n.* hartshorn; **-hornsalz,** *n.* ammonium carbonate; **-käfer,** *m.pl.* stag beetles (Lucanidae); **-kalb,** *n.* fawn; **-kuh,** *f.* hind, roe; **-leder,** *n.* buckskin; **-zunge,** *f.* hart's-tongue (Scolopendrium).

Hirse, *f.* millet (Panicum); **-fieber,** *n.* miliary fever; **-korn,** *n.* millet seed.

Hirsen-eisenstein, *m.* **-erz,** *n.* oölitic hematite.

Hirt, Hirte, *m.* shepherd, herdsman.

Hirten-tasche, *f.* **-täschchen, -täschel,** *n.* shepherd's-purse (*Capsella bursa-pastoris*).

hissen, to hoist, set (sail).

histogen, congenital.

Histogenese, *f.* histogenesis.

Histologie, *f.* histology.

histologisch, histological.

historisch, historical.

Hitzdraht, *m.* hot wire.

Hitze, *f.* heat, hotness, ardor, fervor, passion; **in der ~ erhärtend,** thermosetting.

Hitze-beständig, heat-resistant, thermostable; **-einwirkung,** *f.* action or influence of heat; **-empfindlich,** sensitive to heat; **-fest,** resistant to heat; **-grad,** *m.* degree of heat; **-härtung,** *f.* baking (resins), thermosetting; **-laubfall,** *m.* leaf drop due to heat; **-messer,** *m.* pyrometer.

hitzen, to heat.

Hitzestrahlung, *f.* heat radiation.

hitzig, hot, heating, hasty, acute, passionate, choleric.

Hitzschlag, *m.* heatstroke.

hob (heben), lifted, raised.

Hobel, *m.* plane.

hobeln, to plane, smooth.

Hobelspäne, *m.pl.* shavings.

hoch, high, tall, intense, bright, deep, great, sublime; **das ist ihm zu ~,** that is too deep for him.

hoch-achten, to esteem highly; **-achtung,** *f.* high(est) regard; **-achtungsvoll,** Yours respectfully; **-ätzung,** *f.* relief engraving; **-bau,** *m.* superstructure; **-bild,** *n.* relief picture; **-bildsam,** highly plastic or flexible; **-blatt,** *n.* hyposophyll, subtending leaf, spath, bract; **-artig,** bracteal; **-region,** *f.* bracteal region; **-stamm,** *m.* thalamus.

hoch-blau, bright blue, light blue, azure; **-druck,** *m.-e,* high pressure, relief printing; **-ebene,** *f.* tableland, plateau; **-email,** *n.* embossed enamel; **-empfindlichkeit,** *f.* greatest sensitiveness; **-entwickelt,** highly developed; **-erhaben,** in high relief, sublime; **-farbig,** highly colored; **-fein,** superfine, very choice; **-flut,** *f.* high tide, boom.

hoch-frequent, highly frequent; -frequenz-strom, m. high-frequency current; -gebirge, n. high mountains; -gebirgspflanze, f. alpine plant; -geehrt, highly honored; -geladen, highly charged; -geschätzt, highly esteemed; -gespannt, at high tension, highly superheated; -glanz, m. high polish, brilliancy; -gradig, in high degree.

hoch-grün, bright green; -herzig, noble-minded; -kante, f. edge; -kantig, on edge, edgewise; -kessel, m. high-pressure boiler; -kette, f. high-twist warp; -konzentriert, highly concentrated; -kultur, f. culture of optimum state; -lage, f. high altitude.

hoch-lagern, to raise, elevate; -leistung, f. high capacity, heavy duty; -molekular, of high molecular weight; -moor, n. high moor, high peat bog; -mütig, haughty, proud, arrogant.

Hochofen, m.-̈, blast furnace; -anlage, f. blast-furnace plant; -betrieb, m. blast-furnace operation; -schlacke, f. blast-furnace slag; -schmelze, f. blast-furnace smelting; -wesen, n. blast-furnace technique.

hoch-prozentig, of high percentage; -ragend, very lofty, procerus, towering; -rot, bright red; -rund, convex; -scharlach, m. cochineal scarlet; -schmelzend, high-melting; -schule, f. a German higher school, college, institute, university (not high school as in U. S. A.); -selig, late, deceased; -siedend, high-boiling; -sommer, m. midsummer.

Hochspannung, f. high tension.

Hochspannungsleitung, f. high-tension line.

höchst, highest, utmost, maximum, extremely, exceedingly, very.

hochstämmig, long-boled, tall.

Hochstauden-flur, f. vegetation of tall perennial herbs; -gesellschaft, f. community of high perennial herbs.

Höchst-belastung, f. maximum duty, peak load; -besetzungszahl, f. maximum number; -betrag, m. maximum amount; -druck, m. maximum pressure; -empfindlich, extremely sensitive.

höchstens, at most, at best.

Höchst-fall, m.-̈e, maximum case; -last, f. maximum load; -leistung, f. maximum output, peak load; -mass, n. greatest measure, maximum; -prozentig, highest percentage; -siedend, highest-boiling; -sommer, m. midsummer; -spannung, f. maximum tension; -standort, m. highest altitude station; -temperatur, f. maximum temperature.

höchstwahrscheinlich, in all probability, most likely.

Höchst-wert, m.-e, maximum value; -zahl, f. highest number.

hoch-trabend, pompous, bombastic; -vakuum, n. low absolute pressure; -vergärend, top-fermenting; -vergärung, top fermentation; -Volt-Röhre, f. high-voltage tube; -wald, m. high forest, seedling forest; -weiss, very white; -wertig, of high value or high valence; -wild, n. large game, deer; -wüchsig, growing tall.

Hochzeit, f.-en, wedding.

Hochzeitsflug, m. nuptial flight.

Hochzucht, f. selection inside a pure line.

Hocke, f. heap of sheaves.

Höcker, m.-, hump, eminence, bump, protuberance, tubercle, huckster.

höckerig, humpy, knotty, knobby, rough, tuberculate, gibbous, nodulated; ~ aufgeblasen, apophysate.

Höcker-kreuzbeinband, n. sacrosciatic ligament; -landschaft, f. hummock growth.

Hode, f. testicle.

Hoden-drüse, f. testicle; -kanälchen, n. seminal canal; -sack, m. scrotum; -sackbruch, m. scrotal (or inguinal) hernia.

Hof, m.-̈e, areola, corona, halo, court, area, estate, yard, farm, aureole.

hoffen, to hope (for).

hoffentlich, it is to be hoped.

Hoffnung, f. hope, expectation.

Hoffnungsstrahl, m. ray of hope.

höflich, polite, civil, courteous.

Hoftüpfel, m. pit; einseitiger ~, half-bordered pit; zweiseitiger ~, full-bordered pit.

Höhe, f. height, altitude, elevation, intensity, amount, summit, latitude, level; in gleicher ~ mit, on the same level with; in der ~, on high; auf der ~, on the summit, zenith, up to date; in die ~, up (ward).

hohe, high.

Hoheit, f. highness, sublimity, greatness.

Höhen-gürtel, m. altitude line; -hochmoor, n. high moor of crests or slopes; -kreis, m. parallel of altitude; -messer, m. hypsometer, altimeter; -region, f. region of altitude; -schichtlinie, f. altitude line; -sonne, f. (künstliche) ultraviolet lamp; -strahlung, f. cosmic radiation; -stufe, f. altitude line; -trieb, m. annual height increment.

Höhen-verstellung, *f.* vertical motion; **-winkel,** *m.* apex, vertical angle, angle of altitude; **-wuchs,** *m.* height growth; **-zug,** *m.* ridge, range; **-zuwachs,** *m.* height increment.

Höhepunkt, *m*-e, high point, peak, climax, altitude.

höher, higher, superior; **-liegend,** more elevated.

hohl, hollow, concave, fistulous; **-ader** *f.* vena cava; **-ausgeschliffen,** hollow ground; **-beil,** *n.* trimming (hollow) ax; **-blutader,***f.* vena cava; **-bohrer,** *m.* hollow auger, hole digger, gimlet, circular spade; **-dotter,** *m. Myagrum perfoliatum;* **-druck,** *m.* cast, fossil imprint; **-drüse,** *f.* follicle.

Höhle, *f.* cave, cavern, hole, den, cavity, ventricle.

höhlen, to hollow, excavate; **-tier,** *n.* cave animal; **-wandung,** *f.* wall of a cavity.

hohl-erhaben, concavo-convex; **-gang,** *m.* fistula, passage, canal; **-geschliffen,** hollow-ground, concave; **-glas,** *n.* hollow glassware, concave glass; **-guss,** *m.* hollow casting.

Hohlhand, *f.* palm; **-band,** *n.* palmar ligament; **-bogen,** *m.* palmar arch; **-fläche,** *f.* palmar surface.

höhlig, containing cavities, cavernous, hollow, honeycombed, porous.

Hohl-keil, *m.* saddle key; **-kugel,** *f.* hollow sphere, ball or shell; **-linse,***f.* concave lens; **-mass,** *n.* measure of capacity; **-nadel,** *f.* hollow needle; **-organ,** *n.* crypt, hollow organ; **-prisma,** *n.* hollow prism; **-raum,** *m.* hollow space, cavity, black body, void, pore space; **-raumschiessen,** *n.* cushioned blasting; **-raum-volumen,** *n.* pore space.

Hohl-rund, concave, **-samig,** coelospermous (hollow seeds); **-schicht,** *f.* air space; **-schuppe,** *f.* scale in throat or corolla; **-sog,** *m.* cavitation (ultrasonics), hollow wake of a ship; **-spat,** *m.* chiastolite; **-spiegel,** *m.* concave mirror; **-stempel,** *m.* matrix; **-tiere,** *n.pl.* Coelenterata.

Höhlung,*f.* cavity, hollow, chamber, fistula, excavation.

Hohl-vene, *f.* vena cava; **-venenloch,** *n.* foramen of vena cava; **-walze,** *f.* cylinder; **-welle,***f.* hollow shaft; **-werden,** to become hollow, decay; **-zahn,** *m.* hemp nettle (Galeopsis); **-zellig,** alveolate; **-ziegel,** *m.* hollow (brick) tile; **-zirkel,** *m.* inside calipers; **-zylinder,** *m.* hollow cylinder.

Hohn, *m.* scorn, disdain.

höhnisch, scornful.

hold, (*dat.*) kind, pleasant, friendly, lovely, pleasing, charming.

Holder, *m.* (Holunder) elder.

holen, to fetch, go for, get, come for; sich etwas ∼, to contract something; ∼ lassen, to send for; da ist nichts zu ∼, there is nothing to be gained there.

Holländer, *m.,* Dutch-man, hollander (engine); **Holländerin,** *f.* Dutchwoman.

holländern, to pulp (in a hollander).

Holländer Weiss, *n.* Dutch white.

holländisch, Dutch; **holländisches Geschirr,** *n.* hollander.

Hölle, *f.* hell.

Höllen-öl, *n.* oil from *Jatropha curcas,* castor oil; **-stein,** *m.* lunar caustic, silver nitrate.

Holm, *m.* spar, hillock, small island.

Holo-eder, *n.* holohedral form; **-edrie,** *f.* holohedrism; **-edrisch,** holohedral.

holp(e)rig, uneven, rough.

Holunder, *m.* elder (*Sambucus canadensis*); **spanischer** ∼, lilac.

Holunder-beere, *f.* elderberry; **-blüte,** *f.* elder blossom; **-kugel,** *f.* elderberry pith ball; **-wein,** *m.* elder(berry) wine.

Holz, *n.*¨er, wood, timber, forest, lumber, thicket, xylem; **-abfall,** *m.* wood waste; **-abfuhr,** *f.* transportation of wood; **-abgabe,** *f.* disposal of wood; **-ader,** *f.* vein in wood; **-ähnlich,** woodlike, ligneous, silvicultural; **-alkohol,** *m.* wood alcohol; **-amiant,** *m.* ligneous asbestos; **-anbau,** *m.* cultivation of forests; **-anweisung,** *f.* marking trees (for cutting).

Holz-apfel, *m.*¨e, crab apple; **-apfelwein,** *m.* crab cider; **-art,** *f.* species of wood; **-artig,** woody, ligneous; **-asbest,** *m.* ligneous asbestos; **-asche,** *f.* wood ashes; **-aschenlauge,***f.* lye (from wood ashes); **-äther,** *m.* methyl ether; **-auszeichnung,** *f.* marking; **-beize,***f.* wood (stain) mordant.

Holz-beizen, *n.* wood staining; **-berechtigung,** *f.* wood right; **-bestand,** *m.* standing crop, stand; **-bewohnend,** wood-inhabiting; **-birne,** *f.* wild pear (*Pirus communis*); **-bock,** *m.* sawing horse, sawing trestle, capricorn beetle; **-boden,** *m.* productive wooded area, wood loft; **-bohrer,** *m.pl.* Cossidae; **-branntwein,** *m.* wood spirit; **-büchse,** *f.* wooden box.

Hölzchen, *n.* splint(er), small piece of wood.

Holz-destillieranlange, *f.* wood-distilling plant; **-element,** *n.* xylem element.

hölzern, wooden, ligneous, clumsy.

Holz-ernte, *f.* wood harvest; **-essig,** *m.* wood vinegar, acetic acid, pyroligneous acid; **-farbig,** of the color of wood; **-faser,** *f.* wood fiber, grain, ligneous fiber; **-faserstoff,** *m.* lignin, cellulose, lignocellulose, wood (fiber) pulp; **-fäule,** *f.* dry rot; **-feuer,** *n.* wood fire; **-frei,** without wood (pulp); **-fresser,** *m.pl.* Xylophagae; **-fuss,** *m.* wooden stand or base.

Holz-geist, *m.* wood spirit, methyl alcohol; **-gestell,** *n.* wooden stand or frame; **-gewächs,** *n.* woody (ligneous) plant; **-gewebe,** *n.* ligneous (woody) tissue, texture of wood; **-griff,** *m.* wooden handle; **-gummi,** *n.* wood (gum) resin; **-haft,** *m.* wooden handle; **-handel,** *m.* timber trade; **-händler,** *m.* lumberman, timber merchant; **-harz,** *n.* wood resin.

Holz-hauer, *m.* woodcutter, lumberer, logger; **-hauergeräte,** *n.pl.* woodcutters' tools; **-hauerhütte,** *f.* logging camp; **-hieb,** *m.* felling, cutting; **-hof,** *m.* woodyard, lumberyard.

holzicht, woody, ligneous.

holzig, woody, ligneous.

Holz-käfer, *m.pl.* Anobiidae, Ptinidae, Lymexylonidae; **-kalk,** *m.* pyrolignite of lime, calcium acetate; **-kassie,** *f. Cassia lignea;* **-kasten,** *m.* wooden box; **-kirsche,** *f.* wild cherry (Cerasus); **-kiste,** *f.* wooden box; **-klotz,** *m.* wood(en) block; **-kohle,** *f.* charcoal.

Holzkohlen-eisen, *n.* charcoal iron; **-klein,** *n.* charcoal dust; **-lösche,** *f.* charcoal dust, small charcoal; **-ofen,** *m.* charcoal oven; **-roheisen,** *n.* charcoal pig iron.

Holz-konservierung, *f.* timber (wood) preservation; **-konservierungsmittel,** *n.* wood preservative.

Holzkörper, *m.* woody tissue, xylem; **geflammter ∼,** rippled or flecked grain of wood.

Holz-kupfer, *n.* wood copper; **-kupfererz,** *n.* wood copper, fibrous olivenite; **-lack,** *m.* stick-lac, wood varnish; **-lager,** *n.* forest depot, woodyard; **-lamelle,** *f.* lignified lamella; **-latte,** *f.* lath of wood, board; **-mangold,** *m.* shinleaf, false wintergreen (Pyrola); **-markstrahl,** *m.* medullary ray in wood; **-markt,** *m.* lumber market; **-masse,** *f.* wood paste, volume of wood, lignolite, xylolite.

Holz-mehl, *n.* wood (flour) powder or meal, sawdust; **-not,** *f.* wood famine; **-nutzung,** *f.* forest cropping; **-öl,** *n.* wood oil; **-ölschleiflack,** *m.* wood-oil rubbing

varnish; **-papier,** *n.* paper from wood pulp; **-pappe,** *f.* wood-pulp board; **-pech,** *n.* wood pitch; **-pflanze,** *f.* woody plant; **-pflaster,** *n.* wood pavement; **-pore,** *f.* xylem vessel (pore).

Holz-reif(en), *m.* wooden ring or hoop; **-rot,** *n.* redwood extract; **-säure,** *f.* pyroligneous acid; **-schlag,** *m.* cutting wood, clearing (in a forest); **-schleifer,** *m.* woodpulp grinder, skidder; **-schliff,** *m.* mechanical wood pulp; **-schnitt,** *m.* wood engraving, woodcut; **-schnitzerei,** *f.* wood carving; **-schutzmittel,** *n.* wood preservative; **-sortierung,** *f.* timber classification.

Holz-span, *m.* wood shaving, chip; **-spiritus,** *m.* wood spirit or alcohol, methyl alcohol; **-stein,** *m.* petrified (fossil) wood; **-stich,** *m.* wood engraving; **-stoff,** *m.* wood pulp, cellulose; **-stoss,** *m.* stack, pile of wood; **-tafel,** *f.* board; **-taube,** *f.* wood pigeon; **-taxe,** *f.* timber royalty; **-tee,** *m.* wood drink.

Holz-teer, *m.* wood tar; **-teeröl,** *n.* wood-tar oil; **-teil,** *m.* xylem; **-trank,** *m.* wood drink; **-tränkung,** *f.* wood (pickling) impregnation; **-trieb,** *m.* unfertile shoot.

Holzung, *f.* (small) wood, felling, cutting; *pl.* felling areas.

Holz-verkohlung, *f.* carbonization of wood; **-ware,** *f.* articles in wood, wooden ware; **-watte,** *f.* wood wool; **-wespen,** *f.pl.* wood wasps (Uroceridae); **-wolle,** *f.* excelsior, wood fiber; **-zellstoff,** *m.* wood pulp, lignocellulose; **-zerstörung,** *f.* wood destruction; **-zeug,** *n.* wood pulp; **-zimt,** *m.* cassia bark.

Holz-zucht, *f.* silviculture, **-züchter,** *m.* silviculturist, forest grower; **-zucker,** *m.* wood sugar, xylose.

Homobrenzcatechin, *n.* homopyrocatechol.

homochrom, of uniform color, homochromous.

homoedrisch, homohedral.

homogametisch, monogametic.

homogen, homogeneous, uniform as to grain size.

homogenisieren, to homogenize.

Homogenität, *f.* homogeneity.

Homokaffeesäure, *f.* homocaffeic acid.

homokline Bestäubung, *f.* autogamy (self-pollination).

homolog, homologous.

Homologie, *f.* homology.

homöomorph, homeomorphous, apparently similar.

homozentrisch, homocentric.

Homozygote, *f.* homozygote, monozygote.

homozygotish, homozygous.

Honig, *m.* honey; **-ähnlich, -artig,** honeylike, melleous; **-biene,** *f.* honeybee; **-blume,** *f.* honeyflower (*Melianthus*); **-drüse,** *f.* nectar gland; **-ertrag,** *m.* yield of honey; **-essig,** *m.* oxymel; **-farbig,** honey-colored; **-gefäss,** *n.*-e, nectary, honey cup; **-geschmack,** *m.* taste of honey.

Honig-gras, *n.* velvet grass (*Holcus lanatus*); **-harnruhr,** *f.* diabetes mellitus; **-klee,** *m.* Melilotus; **-kuchen,** *m.* honeycake, gingerbread; **-lippe,** *f.* labellum; **-pilz,** *m.* honey fungus; **-röhre,** *f.* honey tube, siphuncle; **-saft,** *m.*-e, nectar; **-säure,** *f.* oxymel; **-scheibe,** *f.* honeycomb.

Honig-seim, *m.* liquid honey; **-stein,** *m.* mellite, honeystone; **-strauch,** *m.* Melianthus; **-süss,** sweet as honey; **-tau,** *m.* honeydew; **-topf,** *m.* pot of honey, honeypot; **-trank,** *m.* mead; **-wasser,** *n.* hydromel; **-wein,** *m.* mead, mulse.

hopfen, to hop.

Hopfen, *m.* hop, hops; **-abkochung,** *f.* hop decoction; **-ähnlich, -artig,** like hops; **-aufguss,** *m.* infusion of hops; **-baum,** *m.* hop tree (*Ptelea trifoliata*); **-bitter,** *n.* lupulin; **-buche,** *f.* hop hornbeam (Ostrya); **-darre,** *f.* malt kiln, hop kiln; **-drüssen,** *f.pl.* lupulin; **-klee,** *m.* shamrock (*Medicago lupulina*).

Hopfen-mehl, *n.* lupulin; **-mehltau,** *m.* hop blight; **-öl,** *n.* hop oil; **-schneckenklee,** *m.* shamrock (*Medicago lupulina*); **-staub,** hop dust, lupulin; **-stange,** *f.* hop pole; **-stopfen,** *n.* dry hopping; **-treber,** *f.pl.* spent hops; **-trieb,** *m.* frothy head, first stage of fermentation.

Hör-apparat, *m.* hearing apparatus, receiver (telephone).

hörbar, audible.

Hör-bläschen, *n.* auditory vesicle, otocyst; **-nerve,** *m.* auditory nerve.

horchen, to listen, hearken.

Horde, *f.* hurdle, latticed screen, horde, band, troop, shelf.

hören, to hear.

Hörensagen, *n.* hearsay, rumor.

Hörer, *m.* receiver, auditor, hearer, listener.

Hör-faden, *m.* auditory cilium; **-grübchen,** *n.* auditory pit; **-haar,** *n.* auditory cilium.

Horizont, *m.* horizon.

Horizontale, *f.* horizontal line.

Hör-kölbchen, *n.* auditory tentacle; **-leiste,** *f.* auditory crest.

Hormon, *n.*-e, hormone; **-absonderung,** *f.* hormone secretion; **-artig,** like a hormone; **-drüse,** *f.* hormonal gland; **-haltig,** containing hormone(s).

Horn-abfall, *m.*-e, horn chippings; **-ähnlich, -artig,** hornlike, horny, corneous; **-ast,** *m.* horny knot, looseknot; **-ballen,** *n.* heel or bulb of the frog (hoof of horse), torus corneus; **-blatt,** *n.* horn blade, horny, layer; **-blei,** *n.* phosgenite; **-blende,** *f.* hornblende, amphibole; **-endosperm,** *n.* horny endosperm.

hörnern, of horn, horny.

Hörnerv, *m.*-en, auditory nerve.

Hörnervenloch, *n.* auditory (nerve) foramen.

Horn-erz, *n.* horn silver; **-flügel,** *m.* elytra; **-gebilde,** *n.* horny or cuticular structure; **-gewebe,** *n.* horny tissue.

Hornhaut, *f.* cornea, horny layer of epidermis; **-breite,** *f.* width of the cornea; **-dicke,** *f.* thickness of the cornea; **-fläche,** *f.* surface of the cornea; **-krümmung,** *f.* curved profile or curvature of the cornea; **-narbe,** *f.* corneal scar, cicatrix; **-rand,** *m.* border of the cornea.

hornig, hornlike, horny, corneous, callous.

hornisieren, to vulcanize.

Hornisse, (Hornis), *f.* hornet.

Horn-kamm, *m.* horn comb, ctenidium, a comblike structure; **-kapsel,** *f.* horny capsule; **-klee,** *m.* bird's-foot trefoil (*Lotus corniculatus*); **-kobalt,** *n.* asbolite; **-kraut,** *n.* chickweed (Cerastium); **-krautgewächse,** *n.pl.* Ceratophyllaceae; **-kröte,** *f.* horned toad.

Horn-leiste, *f.* ventral ridge (feather); **-losigkeit,** *f.* absence of horn(y substance); **-mohn,** *m.* poppy (*Galucium luteum*); **-saum,** *m.* coronary margin (of hoof), perioplic or coronary band; **-scheibe,** *f.* horny plate; **-scheitel,** *m.* corneal vertex; **-schicht,** *f.* horny layer, epidermis.

Horn-schwamm, *m.*-e, horny sponge; **-silber,** *n.* cerargyrite, horn silver, silver chloride; **-sohle,** *f.* horny sole (of hoof); **-spatel,** *m.* horn spatula; **-stoff,** *m.* keratin, horny substance; **-strahl,** *m.* cuneus corneus, horny frog (of hoof).

Horn-vieh, *n.* horned cattle; **-vorderfläche,** *f.* front surface of the cornea; **-wand,** *f.* wall of the cornea; **-warze,** *f.* chestnut (of horse), horny wart; **-zapfen,** *m.* horny peg; **-zungenmuskel,** *m.* keratoglossus muscle.

Hör-platte, *f.* auditory plate; **-saal,** *m.* lecture room, auditorium.

Hörsamkeit, *f.* acoustics.

Horst, *m.* cluster of trees, group, nest, retreat.

Hörstein, *m.* ear stone, otolith.

Hortensie, *f.* hydrangea.

Hörzelle, *f.* auditory cell.

Höschen, *n.pl.* pollen-covered legs (of bees).

Hosen, *f.pl.* feathered legs (of birds), trousers; **-rohr,** *n.* Y siphon pipe; **-träger,** *m.pl.* suspenders.

Huaco, *m.* gauco.

Huano, *m.* guano.

hub (heben), raised, lifted.

Hub, *m.* lift(ing), heaving stroke (of piston); **aufgehender** ∼, upstroke.

Hub-höhe, *f.* up-and-down stroke; **-stange,** *f.* pitman rod; **-vergrösserung,** *f.* increasing stroke; **-verlegung,** *f.* stroke; displacement; **-verminderung,** *f.* decreasing stroke; **-werk,** *n.* hoisting gear.

Hübel, *m.* hillock, mound.

hübsch, pretty, charming, handsome.

Huf, *m.* hoof; **-bein,** *n.* bone of the hoof, coffin bone.

Hufeisen, *n.* horseshoe; **-förmig,** horseshoe-shaped; **-fuss,** *m.* horseshoe base; **-magnet,** *m.* horseshoe magnet.

Huf-fett, *n.* hoof ointment, grease; **-gänger,** *m.pl.* Ungulae; **-knorpel,** *m.* lateral cartilage of the hoof; **-knorpelbeinband,** *n.* ligament tying lateral cartilages to coronary bone.

Huf-lattich, *m.* coltsfoot (*Tussilago farfara*); **-nagel,** *m.* horseshoe nail, hobnail; **-polster,** *n.* torus digitalis, plantar cushion, fleshy frog (hoof); **-schlag,** *m.* hoofbeat, horseshoeing.

Hüft-ader, *f.* iliac vein; **-angel,** *f.* subcoxa; **-band,** *n.* cotyloid ligament.

Hüftbein, *n.* hip bone; **-fuge,** *f.* pubic symphysis; **-grube,** *f.* iliac fossa; **-kamm,** *m.* iliac crest; **-lendenband,** *n.* iliolumbar ligament; **-loch,** *n.* obturator foramen; **-lochfurche,** *f.* obturator groove; **-lochkerbe,** *f.* sciatic notch; **-stachel,** *m.* iliac spine.

Hüft-blatt, *n.* ilium, epimerum (insects); **-darm,** *m.* small intestine, intestinum ilium.

Hüfte, *f.* hip, haunch, coxa.

Hüftengegend, *f.* region of the hip.

Hüftgelenk, *n.* hip joint; **-kapselband,** *n.* capsular ligament of the hip; **-pfanne,** *f.* acetabulum.

Hüft-glied, *n.* coxa; **-griffel,** *m.* coxal stylus; **-höhle,** *f.* coxal cavity.

Huftiere, *n.pl.* hoofed animals, Ungulatae.

Hüft-kamm, *m.* iliac crest; **-kreuzfuge,** *f.* sacroiliac symphysis; **-lendenband,** *n.* iliolumbar ligament; **-loch,** *n.* obturator foramen; **-lochfurche,** *f.* obturator canal; **-muskel,** *m.* iliac muscle; **-nerv,** *m.* sciatic nerve; **-pfanne,** *f.* acetabulum, coxal cavity.

Hufträger, *m.pl.* Ungulatae.

Hüftsporn, *m.* coxal spur.

Hügel, *m.* hill, hillock, knob, nodule, knoll, protuberance; **-bewohnend,** collinus, growing on low hills.

hügelig, hilly.

Hügel-pflanzung, *f.* mound planting; **-saat,** *f.* sowing on mounds.

Huhn, *m.* hen fowl.

Hühnchen, *n.* chicken, pullet.

Hühner-artig, gallinaceous; **-auge,** *n.* corn (on the foot), clavus; **-cholera,** *f.* chicken cholera; **-eiweiss,** *n.* egg albumen, white of egg; **-eiweissartig,** albuminous; **-embryo,** *m.* fowl embryo.

Hühner-fett, *n.* chicken fat; **-habicht,** *m.* goshawk; **-keim,** *m.* fowl embryo; **-sarkom,** *n.* fowl sarcoma; **-tuberkulose,** *f.* tuberculosis in the fowl; **-vögel,** *m.pl.* gallinaceous birds.

Huld, *f.* grace, affection, kindness, favor.

huldigen, (*dat.*) to pay homage, devote oneself.

Hülfe, *f.* (Hilfe), help.

Hüll-blatt, *n.* involucral leaf; **-blättchen,** *n.* small involucral leaf; **-borste,** *f.* subtending (awn) bristle.

Hüllchen, *n.* involucre.

Hülle, *f.* cover(ing), tunic, cortex, casing, case, jacket, involucre, wrapper, envelope, sheath integument, peridium; **in** ∼ **und Fülle,** in abundance.

hüllen, to cover, wrap; **-schicht,** *f.* cortical layer.

hüll-förmig, involucriform; **-frucht,** *f.* angiocarpous fruit; **-gewebe,** *n.* periblem, tissue of the envelope; **-kätzchenträger,** *m.* cupuliferous plant; **-kelch,** *m.* periclinium, involucre, calyculus.

Hüll-rohr, *n.* encasing tube; **-schläuche,** *m.pl.* spiral jacket cells (sporostegium in

Chara); **-spelze,** *f.* empty glume, scale; **-ständig,** involucral; **-zellen,** *f.pl.* spiral cortical cells.

Hülse, *f.* hull, husk, pod, case, shell, socket, legume(n), capsule, collar, perisarc, holly.

hülsen-artig, like a hull, socket, leguminous, podlike; **-baum,** *m.* locust tree; **-frucht,** *f.* legume; **-fruchtartig,** leguminous; **-früchtig,** leguminous; **-früchtler,** *m.pl.* Leguminosae; **-gewächse,** *n.pl.* Leguminosae; **-kapsel,** *f.* cyanium; **-kranz,** *m.* involucre of husks; **-träger,** *m.* leguminous plant; **-windung,** *f.* a spiral turn in the seed pod (Leguminosae).

Humate, *n.pl.* soil ingredients.

Humin-säure, *f.* humic acid; **-stoffe,** *m.pl.* humic substances.

Hummel, *f.* bumblebee; **-blume,** *f.* flower pollinated by bumblebee.

Hummer, *m.* lobster.

humös, humic.

humpeln, to hobble, limp.

Humulochinon, *n.* humuloquinone.

Humus, *m.* humus, vegetable mold; **-anzeiger,** *m.* plant which (indicates) requires humus; **-bewohner,** *m.* plant growing on humous soil; **-bildung,** *f.* humus formation; **-decke,** *f.* leaf mold, surface mulch, mold cover; **-erde,** *f.* arable land; **-reich,** rich in humus; **-säure,** *f.* humous acid; **-schicht,** *f.* humus layer; **-stoff,** *m.* humous substance; **-zehrer,** *m.* plant growing on (consuming) humous soil.

Hund, *m.* dog, hound.

Hunde-gattung, *f.* dog species; **-kot,** *m.* canine feces; **-krankheit,** *f.* canine distemper.

hundert, hundred; **-fach,** hundredfold; **-füssig,** centipedal.

hundertgradig, centigrade.

Hundertsatz, *m.* percentage.

Hundertstel, *n.* hundredth (part).

hundertteilig, centesimal, centigrade.

Hunde-seuche, *f.* canine distemper; **-staupe,** *f.* canine distemper; **-zahnspat,** *m.* dogtooth spar.

Hunds-dolde, *f.* fool's-parsley; **-fisch,** *m.* mud minnow; **-gleisse,** fool's parsley; **-hai,** *m.* dogfish, dog shark; **-kamille,** *f.* *Anthemis cotula;* **-petersilie,** *f.* fool's-parsley (*Aethusa cynapium*); **-rose,** *f.* wild brier, dog rose (*Rosa canina*).

Hunds-wolle, *f.* dogbane (Apocynum); **-würger,** *m.* dogbane (*Cynanchum vincetoxicum*); **-wut,** *f.* rabies; **-zahn,** *m.* dog's-tooth (Erythronium), Bermuda grass; **-zunge,** *f.* hound's-tongue (Cynoglossum).

Hunger, *m.* hunger, starvation, appetite.

Hungerkorn, *n.* ergot (of rye).

hungern, to hunger.

Hungersnot, *f.* famine.

Hunger-stein, *m.* salt-pan scale; **-stoffwechsel,** *m.* metabolism during starvation; **-tod,** *m.* starvation; **-warze,** *f.* sublingual caruncle.

hungrig, hungry.

Hupe, *f.* horn, siren.

hüpfen, to hop, skip, jump.

Hüpffuss, *m.* pes saliens, gressorial leg.

hürnen, horny.

hurtig, quick, agile, nimble, swift, speedy.

Husarenknopf, *m.* Spilanthes.

husten, to cough; **-mittel,** *n.* cough remedy; **-reiz,** *m.* throat irritation (causing coughing).

Hut, *m.* ⁼e, hat, cap, pileus, cover, loaf (sugar).

Hut, *f.* guard, pasture.

Hutanlage, *f.* primordium of the pileus.

Hütchen, *n.* capsule.

hüten, to guard, keep, take care, watch; **sich ~,** to be on one's guard.

Hüter, *m.* warden.

Hut-filz, *m.* felt for hats; **-pilz,** *m.* (pileated) mushroom; **-spelze,** *f.* glume.

Hütte, *f.* cabin, hut, shelter, shed, mill, smelting house, foundry, metallurgical plant.

Hütten-after, *m.* residue (tailings) from a smelter; **-arbeit,** *f.* smelting operation, foundry work; **-glas,** *n.* pot metal; **-kunde,** *f.* metallurgy; **-männisch,** metallurgical; **-mehl,** *n.* white-arsenic powder.

Hütten-rauch, *m.* factory fumes, arsenical fumes; **-reise,** *f.* campaign; **-speise,** *f.* ores to be smelted; **-werk,** *n.* smelting works, foundry, mill; **-wesen,** *n.* smelting, metallurgy; **-zinn,** *n.* grain tin.

Hutzucker, *m.* loaf sugar (cone shape).

Hyäne, *f.* hyena.

Hyänsäure, *f.* hyenic acid.

Hyazinthe, *f.* hyacinth.

Hyazinthen-rotz, *m.* hyacinth rot; **-zwiebel,** *f.* hyacinth bulb.

Hyazinthgranat, *m.* essonite.

Hybrid, *n.* hybrid.

Hydathode, *f.* hydathode, water opening.

Hydathodenstrom, *m.* excretion current.

Hydra, *f.* hydra, water snake.

Hydrargyrum, *n.* mercury.

Hydrat, *n.* hydrate, hydroxide.

Hydratation, *f.* hydration.

Hydratationswärme, *f.* heat of hydration.

Hydrat-bildung, *f.* hydrate formation; -haltig, hydrated.

hydratisieren, to hydrate, become hydrated.

Hydratisierungsgrad, *m.* degree of hydration.

Hydratropasäure, *f.* hydratropic acid.

Hydratwasser, *n.* water of hydration; -haltig, containing water of hydration.

Hydraulik, *f.* hydraulics.

hydraulisch, hydraulic.

Hydrazoverbindung, *f.* hydrazo compound.

Hydrid, *n.* hydride.

hydrieren, to hydrogenize, hydrogenate.

Hydrierung, *f.* hydrogenation.

Hydro-bromsäure, *f.* hydrobromic acid; -chinon, *n.* hydroquinone; -chlorsäure, *f.* hydrochloric acid; -cyansäure, *f.* hydrocyanic acid.

hydrogenisieren, to hydrogenate.

Hydrogenisation, *f.* hydrogenation.

Hydrogenschwefel, *m.* hydrogen sulphide.

Hydroiden-generation, *f.* polype generation; -stöckchen, *n.* hydroid colony.

Hydrojodsäure, *f.* hydriodic acid.

Hydrokette, *f.* hydrocell, hydroelement.

Hydrolyse, *f.* hydrolysis.

hydrolysieren, to hydrolyze.

hydropathisch, hydropathic.

Hydroperoxyd, *n.* hydrogen peroxide.

hydrostatisch, hydrostatic.

Hydrothionsäure, *f.* hydrosulphuric acid, hydrogen sulphide.

Hydroxyd, *n.* hydroxide.

Hydroxydul, *n.* hydroxide.

hydroxylhaltig, containing hydroxyl.

hydroxylieren, to hydroxylate.

Hydrozellulose, *f.* hydrocellulose.

Hydrozimtsäure, *f.* hydrocinnamic acid.

Hydrür, *n.* hydride.

Hygiene, *f.* hygiene.

hygienisch, hygienic.

hygroskopisch, hygroscopic.

Hymenialdrüse, *f.* cystidium.

Hymenopterenblume, *f.* flower pollinated by bees.

Hyperamie, *f.* hyperemia.

Hyperbel, *f.* hyperbola.

Hyper-chlorat, *n.* perchlorate; -chlorid, *n.* perchloride; -chlorsäure, *f.* perchloric acid; -jodat, *n.* periodate; -oxyd, *n.* hyperoxide, peroxide; -plasieren, to tend to hyperplasia.

Hyphe, *f.* hypha.

Hyphen-gewebe, *n.* plectenchyma, hyphal tissue; -haut, *f.* membrane of hyphal tissue; -schlauch, *m.* hyphal tube; -sprossung, *f.* hyphal budding.

Hypo-branchialrinne, *n.* endostyle; -chordalbogen, *m.* hypochordal arch; -gäasäure, *f.* hypogeic acid; -glossus, hypoglossal, situated under the tongue; -hirnsäure, *f.* hypocerebric acid; -phosphorig, hypophosphorous; -physe, *f.* hypophysis, pituitary body; -physenvorderlappen, *m.* anterior lobe of hypophysis, anterior pituitary; -sulfit, *n.* thiosulphate.

Hypotenusenfläche, *f.* hypotenuse plane or surface.

hypothallisch, hypothalline.

Hypothek, *f.* mortgage.

Hypothese, *f.* hypothesis.

hypothesieren, to mortgage.

hypothetisch, hypothetical.

I

Iatrochemie, *f.* iatrochemistry.

ich, I.

Ichneumon, *m.* ichneumon wasp, fly.

Ichthyolseife, *f.* ichthyol soap.

Ichthyosismus, *m.* fish poisoning.

Jdeal, *n.* ideal.

Idealismus, *m.* idealism.

Idee, *f.* idea, notion, conception.

Ideenverbindung, *f.* association of ideas.

identifizeren, to identify.

identisch, identical.

Identität, *f.* identity.

Idioplasma, *n.* idioplasm, germ plasm.

Idiot, *m.* idiot.

Idozuckersäure, *f.* idosaccharic acid.

Igel, *m.*-, hedgehog, porcupine (mixer), drag, harrow; **-borstig,** echinate; **-stachel,** *m.* porcupine spicule; **-stachelig,** echinate.

Ignorant, *m.* ignoramus.

ignorieren, to ignore.

ihm, (to) him, (to) it.

ihn, him, it.

ihnen, (to) them.

Ihnen, (to) you.

ihr, you, (to) her, (to) it, their.

Ihr, your.

ihrer, of her, of them, hers, theirs.

Ihrer, (of) you.

ihrerseits, on her, their, your part, in her, their or your turn.

ihresgleichen, the like(s) of her, them, you, her, their, your kind or equal.

ihres-teils, on her, their part.

ihret-halben, -wegen, -willen, on her, their account, for her, their sake.

ihrige, hers, theirs.

Ihrige, yours.

Ikositetraeder, *n.* icositetrahedron.

Ikterus, *m.* jaundice, chlorosis.

illegitim, illegitimate.

illuminieren, to illuminate.

illusorisch, illusory.

illustrieren, to illustrate.

Ilmenitentmischungstafel, *f.* ilmenite disintegration flake.

Iltis, *m.* polecat, skunk, fitchew (Putorius).

im (in dem), in the.

Imaginalscheibe, *f.* imaginal bud or disk.

imaginär, imaginary.

Imber, *m.* (Ingwer), ginger.

imbibieren, to imbibe.

Imbibitionsbewegung, *f.* imbibition movement.

Imbiss, *m.* light meal, lunch(eon).

Imido-äther, *m.* imido ester; **-sulfonsäure,** *f.* imidosulphonic acid.

Imker, *m.* bee keeper, apiarist.

immatrikulieren, to enroll.

Imme, *f.* bee.

Immedialfarbe, *f.* immedial color.

Immen, *f.pl.* Hymenoptera; **-falterblume,** *f.* flower pollinated by bees or butterflies.

immer, always, ever, (with a comparative) more and more; **auf** ~, forever; **noch** ~, still; **wie** ~, as usual; **wann auch** ~, whenever; **wenn auch** ~, although; **wer auch** ~, who(so)ever; **wo auch** ~, where-(so)ever; ~ **reicher,** richer and richer.

immerfort, continually, constantly.

Immergrün, *n.* myrtle, periwinkle (Vinca).

immer-grünend, evergreen; **-hin,** still, nevertheless, after all, forever; **-länger,** longer and longer; **-mehr,** more and more.

Immersions-flüssigkeit, *f.* immersion fluid; **-öl,** *n.* immersion oil.

immer-während, everlasting, perpetual; **-wieder,** repeatedly, again and again; **-zu,** always.

Immortelle, *f.* everlasting (flower).

immunisieren, to immunize.

Immunisierung, *f.* immunization.

Immunisierungs-dauer, *f.* permanence of immunity; **-einheit,** immunization unit; **-rezept,** *n.* scheme of immunization; **-wert,** *m.* immunization value.

Immunität, *f.* immunity

Immunitäts-dauer, *f.* permanence of immunity; **-einheit,** *f.* unit of immunity; **-forschung,** *f.* investigation of immunity.

Immunkörper, *m.* immune body.

Immunochemie, *f.* immunochemistry.

Immunserum, *n.* immune serum.

Impfausbeute, *f.* yield of culture.

impfbar, inoculable.

impfen, to inoculate, vaccinate, graft plants; seed, form (crystals).

Impf-flüssigkeit, *f.* vaccine or inoculation lymph; **-rotz,** *m.* inoculated glanders; **-stich,** *m.* line of inoculation in stab culture; **-stift,** *m.* inoculating pencil; **-stoff,** *m.* vaccine, inoculum, inoculation serum; **-strich,** *m.* line of inoculation in streak culture.

Impfung, *f.* inoculation, vaccination.

Impfversuch, *m.* inoculation experiment.

Implantat, *n.* implant.

implantieren, to implant.

imponieren, (*dat.*) to impress, impose.

importieren, to import.

imposant, imposing, impressive.

impotent, impotent.

imprägnierbar, impregnable.

imprägnieren, to impregnate, imbibe.

Imprägnierung, f. impregnation.

Imprägnierungsmittel, n. impregnating material, stiffener.

Imprägnierverfahren, n. impregnation process.

Impressionszeit, f. presentation time.

Improvisieren, to improvise.

Impuls, m. impulse, impulsion.

imstande sein, to be able, capable of.

in, in, at, into, to.

inaktiv, inactive.

inaktivieren, to put out of action, render inactive, incapacitate.

Inaktivierung, f. inactivation.

Inaktivität, f. inactivity.

Inangriffnahme, f. beginning.

Inanspruchnahme, f. requisition, claim, use.

Inbegriff, m. total, sum, aggregate, inclusion, summary, essence, substance.

inbegriffen (einbegreifen), included, inclusive, implied.

Inbetriebsetzung, f. setting in motion, or working order, starting.

inbezug auf, in (with) regard to, in relation to.

Inbrunst, f. ardor, fervor.

incarnat (inkarnat), flesh-colored, pink.

indem, while, when, as, since, by or in that, because; ~ man . . . arbeitet, by working; als ~, except when.

indes (indessen), meanwhile, however, in the meantime, yet.

Indexstrich, m. index mark or line.

indifferent, inert, neutral.

Indig, m. indigo; -blau, n. indigo blue.

indigen, indigenous, native.

indigo-artig, indigoid; -auszug, m. indigo extract; -blauschwefelsäure, f. indigosulphuric acid; -farbe, f. indigo (dye); -farbstoff, m. indigotin; -karmin, n. indigo carmine; -küpe, f. indigo vat; -leim, m. indigo gelatin or gluten; -liefernd, indigo (bearing) producing; -lösung, f. indigo solution.

Indigo-rot, n. indirubin; -stoff, m. indigo blue, indigotin; -sulfosäure, f. indigosulphonic acid; -weiss, n. indigo white, reduced indigo.

Indikator, m. indicator.

Indioxyd, n. indium oxide.

indisch, (East) Indian; indische Bohne, St. Ignatius's bean; indische Feige, prickly pear, Indian fig; indischer Flachs, jute.

Indisch-gelb, n. Indian yellow; -hanftinktur, f. tincture of Indian hemp.

indiskret, indiscret.

Indiumsulfür, n. indium monosulphide.

Individual-abstand, m. spacing; -züchtung, f. individual selection.

Individualisationsgrenze, f. limitation individualization.

individuell, individual.

Individuum, n. individual.

Indizes, m.pl. indices.

indizieren, to indicate.

Indochinolin, n. indoquinoline.

Indolbildung, f. formation of indole.

indoloid, indol odor (in flowers).

Induktions-rolle, f. induction coil; -spule, f. induction coil; -strom, m. induction current; -vermögen, n. inductive capacity; -wirkung, f. inducing action; -zeit, f. period of induction, latent period.

Induktorspannung, f. voltage (tension) of induction coil.

indurieren, to indurate, make durable, harden.

Industrie-abfallstoff, m. industrial waste material; -abwasser, n. trade waste, manufactory effluent.

Industrielle(r), m. industrial, large manufacturer.

Industrie-wasser, n. industrial water; -zentrum, n. center of industry, industrial center; -zweig, m. branch of industry.

induzieren, to induce.

ineinander, into each other, into one another; -fliessen, to flow or run into one another; -greifen, to interlace, gear, be linked together; -passen, to fit into each other; -wachsen, to interlace by growth.

Inertia, f. inertia.

infam, infamous, atrocious.

Infektion, f. infection.

Infektions-erreger, m. cause of disease, virus; -faden, m. infection hypha, germ tube; -herd, m. focus of infection; -krankheit, f. infectious disease; -pforte, f. infection portal or court; -quelle, f. source of infection; -schlauch, m. germ tube, infection (hypha) thread; -träger, m. conveyer or carrier of infection; -versuch, *m.* infection experiment; **-vorgang,** *m.* process of infection; **-widrig,** anticontagious.

infektiös, infectious.

infiltrieren, to infiltrate.

Infizierung, *f.* infection.

Inflation, *f.* inflation.

Influenza, *f.* influenza; **-bazillus,** *m.* influenza bacillus.

infökund, sterile.

infolge, on account of, owing to; ～ **dessen,** consequently, because of this.

informieren, to inform.

Infra-orbitalrand, *m.* infraorbital border; **-rot,** infrared; **-schall,** *m.* subsonant.

Infundier-apparat, *m.* infusion apparatus; **-büchse,** *f.* infusion vessel, percolater.

infundieren, to infuse.

Infusion, *f.* infusion.

Infusionstierchen, *n.pl.* Infusoria.

Infusorienerde, *f.* infusorial earth.

Ing., *abbr.* (Ingenieur), engineer; **Dr. Ing. habil. Schmidt,** Dr. (of Engineering) Schmidt (qualified as full professor).

Ingangsetzung, *f.* starting.

Ingenieur, *m.* engineer; **-wesen,** *n.* engineering.

ingeniös, ingenious.

Ingrediens, *n.* **Ingredienz,** *f.* ingredient.

ingrimmig, angry.

Inguss, *m.* ingot.

Ingwer, *m.* ginger; **-artig,** like ginger; **-gewürz,** *n.* ginger; **-wurzel,** *f.* whole ginger(root).

Inhaber, *m.* holder, owner, occupant.

inhalieren, to inhale.

Inhalt, *m.* content(s), area, volume, capacity, substance, index.

inhaltlich, as to content.

Inhalts-angabe, *f.* table of contents; **-ermittlung,** *f.* determination of volume; **-leer,** empty; **-reich,** significant; **-übersicht,** *f.* table of contents; **-verzeichnis,** *n.* table of contents, index.

inhomogen, inhomogeneous.

Inhomogenität, *f.* inhomogeneity.

Initiale, *f.* initial, apical cell.

Initial-sprengstoff, *m.* priming explosive; **-strang,** *m.* procambium strand; **-zelle,** *f.* initial cell; **-zünder,** *m.* primer.

Initiative ergreifen, to take the initiative.

initiieren, to initiate.

Injektion, *f.* injection.

Injektions-erreger, *m.* virus; **-spritze,** *f.* injection syringe.

injizieren, to inject.

Injurie, *f.* insult.

inkarnat, flesh-colored, pink; **-klee,** *m.* crimson clover (*Trifolium incarnatum*).

inkl., *abbr.* (inklusive), inclusive.

Inklination, *f.* inclination.

Inklinationsnadel, *f.* dipping needle.

Inkohärens, *f.* incoherence.

Inkrafttreten, *n.* coming into force.

Inkretion, *f.* internal secretion, endocrine product.

inkrustieren, to incrust, become incrusted.

Inkrustierung, *f.* incrustation.

Inkubationszeit, *f.* period of incubation.

Inland, *n.* inland, interior.

Inländer, *m.* native.

inländisch, native, indigenous, internal, domestic, homemade.

inliegend, enclosed.

inmitten, in the midst.

inne, in, within; **-haben,** to hold, have, occupy, possess, keep; **-halten,** to stop, pause, keep (with)in, maintain.

innen, within, in, inside, indoors, at home; **nach** ～, inward; **von** ～ **nach aussen,** from within outward.

Innen-ansicht, *f.* interior view; **-ast,** *m.* endopodite (Crustacea); **-druck,** *m.* internal pressure; **-durchmesser,** *m.* inside diameter; **-fahne,** *f.* inner vane or web; **-fläche,** *f.* inner surface; **-galle,** *f.* inner tissue of a gall; **-haut,** *f.* inner membrane, middle lamella; **-kelch,** *m.* true calyx; **-knospung,** *f.* calycinal gemmation.

Innen-lade, *f.* lacinia, inner lobe or plate; **-leben,** *n.* inner life; **-leitung,** *f.* interior wiring, piping; **-rand,** *m.* inner margin; **-raum,** *m.* inner cavity, lumen; **-rinde,** *f.* inner (secondary) bark, inner phloem, secondary cortex; **-skelett,** *n.* endoskeleton, endophragmal skeleton; **-temperatur,** *f.* internal temperature; **-wand,** *f.* inner wall.

Innen-wäsche, *f.* vacuum wash, internal washing; **-winkel,** *m.* internal angle, interior angle; **-wendig,** introrse; **-zahnkranzantrieb,** *m.* driven by inner gearing; **-zehe,** *f.* inner toe.

inner, interior, inward, internal, inner, intrinsic, central.

Innere, *n.* interior, inside, midst, heart, center; **im Innern,** in the interior.

innere Lade, *f.* lacinia of maxilla, inner plate; **innere Plasmahaut,** *f.* vacuolar membrane, tonoplast; **inneres Seitenfeld,** *n.* lateral (line) cord (of nematodes).

innerhalb, inside, within.

innerlich, inward, internal, interior, profound, sincere, cordial.

inner-molekular intramolecular; **-sekretorisch,** excretory; **-vieren,** to innervate.

innerst, inmost, most intimate.

Innerste(s), *n.* innermost part.

innewerden, to perceive.

innewohnend, inherent.

innig, intimate, cordial, fond, earnest, fervent, sincere.

Innigkeit, *f.* intimacy.

inokulieren, to inoculate.

Inosinsäure, *f.* inosic acid.

Insass, Insasse, *m.* inmate, inhabitant.

insbesondere, particularly, (e)specially.

Insbewusstseinrufen, *n.* recalling to consciousness.

Inschrift, *f.* inscription.

Insekt, *n.* insect, imago.

Insekten-besuch, *m.* visit of an insect; **-blütler,** *m.pl.* Entomophilae; **-frass,** *m.* damage by insects, insect ravage; **-fressend,** insectivorous; **-fresser,** *m.* insectivorum, insect eater; **-kunde,** *f.* entomology; **-larve,** *f.* insect larva; **lehre,** *f.* entomology; **-nadel,** *f.* mounting or insect pin.

Insekten-plage, *f.* insect pest; **-pulver,** *n.* insect powder; **-stich,** *m.* sting (or) bite of an insect; **-verheerung,** *f.* insect pest, devastation by insects; **-vertilgungsmittel,** *n.* insecticide; **-vertreibungsmittel,** *n.* insectifuge.

Insektizid, *n.* insecticide.

Insel, *f.* island; **Inseln im Film,** spots on film, cessing, running.

Insel-meer, *n.* archipelago; **-rasse,** *f.* insular race.

Inserat, *n.*-e, advertisement, insertion.

inserieren, to insert, advertise.

Insertionsfläche, *f.* plane of insertion.

ins-geheim, secretly; **-gemein,** generally; **-gesamt,** all together.

insofern, so far as, inasmuch as.

insoweit, in so far.

inspirieren, to inspire.

inspizieren, to inspect.

instabil, unstable.

instand-halten, to keep up; **-haltung,** *f.* maintenance, keeping in good repair.

inständig, earnest, urgent, pressing.

instand-setzen, to enable, repair; **-setzung,** *f.* restoration, reconditioning, repairing.

instinktiv, instinctive.

instinktmässig, instinctive.

instruieren, to instruct.

instruktiv, instructive.

Instrument, *n.* instrument.

Insulin-kur, *f.* insulin treatment; **-zufuhr,** *f.* administration of insulin.

Integralrechnung, *f.* integral calculus.

integrieren, to integrate.

integrierend, integrating, integrant.

Intelligenzprüfung, *f.* intelligence test.

Intensität, *f.* intensity.

intensiv, intensive, intense.

Intercostal-band, *n.* intercostal ligament; **-feld,** *n.* intercostal plane; **-raum,** *m.* intercostal space.

interessant, interesting.

Interesse, *n.* interest.

Interessent, *m.* interested person.

interessieren, to interest.

Interferenz-bild, *n.* interference figure; **-erscheinung,** *f.* appearance or effect of interference; **-wirkung,** *f.* interferential action.

interferieren, to interfere.

inter-mediär, intermediary, intermediate; **-mittierend,** intermittent; **-pellieren,** to interpellate; **-plantation,** *f.* interplantation; **-polieren,** to interpolate; **-poniert,** interpolated; **-punktieren,** to punctuate; **-segmentalspalte,** *f.* intersegmental fissure; **-specialkampf,** *m.* interspecies struggle; **-stitialstreifen,** *m.* interstice, small intercellular space.

Intervall, *n.* interval.

Inter-vertebralscheibe, *f.* intervertebral disk; **-zellularraum,** *m.* intercellular space.

intim, intimate.

intrathorakal, intrathoracic.

intravenös, intravenous.

intrigant, intriguing, plotting, designing.

Inulin, *n.* inulin.

Inundationsgebiet, *n.* innundation area.

Invaginationsvorgang, *m.* process of invagination.

Inventar, *n.* inventory.

Inventur, *f.* taking inventory.

Inversionsgeschwindigkeit, *f.* inversion velocity.

invertieren, to invert.

Invertierung, *f.* inversion.

Invertzucker, *m.* invert sugar, inverted sugar.

investieren, to invest.

inwärds, inwards.

inwendig, internal, inside, within.

inwie-fern, -weit, in what respect, (in) how far.

inwohnend, inherent.

Inzest, *m.* incest, endogamy, inbreeding.

inzidieren, to incise.

Inzision, *f.* incision.

Inzucht, *f.* inbreeding, endogamy.

inzwischen, meantime, nevertheless.

Iod, *n.* (Jod), iodine.

Ion, *n.*-en, ion.

Ionen-beweglichkeit, *f.* ionic mobility; **-bildend,** forming ions; **-bildung,** *f.* formation of ions; **-gehalt,** *m.* content of ions; **-geschwindigkeit,** *f.* ionic velocity; **-gleichung,** *f.* ionic equation.

Ionen-leitungsstrom, *m.* ionic (conductive) current; **-reibung,** *f.* ionic friction; **-rohr,** *n.* ion tube; **-spaltung,** *f.* ionic cleavage, ionization; **-stoss,** *m.* ionic impulse, ionization current; **-wanderung,** *f.* ionic migration; **-zustand,** *m.* ionic state.

Ionisations-störung, *f.* disturbance of ionization; **-wärme,** *f.* heat of ionization; **-zustand,** *m.* condition of ionization.

Ionisator, *m.* ionizer.

ionisch, ionic.

ionisierbar, ionizable.

ionisieren, to ionize.

ionisierung, *f.* ionization.

irden, earthen; **irdenes Geschirr,** earthenware.

Irden-ware, *f.* earthenware.

irdisch, earthly, terrestrial, perishable.

irgend, any, at all, some, possible; ~ **ein,** some(one); any (whatsoever), any(body), any(one); ~ **einmal,** at any time, at some time or other; ~ **jemand,** some one; ~ **wie,** anyhow, somehow; ~ **welcher,** some(one), any(one); ~ **welch,** any kind of, any, some; ~ **wo,** anywhere, somewhere; ~ **womit,** with whatever; ~ **worin,** in anything whatever; **wenn es** ~ **geht,** if at all possible.

iridisieren, to irisate, iridize.

iridisierend, iridescent.

Iris, *f.* iris; **-blende,** *f.* iris diaphragm; **-epithel,** *n.* iris epithelium; **-haut,** *f.* iris.

irisieren, to irisate, iridize.

irisierend, iridescent.

Irisierung, *f.* iridescence.

Iris-öl, *n.* iris (orris) oil; **-zylinderblende,** *f.* iris cylinder diaphragm.

Iron, *n.* irone.

ironisch, ironic.

irre, astray, lost, wrong.

Irre, *f.* wandering, error, labyrinth.

Irre, *m.&f.* insane person, lunatic.

irreführen, to mislead, deceive.

irremachen, to mislead, puzzle, disturb.

irren, to err, go astray, be wrong; **sich** ~, to have illusions or delusions, be mistaken.

Irren-anstalt, *f.* lunatic asylum; **-arzt,** *m.* alienist, psychopathist.

Irresein, *n.* insanity.

irreversible, irreversible.

Irr-fahrt, *f.* wandering, vagary; **-gang,** *m.* **-garten,** *m.* labyrinth.

irrgläubig, heretical.

irrig, erroneous, false.

Irr-lehre, *f.* false teaching, heresy; **-licht,** *n.* will-o'-the-wisp; **-sinn,** *m.* insanity, delirium; **-sinnig,** mad, lunatic, insane; **-strom,** *m.* stray current.

Irrtum, *m.* error, mistake, fault.

irrtümlich, erroneous, mistaken, false.

irrtümlicherweise, by mistake, erroneously.

Irrung, *f.* error, mistake.

isabellenfarbig, cream-colored, light buff.

ischämisch, ischemic.

Isobaren, *m.pl.* curves of equal pressure.

Iso-butan, *n.* isobutane; **-buttersäure,** *f.* isobutyric acid; **-chinolin,** *n.* isoquinoline; **-chrom,** isochromatic; **-chromatisch,** isochromatic; **-cumarin,** *n.* isocumarin; **-cyansäure,** *f.* isocyanic acid; **-cyclisch,** isocyclic; **-elektrisch,** isoelectric.

Isogen, *n.* polygon of equal sides and equal angles.

Isokline, *f.* isoclinical line.

Isolation, *f.* isolation, insulation.

Isolations-material, *n.* insulating material; **-schicht,** *f.* insulating layer; **-vermögen,** *n.* insulating power; **-zustand,** *m.* state of isolation (insulation).

Isolator, *m.* insulator.

Isolierband, *n.* insulating tape.

isolieren, to isolate, insulate.

Isolier-fähigkeit, *f.* ability to insulate; **-mittel,** *n.* insulating agent, insulator, lagging compound; **-rohr,** *n.* insulating tube, conduit; **-röhre,** *f.* insulating tube, conduit; **-schicht,** *f.* insulating layer.

isoliert, isolated; **isolierte Färbung,** *f.* differential straining.

Isolierung, *f.* isolation, insulation, lagging.

isolog, isologous.

isomer, isomeric.

Isomerie, *f.* isomerism; **-fall,** *m.* case of isomerism; **-möglichkeit,** *f.* possibility of isomerism.

isomerisch, isomeric.

isomerisieren, to isomerize.

Isomerisierung, *f.* isomerization.

Isomerismus, *m.* isomerism.

iso-metrisch, isometric; **-morph,** isomorphous.

isospor, isospore.

Isotherme, *f.* isothermal line.

isotherm(isch), isothermal.

isotonisch, isotonic.

Isotope, *f.* isotope.

isotrop, isotropic.

Iso-valeriansäure, *f.* isovaleric acid; **-zimmtsäure,** *f.* isocinnamic acid.

isst (essen), eats.

Ivakraut, *n.* iva (*Achillea moschata*).

J

ja, yes, of course, indeed, certainly; **ja doch,** surely; **ja freilich,** of course; **jawohl,** yes, indeed; **ja gewiss,** certainly.

jach, hasty, precipitous, steep, sudden.

Jagarazucker, *m.* jaggery (sugar).

Jagd, *f.* hunt(ing), chase, pursuit, shooting, game; **-bezirk,** *m.* game preserve; **-büchse,** sporting rifle; **-flinte,** *f.* sporting rifle; **-horn,** *n.* hunting horn, bugle; **-karte,** *f.* game license; **-schein,** *m.* game license; **-schutz,** *m.* protection of game.

jagen, to hunt, drive, chase.

Jäger, *m.* hunter, huntsman, forest ranger.

jäh, sudden, hasty, abrupt, steep.

jählings, precipitously, abruptly, headlong.

Jahr, *n.*-e, year; **alle Jahre,** every year; **nach Jahren,** after many years; **seit einigen Jahren,** for some years; **über ~ und Tag,** in years, to come; **ein ~ ums andere,** every year; **vor einem Jahr,** a year ago; **vor Jahren,** years ago; **in den achtziger Jahren,** in the eighties; **~ aus ~ ein,** year in year out; **in den letzten Jahren,** in the last few years, recently.

Jahr-buch, *n.*-er, yearbook, almanac; **-bücher,** *n.pl.* annuals.

jahrelang, for years.

Jahres-ausbeute, *f.* annual yield; **-bericht,** *m.* annual report; **-frist,** *f.* space of a year;

-periode, *f.* annual (increment), period of growth; **-ring,** *m.* annual ring; **-schrift,** *f.* annual publication; **-spross,** *m.* year's shoot.

Jahres-tag, *m.*-e, anniversary, birthday; **-trieb,** *m.* present year's growth, annual shoot; **-wechsel,** *m.* (coming of the) new year; **-wertzuwachs,** *m.* annual increase in value; **-zeit,** *f.* season; **-zuwachs,** *m.* annual growth; **-zyklus,** *m.* annual cycle.

Jahrg., *abbr.* (Jahrgang), year's set (publication).

Jahr-gang, *m.*⸚e, year's growth or vintage, year's set; **-hundert,** *n.* century; **-hundertwende,** *f.* turn of the century.

jährlich, yearly, annual.

Jährling, *m.* yearling, one-year seedling.

Jahr-ring, *m.*-e, annual ring; **-tausend,** *n.* a thousand years, millennium; **-tausendelang,** for thousands of years; **-zehnt,** *n.* decade; **-zeitlich,** seasonal.

jähzornig, furious, passionate, hot-tempered.

Jakobs-kraut, *n.* groundsel (*Senecio vulgaris*); **-leiter,** *f.* Greek valerian (*Polemonium caeruleum*).

Jalape, Jalappe, *f.* jalap.

Jalapaharz, *n.* jalap resin.

Jalappenwurzel, *f.* jalap root.

Jalousien, *f.pl.* Venetian blinds.

jammern, to lament, despair, move to pity.

jammervoll, deplorable.

Janusgrün, *n.* Janus green.

Japanholz, *n.* sapanwood.

japanieren, to japan.

Japan-wachs, -talg, *n.* Japan wax, Japan tallow.

jappen, to gasp, pant.

Jasmin, *m.* jasmine, jessamine; **gemeiner ~,** white syringa; **wilder ~,** white syringa.

Jasminblütenöl, *n.* jasmine-flower oil.

Jaspachat, *m.* jasper agate.

Jaspis, *m.* jasper; **-gut,** *n.* jasper ware.

Jaspopal, *m.* jasper opal.

jäten, to weed.

Jauche, *f.* dung water, liquid manure, ichor, sanies; **-grube,** *f.* liquid-manure pit, depositing pit; **-herd,** *m.* focus of ichorous suppuration.

jauchzen, to shout, rejoice.

Javelle'sche Lauge, Javelle water.

jawohl, yes indeed.

Jawort, *n.* consent.

je, always, ever, every, each, per, each time, **~ . . . desto,** the . . . the; **~ . . . ~,** the . . . the; **~ . . . um so,** the . . . the; **~ nach,** depending on, according to; **~ nachdem,** according as; **~ zwei,** two each.

jedenfalls, in any case, by all means.

jeder, every, each, any, everyone; **ein ~** each one.

jeder-mann, everyone, anybody; **-seits,** on each side; **-zeit,** at any time, always.

jedesmal, every time.

jedesmalig, existing, actual, then being.

jedoch, however, yet, nevertheless.

jeglich-er, -e, es, every, each.

jeher, von ~, ever since, all along, from time immemorial.

Jelängerjelieber, *n.* woodbine, honeysuckle (*Lonicera periclymenum*).

jemals, every, at any time.

jemand, somebody, someone, anybody, anyone.

Jenaer Glas, Jena glass.

jener, that (one), the other, that person, the former.

jenseit, jenseits, beyond, on the other side of.

jenseitig, opposite.

Jerusalemsblume, *f.* scarlet lychnis.

Jesuitenrinde, *f.* Jesuit's bark (cinchona bark).

jettschwarz, jetblack.

jetzig, present, actual.

jetzt, now, at present; **bis ~,** until now, hitherto.

Jetzt-wert, *m.***-e,** present value; **-zeit,** *f.* present time, recent period.

jeweilen, from time to time, for the time being.

jeweilig, for the time being, at times, occasional(ly), existing, actual, respectively, corresponding.

jeweils, for the time being, at times, occasionally, as the case may be, in each case, in turn, at times, for the time being, each time, always.

Joch, *n.***-e,** yoke, juga, girder, tie beam, pair of opposite leaflets, team of oxen.

Jochbein, *n.* malar bone, zygomatic bone; **-naht,** *f.* zygomatic suture; **-winkel,** *m.* jugal point.

Joch-bogen, *m.* zygomatic arch; **-brücke,** *f.* zygomatic arch; **-fortsatz,** *m.* zygomatic process; **-fractur,** *f.* fracture of zygoma; **-knochen,** *m.* zygomatic bone.

Jod, *n.* iodine; **-ammonium,** *n.* ammonium iodide; **-amylum,** *n.* starch iodide; **-antimon,** *n.* antimony iodide; **-artig,** iodinelike.

Jodat, *n.* iodate.

Jod-äthyl, *n.* ethyl iodide; **-benzin,** *n.* iodized benzine; **-benzol,** *n.* iodobenzene; **-blei,** *n.* lead iodide; **-bromid,** *n.* iodine bromide; **-bromür,** *n.* iodine monobromide; **-chinolin,** *n.* iodoquinoline; **-chlorür,** *n.* iodine monochloride; **-dampf,** *m.* iodine vapor; **-eisen,** *n.* iron iodide.

Jod-eiweiss, *n.* iodated albumen; **-gehalt,** *m.* iodine content; **-gorgosäure,** *f.* iodogorgic acid, diiodotyrosine; **-haltig,** iodiferous, containing iodine; **-hydrin,** *n.* iodohydrin.

Jodid, *n.* iodide; **-chlorid,** *n.* iodochloride.

jodieren, to iodize, iodate.

jodimetrisch, iodiometric.

Jodinrot, *n.* mercurous iodide.

Jodit, *n.* iodite.

Jodjodkalium, *n.* iodine potassium iodide; -**lösung,** *f.* potassium iodide solution of iodine.

Jod-kali(um), *n.* potassium iodide; -**kali-(um)lösung,** *f.* potassium iodide solution; -**kupfer,** *n.* iodide of copper; -**lösung,** *f.* iodine solution; -**menge,** *f.* amount of iodide; -**methyl,** *n.* methyl iodide, iodomethane; -**mittel,** *n.* iodiferous remedy; -**natrium,** *n.* sodium iodide.

Jodo-benzoesäure, *f.* iodoxybenzoic, acid; -**benzol,** *n.* iodoxybenzene; -**form,** *n.* iodoform; -**formgaze,** *f.* iodoform gauze.

Jodol, *n.* iodol.

Jodometrie, *f.* iodometry.

Jodonaphthalin, *n.* iodoxynaphthalene.

Jodonium, *n.* iodonium.

Jodosobenzol, *n.* iodosobenzene.

Jod-phosphonium, *n.* phosphonium iodide. -**präparat,** *n.* iodine preparation; -**probe,** *f.* iodine test; -**quecksilber,** *n.* mercuric iodide; -**salbe,** *f.* iodine ointment; -**sauer,** iodate of; -**säure,** *f.* iodic acid; -**serum,** *n.* iodized serum.

Job-silber, *n.* silver iodide; -**silizium,** *n.* silicon iodide; -**stärke,** *f.* starch iodide; -**stickstoff,** *m.* nitrogen iodide; -**tinktur,** *f.* tincture of iodine; -**tinkturanstrich,** *m.* painting with tincture of iodine; -**toluol,** *n.* iodotoluene; -**überträger,** *m.* iodine carrier.

Jodür, *n.* iodide.

Jod-verbindung, *f.* iodine compound; -**vergiftung,** *f.* iodine poisoning.

Jodwasserstoff, *m.* hydrogen iodide; -**äther,** *m.* ethyl iodide; -**säure,** *f.* hydriodic acid.

Jodwismut, *m.&n.* bismuth iodide.

Jodyrit, *m.* iodyrite.

Jod-zahl, *f.* iodine number; -**zink,** *n.* zinc iodide; -**zinnober,** *m.* iodide of mercury.

Joghurt, *n.* yoghurt.

Johannis-beere, *f.* currant; -**brache,** *f.* late summer fallow; -**brot,** *n.* carob, St.-John's-bread, carob bean; -**kraut,** *n.* St.-John's-wort (*Hypericum perforatum*); -**trieb,** *m.* lammas shoot, shoot of second sap, after sprig ("Johannes" is June 24); -**wurm,** *m.* glowworm; -**wurzel,** *f.* male fern, aspidium.

Jon, *n.* ion.

Jonan, *n.* ionan.

Jonendissoziation, *f.* ionic dissociation.

Jonium, *n.* ionium.

Jonon, *n.* ionone.

Journal, *n.* newspaper, journal.

Jubel, *m.* jubilation, exultation; -**feier,** *f.* jubilee; -**fest,** *n.* jubilee.

Jubiläum, *n.* jubilee, anniversary.

Jucht, Juchten, *m.*, **Juchtenleder,** *n.* Russia leather.

Juchten-öl, *n.* birch-tar oil, birch oil; -**rot,** *n.* Janus red.

jucken, to itch, irritate, scratch, rub.

Jucken, *n.* itching, pruritus.

Juden, *m.pl.* Jews; -**dornbeere,** *f.* jujube (Zizyphus); -**harz,** *n.* Jew's pitch (asphalt); -**kirsche,** *f.* alkekengi (*Physalis alkekengi*); -**pech,** *n.* Jew's pitch (asphalt); -**pilz,** alkekengi; -**schwamm,** *m. Boletus luridus.*

Jugend, *f.* youth, juvenile period, early stage, adolescence; -**blatt,** *n.* protophyll, seeding leaf; -**form,** *f.* juvenile form; -**kraft,** *f.* youthful strength.

jugendlich, youthful, young, juvenile.

Jugend-stadium, *n.* sapling stage, brush stage; -**wachstum,** *n.* reproduction, early growth; -**zustand,** *m.* state of youth.

Jugular-klappe, *f.* jugular valve; -**platte,** *f.* jugular plate.

Juli, *m.* July.

jung, young, fresh, early, recent, new.

Junge, *m.* boy, lad, youth, apprentice, young cub, puppy, calf.

jungen, to bring forth young.

Jünger, *m.* disciple, follower.

Jungfer, *f.* virgin, maid, spinster.

Jungfern-erde, *f.* virgin soil; -**früchtigkeit,** *f.* parthenocarpy; -**geburt,** *f.* parthenogenesis; -**glas,** *n.* selenite; -**metall,** *n.* native metal; -**öl,** *n.* virgin oil, olive oil; -**pergament,** *n.* vellum, thin parchment; -**quecksilber,** *n.* native mercury; -**schwefel,** *m.* virgin sulphur, native sulphur; -**wachs,** *n.* virgin wax; -**zeugung,** *f.* parthenogenesis.

Jung-frau, *f.* virgin, maid; -**geselle,** *m.* bachelor; -**kuckuck,** *m.* cuckoo fledgling; -**kultur,** *f.* young culture.

Jüngling, *m.* young man.

jüngst, youngest, last, latest, recently; in jüngster Zeit, in recent times.

Jung-steinzeit, *f.* neolithic age; -**storch,** *m.* stork fledgling.

Jungtertiär, *n.* Miocene (period).

Jungwuchs, *m.* young growth; -**grenze,** *f.* timber line.

jungzeitlich, recent.

Juni, *m.* June; **-käfer,** *m.* June chafer.

Junker, *m.* nobleman.

Jura, *m.* Jurassic; **-ablagerung,** *f.* deposit or deposition of jura; **-formation,** *f.* jura formation; **-kalk,** *m.* Jurassic limestone; **-zeit,** *f.* Jura period.

just, just, even now.

justieren, to adjust, justify.

Justier-schraube, *f.* set (adjusting) screw; **-tisch,** *m.* adjusting table.

Justierung, *f.* adjustment, justification.

Justiz, *f.* justice; **-wesen,** *n.* law, legal affairs.

Jute, *f.* jute; **-faden,** *m.* jute, fiber; **-faser,** jute fiber.

Juwel, *n.* jewel.

Juwelier, *m.* jeweler.

Jux, *m.* spree, frolic, lark, filth.

K

Kabel, *n.* cable.

Kabeljau, *m.* codfish; **-lebertran,** *m.* cod-liver oil.

Kabelschub, *m.* lug.

Kachel, *f.* Dutch (glazed) tile.

Kadaver, *m.* carcass, cadaver, corpse.

Kaddig, Kaddich, *m.* cade, juniper.

Kaddigöl, Kadeöl, *n.* oil of cade.

Kadmium, *n.* cadmium; **-gelb,** *n.* cadmium sulphide; **-haltig,** cadmiferous, containing cadmium; **-jodid,** *n.* cadmium iodide; **-legierung,** *f.* cadmium alloy; **-oxyd,** *n.* cadmic oxide.

Käfer, *m.pl.* beetles, chafers, Coleoptera; **-artig,** coleopterous; **-blumen,** *f.pl.* flowers pollinated by beetles (Cantharophilae); **-sammlung,** *f.* collection of beetles.

Kaff, *n.* chaff.

Kaffee, *m.* coffee; **-baum,** *m.* coffee tree; **-bohne,** *f.* coffee bean; **-brand,** *m.* coffee blight; **-gerbsäure,** *f.* caffetannin, caffetannic acid; **-kanne,** *f.* coffee pot; **-satz,** *m.* coffee grounds; **-säure,** *f.* caffeic acid; **-surrogat,** *n.* coffee substitute; **-wicke,** *f.* milk vetch (*Astragalus baeticus*).

Kaffein, *n.* caffeine.

Käfig, *m.*-e, (bird) cage.

kahl, bare, denuded, bald, barren, leafless, threadbare, poor, glabrous; ~ **gehen,** to require no flux.

kahl-ährig, barespiked; **-fläche,** *f.* clear-cut area, denuded area, clearing, area devoid of vegetation; **-flächeninsel,** *f.* area (island) devoid of vegetation; **-frass,** *m.* complete defoliation; **-hauen,** to cut clear, to clear.

Kahlheit, *f.* baldness, barrenness, alopecia.

Kahl-hiebwirtschaft, *f.* clear-cutting system; **-kopf,** *m.* baldhead; **-schlag,** *m.* clear-cutting; **-schlagfläche,** *f.* clear-cut area.

Kahm, *m.* mold.

kahmen, to mold.

Kahmhaut, *f.* zoogloea, pellicle (covering) of mold, scum.

kahmicht (kamig), moldy.

Kahmpilz, *m.* mycoderm, yeastlike fungus producing a pellicle.

Kahn, *m.* boat, canoe.

Kahnbein, *n.* scaphoid bone; **-gelenk,** *n.* cuneoscaphoid articulation; **-höcker,** *m.* tuberosity of scaphoid bone.

kahnförmig, boat-shaped, scaphoid, navicular, cymbiform.

Kai, *m.* quay, wharf.

Kaiman, *m.* alligator, cayman.

Kaiser, *m.* emperor; **-adler,** *m.* imperial eagle; **-blau,** *n.* smalt; **-gelb,** *n.* mineral yellow; **-grün** *n.* imperial green, Paris green.

kaiserlich, imperial.

Kaiser-reich, *n.* empire; **-schnitt,** *m.* Caesarean section; **-wurz,** *f.* masterwort (*Imperato ria ostruthium*).

Kajeputöl, *n.* cajuput oil.

Kakadu, *m.* cockatoo.

Kakao, *m.* cacao, cocoa; **-bohne,** *f.* cocoa bean; **-butter,** *f.* cocoa butter, fat; **-masse,** *f.* cocoa poaste; **-pulver,** *n.* cocoa powder; **-schalen,** *f.pl.* cocoa shells.

Kakerlak, *m.* cockroach, albino.

Kakodylsäure, *f.* cacodylic acid.

Kaktus, *m.* cactus.

Kalabarbohne, *f.* Calabar bean.

Kalamität, *f.* calamity.

Kalander, *m.* calender, glazing rollers; **-saal,** *m.* finishing room; **-schäden,** *m.pl.* calender spots; **-walzenpapier,** *n.* woolen paper, bowl paper, paper for lining calender rolls.

Kalb, *n.*⁼er, calf, fawn.

kalben, to calve.

Kälber-diphtherie, *f.* diphtheria of calves; **-kerbel,** *m.* cowweed (Anthriscus); **-kropf,** *m.* chervil, cow parsley (Chaerophyllum); **-lab,** *n.* rennet; **-lymphe,** *f.* calf lymph; **-magen,** *m.* rennet; **-ruhr,** *f.* calf dysentery, white scour.

Kalb-fell, *n.* calfskin; **-fleisch,** *n.* veal; **-leder,** *n.* calf leather.

Kalbspergament, *n.* vellum.

Kalcit (Kalzit), *m.* calcite.

Kalcium (Kalzium), *n.* calcium.

Kaldaune, *f.* tripe; *pl.* guts.

Kalender, *m.* calendar, almanac.

kalfatern, to caulk.

Kali, *n.* potash; **ätzendes** ~, caustic potash; **blausaures** ~, potassium cyanide; **essigsaures** ~, potassium acetate; **salpetersaures** ~, potassium nitrate.

Kali-alaun, *n.* potash alum; **-ammoniaksuperphosphate,** *n.* potassium ammonium superphosphate; **-ammonsalpeter,** *m.* potassium ammonium nitrate.

Kaliaturholz, *n.* sandalwood, caliatour wood.

Kaliber, *n.* caliber, sort, capacity, gauge, groove.

Kaliblau, *n.* Prussian blue.

kalibrieren, to calibrate, gauge, groove.

Kali-dünger, *m.* fertilizer, potash manure; **-düngesalz,** *n.* potassium salt for fertilizing; **-eisencyanür,** *n.* potassium ferrocyanide; **-haltig,** containing potash; **-hydrat,** *n.* potassium hydroxide, caustic potash.

Kaliko, *m.* calico; **-druck,** *m.* calico printing.

Kali-kugel, *f.* potash bulb; **-lauge,** *f.* potash lye, solution of caustic potash; **-metall,** *n.* potassium; **-pflanze,** *f.* glasswort, alkaline plant; **-rohsalz,** *n.* potassium salt (as mined); **-salpeter,** *m.* saltpeter, niter, potassium nitrate.

Kali-salz, *n.* potash (potassium) salt; **-salzlager,** *n.* bed of potash salts; **-schwefelleber,** *f.* sulphuretted potash, potassium sulphide; **-seife,** *f.* potash soap; **-siederei,** *f.* potash works; **-sulfat,** *n.* potassium sulphate.

Kalium, *n.* potassium; **chlorsaures** ~, potassium chlorate; **essigsaures** ~, potassium acetate.

Kalium-acetat, *n.* potassium acetate; **-alaun,** *m.* potassium alum: **-aurat,** *f.* aureate of potassium; **-azetat,** *n.* potassium acetate;

-brechweinstein, *m.* antimonyl potassium tartrate; **-bromid,** *n.* potassium bromide; **-chlorid,** *n.* potassium chloride; **-eisencyanid,** *n.* potassium ferricyanide; **-formiate,** *n.* potassium formate; **-gehalt,** *m.* potassium content.

Kalium-goldbromür, *n.* potassium bromoaurite; **-goldcyanid,** *n.* potassium auricyanide; **-halogen,** *n.* potassium halide; **-hydrat,** *n.* potassium hydroxide, potassium hydrate; **-hydrid,** *n.* potassium hydride; **-hydroxyd,** *n.* potassium hydroxide; **-hydrür,** *n.* potassium subhydride; **-jodid,** *n.* potassium iodide; **-kobaltinitrit,** *n.* potassium cobaltinitrite; **-nitrat,** *n.* potassium nitrate.

Kalium-oxydhydrat, *n.* potassium hydroxide, potassium oxyhydrate; **-permanganat,** *n.* potassium permanganate; **-platinchlorid,** *n.* potassium platinichloride; **-platinchlorür,** *n.* potassium platinochloride; **-rhodanid,** *n.* potassium thiocyanate; **-seife,** *f.* potassium soap; **-sulfat,** *n.* potassium sulphate; **-sulfid,** *n.* potassium sulphide; **-verbindung,** *f.* potassium compound; **-wasserstoff,** *m.* potassium hydride; **-zyanid,** *n.* potassium cyanide.

Kali-verbindung, *f.* potash compound; **-wasserglas,** *n.* potassium silicate, potash water glass.

Kalk, *m.* lime, chalk, limestone; **gebrannter** ~, quicklime; **gelöschter** ~, slaked lime; **kieselsauer** ~, silicate of lime; **kohlensaurer** ~, calcium carbonate; **phosphorsauer** ~, phosphate of lime; **ungelöschter** ~, quicklime.

Kalk-ablagerung, *f.* lime deposit; **-algen,** *f.pl.* calcareous algae; **-ammonsalpeter,** *m.* nitrate of lime and ammonia; **-anlagerung,** *f.* calcification; **-ansammlung,** *f.* accumulation of lime; **-anstrich,** *m.* whitewash; **-arm,** poor (deficient) in lime; **-artig,** calcareous, limy; **-äscher,** *m.* soap waste, lime pit; **-bedürfnis,** *n.* lime requirement.

Kalk-bestimmung, *f.* determination of lime; **-beuche,** *f.* lime boil; **-beule,** *f.* chalk nodule; **-bewurf,** *m.* coat of plaster; **-blau,** *n.* azurite blue, blue verditer; **-boden,** *m.* lime soil, calcareous soil; **-brei,** *m.* lime paste, lime cream, limewash, detritus of lime salts; **-brennen,** *n.* lime burning; **-brennerei,** *f.* limekiln; **-bruch,** *m.* limestone quarry.

Kalk-brühe, *f.* milk of lime, whitewash; **-drüse,** *f.* chalk gland; **-düngung,** *f.* manuring with lime; **-echt,** fast to lime; **-ei,** *n.* preserved egg; **-einlagerung,** *f.* calcareous deposit; **-eisenstein,** *m.* ferruginous limestone.

kalken, kälken, to lime.

Kalk-entartung, *f.* calcareous degeneration; **-erde,** *f.* lime, calcareous earth; **-erdig,** calcareous; **-faktor,** *m.* lime factor; **-fällung** *f.* precipitation of lime; **-feindlichkeit,** *f.* aversion to lime; **-fliehend,** calciphobous; **-frei,** free from lime; **-führend,** lime-bearing, containing lime; **-gebirge,** *n.* limestone mountains.

Kalk-gehalt, *m.* lime content; **-geröll,** *n.* limestone (detritus) debris; **-glimmer,** *m.* margarite; **-grasflur,** *f.* grassy limestone plain, chalk grassland; **-grube,** *f.* lime pit; **-guss,** *m.* thin lime mortar; **-haltig,** containing lime, calcareous; **-hold,** calciphilous (lime loving); **-hügel,** *m.* limestone hill; **-hütte,** *f.* limekiln; **-hydrat,** *n.* hydrate of lime.

Kalkierpapier, *n.* tracing paper.

kalkig, limy, calcareous.

Kalk-kies, *m.* limestone gravel; **-körperchen,** *n.* calcareous body, granule; **-lager,** *n.* lime deposit; **-lauge,** *f.* lime lye; **-leiste,** *f.* calcareous ridge; **-licht,** *n.* limelight, calcium light; **-liebend,** calcicolous; **-löschen,** *n.* lime slaking; **-lösung,** *f.* solution of lime, calcium hydroxide; **-mangel,** *m.* deficiency of lime; **-mehl,** *n.* lime powder.

kalkmeidend, avoiding calcareous soil, calcifugous; **kalkmeidende Gewächse,** *n.pl.* calcifuges.

Kalk-menge, *f.* amount of lime; **-mergel,** *m.* lime marl; **-messer,** *m.* calcimeter; **-milch,** *f.* slaked lime, milk of lime; **-mörtel,** *m.* lime mortar; **-nadel,** *f.* calcareous spicule, rhabdus; **-niederschlag,** *m.* lime precipitate; **-ofen,** *m.* limekiln; **-pflanze,** *f.* calcareous plant; **-platte,** *f.* shell plate.

Kalk-rädchen, *n.* calcareous wheel; **-rahm,** *m.* cream of lime; **-reich,** rich in lime; **-salpeter,** *m.* calcium nitrate; **-salz,** *n.* lime salt, calcium salt; **-sand,** *m.* calcareous sand; **-schale,** *f.* calcareous shell; **-schaum,** *m.* lime (froth) scum; **-scheibe,** *f.* calcareous disk; **-scheu,** calciphobous.

Kalk-schicht, *f.* chalk layer; **-schiefer,** *m.* calcareous slate; **-schlamm,** *m.* lime sludge; **-schwefelleber,** *f.* sulphurated lime; **-schwiele,** *f.* calcareous callus; **-seife,** *f.* calcium soap; **-spange,** *f.* calcareous arch; **-spat,** *m.* calcite, calcspar; **-spindel,** *f.* calcareous pillar; **-stein,** *m.* limestone.

Kalk-steinablagerung, *f.* limestone deposit; **-steingebiet,** *n.* limestone region; **-stein-**

zuschlag, *m.* addition of limestone; **-stickstoff,** *m.* calcium cyanamide, lime nitrogen; **-sulfat,** *n.* sulphate of lime, calcium sulphate; **-talkspat,** *m.* dolomite; **-tiegel,** *m.* lime crucible; **-tünche,** *f.* whitewash.

kalkulatorisch, by calculation, mathematically.

kalkulieren, to calculate.

Kalk-verbindung, *f.* lime (calcium) compound; **-verseifung,** *f.* saponification with lime; **-wasser,** *n.* limewater; **-werk,** *n.* lime works; **-zufuhr,** *f.* supply of lime; **-zuschlag,** *m.* limestone flux; **-zustand,** *m.* state of lime.

Kallitypie, *n.* callityping.

Källus, *m.* callus.

Kalmen-gürtel, *m.* **-zone,** *f.* calm zone.

Kalmie, *f.* mountain laurel (*Kalmia latifolia*).

Kalmus, *m.* calamus; **-wurzel,** *f.* calamus root.

Kalorescenz, *f.* calorescence.

Kalorie, *f.* calorie.

Kalorien-gehalt, *m.* caloric content; **-lieferant,** *m.* provider of calories; **-zufuhr,** *f.* caloric intake.

Kalorifer, *n.* heater, radiator.

Kalorimeter, *n.&m.* calorimeter.

kalorimetrisch, calorimetric(al).

kalorisch, caloric.

kalt, cold, cool, frigid, chilly, reserved, calm, indifferent, callous; **-bläsig,** refractory; **-blüter,** *m.pl.* cold-blooded animals; **-blütig,** cold-blooded; **-brüchig,** cold-short.

Kälte, *f.* cold, chill, frigidity, indifference, coolness; **-beständig,** resistant to cold; **-empfindlich,** sensitive to cold; **-empfindung,** *f.* sensation of cold; **-erzeugend,** frigorific; **-erzeuger,** *m.* refrigerator; **-erzeugung,** *f.* artificial freezing; **-erzeugungsmachine,** *f.* refrigerating machine; **-festigkeit,** *f.* resistance to cold, cold hardiness; **-grad,** *m.* degree below zero, degree of cold.

Kälte-leistung, *f.* refrigerating capacity; **-mischung,** *f.* freezing mixture; **-reiz,** *m.* low-temperature stimulus, irritation due to cold; **-starre,** *f.* rigor due to low temperature; **-träger,** *m.* cooling medium, cold conductor; **-wüste,** *f.* cold desert, tundra.

kalt-gezogen, cold-drawn; **-gründig,** cold (soil); **-umsetzungsverfahren,** *n.* cold double-decomposition process; **-wasser-**

heilanstalt, *f.* hydropathic establishment; -werden, *n.* becoming cold, refrigeration.

kalzinieren, to calcine.

Kalzit, *n.* calcite.

Kalzium, *n.* calcium; -hydroxyd, *f.* calcium hydroxide; slaked lime, lime hydrate; -karbonat, *n.* calcium carbonate; -oxyd, *n.* calcium oxide, dehydrated lime, burnt lime, -seife, *f.* calcium soap; -verbindung, *f.* calcium compound.

kam, came, was coming.

Kambium, *n.* cambium; -schicht, *f.* cambium zone.

kambrisch, Cambrian (formation).

käme, would come, came, comes.

Kamee, *f.* cameo.

Kamel, *n.* camel; -garn, *n.* mohair; -heu, *n.* camel grass.

Kamelie, *f.* camellia.

Kamelziege, *f.* Angora goat.

Kamerad, *m.* comrade.

Kamfer (Kampfer), *m.* camphor.

kamig (kahmicht), moldy.

Kamille, *f.* camomile.

Kamin, *m.* chimney, fireplace, gut.

Kamm, *m.* crest, ridge, bit, comb, mane, cog, cam, tappet; -artig, crested, pectinate, ctenoid; -blase, *f.* ctenocyst (comb bladder).

kämmen, to comb, card.

Kammer, *f.* chamber, ventricle.

Kämmerchen, *n.* little chamber, locule.

Kämmerei, *f.* combing, exchequer.

Kammer-faser, *f.* septate fiber; -klappe, *f.* ventricular valve; -raum, *m.* ventricular cavity; -säure, *f.* chamber acid, crude sulphuric acid; -scheidewand, *f.* ventricular septum, partition wall; -schiessen, *n.* chambering (explosives); -schlamm *m.* chamber sludge; -schleifer, *m.* pocket grinder; -sohle, *f.* chamber floor; -tiefe, *f.* depth of chamber.

Kammer-tuch, *n.* cambric; -wand, *f.* trama plate (fungi); -wasser, *n.* aqueous humor (of eye).

Kamm-fett, *n.* melted horse grease; -förmig, pectinate, ctenoid; -garn, *n.* worsted yarn; -gewimpert, pectinately fringed or ciliated; -gras, *n.* crested dog's-tail (grass) (*Cynosurus cristatus*); -haar, *n.* horse's mane; -kieme, *f.* ctenidium, comblike gill; -kiemer, *m.pl.* ctenidio branchia; -kies, *m.*

cockscomb pyrites or marcasite; -knorpel, *m.* pectinate cartilage.

Kamm-krabbe, *f.* box crab; -muschel, *f.* scallop; -muskel, *m.* pectineus (muscle); -naht, *f.* pectinate suture; -qualle, *f.* comb jelly (Physalia); -rad, *n.* cogwheel; -saat, *f.* ridge sowing; -schmiele, *f.* comblike meadow grass (*Poa cristata*); -schuppig, ctenoid; -wolle, *f.* carded wool, worsted.

Kamp, *m.* enclosure, nursery, field, area.

Kampagne, *f.* campaign, season.

Kampane, *f.* bell jar.

Kampesch(e)holz, *n.* campeachy wood, logwood.

Kampf, *m.≃e*, combat, action, struggle, effort, contest, fight; ~ ums Dasein, struggle for life.

kämpfen, to fight, strive, struggle, battle, contend.

Kämpfer, *m.* combatant, fighter.

Kampfer, *m.* camphor; -artig, camphorlike; -essig, *m.* camphorated vinegar; -geist, *m.* spirit of camphor.

kampfern, to camphorate.

Kampfer-säure, *f.* camphoric acid; -spiritus, *m.* spirit of camphor.

Kampf-gas, *n.* gas used in warfare; -hahn, *m.* gamecock; -massnahmen, *f.pl.* control measures; -mittel, *n.* means of combat; -platz, *m.* scene of action, battlefield; unfähig, defenseless; -wagen, *m.* armored car, tank; -wütig, aggressive, infuriated.

Kamphen, *n.* camphene.

Kampher, *n.* camphor.

Kanadabalsam, *n.* Canada balsam.

Kanal, *m.≃e*, canal, channel, sewer, drain, conduit.

Kanälchen, *n.* canalicule, canaliculus.

Kanalgas, *n.* sewer gas.

Kanalisation, *f.* canalization, sewerage.

Kanal-jauche, *f.* sewage liquid; -kühler, *m.* tunnel (cooler) condenser; -ofen, *m.* tunnel kiln; -strahl, *m.* canal ray; -strahlbündel, *n.* pencil of canal rays; -wasser, *n.* sewage.

Kanarien-farbe, *f.* canary color; -gelb, canary yellow; -vogel, *m.* canary bird.

Kandare, *f.* curb bit.

kandeln, to channel, flute, groove.

Kandidat, *m.* candidate.

kandieren, to candy, coat (seed grain), treat seed with copper sulphate.

Kandis (-zucker), *m.* sugar candy.

Kaneel, *m.* cinnamon.

Kanevas, *m.* canvas.

Känguruh, *n.* kangaroo.

Kaninchen, *n.* rabbit; **-bau,** *m.* rabbit burrow; **-gehege,** *n.* rabbit warren; **-passage,** *f.* passage through rabbit; **-septi-kämie,** *f.* septicemia in rabbit; **-stall,** *m.* rabbit hutch.

kann (können), can, is able.

Kännchen, *n.* small can.

Kanne, *f.* can, jug, pot, pitcher, liter, ascidium, canister.

kannelieren, to channel, flute, groove.

Kannelierung, *f.* channeling, fluting.

Kannen-kraut, *n.* scouring rush, shave grass (*Equisetum arvense*); **-pflanze,** *f.* pitcher plant; **-strauch,** *m.* nepenthes; **-zinn,** *n.* pewter.

kannettieren, to cap.

kannte (kennen), knew.

Kanone, *f.* cannon, gun.

Kanonen-bein, *n.* cannon bone; **-gut,** *n.* gunmetal; **-ofen,** *m.* sealed tube furnace (high pressure); **-rohr,** *n.* sealed pressure tube.

kanonisch, canonical.

Kantalupe, *f.* cantaloupe.

Kante, *f.* edge, corner, border, margin, brim, lace.

Kantel, *n.* square ruler.

kanten, to edge, square, border, cant, tilt, set (up) on edge; **-länge,** *f.* length of edge, length of side; **-weise,** edgewise, on edge; **winkel,** *m.* angle formed by two planes.

Kantharide, *f.* Spanish fly.

Kantharidenlack, *m.* varnish with sheen of gold beetles.

Kantholz, *n.* squared timber.

kantig, edged, angular, squared; **-be-schlagen,** square-cut.

Kanüle, *f.* tubule, cannule, canula.

Kanzlei, *f.* chancellery, chancery.

kaolinisieren, to kaolinize.

Kap, *n.* cape.

Kapaun, *m.* capon.

Kapazität, *f.* capacity.

kapazitiv, capacitive.

Kapelle, *f.* cupel, sand bath, capsule, chapel, band.

Kapellen-abfall, *m.* loss in cupellation; **-asche,** *f.* bone ash; **-gold,** *n.* fine gold; **-kläre,** *f.* cupel dust; **-ofen,** *m.* cupeling (assay) furnace; **-probe,** *f.* cupel test; **-pulver,** *n.* cupel dust, bone ash; **-raub,** *m.* loss in cupellation; **-träger,** *m.* cupel holder; **-zug,** *m.* loss in cupellation.

kapellieren, to cupel, refine.

Kaper, *f.* caper.

Kapern-gewächse, *n.pl.* Capparidaceae; **-strauch,** *m.* caperbush.

Kapillar, *n.* capillary; **-affinität,** *f.* capillary affinity; **-aktiv,** surface-active, lowering surface tension; **-attraktion,** *f.* capillary attraction.

Kapillare, *f.* capillary, capillary tube.

Kapillar-flasche, *f.* capillary flask; **-gang,** *m.* capillary passage; **-gebiet,** *n.* capillary region; **-gefäss,** *n.* capillary vessel; **-gefässnetz,** *n.* capillary network; **-inaktiv,** increasing surface tension.

Kapillarität, *f.* capillarity.

Kapillaritätsanziehung, *f.* capillary attraction.

Kapillar-kreislauf, *n.* capillary circulation; **-masche,** *f.* capillary network; **-röhrchen,** *n.* capillary tube; **-röhre,** *f.* capillary tube, **-schicht,** *f.* capillary layer; **-span-nung,** *f.* capillary tension: **-wirkung,** *f.* capillary action.

Kapital, *n.* capital, stock.

Kapitalist, *n.* insect-fertilized plant, capitalist.

Kapitel, *n.* chapter.

Kapoköl, *n.* kapokoil.

Kappe, *f.* cap, hood, sheath, top, calyptra.

kappeln, to top.

kappen, to top, lop, cut, caponize; **-flasche,** *f.* bottle with cap; **-förmig,** cucullate, hood-shaped; **-pfeffer,** *m.* Guinea pepper; **-robbe,** *f.* hooded seal; **-steife,** *f.* box-toe cement; **-zelle,** *f.* cap cell.

Kapphahn, *m.* capon.

Kaprylsäure, *f.* caprylic acid.

Kaprinsäure, *f.* capric acid.

Kapsel, *f.-n,* cap, capsule, case, box; **-artig,** capsular, like a capsule; **-band,** *n.* capsular ligament; **-bazillus,** *m.* capsulated bacillus; **-diplokokken,** *m.pl.* capsulated diplococci; **-färbung,** *f.* staining of the capsule; **-faser,** *f.* capsular fiber; **-förmig,** capsular, like a capsule; **-frucht,** *f.* capsule; **-gewebe,** *n.* capsular tissue.

Kapsel-guss, *m.* casting in chills; **-hals,** *m.* apophysis; **-schnitt,** *m.* capsular incision; **-ton,** *m.* sagger clay; **-tragend,** capsuliferous, capsulated.

kaputt, broken.

Kapuze, *f.* hood, cowl.

kapuzenförmig, hoodlike.

Kapuziner, *m.* Capuchin (monk); **-kresse,** *f.* Indian cress, nasturtium (*Tropaeolum majus*).

Kapyr, *n.* kefir.

Karabinerhaken, *'a.* spring hook.

Karaffe, *f.* carafe, decanter.

Karaghenmoos, *n.* carrageen, Irish moss.

karaibisch, Caribbean.

Karamel, *m.* caramel.

karamelisieren, to caramelize.

Karat, *n.* carat; **-gewicht,** *n.* troy weight.

karatieren, to alloy gold.

Karatierung, *f.* alloying of gold.

-karatig, carat.

Karausche, *f.* crucian carp (*Carassius vulgaris*).

Karbe, *f.* common caraway.

Karbid, *n.* carbide.

Karbol-fuchsin, *n.* carbolfuchsin; **-fuchsinlösung,** *f.* carbolfuchsin solution; **-säure,** *f.* carbolic acid, phenol; **-seife,** *f.* carbolic soap; **-vergiftung,** *f.* carbolic acid poisoning; **-wasser,** *n.* aqueous solution of phenol or of carbolic acid; **-watte,** *f.* carbolized cotton wool.

Karbonat, *n.* carbonate.

Karbunkel, *m.* carbuncle, anthrax, furuncle; **-krankheit,** *f.* anthrax.

karburieren, to carbonize.

Kardamom, *m.* cardamom

Kardätsche, *f.* card, screed, striking edge, currycomb, horse brush.

Karde, *f.* teasel (Dipsacus).

Kardobenedikt, *m.* blessed or holy thistle.

Karfunkel, *m.* carbuncle, almandite.

karg, economical, stingy, close, scanty, poor, spare, parsimonious.

kargen, to be sparing, economical, stingy.

Kargheit, *f.* stinginess.

kärglich, sparing, scanty, piteous, paltry.

karibisch, Caribbean.

kariert, checked, checkered.

Kariteöl, *n.* karite oil, shea butter.

Karmelitergeist, *m.* Carmelite water.

karmesin, crimson; **-beeren,** *f.pl.* kermes berries, kermes; **-farbig,** crimson; **-rot,** crimson.

Karmin, *m.-e,* carmine; **-blau,** *n.* indigo carmine; **-lack,** *m.* carmine (cochineal) lake; **-rot,** *n.* carmine red; **-säure,** *f.* carminic acid.

Karminochinon, *n.* carminoquinone.

karmoisin, crimson.

Karnallit, *m.* carnallite.

Karneol, *n.* carnelian.

Karnickel, *n.* "rabbit," concealed motive or factor.

kärntisch, Carinthian.

Karo, *n.* check, checker, square.

Karobe, *f.* carob, carob bean.

Karotide, *f.* carotid artery.

Karotin, *n.* carotene.

Karotte, *f.* carrot.

Karpfen, *m.-,* carp; **-rücken,** *m.* roachback, high back.

Karragheenmoos, *n.* carrageen, Irish moss.

Karre, *f.* wheelbarrow, cart.

Karree, *n.* square.

Karren, *m.* cart, wheelbarrow, truck, car; **-gaul,** *m.* cart horse; **-pflug,** *m.* wheel plow.

Karriere, *f.* career.

Karst, *m.* mattock, prong hoe, bare Alpine tract.

Kartäuser-likor, *m.* chartreuse; **-nelke,** *f.* Carthusian pink; **-pulver,** *n.* Carthusian powder.

Karte, *f.* card, map, chart, menu, charter, ticket; **alles auf eine ~ setzen,** to stake everything on one card.

Kartei, *f.* card index, filing cabinet.

Karten-blatt, *n.* (single) card; **-papier,** *n.* cardboard; **-wesen,** *n.* card indexes.

kartieren, to trace out.

Kartierung, *f.* preparation of a survey sheet.

Kartoffel, *f.-n,* potato; **-anerkennung,** *f.* certification of seed potatoes; **-aushebepflug,** *m.* potato digger; **-ausschuss,** *m.* small potatoes; **-bauversuch,** *m.* potato-breeding experiment; **-bazillus,** *m.* potato bacillus; **-beizung,** *f.* seed-potato disinfection; **-blattrollkrankheit,** *f.* leafcurl (leafroll) of potatoes; **-branntwein,** *m.* potato spirit(s); **-brei,** *m.* mashed potatoes.

Kartoffel-erntemaschine, *f.* potato digger; -käfer, *m.* potato beetle, Colorado potato beetle; -keil, *m.* wedge of potato for medium; -keller, *m.* potato or root cellar; -knollenfäule, *f.* potato blight; -kraut, *n.* potato tops; -krautfäule, *f.* late blight of potatoes; -krebs, *m.* potato wart, black scab; -kultur, *f.* culture on potato medium; -laub, *n.* potato foliage.

Kartoffel-legemaschine, *f.* potato planter; -mehl, *n.* potato flour; -miete, *f.* potato pit; -motte, *f.* potato tuber worm; -nährboden, *m.* potato culture medium; -pest, *f.* potato rot; -pflanzmaschine, *f.* potato-planting machine; -pflug, *m.* plow used in potato culture; -puffer, *m.* potato pancake; -quetschmaschine, *f.* potato pulper.

Kartoffel-rollkrankheit, *f.* potato leafroll; -schale, *f.* potato (peel) skin; -schorf, *m.* potato scab; -sortierzylinder, *m.* potato (grader) sorter; -sortiermaschine, *f.* potato (grader) sorter; -spritzen, *n.* potato-vine spraying; -stärke, *f.* potato starch; -trieb, *m.* potato sprout; -walzmehl, *n.* potato flour from roller mill; -zucker, *m.* potato sugar; -zwiebel, *f.* potato onion.

Karton, *m.* pasteboard box.

Kartonage, -arbeit, *f.* cardboard work.

kartonieren, to bind in boards.

Kartothek, *f.* card collection, card index.

Kartusche, *f.* cartridge, cartouche.

Karub, *m.* Karube, *f.* carob.

Karussel, *n.* merry-go-round, turntable.

Karyokinese, *f.* karyokinesis, cell division.

Karzinom, *n.* carcinoma.

karzinomatös, carcinomatous.

Kaschierung, *f.* lining.

Kaschmir, *m.* cashmere.

Kaschu (Katechu), catechu.

Käse, *m.* cheese, curds; -artig cheesy, caseous.

Kasein, *n.* casein.

Käse-fliege, *f.* cheese fly; -lab, *n.* rennet; -made, *f.* cheese maggot; -magen, *m.* rennet bag, abomasum; -milbe, *f.* cheese mite.

käsen, to curd, curdle, coagulate.

Käsepappel, *f.* mallow; -gewächse, *n.pl.* Malvaceae.

Käserei, *f.* cheese dairy.

Käse-reifung, *f.* curing; -säure, *f.* lactic acid, caseic acid; -spirillen, *n.pl.* spirilla

cultivated in cheese; -stoff, *m.* casein; -vergiftung, *f.* poisoning by cheese; -wasser, *n.* whey.

käsig, cheesy, caseous, curdy.

Kaskarillenrinde, *f.* cascarilla bark.

Kassawamehl, *n.* cassava starch, cassava.

Kasse, *f.* cash, money box, chest, safe, cashier's (ticket) office.

Kasseler Erde, *f.* Cassel earth.

Kasselergelb, *n.* Cassel yellow.

Kasserolle, *f.* casserole.

Kassette, *f.* cash box, coffer, casket, film or plate holder.

Kassettenplatte, *f.* plate in plate holder, precast (concrete) slab unit.

Kassia, *f.* cassia.

Kassienblüten, *f.pl.* cassia buds.

kassieren, to cash, dismiss, annul.

Kassierer, *m.* cashier, treasurer.

Kastanie, *f.* chestnut, horse chestnut.

kastanienbraun, chestnut-brown, auburn, maroon.

Kästchen, *n.-*, little chest or case, casket, alveolus.

kasteien, to chastise, mortify.

Kasten, *m.-*, chest, box, trunk, vat, cold frame, crucible, flask, coffer, safe, alveolus; -speiser, *m.* hopper feed; -träger, *m.* box girder.

Kastoröl, *n.* castor oil.

Kastrat, *m.* eunuch.

Kastration, *f.* castration.

kastrieren, to castrate.

Katabolismus, *m.* catabolism.

Katalase-gehalt, *m.* content of catalase; -probe, *f.* catalase test.

Katalog, *m.-e*, catalogue.

katalogisieren, to catalogue.

Katalysator, *m.-en*, catalyst.

Katalyse *f.* catalysis.

katalysieren, to catalyze.

katalytisch, catalytic.

Kataphorese, *f.* cataphoresis.

Katarrh, *m.* catarrh.

Katarrhalfieber, *n.* malignant catarrh, catarrhal fever.

katarrhalisch, catarrhal.

Katastrophe, *f.* catastrophe.

Katechin, *n.* catechol, catechin.

Katechu, *n.* catechu; **-palme,** *f.* areca; **-säure,** *f.* catechuic acid, catechin tannin.

Kategorie, *f.* category.

kategorisch, categorical.

Kater, *m.*-, tomcat.

Katgut, *n.* catgut.

kathartisch, cathartic.

Katheten, *f.pl.* short sides of a rectangular triangle.

Katheter, *m.* catheter, lecturer's desk.

Kathode, *f.* cathode.

Kathoden-dichte, *f.* cathode density; **-raum,** *n.* cathode space; **-strahl,** *m.* cathode ray; **-strahlenbündel,** *n.* (cathode) ray bundle; **-strahlenenergie,** *f.* energy of cathode rays; **-strahlenröhre,** *f.* cathode ray; **-strahlung,** *f.* cathode radiation; **-zerstäubung,** *f.* cathode sputtering; **-zuckung,** *f.* cathodal contraction.

kathodochemisch, cathodochemical.

Kation, *n.*-en, cation, kation, positive ion.

Kationenbelegung, *f.* attached cations.

Kattun, *m.* calico, cotton; **-druck,** *m.* calico printing; **-druckerei,** *f.* calico printing; **-fabrik,** *f.* cotton mill; **-presse,** *f.* calico press.

Kätzchen, *n.*-, kitten, catkin, ament; **-blätterig,** amentiferous; **-blumig,** amentaceous; **-blütler,** *m.* amentaceous plant; **-form,** *f.* catkinlike form; **-träger,** *m.* amentaceous plant; **-tragend,** amentaceous.

Katze, *f.* cat.

Katzen-auge, *n.* cat's-eye, reflector; **-baldrian,** *m.* valerian; **-darm,** *m.* catgut; **-glimmer,** *m.* cat gold, yellow mica; **-gold,** *n.* cat gold, yellow mica; **-kraut,** *n.* cat thyme (*Teucrium marum*); **-minze,** *f.* catnip (*Nepeta cataria*); **-pfötchen,** *n.* cat's-foot (*Gnaphalium dioicum*); **-silber,** *n.* Argentine mica.

Kau-akt, *m.*-e, act of chewing; **-apparat,** *m.* masticating apparatus; **-äste,** *m.pl.* masticatory branches.

kaubar, masticable.

Kaubewegung, *f.* masticatory movement.

kauen, to chew, bite, masticate.

kauern, to cower.

Kauf, *m.* buying, purchase, bargain; in den ∼ **nehmen,** to make allowance of.

kaufen, to buy, purchase.

Käufer, *m.* buyer, purchaser.

Kauf-gut, *n.* merchandise; **-handel,** *m.* commerce, trade.

Kaufläche, *f.* masticating surface.

Kauf-laden, *m.*:, store, shop; **-leute,** *pl.* merchants, tradesmen.

käuflich, purchasable, marketable, for sale, venal.

Kaufmann, *m.*:er, merchant.

kaufmännisch, mercantile, commercial.

Kaufmuster, *n.* salesman's sample.

Kau-füsse, *m.pl.* masticatory (oral) appendages, chewing feet (of Crustacea); **-gelenk,** *n.* temporomaxillary joint; **-gummi,** *n.* chewing gum; **-lade,** *f.* chewing lobe, masticatory ridge or blade; **-lade,** (innere), *f.* lacina of maxilla, inner plate; **-lade** (äussere), *f.* galea of maxilla, outer plate.

Kaulquappe, *f.* tadpole.

kaum, scarcely, hardly; ∼ **noch,** just a moment ago, barely.

Kau-magen, *m.* gizzard, mastax; **-mittel,** *n.* masticatory; **-muskel,** *m.* masseter muscle; **-muskelgrube,** *f.* masseter fossa; **-organ,** *n.* organ of mastication; **-pfeffer,** *m.* betel; **-platten,** *f.pl.* chewing plates.

Kaupren, *n.* cauprene.

Kau-probe, *f.* mastication test.

Kauriharz, *n.* kauri (kaury) resin.

Kausalität, *f.* causality.

kaustisch, caustic.

kaustifizieren, to causticize, cauterize, corrode.

Kaustizität, *f.* causticity.

Kautabak, *m.* chewing tobacco.

Kautel, *f.* precaution.

Kauter, *m.* cautery.

Kauterien, *n.pl.* cauteries, caustics.

kauterisieren, to cauterize.

kautschen, to couch.

Kautschin, *n.* caoutchene.

Kautschuk, *m.&n.* caoutchouc, rubber, India rubber; **-ballon,** *m.* India-rubber syringe; **-band,** *n.* India-rubber bandage; **-feigenbaum,** *m.* rubber plant, rubber fig; **-gewebe,** *n.* elastic (webbing) tissue; **-milchsaft,** *m.* rubber latex; **-pflanze,** *f.* rubber-yielding plant; **-schlauch,** *m.* India-rubber tube; **-waren,** *f.pl.* rubber goods.

Kauwerkzeuge, *n.pl.* organs for mastication.

Kauz, *m.* little owl, a queer fellow.

Kauzahn, *m.* molar tooth.

Kaverne, *f.* cavity, cavern.

Kawapfeffer, *m.* kava pepper.

keck, bold, audacious.

Keckheit, *f.* boldness.

Kefir, *m.* kephir; **-körner,** *n.pl.* kephir grains; **-pilz,** *m.* kephir fungus.

Kegel, *m.-,* cone, ninepin, skittle, phragmocone; **-fläche,** *f.* conical surface; **-flasche,** *f.* conical flask; **-förmig, kegelig,** conical, cone-shaped, tapering; **-früchtig,** conocarpous; **-rad,** *n.* bevel gear, cone wheel; **-robbe,** *f.* gray seal; **-schnitt,** *m.* conic section, infundibular incision; **-stumpf,** *m.* obtuse cone; **-zelle,** *f.* cell of the crystalline cone.

Kehl-ader, *f.* jugular (laryngeal) vein; **-brustplatte,** *f.* interclavicle; **-deckel,** *m.* epiglottis; **-deckelbändchen,** *n.* frenulum of epiglottis, epiglottic fold; **-deckeldrüse,** *f.* gland of epiglottis; **-deckelknorpel,** *m.* cartilage of epiglottis; **-drüse,** *f.* thyroid gland.

Kehle, *f.* throat, larynx, gula, gullet, groove.

kehlen, to flute, groove.

Kehl-entzündung, *f.* laryngitis; **-füssler,** *m.pl.* Laemodipoda; **-gang,** *m.* esophagus, intermaxillary space; **-geschwulst,** *f.* swelling of the throat; **-grube,** *f.* suprasternal fossa; **-knochen,** *m.* hyoid bone; **-knorpel,** *m.* laryngeal cartilage.

Kehlkopf, *m.* larynx; **-band,** *f.* laryngeal ligament; **-deckel,** *m.* epiglottis, laryngeal cover; **-drüse,** *f.* laryngeal gland; **-eingang,** *m.* orifice of larynx, glottis, entrance to larynx; **-fistel,** *f.* laryngeal fistula.

Kehlkopf-gegend, *f.* laryngeal region; **-knorpel,** *m.* cartilage of the larynx; **-krampf,** *m.* laryngospasm; **-laut,** *m.* guttural sound; **-öffnung,** *f.* upper orifice of larynx; **-spiegel,** *m.* laryngoscope, laryngeal mirror; **-tasche,** *f.* laryngeal ventricle.

Kehl-lappen, *m.pl.* lobes, gills; **-naht,** *f.* throat seam, fillet weld, gular suture; **-zäpflein,** *n.* uvula.

Kehlung, *f.* haunch (of beam), fillet.

Kehr-bild, *n.* negative (of photograph).

Kehre, *f.* turn(ing), direction, way.

kehren, to turn, sweep, dust, brush; **sich ~,** to turn (about); **sich an etwas ~,** to pay attention to something.

Kehricht, *m.&n.* sweepings, dirt, rubbish.

Kehr-platz, *m.* turning place; **-punkt,** *m.* apsis; **-salpeter,** *f.* saltpeter sweepings; **-seite,** *f.* reverse, back, wrong side; **-wert,** *m.* reciprocal value.

keifen, to scold.

Keil, *m.-e,* wedge, cuneus, key, keystone, dowel, cotter pin; **-ähnlich, -artig,** wedge-shaped, cuneiform, sphenoid(al).

Keilbein, *n.* sphenoid bone, cuneiform bone; **-dorn,** *m.* spine of sphenoid; **-flügel,** *m.* wing of sphenoid; **-flügelknochen,** *m.* pterygoid (bone); **-fortsatz,** *m.* sphenoidal process of apophysis; **-höhle,** *f.* sphenoidal sinus; **-horn,** *n.* sphenoid process; **-kamm,** *m.* sphenoid crest.

Keilbein-kieferspalte, *f.* sphenomaxillary fissure; **-körper,** *m.* body of the sphenoid; **-loch,** *n.* sphenoidal foramen; **-naht,** *f.* sphenoidal suture; **-schläfenflügel,** *m.* great wing of sphenoid; **-schnabel,** *m.* rostrum sphenoidale; **-sessel,** *m.* sella turcica; **-spalte,** *f.* sphenoidal fissure; **-stachel,** *m.* spine of sphenoid.

Keil-berechnung, *f.* key proportioning; **-blättrig,** having cuneate leaves; **-color-imeter,** *n.* wedge calorimeter.

keilen, to wedge, key.

Keiler, *m.* wedger, wild boar, cleaving ax, cleft stick.

keil-förmig, wedge-shaped, cuneate, sphenoid; **-fortsatz,** *m.* sphenoidal apophysis or process; **-hacke,** *f.* pickax; **-paar,** *n.* pair of wedges, double wedge; **-pfropfen,** *n.* cleft grafting; **-riemen,** *m.* V belt; **-schnabel,** *m.* sphenoidal rostrum; **-strangkern,** *m.* cuneate nucleus; **-wirkung,** *f.* wedge effect; **-würfelbeinband,** *n.* cuneocuboid ligament.

Keim, *m.-e,* embryo, germ, nucleus, bud, sprout, spore, ~hoot; **-anhang,** *m.* embryonic appendage; **-anlage,** *f.* germinal layer, embryonic rudiment, blastoderm; **-apparat,** *m.* germinating apparatus; **-bahn,** *f.* germ tract; **-bett,** *n.* germinating bed; **-bezirk,** *m.* part of embryo; **-bildung,** *f.* germ formation; **-bläschen,** *n.* germinal vesicle, egg apparatus; **-blase,** *f.* blastoderm, blastocyst.

Keimblatt, *n.-er,* cotyledon, germinal layer; **-äusseres ~,** ectoderm, epiblast; **inneres ~,** entoderm, hypoblast; **mittleres ~,** mesoderm.

Keim-blätterbildung, *f.* formation of germ layers; **-blätterig,** cotyledonous; **-blätterumkehr,** *f.* inversion of germ layers; **-blattlos,** acotyledonous; **-blattstamm,** *m.* primordium (cotyledon); **-blosslegung,** *f.* nucleus denudation.

Keimchen, *n.pl.* gemmules.

Keim-dauer, *f.* duration of germination; **-drüse,** *f.* germ gland, gonad; **-drüsenhormon,** *n.* sex hormone, hormone of germ gland.

keimen, to germinate, develop, bud, sprout.

Keim-entwicklung, *f.* germ development; **-epithel,** *n.* germinal epithelium.

Keimmaterial, *n.* embryonic material.

Keim-faden, *m.*-, germ tube; **-fähig,** capable of germinating; **-fähigkeit,** *f.* capability of germinating, germinating power, viability; **-falte,** *f.* germinal fold, ridge; **-fäule,** *f.* sprout blight; **-flechte,** *f.* blastospore.

Keim-fleck, *m.* germinal spot or macula, chalaza; **-flüssigkeit,** *f.* blastema, fluid of vesicular blastoderm; **-frei,** sterile, free from germs or living organisms; **-freiheit,** *f.* sterility; **-frucht,** *f.* sporangium.

Keim-gang, *m.* germinal duct, funiculus; **-gebilde,** *n.* embryo; **-gewebe,** *n.* germinal tissue, nucellus; **-gift,** *n.* poison from germs, toxins; **-grube,** *f.* germinal fossa (hilum); **-hälfte,** *f.* half-embryo; **-haltig,** containing germs.

Keim-häufchen, *n.* accumulation of germs, soredium; **-haut,** *f.* blastoderm; **-hof,** *m.* germinal area; **-höhle,** *f.* germinal cavity; **-hormon,** *n.* sex hormone, hormone of germination; **-hügel,** *m.* germinal swelling or mound; **-hülle,** *f.* germinal capsule, perisperm; **-isolierung,** *f.* nucleus isolation.

Keim-kapsel, *f.* capsular membrane of ovum; **-kern,** *m.* germinal nucleus; **-knospe,** *f.* embryonic bud, ovule; **-korn,** *n.* germinal spore, granule, brood cell; **-körperchen,** *n.* nucleolus; **-kraft,** *f.* germinating power; **-kugel,** *f.* germinal globule, embryonic sphere; **-lager,** *n.* germinal layer, stroma, hypoblast; **-leben,** *n.* embryonic life.

Keimling, *m.* seedling, germ, embryo.

Keimlings-fäule, *f.* seedling rot; **-krankheit,** *f.* seedling disease, damping off, blight; **-wurzel,** *f.* seminal root.

Keim-loch, *n.* micropyle; **-los,** germless; **-mund,** *m.* micropyle; **-pflanze,** *f.* seedling, embryo; **-pförtchen,** *n.* blastopore; **-pilz,** *m.* blastomyces; **-plasma,** *n.* germplasm; **-pore,** *f.* germ pore; **-probe,** *f.* germinating test; **prüfung,** *f.* germination test.

Keim-sack, *m.*-e, embryo sac, amnion; **-saft,** *m.* fluid contents of germ, blastema; **-schädigung,** *f.* damage to germ; **-scheibe,** *f.* germinal disk, embryonic disk; **-scheide,** *f.* coleoptile; **-schicht,** *f.* germinal layer; **-schild,** *m.* germinal plate; **-schlauch,** *m.* germ tube, sporocyst, blastospore.

Keim-stätte, *f.* germinal center, gonad; **-stock,** *m.* generative gland, ovary; **-stoff,** *m.* germinal matter, blastema; **-streifen,** *m.* germ band; **-tötend,** germicidal; **-töter,** *m.* sterilizator, sterilizer; **-träger,** *m.* carrier; **-unfähig,** incapable of germinating.

Keimung, *f.* germination.

Keimungs-bedingungen, *f.pl.* conditions for germination; **-bild,** *n.* bud formation in yeast; **-dauer,** *f.* duration of germination; **-fähigkeit,** *f.* germinating power.

Keim-versuch, *m.*-e, germination test; **-verzug,** *m.* delayed germination; **-voll,** full of germs; **-weiss,** *n.* endosperm; **-wulst,** *m.* germinal swelling; **-wurzel,** *f.* radicle; **-zählung,** *f.* bacterial count; **-zelle,** *f.* germ cell; **-zelle,** *f.* megaspore, macrospore.

kein, no, not any.

keinenfalls, in no case.

keiner, no one, not anyone, none; ~ von beiden, neither.

keinerlei, not any, of no sort; auf ~ Weise, in no way or manner.

keinesfalls, in no case.

keineswegs, by no means.

keinmal, not once, never.

Keks, *m.* small cake, cookie.

Kelch, *m,* calyx, cup, infundibulum; **-abschnitt,** *m.* calyx lobe or section; **-achsensporn,** *m.* spur of calyx; **-balg,** *m.* empty glume; **-becher,** *m.* receptacle of perigynous flower; **-blatt,** *n.* sepal;- **blättrig,** sepaloid; **-blüte,** *f.* calycinal flower; **-blüter,** *m.pl.* Calyciflorae; **-blütig,** calycanthemous.

Kelch-borste, *f.* awn on calyx (limb); **-decke,** *f.* tegmen calycis, epicalyx; **-deckel,** *m.* calyx lid, paten; **-einsatz,** *m.* insertion of the calyx; **-förmig,** cup-shaped, calyciform; **-glas,** *n.* cup-shaped glass; **-horn,** *n.* wax cup Calycera; **-hüllblatt,** *n.,* **-hülle,** *f.* calycle.

kelchig cuplike, calycinal.

Kelch-larve, *f.* scyphistoma or scyphula; **-los,** acalycinous; **-mensure,** *f.* measuring cup; **-narbe,** *f.* umbril; **-rand,** *m.* calicinal margin; **-röhre,** *f.* calyx tube.

Kelch-saum, *m.* lobe of calyx; **-schwamm,** *m.* cup fungus (Peziza); **-spelze,** *f.* empty glume; **-ständig,** calyciflorous; **-staubfaden,** *m.pl.* epipetals; **-tragend,** calyciflorous; **-zipfel,** *m.* calyx lobe.

Kelen, *n.* kelene, ethyl chloride.

Kelle, *f.* scoop, ladle, trowel.

Keller, *m.* cellar; **-assel,** *f.* sow bug, wood louse; **-geschoss,** *n.* basement; **-hals,** *m.* mezereum (*Daphne mezereum*); **-spinne,** *f.* cave spider.

Kellner, *m.* waiter.

Kelp, *n.* ashes of seaweed.

Kelter, *f.* wine press.

keltern, to press (grapes).

kennbar, knowable, recognizable, discernible.

kennen, to know, be acquainted with, understand; ∼ **lernen,** to become acquainted with, learn.

Kenner, *m.-*, connoisseur, expert, specialist.

Kenn-linie, *f.* graph, curve, diagram, characteristic; **-merkmal,** *n.* characteristic, feature.

kennte, would know, knew, knows.

kenntlich, knowable, distinguishable, conspicuous, marked; ∼ **machen,** make known.

Kenntlichmachung, *f.* characterization, labeling.

Kenntnis, *f.-se,* knowledge, information.

Kennung, *f.* characteristic.

Kenn-wort, *n.-e,* code word; **-zahl,** *f.* index, code number, characteristic; **-zeichen,** *n.* mark, sign, symptom; **-zeichnen,** to mark, characterize; **-zeichnend,** characteristic; **-zeichnung,** *f.* marking; **-ziffer,** *f.* index of a logarithm, coefficient, numerical characteristic.

Keramik, *f.* ceramics.

Keratenchym, *f.* nonfunctional sieve tube of horny texture.

Kerbe, *f.* kerf, notch, groove, depression, constriction, indentation, nick.

Kerbel, *m.* chervil (Anthriscus).

kerben, to notch, (in)dent, groove, channel; **gekerbt,** crenate(d).

kerbig, jagged, notched, indented, grooved.

Kerb-schlag, *m.* notched-bar impact test; **-tiere,** *n.pl.* insects; **-wirkung,** *f.* notch effect; **-zähigkeit,** *f.* notched-bar toughness, notch (strength) tenacity, impact resistance; **-zahn,** *m.* crenature.

Kerf, *m.* insect; **-kunde,** *f.* entomology

Kerl, *m.* fellow.

Kermes-beerengewächse, *n.pl.* Phytolaccaceae; **-rot,** scarlet, cochineal; **-schildlaus,** *f.* kermes insect, coccus.

Kern, *m.-e,* kernel, nucleus, pip, stone, pith, newel, heartwood, grain, core, granule; **falscher** ∼, red heartwood.

Kern-abstand, *m.ᵁe,* nuclear distance; **-achse,** nuclear axis; **-anhäufung,** *f.* accumulation of nuclei; **-artig,** kernel-like, nuclear; **-aufbau,** *m.* nuclear synthesis; **-bewegung,** *f.* nuclear motion; **-bläschen,** *n.* nucleus, nuclear vesicle; **-durchmesser,** *m.* diameter at root, nuclear diameter; **-echt,** breeding true to type; **-eisen,** *n.* mottled white pig iron, core iron.

kernen, to take the kernel.

Kern-epithel, *n.* germinal epithelium; **-faden,** *m.* nuclear (chromatin) thread; **-farbe,** *f.* nuclear stain; **-färbemittel,** *n.* nucleus staining material; **-färbung,** *f.* nuclear staining; **faser,** *f.* nuclear fiber, filament; **-faul,** rotten at the core; **-fäule,** *f.* stem rot; **-fest,** very solid; **-figur,** *f.* nuclear figure, mitotic figure.

kern-frisch, quite fresh; **-frucht,** *f.* kernel, (seed) fruit, pome; **-gebunden,** attached to the nucleus; **-gehäuse,** *n.* (apple) core; **-gerüst,** *n.* nuclear reticulum, framework; **-gesund,** thoroughly healthy (sound); **-guss,** *m.* cored (work) casting.

kernhaft, full of pips, pithy, solid.

kern-haltig, containing a nucleus, nucleate(d); **-hauskammer,** *f.* locule, chamber (cavity) of ovary; **-haut,** *f.* tegumen; **-hefe,** *f.* seed yeast, bacterium; **-höhle,** *f.* nuclear vacuole; **-holz,** *n.* heartwood.

kernig, firm, strong, robust, hard, solid, forcible, vigorous, sound, healthy, pithy, full of pips, granular.

Kernigkeit, *f.* pithiness, strength.

Kern-isomerie, *f.* nucleus (or nuclear) isomerism; **-kasten,** *m.* core box; **-kiemer,** *m.pl.* Nucleobranchiatae; **-körper(chen),** *m.* nucleolus; **-ladung,** *f.* nuclear charge; **-ladungszabl,** *f.* atomic number; **-lähmung,** *f.* nuclear paralysis; **loch,** *n.* cored hole; **-los,** anucleate, without nucleus; **-masse,** *f.* endosperm, nuclear substance.

Kern-mehl, *n.* best grade of flour, firsts; **-membran,** *f.* nuclear membrane; **-milch,** *f.* buttermilk; **-oberfläche,** *f.* nuclear surface; **-obst,** *n.* stone fruit; **-paarung,** *f.* pairing of nuclei, conjugation; **-pflanze,** *f.* seedling plant; **-pilze,** *m.pl.* Pyrenomyces; **-platte,** *f.* nuclear chromatin plate; **-punkt,** *m.* essential point.

Kernpulver, *n.* (rauchloses), coated smokeless powder; **-riss,** *m.* heart shake; **-rissig,** heart-shaken; **-saft,** *m.ᵁe,* nuclear sap or fluid, enchylema; **-salz,** *n.* rock salt; **-sand,** *m.* core sand; **-schäle,** *f.* ring shake, cup shake, internal annular shake; **-schatten,** *m.* deep shadow, umbra;

-scheide, *f.* sheath of nucleus, endodermis; **-schwarz,** *n.* nuclear black.

Kern-segment, *n.* nuclear fragment; **-segmentierung,** *f.* nuclear fragmentation; **-seife,** *f.* curd (grain) soap; **-spindel,** *f.* nuclear spindle; **-spur,** *f.* fang hole; **-stäbchen,** *n.* chromosome; **-stück,** *n.* principal item; **-substanz,** *f.* nuclear substance; **-teilung,** *f.* nuclear division, segmentation; **-tinktion,** *f.* coloring shown by nucleus.

Kern-tonne, *f.* spingle rest (karyokinesis); **-trocken,** thoroughly dry; **-übertritt,** *m.* nuclear migration; **-ursprung,** *m.* origin; **-vermehrung,** *f.* nuclear increase; **-verschmelzung,** *f.* nuclear fusion; **-wand,** *f.* nuclear membrane; **-warze,** *f.* tip of nucleus; **-wolle,** *f.* prime wool; **-wucherung,** *f.* proliferation of the nucleus.

Kern-wuchs, *m.* seedling; **-wüchsig,** sprung from seed; **-zelle,** *f.* cytoplast, elementary cell; **-zerfall,** *m.* disintegration of the nucleus; **-zone,** *f.* nuclear zone.

Kerze, *f.* candle, spark plug.

Kerzenstärke, *f.* candle power.

Kessel, *m.*-, kettle, caldron, copper, retort, boiler, cover (of wild boar), burrow, basin, kennel, narrow valley; **-betrieb,** *m.* boiler operation; **-blech,** *n.* boiler plate; **-dampf,** *m.* live steam; **-druck,** *m.* boiler pressure; **-fallenblumen,** *f.pl.* flowers that are insect traps; **-förmig,** kettleshaped; **-haus,** *n.* boiler house; **-jagen,** *n.* battue shooting; **-kohle,** *f.* steam coal; **-niederschlag,** *m.* deposit in a (kettle) boiler.

Kessel-schuss, *m.* chambering shot, section of boiler shell; **-speisewasser,** *n.* boiler feed water; **-speisung,** *f.* boiler feeding.

Kesselstein, *m.* boiler scale; **-(gegen)mittel,** *n.* boiler compound,disincrustant; **-schicht,** *f.* layer of boiler scale; **-verhütung,** *f.* boiler-scale prevention.

Kessel-treiben, *n.* battue shooting; **-wagen,** *m.* tank car, tank truck.

Keton, *n.* ketone; **-spaltung,** *f.* ketonic cleavage.

Ketoverbindung, *f.* keto compound.

Kette, *f.* chain, warp, train, series, covey.

Ketten, to link, tie, chain; **-bruch,** *m.* continued fraction; **-druck,** *m.* warp printing; **-förmig,** shaped like a chain; **-gelenk,** *n.* link of a chain; **-glied,** *n.* link of a chain; **-isomerie,** *f.* chain isomerism; **-kokken,** *m.pl.* streptococci; **-rad,** *n.* sprocket.

Ketten-linie, *f.* catenary; **-reaktion,** *f.* chain reaction; **-rechnung,** *f.* compound

rule of three; **-spanner,** *m.* take-up device, tensioning device.

Kettspanner, *m.* warp shiner.

keuchen, to gasp, pant, wheeze, roar.

Keuchhusten, *m.* whooping cough, pertussis.

Keule, *f.* club, pestle, leg, shoulder (of meat), quarter, drumstick, clava.

keulen-förmig, club-shaped, clavate, claviform; **-früchtig,** cladocarpous; **-granne,** *f.* club grass, corynephorus; **-haar,** *n,* clavate hair; **-käfer,** *m.pl.* Clavigeridae; **-lilie,** *f.* Cordyline; **-palme,** *f.* palm lily (*Zamia*); **-papillum,** *n.* clavate papillum; **-pilz,** *m.* goatsbeard (Clavaria); **-wespe,** *f.* willow cimbex.

keusch, chaste, pure, modest; **-baum,** *m.* agnus castus, chaste tree (*Vitex agnuscastus*).

Khakifarbe, *f.* khaki color.

Kicher(erbse), *f.* chick-pea (*Cicer arietinum*).

kichern, to giggle, titter.

Kiebitz, *m.* pewit, plover, *Vanellus cristatus.*

Kiefer, *f.* Scotch pine (*Pinus silvestris*).

Kiefer, *m.* jaw(bone), maxilla; **-apparat,** *m.* maxillary apparatus; **-ast,** *m.* maxillary branch; **-ausschnitt,** *m.* maxillary notch· **-bein,** *n.* maxillary bone, maxilliped, gnathopod; **-bogen,** *m.* mandibular arch, inferior maxillary arch; **-deckel,** *m.* gill cover; **-drüse,** *f.* submaxillary process.

Kiefer-egel, *m.* jawless leech (Gnathobdellidae); **-fortsatz,** *m.* maxillary process; **-fühler,** *m.* chelicere, expodoite of maxilliped, extremities of the jaws of arachnoids; **-füsse,** *m.pl.* maxillipeds, accessory jaws; **-gaumenapparat,** *m.* avian palate; **-gaumenspalte,** *f.* cleft of hard palate; **-gelenk,** *n.* temporomaxillary joint, hinge of the jaws; **-gerüst,** *n.* maxilla, jaw.

Kiefer-keilbeingrube, *f.* sphenomaxillary fossa, zygomatic fossa; **-knochen,** *m.* maxillary bone, jawbone; **-leiste,** *f.* maxillary crest, ridge, or groove; **-loch,** *n.* mandibular foramen; **-los,** jawless; **-lympfdrüse,** *f.* submaxillary lymph gland; **-muskel,** *m.* masseter muscle.

Kiefer(n)-bestand, *m.* pinewoods, stand of pines; **-blasenrost,** *m.* blister rust of pine; **-blattwespe,** *f.* pine sawfly (Lophyrus); **-bock,** *m.* capricorn bettle; **-dreher,** *m.* pine branch twist (Melampsora); **-gehölz,** *n.* pine beauty (Panolis); **-gehölz,** *n.* pine grove; **-harzgallenwickler,** *m.* resin gall moth; **-nadel,** *f.* pine needle; **-nadelöl,** *n.*

pine-needle oil; **-nadelrost,** *m.* blister rust (*Peridermium pini*).

Kiefer(n)-ritzenschorf, *m.* pine scab, blight; **-rüssler,** *m.* pine weevil; **-schwärmer,** *m.* pine hawkmoth (*Sphinx pinastri*); **-spanner,** *m.* pine looper moth; **-triebwickler,** *m.* pine-shoot moth, tortrix; **-wald,** *m.* pine grove; **-wurzelschwamm,** *m.* pine redrot; **-zapfen,** *m.* pine cone.

Kiefer-platten, *f.pl.* jaw plates; **-rand,** *m.* edge of jaw; **-schlundmuskel,** *m.* mylopharyngeus muscle; **-sperre,** *f.* lockjaw; **-spitzen,** *f.pl.* jawteeth; **-stiel,** *m.* suspensor of the jaw (in fish); **-taster,** *m.pl.* pedipalpi, maxillary palpi; **-winkel,** *m.* angle of the jaw; **-wölbung,** *f.* palatine arch, roof of mouth; **-zungenbeinmuskel,** *m.* mylohyoid muscle; **-zyste,** *f.* cyst of jaw.

Kiel, *m.*-e, keel, crest of sternum, carine, quill; **auf ebenem** ∼, on even keel.

Kiel-blätter, *n.pl.* keel petals; **-brust,** *f.* chicken breast; **-förmig,** carinate; **-schnecken,** *f.pl.* Heteropodae.

Kieme, *f.* gill, ctenidium, branchia.

Kiemen-achse, *f.* gill axis; **-anhang,** *m.* appendage of gill; **-apparat,** *m* gill apparatus; **-aterie,** *f.* (afferent) gill artery; **-atmend,** breathing through the gills; **-atmer,** *m.pl.* gill breathers; **-atmung,** *f.* gill breathing.

Kiemen-balken, *m.* branchial bar; **-baum,** *m.* dendriform gill; **-blatt,** *n.* gill lamella; **-blättchen,** *n.* branchial leaf, gill filament; **-bogen,** *m.* branchial or visceral arch, gill arch; **-büschel,** *m.pl.* gill plume; **-darm,** *m.* pharynx, branchial region of intestine; **-deckel,** *m.* gill cover or lid, operculum, branchiostegite; **-deckelkieme,** *f.* spiracle; **-deckel-spalt,** *m.* opercular opening.

Kiemen-faden, *m.pl.* gill filaments; **-faser,** *f.pl.* gill filaments; **-fistel,** *f.* branchial fistula; **-förmig,** branchiform; **-furche,** *f.* branchial cleft; **-füsser,** *m.pl.* branchiopodae, water fleas; **-füssler,** *m.pl.* Branchiopodae; **-gang,** *m.* branchial canal; **-gefäss,** *n.* branchial vessel; **-gerüst,** *n.* gill apparatus.

Kiemen-haut, *f.* gill flap, branchiostegite, branchial membrane; **-hautfisch,** *n.* branchiostegan; **-hautstrahl,** *m.* branchiostegal ray; **-herz,** *n.* branchial heart; **-höhle,** *f.* gill cavity; **-kammer,** *f.* branchial or gill chamber; **-loch,** *n.* gill aperture, porus branchialis; **-los,** abranchiate.

Kiemen-öffnung, *f.* branchial cleft, gill opening; **-plättchen,** *n.* gill plate; **-region,**

f. branchial region; **-rest,** *m.* gill remnant; **-rinne,** *f.* endostyle; **-sack,** *m.* gill sac; **-schnecke,** *f.* inferobranchian; **-schwänze,** *m.pl.* Branchiura; **-siphon,** *m.* siphon.

Kiemen-spalte, *f.* branchial cleft, gill slit; **-spaltenorgan,** *n.* branchial groove organ; **-strahl,** *m.* gill ray; **-tiere,** *n.pl.* ichthyoids; **-tragend,** branchiferous; **-träger,** *m.* gill support; **-vene,** *f.* (efferent) gill artery; **-wurm,** *m.* Lernea branchialis.

Kien, *m.* resinous (pine) wood; **-apfel,** *m.* pine cone; **-baum,** *m.* pine tree; **-harz,** *n.* pine resin; **-holz,** *n.* resinous (pine) wood.

kienig, piny, resinous.

Kien-öl, *n.* pine oil; **-russ,** *m.* pine soot, lampblack; **-russpilz,** *m.* fuligo; **-stock,** *m.* carcass.

Kies, *m.* gravel, shingle, pyrites; **-abbrand,** *m.* roasted pyrites; **-äbnlich,** **-artig,** gravelly, pyritous; **-boden,** *m.* gravelly soil, **-brenner,** *m.* pyrites burner.

Kiesel, *m.* pebble, flint, silica, silex; **-algen,** *f.pl.* diatoms; **-anzeiger,** *m.pl.*, calciphobous plants (lime indicator); **-artig,** flinty, siliceous; **-chlorid,** *n.* silicon chloride; **-erde,** *f.* siliceous earth, silica; **-erdehaltig,** siliceous, siliciferous; **-erde-hydrat,** *n.* hydrated silica.

Kiesel-fluorbaryum, *n.* barium silicate; **-fluorblei,** *n.* lead fluosilicate; **-fluorkalium,** *n.* potassium fluosilicate; **-fluorsalz,** *n.* fluosilicate; **-fluorsäure,** *f.* fluosilicic acid; **-fluorwasser-stoffsäure,** *f.* hydrofluosilicic acid; **-fluss,** *m.* siliceous flux; **-flussäure,** *f.* fluosilicic acid; **-galmei,** *m.* siliceous calamine; **-gips,** *m.* vulpinite, anhydrite.

Kiesel-glas, *n.* flint glass, siliceous calamine; **-gur,** *f.* siliceous earth, infusorial earth; **-haltig,** siliceous, siliciferous, flinty; **-hart,** hard as flint; **-hold,** friendly to flint; **-hornschwamm,** *m.* siliceous sponge (Ceraospongiae).

kieselig, siliceous, flinty, pebbly.

Kiesel-kalk, *m.* siliceous limestone; **-kalkeisen,** *n.* ilvaite; **-kalkspat,** *m.* wollastonite; **-knolle,** *f.* flint; **-körper,** *m.* siliceous body; **-kreide,** *f.* siliceous chalk; **-kupfer,** *n.* chrysocolla; **-mangan,** *n.* rhodonite; **-nadel,** *f.* siliceous spicule; **-reich,** flinty, siliceous, pebbly; **-sandstein,** *m.* siliceous sandstone.

Kieselsäure, *f.* silicic acid; **-anhydrid,** *r.* silicic anhydride; **-düngung,** *f.* fertilization with silica salts; **-gallerte,** *f.* silica gel; **-haltig,** containing silicic acid; **-reich,** rich in silicic acid; **-salz,** *n.* silicate.

Kiesel-scheide, *f.* spore membrane of diatoms; **-schiefer,** *m.* siliceous schist; **-schwämme,** *m.pl.* siliceous sponges; **-skelett,** *n.* siliceous skeleton; **-stäbchen,** *n.* siliceous spicule; **-stein,** *m.* pebble, gravelstone, flint; **-stet,** flint stable; **-tuff,** *m.* siliceous sinter; **-verbindung,** *f.* silicate; **-wasserstoff,** *m.* hydrogen silicide.

Kiesel-wasserstoffsäure, *f.* hydrosilicic acid; **-zinkerz,** *n.* siliceous calamine, willemite; **-zuschlag,** *m.* siliceous flux.

Kies-filter, *n.*-, gravel filter; **-grube,** *f.* gravel pit; **-haltig,** gravelly.

kiesig, gravelly, gritty.

Kies-lager, *n.*-, gravel deposit; **-ofen,** *m.* pyrites (burner) kiln; **-weg,** *m.* gravel road.

Kiff, *m.* tan(bark).

Kilo, *n.* **(Kilogramm),** kilogram.

Kilowattstunde, *f.* kilowatt-hour.

Kimme, *f.* notch, chime (of a cask), kerf.

Kind, *n.* child, offspring.

Kindel, *f.* small secondary tuber (of potatoes).

Kinder-balsam, *m.* soothing syrup; **-ernährung,** *f.* infant feeding; **-husten,** *m.* whooping cough, pertussis; **-lähmung,** *f.* infantile paralysis, acute anterior poliomyelitis; **-los,** childless; **-mehl,** *n.* infant food; **-pech,** *n.* meconium; **-pulver,** *n.* soothing powder for children; **-schleim,** *m.* vernix caseosa; **-schmiere,** *f.* vernix caseosa; **-spiel,** *n.* trifle; **-zahn,** *m.* milk tooth.

Kindes-pech, *n.* meconium; **-wasser,** *n.* amniotic fluid.

Kindheit, *f.* childhood, infancy.

kindisch, childish.

kindlich, childlike.

Kinematograph, *m.* cinematograph.

Kinetik, *f.* kinetics.

kinetisch, kinetic; **kinetisches Zentrum,** *n.* centrosphere, centrosome.

Kinn, *n.* chin, mentum; **-auschnitt,** *m.* emargination of mentum; **-backen,** *m.* jaw, maxilla; **-backendrüse,** *f.* submaxillary gland; **-backenknochen,** *m.* jawbone; **-backenkrampf,** *m.* lockjaw, trismus; **-backenzahn,** *m.* molar tooth; **-bart,** *m.* goatsbeard; **-gegend,** *f.* mental region; **-grube,** *f.* mental fossa, dimple; **-höcker,** *m.* maxillary tuberosity.

Kinn-lade, *f.* jaw, maxilla; **-ladenast,** *m.* branch (ramus) of jaw; **-ladenhelm,** *m.* galea; **-ladenscheide,** *f.* gnathotheca; **-ladentaster,** *m.* maxillary palpus; **-loch,** *n.*

mental foramen; **-naht,** *f.* symphysis of lower jaw; **-stütze,** *f.* chin rest; **-winkel,** *m.* mental angle, interamal space; **-zungenbeinmuskel,** *m.* geniohyoid (mylohyoid) muscle; **-zungenmuskel,** *m.* geniglossus muscle.

Kino, *n.* motion pictures, cinema, kino; **-gerbsäure,** *f.* kinotannic acid; **-tinktur,** *f.* tincture of kino.

Kippe, *f.* tilt, hinge; **auf der** ∼, on the verge of (disaster).

kippen, to tip (over), abort, dump.

Kipplager, *n.* rocker (hinged) bearing.

Kippvorrichtung, *f.* tipper, hinge fitting

Kirche, *f.* church.

kirre, tame, familiar.

kirren, to tame, bait, decoy.

Kirrung, *f.* allurement, bait.

Kirsch-baum, *m.* cherry tree; **-blüte,** *f.* cherry blossom; **-branntwein,** *m.* cherry brandy.

Kirsche, *f.* cherry.

Kirsch-gummi, *n.* cherry gum; **-harz,** *n.* cherry gum; **-kern,** *m.* cherry stone; **-lorbeer,** *m.* cherry (bay) laurel; **-rotglut,** *f.* cherry-red heat; **-saft,** *m.* cherry juice; **-wasser,** *n.* cherry water, brandy; **-wurzelkraut,** *n.* athamanta.

Kissen, *n.*-, cushion, pillow, bolster, pad(ding).

Kistchen, *n.*-, small box or chest.

Kiste, *f.* box, chest, case.

Kisten-ausschlagpapier, *n.* casing paper; **-zucker,** *m.* muscovado.

Kitsch, *m.* trash.

Kitt, *m.* cement, putty, lute, mastic; **-drüse,** *f.* colleterial gland.

Kittel, *m.*-, smock, frock.

kitten, to cement, putty, lute, glue.

Kitt-erde, *f.* luting, clay, pozz(u)olana; **-fuchs,** *m.* kit fox; **-harz,** *n.* propolis; **-leiste,** *f.* cement edge; **-masse,** *f.* cement (intercellular) substance; **-schicht,** *f.* connecting callus between stock and scion (of graft); **-substanz,** *f.* cement substance.

Kitzel, *m.* tickling, itching, desire.

kitzeln, to tickle.

kitzlich, ticklish.

Kladstein, *m.* place brick.

klaffen, to gape, yawn, split, chap.

kläffen, to yelp, bark, clamor.

klaffend, (wide) apart, dehiscent.

Klafter, *f.* cord (of wood), fathom; **-holz,** *n.* cordwood.

klaftern, to stack, cord.

Klage, *f.* complaint, lament(ation), grievance, action, suit.

klagen, to complain, lament, bemoan, sue.

kläglich, deplorable, pitiable, plaintive.

Klai, (Klei) *m.* clay.

klamm, tight, close, scarce, narrow, clammy.

Klammer, *f.*-n, clamp, clasp, cramp, bracket, parenthesis; **eckige** ∼, bracket; **runde** ∼, round bracket, parenthesis.

Klammer-ausdruck, *m.* parenthetical expression; **-epithel,** *n.* bracket epithelium; **-fuss,** *m.* grasping leg; **-gänge,** *m.pl.* nuptial chambers; **-haken,** *m.* clasping or grasping hook.

klammern, to cramp, clasp, brace, clinch, rivet, fasten.

Klammer-organ, *n.* clasping organ; **-wurzel,** *f.* clinging rootlet; **-zelle,** *f.* bracket cell, brace.

Klampe, *f.* clamp, cramp, clasp.

klang (klingen), rang, sounded.

Klang, *m.* ∸e, sound, tone, ring, timbre; **einfacher** ∼, a sound composed of several harmonics.

klänge, would sound, sounded, sounds.

Klang-farbe, *f.* tone color, timbre; **-gemisch,** *n.* a sound composed of fundamentals of varying frequencies; **-lehre,** *f.* acoustics; **-los,** soundless; **-reich,** rolling, sonorous; **-wirkung,** *f.* acoustics; **-zinn,** *n.* fine (sonorous) tin.

klappbar, hinged.

Klappe, *f.* flap, trap, theca valve, lid, damper, stop, door, gate.

klappen, to clap, flap, click, strike, clatter, work, succeed, tally; **das klappt,** that fits well, works well.

Klappen-fehler, *m.* valvular defect; **-fläche,** *f.* surface of valve; **-saum,** *m.* edge of valve; **-schrank,** switchboard; **-segel,** *n.* flap of valve; **-spaltig,** loculicidal; **-ventil,** *n.* valve.

Klapper, *f.* rattle, clap(per); **-hülse,** *f.* rattlebox (Crotalaria).

klappern, to rattle, clatter, clapper, chatter.

klapp(e)rig, shaky, rickety, rattling.

Klapper-rose, *f.* corn poppy (*Papaver rhoeas*); **-schlange,** *f.* rattlesnake.

Klapp-falle, *f.* trap; **-kamera,** *f.* folding camera.

Klaps, *m.* slap, smack.

klapsen, to clap, slap, smack.

klar, clear, limpid, distinct, transparent, bright, lucid, evident.

Klär-anlage, *f.* purification (filter) plant; **-apparat,** *n.* clarifying (settling) apparatus; **-becken,** *n.* settling tank, filter bed.

klarblickend, clear-sighted.

Kläre, *f.* clarifier, clear liquid, clearness, coal dust.

klären, to clear (up), clarify, purify, percolate, defecate, settle.

Klär-fass, *n.* clearing cask; **-flasche,** *f.* decanting (bottle) flask.

Klar-gefäss, *n.* clarifier.

Klarheit, *f.* clearness, brightness, clarity, light, evidence.

klarieren, to clear, straighten out.

Klär-kasten, *m.* settler, clarifying tank; **-kessel,** *m.* clarifier.

klar-kochen, to boil till clear; **-legen,** to clear up.

Klär-mittel, *n.* clarifying or clearing agent; **-pfanne,** *f.* clearing (defecating) pan.

klarschleifen, to grind smooth.

Klär-sel, *n.* clarified sugar, fine liquor; **-staub,** *m.* bone ash.

klarstellen, to clear up.

Klärung, *f.* clearing, clarifying, clarification.

Klasse, *f.* class, division, grade, quality.

Klassen-ordnung, *f.* **-einteilung,** *f.* classification.

klassieren, to size (ore).

klassifizieren, to classify.

Klassiker, *m.* classic.

klassisch, classic(al).

klastisch, clastic, fragmental.

Klatsch, *m.* gossip, scandal.

Klatsche, *f.* fly trap.

klatschen, to smack, pop, clap, chat, gossip.

Klatsch-mohn, *m.* corn poppy (*Papaver rhoeas*); **-präparat,** *n.* dab (impression) preparation; **-rose,** *f.* corn poppy (*Papaver rhoeas*).

klauben, to pick, cull, sort.

Klaue, *f.* claw, paw, hoof, fang, clutch, pounce, grasp, foot.

Klauen-apparat, *m.* pretarsus; **-drüse,** *f.* hoof gland; **-entzündung,** *f.* foot rot, whitlow; **-fett,** *n.* **-öl,** *n.* neat's-foot oil; **-seuche,** *f.*

foot disease; **-taster,** *m.pl.* pedipalpi (terminating in a claw).

klauig, having fangs or claws.

Klause, *f.* cell, closet, den, chamber, carcerule, eremus.

Klavier, *n.* piano.

Klebäther, *m.* collodion.

Kleb-drüse, *f.* adhesive gland; **-faden,** *m.* mucous thread secreted by byssus glands; **-fähig,** adhesive; **-fähigkeit,** *f.* adhesiveness; **-kraft,** *f.* adhesive power; **-kraut,** *n.* cleavers (*Galium aparine*); **-masse,** *f.* glandula.

Klebe, *f.* dodder; **-grenze,** *f.* limit of adhesion; **-korn,** *n.* microsome; **-mittel,** *n.* adhesive, agglutinant.

kleben, to glue, paste; ∼ **bleiben,** to stick, adhere.

klebend, adhesive, agglutinant.

Klebepflaster, *n.* adhesive plaster.

Kleber, *m.* gluten, gum, adhesive, sticker, gluer; **-brot,** *n.* gluten bread; **-gries,** *m.* gluten grits; **-haltig,** containing gluten; **-leim,** *m.* gluten glue; **-mehl,** *n.* aleurone, protein granules; **-schicht,** *f.* aleuron layer.

Kleb-kraut, *n.* cleavers, goose grass; **-lack,** *m.* adhesive lacquer.

klebrig, sticky, adhesive, viscid, glutinous, ropy.

Klebrigkeit, *f.* stickiness, viscidity, viscosity.

Kleb-sand, *n.* luting sand; **-scheibe,** *f.* adhesive disk; **-stoff,** *m.* adhesive substance; **-taf(fe)t,** *m.* court plaster; **-wachs,** *n.* adhesive wax, sticking wax.

Klecks, *m.*-e, blot, blotch.

klecksen, to blot, blur, daub.

Klee, *m.* clover, trefoil; **ewiger** ∼, **Luzerner** ∼, alfalfa, lucern.

Klee-baum, *m.* hop trefoil, shrubby trefoil (*Ptelea trifoliata*); **-blatt,** *n.* trefoil leaf, shamrock; **-dreschmaschine,** *f.* clover (thrasher) huller; **-farn,** *m.* nardoo (*Marsilea macropus*); **-futter,** *n.* clover; **-grasbestand,** *m.* clover grass, pasture; **-heu,** *n.* clover hay; **-krebs,** *m.* clover canker, wilt; **-rot,** clover-red, purplish red.

Klee-salz, *n.* salt of sorrel, potassium acid oxalate; **-samen,** *m.* clover seed; **-säure,** *f.* oxalic acid; **-seide,** *f.* clover, dodder; **-stengelbrenner,** *m.* anthracnose of clover; **-strauch,** *m.* hop trefoil, shrubby trefoil (*Ptelea trifoliata*); **-würger,** *n.* chokeweed, broomrape (Orobanche).

Klei, *m.* clay, loam, marl; **-absudbad,** *n.* bran decoction (dye).

Kleid, *n.*-er, garment, dress, clothing, garb,

kleiden, to dress, clothe, suit, fit; **jemanden** ∼, to suit someone.

Kleider-färber, *m.* clothes dyer; **-laus,** *f.* body louse (*Pediculus vestimenti*); **-motte,** *f.* (clothes) moth; **-stoff,** *m.* dress material, cloth.

Kleidung, *f.* clothing, dressing, costume.

Kleidungsstück, *n.* clothing material, article of clothing.

Kleie, *f.* bran, pollard.

kleien-artig, branny, furfuraceous; **-bad,** *n.* bran drench, bath; **-beize,** *f.* bran steep; **-brot,** *n.* bran bread; **-förmig,** branlike; **-mehl,** *n.* pollard; **-sucht,** *f.* pityriasis.

Kleierde, *f.* clay earth.

kleiig, clayey, branny.

klein, small, little, short, narrow; **von** ∼ **ab,** from an early age; **im Kleinen,** in detail, on a small scale; **kleiner werden,** to lessen.

Kleinasien, *n.* Asia Minor.

kleinauf, von ∼, from childhood.

Klein-bauer, *m.* small farmer; **-becken,** *n.* true pelvis; **-bessemerei,** *f.* small Bessemer steel plant; **-bestand,** *m.* small stand, woodlot; **-betrieb,** *m.* small business, work on a small scale; **-blütig,** with small flowers; **-borstig,** setulose (like a fine bristle); **-dornig,** spinulose (like a fine thorn); **-eisenzeug,** *n.* small iron product.

kleinen, to crush, pulverize.

kleinern, to reduce (fractions).

Klein-färber, *m.* clothes dyer; **-finger,** *m.* the little finger; **-fliegenblume,** *f.* flower pollinated by flies; **-gärmethode,** *f.* microfermentation method; **-gefüge,** *n.* fine structure; **-gehornt,** corniculate (like small horns); **-gelappt,** lobulate; **-gepulvert,** finely powdered; **-gestreift,** marked with fine furrows; **-grubig,** foveolate (having small pits); **-handel,** *m.* retail trade.

Kleinheit, *f.* littleness, minuteness.

Kleinhirn, *n.* cerebellum; **-arm,** *m.* peduncle of cerebellum; **-bahn,** *f.* cerebellar tract; **-brückenbahn,** *f.* pontocerebellar tract; **-brückenwinkel,** *m.* cerebellar bulbar angle, cerebellopontile angle; **-bündel,** *m.* cerebellar fasciculus; **-einschnitt,** *m.* fissure of cerebellum; **-hälfte,** *f.* cerebellar hemisphere; **-lappen,** *m.* cerebellar lobe.

Kleinhirn-oberfläche, *f.* cerebellar surface; **-platte,** *f.* cerebellar plate; **-rinde,** *f.* cerebellar cortex; -schenkel, *m.* peduncle of cerebellum; -seitenstrang, *m.* lateral (direct) cerebellar tract; -sichel, *f.* falx cerebelli; -stiel, *m.* peduncle of cerebellum; -verbindung, *f.* cerebellar connection; -windung, *f.* cerebellar convolution.

Kleinholz, *n.* matchwood.

Kleinigkeit, *f.* trifle, small matter.

klein-kelchig, calyculate (having small calyx); -kerfblume, *f.* flower pollinated by small insects; -köpfig, microcephalic (having a small head); -körnig, small (fine) grained; -kristallinisch, finely crystalline; -kronig, small-crowned; -laut, dejected; -lebewesen, *n.* microorganism.

kleinlich, petty, narrow-minded, mean.

Klein-lichtbildkunst, *f.* photomicrography; -lückig, finely porous, close-grained; -mühle, *f.* crushing (pulverizing) mill; -mut, *m.* faint-heartedness; -mütig, faint-hearted.

Kleinod, *n.* jewel, gem, treasure, ornament.

Klein-reisig, *n.* small twigs, spray wood; -schmetterlinge, *m.pl.* Microlepidoptera; -schnablig, parvirostrate (small-beaked); -schuppe, *f.* small scale; -schuppig, squamolose (having minute scales); -species, *f.* monotypic genus; -spore, *f.* microspore; -stachelig, aculeate (sharp-pointed); -städtisch, provincial.

Klein-steller, *m.* by-pass (in Bunsen burner); -sternig, stellulate (shaped like a small star); -traubig, racemulose (in small clusters); -verkauf, *m.* retail business; -vieh, *n.* small cattle; -wild, *n.* small game; -wirtschaft, *f.* small holding; -wulstig, torulose (with small swellings).

Kleister, *m.* paste, size; -älchen, *n.* paste eel (*Anguillula glutinosa*).

kleisterig, pasty, sticky.

kleistern, to paste size (with paste).

Klemmbacke, *f.* jaw, clamp.

Klemme, *f.* clamp, terminal, nippers, tongs, (screw) vise, dilemma, pinch, tight corner, narrow pass.

klemmen, to pinch, squeeze; sich ∼, to jam, bind.

Klemmen-fallenblume, *f.* flower possessing a retinaculum (orchids and milkweed); -spannung, *f.* terminal voltage.

Klemmer, *m.* pinchcock, pince-nez, nose glasses.

Klemm-hebel, *m.* clamping lever; -körper, *m.* retinaculum; -länge, *f.* clamped length (rivet); -pflanzung, *f.* wedge planting,

notching; -platten, *f.pl.* clamping plate, iron tongs; -ring, *m.* clamping collar or ring; -schraube, *f.* binding screw, set screw; -verbindung, *f.* clamp connection.

Klempner, *m.* tinsmith, sheet-metal worker.

klengen, to husk, shell, extract (seed).

Klepper, *m.* nag, hack.

Klette, *f.* burr fruits (Arctium), bur, burdock.

Kletten-distel, *f.* burr thistle; -pflanze, *f.* plant with hooked appendages (on fruit); -wurzel, *f.* burdock root.

Kletterer, *m.* climber.

Kletter-farn, *m.* climbing fern; -fisch, *m.* climbing fish; -fuss, *m.* scansorial leg, climbing foot; -füssig, yoke-footed, zygodactylous; -haar, *n.* barbule, hooked hair; -klette, *f.* climbing appendage (emergence).

klettern, to climb.

kletternd, scandent, climbing.

Kletter-pflanze, *f.* climber, creeper, liana; -prinzip, *n.* cascade principle; -rose, *f.* rambler; -stange, *f.* climbing pole; -vogel, *m.pl.* climbers, scansorial birds (woodpeckers); -wurzel, *f.* climbing root.

Klettfrucht, *f.*∺e, burr fruit.

Klima, *n.* climate; -kunde, *f.* climatology.

klimatisch, climatic.

Klimatisierung, *f.* air conditioning.

klimmen, to climb.

Klimmfuss, *m.* climbing foot.

klimpern, to jingle, tinkle, strum.

Klinge, *f.* blade, sword.

Klingel, *f.* (small) bell.

klingeln, to ring, tinkle; es klingelt, the bell is ringing.

klingen, to sound, ring, clink, resound.

Kling-glas, *n.* flint glass; -stein, *m.* clinkstone, phonolite.

Klinik, *f.*-en, clinical hospital.

klinisch, clinical.

Klinke, *f.* latch, door handle.

Klinker, *m.*- clinker, hard brick.

Klino-achse, *f.* clinoaxis; -edrit, *n.* clinohedrite; -klasit, *m.* clinoclasite; -morph, inclined, asymmetric (of organs).

Klippe, *f.* cliff, rock, reef, crag, bluff.

Klippen-bucht, *f.* rocky bay; -dachs, *m.* rock badger; -fisch, *m.* klipfish, dry cod; -form, *f.* rock form; -küste, *f.* craggy coast; -wand, *f.* rocky wall, escarpment.

klippig, craggy.

klirren, to clink, clatter, clash.

Klischee, *n.* engraved plate, stereotype, cliché.

klischieren, to stereotype, dab.

Klistier, *n.* enema, clyster.

klitschig, doughy.

Kloake, *f.* cloaca, sewer, drain, cesspool.

Kloaken-bläschen, *n.* atrial vessel; -gas, *n.* sewer gas; -röhre, *f.* cloacal tube, pseudogaster of sponges; -spalte, *f.* cloacal opening; -tier, *n.* monotreme; -wasser, *n.* sewage.

Kloben, *m.* log, bottle, pulley, block, vise, pincers, split billet.

klobig, clumsy.

klomm (klimmen), climbed.

klömme, would climb, climbed, climb.

klonisch, clonic.

klopfen, to knock, beat, tap, rap, drive, break, crush.

klopf-fest, antiknock; -festigkeit, *f.* antiknocking properties; -holz, *n.* mallet beater; -käfer, *m.* deathwatch (Anobium); -sieb, *n.* shaking (tapping) sieve.

Klöppel, *m.* clapper, beater, knocker, lace bobbin; -förmig, bobbin shaped.

Klops, *m.*-e, mincemeat ball.

Klosett, *n.* toilet.

Kloss, *m.*-e, lump, clod, dumpling.

Kloster, *n.*-, convent, monastery, cloister.

Klotz, *m.*-e, block, log, butt, stump; -holz, *n.* knotty firewood.

klotzen, to stare; slop-pad (textile).

klotzig, unpolished, knotty, coarse-grained, in chunks.

Kluft, *f.*-e, cleft, fissure, cleavage, chasm, gap, abyss, split timber.

klüften, to cleave, split.

klüftig, cleft, split, cracked, creviced.

Klüftung, *f.* cleaving, segmentation.

klug, clever, smart, intelligent, wise, skillful, prudent.

Klugheit, *f.* prudence, cleverness.

klüglich, wisely.

Klümpchen, *n.* little lump, clod, globule, particle.

Klumpen, *m.* lump, clot, heap, bulk, ingot, nugget; -frucht, *f.* syncarp.

Klumpfuss, *m.* clubfoot.

klumpig, lumpy, cloddy.

klümprig, clotted, clod, lumpy.

Kluppe, *f.* pincers, tongs, nippers, caliper.

kluppieren, to caliper, take girth of tree.

Kluppzange, *f.* forceps.

Klystier, *n.* enema, clyster.

Knabbelkoks, *m.* crushed coke

knabbern, to gnaw, nibble.

Knabe, *m.* boy.

Knabenkrautgewächse, *n.pl.* Orchidaceae.

Knack, *m.* crack; -beere, *f.* wild strawberry (*Fragaria viridis*).

knacken, to crack(le), crepitate, click.

Knack-mandel, *f.* shell almond; -wurst, *f* saveloy, smoked sausage.

Knagge, *f.* cam, tappet, knot, knag bracket.

Knall, *m.* detonation, explosion, clap c" sound pulse, report, crack, pop; -aufsatz, *m.* initiator (explosive); -blei, *n.* fulminating lead.

knallen, to detonate, fulminate, crack, explode.

Knall-erbse, *f.* toy torpedo, detonating ball; -flamme, *f.* oxyhydrogen flame; -gas, *n.* detonating gas, oxhydrogen gas; -gasflamme, *f.* oxyhydrogen flame; -gasgebläse, *n.* oxyhydrogen blowpipe; -gold, *n.* fulminating gold; -kraft, *f.* explosive force; -quecksilber, *n.* fulminating mercury mercuric fulminate; -salpeter, *m.* ammonium nitrate; -satz, *m.* detonating composition.

Knall-säure, *f.* fulminic acid; -schote, *f.* bladder senna (Colutea); -silber, *n.* fulminating silver, silver fulminate; -zucker, *m.* nitrosaccharose; -zündmittel, *n.* detonating primer.

knapp, close, tight, scant, narrow, shabby, meager, exact.

Knappheit, *f.* tightness, conciseness, scarcity.

Knappschiessen, *n.* tight shooting.

Knarre, *f.* rattle, ratchet.

knarren, to creak, squeak, rattle, crackle.

Knast, *m.* knot in wood, stub, stump.

Knaster, *m.* canaster (tobacco).

knattern, to rattle, crackle.

Knäuel, *m.* ball, knob, gnarl, coil, convolution, glomerule, spireme, fascicle, skein, knawel (Scleranthus); -binse, *f.* common rush (*Juncus conglomeratus*); -drüse, *f.* coil or sweat gland, sudoriferous gland; -form, *f.* spireme, glomerule; -förmig, convoluted, ball-shaped, globular, coiled, glomerate.

knäueln, to ball up, snarl.

Knauf, *m.* knob, capital (of a column).

Knaulgras, *n.* orchard grass, cocksfoot (grass) (*Dactylis glomerata*).

knauserig, stingy.

Knebel, *m.* stick, crossbar, club, shoot, slip, mastax.

knebeln, to fasten with a short stick, gag.

Knecht, *m.-e,* servant, hand, trestle.

knechten, to enslave.

knechtisch, slavish.

Knechtschaft, *f.* slavery, servitude.

kneifen, to pinch, nip, gripe, squeeze.

Kneifer, *m.-,* pince-nez, eyeglasses.

Kneifzange, *f.* nippers, tweezers.

Kneipe, *f.* pincers, nippers, beer party, country inn, tavern.

kneipen, to pinch, squeeze, drink (beer).

knetbar, plastic.

kneten, to knead, remold.

Knetmaschine, *f.* kneading machine, masticator, malaxator.

Knick, *m.* flaw, crack, break, sharp bend; **-beinig,** knock-kneed; **-bruchfestigkeit,** *f.* loop strength; **-festigkeit,** *f.* resistance to buckling.

knicken, to crack, break, split, burst, buckle, collapse.

Knick-festigkeit, *f.* breaking strength, resistance to snapping; **-länge,** *f.* effective length; **-last,** *f.* buckling load; **-schwingung,** *f.* bending ("buckling," "kink") vibration.

Knickung, *f.* bending, flexion, buckling.

Knie, *n.* knee, angle, bend, elbow; **-band,** *n.* ligament of the knee; **-beuge,** *f.* bend of the knee, popliteal space; **-beugung,** *f.* genuflexion; **-beule,** *f.* knee hygroma.

knie(e)n, to kneel.

knie-förmig, knee-shaped, geniculate; **-gelenk,** *n.* knee joint; **-gelenkband,** *n.* ligament of the knee joint; **-gelenkbeuger,** *m.* flexor of knee joint; **-gelenkkapsel,** *f.* capsule of the knee joint; **-gelenkkapselspanner,** *m.* subcrural muscle; **-geschwulst,** *n.* swelling of knee: **-höcker,** *m.* geniculate body; **-holz,** *n.* knee timber, elfin wood; **-kehle,** *f.* popliteal space, hollow of the knee.

Knie-kehlenband, *n.* popliteal ligament; **-knochen,** *m.* bone of the knee; **-knoten,** *m.* geniculate ganglion; **-rohr,** *n.* elbow pipe, bent tube; **-scheibe,** *f.* knee cap, patella; **-sehnenreflex,** *m.* knee jerk; **-sehnenstrang,** *m.* hamstring; **-stück,** *n.* elbow, knee, angle.

kniff (kneifen), pinched.

Kniff, *m.* pinch, crease, trick, device, artifice.

kniffen, to fold.

knipsen, to snap, clip.

Knirps, *m.* dwarf, pigmy.

knirschen, to crackle, gnash, grate, crunch, rustle, scroop; **knirschender Griff,** *m.* scroopy feel.

Knistergold, *n.* Dutch gold, tinsel.

knistern, to crackle, crepitate, rustle.

Knitter, *m.* crease; **-gold,** *n.* Dutch gold.

knitt(e)rig, creased, crumpled, irritable.

knittern, to crackle, crumple, crease.

Knitterzahl, *f.* fold-test characteristic.

Knoblauch, *m.* garlic; **-artig,** garliclike, garlicky; **-erz,** *n.* scorodite; **-gamander,** *m.* water germander; **-hederich,** *m.* hedge garlic; **-strauch,** *m.* garlic shrub; **-zehe,** *f.* clove of garlic.

Knöchel, *m.* knuckle, ankle, malleolus (*pl.*) bones, dice; **-band,** *n.* ligament of the ankle, **-bein,** *n.* bone of the ankle.

Knöchelchen, *n.* ossicle, small bone.

Knöchel-fortsatz, *m.* malleolar apophysis (process); **-gelenk,** *n.* ankle joint; **-haar,** *n.* nodulose hair; **-verletzung,** *f.* injury of ankle joint.

Knochen, *m.* bone; **-abfall,** *m.* bone waste; **-ähnlich,** bonelike, osseous; **-ansatz,** *m.* epiphysis of bone; **-artig,** osseous; **-asche,** *f.* bone ash; **-balken,** *m.* trabeculum or spicule of bone; **-band,** *n.* ligament; **-bau,** *m.* framework or structure of the body or bone; **-beschreibung,** *f.* osteology.

Knochen-bildend, bone-forming; **-bildung,** *f.* bone formation; **-bildungselement,** *n.* bone formative element; **-blatt,** *n.* lamella of bone; **-bogen,** *m.* bone arch; **-brand,** *m.* caries, cariosis; **-bruch,** *m.* fracture of bone; **-dünger,** *m.* bone manure; **-dungmehl,** *n.* fertilizer consisting of bone meal; **düngung,** *f.* manuring with bone; **-entwicklung,** *f.* development of bone.

Knochen-erde, *f.* bone earth (bone ash), earth, phosphates of bone; **-fett,** *n.* bone fat, bone grease; **-fische,** *m.pl.* Teleostae; **-fortsatz,** *m.* bony process; **-frass,** *m.*

caries, -füge, *f.* symphysis; -gallerte, *f.* bone gelatin, ossein; -gebäude, *n.* skeleton; -gebilde, *n.* bone formation; -geist, *m.* bone spirit; -gelenk, *n.* articulation.

Knochen-gelenkband, *n.* ligament; -gelenkfläche, *f.* articular surface of bone; -gerippe, *n.* osseous framework, skeleton; -gerüst, *m.* skeleton; -gewebe, *n.* bony tissue; -grundsubstanz, *f.* fundamental tissue or matrix of bone; -haut, *f.* periosteum; -hebel, *m.* bone elevator; -höhle, *f.* cavity of the bone; -impression, *f.* depression of a bone.

Knochen-kapsel, *f.* bony capsule; -kern, *m.* osseous nucleus, center of ossification; -knorpel, *m.* primitive cartilage; -knoten, *m.* bony condyle, bony prominence; -kohle, *f.* bone black, animal charcoal; -kopf, *m.* head of the bone; -krebs, *m.* cancer of bone; -kunde, *f.* osteology; -lappen, *m.* bone flap; -leim, *m.* gelatin, bone glue, osteocolla.

Knochen-mantel, *m.* covering of the bone; -mark, *m.* marrow of the bone; -mehl, *n.* bone meal; -naht, *f.* bone suture; -narbe, *f.* callus; -oberfläche, *f.* surface of a bone; -öl, *n.* neat's-foot oil; -paar, *n.* pair of bones; -partie, *f.* part of a bone; -pfanne, *f.* glenoid cavity.

Knochen-rinne, *f.* bony furrow; -röhre, *f.* cylindrical bone, osseous tube; -säge, *f.* bone saw; -salze, *n.pl.* inorganic matter of bone; -säure, *f.* phosphoric acid; -schale, *f.* osseous envelope; -schrot, *m.* coarsely crushed bones; -schuppe, *f.* bony scale; -schwarz, *n.* bone black; -splitter, *m.* bone splinter.

Knochen-stichwunde, *f.* stab wound in a bone; -verbindung, *f.* articulation of bones, joint; -vertiefung, *f.* glenoid cavity, bone cup; -vorsprung, *m.* body process, prominence; -wand, *f.* wall of the bone; -wirbel, *m.* vertebra; -wucherung, *f.* hypertrophy; -zapfen, *m.* tab-shaped piece of bone, bony pivot; -zelle, *f.* bone cell, stone cell.

knöchern, bony, osseous.

knochig, bony, osseous.

Knöchlein, *n.* small bone.

Knödel, *m.* dumpling.

Knöllchen, *n.* root tubercle, bulblet, nodule, little knob; -bakterien, *n.pl.* nodule bacteria.

Knolle, *f.* Knollen, *m.* lump, clod, knob, nodule, tuber, tubercle, knot.

Knollen-baselle, *f.* (*Ullucus tuberosus*); -blätterschwamm, *m.* death cup, deadly amanita, (*Amanita phalloides*); -bildung, *f.* tuber formation; -fäule, *f.* tuber rot; -gewächse, *n.pl.* tuberiferous plants.

Knollen-kohl, *m.* kohlrabi; -krankheit, *f.* tuber disease, elephantiasis; -krebs, *m.* keloid; -kümmel, *m.* earthnut; -maser, *f.* figured wood, bur; -pflanze, *f.* tuberous or bulbous plant; -wurz, *f.* Amorphophallus; -wurzel, *f.* tuberous root; -zwiebel, *f.* corm, bulbotuber.

knollig, knotty, knobby, tuberous, bulbous.

Knopf, *m.-e*, button, knob, head, knot, stud, bud, condyle; -artig, button-shaped, knobbed; -binse, *f.* common rush (*Juncus*).

Knöpfchen, *n.* small button.

Knopfdeckel, *m.* cover with knob.

knöpfen, to button.

knopf-förmig, button-shaped, condyloid; -fortsatz, *m.* condyloid process; -klette, *f.* button bur; -kraut, *n.* Galinsoga; -loch, *n.* buttonhole; -maschine, *f.* button machine, button breaker (textile); -naht, *f.* button suture, interrupted suture.

Knopper, *f.* fruit, gall of oak, gallnut, valonia; -eiche, *f.* egilops, valonia.

Knorpel, *m.* cartilage, gristle; -ähnlich, cartilaginous; -ansatz, *m.* cartilaginous epiphysis; -arm, *m.* arm of cartilage; -artig, cartilaginous; -band, *n.* synchondrosis, fibrocartilage; -beinfügung, *f.* synchondrosis; -belag, *m.* cartilaginous covering; -bildung, *f.* formation of cartilage; -brücke, *f.* bridge of cartilage.

Knorpel-collenchym, *n.* cartilaginous collenchyma; -ernährung, *f.* nutrition of cartilage; -fisch, *m.* cartilaginous fish; -flosse, *f.* cartilaginous fin; -fortsatz, *m.* cartilaginous process; -gelenk, *n.* symphysis, cartilaginous joint; -gerüst, *n.* framework of cartilage; -gewebe, *f.* cartilaginous tissue; -haut, *f.* perichondrium; -kohle, *f.* nodular coal.

knorpelig, cartilaginous.

Knorpel-leim, *m.* chondrin; -schädel, *m.* chondrocranium; -schale, *f.* cartilaginous shell; -scheibe, *f.* cartilaginous disk; -skelett, *n.* cartilaginous skeleton; -spange, *f.* tongue of cartilage; -strahl, *m.* cartilaginous ray; -streif, *m.* cartilaginous band or strip; -stütze, *f.* cartilage support; -tang, *m.* carragaen, Irish moss (*Chondrus*).

Knorpel-verbindung, *f.* synchondrosis; -wirbel, *m.* cartilaginous vertebra; -zerlegung, *f.* cartilage dissection; -zungenbeinmuskel, *m.* chondroglossal muscle.

knorplich, cartilaginous.

Knorren, *m.* knot, gnarl, protuberance, excrescence, snag, tuberosity, condyle; **-muskel,** *m.* anconeus muscle.

knorrig, gnarled, knotty.

Knöspchen, *n.* plumule, small bud, gemmule.

Knospe, *f.* bud, burgeon, gemmule.

knospen, to bud; **-anlage,** *f.* rudimentary bud, "anlage," vernation, foliation, leafing; **-artig,** budlike; **-bildung,** *f.* gemmation; **-decke,** *f.* bud scale, estivation; **-drang,** *m.* blastomania, the production of an abnormal number of leaf shoots; **-grund,** *m.* chalaza (base of nucellus); **-hülle,** *f.* integument, bud covering; **-kern,** *m.* nucellus; **-knöllchen,** *n.* budlike tuber; **-koralle,** *f.* oculina; **-lage,** *f.* vernation, estivation.

Knospen-mutation, *f.* bud mutation; **-schuppe,** *f.* bud scale; **-schuppig,** ramentaceous (having scales); **-schutz,** *m.* bud protection; **-strahler,** *m.pl.* Blastoidea; **-tragend,** bud-bearing, gemmiferous; **-träger,** *m.* funiculus; **-warze,** *f.* nucellus; **-zeit,** *f.* budding season; **-zwiebel,** *f.* bulbil, bulblet.

knospig, budlike, full of buds.

Knospungs-vorgang, *m.* budding process; **-zone,** *f.* budding zone.

Knötchen, *n.* little knot, nodule, tubercle, knob, pimple.

knoten, to tie in knots.

Knoten, *m.*- knot, joint, node, articulation, nodule, tubercle, condyle, ganglion, knob, plot; **-ader,** *f.* sciatic vein; **-blech,** *n.* gusset plate; **-blümchen,** *n.* snowflake (Leucoium); **-borste,** *f.* nodulose bristle; **-festigkeit,** *f.* loop strength; **-fuchsschwanz,** *m.* bluegrass (*Poa pratensis*); **-hülle,** *f.* lodicule (nodular cover).

Knoten-punkt, *m.* nodal point, point of junction; **-scheibe,** *f.* disk of nodal cells; **-skorbut,** *m.* nodular scurvy; **-stock,** *m.* knotty stick; **-wurm,** *m.* hairworm; **-wurz,** *f.* figwort (Scrophularia); **-zahl,** *f.* nodal number; **-zelle,** *f.* cells underneath egg cell (in Chara).

Knöterich, *m.* knotgrass (*Polygonum*).

Knotfestigkeit, *f.* tensile strength at knot; **-gewächse,** *n.pl.* Polygonaceae.

knotig, knotty, gnarled, nodular, tubercular, caddish, jointed, articulate.

Knotpunkt, *m.*-e, junction.

Knotstock, *m.* knotty stick.

knüpfen, to tie, knot, knit, unite, attach, fasten.

Knüppel, *m.*-, billet, cudgel, club, stick, French roll.

knurren, to growl, snarl, (g)rumble.

knurrig, grumblingly.

knusperig, crisp.

Knute, *f.* knout.

Knüttel, *m.*-, cudgel, club.

Koagulat, *n.* clot, coagulum.

Koagulationswärme, *f.* heat of coagulation

koagulierbar, coagulable.

koagulieren, to coagulate.

Koagulierung, *f.* coagulation.

Koagulierungs-fähigkeit, *f.* coagulability; **-mittel,** *n.* coagulating agent, coagulant.

Kobalt, *m.*-e, cobalt; **-a(m)min,** *n.* cobalt-ammine; **-beschlag,** *m.* earthy erythrite; **-bleierz,** *n.* **-bleiglanz,** *m.* clausthalite; **-blume,** *f.* **-blüte,** *f.* cobalt bloom, erythrite: **-chlorür,** *n.* cobaltous chloride.

Kobalt-farbe, *f.* powder blue; **-gelb,** *n.* cobalt yellow; **-gehalt,** *m.* cobalt content; **-glanz,** *m.* cobalt glance, cobaltite; **-haltig,** cobaltiferous.

Kobaltiak, *n.* cobaltiac, cobaltammine.

Kobalti-chlorid, *n.* cobaltic chloride; **-kaliumnitrit,** *n.* potassium cobaltinitrite; **-sulfid,** *n.* cobaltic sulphide; **-verbindung,** *f.* cobaltic compound.

Kobalt-manganerz, *n.* asbolite; **-nickelkies,** *m.* cobalt pyrites, linnaeite.

Kobalto-chlorid, *n.* cobaltous chloride; **-nitrat,** *n.* cobaltous nitrate.

Kobalt-oxyd, *n.* cobalt oxide, cobaltic oxide; **-oxydul,** *n.* cobaltous oxide; **-oxydulverbindung,** *f.* cobaltous compound; **-spat,** *m.* sphaerocobaltite; **-speise,** *f.* cobalt speiss; **-verbindung,** *f.* cobalt compound; **-vitriol,** *m.* cobalt vitriol, cobaltous sulphate.

Koben, *m.* pigsty.

Kober, *m.* basket.

Koch, *m.*-e, cook; **-apparat,** *m.* cooking apparatus; **-becher,** *m.* beaker; **-beständig,** fast to boiling; **-birne,** *f.* stewing pear; **-dauer,** *f.* duration of boiling; **-echt,** fast to boiling.

kochen, to boil, cook, seethe.

Kochen, *n.* cooking, cookery, boiling.

Kocher, *m.*-, cooker, kettle.

Kocherei, *f.* boiling, cooking.

Koch-flasche, *f.* boiling flask; **-gefäss,** *n.* boiling vessel; **-gerät,** *n.* **-geschirr,** *n.* cooking utensils; **-hitze,** *f.* boiling heat; **-kessel,** *m.* boiling kettle, boiler, pulp boiler; **-kläre,** *f.* filtered liquor; **-kölbchen,** boiling flask; **-lauge,** *f.* boiling lye; **-puddeln,** *n.* pig boiling; **-punkt,** *m.* boiling point.

Koch-rohr, *n.* boiling tube; **-röhre,** *f.* boiling tube; **-salz,** *n.* sodium chloride, table salt; **-salzlösung,** *f.* sodium chloride solution; **-topf,** *m.* boiler, cooker; **-wasser,** *n.* boiling water; **-zeit,** *f.* period of boiling; **-zucker,** *m.* brown (powdered) sugar; **-zwecke,** *m.pl.* culinary operations.

Kockelskörner, *n.pl.* Indian berries, cocculus indicus.

Kodäthylin, *n.* codethyline.

Kodein, *n.* codeine.

Köder, *m.* bait, decoy; **-gast,** *m.* bait visitor; **-fang,** *m.* catching by means of bait; **-kasten,** *m.* bait container.

ködern, to bait, lure.

Köder-rezept, *n.* bait formula; **-sandwurm,** *m.* worm for baiting; **-schnur,** *f.* string with bait attached.

Kodex, *m.* old manuscript, code.

Kodol, *n.* cod-liver oil.

Koeffizient, *m.* coefficient.

Koenzym, *n.* coenzyme.

Köerzitivkraft, *f.* coercive force.

koexistieren, to coexist.

Koffein, *n.* caffeine; **-anreicherungsverfahren,** *n.* caffeine enrichment procedure.

Koffer, *m.* trunk, coffer, box.

Kognak, *m.* cognac.

kohärent, coherent.

Kohärenz, *f.* coherence, coherency.

kohärieren, to cohere.

Kohäsion, *f.* cohesion, coherence.

Kohäsionsvermögen, *n.* cohesiveness.

kohäsiv, cohesive.

Kohl, *m.* cabbage; **-amsel,** *f.* blackbird, ouzel; **-arten,** *f.pl.* brassicaceous plants; **-blatt,** *n.* cabbage leaf.

Kohle, *f.* coal, charcoal, carbon; **A ~,** activated carbon.

Kohle-chemie, *f.* coal (-tar) chemistry; **-fadenlampe,** *f.* carbon-filament lamp; **-förderung,** *f.* coal output; **-klemme,** *f.* carbon terminal.

kohlen, to char, carbonize, burn charcoal, carburize.

Kohlen-abbrand, *m.* consumption of carbon; **-ähnlich,** coallike, carbonlike, carbonaceous; **-artig,** coallike, carbonlike, carbonaceous; **-becken,** *n.* coal field; **-bergwerk,** *n.* mine, colliery; **-beule,** *f.* carbuncle; **-bleispat,** *m.* cerussite, white lead ore; **-bleivitriolspat,** *m.* lanarkite; **-blende,** *f.* anthracite; **-bogenlampe,** *f.* carbon-arc lamp.

Kohlen-brennerei, *f.* charcoal works or burning; **-dioxyd,** *n.* carbon dioxide; **-dunst,** *m.* vapor from coals; **-eisenstein,** *m.* blackband, carbonaceous ironstone; **-faden,** *m.* carbon filament; **-filter,** *n.* charcoal filter; **-flöz,** *n.* coal seam, coal measure; **-futter,** *n.* carbonaceous lining; **-gas,** *n.* coal gas; **-gestübbe,** *n.* **-griess,** *m.* **-grus,** *m.* coal slack.

Kohlen-grube, *f.* coal mine; **-haltig,** carboniferous; **-hydrat,** *n.* carbohydrate; **-hydratabbau,** *m.* carbohydrate metabolism; **-hydratverwertung,** *f.* carbohydrate utilization; **-kalk,** *m.* carboniferous limestone; **-kalkspat,** *m.* anthraconite; **-kalkstein,** *m.* carboniferous limestone; **-karbonit,** *n.* kohlencarbonite; **-klein,** *n.* small coal.

Kohlen-klemme, *f.* carbon terminal; **-lampe,** *f.* carbon lamp; **-lösche,** *f.* coal dust; **-meiler,** *m.* charcoal pile or kiln; **-monoxyd,** *n.* carbon monoxide; **-mulm,** *m.* coal dust, slack.

Kohlenoxyd, *n.* carbon monoxide; **-gas,** *n.* carbon monoxide gas; **-kalium,** *n.* potassium (carboxide), hexacarbonyl; **-knallgas,** *n.* explosive gas (carbon monoxide and oxygen); **-nickel,** *n.* nickel carbonyl; **-reich,** rich in carbon monoxide; **giftung,** *f.* carbon monoxide poisoning.

Kohlen-oxyhämoglobin, *n.* carbohemoglobin; **-papier,** *n.* carbon paper; **-sandstein,** *m.* carboniferous sandstone; **kohlensauer,** carbonate of; **kohlensaurer Kalk,** *m.* calcium carbonate; **kohlensaures Natrium,** *n.* sodium carbonate.

Kohlensäure, *f.* carbonic acid; **-anhydrid,** *n* carbonic anhydride; **-anreicherung,** *f* increase of carbon dioxide; **-ausscheidung,** *f.* carbon dioxide output, excretion of carbon dioxide; **-bad,** *n.* carbon dioxide bath; **-bläschen,** *n.* little bubble of carbon dioxide; **-chlorid,** *n.* carbonyl chloride; **-entwicklung,** *f.* evolution of carbonic acid; **-ester,** *m.* carbonic ester; **-gas,** *n.* carbonic acid gas, carbon dioxide.

Kohlensäure-gehalt, *m.* carbon dioxide content; -haltig, containing carbonic acid; -messer, *m.* anthracometer, carbonometer; -mikrotom, *n.* freezing (carbon dioxide) microtome; -salz, *n.* carbonate; -schnee, *m.* dry ice, carbon dioxide snow.

Kohlensäure-spannung, *f.* carbon dioxide tension; -strom, *m.* current of carbon dioxide; -verlust, *m.* loss of carbon dioxide; -versorgung, *f.* carbon dioxide supply; -wasser, *n.* carbonated water; -zusatz, *m.* addition of carbon dioxide.

Kohlen-schiefer, *m.* bituminous shale, coal-bearing shale; -schlacke, *f.* cinder, clinker; -schlichte, *f.* black wash; -schwarz, *n.* carbon black, charcoal black; -spat, *m.* anthraconite, whewellite; -spitze, *f.* carbon point; -staub, *m.* coal dust, pulverized coal, charcoal dust; -stickstoff, *m.* cyanogen; -stickstoffsäure, *f.* picric acid.

Kohlenstoff, *m.* carbon; -arm, poor in carbon; -art, *f.* variety of carbon; -atom, *n.* carbon atom; -ausscheidung, *f.* separation of carbon; -bestimmung, *f.* carbon determination; -bindung, *f.* carbon linkage; -eisen, *n.* iron carbide; -entziehung, *f.* removal of carbon, decarbonization; -gehalt, *m.* carbon content.

Kohlenstoff-gerüst, *n.* carbon skeleton; -haltig, carbonaceous; -kalium, *n.* potassium carbide; -kern, *m.* carbon nucleus; -kette, *f.* carbon chain; -legierung, *f.* carbon alloy; -metall, *n.* carbide; -reich, rich in carbon; -silizium, *n.* carbon silicide; -stein, *m.* carbon brick.

Kohlenstoff-sulfid, *n.* carbon disulphide; -tetrachlorid, *n.* carbon tetrachloride; -verbindung, *f.* carbon compound.

Kohlen-sulfid, *n.* carbon disulphide; -sulfidsalz, *n.* thiocarbonate, sulphocarbonate; -teer, *m.* coal tar; -teerfarbe, *f.* coal tar color; -tiegel, *m.* carbon (charcoal) crucible; -verbrauch, *m.* coal consumption; -vergasung, *f.* coal distillation; -wassergas, *n.* hydrocarbon gas; -wassergemisch, *n.* hydrocarbon mixture; -wasserstoff, *m.* hydrocarbon.

Kohlenwasserstoffgas, *n.* hydrocarbon gas; leichtes ~, methane; schweres ~, ethylene.

Kohlenwasserstoff-haltig, hydrocarbonaceous; -verbindung, *f.* hydrocarbon.

Kohlenziegel, *m.* coal briquet.

Kohlepapier, *n.* carbon paper.

Köhler, *m.* charcoal burner.

Köhlerei, *f.* charcoal burning, charcoal works.

Kohl-eule, *f.* cabbage moth; -fliege, *f.* cabbage fly (*Athomyia brassicae*); -floh, *m.* cabbage flea; -hernie, *f.* clubroot.

kohlig, like coal, coal-bearing.

Kohl-käfer, *m.* cabbage beetle; -kopf, *m.* head of cabbage; -lauch, *m.* cabbage garlic; -meise, *f.* great titmouse; -palme, *f.* cabbage (palm) palmetto; -palmöl, *n.* cabbage-palm oil; -rabe, *m.* common raven; -rabi, *m.* kohlrabi; -raps, *m.* rape, rapeseed; -raupe, *f.* cabbage caterpillar.

Kohl-rübe, *f.* rutabaga, turnip; -saat, *f.* colza, rapeseed; -schwarz, coal black; -setzlinge, *m.pl.* young cabbage plants; -sprossen, *m.pl.* Brussels sprouts; -stengel, *m.* cabbage stalk.

Kohlung, *f.* carbonization, carburization, charring.

Kohlweissling, *m.* cabbage (white) butterfly.

kohobieren, to cohobate, distill repeatedly.

Kohunennussöl, *n.* cohune-nut oil.

Kok (Koks), *m.* coke.

Koka, *f.* coca.

Kokain, *n.* cocaine; -vergiftung, *f.* cocainism

Kokardenblume, *f.* Gaillardia.

Koker, *m.* sagger.

Kokerei, *f.* coke plant; -ofen, *m.* coke oven.

Kokillen-hartguss, *m.* chill casting; -rand, *m.* chill-mold collar.

Kokkelskörner, *n.* Indian berry, cocculus indicus.

Kokken, *m.pl.* cocci; -ähnlich, resembling cocci; -ketten, *f.pl.* streptococci; -träger, *m.* carrier of cocci.

Kokkus, *m.* coccus.

Kokon, *m.* cocoon; -faden, *m.* cocoon thread, silk thread.

Kokos-baum, *m.*˸e, coco, cocoa palm, coconut tree; -butter, *f.* coconut (oil) butter; -faser, *f.* coconut fiber, coir; -fett, *n.* coconut oil.

Kokosnuss, *f.*˸e, coconut; -bast, *m.* coconut fiber; faser, *f.* coconut fiber; -milch, *f.* coconut milk; -öl, *n.* coconut oil; -palme, *f.* coco palm; -seife, *f.* coconut-oil soap; -stearinsäure, *f.* cocinic acid, cocinin; -talg, *m.* coconut oil; -talgsäure, *f.* cocinic acid.

Koks, *m.* coke; -abfall, *m.* refuse coke; -ähnlich, cokelike; -ausbeute, *f.* yield of coke; **-bereitung,** *f.* coke making, coking; **-brennen,** *n.* coke burning; **-erzeugung,** *f.* coke production; **-filter,** *m.* coke filter; **-gas,** *n.* coke gas; **-heizung,** *f.* heating with coke.

Koks-hochofen, *m.* coke blast furnace; **-klein,** *n.* small coke; **-kohle,** *f.* coking coal; **-lösche,** *f.* coke dust; **-ofen,** *m.* coke oven; **-schicht,** *f.* layer of coke; **-staub,** *m.* coke dust.

Kolanuss, *f.* kola nut.

Kolatorium, *n.* colatorium.

Kölbchen, *n.* little flask, small club, spikelet.

Kolben, *m.* flask, demijohn, butt (end), club, mallet, force, bulb, nodule, piston, soldering iron, bloom, bolthead, matrass, cucurbit, head, spike, club, knob, alembic, retort, spadix; **-anhang,** *m.* clublike appendage; **-brand,** *m.* cobsmut; **-förmig,** club-shaped, spadiceous; **-hals,** *m.* neck of a flask; **-hirse,** *f.* Italian millet; **-hub,** *m.* stroke of a piston; **-kissen,** *n.* bulb cushion; **-maschine,** *f.* reciprocator; **-moos,** *n.* club moss (Lycopodium).

Kolben-schieber, *m.* piston valve; **-schimmel,** *m.* club mold (Aspergillus); **-stange,** *f.* piston rod; **-stoss,** *m.* piston stroke; **-tragend,** spadiceous; **-träger,** *m.* flask (support) stand; **-wasserkäfer,** *m.pl.* Hydrophillidae.

kolbig, knobby, knotty, clublike, nodular.

Koli-arten, *m.pl.* races of colon bacilli; **-bakterien,** *n.pl.* coliform bacteria; **-bazillus,** *m.* colon bacillus.

Kolibri, *m.* humming bird; **-blume,** *f.* flower pollinated by humming birds.

kolieren, to filter, strain, percolate.

Kolier-rahmen, *m.* filter(ing) frame; **-tuch,** *n.* filter(ing) cloth.

Koligruppe, *f. Bacillus coli* group.

Kolik, *f.* colic.

Koli-reinkultur, *f.* pure culture of colon bacillus; **-titer,** *m.* count of colon bacilli.

Kolk, *m.* deep pool, eddy, scour.

Kolkrabe, *n.* raven (*Corvus corax*).

Kollargolpräparate, *n.pl.* collargol preparations.

Kolleg, *n.-e,* course (of lectures).

Kollege, *m.-n,* colleague.

Kollegienheft, *n.* student's notebook.

Kollegium, *n.* council, board, staff.

Kollekte, *f.* collection.

kollektiv, collective.

Kollektor, *m.* commutator.

Koller, *m.* staggers, choler; **-ader,** *f.* frontal vein; **-distel,** *f.* Eryngium; **-gang,** *m.* edge mill; **-mühle,** *f.* edge mill.

kollern, to rumble, gobble, roll, rave, have staggers.

Koller-stoff, *m.* waste(paper); **-wuchs,** *n.* wide-spreading crown.

kollidieren, to collide.

Kollidin, *n.* collidine.

Kollimation, *f.* collimation.

Kollision, *f.* collision.

Kollo, *n.* parcel, bale, bundle.

kollodisieren, to collodionize.

Kollodium, *n.* collodion; **-ersatz,** *m.* collodion substitute; **-häutchen,** *n.* collodion film; **-lösung,** *f.* collodion solution; **-säckchen,** *n.* collodion sac; **-seide,** *f.* collodion silk; **-überzug,** *m.* coat or skin of collodion; **-verfahren,** *n.* collodion method; **-wolle,** *f.* collodion cotton, celloidin, pyroxylin.

kolloid(al), colloid, colloidal.

Kolloid-chemie, *f.* colloid chemistry; **-chemisch,** colloidochemical; **-fällung,** *f.* colloid precipitation; **-grad,** *m.* colloidal refinement; **-hydrat,** *n.* colloid hydrate; **-reaktion,** *f.* colloid reaction; **-substanz,** *f.* colloid substance, colloid; **-teilchen,** *n.* colloid particle; **-zustand,** *m.* colloidal state.

Kolmation, *n.* deposition of soil (from flowing water).

Kölner, Cologne; **-wasser,** *n.* Cologne water, eau de Cologne.

kölnisch, Cologne.

Kolon, *n.* colon; **-bazillus,** *m.* colon bacillus.

Kolonial-waren, *f.pl.* groceries. colonial produce; **-zucker,** *m.* cane sugar

Kolonie, *f.* colony.

kolonienbildend, colonial.

kolonisieren, to colonize.

Kolonne, *f.* column, gang.

Kolophoneisenerz, *m.* pitticite.

Kolophonium, *n.* colophony, rosin.

Kolophonsäure, *f.* colophonic acid.

Koloquinte, *f.* colocynth, bitter apple (*Citrullus colocynthis*).

Koloquintin, *n.* colocynthin.

kolorieren, to color.

Kolorimetrie, *f.* colorimetry.

kolorimetrisch, colorimetric.

Kolorit, *n.* color(ing), hue.

kolossal, huge.

Kolostrumkörperchen, *n.* colostral cell.

Kolter, *n.* colter.

Kolumbowurzel, *f.* calumba (columbo) (root).

Komansäure, *f.* comanic acid.

Kombinationsfärbung, *f.* differential staining.

kombinieren, to combine.

Komensäure, *f.* comenic acid.

Komet, *m.* comet.

komisch, comic, funny.

Komma, *n.* comma, decimal point; **-bazillus,** cholera vibrio; **-förmiger Bazillus,** comma-shaped bacillus.

kommandieren, to command.

kommen, to come, happen, be, arise, approach, spring up, get to, proceed from, come out, arrive at; ∼ **lassen,** to have come, let come; **dazu** ∼, to be added; **es kommt . . . auf,** there is used . . . with (to); **gleich** ∼, to be equal to; **zustande** ∼, to come about; **zu stehen** ∼, to amount to; **dazu kommt, dass,** it must be added that, moreover; **zum Ausdruck** ∼, to be expressed; **zum Vorschein** ∼, to appear; **zur Ausbildung** ∼, to develop; **zur Verwendung** ∼, to be used; **zu etwas** ∼, to come to something, arrive at something.

Kommentar, *m.* -e, commentary.

kommentieren, to comment on, annotate.

Kommerz, *m.* commerce.

Kommis, *m.* clerk.

Kommission, *f.* commission, committee.

Kommisuralsiebröhre, *f.* commissural sieve tube.

Kommisurenfasern, *f.pl.* commisural (tracts) fibers.

Kommode, *f.* (chest of) drawers.

kommunizieren, to commute.

Komödie, *f.* comedy.

kompakt, compact, solid, rugged.

Kompass, *m.* -e, compass; **-häuschen,** *n.* binnacle; **-rose,** *f.* compass card.

Kompendium, *n.* manual, compendium, abridged treatise, abstract.

kompensieren, to compensate.

Komplement, *n.* complement; **-ablenkung,** *f.* deviation of the complement.

komplementär, complementary.

Komplement-bindung, *f.* complement fixation; **-fixierung,** *f.* fixation of complement; **-wirkung,** *f.* complement action.

komplet, complete.

komplettieren, to complete.

Komplexverbindung, *f.* complex compound

Kompliment, *n.* compliment.

komplizieren, to complicate.

kompliziert, complicated, intricate.

Komplott, *n.*-e, plot.

Komponente, *f.* component (of a) force.

komponieren, to compose.

Komposition, *f.* composition.

Kompost, *n.* compost, mulch; **mit** ∼ **düngen,** to compost, mulch.

Kompott, *n.*-e, stewed (or preserved) fruit; jam.

Kompressibilität, *f.* compressibility.

Kompressions-reiz, *m.* compression stimulus; **-welle,** *f.* compression wave.

komprimierbar, compressible.

komprimieren, to compress.

Kompromiss, *m.* compromise.

kompromittieren, to compromise.

Konchylien, *f.pl.* shells, shellfish.

Kondensat, *n.* condensate.

Kondensations-apparat, *m.* condenser, condensing apparatus; **-betrieb,** *m.* pass-out operation; **-druck,** *m.* condensation pressure; **-ergebnis,** *n.* condensation product; **-gefäss,** *n.* condensation vessel, receiver; **-rohr,** *n.* condensing tube, adapter; **-röhre,** *f.* condensing tube, adapter; **-verlust,** *m.* loss from condensation; **-wasser,** *n.* water of condensation.

Kondensator, *m.*-en, condenser.

kondensierbar, condensable.

kondensieren, to condense.

Kondens-topf, *m.*-e, condensing pot, steam trap; **-wasser,** *n.* water of condensation.

konditionieren, to condition.

Konditor, *m.* confectioner.

Konditorei, *f.* confectionery; **-waren,** *f.* confectionery.

Konfekt, *n.*-e, confectionery.

konferenz, *f.* conference.

konferieren, to confer.

konfiszieren, to confiscate

Konfitüren, *f.pl.* confectionery, candied fruits.

Konflikt, *m.*-e, conflict.

konfokal, confocal, having the same foci.

konfrontieren, to confront.

konfus, confused.

kongelieren, to congeal.

kongruent, congruent, (math.) equal

Kongruenz, *f.* congruity.

kongruieren, to coincide.

Konifere, *f.* conifer.

Koniferen-holz, *n.* conifer wood; **-stamm** *m.* stem of conifer.

König, *m.*-e, king, regulus.

Königin, *f.* queen.

Königinnenzelle, *f.* cell of the queen (bee).

königlich, kingly, regal, royal.

König-reich, *n.* kingdom, realm; **-salbe,** *f.* resin cerate, basilicon ointment.

Königs-adler, *m.* golden eagle; **-apfel,** *m.* pomeroy (*Bromelia*); **-blau,** *n.* smalt; **blume,** *f.* peony; **-chinarinde,** *f.* calisaya bark, yellow cinchona bark; **-farn,** *m.* royal fern (*Osmunda regalis*).

Königs-gelb, *n.* chrome yellow; **-grün,** *n.* Paris green; **-kerze,** *f.* common (great) mullein (*Verbascum thapsus*); **-krankheit,** *f.* king's evil, scrofula; **-salbe,** *f.* basilicon, resin cerate; **-säure,** *f.* aqua regia; **-wasser,** *n.* aqua regia.

Koniin, *n.* conine, coniine.

konisch, conic, conical, coniform; **konische Kreuzspule,** *f.* cone.

konjugieren, to conjugate.

Konjunktiva, *f.* conjunctiva.

konkav, concave; **-konvex,** concavo-convex.

Konkavspiegel, *m.* concave mirror.

Konkrement, *n.* concrement, concretion.

konkret, concrete.

Konkurrenz, *f.* competition; **-kampf,** *m.* struggle for survival, antagonistic action; **-los,** exclusive.

konkurrieren, to compete.

konkurrierend, concurrent.

Konkurs, *m.* bankruptcy, failure, assignment.

könne, could, can.

können, to be able, can, may.

konnte (können), could, was able, might, can.

Konoden, *f.pl.* conodes, tie lines.

konsequent, consistent, consequent.

Konsequenz, *f.* conclusion.

konservativ, conservative.

Konserve, *f.* preserved food, conserve, confection, electuary.

Konserven-büchse, *f.* -dose, *f.* can, tin; **-fabrik,** *f.* cannery, preserve factory.

konservieren, to preserve.

Konservierung, *f.* preservation, conservation.

Konservierungs-firnis, *m.* preserving varnish; **-mittel,** *n.* preservative; **-verfahren,** *n.* preserving method.

konsistentes Fett, *n.* grease, solid lubricant.

Konsistenz, *f.* consistency, body (lacquer); **-messer,** *m.* viscosimeter.

Konsole, *f.* bracket, console.

konsolidieren, to consolidate.

Konsortium, *n.* association, syndicate.

Konstante, *f.* constant.

Konstant-(er)haltung, *f.* keeping constant, maintenance; **-halten,** to maintain.

Konstanz, *n.* constancy.

konstatieren, to ascertain, establish, prove, verify.

konstituieren, to constitute.

Konstitutions-formel, *f.* constitutional formula; **-wasser,** *n.* water of consti ution.

konstruieren, to construct, design.

konsultieren, to consult.

Konsum, *m.* consumption.

Konsument, *m.* consumer.

konsumieren, to consume.

Kontagiostät, *f.* infectivity, contagiousness

Kontagium, *n.* contagion.

Kontakt, *m.* contact, terminal; **-fläche,** *f.* surface of contact; **-gift,** *n.* contact poison; **-oberfläche,** *f.* surface of contact; **-potential,** *n.* interface potential; **-substanz,** *f.* contact substance, catalyst; **-verfahren,** *n.* contact process; **-wirkung,** *f.* contact action, catalysis.

Kontinent, *m.*-e, continent.

kontinuierlich, continuous.

Kontinuität, *f.* continuity.

Konto, *n.* account.

Kontor, *n.* office.

kontrahieren, to contract.

kontraktil, contractile.

kontrollierbar, controllable.

kontrollieren, to control, check, supervise, converge.

Kontrollprobe, *f.* duplicate (control) sample.

Konus, *m.* cone.

Konvektionsstrom, *m.* convex stream (current).

Konvergenz, *f.* convergence.

konvergierend, convergent.

konvertieren, to convert.

konvex, convex; -konkav, convexo-concave.

Konzentrations-änderung, *f.* change in concentration; -gefälle, *n.* concentration (gradient) fall; -spannung, *f.* concentration potential; -stein, *m.* white metal; -verhältnis, *f.* ratio of concentration; -viereck, *n.* quarternary system.

konzentrieren, to concentrate.

Konzentrierung, *f.* concentration.

konzentrisch, concentric.

Konzeption, *f.* conception.

Konzession, *f.* concession, patent, license.

Koordinate, *f.* coordinate.

Koordinatenzahl, *f.* index of coordination.

Koordinationslehre, *f.* coordination theory.

Kopaiva-balsam, *m.* (balsam of) copaiva.

Kopal-baum, *m.* copal tree (*Valeria indica*), -fichte, *f.* Agathis; -firnis, *m.* -lack, *m.* copal varnish.

Köper (Weben), *m.* twill (weaving).

köpern, to twill.

Kopf, *m.*ˑe, head, top, crown, summit; aus dem ∼, by heart; sich den ∼ zerbrechen, to rack one's brain.

Kopf-ader, *f.* vein of the head, cephalic vein; -amnionhöhle, *f.* head amniotic cavity; -arme, *m.pl.* head tentacles; -armpulsader, *f.* brachiocephalic (artery) trunk; -bau, *m.* structure of the head; -bedeckung, *f.* scalp; -blase, *f.* cephalic vesicle; -blüten, *f.pl.* aggregate flowers; -brust, *f.* cephalothorax; -brustschild, *m.* carapace; -brustück, *n.* cephalothorax; -buckel, *m.* glabella.

Köpfchen, *n.* capitulum, condyle, cluster; -darm, *m.* upper part of foregut; -diachasium, *n.* botryose cyme; -haar, *n.* capitate hair; -rispe, *f.* compound inflorescence of Compositae; -sichel, *f.* drepanium (a sickel-shaped cyme); -schraubel, *f.* a botryose cyme; -spirre, *f.* anthela (a pani-

cle of Juncus); -stiel, *m.* pedicel; -wickel, *m.* cincinnus; -zelle, *f.* head cell.

Kopf-darm, *m.* head gut, cephalic duct, capitulum; -decke, *f.* scalp; -drüse, *f.* cephalic gland; -düngung, *f.* top dressing (fertilization); -eibe, *f.* Cephalotaxus.

köpfen, to top, behead, poll(ard), truncate.

Kopf-fortsatz, *m.* cephalic appendage, head process; -füsser, *m.pl.* Cephalopoda, cuttlefish; -gelenk, *n.* articulation of head with spine; -gipfel, *m.* vertex, fastigium; -gliedmassen, *n.pl.* cephalic appendages; -grind, *m.* scald head, porrigo.

Kopf-haar, *m.* hair of the head; -haube, *f.* crest, tuft, hood; -haut, *f.* scalp, skin of the head; -hautverletzung, *f.* scalp injury; -heber, *m.* splenius muscle; -holz, *n.* lopped tree, pollard; -holzbetrieb, *m.* pollarding, topping.

köpfig, capitate, cephalous, -headed.

Kopf-kappe, *f.* head fold, anter or layer of head, cephalic veil, hood; -kegel, *m.* oral bone; -keilbein, *n.* sphenoid bone; -keim, *m.* head germ; -kiemer, *m.pl.* Cephalobranchia; -kissen, *n.* pillow; -knorpel, *m.* cephalic cartilage; -kohl, *m.* common white (headed) cabbage; -lappen, *m.* cephalic love, preoral segment; -larve, *f.* nauplius.

Kopf-laus, *f.* head louse (*Pediculus capitis*); -los, headless, acephalous, brainless, silly, stupid; -naht, *f.* cranial suture; -neiger, *m.* flexor muscle of head; -niere, *f.* head kidney, pronephros; -platte, *f.* cephalic plate; -rain, *m.* apterium capitis, head border or ridge; -ring, *m.* nozzle block (zinc); -rose, *f.* erysipelas; -salat, *m.* head lettuce.

Kopf-scheibe, *f.* cephalic disk; -scheide, *f.* cephalic sheath; -scheu, shy, skittish, restive; -schild, *m.* clypeus, cephalic shield; -schimmel, *m.* mold (Mucor); -schmerz, *m.* headache; -seite, *f.* cranial end; -stand, *m.* head (Compositae); -steuer, *m.* poll tax; -träger, *m.* atlas.

Kopf-überschrift, *f.* principal heading; -wasser, *m.* hair wash; -wassersucht, *f.* hydrocephalus; -weh, *n.* headache; -weide, *f.* pollard willow; -wirbel, *m.* atlas, cephalic vertebra; -zapfen, *m.* prostomium; -zerbrechen, mental strain, "headache."

Kopie, *f.* copy.

kopieren, to copy.

Kopier-farbe, *f.* copying ink; -presse, *f.* copying press; -tinte, *f.* copying ink.

Koppel, *f.* coupling, belt, leash, enclosure.

koppeln, to couple, tie, unite.

Köppeln, *n.* afterfermentation.

Koppelung, *f.* linkage, coupling.

Koppelungs-stetigkeit, *f.* linkage permanency; **-untersuchung**, *f.* linkage (study) investigation; **-verhältnis**, *n.* linkage relations; **-wechsel**, *m.* change in linkage; **-zahl**, *f.* linkage number; **-ziffer**, *f.* linkage number.

Koppel-weide, *f.* enclosed pasture land; **-wirtschaft**, *f.* rotation of crops.

Koprafett, *n.* **-öl**, *n.* copra (coconut) oil.

Koprolith, *m.* coprolite.

kopulieren, to graft, pair, marry, copulate.

Koralle, *f.* coral.

korallen-artig, coral-like, coralloid; **-bank**, *f.* coral reef; **-gerüst**, *n.* polyparium, coral structure; **-moos**, *n.* coral moss (Corallina); **-riff**, *n.* coral reef; **-stock**, *m.* coral colony; **-strauch**, *m.* Erythrina; **-tiere**, *n.pl.* Anthozoa; **-wurzel**, *f.* polypody root.

Korb, *m.*-ᵉe, basket, hamper, crate, pannier, canister, rejection, dismissal; **-binse**, *f.* frail; **-blütler**, *m.pl.* Compositae.

Körbchen, *n.* small basket, corbicula.

Korb-flasche, *f.* carboy, demijohn; **-flechterei**, *f.* basketwork; **-weide**, *f.* basket willow, (velvet) osier (*Salix viminalis*).

Kordel, *f.* twine, string, cord.

Kordit, *n.* cordite.

Kordon, cordon, line.

kören, to assay, inspect.

Koriander, *m.* coriander.

Korinthe, *f.* currant.

Kork, *m.*-e, cork, suber, stopper; **-ähnlich**, corklike; **-artig**, corklike, suberose; **-asbest**, *m.* mountain cork, rock cork, cork fossil; **-baum**, *m.* cork tree; **-bohrer**, *m.* cork borer; **-eiche**, *f.* cork oak, cork tree (*Quercus suber*).

korken, to cork; **-zieher**, *m.* corkscrew.

Kork-gewinnung, *f.* removal of cork; **-haut**, *f.* periderm; **-höcker**, *m.* corky wart or knob.

korkig, suberous.

Kork-kohle, *f.* cork charcoal, burnt cork; **-kruste**, *f.* cork crust; **-leiste**, *f.* cork ridge; **-mehl**, *n.* cork (meal) powder; **-mutterschicht**, *f.* phellogen; **-pfropfen**, *m.* cork stopper, cork; **-rissigkeit**, *f.* cracking of the periderm; **-säure**, *f.* suberic acid; **-schicht**, *f.* periderm; **-schwarz**, *n.* cork black.

Kork-spund, *m.* cork stopper, cork; **-stein**, *m.* corkboard, cork brick; **-stoff**, *m.* suberin; **-stopfen**, *m.* **-stöpsel**, *m.* cork stopper, cork; **-substanz**, *f.* suberin; **-sucht**, *f.* formation of excessive amounts of cork; **-teppich**, *m.* linoleum; **-warze**, *f.* lenticel.

Kork-wucherung, *f.* callus formation, proliferation of the periderm; **-zelle**, *f.* cork cell, periderm cell; **-zieher**, *m.* corkscrew.

Kormophyt, *m.* cormophyte.

Korn, *n.* grain, seed, chondrium, kernel, standard, corn, rye, fineness, gunsight, boon (of flax); **-ähre**, *f.* ear of corn, spike, head; **-alkohol**, *m.* grain alcohol; **-anteile**, *m.pl.* grain-size (distribution) fraction; **-art**, *f.* kind of grain; **-bau**, *m.* growing of grain; **-bildung**, *f.* granulation, crystallization; **-bildungspunkt**, *m.* granulating point; **-blau**, cornflower blue; **-blei**, *n.* grain lead.

Korn-blume, *f.* bluebottle, cornflower (*Centaurea cyanus*); **-boden**, *m.* granary; **-brand**, *m.* blight, smut; **-branntwein**, *m.* grain spirits, whisky; **-bürste**, *f.* button brush.

Körnchen, *n.* little grain, granule, spore of a mold; **-flieger**, *m.* poppy type of seed or pollen (wind dissemination); **-schlauch**, *m.* cell containing granules.

Kornea, *f.* cornea.

Kornealreflex, *m.* corneal reflex.

Kornelkirsche, *f.* cornelian cherry.

körneln, to granulate.

Körnelung, *f.* granulation.

körnen, to granulate, grain, corn, run to seed.

Körner, *n.pl.* hard seeds; **-asant**, *m.* granular asafetida; **-form**, *f.* granular shape or form; **-fresser**, *m.* granivorous bird; **-frucht**, *f.* cereal, grain; **-futter**, *n.* grain; **-haufen**, *m.* mass of granules; **-lack**, *m.* seed-lac, **-plasma**, *n.* granular protoplasm; **-reich**, grainy; **-tragend**, graniferous; **-zinn**, *n.* grain (granular) tin.

Korn-förmig, granular; **-frucht**, *f.* caryopsis; **-fuselöl**, *n.* fusel oil from grain; **-garbe**, *f.* sheaf; **-gemenge**, *n.* mixture of grain sizes; **-grenze**, *f.* grain boundary; **-grösse**, *f.* grain size.

Korngrössen-einteilung, *f.* grain-size classification; **-verteilung**, *f.* particle-size distribution.

Körnhaus, *m.* granulating house or mill.

körnig, granular, granulated, grainy, pebbly, gritty, grained.

Körnigkeit, *f.* granularity.

körnigkristallinisch, granular-crystalline.

Korn-käfer, *m.* grain weevil; **-kammer,** *f.* granary; **-kluft,** *f.* assayer's tongs; **-kochen,** *n.* boiling to grain (sugar); **-kupfer,** *n.* granulated copper; **-mutter,** *f.* ergot; **-prüfer,** *m.* grain tester; **-puddeln,** *n.* puddling of granular iron; **-rade,** *f.* corn cockle, corn campion (*Agrostemma githago*); **-schnaps,** *m.* grain spirits, whisky; **-sieb,** *n.* granulating sieve, grain sieve.

Kornung, *f.* range of grain sizes.

Körnung, *f.* granulation, graining.

Korn-spitze, *f.* dead center; **-waage,** *f.* button (assay) balance, grain scales; **-wurm,** *m.* weevil; **-zucker,** *m.* granulated sugar; **-zusammensetzung,** *f.* gradation of grain sizes.

korollinisch, like a corolla.

Körper, *m.-,* body, substance, compound, carcass, corpse; **-achse,** *f.* axis of the body; **-bau,** *m.* structure of the body; **-behaarung** *f.* pilosity, vestiture; **-beschaffenheit,** *f.* constitution, disposition, physique.

Körperchen, *n.* corpuscle, particle.

körpereigen, belonging to own body; **-farbe,** *f.* body color, pigment; **-flüssigkeit,** *f.* body fluid; **-fülle,** *f.* corpulence; **-gewebe,** *n.* connective tissue of the body; **-gewicht,** *n.* body weight.

Körper-gliederung, *f.* segmentation of the body; **-grösse,** *f.* stature; **-gruppe,** *f.* group of bodies; **-haltung,** *f.* deportment, carriage, bearing; **-herz,** *n.* systemic heart, the left side of the heart; **-höhle,** *f.* body cavity; **-hülle,** *f.* body covering; **-kraft,** *f.* physical strength; **-kreislauf,** *m.* systemic circulation; **-lehre,** somatology.

körperlich, bodily, corporeal, substantial, material, corpuscular, solid.

Körper-mass, *n.* cubic measure; **-mitte,** *f.* middle of body; **-oberfläche,** *f.* body surface; **-öffnung,** *f.* aperture of the body; **-pulsader,** *f.* aorta; **-saft,** *m.* body liquids or humors; **-schaft,** *f.* corporation; **-scheibe,** *f.* body (central) disk; **-schlagader,** *f.* aorta; **-schwäche,** *f.* bodily weakness.

Körper-stellung, *f.* posture; **-stoff,** *m.* organic matter; **-teil,** *m.* organ, part of body; **-teilchen,** *n.* particle, molecule; **-umriss,** *m.* body outline; **-unterseite,** *f.* ventral part of the body; **-wärme,** *f.* body heat; **-zusammensetzung,** *f.* body composition.

Korps, *n.* corps, body of things

korpuskuliar, corpuscular.

korrekt, correct.

Korrektivmittel, *n.* corrigent.

Korrektur, *f.* correction, proof.

Korrelat, *n.* correlative.

Korridor, *m.-e,* passage, hallway, corridor.

korrigieren, to correct.

korrodieren, to corrode.

korrosions-beständig, corrosion-resistant; **-mittel,** *n.* corrosive.

Korund, *m.* corundum.

Körung, *f.* inspection, sampling, trying.

Koschenille, *f.* cochineal.

Kosekante, *f.* cosecant.

Kosinus, *m.* cosine; **-satz,** *m.* cosine theorem.

kosmetisch, cosmetic.

Kosmos, *m.* cosmos.

Kosoblüten, *f.pl.* brayera, cusso (flowers).

Kost, *f.* food, fare, diet, board.

kostbar, precious, splendid, costly, expensive.

Kostbarkeit, *f.* precious object.

kosten, to cost, taste, try, experience.

Kosten, *f.pl.* costs, expenses, charges; **auf ~,** at the expense.

Kosten-anschlag, *m.-e,* estimate; **-aufwand,** *m.* expenditure; **-frei,** free of charge; **-los,** free of charge; **-wert,** *m.* cost value.

köstlich, costly, delicious, dainty, excellent.

Kost-probe, *f.* sample; **-spielig,** expensive.

Kostüm, *n.* costume, dress, suit.

Kostwurz, *f.* cotusroot, pachak.

Kot, *m.* feces, excrement, droppings, mud, silt, filth, dirt; **-abgang,** *m.* defecation; **-artig,** fecal, deculent, excremental; **-ausführend,** asperient, purgative, cathartic; **-ausleerung,** *f.* evacuation of feces; **-bad,** *n.* dung bath; **-blech,** *n.* mudguard; **-brett,** *n.* dropping board; **-flügel,** *m.* mudguard.

Kotelett, *n.* cutlet, chop.

Kotenschopf, *m.* fetlock.

Köter, *m.* cur.

Kot-flügel, *m.-,* mudguard; **-geruch,** *m* fecal odor; **-grube,** *f.* cesspool.

kotig, fecal, stercoraceous, dirty, filthy.

kotonisieren, to degum (silk).

Kotorinde, *f.* coto (bark).

Kot-porphyrin, *n.* coproporphyrin; **-stein,** *m.* fecal concretion.

Kouvert, *n.* envelope, cover.

Kovolum(en), *n.* covolume.

Koxal-fortsatz, *m.* process of the coxa; **-glied,** *n.* coxal segment; **-platte,** *f.* coxal plate.

Krabbe, *f.* crab.

krabbecht, fast to crabbing.

krabbeln, to crawl, tickle, itch.

Krabbenschere, *f.* pincers of the crab.

Krach, *m.* crack, crash, crisis.

krachen, to crash, crack, crackle, crepitate, rustle.

krächzen, to croak, caw.

kraft, by virtue of, on the strength of.

Kraft, *f.-̈e,* power, force, strength, vigor, energy, virtue, stress; **-abgabe,** *f.* supply of power; **-anlage,** *f.* power plant; **-anstrengung,** *f.* effort; **-aufwand,** *m.* expenditure of energy, effort; **-ausdruck,** *m.* strong expression or language; **-äusserung,** *f.* manifestation of energy.

Kraft-bedarf, *m.* power demand or requirement; **-brühe,** *f.* strong broth; **-dehnungsmesser,** *n.* stress-strain tester; **-eck,** *n.* force polygon; **-einheit,** *f.* unit of force or work; **-empfindung,** *f.* sensation of tension; **-entwicklung,** *f.* expenditure of force; **-epolygon,** *n.* polygon of forces; **-erzeugung,** *f.* power production.

Kräfte-system, *n.* system of forces; **-verteilung,** *f.* division of forces; **-vieleck,** *n.* force polygon; **-zerfall,** *m.* disintegration of strength.

Kraft-futter, *n.* concentrates, concentrated feed; **-gas,** *n.* power gas, producer gas.

kräftig, strong, heavy, severe, vigorous, effective, valid, nourishing, powerful.

kräftigen, to strengthen.

Kraft-knospe, *f.* winter bud of herbaceous plants (initiating new growth); **-lehre,** dynamics; **-leitung,** *f.* power circuit; **-linie,** *f.* line of force; **-los,** forceless, powerless, feeble; **-mehl,** *n.* starch, amylum; **-messer,** *m.* dynamometer; **-mittel,** *n.* forceful means, tonic remedy; **-probe,** *f.* trial of strength; **-quelle,** *f.* source of power.

Kraft-röhre, *f.* tube of force; **-sammler,** *m.* accumulator; **-schalter,** *m.* pilot; **-spiritus,** *m.* motor spirit; **-spross,** *m.* shoot which elongates; **-stoff,** *m.* fuel; **-strom,** *m.* power (tension) current; **-übertragung,** *f.* power transmission; **-verbrauch,** *m.* power consumption; **-voll,** powerful, vigorous.

Kraft-wagen, *m.* automobile, motor car; **-wechsel,** *m.* energy exchange; **-werk,** *n.*

power station; **-wirkung,** *f.* dynamic effect, action of a force; **-zentrale,** *f.* power station; **-zweig,** *m.* branch which elongates.

Krag-balken, *m.* cantilever beam; **-träger,** *m.* console.

Kragen, *m.-,* collar, involucre, cape, flange; **-kolben,** *m.* collared (flanged) flask; **-zelle,** *f.* collar cell (sponges).

Krähe, *f.* crow.

krähen, to crow; **-augen,** *n.pl.* nux vomica; **-beere,** *f.* crowberry (*Empetrum*); **-förmig,** corviform.

Krahle, *f.* rake.

Kralle, *f.* claw, ungula, dactyl, flipper, talon, clutch.

krallen-förmig, claw-shaped; **-hieb,** *m.* stroke with a claw; **-paar,** *n.* pair of claws; **-platte,** *f.* the upper (curved) part of the claw; **-ranke,** *f.* clawlike tendril; **-sohle,** *f.* the sole of the claw; **-winde,** *f.* Cobaea.

Kram, *m.* retail (trade), store, shop, retail articles, stuff, lot, odds and ends, trash.

kramen, to rummage.

Krämer, *m.* retailer, shopkeeper; **-gewicht,** *n.* avoirdupois.

Krammenzelle, *f.* anchor cell at base of commissure.

Krammetsvogel, *m.* fieldfare (*Turdus pilaris*).

Krampe, *f.* cramp (iron), clamp, staple, wood pick, flap, flange.

Krampf, *m.-̈e,* cramp, spasm, convulsion, fits; **-ader,** *f.* varicose vein; **-artig,** spasmodic; **-arznei,** *f.* antispasmodic; **-gift,** *n.* convulsive poison; **-haft,** spasmodic, convulsive, spastic; **-mittel,** *n.* antispasmodic; **-wurzel,** *f.* valerian root.

Kran, *m.* cock, faucet, crane.

Kranewitbeere, *f.* juniper berry.

Kranich, *m.-e,* common crane; **-schnabel,** *m.* crane's-bill (Geranium), stork's-bill (Pelargonium).

krank, ill, sick.

kränkeln, to be ailing, be sickly, suffering.

Kranken-anstalt, *f.* **-haus,** *n.* hospital: **-kost,** *f.* diet; **-serum,** *n.* serum of a sick person.

krankhaft, diseased, morbid, abnormal.

Krankheit, *f.* illness, disease, sickness.

Krankheits-bild, *n.-er,* diagnosis of the illness, aspect of a disease; **-erregend,** disease-producing, exciting disease, path ɔ genic; **-erreger,** *m.* cause of disease, pathogenic agent; **-erscheinung,** *f.* pathological symptom; **-erzeugend,** pathogenic; **-keim,** *m.* disease germ; **-kunde,** pathology; **-lehre,** *f.* pathology; **-stoff,** *m.* contagious matter; **-verlauf,** *m.* course of a disease; **-vorgang,** *m.* course of disease; **-widerständig,** disease-resistant.

kränklich, sickly, in poor health.

Kränkung, *f.* insult, vexation.

Kranz, *m.*-̈e, wreath, crown, corona, areola, ring, circle, border, rim, brim; **-blume,** *f.* garland flower (Hedychium); **-brenner,** *m.* ring burner.

Kränzchen, *n.* little wreath, private circle, bee.

Kranzdarm, *m.* peripheral intestine.

Krapfen, *m.* apple fritter.

Krapp, *m.* madder (*Rubia tinctorum*); **-farbe,** *f.* madder color; **-farbstoff,** *m.* alizarin; **-gewächse,** *n.pl.* Rubiaceae; **-stoff,** *m.* alizarin; **-wurzel,** *f.* madder root.

Krater, *m.* crater; **-bildung,** *f.* blotching, pitting.

Kratte, *f.* crate.

Kratz, *m.* scratch; **-artig,** resembling the itch; **-beere,** *f.* brambleberry, blackberry, dewberry; **-blei,** *n.* slag head; **-bürste,** *f.* stiff brush, scraper, cross (irritable) person; **-bürstig,** irritable, cross; **-distel,** *f.* horse thistle (*Cirsium arvense*).

Kratze, *f.* scraper, rake, card (for cotton).

Krätze, *f.* scabies, itch, waste metal.

Kratzeisen, *n.* scraper.

kratzen, to scrape, scratch, irritate, have a harsh and tart taste.

Kratzer, *m.* scraper, scratcher.

Kratzer, *m.pl.* Acanthocephala.

Krätzer, *m.* bad wine.

Krätzfrische, *n.* refining of waste.

krätzig, itchy, scabious, fibrous.

Krätzmessing, *n.* brass (cuttings) filings.

Krätzmilben, *f.pl.* Sarcoptiden.

Kratzstelle, *f.* scratched place.

kraus, crisp, curly, curled, corrugated, nappy, ruffled; **-blättrig,** crispifolious.

Kräuschung, *f.* crinkling.

Krause, *f.* frill, ruff.

Kräusel-haar, *n.* curled hair; **-krankheit,** *f.* curly leaf (disease).

kräuseln, to curl, crinkle, crisp, crimp, mill.

Krauseminze, *f.* spearmint.

Kräusen, *f.pl.* head (in brewing).

Kraus-gummi, *n.* crepe rubber; **-haarig,** curly-haired; **-kopf,** *f.* curlyhead; **-putz,** *m.* rough plaster, rough cast; **-tabak,** *m.* shag.

Kraut, *n.*-̈er, herb, vine, plant, weed, tops (leaves) of beets, cabbage; **-artig,** herbaceous.

Kräuter-bier, *n.* medicated ale; **-essig,** *m.* aromatic vinegar; **-käse,** *m.* green cheese; **-kunde,** *f.* botany; **-mittel,** *n.* vegetable remedy; **-tee,** *m.* herb tea; **-verein,** *m.* herb community; **-wein,** *m.* medicated wine; **-zucker,** *m.* conserve.

Kraut-flur, *f.* herb vegetation or meadow; **-garten,** *m.* kitchen garden; **-halde,** *f.* mat herbage, herb field, hillside; **-matte,** *f.* mat herbage, meadow; **-schicht,** *f.* herb strata (in a vegetation).

Krawatte, *f.* tie, scarf, cravat.

Kreatin, *n.* creatine.

Kreatinin, *n.* creatinine.

Kreatur, *f.* creature.

Krebs, *m.*-e, cancer, wart, ulcer, crayfish, grain, canker, crab; **-artig,** cancerous, cankerous, crablike, crustaceous; **-behandlung,** *f.* cancer treatment; **-beule,** *f.* cancerous excrescence; **-distel,** *f.* cotton thistle (*Onopordon acanthium*).

Krebse, *m.pl.* crustaceans.

krebs-fest, wart-resistant; **-geschwulst,** *f.* cancerous swelling, tumor; **-gewebe,** *n.* cancer tissue.

krebsig, cancerous, affected with cancer, cankered.

Krebs-milch, *f.* cancer juice; **-pest,** *f.* crayfish pest; **-schere,** *f.* claw of a crayfish; **-tiere,** *n.pl.* Crustacea; **-widerstandsfähigkeit,** *f.* wart resistance; **-wurz,** *f.* beechdrops (*Leptamnium virginianum*); **-wurzel,** *f.* squawroot (*Conopholis americana*).

kredenzen, to taste (wine).

Kredit, *m.* credit.

kreditieren, to credit, give credit.

Kreide, *f.* chalk, cretaceous flora; **-artig,** chalky, cretaceous; **-boden,** *m.* chalky soil; **-formation,** *f.* chalk formation; **-gur,** *f.* mineral agaric, lithomarge; **-haltig,** containing chalk, cretaceous; **-mehl,** *n.* powdered chalk.

kreiden, to chalk.

Kreide-papier, *n.* enameled paper; **-pulver,** *n.* chalk powder; **-stein,** *m.* chalkstone;

-stift, *m.* crayon; -weiss, as white as a sheet.

kreidig, chalky, cretaceous.

Kreis, *m.*-e, circle, circuit, ring, orbit, sphere, electric current, span of life, zone, district, areola, range; -abschnitt, *m.* segment; -artig, circular; -ausschnitt, *m.* sector; -bahn, *f.* circular path, orbit; -bewegung, *f.* circular (rotary) motion, circumnutation; -bogen, *m.* arc (of a circle), circular arch.

kreischen, to shriek, scream, hiss, sizzle, grate.

Kreisel, *m.*-, spinning top, gyroscope; -bewegung, *f.* motion of a top; -förmig, turbinate, top-shaped; -frequenz, *f.* angular velocity; -gang, *m.* revolution, rotation, labyrinth; -molekül, *n.* spinning molecule.

kreiseln, to spin (like) a top, revolve.

Kreisel-pumpe, *f.* centrifugal pump; -rad, *n.* turbine, impeller, rotor.

kreisen, to circle, revolve, rotate, circulate.

kreisende (Bewegung), nutation (movement).

Kreis-fläche, *f.* basal (circular) area; -förmig, circular, round, orbicular; -kegel, *m.* circular cone; -lauf, *m.* circulation, rotation, cycle, circuit; -laufdrüse, *f.* circulatory gland; -laufend, circulatory.

Kreis-linie, *f.* circular line, circumference; -prozess, *m.* cyclic process, cycle; -ring, *m.* ring-shaped area, annular shape; -rund, circular, orbicular; -säge, *f.* circular saw, disk saw; -schicht, *f.* circular layer, (of a tree) annual ring; -schuppe, *f.* round scale.

kreissend, parturient.

kreis-ständig, cyclic; -umfang, *m.* circumference, periphery.

Krem, *n.* cream.

Krempe, *f.* wood pick, kremp, flange, edge, flap, cramp iron, border.

krempeln, to card.

Krensäure, *f.* crenic acid.

Kreosol, *n.* creosol.

Kreosot, *n.* creosote.

kreosotieren, to creosote.

Kreosotöl, *n.* creosote oil.

krepieren, to die, burst, vex.

krepitieren, to crepitate, crackle.

Krepp, *m.* crape, crêpe.

Kresol, *n.* cresol; -natron, *n.* sodium cresylate; -seife, *f.* cresol soap.

Kresorcin, *n.* cresorcinol.

Kresotinsäure, *f.* cresotic (cresotinic) acid.

Kresse, *f.* cress, garden peppergrass (Lepidium).

Kresyl, *n.* cresyl; -säure, *f.* cresylic acid.

Kreuz, *n.* -e cross, affliction, decussation, sacral region, loin, rump, croup, club (cards); -beere, *f.* buckthorn berry.

Kreuzbein, *n.* sacrum; -flügel, *m.* wing of the sacrum; -horn, *n.* sacral corner, process of the sacrum; -hüftbeinband, *n.* sacroiliac ligament; -krümmung, *f.* sacral flexure; -spitze, *f.* apex of the sacrum; -wirbel, *m.* sacral vertebra.

Kreuz-befruchtung, *f.* cross-fertilization; -bestäubung, *f.* cross-pollination; -blume, *f.* milkwort (Polygala); -blumengewächse, *n.pl.* Polygalaceae; -blütler, *m.* cruciferous plant, -blütlergewächse, *n.pl.* Crucifera; -deckflügler, *m.pl.* Staphylinidae.

Kreuzdorn, *m.* buckthorn (*Rhamnus cathartica*); -beeren, *f.pl.* buckthorn berries; -gewächse, *n.pl.* Rhamnaceae.

kreuzen, to hybridize, cross; sich ~, to cross, intersect.

kreuz-förmig, cross-shaped, decussate, cruciform, cruciate; -geflecht, *n.* sacral plexus; -gegend, *f.* sacral (lumbar) region; -gitter, *n.* cross (grating), lattice; -gras, *n.* Eleusine; -hahn, *m.* four-way cock; -haue, *f.* pickax; -knochen, *m*, sacrum; -knoten, *m.* sacral ganglion. -kraut, *n.* groundsel (Senecio); -kümmel, *m.* cumin; -muskel, *m.* sacrolumbar muscle.

Kreuz-otter, *f.* common viper or adder; -pflanzung, *f.* quincunx planting; -punkt, *m.* intersection; -schmerz, *m.* lumbago; -schnabel, *m.* crossbill (*Loxia curvirostra*); -sitzbeinband, *n.* sacrosciatic ligament; -spinne, *f.* garden spider; -ständig, decussate; -stein, *m.* cross-stone; -steissbeingegend, *f.* sacrococcygeal region; -strauch, *m.* Baccharis; -tisch, *m.* mechanical stage (microscope).

Kreuzung, *f.* diamond (skein), wind, crossing, hybridization; echte ~, gnesiogamy; einartige ~, xenogamy (cross-fertilization).

Kreuzungs-knoten, *m.* spicular node (sponges); -partner, *m.* mate, one of the parents in crossing; -punkt, *m.* intersection, part of decussation.

Kreuzverweisung, *f.* cross reference.

kreuzweise, crosswise, transverse.

kribbeln (kriebeln), to tickle, itch, irritate, tingle.

Kriechbein, *n.* walking (crawling) leg.

kriechen, to creep, crawl.

kriechend, creeping, repeat, reptant, decumbent.

Kriech-funken, *m.* flashover (surface discharge across insulation); -fuss, *m.* foot adapted for crawling; -pflanze, *f.* creeper; -sohle, *f.* creeping (disk) sole of snails; -spur, *f.* trail; -staude, *f.* herbaceous perennial with creeping stolons; -tier, *n.* reptile.

Krieg, *m.*-e, war.

kriegen, to seize, catch, wage war, get.

kriegerisch, warlike.

Kriegführung, *f.* warfare.

krimpen, to shrink, sponge.

Krimpfähigkeit, *f.* property of shrinking, felting property.

Krimstecher, *m.* field glass.

Kringel, *m.* cracknel.

Krippe, *f.* crib, manger.

Krise, *f.* crisis, depression.

krisenhaft, critical.

Krisis, *f.* crisis.

krispelig, blistered, grained, pebbled.

krispeln, to crimple, grain, pebble.

Kristall, *m.*-e, crystal; -abscheidung, *f.* separation of crystals; -achse, *f.* crystal axis, crystallographic axis; -ähnlich, -artig, crystal-like, crystalline; -ausscheidung, *f.* separation of crystals; -bau, *m.* crystal structure; -behälter, *m.*-, crystal-containing cell; -benzol, *n.* benzene of crystallization; -bildung, *f.* formation of crystals, crystallization, (sugar) granulation; -brei, *m.* crystal sludge.

Kristall-chloroform, *n.* chloroform of crystallization; -drüse, *f.* clustered crystals; -ecke, *f.* solid angle of a crystal.

kristallen, crystalline.

Kristall-faser, *f.* (septate) fiber containing crystals; -feuchtigkeit, *f.* crystalline humor; -fläche, *f.* crystal face; -förmig, crystalline; -gerippe, *n.* bonding laver; -gitter, *n.* crystal lattice; -glasur, *f.* crystalline glaze; -haltig, containing crystals, crystalliferous; -haut, *f.* crystalline crust; -häutchen, *n.* crystalline film; -hell. (as clear as) crystal, transparent.

kristallin, crystalline.

kristallinisch, crystalline.

Kristallinse, *f.* crystalline lens.

Kristallisations-bassin, *n.* crystallizing basin; -fähig, crystallizable; -fähigkeit, *f.* crystallizability; -gefäss, *n.* crystallizing vessel, crystallizer; -wärme, *f.* heat of crystallization.

kristallisierbar, crystallizable.

Kristallisierbarkeit, *f.* crystallizability; -behälter, *m.* crystallizing receptacle or tank.

kristallisieren, to crystallize.

Kristallisier-gefäss, *n.* crystallizing vessel, crystallizer; -schale, *f.* crystallizing dish.

Kristallisierung, *f.* crystallization, crystallizing.

Kristall-kammerfaser, *f.* septate fiber containing crystals; -keim, *m.* crystal nucleus, seed crystal; -kern, *m.* nucleus of crystallization; -lehre, *f.* crystallography; -linse, *f.* crystalline lens; -mehl, *m.* crystal sand (calcium oxalate), crystal powder, acicular crystal; -nädelchen, *n.* acicular crystal; -oberfläche, *f.* crystal surface.

Kristallographie, *f.* crystallography.

kristallographisch, crystallographic.

Kristall-sand, *m.* crystal sand; -säure, *f.* fuming sulphuric acid in crystalline form; -soda, *f.* soda crystals; -stein, *m.* rock crystal; -waren, *f.pl.* crystal (glass) ware.

Kristallwasser, *n.* crystal water, water of crystallization; -frei, free from water of crystallization; -haltig, containing crystal water.

Kristallzucker, *m.* refined sugar in crystals.

Kriterium, *m.* criterion.

Kritik, *f.* criticism, review.

Kritiker, *m.* critic.

kritiklos, without criticism, undiscriminating.

kritisch, critical.

kritisieren, to criticize.

kritteln, to carp at, criticize.

kritzeln, to scribble, scratch.

kroch (kriechen), crept, crawled.

Krokodil, *n.* crocodile; -narben, *f.pl.* alligatoring (severe crisscross cracking).

Krokodilier, *pl.* Crocodilia.

Krokonsäure, *f.* croconic acid.

Krönchen, *n.* (small) crown, paracorolla.

Krone, *f.* crown, corolla, coronet, corona, perianth, wreath, crest, top.

Kronen-achsensporn, *m.* spur in lip of orchid flower; **-ansatz,** *m.* top of bole, point where crown of tree commences; **-artig,** like a crown, coronal, coronary; **-aufsatz,** *m.* column; **-band,** *n.* coronary ligament; **-bäume,** *m.pl.* trees having a (corolla) branched trunk; **-bein,** *n.* frontal bone; **-blatt,** *n.* petal; **-brenner,** *m.* ring burner; **-fäule,** *f.* crown rot, collar rot of trees.

Kronen-fortsatz, *m.* coronoid process; **-gerüst,** *n.* framework of crown; **-gold,** *n.* 18-carat gold; **-lederhaut,** *f.* corium coronarium; **-naht,** *f.* coronal suture; **-rinne,** *f.* coronary sulcus or groove; **-röhre,** *f.* perianth tube, tube of (gamopetalous) corolla; **-rost,** *m.* crown rust; **-spelze,** *f.* lemma; **-ständig,** epipetalous; **-tragend,** corolliferous.

Kronglas, *n.* crown glass; **-wicke,** *f.* sicklewort (Coronilla).

Kronkümmel, *m.* cumin.

Krönung, *f.* coronation.

Kropf, *m.*⸚e, goiter, bronchocele, craw, crop, swelling, band, excrescence, breasting; **-drüse,** *f.* thyroid gland.

kröpfen, to gorge, cram, bend (at angles).

Kropf-haar, *n.* unicellular hair widened at either end; **-höhle,** *f.* crop cavity (of a bird).

kropfig, goitrous, strumose.

Kropf-maser, *f.* wen, burr; **-rohr,** *n.* bent tube; **-schnitt,** *m.* incision (of bird's crop); **-taube,** *f.* pouter.

Kröpfung, *f.* crimping.

Kropf-wurz, *f.* figwort; **-wurzel,** *f.* polypody root; **-zylinder,** *m.* glass cylinder with a wider upper part.

kröseln, to crumble (glass), groove.

Kröte, *f.* toad.

Kroton-öl, *n.* croton oil; **-säure,** *f.* crotonic acid.

Krücke, *f.* crutch, rake, rabble, scraper.

Krückstock, *m.* crutched stick.

Krug, *m.*⸚e, jug, mug, pitcher, jar, pot, urn; **-farn,** *m.* Davallia; **-förmig,** in the shape of a jug, urceolate.

Kruke, *f.* stone (earthenware) pot or pitcher.

krüllen, to crumple.

Krullfarn, *m.* maidenhair (Adiantum).

Krülltabak, *m.* shag (tobacco).

Krümchen, *n.* crumb.

Krume, *f.* crumb, black earth, young shoots.

krüm(e)lig, crumbly, crumbling, friable.

krümeln, to crumble.

Krümel-pflug, *m.* plow with cylindrical moldboard; **-struktur,** *f.* crumb structure; **-zucker,** *m.* dextrose, (dextro)glucose, granular sugar.

krumig, crumby.

krumm, crooked, curved, bent, arched, sinuous; **-baum,** *m.* -fichte, -kiefer, *f.* knee pine, mugho pine, dwarf mountain fir; **-beinig,** bowlegged; **-blätt(e)rig,** curvifoliate; **-darm,** *m.* ileum.

krümmen, to crook, bend, curve, warp.

Krümmer, *m.* bend, elbow, bent piece.

krumm-faserig, cross (twisted) grained; **-früchtig,** campylocarpous (crooked fruit); **-gebüsch,** *n.* dwarf scrub, elfin wood; **-kolz,** *n.* curved (compass) timber, elfin wood; **-läufig,** campylotropous (running crooked); **-linig,** curvilinear, curved, nonlinear; **-öl,** *n.* templin oil.

Krümmung, *f.* curvature, curve, bend, bending, turn, winding, sinuosity, crookedness, flexure.

Krümmungshalbmesser, *m.* radius of curvature.

Krummzirkel, *m.* calipers, bow compasses.

krümpeln, to crumple, ruffle, pucker, crinkle.

Krupp, *m.* croup.

Kruppe, *f.* croup, crupper.

Krüppel, *m.* cripple; **-form,** *f.* (dwarfed) form, stunted; **-grenze,** *f.* (Baumgrenze), timberline; **-haft,** crippled, deformed, stunted.

krüppelig, crippled, stunted, maimed.

Krüppelwuchs, *m.* crippled growth, scrub.

Kruste, *f.* crust, scab, scale, incrustation.

krusten-artig, crustlike, crusty, crustaceous; **-bildung,** *f.* crust formation, incrustation; **-flechte,** *f.* crustaceous lichen; **-tier,** *n.* crustacean.

krustieren, to (in)crust.

krustig, crusty, crusted.

kryohydratisch, cryohydric.

Kryo-lith, *m.* cryolite; **-phor,** *n.* cryophorus; **-skopie,** *f.* cryoscopy.

Krypta, *f.* crypt.

Kryptogame, *f.* cryptogam.

kryptogamisch, cryptogamous.

Krystall, *m.* crystal.

Kuba-kiefer, *f.* Cuban pine; **-holz,** *n.* Cuba wood.

Kubebe, *f.* cubeb.

Kübel, *m.* tub, vat, pail, bucket.

kubieren, to cube, calculate volume.

Kubierungsformel, *f.* cubing formula.

Kubik-gehalt, *m.* solid contents, volume; **-inhalt,** *m.* cubic content; **-wurzel,** *f.* cube root; **-zahl,** *f.* cube; **-zentimeter,** *m.&n.* cubic centimeter.

kubisch, cubic(al).

Küblerware, *f.* hollow ware, cooperage.

Kubus, *m.* cube.

Küche, *f.* kitchen, cooking, cookery.

Kuchen, *m.* cake, placenta; **-bildend,** cakeforming, caking; **-förmig,** placentiform.

Küchen-gewächs, *n.* vegetables; **-salz,** *n.* common salt; **-schabe,** *f.* cockroach; **-schelle,** *f.* pasqueflower (Pulsatilla); **zettel,** *m.* menu, bill of fare.

Kuckuck, *m.* cuckoo.

Kuckucksblume, *f.* ragged robin (*Lychnis flos-cuculi*).

Kufe, *f.* vat, tub.

Küfer, *m.* cooper.

Kugel, *f.***-n,** ball, globe, sphere, bulb, shot; **-abschnitt,** *m.* spherical segment; **-ähnlich,** spheroidal, spherical; **-apparat,** *m.* bulb apparatus; **-bakterien,** *n.pl.* sphero bacteria, cocci; **-blume,** *f.* globe daisy (Globularia).

Kügelchen, *n.* small (ball) bulb, globule, pellet.

Kugel-distal, *f.* globe thistle (Echinops); **-dreieck,** *n.* spherical triangle; **-fadenform,** *f.* streptococcus form; **-fallmethode,** *f.* falling-ball method; **-fest,** bulletproof; **-fläche,** *f.* spherical surface; **-flasche,** *f.* spherical (balloon) flask; **-förmig,** globular, spherical, globose; **-früchtig,** spherocarpous (spherical fruit); **-funktion,** *f.* spherical harmonic.

Kugel-gelenk, *n.* ball (and socket) joint, arthrodia; **-gestalt,** *f.* spherical form, sphericity; **-hefe,** *f.* spherical yeast cell.

kugelig, globular, spherical, globose.

kugel-köpfig, having flowers in a (close) globular head; **-kühler,** *m.* ball condenser; **-lage,** *f.* position of a bullet; **-lager,** *n.* ball bearing; **-linse,** *f.* spherical lens; **-mühle,** *f.* ball mill.

kugeln, to roll, bowl, form into a ball.

Kugel-rohr, *n.* **-röhre,** *f.* bulb tube; **-schale,** *f.* spherical shell; **-schliff,** *m.* ground ball-and-socket joint.

kugelsicher, bulletproof; **kugelsicheres Glas,** *n.* bulletproof glass.

Kugel-spiegel, *m.* spherical mirror; **-stamm,** *m.* globular trunk; **-stopfen,** *m.* bulb stopper; **-tee,** *m.* gunpowder tea; **-textur,** *f.* orbicular (spheroidal) structure; **-trieb,** *m.* globular shoot; **-ventil,** *n.* ball valve; **-vorlage,** *f.* spherical receiver; **-welle,** *f.* spherical wave; **-zange,** *f.* ball extractor, bullet forceps.

Kuh, *f.***-e,** cow; **-blume,** *f.* marsh marigold; **-dünger,** *m.* cow dung; **-euter,** *n.* cow udder; **-fladen,** *m.* cow dung; **-hirt,** *m.* cowherd; **-kot,** *m.* cow dung.

kühl, cool; **-anlage,** *f.* cooling (refrigerating) plant; **-apparat,** *m.* cooling apparatus, refrigerator, condenser; **-bottich,** *m.* cooler, cooling tub.

Kühle, *f.* coolness, freshness.

kühlen, to cool, chill, refrigerate.

Kühler, *m.* condenser, cooler, refrigerator, (automobile) radiator; **-ende,** *n.* end of cooler; **-gestell,** *n.* cooler support; **-mantel,** *m.* cooler jacket; **-retorte,** *f.* condenser retort.

Kühl-fass, *n.***-er,** cooling (vat) vessel; **-fläche,** *f.* cooling surface; **-flüssigkeit,** *f.* cooling liquid; **-gefäss,** *m.* cooling vessel, refrigerator, condenser; **-geläger,** *n.* wort sediment, dregs; **-kammer,** *f.* cooling chamber; **-mantel,** *m.* cooling jacket; **-maschine,** *f.* refrigerating machine; **-mittel,** *n.* refrigerant; **-ofen,** *m.**-*, annealing oven.

Kühl-pfanne, *f.* cooling pan; **-raum,** *m.* cold-storage chamber; **-rohr,** *n.*, **-röhre,** *f.* condenser tube; **-salz,** *n.* refrigerating salt; **-schiff,** *n.* cooling (pan) back, cooler; **-schlange,** *f.* cooling coil; **schrank,** *m.* refrigerator, cooling cabinet; **-spirale,** *f.* spiral cooler; **-tasche,** *f.* cooling chamber.

Kühlung, *f.* cooling, refrigeration.

Kühlungsgrad, *m.* degree of cooling.

Kühl-verfahren, *n.* cooling process; **-vorrichtung,** *f.* refrigerating apparatus; **-wagen,** *m.* refrigerator car; **-wasser,** *n.* cooling water, lead water; **-werk,** *n.* refrigerating plant; **-wirkung,** *f.* cooling effect.

Kuhmist, *m.* cow dung.

kühn, bold.

Kühnheit, *f.* boldness.

Kuhpocken, *f.pl.* cowpox; **-erreger,** *m.* cowpox bacillus; **-gift,** *n.* vaccine virus; **-impfung,** *f.* vaccination; **-stoff,** *m.* vaccine (matter) lymph; **-virus,** *m.* cowpox virus.

Kuhstall, *m.* cow barn.

Kukabrühe, *f.* Bordeaux mixture.

Küken, *n.* chick, stopcock.

Kukuruz, *m.* corn, maize.

Külbchen, *n.* ball, piece, lump (glass).

Kulilawanöl, *n.* culilawan oil.

kulinarisch, culinary.

Kulisse, *f.* wing, movable scene, corridor.

kulminieren, to culminate.

kultivierbar, capable of cultivation, tillable.

Kultivierbarkeit, *f.* susceptibility of cultivation.

kultivieren, to cultivate, culture.

Kultivierung, *f.* culture, cultivation.

Kultur, *f.* culture, cultivation, plantation, civilization; **-arbeit,** *f.* cultural work; **-bedingung,** *f.* culture requirement; **-betrieb,** *m.* forest planting, artificial regeneration; **-dauer,** *f.* duration of cultural experiment.

kulturell, cultural.

kultur-fähig, arable, tillable; **-filtrat,** *n.* filtrate from culture; **-fläche,** *f.* area to be stocked or planted (with trees); **-form,** *f.* cultivated strain, culture form; **-gebiet,** *n.* civilized region; **-geräte,** *n.pl.* agricultural implements; **-geschichtlich,** with relation to the history of civilization; **-hefe,** *f.* culture yeast; **-kolben,** *m.* culture flask; **-kosten,** *f.pl.* cultural expenses.

Kultur-landschaft, *f.* cultivated land; **-medien,** *n.pl.* culture media; **-methode,** *f.* method of culture; **-opfer,** *n.* victim (sacrifice) of civilization (culture); **-pflanze,** *f.* cultivated plant; **-röhre,** *f.* culture tube; **-schale,** *f.* culture plate; **-schicht,** *f.* culture stratum; **-staat,** *m.* civilized state; **-stamm,** *m.* stock culture.

Kultur-stufe, *f.* stage of civilization; **-verfahren,** *n.* cultural method, procedure; **-versuch,** *m.* cultivation (cultural) experiment; **-volk,** *n.* civilized race or people; **-zweck,** *m.* cultural purpose.

Kumarinsäure, *f.* coumaric acid.

Kuminsäure, *f.* cumic (cuminic) acid.

Kümmel, *m.* caraway, cumin, kümmel (liqueur); **-öl,** *n.* caraway oil, cumin oil.

Kummer, *m.* grief, sorrow, care, trouble.

kümmerlich, poor, stunted, scrubby, needy, crippled.

Kümmerling, *m.* dying tree.

kümmern, to trouble, grieve, concern, wilt, suffer, be stunted, starve; **sich ~,** to be worried; **sich um etwas ~,** to pay heed (attention) to something.

Kümmernis, *f.* affliction.

kummervoll, sorrowful.

Kum(me)t, *n.* (horse) collar.

Kumol, *n.* cumene.

Kumpan, *m.* companion, fellow.

Kumpe, *f.* basin, vessel.

Kumys, *m.* kumiss.

kund, known, public; **~ und zu wissen sei,** take notice that.

kundbar, known, notorious.

Kunde, *m.-n,* customer, patient, client.

Kunde, *f.* science, knowledge, information, news.

kundgeben, to make known, publish, manifest, declare.

Kundgebung, *f.* announcement, demonstration.

kundig, *(gen.)* skillful, intelligent, learned, expert.

kündigen, to give notice of, give warning, recall, resign.

Kündigung, *f.* (previous) notice, warning.

Kundschaft, *f.* custom, patronage, information, knowledge.

kundschaften, to reconnoiter.

Kundschafter, *m.* spy, explorer.

künftig, future; **~ hin,** henceforth, after that.

Kunigundenkraut, *n.* boneset (*Eupatorium perfoliatum*).

Kunst, *f.* art, ingenuity, profession, skill, work (of art).

Kunst-, artificial, synthetic, (in compounds); **-ausdruck,** *m.* technical term; **-brut,** *f.* artificial incubation; **-butter,** *f.* artificial butter, (oleo)margarine; **-druckpapier,** *n.* art paper; **-dünger,** *m.* artificial (manure) fertilizer; **-eis,** *n.* artificial ice; **-faden,** *m.* artificial fiber; **-fehler,** *m.* technical error; **-fertig,** skillful.

Kunst-fertigkeit, *f.* technical skill; **-fett,** *n.* artificial (fat) grease; **-fleiss,** *m.* industry; **-gärtnerei,** *f.* horticulture, nursery; **-gewerbe,** *n.* useful art; **-gewerbeschule,**

f. school of arts and crafts; **-glanz,** *m.*
artificial luster; **-griff,** *m.* artifice, knack,
trick, device; **-guss,** *m.* art casting;
-harz, *n.* artificial (synthetic) resin.

Kunst-harzpressstoff, *m.* synthetic plastic
material; **-hefe,** *f.* artificial yeast; **-heil-
mittel,** *n.* artificial (synthetic) remedy;
-holz, *n.* artificial wood; **-honig,** *m.*
artificial honey; **-horn,** *n.* celluloid;
-lehre, *f.* technology, technics.

Künstler, *m.* artist.

künstlerisch, artistic.

künstlich, artistic, artificial, artful, ingenious.

Kunst-mittel, *n.* artificial means; **-produkt,**
n. artificial product; **-richter,** *m.* critic;
-seide, *f.* artificial silk; **-seideverarbeitung,**
f. rayon processing; **-spinnfaser,** *f.* staple
fiber; **-sprache,** *f.* technical language;
-stoff, *m.* plastic, artificial substance or
material; **-stück,** *n.* clever feat, trick;
-voll, artistic, ingenious, clever.

Kunst-wabe, *f.* comb foundation; **-wiese,** *f.*
cultivated (tame) pasture; **-werk,** *n.*
work of art; **-wolle,** *f.* artificial wool,
shoddy; **-wort,** *n.* technical term.

kunterbunt, parti-colored, gaudy, topsy-
turvy.

Kuoxam, *n.* cuprammonium solution.

Küpe, *f.* copper, boiler, vat.

kupellieren, to cupel.

küpen, to vat (dye); **-artikel,** *m.* vat style
(calico); **-färberie,** *f.* vat dyeing.

Kupfer, *n.* copper; **-abfall,** *m.* waste
copper; **-alaun,** *m.* cuprum aluminatum,
lapis divinus; **-ammonium,** *n.* cupr(o)-
ammonium; **-antimonglanz,** *m.* chalco-
stibite; **-artig,** (kupferig), copperlike;
-asche, *f.* copper scale; **-blatt,** *n.* copper
foil; **-blau,** *n.* blue verditer, azurite; **-blech,**
n. sheet copper.

Kupferblei, *n.* copper-lead alloy; **-glanz,** *m.*
cuproplumbite; **-vitriol,** *m.* linarite.

Kupfer-blende, *f.* tennantite; **-blüte,** *f.*
copper bloom; **-braun,** *n.* tile ore, earthy
ferruginous cuprite; **-bromid,** *n.* cupric
bromide; **-bromür,** *n.* cuprous bromide;
-chlorid, *n.* copper chloride, cupric chloride;
-chlorür, *n.* cuprous chloride; **-cyanid,** *n.*
copper cyanide, cupric cyanide; **-cyanür,** *n.*
cuprous cyanide; **-dorn,** *m.* liquated
copper slag.

Kupfer-draht, *m.* copper wire; **-drahtnetz,**
n. copper gauze; **-druck,** *m.* copperplate
(printing); **-elektrode,** *f.* copper electrode;
-erz, *n.* copper ore; **-fahlerz,** *n.* tetra-

hedrite, tennantite; **-farbe,** *f.* copper
color; **-federerz,** *n.* copper bloom; **-feilicht,**
n. copper filings; **-folie,** *f.* copper foil.

kupfer-führend, copper-bearing; **-gare,** *f.*
copper refining; **-garmachen,** *n.* copper
refining; **-gefäss,** *n.* copper vessel; **-gehalt,**
m. copper content; **-geist,** *m.* spirit of
verdigris; **-gewinnung,** *f.* extraction of
copper; **-glanz,** *m.* copper glance; **-glas,** *n.*
-glaserz, *n.* chalcocite; **-glimmer,** *m.*
chalcophyllite, copper mica.

Kupfer-glühspan, *m.* copper scale; **-gold,**
n. Mannheim gold, similor; **-grün,** *n.*
copper green, verdigris; **-haltig,** cuprif-
erous, cupreous, containing copper; **-ham-
merschlag,** *m.* copper scale; **-hydrat,** *n.*
copper hydroxide; **-hydrid,** *n.* copper
hydride; **-hydroxyd,** *n.* copper (cupric)
hydroxide; **-hydroxydul,** *n.* cuprous
hydroxide.

kupferig, copperlike, cupreous.

Kupfer-indig, *m.* indigo copper; **-jodid,** *n.*
copper iodide, cupric iodide; **-jodür,** *n.*
cuprous iodide; **-kalk,** *m.* copper oxide;
-kalkbrühe, *f.* Bordeaux mixture; **-kies,**
m. copper pyrites, chalcopyrite.

kupfer-kieshaltig, containing copper pyrites; **-könig,** *m.* copper regulus; **-lasur,**
f. azurite; **-legierung,** *f.* copper alloy;
-lösung, *f.* copper solution; **-münze,**
copper coin.

kupfern, to treat with copper.

Kupfer-nickel, *n.* copper nickel; **-nieder-
schlag,** *m.* copper precipitate.

Kupferoxyd, *n.* cupric oxide, copper oxide;
-hydrat, *n.* cupric hydroxide; **-salz,** *n.*
cupric salt; **-verbindung,** *f.* cupric compound.

Kupferoxydul, *n.* cuprous oxide; **-hydrat,** *n.*
cuprous hydroxide; **-salz,** *n.* cuprous salt;
-verbindung, *f.* cuprous compound.

Kupfer-platte, *f.* copperplate; **-pol,** *m*
copper pole; **-probe,** *f.* copper assay, test
for copper; **-rauch,** *m.* copper smoke.
copper fumes; **-reinigung,** *f.* copper refining; **-rhodanat,** *n.* **-rhodanid,** *n.* copper
(cupric) thiocyanate; **-rohr,** *n.,* **-röhre,** *f.*
copper (tube) pipe; **-rohstein,** *m.* law
copper matte; **-rost,** *m.* copper rust,
verdigris.

kupfer-rot, copper-red, copper-colored; **-rot,**
n. red copper; **-salz,** *n.* copper salt;
-sam(me)terz, *n.* velvet copper ore.
cyanotrichite; **-säure,** *f.* cupric acid;
-schaum, *m.* copper scum; **-scheibe,** *f.*
copper disk; **-schiefer,** *m.* copper slate;

-schlacke, *f.* copper slag; -schlange, *f.* copper coil.

Kupfer-schmied, *m.* coppersmith; -schwärze, *f.* black copper (melaconite); -schwefel, *m.* copper sulphide; -seide, *f.* cuprammonium silk; -silberglanz, *m.* stromeyerite; -sinter, *m.* copper scale; -smaragd, *m.* emerald copper, dioptase; -stahl, *m.* copper steel; -stechen, *n.* copper engraving; -stein, *m.* copper matte.

Kupfer-stich, *m.* copper engraving; -sulfat, *n.* copper sulphate, cupric sulphate; -sulfid, *n.* copper sulphide, cupric sulphide; -sulfür, *n.* cuprous sulphide; -überzug, *m.* copper coating; -verbindung, *f.* copper compound; -vergiftung, *f.* copper poisoning; -vitriol, *m.* copper sulphate, blue vitriol, cupric sulphate; -wasser, *n.* copper water; -wasserstoff, *m.* copper hydride.

Kupfer-zuschlag, *m.* copper flux; -zyanür, *m.* cuprous cyanide.

kupfrig, copperlike.

kupieren, to dock, abort.

Kupol(hoch)ofen, *m.* cupola (blast) furnace.

Kuppe, *f.* top, summit, tip, head, peak.

Kuppel, *f.* cupola, cupel, dome; -artig, dome-shaped; -blindsack, *m.* blind sac of the cupola, apex of cochlea.

kuppeln, to couple, leash, tie.

kuppenförmig, dome-shaped.

Kuppler, *m.* coupler, (dye) developer.

Kupplung, *f.* coupling, (automobile) clutch.

Kupplungs-bad, *n.* developing bath; -flotte, *f.* developing liquor.

Kuprichlorid, *n.* cupric chloride.

Kuprit, *m.* cuprite.

Kuprochloride, *n.* cuprous chloride.

Kur, *f.* cure, treatment.

kurativ, curative.

Kurbel, *f.* crank, (winch) handle; -pumpe, *f.* reciprocating pump.

kurbeln, to run, work, wind, turn, crank.

Kürbis, *m.*-e, gourd, pumpkin; -baum, *m.* gourd (calabash) tree; -frucht, *f.* pepo (-nium); -gewächse, *n.pl.* Cucurbitaceae; kern, *m.* korn, *n.* -samen, *m.* pumpkin seed.

küren, to choose, elect.

kurieren, to cure, restore, mend.

Kurkuma, *f.* curcuma, turmeric; -gelb, *n.* curcumin; -wurzel, *f.* turmeric (root).

Kurort, *m.*-e, health resort.

Kurrentbuchstaben, *m.pl.* script, italics.

Kurs, *m.*-e, circulation, course, exchange. currency; -buch, railway guide.

Kürschner, *m.* furrier.

kursieren, to be current.

kursiv, italic; -schrift, *f.* italics.

Kursus, *m.* course (of lectures).

Kurswert, *m.* exchange value.

Kurve, *f.* curve.

Kurven-ast, *m.* branch of a curve; -bild, *n.* curve, graph; -gipfel, *m.* apex of a curve; -schar, *f.* group (system) of curves; -schnittpunkt, *m.* intersection of a curve; -verlauf, *m.* course of the curve.

kurz, short, brief; sich ~ fassen, to express oneself briefly; zu ~ kommen, to come off badly; ~ und klein schlagen, to smash; über ~ oder lang, sooner or later; binnen kurzem, within a short time; vor kurzem, recently; in kurzem, shortly; seit kurzem, lately; bis vor kurzem, until quite recently; ~ und gut, in short.

kurz-armig, short-armed, short-beam; -astig, short-branched; -borstig, hirtellous, minutely (short) hirsute; -brüchig, short, brittle; -dauernd, short (lived), brief; -dornig, brachyacanthus, short-thorned.

Kürze, *f.* shortness, brevity; in ~, briefly

kürzen, to shorten, abridge, curtail.

Kurz-flügler, *m.pl.* Staphylinidae; -gefasst, brief, concise; -gestielt, petiolate, with a short pedicel, subsessile; -griffelig, short-styled; -haarig, short-haired; -hacken, *n.* superficial hoeing; -halsig, short-necked; -lebig, short-lived.

kürzlich, late, recent.

kurz-schäftig, short-bodied; -schliessen, to short-circuit; -schluss, *m.* short circuit; -schlussklemme, *f.* shunt; -schrift, *f.* shorthand, stenography; -sichtig, near (short)sighted.

Kurz-sichtigkeit, *f.* shortsightedness, myopia; -stäbchen, *n.* bacillus; -steifhaarig, hirtus; -stengelig, brachycaulic, having short stems; -strecke, *f.* short distance; -trieb, *m.* short shoot, brachyblast.

kurzum, in short, in brief.

Kürzungsfette, *n.pl.* shortening.

Kurzwaren, *f.pl.* small wares, hardware.

kurzweg, in short, for short, simply.

Kurz-weil, *f.* amusement, pastime; -wellig, of short wave length, short-wave; -wollig, short nap(ped), lanuginose.

Kuscheln, *f.pl.* scrubby growth forms of mountain pine.

küssen, to kiss.

Kussin, n. kosin.

Kussoblumen, f.pl. brayera, cusso (flowers).

Küste, f. coast, shore.

küsteliebend, littoral (loving the shore).

Küsten-bewohner, m.pl. inhabitants of rocky coasts, shore forms; **-land,** n. coast land; **-strich,** m. shore line, strip of coast; **-strömung,** f. littoral current; **-vegetation,** f. coastal vegetation; **-versetzung,** f. change in the coast line.

Kustos, m. keeper, custodian, curator.

kutan, cutaneous.

Kutikular-erhebung, f. cuticular elevation; **-leiste,** f. ridge in cuticle.

Kutschbock, m. coach box.

Kutsche, f. coach, carriage.

Kutscher, m. coachman, driver.

Kutte, f. cowl.

Kutteln, f. tripe.

Kuvert, n.-e, envelope, cover.

kuvertieren, to put in an envelope.

Küvette, f. bulb, vessel, tray, cuvette, trough, narrow test flume.

Kyanäthin, n. kyanethine.

kyanisieren, to kyanize.

Kyanisierung, f. kyanization.

Kyaphenin, n. kyaphenine.

Kynurensäure, f. kynurenic acid.

Kyste, f. cyst.

L

Lab, n. rennet.

Labdan-gummi, -harz, n. labdanum, ladanum.

Labdrüse, f. peptic gland.

laben, to curdle with rennet, refresh, restore.

Laberdan, m. salted codfish.

Labessenz, f. (essence of) rennet.

Labialtaster, m. labial palpus.

Labiat, n. labiate.

labil, labile, unstable.

Labkraut, n. Galium.

Labmagen, m. abomasum, rennet bag.

Laborant, m. laboratory helper, technician.

Labor(atorium), n. laboratory.

laborieren, to do laboratory work, labor, suffer from.

Lab-probe, f. curd test; **-pulver,** n. rennet powder; **-saft,** m. gastric juice.

Labradorisieren, n. aventurism, iridescence, schillerization.

Labradorstein, m. Labrador stone, labradorite.

Labyrinth, n. labyrinth, maze; **-bläschen,** n. otic vessel; **-fenster,** n. fenestra of labyrinth; **-flüssigkeit,** f. endolymph; **-vorhof,** m. vestibule of labyrinth.

Lache, f. laugh, pool, puddle, groove, face, blaze.

lächeln, to smile.

lachen, to laugh.

lächerlich, laughable, ridiculous.

Lach-gas, n. laughing gas; **-krampf,** m. paroxysm of laughter, convulsive laughter.

Lachs, m. salmon; **-farbig,** salmon-colored; **-forelle,** f. salmon trout.

Lacht, m. slag, finery slag.

Lack, m. lac, lacquer, japan, primer, varnish, lake; **-anstrich,** m. coat of lacquer; **-auflösungsmittel,** n. varnish remover; **-bildner,** m. lake former; **-farbe,** f. lake, lac dye, enamel, varnish color; **-farbig,** lake-colored; **-firnis,** m. lac varnish; **-harz,** n. gum-lac.

lackieren (lacken), to lacquer, varnish.

Lack-lack, m. lac (lake) dye; **-lasurfarbe,** f. transparent varnish color; **-leder,** n. japanned leather, patent leather.

Lackmus, m. litmus; **-farbstoff,** m. litmus (dye) coloring matter; **-flechte,** f. litmus lichen, archil; **-lösung,** f. litmus solution; **-molke,** f. litmus milk (whey); **-papier,** n. litmus paper; **-reaktion,** f. reaction to litmus; **-tinktur,** f. litmus tincture.

Lacküberzug, m. coat of lacquer.

Lacmus, m. litmus.

Lactar-insäure, f. lactarinic acid; **-säure,** f. lactaric acid.

Lactonbindung, f. lactonic linkage.

Lacunargewebe, n. trabecular tissue.

Ladangummi, n. labdanum, ladanum.

Lade, f. drawer, maudible, box, case, chest, plate; **-äussere ~,** galea of maxilla, outer plate; **innere ~,** lacinia of maxilla, inner plate.

Lade-baum, *m.* derrick; **-dichte,** *f.* charge density; **-kapazität,** *f.* loading (charging) capacity; **-löffel,** *m.* loading plate; **-marken,** *f.pl.* load line, Plimsoll mark.

laden, to load, charge, freight, summon, invite.

Laden, *m.⸗,* store, shop, shutter; **-preis,** *m.* retail price.

Lader, *m.* loader, charger, filler.

Lade-raum, *m.⸗e,* loading space, exploding chamber; **-schaltung,** *f.* charging connection; **-spannung,** *f.* charging voltage; **-strom,** *m.* charging current; **-widerstand,** *m.* resistance during charge.

lädieren, to hurt, injure.

Ladung, *f.* load, cargo, charge, shoot, charging; **geballte** ∼, concentrated charge; **gestreckte** ∼, distributed charge.

Ladungs-änderung, *f.* change in potential; **-dichte,** *f.* density of charge; **-empfindlichkeit,** *f.* charge sensitivity; **-flasche,** *f.* Leyden jar; **-gemisch,** *n.* mixed charge; **-sinn,** *m.* nature of a charge; **-träger,** *m.* charge carrier; **-wolke,** *f.* charge cloud.

iag (liegen), lay.

Lage, *f.* situation, position, attitude, exposure, aspect, layer, deposit, stratum, bed, coat(ing), state, location, condition, stroma; **in der** ∼ **sein,** to be in a position.

Lagebeziehung, *f.* relative position.

lagefest, stable; ∼ **machen,** to stabilize.

Lagefestigkeit, *f.* stability.

Lägel, *n.* (small) barrel, keg.

lagen-förmig, -weise, in layers (of beds).

Lager, *n.-,* bed, layer, stroma, stratum, couch, depot, deposit, store, stock, supply, sediment, dregs, thallus, camp, lair, bearing; **-bestand,** *m.* stock inventory; **-bock,** *m.* bearing stand, pedestal; **-buchse,** *f.* **-büchse,** *f.* bearing bush(ing); **-butter,** *f.* cold-storage butter; **-echt,** fast to storing; **-fass,** *n.* storage cask, stock tub.

Lägerflora, Alpine pasture flora.

Lager-festigkeit, *f.* stability in storage; **-förmig,** in layers or strata; **-frucht,** *f.* lodged grain field (laid by rain or wind); **-gang,** *m.* sill, bedded vein; **-haus,** *n.* warehouse; **-holz,** *n.* fallen trunk (tree uprooted by storm); **-keller,** *m.* storage cellar; **-metall,** *n.* bushing metal, babbitt.

lagern, to be stored, be deposited, store, pile, place, lay down, deposit, lie (down), camp, rest, repose.

Lagern, *n.* warehousing, storing, stratification, lodging, deposition.

Lager-pflanzen, *f.pl.* Thallophytae; **-platz,** *m.* storage place, camp site, landing depot; **-prozess,** *m.* storage process; **-raum,** *m.* storeroom warehouse; **-reif,** aged; **-schale,** *f.* bearing bush(ing), shells of bearing; **-schmieröl,** *n.* film of lubricating oil; **-stätte,** *f.* deposit.

Lagerung, *f.* lying down, arrangement, orientation, stratification, bed(ding), storage, packing.

Lagerungs-form, *f.* structure and nature of residual layer; **-verhältnis,** *n.* state of stratification.

Lagesinn, *m.* sense of position, static sense.

Lagerverschiebung, *f.* change in position.

lageweise, in layers, in strata.

lahm, lame, paralyzed.

lähmen, to paralyze, cripple, lame.

Lähmung, *f.* lameness, paralysis.

Lähmungserscheinung, *f.* symptom of paralysis.

Lahn, *m.* flattened (fine) wire, tinsel.

Laib, *m.-e,* loaf (of bread).

Laich, *m.-e,* spawn.

laichen, to spawn.

Laich-kraut, *m.* pondweed (Pontamogeton); **-krautgewächse,** *n.pl.* Potamogetonaceae; **-platz,** *m.* spawning place; **-teich,** *m.* breeding pond; **-zeit,** *f.* spawning time.

Laie, *m.* layman, novice.

Lake, *f.* brine, pickle.

Laken, *n.* linen, cloth, sheet, shroud.

Lakmus, *m.* litmus.

Lakritze, *f.* licorice.

Lakritzensaft, *m.* (extract of) licorice.

Laktalbumin, *n.* lactalbumin.

Laktat, *n.* lactate.

Laktation, *f.* lactation.

Lakton, *n.* lactone.

Laktose, *f.* lactose.

Lambertsnuss, *f.* filbert, hazelnut.

Lamelle, *f.* lamel(la), lamina, layer, segment, reed, lip film.

lamellieren, to laminate.

Lamellenkörperchen, *n.* lamellate corpuscle.

laminieren, to laminate.

Lamm, *n.⸗er,* lamb.

Lämmerwolle, *f.* lamb's wool.

Lampe, *f.* lamp.

Lampen-arbeit, *f.* blast-lamp work; **-docht,** *m.* lampwick; **-faden,** *m.* lighting filament; **-fassung,** *f.* lamp (mount) fitting; **-fieber,** *n.* stage fright; **-licht,** *n.* lamp light; **-russ,** *m.* lampblack; **-schwarz,** *n.* lampblack.

Land, *n.*ᴢer, land, country, ground, soil; **-abdachung,** *f.* downstream slope; **-arbeit,** *f.* argricultural labor; **-arbeiter,** *m.* farm laborer; **-bau,** *m.* agriculture; **-bauer,** *m.* farmer; **-besitz,** *m.* landed property; **-besitzer,** *m.* landholder; **-bewohner,** *m.* one living in the country; **-eigentum,** *m.* landed property.

Land-eigentümer, *m.* landed proprietor; **-einwärts,** inland; **-enge,** *f.* isthmus.

Landes-aufnahme, *f.* topographic mapping; **-erzeugnis,** *n.* agricultural product, home produce.

Land-gut, *n.*ᴢer, (country) estate; **-innere,** *n.* inland, interior; **-karte,** *f.* map; **-krankheit,** *f.* endemic disease; **-kundig,** notorious; **-läufig,** customary, current.

ländlich, rural, rustic, countrylike.

Land-mann, *m.*ᴢer, farmer, countryman; **-messer,** *m.* surveyor; **-rasse,** *f.* native breed, indigenous breed.

Landschaft, *f.* province, district, state, landscape.

landschaftlich, scenic, relating to landscape, rural.

Landschafts-bild, *n.*-er, landscape, scene; **-element,** *n.* feature (element) of the landscape.

Land-schnecke, *f.* land snail; **-see,** *m.* inland lake; **-seuche,** *f.* epidemic; **-strasse,** *f.* highway; **-strich,** *m.* region, district, climate; **-sturm,** *m.* general levy (of troops); **-tag,** *m.* diet, legislature; **-tier,** *n.* terrestrial animal (living on land); **-verbindung,** *f.* isthmus; **-vogel,** *m.* terrestrial bird; **-volk,** *n.* country people, peasants.

landw., *abbv.* (landwirtschaftlich), agricultural.

Land-wirt, *m.*-e, farmer; **-wirtschaft,** *f.* agriculture; **-wirtschaftlich,** agricultural; **-wirtschaftskrise,** *f.* agricultural depression; **-zunge,** *f.* spit (of land).

lang, long, tall, lengthy, prolonged, ropy; **Jahre** ~, for years; **eine Zeit** ~, for a time; **drei Jahre** ~, for three years; **seit langem,** for a long time.

lang-anhaltend, long, continuous; **-blättrig,** macrophyllous, long-leaved; **-brennweitig,** long-focus; **-dauernd,** long (lasting), continued.

lange, long, far, by far; **so** ~ (als), as long (as).

Lange, *f.* (Tuchmuster, *n.*) swatch (sample of fabric).

Länge, *f.* length, duration, longitude, tallness; **in die** ~ **ziehen,** elongate, draw out, prolong; **der** ~ **nach,** lengthwise.

Längebruch, *m.* longitudinal fracture.

langeiförmig, of extended oval shape.

Langel, *n.* slack thread.

langen, to suffice, go far, reach, seize, take, pass on.

Längen-ausdehnung, *f.* linear expansion; **-bruch,** *m.* longitudinal fracture; **-dimension,** *f.* dimension of length; **-durchschnitt,** *m.* longitudinal section; **-einheit,** *f.* unit of length; **-grad,** *m.* degree of longitude; **-mass,** *n.* linear measure.

Längen-profil, *n.*-e, longitudinal fissure; **-schnitt,** *m.* longitudinal section or incision; **-spalt,** *m.* longitudinal fissure; **-trieb,** *m.* leading shoot, leader; **-wachstum,** *n.* growth in length, longitudinal growth; **-zuwachs,** *m.* height increment.

länger, longer; **längere Zeit,** for rather a long (considerable) time; **immer** ~, longer and longer.

Langerhanssche Inseln, islands of Langerhans.

längerwellig, of greater wave length.

Langeweile, *f.* boredom, tediousness.

lang-flüg(e)lig, longipennate, macropteran; **-fristig,** of long duration, long-time; **-geschnäbelt,** long-billed; **-geschwänzt,** longicaudate; **-gespitzt,** acuminous running to a point; **-gestielt,** long handled, long stalked; **-gestreckt,** extended, elongated.

lang-gezogen, elongated, extended, long-drawn-out; **-griffelig,** macrostylous, stylose; **-haarig,** long-haired, shaggy, flossy, long-staple; **-halsig,** long-necked; **-holz,** *n.* long wood, log.

langj., *abbv.* (langjährig), of many years.

lang-jährig, of many years (duration); **-lebig,** long-lived, macrobiotic.

länglich, oblong, longish, longitudinal; **-blättrig,** with oblong leaves; **-herzförmig,** cordate-oblong; **-lanzettlich,** oblong lanceolate; **-rund,** elliptical, oval, oblong-ovate.

Lang-loch, *n.* oblong hole, slot; **-mut,** *f.* forbearance, patience; **-rund,** oval.

Langrüssler, *m.pl.* Rhynchophora.

längs, along.

Längsachse, *f.* longitudinal axis.

langsam, slow; **-binder,** *m.* slow-setting cement.

Langsamkeit, *f.* slowness.

langsamwüchsig, slow-growing.

Längsaufspaltung, *f.* longitudinal splitting.

Längs-band, *n.*-er, longitudinal ligament: **-bruch,** *m.* longitudinal fracture; **-bündel,** *n.* longitudinal bundle; **-durchschnitt,** *m.* longitudinal section; **-ebene,** *f.* longitudinal plane.

lang-schäftig, long-boled; **-schiff,** *m.* long-fibe-ed mechanical pulp; **-schnauzig,** with a long beak; **-schwänze,** *m.pl.* Macrura, long-tailed tomtits.

Langsein, *n.* ropiness (of wine).

Langs-faser, *f.* longitudinal fiber; **-furche,** *f.* longitudinal groove or furrow; **-geissel,** *f.* longitudinal flagellum; **-geteilt,** longitudinally (cruciately) divided.

langsichtig, long-sighted.

Langsiebmaschine, *f.* Fourdrinier, wet machine, wet press.

längs-laufend, longitudinal; **-läufig,** axio-dromous; **-leiste,** *f.* longitudinal ridge; **-muskel,** *m.* longitudinal muscle; **-muskelschicht,** *f.* longitudinal muscle layer; **-richtung,** *f.* long axis longitudinally.

Längs-schlitz, *m.* longitudinal fissure; **-schnitt,** *m.* longitudinal section; **-schwingend,** longitudinally oscillating; **-spalte,** *f.* longitudinal cleft; **-spaltung,** *f.* longitudinal splitting; **-streifen,** *m.* longitudinal (strip) stripe or stria.

längst, longest, long ago.

Lang-stäbchen, *n.* bacillus; **-stapelig,** long staple; **-staubfädig,** having long anthers.

längstens, at the (latest) longest, most.

langstielig, long-stemmed or stalked, long-handled.

langstrecken, to stretch out.

Längs-wand, *f.*-e, longitudinal wall; **-zeichnung,** *f.* longitudinal marking; **-zerreissfestigkeit,** *f.* (longitudinal) tensile strength; **-zug,** *m.* longitudinal tract.

Lang-teilung, *f.* longitudinal cleavage; **-trieb,** *m.* long shoot; **-wanzen,** *f.pl.* Lygaeidae; **-weilen,** to weary, tire, bore; **-weilig,** tiresome; **-wellig,** of long wave length, long-wave; **-wierig,** protracted, wearisome, **-ziehen,** to draw out.

Lanthan, *n.* lanthanum; **-salz,** *n.* lanthanum salt.

Lanze, *f.* lance, harpoon.

lanzenförmig, lanceolate.

Lanzett-fisch, *m.* lancelet (Amphioxus); **-förmig,** lanceolate.

Lanzettier, *n.* Amphioxus.

lanzettlich, lanceolate.

Lapisdruck, *m.* lapis style.

Läppchen, *n.* flap, rag, lobe.

Läppmaschine, *f.* lapping machine.

Lappen, *m.*-, flap, rag, lobe, wattle, gill; **-bildung,** *f.* lobulation; **-förmig,** flaplike; **-fuss,** *m.* finfoot, lobefoot, scalloped leg (pedes lobati); **-häute,** *f.pl.* web, skin between toes; **-quallen,** *f.pl.* Lobomedusa; **-tasche,** *f.* lobe pouch.

lappig, lobed, lobate, glomerate, limp, flabby, flaccid, tattered.

Lappung, *f.* serration.

Lärche, *f.* larch, tamarack.

Lärchen-baum, *m.* larch; **-harz,** *n.* larch resin (Venetian turpentine); **-holz,** *n.* larch wood; **-krebs,** *m.* larch canker (blister); **-pilz,** *m.* schwamm, *m.* purging or larch agaric (Polyporus); **-rindenlaus,** *f.* larch (bug) louse; **-stoff,** *m.* coniferin; **-terpentin,** *m.* Venice (larch or Venetian) turpentine; **-wald,** *m.* larch (tamarack) forest.

Lardöl, *n.* lard oil.

Laricin, *n.* larixinic acid, larixin.

Lärm, *m.* noise, alarm, any sound that disturbs calm.

Larve, *f.* larva, grub, mask.

Larven-blütler, *m.* plant with a personate corolla; **-faden,** *m.* larval filament.

larvizid, larvicidal.

las (lesen), read.

Lasche, *f.* fish, fishplate, cover plate, butt strap, side bar.

lasieren, to glaze.

Lasierfarbe, *f.* glazing color.

Läsion, *f.* lesion.

lassen, to let, leave, yield, permit, allow, cause, have, desist, look, suit; **Blut ~,** to let blood; **es lässt sich,** it can be; **es liess sich,** it could be; **gelassen,** calm, collected, patient; **es lässt sich sehen,** it can be seen; **das lässt sich denken,** I should think so; **er liess sich nichts merken,** he did not show it; **etwas tun ~,** to have something done; **das lässt sich tun,** that can be done.

lässig, idle, negligent, lazy, neglectful, careless.

lässt (lassen), let, permit, has.

Last, *f.*-**en,** load, burden, weight, charge, trouble; -**arm,** *m.* load arm; -**aufnahme,** *f.* bearing pressure.

lasten, to weigh, load, encumber, burden.

Lastenzug, *m.* series of loads, train of loads.

lästig, (*dat.*) burdensome, troublesome, irksome.

Last-senkung, *f.* load settlement; lowering of load; -**steigerungt,** *f.* -**stufe,** *f.* load increment; -**übertragung,** *f.* transmission of load.

Lastwagen, *m.*-, truck, freight car, lorry.

Lasur, *f.* azure; -**blau,** azure, sky-blue; -**fähigkeit,** *f.* opacity, transparent coating; -**farbe,** *f.* azure, ultramarine; -**farben,** azure, sky-blue; -**lack,** *m.* transparent varnish; -**spat,** *m.* lazulite; -**stein,** *m.* (lapis) lazuli.

lateinisch, Latin, roman (letters).

latent, latent.

Latenz, *f.* latency; -**zeit,** *f.* latent period.

Laterne, *f.* lantern, street lamp.

Latex, *m.* rubber latex.

Latierbaum, *m.* bar, barrier.

Latschenhochmoor, *n.* high moor covered with scrubby growth of pine.

Latsche(n-kiefer), *f.* dwarf (knee) pine.

Latschenöl, *n.* templin oil.

Latte, *f.* lath.

Latten-werk, *n.* trellis; -**zaun,** *m.* railing.

Lattich, *m.* lettuce; -**säure,** *f.* lactucic acid.

Latwerge, *f.* electuary, confection.

lau, lukewarm, tepid, mild, indifferent.

Laub, *n.* foliage, leaves; -**abfall,** *m.* leaf fall; -**abwerfen,** *n.* defoliation; -**artig,** foliaceous; -**ausbruch,** *m.* leafing; -**baum,** *m.* deciduous tree, broad-leaved tree; -**blatt,** *n.* foliage leaf; -**blattrosette,** *f.* rosette of foliage leaves; -**dach,** *n.* leaf canopy, leaf ceiling; -**decke,** *f.* soil-covering of leaves.

Laube, *f.* arbor, bower.

Laub-entfaltung, *f.* foliation; -**erde,** *f.* leaf mold; -**fall,** *m.* defoliation; -**flechte,** *f.* foliaceous lichen; -**grün,** *n.* leaf green, pigment; -**heuschrecken,** *f.pl.* Locustidae; -**holz,** *n.* deciduous or foliage trees; -**holzkohle,** *f.* hardwood charcoal; -**knospe,** *f.* leaf bud.

Laub-krone, *f.* leaf crown; -**moose,** *n.pl.* Musci, mosses; -**sporophyll,** *n.* leafy sporophyll; -**spross,** *m.* shoot; -**streu,** *f.* leaf litter; -**verlierend,** deciduous; -**verwehung,** *f.* dispersion of leaves; -**wald,** *m.* deciduous forest, broadleaf wood; -**wechsel,** *m.* change of foliage; -**wechselnd,** deciduous; -**werk,** *n.* foliage.

Lauch, *m.* leek (Alium); -**artig,** leeklike: -**grün,** leek green.

Lauer, *f.* ambush, lookout, lying in wait. low (press) wine.

lauern, to lie in wait.

Lauf, *m.*-̈e, course, track, path, flow, run(ning), action, work, rutting season, stream, race, progress, current, gun barrel, tarsus, orbit; -**bahn,** *f.* racecourse, tract, run(way), career; -**bein,** *n.* cursorial leg; -**bekleidung,** *f.* tarsal covering; -**bild,** *n.* moving picture.

Läufe, *m.pl.* feet of furred game.

laufen, to run, flow, go, move, elapse, turn, operate, act, travel, extend, leak, pass; ~ **lassen,** to let go, set free.

laufend, running, current, consecutive, linear.

Läufer, *m.*-, runner, tendril, sucker, shoot, carpet, slider, stretcher, traveler, rotor, -**gewicht,** *n.* sliding weight.

Lauf-feuer, *n.* surface fire; -**fläche,** *f.* bearing surface, journal; -**fuss,** *m.* cursorial leg; -**geschwindigkeit,** *f.* speed in running; -**gewicht,** *n.* sliding weight, counterpoise; -**glazur,** *f.* flow glaze; -**graben,** *m.* trench.

läufig, ruttish, in heat.

Läufigkeit, *f.* time of rutting.

Lauf-käfer, *m.pl.* ground beetles (Carabidae); -**katze,** *f.* crane carriage, trolley; -**knochen,** *m.* metatarsus; -**kran,** *m.* traveling crane; -**pass,** *m.* dismissal; -**pfanne,** *f.* (sugar) cooler; -**richtung,** *f.* direction of motion; -**rolle,** *f.* roller; -**schuppe,** *f.* scale of bird's leg; -**schwein,** *n.* porker.

Lauf-vogel, *m.* running bird; -**werk,** *n.* mechanism, power plant; -**wert,** *m.* peripheral speed of wheel; -**zahl,** *f.* continuous variable, variable number.

Lauge, *f.* lye, liquor, steep, lixivium, buck, brine.

laugen, to lye, steep (in lye), buck, lixiviate; -**artig,** resembling lye, alkaline, lixivila; -**asche,** *f.* potash, leached, ashes; -**bad,** *n.* lye (bath) liquor, alkaline bath; -**blume,** *f.* brass buttons, buck's-horn (*Cotula coronopifolia*); -**echt,** fast to lye.

Laugen-eiweiss, *n.* basic protein; -**flüssigkeit,** *f.* liquor; -**haft,** like lye, alkaline; -**messer,** *m.* alkalimeter; -**salz,** *n.* alkaline (lixivial) salt; -salzig, alkaline, lixivial; -sprödigkeit, *f.* caustic embrittlement; -wasser, *n.* liquor, alkaline solution; -zusatz, *m.* addition of lye.

Laugerei, *f.* lixiviation, steeping.

Laugerückstand, *m.* residue from lixiviation.

Laugflüssigkeit, *f.* liquor, alkaline solution.

laugig, resembling lye.

Laugung, *f.* lyeing, bucking, leaching.

Laune, *f.* humor, mood, temper, frame of mind.

Laurin-fett, *n.* laurin; -säure, *f.* lauric acid.

Laus, .:e, louse.

lauschen, to listen, spy.

Läuse-körner, *n.pl.* stavesacre seed, cocculus indicus, sabadila seed; -kraut, *n.* lousewort (Pedicular i); -pulver, *n.* insect powder; -sucht, *f.* lousiness, pediculols.

Lausfliegen, *f.pl.* Pupipara.

laut, loud, in accordance with.

Laut, *m.*-e, sound, tone, note; -apparat, *m.* sound-producing organ.

lautbar, known, public, notorious, audible.

Laute, *f.* lute, crutch.

lauten, to sound, run, read.

läuten, to ring, peal.

lauter, pure, clear, candid, true, genuine, unalloyed, mere, only; -beize, *f.* white liquor (in Turkey-red dyeing).

Läuter-batterie, *f.* underlet; -boden, *m.* false bottom, strainer; -bottich, *m.* straining (clarifying) vat; -feuer, *n.* refining fire; -maische, *f.* liquid part of mash.

läutern, to purify, refine, clear, clarify, purge, filter, rectify, defecate, wash, ennoble, mend, clean, weed out.

Läuter-ofen, *m.* refining furnace; -pfanne, *f.* clearing pan, clarifier, defecator.

Läuterung, *f.* purification, rectification.

Läuterungs-hieb, *m.* cleaning in young crops; -mittel, *n.* purifying agent.

Läuter-vorrichtung, *f.* purifying apparatus.

Laut-erzeugung, *f.* sound production; -lehre, *f.* phonetics; -sprache, *f.* articulate language; -stärke, *f.* loudness, sound intensity; -verstärkungsmethode, *f.* method of increasing intensity of sound, amplifying.

lauwarm, lukewarm.

Lava, *f.* lava.

Lavendel, *m.* lavender; -blüte, *f.* lavender flower; -öl, *n.* lavender oil.

Lavezstein, *m.* potstone.

lävogyr, levorotatory.

Lävulin, *n.* levulin; -säure, *f.* levulinic acid.

Lävulose, *f.* levulose.

Lawine, *f.* avalanche, snowslide.

Lawinenschutt, *m.* snow-slide debris.

Laxanz, *n.* laxative, purgative.

laxieren, to purge.

laxierend, purging, laxative.

Laxiermittel, *n.* laxative, purgative.

Laxiersalz, *n.* purging or laxative salt; englisches ∼, Epsom salt (magnesium sulphate).

Lazarett, *n.* (military) hospital.

leben, to live, exist.

Leben, *n.* life, existence; ums ∼ kommen, to lose one's life; ums ∼ bringen, to kill.

lebend, living; -gewicht, *n.* live weight.

lebendig, living, live, alive; lebendige Kraft, kinetic energy, inertia.

lebendiggebärend, viviparous.

Lebens-alter, *n.* age, period of life; -art, *f.* way (manner) of living; -aufgabe, *f.* vital task; -äusserung, *f.* manifestation of life; -baum, *m.* arborvitae; -bedingung, *f.* essential condition for life; -bezirk, *m.* life zone; -cyklus, *m.* life cycle; -dauer, *f.* life (period) span, durability, lifetime, longevity; -eigenschaft, *f.* property of living matter, attribute of life, vital activity.

Lebens-erhaltung, *f.* preservation of life; -erklärung, *f.* explanation of life; -erscheinung, *f.* appearance of life, phenomenon of life; -fähig, capable of living, viable; -fähigkeit, *f.* capacity for living, vitality, viability; -form, *f.* growth form, form of life; -führung, *f.* conduct of life, manner of living; -funktion, *f.* vital function; -gefährlich, dangerous (to life), perilous; -gemeinschaften, *f.pl.* biological communities.

Lebens-geschehen, *n.* course of life; geschichte, *f.* life history, biography; -gewohnheit, *f.* habit; -haltung, *f.* retention or preservation of life, standard of living; -holz, *n.* lignum vitae; -jahr, *n.* year of one's life; -keim, *m.* vital germ; -kraft, *f.* vitality, vigor, vital force; -kunde, *f.* -lehre, *f.* biology.

lebens-lang, -länglich, lifelong, for life; -luft, *f.* vital air (oxygen); -mittel, *n.pl.* provisions, victuals, food, nourishment; -mitteluntersuchung, *f.* investigation of foods, food research; -notwendigkeit, *f.* vital necessity; -ordnung, *f.* regimen, diet;

-prozess, *m.* vital process; -raum, *m.* environment, milieu, living space; -saft, *m.* vital fluid, latex; -strahl, *m.* life ray.

Lebens-strahlung, *f.* life radiation, radiation of living tissue; -substanz, *f.* vital substance; -tätig, vital active; -tätigkeit, *f.* vital action, vitality; -träger, *m.* biophore; -trieb, *m.* vital impulse; -unfähig, incapable of living; -unterhalt, *m.* living, subsistence; -verhältnis, *n.* condition of life; -verrichtung, *f.* vital function.

Lebens-versicherung, *f.* life insurance; -vorgang, *m.* vital process; -wahrscheinlichkeit, *f.* expectation (expectancy) of life; -wandel, *m.* life, conduct; -weise, *f.* mode of life, habit.

lebenswichtig, essential for life; lebenswichtige Anlageteile, *n.pl.* key equipment.

lebens-zäh, hardy; -zeit, *f.* lifetime, age; -zusammenhang, *m.* vital connection; -zyklus, *m.* life cycle.

Leber, *f.* liver, hepar; -ausfluss, *m.* discharge from the liver; -band, *n.* ligament of the liver; -blasengang, *m.* hepatocystic (bile) duct; -blende, *f.* zinc blende, reniform sphalerite; -blindschläuche, *m.pl.* hepatic caeca; -blümchen, *n.* liverwort (Hepatica); -blutader, *f.* hepatic vein; -braun, liver brown; -brei, *m.* liver pulp.

Leber-drüse, *f.* hepatic (lymph) gland; -egelseuche, *f.* liver rot, (liver) fluke disease; -eisenerz, *n.* pyrrhotite; -erz, *n.* hepatic ore; -farbe, *f.* liver color; -fäule, *f.* -fleck, *m.* liver spot, chloasma; -galle, *f.* hepatic bile; -gallengang, *m.* hepatic duct; -gefäss, *n.* hepatic vessel.

Leber-gefässhülle, *f.* Glisson's capsule; -gegend, *f.* hepatic region; -grube, *f.* hepatic fossa; -haut, *f.* tunic of the liver; -hülle, *f.* Glisson's capsule; -kies, *m.* hepatic marcasite, pyrrhotite; -klette, *f* Agrimonia; -kraut, *n.* liverwort (Marchantia); -läppchen, *n.* hepatic lobe (lobule); -mittel, *n.* liver remedy.

Leber-moose, *n.pl.* Hepaticae; -pforte, *f.* porta hepatis; -stärke, *f.* glycogen; -stein, *m.* hepatite, biliary calculus, gallstone; -tran, *m.* cod-liver oil; -zelle, *f.* hepatic cell; -zellenbalken, *m.pl.* cord (trabecula) of liver cells.

Lebewesen, *n.* living being, organism; kleinstes ∼, microörganism.

Lebewohl, *n.* farewell.

lebhaft, lively, vivacious, brisk, birght, gay, vivid, cheerful, active.

Lebhaftigkeit, *f.* liveliness.

Lebkuchen, *m.* gingerbread.

leblos, lifeless, inanimate, dull, quiet, inactive.

Lebzeit, *f.*-en, lifetime; zur ∼, while alive.

Lech, *m.* regulus, matte, metal.

Leck, *m.&n.* leak(age).

Leckage, *f.* leaking, leakage.

lecken, to leak, drip out, trickle out, lick.

lecker, dainty, delicious, delicate, nice; -bissen, *m.* dainty morsel.

Leckerei, *f.* daintiness.

Leck-salz, *n.* rock salt in blocks; -sucht, *f.* pica.

Leder, *n.* leather; -abfall, *m.* leather (cuttings) waste; -ähnlich, -artig, leatherlike, leathery, coriaceous; -band, *m.* leather binding (in calf); -etui, *n.* leather case; -farbe, *f.* leather color; -gelb, buff; -gummi, *n.* (India) rubber; -handel, *m.* leather trade; -harz, *n.* (India) rubber.

Leder-haut, *n.* true skin, corium, derma; -holz, *n.* leatherwood (*Dirca palustus*); -kohle, *f.* charcoal from leather; -mehl, *n.* ground leather.

ledern, of leather.

Leder-pappe, *f.* leather board; -riemen, *m.* leather strap, or belt; -schmiere, *f.* (leather) dégras, polish, dubbing; -strauch *m.* hop tree (*Ptelea trifoliata*); -zucker, *m.* marshmallow paste; (brauner) ∼, licorice paste.

ledig, free, exempt, empty, devoid, vacant, single, unmarried.

lediglich, only, solely, purely, merely, entirely, simply.

leer, empty, blank, clean, void, vacant; -darm, *m.* jejunum.

Leere, *f.* vacuum, emptiness, gap, vacancy, void.

leeren, to empty, evacuate.

Leer-fass, *n.*̈er, emptying vat; -gang, *m.* running without load; -gerüst, *n.* scaffold; -gewicht, *n.* empty weight, tare; -lauf, *m.* running without load, -taste, *f.* space bar.

Leerung, *f.* emptying, evacuation, clearance.

Lefze, *f.* lip.

Lege-bohrer, *m.* terebra, ovipositor; -halle, *f.* laying house; -henne, *f.* layer (hen).

legen, to lay (down), put, place, deposit, plant, abate; sich ∼, to lie down, calm, abate, slacken; sich auf etwas ∼, to devote oneself to something; von sich ∼, to lay aside; **sich ~ an,** to become attached to, join.

Lege-nest, *m.* laying nest; **-rinne,** *f.* groove in ovipositor; **-röhre,** *f.* ovipositor.

Legföhre, *f. Pinus montana.*

Legföhrengstrüpp, *n.* elfin woodland (mountain-pine brushwood).

legierbar, alloyable.

legieren, to alloy, bequeath, be mixed with.

Legierung, *f.* alloy(ing).

Legierungsstahl, *m.* alloy steel.

Legionär, *m.* legionary.

Legschindel, *f.* clapboard.

Legumin, *n.* legumin.

Leguminose, *f.* legume, pea meal, leguminous plant

Lehm, *m.* loam, yellow-brown or lean or very sandy clay, mud; **-artig,** loamy, argillaceous; **-boden,** *m.* loamy soil, clay soil; **-(form)guss,** *m.* loam casting; **-grube,** *f.* loam (clay) pit.

lehmig, loamy, clayey, argillaceous.

Lehm-kalk, *m.* argillaceous limestone; **-kern,** *m.* loam core; **-kitt,** *m.* loam lute; **-mergel,** *m.* loamy marl; **-schicht,** *f.* loam coat; **-stein,** *m.* unburnt brick.

Lehne, *f.* back, support, railing, slope, inclined plane, declivity.

lehnen, to lean.

Lehramt, *n.* teaching profession.

Lehr-anstalt, *f.*-en, educational institution; **-buch,** *n.* textbook.

Lehre, *f.* instruction, teaching, doctrine, science, theory, lesson, apprenticeship, pattern, gauge, balance, centering, conclusion, caliber, staff, rule.

lehren, to teach, instruct, inform, prove, show; **gelehrt,** learned.

Lehrer, *m.*-, teacher.

Lehr-fach, *n.*-er, teaching, branch of study; **-forst,** *m.* demonstration (training) forest; **-gang,** *m.* curriculum; **gebäude,** *n.* system of instruction; **-gerüst,** *n.* false work, molding frame; **-kursus,** *m.* course of study.

Lehrling, *m.*-e, apprentice, pupil.

Lehr-mittel, *n.* material (means) of instruction; **-plan,** *m.* curriculum; **-reich,** instructive; **-satz,** *m.* theorem, doctrine; **-stelle,** *f.* teaching position; **stuhl,** *m.* professorship.

Leib, *m.*-er, abdomen, belly, body, womb, trunk waist.

Leibes-decke, *f.* integument; **-frucht,** *f* fetus; **-höhle,** *f.* body or gastric cavity, coelom; **-ring,** *m.* body segment.

leiblich, bodily, material, corporal, somatic, in person.

Leibungsdruck, *m.* bearing pressure.

Leichdorn, *m.* corn (on the foot).

Leiche, *f.* corpse, cadaver.

Leichen-alkaloid, *n.* putrefactive alkaloid, ptomaine; **-base,** *f.* putrefactive base, ptomaine; **-begängnis,** *n.* funeral; **-fett,** *n.* adipocere; **-gift,** *n.* ptomaine; **-verbrennung,** *f.* cremation; **wachs,** *n.* adipocere; **-wurm,** *m.* maggot.

Leichnam, *m.* corpse, cadaver.

leicht, (*dat.*) light, easy, mild, slight, easily, readily; **-beweglich,** very mobile, easily movable; **-entzündlich,** easily inflammable; **-fertig,** thoughtless, careless; **-flüchtig,** readily volatile; **-flüchtigkeit,** *f.* volatility.

leicht-flüssig, easily (dissolved) liquefiable, mobile; **-flüssigkeit,** *f.* easy fusibility, fluidity, mobility; **-frucht,** *f.* light grain; **-gläubig,** credulous; **-hin,** lightly, casually, **-horn,** *n.* light horn.

Leichtigkeit, *f.* lightness, readiness, facility, ease.

leichtlich, easily.

leicht-löslich, easily (dissolved) soluble; **-metall,** *n.* light metal; **-öl,** *n.* light oil; **-schmelzbar,** easily fusible; **-siedend,** low-boiling; **-sinnig,** light-minded, careless, thoughtless; **-verderblich,** corruptible, perishable.

Leid, *n.*-en, sorrow, grief, pain, regret, wrong, harm, mourning, misfortune; **es tut mir ~,** I am sorry.

leiden, to suffer, undergo, allow, permit, admit; **an etwas ~,** to be subject to, suffer from.

Leiden, *n.* suffering, affliction, distress, ailment, malady, disease, pain.

Leidener Flasche, *f.* Leyden jar.

Leidenschaft, *f.* passion; **-lich,** enthusiastic.

leidenschaftslos, dispassionate.

leider, unfortunately, alas.

leidig, fatal, unpleasant, disagreeable, evil, tiresome, pitiful.

leidlich, tolerable, passable, mediocre, fair.

leierförmig, lyrate(d), lyre-shaped.

leihen, to lend, loan, borrow.

Leim, *m.* glue, birdlime, caterpillar grease, gelatin, size, paste, grease; **farbloser** ~, gelatin; **pflanzlicher** ~, vegetable glue.

leim-artig, gluelike, gelatinous; **-aufstrich,** *m.* coat of glue.

leimen, to glue, size, encircle trees with grease.

leimend, adhesive, agglutinative.

Leim-farbe, *f.* distemper, size color; **-fass,** *n.* size (glue) tank; **-festigkeit,** *f.* size test, resistance due to sizing; **-flüssigkeit,** *f.* size; **-form,** *f.* size mold; **-gebend,** yielding glue, gelatinous, collagenous; **-gewebe,** *n.* collenchyma; **-glanz,** *m.* size (for leather); **-gut,** *m.* material for making glue.

leimig, gluey, glutinous, adhesive.

Leim-kitt, *m.* putty, joiner's cement; **-kraut,** *n.* catchfly (Silene); **-leder,** *n.* leather scraps for glue making; **-lösung,** *f.* solution of glue; **-niederschlag,** *m.* lye (soap) precipitate; **-pflaster,** *n.* adhesive plaster.

Leim-ring, *m.* grease band; **-seife,** *f.* filled soap (with glycerin and lye); **-sieder,** *m.* glue boiler; **-stoff,** *m.* sizing material, gluten; **-substanz,** *f.* gelatinous substance; **-süss,** *n.* glycine.

Leimung, *f.* glueing, sizing.

Leim-zotte, *f.* complex of glands; **-zucker,** *m.* glycine, glycocoll.

Lein, *m.* flax, linseed; **-dotter,** *m.* gold-of-pleasure (*Camelina sativa*); **-dotteröl,** *n.* cameline oil.

Leine, *f.* line, cord, rope.

leinen, linen.

Leinen, *n.* linen; **-faden,** *m.* linen (fiber) thread; **-stoff,** *m.* linen material.

Lein-firnis, *m.* linseed varnish; **-gewächse,** *n.pl.* Linaceae; **-kraut,** *n.* toadflax, flaxweed (*Linaria vulgaris*); **-kuchen,** *m.* linseed (oil) cake; **-mehl,** *m.* linseed meal.

Leinöl, *n.* linseed oil; **-ersatz,** *m.* linseed-oil substitute; **-firnis,** *m.* linseed-oil varnish; **-kuchen,** *m.* linseed (oil) cake; **-säure,** *f.* linoleic acid; **-trockenprozess,** *m.* drying of linseed oil.

Lein-pfad, *m.* towpath (at canal); **pflanze,** *f.* flax; **-saat,** *f.* linseed; **-samen,** *m.* flaxseed, linseed; **-samenmehl,** *n.* flaxseed meal; **-seide,** *f.* flax dodder; **-wand,** *f.* linen (cloth), canvas; **-wandband,** *m.* cloth binding.

leise, low, soft, gentle, slight, imperceptible.

Leiste, *f.* ridge, groin, helix, ledge, border, lip, carina, crest, list, selvage.

leisten, to do, perform, carry out, accomplish, execute, effect, realize, render, pay, give, fulfill; **Beistand** ~, to lend aid; **sich etwas** ~, to afford treat oneself to something; **Folge** ~, to obey.

Leisten-bein, *n.* puboischiac bone; **-beuge,** *f.* the flexure of the groin; **-bruch,** *m.* groin rupture, inguinal hernia; **-drüse,** *f.* inguinal gland; **-falte,** *f.* inguinal fold; **-förmig,** ledged, ledge-shaped; **-furche,** *f.* inguinal fossa, furrow; **-geflechte,** *n.* inguinal plexus; **-gegend,** *f.* inguinal region; **-grube,** *f.* inguinal fossa.

Leisten-muster, *n.* ridge pattern; **-netz,** *n.* projections of wall into the cells of the epidermis; **-öffnung,** *f.* inguinal aperture; **-presse,** *f.* press brake; **-trommel,** *f.* beater drum; **-wirbel,** *m.* lumbar whorl (hair center).

Leistung, *f.* work, performance, production, obligation, accomplishment, output, capacity, power, service.

leistungs-fähig, efficient, productive; **-fähigkeit,** *f.* productive power, ability to perform, capacity, efficiency; **-formel,** *f.* efficiency formula; **-kern,** *m.* vital center of protein substances; **-messer,** *m.* wattmeter, output meter; **-rechnung,** *f.* calculation of performance.

Leit-apparat, *m.* conducting apparatus; **-bahngefüge,** *n.* channel fabric; **-band,** *n.* gubernaculum.

Leitbarkeit, *f.* ductility, conductibility, versatility, flexibility.

Leit-blech, *n.* baffle, fin; **-bündel,** *n.* vascular bundle; **-bündel-anatomie,** *f.* vascular anatomy; **-bündel-kryptogamen,** *pl.* vascular cryptogams.

leiten, to conduct, lead, direct, guide, convey, govern, preside over.

leitend, leading, conducting.

Leiter, *m.* conductor, leader, guide, director.

Leiter, *f.* ladder; **-förmig,** scalariform, ladder-shaped; **-gefäss,** *n.* scalariform vessel; **-kreis,** *m.* conductor ring; **-netz,** *n.* network of conductors; **-stange,** *f.* side of a ladder, pole, ladder wood; **-weg,** *m.* path formed by the conductor.

Leit-faden, *m.* clue, guide, manual, textbook, compendium, introduction; **-fähig,** conducting, conductive; **-fähigkeit,** *f.* conductivity; **-fähigkeitsmessung,** *f.* conductivity measurement; **-fläche,** *f.* conducting surface, guiding surface; **-fossilien,** *pl.* index fossils (showing earth layers).

Leit-hammel, *m.* bellwether; **-linie,** *f.* directrix; **-parenchym,** *n.* conducting parenchyma; **-satz,** *m.* guiding principle; **-scheide,** *f.* mestome sheath; **-stern,** *m.* polestar, guiding star; **-strahl,** *m.* radius vector; **-trieb,** *m.* leader.

Leitung, *f.* conduction, conducting, transmission, circuit, wire, cable, lead, conduit, piping, tubing, supply, direction, guide, control, management, main, duct.

Leitungs-abzweigung, *f.* branching of a conductor; **-bahn,** *f.* path of conduction; **-draht,** *m.* conducting wire; **-fähig,** conductive; **-fähigkeit,** *f.* conductivity; **-gewebe,** *n.* conducting tissue; **-kraft,** *f.* conducting power; **-rohr,** *m.* **-röhre,** *f.* conducting tube or pipe, delivery tube, conduit (pipe).

Leitungs-spannung, *f.* voltage of the line; **-strom,** *m.* conduction current; **-system,** *n.* vascular system; **-vermögen,** *n.* conductivity; **-verzögerung,** *f.* delayed conduction; **-wärme,** *f.* heat of conduction; **-wasser,** *n.* tap (hydrant) water; **-widerstand,** *m.* (line) resistance; **-zweig,** *m.* branch conductor.

Leit-vermögen, *n.* conducting power, conductivity; **-werk,** *n.* training wall, diversion structure; **-zelle,** *f.* conducting cell.

Lektion, *f.* lesson.

Lektüre, *f.* reading.

Lemnische Erde, Lemnian bole (earth).

Lemongrasöl, *n.* lemon-grass oil.

Lende, *f.* loin, hip, haunch, lumbar region.

Lendendarmbein-band, *n.* iliolumbar ligament; **-muskel,** *m.* iliopsoas muscle.

Lenden-drüse, *f.* lumbar gland; **-geflecht,** *n.* lumbar plexus; **-gegend,** *f.* lumbar region; **-knochen,** *m.* hipbone, ischium; **-kreuzgegend,** *f.* lumbosacral region; **-muskel,** *m.* psoas muscle; **-rippenband,** *n.* external arcuate ligament; **-schenkel,** *m.* crura of the diaphragm; **-wirbel,** *m.* lumbar vertebra; **-wirbelsäule,** *f.* lumbar portion of the spine; **-zwischenwirbelscheibe,** *f.* lumbar intervertebral disk.

lenkbar, dirigible, flexible, manageable, docile.

lenken, to turn, bend, lead, guide, conduct, direct, drive, steer, control.

Lenz, *m.* spring.

Lenzin, *n.* a white pigment, light spar, gypsum.

Lepidopteren, *f.pl.* lepidopters.

Lepra, *f.* leprosy; **-bazillus,** *m.* leprosy bacillus; **-heilserum,** *n.* curative serum for leprosy.

lepto-centrisch, amphivasal; **-parenchym,** phloem parenchyma; **-thrixartig,** resembling leptothrix.

Lerche, *f.* lark, larch.

Lerchensporn, *m.* holewort, hollowwort Corydalis.

lernbar, learnable.

lernen, to learn; **kennen** ~, to become acquainted with.

Lesart, *f.* reading, manner of reading.

lesbar, legible, readable.

Lesbarkeit, *f.* legibility, readability.

Lese, *f.* vintage, gleaning, gathering; **-abstand,** *m.* reading distance; **-buch,** *n.* reader; **-glas,** *n.* reading glass; **-holz,** *n.* dry fallen wood; **-lupe,** *f.* reading lens.

lesen, to read, lecture, gather, pick, select, cull.

Leser, *m.* reader.

leserlich, legible.

Lesestein, *m.* bog (brown) iron ore, boulder, float, fragment of bedrock.

letal, lethal, fatal; **-faktor,** *m.* lethal factor; **-gene,** *m.pl.* lethals.

Letten, *m.* loam, potter's clay, very pure clay, fat clay; **-nudel,** *f.* tamping cartridge of clay.

Letter, *f.* letter, character, type.

Lettern-gut, *n.* **-metall,** *n.* type metal.

lettig, clayey, loamy.

letztangeführt, last-quoted.

letzte, last, ultimate, latest, final, lowest, extreme; **der (die, das) letztere,** the latter; **in letzter Zeit,** recently, lately; **letztens,** of late; **letzthin,** of late; **im letzten Grunde,** in the last analysis; **letzten Endes,** in the last analysis.

Letztere, *n.* the latter.

letzt-erwähnt, last-mentioned; **-genannt,** last-named, latter; **-gerichtet,** in the latter direction; **-hin,** lastly, in the last analysis.

Leu, *m.* lion.

Leuchämie, *f.* leukemia.

Leucht-bakterien, *n.pl.* photogenic bacteria; **-bombe,** *f.* flash bomb; **-brenner,** *m.* illuminating burner; **-dichte,** *f.* luminous density.

Leuchte, *f.* light, lamp.

Leuchtelektron, *n.* emitting electron.

leuchten, to (give) light, shine, glow, beam, radiate, illuminate.

Leuchten, *n.* shining, burning, coruscation, phosphorescence (sea).

leuchtend, luminous, bright, shining, lustrous, photogenic.

Leuchterscheinung, *f.* luminous phenomenon.

leuchtfähig, capable of luminescence.

Leuchtfarbe, *f.* luminous paint or color.

Leuchtgas, *n.* illuminating (coal) gas; **-anstalt,** *f.* illuminating-gas plant; **-erzeugung,** *f.* production of illuminating gas.

Leucht-hülle, *f.* luminous envelope; **-käfer,** *m.* firefly, glowworm; **-kraft,** *f.* illuminating power; **-kraftbestimmung,** *f.* photometry; **-masse,** *f.* luminous mass; **-material,** *n.* illuminating medium or material; **-mittel,** *n.* illuminant; **-organ,** *n.* luminous organ; **-petroleum,** *n.* kerosene; **-punkt,** *m.* luminous point.

Leucht-röhre, *f.* illuminating tube, neon tube, fluorescent tube; **-schild,** *n.* illuminated sign; **-schirm,** *m.* fluorescent screen; **-stärke,** *f.* brightness; **-stein,** *m.* phosphorescent stone; **-spurgeschoss,** *n.* **-spurgranate,** *f.* tracer shell; **-stab,** *m.* flashlight, torch; **-steifen,** *m.* luminous streak (layer); **-vermögen,** *n.* illuminating power; **-wert,** *m.* illuminating value; **-wurm,** *m.* glowworm.

Leucin, *n.* leucine.

leugnen, to deny, disavow, retract.

Leukämie, *f.* leukemia.

Leukolyse, *f.* leucocytolysis.

Leuko-phan, *m.* leucophane; **-verbindung,** *f.* leuco compound; **-zyt,** *n.* leucocyte; **-zyten,** *pl.* white blood corpuscles; **-zytenzahl,** *f.* leucocyte count; **-zytose,** *f.* leucocytosis.

Leute, *pl.* people, persons, men, the world, public, lives, hands, servants, crowd.

leutselig, affable, familiar, humane, popular, kind, gentle.

Leuzit, *m.* leucite.

levigieren, to levigate, pulverize.

Levkoje, *f.* sea stock, gillyflower (*Matthiola sinuata*).

lexikal(isch), lexical, lexicographic.

Lexikon, *n* dictionary, lexicon.

Leydner Flasche, Leyden jar.

Lezithin, *n.* lecithin.

Libell, *f.* dragonfly, (water) level.

Libriformgewebe, *n.* libriform tissue.

Libroplast, *m.* elaioplast.

Licht, *n.* light, candle, brightness, clearing; auffallendes $\sim$, reflected light; durchfallendes $\sim$, transmitted light; zurückgeworfenes $\sim$, reflected light.

licht, light, bright, luminous, light, thin, pale (in the) clear, interior, open (space); **-abschluss,** *m.* exclusion of light; **-absorption,** *f.* light absorption; **-art,** *f.* kind of light; **-äther,** *m.* luminiferous ether; **-ausschluss,** *m.* exclusion (absence) of light; **-baum,** *m.* light-demanding tree, intolerant tree; **-bedarf,** *m.* light requirement; **-bedingung,** *f.* condition of light; **-bedürfnis,** *n.* light requirement.

licht-bedürftig, light-needing, intolerant, light-demanding; **-belaubt,** light foliaged; **-beständig,** stable in light, fast to light, photostable; **-bestockt,** scantily stocked or wooded; **-beugung,** *f.* refraction of light; **-bild,** *n.*-er, photograph; **-bildlich,** photographic; **-bildkunst,** *f.* photography; **-bildung,** *f.* production of light, photogenesis; **-blatt,** *n.* sun leaf, heliophilous leaf.

licht-blau, light (pale) blue; **-bogen,** *m.* (luminous) arc; **-bogenschweissung,** *f.* arc welding; **-bogenzündung,** *f.* arc or plug ignition; **-braun,** light brown; **-brechend,** refracting, refractive, diaptric(al); **-brechung,** *f.* refraction of light; **-brechungsvermögen,** *n.* refractive power, refractivity; **-bündel,** *n.* pencil of rays; **-chemisch,** photochemical.

licht-dicht, lighttight, lightproof; **-druck,** *m.* photographic printing; **-druckgelatine,** *f.* heliographic gelatin; **-durchlässig,** translucent, transmitting light; **-durchlässigkeit,** *f.* permeability, transparency; **-echt,** resistant (fast) to light, nonfading; **-echtheit,** *f.* fastness to light; **-effekt,** *m.* luminous effect; **-eindruck,** *m.* luminous impression; **-einfall,** *m.* incidence of light.

Licht-einwirkung, *f.* action (effect) of light; **-elektrisch,** photoelectric; **-empfindlich,** sensitive to light, sensitized; **-empfindung,** *f.* sensation of light, impression caused by light.

lichten, to clear, open, thin (out), weigh (anchor), light(en) (a ship), to isolate.

licht-entwickelnd, emitting light, photogenic; **-entwicklung,** *f.* evolution of light, photogenesis; **-entzug,** *m.* reducing the supply of light.

lichter Durchmesser, *m.* inside diameter.

Lichter, *n.pl.* highlights; **-fabrik,** *f.* candle factory.

lichterloh, blazing, all ablaze.

Licht-erscheinung, *f.* luminous phenomenon; **-erzeugend,** producing light, photogenic; **-faden,** *m.* electric (light) filament; **-fangend,** diaphototropic; **-fanglaterne,** *f.* trapping lantern; **-farben,** light-colored; **-farbendruck,** *m.* photomechanical color printing; **-filter,** *n.* color filter (screen); **-form,** *f.* candle mold; **-fortpflanzung,** *f.* transmission of light.

Licht-funk, *m.* telephoto; **-gebend,** giving light, luminous; **-gebilde,** *n.* phenomenon (form) of light; **-gefördert,** light-favored; **-gelb,** light yellow; **-genuss,** *m.* light utilization, photic ration; **-genussverteilung,** *f.* distribution of photic ration; **-geschwindigkeit,** *f.* velocity of light; **-giessen,** *n.* candle molding; **-glanz,** *m.* brilliant luster, brightness.

Licht-güte, *f.* quality of light; **-hieb,** *m.* thinning, light felling; **-hof,** *m.* halation; **-hofsicher,** nonhalation; **-holz,** *n.* light-loving tree, light demander; **-hülle,** *f.* luminous envelope; **-kegel,** *m.* cone of light, luminous core; **-kranz,** *m.* corona (of the sun); **-kreis,** *m.* circle of light, halo; **-kronig,** thin-crowned.

Licht-lage, *f.* position in relation to light; **-lehre,** *f.* optics, science of light; **-leimdruck,** *m.* collotypy; **-leitung,** *f.* lighting circuit; **-liebend,** light-loving euphotic; **-loch,** *n.* opening for light, pupil; **-los,** without light, dark; **-menge,** *f.* quantity of light; **-messer,** *m.* photometer; **-messkunst,** *f.* photometry.

Licht-messung, *f.* photometry; **-motte,** *f.* pyralidid; **-nelfe,** *f.* campion (Lychnis); **-pause,** *f.* photographic tracing, blueprint phototype; **-pauspapier,** *n.* blueprint paper; **-punkt,** *m.* luminous (point), spot; **-quantum,** *n.* quantum (quantity) of light; **-quelle,** *f.* source of light; **-reflektierend,** light-reflecting; **-region,** *f.* light region; **-reiz,** *m.* light stimulus.

Licht-scheibe, *f.* disk of light; **-schein,** *m.* gleam, shine; **-scheu,** afraid of light, heliophobous, aphotic; **-schirm,** *m.* screen; **-schlag,** removal cutting, light felling; **-schluckend,** light-absorbing; **-schwach,** dull, giving off feeble light; **-sinnesorgan,** *n.* light-perceptive organ; **-spiegler,** *m.* reflector of light; **-stand,** *m.* open stand.

Licht-stärke, *f.* intensity of light; **-steindruck,** *m.* photolithography; **-strahl,** *m.* light ray, beam of light, luminous ray; **-strahlung,** *f.* light radiation; **-summe,** *f.*

light summation; **-talg,** *m.* candle tallow; **-teilchen,** *n.* particle of light; **-undurchlässig,** opaque to light; **-unechtheit,** *f.* lack of fastness to light; **-unempfindlich,** insensitive to light.

Lichtung, *f.* lumen, clearing, glade, thinning.

Lichtungszuwachs, *m.* open-stand increment.

Licht-unterschied, difference of light intensification; **-vag,** heliophobic, aphotic; **-verminderung,** *f.* decrease of light; **-voll,** luminous, lucid; **-weg,** *m.* course or path of light; **-weite,** *f.* width in the clear, clearance.

Licht-welle, *f.* light wave; **-wendig,** photometric; **-wirkung,** *f.* action of light, luminous effect; **-wulst,** *m.* ring of light; **-zelle,** *f.* visual cell; **-zerstreuung,** *f.* dispersion of light.

Lid, *n.* eyelid; **-bindehaut,** *f.* conjunctiva of the eye.

Liderung, *f.* packing, washer gasket.

Lid-rand, *m.* margin of the eyelid; **-talgdrüse,** *f.* tarsal (sebaceous) gland.

lieb, (*dat.*) dear, beloved, esteemed, agreeable.

Liebe, *f.* love, affection, favor.

lieben, to love, like, cherish.

Liebenswürdigkeit, *f.* amiability, kindness.

lieber, rather, sooner, better, more agreeable.

Liebes-apfel, *m.* tomato; **-gras,** *n.* quaking grass (Briza); **-pfeil,** *m.* dart; **-stöckel,** *n.* lovage (*Levisticum officinale*).

liebevoll, loving, affectionate.

Liebhaber, *m.* lover, amateur, buyer.

Liebig'scher Kühler, Liebig condenser.

lieblich, lovely, graceful, sweet, charming.

Lieblingsnahrung, *f.* favorite food.

Liebstöckel, *m.* lovage (*Levisticum officinale*).

Lied, *n.* song.

liederlich, careless, negligent, disorderly, dissolute.

lief (laufen), ran.

Lieferant, Lieferer, *m.* purveyor, caterer, contractor.

lieferbar, deliverable, available.

liefern, to yield, produce, deliver, supply, furnish, afford, provide.

Lieferung, *f.* supply(ing), providing, delivery, issue, number, part, cargo, parcel, lot, carload.

lieferungsweise, in parts or numbers.

liegen, to lie, be, placed or situated, matter, signify; **zugrunde** ∼, to underlie; **es liegt auf der Hand,** it is obvious (plain); **am Herzen** ∼, to be of interest to; **es liegt nahe,** it is natural, it suggests itself; **mir liegt viel daran,** that matters a great deal to me; **das liegt nun einmal daran, dass . . .** this is due to the fact that **. . . ; an wem liegt es,** whose fault is it?; **es liegt an ihm,** it is his fault; **soviel an mir liegt,** as far as it lies in my power; **tief** ∼, to range low; **wie liegt die Sache,** what is the situation?

liegend, lying, extended, horizontal, procumbent, prostrate; **liegende Schrift,** italics; **gelegen,** situated, convenient, important.

lieh, (leihen), loaned.

Liesch(gras), n. cat's-tail, timothy (grass) (*Phleum pratense*).

lieschen, to husk.

liess (lassen), left, had; ∼ **sich,** could be.

liest (lesen), reads.

Ligatur, f. ligature.

Lignin, n. lignin; **-haltig,** containing lignin; **-reich,** rich in lignin.

Lignit, m. lignite.

Ligroin, n. ligroin, petroleum ether.

Ligulargrube, f. ligular pit.

Liguster, m. privet.

Likör, m. liqueur; **-artig,** liqueurlike.

lila, lilac (colored), pale violet; **-farbe,** f. lilac color.

Lilie, f. lily.

Lilienbaum, m. magnolia, beaver tree, swampwood; **-gewächse,** n.pl. Liliaceae; **-hähnchen,** n. lily beetle.

Lima-bohne, f. Lima bean; **-holz,** n. Lima wood.

Limbus, m. lower plate of transit.

Limes, m. limit.

Limette, f. lime.

Limettenessenz, f. lime juice.

Limone, f. citron, cedrat (*Citrus limonum*); (süsse) ∼, lime; (saure, eigentliche) ∼, lemon.

Limonen, n. limonene.

Limongras, n. lemon grass.

Linaloeholz, n. linaloa (wood).

lind, soft, gentle, mild, smooth, scoured.

Lindausche Zelle, f. primordium of apothecium.

Linde, f. linden basswood, lime tree.

Linden-bast, m. lime bast; **-blüte,** f. linden flower; **-frucht,** f. carcerule; **-gewächse,** n.pl. Tiliaceae; **-holz,** n. linden wood, basswood; **-kohle,** f. lime charcoal, lindenwood charcoal; **-schwärmer,** m. limehawk moth (*Smerinthus tiliae*); **-schwärmerraupe,** f. caterpillar of the limehawk moth.

lindern, to soften, ease, alleviate, relieve, moderate, calm.

lindernd, soothing, palliative, lenitive.

Linderungsmittel, n. soothing remedy, palliative, lenitive.

Lineal, n. straightedge, rule, ruler.

linealisch, linear, lineal, lineate.

Linie, f. line, lineage, descent, ancestry; **in erster** ∼, first of all, above all; **in letzter** ∼, finally, in the last analysis.

linien-förmig, linear; **-mitte,** f. middle of a line; **-paar,** n. pair of lines; **-spannung,** f. line (tension) voltage; **-spektrum,** n. line spectrum; **-verschiebung,** f. displacement of lines; **-zahl,** f. number of lines; **-zug,** m. (plotted) line, trace, curve (in a graph).

liniieren, to rule.

Liniierfarbe, f. ruling ink.

Linin, n. linen; **-gerüst,** n. linen meshwork.

link, left, wrong.

linkisch, awkward, clumsy, left-handed.

links, to the left, (on the) left.

linksdr., abbr. (linksdrehend), turning to the left, levorotatory.

links-drehend, levorotatory; **-drehung,** f. levorotation; left-handed polarization; **-fruchtzucker,** m. levulose; **-gedreht,** left contorted; **-griffelig,** aristerostylic (style on the left); **-läufig,** to the left, counterclockwise.

links-kreisende Pflanze, f. left-hand climber; **-milchsäure,** f. levolactic acid; **-säure,** f. levo acid; **-schraube,** f. lefthanded screw; **-spirale,** f. left spiral; **-weinsäure,** f. levotartaric acid.

Linolensäure, f. linolenic acid.

Linoleum, n. linoleum.

Linolsäure, f. linoleic acid.

Linse, f. lens, lentil, bob (of pendulum).

linsen, lenticular; **-ähnlich, -artig,** lenticular, lens-shaped; **-bein,** n. sesamoid bone; **-bläschen,** n. lens vesicle; **-drüse,** f. lenticular gland; **-erz,** n. oolitic limonite;

-faser, *f.* crystal-line fiber; **-fassring,** *m.* lens mount (on microscope); **-förmig,** lens-shaped, lenti- form.

Linsen-glas, *n.* lens; **-gross,** lentil-sized; **-grube,** *f.* lens pit; **-halter,** *m.* lens holder; **-haut,** *f.* crystalline capsule; **-kern,** *m.* lenticular nucleus; **-knochen,** *m.* lenticular bone; **körper,** *m.* body of the (crystalline) lens; **-paar,** *n.* paired lenses; **-rand,** *m.* edge of a lens.

Linsen-raster, *m.* lenticular screen; **-system,** *n.* system of lenses; **-zusammenstellung,** *f.* lens combination.

lipoidlöslich, soluble in oily or fatty substances.

Lipolyse, *f.* lipolysis.

Lippe, *f.* lip, labium, label(lum), edge, border.

lippen-artig, liplike; **-band,** *n.* ligament of the lip; **-bändchen,** *n.* frenulum labii; **-blüte,** *f.* labiate flower; **-blütler,** *m.pl.* Labiatae; **-bogen,** *m.* labial arch; **-drüse,** *f.* gland of the lip; **-fläche,** *f.* surface of the lip; **-furche,** *f.* labial groove.

Lippen-füsser, *m.pl.* Chilopodae; **-gegend,** *f.* labial region; **-knorpel,** *m.* labial cartilage; **-membran,** *f.* peristomial membrane; **-rand,** *m.* margin of the lip, labrum; **-spalte,** *f.* lip cleft, rima oris; **-taster,** *m.* labial palpus; **-vorhof,** *m.* labial vestibule; **-wunde,** *f.* wound on the lip.

liqueszieren, to liquefy, melt.

liquid, liquid, payable, due.

liquidieren, to liquidate, settle.

lischt (löschen), puts out, blots.

List, *f.* cunning, device, craftiness, artifice, trick.

Liste, *f.* list, register, roll, catalogue.

Listenpreis, *m.* list (catalogue) price.

literarisch, literary.

Literaturangaben, *f.pl.* bibliographical data.

Liter-kolben, *m.* liter flask; **-mass,** *n.* liter measure.

Lithargyrum, *n.* litharge.

Lithion, *n.* lithia; **-glimmer,** *m.* lithia mica.

lithium-haltig, containing lithium; **-jodid,** *n.* lithium iodide; **-salz,** *n.* lithium salt.

litt (leiden), suffered.

Litze, *f.* lace, cord, braid, string, thread, strand.

Lixiv, *n.* lixivium, lye.

Lizenz, *f.* license (poetic).

Lob, *n.* praise, applause, fame.

Lobelie, *f.* lobelia.

loben, to praise, commend.

löblich, praiseworthy, commendable, estimable.

Lobrede, *f.* eulogy.

Loch, *n.*⁻**er,** hole, opening, foramen, eye, pore, cavity, slot, pocket, prison, orifice, aperture, perforation; **-abstand,** *m.* perforation pitch; **-blende,** *f.* perforated screen, diaphragm.

lochen, to pierce, perforate, punch.

Löcherhieb, *m.* gap cutting.

löcherig, full of holes, perforated, porous.

Löcher-pflanzung, *f.* hole planting; **-pilze,** *m.pl.* Polyporaceae; **-reihe,** *f.* ambulacra; **-saat,** *f.* sowing in holes; **-schwamm,** *m.* Polyporus.

Loch-frass, *m.* corrosions, pitting; **-kultur,** *f.* stab culture; **-säge,** *f.* compass saw, pad saw.

Lochung, *f.* perforation, punching.

Lochweite, *f.* width of opening, inside diameter.

locken, to bait, decoy, entice, attract, curl.

Lockente, *f.* decoy duck.

locker, lax, loose, slack, not compact, spongy, porous, light, distant.

Lockerheit, *f.* porosity, looseness.

lockern, to loosen, make loose, lighten, slacken, relax.

Lockerung, *f.* loosening.

Lock-farbe, *f.* color used as bait or lure; **-mittel,** *n.* bait, lure; **-pfeife,** *f.* birdcall; **-speise,** *f.* lure, bait.

Lode, *f.* shoot, sprout, sprig, deciduous transplant, rag, tuft, coarse woolen cloth.

lodern, to blaze, flame, flare, burst forth.

Löffel, *m.-,* spoon, ladle, curette, bucket of excavator, dipper, scoop; **-artig,** cochlear(iform), spoon-shaped; **-bohrer,** *m.* center bit (spoon auger); **-ente,** *f.* shoveler; **-förmig,** cochlear(iform), spoon-shaped; **-kraut,** *n.* scurvy grass (Cochlearia); **-stiel,** *m.* spoon handle; **-weise,** by spoonfuls.

Löffler'scher Diphtherienährboden, *m.* Loef·fler's serum.

log (lügen), lied.

Logarithmus, *m.* logarithm.

Logik, *f.* logic.

logisch(erweise), logically.

loh, blazing, burning; **-beize,** *f.* tan liquor, tanning; **-blüte,** *f.* flower of tan (*Fuligo*); **-brühe,** *f.* bark liquor, ooze.

Lohe, *f.* tanbark, tan (liquor), ooze, flame, flare, blaze; **-artig,** tanlike.

Loh-eiche, *f.* common (tanbark) oak; **-eisen,** *n.* barking iron, spud.

lohen, to tan, steep (in tan liquor), blaze, flame.

Loh-farbe, *f.* tan color; **-fass,** *n.* tan vat; **-gare,** *f.* (bark) tanning, dressing; **-gerber,** *m.* (bark) tanner; **-gerberei,** *f.* tannery; **-hecke,** *f.* strip of oak (coppice) wood; **-krankheit,** *f.* abnormal lenticel formation.

Lohn, *m.*-̈e, compensation, reward, wages, pay, salary; **-arbeiter,** *m.* common workman.

lohnen, to pay, recompense, reward.

lohnend, profitable, advantageous.

Löhnung, *f.* pay, payment.

Loh-probe, *f.* bark test; **-rinde,** *f.* tanbark.

Lokal, *n.* locality, place, tavern, shop; **-empfindlichkeit,** *f.* local sensitiveness; **-ertragstafel,** *f.* local yield table; **-farbe,** *f.* natural color.

lokalisieren, to localize.

Lokal-wirkung, *f.* local action or effect.

Lokomobile, *n.* traction engine, portable engine.

Lokomotive, *f.* locomotive.

Lolchgräser, *n.pl.* Loliae (darnel).

Longitudinalschwingung, *f.* longitudinal oscillation.

Loofafasern, *f.pl.* luffa (loofah) fibers.

lopotrich, lophotrichic.

Lorbeer, *m.* laurel, bay; **-baum,** *m.* laurel; **-blatt,** *n.* laurel (bay) leaf.

Lorbeere, *f.* berry of the laurel tree.

Lorbeer-gewächse, *n.pl.* Lauraceae; **-kampher,** *m.* laurin; **-kraut,** *n.* spurge laurel; **-öl,** *n.* laurel oil; **-rose,** *f.* oleander; **-spiritus,** *m.* bay rum.

Los, *n.*-e, lot, share, portion, fate, destiny, prize.

los, loose, free; **was ist los,** what is up, what is going on; **es ist etwas los,** something (important) in going on; **ich bin es los,** I am rid of it; **-werden,** to get rid of.

lösbar, soluble, dissoluble, resolvable.

Lösbarkeit, *f.* (dis)solubility.

Losbaum, *m.* Clerodendron.

losblättern, to exfoliate.

losch (löschen), put out.

Lösch-arbeit, *f.* unloading, charcoal fining process; **-blatt,** *n.*-̈er, (sheet of) blotting paper.

Lösche, *f.* charcoal (dust), coal dust, slack, cinder, clinker.

löschen, to extinguish, liquidate, quench, slake (lime), blot, cancel, discharge, unload, clear, go out.

Löscher, *m.* extinguisher, quencher, unloader.

Lösch-kalk, *m.* quicklime, slaked lime; **-kohle,** *f.* quenched charcoal; **-papier,** *n.* blotting paper.

Löschung, *f.* extinguishing, canceling.

Löschwasser, *n.* quenching (tempering) water.

losdrücken, to push off, fire off.

lose, loose, slack, movable.

lösekräftig, strongly solvent.

Lösemittel, *n.* solvent.

lösen, to dissolve, solve, loosen, relax, untie, detach, release, redeem, fire (a gun), make (money), get loose, cancel.

lösend, dissolving, solvent, expectorant, purgative.

Löse-vermögen, *n.* dissolving power; **-wirkung,** *f.* dissolving (solvent) action.

los-gehen, to become loose, come (go) off; **-gelöst** (loslösen), detached; **-hieb,** *m.* severance, cutting; **-kitten,** detach, unseal.

Losgehen, *n.* deflagration, explosion; **-verspätetes** ∼, delayed explosion, hangfire; **vorzeitiges** ∼, premature explosion or deflagration.

loslassen, to let loose, release.

löslich, soluble.

Löslichkeit, *f.* solubility.

Löslichkeits-beeinflussung, *f.* influencing solubility; **-bestimmung,** *f.* solubility determination; **-produkt,** *n.* solubility product; **-steigerung,** *f.* increasing solubility; **-verhältnis,** *n.* ratio of solubility; **-verminderung,** *f.* decreasing solubility; **-zahl,** *f.* dilution value, solubility value.

Löslichmachung, *f.* rendering soluble.

los-lösen, to set free, liberate, separate, untie, detach; **-lösung,** *f.* freeing, releasing, dissociation, separation; **-löten,** unsolder; **-platzen,** to explode, burst out; **-reissen,** to tear off or away; **-ringen, sich** ∼, to free oneself.

Löss, *m.* loess.

lossagen, to renounce.

Lössboden, *m.* loess.

Losscheibe, *f.* idler pulley.

los-sprechen, to release, acquit; **-sprengen,** to blast loose, burst off; **-trennen,** to separate, sever, tear apart, unstitch.

Losschnellende (Pflanzen), *f.pl.* Explodiflorae.

Lostvergiftete, *m.* person poisoned by Lost (mustard) gas.

Losung, *f.* casting of lots, excrement, droppings, watchword, signal, alarm.

Lösung, *f.* solution, discharge, loosening.

Lösungs-benzol, *n.* solvent benzol, a distillate containing alkylated benzenes; **-erscheinung,** *f.* phenomenon of solution; **-fähig,** capable of solution; **-fähigkeit,** *f.* dissolving capacity; **-flüssigkeit,** *f.* solvent liquid, solvent; **-koeffizient,** *m.* coefficient of solubility; **-mittel,** *n.* solvent.

Lösungs-stärke, *f.* strength of solution; **-tension,** *f.* solution tension; **-theorie,** *f.* theory of solution; **-vermögen,** *n.* dissolving power; **-wärme,** *f.* heat of solution; **-wasser,** *n.* solvent water.

Lot, *n.* solder, plummet, plumb, a weight (now 10 grams), perpendicular (line).

Löt-apparat, *m.* soldering apparatus.

lötbar, solderable.

Lötblei, *n.* lead solder; **-brenner,** *m.* soldering burner, gas blowpipe.

Löte, *f.* solder, soldering.

loten, to plumb, sound.

löten, to solder, braze, agglutinate.

Löten, *n.* soldering, brazing.

Lötflamme, *f.* blowpipe flame.

Lotgang, *m.* vertical gallery (beetles).

lötig, fine, pure, weighing half an ounce or ten grams (of ore).

Lötigkeit, *f.* fineness (of silver).

Löt-kolben, *m.* soldering (bit) iron; **-lampe,** *f.* soldering torch; **-material,** *n.* soldering material; **-metall,** *n.* soldering metal; **-mittel,** *n.* solder.

lot-recht, perpendicular, vertical; **-richtung,** *f.* perpendicular direction.

Lötrohr, *n.* blowpipe; **-analyse,** *f.* blowpipe analysis; **-beschlag,** *m.* encrustation on charcoal (coating) before the blowpipe; **-flamme,** *f.* blowpipe flame; **-gebläse,** *n.* bellows blowpipe, blast lamp; **-probe,** *f.* blowpipe test; **-versuch,** *m.* blowpipe (experiment) test.

Löt-salz, *n.* soldering salt; **-säure,** *f.* soldering acid; **-stelle,** *f.* soldered place.

Lotte, *f.* ball, bloom of steel.

Lötung, *f.* soldering, agglutination, adhesion.

Lotus-blume, *f.* Nelumbo; **-pflaume,** *f.* Diospyros.

Löt-wasser, *n.* soldering fluid; **-zinn,** *n.* soldering tin.

Loupe, *f.* magnifying glass.

Löwe, *m.* lion.

Löwenmaul, *n.* snapdragon (Antirrhinum).

Löwenzahn, *m.* dandelion; **-bitter,** *n.* taraxacin; **-wurzel,** *f.* dandelion root.

Loxachina, *f.* pale bark.

Luch, *n.* marsh bog.

Luchs, *m.* lynx.

Lücke, *f.* gap, void, interstice, space, lacuna, blank, deficit, deficiency.

Lückenbindung, *n.* unsaturated linkage.

lückenhaft, having gaps, meager, defective, fragmentary, interrupted, broken, incomplete.

Lücken-kollenchym, *n.* tubular collenchyma; **-los,** complete, unbroken, uninterrupted, consistent; **-parenchym,** *n.* spongy parenchyma.

lückig, porous, honeycombed.

lud (laden), invited, loaded.

Luder, *n.* carrion.

Luft, *f.=e,* air, atmosphere; **-abschluss,** *m.* exclusion of air; **-abzug,** *m.* air exhaust; **-ähnlich,** gaseous; **-artig,** gaseous, aeriform; **-atmend,** air breathing; **-auftrieb,** *m.* air buoyancy, distension, swelling; **-ausdehnungsmaschine,** *f.* hot-air engine; **-ausschluss,** *m.* exclusion of air; **-ausströmung,** *f.* passage or outlet of air.

Luft-austausch, *m.* exchange of air; **-bad,** *n.=er,* air bath; **-ballon,** *m.* air balloon; **-befeuchter,** *m.* air moistener; **-behälter,** *m.* air chamber, lungs; **-beschaffenheit,** *f.* condition of the air; **-beständig,** stable in air, not affected by air; **-beständigkeit,** *f.* resistance to atmospheric action, stability in air; **-bestandteil,** *m.-e,* constituent of air; **-bewegung,** *f.* flow of air.

Luft-bläschen, *n.* (small) air bubble; **-blase,** *f.* air (bubble) bladder, vesicle; **-dicht,** airtight, airproof, hermetical(ly); **-dichtheit,** *f.* airtightness, impermeability to air; **-dichtigkeit,** *f.* atmospheric density; **-dichtschliessend,** forming an airtight seal, hermetic; **-druck,** *m.* atmospheric (barometric) pressure; **-druckgang,** *m.* course of amospheric (air) pressure; **-druckmesser,** *m.* barometer; **-druckpumpe,** *f.* pneumatic pump, air compressor.

Luft-druckverteilung, *f.* distribution of atmospheric (air) pressure; **-durchlässig-keit,** perviousness to air, porousness; **-echt,** fast to air or atmospheric influences; **-eintritt,** *m.* entrance of air; **-einwirkung,** *f.* action or effect of air; **-empfindlich,** sensitive to air.

lüften, to air, aerate, ventilate, weather, raise.

Luft-entkeimung, *f.* sterilization of the air; **-entstäubung,** *f.* removal of dust from the air; **-entzündlich,** inflammable in contact with air.

Lüfter, *m.* ventilator.

Luft-erhitzer, *m.* air heater; **-erscheinung,** *f.* atmospheric phenomenon; **-fahrt,** *f.* balloon ascent, airplane trip; **-fahrzeug,** *n.* aircraft; **-feuchtigkeit,** *f.* atmospheric moisture or humidity; **-filter,** *n.* air filter; **-flasche,** *f.* float (of Siphonophora), pneumatocyst; **-förderung,** *f.* transport or displacement of air; **-förmig,** gaseous, aeriform; **-führend,** air-containing.

Luft-gang, *m.* air canal; **-gas,** *n.* air gas; **-gefäss,** *n.*-e, air vessel; **-gefüllt,** filled with air, pneumatic; **-gehalt,** *m.* air content; **-gekühlt,** air-cooled; **-gütemesser,** *m.* eudiometer; **-haltig,** containing air; **-heizung,** *f.* hot-air heating; **-höhle,** *f.* air cavity; **-hülle,** *f.* atmosphere.

luftig, aerial, airy, gaseous, flighty, light, voluminous, windy.

Luft-inhalt, *m.* volume of air, contents of air; **-ion,** *n.* atmospheric ion; **-kalk,** *m.* air-hardening lime, gypsum; **-kammer,** *f.* air chamber, pneumatophore, air canal, float; **-kanal,** *m.* air canal, trachea, air duct; **-kessel,** *m.* air reservoir; **-keimer,** *m.pl.* Pneumobrachia; **-knochen,** *m.* air (pneumatic) bone; **-knolle,** *f.* aerial tuber; **-kraftmaschine,** *f.* hot-air engine.

Luft-kreis, *m.*-e, atmosphere; **-kühler,** *m.* air cooler; **-kühlung,** *f.* air cooling; **-lack,** *m.* airproof varnish; **-leer,** exhausted, void (of air); **-leere,** *f.* vacuum, air exhaustion.

luftleer, vacuum; **luftleerer Raum,** *m.* vacuum (space).

luft-leitend, air-conducting; **-loch,** *n.* air (vent) hole; **-lücke,** *f.* air space; **-mangel,** *n.* lack of air; **-masse,** *f.* body (mass) of air; **-menge,** *f.* amount of air; **-messer,** *m.* aerometer; **-molekül,** *n.* air molecule; **-mortel,** *m.* air mortar, lime mortar;

-mycel, *n.* aerial mycelium; **-nitrit,** *n.* atmospheric nitrogen.

Luft-pflanze, *f.* epiphyte; **-pilz,** organism in the air; **-prüfer,** *m.* air tester; **-pumpe,** *f.* air pump; **-raum,** *m.* air space or cavity; **-reibung,** *f.* friction of the air; **-reinigend,** purifying the air; **-reiniger,** *m.* air purifier; **-rohr,** *n.* vent pipe; **-röhre,** *f.* air (tube) pipe, windpipe, trachea.

Luftröhren-ast, *m.* bronchus; **-deckel,** *m.* epiglottis; **-entzündung,** *f.* bronchitis; **-katarrh,** *m.* tracheal catarrh; **-knorpel,** *m.* tracheal (ligament) cartilage; **-kopf,** *m.* larynx; **-spalt,** *m.* glottis.

Luft-rohrflamme, *f.* blowpipe flame; **-rück-stand,** *m.* residual atmosphere; **-sack,** *m.* air sac; **-sättigung,** *f.* saturation of the air; **-sauerstoff,** *m.* atmospheric oxygen; **-saugapparat,** *m.* **-sauger,** *m.* aspirator; **-säule,** *f.* air column; **-säure,** *g.* carbonic acid; **-schicht,** *f.* layer (film) of air; **-schiff,** *n.* airship.

Luft-schiffer, *m.* aeronaut; **-schlag,** *m.* petard; **-schöpfen,** *n.* respiration; **-schraube,** *f.* propeller; **-schutz,** *m.* air defense; **-schutzgerätschaften,** *f.pl.* equipment for air-raid protection; **-schwärmer,** *m.* serpent; **-schwebergesellschaften,** *f.pl.* (aero) plankton; **-spalte,** *f.* air chamber; **-spiegelung,** *f.* mirage; **-stickstoff,** *m.* atmospheric nitrogen.

Luft-störung, *f.* static; **-strecke,** *f.* air travel; **-strom,** *m.* air current; **-strömung,** *f.* current of air; **-teilchen,** *n.* air particle; **-tier,** *n.* animal of the air.

Luft-trennung, *f.* separation of air; **-trocken,** air-dry, air-dried; **-trockengewicht,** *n.* air-dry weight; **-trocknen,** to dry in air, air-condition, air-dry; **-trocknung,** *f.* air-drying; **-überschuss,** *m.* excess air.

Lüftung, *f.* airing, ventilation, aeration

Luft-untersuchung, *f.* air (atmospheric) research, examination of the air; **-ver-dichter,** *m.* air compressor; **-verdichtung,** *f.* air compression; **-verdorben,** weathered, deteriorated; **-verdrängung,** *f.* displacement of air; **-verdünnung,** *f.* rarefaction of air; **-versetzung,** *f.* shifting of air, transport of air; **-volumen,** *n.* volume of air; **-waage,** *f.* aerometer; **-wechsel,** *m.* ventilation.

Luft-weg, *m.*-e, air (way), passage, respiratory tract; **-welle,** *f.* air wave; **-wider-stand,** *m.* air resistance; **-wirbel,** *m.* vortex, whirl; **-wirkung,** *f.* atmospheric effect; **-wurzel,** *f.* aerial root; **-ziegel,** *m.* air-dried brick; **-zufluss,** *m.* air supply, influx of air; **-zufuhr,** *f.* air supply; **-zu-führung,** *f.* supply of air.

Luft-zug, *m.*ᴗe, draft, (air) current; **-zünder,** *m.* pyrophorus; **-zurichtung,** *f.* airconditioning.

Luftzutritt, *m.* access of air; **unter** ∼, with access of air.

Luftzwischenraum, *m.*ᴗe, air gap.

lugen, to look out.

lügen, to (tell a) lie, deceive, be affected.

Luke, *f.* trap door, hatch.

lullen, to lull (to sleep).

Lumen, *n.* lumen.

Luminal, *n.* phenobarbital.

Lumpen, *m.*-, rag, tatter; **-brei,** *m.* first stuff, pulp (paper); **-wolf,** *m.* rag-tearing machine, devil; **-wolle,** *f.* shoddy; **-zucker,** *m.* titler (coarse loaf sugar).

Lunge, *f.* lung, lungs.

Lungen-abschnitt, *m.* section of the lung; **-arterie,** *f.* pulmonary artery; **-arterienklappe,** *f.* pulmonary valve; **-ast,** *m.* pulmonary branch; **-atmer,** *m.* pulmonary breather; **-atmung,** *f.* pulmonary respiration; **-band,** *n.* ligament of the lung; **-bläschen,** *n.* lung vesicle; **-blase,** *f.* pulmonary vesicle; **-blatt,** *n.* pulmonary lobe.

Lungen-blutader, *f.* pulmonary vein; **-entzündung,** *f.* pneumonia; **-fell,** *n.* pleura pulmonalis, visceral pleura; **-fellentzündung,** *f.* (pulmonary) pleurisy, inflammation of visceral pleura; **-flügel,** *m.* pulmonary lobe; **-gefäss,** *n.* pulmonary vessel; **-geflecht,** *n.* pulmonary plexus; **gerüst,** *n.* lung stroma; **-herz,** *n.* right side of the heart.

Lungen-kammer, *f.* right ventricle; **-komplikation,** *f.* complication in the lungs; **-kraut,** *n.* lungwort (Pulmonaria); **-kreislauf,** *m.* pulmonary circulation; **-lappen,** *m.* lobe of the lung; **-leidende,** *m.* tubercular person; **-leiste,** *f.* pulmonary ridge; **-nervenstamm,** *m.* pulmonary vein trunk; **-pfeifchen,** *n.pl.* parabronchi.

Lungen-pfeifer, *m.* roarer, whistler (horse); **-pforte,** *f.* hilum of lung; **-rand,** *m.* margin of the lung; **-sack,** *m.* pulmonary sac; **-schädigend,** harmful to the lungs; **-schnecken,** *f.pl.* Pulmonata, air-breathing snails; **-schützer,** *m.* respirator, lung protector; **-schwindsucht,** *f.* tuberculosis; **-spitze,** *f.* apex of the lung; **-sucht,** *f.* (pulmonary) consumption; **-tuberkel,** *f.* lung tubercle; **-vene,** *f.* pulmonary vein; **-venenblutung,** *f.* hemorrhage of the lungs.

lungern, to loiter.

Lunker, *n.* pipe, cavity.

lunkern, to pipe, develop cavities.

Lunte, *f.* slow match, fuse, slubbing, raving.

Lupe, *f.* magnifying glass.

Lupine, *f.* lupine.

Luppe, *f.* loop, lump (iron), ore bloom.

Luppen-frischhütte, *f.* bloomery; **-stahl,** *m.* bloom steel.

Lupulinsäure, *f.* lupulinic (lupulic) acid.

Lupus, *m.* lupus.

Lurche, *m.pl.* Anura.

Lurchfische, *m.pl.* lungfish (Dipnoi).

Lust, *f.* pleasure, joy, mirth, desire, blight, inclination, lust; **-gas,** *n.* laughing gas (nitrous oxide).

lustig, gay, joyous, merry, jolly, amusing, funny.

lustlos, inactive (of a market).

lustrieren, to luster.

Lust-seuche, *f.* syphilis; **-spiel,** *n.* comedy.

Luteo-kobaltchlorid, *n.* luteocobaltic chloride.

Lutidinsäure, *f.* lutidinic acid.

lutieren, to lute.

Lutte, *f.* ventilating tube, vent tube.

Lutter, *m.* low wine, singlings; **-blase,** *f.* low-wine still.

luttern, to distill low wine.

Luxus, *m.* luxury.

luzerne, *f.* Luzernerklee, *m.* lucerne, alfalfa (*Medicago sativa*).

Lymph-adenitis, *f.* lymphadenitis; **-angitis,** *f.* lymphangitis; **-bahn,** *f.* lymph tract; **-bildung,** *f.* formation of lymph; **-drüse,** *f.* lymphatic gland; **-drüsenpaket,** *n.* lymphatic vessel.

Lymphe, *f.* lymph, vaccine.

Lymph-gefäss, *n.* lymphatic vessel; **-gefässtamm,** *m.* lymphatic trunk; **-knoten,** *m.* lymphatic ganglion; **-körperchen,** *n.* leucocyte, lymph corpuscle; **-röhre,** *f.* lymph canal; **-strom,** *m.* lymphatic current.

Lyse, *f.* lysis.

Lysol, *n.* lysol.

Lyssa, *f.* rabies; **-virus,** *m.* rabies virus.

lytisch, lytic, disintegrating.

M

Maal, *n.* spot, mole, mark.

Mäander, *m.* meander.

macerieren, to macerate.

Machart, *f.*-en, pattern, fashion, type.

Mache, *f.* manufacture, make, workmanship; **-einheit,** *f.* Mache unit (of radioactive substances).

machen, to make, do, create, form, erect, cause, procure, get, deal, trade, perform, manufacture, construct; **Anspruch auf etwas ~,** to lay claim to something; **sich ~,** to happen, come about, appear; **sich aus der Sache etwas ~,** to attach importance to the matter, **sich an etwas ~,** to apply oneself to.

Macherei, *f.* making, make, bungling.

Macht, *f.*-̈e, power, might, force, authority; **-haber,** *m.* authority.

mächtig, (*gen.*) powerful, mighty, immense, strong, huge, big, large, thick, ~ **sein,** to be master of, have command of.

Mächtigkeit, *f.* mightiness, thickness, size, power, depth, extent.

machtlos, powerless, impotent, weak.

Machwerk, *n.* inferior (poor) work, bungling work.

Macis, *f.* mace; **-öl,** *n.* oil of mace.

Madarwurzel, *f.* mudar root.

Mädchen, *n.*-, girl, maid.

Made, *f.* maggot, mite.

Madenwurm, *m.* common pinworm.

madig, maggoty, grubby, wormy.

Madreporenplatte, *f.* madreporic plate (of starfish).

Mafuratalg, *m.* mafura tallow.

mafurisch, mafura (from kernels of *Trichilia emetica*); **mafurische Butter,** *f.* mafura (butter) tallow.

mag (mögen), likes to, may.

Magazin, *n.* warehouse, store, depot.

Magdalarot, *n.* Magdala red.

Magen, *m.*-, stomach, maw, gizzard; **-abschnitt,** *m.* part or section of stomach, centrogaster; **-arznei,** *f.* stomachic; **-ausgang,** *m.* outlet of stomach, pyloris; **-bewegung,** *f.* gastric movement; **-blindsack,** *m.* gastric caecum; **-brei,** *m.* chyme; **-bremse,** *f.* horse botfly.

Magen-brennen, *n.* pyrosis; **-darm,** *m.* intestine, archenteron; **-drüse,** *f.* gastric

gland; **-ebene,** *f.* gastral plane; **-eingang,** *m.* inlet of stomach, cardia; **-entzündung,** *f.* gastritis; **-falte,** *f.* mesenteric septum; **-flüssigkeit,** *f.* gastric fluid.

Magen-gefäss, *n.* gastric vessel; **-geflecht,** *n.* gastric plexus; **-gegend,** *f.* gastric region, epigastrium; **-grimmdarmnetz,** *n.* gastrocolic omentum; **-grube,** *f.* pit of the stomach; **-grund,** *m.* fundus ventriculi; **-haut,** *f.* coat (membrane) of the stomach; **-höhle,** *f.* cavity of the stomach, paragaster; **-inhalt,** *m.* contents of the stomach.

Magen-lab, *n.* rennet; **-labdrüse,** *f.* gastric peptic gland; **-lähmung,** *f.* paralysis of stomach; **-lipase,** *f.* pepsin; **-lymphdrüse,** *f.* lymphatic gland; **-mittel,** *n.* stomachic; **-mund,** *m.* esophageal orifice, cardia; **-muskel,** *m.* muscle of the stomach.

Magen-pförtner, *m.* pylorus; **-pförtnerklappe,** *f.* pyloric sphincter or valve; **-rinne,** *f.* gastral furrow; **-rohr,** *n.* esophagus; **-saft,** *m.* gastric juice; **-schlauch,** *m.* gastric tube, polypite; **-schleimhaut,** *f.* mucous membrane of stomach, gastric mucosa; **-schlund,** *m.* esophagus; **-schnitt,** *m.* gastrotomy; **-schwäche,** *f.* dyspepsia.

Magen-stärkend, stomachic; **-stärkungsmittel,** *n.* stomachic; **-stein,** *m.* gastric concretion; **-stiel,** *m.* manubrium; **-tasche,** *f.* gastric pouch (mesentery); **-verdauung,** *f.* gastric digestion; **-wand,** *f.* wall of the stomach; **-zwerchfellband,** *n.* gastrophrenic ligament; **-zwölffingerdarm,** *m.* gastroduodenum.

mager, lean, thin, slender, meager, frugal, poor, sterile; **magerer Lack,** *m.* light varnish, low-grade varnish; **mageres Öl,** mineral oil.

Mager-beton, *m.* lean concrete; **-kalk,** *m.* lime containing magnesia salts.

Magerkeit, *f.* leanness, meagerness, thinness.

Magerkeitsanzeiger, *m.* indicator of lime exhaustion in soil.

Mager-kohle, *f.* noncoking coal, semibituminous coal; **-matte,** *f.* poor (unfertile) meadow; **-milch,** *f.* skim milk.

magern, to make (become, grow) lean, thin, or poor.

Magerungsmittel, *n.* thinning material, lean clay.

Magerwiese, *f.* unfertile or sparse meadow.

magisch, magic(al).

Magnesia-gehalt, *m.* magnesia content; **-glimmer,** *m.* magnesium mica; **-haltig,** containing magnesia, magnesian; **-hydrat,** *n.* magnesium hydroxide; **-milch,** *f.* milk of magnesia; **-mischung,** *f.* magnesia mixture; **-salz,** *n.* magnesia salt.

Magnesit-spat, *m.* magnesite; **-stein,** *m.* magnesite brick.

Magnesium, *n.* magnesium; **-haltig,** containing magnesium; **-jodid,** *n.* magnesium iodide; **-pulver,** *n.* magnesium powder; **-sulfat,** *n.* magnesium sulphate; **-verbindung,** *f.* magnesium compound.

Magnet, *m.*-e, magnet; **-eisenerz,** *n.* magnetite.

magnetisch, magnetic.

magnetisier-bar, -fähig, magnetizable.

Magnetismus, *m.* magnetism.

magnetisieren, to magnetize.

Magnet-nadel, *f.*-n, magnetic (compass) needle; **-stab,** *m.* magnetic bar, bar magnet; **-stein,** *m.* magnetic iron ore, lodestone.

Magnolie, *f.* magnolia.

Magsamen, *m.* poppy seed.

Mahagoni, *n.* mahogany; **-baum,** *m.* mahogany tree; **-holz,** *n.* mahogany.

Mahd, *f.* mowing, hay crop.

mähen, to mow.

Mahl, *n.* meal, mark, mole.

mahlen, to grind, mill, crush, beat (paper manufacturing).

Mahl-feinheit, *f.* fineness of grinding; **-fläche,** *f.* rubbing surface, crown of molar tooth; **-gut,** *n.* material to be ground; **-korn,** *n.* grist; **-rückstand,** *m.* grinding residue.

Mahlungsgrad, *m.* (pulp) freeness; **-prüfer,** *m.* beaten-stuff tester, freeness tester.

Mahl-werk, *n.* grinder, grinding mill; **-zahn,** *m.* molar; **-zeit,** *f₂* meal, repast.

Mähmaschine, *f.* mower.

mahnen, to remind, urge, exhort, dun.

Mahonie, *f.* Berberis.

Mai, *m.* May; **-baum,** *m.* birch, pole; **-blume,** *f.* lily of the valley; **-fisch,** *m.* shad; **-glöckchen,** *n.* lily of the valley; **-käfer,** *m.* cockchafer (*Melolontha vulgaris*); **-kätzchen,** *n.* catkin (birches); **-rübe,** *f.* early garden turnip.

Mais, *m.* maize, Indian corn; **-brand,** *m.* corn smut; **-branntwein,** *m.* whisky from maize.

Maisch-apparat, *m.*-e, mashing apparatus; **-bottich,** *m.* mash (mashing) tub.

Maische, *f.* mash; **weingare** ∼, (distilling) mash.

maischen, to mash.

Maisch-gitter, *n.* stirrer, rake (in brewing); **-kessel,** *m.* mash copper; **-kolonne,** *f.* beer still; **-pfanne,** *f.* mash copper.

Maischung, *f.* mashing, mash.

Maisch-ventil, *f.* grains (trap) valve; **-wasser,** *n.* mash liquor; **-würze,** *f.* mash wort.

Mais-dibbler, *m.* corn planter; **-geist,** *m.* corn spirit; **-kleber,** *m.* zein(e); **-kolben,** *m.* corncob; **-krankheit,** *f.* pellagra, maize poisoning; **-mehl,** *n.* Indian (corn) meal; **-mehlkleber,** *m.* zein; **-öl,** *n.* maize oil; **-pistille,** *n.pl.* corn silk, zea; **-stärke,** *f.* maize starch, cornstarch.

Mai-trank, *m.* wine seasoned with woodruff; **-trieb,** *m.* early growth; **-wein,** *m.* wine seasoned with woodruff.

Marjoran, *m.* marjoram.

majorenn, of age.

makadamisieren, to macadamize.

Makadamstrasse, *f.* macadam road.

Makel, *m.* stain, spot, blemish, flaw.

Maker, *m.* maul, sledge.

Makler, Mäkler, *m.* broker, agent, jobber, faultfinder.

Makrele, *f.* mackerel.

Makroanalyse, *f.* macroanalysis.

Makrone, *f.* macaroon.

makroskopisch, macroscopic.

Makulatur, *f.* waste(paper) sheets.

Mal, *n.*-e, time, mark, spot, mole, sign, token, boundary, (ptera)stigma; **ein** ∼, once.

mal, time(s), once, just.

Malachit-grün, *n.* malachite green; **-grünagar,** *m.* malachite-green agar; **-grünnährboden,** *m.* malachite-green medium (nutrient medium); **-kiesel,** *m.* chrysocolla.

Malakkanuss, *f.* Malacca bean, marking nut.

Malaria, *f.* malaria.

malaxieren, to malaxate, knead, soften.

Malbaum, *m.* boundary tree.

Malein-aldehyd, *n.* maleic aldehyde; **-säure,** *f.* maleic acid.

malen, to paint, sketch, depict, picture.

Maler, *m.* painter, artist.

Malerei, *f.* painting (art).

Maler-farbe, *f.* painter's color; **-firnis,** *m.* painter's varnish; **-gold,** *n.* painter's gold, ormolu.

malerisch, picturesque.

Maler-kolik, painter's colic, plumbism; **-krankheit,** *f.* painter's colic, plumbism; **-leinwand,** *f.* canvas; **-tuch,** *n.* canvas.

Mallein, *n.* mallein; **-dosis,** *f.* dosage of mallein; **-impfung,** *f.* injection of mallein; **-reaktion,** *f.* mallein reaction.

Malleus, *m.* glanders; **-knoten, m.** glanders nodule.

malnehmen, to multiply.

malon-sauer, malonate of; **-säure,** *f.* malonic acid.

Malve, *f.* mallow.

Malven-farbe, *f.* mauve; **-kraut,** *n.* mallow.

Malz, *n.* malt; **-aufguss,** *m.* infusion of malt; **-auszug,** *m.* malt extract; **-bottich,** *m.* malt vat; **-darre,** *f.* malt kiln; **-eiweiss,** *n.* diastase, malt protein.

malzen, mälzen, to (make) malt.

Mälzer, *m.* maltman.

Mälzerei, *f.* malting, malthouse.

Malz-essig, *m.* malt vinegar; **-extrakt,** *m.* malt extract; **-fabrik,** *f.* malthouse, malting; **-gerste,** *f.* malting barley; **-häufen,** *n.* couching, **-keime,** *m.pl.* sprouts of malt; **-probe,** *f.* malt (test) testing; **-schrot,** *n.* crushed malt, malt grist; **-stärke,** *f.* malt starch; **-tenne,** *f.* malt floor; **-treber,** *pl.* grains, spent malt.

Mälzung, *f.* malting.

Mälzungsschwund, *m.* malting shrinkage.

Malzzucker, *m.* malt sugar, maltose.

Mammutsbaum, *m.* giant sequoia, mammoth tree (*Sequoia gigantea*).

man, (some)one, a person, they, somebody, people, we, you, only.

manch (-er, -e, -es) many a, many a one, some.

mancherlei, various, of several sorts.

manches, many a thing, many things.

manchmal, sometimes, often.

Mandarindruck, *m.* mandarining.

Mandarine, *f.* mandarin (*Citrus nobilis*).

Mandel, *f.-n,* almond, tonsil, (set of) fifteen, shock (of sheaves), geode; **-artig,** almond-like, amygdaline; **-baum,** *m.* almond tree (*Prunus amygdalus*); **-blüte,** *f.* almond blossom; **-bräune,** *f.* quinsy; **-drüse,** *f.* tonsil; **-entzündung,** *f.* tonsillitis; **-förmig,**

almond-shaped, amygdaloid; **-füllung,** *f.* amygdaloidal infillings; **-kern,** *m.* almond kernel.

Mandel-milch, *f.* emulsion of almond; **-säure,** *f.* mandelic acid; **-säureamid,** *n.* mandelamide; **-seife,** *f.* almond soap; **-stein,** *m.* amygdaloid, tonsillar (calculus) concretion.

Mangan, *n.* manganese; **-alaun,** *m.* manganese alum; **-bister,** *m.* manganese (bister) brown; **-blende,** *f.* alabandite; **-chlorid,** *n.* manganic chloride; **-chlorür,** *n.* manganous chloride; **-dioxyd,** *n.* manganese dioxide; **-eisen,** *n.* ferromanganese; **-eisenstein,** *m.* triplite; **-erz,** *n.* manganese ore.

Mangan-gehalt, *m.* manganese content; **-glanz,** *m.* alabandite; **-granat,** *m.* manganese garnet, spessartite; **-haltig,** manganiferous.

Manganichlorid, *n.* manganic chloride.

manganig, manganous; **-sauer,** manganite of; **-säure,** *f.* manganous acid.

Mangani-hydroxyd, *n.* manganic hydroxide; **-verbindung,** *f.* manganic compound.

Mangan-jodür, *n.* manganous iodide; **-kiesel,** *m.* rhodonite, manganiferous quartzite; **-legierung,** *f.* manganese alloy.

Mangano-chlorid, *n.* manganous chloride; **-ferrum,** *n.* ferromanganese; **-ion,** *n.* manganous ion; **-verbindung,** *f.* manganous compound.

Manganoxyd, *n.* manganese (manganic) oxide.

Manganoxydhydrat, *n.* manganic hydroxide.

Manganoxydul, *n.* manganous oxide; **-hydrat,** *n.* manganous hydroxide; **-oxyd,** *n.* mangano-manganic oxide.

Mangan-oxydverbindung, *f.* manganic compound; **-pecherz,** *n.* triplite; **-säure,** *f.* manganic acid; **-säureanhydrid,** *n.* manganic anhydride; **-schaum,** *m.* bog manganese; **-spat,** *m.* rhodochrosite; **-stahl,** *m.* manganese steel; **-sulfür,** *n.* manganous sulphide; **-superoxyd,** *n.* manganese (dioxide) peroxide; **-verbindung,** *f.* manganese compound; **-vitriol,** *m.* manganese (sulphate) vitriol.

Mangel, *m.∴,* defect, fault, flaw, lack, want. scarcity, deficiency, distress; **-haft,** defective, deficient, imperfect, incomplete.

mangeln, (*dat.*) to be (deficient) wanting, lack, mangle.

mangels, in default of, for want of.

Mangfutter, *n.* mixed grain.

Mangold, *m.* beet(root), mangel-wurzel, stock beet.

Manie, *f.* mania.

Manier, *f.* manner, fashion, mode.

Manilahanf, *m.* Manila (Menado, Siam) hemp (*Musatextilis*).

manipulieren, to manipulate.

Manko, *n.* deficiency, deficit, shortage.

Mann, *m.:er,* husband.

Manna-gras, *n.* floating fescue (*Glyceria fluitans*); **-schwaden,** *m.* floating fescue (*Glyceria fluitans*); **-stoff,** *m.* **-zucker,** *m.* mannitol, manna sugar.

mannbar, able to bear fruit, marriageable.

Mannbarkeit, *f.* sexual maturity.

Männchen, *n.* little man, manikin, male.

Mannesreife, *f.* puberty, maturity.

mannig-fach, manifold, various, varied; **-faltig,** manifold, various, varied; **-faltigkeit,** *f.* manifoldness, variety, diversity, multiplicity, number.

Mannit, *n.* mannitol, mannite.

männlich, male, masculine, brave, manly, staminate; **männliche Keimzelle,** *f.* male germ cell, microspore, pollen grain.

Männlichkeitsgen, *n.* gene producing maleness.

Mannloch, *n.* manhole.

Mannozuckersäure, *f.* mannosaccharic acid.

Mannschaft, *f.* men, forces, staff, crew.

Mannschild, *m.* Androsace.

mannshoch, as tall as a man.

Mannstreu, *m.* Eryngium.

Mannweib, *n.* masculine type of woman, virago.

mannweibig, gynandrous (both sexes).

Mannweibigkeit, *f.* hermaphroditism.

Manometer, *m.* pressure gauge.

manometrisch, manometric.

Manöverpulver, *n.* blank-fire powder.

Manschette, *f.* cuff, collar, flap, armilla (frill), sleeve.

Mantel, *m.:,* mantle, pallium, belt, case, sleeve, casing jacket, shell, convex surface, sheet; **-bucht,** *f.* umbo (sinupalliata); **-chimäre,** *f.* periclinal chimera; **-eindruck,** *m.* mantle scar (impression); **-falten,** *f.pl.* mantle (lobes) folds; **-fläche,** *f.* superficies, surface of the mantle or shell; **-geschoss,** *n.* metallic cartridge; **-herz,** *n.* cor villosum; **-höhlenflüssigkeit,** *f.* pallial sinus fluid;

-höhlenkiemen, *f.pl.* the gills of the mantle cavity.

mantel-kiemig, palliobranchiate; **-lappen,** *m.* mantle lobe or lappet; **-linie,** *f.* pallial line; **-narbe,** *f.* mantle scar; **-öffnung,** *f.* pallial aperture; **-rand,** *m.* edge of the mantle; **-raum,** *m.* mantle cavity; **-reibung,** *f.* skin friction; **-rohr,** *n.* casing; **-schicht,** *f.* protective layer.

Mantel-schlitz, *m.* mantle slit; **-sinus,** *m.* pallial sinus; **-spalte,** *f.* mantle slit; **-sprengstoff,** *m.* sheathed explosive; **-tasche,** *f.* posterior transverse cerebral fissure; **-tiere,** *n.pl.* Tunicata; **-wulst,** *f.* mantle swelling.

Manufaktur, *f.* manufacture.

Mappe, *f.* portfolio, case, bag.

Maräne, marane (*Coregonus maraena*).

Marantastärke, *f.* maranta starch, arrowroot.

Märchen, *n.* fairy tale, legend; **-haft,** fabulous, fictitious, legendary.

Marder, *m.* pine marten; **-artig,** martenlike.

Märe, *f.* news, rumor, report, tradition.

Margarine, *f.* margarine; **-butter,** *f.* margarine.

margarinsauer, margarate of; **-säure,** *f.* margaric acid.

Marien-bad, *n.:er,* water bath; **-distel,** *f.* milk thistle (*Silybum marianum*); **-flachs,** *m.* toadflax (*Linaria*); **-glas,** *n.* selenite, mica; **-gras,** *n.* Hierochloa, Phalaris; **-käfer,** *m.pl.* ladybirds (Coccinellidae).

marinieren, to marinate, pickle.

Marine, *f.* navy; **-leim,** *m.* marine glue.

Mark, *f.* mark (German currency), boundary.

Mark, *n.* marrow, pith, pulp, core, medulla; verlängertes ∼, medulla oblongata.

markant, striking, characteristic, well cut.

markartig, marrowlike, myeloid, pithlike, medullary.

Markasitglanz, *m.* tetradymite.

Mark-bildung, *f.* myelinization; **-blatt,** *n.* medullary lamina; **-bogen,** *m.* fornix, medullary (cerebral) triangle; **-brücke,** *f.* branch gap; **-bündel,** *n.* medullary fascicle, pith bundle.

Marke, *f.* mark, stamp, token, sort, quality, brand.

Markenfaden, *m.* identification thread (in fuse or electric cable).

Markette, *f.* virgin wax in cake form.

Mark-fleck, *m.* medullary spot, pith fleck; **-flüssigkeit,** *f.* spinal fluid; **-fortsatz,** *m.* cerebellar peduncle; **-furche,** *f.* medullary groove; **-haltig,** medullated; **-haut,** *f.* endosteum; **-höhle,** *f.* pith cavity, medullary (marrow) cavity; **-holz,** *n.* pithy wood; **-hügel,** *m.* corpus mammillare, optic disk.

markieren, to mark, brand, label.

Mark-kanal, *m.* medullary canal; **-kegel,** *m.* medullary cone; **-knopf,** *m.* medulla oblongata; **-knopfschenkel,** *m.* peduncle of cerebellum; **-krebs,** *m.* medullary cancer; **-lager,** *n.* medullary layer; **-lamelle,** *f.* medullary lamina, element of the marrow; **-los,** nonmedullated.

Mark-lücke, *f.* medullary space; **-masse,** *f.* medullary substance; **-plättchen,** *n.* giant cells of bone marrow, element of the marrow; **-raum,** *m.* medullary space; **-rohr,** *n.* medullary canal; **-saft,** *m.* medullary sap; **-scheide,** *f.* pith sheath, medullary (myelin) sheath, boundary, limit.

Mark-scheidenbildung, *f.* myelinization; **-schicht,** *f.* medullary layer, medulla (of lichen thallus); **-segel,** *n.* medullary veil; **-ständig,** medullary; **-stoff,** *m.* medullary substance; **-strahl,** *m.* medullary (pith) ray; **-strahlzelle,** *f.* medullary-ray cell; **-strang,** *m.* medullary cord, medullary fasciculus.

Markt, *m.*ːe, market, trade, fair, business, mart; **auf den** ∼ **bringen,** to put on the market.

markten, to market, bargain.

markt-fähig, marketable; **-gängig,** market (-able), current; **-preis,** *m.* market price; **-reif,** ready for market, marketable; **-tasche,** *f.* market bag; **-zettel,** *m.* market report, list.

Markung, *f.* field (marked off).

Mark-verbindung, *f.* pith connection; **-wald,** *m.* border forest; **-wiederholung,** *f.* pith fleck; **-wulst,** *m.* medullary eminence; **-zapfen,** *m.* medullary cone.

Marmelade, *f.* jam, marmalade.

Marmor, *m.* marble; **-ähnlich,** **-artig,** marblelike, marmoraceous.

marmorieren, to marble, grain, vein, mottle.

Marmor-kalk, *m.* marble lime; **-kiesel,** *m.* a kind of hornstone; **-mehl,** *n.* marble dust; **-papier,** *m.* marbled paper.

marode, exhausted, tired.

Marone, *f.* (sweet) chestnut.

Maroquin, *m.* morocco (leather).

Marsch, *m.*ːe, march (military).

Marsch, *f.* moor, fen, swamp; **-boden,** *m.* marshland, marshy soil, swamp; **-land,** *n.* moorland, marsh; **-ton,** *m.* sea clay.

Marshische Probe, *f.* Marsh test.

Marstall, *m.* stud, stable.

Martinstahl, *m.* Martin steel.

Martitisierung, *f.* conversion of magnetite into martite.

Martiusgelb, *n.* Martius yellow.

März, *m.* March.

Masche, *f.* mesh, interstice, stitch, compartment, number of mesh per square centimeter.

Maschen-gewebe, *n.* retiform tissue; **-grösse,** *f.* size of mesh; **-raum,** *m.* retiform space, meshlike space in spongy tissue; **-weite,** *f.* width of mesh; **-werk,** *n.* network.

maschig, meshed, netted, reticulated.

Maschine, *f.* machine, engine.

maschinell, mechanical(ly), with machinery.

Maschinen-bauer, *m.* machine builder, machinist; **-element,** *n.* machine part; **-fett,** *n.* machine (grease), lubricant; **-gewehr,** *n*; machine gun; **-kunde,** *f.* **-lehre,** *f.* (science of) engineering; **-mässig,** machinelike, mechanical; **-schmiere,** *f.* lubricating grease; **-schrift,** *f.* typewriting; **-torf,** *m.* machine-cut peat; **-werk,** *n.* machinery.

Masel, *f.* scar, mark, spot, rash.

Maser, *f.* speckle, spot, mark, vein, gnarled, streaked or grained wood, burr, knot (of wood); **-bildung,** *f.* gnarl formation; **-holz,** *n.* curled or veined wood.

maserig, speckled, streaked, grained, curled.

Maser-kegel, -knollen, -knoten, *m.* burr.

Masern, *f.pl.* measles, rubeola.

Maserpapier, *n.* speckled paper.

Maserung, *f.* speckling, veining, graining, *f.* periodical flame effect.

Maske, *f.* mask, galeotheca, disguise, pretext.

Maskenblume, *f.* (*Mimulus cardinalis*).

maskieren, to mask, disguise.

mass (messen), measured, was measuring.

Mass, *n.*-e, measure, standard, proportion, dimension, index, degree, manner, rate, extent, size, height, measurement, bounds; **in dem Masse als,** in the same manner as; **alles mit Massen,** everything in moderation; **in hohem Masse,** in a high degree.

very; **in grossem Masse,** to a large extent; **auf Mass,** to size.

Mass-analyse, *f.* volumetric analysis; **-analytisch,** volumetric; **-bürette,** *f.* measuring burette.

Masse, *f.* mass, substance, volume, amount, pulp, paste, composition, bulk, quantity, stock, assets; **-frei,** free of mass.

Masseinheit, *f.* unit of measure.

Masse-kern, *m.* magnetic core. dust core (powder and binder).

Massel, *f.* pig, slab, bloom.

Massen-alter, *n.* volume age; **-analyse,** *f.* volumetric analysis; **-angst,** *f.* mass psychosis, fear of the masses; **-aufnahme,** *f.* estimate of standing crop; **-auftreten,** *n.* epidemic, widespread appearance; **-berechnung,** *f.* gross calculations, mensuration of earthwork; **-ertrag,** *m* volume production, volumetric yield; **-ertragsregelung,** *f.* method of determining yield by volume; **-erzeugung,** *f.* mass production; **-gestein,** *n.* unstratified rock, massive (solid) rock.

Massen-guss, *m.* dry-sand casting; **-haft,** massive, massy, voluminous, numerous, abundant, in a lump; **-kraft,** *f.* force of mass; **-los,** without mass, imaginary; **-mittelpunkt,** *m.* mid-point of the whole, center of gravity; **-moment,** *m.* moment of inertia; **-punkt,** *m.* center of gravity, material point; **-sterben,** *n.* widespread dying off; **-tafel,** *f.* volume table; **-teilchen,** *n.* physical unit, *n.* corpuscle (molecule).

Massen-verhältnis, *n.* relative mass, mass proportion; **-wirkung,** *f.* mass action; **-wirkungsgesetz,** *n.* law of mass action; **-wirtschaft,** *f.* management based on the greatest production; **-wuchs,** *m.* volume increment, growth in yield; **-zucht,** *f.* growing in large quantities; **-zuwachs,** *m.* volume increment, mass accretion, growth in volume.

Masse-schlanm, *m.* body slip; **-schlicker,** *m.* body (slip) paste.

Mass-flasche, *f.* measuring flask; **-flüssigkeit,** *f.* standard solution; **-formel,** *f.* standard formula.

Massgabe, *f.* measure, proportion; **nach ~,** according to, in proportion to.

mass-gebend, determinative, decisive, controlling, authoritative, conclusive, standard; **-gefäss,** *n.* measuring vessel, graduate; **-gerecht,** mathematical, of proper size, true to size; **-holder,** *m.* field maple (*Acer campestre*).

massig, massy, massive, bulky, solid.

mässig, moderate, temperate, reasonable (price).

mässigen, to moderate, temper, restrain, ease.

Mässigkeit, *f.* moderation, temperance.

Mässigung, *f.* moderation.

massiv, massive, solid, unalloyed, clumsy.

Massliebchen, *n.* daisy, oxeye daisy (*Chrysanthemum leucanthemum*).

mass-mässig, by measurement.

Mass-nahme, *f.* precaution, measure, mode of action; **-regel,** *f.* step, measure, expedient; **-röhre,** *f.* measuring tube, graduated tube, burette; **-stab,** *m.* scale, rule, measure, criterion, standard proportion; **-stäblich,** according to scale; **-system,** *n.* system of measurement; **-teil,** *m.* part by measure; **-zahl,** *f.* unit of measurement, scalar number.

Mast, *f.* feeding, fattening, mast.

Mastdarm, *m.* rectum; **-gegend,** *f.* rectal region; **-gekröse,** *n.* mesorectum; **-schleimhaut,** *f.* rectal mucous membrane; **-sitzbeingrube,** *f.* ischiorectal fossa.

mästen, to fatten, feed (well).

Mast-fähigkeit, *f.* fattening capacity; **-feder,** *f.* tail feather.

Mastikation, *f.* mastication, compression (of rubber).

Mastitis, *n.* mastitis.

Mastix, *m.* (gum) mastic; **-firnis,** *m.* mastic varnish; **-harz,** *n.* mastic (resin); **-kitt,** *m.* mastic (cement); **-lösung,** *f.* resin solution.

mastizieren, to masticate, chew.

Mast-jahr, *n.* mast year; **-kraut,** *n.* (Sagina).

Mastnutzung, *f.* pannage.

Mastnutzungsrecht, *n.* right to pannage.

Mastordnung, *f.* pannage regulation.

Mästung, *f.* fatness.

Mastvieh, *n.* fattening cattle.

Masut, *n.* (Russian) fuel oil.

Material, *n.* material, matter, substance, experimental data; **-ertrag,** *n.* yield in material; **-förderung,** *f.* material handling; **-gewinnung,** *f.* recovery or extraction of material.

Materialien, *n.pl.* (raw) materials(s).

Material-prüfung, *f.* testing of materials; **-prüfungsamt,** *n.* laboratory for testing materials; **-vorrat,** *m.* supply of substance; **-waren,** *f.pl.* groceries, drugs.

Materie, *f.* matter. stuff; **-atom,** *n.* atom of matter.

materiell, material (cause).

Materie-teilchen, *n.* particle of matter; **-welle,** *f.* wave of matter.

Mathematik, *f.* mathematics.

mathematisch, mathematical.

Matjeshering, *m.* young or white herring, matie.

Matratze, *f.* mattress.

matrisieren, to damp (paper).

Matrize, *f.* matrix, mold, bottom die, dry mat.

Matrizenuntersatz, *m.* die block.

Matsch, *m.* pulp, squash, mash, slush, mire.

Matt, *n.* dullness, deadness (of surface).

matt, dull, dead, mat, ground (glass), faint, feeble, weak, dull, insipid, dim, flat, exhausted, pasty; **-beize,** *f.* pickle (to give a dull surface); **brenne,** *f.* dull pickling, tarnishing.

Matte, *f.* mat, meadow, matting.

Matt-eisen, *n.* white pig iron; **-farbe,** *f.* matt (deadening) color; **-gelb,** pale-yellow, cream-colored; **-geschliffen,** ground, frosted; **-glanz,** *m.* dull finish; **-glas,** *n.* ground (frosted) glass; **-heit,** *f.* dullness.

mattieren, to dull, tarnish, deaden, give a mat finish to, deluster.

Mattierungsmittel, *n.* delusterant.

Mattigkeit, *f.* exhaustion.

Matt-kohle, *f.* dull or grayish-black coal; **-rot,** dull red; **-scheibe,** *f.* ground glass (plate); **-schleifen,** to grind, frost (glass); **-schwarz,** dull black; **-sein,** *n.* dullness, deadness, dimness; **-setzen,** to checkmate, deprive of influence; **-weiss,** dull white.

Maturitätsexamen, *n.* final examination.

Mauer, *f.* wall, theca; **-blatt,** *n.* theca; **-gelb,** *n.* yellow badigeon; **-kalk,** *m.* mortar; **-kraut,** *n.* wall pellitory.

mauern, to build or construct walls, wall in.

Mauer-parenchym, *n.* muriform parenchyma; **-pfeffer,** *m.* stonecrop (Sedum); **-raute,** *f.* Asplenium; **-salpeter,** *m.* calcium nitrate; **-stein,** *m.* brick; **-werk,** *n.* masonry; **-ziegel,** *m.* building brick.

Mauke, *f.* scurf.

Mauken, *n.* fermenting, aging (of ceramics).

Maul, *n.* mouth, jaws; **-band,** *n.* bändchen, *n.* labial frenulum; **-beerbaum,** *m.* mulberry tree (Morus); **-beerdrüse,** *f.* moru-lose gland; **-beere,** *f.* mulberry;- **beergewächse,** *n.pl.* Moraceae.

Maul-drüse, *f.* labial gland; **-esel,** *m.* mule; **-füsser,** *m.pl.* Stomatopa; **-rinne,** *f.* philtrum (depression); **-spalte,** *f.* rima oris (mouth cleft); **-sperre,** *f.* tetanus, lockjaw; **tier,** *n.* mule.

Maul- und Klauen-seuche, *f.* foot-and-mouth disease.

Maul-winkel, *m.* angle of the mouth; **-wurf,** *m.* mole; **-wurfsdränung,** *f.* mole drainage; **-wurfsgrille,** *f.* mole cricket

Maurer, *m.* mason, bricklayer.

Maus, *f.*: **-e,** mouse.

Mause, *f.* molt(ing season).

Mäuse-dreck, *m.* mouse dung; **-gift,** *n.* ratsbane, white arsenic.

Mauser, *f.* molt(ing season).

mausern, to molt.

Mäuse-septikämie, *f.* mouse septicemia; **-typhus,** *m.* mouse plague.

maus-fahl, -farben, mouse-colored, mouse-gray.

Mauvein, *n.* mauve.

Maxillar-drüse, *f.* shell gland; **-lade,** *f.* maxillae; **-taster,** *m.* maxillary palpus.

Maxillendrüsen, *f.pl.* maxillary (shell) glands.

maximal, maximum, maximal; **-spannung,** *f.* maximum voltage; **-wertigkeit,** *f.* maximum valence; **-zahl,** *f.* maximum number.

mazerieren, to macerate.

Mechanik, *f.* mechanics, mechanism.

Mechaniker, *m.* mechanic, machinist.

mechanisch, mechanical; **mechanische Feuerung,** *f.* stoker; **mechanische Zelle,** *f.* stereome cell (supporting cell).

Mechanismus, *m.* mechanism, works.

Meconsäure, *f.* meconic acid.

med., *abbr.* (medizinisch), medical.

Medaille, *f.* medal.

Medialrandfortsatz, *m.* endite.

Median-furche, *f.* median groove; **-septum,** *n.* median septal ridge; **-wulst,** *f.* median fold.

Medien, *n.pl.* mediums, media.

Medikament, *n.* medicament, medicine, drug.

Mediterranfieber, *n.* undulant (Malta Mediterranean) fever.

Medium, *n.* medium.

Medizin, *f.* medicine.

Medizinal-rinde, *f.* officinal bark.

Mediziner, *m.* medical man or student.

mediziniert, medicated.

medizinisch, medicinal, medical.

Medullar-bezirk, *m.* neural region; -furche, *f.* medullary groove; -platte,*f.* neural plate; -rinne, *f.* -rohr, *n.* embryonic medullary tube; -wulst, *f.* embryonic medullary eminence or fold.

Meduse, *f.* jellyfish.

Medusenkörper, *m.* body of medusa.

Meer, *n.*-e, sea, ocean; -bewohnend, marine; -blau, greenish-blue, glaucous; -busen, *m.* bay, gulf.

Meeres-alge, *f.* sea alga; -bildung, *f.* marine formation; -boden, *m.* sea bottom; -einbruch, *m.* oceanic inroad; -fläche, *f.* (surface) level; -gebiet, *n.* marine region; -grund, *m.* sea bottom; -höhe, *f.* altitude, sea level; -küste, *f.* seacoast; -leuchten, *n.* marine phosphorescence.

Meeres-niveau, *n.* sea level, surface of the sea; -oberfläche, *f.* surface of the sea; -spiegel, *m.* sea level, surface of the sea; -strand, *m.* seashore.

Meer-farbe, *f.* sea-green; -fenchel, *m.* Crithmum; -kohl, *m.* sea kale; -linse, *f.* *Lemna maritimum;* -rettich, *m.* horseradish; -salz, *n.* sea salt; -schaum, *m.* meerschaum, sea foam; -schlamm, *m.* sea ooze; -schwein, *n.* porpoise; -schweinchen, *n.* guinea pig; -schweintran, *m.* porpoise oil.

meer-strandbewohnend, maritimus, maritime; -tang, *n.* seaweed, alga; -traube, *f.* *Coccoloba uvivera;* -träubel, *f.* *Ephedra;* -wasser, *n.* sea water; -wasserecht, fast to sea water; -zwiebel,*f.* squill, sea onion.

Megerg, *n.* megerg.

Megerkraut, *n.* yellow bedstraw (*Galium verum*).

Megohm, *n.* megohm.

Mehl, *n.* meal, flour, dust, powder; -artig, like meal or flour, farinaceous; -beerbaum, *m.* whitebeam tree (*Sorbus aria*); -beere,*f.* haw; -beutel, *m.* bolter, sifter; -fein, as fine as flour; -früchte, *f.pl.* cereals; -haltig, containing flour, farinaceous.

mehlig, floury, mealy, farinose.

Mehligkeit,*f.* kernal starchiness.

Mehl-käfer, *m.* meal beetle; -kleister, *m.* flour paste; -körper, *m.* endosperm; -kreide, *f.* earthy calcite, infusorial earth; -sand, *m.* very fine sand, rock flour;

-speise, *f.* farinaceous food; -tau, *m.* mildew; -taupilze, *m.pl.* mildews; -wurm, *m.* meal worm; -wurmpuppe, *f.* meal-worm pupa; -zucker, *m.* powdered sugar.

mehr, more; nicht ~, no (more) longer; nicht ~ lange, not much longer; und andere ~, and a few others; und dergleichen ~, and the like; u.a. ~, etc.; noch ~, even more, still more; um so viel ~ als, all the more as; ~ oder weniger, more or less; immer ~, more and more.

mehr-ährig, many-eared, multiheaded; -atomig, polyatomic; -aufwand, *m.* increased expenditure; -ausscheidung, *f.* increased secretion; -bändig, of several volumes; -basigkeit, *f.* polybasicity; -basisch, polybasic; -belastung, *f.* surcharge, increased (extra) load or burden; -betrag, *m.* increased yield, extra amount, excess; -blütig, multiflowered.

Mehr-deutigkeit, *f.* ambiguity; -dimensional, multidimensional, -drehung, *f.* multirotation.

mehren, to increase, multiply, augment, propagate.

mehrere, several.

mehrerlei, several kinds, sundry.

mehr-fach, manifold, multiple, numerous, repeated; -fächerig, multilocular; -fachfärbung,*f.* multiple staining; -fältig, manifold, multiple, numerous, repeated; -farbig, polychromatic, pleochroic; -farbigkeit, *f.* polychromatism, pleochroism.

mehr-feldrig, with multiple spans; -flammig, having more than one flame; -gablig, many-toothed, many-forked; -gewicht, *n.* excess weight, overweight; -gipfelig, many-pointed, multimodal; -gliedrig, having several (more) members.

Mehrheit,*f.* majority, plural(ity).

mehr-jährig, several years old; -kammerig, multilocular; -kernig, polynuclear, having more than one nucleus; -lappig, manylobed; -malig, repeated; -mals, several times, repeatedly.

Mehr-phasenstrom, *m.* polyphase current; -phasig, polyphase, multiphase; -polig, multipolar; -reihig, in multiple row; -samig, many-seeded, polyspermous; -scharpflug, *m.* multiple plow, gang plow; -schichtig, multilayered.

mehrstellig, with more than one figure; mehrstellige Zahl, *f.* number with more than one figure.

mehr-stufig, of several grades; -stündig, of several hours' duration; -tägig, of several days' duration; **-verbrauch,** *m.* greater consumption, more general use; **-wert,** *m.* surplus value, revenue; **-wertig,** polyhydroxy, multivalent, polyvalent; **-zahl,** *f.* majority, plural(ity); **-zellig,** multicellular; **-zellreihig,** multiseriate; **-zinkig,** many-fluked (-pronged).

meiden, to avoid, shun.

Meierei, *f.* (dairy) farm.

Meile, *f.* mile.

Meiler, *m.* charcoal (kiln) pile; **-kohle,** *f.* charcoal; **-stätte,** *f.* charring place; **-verfahren,** *n.* pile charring; **-verkohlung,** *f.* kiln burning.

mein, my, mine.

meinen, to think, mean, believe, deem fitting.

meinerseits, for (on) my part.

meines Wissens, as far as I know.

meinet-halben, -wegen, for my (part) sake,

Meinung, *f.* opinion, belief, idea, view, meaning, intention.

Meiran, *m.* marjoram.

Meisch, *m.* mash, grape must.

Meissel, *m.* chisel, pledget; **-förmig,** chisel-shaped; **-schar,** *f.* knife colter (of plow).

meist, most, mostly, usually; **am meisten,** most (highly), for the most part.

Meistbietender, *m.* highest bidder.

meistens, meistenteils, for the most part, generally, as a rule.

Meister, *m.* master; **-haft,** masterly; **-stück.** *n.* masterpiece; **-wurz,** *f.* masterwort (*Imperatoria ostruthium*); **-wurzel,** *f.* masterwort (*Imperatoria ostruthium*).

Meistgebot, *n.* highest bid.

Mekoninsäure, *f.* meconinic acid.

Mekonsäure, *f.* meconic acid.

Melangallussäure, *f.* metagallic (melanogallic) acid.

Melange, *f.* mixture.

melangieren, to mix.

Melanglanz, *m.* stephanite.

Melasse, *f.* molasses, treacle.

Melassensäure, *f.* melassic acid.

Melde, *f.* Atriplex; **-amt,** *n.* registration, (recording) office.

melden, to advise, announce, inform, notify, mention, present, apply; **-gewächse,** *n.pl.* Chenopodiaceae.

Meldung, *f.* advice, notification.

melieren, to mix, mottle.

Melier-fasern, *f.pl.* mottling fibers; **-papier,** *n.* mottled paper.

Melilotenklee, *m.* melilot, sweet clover.

Melinit, *n.* picric acid.

Melioration, *f.* soil improvement.

meliorieren, to (a)meliorate.

Meliszucker, *m.* coarse loaf sugar.

Melisse, *f.* balm, balm leaf or mint.

Melissen-geist, *m.* balm, spirit, Carmelite water; **-kraut,** *n.* balm, balm leaf or mint.

Melissinsäure, *f.* melissic acid.

melken, to milk.

Melk-maschine, *f.* milking machine; **-stuhl,** *m.* milking stool.

Mellithsäure, *f.* mellitic acid.

Melone, *f.* melon.

Meltau, *m.* mildew; **-fest,** resistant to mildew; **-pilze,** *m.pl.* Erysiphaceae.

Membran, *f.* membrane, diaphragm, lamella; **-abhebung,** *f.* membrane separation; **-fortsatz,** *m.* membrane process, prolongation of cell wall; **-gleichgewicht,** *n.* equilibrium in membrane charge; **-ladung,** *f.* membrane charge; **-schleim,** *m.* membrane mucilage.

Mendelsch, Mendelian.

mengbar, capable of being mixed, miscible.

Menge, *f.* quantity, multitude, mass, crowd, amount, abundance, plenty, rate, variety; **eine ganze ∼,** quite a lot.

mengen, to mix, blend, mingle, admix, meddle; **-anteil,** *m.* quantity proportion, constituent amount; **-bestimmung,** *f.* quantitative determination; **-einheit,** *f.* unit of quantity, mass unity; **-mässig,** quantitative; **-untersuchung,** *f.* quantitative examination; **-verhältnis,** *n.* quantitative relation, proportion, ratio, relative proportions.

Meng-futter, *n.* mixed food; **-gestein,** *n.* conglomerate; **-kapsel,** *f.* mixing capsule; **-korn,** *n.* wheat and rye mixed; **-saat,** *f.* mixed seeds; **-spatel,** *m.* mixing spatula; **-teil,** *m.* ingredient.

Mengung, *f.* mixing, mixture, blend(ing), hybridization.

Mengungsverhältnis, *n.* proportion of ingredients.

Menhadenöl, *n.* menhaden oil.

Meningen, *pl.* meninges.

Meningitis, *f.* meningitis.

Meningokokkus, *m.* meningococcus.

Meniskus, m. meniscus.

Mennig, m. Mennige, f. minium, red lead.

mennigen, to paint with minium.

Mensch, m.-en, man, human being, person.

Menschen-affe, m. anthropoid ape; -ähnlich, anthropoid; -alter, n. generation; -bedürfnis, n. human need, men required; -blut, n. human blood; -freund, m. philanthropist; -geschlecht, n. human race; -kind, n. child of man.

Menschen-körper, m. human body; -krankheit, f. human illness; -lehre, f. anthropology; -pocken, f.pl. smallpox, variola; -schädel, m. human skull; -serum, human serum; -verstand, m. human understanding, mind; -werdung, f. transformation into human species, anthropogenesis, evolution.

Menschheit, f. mankind, human race.

menschlich, human, humane.

Mensur, f. measure, measuring vessel, duel (student); -glas, n. measuring (graduated) glass.

Menthakampher, m. mint camphor, menthol.

mephitisch, mephitic.

mercerisieren, to mercerize.

Mercur, m. mercury.

Mergel, m.-, marl; -art, f. kind of marl; -artig, marly; -boden, m. marly soil; -düngung, f. marling; -erde, f. earthy marl; -haltig, marly.

mergelig, marly.

Mergelkalk, m. marly limestone.

mergeln, to (manure with) marl.

Mergel-sand, m. marl sand; -ton, m. argillaceous marl.

Mergelung, f. liming, chalking, fertilizing with marl.

merkbar, perceptible, noticeable, evident.

merken, to mark, note, notice, perceive, bear in mind, observe; ~ lassen, to betray, divulge.

merkenswert, noteworthy.

Merkfähigkeit, f. memory.

merklich, perceptible, noticeable, appreciable, visible.

Merkmal, n. characteristic, mark, sign, earmark, symptom, indication, criterion, particular feature.

Merkmals-analyse, f. character analysis; -gruppe, f. character group (of class); -paar, n. character pair, allelomorphs;

-träger, m. gene; -unterschiedlichkeit, f. character difference.

Merktinte, f. marking ink.

Merkur, m. mercury; -blende, f. cinnabar; -chlorid, n. mercuric chloride; -chlorür, n. mercurous chloride; -haltig, containing mercury, mercurial; -hornerz, n horn quicksilver, calomel.

Merkurialien, n.pl. mercurials.

Merkurialmittel, n. mercurial preparation.

Merkuri-ammoniumchlorid, n. mercuriammonium chloride; -chlorid, n. mercuric chloride; -cyanid, n. mercuric cyanide.

merkurieren, to mercurize, combine with mercury.

Merkurierung, f. mercurization.

Merkuri-jodid, n. mercuric iodide; -nitrat, n. mercuric nitrate; -oxyd, n. mercuric oxide; -sulfat, n. mercuric sulphate; -sulfid, n. mercuric sulphide; -verbindung, f. mercuric compound.

Merkuro-acetat, n. mercurous acetate.

Merkur-oxyd, n. mercuric oxide; -silber, n. silver amalgam; -sulfid, n. mercuric sulphide.

merk-würdig, noteworthy, remarkable; -würdigerweise, strange to say; -zeichen, n. mark, sign, memorandum.

Mero-chinen, n. meroquinine; -tropie. f merotropism, merotropy.

Merzerisation, f. mercerization.

merzerisieren, to mercerize.

mesenchymal, mesenchymic.

Mesenchymzelle, f. mesenchyme cell.

Mesenterialfalte, f. mesenteric fold.

Mesoblasthof, m. mesoblast area.

Mesoderm, n. mesoderm; -anhäufung, f. mesoderm mass; -höhle, f. coelom; -streifen, m. mesoderm band.

Meso-phytengebüsch, n. mesophytic bushland; -weinsäure, f. mesotartaric acid.

Mesoxalsäure, f. mesoxalic acid.

Mess-analyse, f. volumetric analysis; -apparat, m. measuring apparatus; -band, n. tape measure.

messbar, measurable.

Mess-bereich, m. measuring range; -dose, f. pressure cell; -einteilung, f. graduation.

messen, to measure, survey, contain, gauge.

Messer, n.-, knife, cutter, meter

Messer, *m.*-, measurer, meter.

Messergebnis, *n.*-se, result of measurement.

Messer-griff, *m.* -klinge, *f.* knife blade; -spitze, *f.* knife point; -stahl, *m.* knife steel.

Mess-fehler, *m.*-, error in measurement; -flasche, *f.* measuring or graduated flask; -flüssigkeit, *f.* measuring liquid; -gefäss, *n.* measuring vessel; -genauigkeit, *f.* accuracy of measurement; -geräte, *n.pl.* measuring apparatus; -glas, *n.* measuring glass, graduated glass vessel; -glied, *n.* metering element; -grenze, *f.* limit of measurement; -heber, *m.* pipette; -holz, *n.* dimension timber.

Messing, *n.* brass; -artig, like brass, brassy; -blech, *n.* brass plate, sheet brass; -blüte, *f.* aurichalcite; -brennen, *n.* brass making; -draht, *m.* brass wire; -farben, brass-colored; -fassung, *f.* brass mounting, casing; -giesser, *m.* brass founder; -kugel, *f.* brass ball.

Messing-netz, *n.* brass netting, brass gauze; -rohr, *n.* -röhre, *f.* brass tube or pipe; -schlaglot, *n.* brass solder; -späne, *m.pl.* brass shavings, brass turnings.

Mess-instrument, *n.*-e, measuring instrument; -keil, *m.* measuring wedge, inside caliper for pipes; -kölbchen, *n.* little measuring flask; -kolben, *m.* measuring flask; -länge, *f.* gauge length; -latte, *f.* measuring (staff) rod; -mittel, *n.* means of measuring, measuring instrument; -okular, *n.* micrometric eyepiece; -pipette, *f.* graduated (scale) pipette; -reihe, *f.* series of measurements.

Mess-rohr, *n.* -röhre, *f.* measuring tube, burette; -strecke, *f.* measured train, measured trajectory (of projectile); -tisch, *m.* surveyor's table; -trichter, *m.* measuring funnel; -trommel, *f.* graduated drum; -uhr, *f.* dial gauge.

Messung, *f.* measurement, measuring, mensuration.

Messungsergebnis, *n.* result of measurement.

Mess-verfahren, *n.*-, method (process) of measurement; -vorrichtung, *f.* measuring device; -zylinder, *m.* measuring (graduated) cylinder.

Met, *m.* mead.

Meta-antimonsäure, *f.* metantimonic acid; -arsenig, metarsenious; -bleisäure, *f.* metaplumbic acid; -bolie, *f.* metabolism; -bolisch, metabolic; -bolismus, *m.* metabolism; -borsäure, *f.* metaboric acid;

-chromatisch, metachromatic; -cymol, *n.* metacymene; -eisenoxyd, *n.* metaferric oxide; -kohlensäure, *f.* metacarbonic acid.

Metall, *n.*-e, me⁺al; -abfall, *m.* waste metal; -ader, *f.* metallic (metalliferous) vein; -ähnlich, metallic, metalline; -amid, *n.* metallic amide; -artig, metallic, metalline; -auftrag, *m.* metallic coating or plating; -azid, *n.* metallic azide.

Metall-beschwerung, *f.* loading with metallic salts; -blatt, *n.* sheet of metal; -carbid, *n.* metallic carbide; -chlorid, *n.* metallic chloride; -dampf, *m.* metallic vapor; -draht, *m.* metal wire; -eigenschaft, *f.* metallic property; -einkristall, *m.* metal single crystal; -faden, *m.* metal thread, metal filament; -farbe, *f.* metallic color.

Metall-färbung, *f.* coloring of metal; -fassung, *f.* metal casing or mounting; -folie, *f.* metal foil; -führend, metalliferous; -gehalt, *m.* metal(lic) content; -gekrätz, *n.* metal waste, dross; -gemisch, *n.* metallic mixture, alloy; -gewebe, *n.* wire (gauze) cloth; -gewinnung, *f.* extraction of metals, metallurgy; -gift, *n.* metallic poison.

Metall-glanz, *m.* metallic luster; -glas, *n.* enamel; -gold, *n.* Dutch metal; -guss, *m.* metal founding; -haltig, containing metal, metalliferous; -hütte, *f.* nonferrous smelter; -ion, *n.* ion of metal; -lehre, metallurgy.

metallisch, metallic.

metallisieren, to metallize.

Metallität, *f.* metallic nature.

Metall-keramik, *f.* powder metallurgy; -könig, *m.* metallic (button) regulus; -korn, *n.* globule, regulus, silver head, metal grain; -körner, *n.pl.* granulated metal; -kunde, *f.* metallography, science of metals; -legierung, *f.* metallic alloy; -membran, *f.* metal diaphragm; -mohr, *m.* metallic moiré; -mutter, *f.* matrix; -niet, *n.* metal strip, rivet; -oxyd, *n.* metallic oxide.

Metall-probe, *f.* assay (test) for metal; -rohr, *n.*, -röhre, *f.* metal tube or pipe; -safran, *m.* saffron (crocus) of antimony; -scheibe, *f.* metal disk; -schlauch, *m.* (flexible) metallic hose; -silber, *n.* imitation silver foil; -späne, *m.pl.* shavings, turnings, or chips; -spritzverfahren, *n.* metallization; -sulfid, *n.* metallic sulphide.

Metall-teil, *m.* metal part; -tuch, *n.* wire cloth; -überziehung, *f.* metal plating; -überzug, *m.* metallic coating, wash.

Metallurg, *m.* metallurgist.

Metall-verarbeitung, *f.* metal working;
-verbindung, *f.* metallic compound; **-ver-
giftung,** *f.* metallic poisoning; **-versetzung,**
f. alloying, alloy; **-verwandlung,** *f.* metal
transformation; **-waren,** *f.pl.* metal wares,
hardware; **-wolle,** *f.* metal wool.

Metamerie, *f.* metamerism, metamery.

Metanilgelb, *n.* metanil yellow.

metantimonig, metantimonious.

Meta-phosphorsäure, *f.* metaphosphoric
acid; **-physik,** *f.* metaphysics; **-säure,** *f.*
meta acid; **-stabil,** metastable; **-ständig,**
in the meta position; **-stase,** *f.* metastasis.

Meta-stasenbildung, *f.* metastatic formation; **-stellung,** *f.* meta position; **-tarsus-
bürste,** *f.* sarothrum, pollen brush of bee;
-verbindung, *f.* meta (compound) derivative; **-wolframsäure,** *f.* metatungstic
acid; **-zuckersäure,** *f.* metasaccharic acid.

Meteoreisen, *n.* meteoric iron.

meteorisch, meteoric, meteoristic.

Meterologe, *m.* meterologist.

Meteor-schwarm, *m.* host of meteors,
meteoric shower; **-staub,** *m.* meteoric dust;
-stein, *m.* meteoric stone, aerolite.

Meter, *m.&n.* meter; **-kerze,** *f.* meter
candle; **-mass,** *n.* metric measure, pocket
rule.

Methan, *n.* methane.

Methode, *f.* method.

Methodik, *f.* methodics, methodology.

methodisch, methodical.

Methyl-alkohol, *m.* ethyl alcohol; **-äther,**
m. methyl ether; **-chlorid,** *n.* methyl
chloride.

Methylenblau, *n.* methylene blue.

Methyl-gallusäthersäure, *f.* ortho methyl-
gallic acid; **-grün,** *n.* methyl green; **-hy-
drür,** *n.* methyl hydride, methane.

methylieren, to methylate.

Methyl-jodid, *n.* methyl iodide, iodomethane; **-kautschuk,** *m.* methyl rubber;
-nitrit, *n.* methyl nitrite; **-verbindung,** *f.*
methyl compound; **-violett,** *n.* methyl
violet; **-wasserstoff,** *m.* methyl hydride,
methane; **-zahl,** *f.* methyl (number)
value.

Metochinon, *n.* metoquinone.

metrisch, metric(al).

Metze, *f.* peck.

Metzelsuppe, *f.* meat broth.

Metzger, *m.* butcher.

Meute, *f.* pack of hounds.

miasmatisch, miasmatic(al).

Micell, *n.* micelle.

mich, me, myself.

mied (meiden), avoided.

Miene, *f.* air, mien, feature, look.

Mienenspiel, *n.* play of the features.

Miere, *f.* chickweed (Alsine).

Miesmuschel, *f.* sea mussel.

Miete, *f.* mite, hire, lease, rent, stack, shock.

mieten, to hire, charter, lease, rent.

Mieter, *m.*-, renter, tenant, lessee.

Migräne, *f.* migraine, (sick) headache.

Mikroanalyse, *f.* microanalysis.

Mikroben, *f.pl.* microbes; **-forschung,** *f.*
investigation of microbes; **-impfung,** *f.*
microbe inoculation; **-tätigkeit,** *f.* bacterial
activity.

Mikrobien, *f.pl.* microbes.

Mikro-biologie, *f.* microbiology, bacteriology; **-brenner,** *m.* microburner; **-chemie,**
f. microchemistry; **-chirurgisch,** micro-
surgical; **-flora,** *f.* microflora; **-gonidien,**
f.pl. microgonidia; **-kokkus,** *m.* micro-
coccus; **-meter,** *m.* micrometer; **-meter-
schraube,** *f.* micrometric screw, fine
adjustment; **-metrisch,** micrometric.

Mikron, *n.* micron.

Mikro-nutsche, *f.* microsuction filter; **-or-
ganismus,** *m.* microorganism; **-parasit,** *m.*
microparasite; **-photographic,** *f.* photomicrography; **-schnell-bestimmung,** *f.*
rapid microdetermination; **-skop,** *n.* microscope; **-skopieren,** to examine with the
microscope; **-skopisch,** microscopic(al);
-skoplinse, *f.* lens of microscope; **-spo-
ridien,** *f.pl.* microsporidia.

Mikro-tom, *n.* microtome; **-tomschnitt,**
m. microtome section; **-verbrennung,** *f.*
microincineration; **-volumetrisch,** micro-
volumetric; **-waage,** *f.* microbalance.

Milbe, *f.* mite (Acarus).

Milch, *f.* milk, emulsion, milt, soft roe;
-abscheidend, milk secreting; **-absondernd,**
milk secreting; **-absonderung,** *f.*
milk secretion; **-abtreibend,** antigalactic;
-achat, *m.* milk-white agate; **-ader,** *f.*
lacteal vessel, vein; **-ähnlich, -artig,** milk-
like, milky, lacteal; **-ausstrich,** *m.* smear of
milk sediment.

Milch-backzahn, *n.* milk molar; **-bestand-
teil,** *m.* constituent of milk; **-bier,** *n.* kumiss;
-brustgang, *m.* thoracic canal; **-drüse,** *f.*
mammary (lacteal) gland; **-drüsengang,** *m.*

milk duct; **-eimer,** *m.* milk pail, bucket; **-eischimmel,** *m.* *Oïdium lactis.*

milchen, to milk, give a milky juice, emulsify.

Milch-fälschung, *f.* adulteration of milk; **-farbe,** *f.* milk color; **-fehler,** *m.* *pl.* milk diseases; **-ferkel,** *n.* suckling pig; **-ferment,** *n.* milk ferment; **-fett,** *n.* milk fat; **-fettkügelchen,** *n.pl.* fat globules; **-führend,** lactiferous; **-gang,** *m.* lactiferous duct, milk duct; **-gärung,** *f.* fermentation of milk.

Milch-gebiss, *n.* milk dentition; **-gefäss,** *n.* lacteal, chyliferic (chyle) vessel; **-gerinnung,** *f.* curdling of milk; **-gewinnung,** *f.* production of milk; **-glanzkrankeit,** *f.* silverleaf disease; **-güte,** *f.* quality of milk; **-harnen,** *n.* chyluria; **-harnfluss,** *m.* chyluria.

milchicht, milky, lacteal.

milchig, milky, lacteal; **-trüb,** milky, turbid.

Milch-kanal, *m.* lactiferous duct; **-kotbakterien,** *f.pl.* bacteria of dirt (dung) in milk; **-kraut,** *n.* sea milkwort (*Glaux maritima*); **-kügelchen,** *n.* milk globule or corpuscle; **-kuh,** *f.* milch cow, cow in milk; **-lab,** *n.* rennet; **-leistung,** *f.* milk yield; **-messer,** *m.* galactometer, lactometer; **-nährboden,** *m.* milk nutrient medium; **-porzellan,** *n.* milk glass.

Milch-prober, *m.,* **-prüfer,** *m.* milk tester; **-prüfung,** *f.* milk testing; **-pulver,** *n.* milk powder; **-rahm,** *m.* cream; **-röhre,** *f.* lactiferous duct, latex tube.

Milch-saft, *m.* milky juice, latex, chyle; **-saftführend,** lactiferous; **-saftgang,** *m.* chyliferous vessel; **-saftig,** chylous; **-saftschlauch,** *m.* latex tube; **-sauer,** of or combined with lactic acid, lactate of.

Milchsäure, *f.* lactic acid; **-bacillus,** *m.* lactic-acid bacillus; **-bakterie,** *f.* lactic-acid bacterium; **-ferment,** *n.* lactic ferment; **-gärung,** *f.* lactic-acid fermentation; **-menge,** *f.* amount of lactic acid; **-pilz,** *m.* lactic-acid bacillus; **-salz,** *n.* lactate; **-stäbchen,** *n.* lactic-acid bacillus.

Milch-stern, *m.* Ornithogalum; **-strasse,** *f.* Milky Way; **-tier,** *n.* lactating animal (giving milk); **-treibend,** lactiferous; **-untersuchung,** *f.* examination of milk, milk analysis; **-verfälschung,** *f.* adulteration of milk; **-vermehrend,** galactagog; **-vertreibend,** antigalactic; **-vieh,** *n.* cattle giving milk, dairy cattle; **-viehhaltung,** *f.* dairy husbandry.

Milch-viehzüchter, *m.* dairy farmer; **-waage,** *f.* lactometer; **-warze,** *f.* nipple; **-wein,** *m.* kumiss; **-weiss,** milk-white;

-wicke, *f.* Astragalus; **-wirtschaft,** *f.* dairy farm(ing); **-zahn,** *m.* milk tooth, temporary tooth, deciduous tooth; **-zeichen,** *n.pl.* lacteal marks; **-zelle,** *f.* latex cell; **-zersetzung,** *f.* decomposition of milk.

Milchzucker, *m.* milk sugar, lactose; **-agar,** *m.* lactose agar; **-säure,** *f.* saccholactic (mucic) acid.

mild, milde, mild, soft, lenient, gentle, mellow, kind.

mildern, to soften, temper, moderate, alleviate, mitigate, correct.

mildernd, mitigant, alleviating.

Milderung, *n.* softening, tempering, correction.

Milderungsmittel, *n.* mitigant, demulcent, corrective, lenitive.

Miliartuberkulose, *f.* miliary tuberculosis.

Milieu, *n.* surroundings, environment, medium; **-bedingt,** determined by environment.

Militär, *n.* soldiers, military, army.

militärisch, military.

Milliarde, *f.* thousand millions, billion (U. S.).

Millimeter, *m.* millimeter.

Million, *f.* million.

millionstel, millionth (part), micro-.

Milz, *f.-e,* spleen.

Milzbrand, *m.* anthrax; **-bazillus,** anthrax bacillus; **-fieber,** *n.* anthrax; **-krank,** affected with anthrax; **-schutzimpfung,** *f.* prophylactic inoculation against anthrax; **-sporen,** *m.pl.* spores of anthrax bacillus.

Milz-drüse, *f.* spleen; **-farn,** *m.* spleenwort (*Asplenium ceterach*); **-magenband,** *n.* gastrolienal (splenic) ligament; **-nierenband,** *n.* renolienal ligament; **-rinne,** *f.* hilum of the spleen; **-saft,** *m.* spleen pulp; **-tumor,** *m.* tumor due to anthrax.

Mimose, *f.* mimosa.

Mimosen-gummi, *n.* gum arabic; **-zweig,** *m.* mimosa twig.

minder, less, smaller, inferior, minor; **-druck,** *m.* reduced pressure; **-ertrag,** *m.* decreased yield; **-gehalt,** *m.* lesser (short) content; **-gewicht,** *n.* underweight; **-haltig,** inferior, low-grade, of less value.

Minderheit, *f.* minority.

minderjährig, underage, minor.

mindern, to diminish, lessen, decrease.

Minder-wert, *m.-e,* lesser value, inferiority; **-wertig,** of lower valence, inferior; **-wert r-**

keit, *f.* lower valence, inferior value; **-zahl,** *f.* minority.

mindest, least, smallest, minimum, lowest.

mindestens, zum mindesten, at least, at the (very) least.

Mindestwert, *m.* least value, minimum value.

Mine, *f.* mine, crayon (for colored pencils).

Minen-gas, *n.* mine gas; **-pulver,** *n.* blasting powder.

Mineral-ablagerung, *f.* deposit(ion) of minerals; **-bestandteil,** *m.* mineral constituent; **-blau,** *n.* mineral blue; **-boden,** *m.* mineral soil; **-farbstoff,** *m.* mineral dye; **-fettwachs,** *n.* mineral tallow.

Mineralienkunde, *f.* mineralogy.

mineralisch, mineral.

Mineralmohr, *m.* black (amorphous) mercuric sulphide.

Mineraloge, *m.* mineralogist.

Mineralogie, *f.* mineralogy.

Mineral-pech, *n.* mineral pitch; **-quelle,** *f.* mineral spring; **-reich,** *n.* mineral kingdom; **-rot,** *n.* cinnabar; **-schmiermittel,** *n.* mineral lubricant; **-schwarz,** *n.* mineral black; **-seife,** *f.* mineral soap; **-(stoff)-wechsel,** *m.* inorganic metabolism; **-substanz,** *f.* mineral matter.

Miniatur, *f.* miniature; **-ausgabe,** *f.* miniature edition; **-bild,** *n.* miniature picture.

minimal, minute, minimum; **-betrag,** *m.* lowest amount, lowest rate; **-dosis,** minimal dose; **-gehalt,** *m.* minimum content; **-oberfläche,** *f.* minimum surface; **-wert,** *m.* minimum value.

Ministerium, *n.* ministry, administration.

minus, minus, less; **-zeichen,** *n.* minus sign.

Minute, *f.* minute.

minutenlang, lasting a minute, lasting for minutes.

Minze, *f.* mint (Mentha).

Mipolid, *n.* mixed polyamide.

mir, to me, me.

Mirban-essenz, *f.* essence of mirbane, nitrobenzene; **-öl,** *n.* oil of mirbane.

Mirrhe, *f.* myrrh.

Mirte, *f.* myrtle.

Mischapparat, *m.* mixing apparatus, mixer.

mischbar, miscible, mixable.

Mischbarkeit, *f.* miscibility.

Misch-behälter, *m.* mixing tank; **-bestand,** *m.*-e, mixed stand or crop; **-bildung,** *f.*

mixed formation; **-dünger,** *m.* mixed commercial fertilizer.

mischen, to mix, mingle, combine, blend, adulterate, alloy, interfere, shuffle, compound; **sich** ∼, to be miscible.

Mischer, *m.* mixer, mixing vessel.

Misch-farbe, *f.* mixed color, combination color; **-färbung,** *f.* mixed staining; **-flasche,** *f.* mixing bottle; **-frucht,** *f.* interspecies hybrid; **-gefäss,** *n.* mixing vessel; **-glas,** *n.* mixing glass; **-hefe,** *f.* composite yeast; **-infektion,** *f.* mixed infection; **-kultur,** *f.* mixed planting; **-laubregion,** *f.* mixed deciduous wood.

Mischling, *m.* hybrid, crossbreed.

Misch-masch, *m.* mixup, confusion; **-metall,** *n.* mixed metal, alloy; **-moor,** *n.* moor with a complex surface vegetation; **-pipette,** *f.* mixing pipette; **-rasse,** *f.* crossbreed; **-regel,** *f.* rule for mixing; **-rohr,** *n.* mixing tube; **-typus,** *m.* mixed type, hybrid type.

Mischung, *f.* composition, mixture, mixing, blend, alloy, adulteration, combination, compound.

Mischungs-bestandteil, *m.* ingredient (constituent) of a mixture; **-fähig,** miscible; **-gewicht,** *n.* combining weight; **-lücke,** *f.* miscibility gap; **-rechnung,** *f.* alligation; **-regel,** *f.* rule (law) of mixtures; **-verhältnis,** *n.* mixing proportion, ratio; **-wärme,** *f.* heat of (mixing) mixture.

Misch-ventil, *n.* mixing valve; **-wald,** *m.* mixed (wood) stand, forest of various types of trees; **-walzwerk,** *n.* mixing rollers; **-wuchs,** *m.* mixed growth.

Mispel, *f.* medlar (*Mespilus germanica*).

miss-achten, to disregard, despise, disdain, undervalue, neglect; **-arten,** to degenerate; **-artung,** *f.* degeneracy; **-bildung,** *f.* malformation, monstrosity, deformity, anomaly, defect; **-billigen,** to disapprove (of), object to, oppose, condemn, reject; **-brauch,** *m.* misuse, abuse, malpractice; **-brauchen,** to misuse.

missen, to miss, dispense with, want, lack.

Miss-erfolg, *m.*-e, failure; **-ernte,** *f.* crop failure; **-fallen,** to be displeasing; **-fällig,** disagreeable, unpleasant; **-farbig,** discolored; **-färbung,** *f.* discoloration; **-geburt,** *f.* abortion, monster.

Miss-geschick, *n.* misfortune, mishap; **-gestaltet,** deformed, misshapen; **-glücken,** to fail; **-griff,** *m.* mistake, blunder; **-gunst,** *f.* disfavor, jealousy; **-handeln,** to mistreat.

misslang (misslingen), **es** ∼, it was unsuccessful, it failed.

miss-lich, uncertain, doubtful, precarious; **-lingen,** to fail, to be unsuccessful; **-lungen,** failed; **-raten,** to fail.

Miss-stand, m.-̈e, inconvenience, grievance, defect, bad state, impropriety, abuse; **-trauen,** to distrust, suspect; **-verhältnis,** n. asymmetry, disproportion, inadequacy, disparity; **-verständlich,** by misunderstanding; **-verständnis,** n. misunderstanding, difference, mistake; **-verstehen,** to misunderstand; **-wachs,** m. crop failure, scarcity, anomalous growth; **-wüchsig,** badly grown, unthriftily grown.

misst (messen), measures.

Mist, m. manure, dung; **-beet,** n. hotbed; **-beetkasten,** m. forcing frame; **-beize,** f. dung bate.

Mistel, f. mistletoe; **-drossel,** f. missel (bird) thrush; **-gewächse,** n.pl. Loranthaceae.

misten, to manure, dung, fertilize.

Mist-haufen, m. dunghill; **-jauche,** f. liquid manure; **-käfer,** m. dorbeetle, dung beetle; **-pulver,** n. powdered manure, poudrette.

mit, with, by, in, at, together, jointly, along, also; **-anführen,** to include; **-arbeiten,** to assist, co-operate, collaborate; **-arbeiter,** m. coworker, contributor, assistant, co-operative expert, collaborator; **-begreifen,** to comprise, include, comprehend; **-bewegt,** in relative motion, moving; **-bewegung,** f. comovement, collateral (associated) movement; **-bewerber,** m. competitor; **-bewohner,** m. coinhabitant, associate; **-bringen,** to bring along; **-einander,** with one another, together.

mit-einbegriffen (miteingreifen), included in; **-erleben,** to witness, experience; **-esser,** m. comedo, acne punctata; **-führen,** to carry (take) along, entrain; **-geben,** to impart, give along with; **-gefühl,** n. sympathy; **-geführt,** carried along; **-gerissen** (mitreissen), carried over (down or along), entrained, entrapped; **-gerissenwerden,** n. being carried along; **-glied,** n. member, fellow.

Mit-gliedschaft, f. membership; **-helfen,** to assist; **-helfer,** m. accomplice, coworker, assistant; **-herrschend,** codominant; **-hilfe,** f. aid, cooperation; **-hin,** hence, therefore, consequently, of course.

Mitisgrün, n. Paris green, emerald green, Vienna green.

mit-klingen, to sound at the same time; **-leid,** n. pity; **-leidig,** sympathetic, compassionate; **-machen,** to participate, join

in, take part in, conform to; **-nehmen,** to take (along), share, weaken, exhaust, wear, criticize; **-nehmer,** m. driver, lathe dog; **-nehmerwendeisen,** n.pl. bangers; **-niederreissen,** to carry down.

Mitose, f. mitosis; **-beeinflussung,** f. influencing the process of cell (nuclear) division (mitosis, karyokinesis).

mit-reissen, to carry over, distill, carry (pull) along; **-samt,** together with; **-schleppen,** to drag along; **-schwingen,** to covibrate; **-spielen,** to participate, be involved, be a factor.

Mittag, m. midday, noon, south.

Mittags-blume, f. Mesembryanthemum; **-essen,** n. noon meal; **-kreis,** m. meridian; **-linie,** f. meridian; **-pause,** f. midday relaxation (rest).

Mitte, f. middle, center, midst, mean.

mitteilen, to communicate, inform, impart, convey, give, advise.

Mitteilung, f. communication, report.

Mitteilungsvermögen, n. ability to communicate.

Mittel, n.-, means, middle, medium, expedient, agent, remedy, mean, average, capital, mediation; **im ∼,** on the average.

mittel, middle, central, mean, average, medium, intermediate; **-ader,** f. media, median vein; **-alterlich,** medieval.

mittelbar, indirect, mediate.

Mittel-bauch, m. mesogastrium; **-bauchgegend,** f. mesogastric region; **-bein,** n. intermediate leg; **-bildung,** f. intermediate hybrid; **-binder,** m. medium-setting cement; **-blatt,** n. foliage leaf; **-blattstamm,** m. part of stem bearing foliage leaves; **-blech,** n. medium plate.

Mittelbrust, f. mesothorax; **-bein,** n. body of the sternum; **-fortsatz,** m. process of the mesothorax; **-ring,** m, **-stück,** n. mesothorax.

Mittel-darm, m. mid-intestine, mid-gut, mesenteron, mesogaster, intestine; **-darmdrüse,** f. intestinal gland; **-ding,** n. intermediate, cross (between); **-druck,** m. medium pressure; **-eck,** n. **-ecke,** f. lateral summit; **-farbe,** f. intermediate (secondary) color; **-faser,** f. central fiber; **-fehler.** m. average (mean) error; **-fell,** n. mediastinum; **-felldrüse,** f. mediastinal gland.

Mittel-finger, m. middle finger; **-fleisch,** n. perineum; **-flüssig,** semifluid; **-form,** f. intermediate type.

Mittelfuss, *m.* metatarsus; **-band,** *n.* metatarsal ligament; **-gelenk,** *n.* metatarsal joint; **-knochen,** *m.* metacarpal bone; **-rückenband,** *n.* dorsal metatarsal ligament; **-sohlenband,** *n.* metatarsal plantar ligament.

Mittel-gebirge, *n.* secondary chain of mountains; **-gehirn,** *n.* midbrain, mesocephalon; **-geschwindigkeit,** *f.* mean velocity; **-glied,** *n.* middle phalanx, intermediate member; **-griffelig,** pistil of medium size, medium-styled; **-gross,** medium-sized; **-grösse,** *f.* medium size.

Mittelhand, *f.* metacarpus; **-band,** *n.* metacarpal ligament; **-gelenk,** *n.* metacarpal joint.

mittel-hart, medium (moderately) hard; **-haut,** *f.* middle layer or coat, middle tunic, tunica media.

Mittelhirn, *n.* midbrain; **-beuge,** *f.* midbrain flexure, mesencephalic bend; **-bläschen,** *n.* mesencephalon; **-falte,** *f.* midbrain fold.

Mittel-höhe, *f.* mean height; **-hüfte,** *f.* middle coxa; **-keim,** *m.* mesoblast; **-kiefer,** *m.* intermaxillary (premaxillary) bone, first maxilla, maxillule (Crustaceae); **-kiefertaster,** *m.* endopodite of maxillule; **-knochen,** *m.* metacarpal bone; **-kraft,** *f.* resultant force; **-lage,** *f.* middle position; **-lang,** of medium length; **-leib,** *m.* thorax.

Mittel-lauf, *m.* middle (runnings) fraction (in distilling); **-lauge,** *f.* medium strong (weak) lye; **-linie,** *f.* median (center) line, axis, equator; **-los,** without means; **-mässig,** mediocre, middling, indifferent, average, fair.

Mittelmeer, *n.* Mediterranean Sea; **-fieber,** *n.* undulant (Malta) fever.

Mittel-nerv, *m.* midrib (far), median nerve; **-öl,** *n.* middle fraction; **-partei,** *f.* Center (party); **-platte,** *f.* middle lamella, median plate (of coelom); **-punkt,** *m.* center, central point, focus; **-punktsfläche,** *f.* central plane; **-punktslage,** *f.* position of the center; **-rasse,** *f.* intermediate race; **-rinde,** *f.* primary cortex; **-rippe,** *f.* midrib; **-rücken,** *m.* mesonotum.

mittels, by means of.

Mittel-salz, *n.* neutral salt; **-schicht,** *f.* intermediate layer; **-schlächtig,** middle-shot (water); **-schwer,** medium heavy; **-spalt,** *m.* longitudinal (middle) fissure.

mittelst, by means of, through.

Mittel-stamm, *m.* average (mean) stem; **-stand,** *m.* middle class; **-ständig,** occupying a middle position, perigynous, central,

middle; **-stark,** moderately strong; **-stärke,** *f.* mean diameter; **-steinzeit,** *f.* mesolithic stone age; **-steinzeitlich,** eolithic; **-stellung,** *f.* intermediary, balance; **-stengel,** *m.* central stem; **-strasse,** *f.* middle course; **-strecke,** *f.* medium distance, middle stretch.

Mittel-stück, *n.* middle piece, central portion, hyoid bone, diaphysis, shaft of bone; **-stufe,** *f.* intermediate stage; **-wand,** *f.* mediastinum, middle wall; **-weich,** medium (moderately) soft; **-wert,** *m.* average, mean, mean value; **-zahl,** *f.* -en, mean; **-zahn,** *m.* incisor (tooth); **-zehe,** *f.* median digit, middle toe; **-zehenknochen,** *m.* middle phalanx of toe; **-zeug,** *n.* middle (second) stuff.

mitten, in the middle or midst, amid(st), midway (between); **-durchmesser,** *m.* mid-diameter.

Mitternacht, *f.* midnight, north.

mittig, central, centric, centrally located.

mittler, middle, central, inner, medium, average; **mittlere Abweichung,** *f.* **mittlere Streuung,** *f.* standard deviation, scattering average.

mittlerweile, meanwhile.

mit-übernehmen, to take over with; **-unter,** occasionally, at times; **-verarbeiten,** to process together with; **-welt,** *f.* present age; **-wirken,** to cooperate, contribute, take part, assist; **-wirkung,** *f.* cooperation, participation, assistance; **-zählen,** to number with or among.

Mizelle, *f.* colloidal salt or electrolite.

Möbel, *n.* piece of furniture; **-mattierung,** *f.* rubbed finish of furniture.

mobil, mobile, quick, nimble, active.

mobilisieren, to mobilize.

Mobilität, *f.* mobility, motility.

möblieren, to furnish, fit up.

mochte (mögen), liked to.

möchte (mögen), would like to.

Mockstahl, *m.* semisteel.

Mode, *f.* fashion, mode, vogue; **-gewürz,** *n.* allspice, pimento.

Model, *m.* modulus, block.

Modell, *n.* model, pattern, mold.

modellieren, to model, mold.

Modellier-holz, *n.* modeling tool; **-ton,** *m.* modeling clay.

modeln, to model, mold, figure.

Moder, *n.* mold, putrefaction, decay, humus, mud, silt, mire; **-duft,** *m.* musty (moldy) smell, smell of decay, cadaverous smell; **-erde,** *f.* soil humus derived from (decayed) decomposing vegetable matter; **-geruch,** *m.* musty (moldy) smell, smell of decay, cadaverous smell; **-haft,** moldy, musty, molded, moldering, putrid.

moderieren, to moderate.

moderig, musty, moldy, putrid, decayed.

modern, to molder, rot, decay, putrefy.

modern, modern, fashionable.

Moder-pilz, *m.* saprophytic fungus; **-stein,** *m.* rottenstone; **-stoff,** *m.* humus; **-torf,** *m.* moldy peat.

Modifikations-breite, -weite, *f.* amplitude of variation.

modifizieren, to modify.

Modul, *m.* modulus.

Modus, *m.* mode, method, mood (of verbs).

mögen, may, like to; **gern** ∼, to be fond of; **lieber** ∼, to prefer.

möglich, possible, feasible, practicable, eventual.

möglicherweise, possibly, perhaps, as far as possible.

Möglichkeit, *f.* possibility, eventuality, feasibility, practicability; **nach** ∼, as far as possible.

möglichst, (as much) as possible.

Mohn, *m.* poppy (Papaver); **-gewächse,** *n.pl.* Papaveraceae; **-kapsel,** *f.,* **-kopf,** *m.* poppy capsule, poppyhead; **-ling,** *m.* Meconopsis; **-öl,** *n.* poppy-seed oil; **-salt,** *m.* poppy juice, opium; **-samen,** *m.* poppy seed; **-säure,** *f.* meconic acid; **-stoff,** *m.* narcotine; **-typ** (der Flugorgane), *m.* poppy type (of flying organs of seed).

Mohr, *m.* black, Ethiopian, Moor, Negro.

Möhre, *f.* carrot.

Möhrenfarbstoff, *m.* carotene.

Mohrenhirse, *f.* kaffir (caffre) corn (Sorghum).

Mohrrübe, *f.* carrot.

Mohrsches Salz, *n.* Mohr's salt (ammonium ferrous sulphate).

moirieren, to cloud, water.

Mol, *n.* mol.

Molargewicht, *n.* molar weight.

Molch, *m.* salamander.

Molekelgewicht, *n.* molecular weight.

Molekül, *n.* **Molekel,** *f.* molecule.

Molekular-abstossung, *f.* molecular repulsion; **-anziehung,** *f.* molecular attraction; **-bewegung,** *f.* molecular motion or movement; **-brechung,** *f.,* **-brechungsvermögen,** *n.* molecular refraction; **-drehung,** *f.* molecular rotation; **-druck,** *m.* molecular pressure; **-erscheinung,** f. molecular appearance, phenomenon, or effect; **-formel,** *f.* molecular formula.

Molekular-gewicht, *n.* molecular weight; **-gewichtsbestimmung,** *f.* molecular-weight determination; **-grösse,** *f.* molecular (weight) magnitude; **-reibung,** *f.* molecular friction; **-störung,** *f.* molecular disturbance; **-verbindung,** *f.* molecular compound; **-wärme,** *f.* molecular heat; **-wirkung,** *f.* molecular action.

molekularzertrümmernd, molecule-disintegrating; **molekularzertrümmernde Stosskraft,** *f.* molecule-disintegrating impact or energy.

Molekularzustand, *m.* molecular condition or state, molecularity.

Molekül-schicht, *f.* layer of molecules; **-sieb,** *n.* microfilter; **-strahl,** *m.* molecular ray.

Molen-bruch, *m.* mole fraction; **-verhältnis,** *n.* mole ratio.

Mol-gewicht, *n.* molar weight; **-grösse,** *f.* molar magnitude; **-ion,** *n.* mole ion.

Molisierung, *f.* molization (union of ions to form a molecule).

molk (melken), milked.

Molke, *f.* **Molken,** *f.pl.* whey.

Molken-butter, *f.* whey butter; **-eiweiss,** *n.* whey protein; **-säure,** *f.* lactic acid; **-wesen,** *n.* **-wirtschaft** *f.* dairy.

Molkerei, *f.* dairy; **-produkt,** *n.* dairy product.

molkig, wheyey, like whey.

Möller, *m.* mixture (of ores), burden (of blast furnace).

Möllerung, *f.* mixing the ores.

mollig, pleasant, comfortable, cosy, snug, soft.

Molluske, *f.* mollusk.

Molluskengehäuse, *n.* shell of mollusk.

Molluskumkörperchen, *n.pl.* molluscum bodies.

Molrefraktion, *f.* molar refraction.

Molterbrett, *n.* moldboard plowshare tail.

Mol-verhältnis, *n.* molar ratio; **-volum,** *n.* molal volume, molar volume.

Molybdän, *n.* molybdenum; **-blau,** *n.* molybdenum blue; **-bleispat,** *m.* wulfenite; **-glanz,** *m.* molybdenite; **-haltig,** molybdeniferous; **-kies,** *m.* molybdenite; **-ocker,** *m.* molybdic ocher, molybdite; **-oxyd,** *n.* molybdenum oxide; **-säure,** *f.* molybdic acid.

Molzustand, *m.* molecular condition.

Moment, *m.*-e, moment; **-zünder,** *m.* instantaneous fuse; **-zündpille,** *f.* flash composition.

Moment, *n.*-e, reason, motive, momentum, feature, force, instance, impetus.

momentan, momentary, instantaneous.

Moment-aufnahme, *f.* **-bild,** *n.* instantaneous photograph, snapshot.

monalkyliert, monalkylated.

Monat, *m.*-e, month.

monat(e)lang, lasting a month or months, for months.

Monats-bericht, *m.*-e, monthly report; **-fluss,** *m.* menstruation; **-heft,** *n.* monthly part or number; **-schrift,** *f.* monthly publication.

Mönch, *m.* monk.

Mönchs-kappe, *f.* monkshood, aconite, cowl; **-pfeffer,** *m.* monk's pepper tree, agnus castus.

Mond, *m.* moon; **-förmig,** moon (crescent) shaped, lunate; **-glas,** *n.* crown glass; **-milch,** *f.* agaric mineral; **-periode,** *f.* lunar periodicity; **-raute,** *f.* moonwort (Botrychium); **-ring,** *m.* pith fleck; **-same,** *f.* moonseed (Menispermum); **-stein,** *m.* moonstone; **-viole,** *f.* Lunaria.

Mono-carbonsäure, *f.* monocarboxylic acid; **-cyclisch,** monocyclic; **-derivat,** *n.* monosubstituted derivative, monoderivative; **-gamie,** *f.* monogamy; **-gonie,** *f.* asexual reproduction; **-graphie,** *f.* monograph; **-hydratisch,** monohydric; **-klinisch,** monoclinic; **-log,** *m.* monologue.

monomer, monocarpellary, monomer.

mono-phasisch, monophase, single-phase; **-stemon,** *n.* having only one cycle of stamens; **-ton,** monotonous; **-trich,** monotrichic; **-tricha,** monotricha.

Monoxyd, *n.* monoxide.

monozyklisch, monocyclic.

Montage, *f.* mounting, assemblage, setting up.

Montan-industrie, *f.* mining industry; **-wachs,** *n.* montan wax.

montieren, to mount, fit up, erect, equip, assemble.

Moor, *n.*-e, moor, bog, fen; **-boden,** *m.* marshy soil; **-erde,** *f.* bog earth, peaty soil, muck soil; **-heide,** *f.* heath, moorland; **-lauge,** *f.* marsh lye, extract from bog earth; **-mergel,** *m.* marl found in peat deposits; **-salz,** *n.* marsh salt; **-strauch,** *m.* Itea; **-teich,** *m.* pond in a moor country; **-torf,** *m.* molded peat; **-wasser,** *n.* peat water.

Moos, *n.* moss (lichen), peat bog; **-achat,** *m.* moss agate; **-artig,** mosslike, mossy; **-beere,** *f.* cranberry, moor-(moss-) berry (*Vaccinium oxycoccus*); **-bestand,** *m.* stand on mossy ground; **-büchse,** *f.* moss capsule, theca; **-farn,** *m.* Selaginella; **-frucht,** *f.* moss sporangium; **-glöckchen,** *n.* Linnaea; **-grün,** *n.* moss green; **-haube,** *f.* veil, calyptra; **-heide,** *f.* moss heath.

moosig, mossy, sphagnous.

Moss-kelch, *m.* perichaetium; **-kunde,** *f.* muscology, bryology; **-moor,** *n.* sphagnum moor; **-pflanzen,** *f.pl.* Bryophyta; **-pulver,** *n.* lycopodium powder; **-rohhumus,** *m.* moss peat, moss raw humus; **-schicht,** *f.* layer of moss; **-stempel,** *m.* podetium of certain lichens.

Moos-stärke, *f.* lichen starch, lichenin; **-sumpf,** *m.* moss bog; **-teppich,** *m.* carpet of moss; **-tierchen,** *n.* moss animal (Polyzoa or Bryozoa); **-tierwelt,** *f.* moss fauna; **-torf,** *m.* peat (turf), sphagnum peat; **-urne,** *f.* theca of moss; **-vorkeim,** *m.* protonema of moss; **-wuchs,** *m.* mossy growth.

Moräne, *f.* moraine; **-material,** *n.* moraine deposit.

Morast, *m.* bog, fen, marsh, mud, swamp, morass; **-erz,** *n.* bog ore.

Morbillen, *f.pl.* measles, rubella.

Morchel, *f.* morel.

Mord, *m.* murder.

mordanzieren, to mordant.

Mord-fliege, *f.* tachina fly; **-luft,** *f.* musty air, cadaverous smell; **-raupen,** *f.pl.* carnivorous caterpillars.

morganatisch, morganatic (marriage).

morgen, tomorrow.

Morgen, *m.* morning, dawn, East, Orient, measure of land, acre; **-brot,** *n.* breakfast.

morgend, of tomorrow.

Morgen-land, *n.* East, Orient; **-röte,** *f.* red sky, aurora.

morgens, in the morning, every morning.

Morgenstunde, *f.* morning hour.

Morin(ga)gerbsäure, *f.* moringatannic acid.

Morphium, *n.* morphine, morphia.

Morphogen, *m.* formative (evolution of form).

Morphologie, *f.* morphology.

morsch, rotten, decayed, moldy, decomposed, tender, frail, fragile.

morschen, to rot, decay.

Morschheit, *f.* rottenness, decay.

Morselle, *f.* lozenge.

Mörser, *m.*-, mortar; **-keule,** *f.* pestle.

Mörtel, *m.* mortar, plaster; **-kranz,** *m.* "wreath of mortar"; **-wäsche,** *f.* thin mortar, grout.

mosaik-artig, mosaiclike; **-pflaster,** *n.* fancy pavement, shagreen

mosaisch, mosaic.

Moschus, *m.* mush; **-distel;** *f.* musk thistle; **-drüse,** *f.* musk gland; **-korn,** *n.* musk seed; **-kraut,** *n.* cat thyme, Adoxa; **-wurzel,** *f.* muskroot (*Ferula sumbul*).

Mosel, *f.* Moselle; **-wein,** *m.* Moselle (wine).

Moskovade, *f.* muscovado.

Most, *m.* must, fruit juice.

Mostrich, *m.* mustard.

Most-sirup, *m.* arrope; **-waage,** *f.* must gauge.

motivieren, to motivate.

Motorenbetriebsstoff, *m.* motor fuel.

Motor-pflug, *m.* motor plow; **-rad,** *n.* motorcycle; **-walze,** *f.* motor roller.

Motring, *m.* skein, hank.

Motte, *f.* moth.

Motten-pulver, *n.* moth (insect) powder; **-schutzmittel,** *n.* moth preventative; **-strauch,** *m.* Plectranthus.

Motze, *f.* marver.

moussieren, to effervesce, froth, sparkle, fizz.

Möwe, *f.* (sea) gull.

Mowrasäure, *f.* mowric acid.

Mücke, *f.* gnat, midge, mosquito.

Mucor, *m.* micro; **-mykose,** *f.* mucor mycosis.

Mudde, *f.* mud.

müde, (*gen.*) tired, exhausted, weary, worn out, fatigued.

Müdigkeit, *f.* fatigue, weariness, exhaustion.

Muff, *m.* muff, sleeve, socket (joint), clamp, coupling box, moldiness, mustiness.

Muffel, *f.* muffle, mouth, snout; **-farbe,** *f,* muffle color.

Muffen-eisen, *n.* socket iron; **-rohr,** *n.* socket pipe.

muffig, musty, moldy.

Mühe, *f.* pains, trouble, exterior, effort, care; **sich ~ geben,** to take pains.

mühelos, without trouble, effortless, easy.

mühen, to trouble, toil, take pains.

mühevoll, troublesome, difficult, laborious.

Mühle, *f.* mill, crusher, grinder, pulverizer.

Mühlen-bauer, *m.* millwright; **-staub,** *m.* mill dust.

Mühlstein, *m.* millstone.

Muhr, *f.* moraine.

Mühsal, *n.* difficulty, trouble.

mühsam, troublesome, laborious, hard.

mühselig, laborious, hard, toilsome.

Mühseligkeit, *f.* hardship, misery.

Muldbrett, *n.* moldboard, leveling machine.

Mulde, *f.* trough, basin, bowl, hollow, valley, pig mold, pig (of lead).

Mulden-blei, *n.* pig lead; **-presse,** *f.* cylinder press (for textiles).

Müll, Mull, *n.* dust, (dry) mold, refuse, sweepings, humus.

Müller, *m.* miller.

Mull-erde, *f.* humus soil, leaf mold; **-krapp,** *m.* mull madder.

Mulm, *m.* ore dust, mold humus, decay, rot.

mulmen, to pulverize.

mulmig, dusty, earthy, decayed, wormeaten.

multipel, multiple.

Multiplikand, *m.* factor.

Multiplikationseffekt, *m.* effect of multiplication.

Multiplikator, *m.* multiplier.

multiplizieren, to multiply.

multrig, moldy.

Mumie, *f.* mummy.

Mumienbildung, *f.* mummification.

mumifizieren, to mummify.

Mumme, *f.* mum (a strong beer), mask.

Mummelblume, *f.* nuphar (aquatic plant).

Mund, *m.* mouth, opening, os, orifice, muzzle, vent, aperture, stoma, ostiole; **-art,** *f.* dialect, idiom; **-besatz,** *m.* peristome; **-boden,** *m.* floor of the mouth; **-bucht,**

f. buccal cavity, oral sinus, stomodaeum; **-darm,** *m.* stomodaeum, esophagus; **-dolche,** *m.pl.* styluses; **-drüse,** *f.* buccal (oral) gland; **-einstülpung,** *f.* oral invagination.

munden, to taste good.

münden, to discharge, run into, empty, open.

Mund-feld, *n.* peristome; **-gegend,** *f.* oral region; **-gerecht,** fit for eating, suitable; **-gliedmassen,** *n.pl.* mouth parts; **-grube,** *f.* oral diverticulum; **-höhle,** *f.* mouth cavity.

Mundhöhlen-boden, *m.* floor of mouth cavity; **-dach,** *n.* hard or bony palate, roof of mouth cavity; **-drüse,** *f.* buccal gland; **-eingang,** *m.* entrance into oral cavity; **-zahn,** *m.* pharyngeal tooth.

mündig, of age.

Mund-kapselbewaffnung, *f.* armature of mouth capsule; **-kegel,** *m.* orifice of mouth, hypostome, oral cone, peristome; **-klappe,** *f.* epiglottis; **-klemme,** *f.* lockjaw; **-lappen,** *m.* labial palpus, oral lobe; **-leim,** *m.* mouth glue (to be moistened by licking).

mündlich, oral, verbal.

Mund-masse, *f.* buccal mass; **-öffnung,** *f.* orifice of mouth, oral aperture; **-rachen,** *m.* isthmus of fauces; **-rachenhöhle,** *f.* oropharyngeal cavity; **-rand,** *m.* edge of mouth; **-region,** *f.* mouth region; **-saugnapf,** *m.* oral sucker; **-saum,** *m.* peristome, aperture.

Mund-scheibe, *f.* peristome, oral disk; **-schleim,** *m.* oral mucus; **-schleimhaut,** *f.* mucous membrane of mouth; **-schliesser,** *m.* orbicularis; **-schiltz,** *m.* oral slit; **-schlund,** *m.* fauces; **-segel,** *n.pl.* labial palpi, velum; **-segment,** *n.* oral segment.

Mund-skelett, *n.* visceral skeleton; **-spalte,** *f.* buccal cleft, fissura oris; **-speichel,** *m.* saliva of the mouth; **-speicheldrüse,** *f.* salivary gland; **-stück,** *n.* mouthpiece; **-teile,** *m.pl.* organs of the mouth; **-tentakel,** oral tentacle; **-trichter,** *m.* oral funnel.

Mündung, *f.* mouth, opening, aperture, orifice, ostiole, outlet, estuary.

Mündungs-energie, *f.* muzzle energy; **-feuer,** *n.* muzzle flash.

mündungsfeuerfrei, flashless; **mündungsfeuerfreies Pulver,** *n.* flashless powder.

Mündungs-knall, *m.* muzzle sound; **-paraphysen,** *f.pl.* paraphyses surrounding an orifice.

Mund-verdauung, *f.* oral digestion **-vorhof,** *m.* vestibule of mouth; **-wasser,** *n.* gargle, mouthwash; **-werkzeuge,** *n.pl.* implements

of the mouth; **-winkel,** *m.* corner of the mouth; **-wulst,** *f.* peristome; **-zahn,** *m.* tooth (of the mouth).

munter, brisk, lively, cheerful, vigorous.

Münz-anstalt, *f.* mint; **-beschickung,** *f.* alloyage.

Munze, *f.* mint (Mentha).

Münze, *f.* coin, money, medal, mint.

münzen, to mint, coin.

Münz-gehalt, *m.* fineness (of coins); **-wesen,** *n.* coinage, minting.

mürbe, tender, soft, delicate, mellow, brittle, friable, short, pliable, affected with dry rot; **-machemittel,** *n.* shortening or softening agents.

Mürbigkeit, *f.* mellowness.

Mure, *f.* rockslide.

Murgang, *m.* (wet) landslide.

murmeln, to murmur.

Murmeltier, *n.* marmot.

Mus, *n.* jam, marmalade, pulp, (fruit) sauce; **-artig,** like jam, pulpy, thick.

Muschel, *f.* mussel, shell, concha, turbinate bone, external ear; **-bein,** *n.* turbinate bone; **-förmig,** shell-shaped; **-höhle,** *f.* hollow of concha, cavity of the turbinated bone.

muschelig, conchoidal, shelly, shell-like.

Muschel-kalk, *m.* shell lime(stone); **-kalkformation,** *f.* ostracite formation; **-krebse,** *m.pl.* Ostracoda; **-marmor,** *m.* shell marble, lumachel; **-mergel,** *m.* shell marl; **-schieber-Steurung,** *f.* slide-valve gear; **-tiere,** *p.* Lamellibranchiata, shellfish, Conchifera, mollusks.

Musiker, *m.* musician.

Musiv-arbeit, *f.* mosaic work; **-gold,** *n.* mosaic gold.

Muskarin, *n.* muscarine.

Muskat, balsam, *m.* nutmeg butter.

Muskate, *f.* nutmeg.

Muskateller, *m.* muscatel.

Muskatenblüte, *f.* mace.

Muskatnuss, *f.* nutmeg, Myristica.

Muskel, *m.* muscle; **-ansatz,** *m.* insertion of muscle, strenuous work; **-arbeit,** *f.* work on muscles, study of muscles; **-bau,** *m.* structure of muscle; **-bauch,** *m.* belly of a muscle; **-bewegung,** *f.* movement of muscle; **-binde,** *f.* ligament, fascia; **-bündel,** *n.* fascicle of muscle.

Muskel-eindruck, *m.* muscular impression; **-eiweiss,** *n.* myosin; **-empfindung,** *f.*

muscular sensation; **-farbstoff,** *m.* muscle pigment; **-faser,** *f.* muscular (muscle) fiber; **-fleisch,** *n.* muscular substance; **-gewebe,** *n.* muscular tissue.

Muskel-gift, *n.* muscle poison; **-gleichgewicht,** *n.* muscular balance; **-gräte,** *f.* small fishbone; **-haut, -hülle,** *f.* muscular coat; **-interstitien,** *n.pl.* interstices in the muscles; **-kopf,** *m.* head of muscles; **-körper,** *m.* body of muscle.

Muskel-lähmung, *f.* paralysis of the muscles; **-lehre,** *f.* myology; **-leistung,** *f.* muscular efficiency; **-magen,** *m.* gizzard; **-masse,** *f.* muscular substance; **-narbe,** *f.* scar of muscle; **-reifen,** *m.* muscle hoop.

Muskel-scheide, *f.* sheath of muscle; **-schicht,** *f.* muscular layer; **-schwanz,** *m.* tail of muscle; **-sehne,** *f.* tendon; **-spannung,** *f.* muscular tension; **-stoff,** *m.* sarcosine; **-tätigkeit,** *f.* muscle activity; **-trichine,** *f.* muscle trichina; **-ursprung,** *m.* origin of a muscle.

Muskel-wand, *f.* muscle wall; **-wulst,** *f.* muscular prominence; **-zelle,** *f.* muscle cell; **-ziehen,** *n.* muscular contraction; **-zucker,** *m.* inositol; **-zuckung,** *f.* muscle twitch, spasm or contraction; **-zug,** *m.* muscular fasciculus; **-zusammenziehung,** *f.* contracture of the muscle.

Muskovit, *m.* muscovite, potassium mica.

Muskulatur, *f.* musculature.

muskulös, muscular.

muss (müssen), must, has to.

Muss, *n.* (absolute) necessity.

Musse, *f.* leisure.

Musselin, *m.* muslin.

müssen, must, be obliged to.

müssig, idle, lazy.

musste (müssen), had to, was forced to.

müsste (müssen), would have to.

Muster, *n.* model, type, standard, ideal, pattern, design, sample, specimen, test, example; **-brief,** *m.* pattern card; **-fläche,** *f.* representative area; **-flasche,** *f.* sample bottle; **-gültig,** model, standard, typical, ideal, classic; **-haft,** exemplary, standard, typical; **-karte,** *f.* pattern card, sample card; **-mässig,** standard, typical.

mustern, to examine, inspect, figure, emboss, muster, criticize.

Muster-sammlung, *f.* specimen collection; **-schutz,** *m.* registered pattern, copyright.

Mut, *m.* courage, spirit, heart, mood, humor, wrath, anger, pluck.

Mutation, *f.* mutation.

Mutationstheorie, *f.* theory of discontinuous variations.

mutig, spirited, courageous.

mut-massen, to guess, presume, suppose, conjecture; **-masslich,** supposed, probably, conjectural, apparent; **-massung,** *f.* presumption, conjecture, supposition.

Mutter, *f.* mother, matrix, womb, uterus, nut; **-balg,** *m.* uterine cyst; **-band,** *n.* ligament of uterus; **-baum,** *m.* nurse tree, parent tree; **-bestand,** *m.* shelter wood, parent stand; **-biene,** *f.* queen bee; **-boden,** *m.* parent tissue, stoma, native soil, topsoil, foundation; **-erde,** *f.* garden mold, native soil; **-fass,** *n.* mother vat; **-fieber,** *n.* puerperal fever.

Mutter-form, *f.* parent form; **-gänge,** *m.pl.* parent galleries (of beetles); **-gestein,** *n.* gangue, matrix, parent rock; **-gewebe,** *n.* mother tissue, matrix, uterine tissue; **-gewinde,** *f.* female thread; **-grund,** *m.* base of uterus; **-gummi,** *n.* galbanum (gum resin); **-hals,** *m.* neck of uterus; **-korn,** *n.* ergot, blighted corn (*Sclerotium clavus*); **-harz,** *n.* galbanum.

Mutter-kornpilz, *m.* ergot of rye; **-kraut,** *n.* fever-few (*Chrysanthemum parthenium*); **-kuchen,** *m.* placenta; **-kümmel,** *m.* cumin; **-lauge,** *f.* mother liquor; **-leib,** *m.* womb, uterus; **-mund,** *m.* orifice of uterus; **-nelke,** *f.* mother clove; **-organismus,** *m.* donor organism; **-pech,** *n.* meconium.

Mutter-rohr, *n.* Fallopian tube; **-scheide,** *f.* vagina; **-schlüssel,** *m.* nut wrench; **-substanz,** *f.* mother substance, stroma, matrix; **-tier,** *f.* mother (parent) cell; **-zimt,** *m.* cassia.

Mütze, *f.* calyptra, cap.

mützenförmig, cap-shaped.

Mycelast, *m.* **Mycelfaden,** *m.* mycelial hypha.

myceliar (Rand), mycelial (border).

Mycelium, *n.* spawn, mycelium.

Mycel-pilze, *m.pl.* Hyphomycetes; **-rasen,** *m.* fur of a mold; **-überwinterung,** *f.* mycelial hibernation.

mydriatisch, mydriatic.

Myelin, *n.* myelin.

Mykologie, *f.* mycology.

Mykorrhiza, *f.* combination of mycelium and suckers (roots).

Mykose, Mykosis, *f.* mycosis.

mykotisch, mycotic.

mykotroph, mycotrophic.

Myocarditis, *f.* myocarditis.

Myrikawachs, *n.* myrtle wax.

Myronsäure, *f.* myronic acid.

Myrosinbehälter, *m.* myrosin cell.

Myrrhe, *f.* **Myrrhenharz,** *n.* myrrh.

Myrte, *f.* myrtle.

Myrten-gewächse, *n.pl.* Myrtaceae; **-wachs,** *n.* myrtle wax.

mystisch, mystic(al).

Mytilotoxin, *n.* mytilotoxine.

Myxomyzeten, *f.pl.* Myxomycetes.

Myzel, *n.* mycelium; **-ast, -faden,** *m.* mycelial hypha.

N

Nabe, *f.* hub, nave (of wheel), boss.

Nabel, *m.* hilum, navel, umbilicus; **-blase,** *f.* umbilical vesicle; **-fleck,** *m.* hilum, chalaza; **-gegend,** *f.* umbilical region; **-kraut,** *n.* navelwort; **-ritze,** *f.* umbilical fissure; **-schnur,** *f.* umbilical cord, funiculus; **-schwiele,** *f.* umbilical callus; **-strang,** *m.* umbilical cord, funiculus; **-tiere,** *n.pl.* Amniota.

nach, to, toward, after, according to, (taste) of, behind, subsequent, next to; $\sim$ **und** $\sim$, little by little, gradually, by degrees; $\sim$ **vorn,** toward the front, forward; $\sim$ **wie vor,** just the same as before, now as ever, as usual; $\sim$ **aussen,** outward; externally; . . . $\sim$ **hin-(zu),** toward; $\sim$ **unten,** downward; der Färbung $\sim$, as regards the color; eine Frage $\sim$, a question as to; je $\sim$, according to; $\sim$ **mehr, des schmeckt** $\sim$ **mehr,** it tastes like more; er verlangt $\sim$ **mehr,** he longs (is anxious) for more.

nach-ahmen, to imitate, copy, counterfeit, adulterate; **-ahmung,** *f.* imitation; **-arbeit,** *f.* retouching, repair, maintenance, afterwork.

Nachbar, *m.*-n, neighbor; **-bestäubung,** *f.* geitonogamy; **-gebiet,** *n.* neighboring territory, related subject; **-kreuzung,** *f.* vicinism (due to hybridization); **-linie,** *f.* adjacent line; **-schaft,** *f.* neighborhood, vicinity; **-zelle,** *f.* adjacent cell.

Nach-behandlung, *f.* after or subsequent treatment; **-beizen,** to redye, sadden; **-beschickung,** *f.* aftercharging, aftercharge; **-bessern,** to improve, touch up, replant, retouch, repair, mend; **-besserung,** *f.* afterculture, replant; **-bild,** *n.* copy, afterimage, imitation; **-bilden,** to copy, reproduce, imitate, counterfeit; **-bleichen,** to bleach again; **-blutung,** *f.* secondary bleeding; **-brand,** *m.* second (burning) fire.

nach-brennen, to smolder, burn again; **-dampf,** *m.* afterdamp, chokedamp; **-dauern,** to continue, last.

nachdem, afterward, hereafter, after, when, according to; je $\sim$, according as.

nach-denken, to meditate, reflect; **-druck,** *m.* energy, firmness, emphasis, reprinting, reproduction; **-dunkeln,** to darken, grow darker, deepen, sadden; **-eifer,** *m.* emulation; **-eilen,** to hasten after, pursue, lag, retard, follow; **-eilend,** lagging; **-einander,** *n.* succession; **-einander,** one after another, successively; **-eiszeit,** *f.* postglacial time.

Nachen, *m.* boat.

Nachf., *abbr.* (Nachfolger), successor(s).

nach-färben, to dye again, counterstain; **-filter,** *m.* second filter; **-filtern,** to filter again, refilter; **-fixieren,** to fix again; **-folge,** *f.* succession, sequence; **-folgen,** to follow, pursue, succeed; **-folgend,** following, subsequent, continuous, consecutive, secondary; **-folger,** *m.*-, successor, follower, imitator; **-forschen,** to search, examine, investigate; **-forschung,** *f.* research, investigation, examination, search, scrutiny.

Nach-frage, *f.* demand, inquiry; **-fragen,** to inquire about, demand, investigate; **-frischen,** to refine; **-frucht,** *f.* succeeding crop in a rotation, aftercrop; **-führen,** to introduce later; **-füllen,** to fill up, replenish, add to; **-gären,** to ferment again, undergo afterfermentation; **-gärung,** *f.* afterfermentation, secondary fermentation; **-gärungshefe,** *f.* secondary yeast fermentation; **-geahmt,** imitated, counterfeit, fictitious.

nach-geben, to give in, give way, stretch, submit; **-geben,** *n.* submission, yielding; **-geburt,** *f.* afterbirth; **-gehen,** to follow, pursue, lose, perform; **-gerben,** to tan again; **-geruch,** *m.* aftersmell; **-geschmack,** *m.* aftertaste; **-gewiesen** (nachweisen) detected; **-giebig,** flexible, pliable, compliant; **-giessen,** to pour again, add more, refill, replenish.

Nach-glühen, *n.* afterglow; **-guss,** *m.*-e, second pouring, refilling replenishing; **-hall,** *m.* reverberation, resonance, echo; **-haltig,** lasting, enduring, sustained, persevering; **-haltigkeit,** *f.* permanence, durability, lastingness, perseverance, prolonged action; **-her,** afterward, subsequently, hereafter, later (on); **-herig,** later, subsequent, future; **-hieb,** *m.* secondary felling; **-hilfe,** *f.* assistance, aid; **-hirn,** *n.* metencephalon.

Nach-hinken, *n.* time lag; **-holen,** to recover, make up; **-hut,** *f.* rear, rear guard; second pasture (pasturage); **-impfung,** *f.* reinoculation; **-infektion,** *f.* reinfection; **kochen,** to boil again, reboil; **-komme,** *m.* descendant, offspring, successor; **-kommen,** to follow, overtake, comply with, perform, accede to, come later; **-kommenerwartung,** *f.* perjugate expectancy; **-kommenschaft,** *f.* progeny, offspring.

Nach-kondensator, *m.* secondary condenser; **-kühlen,** to cool again, recool; **-ladung,** *f.* additional charge, recharge; **-lass,** *m.* relaxation, intermission, annealing, discount, rebate, reductions, diminution, deduction; **-lassen,** to leave behind, slow up, bequeath, pour after, temper, anneal, loosen, slacken, relax, abate, quiet off (market), deduct, fail, subside, soften, fall off; **-lässig,** negligent, careless, remiss.

Nach-lässigkeit, *f.* negligence, indolence; **-lasskette,** *f.* extension chain; **-lauf,** *m.* second(ary) running, chase, tails (distilling); **-laufen,** to pursue, run after; **-lese,** *f.* gleaning, remains, rereading, later selection; **-leuchten,** to shine afterward, phosphoresce; **-liefern,** to furnish subsequently, supplement.

nachmachen, to imitate, counterfeit; **nachgemacht,** imitated, counterfeit, artificial.

nach-malig, subsequent; **-mark,** *n.* medulla oblongata; **-mast,** *f.* afterpannage; **-mattieren,** *n.* ultimate delustering; **-mittag,** *m.* afternoon; **-nahme,** *f.* cash reimbursement; **-niere,** *f.* metanephros; **-nuancieren,** to shade (colors); **-pflanzen,** *n.* replanting; **-pressen,** to repress.

nach-präfen, to re-examine, control, check; **-prüfung,** *f.* aftertrial, re-examination; **-putzen,** to repolish, finish off; **-rechnen,** to check, verify, examine; **-reifen,** *n.* subsequent (secondary) ripening; **-reifung,** *f.* finishing (photographic emulsion); **-richt,** *f.* news, information, notice; **-rücken,** *n.* progress, advance; **-rühmen,** to accredit, say in praise of; **-sacken,** to sag, subside, settle; **-sagen,** to say after, repeat after, report.

nach-salzen, to salt again, resalt; **-schieben,** to push after; **-schieber,** *m.* proleg, caudal disk (of caterpillars); **-schiessen,** *n.* aftershooting (in quarries); **-schlagen,** to look

up, refer to, consult; **-schlagewerk,** *n.* reference work; **-schleifen,** to regrind, resharpen; **-schlüssel,** *m.* master key, skeleton key; **-schmecken,** to leave an aftertaste; **-schrift,** *f.* postscript, transcript, copy.

nach-schrumpfen, to aftershrink; **-schub,** *m.* relief, convoy; **-schwaden,** *m.* afterdamp; **-schwelen,** to continue to smolder; **-sehen,** to look, inspect, search, examine, see (to), investigate, overhaul, overlook, excuse; **-setzen,** to add, put after, pursue, postpone; **-sicht,** *f.* inspection, forbearance, indulgence, respite; **-spülen,** to rinse after, wash again; **-spüren,** to trace.

nächst, next, nearest; **-ältest,** next eldest: **∼ dem,** after that, besides; **-folgend,** succeeding, immediately succeeding; **-liegend,** nearest, next following; **am nächsten,** nearest, next.

nach-stechen, to refeed, repass, top up; **-stehen,** to follow, be inferior; **-stehend,** following, below; **-stellbar,** regulable, adjustable; **-stellen,** to regulate, put back, set traps.

nächstens, next time, shortly.

nächstniedrig, next lower.

nachsuchen, to search after, look for, seek, apply for.

Nachsud, *m.* second (boiling) evaporation.

Nacht, *f.* night; **-blume,** *f.* nocturnal flower; **-blütler,** *m.pl.* night-flowering plants.

Nach-teil, *m.* disadvantage, detriment, inconvenience, drawback, damage; **-teilig,** disadvantageous, detrimental, injurious.

Nach-falter, *m.* moth (Heterocera); **-fang,** *m.* night collecting.

Nachtigall, *f.* nightingale.

Nachtisch, *m.* dessert.

Nacht-kerze, *f.* night light, evening primrose (*Oenothera biennis*); **-kerzengewächse,** *n.pl.* Onagraceae.

nächtlich, nightly, by night.

Nacht-mahl, *n.* supper; **-pfauenauge,** *n.* emperor moth.

Nach-trag, *m.:e,* supplement, postscript, addendum; **-tragen,** to add, append, carry a thing after; **-träglich,** supplementary, additional, further, extra, subsequent, later, ultimately; **-tripper,** *m.* gleet.

nachts, in the night.

Nacht-schatten, *m.* nightshade (Solanum); **-schattengewächse,** *n.pl.* Solanaceae; **-stellung,** *f.* night position (of leaves); **-tau,** *m.* night dew.

nach-verdampfen, to evaporate again, re-evaporate; **-verjüngung,** *f.* regeneration after removal of old growth; **-walzen,** to dress, finish; **-waschen,** to wash again, rewash; **-weichen,** to couch; **-weis,** *m.* detection, identification, proof, demonstration, information; **-weisbar,** detectable, demonstrable, manifest, evident; **-weisen,** to detect, prove, demonstrate, indicate, establish, identify, refer to; **-weislich,** demonstrable; **-weismethode,** *f.* method of determination or detection.

Nach-weismittel, *n.* means of detection or determination; **-weisung,** *f.* detection, proof, demonstration; **-welt,** *f.* posterity; **-wert,** *m.*-e, later (future) value; **-wiegen,** to weigh again, reweigh; **-wirkung,** *f.* after-effect, secondary effect; **-wirkungsbewegung,** *f.* aftereffect movement; **-wuchs,** *m.* rising generation, second growth; **-würze,** *f.* second wort; **-ziehen,** to pull after.

Nach-zucht, *f.* regeneration; **-zügler,** *m.* straggler, laggard, retarded tree; **-zündung,** *f.* retarded ignition.

Nacken, *m.* nape of the neck; **-band,** *n.* cervical ligament; **-beuge,** *f.* nape bend, cervical flexure; **-drüse,** *f.* cervical ganglion; **-furche,** *f.* neck furrow; **-gabel,** *f.* scent horns (of caterpillars); **-gegend,** *f.* cervical region; **-höcker,** *m.* nape prominence; **-knorpel,** *m.* nuchal cartilage.

Nacken-kreuz, *n.* nape cross (meeting of hair lines); **-krümmung,** *f.* curvature of the neck; **-linie,** *f.* nape line; **-mark,** *n.* cervical portion of spinal cord; **-platte,** *f.* neck plate; **-quermuskel,** *m.* transverse cervical muscle; **-stachel,** *m.* dorsal spine; **-steisslänge,** *f.* nape-breechlength; **-strang,** *m.* cord of cervical ligaments.

Nacken-tentakeln, *f.pl.* cervical tentacles; **-warzenbeinmuskel,** *m.* trachelomastoid muscle; **-winkel,** *m.* cervical angle; **-wirbel,** *m.* cervical vertebra; **-wulst,** *f.* neck swelling.

nackt, naked, bare, nude, plain, open; **-blütig,** nudifloral; **-farn,** *m.* silver fern (Gymnogram); **-früchtig,** gymnocarpous; **-füssiger Zweig,** *m.* bulbil, small axillary bulb; **-samig,** gymnospermous; **-schnecke,** *f.* naked snail; **-stengelig,** nonleafy.

Nadel, *f.* needle, pin, needle leaf; **-abfall,** *m.* needle shedding; **-artig,** needlelike, acicular; **-ausschlag,** *m.* deflection of the needle; **-baum,** *m.* coniferous tree; **-blatt,** *n.* needle (leaf), gymnosperm leaf, acerose leaf.

Nädelchen, *n.* little needle (or pin).

Nadel-decke, *f.* matting of needles; **-eisenerz,** *n.* needle iron ore; **-erz,** *n.* needle ore; **-faser,** *f.* acicular fiber; **-förmig,** needle-shaped, acicular; **-funkenstrecke,** *f.* needle gap, distance; **-galvanometer,** *n.* needle galvanometer; **-holz,** *n.* coniferous wood, pines and firs; **-hölzer,** *n.pl.* Coniferae.

Nadelholz-gebiet, *n.* region of coniferous woods; **-kohle,** *f.* softwood (pine) charcoal; **-sämling,** *m.* conifer seedling.

Nadel-mischwald, *m.* mixed coniferous forest; **-streu,** *f.* litter from dead needles; **-wald,** *m.* coniferous forest; **-wehr,** *n.* needle weir; **-zeolith,** *m.* needle zeolite (natrolite); **-zinnerz,** *n.* acicular cassiterite.

Nafta, *f.* naphtha.

Nagel, *m.* nail, unguis, onyx, spur, clawlike petal, pine, thorn.

Nagelbein, *n.* lachrymal bone.

Nägelchen, *n.* little nail, brad, carnation, syringa, clove.

Nägelein, *n.* little nail, tack, clove, pink; **-gras,** *n.* chickweed; **-pfeffer,** *m.* allspice: **-rinde,** *f.* clove bark (cinnamon); **-zimt,** *m.* clove (bark), cinnamon.

Nagel-falz, *m.* nail groove, nail fold; **-feld,** *n.* nail field; **-fläche,** *f.* surface of nail; **-fluh,** *f.* gompholite, Nagelfluh, conglomerate; **-förmig,** nail-shaped, unguiform; **-grund,** *m* .nail base; **-kultur,** *f.* nailhead culture.

nageln, to nail, spike, tack.

nagel-neu, brand-new; **-saum,** *m.* nailfringe; **-weiss,** *n.* lunula; **-wurzel,** *f.* root of nail.

nagen, to gnaw, nibble, eat into, corrode.

Nager, *m.*-, rodent, gnawer; **-carcinom,** *n.* rodent carcinoma.

Nagetier, *n.*-e, rodent, gnawer.

Nagezahn, *m.*-e, gnawing tooth.

nahe, (*dat.*) near, adjoining, adjacent, imminent, impending, close; ~ **legen,** make plain, bring home; ~ **an** (25), nearly or about (25); **es war** ~ **daran, dass,** it nearly happened that; ~ **zu,** almost, nearly; **es liegt** ~ **. . . ,** it is obvious, urgent, pertinent, or desirable to . . .

Nähe, *f.* nearness, closeness, surroundings, vicinity, presence; **in der** ~, near to.

nahe-kommen, to approach, resemble; **-liegen,** to be near, lie close, be natural, be obvious, suggest itself; **-liegend,** near-by, adjacent, neighboring, obvious, manifest.

nahen, (*dat.*) to approach, come near.

nähen, to sew.

näher, nearer, closer, more precise.

Nähere(s), *n.* particulars, details.

näherkommen, to approach.

nähern, to bring near, approach, draw near; **sich ~,** to come nearer, approach.

Näherung, *f.* approach, approximation.

Näherungs-methode, *f.* method of approximation; **-wert,** *m.* approximate value.

nahe-stehend, close (related) connected; **-zu,** almost, nearly, well-nigh.

nahm (nehmen), took, was taking.

Nähnadel, *f.*-n, (sewing) needle.

Nahpunkt, *m.*-e, nearest point of clear vision.

Nähr-agar, *m.* nutrient agar; **-blatt,** *n.* storage leaf; **-boden,** *m.* culture medium, nutrient substratum; **-bodenbereitung,** *f.* preparation of culture medium; **-bodenklärung,** *f.* clarification of culture medium; **-bouillon,** *f.* nutrient broth; **-brühe,** *f.* nutrient bouillon.

nähren, to feed, provide, nourish, support.

nährend, nourishing, nutritive, nutritious, nutrient.

Nähr-flüssigkeit, *f.* nutrient or fluid; **-gang,** *m.* alimentary canal, nutrient duct; **-gelatine,** *f.* nutrient gelatin; **-geschäft,** *n.* nutrition; **-gewebe,** *n.* endosperm, nutrient tissue; **-haar,** *n.* nutrient hair.

nahrhaft, nutritive, nourishing, nutritious, lucrative, alimentary.

Nähr-hefe, *f.* nutrient yeast; **-kraft,** *f.* nutritive power; **-kräftig,** nutritious; **-lösung,** *f.* nutrient solution; **-medium,** *n.* nutrient medium; **-mediumwechsel,** *m.* change of nutrient medium; **-mittel,** *n.* food, nutriment, nutrient.

Nähr-mutter, *f.* nursing mother (bird); **-mycel,** *n.* vegetative mycelium; **-pflanze,** *f.* host (food) plant; **-plasma,** *f.* trophoplasm; **-präparat,** *n.* food preparation; **-saft,** *m.* nutrient juice, chyle, sap; **-salz,** *n.* nutrient salt; **-schicht,** *f.* nutritive layer, endosperm.

Nährstoff, *m.*-e, nutritive substance, nutrient food(stuff); **-arm,** poor in food material; **-gehalt,** *m.* nutrient content; **-leitung,** *f.* conducting of nourishment; **-reich,** rich in nutritive substance, fertile.

Nähr-substanz, *f.*-en, nutrient (medium) substance; **-substrat,** *n.* nutrient (substratum) base or medium.

Nahrung, *f.* nourishment, nutriment, food.

Nahrungs-aufnahme, *f.* absorption of food; **-aufwand,** *m.* nutritional expenditure; **-bedarf,** *m.* food requirement; **-bedürfnis,** *m.* need of nourishment; **-brei,** *m.* chyme; **-dotter,** *m.* nutritive (food) yolk, deutoplasm; **-flüssigkeit,** *f.* chyle; **-kanal,** *m.* alimentary canal; **-kreislauf,** *m.* nutrition cycle; **-milch,** *f.* chyle.

Nahrungsmittel, *n.* food, nutrient, foodstuff; **-chemiker,** *n.* food chemist; **-fälschung,** *f.* food adulteration; **-kunde,** *f.* (science of) nutrition; **-untersuchung,** *f.* food research; **-verfälschung** *f.* food adulteration.

Nahrungs-rohr, *n.,* **-röhre,** *f.* alimentary canal; **-saft,** *m.* nutrient juice, chyle, sap; **-schlauch,** *m.* alimentary tube; **-stoff,** *m.* nutritive substance; **-störung,** *f.* disturbance of nutrition, alimentary disorder; **-teilchen,** *n.* nutritive element; **-trieb,** *m.* food urge; **-untersuchung,** *f.* food research.

Nahrungs-vergiftung, *f.* food poisoning; **-verweigerung,** *f.* refusal to take food, sitiophobia, hunger strike; **-weg,** *m.* channel of nutrition; **-wert,** *m.* nutritive value, food value; **-wettbewerb,** *m.* struggle for food; **-zerkleinerung,** *f.* mastication of food; **-zufuhr,** *f.* intake of food.

Nähr-vorrat, *m.*-̈e, reserve food; **-wasser,** *n.* nutrient solution; **-wert,** *m.* nutrient value; **-wurzel,** *f.* absorbing root; **-zelle,** *f.* nurse cell, nutritive cell.

Naht, *f.* seam, joint, suture, raphe; **-knochen,** *m.* Wormian bone; **-knorpel,** *m.* interarticular cartilage; **-los,** seamless; **-spur,** *f.* blastemal suture; **-stärke,** *f.* strength or dimension of seam.

Nähwachs, *n.* sewing wax.

naiv, naïve.

Name, *m.* name, denomination, reputation title.

Namen-gebung, *f.* naming, nomenclature; **-register,** *n.* name index, list of names.

namens, by the name of, called, in the name (behalf) of.

namentlich, by name, especially, particularly.

Namenverzeichnis, *n.* name index.

namhaft, named, renowned, well-known, considerable, worth mentioning.

nämlich, identical, same, namely, that is.

nannte (nennen), named.

Nanzigersäure, *f.* lactic acid.

Napf, *m.* bowl, basin, pan, cupful.

Näpfchen, *n.* cup, little bowl or basin, blank (for blasting caps), cupule; **-kobalt,** *m.* flaky metallic arsenic.

Napf-flieger, *m.pl.* biconcave (concave-convex) seeds or fruits with membrane wings; **-förmig,** acetabuliform, bowl-(cup-) shaped; **-schnecke,** *f.* cup-shell (Patella).

Napht(h)a, *f.* naphtha, petroleum.

Napht(h)acen, *n.* naphthacene.

Napht(h)afeld, *n.* oil field.

Napht(h)aldehyd, *n.* naphthaldehyde.

Napht(h)alin, *n.* naphthalene; **-derivat,** *n.* derivative of naphthalene.

Napht(h)aquelle, *f.* oil well.

Napht(h)-azarin, *n.* naphthazarin; **-azin,** *n.* naphthazine.

Napht(h)en, *n.* naphthene.

Napht(h)idin, *n.* naphthidine.

Napht(h)o-brenzcatechin, *n.* naphthopyrocatechol; **-chinon,** *n.* naphthoquinone; **-cumarin,** *n.* naphthocoumarin.

Napht(h)ol, *n.* naphthol.

napht(h)olieren, to naphtholize, naphtholate.

napht(h)olsauer, naphtholsulphonate of.

Napht(h)oyl, *n.* naphthoyl.

Napht(h)sultam, *n.* naphthosultam.

Napht(h)yl, *n.* naphthyl; **-amin,** *n.* naphthylamine.

Napht(h)yridin, *n.* naphthyridine.

Narbe, *f.* scar, cicatrix, stigma, hilum, seam, grain, topsoil.

narben, to scar, grain; **-bildung,** *f.* cicatrization, pitting; **-bindegewebe,** *n.,* **-gewebe,** *n.* scar (cicatricial) tissue; **-fortsatz,** *m.,* **-lappen,** *m.* stigmatic lobe; **-nachreif,** protandrous; **-papilla,** *f.* stigmatic papilla; **-schleim,** *m.* stigmatic mucus; **-seite,** *f.* grain side; **-vorreif,** protogynous.

narbig, scarred, pitted, scarry, cicatrized, grained.

Narde, *f.* spikenard, nard, lavandula.

Narkose, *f.* narcosis.

Narkotin, *n.* narcotine.

narkotisch, narcotic.

narkotisieren, to narcotize.

närrisch, foolish, eccentric, crazy, odd, funny.

Narzisse, *f.* narcissus.

nascierend, nascent.

Nase, *f.* nose, snout, proboscis, beak. cam, tappet, spout, nozzle.

näseln, to nasalize, sniff, scent.

Nasen-bein, *n.* bone of the nose; **-bluten,** *n.* epistaxis, bleeding of the nose; **-dach,** *n.* nasal arch, roof; **-feld,** *n.* olfactory (nasal) area; **-fläche,** *f.* nasal surface; **-flügel,** *m.* side (wing) of nose, ala nasi; **-flügelknorpel,** *m.* nasoalar cartilage; **-fortsatz,** *m.* nasal process; **-furche,** *f.* nasal groove.

Nasen-gang, *m.* nasal duct; **-gaumengang,** *m.* nasopalatine canal; **-grube,** *f.* nostril, nasal (pit) fossa, nasal groove; **-höhle,** *f.* nasal cavity; **-kamm,** *m.* nasal crest; **-kanal,** *m.* nasal canal; **-knorpel,** *m.* cartilage of the nose; **-koppe, -kuppe,** *f.* tip of the nose; **-lappen,** *m.pl.* sides (wings) of the nose, ala nasi.

Nasen-lippenfalte, *f.* nasolabial groove or fold; **-loch,** *n.* nostril, narial opening, nare; **-muschel,** *f.* turbinated bone, concha; **-polyp,** *m.* nasal polypus; **-rachengang,** *m.* nasopharyngeal canal; **-rand,** *m.* contour of the nose; **-rücken, -sattel,** *m.* bridge of the nose; **-scheidewand,** *f.* nasal partition or septum.

Nasen-schleim, *m.* nasal mucus; **-schleimhaut,** *f.* mucous membrane of the nose; **-schlund,** *m.* nasopharyngeal cavity; **-sekret,** *n.* nasal secretion; **-stachel,** *m.* nasal spine; **-steg,** *m.* bridge; **-vorhof,** *m.* nasal vestibule; **-wurzel,** *f.* root of the nose; **-wurzelkreuz,** *n.* nasal cross (meeting of hair lines).

Nashorn, *n.* rhinoceros.

Nasolabialfalte, *f.* nasolabial fold.

nass, wet, green, unseasoned, moist, low marshy, humid, damp; **nasser Boden,** low or marshy soil; **nasser Weg,** wet way, wet process, humid analysis.

Nass-beize, *f.* liquid disinfection, seed steep; **-beizmittel,** *n.* liquid disinfectant; **-dehnung,** *f.* (ND) wet elongation (WE).

Nässe, *f.* wetness, moisture, humidity.

nässen, to wet, soak, moisten, ooze, discharge.

Nass-fäule, *f.* wet rot of potatoes; **-festigkeit,** *f.* (NF) wet strength (WS).

Näss-gehalt, *m.* moisture content; **-probe,** *f.* moisture test or determination.

Nassverfahren, *n.* wet process.

naszierend, nascent.

Nativpräparat, *n.* untreated (unstained) specimen.

Natracetessigester, *m.* sodioacetoacetic ester.

Natrium, *n.* sodium; **-acetat,** *n.* sodium acetate; **-alaun,** *n.* sodium alum; **-alkoholat,** *n.* sodium alcoholate; **-amid,** *n.* sodium amide, sodamide; **-äthylat,** *n.* sodium ethylate; **-benzoat,** *n.* sodium benzoate; **-bikarbonat,** *n.* sodium bicarbonate; **-bisulfat Kuchen,** *m.* niter cake; **-borat,** *n.* borax, sodium borate.

Natrium-brechweinstein, *m.* antimonyl sodium tartrate; **-bromid,** *n.* sodium bromide; **-chlorid,** *n.* sodium chloride; **-citrat,** *n.* sodium citrate; **-dampf,** *m.* sodium vapor of fumes; **-flamme,** *f.* sodium flame; **-formiat,** *n.* sodium formate; **-gehalt,** *n.* sodium content; **-hydrat,** *n.* sodium hydroxide; **-hydroxyd,** *n.* sodium hydroxide, caustic soda.

Natrium-hyperjodat, *n.* sodium periodate; **-hypochlorid,** *n.* sodium hypochloride. **-jodat,** *n.* sodium iodate; **-jodid,** *n.* sodium iodide; **-kaliumtartrat,** *n.* sodium potassium tartrate; **-karbonat,** *n.* sodium carbonate; **-kieselfluorid,** *n.* sodium fluosilicate; **-metall,** *n.* sodium metal; **-nitrat,** *n.* sodium nitrate; **-nitritlösung,** *f.* solution of nitrite of sodium.

Natrium-oxyd, *n.* sodium oxide; **-oxydhydrat,** *n.* sodium hydroxide; **-phenolat,** *n.* sodium phenolate; **-phosphat,** *n.* sodium phosphate; **-salz,** *n.* sodium salt; **-seife,** *f.* sodium soap; **-sulfat,** *n.* sodium sulphate; **-sulfat Kuchen,** *m.* salt cake; **-sulfit,** *n.* sodium sulphite; **-superoxyd,** *n.* sodium superoxide (sodium peroxide).

Natrium-thiosulfat, *n.* sodium thiosulphate; **-verbindung,** *f.* sodium compound; **-wasserstoff,** *m.* sodium hydride.

Natron, *n.* caustic soda, sodium hydroxide, soda; **-alaun,** *m.* soda alum; **-ätzlauge,** *f.* caustic soda (solution); **-cellulose,** *f.* soda pulp; **-haltig,** containing soda; **-hydrat,** *n.* sodium hydroxide; **-hydratlösung,** *f.* sodium hydroxide solution; **-hyperoxyd,** *n.* sodium peroxide; **-kalk,** *m.* soda lime; **-kalkglas,** *n.* soda-lime glass.

Natron-lauge, *f.* soda lye, sodium hydroxide, caustic soda solution; **-metall,** *n.* (metallic) sodium; **-pastille,** *f.* troche of sodium bicarbonate; **-salpeter,** *m.* sodium nitrate; **-salz,** *n.* soda (sodium) salt; **-seife,** *f.* soda soap, hard soap; **-stoff,** *m.* soda pulp; **-wasserglas,** *n.* soda-water glass, sodium

silicate; **-weinstein,** *m.* sodium tartrate; **-zellstoff,** *m.* soda pulp.

Natter, *f.-,* adder, viper; **-kopf,** *m.* blueweed (*Echium vulgare*); **-wurz,** *f.,* **-wurzel,** *f.* bistort; **-zunge,** *f.* adder's-tongue (Ophioglossum).

Natur, *f.* nature, constitution, disposition, temper, frame of mind; **von ~ aus,** by nature.

Natur-anlage, *f.* natural disposition; **-banngebiet,** *n.* nature preserve; **-erkenntnis,** *n.* scientific knowledge, perception of nature; **-erscheinung,** *f.* natural phenomenon; **-erzeugnis,** *f.* natural product; **-farbe,** *f.* natural color; **-fehler,** *m.* natural defect; **-forscher,** *m.* investigator of nature, naturalist; **-forschung,** *f.* investigation of nature, scientific research; **-gabe,** *f.* gift of nature.

natur-gemäss, according to nature, natural; **-geschichte,** *f.* nature history, natural history; **-gesetz,** *n.* law of nature, natural law; **-härte,** *f.* natural hardness; **-heilung,** *f.* spontaneous cure; **-kausalität,** *f.* natural causality; **-körper,** *m.* natural body; **-kraft,** *f.* natural force or power; **-lab,** *n.* natural rennet; **-lehre,** *f.* natural (science) philosophy, physics.

natürlich, natural, native, innate, normal, of course.

Natur-papier, *n.* stuff-colored paper, imitation art paper; **-produkt,** *n.* native substance, natural product; **-reich,** *n.* kingdom of nature; **-rostung,** *f.* natural corrosion; **-schutz,** *m.* nature conservation; **-schutzgebiet,** *n.* nature reserve; **-stoff,** *m.* natural substance; **-treue,** *f.* lifelikeness (true to life); **-trieb,** *m.* instinct; **-verehrung,** *f.* worship of nature.

Natur-verjüngungswirtschaft, *f.* natural reproduction system; **-volk,** *n.* primitive race; **-widrig,** unnatural, abnormal; **-wissenschaft,** *f.* natural science; **-wissenschaftler,** *m.* natural scientist; **-wissenschaftlich,** scientific, pertaining to natural science; **-zustand,** *m.* natural state.

Neapel-gelb, *n.* Naples yellow; **-rot,** *n.* Naples red.

Neapler Cholerabakteria, *f. Bacillus neapolitanus.*

Nebel, *m.* mist, haze, fog; **-apparat,** *m.* atomizer; **-artig,** mistlike, misty, foggy; **-decke,** *f.* misty veil; **-fleck,** *m.* nebula; **-form,** *f.* form of mist or dew; **-geschoss,** *n.* smoke (projectile) shell.

nebelig, misty, foggy.

Nebel-kasten, *m.* smokebox; **-spurauf-nahme,** *f.* cloud-chamber photograph; **-streif,** *m.* streak of mist, cloud; **-topf,** *m.* smoke pot; **-trommel,** *f.* smoke drum; **-tröpfchen,** *n.* fog particle, minute drop.

neben, beside, by, in addition to, as well as, near, besides, in; ∼ **an,** next door, close by; ∼ **bei,** besides, by the way, incidental.

Neben-achse, *f.* lateral or secondary axis; **-ader,** *f.* spurious vein, accessory blood vessel; **-ast,** *m.* collateral branch, epipodite; **-augen,** *n.pl.* ocelli; **-bahn,** *f.* side track, siding; **-band,** *n.* accessory ligament; **-bedeutung,** *f.* secondary meaning; **-bedingung,** *f.* accessory condition, secondary factor; **-begriff,** *m.* collateral idea; **-beruf,** *m.* side line.

Neben-bestand, *m.* secondary stand; **-bestandteil,** *m.* secondary ingredient, subsidiary member, accessory constituent; **-betrieb,** secondary process, side line, extra activity (collateral); **-bewegung,** *f.* secondary or minor movement; **-beweis,** *m.* additional proof; **-biegung,** *f.* lateral bend; **-bindung,** *f.* secondary union or linkage; **-blatt,** *n.* bract, ligule, stipule, supplement; **-blättchen,** *n.* bract, bracteole, stipule, ligule; **-blattförmig,** stipuliform.

neben-blattlos, exstipulate; **-blättrig,** stipuliform, stipulate; **-blattständig,** beside or near the leaf, laterifolious; **-blumenkrone,** *f.* paracorolla, corona, crown of corolla; **-buhler,** *m.* rival; **-dotter,** *m.* accessory yolk; **-drüse,** *f.* accessory gland; **-durchmesser,** *m.* conjugate diameter.

nebeneinander, side by side, coordinated (associations), near each other, close together, in proximity, in juxtaposition, opposite; **-schalten,** to connect in parallel; **-stellung,** *f.* juxtaposition, comparison.

Neben-einteilung, *f.* subdivision; **-erhabenheit,** *f.* accessory protuberance; **-erzeugnis,** *n.* by-product; **-farbe,** *f.* secondary color; **-feder,** *f.* aftershaft; **-feld,** *n.* adjoining field; **-fläche,** *f.* secondary face; **-fluss,** *m.* tributary; **-folge,** *f.* indirect result, secondary effect; **-frucht,** *f.* paracarpium, imperfect stage.

Neben-gang, *m.* byway, lateral vein; **-geissel,** *f.* paraflagellum; **-gemengteil,** *n.* secondary constituent of a mixture; **-geschmack,** *m.* aftertaste; **-gestein,** *n.* country (partition) rock; **-gewebe,** *n.* accessory tissue; **-handlung,** *f.* subordinate action, episode, side show; **-häutchen,** *n.* accessory membrane.

nebenher, besides, by the way, moreover; **-gehend,** accessory, additional, secondary, minor.

Neben-höcker, *m.* accessory condyle or eminence; **-hoden,** *m.* epididymis; **-kammer,** *f.* accessory (small) chamber, auricle of heart; **-keim,** *m.* parablast; **-keimbahn,** *f.* secondary germ tract; **-keimstätte,** *f.* epigonad; **-kelch,** *m.* calycle, calyculus, involucre; **-kern,** *m.* paranucleus; **-kette,** *f.* side (subordinate) chain; **-kieme,** *f.* pseudogill, pseudobranch.

Neben-klaue, *f.* accessory claw; **-korn,** *n.* secondary kernel; **-krone,** *f.* paracorolla, crown of corolla; **-kuchen,** *m.* supplementary liver; **-lappen,** *m.pl.* accessory lobes; **-leber,** *f.* supplementary liver; **-leiter,** *m.* branch conductor; **-linie,** *f.* secondary (branch) line; **-luft,** *f.* secondary air; **-magen,** *m.* accessory stomach.

Neben-milchdrüse, *f.* accessory mammary gland; **-milz,** *f.* accessory spleen; **-mittelfussknochen,** *m.* splint bone; **-nerv,** *m.* accessory vein; **-niere,** *f.* suprarenal capsule.

Nebennieren-arterie, *f.* suprarenal artery, adrenal vessel; **-ast,** *m.* adrenal branch; **-leiste,** *f.* suprarenal ridge; **-mark,** *n* medulla of suprarenal gland; **-rinde,** *f.* adrenal cortex.

Neben-nutzung, *f.* secondary utilization, minor produce, byproduct; **-organ,** *n.* accessory organ; **-produkt,** *n.* by-product; quantenzahl, *f.* secondary quantum number; **-reaktion,** *f.* side reaction; **-reihe,** *f.* accessory row; **-rohr,** *n.* side (branch) tube; **-rolle,** *f.* subordinate role; **-rückenlinie,** *f.* lateral line; **-sache,** *f.* secondary matter.

neben-sächlich, incidental, accidental, subsidiary, accessory; **-schaft,** *m.* aftershaft, hyporhachis; **-schilddrüse,** *f.* parathyroid gland; **-schliessung,** *f.* shunt.

Nebenschluss, *m.*⁼e, shunt; **-schaltung,** *f.* shunt connection; **-sonne,** *f.* parhelion; **-spannung,** *f.* secondary stress; **-stehend,** annexed, in the margin, following; **-strom,** *m.* shunt current; **-widerstand,** *m.* shunt resistance.

Neben-schössling, *m.* sucker, offshoot; **-schwarm,** *m.* afterswarm; **-serie,** *f.* secondary (subordinate) series; **-spirale,** *f.* secondary coil; **-sporangium,** *n.* reduced conidiumlike sporangium; **-spross,** *m.* secondary shoot; **-ständig,** collateral, accessory; **-stehend,** standing (near) beside; **-symbiose,** *f.* parasymbiosis; **-sympodium,** *n.* secondary sympodium.

Neben-taster, *m.* maxillary palpus; -teil, *m.* accessory part; -titel, *m.* subtitle; -typus, *m.* secondary type, facies; -umstand, *m.* accessory detail, circumstance; -valenz, *f.* secondary valence; -weg, *m.* byroad; -weibig, perigynous; -widerstand, *m.* shunt; -winkel, *m.* adjacent angle.

Neben-wirkung, *f.* secondary action; -wirtspflanze, *f.* secondary host; -wort, *n.* adverb; -wurzel, *f.* lateral root, adventitious root; -zacke, *f.* lateral denticle; -zeile, *f.* parastichy; -zelle, *f.* accessory cell; -zunge, *f.* paraglossa; -zweig, *m.* side (lateral) branch.

neblig, foggy, misty, confused.

nebst, besides, including, in addition to.

negativ, negative.

Neger, *m.* Negro.

nehmen, to take, receive, get, accept, capture; ein Ende ∼, to cease; ∼ wir den Fall, dass, let us assume that; auf sich ∼, to assume (a burden); es ernst mit etwas ∼, to be serious about a thing; in Anspruch ∼, to make demands upon.

Neige, *f.* inclination, propensity, version, declivity, slope, dregs, sediment, decline, wane, depression.

neigen, to slope, incline, bend, lean, dip, tend, decline, bow; geneigt, inclined, disposed, favorable.

Neigung, *f.* inclination, bending, gradient, slope, slant, pitch, dip, tendency.

Neigungs-ebene, *f.* inclined plane; -linie, *f.* gradient; -winkel, *m.* angle of inclination.

nein, no.

Nekrolog, *m.* obituary.

Nekrose, *f.* necrosis; -bazillus, *m.* Bang's necrosis bacillus.

Nektarium, *n.* nectary.

Nelke, *f.* pink, carnation, clove.

Nelken-gewächse, *n.pl.* Caryophyllaceae; -öl, *n.* clove oil; -pfeffer, *m.* allspice, pimento; -säure, *f.* eugenol, caryophyllic acid; -stein, *m.* iolite; -wurz(el), *f.* avens (*Geum urbanum*), pink (clove) root; -zim(m)t, *m.* clove cinnamon, clove cassia.

Nennbelastung, *f.* nominal load.

nennen, to name, call, mention, term, quote; genannt, above mentioned.

nennenswert, worth mentioning, noteworthy.

Nenner, *m.* denominator.

Nennleistung, *f.* nominal output, rated power.

Nennung, *f.* naming, mentioning, entry (race).

Nenn-wert, *m.* nominal value; -wort, *n.* noun, substantive.

Neodym, *n.* neodymium.

Neonglimmlampe, *f.* neon light (tube).

neoplastich, neoplastic.

Neroliöl, *n.* neroli oil (of orange blossoms).

Nerv, *m.* nerve, sinew, fiber, vein, filament.

Nervatur, *f.* venation.

Nerven-ast, *m.* neural branch; -bahn, *f.* nerve tract; -bogen, *m.* neural arch; -durchschneidung, *f.* cutting or severing of nerves; -eintritt, *m.* nerve entry; -endapparat, *m.* nerve end organ; -endhügel, *m.* motorial end plate, nerve-end structure; -endigung, *f.* termination of a nerve; -entzündung, *f.* neuritis.

Nerven-faser, *f.* nerve fiber; -fasernetz, *n.* reticulum of nerve fibers, network of fibrils; -faserschicht, *f.* nerve-fiber layer; -fortsatz, *m.* nerve process; -gewebe, *n.* nerve tissue; -grenzstrang, *m.* sympathetic nerve chain.

Nerven-haut, *f.* nerve neurilemma, sheath, retina; -hülle, *f.* sheath enclosing the nerve fibers; -kern, *m.* nerve origin nucleus, nerve ganglion; -kitt, *m.* neuroglia; -knoten, *m.* nerve ganglion; -knotenpaar, *n.* pair of nerves; -kunde, *f.* neurology.

Nerven-lähmung, *f.* neuroparalysis; -lehre, *f.* neurology; -leiste, *f.* embryonic neural crest or ridge; -leitung, *f.* nerve conduction; -loch, *n.* foramen of nerve; -mark, *n.* medulla of nerve; -masse, *f.* nerve (neural) substance; -naht, *f.* nerve seam or suture; -netz, *n.* reticulum of nerve fibers, network of nerves, nerve plexus.

Nerven-reiz, *m.* nervous irritation; -röhre, *f.* nerve fiber; -scheide, *f.* sheath enclosing nerve fibers; -schwäche, *f.* nervousness, neurasthenia; -stamm, *m.* nerve trunk; -strang, *m.* nerve fiber; -system, *n.* nervous system; -tätigkeit, *f.* nerve function; -werk, *n.* nervous system; -wurzel, *f.* nerve root; -zart, very delicate, nervous; -zelle, *f.* nerve cell.

nervig, nervous, nerved, nervate, sinewy, vigorous, strong, pithy.

Nervillennetz, *n.* net veins.

nervös, nervous, excitable, forcible; auf nervösem Wege, by way of the nerves.

Nessel, *f.* nettle; **-ausschlag,** *m.* nettle rash; **-blatt,** *n.* Acalypha; **-faden,** *m.* cnidocil; **-fieber,** *n.* nettle rash,urticaria;**-gewächse,** *n.pl.* Urticaceae; **-kapsel,** *f.* stinging capsule or nematocyst, rhabdite; **-quallen,** *f.pl.* Scyphomedusae; **-tiere,** *n.pl.* Hydrozoa, Cnidaria; **-tuch,** *n.* strong, rough, and dense domestic cheesecloth; **-zelle,** *f.* cnidoblast, nematocyst.

Nest, *n.* nest; **-dune,** *f.* nestling feather, down, neoptile; **-ei,** *n.* nest egg; **-farn,** *m.* Asplenium; **-feder,** *f.* nestling feather, down; **-flüchter,** *m.* autophagous bird; **-hocker,** *m.* insessorial bird; **-vogel,** *m.* autophagous bird.

nett, neat, tidy, pretty, pleasant, kind, elegant.

netto, net; **-ertrag,** *m.* net (yield) proceeds; **-gewicht,** *n.* net weight.

Netz, *n.*-e, net, netting, reticulum, gauze, network, plexus, system, omentum, reticle; **-ader,** *f.* omental artery; **-adern,** *f.pl.* checking (slight crisscross cracking); **-ähnlich, -artig,** netlike, reticular, plexiform; **-ätzung,** *f.* autotypy; **-augen,** *n.pl.* faceted eyes of insects; **-bad,** *n.* wetting-out bath; **-beize,** *f.* oil mordant; **-bindung,** *f.* covalence.

netz-blättrig, dictyophyllous; **-blutader,** *f.* omental vein; **-elektrode,** *f.* wire-gauze electrode; **-ebene,** *f.* lattice plane.

netzen, to wet, moisten, steep.

Netz-fass, *n.* steeping tub; **-ferment,** *n.* enzyme of the omentum; **-flieger,** *m.pl.* Neuroptera; **-flotte,** *f.* wetting-out liquor; **-flügler,** *m.pl.* Neuroptera; **-förmig,** net-shaped, reticular; **-früchtig,** dictyocarpous; **-gefäss,** *n.* reticulate vessel.

Netzhaut, *f.* retina; **-bezirk,** *m.* region of the retina; **-bild,** *n.* retinal image; **-ebene,** *f.* retinal plane; **-eindruck,** *m.* retina (image) impression; **-erregung,** *f.* retinal (excitation) stimulation; **-grube,** *f.* macula; **-rand,** *m.* margin of the retina; **-stäbchen,** *n.* rod of the retina; **-stelle,** *f.* retinal point; **-zäpfchen,** *n.* cone of the retina.

Netz-knorpel, *m.* reticular cartilage; **-magen,** *m.* second stomach (reticulum) of ruminants; **-mittel,** *n.* wetting agent; **-nerv,** *m.* omental nerve, nervil; **-nervig,** of reticulate venation; **-schutz,** *m.* protecting gauze; **-spannung,** *f.* line voltage; **-ständer,** *m.* steeping tub; **-strom,** *m.* current from a (network) distributing system; **-werk,** *n.* network; **-zelle,** *f.* reticular cell.

neu, new, original, newly, lately, recent, modern; **aufs neue,** anew, again; **von neuem,** anew, again; **in neuester Zeit,** in most recent time(s), quite recently.

neu-artig, new, of a new kind; **-bearbeiten,** to work over, revise; **-berechnung,** *f.* recalculation; **-bildung,** *f.* new growth, new formation, neoplasm; **-bildungsreiz,** *m.* formative stimulus; **-blau,** *n.* mixture of starch and indigo; **-braun,** *n.* Prussiate of copper; **-bürger,** *m.* neophyte (newly introduced), adventive, newcomer; **-entstehen,** to be newly formed.

neuer, newer, recent, modern, later; **-dings,** recently, newly, again.

neuerlich, new, fresh.

Neuerung, *f.* innovation, recent change.

Neu-erwerbung, *f.* new acquisition; **-erzeugung,** *f.* new production, reproduction; **-gebildet,** newly formed; **-gestaltung,** *f.* reorganization, modification; **-gewürz,** *n.* allspice; **-gier(de),** *f.* curiosity; **-gierig,** curious, inquisitive; **-grün,** *n.* Paris green.

Neuheit, *f.* novelty, newness, fashion.

neuheitsschädlich, anticipatory (of patents).

Neuigkeit, *f.* news, novelty.

neulich, lately, of late, recent.

Neuling, *m.*-e, novice, beginner.

neun, nine; **-auge,** *n.* river lamprey (Petromyzon); **-eckig,** enneagonal, nine-cornered.

neunerlei, of nine kinds.

neun-fach, -fältig, ninefold; **-flächig,** nine-sided (or faced); **-gliedrig,** having nine limbs or members; **-mal,** nine times.

neunte, ninth.

neuntel, ninth (fraction).

neunwertig, nonavalent.

Neuprüfung, *f.* new test, re-examination.

Neural-anlage, *f.* rudiment of neural tube, **-höhle,** *f.* neural canal; **-kanal,** *m.* neural canal; **-leiste,** *f.* neural crest; **-platten,** *f.pl.* neural plates, expanded neural spine; **-rohr,** *n.* neural tube, medullary tube.

Neurit, *n.* neuron, nerve, nerve process.

Neurofibrill, *f.* nerve fibril, neurofibril.

Neurogliagerüst, *n.* neuroglial scaffolding.

Neuronenverbindung, *f.* neuron junction.

Neuschöpfung, *f.* new creation.

Neu-silber, *n.* nickel silver, German silver; **-steinzeitlich,** neolithic.

neutral, neutral, neuter; **-fett,** *n.* neutral fat.

Neutralisation, *f.* neutralization.

Neutralisationswärme, *f.* heat of neutralization.

neutralisieren, to neutralize.

Neutralisierung, *f.* neutralization.

Neutralität, *f.* neutrality.

Neutral-körper, *m.*-, neutral substance; **-punkt,** *m.* neutral point; **-rot,** *n.* neutral red; **-salz,** *n.* neutral salt; **-salzion,** *n.* neutral salt ion; **-salzwirkung,** *f.* neutral salt effect.

Neutuberkulin, *n.* new tuberculin.

Neuwieder Grün, *n.* Paris green.

Neuzeit, *f.* modern times.

neuzeitlich, modern.

Neuzüchtung, *f.* breeding of a new species.

nicht, not; **mit nichten,** not at all; **auch** ～ not either, neither; **gar** ～, not at all; **ganz und gar** ～, not in the least; **durchaus** ～, by no means; ～ **doch!,** certainly not!; ～ **mehr,** no longer; ～ **wenige,** not a few; ～ **weniger als,** no(t) less than; **wo** ～, unless, if . . . not; ～ **wahr?** isn't that so?

nicht-angreifend, noncorroding, inert; **-anlegung,** *f.* nondevelopment, suppression; **-auflösung,** *f.* nonsolution; **-auseinanderweichen,** *n.* nondisjunction; **-bindig,** noncohesive; **-dissoziiert,** undissociated; **-drehend,** nonrotary, nonrevolving, neutral.

Nichte, *f.* niece.

Nicht-eignung, *f.* unsuitableness, unfitness; **-elektrolyt,** *n.* nonelectrolyte; **-entartung,** *f.* nondegeneration; **-existenzfähig,** incapable of existence; **-flüchtig,** nonvolatile; **-gasförmig,** nongaseous; **-gebrauch,** *m.* disuse, lack of use; **-häufig,** infrequent.

nichten, mit, not at all.

nichtig, null, void, invalid, empty, futile, idle.

Nichtigkeit, *f.* nullity, invalidation, voidness, annulment.

Nichtigkeits-klage, *f.* **-verfahren,** *n.* invalidity suit.

nicht-kohärent, noncoherent; **-lebend,** not living; **-leitend,** nonconducting; **-leiter,** *m.* nonconductor; **-leuchtend,** non-(incandescent) luminous, dull, mat; **-metallisch,** nonmetallic; **-mischbarkeit,** *f.* immiscibility; **-oxydierbar,** unoxidizable; **-pathogen,** nonpathogenic; **-periodisch,** aperiodic; **-reduzierbar,** not reducible, irreducible;

-rostend, nonrusting, noncorroding, rustproof.

nichts, Nichts, *n.* nothing, none; **gar** ～, nothing at all; ～ **nützen,** to be of no use.

Nicht-sättigung, *f.* nonsaturation, unsaturation; **-schmelzbar,** nonfusible; **-schnürig,** crooked.

nichtsdestoweniger, nevertheless, notwithstanding.

nichtspaltend, nonsegregating.

nichts-sagend, meaningless; **-würdig,** worthless, base, futile.

Nicht-trennung, *f.* nondisjunction; **-tropfend,** nondripping; **-umkehrbar,** nonreversible; **-umwandelbar,** inconvertible; **-vergrünen,** *n.* ungreenable black; **-wärmeleiter,** *m.* nonconductor of heat; **-wässerig,** nonaqueous; **-zucker,** *m.* nonsugar.

Nickel, *n.* nickel; **-antimonglanz,** *m.* ullmannite; **-arsenik,** *n.* nickel arsenide; **-arsenikglanz,** *m.* **-arsenkies,** *m.* gersdorffite; **-artig,** nickellike; **-blüte,** *f.* nickel bloom; **-chlorür,** *n.* nickel(ous) chloride; **-draht,** *m.* nickel wire; **-drahtnetz,** *n.* nickel gauze; **-erz,** *n.* nickel ore.

Nickel-fahlerz, *n.* studerite, malinowskite; **-flusseisen,** *n.* nickel steel; **-gefäss,** *n.* nickel vessel; **-gehalt,** *m.* nickel content; **-glanz,** *m.* nickel glance; **-haltig,** containing nickel, nickeliferous; **-hydroxydul,** *n.* nickelous hydroxide; **-kies,** *m.* millerite; **-legierung,** *f.* nickel alloy; **-münze,** *f.* nickel coin.

Nickel-ocker, *m.* nickel ocher; **-spiessglanz,** *m.* ullmannite; **-stahl,** *m.* nickel steel; **-sulfür,** *n.* nickelous sulphide; **-tiegel,** *m.* nickel crucible; **-überzug,** *m.* nickel plating; **-vitriol,** *m.* nickel sulphate; **-zusatz,** *m.* addition of nickel.

nicken, to nod.

Nickhaut, *f.* nictitating membrane.

nie, never.

nieder, low, lower, inferior, secondary, down, vulgar, mean; **-bewegung,** *f.* downward motion or movement; **-blasen,** to blow out; **-blatt,** *n.* scale, cataphyll, cataphyllary leaf; **-blattmanschette,** *f.* protective sheath of bud scale; **-blattstamm,** *m.* subex; **-druck,** *m.* low pressure; **-drücken,** to press down, depress; **-durchforstung,** *f.* thinning the suppressed trees, low cut; **-fallen,** to fall down, precipitate, settle.

Nieder-gang, *m.* going down, downstroke, descent, decline; **-gedrückt,** depressed; **-gedrücktkugelig,** spheroidal; **-gehen,** to fall, subside, go down; **-gerissen,** dejec'ed; **-geschlagen,** dejected; **-gestreckt,** stretched down, humifuse, prostrate, decumbent; **-holz,** *n.* undergrowth, brushwood, dwarfed trees; **-holzformation,** *f.* low scrub vegetation; **-lage,** *f.* deposit, warehouse, branch, depot, defeat.

niederlassen, to let down, lower, settle down, establish oneself; **sich ~,** to settle, alight.

nieder-legen, to lay down, put down, deposit, resign; **-liegend,** decumbent, prostrate; **-reissen,** to carry down, drag down, tear down, destroy; **-reissen,** *n.* demolition, pulling down, passive precipitation; **-ringen,** to overcome; **-schlag,** *m.* precipitate, precipitation, rainfall, deposit, sediment; **-schlagbar,** precipitable; **-schlagen,** to precipitate, deposit, beat down, fell, quell, refute, depress, dishearten; **-schlagend,** precipitant, sedative, discouraging, depressing; **-schlaggefäss,** *n.* precipitating vessel.

Niederschlags-bildung, *f.* formation of precipitation; **-membran,** *f.* precipitation membrane; **-menge,** *f.* amount of (precipitate) rainfall; **-mittel,** *n.* precipitant.

Niederschlagung, *f.* precipitation, dismissal.

Niederschlag-verfahren, *n.* precipitation method; **-vorrichtung,** *f.* precipitation apparatus; **-wärme,** *f.* heat of condensation; **-wasser,** *n.* water of condensation; **-zeit,** *f.* time of precipitation.

Nieder-schmelzen, to melt down; **-spannung,** *f.* low pressure; **-spross,** *m.* cataplast, underground shoot.

Niederung, *f.* lowland, low ground, valley, depression.

Niederungsmoor, *m.* lowland moor.

nieder-voltig, low voltage; **-wald,** *m.* coppice, copse, sprout forest, underwood, undergrowth; **-wärts,** downward; **-zieher,** *m.* depressor muscle.

niedrig, low.

niedriger, lower.

niemals, never.

niemand, nobody, no one.

Niere, *f.* kidney, nephridium, nodule, concretion; **bleibende ~,** *f.* metanephros.

Nieren-ausführungsgang, *m.* efferent renal duct; **-baum,** *m.* Anacardium; **-becher,** *m.* calyx of kidney; **-becken,** *n.* pelvis of kidney; **-blättrig,** renifolious; **-drüse,** *f.* renal gland; **-entzündung,** *f.* nephritis; **-förmig,** kidney-shaped, reniform.

Nieren-gefäss, *n.* renal vessel; **-geflecht,** *n.* renal plexus; **-gegend,** *f.* renal region; **-gries(s),** *m.* renal gravel; **-haut,** *f.* renal capsule; **-kelch,** *m.* calyx of kidney; **-lappen,** *m.* kidney lobe; **-mittel,** *n.* kidney remedy; **-mündung,** *f.* nephridial opening.

Nieren-öffnung, *f.* renal aperture; **-pfortadernetz,** *n.* renal portal system; **-sack,** *m.* renal sac; **-schlauch,** *m.* renal tube; **-schuppenfarn,** *m.* Nephrolepis; **-stein,** *m.* kidney stone, renal calculus; **-trichter,** *m.* nephrostome, renal funnel.

nierig, kidney-shaped, reniform, nodular, in pockets.

Niese-fieber, *n.* hay fever; **-mittel,** *n.* sternutative.

niesen, to sneeze.

Nies-kraut, *n.* sneezewort (*Achillea ptarmica);* **-wurz,** hellebore; **-wurzel,** *f.* hellebore.

Niet, *n.* **Niete,** *f.* rivet, pin.

nieten, to rivet.

Nietnagel, *m.* rivet, hangnail.

Nikotin, *n.* nicotine; **-frei,** nicotine-free; **-gehalt,** *m.* nicotine content; **-säure,** *f.* nicotinic (nicotic) acid; **-vergiftung,** *f.* nicotine poisoning.

Nil-blau, *n.* Nile blue; **-pferd,** *n.* hippopotamus.

nimmer, never; **-satt,** insatiable.

nimmt (nehmen), takes, is taking.

Niob, *n.* niobium, columbium.

Niobat, *n.* niobate.

Niob-säure, *f.* niobic acid; **-wasserstoff,** *m.* niobium hydride.

nippen, to sip.

nirgend, nirgends, nowhere.

Nische, *f.* niche, recess, small pocket.

Nischenblatt, *n.* basal sheathing leaf ot fern, pocket leaf.

Nist-eingangsmündung, *f.* nest entrance; **-gewohnheit,** *f.* nesting habit.

Nitragin, *n.* nitragin, nitrogenous manure or fertilizer.

Nitrat, *n.* nitrate; **-ion,** *n.* nitrate ion; **-reduzieren,** to reduce nitrate.

Nitrid, *n.* nitride.

Nitrierapparat, *m.* nitrating apparatus.

nitrierbar, nitratable, nitrifiable.

nitrieren, to nitrate, nitrify.

Nitrier-gemisch, *n.* nitrating mixture; **-säure,** *f.* nitric-sulphuric acid.

Nitrierung, *f.* nitration, nitrification.

nitrifizieren, to nitrify.

Nitrit, *n.* nitrite; **-bildner,** *n.* nitrous bacterium; **-frei,** nitrite-free.

Nitro-bakterien, *n.pl.* nitrobacter, nitric organisms; **-benzin,** *n.* nitrobenzene; **-benzol,** *n.* nitrobenzene; **-cocussäure,** *f.* nitrococcic acid; **-derivat,** *n.* nitro derivative; **-farbstoff,** *m.* nitro dye; **-fettkörper,** *m.* aliphatic nitro compound; **-fettsäure,** *f.* nitro fatty acid; **-glyzerin,** *n.* nitroglycerin; **-gruppe,** *f.* nitro group.

Nitro-halogenbenzol, *n.* halonitrobenzene; **-kohlenstoff,** *m.* tetranitromethane; **-körper,** *m.* nitro substance, nitro compound.

Nitrolsäure, *f.* nitrolic acid.

Nitro-pentaerythrit, *n.* pentaerythritol tetranitrate; **-prussidnatrium,** *n.* sodium nitroprusside.

nitros, nitrous.

Nitroschwefelsäure, *f.* nitrosulphuric acid.

Nitrose, *f.* nitrosylsulphuric acid.

nitrosieren, to treat with nitrous acid, introduce the nitroso group.

Nitroso-bakterien, *n.pl.* nitrous organisms; **-benzol,** *n.* nitrosobenzene; **-indolreaktion,** *f.* cholera-red reaction; **-kobaltwasserstoffsäure,** *f.* cobaltinitrous acid; **-verbindung,** *f.* nitroso compound.

Nitro-sprengstoff, *m.* nitro explosive; **-stärke,** *f.* nitrostarch.

Nitrosyl-säure, *f.* nitrosylic acid; **-schwefelsäure,** *f.* nitrosylsulphuric acid.

Nitroverbindung, *f.* nitro compound.

Nitroxyd, *n.* nitrogen oxide.

Nitroxylgruppe, *f.* nitroxyl group.

Nitroxylol, *n.* nitroxylene.

Niveau, *n.* surface, level; **-fläche,** *f.* level surface; **-linie,** *f.* potential line, grade line; **-pfahl,** *m.* grade peg or stake; **-rohr,** *n.* **-röhre,** *f.* leveling tube; **-schwankung,** *f.* change in depth or level; **-senkung,** *f.* lowering of depth or level.

nivellieren, to level, grade.

Nivellier-instrument, *n.* level, transit, leveling instrument; **-latte,** *f.* leveling staff, stadia rod.

Nivellierung, *f.* leveling.

Nixkrautgewächse, *n.pl.* Najadaceae.

noch, still, yet, more, in addition to, else, however, further, even, nor; ~ **ein,**

another; ~ **einmal,** once more; **nur** ~, only; ~ **immer,** still; ~ **nicht,** not yet; **weder . . .** ~, neither . . . nor.

noch-malig, repeated; **-mals,** once more, once again, again.

Nocken, *m.* cam, lifter; **-welle,** *f.* camshaft.

Nodus, *m.* node.

Nomenklatur, *f.* nomenclature.

Nonius, *m.* vernier; **-einteilung,** *f.* vernier scale.

Noppe, *f.* nap, burl, nub.

Noppenbeize, *f.* burl dye.

Nord, Norden, *m.* north.

nördlich, northerly, northern, arctic.

Nord-licht, *n.* aurora borealis; **-ost,** *m.* northeast; **-pol,** *m.* north pole.

Norm, *f.* norm, standard.

normal, normal, standard, at right angles, perpendicular to.

Normal-bedingungen, *f.pl.* normal conditions, standard specifications; **-druck,** *m.* normal pressure, standard pressure; **-einstellung,** *f.* normal position; **-element,** *n.* standard cell.

normalerweise, normally.

Normal-essig, *m.* standard vinegar, proof vinegar; **-fall,** *m.* normal case; **-feuchtigkeit,** *f.* normal amount of moisture; **-flüssigkeit,** *f.* standard solution; **-gewicht,** *n.* standard weight; **-grösse,** *f.* normal size, standard size.

normalisieren, to standardize, normalize.

Normalisierung, *f.* standardization.

Normalität, *f.* normality.

Normal-kerze, *f.* standard candle; **-klafter,** *n.* sample cord of wood; **-kraft,** *f.* force at right angles; **-lösung,** *f.* normal solution, standard solution; **-masstab,** *m.* normal standard of measurement; **-menschenserum,** *n.* normal human serum; **-null,** *f.* sea level (not open sea, but at a point in Holland); **-platinöse,** *f.* standard platinum loop; **-profil,** *n.* standard cross section; **-schliff,** *m.* standard ground joint.

Normal-serum, *n.* normal serum, standard; **-spannung,** *f.* normal voltage; **-stärke** *f.* normal strength, standard strength; **-temperatur,** *f.* standard temperature; **-tiefe,** *f.* normal depth; **-vorrat,** *m.* normal growing stock; **-wald,** *m.* normal forest, ideal forest; **-weingeist,** *m.* proof spirit; **-wert,** *m.* normal value, standard value; **-widerstand,** *m.* normal or standard resistance; **-zustand, _m._** normal or standard state or condition.

normen, to standardize.

Normen-ausschuss, _m._ committee on standards; **-vorschrift, _f._** standard specification.

normieren, to standardize, gauge, regulate.

Norm-kultur, _f._ typical culture; **-recht,** normal.

Normung, _f._ standardization.

normwidrig, abnormal.

Not, _f._ need, necessity, urgency, want, emergency, trouble, distress, peril, effort, sorrow, care; ∼ **haben,** to find it difficult; **es tut** ∼, **dass,** it is needful (essential); **es täte** ∼, it would be best; **mit** ∼, barely, with difficulty; **zur** ∼, on (in) an emergency.

Not-auslass, _m._ emergency outlet; **-behelf, _m._** makeshift, last (resort) resource; **-dürftig,** scanty, needy; **-fall, _m._** emergency; **-gar,** undertanned; **-gedrungen,** compulsory, forced, necessarily.

Notenlinien, _f.pl._ streaks.

notieren, to note, notify, quote.

nötig, necessary, required, needful; ∼ **haben,** to want, be in need of.

nötigen, to necessitate, force, invite, urge; **-falls,** if need be, if necessary, eventually.

Notiz, _f._ notice, note; **-buch, _n._** notebook.

Not-mittel, _n._ expedient, shift; **-reif,** forced, prematurely ripe, unripe, immature; **-reife, _f._** premature ripening, incomplete ripeness, immaturity; **-stand, _m._** urgent (critical) state, urgency, relief, need; **-wehr, _f._** self-defense; **-wendig,** necessary, essential; **-wendigerweise,** necessarily; **-wendigkeit, _f._** necessity.

Novojodin, _n._ novoiodin.

Nu, _m._ moment, trice; **im** ∼, in an instant.

Nuance, Nüance, _f._ shade, tint.

nuancieren, to shade (off), modulate.

nüchtern, empty, fasting, sober, temperate, moderate, cool, flat, insipid, stale, calm.

Nucleinsäure, _f._ nucleic acid.

Nudeln, _f.pl._ noodles, vermicelli, macaroni.

Nukleoproteid, _n._ nucleoprotein.

Nukleus, _m._ nucleus, initial point of growth.

Null, _f._ zero, naught, cipher; ∼ **und richtig,** null and void, invalid.

Null-ablesung, _f._ zero reading; **-achse, _f._** neutral axis; **-einstellung, _f._** initial adjustment; **-grad, _m._** zero; **-lage, _f._** zero position; **-leiter, _m._** return wire (electricity);

-linie, _f._ zero line; **-methode, _f._** zero method; **-niveau, _n._** zero level.

Nullpunkt, _m._ zero point, zero; **-abweichung, _f._** zero error.

Null-reibung, _f._ absence of friction; **-setzen, _n._** setting equal to zero; **-spannung, _f._** zero voltage; **-stellung, _f._** zero position; **-strich, _m._** zero mark.

nullte Spalte, _f._ zero column.

Nullung, _f._ zero voltage.

Null-verfahren, _n._ zero method; **-wert, _m._** zero, nought; **-wertig,** nonvalent, avalent.

numerieren, to number.

Numerierung, _f._ numbering, numeration, notation.

numerisch, numerical.

Nummer, _f._ number.

nummern, to number.

nun, now, well, why, so, now since; **-mehr,** at present, now, by this time, henceforth; **-mehrig,** present.

nur, only, but, scarcely; ∼ **immer,** still; ∼ **nicht,** but, solely; ∼ **etwas,** only about; ∼ **noch,** only just; ∼ **mehr** only just; **fast** ∼ **noch,** hardly any(thing) but; ∼ **zu sehr,** only too well (much); **nicht** ∼, **sondern auch,** not only . . . but also; . . . , ∼ **dass** . . . , except that; **wenn** ∼, if only, provided that; **was** ∼, whatever; **wer** ∼, whoever; **wohin** ∼, wherever.

Nuss, _f._ nut, walnut; **-baum, _m._** nut tree, walnut; **-braun,** nut-brown.

Nüsschen, _n._ small nut, nucule.

Nuss-kern, _m._ kernel of a nut; **-kernmehl, _n._** nut meal; **-knacker, _m._** nutcracker; **-kohle, _f._** nut coal; **-öl, _n._** nut oil.

Nüstern, _f.pl._ nostrils.

Nut(e), _f._ groove, slot, flute, rabbet; ∼ **und Feder,** splined connection.

Nutschapparat, _m._ suction apparatus.

Nutsche, _f._ suction filter.

nutschen, to filter (by suction), suck; **-becher, _m._** suction-filter cup; **-sieb, _n._** suction-filter sieve; **-trichter, _m._** suction funnel.

Nutsharz, _n._ acaroid (resin) gum.

Nutz-anwendung, _f._ economic (practical) application; **-arbeit, _f._** useful work.

nutzbar, useful, profitable, available, productive, effective.

Nutzbarkeit, _f._ exploitability.

nutzbar-machen, to utilize; **-machung,** *f.* utilization.

nutzbringend, profitable.

nutze, nütze, useful, of use, profitable.

Nutzeffekt, *m.* useful effect, efficiency, effective power.

nutzen, (*dat.*) to be of use, use, exploit, crop.

Nutzen *m.* use, utility, advantage, gain, profit.

Nutz-feld, *n.* useful field; **-gras,** *n.* grass for fodder; **-höhe,** *f.* effective depth (height); -**holz,** *n.* commercial timber; **-last,** *f.* live (useful) load; **-leistung,** *f.* useful (work) effect, effective force.

nützlich, (*dat.*) useful, profitable, advantageous, serviceable.

Nützlichkeit, *f.* usefulness, utility, advantage.

nutz-los, useless, unprofitable; **-niesser,** *m.* usufructuary; **-niessung,** *f.* usufruct; **-pflanze,** *f.* food (fodder) plant; **-strom,** *m.* useful current; **-tier,** *n.* useful animal.

Nutzung, *f.* revenue, produce, yield, harvest.

Nutzungs-dauer, *f.* useful life; **-periode,** *f.* utilization period; **-prozent,** *n.* utilization percentage; **-recht,** *n.* right of use; **-satz,** *m.* yield.

Nutz-wert, *m.* **-e,** economic value; **-wirkung,** *f.* useful effect.

O

Oase, *f.* oasis.

ob, whether, if, beyond; ∼ **auch,** although.

Obacht, *f.* heed, attention.

Obdach, *n.* shelter, lodging.

oben, above, upstairs, overhead, before; **von ∼ nach unten,** from above downward; **nach ∼,** upstairs, up, on high, upward; **von ∼,** from the top.

oben-an, at the top; **-auf,** at the top, head; **-drein,** over and above; **-erwähnt,** above-mentioned; **-hin,** superficially, slightly.

ober, superior, upper, higher; **-antenne,** *f.* antennule, first pair of antenna; **-arm,** *m.* upper arm.

Oberarmbein, *n.* humerus; **-gelenkkopf,** *m.* head of humerus; **-gelenkrolle,** *f.* glenoid surface of humerus; **-hals,** *m.* neck of humerus; **-narbe,** *f.* tuberosity of humerus.

Oberarm-gelenk, *n.* shoulder joint; **-gelenkgrube,** *f.* glenoid fossa of scapula; **-höcker,** *m.* deltoid tuberosity; **-knochen,** *m.* humerus; **-knorren,** *m.* condyle of humerus; **-kopf,** *m.* head of humerus; **-leiste,** *f.* deltoid ridge; **-muskel,** *m.* deltoid muscle of upper arm.

Oberaugenhöhle, *f.* supraorbital fossa.

Oberaugenhöhle-loch, *n.* supraorbital foramen; **-rand,** *m.* supraorbital arch.

Oberbau, *m.* superstructure.

Oberbauch, *m.* epigastrium, upper part of abdomen; **-gegend,** *f.* epigastric region.

Ober-begriff, *m.* superimposed concept; **-bewusstsein,** *n.* superconsciousness, conscious self; **-blatt,** *n.* epiphyll; **-boden,** *m.* topsoil.

obere, upper, higher, superior, head, chief.

Ober-faltenhöhle, *f.* metapleural canal; **-feder,** *f.* tectrix, covert; **-fläche,** *f.* surface, area.

oberflächen-aktiv, surface active, readily absorbable, referring to substances that lower surface tension; **-bau,** *m.* surface structure; **-bearbeitung,** *f.* finish: **-behandlung,** *f.* surface treatment; **-bildung,** *f.* surface marking, formation; **-druck,** *m.* surface pressure; **-einheit,** *f.* unit of area; **-energie,** *f.* surface energy, surface tension; **-erscheinung,** *f.* surface phenomenon.

Oberflächen-farbe, *f.* surface color; **-furchung,** *f.* superficial cleavage; **-härtung,** *f.* casehardening; **-häutchen,** *n.* surface membrane or pellicle; **-inaktiv (-kapillarinaktiv)** referring to substances increasing surface tension; **-kondensator,** *m.* surface condenser; **-kultur,** *f.* surface cultivation; **-ladung,** *f.* surface charge; **-lösung,** *f.* surface solution.

Oberflächen-nadel, *f.* dermal spicule; **-niederschlag,** *m.* surface precipitate; **-periderm,** *n.* surface (superficial) periderm; **-pflanzen,** *f.pl.* exochomophytes (surface-rooting and mat-forming plants), hemikryptophytes.

Oberflächen-scheibe, *f.* disk from dermal layer; **-schicht,** *f.* surface layer or membrane; **-schnitt,** *m.* surface section; **-schrumpfung,** *f.* shrinkage of the surface; **-spannung,** *f.* surface tension; **-verminderung,** *f.* decrease (in size) of the surface; **-wirkung,** *f.* surface (action) effect.

ober-flächlich, superficial, on the surface, shallow; **-flügel,** *m.* upper wing, anterior part of wing; **-flügeldecken,** *f.pl.* subalary feathers; **-förster,** *m.* forest superintendent; **-fuss,** *m.* instep, tarsus.

obergärig, top; **obergärige Hefe,** *f.* top yeast.

Ober-gärung, *f.* top fermentation; **-grätengrube,** *f.* supraspinal fossa; **-grund,** *m.* superficial soil, surface soil.

ober-halb, above; **-hals,** *m.* dorsal (cervical) region; **-hand,** *f.* back of the hand, metacarpus, predominance; **-haupt,** *n.* vertex, head, chief; **-haut,** *f.* epidermis: **-häutchen,** *n.* cuticle.

Ober-hautgebilde, *n.* epidermic formation; **-hautleiste,** *f.* epidermal ridge; **-hefe,** *f.* top yeast; **-holz,** *n.* overwood, timber; **-hüftgegend,** *f.* upper-hip region; **-irdisch,** overground, epigeous, aerial part; **-keim,** *m.* epiblast, ectoderm.

Oberkiefer, *m.* superior maxilla, upper jaw, upper back; **-ast,** *m.* supramaxillary branch; **-bein,** *n.* superior maxilla; **-fortsatz,** *m.* process of superior maxilla; **-gaumenfortsatz,** *m.* palatine process of superior maxilla; **-gerüst,** *n.* superior maxilla (frame).

Oberkiefer-grube, *f.* canine fossa; **-höhle,** *f.* maxillary cavity; **-knochen,** *m.* superior maxilla; **-körper,** *m.* body of superior maxilla; **-lappen,** *m.pl.* maxillary plates, processes; **-taster,** *m.* mandibular palp.

Ober-kinnbacken, *m.* upper jaw, superior maxilla; **-kinnlade,** *f.* upper jaw; **-lappen,** *m.* superior lobe; **-lauf,** *m.* upper course (of river); **-leib,** *m.* upper part of body or trunk; **-licht,** *n.* light from above, skylight.

Ober-lippe, *f.* upper lip, labrum, epistome; **-lippendrüse,** *f.* labial gland; **-niere,** *f.* suprarenal gland; **-ohrenkreuz,** *n.* supraauricular cross (meeting of hairlines); **-rinde,** *f.* outer bark; **-schädel,** *m.* epicranium.

Oberschenkel, *m.* thigh; **-anzieher,** *m.* adductor muscle of femur; **-bein,** *n.* femur; **-beuger,** *m.* flexor of the thigh; **-bruch,** *m.* fracture of femur; **-flur,** *f.* femoral tract; **-gegend,** *f.* femoral region; **-hals,** *m.* neck of the femur; **-knorren,** *m.* condyle of femur; **-kopf,** *m.* head of the femur.

Ober-schicht, *f.* upper layer or stratum; **-schlächtig,** incubous, the oblique insertion of distichous leaves of Hepaticae (Jackson); **-schlundganglion,** *n.* supraesophageal ganglion; **-schlüsselbeingrube,** *f.* supraclavicular fossa; **-schnabel,** *m.*

upper jaw of bird; **-schulterblattgegend,** *f.* suprascapular region; **-schwanzdecken,** *f.pl.* upper tail coverts; **-schwingung,** *f.* overtone, oscillation, harmonic; **-seite,** *f.* upper side; **-spannung,** *f.* high-tension voltage.

oberst, uppermost, topmost, highest

oberständig, hypogynous superior.

Ober-tasse, *f.* cup; **-teig,** *m.* upper dough; **-teil,** *m.* upper part, top part; **-ton,** *m.* overtone, harmonic; **-wasser,** *n.* headwater; **-welle,** *f.* harmonic vibration; **-zahn,** *m.* upper tooth.

obgleich, although.

Obhut, *f.* protection, care.

obig, above, foregoing, above-mentioned.

Objekt-abstand, *m.* working distance; **-glas,** *n.* (microscopic) slide, mount.

Objektiv, *n.-e,* objective; **-wechsler,** *m.* revolving nosepiece (of microscope).

Objekt-raum, *m.* object distance; **-sucher,** *m.* object finder; **-tisch,** *m.* stage, stand.

Objektträger, *m.-,* slide, stand, mount; **-halter,** *m.* slide forceps; **-präparat,** *n.* film made on slide.

Objektträger mit Vertiefung, hollow-ground slide.

Oblate, *f.* wafer.

obliegen, to cultivate, be incumbent (on), apply (to), attend (to).

Obliegenheit, *f.* obligation, duty.

obligat, obligatory.

obligatorisch, obligatory, compulsory.

Obmann, *m.* chairman, head man.

obschon, although.

Observatorium, *n.* observatory.

Obst, *n.* fruit; **-art,** *f.* kind of fruit; **-bau,** *m.* horticulture; **-baum,** *m.* fruit tree; **-baumkrebs,** *m.* fruit-tree canker; **-baumschädiger,** *m.* orchard pest; **-branntwein,** *m.* fruit (brandy) spirit; **-essig,** *m.* fruit vinegar; **-frucht,** *f.* fruit, stone fruit; **-garten,** *m.* orchard.

Obst-kern, *m.* fruit (kernel) stone; **-konserve,** *f.* preserved fruit; **-made,** *f.* fruit worm, larva; **-most,** *m.* fruit juice; **-mus,** *n.* fruit (sauce) butter, jam, marmalade; **-saft,** *m.* fruit juice; **-wein,** *m.* cider, fruit wine; **-zucker,** *m.* fruit sugar, levulose, fructose.

obwalten, to rule, control, exist, prevail, predominate.

obwohl, obzwar, although, though.

ocherig, ocherous.

Ochras, *m.* black salt, crude potash, melted ashes.

Ochs, Ochse, *m.* ox.

Ochsen-fleisch, *n.* beef; **-frosch,** *m.* bull-frog; **-galle,** *f.* ox (gall) bile; **-klauenfett,** *n.* neat's-foot oil; **-leder,** *n.* neat's leather; **-zunge,** *f.* oxtongue, bugloss (*Anchusa*), borage; **(färbende) Oschenzunge,** alkanet.

Ocker, *m.* ocher; **-artig,** like ocher, ocherous; **-farbig,** ocher-colored, ocherous; **-gelb,** ocher, ocher yellow.

Oculieren, *n.* budding, grafting.

od., *abbr.* (oder), or.

öde, waste, deserted.

Odem, *n.* edema.

oder, or.

Odermennig, *m.* agrimony.

Ödland, *n.* wasteland, barren land; **-fläche,** *f.* wasteland.

Odometer, *m.&n.* consolidation device, odomata.

Öfchen, *n.* little (furnace) stove.

Ofen, *m.⸚,* furnace, oven, kiln, stove; **-bruch,** *m.* tutty (zinc); **-futter,** *n.* furnace lining; **-galmei,** *m.* furnace cadmia, tutty; **-gang,** *m.* working order of a furn ce; **-kachel,** *f.* stove tile; **-russ,** *m.* furnace (oven) soot; **-sau,** *f.* furnace sow; **-schlacke,** *f.* furnace slag; **-schwamm,** *m.* furnace cadmia, tutty; **-trocken,** kiln-dried; **-tür,** *f.* door (of stove), wicket; **-ziegel,** *m.* fire brick, stove tile.

offen, open, clear, vacant, clever, frank, denuded, bare.

offenbar, manifest, obvious, evident, plain.

offen-baren, to disclose, reveal, manifest; **-kundig,** well-known, public, notorious, evident; **-sichtlich,** obvious(ly), apparent.

öffentlich, public, open.

Öffentlichkeit, *f.* publicity; **an die ∼ treten,** to appear publicly, be published.

Offerte, *f.* offer, proposal, proffer, bid.

offiziell, official.

Offizier, *m.* officer.

Offizin, *f.* dispensary, apothecary's shop, printing shop.

offizinell, officinal.

öffnen, to open, disclose, reveal.

öffnend, aperient, opening, laxative.

Öffnung, *f.* opening, aperture, gap, dehiscence, orifice, mouth, incision, dis-section, evacuation, hole; **zur ∼ bringen,** to cause to open.

Öffnungs-kappe, *f.* opening device, opener; **-mittel,** *n.* aperient; **-stoss,** *m.* initial (opening) stimulus; **-verhältnis,** *n.* aperture ratio, relative aperture; **-weise,** *f.* manner of dehiscence (of capsule); **-winkel,** *m.* angular aperture, generating angle, vertex angle, aperture angle.

oft, often.

öfter, oftener, more frequently, repeated.

öfters, often, frequently, sometimes, several times; **des (zum) öfteren,** oftentimes.

oft-malig, frequent, repeated; **-mals,** frequent.

ohne, without, but that; **∼ dass,** without; **∼ dem, ∼ dies,** without (apart from) that, besides; **∼ hin,** besides; **∼ weiteres,** without further ado, at once, forthwith, directly.

ohngefähr, approximately.

Ohnmacht, *f.* weakness, fainting, syncope, swoon.

ohnmächtig, weak, faint, unconscious.

Ohr, *n.*-en, ear, auricle, wing of shell.

Öhr, *n.*-e, eye (of needle), handle, lug, catch.

Ohr-band, *n.* ligament of the ear; **-bläschen,** *n.* auditory vesicle, otocyst; **-blatt,** *n.* lobe of the ear, pinna; **-drüse,** *f.* parotid gland; **-ecke (hintere)** *f.* antitragus; **-ecke (vordere)** *f.* tragus.

Ohren-höhle, *f.* cavity of the ear; **-knorpel,** *m.* auricular cartilage; **-qualle,** *f.* jellyfish (Aurelia); **-schmalz,** *n.* cerumen, earwax; **-stein,** *m.* otolith; **-trommel,** *f.* eardrum; **-trompete,** *f.* Eustachian tube.

Ohr-falte, *f.* auricular fold; **-finger,** *m.* little finger; **-förmig,** auriform; **-fortsatz,** *m.* auditory process; **-gang,** *m.* auditory canal; **-gegend,** *f.* region of the ear, ear coverts; **-halskanal,** *m.* Eustachian tube; **-hammer,** *m.* mallet; **-hügel,** *m.* auditory hillock.

Ohr-kanal, *m.* auditory canal; **-kiemen-spalte,** *f.* first branchial cleft; **-knöchel-chen,** *n.* auditory ossicle; **-knorpel,** *m.* cartilage of the ear; **-knoten,** *m.* otic ganglion; **-kreis,** *m.* helix; **-kreis (innerer),** *m.* anthelix; **-läppchen,** *n.* lobule of the ear; **-leiste,** *f.* helix; **-loch,** *n.* external auditory meatus.

Ohrmuschel, *f.* external ear, pinna, auricle, ear conch; **-leiste,** *f.*, **-rand,** *m.* helix.

Ohr-scheibe, *f.* external ear (of birds); **-schnecke,** *f.* cochlea of inner ear; **-speicheldrüse,** *f.* parotid gland; **-stein,** *m.*

otolith; **-trommel,** *f.* eardrum; **-trompete,** *f.* Eustachian tube; **-wachs,** *n.* earwax, cerumen; **-wasser,** *n.* endolymph; **-wurm,** *m.* earwig.

Oidiumkette, *f.* oïdium chain.

Oker, *m.* ocher.

okkludieren, to occlude.

ökologische Art, *f.* biologic species.

ökonomisch, economical, thrifty, agricultural.

Oktaeder, *n.* octahedron.

oktaedrisch, octahedral.

oktocarbocyclisch, octacarbocyclic.

Okular, *n.* eyepiece; **-blende,** *f.* eyepiece diaphragm; **-brennweite,** *f.* focal length of the eyepiece; **-mikrometer,** *n.* eyepiece micrometer; **-muschel,** *f.* eyepiece cup; **-schätzung,** *f.* ocular estimate.

okulieren, to graft, inoculate.

Okulieren, *n.* budding, grafting.

Öl, *n.*-e, oil; **-abscheider,** *m.* oil separator, oil trap; **-artig,** oily; **-ausscheider,** *m.* oil separator; **-bad,** *n.* oil bath.

Ölbaum, *m.* ⁼e, olive tree; falscher ∼, oleaster.

Ölbaum-gummi, -harz, *n.* elemi.

Öl-beere, *f.* olive; **-behälter,** *m.* oil container, oil-storing organ; **-beize,** *f.* oil mordant; **-bildend,** oil-forming, olefiant; **-blau,** *n.* smalt, Saxon blue, indigo copper; **-bodensatz,** *m.* oil sediment; **-bohrung,** *f.* oil well; **-brenner,** *m.* oil burner; **-drass,** *m.* oil dregs; **-druck,** *m.* oil pressure, oleography.

Oleaster, *m.* wild olive.

Olefin, *n.* olefin.

olefinisch, olefinic.

Olein, *n.* olein; **-säure,** *f.* oleic acid.

ölen, to oil.

Oleokreosot, *n.* creosote oleate.

Ölerglas, *n.* glass oil cup.

Öl-ersatz, *m.* oil substitute; **-fabrik,** *f.* oil factory; **-farbe,** *f.* oil color; **-farbendruck,** *m.* oleography, oleograph.

Oleum, *n.* fuming sulphuric acid.

ölgar, oiled, chamois.

Öl-gas, *n.* oil gas; **-gasteer,** *m.* oil-gas tar; **-geläger,** *n.* oil dregs, sediment; **-geschmack,** *m.* oily taste; **-gewinnung,** *f.* oil production; **-haltig,** containing oil, oleiferous; **-handel,** *m.* oil trade; **-hefen,** *f.pl.* oil (dregs) lees; **-hypha,** *f.* oil hypha.

Oliban, *n.* olibanum, frankincense.

ölicht, oily, oleaginous.

ölig, oily, oleaginous.

Öligkeit, *f.* oiliness.

Oligozän, *n.* oligocene.

Oligoklas, *m.* oligoclase.

Öl-immersion, oil-immersion; **-industrie,** *f.* oil industry; **-isolation,** *f.* oil insulation.

Olive, *f.* olive.

oliven-artig, olivary; **-baum,** *m.* olive tree; **-braun,** olive brown; **-farbe,** *f.* olive color; **-förmig,** olivary; **-kern,** *m.* olivary nucleus; **-kernöl,** *n.* olive-kernel oil; **-öl,** *n.* olive oil.

Olivin, *m.* silicate of magnesium, olivine, chrysolite.

Öl-kautschuk, *m.* rubber substitute; **-kitt,** *m.* putty; **-körper,** *n.* oil body; **-kuchen,** *m.* oil cake; **-kugel,** *m.* oil (globule) drop; **-lack,** *m.* oil varnish; **-leder,** *n.* chamois; **-madie,** *f.* melosa (*Madia saliva*); **-malerei,** *f.* oil painting.

Öl-menge, *f.* amount of oil; **-messer,** *m.* oleometer; **-milch,** *f.* oil emulsion; **-nussbaum,** *m.* butternut tree, horse-radish tree (*Moringa*); **-palme,** *f.* Elaeis; **-papier,** *n.* oilpaper; **-reinigung,** *f.* purification of oil; **-rettich,** *m.* radish (*Raphanus sativus*); **-rückstand,** *m.* oil residue; **-same(n),** *m.* rapeseed, linseed; **-satz,** *m.* oil sediment, oil foots.

Öl-säure, *f.* oleic acid; **-schiefer,** *m.* oil shale; **-schlagen,** *n.* oil pressing; **-schmierung,** *f.* oil lubrication; **-schwarz,** *n.* oil black, lampblack; **-seife,** *f.* oil soap; **-sodaseife,** *f.* Castile soap; **-spur,** *f.* trace of oil; **-staub,** *m.* oil spray; **-stoff,** *m.* olein; **-striemen,** *m.* oil (secretion) canal; **-süss,** *n.* glycerol, glycerin; **-trester,** *m.pl.* oil marc (residue from pressing); **-tuch,** *n.* oilcloth; **-umlauf,** *m.* oil circulation.

Ölung, *f.* oiling.

Öl-verbrauch, *m.* oil consumption; **-waage,** *f.* oil hydrometer, oleometer; **-weidengewächse,** *n.pl.* Elaeagnaceae; **-zelle,** *f.* oil cell; **-zucker,** *m.* oleosaccharum; **-zufluss,** *m.* oil inflow, oil feed; **-zusatz,** *m.* addition of oil.

Önanthäther, *m.* enanthic ether.

Ooblastemfortsatz, *m.* conjugation tube.

Öogenese, *f.* formation of an egg.

Oogoniumstand, *m.* oögoniophore.

Oolith, *m.* oölite.

oolithisch, oölitic.

Ooplasmarinde, *f.* oöplasmic cortex.

opak, opaque.

opal-artig, opallike, opaline; -blau, *n.* opal blue.

opaleszieren, to opalesce.

Opal-farbe, *f.* opal color; -glanz, *m.* opaline luster, opalescence; -glänzend, opalescent.

opalisieren, to opalesce.

opalschillernd, opalescent.

Opazität, *f.* opacity.

Oper, *f.* opera.

Operation, *f.* operation, process.

operieren, to operate.

Operkularborsten, *f.pl.* opercular setae.

Operment, *n.* orpiment.

Opfer, *n.* offering, sacrifice, victim.

opfern, to sacrifice.

Ophthalmie, *f.* ophthalmia.

Opiansäure, *f.* opianic acid.

Opiumsäure, *f.* meconic acid.

Opsoninuntersuchung, *f.* opsonic investigation.

opsonisch, opsonic.

Optik, *f.* optics.

optimistisch, optimistic.

optisch, optic, optical.

Optogramm, *n.* optogram.

Orange, *f.* orange (fruit).

Orangen-blüte, *f.* orange blossom; -farbe, *f.* orange color; -frucht, *f.* hesperidium, citrus fruit; -gelb, *n.* orange yellow; -rot, orange-red; -samenöl, *n.* orange-seed oil; -schale, *f.* orange peel.

Orang-Utaug, *m.* orangutan.

Orbita, *f.* orbit, eye socket.

Orbital-borste, *f.* orbital bristle; -flügel, *m.* wing of the sphenoid; -lappen, orbital lobe; -spalte, *f.* orbital cleft.

Örchen, *n.* auricle.

Orchideenblüte, *f.* orchid flower.

Orden, *m.* order, decoration, medal.

ordentlich, ordinary, regular, orderly, respectable, steady, downright, really, seriously.

ordinär, ordinary, mean, regular, common, inferior.

Ordinate, *f.* ordinate, offset; -achse, *f.* ordinate axis; -strecke, *f.* distance on the ordinate.

Ordinierung, *f.* prescription.

ordnen, to order, organize, arrange, classify, regulate, settle.

Ordnung, *f.* order, arrangement, regulation, classification, class, succession, series, division.

ordnungs-gemäss, orderly, regular, well; -mässig, orderly, methodical, duly, lawful, well; -widrig, irregular, disorderly.

Ordnungszahl, *f.* ordinal number, atomic number, serial number, test number, order number, concentration factor.

Organ, *n.* organ, agent, agency; -anlage, *f.* organ rudiment; -bildung, *f.* organ formation; -brei, *m.* tissue pulp; -eiweiss, *n.* organ protein.

Organiker, *m.* organic chemist.

Organisationslaufplan, *m.* organization, guiding plan.

organisatorisch, organizing.

organisch, organic.

organisieren, to organize.

Organismus, *m.* organism.

Organometall, *n.* organometallic compound.

organometallisch, organometallic.

Organreserve, *f.* organic reserve.

Organteil, *m.-e,* part of an organ.

Orgel, *f.* organ (the instrument); -korallen, *f.pl.* Tubipora.

orientalisch, oriental.

orientieren, to orient, inform, right.

Orientierung, *f.* orientation, survey.

Orientierungsbewegung, *f.* orientation movement.

Orkan, *m.-e,* hurricane, gale.

Orseille, *f.* archil, orchil; -flechte, *f.* archil, rock moss.

Orsellinsäure, *f.* orsellinic acid.

Ort, *m.* place, point, locus, region, locality, spot; an ～ und Stelle, on the spot.

Orterde, *f.* loose accumulations of humic substances.

Ortho-ameisensäure, *f.* orthoformic acid; -antimonigsäure, *f.* orthoantimonious acid; -arsenigsäure, *f.* orthoarsenious acid; -chinon, *n.* orthoquinone; -kieselsäure, *f.* orthosilicic acid; -klas, *m.* orthoclase; -rhombisch, orthorhombic; -salpetersäure, *f.* orthonitric acid; -säure, *f.* ortho acid; -stellung, *f.* ortho position.

orthotomisch, in straight sections, straight edges.

Orthoverbindung, *f.* ortho compound.

Ortisomerie, *f.* position isomerism.

örtlich, local, topical, endemic.

Orts-abteilung, *f.* compartment; **-anruf,** *m.* local call; **-bestände,** *m.pl.* society, facies; **-bewegung,** *f.* locomotion.

Ortschaft, *f.* place, village.

orts-fest, stationary; **-funktion,** *f.* position function; **-isomerie,** *f.* place (position) isomerism; **-sässig,** local.

Ortstein, *m.* hardpan, moor pan, boundary stone.

Orts-veränderung, *f.* change of position; **-vereine,** *m.pl.* society, facies; **-wechsel,** *m.* change of position, migration.

os (Latin), mouth; **per** ∼, through the mouth.

Oschakkpflanze, *f.* oshac, ammoniac plant.

Öse, *f.* loop, ring, eye, hook, lug, ear, catch, platinum-wire loop.

Ösen-blatt, *n.* flange, tongue, lip; **-schraube,** *f.* eyebolt.

Osmium, *n.* osmium; **-haltig,** containing osmium; **-oxydul,** *n.* protoxide of osmium; **-säure,** *f.* osmic acid; **-verbindung,** *f.* osmium compound.

Osmose, *f.* osmosis, osmose.

osmosieren, to osmose.

osmotisch, osmotic.

Ost, Osten, *m.* east, Orient.

Osterluzei, *f.* birthwort (*Aristolochia clematitis);* **-gewächse,** *n.pl.* Aristolochiaceae.

Ostern, *n.* Easter.

Österreich, *n.* Austria.

östlich, eastern, oriental, easterly.

Ostritzwurzel, *f.* masterwort, Imperatoria root.

Ostsee, *f.* Baltic (Sea).

oszillieren, to oscillate.

Otter, *f.* adder, viper.

Otter, *m.* otter.

Ovarialkapsel, *f.* ovarian capsule, gonotheca.

Oxalat, *n.* oxalate.

Oxal-äther, *m.* oxalic ether, ethyl oxalate; **-essigester,** *m.* oxalacetic ester; **-ester,** *m.* oxalic ester, ethyl oxalate; **-salz,** *n.* oxalate.

oxalsauer, oxalate of; **oxalsaurer Kalk,** *m.* calcium oxalate.

Oxalsäure, *f.* oxalic acid; **-lösung,** *f.* oxalic acid; **-lösung,** *f.* oxalic acid solution; **-salz,** *n.* oxalate.

Oxalursäure, *f.* oxaluric acid.

Oxamidsäure, Oxaminsäure, *f.* oxamic acid.

Oxhämoglobin, *n.* oxyhemoglobin.

Oxhoft, *n.* hogshead.

Oxy-aldehyd, *n.* hydroxy aldehyde; **-ammoniak,** *n.* oxyammonia, hydroxylamine; **-azoverbindung,** *f.* hydroxyazo compound; **-carbonsäure,** *f.* hydroxycarboxylic acid; **-chinolin,** *n.* hydroxyquinoline; **-chlorkupfer,** *n.* copper oxychloride.

Oxyd, *n.* oxide.

oxydabel, oxidizable.

oxydartig, of the nature of, (like) an oxide.

Oxydase, *f.* oxidase.

Oxydation, *f.* oxidation.

Oxydations-artikel, *m.* oxidation style; **-bestreben,** *n.* tendency to oxidize; **-fähig,** capable of oxidation; **-flamme,** *f.* oxidizing flame; **-grad,** *m.* degree of oxidation; **-mittel,** *n.* oxidizing agent; **-stoffwechsel,** *m.* oxidation metabolism; **-stufe,** *f.* stage of oxidation; **-vorgang,** *m.* oxidation process; **-wirkung,** *f.* oxidizing action or effect.

Oxyd-beschlag, *m.* coating of oxide; **-bildend,** oxide-forming; **-haltig,** containing oxide or oxides, oxidic; **-haut,** *f.* film of oxide; **-hydrat,** *n.* hydrated oxide, hydroxide.

Oxydierbarkeit, *f.* oxidizability.

oxydieren, to oxidize.

Oxydiermittel, *n.* oxidizing agent.

Oxydierung, *f.* oxidation.

oxydisch, oxidic, oxygenic.

Oxyd-oxydul, *n.* (-oso, -ic) oxide; **-rot,** *n.* Turkey red, purple oxide of iron; **-schicht,** *f.* layer (film) of oxide.

Oxydul, *n.* protoxide, (-ous) oxide, suboxide.

Oxy-essigsäure, *f.* hydroxyacetic acid; **-fettsäure,** *f.* hydroxy-fatty acid.

oxygenieren, to oxygenate, oxygenize.

Oxygenierung, *f.* oxygenation.

Oxyketon, *n.* hydroxyketone; **-carbonsäure,** *f.* hydroxyketocarboxylic acid.

Oxymethyl-gruppe, *f.* hydroxymethyl group.

Oxy-salz, *n.* oxysalt; **-säure,** *f.* oxyacid; **-schwefelsäure,** *f.* oxysulphuric acid; **-toluol,** *n.* hydroxytoluene; **-zellulose,** *f.* oxycellulose.

Ozäna, *f.* ozena.

Ozean, *m.* ocean.

Ozellenplatte, *f.* ocellar plate.

Ozobenzol, *n.* ozobenzene.

Ozokerit, *m.* ozocerite.

Ozon, *n.* ozone; **-erzeugend,** producing ozone, ozoniferous; **-haltig,** containing ozone, ozoniferous.

Ozonisator, *m.* ozonizer.

ozonisieren, to ozonize.

Ozonsauerstoff, *m.* ozonized oxygen.

P

paar, even; ∼ **oder unpaar,** even or odd.

Paar, *n.*-e, pair, two, couple, a few.

paaren, to conjugate, pair, copulate, couple, join, unite, mate, match; **gepaart,** conjugated, geminate, didymous.

Paarhufer, *m.pl.* Artiodactyla (even number of toes).

paarig, in pairs, paired, even.

Paarling, *m.* one of a pair, allelomorph.

paar mal, ein paar mal, a few times.

Paarung, *f.* pairing, copulation, mating, coupling, conjugation.

Paarungsausfall, *m.* product of mating.

paarweise, in pairs, in couples, by twos.

Paarzeher, *m.pl.* Artiodactyla.

Paarzeit, *f.* mating season.

Pacht, *f.* lease, tenure, rent.

Pächter, *m.*-, tenant, leaseholder.

Pachtvertrag, *m.* lease.

Pack, *m.* pack, bale, packet, package, bundle.

Pack, *n.* rabble.

Packdarm, *m.* rectum.

packen, to pack, seize, claw, pounce.

Pack-haus, *n.* ⁼er, **-hof,** *m.* warehouse, customhouse; **-leinen,** *n.* sacking, packing cloth; **-leinwand,** *f.* packing cloth; **-papier,** *n.* wrapping paper; **-stoff,** *m.* packing material; **-tuch,** *n.* packing cloth.

Packung, *f.* packing, loading, seizure, structure, densification.

Packzeug, *n.* packing material.

Paket, *n.*-e, packet, parcel, bundle.

paläontologisch, palaeontological.

Palatinspange, *f.* palatine arch.

Palisaden-drüse, *f.* palisade gland; **-gewebe,** *n.* palisade tissue; **-wurm,** *m.* Strongylous; **-zellbüschel,** *n.* group of palisade cells.

Palisanderholz, *n.* rosewood.

Palladichlorwasserstoffsäure, *f.* chloropalladic acid.

Palladium-bromür, *n.* palladous bromide; **-chlorid,** *n.* palladium chloride; **-gehalt,** *m.* palladium content; **-jodür,** *n.* palladous iodide; **-mohr,** palladium black; **-oxydul,** *n.* palladous oxide; **-reihe,** *f.* palladium series.

Pallado-chlorwasserstoffsäure, *f.* chloropalladous acid; **-hydroxyd,** *n.* palladous hydroxide.

Palmatinseife, *f.* palmatin soap.

Palme, *f.* palm.

Palmen-öl, *n.* palm oil; **-stärke,** *f.* palm starch, sago; **-typus,** *m.* palm type.

Palmfarn, Angiopteris, Cycas.

Palmfett *n.* palm (oil) butter.

Palmin, *n.* coconut butter.

Palmitinsäure, *f.* palmitic acid.

Palm-kernöl, *n.* palm-kernel oil; **-lilie,** *f.* yucca; **-nussöl,** *n.* palm-kernel oil, coconut oil; **-öl,** *n.* palm oil; **-stärke,** *f.* palm starch, sago; **-wachs,** *n.* palm wax; **-zucker,** *m.* palm sugar, jaggery.

palpierbar, palpable.

Panaschierung, *f.* variegation, mottling.

pandemisch, pandemic.

Pankreas, *n.* pancreas; **-drüse,** *f.* pancreas; **-insel,** *f.* island of the pancreas; **-saft,** *m.* pancreatic juice.

pankreatisch, pancreatic.

Panne, *f.* breakdown, mishap.

Pansen, *m.* rumen (of the ruminants), paunch.

pantoffel-artig, in the shape of a slipper; **-tierchen,** *n.* Paramecium.

Panzer, *m.*-, armor, shell, (coat of) mail, cuirass; **-blech,** *n.* armor plate; **-fische,** *m.pl.* Ostraceodermi, Placodermi; **-kopfgranate,** *f.* armor-piercing shell; **-krebse,** *m.pl.* Thoracostraca.

panzern, to armor, armor plate.

Panzer-platte, *f.* armor plate; **-technik,** technique of armored protection.

Päonie, *f.* peony.

Papagei, *m.* parrot.

Papau, *m.* Asimina (papaw, etc.).

Papel, *f.* papule, pimple.

Papier, *n.*-e, paper; **-abfall,** *m.* paper waste; **-abgang,** *m.* paper waste; **-blatt,** *n.* sheet or leaf of paper; **-bogen,** *m.* sheet of paper; **-brei,** *m.* paper pulp.

papieren, (of) paper, papery.

Papier-fabrik, *f.* paper factory, paper mill; **-fabrikant,** *m.* papermaker; **-filter,** *n.* paper filter; **-fläche,** *f.* paper surface; **-handel,** *m.* paper trade; **-handlung,** *f.* stationer's shop; **-holz,** *n.* pulpwood; **-knochen,** *m.* papyraceous lamina of ethmoid bone; **-kohle,** *f.* paper coal; **-leim,** *m.* paper size.

Papier-masse, *f.* paper pulp; **-prüfung,** *f.* paper testing; **-scheibe,** *f.* paper disk; **-schlauch,** *m.* paper bag (for tamping); **-sorte** *f.* quality of paper; **-stoff,** *m.* paper pulp.

Papier-stoffbrei, *m.* paper pulp (in water); **-streifen,** *m.* paper (strip) web; **-teig,** *m.* papier-mâché; **-überseite,** *f.* felt side (in paper manufacturing); **-zeichen,** *n.* watermark; **-zeug,** *n.* wood pulp, paper pulp.

Papille, *f.* papilla, pimple, nipple.

Papin'scher Topf, *m.* pressure cooker.

Papillen-hals, *m.* papillary neck; **-polster,** *n.* papillary cushion.

Papp, *m.* paste, pap.

Pappatacifieber, *n.* sand-fly (phlebotomus) fever.

Papp-band, *m.* board binding; **-bogen,** *m.* sheet of pasteboard or cardboard; **-deckel,** *m.* pasteboard, paperboard cover.

Pappe, *f.* pasteboard, cardboard, pap, paste, pulp sheet; **geformte** ∿, millboard.

Pappel, *f.* poplar, mallow **-schwärmer,** *m.* poplar hawkmoth; **-spinner,** *m.* species of lappet moth.

pappen, to paste, work in pasteboard; **-art,** *f.* **-deckel,** *m.* pasteboard; **-fabrik,** *f.* paperboard mill; **-leim,** *m.* pasteboard glue; **-stiel,** *m.* trifle.

Papphülse, *f.* pasteboard case.

pappig, pasty, sticky.

Papp-karton, *m.* cardboard box, carton; **-masse,** *f.* papier-mâché; **-schachtel,** *f.* pasteboard box; **-schirm,** *m.* pasteboard screen.

Paraband, *n.* rubber tape.

Parabel, *f.* parabola, parable.

parabolisch, parabolic, allegorical.

Paracyan, *n.* paracyanogen.

Paradies, *n.* paradise; **-apfel,** *m.* tomato; **-feige,** *f.* banana; **-holz,** *n.* agalloch, aloeswood; **-körner,** *n.pl.* grains of paradise; **-vogel,** *m.* bird of paradise.

paradox, paradoxical.

Paraffin, *n.*-e, paraffin; **-bad,** *n.* paraffin bath; **-durchtränkung,** *f.* paraffin, impregnation; **-einbettung,** *f.* imbedding in paraffin.

paraffinieren, to coat with paraffin.

Paraffin-kerze, *f.* paraffin candle; **-öl,** *n.* liquid paraffin; **-reihe,** *f.* paraffin series; **-salbe,** *f.* petrolatum, paraffin ointment; **-säure,** *f.* paraffinic acid; **-schnittbänder,** *n.pl.* ribbons of paraffin, serial sections.

Para-fuchsin, *n.* pararosaniline; **-glossumspangen,** *f.pl.* paraglossa; **-gummi,** *n.,* **-kautschuk,** *m.* Para rubber; **-kolibacillose,** *f.* infection with paracolon bacilli; **-kresse,** *f.* Spilanthes.

Parallel-achse, *f.* parallel axis; **-erscheinnung,** *f.* analogous form, parallel phenomenon; **-parzelle,** *f.* parallel experimental plot; **-probe,** *f.* parallel test; **-schaltung,** *f.* connection in parallels; **-versuch,** *m* parallel experiment, duplicate determination.

Paralysator, *m.* anticatalyst.

Paralyse, *f.* paralysis.

paralysieren, to paralyze.

para-magnetisch, paramagnetic; **-milchsäure,** *f.* dextrolactic acid (paralactic acid); **-nuss,** *f.* Brazil nut; **-podialfortsätze,** *m.pl.* epipodites; **-septalknorpel,** *m.* paraseptal cartilage.

Parasit, *m.*-en, parasite.

parasitär, parasitic.

Parasitenkunde, *f.* parasitology.

parasitentötend, parasiticide.

parasitisch, parasitic.

Parasitologie, *f.* parasitology.

paraständig, in the para position.

Parastellung, *f.* para position.

parat, ready.

Paratyphus, *m.* paratyphoid fever; **-bazillen,** *m.pl.* paratyphoid bacilli.

Para-verbindung, *f.* para compound; **-weinsäure,** *f.* paratartaric (racemic) acid.

Parenchym, *n.* parenchyma.

parenchymatisch, parenchymatous.

Parenchymscheide, *f.* parenchymatous sheath.

Parenthese, *f.* parentheses, brackets.

Parforce-jagd, *f.* hunting with hounds and on horseback.

Parfüm, *n.* perfume.

Parfümerie, *f.* perfumery.

parfümieren, to perfume, scent.

Pari, *n.* par; **auf** ∼, at par; **über** ∼, above par.

Parisergrün, *n.* Paris green.

Pariwert *m.* par value.

Park, *m.* park.

Parkettwachs, *n.* floor wax.

Paröken, *n.* commensal living on another organism.

Partei, *f.* part, party, faction, side, following.

parteiisch, partial, biased, prejudiced, taking sides.

Parthenogenese, *f.* parthenogenesis.

Partial-antigene, *f.* partial antigens; **-bruch,** *m.* partial fraction; **-druck,** *m.* partial pressure; **-explantat,** *n.* explant of part of organism.

Partie, *f.* party, company, parcel, lot, portion, batch, picnic, game, match, shipment.

partiell, partial.

Partieware, *f.* off-standard goods.

Partikel, *f.* particle.

Partikelchen, *n.* small particle.

Parzelle, *f.* parcel, compartment, lot.

parzellieren, to parcel out.

Passagen-kulture, *f.* **weiterimpfung,** *f.* culture transfer.

Passagier, *m.*-e, passenger.

passen, (*dat.*) to fit, be fit, be (convenient) suited, harmonize, wait, adjust, adapt, measure.

passend, fit, suitable, appropriate.

Passglas, *n.* graduated glass.

passieren, to pass, cross, happen, occur, take place.

Passionblume, *f.* Passiflora.

passiv, passive, inactive.

passivieren, to render inactive, passivate.

passivierend, passively, inactively.

Passivität, *f.* passivity.

Pastellfarbe, *f.* pastel color.

Pastete, *f.* pastry, pie.

Pasteurellose, *f.* pasteurellosis.

pasteurisieren, to pasteurize.

pastig, pasty.

Pastille, *f.* tablet.

Pastinakwurzel, *f.* parsnip.

pastös, pasty.

Patent, *n.*-e, patent; **-amt,** *n.* patent office; **-anmeldung,** *f.* application for a patent; **-anspruch,** *m.* patent claim; **-anwalt,** *m.* patent attorney; **-beschreibung,** *f.* patent (description) specification; **-dauer,** *f.* life of a patent.

patentierbar, patentable.

Patent-inhaber, *m.* patentee; **-recht,** *n.* patent (right) law; **-salz,** *n.* ammonium antimony fluoride; **-schrift,** *f.* patent, patent specification; **-schutz,** *m.* protection by patent; **-verletzung,** *f.* patent infringement; **-zement,** *m.* Roman cement.

Paternostererbse, *f.* Indian licorice (*Abrus precatorius*).

pathogen, pathogenic.

Pathogenese, *f.* pathogenesis.

Pathologie, *f.* pathology.

pathologisch, pathological.

Pathotropismus, *m.* pathotropism.

patinieren, to patinate.

Patrone, *f.* cartridge, pattern, stencil, mandrel, shell.

Patronenhülse, *f.* cartridge case.

Patsche, *f.* fix, difficulty, mess, dilemma, slush, mud.

patschen, to splash, clap. smack, slap.

Patschuli, *n.* patchouli.

pattinsonieren, to pattinsonize.

Pauke, *f.* drum, tympanum, harangue.

Pauken-bein, *n.* tympanic (supratemporal) bone; **-decke,** *f.* covering of tympanum; **-drüse,** *f.* glandula tympanum.

Paukenfell, *n.* tympanic membrane, drumhead; **-fenster,** *n.* tympanic fenestra; **-saite,** *f.* chorda tympani; **-tasche,** *f.* tympanic cavity, recess (pouch) of tympanic membrane.

Pauken-gang, *m.* tympanic canal; **-höhle,** *f.* tympanic cavity; **-höhlendach,** *n.* roof of tympanum; **-höhlenenge,** *f.* isthmus of tympanum; **-rinne,** *f.* tympanum groove; **-treppe,** *f.* scala tympani.

Pauschalsumme, *f.* total (lump) sum.

pauschen, to swell, refine.

Pauscht, *m.* post (paper).

Pause, *f.* tracing, pause; ∼ **machen,** to rest.

pausen, to trace, calk.

Paus-leinen, *n.* tracing cloth; **-leinwand,** *f.* tracing cloth; **-papier,** *n.* tracing paper.

Pe Ce Faser, *f.* polyvinyl chloride fiber.

Pech, *n.* pitch; ~ **haben,** to have hard luck.

Pech-art, *f.* variety of pitch; **-artig,** pitchlike, bituminous; **-blende,** *f.* pitchblende; **-draht,** *m.* pitched (shoemaker's) thread.

pecheln, to smell pitchy, make pitch.

pechen, to pitch, coat with pitch.

Pech-erde, *f.* bituminous earth; **-finster,** pitch-dark; **-geschmack,** *n.* pitchy taste; **-glanz,** *m.* pitchy luster; **-granat,** *m.* colophonite; **-griess,** *m.* pitch cake, pitch grit; **-harz,** *n.* pitch resin.

pechig, pitchy.

Pech-kiefer, *f.* pitch pine; **-kohle,** *f.* pitch (bituminous) coal; **-öl,** *n.* tar oil; **-pflaster,** *n.* asphalt (tar) paving; **-schwarz,** pitch-black; **-stein,** *m.* pitchstone; **-steinkohle,** *f.* pitch coal, jet; **-tanne,** *f.* pitch pine; **-torf,** *m.* pitch peat, black fuel peat; **-uran,** *n.* pitchblende.

Pedalganglion, *n.* pedal ganglion (in the feet of mollusks).

Pegel, *m.* water gauge, gauge rod, depth indicator.

Peilfunk, *m.* beam.

Peilung, *f.* sounding.

Pein, *f.* pain, trouble, torment, torture.

peinigen, to torment, trouble.

peinlich, painful, painstaking, careful, precise, penal.

Peitsche, *f.* whip.

peitschen, to whip, beat, lash, scourge; **-förmig,** whip-shaped, flagelliform; **-haar,** *n.* whiplike hair.

Pekannuss, *f.* pecan.

pektinartig, pectinlike.

pektinig, pectinous.

Pektin-säure, *f.* pectic acid; **-stoff,** *m.* pectin substance; **-zucker,** *m.* arabinose.

Pelargonsäure, *f.* pelargonic acid.

Peligot-rohr, *n.* **-röhre,** *f.* Peligot tube.

Pellagra, *f.* pellagra.

Pelle, *f.* pell, husk, skin.

Peloteuse, *f.* plodder (soap).

Pelz, *m.* pelt, skin, fur; **-dune,** *f.* plume; **-farn,** *m.* Notholaena.

pelzig, furry, nappy, cottony, fleecy.

Pendel, *n.* pendulum; **-artig,** like a pendulum; **-changierung,** *f.* swing-arm traverse motion.

pendeln, to oscillate, swing, vibrate, undulate.

penetrieren, to penetrate.

Penisstachel, *m.* penis.

Pensee, *n.* pansy.

Pension, *f.* pension, board, boardinghouse, boarding school.

pentacarbocyclisch, pentacarbocyclic.

Pentathionsäure, *f.* pentathionic acid.

Pentinsäure, *f.* pentinoic acid.

Pentosurie, *f.* pentosuria.

Pentoxyd, *n.* pentoxide.

Pentrinit, *n.* pentaerythritol tetranitrate nitroglycerin.

Pentrit, *n.* pentaerythritol tetranitrate.

Pepsin, *n.* pepsin; **-drüse,** *f.* peptic gland. **-haltig,** containing pepsin.

Peptisator, *m.* peptizer, peptizing agent.

peptisch, peptic.

peptisieren, to peptize.

Peptisierung, *f.* peptization.

peptolytisch, peptolytic.

Pepton, *n.* peptone; **-fleischbrühe,** *f.* peptone-beef broth.

peptonisieren, to peptonize.

Per-acidität, *f.* superacidity; **-borsäure,** *f.* perboric acid; **-bromsäure,** *f.* perbromic acid.

Perchagummi, *m.* & *n.* gutta-percha.

Perchlorsäure, *f.* perchloric acid.

perennierend, perennial.

Perforationsschlauch, *m.* penetration tube.

perforieren, to perforate.

Pergament, *n.* parchment; **-ähnlich,** parchmentlike.

pergamentieren, to parchmentize.

Pergamentpapier, *n.* parchment paper.

Pergamyn, *n.* pergamyn, glassine, imitation parchment.

perhydrieren, to perhydrogenize.

Perhydrol, *n.* hydrogen peroxide.

Peribranchialraum, *m.* atrial cavity.

Pericardialeinstülpung, *f.* pericardial invagination.

Perichaetialblatt, *n.* involucral leaf (around the base of the seta in mosses) (Jackson).

Periclinalchimäre, *f.* periclinal chimera, graft hybrid.

Periderm, *n.* periderm, perisarc (of Hydrozoa); **-bekleidung,** *f.* perisarc: **-dauer-**

gewebe, *n.* phellem (cork); **-hülle,** *f.* perisarcal envelope; **-napf,** *m.* perisarc cup.

Perigonialblätter, *n.pl.* involucral leaves surrounding the antheridia.

Perihel, *n.* perihelion.

Perikard, *n.* pericardium.

Periklas, *m.* periclase, periclasite.

Perillasäure, *f.* perillic acid.

Periode, *f.* period, repetend, interval.

Perioden-einteilung, *f.* division into periods; **-fläche,** *f.* periodic block, affectation.

periodisch, periodical.

Periodizität, *f.* periodicity.

peripher, peripheral.

Peripherie, *f.* circumference, periphery, outskirts.

peripherisch, peripheral.

Peripneumonia, pleuropneumonia.

peristaltisch, peristaltic.

Peristomfeld, *n.* peristomal area, peristome.

Peritonealhöhle, *f.* peritoneal cavity.

peritrich, peritrichic.

Peritricha, *f.* peritricha.

Per-jodat, *n.* periodate; **-jodsäure,** *f.* periodic acid.

Perkussionszündhütchen, *n.* percussion cap.

perl-artig, pearly, nacreous, beadlike; **-asche,** *f.* pearlash; **-blase,** *f.* bladderlike hair; **-drüse,** *f.* pearl gland.

Perle, *f.* pearl, bead.

perlen, to rise in pearls, effervesce, form bubbles, sparkle, form drops, glisten; **-glanz,** *m.* pearly (nacreous) luster; **-schnur,** *f.* string of pearls (beads); **-schnurhaar,** *n.* nodulose hair.

perl-farben, pearl-colored; **-farn,** *m.* Onoclea; **-glimmer,** *m.* margarite; **-gras,** *n.* Melica; **-grau,** pearl-gray; **-graupen,** *f.pl.* pearl barley; **-huhn,** *n.* guinea fowl.

Perlitreaktion, *f.* pearlite reaction.

Perl-kohle, *f.* pea coal; **-koks,** *m.* coke breeze, culm coke; **-moos,** *n.* pearl moss, carrageen; **-muschel,** *f.* pearl oyster.

Perlmutter, *f.* mother-of-pearl, nacre; **-artig,** like mother-of-pearl, nacreous; **-blech,** *n.* crystallized tinplate; **-glanz,** *m.* mother-of-pearl luster; **-glänzend,** having a mother-of-pearl luster, pearly.

Perl-rohr, *n.* **-röhre,** *f.* tube filled with beads; **-sago,** *m.* pearl sago; **-salz,** *n.* microcosmic

salt, sodium phosphate; **-samen,** *m.* seed pearl; **-schicht,** *f.* nacreous layer of a shell; **-schnurförmig,** moniliform, like a string of beads; **-seide,** *f.* ardassine; **-stein,** *m.* perlite, adularia; **-sucht,** *f.* bovine tuberculosis.

Permanganatlösung, *f.* permanganate solution.

Permanganasäure, *f.* permanganic acid.

Permeabilität, *f.* permeability.

Permeabilitätsänderung, *f.* change of permeability.

permutieren, to permute.

Permutitverfahren, *n.* permutite process.

perniciös, pernicious.

Peroxyd, *n.* peroxide.

Peroxydase, *f.* peroxidase.

Perpendikel, *n.* perpendicular (line) pendulum.

Per-salz, *n.* persalt; **-säure,** *f.* peracid; **-schwefelsäure,** *f.* persulphuric acid.

Perseit, *n.* perseitol, perseite.

Personal, *n.* personnel, staff, assistants.

persönlich, personal.

Perstoff, *m.* diphosgene.

Persulfocyansäure, *f.* persulphocyanic acid, perthiocyanic acid.

Peru-rinde, *f.* cinchona, Peruvian bark; **-salpeter,** *m.* nitrate of soda.

Pest, *f.* plague, pest, pestilence; **-ähnlich,** resembling plague, pestilential, contagious, infectious; **-bakterien,** *n.pl.* plague bacilli; **-bazillus,** *m.* plague bacillus; **-fieber,** *n.* anthrax.

Pestilenzkraut, *n.* Galega.

pest-krank, plague-infected; **-wurz,** *f.* Pedasites.

Petersilie, *f.* parsley.

petersilienähnlich, parsleylike.

Peterskraut, *n.* wall pellitory.

Petrischale, *f.* Petri dish.

Petrol, *n.* petroleum; **-äther,** *m.* petroleum ether.

Petroleum, *n.* petroleum, mineral oil; **-äther,** *m.* petroleum ether; **-behälter,** *m.* petroleum container; **-dampf,** *m.* petroleum vapor; **-destillationsgefäss,** *n.* petroleum still; **-geruch,** *m.* petroleum odor; **-haltig,** containing petroleum; **-handel,** *m.* petroleum trade; **-seifenbrühe,** *f.* kerosene emulsion.

Petrol-koks, *m.* petroleum coke, oil coke; -**säure,** *f.* petrolic acid.

Petschaft, *n.* seal, signet.

Petsche, *f.* drying (room) frame.

Pfad, *m.* path.

Pfaff, *m.* rivet stamp, nut driver.

Pfaffe, *m.* priest.

Pfaffenhütchen, *n.* Evonymus.

Pfahl, *m.* stake, pile, prop, post, pole, stick, picket.

Pfählchen, *n.pl.* pali (of Anthozoa); -**kranz,** *m.* circle of pali.

pfählen, to prop, support, empale.

Pfahl-gründung, *f.* pile foundation; -**rohr,** *n.* giant reed (*Arundo donax*); -**rost,** *m.* pile cluster or cap; -**wurzel,** *f.* taproot; **zaun,** *m.* paling, picket fence.

Pfalz, *f.* the Palatinate.

Pfand, *n.* pledge, deposit, security, forfeit.

Pfanne, *f.* pan, copper, boiler, pantile, bearing, socket, acetabulum.

pfannen-artig, acetabular; -**gras,** *n.* knotgrass, Paspalum; -**grube,** *f.* acetabular fossa; -**knorpel,** *m.* acetabular cartilage; -**rand,** *m.* acetabular (cotyloid) margin; -**stein,** *m.* pan scale, boiler scale; -**werk,** *n.* saltworks; -**ziegel,** *m.* pantile.

Pfänner, *m.* salt manufacturer.

Pfau, *m.* peacock; -**blau,** peacock-blue.

Pfeffer, *m.* pepper; -**artig,** like pepper, peppery; -**kraut,** *n.* savory (Satureia); -**kuchen,** *m.* gingerbread; -**minze,** *f.* peppermint.

Pfefferminz-geruch, *m.* peppermint odor; -**öl,** *n.* peppermint oil.

Pfefferstein, *m.* peperino.

Pfeife, *f.* pipe, whistle, fife, blown-out shot.

pfeifen, to pipe, fife, whistle; -**erde,** *f.* pipe clay; -**knochen,** *m.* tibia; -**rohr,** *n.* pipestem; -**strauch,** *m.* syringa, mock orange, Philadelphus; -**ton,** *m.* pipe clay.

Pfeil, *m.* arrow, dart, rise (of a curve), camber (of an arch); -**drüse,** *f.* dart gland.

Pfeiler, *m.* pillar, pier, post, prop; -**zelle,** *f.* rod cell.

pfeil-förmig, arrow-shaped, sagittate; -**gift,** *n.* curare, arrow poison; -**höhe,** *f.* height (of a miniscus, arch); -**höhle,** *f.* sagittal sinus; -**kraut,** *n.* arrowhead (*Sagittaria sagittifolia*); -**sack,** *m.* dark sac; -**würmer,** *m.pl.* Chaetognathi; -**wurz,** *f.* arrowfoot 'Maranta arundinaceae); -**verhältnis,** *n.*

ratio of rise to span; -**wurzelmehl,** *n.* arrowroot flour.

Pfennig, *m.* penny, pfennig (1/100 of mark); -**kraut,** *n.* pennycress (*Thlaspi arvense*).

Pferd, *n.* horse.

Pferde-bohne, *f.* horse bean; -**dünger,** *m.* horse manure; -**harnsäure,** *f.* hippuric acid; -**kraft,** *f.* horsepower; -**kraftstunde,** *f.* horsepower-hour; -**magenfliegen,** *f.pl.* botflies (Gastrophillidae); -**milch,** *f.* mare's milk; -**minze,** *f.* horsemint; -**mist,** *m.* horse manure.

Pferde-pneumonie, *f.* acute pneumonia of the horse; -**sattel,** *m.* sella turcica, saddle; -**schweif,** *m.* horse s tail; -**serum,** *n.* horse serum; -**stärke,** *f.* horsepower; -**zucht,** *f.* horse breeding.

pfiff (pfeifen), whistled, piped.

Pfiff, *m.* whistle, trick.

Pfifferling, *m.* mushroom.

Pfingstrose, *f.* peony.

Pfirsich, *m.* peach; -**blüte,** *f.* peach blossom; -**holz,** *n.* peachwood; -**kern,** *m.* peach kernel; -**palme,** *f.* Bactris.

Pflanz-beet, *n.* -e, planting bed; -**beil,** *n.* planting hatchet; -**bohrer,** *m.* tree planter, semicircular spade; -**brett,** *n.* planting board.

Pfländzchen, *n.* little plant, plantlet, seedling.

Pflanzdolch, *m.* planting dagger, dibble.

Pflanze, *f.* plant, vegetable.

Pflanz-eisen, -**holz,** *n.* planting peg, dibble.

pflanzen, to plant; -**abfälle,** *m.pl.* plant debris, vegetable remains; -**alkali,** *n.* vegetable alkali; -**alkaloid,** *n.* plant (vegetable) alkaloid; -**art,** *f.* species of plant; -**artig,** plantlike, vegetable; -**asche,** *f.* plant ash; -**aufguss,** *m.* (plant) infusion; -**base,** *f.* vegetable (base), alkaloid; -**beschreibung,** *f.* description of plants.

Pflanzen-beschützer, *m.* protector of plants; -**bestand,** *m.* plant formation; -**bestandteil,** *m.* vegetable constituent; -**butter,** *f.* vegetable butter; -**chemie,** *f.* plant chemistry; -**chemisch,** phytochemical; -**decke,** *f.* covering of vegetation; -**dekokt,** *n.* plant decoction, juice of vegetables; -**eiweiss,** *n.* vegetable (albumin) protein.

Pflanzen-erde, *f.* vegetable mold, humus; -**ernährung,** *f.* nourishment of plants; -**farbe,** *f.* vegetable color; -**farbstoff,** *m.* plant pigment, vegetable dye; -**faser,** *f.* vegetable (plant) fiber; -**faserstoff,** *m.* vegetable fibrin; -**fett,** *n.* vegetable fat; -**fibrin** *n.* vegetable gluten, cellulose fibrin; **-forscher,** *m.* botanist; **-fressend,** herbivorous.

Pflanzen-fresser, *m.* herbivorous animal, herbivore; **-führend,** plant-yielding, containing plant remains; **-fund,** *m.* plant findings, remains, fossil; **-fundpunkt,** *m.* plant station, plant locality; **-gallert,** *n.* vegetable gelatin, pectin; **-gattung,** *f.* genus of plants; **-gemeinschaft,** *f.* plant community; **-geschwulst,** *f.* plant tumor; **-gesellschaft,** *f.* plant association, plant society.

Pflanzen-grün, *n.* chlorophyll; **-haar,** *n.* vegetable (horse)hair; **-händler,** *m.* nurseryman; **-kasein,** *n.* legumin, vegetable casein; **-kleber,** *m.* gluten; **-kleid,** *n.* flora; **-kohle,** *f.* vegetable charcoal; **-krankheit,** *f.* plant disease; **-kunde,** *f.* botany; **-laugensalz,** *n.* potash; **-läuse,** *f.pl.* plant lice, aphides.

Pflanzen-leben, *n.* plant life; **-lehre,** *f.* botany; **-leim,** *m.* plant gum, vegetable glue, gliadin, gluten; **-nahrung,** *f.* plant food; **-pathologie,** *f.* plant pathology; **-pech,** *n.* vegetable pitch; **-reich,** *n.* vegetable (plant) kingdom; **-rest,** *m.* plant remains; **-rot,** *n.* carthamin; **-saft,** *m.* vegetable (plant) juice; **-schädling,** *m.* plant pest; **-schleim,** *m.* mucilage.

Pflanzenschutz, *m.* plant protection, quarantine; **-bestimmung,** *f.* plant-protection regulation; **-dienst,** *m.* plant-protection service; **-düngung,** *f.* fertilizer application against plant pests; **-mittel,** *n.* plant-disinfectant or -protective agent.

Pflanzen-seide, *f.* vegetable silk; **-stoff,** *m.* vegetable matter; **-talg,** *m.* vegetable tallow; **-teil,** *m.* part of plant; **-tier,** *n.* zoophyte; **-verband,** *m.* arrangement of plants; **-verbreitung,** *f.* distribution of plants.

Pflanzen-verein, *m.* plant community; **-wachs,** *n.* vegetable wax; **-wachstum,** *n.* **-wuchs,** *m.* plant growth; vegetation; **-zelle,** *f.* plant (vegetable) cell; **-zellenstoff,** *m.* cellulose; **-zucht,** *f.* plant breeding.

Pflanzer, *m.* planter, settler.

Pflanz-erde, *f.* compost; **-garten,** *m.* nursery; **-holz,** *n.* planting peg, dibble; **-kartoffel,** *f.* seed potato.

pflanzlich, plant, vegetable.

Pflanzling, *m.* plantlet.

Pflanz-loch, *n.* plant hole, pit; **-reihe,** *f.* planting row; **-schule,** *f.* nursery; **-stätte,** *f.* place for planting, colony; **-tauglichkeit,** *f.* agronomic value (fitness for planting);

-verfahren, *n.* method of planting; **-weite,** *f.* planting distance, spacing.

Pflanzzeit, *f.* season for planting.

Pflaster, *n.* plaster, pavement, paving; **-epithel,** *n.* pavement epithelium; **-käfer,** *m.pl.* Spanish flies, blister beetles (Meloidae).

pflastern, to plaster, dress with plaster, pave.

pflaster-steinartig, pavementlike; **-ziegel,** *m.* paving brick.

pflatschen, to pad (calico).

Pflatschfarbe, *f.* padding liquor.

Pflaume, *f.* plum, prune.

Pflaumen-baum, *m.* plum tree; **-farbig,** plum-colored; **-sieder,** *m.* plum distiller.

Pflege, *f.* care, nursing, tending, rearing, education, culture, cultivation.

pflegen, to be accustomed, be in the habit of, indulge, attend to, care for, tend, cultivate, nurse; **das pflegt so zu sein,** that is usually the case; **der Ruhe ∼,** to take a rest, take it easy; **wie man zu sagen pflegt,** as one is accustomed to say; **Rats ∼,** keep counsel.

pfleglich, careful.

Pflegetier, *n.* foster mother, phorozoid.

Pflicht, *f.***-en,** duty, obligation; **-gemäss,** conformable to (one's) duty; **-schuldig,** in duty bound, obligatory.

Pflock, *m.***-e,** peg, pin, stake, picket, plug, tampon, embolus.

pflog (pflegen), took care to, attended to.

pflücken, to pluck, pick, gather.

Pflücksalat, *m.* leaf lettuce.

Pflug, *m.*:̈e, plow; **-balken,** *m.* plow beam, furrow ridge.

pflügen, to plow.

Pflug-karren, *m.* plow truck; **-körper,** *m.* body of the plow.

Pflugschar, *m.* vomer, plowshare; **-ausschnitt,** *m.* notch of vomer; **-bein,** *n.* vomer; **-flügel,** *m.* wing of vomer; **-knochen,** *m.* vomer; **-loch,** *n.* foramen of vomer; **-rinne,** *f.* sulcus of vomer.

Pflug-sterz, *m.* plow handle; **-tiefe,** *f.* depth of furrow.

Pfortader, *f.* portal vein; **-kreislauf,** *m.* portal circulation.

Pforte, *f.* orifice, opening, entrance, door gate.

Pförtner, *m.* pylorus, porter, doorkeeper; **-anhänge,** *m.pl.* pyloric appendages; **-klappe,** *f.* pyloric sphincter, valve.

Pfosten, *m.* post, support, plank, door jamb.

Pfote, *f.* paw.

Pfriem, *m.-e,* **Pfrieme,** *f.* **Pfriemen,** *m.,* punch, awl.

Pfriemenborste, *f.* acicular bristle.

pfriem-förmig, subulate, awl-shaped; **-gras,** *n.* matgrass, matweed (*Nardus stricta*); **-kraut,** *n.* Spanish broom (*Spartium junceum*).

pfriemlich, subulate, awl-shaped.

pfriemstachelig, erinous, with sharp points.

Pfropf, *m.-e,* **Pfropfen,** *m.,* stopper, plug, wad, cork, graft, clot, tampon, thrombus, embolus; **-artig,** stopperlike; **-bastard,** *m.* graft hybrid.

pfropfen, to graft, stopper, plug, cork, cram; **-zieher,** *m.* corkscrew.

Pfropf-hybrid, *m.* graft hybrid; **-messer,** *n.* grafting knife; **-reis,** *n.* graft scion; **-spalt** *m.* grafting slit; **-stelle,** *f.* graft union; **-wachs,** *n.* grafting wax; **-werkzeug,** *n.* grafting tool.

Pfuhl, *m.* pool, puddle, slough.

Pfühl, *m.&n.-e,* pillow, bolster, cushion.

Pfund, *n.-e,* pound; **-leder,** *n.* sole leather.

pfuschen, to bungle, blunder, meddle.

Pfütze, *f.* puddle, wallow, mud hole, slough.

phagedänisches Wasser, *n.* yellow mercurial lotion.

Phagozyt, *m.* phagocyte.

phagozytär, depending on action of phagozytes.

Phagozytentheorie, *f.* phagocytosis theory.

Phagozytose, *f.* phagocytosis.

phanerogamisch, phanerogamous.

Phänomen, *n.* phenomenon.

Phantasie, *f.* imagination, fancy, vision.

phantasieren, to imagine, dream, muse, ramble, be delirious.

phantasievoll, imaginative, fanciful.

Phantast, *m.* dreamer, visionary.

Pharmako-log, *m.* pharmacologist; **-logie,** *f.* pharmacology; **-logisch,** pharmacological; **-pöe,** *f.* pharmacopeia.

Pharmazeut, *m.* pharmaceutist.

Pharmazeutik, *f.* pharmaceutics.

pharmazeutisch, pharmaceutical.

Pharmazie, *f.* pharmacy.

Pharynx-anschwellung, *f.* pharyngeal bulb (swelling); **-krone,** *f.* crown of pharynx.

Phase, *f.* phase.

Phasen-änderung, *f.* phase change; **-gesetz,** *n.* phase law; **-gleich,** of like phase; **-gleichgewicht,** *n.* equilbrium between phases, phase coincidence; **-grenze,** *f.* phase boundary; **-lehre,** *f.* doctrine of phases; **-regel,** *f.* phase rule.

Phasen-spannung, *f.* phase voltage; **-unter-schied,** *m.* phase difference; **-verkettung,** *f.* interlinking of phases; **-verschiebung,** *f.* phase displacement; **-verzögerung,** *f.* phase lagging; **-zahl,** *f.* number of phases.

Phasotropie, *f.* phasotropy.

Phenol-äther, *m.* phenol ether; **-gruppe,** *f.* phenol group; **-kalium,** *n.* potassium phenolate; **-lösung,** *f.* phenol solution; **-natrium,** *n.* sodium phenolate; **-öl,** *n.* carbolic acid, phenol; **-phtalein,** *n.* phenolphthalein; **-schwefelsäure,** *f.* phenolsulphuric acid.

Phenyl-anilin, *n.* phenylaniline; **-arsen-chlorür,** *n.* phenylarsenious chloride.

Phenylenblau, *n.* phenylene blue.

Phenylessigsäure, *f.* phenylacetic acid.

phenylieren, to phenylate.

Phenyl-milchsäure, *f.* phenyllactic acid; **-purpursäure,** *f.* isopurpuric acid; **-säure,** *f.* phenylic acid, carbolic acid; **-schwefel-säure,** *f.* phenylsulphuric acid, sulphocarbolic acid; **-siliciumchlorid,** *n.* phenylsilicon chloride; **-wasserstoff,** *m.* phenyl hydride, benzene.

Philosoph, *m.-en,* philosopher.

philosophisch, philosophical.

Phiole, *f.* vial, phial.

Phlegma, *n.* phlegm, sluggishness.

phlegmatisieren, to desensitize (explosives).

Phloem, *n.* phloem (bast elements); **-insel,** *f.* island of phloem.

phlogistisch, phlogistic.

Phlorchinyl, *n.* phloroquinyl.

Phloroglucid, *n.* phloroglucide.

Phonetik, *f.* phonetics.

Phönizin, *n.* phenicin, phoenicin.

Phosgen, *n.* phosgene, carbonyl chloride.

Phosphat, *n.* phosphate; **-dünger,** *m.* phosphate fertilizer.

Phosphatese, *f.* phosphatese.

phosphatführend, phosphate-bearing.

phosphatisch, phosphatic.

phosphenylig, phosphenylous.

Phosphenylsäure, *f.* phosphenylic acid.

Phosphinigsäure, *f.* phosphinous acid.

Phosphinsäure, *f.* phosphinic acid.

Phosphor, *m.* phosphorus; -artig, like phosphorus; -basis, phosphorus base; -bestimmung, *f.* determination of phosphorus; -blei, *n.* lead phosphide; -bromid, *n.* phosphorus bromide; -bromür, *n.* phosphorus (tri)bromide; -chlorür, *n.* phosphorus (tri)chloride; -dampf, *m.* phosphorus vapor; -eisen, *n.* ferrophosphorus, iron phosphide.

Phosphorescenz, *f.* phosphorescence.

phosphoreszieren, to phosphoresce.

phosphoreszierend, phosphorescent.

Phosphoreszierung, *f.* phosphorescence.

Phosphor-fleischsäure, *f.* phosphocarnic acid; -frei, free from phosphorus; -gehalt, *m.* phosphorus content; -haltig, containing phosphorus, phosphorated.

phosphorig, phosphorous; -sauer, phosphite of.

phosphorisch, phosphoric.

phosphorisieren, to phosphorize, phosphorate.

Phosphorit, *m.* phosphate of lime.

Phosphor-jodid, *n.* phosphorus (tri)iodide; -jodür, *n.* phosphorus diiodide; -kerzchen, *n.* wax match, vesta; -kupfererz, *n.* libethenite; -löffel, *m.* phosphorus spoon; -masse, *f.* phosphorus paste.

Phosphor-metall, *n.* phosphide; -natrium, *n.* sodium phosphide; -öl, *n.* phosphorated oil; -oxydul, *n.* phosphorus trioxide; -salz, *n.* microcosmic salt; -sauer, phosphate of.

Phosphorsäure, *f.* phosphoric acid; -anhydrid, *n.* phosphoric anhydride; -lösung, *f.* phosphoric acid solution.

Phosphor-stange, *f.* stick of phosphorus; -sulfid, *n.* phosphorus sulphide; -verbindung, *f.* phosphorus compound; -vergiftung, *f.* phosphorus poisoning; -wasserstoff, *m.* hydrogen phosphide; -zinn, *n.* tin phosphide; -zündhölzchen, *n.* phosphorus match.

Photo-bakterien, *n.pl.* photogenic bacteria; -chemie, *f.* photochemistry; -chemisch, photochemical; -effekt, *m.* photo effect, photokinesis; -elektrisch, photoelectric.

photogen, photogenic.

Photo-gramm, *n.* photograph; -graph, *m.* photographer; -graphie, *f.* photography,

photograph; -graphieren, to photograph; -graphisch, photographic; -kopie, *f.* photographic copy, photoprint.

photo-kopieren, to photostat; -lyse, *f.* photolysis; -metrisch, photometric; -physik, *f.* photophysics; -sphäre, *f.* photosphere; -tropie, *f.* phototropism.

Phtal-amidsäure, *f.* -aminsäure, *f.* phthalamic acid; -azin, *n.* phthalazine.

Phtalein, *n.* phthalein.

Phtalmonopersäure, *f.* monoperphthalic acid.

Phtalonsäure, *f.* phthalonic acid.

Phtalsäure, *f.* phthalic acid; -anhydrid, *n.* phthalic anhydride.

phthisisch, phthisical.

Phykomyzeten, *pl.* Phycomycetes.

phylogenetisch, phylogenetic.

Phylogenie, *f.* doctrine of descent, phylogeny.

Physik, *f.* physics, tin composition.

physikalisch, physical; -chemisch, physical-chemical, physicochemical.

Physikbad, *n.* tin composition.

Physiker, *m.* physicist.

Physiksalz, *n.* red spirit.

Physiognomie, *f.* physiognomy.

Physio-log, *m.* physiologist; -logie, *f.* physiology; -logisch, physiological.

physisch, physical.

Phytochemie, *f.* phytochemistry.

phytochemisch, phytochemical.

Pichapparat, *m.* pitching machine.

pichen, to pitch.

Pich-pech, *n.* common pitch; -wachs, *n.* propolis.

Picke, *f.* pickax, pick.

Pickel, *m.* pimple, pickax, pick.

picken, to peck, pick.

Pickharz, *n.* galipot.

Picolinsäure, *f.* picolinic acid.

Piezo-chemie, *f.* piezochemistry; -elektrizität, *f.* piezoelectricity.

Pigment, *n.* pigment.

pigmentarisch, pigmentary.

Pigment-bakterien, *pl.* chromogenic bacteria; -bazillen, *pl.* chromogenic bacilli; -bildung, *f.* pigment formation, chromogenesis; -blatt, *n.* pigment layer; -farbe, *f.* pigment color; -farbstoff, *n.* pigment, toner; **-frei,** free from pigment; **-haltig,** containing pigment, pigmented.

pigmentieren, to pigment, become pigmented.

pigment-los, without pigment; **-papier,** *n.* pigment (carbon) paper; **-verteilung,** *f.* distribution of pigment.

Pik, *m.* -s, peak, pique, *n,* spades (cards).

pikant, piquant, pungent.

Pikraminsäure, *f.* picramic acid.

Pikrinsäure, *f.* picric acid.

Pikro-karmin, *n.* picrocarmine; **-toxinsäure,** *f.* picrotoxinic acid.

Pikryl, *n.* picryl.

Pilee, *f.* -zucker, *m.* crushed sugar.

Pilgerschrittchangierung, *f.* pilgrim step variation on traverse motion.

pilieren, grind, mill (soap).

Pille, *f.* pill.

Pillen-farn, *m.* Pilularia; **-schachtel,** *f.* pillbox.

Pilz, *m.*-e, fungus, mushroom; **-ähnlich,** like a mushroom, fungoid; **-art,** *f.* species of mushroom or fungus; **-artig,** like a mushroom, fungoid; **-blume,** *f.* fungus fructification; **-entwickelung,** *f.* fungus development; **-faden,** *m.* fungal thread, mycelium; **-fliegen,** *f.pl.* Platypezidae; **-förmig,** fungiform; **-fressend,** mycophagous; **-gattung,** *f.* fungus family.

pilzicht, fungous, fungoid.

pilzig, fungous, fungoid.

Pilz-käfer, *m.pl.* fungus beetles (Endomychidae); **-keim,** *m.* spore of fungus, fungus germ; **-krankheit,** *f.* fungus disease; **-kunde,** *f.* mycology; **-mantel,** *m.* coat or cover of fungus; **-mücken,** *f.pl.* fungus gnats (Mycetophilidae); **-stoff,** *m.* fungin; **-tiere,** *n.pl.* Mycetozoa, Myxomycetes; **-tötend,** fungicidal, germicide; **-verdauende Pflanze,** *f.* plant with endotrophic mycorrhiza; **-wurzel,** *f.* mycorrhiza.

Pimarsäure, *f.* pimaric acid.

Pimelinsäure, *f.* pimelic acid.

Piment, *n.* -e, pimento, allspice; **-pfeffer,** *m.* pimento, allspice; **-rum,** *m.* bay rum.

Pimpernuss, *f.* ⸚e, bladdernut (Staphylea), pistachio nut.

Pimpinelle, *f.* burnet saxifrage (*Pimpinella*).

Pinakon, *n.* pinacol; **-bildung,** *f.* pinacol formation.

Pinaldrüse, *f.* pineal gland.

Pinen, *n.* pinene.

Pineytalg, *m.* piney tallow.

Pinguin, *m.* -e, penguin (Aptenodytes).

Pinie, *f.* (stone) pine, pine kernel or seed.

Pinit, *n.* pinitol, pinite.

pinken, to treat with pink salt, hammer on anvil.

Pinksalz, *n.* pink salt, double chloride of zinc and ammonium.

Pinne, *f.* pin, peg, quill feather, tack, pivot.

Pinsäure, *f.* pinic acid.

Pinsel, *m.* -, (painter's) brush, pencil, tuft of hair; **-feder,** *f.* oil-gland feather; **-förmig,** brushlike, pencil-shaped.

pinseln, to pencil, paint, daub.

Pinsel-schimmel, *m.* Penicillium; **-zotte,** *f.* brushlike (bushy), shaggy hair.

Pinusharz, *n.* pine resin.

Pinzette, *f.* forceps, tweezers, pincers.

Pionier, *m.* pioneer.

Piperinsäure, *f.* piperic acid.

Pipette, *f.* pipette.

Pipetten-flasche, *f.* pipette; **-gestell,** *n.* pipette stand.

pipettieren, to introduce into or measure with a pipette, pipette.

Piroplasma, *n.* piroplasma.

Piroplasmose, *f.* piroplasmosis.

Pistazie, *f.* pistachio (nut).

Pistaziengrün, *n.* pistachio green.

Pistill, *n.* pestle, pistil.

Pita-hanf, *m.* -faser, *f.* pita hemp, pita.

Pitotrohr, *n.* Pitot (impact) tube.

Placenta, *f.* placenta.

placken, to flatten, ram, pester, torment, slave.

Plackerei, *f.* drudgery, oppression.

Plage, *f.* trouble, bother, torment, vexation, plague, pest, drudgery, epizootic, contagious disease.

plagen, to plague, torment, vex, annoy, trouble, bother, worry.

Plagge, *f.* sod.

Plaggen-haue, *f.* grub hoe; **-hieb,** *m.* removal of sod.

Plagioklas, *m.* plagioclase.

Plakat, *n.* placard, poster; **-farbe,** *f.* lithographic color.

Plan, *m.* plan, design, intention, plain, plane, glade.

Planet, *m.* planet, asteroid.

planieren, to plane, grade, planish, plain, smooth, level, size.

Planier-löffel, *m.* skimmer; **-masse,** *f.* size (paper).

Planierung, *f.* leveling, grading.

Planierwasser, *n.* glue water, size.

Planke, *f.* plank, board.

Plankengerüst, *n.* scaffolding, plank buttress.

plan-konkav, plano-concave; **-konvex,** plano-convex; **-mässig,** systematic, according to plan, methodical; **-mühle,** *f.* grinding mill; **-voll,** carefully planned.

planschen, to splash.

Planspiegel, *m.* plane mirror.

plansymmetrisch, planisymmetric(al).

Plantage, *f.* plantation.

Planum, *n.* bed, subgrade.

Plasma-bezirk, *m.* cytoplasmic region; **-brücke,** *f.* plasmodesma; **-haut,** *f.* plasma membrane; **-klümpchen,** *n.* small particle or globule of plasma; **-körper,** **-leib,** *m.* plasmatic body; **-medium,** *n.* plasma medium; **-strömung,** *f.* plasma streaming, protoplasmic current; **-verbindung,** *f.* plasmodesma.

Plasmolyse, *f.* plasmolysis; **-rückgang,** *m.* recovery from plasmolysis.

plasmolytisch, plasmolytic.

Plastik, *f.* plastic art.

plastisch, plastic.

plastizieren, to plasticize.

Plastizierer, *m.* plasticizer.

Plastizität, *f.* plasticity.

Platane, *f.* plane, plane tree, sycamore.

Platin, *n.* platinum; **-abfall,** *m.* platinum waste, residue; **-artig,** like platinum, platinoid; **-asbest,** *m.* platinized asbestos; **-bad,** *n.* platinum bath; **-blase,** *f.* platinum still; **-blech,** *n.* platinum sheet; **-chlorid,** *n.* platinum chloride; **-chlorür,** *n.* platinous chloride; **-chlorwasserstoff,** *m.* chloroplatinic acid; **-cyanür,** *n.* platinocyanide.

Platin-draht, *m.* platinum wire; **-drahtöse,** *f.* platinum-wire loop; **-dreieck,** *n.* platinum triangle; **-gefäss,** *n.* platinum vessel; **-gerät,** *n.* platinum apparatus; **-haltig,** containing platinum, platiniferous.

Platine, *f.* plate, mill bar.

Platin(i)chlorid, *n.* platinic chloride; **-chlorwasserstoff,** *m.* chloroplatinic acid.

platinieren, to platinize.

Platini-salz, *n.* platinic salt; **-verbindung,** *f.* platinic compound.

Platin-löffel, *m.* platinum spoon; **-mohr,** *m.* platinum black; **-nadel,** *f.* platinum needle, platinum wire.

Platino-chlorid, *n.* platinous chloride; **-chlorwasserstoff,** *m.* chloroplatinous acid.

Platinöse, *f.* platinum-wire loop.

Platinoverbindung, *f.* platinous compound.

Platin-oxyd, *n.* platinum oxide; **oxydverbindung,** *f.* platinic compound; **-reihe,** *f.* platinum series; **-rückstand,** *m.* platinum residue; **-salmiak,** *m.* ammonium chloroplatinate; **-säure,** *f.* platinic acid; **-schale,** *f.* platinum dish.

Platin-schiffchen, *n.* platinum boat; **-schwarz,** *n.* platinum black or mohr; **-spatel,** *m.* platinum spatula; **-spitze,** *f.* platinum point; **-stern,** *m.* platinum star; **-tiegel,** *m.* platinum crucible; **-verbindung,** *f.* platinum compound.

plätschern, to splash, plash, ripple, murmur.

platt, flat, plain, even, level, low, stale, insipid.

Plättchen, *n.* little plate, platelet, lamella.

Platte, *f.* plate, plot, patch, spot, slab, lamina, planchet, leaf, flagstone, plate culture, tray, blaze, mark, lamella, plateau, tableland.

Plätte, *f.* ironing, flatiron.

plätten, to flatten, iron, laminate, flag.

Platten-beschuss, *m.* plate test; **-collenchym,** *n.* lamellar collenchyma; **-drehflügler,** *m.* plant with ailanthus type of flying organs of seed (*Bignonia unguis*); **-druck,** *m.* stereotype, printing from plates; **-epithel,** *n.* flattened epithelium; **-epithelgeschwulst,** *n.* lamellar epithelioma; **-fläschchen,** *n.* flat bottle used for plate culturing; **-förmig,** platelike, lamellar, lamelliform; **-gewebe,** *n.* lamellar tissue; **-giessen,** *n.* pouring plates.

Platten-glimmer, *m.* sheet mica; **-kalk,** *m.* slab limestone; **-knochen,** *m.* lamellar bone, flat bone; **-kultur,** *f.* Petri-dish (plate) culture; **-kupfer,** *n.* skeet copper; **-pulver,** *n.* rolled powder; **-saat,** *f.* sowing in patches; **-schale,** *f.* flat dish, Petri dish; **-turm,** *m.* plate (column), tower; **-würmer,** *m.pl.* Platyhelminthes.

plattgedrückt, flattened.

Platthufer, *m.pl.* Hyracoidae.

plattieren, to plat, plait.

Plattierung, *f.* plating, plate.

Platt-käfer, *m.pl.* corn beetle (Cucudidae); **-würmer,** *pl.* flatworms (Platyhelminthes).

Platz, *m.* ̈e, place, room, spot, site, seat, town square, locality, plot.

Plätzchen, *n.* little (raisin) cake, lozenge, troche, tablet, tabloid, tabella.

platzen, to burst, crash, rupture, explode, crack.

plätzen, to blaze, mark, pop, spot.

Platz-nummer, *f.* atomic number; **-regen,** *m.* pelting rain; **-wechsel,** *m.* change of place, migration.

plausibel, plausible.

plazentenbrüchig, placental dehiscence (of capsule).

Pleistozän, *n.* Pleistocene.

Plejade, *f.* pleiad.

Plenter-betrieb, *m.* selection (femel, plenter) system; **-durchforstung,** *f.* selection thinning.

plentern, tocut, select, practice selection.

Plenter-wald, *m.* selection forest; **-wirtschaft,** *f.* selection system.

Pleochroismus, *m.* pleochroism.

pleomorph, pleomorphic.

Pleuelstange, *f.* connecting rod.

Pleurasack, *m.* pleural sac.

pleuritisch, pleuritic.

pliant, flexible.

Plombe, *f.* plug, filling (for teeth), lead seal.

plombieren, to fill, plug.

Plotz, *m.* explosion.

Plötze, *f.* roach (*Leuciscus rutilus*).

plotzen, explode.

plötzlich, sudden.

Plumbisalz, *n.* plumbic salt.

Plumboverbindung, *f.* plumbous compound.

plump, bulky, clumsy, heavy, gross, awkward.

Plunger, *m.* plunger.

Plüsch, *m.* plush.

Pluszeichen, *n.* plus sign.

Pneu, *n.* tire.

pneumatisch, pneumatic.

Pneumokokkus, *m.* pneumococcus.

Pneumonie, *f.* pneumonia; **-Mikrokokken,** *pl.* pneumococci.

pneumonisch, pneumonic.

Pneumonomykosis, *f.* affection of the lungs due to molds.

pochen, to pound, batter, stamp, beat, knock, rap, brag, boast.

Poch-erz, *n.* ore (as mined); **-gestein,** *n.* stamp rock; **-käfer,** *m.pl.* Anobiidae, Ptinidae; **-mehl,** *n.* pulverized ore; **-mühle,** *f.* stamp mill; **-satz,** *m.* **-schlamm,** *m.* **-schlich,** *m.* ore slime, sludge; **-stempelreihe,** *f.* stamp battery; **-werk,** *n.* stamp mill.

Pocke, *f.* pock.

Pocken, *f.pl.* smallpox; **-erreger,** *m.* exciting cause of smallpox; **-exanthem,** *n.* exanthema of smallpox; **-gift,** *n.* virus of smallpox; **-holz,** *n.* lignum vitae, pockwood; **-impfung,** *f.* vaccination; **-krankheit,** *f.* black scurf and stem canker; **-lymphe,** *f.* vaccine lymph; **-virus,** *m.* smallpox virus; **-wurzel,** *f.* chinaroot.

Pockholz, *n.* pockwood, lignum vitae, guaiacum wood.

Podest, *m.* landing (of staircase).

Poikilothermen, *pl.* poikilothermic animals.

Pokal, *m.* goblet, cup.

Pökel, *m.* pickle, brine; **-fass,** *n.* pickling tub; **-fleisch,** *n.* pickled (salted) meat.

Pökelei, *f.* (meat) salting house.

Pökelkufe, *f.* pickling (vat) tub.

pökeln, to pickle.

Pökeltrog, *m.* pickling trough.

Pol, *m.* pole; **-anziehung,** *f.* polar attraction.

Polar-dreieck, *n.* polar triangle; **-gegend,** *f.* polar region.

Polarisations-apparat, *m.* polarizing apparatus; **-ebene,** *f.* plane of polarization; **-einrichtung,** *f.* polarizing attachment; **-erscheinung,** *f.* polarization phenomenon; **-prisma,** *n.* polarizer; **-strom,** *m.* polarization current; **-vorrichtung,** *f.* polarizing attachment; **-winkel,** *m.* angle of polarization.

Polarisator, *m.* polarizer.

polarisierbar, polarizable.

polarisieren, to polarize.

Polarität, *f.* polarity.

Pol-bahn, *f.* path, orbit or progression of a pole; **-bildung,** *f.* pole formation, polarization; **-draht,** *m.* wire pole; **-eck,** *n.* **-ecke,** *f.* summit; **-höhe,** *f.* latitude.

Polei, *m.* pennyroyal.

Polemik, *f.* controversy, polemics.

polen, to pole.

Polende, *n.* electrode.

Polfaden, *m.* polar thread.

Police, *f.* (insurance) policy.

polierbar, capable of being polished.

polieren, to polish, burnish.

polier-fähig, capable of being polished; **-flüssigkeit,** *f.* liquid polish; **-kalk,** *m.* polishing chalk; **-masse,** *f.* polishing paste; **-mittel,** *n.* polishing substance; **-papier,** *n.* sandpaper, polishing paper; **-pulver,** *n.* polishing powder; **-rot,** *n.* colcothar, crocus, rouge; **-wachs,** *n.* polishing wax.

Politur, *f.* polish, gloss, luster, varnish; **-fähig,** polishable; **-lack,** *m.* polishing (shellac) varnish.

Polizei, *f.* police, police station.

Pol-kappe, *f.* polar cap; **-kern,** *m.* polnucleus; **-klemme,** *f.* binding post, connection clamp; **-körner,** *n.pl.* polar granules; **-körper,** *m.* polar (body) cell.

Pollen, *m.* pollen; **-analyse,** *f.* pollen analysis; **-blume,** *f.* flower producing pollen but not nectar; **-fach,** *n.* pollen sac; **-korn,** *n.* pollen grain; **-körper,** *m.* pollen; **-sack,** *m.* pollen sack; **-schlauch,** *m.* pollen tube; **-schlauchkern,** *n.* (vegetative) nucleus of pollen grain; **-übertragung,** *f.* transfer of pollen, pollination.

Pollinationstropfen, *m.* liquid excreted by micropyle.

Pollinium, *n.* pollen mass, pollinium.

pol-los, poleless, without poles; **-plasma,** *n.* pole plasma; **-platte,** *f.* pole field; **-reagenzpapier,** *n.* pole paper.

Polster, *n.* cushion, bolster, pad(ding), hummock, pulvinus, compress; **-artig,** pulvinate; **-bildner,** *m.* bunch grass, cushion-forming plants; **-gewächse,** *n.pl.* cushion plant; **-laubmoos,** *n.* cushion-forming liverwort.

polstern, to pad.

Polsterpflanze, *f.* matplant, cushion plant.

Pol-strahlung, *f.* polar radiation; **-such-papier,** *n.* pole(-finding) paper; **-wärts,** toward the pole; **-wechsel,** *m.* change (reversal) of poles.

poly-chromatisch, polychromatic, polychrome; **-chromsäure,** *f.* polychromic acid; **-cyclisch,** polycyclic; **-eder,** *n.* polyhedron; **-edrisch,** polyhedral; **-gon,** polygonal; **-hyperjodat,** *n.* polyperiodate; **-kieselsäure,** *f.* polysilicic acid.

polymer, polymeric, **-einheitlich,** of similar degree of polymerization.

Poly-merie, *f.* polymerism; **-merisat,** *n.* polymeride; **-merisieren,** to polymerize; **-molybdänsäure,** *f.* polymolybdie acid;

-morph, polymorphous, polymorphic; **-morphie,** *f.* polymorphism, polymorphy.

Polypengehäuse, *n.* polyparium.

Polypnoe, *f.* polypnoea, accelerated respiration.

poly-valent, polyvalent; **-zyklisch,** polycyclic.

Polzelle, *f.* polar body, polar cell.

Pomeranze, *f.* (bitter) orange.

pomeranzen-artig, orangelike; **-bitter,** *n.* hesperidin; **-blütenöl,** *n.* orange-flower oil, neroli; **-gelb,** orange-yellow; **-liqueur,** *m.* curaçao; **-schalenöl,** *n.* orange(-peel) oil.

Pompelmuse, *f.* shaddock, grapefruit.

ponderabel, ponderable, weighable.

Popanz, *m.* bugbear, bogy, scarecrow.

populär, popularly.

Pore, *f.* pore, pit, foramen.

Poren-anteil, *m.* proportion of voids; **-gehalt,** *m.* void or poor content; **-grösse,** *f.* size of pore(s); **-kanal,** *m.* pit channel, pore canal; **-kapsel,** *f.* capsule dehiscing through pores; **-kork,** *m.* strip of periderm in a lenticel; **-platten,** *f.pl.* sensillae placodae; **-volumen,** *n.* porosity; **-weg,** *m.* pore passage, passage through a filter; **-weite,** *f.* diameter of the pore.

Porenzelle, *f.* guard cell; ∼ **der Spalt öffnung,** *f.* guard cell of stomate.

porig, porous.

porös, porous, permeable, penetrable.

Porosität *f.* porosity.

Porphyr, *m.* porphyry; **-ähnlich, -artig,** porphyritic; **-felsen,** *m.,* **-gestein,** *n.* porphyritic rock.

Porsch, Porst, *m.* marsh tea, wild rosemary (*Ledum palus..* .).

Porterwürze, *f.* porter wort (brewing).

Portier, *m.* porter, doorkeeper.

portionsweise, in portions.

Portlandkalk, *m.* Portland limestone.

Porto, *n.* postage; **-frei,** post-free, postpaid.

Portugal-öl, *n.* Portugal oil, orange-peel oil; **-wasser,** *n.* laurel water.

Porzellan, *n.* porcelain, china; **-becher,** *m.* porcelain beaker; **-brennofen,** *m.* porcelain kiln; **-erde,** *f.* porcelain clay, kaolin; **-fabrikation,** *f.* porcelain manufacture; **-filter,** *n.* porcelain filter; **-griff,** *m.* porcelain handle; **-knopf,** *m.* knob of porcelain; **-malerei,** *f.* china painting; **-masse,** *f.* porcelain body.

Porzellan-mörser, *m.* porcelain mortar; **-mörtel,** *m.* pozzuolana mortar; **-schale,** *f.* porcelain dish; **-schiffchen,** *n.* porcelain boat; **-spat,** *m.* scapolite; **-spatel,** *m.* porcelain spatula; **-tiegel,** *m.* porcelain crucible; **-ton,** *m.* porcelain clay, kaolin; **-tonumschlag,** *m.* cataplasm of kaolin; **-trichter,** *m.* porcelain funnel.

Pose, *f.* quill, pose.

positiv, positive; **positive Spannung,** *f.* turgor, positive tension.

Post, *f.* post, mail, post office, news; ~ **wendend,** by return mail.

Postament, *n.* base, pedestal.

Postamt, *n.* post office.

Posten, *m.* post, situation, place, item, batch, entry, amount, sum, lot, parcel, sentry.

post-frei, post-free, postpaid; **-karte,** *f.* postcard, post map; **-lagernd,** general delivery; **-stempel,** *m.* postmark; **-verein,** *m.* postal union; **-wertzeichen.** *n.* stamp; **-zeichen,** *n.* postmark.

Potential-abfall, *m.* fall of potential; **-exponent,** *m.* index; **-gefälle,** *n.* electrical gradient; **-sprung,** *m.* difference of potential; **-unterschied,** *m.* potential difference; **-schwelle,** *f.* potential barrier.

potentiell, potential.

potentiieren, to render potent.

Potenz, *f.* power.

potenzieren, to raise to a higher power.

Potenzreihe, *f.* exponential series.

Pottasche, *f.* potash, potassium carbonate; **-fluss,** *m.* crude potash (from ashes); **-lösung,** *f.* potash solution; **-siederei,** *f.* potash factory.

pottecht, fast to potting.

Pottfisch, *m.* sperm whale.

Pottlot, *n.* graphite, black lead.

poussieren, to court, promote, push.

Pozzolanerde, *f.* pozzolana.

Pracht, *f.* splendor, magnificence, luxury, pomp, display; **-ausgabe,** *f.* edition de luxe.

prächtig, splendid, magnificent, gorgeous, sumptuous, charming.

Pracht-käfer, *m.pl.* metallic beetle (Buprestidae); **-kerze,** *f.* Guara; **-spiere,** *f.* Exochorda; **-voll,** beautiful, glorious, splendid, magnificent.

prädisponieren, to predipose.

Präexistenz, *f.* preexistence.

Präge-anstalt, *f.* mint; **-form,** *f.* matrix.

prägen, to stamp, coin, imprint.

prägnant, significant, exact, precise, pregnant.

Prägung, *f.* coining, stamping, coinage.

prähistorisch, prehistorical.

prahlen, to boast, brag, be loud (colors).

präjudizieren, to prejudge.

Praktikant, *m.* laboratory (worker) student, practitioner, assistant.

Praktiker, *m.* practician, experienced person.

Praktikum, *n.* practice, laboratory (practical) course (not theoretical), laboratory manual.

praktisch, practical, experimental, useful, serviceable, by practice, practiced.

praktizieren, to practice.

Prälabrum, *n.* clypeus (a shield).

Prall, *m.* shock, collision, rebound, reflection, backstroke; **-blech,** *n.* baffle.

prall, tight, stretched, stout, tense, plump, well-rounded.

prallen, to bounce, rebound, dash, be reflected.

Prallheit, *f.* tightness, tension, stoutness.

Prall-kraft, *f.* resiliency, elasticity; **-winkel,** *m.* angle of reflection.

Prämie, *f.* premium, prize, bonus.

prangen, to make a show, look fine, be resplendent, glitter, shine.

Pranke, *f.* clutch, claw, paw.

präoral, preoral.

Präparat, *n.* preparation.

Präparaten-fischer, *m.* section lifter; **-glas,** *n.* specimen tube; **-röhrchen,** *n.* preparation tube; **-schachtel,** *f.* microscope-slide box; **-tafel,** *f.* preparation slab, turntable.

präparieren, to prepare, dissect; **präpariertes Papier,** sensitized paper.

Präparier-lupe, *f.* dissecting magnifier, lens; **-nadel,** *f.* dissecting needle; **-salz,** *n.* preparing salt, sodium stannate; **-tisch,** *m.* dissecting table.

Präsentationszeit, *f.* presentation time.

präsentieren, to present.

Praseodym, *n.* praseodymium.

Präservativ, *n.* preservative.

Präserven, *n.pl.* preserves.

präservieren, to preserve.

Präservierung, *f.* preservation, preserving.

Präservierungsmittel, *n.* preservative.

prasseln, to crackle, rattle, rustle.

präsumptiv, presumptive.

Prätergit, n. protergum, pronotum.

Pravazspritze, f. Pravaz (hypodermic) syringe.

präventiv, preventive; -impfung, f. preventive inoculation; -spross, m. adventitious, shoot, sprout.

Praxis, f. practice, exercise, usage.

Präzession, f. precession.

Präzipitat, n. precipitate.

Präzipitation, f. precipitation.

Präzipitationswärme, f. heat of precipitation.

Präzipitierbottich, m. precipitating vat.

präzipitieren, to precipitate.

Präzipitiermittel, n. precipitant.

Präzipitin, n. precipitin; -methode, f. precipitin (precipitative) method; -reaktion, f. precipitin reaction; -schwund, m. disappearance of precipitin.

präzis, precise.

präzise, precisely, exactly.

präzisieren, to render (make) precise, define.

Präzision, f. precision.

Präzisionswaage, f. precision balance.

predigen, to preach.

Preis, m. -e, price, fee, fare, value, rate, prize, glory, praise.

Preiselbeere, f. red whortleberry, mountain cranberry.

preisen, to praise, glorify, commend, exalt.

preisgeben, to give over, abandon, give up, hand over, expose.

Preissatz, m. valuation, estimate.

Preisselbeere, f. cranberry, red whortleberry.

preiswert, praiseworthy, worth the price.

Prellbock, m. bumping post.

prellen, to toss, make rebound, cheat, dupe, contuse.

Prellstein, m. curbstone.

Pressbeutel, m. pressing (filter) bag.

Presse, f. press, journalism, gloss, luster.

pressen, to press, compress, squeeze, strain, force, pinch, cram, depress, deject, oppress.

Press-filter, n.-, pressure (press) filter; -form, f. mold; -gas, n. compressed gas; -glanz, m. gloss from pressing; -hefe, f. pressed yeast, compressed yeast; -kuchen, n. briquet, -ling, m. something pressed,

pressed article, expressed beet pulp; -luft, f. compressed air; -massen, f.pl. molding preparation; -mischung, f. molding mixture.

Press-naht, f. burr; -rückstand, m. expressed residue; -saft, m. press juice; -span, m. pressboard; -stoff, m. plastic material, molded plastic compound; -torf, m. pressed peat; -tuch, n. filter cloth.

Pressung, f. pressure, pressing, compression.

Press-verfahren, n.-, pressing process; -walze, f. press roll.

Preussen, n. Prussia.

prickeln, to prickle, prick, sting.

prickelnd, sharp, pungent, prickling.

Priemtabak, m. chewing tobacco.

pries (preisen), praised, was praising.

Prima, f. highest class (Gymnasium).

Priman-blatt, n. the primary leaf bud of an embryo (plumule); -blüte, f. the terminal flower of a cymose inflorescence.

primär, primary, idiopathic; primärer Embryosackkern, m. initial nucleus of the embryosac.

Primär-element, n.-e, primary cell; -kreis, m. primary circuit; -strahlung, f. primary radiation.

Prima-soda, f. refined soda; -ware, f. superior (article) goods.

Primel, f. primrose.

primitiv, primitive; -furche, f. primitive furrow; -knoten, m. primitive node; -rinne, f. primitive groove; -streifen, m. primitive streak.

Primordial-blatt, n. leaf primordium; -gefäss, n. protoxylem vessel; -schlauch, m. primordial utricle (vacuole).

Primzahl, f. prime number.

Prinzip, n.-e, -ien, principle.

prinzipiell, in principle, fundamental, of kind.

Prinzipium, n. principle.

Priorität, f. priority.

Prioritätsbeleg, n. certified copy of application.

Prise, f. prize, pinch (snuff).

Prisma, n. prism; -ähnlich, -artig, prismlike, prismoidal, prismatic.

prismatisch, prismat.

Prismen-fläche, f. prismatic face; -förmig, prism-shaped, prismatic; -glas, n. prism glass; -kante, f. prismatic edge; -spektrum, n. prismatic spectrum.

Pritsche, *f.* bat, washing floor, bench, plank.

Privatdozent, *m.* a licensed university lecturer (receiving only student fees).

pro, pro, per.

probat, approved, tried.

Probe, *f.* test, assay, experiment, trial, sample, pattern, specimen, proof, probation, rehearsal, (trade-)mark; **-abdruck,** *m.* proof (print); **-bogen,** *m.* proof sheet; **-brühe,** *f.* test bath, dye test; **-dienstleistung,** *f.* sample service, probation stage; **-druck,** *m.* proof (sheet); **-entnahme,** *f.* sample taking; **-essig,** *m.* proof vinegar; **-färbung,** *f.* test dyeing; **-fläche,** *f.* sample plot, sample area.

Probe-flasche, *f.* sample (specimen) bottle; **-flüssigkeit,** *f.* test liquid; **-glas,** *n.* specimen (test) tube; **-gold,** *n.* standard gold; **-gut,** *n.* sample; **-haltig,** proof, standard; **-holzfällung,** *f.* felling of sample trees; **-korn,** *n.* assay button; **-machen,** *n.* testing, assaying; **-mass,** *n.* standard measure.

probe-mässig, according to sample; **-muster,** *n.* sample for testing; **-nadel,** *f.* touch needle; **-nahme,** *f.* sampling, sample; **-papier,** *n.* test paper.

Prober, *m.* tester, sampler, assayer.

Probe-rohr, *n.-e,* **-röhrchen,** *n.* test tube; **-schachtel,** *f.* sample box; **-scherbe,** *f.* cupel; **-scherben,** *m.* cupel; **-spiritus,** *m.* (standard) proof spirit; **-stamm,** *m.* sample tree, test tree; **-stecher,** *m.* sampler, proof stick; **-stein,** *m.* touchstone, sample stone; **-stoff,** *m.-e,* sample material; **-stück,** *n.* specimen, sample.

Probe-tiegel, *m.* assay crucible, cupel; **-waage,** *f.* assay balance; **-weise,** by way of (testing) trial; **-ziehen,** *n.* sampling; **-zieher,** *m.* sampler; **-zylinder,** *m.* trial jar, test tube.

probieren, to test, assay, try, attempt, prove.

Probierer, *m.* tester, sampler, assayer, analyst.

Probier-gefäss, *n.-e,* vessel; **-geräte,** *n.pl.,* **-gerätschaften,** *f.pl.* assaying apparatus; **-gewicht,** *n.* assay weight; **-glas,** *n.* test tube; **-glätte,** *f.* test litharge; **-hahn,** *m.* try cock, gauge cock; **-kluft,** *f.* assayer's tongs; **-korn,** *n.* assay button, assay grain.

Probier-methode, *f* method of experiment; **-nadel,** *f.* touch needle; **-ofen,** *m.* assay furnace; **-papier,** *n.* test paper; **-röhre,** *f.* test tube; **-röhrengestell,** *n.* test-tube rack;

-tute, *f.* assay crucible; **-waage,** *f.* assay balance; **-zange,** *f.* assayer's tongs.

Problematik, *f.* problems.

procentig, percentage.

Produkt, *n.* product, produce.

Produktionsfähigkeit, *f.* productivity, capacity.

Produzent, *m.* producer, grower.

produzieren, to produce.

Prof. habil., resident professor.

professorisch, professorial.

Professur, *f.* professorship.

Profil, *n.-e,* profile, section, cross section.

profilieren, to set up or draw profiles.

profiliert, side-faced; **profilierter Stab,** *m.* profiled bar.

projektieren, to project, plan, design, propose.

Projektionsmattscheibe, *f.* ground-glass screen.

projizieren, to project.

promillig, per mile, per thousand.

promovieren, to graduate, take a degree.

prophylaktisch, prophylactic.

Prophylaxe, *f.* prophylaxis.

Propiolsäure, *f.* propiolic acid.

propionsauer, *f.* propionate of.

Propionsäure, *f.* propionic acid; **-bakterien,** *n.pl.* propionic acid bacteria.

proportional, proportional, proportionate.

Proportionalität, *f.* proportionality.

Proportionalschlag, *m.* reduced cutting.

Propyl-alkohol, *m.* propyl alcohol; **-wasserstoff,** *m.* propyl hydride, propane.

Prosternalkiel, *m.* prosternal keel.

Protein, *n.-e,* protein; **-haltig,** containing protein; **-körper,** *m.* protein substance, protein; **-stoff,** *m.* protein substance; **-urie,** *f.* albuminuria; **-verbindung,** *f.* protein compound.

Protenparenchym, *n.* protenchyma (ground parenchyma).

Proteolyse, *f.* proteolysis.

proteolytisch, proteolytic.

Proteus-arten, *pl.* species of Proteus; **-gruppe,** *f.* Proteus group of bacilli.

Prothoracalflügel, *m.* wing of the prothorax.

Protokatechusäure, *f.* protocatechuic acid.

Protokokkus, *m.* Protococcus.

Protokoll, *n.* minutes, record, report, protocol, autopsy.

Protonen-beschleunigung, *f.* acceleration of protons; **-geschoss,** *n.* proton projectile; **-wanderung,** *f.* movement of the proton.

Protoplasma, *n.* protoplasm; **-bewegung,** *f.* protoplasmic movement; **-kammer,** *f.* plasma chamber; **-körper,** *m.* protoplasmic body; **-strahl,** *m.* protoplasm ray.

Protoxyd, *n.* protoxide.

protozoaartig, resembling protozoa.

Protozoen, *n.pl.* Protozoa; **-infektion,** *f.* protozoal infection; **-untersuchung,** *f.* examination for (or of) protozoa.

protozoisch, protozoal.

Protozoologie, *f.* protozoology.

Provenienz, *f.* origin, source, derivation, provenance.

Proventiv-knospe, *f.* prolepsis, proventitious bud; **-spross,** *m.* shoot developing from a proventitious bud (prolepsis).

Proviant, *m.* provisions, victuals, forage.

Provision, *f.* provision, commission.

Provisor, *m.* pharmacist's (chemist's) assistant.

provisorisch, provisional.

proximal, proximal.

Prozedur, *f.* procedure.

Prozent, *n.* per cent; **-gehalt,** *m.* percentage content.

prozentig, percent(age).

prozentisch, percent(age).

Prozent-satz, *m.* percentage rate; **-teilung,** *f.* percentage scale.

prozentual, per cent; **prozentuale Fehlergrösse,** *f.* percentage of error.

Prozess, *m.-e,* process, lawsuit.

prozessieren, to litigate.

Prozessionsspinner, *m.pl.* Cnethocampidae.

Prüfapparat, *m.-e,* testing apparatus.

prüfbar, capable of being tested or assayed.

prüfen, to test, try, prove, assay, taste, examine, check, inspect.

Prüfer, *m.-,* tester, assayer, examiner.

Prüf-ergebnis, *n.* test result; **-gerät,** *n.-e,* testing apparatus; **-glas,** *n.* test (glass) tube; **-kelch,** *m.* test (reaction) glass; **-ling,** *m.* test sample, specimen, applicant for an examination; **-mittel,** *n.* testing agent; **-nadel,** *f.* plasticity needle; **-scheibe,** *f.* test disk; **-stein,** *m.* touchstone, test.

Prüfung, *f.* examination, assay, trial, testing, proof.

Prüfungs-bescheid, *m.* test instruction, report on an examination; **-mittel,** *n.* testing agent; **-schein,** *m.* certificate.

Prüfverfahren, *n.* testing method.

Prügel, *m.* cudgel, stick, club, beating, blow.

Prunellensalz, *n.* sal prunellae, fused potassium nitrate.

Prunk, *m.* pomp, state, splendor, show.

Psalter, *m.* rumen.

Pseudo-harnsäure, *f.* pseudouric acid; **-harnstoff,** *m.* pseudourea; **-katalysator,** *m.* pseudocatalyst; **-katalytisch,** pseudocatalytic; **-lösung,** *f.* pseudo solution; **-merie,** *f.* pseudomerism, tautomerism; **-morph,** pseudomorphous; **-ödem,** *n.* pseudoedema; **-podienbildung,** *f.* formation of pseudopodia; **-saftmal,** *n.* false nectar guide.

Psorospermienschläuche, *m.pl.* psorosperm corpuscles.

Psychologie, *f.* psychology.

Ptomain, *n.* ptomain.

publizieren, to publish.

Puddel-arbeiter, *m.-,* puddler; **-eisen,** *n.* puddled iron.

puddeln, to puddle.

Puddel-prozess, *m.-e,* puddling process; **-roheisen,** *n.* forge pig; **-schlacke,** *f.* puddling slag; **-sohle,** *f.* puddling-furnace bed; **-spiegel,** *m.* specular forge pig iron; **-spitze,** *f.* puddler's paddle; **-stab,** *m.* puddle bar; **-verfahren,** *n.* puddling process; **-walze,** *f.* puddle roll; **-werk,** *n.* puddling works.

Pudel, *m.* poodle, drudge, blunder, miss.

Puder, *m.* powder; **-dune,** *f.* powder down.

puderig, powdery.

pudern, to powder.

Puderzucker, *m.* powdered sugar.

Puerperalfieber, *n.* puerperal fever.

Puff, *m.-e,* blow, bang, crash, thump, puff, knock.

puffen, to puff, swell, pop.

Puffer, *m.-,* buffer; **-lösung,** *f.* buffer solution; **-wert,** *m.* buffer value; **-wirkung,** *f.* buffer action.

Pufferung, *f.* cushioning, buffering.

Pulpe, *f.* pulp.

Puls, *m.* pulse; **-ader,** *f.* artery; **-aderblut,** *n.* arterial blood; **-glas,** *n.* cryophorus.

pulse glass, water hammer; **-hammer,** *m.* cryophorus, pulse glass, water hammer.

pulsieren, to pulsate.

Puls-schlag, *m.* pulse beat, pulsation; **-zahl,** *f.* pulse rate.

Pult, *n.*-e, desk; **-feuerung,** *f.* firing on stepped grate bars, inclined stoker; **-ofen,** *m.* back-flame hearth.

Pulver, *n.* powder; **-artig,** powdery; **-band,** *n.* powder strand; **-blättchen,** *n.* powder grain; **-fabrik,** *f.* powder factory; **-fass,** *n.* powder keg; **-flasche,** *f.* powder bottle; **-förmig,** in the form of powder, powdery; **-glas,** *n.* widemouthed bottle.

pulverig, powdery.

pulverisierbar, pulverable.

pulverisieren, to powder, pulverize, grind.

Pulverisierung, *f.* pulverization.

Pulver-korn, *n.* grain of powder; **-ladung,** *f.* powder charge; **-mörser,** *m.* powder mortar.

pulvern, to pulverize.

Pulver-probe, *f.* powder test; **-probiermörser,** *m.* small powder mortar; **-satz,** *m.* powder composition; **-schlag,** *m.* cracker, petard; **-zucker,** *m.* powdered sugar.

Pumpe, *f.* pump.

pumpen, to pump, borrow, lend.

punkt, punctually, on the stroke.

Punkt, *m.*-e, point, dot, spot, fleck, period; **Punkte und Stricke,** dots and dashes.

Punkt-augen, *n.pl.* ocelli; **-förmig,** in the form of points or dots, punctiform.

punktieren, to point, dot, punctuate, puncture.

punktiert, punctuate, marked with dots, dotted.

Punktionsflüssigkeit, *f.* puncture exudate.

pünktlich, punctual, exact, promptly.

punktmechanisch, pertaining to the mechanics of particles.

Punkt-lichtlampe, *f.* tungsten-point source of light; **-reihe,** *f.* row of dots, series of points; **-schweissung,** *f.* spot welding; **-streifen,** *m.* dotted row, strial puncture; **-symmetrisch,** point symmetrical; **-weise,** point by point.

Punktum, *n.* period.

Punsch, *m.* punch (the drink).

Punzen, *m.* punch (the tool).

Pupille, *f.* pupil (of the eye).

Pupillen-abstand, *m.* distance between the pupils; **-entfernung,** *f.* interpupillary distance; **-erweiterung,** *f.* dilation of the pupil, mydriasis; **-weite,** *f.* diameter of the pupil.

Puppe, *f.* pupa, chrysalis, cocoon, doll, puppet.

Puppen-dauer, *f.* period of pupation; **-hülle,** *f.* case of pupa, cocoon; **-kokon,** *m.* cocoon; **-räuber,** *m.* ground beetle, pupivora (*Calosoma sycophanta*); **-wiege,** *f.* puparium, cocoon, pupal chamber.

Purganz, *f.* purgative.

purgieren, to boil off, purge.

Purgier-harz, *n.* scammony; **-kassia,** *f.* purging cassia; **-kassie,** *f.* purging cassia; **-korn,** *n.* purging grain, castor bean; (kleines) **-korn,** croton seed; **-kraut,** *n.* hedge hyssop; **-lein,** *n.* purging flax; **-mittel,** *n.* purgative; **-nuss,** *f.* purging nut; **-paradiesäpfel,** *m.pl.* colocynth pulp.

purifizieren, to purify.

Purin-basen, *f.pl.* purine basis; **-gruppe,** *f.* purine group.

Purpur, *m.* purple; **-färbung,** *f.* purple coloring; **-holz,** *n.* violet wood; **-muschel,** *f.* purple shell.

purpurn, to purple.

purpur-rot, purple-red, crimson; **-rötlich,** purpurascens; **-säure,** *f.* purpuric acid.

purzeln, to tumble.

Pustel, *f.* pustule, pimple; **-artig,** pustulate; **-schorf,** *m.* blister scab.

pusten, blow, pant.

Pust-probe, *f.* blow (bubble) test; **-rohr,** *n.* blowgun; **-span,** *m.* skimmer.

Puter, *m.* turkey.

Putz, *m.* plaster, plastering, dress, toilet, ornament; **-baumwolle,** *f.* cotton waste; **-bein,** *n.* leg used for cleaning.

putzen, to clean, cleanse, scour, polish, adorn, dress, plaster (a wall), lop, decorate.

Putzerei, *f.* dressing.

Putz-füsse, *m.pl.* pedamina (used for cleaning); **-kalk,** *m.* plastering lime, polishing chalk; **-lage,** *f.* coat of plaster; **-leder,** *n.* chamois (leather); **-macherei,** *f.* millinery; **-mittel,** *n.* cleaning (polishing) material; **-organe,** *n.pl.* organs for cleaning.

Putz-präparat, *n.*-e, polishing preparation; **-pulver,** *n.* cleaning powder; **-schicht,** *f.* coat of plaster; **-stein,** *m.* cleaning stone, bath brick; **-tisch,** *m.* dressing (cleaning) table; **-tuch,** *n.* cloth for cleaning; **-wasser,** *n.* dilute acid for scouring; **-wolle,** *f.* waste.

Puzzolane, *f.* pozzuolana.

Pyämie, *f.* pyemia.

pyämisch, pyemic.

Pylorusverschluss, *m.* pyloric block.

pyogen, pyogenic.

Pyoktanin, *n.* methyl violet.

Pyorrhöe, *f.* pyorrhea, suppurative catarrh.

Pyramiden-bahn, *f.* pyramidal tract; -bein, *n.* cuneiform bone of wrist; -förmig, pyramidal; -fortsatz, *m.* pyramidal process; -würfel, *m.* tetrahexahedron.

Pyrit, *m.* pyrite; -abbrände, *m.pl.* pyrites cinders; -haltig, pyritiferous.

pyritisch, pyritic.

Pyritofen, *m.* pyrites (oven) burner.

Pyro-antimonsäure, *f.* pyroantimonic acid; -elektrizität, *f.* pyroelectricity; -gallus-säure, *f.* pyrogallic acid (pyrogallol).

pyrogen, pyrogenic.

Pyro-katechin, *n.* pyrocatechin; -metrisch pyrometric.

Pyrophor, *n.* pyrophorus.

pyro-phor, -phorisch, pyrophoric.

pyro-phosphorsauer, pyrophosphoric; phos-phorsäure, *f.* pyrophosphoric acid; -säure, *f.* pyro acid; -schleimsäure, *f.* pyromucic acid; -schwefelsäure, *f.* pyrosulphuric acid; -schweflig, pyrosulphurous; -technik, *f.* pyrotechnics; -technische Waren, fire-works; -weinsäure, *f.* pyrotartaric acid.

Pyrrol, *n.* pyrrole.

Q

Quabbe, (Quappe) *f.* tadpole, wen, growth.

quabbeln, to shake, quiver, quake, be flabby.

Quacksalber, *m.* quack, charlatan.

Quaddel, *n.* swelling.

Quader, *m.* ashlar, freestone.

Quadrant, *m.* quadrant.

Quadrat, *n.*-e, square; -bein, *n.* quadrate; -centimeter, *n.&m.* square centimeter; -fuss, *m.* square foot.

quadratisch, square, quadratic, tetragonal.

Quadrat-jochbein, *n.* quadratojugal bone; -meter, *m.* square meter; -millimeter, *m.* square millimeter; -pflanzung, *f.* square planting; -pyramide, *f.* square pyramid.

Quadratur, *f.* squaring, quadrature.

Quadrat-verhältnis, *n.* square ratio; -wurzel, *f.* square root; -zahl, *f.* square number, square; -zentimeter, *m.&n.* square centi-meter.

quadrieren, to square (a number).

quälen, to torment, worry, bore, molest, afflict, agonize, distress.

Quälen, *n.* disaggregating, milling to break down the structure.

Qualität, *f.* quality, kind, sort, brand.

qualitativ, qualitative.

Qualle, *f.* jellyfish, medusa.

Quallenpolypus, *m.* jellyfish polyp.

Qualm, *m.* dense smoke, vapor, steam.

qualmen, to emit (give forth) dense smoke or vapor.

qualvoll, very painful, agonizing, excruciat-ing.

Quandel, *m.* flue in center of kiln.

quanten-haft, pertaining to quanta; -hypo-these, *f.* quantum hypothesis; -mässig, in relation to quanta; -theorie, *f.* quantum theory; -zahl, *f.* quantum number.

Quantität, *f.* quantity.

quantitativ, quantitative.

Quantitätsbestimmung, *f.* quantitative de-termination.

Quantum, *n.* quantum, quantity, amount, portion, share, quota.

Quappe, *f.* eelpout, burbot (Lota).

Quark, *m.* curd, curds, trash; -artig, (quarkig), curdlike, curdy.

Quart, *n.* quarto, quart.

Quartal, *n.* quarter of a year.

Quartanblüte, *f.* terminal flower of the fourth axis of a cymose inflorescence.

quartär, quaternary.

Quartband, *m.* quarto volume.

Quarte, *f.* quarter, fourth.

Quartier, *n.*-e, quarter, quarters, lodging.

quartieren, to quarter, lodge, divide into four parts.

Quartierung, *f.* quartation.

Quartscheidung, *f.* separation by quartation.

Quartsextaccord, *m.* chord of the sixth and fourth.

Quarz, *m.* quartz; -ähnlich, -artig, quart-zose; -drüse, *f.* crystallized quartz; -fen-ster, *n.* quartz window; -glas, *n.* quartz glass; -keilsaccharimeter, *m. &n.* Q-wedge saccharimeter; -linse, *f.* quartz lens; -mehl, *n.* quartz flour; -pulver, *n.* quartz powder.

Quarz-rohr, *n.* quartz tube; -schiefer, *m.* quartz shale, schist; -ziegel, *m.* quartz brick.

quasielastisch, quasielastic.

Quassiaholz, *n.* quassia (wood).

Quast, *m.* Quaste, *f.* tassel, tuft, brush, knot, snag.

Quastenflosser, *m.pl.* Crossopterygii.

quaternär, quaternary; -formation, *f.* diluvial formation.

Quebrachit, *n.* quebrachitol, quebrachite.

Quebrachorinde, *f.* quebracho bark.

Quecke, *f.* couch grass (*Agropyrum repens*).

Quecksilber, *n.* mercury, quicksilver; -ähnlich, mercurylike, mercurial; -artig, mercurial; -bad, *n.* quicksilver bath; -barometer, *n.* mercury barometer; -beizmittel, *n.* mercurial disinfectant; -bogen, *m.* mercury arc; -branderz, *n.* idrialite; -chlorid, *n.* mercuric chloride; -chlorür, *n.* mercurous chloride.

Quecksilber-cyanid, *n.* mercuric cyanide; -cyanur, *n.* mercurous cyanide; -dampf, *m.* mercury vapor; -dampflampe, *f.* mercury-vapor lamp; -druck, *m.* mercury pressure; -faden, *m.* mercury thread; -fahlerz, *n.* tetrahedrite containing mercury; -halogen, *n.* mercury halide; -haltig, containing mercury, mercurial; -hornerz, *n.* horn quicksilver.

Quecksilber-jodid, *n.* mercuric iodide; -jodür, *n.* mercurous iodide; -lebererz, *n.* hepatic cinnabar; -legierung, *f.* mercury alloy, amalgam; -luftpumpe, *f.* mercury pump, air pump; -mittel, *n.* mercurial; -mohr, *m.* mercuric sulphide.

quecksilbern, mercury, mercurial.

Quecksilber-näpfchen, *n.* little bowl of mercury; -oxyd, *n.* mercuric oxide; -oxydsalz, *n.* mercuric salt; -oxydul, *n.* mercurous oxide; -oxydulsalz, *n.* mercurous salt; -pflaster, *n.* mercurial plaster; -pille, *f.* blue pill; -präparat, *n.* mercurial preparation; -rhodanid, *n.* mercuric thiocyanate; -salbe, *f.* mercurial ointment.

Quecksilber-salpeter, *n.* nitrate of mercury; -salz, *n.* mercury salt; -säule, *f.* column of mercury; -spat, *m.* horn quicksilver; -spiegel, *m.* meniscus of mercury; -stand, *m.* mercury level; -sublimat, *n.* corrosive sublimate, mercuric chloride; -sulfid, *n.* mercuric sulphide, cinnabar; -sulfur, *n.* mercurous sulphide; -verbindung, *f.* mercury compound.

Quecksilber-verfahren, *n.* mercury process; -vergiftung, *f.* mercury poisoning; -vitriol,

m. mercuric sulphate; -wanne, *f.* mercury trough; -zyanid, *n.* mercuric cyanide.

Quell, *m.* source, spring, fountain, well; -bach, *m.* river source.

quellbar, capable of swelling.

Quellbarkeit, *f.* capability of swelling.

Quellbottich, *m.* steeping vat.

Quelle, *f.* source, origin, spring, well; eine ∼ fassen, to confine a spring.

quellen, to swell, expand, soak, steep, imbibe moisture, spring, well, arise, flow, gush.

quell-fähig, capable of swelling; -flur, *f.* vegetation of springs; -gas, *n.* gas from springs; -gebiet, *n.* headwaters; -gras, *n.* Catabrosa; -niveau, *n.* spring horizon; -reif, sufficiently (steeped) soaked; -reife, *f.* sufficient steeping; -salz, *n.* spring (well) salt; -säure, *f.* crenic acid.

Quell-schicht, *f.* swelling layer; -sole, *f.* spring brine; -stock, *m.* steep tank; -teich, *m.* pond fed by a spring.

Quellung, *f.* swelling, tumefaction, soaking.

Quellungs-wärme, *f.* heat of (swelling) tumefaction; -zustand, *m.* condition of swelling.

Quell-vermögen, *n.* expansive capacity; -wasser, *n.* spring water, well water.

Quendel, *m.* wild thyme.

quer, cross, transverse, diagonal, slanting, oblique; -achse, *f.* transverse axis; -arm, *m.* crossarm, crossbar; -balken, *m.* crossbeam; -bänderung, *f.* bars, parallel cross markings; -bandmuskel, *m.* transverse abdominal muscle; -bewegung, *f.* transverse motion; -binde, *f.* transverse bandage, parallel cross markings; -blatt, *n.* dissepiment (of Anthozoa); -bügel, *m.* curved transverse band, crossbow.

Quer-cit, *n.* quercitol, quercite; -citronrinde, *f.* quercitron bark; -colon, *m.* transverse colon; -damm, *m.* cross dike; -darm, *m.* transverse colon; -dickdarm, *m.* transverse colon; -durchmesser, *m.* transverse diameter; -durchschnitt, *m.* cross section.

Quere, *f.* transverse direction, cross direction, breadth.

Quer-falte, *f.* transverse fold; -faser, *f.* transverse fiber; -faserschicht, *f.* transverse fibrous layer; -fell, *n.* diaphragm; -festigkeit, *f.* lateral strength; -fortsatz, *m.* transverse process; -fortsatzloch, *n.* foramen of transverse process; -furche, *f.* transverse groove, sulcus; -geissel, *f.*

transverse cilium; **-gestreift,** transversely striated.

quer-geteilt, transversely septate; **-grimm-darm,** *m.* transverse colon; **-haupt,** *n.* crosshead; **-haut,** *f.* diaphragm; **-kanal,** *m.* transverse canal; **-kraft,** *f.* transverse (shearing) force; **-krümmung,** *f.* transverse curvature; **-laufend,** transversal, transverse; **-läufig,** plagiodromous, running oblique; **-leiste,** *f.* transverse ridge.

Quer-parenchym, *n.* radial parenchyma; **-profil,** *n.* cross section; **-riss,** *m.* transverse (tear) crack, cross section; **-ruder,** *n.* aileron; **-runzlig,** transversely corrugated or rugose; **-schlag,** *m.* (mining) drifting; **-schleifen,** to grind (wood) across the grain; **-schnitt,** *m.* cross (transverse) section, crosscut.

Querschnitts-ebene, *f.* cross-sectional plane; **-einheit,** *f.* sectional unit; **-serie,** *f.* series of cross sections.

Quer-schwingung, *f.* transverse vibration; **-stabilität,** *f.* resistance to lateral wave action (ship), lateral stability; **-streifung,** *f.* cross striation; **-striemen,** *m.* striga; **-stück,** *n.* crosspiece; **-teilung,** *f.* transverse partition, transfission; **-trennung,** *f.* transverse separation or severance; **-verengt,** obliquely contracted; **-verlaufend,** running transversely; **-verzierung,** *f.* transverse markings.

Quer-wand, *f.* transverse wall, diaphragm, partition; **-zergliederung,** *f.* cross septation; **-zit,** *n.* quercitol, quercite; **-zitronrinde,** *f.* quercitron bark; **-zusammenziehung,** *f.* lateral contraction.

Quetsche, *f.* wild plum, squeezer, presser, crusher, wringer.

quetschen, to pinch, squeeze, bruise, crush, flatten, contuse.

Quetscher, *m.* pincher, squeezer.

Quetsch-hahn, *m.* pinch clip, pinchcock: **-mühle,** *f.* crushing mill.

Questschung, *f.* crushing, contusion.

Quetsch-werk, *n.* crushing mill, crusher; **-wunde,** *f.* contused wound.

Quick-arbeit, *f.* amalgamation; **-beutel,** *m.* amalgamating skin; **-brei,** *m.* amalgam.

quicken, to amalgamate.

Quick-erz, *n.* mercury ore; **-gold,** *n.* gold amalgam; **-wasser,** *n.* quickening liquid, mercurial solution.

quieken, to squeak, squeal.

Quillaja-rinde, *f.* quillai(a) bark.

quillt (quellen), gushes, flows.

Quinte, *f.* fifth (in music).

Quintsextaccord, *m.* chord of the fifth and sixth.

Quirl, *m.* twirling device, agitator, whirl, whorl.

quirlen, to twirl, turn, whirl.

quirl-förmig, verticillate; **-ständig,** whirled, verticillate.

quitt, even, quits, rid.

Quitte, *f.* quince.

Quitten-äther, *m.* quince essence; **-essenz,** *f.* quince essence; **-kern, -samen,** *m.* quince seed.

quittieren, to receipt, quit, leave, retire.

Quittung, *f.* receipt.

quoll (quellen), gushed, flowed.

Quotient, *m.* quotient.

R

Rabatt, *m.* discount, deduction, allowance, rebate.

Rabatte, *f.* ridge, bed, border.

Rabattensaat, *f.* sowing on ridges.

Rabe, *m.* raven, crow.

Raben-bein, *n.* coracoid bone; **-fortsatz,** *m.* coracoid (process) apophysis; **-krähe,** *f.* carrion crow; **-schnabelbein,** *n.* coracoid bone; **-schnabelfortsatz,** *m.* coracoid apophysis; **-schnabelknochen,** *m.* coracoid bone; **-schwarz,** jet black; **-stein,** *m.* gallows.

Rabies, *pl.* rabies.

racemisch, racemic.

racemisieren, to racemize.

Racem-körper, *m.* racemic substance; **-verbindung,** *f.* racemic compound.

Rache, *f.* revenge, vengeance.

Rachen, *m.* throat, cavity of the mouth, jaws, pharynx, fauces.

rächen, to take revenge, avenge.

Rachen-bein, *n.* inferior maxilla; **-blume,** *f.* ringent corolla; **-blüte,** *f.* labiate flower; **-blütig,** ringent, labiate; **-blütler,** *m.* labiate; **-enge,** *f.* isthmus of the fauces. **-förmig,** ringent, labiate(d).

Rachen-haut, *f.* (bucco)pharyngeal membrane; **-höhle,** *f.* pharynx, pharyngeal cavity; **-mündung,** *f.* isthmus of the fauces; **-raum,** *m.* pharyngeal space; **-schleimhaut,**

f. mucous membrane of the pharynx; **-schnürmuskel,** *m.* constructor of pharynx; **-spalte,** *f.* isthmus of the fauces.

Rad, *n.ᐨer,* wheel; **-achse,** *f.* axle of a wheel; **-arm,** *m.* spoke (of wheel); **-band,** *m.* tire; **-bewegung,** *f.* rotary motion, rotation; **-drehung,** *f.* rotation, torsion.

Rädelerz, *n.* wheel ore, bournonite.

Rädelsführer, *m.* ringleader.

rädern, to sift, screen, furnish with wheels.

Räder-organ, *n.* trochal disk, wheel organ; **-tiere,** *n.pl.* Rotifera, wheel animalcules; **-werk,** *n.* wheelwork, gearing, sifting apparatus.

rad-förmig, wheel-shaped, rotate; **-gelenk,** *n.* pivot joint.

Radial-kammer, *f.* radial chamber; **-schnitt,** *m.* radial section.

radiär, actinomorphic, radial, radiating.

Radien, *m.pl.* radii.

radieren, to etch, erase.

Radier-firnis, *m.* etching varnish; **-grund,** *m.* etching ground; **-gummi,** *n.* rubber eraser; **-kunst,** *f.* art of etching; **-messer,** *n.* eraser, penknife.

Radierung, *f.* etching, erasure.

Radieschen, *n.* radish.

radiieren, to radiate.

Radikal, *n.-e,* radical, root; **-achse,** *f.* radical axis; **-essig,** *m.* radical vinegar, glacial acetic acid.

Radikand, *m.* radicand.

Radio-aktivität, *f.* radioactivity; **-chemie,** *f.* radiochemistry; **-tellur,** *n.* radiotellurium; **-thor,** *n.* radiothorium.

Radium, *n.* radium; **-bromid,** *n.* radium bromide; **-jodid,** *n.* radium iodide; **-strahlen,** *m.pl.* radium rays.

Radius, *m.* radius.

radizieren, to extract the root of.

Rad-kranz, *m.ᐨe,* rim, tire (wheel); **-lenker,** *m.* wheel rod, guide; **-linie,** *f.* cycloid; **-reif, -reifen,** *m.* tire, rim; **-scheibe,** *f.* trochal disk; **-schuh,** *m.* brake; **-speiche,** *f.* spoke.

Radula-sack, *m.* radular sac; **-tasche,** *f.* radular sac.

Rad-welle, *f.* axle, wheel and axle, wheel shaft; **-zahn,** *m.* tooth, cog (of a wheel).

raffen, to snatch up, pick up, carry off.

Raffinade, *f.* **-zucker,** *m.* refined sugar.

Raffination, *f.* refining.

Raffinations-ertrag, -wert, *m.* (sugar) rendement, yield.

Raffinatsilber, *n.* refined silver.

Raffinerie, *f.* refinery, finesse.

Raffineur, *m.* refiner.

Raffinieranlage, *f.* refining plant.

raffinieren, to refine.

ragen, to project, tower.

Rahm, *m.* cream, crust, frame, sootᐨ **-ähnlich, -artig,** cream-like, creamy; **-eis,** *n.* ice cream.

rahmen, to skim, remove the cream, form a cream, frame.

Rahmen, *m.* frame, structure, compass, edge, border, bounds, scope, replum; **-binder,** *m.* rigid frame; **-hülse,** *f.* craspedium; **-schenkel,** *m.* batten; **-vortrieb,** *m.* timberwork.

Rahm-erz, *n.-e,* a foamy variety of wad; **-farbe,** *f.* cream color.

rahmig, sooty, creamy.

Rahmkäse, *m.* cream cheese.

Raife, *f.pl.* cerci.

Rain, *m.* ridge, border, bank, edge, headland.

Raine, *m.pl.* apteria.

Rain-farn, *m.* tansy (*Tanacetum vulgare*); **-weide,** *f.* privet (*Ligustrum vulgare*).

rajolen, to trench-plow.

Rakel, *f.* doctor (calico); **-appretiermaschine,** *f.* **-maschine,** *f.* **-stärkemaschine,** *f.* backfilling machine, backfilling starcher.

Rakete, *f.* rocket, firecracker.

Ralle, *f.* (water) rail.

Ramiefaser, *f.* ramie fiber.

ramifizieren, to ramify.

Ramifizierung, *f.* ramification.

Rammbär, *m.* rammer, pile driver.

Ramme, *f.* pile driver, rammer.

Rammelkammer, *f.* nuptial chamber.

rammen, to ram, beat down, drive (piles).

Rammfilterbrunnen, *m.* well points.

Rammler, *m.* buck, male hare, tomcat.

Rammvorrichtung, *f.* ramming apparatus.

Rampe, *f.* ramp, platform, footlights.

ramponieren, to damage, injure.

Ramsch, *m.* lot, refuse, bulk, lump, cheap stuff; **-ware,** *f.* job lot.

Rand, *m.ᐨer,* edge, border, brim, rim, margin, boundary, flange. lip; **äusserer** ∼, extrados, outer surface; **innerer** ~, intrados, inner surface.

Rand-bast, *m.* marginal bast; **-baum,** *m.* border tree; **-bedingung,** *f.* limit, (boundary) condition; **-beschaffenheit,** *f.* shape of the margin; **-bläschen,** *n.* marginal bladder, statocyst.

Rand-blüte, *f.* ray flower, marginal flower; **-bogen,** *m.* marginal arch; **-bündel,** *n.* marginal bundle; **-dicke,** *f.* thickness of the rim or edge; **-drüse,** *f.* marginal gland; **-ebene,** *f.* plane of the rim.

rändeln, rändern, to rim, edge, border, mill.

Ränderscheibe, *f.* edge (cutter) mill.

Rand-fassung, *f.* rim; **-feder,** *f.* marginal (tectrix) feather; **-fläche,** *f.* marginal surface, lateral face; **-gärung,** *f.* rim fermentation; **-gebiet,** *n.* border region; **-kante,** *f.* lateral edge; **-kerbe,** *f.* marginal notch; **-körper,** *m.* marginal sensory body, lithocyst; **-los,** rimless, marginless; **-mal,** *n.* stigma or pterostigma (mark on edge of wing).

rand-nervig, unforked secondary vein of leaf (craspedodromous); **-partie,** *f.* marginal region, periphery; **-pflanzung,** *f.* border planting; **-platten,** *f.pl.* marginals; **-saum,** *m.* craspedon, velum; **-schärfe,** *f.* sharpness of the border; **-schicht,** *f.* marginal zone, peripheral layer; **-schleier,** *m.* marginal zone, peripheral layer; **-spannung,** *f.* edge stress, extreme fiber stress; **-spalte,** *f.* marginal fissure.

rand-ständig, marginal, peripheral; **-träger,** *m.* edge beam, spandrel beam; **-tüpfel,** *m.* marginal pit.

Randung, *f.* edge, shape or form of the edge.

Rand-verjüngung, *f.* regeneration by strip fellings; **-wachstum,** *n.* marginal growth; **-wärts,** in the direction of the margin; **-wert,** *m.* boundary value; **-winkel** *m.* angle of contact; **-wulst,** *f.* marginal (eminence) elevation, mesenteric filament; **-zahn,** *m.* marginal tooth; **-zelle,** *f.* marginal cell; **-zellewachstum,** *n.* marginal growth; **-zone,** *f.* marginal zone.

rang (ringen), wrestled, was wrestling.

Rang, *m.* ⸚e, rank, quality, position, station, row, tier.

rangieren, to rank, arrange, classify.

Rangierlokomotive, *f.* switching engine.

Rank, *n.* winding road, turn, turning.

Ranke, *f.* tendril, climber, runner, cirrus, shoot.

ranken, to creep, climb, run; **-förmig,** cirrhiform, cirrhous; **-füsse,** *m.pl.* cirri of barnacles; **-füsser,** *m.pl.* Cirripedia; **-fusskrebse,** *m.pl.* Cirripedia; **-kletterer,** *m.* tendril climber; **-pflanze,** *f.* climber, runner.

rann (rinnen), ran, was running.

rannte (rennen), ran, was running.

Ränzel, *n.* **Ranzen,** *m.* knapsack, satchel, wallet.

Ranzidität, *f.* rancidity.

ranzig, rancid.

Ranzigkeit, *f.* rancidity, rancidness.

Ranzig-werden, *n.* becoming rancid.

Raphidenschlauch, *m.* raphid cell.

Rapp, *m.* **Rappe,** *f.* rape, grape pomace.

Rappel, *m.* madness, rage.

Rappen, *m.* black horse.

rapportfrei, without periodicity.

Rapputz, *m.* rough coat, plastering.

Raps, *m.* rape (*Brassica napus*); **-kuchen,** *m.* rapeseed cake; **-mehl,** *n.* linseed meal; **-saat,** *f.* **-same(n),** *m.* rapeseed, colza (*Brassica napus*).

Rapünzchen, *n.* lamb's-lettuce (*Valerianella olitoria*).

rasch, quick, brisk, nimble, swift, speedy, rapid, prompt; **rascher Satz,** *m.* mealpowder (common fuse) composition.

rascheln, to rustle, crackle.

rasen, to rave, rage.

Rasen, *m.* turf, sod, lawn, sward, furry coating, fur; **-artig,** grassy, like grass or turf; **-asche,** *f.* turf ashes; **-bekleidung,** *f.* sod revetment; **-bildend,** cespitose, turfing, mat-forming; **-bleiche,** *f.* grass (sun) bleaching.

rasend, furious.

Rasen-eisenerz, *n.* bog iron ore, limonite, meadow ore; **-eisenstein,** *m.* bog iron ore, limonite, meadow ore; **-gesellschaften,** *f.pl.* turf communities; **-narbe,** *f.* thick turf, sod.

rasieren, to shave, raze.

Rasier-flechte, *f.* ringworm, Herpes tonsurans; **-klinge,** *f.* razor blade; **-messer,** *n.* razor; **-pulver,** *n.* shaving powder; **-seife,** *f.* shaving soap.

Raspel, Raspe, *f.* rasp, grater, radula (of snails).

raspeln, to rasp, grate, scrape.

Rasse, *f.* race, breed, strain, type, stock.

rasseln, to rattle, clash, clatter.

Rassen-echtheit, *f.* genuineness of strain; **-hochzucht,** *f.* improved (pure) breeding.

Rast, *f.* rest, repose, relaxation, boshes.

rasten, to rest, repose, halt.

Raster, *m.* screen; **-ätzung,** *f.* **-bild,** *n.* autotypy; **-element,** *n.* screen plate.

Rastgärung, *f.* slow and incomplete fermentation.

rastlos, restless.

Rasur, *f.* erasure.

Rat, *m.*̈e, counsel, advice, suggestion, deliberation, means, remedy, expedient, council, board, councilor; **zu Rate ziehen,** to consult.

rät (raten), advises.

Rata, *f.* **Rate,** *f.* rate, quota, installment.

Ratanhia-wurzel, *f.* rhatany (root).

raten, (*dat.*) to advise, help, aid, assist, guess, solve, **geraten,** advisable.

Rathaus, *n.*̈er, town hall.

rationell, rational, reasonable, economical.

rätlich, advisable, expedient, useful, wholesome.

ratlos, helpless, embarrassed, perplexed.

ratsam, advisable, commendable, expedient, fit.

Ratschlag, *m.*̈e, advice, counsel, suggestion.

ratschlagen, to consult, deliberate.

Ratschluss, *m.*̈e, resolution, decision, decree.

Rätsel, *n.* riddle, puzzle, problem, mystery, enigma; **-haft,** puzzling, enigmatical, mysterious.

Ratte, *f.* rat.

rätten, to screen, sieve, riddle.

Ratten-gift, *n.* rat poison, white arsenic; **-schwanz,** *m.* rattail (file); **-sarkom,** *n.* rat sarcoma; **-vertilgungsmittel,** *n.* vermin killer, vermicide.

Raub, *m.* robbery, rapine, prey, spoil, booty, loot, pillaging; **-bau,** *m.* destructive lumbering; **-bein,** *n.* raptatorial leg.

rauben, to rob, abduct.

Räuber, *m.* robber, sucker (shoot).

räuberisch, predatory, predaceous.

Raub-fliegen, *f.pl.* robber (hornet) flies (Asilidae); **-fuss,** *m.* raptatorial leg; **-käfer,** *m.pl.* Staphylinidae; **-tiere,** *n.pl.* beasts of prey (Carnivora); **-vögel,** *m.pl.* birds of prey (Raptatores); **-wespen,** *f.pl.* Rapientia; **-wirtschaft,** *f.* destructive lumbering, ruinous exploitation.

Rauch, *m.* smoke, soot, fume, vapor; **-achat,** *m.* smoky agate; **-artig,** smoky; **-belästigung,** *f.* smoke nuisance; **-bildung,** *f.* formation of smoke; **-dicht,** smoketight, smokeproof.

rauchen, to fume, smoke, reek.

Räucher-essenz, *f.* aromatic essence; **-essig,** *m.* aromatic vinegar.

räucherig, smoky, dingy, reeking.

Räucher-kerzchen, *n.* fumigating candle; **-kerze,** *f.* fumigating candle; **-mittel,** *n.* fumigant.

räuchern, to fumigate, cure, smoke, perfume, scent.

Räucher-papier, *n.* fumigating paper; **-pulver,** *n.* fumigating powder.

Räucherung, *f.* fumigation, smoking, incense burning.

Räucherwerk, *n.* perfumes, incense, scents.

Rauch-erzeugung, *f.* smudging; **-fang,** *m.* chimney, flue; **-farben,** smoke-colored; **-farbig,** smoke-colored; **fleisch,** *n.* smoked meat; **-frei,** free from smoke, smokeless; **-gas,** *n.* flue gas, gas of combustion; **-gasvorwärmer,** *m.* economizer; **-geschwärzt,** smoke-stained; **-glas,** *n.* smoked (tinted) glass; **-helm,** *m.* smoke helmet.

rauchig, smoky.

Rauch-kalk, *m.* magnesian limestone; **-kanal,** *m.* smoke flue; **-los,** smokeless; **-rohr,** *n.* smoke flue; **-schaden,** *m.* damage by fume; **-schieber,** *m.* damper; **-schleier,** *m.* smoke screen.

rauchschwach, giving little smoke.

rauch-schwaches Pulver, *n.* smokeless powder.

rauch-schwarz, black as soot; **-stärke,** *f.* density of smoke; **-verbrennung,** *f.* smoke (combustion) consumption; **-verbrennungseinrichtung,** *f.* smoke consumer; **-verhütung,** *f.* smoke prevention; **-verzehrung,** *f.* smoke consumption; **-vorhang,** *m.* smoke screen; **-wand,** *f.* smoke screen; **-waren,** *f.pl.* furs, peltry; **-wolke,** *f.* smoke cloud.

Räude, *f.* mange, scab, scurf.

räudig, scabbed, scabby, mangy.

Raufe, *f.* hackle, rack.

raufen, to pull, pluck, scuffle, tussle.

rauh, rough, rugged, raw, coarse, unfinished; **-artikel,** *m.* raised style (in fabrics); **-blatt,** *n.* coarse, often recurved hairy leaf of zoophobic plant; **-blättrig,** asperifolious; **-dach,** *n.* turf cover.

rauhen, to nap (fabrics).

rauhhaarig, hirsute.

Rauhheit, *f.* roughness.

Rauhigkeitsbeiwert, *m.* coefficient of roughness.

Rauhreif, *m.* hoarfrost.

Rauke, *f.* hedge mustard (*Eruca sativa*).

Raum, *m.*-e, space, volume, room, capacity, position, scope, accommodation, hold, opportunity; **-analyse,** *f.* volumetric analysis; **-auffassung,** *f.* interpretation of space; **-beständig,** incompressible, constant volume; **-bestimmung,** *f.* determination of volume; **-bewetterung,** *f.* air conditioning; **-bild,** *n.* space diagram; **-chemie,** *f.* stereochemistry: **-dichte,** *f.* density by volume; **-einheit,** *f.* unit of (space) volume; **-element,** *n.* spatial unit.

räumen, to clear (away), remove, evacuate, retreat, leave, give up, dispatch.

Raum-formel, *f.*-n, spatial formula; **-gebilde,** *n.* space diagram; **-gehalt,** *m.* content by volume, spatial content; **-geometrie,** *f.* solid geometry; **-gewicht,** *n.* volumetric (unit) weight, bulk density; **-gitter,** *n.* space lattice.

räumig, spacious, roomy, undercrowded.

Räumigkeit, *f.* specific volume, roominess.

Raum-inhalt, *m.* volume, content, (cubic) capacity; **-isomerie,** *f.* spatial isomerism, stereoisomerism; **-kurve,** *f.* solid curve; **-lehre,** *f.* geometry, science of space.

räumlich, spatial, steric, relating to volume, three-dimesional, volumetric.

Räumlichkeit, *f.* spaciousness, extension, specific volume, spatiality, roominess, space.

Raum-mass, *n.*-e, measure of capacity, dimensions, volume, stacked measure; **-menge,** *f.* amount of space, volume; **-meter,** *n.* cubic meter; **-orientierung,** *f.* orientation in space; **-sinn,** *m.* spatial (sense) perception; **-teil,** *m.* part by volume, volume.

Räumung, *f.* removal, final cutting.

Räumungshieb, *m.* final cutting.

Raum-urteil, *n.* spatial judgment; **-veränderung,** *f.* change in volume; **-verhältnis,** *f.* volume relation or ratio, proportion by volume; **-verminderung,** *f.* decrease in volume.

raunen, to whisper.

Raupe, *f.* caterpillar, maggot, worm, whim, fancy.

Raupen-fliege, *f.* tachina, larva fly; **-frass,** *m.* destruction by caterpillars; **-kot,** *m.*

larval excrements; **-leim,** *m.* insect paste (for protecting trees).

Rausch, *m.* drunkenness, intoxication, rushing, roar, murmur; **-beere,** *f.* crowberry (*Empetrum nigrum*).

Rauschbrand, *m.* blackleg, symptomatic anthrax; **-bazillus,** *m.* bacillus of blackleg (symptomatic anthrax); **-impfung,** *f.* inoculation against blackleg (symptomatic anthrax).

rauschen, to rush, roar, gurgle, purl, murmur, swirl, rustle, whistle.

Rausch-gelb, *n.* orpiment; **-gold,** *n.* Dutch gold, tinsel; **-mittel,** *n.* intoxicant; **-rot,** *n.* realgar; **-silber,** *n.* imitation silver foil.

Raute, *f.* rue, rhombus, diamond (cards).

rauten-ähnlich, like rue, rhomboid; **-flach,** *n.* rhombohedron; **fläche,** *f.* rhombus; **flächner,** *m.* rhombohedron; **-förmig,** rhombic, diamond-shaped; **-gewächse,** *n.pl.* Rutaceae; **-grube,** *f.* rhomboidal fossa; **-lippe,** *f.* rhomboid lip; **-öl,** *n.* oil of rue; **-spat,** *m.* rhomb spar, dolomite.

Reagens, *n.* reagent; **-glas,** *n.* test tube; **-glashalter,** *m.* test-tube holder; **-glaskultur,** culture in test tube; **-glasstichkultur,** *f.* (test tube) stab culture; **-kelch,** *m.* test glass; **-lösung,** *f.* test solution; **-mittel,** *n.* reagent; **-papier,** *n.* test paper, litmus paper; **-röhrchen,** *n.*, **-röhre,** *f.* test tube.

Reagenzien, *n.pl.* reagents; **-flasche,** *f.* reagent bottle.

reagieren, to react.

reagierend, reactive.

Reagierglas, *n.* test tube; **-bürste,** *f.* test-tube brush; **-gestell,** *n.* test-tube stand; **-halter,** *m.* test-tube holder.

Reagierkelch, *m.* test cup.

Reaktions-ablauf, *m.* expiration (course) of a reaction, result of a reaction; **-bahn,** *f.* path of a reaction; **-fähigkeit,** *f.* capability (power) of reacting, reactivity; **-flüssigkeit,** *f.* reaction liquid; **-fortgang,** *m.* continuation of a reaction; **-gemisch,** *n.* reaction mixture; **-geschehen,** *n.* occurrence of reaction, separate reaction; **-geschwindigkeit,** *f.* reaction velocity; **-gleichung,** *f.* equation of a reaction; **-kette,** *f.* series of reactions.

Reactions-kurve, *f.* curve of reaction; **-los,** reactionless; **-losigkeit,** *f.* absence of reaction, nonreaction; **-masse,** *f.* reaction mass, mass resulting from a reaction; **-mischung,** *f.* reaction mixture; **-mittel,** *n.* reagent; **-papier,** *n.* test paper; **-produkt,** *n.* product of reaction; **-stufe**, *f.* step (stage of a reaction; **-träge**, slow to react.

Reaktions-trägheit, *f.* slowness to reaction, inertness; **-turm,** *m.* reaction tower; **-verlauf,** *m.* course of a reaction; **-wärme,** *f.* heat of reaction; **-zeit,** *f.* period of reaction.

Reaktivität, *f.* reactivity.

real, real, actual.

realisieren, to realize.

Realität, *f.* reality.

Reallast, *f.* real servitude, easement.

Realschule, *f.* German secondary school (for science and modern languages).

Rebe, *f.* vine, tendril, shoot, grape(vine).

Reben-dolde, *f.* earthnut (Oenanthe); **-gewächse,** *n.pl.* Vitaceae; **-russ,** *m.* vine black, Frankfort black; **-saft,** *m.* juice of the grape, wine; **-schädling,** *m.* vine pest; **-schwarz,** *n.* vine black; **-stecher,** *m.* grape beetle, Rhynchitidae.

Reb-huhn, *n.* partridge; **-hühnervolk,** *n.* covey of partridges; **-laus,** *f.* vine louse, phylloxera; **-stecken,** *m.* vine stake, vine prop.

Rechen, *m.* rake, rack; **-fehler,** *m.* error in calculation; **-gut,** *n.* material retained on trash rack; **-kunst,** *f.* arithmetic.

Rechenschaft, *f.* account; $\sim$ **-geben** (ablegen), to give account, answer.

Rechen-schieber, slide rule; **-stab,** *m.* trash-rack bar, slide rule; **-stift,** *m.* slate pencil; **-tafel,** *f.* slate, blackboard, multiplication table.

rechnen, to count, reckon, calculate, figure, compute, estimate, depend on; $\sim$ **zu,** to classify with, group along with, include.

rechnerisch, mathematical(ly), analytically.

Rechnung, *f.* calculation, account, bill, arithmetic, calculus, invoice, computation; $\sim$ **tragen,** to take into account, comply with.

Rechnungs-art, *f.* species, arithmetical species, calculation; **-betrag,** *m.* amount of an account or bill; **-führer,** *m.* bookkeeper, accountant; **-jahr,** *n.* fiscal (financial) year; **-mässig,** in accordance with calculation or books; **-zinsfuss,** *m.* interest rate.

Rechstreu, *f.* litter of dead leaves.

Recht, *n.*-e, right, privilege, claim, justice, law; **mit** $\sim$, rightly, with reason, justly; **ohne** $\sim$, unjustly; **im Rechte sein,** to be in the right; **von Rechts wegen,** by rights, according to justice; $\sim$ **behalten,** to be

right in the end; **mit** $\sim$ **sagen,** to be correct in saying.

recht, right, correct, proper, true, genuine, suitable, befitting, real, legitimate, own, agreeable, very, indeed, exactly, quite, accurate, thorough, solid; $\sim$ **haben,** to be right; **rechter Winkel,** right angle; **zum rechten sehen,** to attend to something; **zur rechten Zeit,** in due time, in the nick of time; $\sim$ **gut,** very good, quite well; $\sim$ **gern,** most willingly, gladly; **erst** $\sim$, all the more, especially, more than ever; **mir ist es** $\sim$, it is agreeable to me; **mit vollem (gutem)** $\sim$, for good reason(s).

Rechte, *f.* right side, right hand, party.

Rechteck, *n.*-e, rectangle.

rechteckig, rectangular.

rechten, to litigate, plead, dispute.

rechterhand, on the right-hand side.

rechtfertigen, to justify, vindicate.

Rechtfertigung, *f.* justification.

recht-geben, to admit, support, prove right. **-gläubig,** orthodox; **-haben,** to be right; **-haberisch,** positive, dogmatical; **-läufig,** running the normal course, clockwise.

rechtlich, legal, judicial, fair, honest.

recht-los, illegal; **-mässig,** legal, lawful.

rechts, (to the) right.

Rechts-anwalt, *m.* attorney; **-beständig,** valid, legal.

recht-schaffen, just, honest, upright; **-schreibung,** *f.* orthography, spelling.

rechts-drehend, dextrorotatory; **-drehung,** *f.* dextrorotation, right-handed polarization; **-gedreht,** dextrorse; **-gelehrte,** *m.* lawyer, jurist; **-griffelig,** dexiostylic; **-gültigkeit,** *f.* validity; **-handel,** *m.* lawsuit; **-kräftig,** valid, legal.

rechtskreisend, turning to the right; **rechtskreisende Pflanze,** *f.* right-hand (dextrorse) climber.

rechts-läufig, to the right, clockwise; **-milchsäure,** *f.* dextrolactic acid; **-mittel,** *n.* legal remedy; **-nachfolgerungserklärung,** *f.* legalized copy of assignment; **-säure,** *f.* dextro acid; **-schraube,** *f.* right-handed screw; **-weinsäure,** *f.* dextrotartaric acid.

recht-winklig, right-angled, rectangular; **-zeitig,** opportune, seasonable, in time, punctually.

Recipient, *m.* recipient, receiver.

reciprok, reciprocal.

Reck, *n.* rack, stretcher, horizontal bar.

Recke, *f.* rack, stretcher, horizontal bar, giant, hero.

recken, to stretch, extend, rack.

Reckung, *f.* expansion, stretching.

Reckwalzen, *f.pl.* **Reckwerk,** *n.* finishing rolls.

Rectaldrüse, *f.* rectal gland.

Redakteur, *m.* editor.

Redaktion, *f.* editing, editorial (staff).

Rede, *f.* speech, language, talk, conversation, discourse, utterance, report, rumor, account; **es wird die ~ davon sein,** we shall speak of it; **es kann keine ~ davon sein,** there can be no question of it; **in ~ stehen,** be under discussion.

reden, to speak, talk, plead, discourse.

Redensart, *f.*-en, expression, phrase, term, idiom.

Redeweise, *f.* manner of speaking, style.

redigieren, to edit.

redlich, upright, honest, open, fair, candid.

Redner, *m.* orator, speaker; **-bühne,** *f.* platform.

redselig, talkative.

Reduktions-arbeit, *f.* process of reducing, reduction; **-fähig,** capable of reduction; **-fähigkeit,** *f.* reductibility; **-faktor,** *m.* reducing factor; **-ferment,** *n.* reducing enzyme; **flamme,** *f.* reducing flame; **-kraft,** *f.* reducing power; **-mittel,** *n.* reducer, reducing agent; **-ort,** *m.* reduction region; **-röhre,** *f.* reduction tube; **-teilung,** *f.* reduction division; **-vermögen,** *n.* reducing power.

reduzierbar, reducible.

reduzieren, to reduce, atrophy.

reduzier-fähig, capable of reduction; **-salz,** *n.* reducing salt.

reduziert, *f.* vestigial, reduced.

Reduzierung, *f.* reduction.

Reduzierventil, *n.* reducing valve.

reell, real, solid, sound, fair, honest.

Reep, *n.* rope.

Referat, *n.*-e, report, abstract, review.

Referent, *m.* reporter, reviewer.

referieren, to report.

reflektieren, to reflect, consider.

Reflektionsvermögen, *n.* reflecting power.

Reflex, *m.*-e, reflex; **-artig,** like a reflex; **-bahn,** *f.* reflex tract; **-beantwortung,** *f.* reflex response; **-bewegung,** *f.* reflex movement; **-hemmung,** *f.* reflex inhibition.

Reflexions-ebene, *f.* plane of reflection; **-winkel,** *m.* angle of reflection.

Reflexkette, *f.* chain of reflexes; **-nerv,** *m.* reflex nerve; **-wirkung,** *f.* reflex effect.

refraktär, refractory.

Refraktionswinkel, *m.* angle of refraction.

refrigieren, to refrigerate, freeze.

Regal, *n.* shelves.

rege, moving, animated, movable, alert, quick, active, lively, enthusiastic, industrious.

Regel, *f.*-n, rule, regulation, principle, standard, menstruation; **in der ~,** as a rule, ordinarily, usually.

regelbar, adjustable.

Regel-belastung, *n.* normal load; **-glied,** *n.* final control element.

regel-los, anomalous, irregular; **-mässig,** regular, ordinary, normal, regularly, actinomorphic; **-mässigkeit,** *f.* regularity, uniformity, conformity to law; **-mischröhre,** *f.* fading mix hexode.

regeln, to regulate, adjust, order, settle, arrange, fix, determine, govern.

regelrecht, regular, correct, normal, in accordance with rule.

Regelung, *f.* regulation, adjustment, control.

Regel-unterschied, *m.* deviation; **-widrig,** irregular, abnormal.

regen, to stir, move, rouse, be active, moving.

Regen, *m.* rain; **-arm,** dry, rainless.

Regenbogen, *m.* rainbow; **-farbig,** rainbow colored, iridescent; **-haut,** *f.* iris; **-hautband,** *n.* ciliary ligament.

Regeneration, *f.* regeneration.

Regeneratgummi, *m.* regenerated (reclaimed) rubber.

regenerieren, to regenerate.

Regenerierung, *f.* regeneration.

Regeneriervorrichtung, *f.* regenerative device.

Regen-fang, *m.* cistern; **-freundlich,** ombrophilous, rain-loving; **-los,** without rain, dry; **-mass,** *n,* rain gauge; **-menge,** *f.* amount of rain; **-messer,** *m.* rain gauge; **-pfeifer,** *m.* golden plover; **-scheu,** ombrophobic, rain shy; **-schirm,** *m.* umbrella; **-tropfen,** *m.* raindrop.

Regen-wald, *m.* tropical rain forest; **-wasser,** *n.* rain water; **-wurm,** *m.* earthworm; **-zeit,** *f.* rainy season.

Regie, *f.* administration; -verschluss, *m.* bond.

regieren, to rule, reign, govern, direct, regulate, conduct, manage, guide.

Regierung, *f.* reign, rule, government, direction

Regierungsrat, *m.* administrative adviser.

Register, *n.* index, table of contents, register, record.

Registratur, *f.* registry.

registrieren, to register, record, enter, file, index.

Regler, *m.* regulator, controller.

Reglisse, *f.* licorice, marshmallow paste.

regnen, to rain.

Regnerdüse, *f.* spray nozzle.

regnerisch, rainy.

regressiv, *f.* regressive, degenerative.

regsam, active, mobile, quick, agile.

Regsamkeit, *f.* alertness, activity, agility.

Regulationsvorgang, *m.* regulatory process.

regulativ, regulating.

regulieren, to regulate, govern.

Regulierhahn, *m.* regulating cock.

Regulierung, *f.* regulation.

Regulierwiderstand, *m.* adjustable resistance.

regulinisch, reguline.

Regung, *f.* motion, stirring, moving, emotion, agitation.

Reh, *n.*-e, deer, roe; -bock, *m.* roebuck; -braun, *n.* fawn color; -farben, -farbig, fawn colored; -geiss, *f.* doe; -kalb, *n.* roe calf, fawn; -leder, *n.* doeskin; -posten, *m.pl.* buckshot; -wild, *n.* roe deer.

Reibahle, *f.* broach.

Reibe, *f.* grater, rasp.

reibecht, fast to rubbing.

Reibeisen, *n.* rasp, grater.

Reibemühle, *f.* grinding mill.

reiben, to rub, grind, triturate, grate, scour, chafe, annoy, provoke, stir, erase.

Reibepulver, *n.* abrasive powder.

Reiber, *m.* grater, rubber, pestle, grinder, brayer, rubber rasp.

Reibezunge, *f.* tongue with a radula.

Reib-festigkeit, *f.* chafing resistance, resistance to abrasion; -fläche, *f.* rubbing or rubbed surface; -kasten, *m.* grinding mill;

-keule, *f.* pestle; -maschine, *f.* grating medium; -membran, *f.* radula; -platte, *f.* grating radula; -schale, *f.* mortar; -stein, *m.* grindstone; -unechtheit, *f.* lack of fastness to rubbing.

Reibung, *f.* friction, rubbing, attrition, grating, difficulty; innere ~, internal friction, viscosity.

Reibungs-beiwert, *m.* coefficient of friction; -elektrizität, *f.* frictional electricity; -frei, without friction; -koeffizient, *m.* frictional index, coefficient of friction; -probe, *f.* friction test; -versuch, *m.* shear test; -wärme, *f.* friction heat; -widerstand, *m.* frictional resistance; -zahl, -ziffer, *f.* coefficient of friction.

Reibzündhölzchen, *n.* friction match.

Reich, *n.* state, realm, empire, kingdom.

reich, rich, wealthy, concentrated, full, abundant; -blühend, abounding in flowers.

reichen, to reach, extend, pass, hand, give, present, suffice, last.

Reich-frischen, *n.* enriching (of copper).

reichhaltig, reichlich, abundant, copious, plentiful, rich, full, well, profuse.

Reichsanstalt, *f.* government institute.

Reich-schaum, *m.* zinc crust, rich in silver; -schlacke, *f.* rich slag; -schmelzen, *n.* smelting of precious metals.

Reichs-gesundheitsamt, *n.* government board of health; -mark, *f.* reichsmark (German money); -patent, *n.* German patent.

Reichtum, *m.*-̈er, wealth, richness, abundance.

Reichweite, *f.* radius of influence, range; ausser ~, out of reach.

Reif, *m.* ring, hoop, tire, circle, collar, bloom, hoarfrost.

reif, ripe, mature, fully developed, ready.

Reife, *f.* ripeness, maturity, age, puberty; -grad, *m.* degree of ripeness or maturity.

Reifei, *n.* mature ovum.

Reifemerkmal, *n.* indicator of ripeness.

reifen, to ripen, mature.

Reifen, *m.*-, ring, hoop, tire, collar; -artig, ringlike, hooplike; -cord, *m.* tire cord.

Reife-teilung, *f.* maturation division; -vorgang, *m.* ripening process; -zeit, *f.* age of maturity; -zustand, *m.* ripe state, ripeness.

Reif-furche, *f.* segment groove (on insects); -holz, *n.* heartwood.

reiflich, careful, mature.

Reifstecken, *m.* hoop pole, straight sapling.

Reifung, *f.* maturing.

Reifungserscheinung, *f.* appearance of ripening.

Reihe, *f.* row, range, suite, series, line, succession, rotation, train, sequence, rank, order, number, progression, file, turn; **der ∼ nach,** in succession; **die ∼ ist an mir,** it is my turn; **ausser der ∼,** out of turn; **in Reih(e) und Glied,** in order, in rank and file.

reihen, to arrange in a series or row, form a row, string, baste, stitch; **-entfernung,** *f.* row distance; **-folge,** *f.* sequence, succession, order, course; **-gemmen,** *f.pl.* chain gemmae; **-pflanzung,** *f.* planting in rows; **-saat,** *f.* sowing in rows; **-schaltung,** *f.* connection in series; **-variabilität,** *f.* variability of different rows.

Reiher, *m.* heron; **-schnabel,** *m.* stork's-bill (Erodium).

rein, pure, clean, neat, tidy, clear, undiluted, sheer, absolutely, mere, quite; **∼ halten,** to keep clean; **darüber ins Reine kommen,** to get to the bottom of that; **ins Reine bringen,** to clear up, put in order.

Rein-bestand, *m.* pure stand, single crop; **-darstellung,** *f.* preparation in a pure condition, purification; **-ertrag,** *m.* net yield, net profit or revenue; **-ertragslehre,** *f.* theory of the highest net revenue; **-gelb,** *n.* pure yellow (flavous); **-gewicht,** *n.* net weight; **-gewinn,** *m.* **-gewinnung,** *f.* purifying, purification.

Reinheit, *f.* purity, pureness, clean(li)ness.

Reinheits-grad, *m.* degree of fineness or purity; **-probe,** *f.* test for purity.

reinigen, to purify, refine, wash, rectify, clarify, lose dead limbs, clean, clear, cleanse, scour, purge, disinfect.

Reiniger, *m.* purifier; **-wasser,** *n.* cleansing water.

Reinigung, *f.* purification, cleaning, self-pruning, rectification, menstruation.

Reinigungs-behälter, *m.* filtering basin or tank; **-mittel,** *n.* purifying agent, purifier, cleansing agent, detergent, purgative; **-möller,** *m.* purifying (blast-furnace) burden; **-prozess,** *m.* natural pruning; **-vermögen,** *n.* detergent (cleansing) power.

Reinkultur, *f.* pure culture.

reinlich, distinct, clean cut, tidy.

Reinschrift, *f.* fair copy, final copy.

reinst, purest.

Reinzucht, *f.* pure culture; **-hefen,** *f.pl.* pure culture of yeasts.

Reinzüchtung, *f.* obtaining a pure culture.

Reis, *m.* rice.

Reis, *n.* twig, sprig, shoot, scion.

Reise, *f.* journey, tour, trip, voyage.

reisen, to travel, journey, go, set out, leave.

Reisermoorgesellschaften, *f.pl.* heath-plant communities.

Reisfuttermehl, *n.* rice flour, ground rice.

Reisgräser, *n.pl.* Oryzae.

Reisig, *n.* brushwood, twigs, deadwood, prunings.

Reis-käfer, *m.* rice weevil; **-körper,** *m.* rice body, melon-seed body; **-mehl,** *n.* rice flour; **-puder,** *m.* rice powder.

Reiss-blei, *n.* graphite; **-brett,** *n.* drawing board.

Reissschleim, *m.* rice water.

Reissebene, *f.* fracture plane.

reissen, to tear, pull, drag, grasp, seize, snatch, split, trace, draw, bruise, burst, break, crack, tear along, scramble, rend, crush, rough-grind (glass).

reissend, tearing, rapacious, carnivorous, rapid, racking, impetuous.

Reisser, *m.* gouge blaze, bark blaze, scratcher.

Reiss-feder, *f.* drawing pen; **-festigkeit,** *f.* resistance to tearing or breaking, tenacity, tensile strength; **-gelb,** *n.* orpiment; **-kohle,** *f.* charcoal crayon; **-korn,** *n.* artificial grain; **-lack,** *m.* crackle leather; **-länge,** *f.* breaking length (of synthetic fibers); **-libelle,** *f.* striding level; **-nagel,** *m.* thumbtack; **-schiene,** *f.* T square.

Reisstärke, *f.* rice starch.

Reiss-verschluss, *m.* slide fastener, zipper closure; **-verschlussglied,** *n.* slide-fastener link; **-wolle,** *f.* reused wool; **-zahn,** *m.* ̈e, fang, carnassial tooth, flesh tooth, canine tooth; **-zeug,** *n.* drawing instruments.

reiten, to ride (horseback).

reitend, equitant.

Reiter, *m.* rider, horseman.

Reiz, *m.* irritant, stimulus, irritation, excitement, charm, attraction, grace; **-bahnung,** *f.* facility for stimulus.

reizbar, irritable, nervous, sensitive.

Reiz-beantwortung, *f.* response to stimulus; **-bedingung,** *f.* condition of stimulation; **-bewegung,** *f.* movement due to stimulation or irritation; **-dauer,** *f.* duration of stimulation; **-empfänglichkeit,** *f.* susceptibility to stimulation.

reizen, to stimulate, irritate, excite, entice, attract, allure, charm.

reizend, irritating, charming, enticing, delicious.

Reiz-erfolg, *m.-e,* resulting stimulation; **-fähig,** irritable; **-feld,** *n.* field of stimulation; **-fortpflanzung,** *f.* conduction of stimulus; **-frequenz,** *f.* frequency of stimulation; **-gift,** *n.* irritant poison; **-gipfel,** *m.* stimulus giving maximum excitation; **-haken,** *m.* irritable hook; **-hemmung,** *f.* retarding stimuli; **-leitung,** *f.* conduction of stimuli.

Reiz-leitungsstoff, *m.* substance for conduction of stimuli; **-los,** nonirritant, nonstimulating, charmless, unattractive, insipid; **-losigkeit,** *f.* nonirritance, unattractiveness; **-menge,** *f.* energy (intensity) of stimulation; **-mittel,** *n.* stimulant, irritant, incentive, inducement; **-perzipierend,** sensitive, tactile; **-schwelle,** *f.* threshold of stimulation; **-stelle,** *f.* place of irritation; **-stoff,** *m.* adjuvant, stimulating substance; **-übertragung,** *f.* transmission of stimuli.

Reizung, *f.* stimulation, irritation, excitation.

Reiz-ursache, *f.* source (cause) of stimulation; **-voll,** alluring, exciting; **-vorgang,** *m.* process (transmission) of stimulation; **-wirkung,** *f.* irritating (stimulating) effect.

rekapitulieren, to recapitulate.

Reklamation, *f.* complaint, claim, protest, objection.

Reklame, *f.* advertisement, advertising.

reklamieren, to (re)claim, object, complain.

Rektaszension, *f.* right ascension.

Rekteseite, *f.* right-hand page, odd (uneven) page.

Rektifikation, *f.* rectification, fractional distillation.

Rektifikations-apparat, *m.* rectifying apparatus, rectifier; **-kolonne,** *f.* rectifying column.

rektifizieren, to rectify.

Rektifizierung, *f.* rectification.

Rekurrenskranke, *m.* relapsing-fever patient.

relativ, relative.

Relativität, *f.* relativity.

Relativitätstheorie, *f.* theory of relativity.

relaxieren, to relax.

Relevanz, *f.* relevance, relevancy.

Relief, *n.* embossment.

Remise, *f.* wagon shed, low cover.

remittieren, to remit.

remontierend, everblooming, perpetual.

Rendant, *m.* accountant.

Rendement, *m.* yield.

Rendita, *f.* extent of weighting (fabrics).

renken, to bend, turn, wrench, sprain.

rennen, to run, race, extract, smelt (iron).

Renn-arbeit, *f.* direct process (of iron extraction); **-feuer,** *n.* bloomery hearth, smelting furnace; **-(feuer)eisen,** *n.* malleable iron; **-(feuer)schlacke,** *f.* direct-process slag; **-fuss,** *m.* cursorial leg; **-stahl,** *m.* direct-process steel; **-tier,** *n.* reindeer; **-tierflechte,** *f.* reindeer lichen, moss.

Renommee, *n.* renown, reputation.

renommieren, to boast, brag.

renommiert, renowned, famous, well-known.

rentabel, profitable, remunerative.

Rentabilität, *f.* profitableness.

Rente, *f.* rent, revenue, income, annuity.

rentieren, to pay, be profitable, yield a revenue.

Rentierungswert, *m.* rental value.

reparativer Wurzelspross, *m.* (Ersatzspross), compensatory shoot.

Reparatur, *f.* repair.

reparieren, to repair.

repassieren, to boil off (silk) a second time.

repetieren, to repeat.

Repetition, *f.* repetition, recapitulation.

Repräsentant, *m.* representative.

repräsentieren, to represent.

Reproduktionskraft, *f.* reproductive power.

reproduzierbar, reproducible.

reproduzieren, to reproduce.

Reps, *m.* rape.

Reptil, *n.* reptile.

Reptilienei, *n.* egg of a reptile.

requirieren, to request, requisition.

Reseda, *f.* mignonette (*Reseda odorata*); **gelbe** ～, dyer's(-weed) rocket (*Reseda luteola*).

Reservage, *f.* resist, reserve; **-artikel,** *m.* resist (reserve) style (of fabrics).

Reserve, *f.* reserve, resist; **-mittel,** *n.* reserve, resist; **-muster,** *n.* reference pattern;

-stärke, *f.* reserve strength or force, reserve starch; -stoff, *m.* reserve material; -stoff, behälter, *m.* endosperm, storage organ; -teil, *m.* spare part.

reservieren, to reserve.

Reservierungsmittel, *n.* resist, reserve (calico).

Residuum, *n.* residuum, residue.

resinogene Schicht, *f.* resinous layer of secretory cell.

Resistenz, *f.* resistance.

Resonanzholz, *n.* resonant (sounding-board) wood.

resorbieren, to reabsorb, resorb.

Resorption, *f.* reabsorption.

Resorzin, *n.* resorcinol, resorcin.

respektive, respectively, or.

Respirationsnahrungsmittel, *n.* respiratory food, heat-producing food.

Respiro, *f.* grace period (on patents).

Rest, *m.*-e, rest, residue, remainder, remains, dregs, remnant, balance, vestige, difference.

Restalblase, *f.* stercoral pocket.

Rest-flüssigkeit, *f.* residual liquid; -glied, *n.* residual term or member, remainder; härte, *f.* residual hardness.

restieren, to remain, be left.

Restitutionsvermögen, *n.* regeneration capacity.

Rest-lauge, *f.* residual liquor; -los, without residue or remainder, completely, entirely, absolutely; -stickstoff, *m.* residual nitrogen; -stickstoff-körper, *m.* nitrogen residual constituents; -strahl, *m.* residual ray; -strom, *m.* residual current; -valenz, *f.* residual valence.

Resultantengesetz, *n.*-e, law of resultants.

Resultat, *n.*-e, result.

resultieren, to result.

resultierend, resulting, resultant.

Reteleiste, *f.* rete ridge.

Retentionstheorie, *f.* retention theory.

Retinablatt, *n.* retinal layer.

Retorte, *f.* retort.

Retorten-bauch, *m.* bulb of a retort; -gestell, *n.* retort stand; -hals, *m.* neck of a retort; -halter, *m.* retort holder, retort stand; -haus, *n.* retort house; -helm, *m.* retort (head) helm; -kitt, *m.* retort (cement) lute; -kohle, *f.* retort carbon.

Retorten-mündung, *f.* mouth of a retort; -rückstand, *m.* retort residue; -verkokung, *f.* retort coking; -vorstoss, *m.* adapter condenser; -zelle, *f.* ampulla.

retouchieren, to retouch.

Retournöl, *n.* recovered oil.

retten, to save, preserve, rescue, set free, recover, escape.

Rettich, Rettig, *m.* black radish.

Rettung, *f.* rescue, recovery, preservation, saving, escape, salvage.

rettungslos, irretrievable, beyond hope.

Rettungsmittel, *n.* remedy, resource, expedient.

reuen, to repent of, regret.

Reugeld, *n.* forfeit.

Reuse, *f.* corona of flower, weir basket, Aristolochia.

Reuthaue, *f.* mattock, hoe.

reverberieren, to reverberate.

reversibel, reversierbar, reversible.

revidieren, to revise, examine, check.

Revier, *n.* district, region.

Revision, *f.* inspection, revision, auditing.

Revolver-Objektivwechsler, *m.* revolving nosepiece of microscope.

Rezension, *f.* review, criticism.

rezent, recent.

Rezept, *n.*-e, recipe, formula, prescription; -buch, *n.* receipt book.

Rezeptor, *m.* receptor, receiver.

Rezeptorenseitenkette, *f.* receptor side chain.

Rezeptur, *f.* dispensing of medicines, receivership.

rezessiv, recessive.

Rezipient, *m.* receiver, recipient.

reziprok, reciprocal(ly), converse(ly).

Rhabarber, *m.* rhubarb; -gelb, *n.* chrysophanic acid; -gerbsäure, *f.* rheotannic acid; -säure, *f.* chrysophanic acid.

Rhachitis, *f.* rickets.

Rhein-säure, *f.* rheic (chrysophanic) acid; -wein, *m.* Rhine wine.

Rheumatismus, *m.* rheumatism.

Rhinosklerom, *n.* rhinoscleroma.

rhizogene Schicht, *f.* pericambium.

Rhizom, *n.* rhizome; -sprossung, *f.* runner formation.

Rhodan, *n.* thiocyanogen, sulphocyanogen; **-aluminium,** *n.* aluminum thiocyanate; **-ammonlösung,** *f.* ammonium thiocyanate solution.

Rhodanat, *n.* thiocyanate; **-lösung,** *f.* thiocyanate solution.

Rhodanid, *n.* thiocyanate.

Rhodanion, *n.* thiocyanogen ion.

Rhodanür, *n.* thiocyanate, sulphocyanate.

Rhodanverbindung, *f.* thiocyanogen compound.

Rhodinasäure, *f.* rhodinic acid.

Rhodium-chlorwasserstoffsäure, *f.* acid containing rhodium, chlorine, and hydrogen; **-metall,** *n.* rhodium metal; **-verbindung,** *f.* rhodium compound.

Rhomben-dodekaeder, *n.* rhombic dodecahedron; **-förmig,** rhomb-shaped, rhombic.

rhombisch, rhombic.

Rhomboeder, *n.* rhombohedron.

rhomboedrisch, rhombohedral.

rhomboidisch, rhomboid, rhomboidal.

Rhuslack, *m.* rhus varnish.

rhythmisch, rhythmical.

Rhythmus, *m.* rhythm.

Richtblei, *n.* plumb line, plummet.

richten, to direct, turn, regulate, arrange, aim, adjust, set (up), straighten, address, raise, erect, judge, rise, conform, guide; **sich nach etwas ~,** to conform to (with) or be governed in something; **sich auf etwas ~,** to keep oneself ready for something; **zugrunde ~,** to ruin.

richtend, formative, directing.

Richter, *m.* judge, justice.

Richtfunkbake, *f.* radio beam.

richtig, right, correct, exact, accurate, suitable, just, fair, true, real.

Richtigkeit, *f.* rightness, correctness, exactness.

Richtigstellung, *f.* rectification, correction.

Richt-linie, *f.* guide line, guiding line, rule, instruction, axis; **-mass,** *n.* standard, gauge; **-platte,** *f.* adjusting (orientation) plate; **-scheit,** *n.* rule, straightedge; **-schnur,** *f.* chalk line, plumb line.

Richtung, *f.* direction, route, course, bearing, orientation, setting, trend, shape; **-gebend,** direction-showing, indicating direction.

Richtungs-änderung, *f.* change of direction; **-bewegung,** *f.* orientation movement;

-körper, *m.* polar (body) globule; **-septen,** *n.pl.* directive mesenteries; **-wahrnehmung,** perception of direction.

Ricinölsäure, *f.* ricinoleic acid.

Ricinus, *m.* castor-oil plant; **-öl,** *n.* castor oil; **-ölsäure,** *f.* ricinoleic acid; **-samen,** *m.* castor bean; **-seife,** *f.* castor-oil soap.

Ricke, *f.* doe.

rieb (reiben), rubbed, was rubbing.

Riechbein, *n.* ethmoid bone; **-loch,** *n.* ethmoidal foramen.

riechen, to reek, smell; **~ nach,** to smell of.

Riechen, *n.* smelling, odor, olfaction, scent.

riechend, smelling, redolent, perfumed, strong, fragrant.

Riech-epithel, *n.* olfactory epithelium; **-essig,** *m.* aromatic vinegar; **-faden,** *m.* olfactory filament; **-feld,** *n.* olfactory area; **-fläschchen,** *n.* smelling bottle; **-furche,** *f.* olfactory sulcus; **-grube,** *f.* olfactory fossa; **-haar,** *n.* olfactory hair; **-haut,** *f.* olfactory membrane; **-hirn,** *n.* olfactory lobe.

Riech-hirnrinde, *f.* olfactory cortex; **-hügel,** *m.* postconcha, bulbus olfactorius; **-kegel,** *m.* olfactory cone; **-kolben,** *m.* olfactory bulb; **-lappen,** *m.* olfactory lobe; **-mittel,** *n.* scent, perfume; **-nerv,** *m.* olfactory nerve; **-organ,** *n.* olfactory organ; **-platte,** *f.* olfactory plate; **-röhrchen,** *n.* olfactory tubule.

Riech-säckchen, *n.* olfactory sac; **-salz,** *n.* smelling salts; **-schleimhaut,** *f.* olfactory mucous membrane; **-stoff,** *m.* odoriferous substance, perfume; **-wasser,** *n.* scented water; **-werkzeug,** *n.* olfactory (apparatus) organ; **-wulst,** *f.* olfactory (fold) tubercle.

Ried, *n.* reed, marsh, moor; **-gras,** *n.* reed, sedge (Carex); **-gräser,** *n.pl.* Cyperaceae; **-moor,** *n.* reed marsh.

rief (rufen), called, was calling.

Rief, *m.* carina, ridge.

Riefe, *f.* groove, channel.

riefeln, to channel, cut, groove, rifle, knurl, mill, striate.

Riegel, *m.* bar, bolt, rail, tie, truss, latch.

Riemen, *m.* strap, thong, band, belt, oar; **-blumengewächse,** *n.pl.* Loranthaceae; **-fett,** *n.* belt dressing; **-scheibe,** *f.* pulley.

Ries, *n.* ream.

Riese, *m.***-n,** giant.

Riese, *f.* slide (for timber).

Riesel-feld, *n.* irrigated (sewage) field; **-geschwindigkeit,** *f.* speed of flow; **-höhe,**

f. packing depth; **-jauche,** *f.* sewage (as a fertilizer).

rieseln, to ripple, gush, percolate, trickle, run.

Riesel-schutt, *m.* fine rolling rock debris; **-turm,** *m.* trickling tower; **-wasser,** *n.* irrigation (trickling) water.

riesen, to slide; **-form,** *f.* gigantic form or species; **-kolonie,** *f.* giant colony; **-schilf,** *m.* giant reed (*Arundo donax*); **-schlange,** *f.* python, boa constrictor, anaconda; **-schnaken,** *f.pl.* Tipulidae; **-zelle,** *f.* giant cell.

riesig, gigantic.

riet (raten), advised.

Riff, *n.*-e, reef, ridge, shelf, ledge, carina.

Riffelglas, *n.* holophane glass.

riffeln, to corrugate, rib, ripple, channel, groove.

Riffeltrichter, *m.*-, ribbed funnel.

rigorös, rigorous.

Rille, *f.* furrow, drill, groove, rill, vallecula.

Rillenpflug, *m.* drill plow.

Rillensaat, *f.* sowing in rills.

Rillenzieher, *m.* drill hoe.

Rind, *n.*-er, neat, ox, cow, bovine animal, cattle.

Rinde, *f.* rind, bark, cortex, crust.

rinden-bewohnend, growing on the outer bark; **-borke,** *f.* outer bark, ross; **-brand,** *m.* bark (blister) scorching, frost canker; **-brüter,** *m.* bark hatcher; **-bündelsystem,** *n.* leaf traces or branches; **-farbstoff,** *m.* phlobaphene (coloring matter of bark); **-flechte,** *f.* lichens growing on the bark; **-gewebe,** *n.* cortical tissue; **-grau,** *n.* gray matter of the cortex.

Rinden-grenze, *f.* phloeoterma (innermost layer); **-haut,** *f.* periderm; **-höcker,** *m.* **-höckerchen,** *n.* gibbosity, lenticel; **-käfer,** *m.pl.* bark-destroying beetles; **-korallen,** *f.pl.* fan corals (Gorgoniidae, Octocoralla); **-markstrahl,** *m.* phloem ray; **-netz,** *n.* cortical plexus.

Rinden-pore, *f.* lenticel; **-pfropfen,** *n.* bark grafting; **-saugstrang,** *m.* cortical haustorium (a sucker); **-säure,** *f.* corticinic acid; **-schicht,** *f.* cortical layer; **-stück,** *n.* piece of bark (crust, rind); **-substanz,** *f.* cortical substance; **-wand,** *f.* the cell wall cutting leaf initials from the axis; **-wulst,** *m.* ridge on a stem.

Rinder-bouillon, *f.* beef broth; **-braten,** *m.* roast beef; **-fett,** *n.* beef suet; **-galle,** *f.* ox-

gall; **-klauenöl,** *n.* neat's-foot oil; **-mark-fett,** *n.* beef-marrow fat; **-pest,** *f.* cattle plague; **-talg,** *m.* beef tallow; **-tuberkulose,** *f.* bovine tuberculosis.

Rind-fleisch, *n.* beef; **-fleischbrühe,** *f.* beef broth, beef tea; **-leder,** *n.* neat's leather, cowhide.

Rinds-auge, *n.* oxeye (Buphthalmum); **-klauenfett,** *n.* neat's-foot oil.

Rindspalte, *f.* split cowhide.

Rindstalg, *m.* beef tallow.

Rindvieh, *n.* cattle.

Ring, *m.*-e, ring, annulus, link, band, hoop, loop, coil, collar; **-ähnlich,** ringlike, circular, cyclic, areolar, cricoid, annular; **-alkohol,** *m.* cyclic alcohol; **-amin,** *n.* cyclic amine; **-artig,** ringlike, circular, cyclic, areolar, cricoid, annular; **-aufspaltung,** *f.* ring cleavage; **-bildung,** *f.* ring formation; **-blume,** *f.* Anacyclus; **-brenner,** *m.* ring burner.

Ringel-blume, *f.* marigold (Calendula); **-borke,** *f.* periderm (peeling off in rings).

ringelig, ringlike, annular.

Ringel-klette, *f.* burr; **-krebse,** *m.pl.* Arthrostaca.

ringeln, to ring, curl, girdle.

Ringel-natter, *f.* common grass snake, ring snake; **-spinner,** *n.* annulary caterpillar, lackey moth.

Ringelung, *f.* girdling.

Ringel-walze, *f.* annular (corrugated) roller; **-würmer,** *m.pl.* Annelida.

ringen, to struggle, strive after, wrestle, grapple with, wring, ring, curl.

Ringerlösung, *f.* Ringer's solution.

Ring-erweiterung, *f.* ring extension; **-faser,** *f.* annular fiber; **-faserhaut,** *f.* middle tunic of vessel; **-faserschicht,** *f.* circular layer of fibers; **-feder,** *f.* annular spring; **-förmig,** cyclic, ring-shaped, annular; **-gefäss,** *n.* annual (vessel) xylem element; **-gürtel,** *m.* body segment; **-glied,** *n.* ring member; **-haube,** *f.* cowling ring.

Ring-keton, *n.* cyclic ketone; **-knochen,** *m.* cricoid bone; **-knorpel,** *m.* cricoid cartilage; **-knorpelgelenk,** *n.* cricoid articulation.

Ringlichkeit, *f.* ring formation.

Ring-muskel, *m.* circular muscle; **-ofen,** *m.* annular kiln; **-öffnung,** *f.* ring opening; **-porig,** ring-porous.

rings, around; **-herum,** on all sides.

Ring-saum, *m.* velum; **-schäle,** *f.* internal annular shake, cup shake; **-schicht,** *f.*

annular layer; **-schliessen,** to form a ring; **-schliessung,** *f.* cyclization, ring closure; **-schlundkopfmuskel,** *m.* cricopharyngeus muscle.

ringsgleich, in the same direction, with equal rings.

Ring-spaltung, *f.* ring cleavage; **-spannung,** *f.* ring tension; **-sprengung,** *f.* ring cleavage.

ringsum, around, all around.

Ring-tracheide, *f.* annual element of xylem; **-ungesättigt,** cyclically unsaturated, containing an unsaturated ring; **-verbindung,** *f.* ring (cyclic) compound; **-verkleinerung,** *f.* reduction of a ring; **-zugfestigkeit,** *f.* annular tensile strength; **-zwirn,** *m.* ring twisting.

Rinne, *f.* furrow, groove, channel, gutter, trough, chute, vallecula, sulcus, flange or recurved margin (of proximal barbule).

rinnen, to run, flow, leak, trickle, drip; **-förmig,** groove-shaped canaliculate.

Rinnsal, *n.* rill, watercourse, channel.

Rinnstein, *m.* sink, gutter (stone), culvert.

Rippe, *f.* rib, costa.

rippen, to rib; **gerippt,** ribbed, fluted, corded.

Rippen-ansatz, *m.* base of the rib; **-atmen,** *n.* thoracic (costal) respiration; **-aufheber,** *m.* levator costae; **-band,** *n.* costal ligament; **-brustbeingelenk,** *n.* sternocostal articulation; **-farn,** *m.* Blechnum; **-fell,** *n.* pleura; **-fortsatz,** *m.* costal process; **-furche,** *f.* costal groove; **-gefässe,** *n.pl.* radial canals.

Rippen-gegend, *f.* costal region; **-glas,** *n.* ribbed glass; **-hals,** *m.* neck of the rib; **-haut,** *f.* costal pleura; **-heber,** *m.* levator costae; **-heizrohr,** *n.* heating coil; **-höcker,** *m.* costal tubercle; **-höckergelenk,** *n.* transverse costal articulation; **-knochen,** *m.* bony part of the rib; **-knorpel,** *m.* costal cartilage.

Rippen-knorpelgelenk, *n.* articulation of the costal cartilages; **-pfanne** *f.* costal fossa; **-quallen,** *f. pl.* Ctenophora; **-rinne,** *f.* costal sulcus; **-rohr,** *n.* ribbed pipe or tube; **-trichter,** *m.* ribbed funnel.

Rippen-verbindung, *f.* costal articulation; **-wand,** *f.* costal wall; **-winkel,** *m.* angle of the ribs; **-wirbel,** *m.* costal vertebra; **-zwischenraum,** *m.* intercostal space; **-zylinder,** *m.* ribbed cylinder.

Risigallum, *n.* realgar.

Risiko, *n.* risk.

riskieren, to risk.

Rispe, *f.* panicle, wild oats.

Rispen-äste, *m.pl.* branches of the panicle; **-farne,** *m.pl.* Osmundaceae; **-gras,** *n.* Poa; **-hirse,** *f.* Panicum; **-spindel,** *f.* rachis of panicle.

riss (reissen), tore, was tearing.

Riss, *m.-e,* fissure, crack, flaw, check, shake, rent, cleft, tear, laceration, gap, draft, sketch, design.

Rissebildung, *f.* formation of cracks, fissuring.

rissig, fissured, cracked, flawy, torn, shaky; ~ **werden,** to crack, get brittle.

Rissigkeit, *f.* cracked state or place, faultiness.

Risstelle, *f.* suture of dehiscence, location of crack.

ritt (reiten), rode, was riding.

Ritter, *m.* knight; **-sporn,** *m.* larkspur (Delphinium); **-stern,** *m.* Hippeastrum.

Ritz, *m.* **Ritze,** *f.* scratch, cleft, fissure, rift, chap, crack, chink, slit.

Ritzel, *n.* pinion.

ritzen, to crack, slit, scratch, graze, etch, tear, cut.

Ritzhärte, *f.* hardness to scratching.

Rizin, *n.* ricin.

Robbe, *f.* seal animal.

Robbentran, *m.* seal oil.

roch (riechen), smelled, was smelling.

Rochellesalz, *n.* Rochelle salt, sodium potassium tartrate.

röcheln, to rattle (in throat).

Rochen, *m.* ray, roach.

Rock, *m.-e,* coat, gown, robe, skirt, frock, dress.

Rodehacke, *f.* mattock, grub hoe.

Rodeland, *n.* clearing, virgin soil.

roden, to root out, grub, clear.

Rodewerkzeug, *n.* grubbing implement.

Rodung, *f.* uprooting, grubbing.

Rogen, *m.* roe, spawn; **-stein,** *m.* oölite; **-steinartig,** oölitic.

Roggen, *m.* rye; **-brot,** *n.* rye bread; **-kleber,** *m.* rye gluten; **-mehl,** *n.* rye flour; **-mutter,** *f.* ergot; **-saatgut,** *n.* rye seed; **-stärke,** *f.* rye starch; **-stengelbrand,** *m.* flat (stripe) smut of rye.

roh, raw, crude, rough, coarse, in native state, gross; **-arbeit,** *f.* ore smelting; **-benzol,** *n.* crude benzene; **-blende,** *f.*

raw blende, crude mix or glance; **-boden-pflanze,** *f.* plant growing on virgin soil; **-breite,** *f.* grège width; **-chlorophyllösung,** *f.* crude chlorophyll extract.

Roheisen, *n.* crude iron, pig iron; **-gans,** *f.* (iron) pig; **-guss,** *m.* pig-iron casting.

Roheit, *f.* crudity.

Roh-ertrag, *m.* **-ze,** gross yield, total revenue; **-erz,** *n.* raw ore; **-erzeugnis,** *n.* raw product; **-faser,** *f.* crude fiber; **-faser-bestimmung,** *f.* determination of crude fiber; **-fett,** *n.* brute fat; **-formel,** *f.* empirical formula; **-frischen,** *n.* first refining; **-frischperiode,** *f.* boil, boiling stage; **-frucht,** *f.* unmalted grain, unprocessed produce.

Roh-gang, *m.* irregular (cold) working; **-gar,** partly refined; **-gegossen** (giessen), crude-cast; **-geschmack,** *m.* raw taste; **-gewicht,** *n.* gross weight; **-gift,** *n.* crude toxin; **-gummi,** *n.* crude rubber; **-haut,** *f.* rawhide.

Roh-humus, *m.* raw humus; **-humusboden,** *m.* virgin humus soil; **-kautschuk,** *m.* raw rubber; **-kohle,** *f.* rough coal, run of mine; **-kost,** *f.* uncooked food; **-kultur,** *f.* cultivation of virgin soil, impure culture; **-kupfer,** *n.* crude copper; **-mallein,** *n.* crude mallein; **-material,** *n.* raw material; **-messing,** *n.* crude brass.

Roh-naphtha, *f.* crude petroleum; **-ofen,** *m.* ore furnace; **-öl,** *n.* crude petroleum; **-paraffin,** *n.* crude paraffin; **-phosphat,** *m.* rock phosphate; **-probe,** *f.* crude sample; **-produkt,** *n.* raw product; **-protein,** crude protein.

Rohr, *n.***-e,** tube, pipe, reed, cane, flue, canal, barrel; **-ammer,** *f.* reed bunting; **-ansatz,** *m.* connecting tube; **-artig,** reedlike, arundinaceous.

Röhrbein, *n.* shank bone, cannon bone.

Rohr-bogen, *m.* tube turn, ell; **-brunnen,** *m.* artesian well, cased well; **-bürste,** *f.* tube brush.

Röhrchen, *n.* little test tube or pipe, tubule, cane, reed; **-pilz,** *m.* toadstool, mushroom.

Rohrdommel, *f.* bittern.

Röhre, *f.* tube, pipe, reed, nozzle, funnel, spout, channel, lumen, duct, conduit, shaft, tunnel.

röhren-artig, tubular, fistular; **-belastung,** *f.* charge on the tube; **-bewohnend,** tube dwelling; **-blatt,** *n.* tubular leaf; **-blumig,** tubiflorous; **-blüte,** *f.* tubular flower; **-bürste,** *f.* tube brush; **-förmig,** tubular, fistular; **-glied,** *n.* tube segment; **-halter,** *m.* tube or pipe (holder).

Röhren-kassie, *f.* purging cassia; **-kiemer,** *m.pl.* Tubularia; **-klemme,** *f.* tube clamp: **-knochen,** *m.* long hollow bone; **-körper,** *m.* tube substance or assembly; **-libelle,** *f.* air (spirit) level; **-lot,** *n.* pipe solder; **-manna,** *f.* flake manna; **-nudeln,** *f.pl.* macaroni; **-ofen,** *m.* pipe still, tube, heater.

Röhren-pilz, *m.* Boletus; **-polypen,** *m.pl.* Tubularia; **-pulver,** *n.* perforated powder; **-quallen,** *f.pl.* Siphonophora; **-spannung,** *f.* tube voltage; **-substanz,** *f.* medullary substance.

Röhren-träger, *m.* tube support; **-werk,** *n.* tubing, piping; **-wischer,** *m.* tube brush; **-würmer,** *m.pl.* Sedentaria, Tubicolae; **-zahn,** *m.* solenoglyphic or tubular tooth (of snakes); **-zellen,** *f.pl.* tracheids (in wood).

rohr-förmig, tubular; **-glanzgras,** *n.* ribbon grass (*Phalaris arundinacea*).

röhrig, tubular, fistular.

Rohrkolben, *m.* cattail (Typha); **-gewächse,** *n.pl.* Typhaceae; **-hirse,** *f.* Pennisetum.

Röhrlinge, *m.pl.* Boletaceae (fleshy tubular fungi).

Rohr-kopfgasolin, *n.* casinghead gasoline; **-leitung,** *f.* tubing, piping, pipe line; **-pulver,** *n.* tubular powder; **-schellen-verbindung,** *f.* sleeve joint of tubing; **-schlange,** *f.* coil, worm, spiral tube; **-schnecken,** *f.pl.* Scaphopoda; **-siel,** *n.* pipe culvert; **-stamm,** *m.* cane, reed; **-stammgebüsch,** *n.* cane or reed thicket; **-sumpf,** *m.* reed swamp.

Rohr-wandung, *f.* wall of the pipe; **-weite,** *f.* bore of a tube or pipe; **-werk,** *n.* tubing, tube mill; **-zange,** *f.* pipe wrench.

Rohrzucker, *m.* saccharose, sucrose, cane sugar; **-saft,** *m.* cane juice; **-verbindung,** *f.* cane-sugar compound.

Roh-saft, *m.* crude sap; **-schlacke,** *f.* raw (ore) slag; **-schmelzen,** *n.* ore smelting; **-schwefel,** *m.* crude sulphur; **-seide,** *f.* raw silk; **-soda,** *f.* crude soda, black ash; **-sole,** *f.* crude brine.

Roh-spiritus, *m.* crude spirit; **-stahl,** *m.* natural steel; **-stein,** *m.* coarse metal; **-stoff,** *m.* raw material; **-sulfat,** *n.* crude sulphate; **-ton,** *m.* grège color; **-wolle,** *f.* raw wool; **-zucker,** *m.* raw (unrefined) sugar.

Roll-bein, *n.* trochlea; **-blatt,** *n.* revolute leaf.

Rolle, *f.* roll, roller, register, caster, pulley, trochlea, calender, reel, spool, role, part.

rollen, to roll, rotate, calender; **-artig,** cylindrical, trochlear; **-förmig,** cylindrical, trochlear; **-gelagert,** mounted on roller bearings; **-lager,** *n.* roller bearing; **-zug,** *m.* block and tackle.

Roll-farn, *m.* Allosurus; **-flasche,** *f.* narrow-necked cylindrical bottle; **-fortsatz,** *m.* trochanter; **-gelenk,** *n.* pivot joint; **-grube,** *f.* trochlear fossa; **-hügel,** *m.* trochanter.

Roll-muskel, *m.* trochlear muscle, rotator muscle; **-röhrchen,** *n.* roll culture; **-rüssel,** *m.* glossa; **-scheibe,** *f.* patella; **-schicht,** *f.* upright course (of bricks set on end); **-stein,** *m.* boulder; **-treppe,** *f.* escalator.

Rollung, *f.* curvature, roll, volution.

Rollwagen, *m.* truck, lorry.

Roman, *m.* novel, romance.

römisch, Roman.

römische Kamille, Roman camomile.

römischer Kümmel, cumin.

römische Minze, spearmint.

rönne (rinnen), would run, ran, runs.

Röntgen-anlage, *f.* X-ray laboratory; **-bild,** *n.* exograph; **-röhre,** *f.* Roentgen (X-ray) tube; **-strahlen,** *m.pl.* X rays, Roentgen rays.

Rosa, *n.* pink, rose (color).

rosa, -farben, -farbig, rose(colored), pink; **-hefe,** *f.* pink yeast.

rösch, brittle, coarse, hard baked or roasted.

röschen, to age or cure, dig a trench.

Rösch-erz, -gewächs, *n.* brittle silver ore, stephanite.

Röschheit, *f.* freeness (in papermaking).

Rose, *f.* rose, rosette, burr, erysipelas.

Rosen-blatt, *n.* rose leaf; **-essenz,** *f.* attar of roses; **-farbe,** *f.* rose color; **-geruch,** *m.* rose odor; **-gewächse,** *n.pl.* Rosaceae; **-holz,** *n.* rosewood; **-honig,** *m.* honey of rose; **-kamm,** *m.* rose comb; **-kohl,** *m.* Brussels sprouts; **-konserve,** *f.* confection of rose.

Rosen-kranz, *m.*-e, rosary, rose garland; **-kranzförmig,** moniliform, streptococcus form, rosarylike; **-lack,** *m.* rose lake; **-lorbeer,** *m.* oleander, mountain rose; **-öl,** *n.* oil (attar) of roses; **-rot,** rose-red, pink; **-schwamm,** *m.* bedeguar, rose gall, **-spat,** *m.* rhodochrosite; **-stock,** *m.* rosebush, base of antlers; **-wasser,** *n.* rose water; **-zweig,** *m.* rose twig.

rosetten-artig, like a rosette; **-gewächse,** *n.pl.* rosette plants; **-kupfer,** *n.* rosette copper; **-staude,** *f.,* **-träger,** *m.* rosette plant.

rosettieren, to make rosette copper.

rosieren, to dye pink or rose.

Rosiersalz, *n.* rose salt, tin composition.

rosig, rosy, rosacic.

Rosine, *f.* raisin.

Rosmarin, *m.* rosemary; **-öl,** *n.* rosemary oil; **-weide,** *f.* Itea.

Rosolsäure, *f.* rosolic acid.

Ross, *n.* horse, steed; **-farn,** *m.* Allosorus; **-fenchel,** *m.* Phellandrium; **-huf,** *m.* coltsfoot (*Tussilago farfara*); **-kastanie,** *f.* horse chestnut; **-kastaniengewächse,** *n.pl.* Hippocastanaceae; **-schwefel,** *m.* sulphur vivum, horse brimstone; **-wurzel,** *f.* carline thistle, carline root.

Rost, *m.* -e rust, smut, mildew, roasting charge, grate, gridiron; liegender ∼, spread footing.

Röst-abgang, *m.* loss (of weight) due to roasting; **-arbeit,** *f.* roasting process: **-betriebsdauer,** *f.* roasting time.

Rostbildung, *f.* rust formation.

Röstbitter, *n.* assamar.

Rost-brand, *m.* rust, mildew, smut; **-braun,** rusty brown.

Röste, *f.* roasting (place), roasting charge, retting, steeping, rettery.

rosten, to rust.

rösten, to roast, torrefy, ret, steep, broil, grill, calcine.

Rösten, *n.* retting.

Rostentfernung, *f.* rust removal.

Röster, *m.* roaster; **-zeugnis,** *n.* product of roasting.

Röst-erzeugnis, *n.* product of roasting.

Rost-farbe, *f.* rust color; **-fläche,** *f.* grate surface; **-fleckig,** rust-spotted, rust-stained; **-frei,** stainless (steel).

Röstgas, *n.*-e, gas from roasting.

Rostgelb, *n.* a buff pigment.

rostgelb, rusty yellow.

Röst-gummi, *n.* dextrin; **-gut,** *n.* roasted material, roasting charge.

rostig, rusty, corroded; **-werden,** *n.* russeting; **-kitt,** *m.* iron-rust cement.

Rostkitt, *m.* iron-rust cement.

Röst-kufe, *f.* retting vat; **-malz,** *n.* roasted malt, black malt.

Rostmittel, *n.* rust preventive.

Röstofen, *m.* roasting (furnace) kiln.

Rostpilz, *m.* rust.

Röst-posten, *m.* roasting charge; **-probe,** *f.* calcination test; **-prozess,** *m.* roasting (calcination) process; **-rückstand,** *m.* residue from roasting; **-scherben,** *m.* roasting dish; **-schlacke,** *f.* slag from roasting.

Röst-schmelzen, *n.* roasting and smelting; **-schutz,** *m.* protection against rust; **-schützend,** rust-preventing; **-schutzmittel,** *n.* antirust agent; **-sicher,** rustproof; **-staub,** *m.* dust of roasted ore.

Röstung, *f.* roasting, calcination, retting.

Röstverfahren, *n.* roasting process.

rostverhütend, rust-preventing.

Röst-verlust, *m.* loss from roasting; **-vorrichtung,** *f.* roasting apparatus; **-wasser,** *n.* steeping water; **-zuschlag,** *m.* flux for roasting.

Rot, *n.* red, rouge; **-algen,** *f.pl.* red algae (Rhodophyceae).

rot, red.

Rotangpalme, *f.* rattan (palm) (Calamus).

Rotation, *f.* rotation, revolution.

Rotations-achse, *f.* axis of rotation; **-bewegung,** *f.* rotary motion; **-frei,** irrotational.

Rot-auge, *n.*-n, roach, redeye, rudd (Leuciscus); **-beize,** *f.* red (mordant) liquor; **-blau,** reddish blue; **-bleierz,** *n.* red-lead ore; **-bleispat,** *n.* red-lead ore; **-braun,** red-brown; **-braunsteinerz,** *n.* rhodonite; **-bruch,** *m.* red-shortness; **-brüchig,** red-short; **-buche,** *f.* red beech.

rotbunt, red and white.

Röte, *f.* redness, red, madder, blush.

Roteiche, *f.* red oak.

Roteisen-erz, *n.* red iron ore, hematite; **-ocker,** *m.* red-iron ocher, earthy hematite; **-stein,** *m.* red iron ore, hematite.

Rötel, *m.* red ocher, ruddle.

Röteln, *f.pl.* German measles, rubella.

röten, to redden, remove coarse bark.

rötend, rubefacient.

Roterle, *f.* red alder (*Alnus glutinosa*).

Rotesche, *f.* red ash.

rot-färben, to color red; **-farbig,** red-colored; **-färbung,** *f.* red coloration, red color; **-fäule,** *f.* red rot; **-feuer,** *n.* red fire; **-fichte,** *f.* red spruce; **-gar,** tanned (to a russet color); **-gelb,** orange, reddish yellow; **-gerben,** to tan; **-gerber,** *m.* tanner.

Rot-giesser, *m.* red caster, brazier; **-glühen,** to heat to redness; **-glühend,** glowing red, red-hot; **-glühhitze,** *f.* red heat.

Rotglut, *f.* red heat; **bei beginnender** ∼, at the start of red heat.

Rot-gültigerz, *n.* red silver ore; **-guss,** *m.* red brass; **-hirsch,** *m.* red deer, stag; **-hitze,** *f.* red heat; **-holz,** *n.* redwood; **-huhn,** *n.* red partridge.

rotieren, to rotate.

rotierend, rotating, rotary.

Rot-kehlchen, *n.* robin; **-kiefer,** *f.* red pine, Norway pine; **-klee,** *m.* red clover; **-kohl,** *m.* red cabbage; **-kohle,** *f.* red charcoal; **-kupfer,** *n.* red copper (ore); **-kupfererz,** *n.* red copper (ore); **-lauf,** *m.* erysipelas.

rötlich, reddish; **-braun,** reddishbrown.

Rotliegendes, *n.* lower new red sandstone.

rotmachend, rubefacient.

Rot-nickelkies, *m.* niccolite; **-ocker,** *m.* red ocher; **-rauschgelb,** *n.* realgar; **-salz,** *n.* sodium acetate; **-säure,** *f.* erythric acid; **-schwanz,** *m.* tussock moth; **-schwingel,** *m.* Festuca rubra; **-silber,** *n.* red silver ore; **-silbererz,** *n.* red silver ore; **-spat,** *m.* rhodonite.

Rot-spiessglanz(erz), *n.* kermesite; **-stein,** *m.* red ocher, ruddle, red brick; **-tanne,** *f.* red fir, Norway spruce.

Rotte, *f.* retting, party, troop, band, gang.

rotten, to ret or steep.

Rotten-feuer, *n.* volley; **-führer,** *m.* head workman.

Rottmeister, *m.* logging boss.

Rötung, *f.* reddening, red tint.

Rot-verschiebung, *f.* displacement toward the red; **-wein,** *m.* red wine; **-wild,** *n.* red deer.

Rotz, *m.* glanders; **-bazillus,** *m.* glanders bacillus; **-krank,** infected with glanders; **-krankheit,** *f.* glanders; **-lyphe,** *f.* mallein; **-pilz,** *m.* glanders bacillus.

Rübe, *f.* (rote), beet, beetroot; (gelbe), carrot; (weisse), turnip, rape.

Rüben-asche, *f.* beet ashes; **-bau,** *m.* cultivation of turnips or beetroot; **-beizen,** *n.* beet-seed disinfection; **-blattwespe,** *f.* turnip sawfly (Athalia spinarum); **-brei,** *m.* beet pulp; **-breiapparat,** *m.* root pulper; **-distel,** *f.* Swiss knapweed (*Rhaponticum cynaroides*); **-essig,** *m.* beet(root) vinegar; **-förmig,** turnip-shaped, napiform; **-land,** *n.* land where beets are cultivated.

Rüben-melasse, *f.* beet(root) molasses; **-pottasche,** *f.* potash from beetroot molasses; **-rohzucker,** *m.* raw beet sugar; **-saft,** *m.* beet(root) juice; **-samen,** *m.* turnip, rape, beet, or carrot seed; **-schlempe,** *f.* beet vinasse; **-schnitzel,** *m.* beet (chip) slice; **-spiritus,** *m.* beet spirit; **-stecher,** *m.* beet sampler; **-wurzelbrand,** *m.* root rot of beets.

Rübenzucker, *m.* beet(root) sugar; **-fabrik,** *f.* beet-sugar factory; **-industrie,** *f.* beet-sugar industry.

Rubeolen, *pl.* German measles, rubella.

Rubidium-alaun, *m.* rubidium alum; **-chlorid,** *n.* rubidium chloride; **-jodid,** *n.* rubidium iodide.

Rubin, *m.* ruby; **-balas,** *m.* balas ruby, ruby spinel; **-blende,** *f.* pyrargyrite; **-farbe,** *f.* ruby color, ruby; **-fluss,** *m.* ruby glass; **-glas,** *n.* ruby glass; **-glimmer,** *m.* gothite; **-granat,** *m.* rock ruby; **-rot,** ruby-red, ruby.

Rüböl, *n.* rape(seed) oil; **-kuchen,** *m.* rapeseed cake.

Rubrik, *f.* heading, column.

Rübsen, *m.* rapeseed *(Brassica rapus);* **-öl,** *n.* rape(seed) oil.

Ruchgras, *n.* (sweet) vernal grass *(Anthoxanthum odoratum).*

ruchlos, scentless, vicious, malicious, wicked, nefarious.

Ruck, *m.-e,* jerk, jolt, sudden, push, tug, shock; **-artig,** jerky.

rück, back, backward; **-ansicht,** *f.* rear view; **-bilden,** to form again, re-form, undergo involution; **-bildung,** *f.* involution, retrogressive metamorphosis; **-bildungsalter,** *n.* age of retrogression; **-blick,** *m.* retrospect; **-druck,** *m.* reaction (pressure).

rücken, to move, bring nearer, push, pull, transport, stir, proceed, haul, skid.

Rücken, *m.-,* back, rear, dorsum, ridge; **-ader,** *f.* dorsal vein; **-ast,** *m.* dorsal branch; **-band,** *n.* dorsal ligament; **-bein,** *n.* backbone, spine; **-cirrus,** *m.* dorsal cirrus; **-decke,** *f.* dorsal surface; **-dreher,** *m.* spinal rotator; **-feld,** *n.* dorsal field; **-fell,** *n.* pleura.

Rücken-fläche, *f.* dorsal surface; **-flosse,** *f.* dorsal fin; **-furche,** *f.* dorsal groove; **-gefäss,** *n.* dorsal vessel; **-gegend,** *f.* dorsal region; **-gelenk,** *n.* vertebral articulation; **-haut,** *f.* dorsal pleura, skin of the back.

Rücken-kamm, *m.* comb of spines; **-kieme,** *f* dorsal gill; **-knickung,** *f.* dorsal flexure;

-kreuz, *n.* lumbar region; **-lage,** *f.* dorsal position; **-lehne,** *f.* back (of chair); **-linie,** *f.* dorsal line; **-mark,** *n.* spinal cord.

Rückenmarks-haut, *f.* membrane (meninx) of the spinal cord; **-hülle,** *f.* membrane (meninx) of the spinal cord; **-kanal,** *m.* spinal canal; **-loch,** *n.* vertebral foramen; **-masse,** *f.* mass of the spinal cord, spinal marrow (cord); **-nerv,** *m.* spinal nerve; **-rinde,** *f.* cortical substance of spinal cord; **-strang,** *m.* tract of spinal cord.

Rücken-mund, *m.* dorsal mouth; **-muskel,** *m.* muscle of the back; **-naht,** *f.* back seam, dorsal suture; **-panzer,** *m.* dorsal shield, carapace; **-platte,** *f.* dorsal plate, tergum, notum, tergite; **-saite,** *f.* chorda dorsalis; **-säule,** *f.* vertebral column; **-schiene,** *f.* tergite; **-schild,** *m.* clypeus, scutellum, carapace; **-schulp,** *m.* cuttlebone; **-seite,** *f.* back, hinder part, rear, dorsal side.

Rücken-ständig, dorsal; **-strang,** *m.* dorsal cord, marginal cord; **-tafel,** *f.* dorsal plate; **-weh,** *n.* lumbago; **-winkel,** *m.* dorsal angle; **-wirbel,** *m.* dorsal vertebra; **-wölbung,** *f.* dorsal curvature; **-wurzelig,** incumbent, notorrhizal; **-zapfen,** *m.* dorsal cone.

Rück-erinnerung, *f.* reminiscence; **-fahrt,** *f.* return journey; **-fall,** *m.* relapse, return, reversion; **-fliessend,** flowing back, reflux.

Rückfluss, *m.* reflux; **-kühler,** *m.* reflux condenser.

Rück-führung, *f.* follow-up device, restoring mechanism; **-gang,** *m.-e,* return, retrogression, relapse, decline, backstroke; **-gängig,** retrograde, declining, retrogressive, null and void; **-gebildet,** degenerate; **-gewinnung,** *f.* recovery, regeneration; **-grat,** *m.* vertebral column, spine.

Rückgrats-band, *n.* spinal ligament; **-bein,** *n.* vertebra; **-flur,** *f.* spinal tract; **-gelenk,** *n.* vertebral articulation; **-höhle,** *f.* vertebral canal; **-krümmung,** *f.* curvature of the spine; **-rain,** *m.* apterium spinale; **-strecker,** *m.* erector muscle of back; **-wirbel,** *m.* vertebra.

Rückhalt, *m.* support, stay, restraint, reserve; **-los,** unreserved, openly, plainly.

Rück-holvorrichtung, *f.* reset device; **-infektion,** *f.* reinfection; **-kehr,** *f.* return; **-kohlung,** *f.* recarbonization; **-kreuzung,** *f.* backcrossing; **-kühlanlage,** *f.* (re)cooling plant; **kunft,** *f.* return; **-lauf,** *m.* recoil; **-laufend, -läufig,** recurrent, retrograde.

Rück-laufzylinder, *m.* recoil cylinder; **-leiter,** *m.* return (conductor) wire; **-leitung,** *f.* return line.

rücklings, backward.

Rück-prall, *m.* rebound, recoil; **-saugung,** *f.* absorption, sucking back; **-schau,** *f.* review, retrospect.

Rückschlag, *m.*-̈e, striking back, backstroke, check, setback, rebound, recoil, return, reverberation, atavism; **-bildung,** *f.* atavism; **-hemmung,** *f.* prevention of (striking back) backfiring; **-ventil,** *n.* nonreturn valve, check valve.

Rück-schluss, *m.*-̈e, inference, conclusion; **-schnitt,** *m.* cutback; **-schreitend,** retrogressive, retrograde; **-schritt,** *m.* backward movement, recession, retrogression, relapse; **-seite,** *f.* back, wrong side, reverse.

Rücksicht, *f.*-en, regard, respect, consideration, motive; **mit ∼ auf,** with regard to, in consideration of.

rücksicht-lich, with regard to; **-nahme,** *f.* consideration.

rücksichtslos, relentless, inconsiderate.

Rück-sprache, *f.* consultation, conference; **-stand,** *m.* residue, sediment, refuse, distillate, remains, arrears, waste, scale; **-ständig,** residual, residuary, in arrears, overdue, outstanding, dorsal, backwards; **-standsgewicht,** *n.* weight of residue; **-stein,** *m.* back stone, crucible bottom; **-stoss,***m.* backstroke, recoil; **-stossmotor,** *m.* jet-propulsion motor; **-strahlkopie,***f.* reflex print; **-strahlung,** *f.* reflection; **-strahlverfahren,** *n.* back-reflection method; **-streuung,** *f.* scattering (of X-rays).

Rück-strom, *m.* reverse (return) current; **-stülpung,** *f.* retraction, reduction; **-treiben,** to drive back; **-tritt,** *m.* retreat, retrogression, resignation, retirement; **-titrieren,** *n.* back titration; **-umwandlung, -verwandlung,** *f.* reversion, reconversion, retransformation; **-verwitterung,** *f.* backward (secondary) erosion; **-wand,** *f.* back wall, rear wall.

rückwärts, backward, back; **-beuger,** *m.* supinator muscle; **-dreher,** *m.* supinator muscle; **-gang,** *m.* back motion; **-gekrümmt,** bent backward, retroverted; **-wender,** *m.* supinator muscle.

Rückweg, *m.* return route, way back.

ruckweise, by jerks, intermittently.

rück-wirken, to react; **-wirkend,** reacting, retroactive, reciprocal, reactive; **-wirkung,** *f.* reaction, retroaction; **-zieher,** *m.* re-

tractor muscle; **-zug,** *m.* retreat, return; **-zündung,** *f.* backfire.

Rüde, *m.* male (of dogs, foxes, etc.).

rude, rough, coarse, vulgar.

Rudel, *n.* flock, crowd, herd, stirring pole.

Ruder, *n.* oar, rudder, helm; **-flosse,** *f.* fin for steering; **-fuss,** *m.* totipalmate leg, pes steganus; **-füssler,** *m.pl.* Copepoda.

rudern, to row, paddle.

Ruder-organ, *n.* swimming foot; **-plättchen,** *n.pl.* combs (Ctenophora); **-schwanz,** *m.* swimming tail; **-schwänzchen,** *n.* vibratile tail.

rudimentär, rudimentary.

Ruf, *m.*-e, call, calling, cry, shout, report, rumor, reputation.

rufen, to call.

Ruhbütte, *f.* storage vat.

Ruhe, *f.* rest, repose, quiet, silence, peace, stagnation, recreation; **-alkinet,** *m.* resting cell; **-bedürfnis,** *n.* rest requirement; **-haltung,** *f.* position at rest; **-lage,** *f.* position of rest.

ruhen, to rest, repose, sleep; **∼ auf,** to be supported by.

ruhend, resting, latent, stagnant, static.

Ruhe-pulver, *n.* sedative power; **-punkt,** *m.* point of rest, center of gravity, fulcrum, pause; **-spannung,** *f.* voltage on open circuit; **-stadium,** *n.* rest, encystment; **-stand,** *m.* retirement; **-stoffwechsel,** *m.* resting metabolism; **-stromelement,** *n.* closed-circuit cell; **-system,** *n.* static system; **-umsatz,** *m.* resting metabolism; **-winkel,** *m.* angle of repose; **-zustand,** *m.* state of rest, dormancy.

ruhig, at rest, quiet, still, calm, serene, cool.

Ruhm, *m.* glory, praise, fame, reputation.

Ruhmasse, *f.* rest (static) mass.

rühmen, to commend, extol, praise, glorify; **sich ∼,** (*gen.*) boast, pride oneself.

Ruhmesblume, *f.* Clianthus.

ruhmvoll, illustrious, famous.

Ruhr, *f.* dysentery, turning up the soil.

Rührapparat, *m.* stirring apparatus, agitator, stirrer.

Ruhrbazillen, *m.pl.* dysentery bacilli.

Rühreisen, *n.* poker, iron stirrer.

rühren, to stir, move, beat, touch, strike, agitate.

Rührer, *m.* stirrer, stirring rod.

Rühr-fass, *n.* churn; **-flügel,** *m.* mashing oar, scoop; **-form,***f.* form of stirrer; **-haken,**

m. rake, rabble; **-holz,** *n.* wooden stirrer, paddle.

rührig, stirring, busy, active, alert, nimble, agile.

Rührkrücke, *f.* stirring crutch.

Ruhr-mittel, *n.* remedy for dysentery; **-rinde,** *f.* Simarouba bark.

Rühr-scheit, *n.* paddle, spatula; **-spatel,** *m.* stirring spatula; **-stab,** *m.* stirring rod; **-stativ,** *n.* stirring stand.

Rührung, *f.* stirring, emotion, feeling, compassion.

Rührwerk, *n.* stirrer, stirring apparatus, agitator.

Ruhrwurzel, *f.-n,* tormentil root, ipecac, calumba.

Rührzeit, *f.-en,* time of stirring.

Ruinenmarmor, *m.* marble ruins.

Rujaholz, *n.* young fustic, Venetian sumac wood.

Rüllöl, *n.* cameline oil.

Rum-äther, *m.* rum ether; **-brennerei,** *f.* rum distillery.

rumpeln, to rumble, rattle.

Rumpf, *m.* body, torso, hull, stump, stalk; **-abschnitt,** *m.* truck section; **-amnionhöhle,** *f.* trunk amniotic cavity; **-beine,** *n.pl.,* **-gliedmassen,** *n.pl.* body legs, thoracopods, pleopods; **-höhle,** *f.* cavity of the trunk.

Rumpf-keim, *m.* trunk term; **-knochen,** *m.pl.* the bones of the trunk; **-ladung,** *f.* body charge; **-länge,** *f.* length of trunk; **-segment,** *n.* body segment or somite; **-seiternraine,** *m.pl.* apteria trunci lateralia; **-skelett,** *n.* axial skeleton.

Rumsprit, *m.* double rum.

rund, round, about, approximately, even (of numbers); **-blättrig,** rotundifolious, round-leaved; **-brecher,** *m.* gyratory crusher; **-brenner,** *m.* ring burner; **-eisen,** *n.* round iron, rod iron.

runderhaben, convex.

Rund-faser, *f.-n,* round fiber (tracheid); **-feile,** *f.* round file; **-flasche,** *f.* round flask; **-funk,** *m.* (radio) broadcasting; **-funksender,** *m.* radio transmitter; **-hohl,** concave; **-holz,** *n.* round (log) timber; **-kolben,** *m.* round-bottomed flask; **-kopfschraube,** *f.* roundhead screw; **-krabben,** *f.pl.* Oxystomata.

rundlich, roundish.

Rund-mäuler, *pl.* Cyclostomata; **-reise,** *f.* round trip, circuit; **-schlüssel,** *m.* hollow key; **-schreiben,** *n.* circular letter; **-schuppe,** *f.* cycloid fish scale; **-stuhl,** *m.* circular knitting machine.

rundweg, plainly, roundly, bluntly, flatly.

Rundwurm, *m.* roundworm (Ascaris).

Runkel-rübe, *f.* beet, beetroot, red beet; **-rübenzucker,** *m.* beet(root) sugar.

Runse, *f.* rivulet, rill, gully, ravine.

Runzel, *f.* wrinkle, fold, rumple; **-bildung,** *f.* shriveling, festooning; **-blatt,** *n.* wrinkled, corrugated, or xerophytic leaf; **-korn,** *n.* distorted grain effect.

runz(e)lig, rugose, wrinkled, puckered, shriveled.

Runzelschorf, *m.* scab, tar-spot disease.

rupfen, to pluck, pick, pull.

Rupffestigkeit, *f.* resistance to pick test.

Ruprechtskraut, *n.* herb Robert (*Geranium robertianum*).

Rusaöl, *n.* ginger-grass oil.

Russ, *m.* soot, lampblack, carbon black, rust; **-artig,** sootlike, fuliginous; **-bildung,** *f.* soot formation; **-braun,** *n.* bister; **-brennerei,** *f.* manufacture of lampback.

Rüssel, *m.* nose, snout, rostrum, nozzle, trunk, proboscis, beak, sucking tube, haustellum; **-artig,** proboscidiform; **-drüse,** *f.* proboscis gland; **-egel,** *m.* jawed leech; **-furche,** *f.* proboscis groove; **-hufer,** *m.pl.* Proboscidae; **-käfer,** *m.pl.* weevils, snout beetles (Curculionidae); **-labellen,** *f.pl.* labial palpi; **-scheide, -tasche,** *f.* proboscis sheath; **-tier,** *n.* proboscidian.

russen, to soot, smut, blacken, to smoke (lamp).

russend, sooty, smoky.

Russfarbe, *f.* bister.

russig, sooty, fuliginous.

Russ-kobalt, *m.* asbolite; **-schwarz,** *n.* lampblack; **-tau,** *m.* sooty mold.

rüsten, to prepare, equip, furnish, mobilize.

Rüster, *f.* elm; **-rinde,** *f.* elm bark.

rüstig, vigorous, robust, hale, active.

Rüstmaterial, *n.* scaffold material.

Rüstung, *f.* preparation, equipment, armament, utensils, scaffolding, armature.

Rüstzeug, *n.* set of tools, implements, crane, scaffolding.

Rute, *f.* rod, measure (16½ ft.), wand, birch, pole, penis, brush (tail).

ruten-förmig, rod-shaped, virgate, twiggy; **-krankheit,** *f.* cane disease; **-spross,** *m.* slender leafy shoot; **-sterben,** *n.* dieback of canes.

Ruthenium-oxyd, *n.* ruthenium oxide; **-oxydul,** *n.* ruthenium monoxide; **-verbindung,** *f.* ruthenium compound.

Rutsche, *f.* shoot, chute, slide, fall.

rutschen, to slide, slip, glide.

Rutschung, *f.* slide.

Rutschpulver, *n.* talc powder.

Rüttelbewegung, *f.* shaking motion.

rütteln, to shake, jolt, vibrate.

Rüttlung, *f.* shaking, vibration.

S

Saal, *m.* Säle, hall, assembly room.

Saat, *f.*-en, seed, sowing; **-beet,** *n.* seedbed; **-beizmittel,** *n.* seed disinfectant.

Saatenanerkennung, *f.* seed certification.

Saat-erbse, *f.* field pea (*Pisum arvense*); **-eule,** *f.* dark moth (*Agrotis segetum*); **-gans,** *f.* bean goose (*Anser segetum*); **-getreide,** *n.* cereal seed; **-gitter,** *n.* lath screen, wire netting for seedbeds.

Saatgut, *n.* seed; **-beize,** *f.* seed disinfection, seed steep; **-krankheit,** *f.* seed-borne disease; **-veredelung,** *f.* improvement of seed grain.

Saat-hammer, *m.* dibbling mallet; **-horn,** *n.* seed horn, sowing drill; **-kamp,** *m.* nursery; **-korn,** *n.* single seed; **-landliebend** segetalis, growing in grain fields; **-latte,** *f.* seed lath; **-rille,** *f.* seed drill, line of seedlings; **-schnellkäfer,** *m.* spring or click beetle (*Agriotes lineatus*); **-schule,** *f.* nursery; **-schulpflanze,** *f.* nursery-grown plant.

Saat-wicke, *f.* vetch (common) tare (*Vicia sativa*); **-wucherblume,** *f.* corn marigold (*Chrysanthemum segetum*); **-zeit,** *f.* sowing season.

Sabadillsamen, *m.* sabadilla seeds.

Säbel, *m.* saber, sword; **-förmig,** sabershaped, ensiform, scimitar-shaped; **-kolben,** *m.* sausage flask.

Sabinerbaum, *m.* savin.

Saccharin, *n.* saccharin.

saccharoidisch, saccharoid, saccharoidal.

Sache, *f.* affair, matter, concern, subject, thing, object, cause, article, case.

Sach-gebiet, *n.* department of knowledge, subject; **-gemäss,** appropriate, pertinent, serviceable; **-kenner,** *m.* expert; **-kenntnis,** *f.* expert knowledge, experience; **-kundig,** experienced, expert, versed; **-lage,** *f.* state of affairs, circumstance.

sachlich, real, positive, objective, essential, material, technical.

Sachlichkeit, *f.* objectivity, reality.

Sachregister, *n.* index, table of contents.

sacht(e), soft, gentle, light, easy, cautiously, gradually.

Sach-verhalt, *m.* state of affairs; **-verhältnis,** *n.* state of affairs; **-verständig,** experienced, versed; **-verständiger,** *m.* expert, authority; **-verzeichnis,** *n.* subject index; **-walter,** *m.* legal adviser, counsel, attorney; **-wörterbuch,** *n.* encyclopedia.

Sack, *m.*-̈e, bag, sack, pocket, sac, cyst, pouch; **-artig,** cystlike, pouchlike; **-band,** *n.* bag string, sack tie.

Säckel, *m.* purse, little bag; **-blume,** *f.* Ceanothus americanus.

sacken, to subside, sag, sink, sack, pack.

Sack-filter, *n.* bag (sack) filter; **-förmig,** sacklike, pouchlike; **-gasse,** *f.* blind alley; **-leinen,** *n.* sackcloth, sacking; **-leinwand,** *f.* sackcloth, sacking; **-loch,** *n.* blind hole; **-pusule,** *f.* main contractile vacuole.

Sackung, *f.* settlement, sagging, subsidence.

Sadebaum, *m.* savin (*Juniperus sabina*).

Säemaschine, *f.* sowing machine, drill.

säen, to sow, seed.

Saffian, *m.* morocco (leather).

Safflor, *m.* safflower (*Cavthamus tinctorius*). **-blüte,** *f.* safflower blossom; **-gelb,** *n;* safflower yellow; **-rot,** *n.* safflower red, carthamin.

Safran, *m.* saffron (*Crocus sativus*); **-ähnlich,** saffronlike, croceous, saffrony; **-farben,** **-farbig,** saffron colored; **-gelb,** saffron yellow, saffron; **-haltig,** containing saffron.

Saft, *m.*-̈e, juice, sap, cell sap, lymph, fluid, moisture, liquor, sirup, gravy, humors (of the body); **-ausfluss,** *m.* exudation of sap; **-bahn,** *f.* course (circulation); of sap; **-behälter,** *m.* somatocyst; **-blume,** *f.* nectar-secreting flower; **-decke,** *f.* nectar cover; **-drüse,** *f.* nectar gland; **-faden,** *m.* succulent filament, paraphysis; **-fluss,** *m.*

exudation of sap; **-hieb,** *m.* felling in the growing season.

saftig, juicy, succulent, sappy, wet.

Saftigkeit, *f.* juiciness, sappiness.

Saft-kanal, *m.* lymph canal; **-kanälchen,** *n.pl.* serous canaliculi; **-leitung,** *f.* sap translocation; **-pflanze,** *f.* succulent plant; **-raum,** *m.* cell cavity, vacuole; **-reich,** rich in juice or sap, succulent.

Saft-röhre, *f.* lymphatic vessel; **-stamm,** *m.* succulent trunk; **-strom,** *m.* sap flow, lymph stream; **-tropfen,** *m.* drop of sap; **-umlauf,** *m.* circulation of sap; **-verkehr,** *m.* movement of sap; **-zeit,** *f.* sap season; **-zelle,** *f.* lymph cell.

Sagapengummi, *n.* sagapenum (a resin).

Sage, *f.* saying, rumor, report, tradition, fable, legend.

Säge, *f.* saw.

sägeartig, sawlike, serrate(d); ~ **gezähnt,** serrate, dentate.

Säge-blatt, *n.* silicious leaf, saw blade; **-fortsatz,** *m.* serrated process; **-gatter,** *n.* frame of saw.

Sägemehl, *n.* sawdust; **-artig,** like sawdust.

sagen, to say, tell, speak; **beiläufig gesagt,** by the way; **offen gesagt,** in plain language; **das hat nichts zu ~,** that is of no great importance; **das will viel ~,** that is saying a great deal.

sägen, to saw.

sagenhaft, legendary, traditionary.

Säge-schnitt, *m.* saw cut; **-späne,** *m.pl.* sawdust; **-zahn,** *m.* saw tooth, indentation.

Sagittalebene, *f.* sagittal plane.

Sagopalme, *f.* Cycas.

Sagradarinde, *f.* cascara sagrada.

sah (sehen), saw.

Sahlband, *n.* selvage, wall (of a lode).

Sahne, *f.* cream.

sahnen, to skim (milk).

Sahnenkäse, *m.* cream cheese.

Saibling, *m.* char (a trout).

saiger, perpendicular, vertical.

saigern, to liquate.

Saite, *f.* catgut, cord, chorda, string.

Saiten-draht, *m.* music wire; **-galvanometer,** *n.* string (thread) galvanometer.

säkulär, secular, of long duration.

säkularisieren, to secularize.

Salat, *m.* salad, lettuce; **-kopf,** *m.* head of lettuce; **-öl,** *n.* salad oil, olive oil.

Salband, *n.* selvage, wall (of a lode).

Salbe, *f.* salve, ointment.

Salbei, *f.* sage (Salvia).

salben, to apply salve, anoint; **-artig,** salvelike, unctuous; **-behandlung,** *f.* salve treatment; **-grundlage,** *f.* ointment base; **-spatel,** *m.* salve spatula.

salbig, salvy, unctuous.

Saldo, *m.* balance (of an account).

Salep, *m.* salep; **-schleim,** *m.* salep mucilage: **-wurzel,** *f.* salep.

Salicoylsäure, *f.* salicylic acid.

salicylieren, to salicylate.

salicylig, salicylous.

salicyl-sauer, salicylate of; **-säure,** *f.* salicylic acid; **-streupulver,** *n.* salicylated (talc) dusting powder; **-talg,** *m.* salicylated grease; **-ursäure,** *f.* salicyluric acid.

Saline, *f.* saltworks, ricks, saltern; **-wasser,** *n.* saline water.

salinisch, saline.

salivieren, to salivate.

Salm, *m.* salmon, long yarn (story).

Salmiak, *m.* sal ammoniac, ammonium chloride; **-geist,** *m.* aqueous ammonia; **-lakritze,** *f.* pastilles of licorice and ammonia; **-lösung,** *f.* ammonium chloride solution; **-pastillen,** *f.pl.* pastilles; **-salz,** *n.* sal volatile, ammonium chloride, sal ammoniac; **-spiritus,** *m.* aqueous ammonia.

Salmrot, *n.* salmon red.

Salomonssiegel, *n.* Solomon's-seal.

Salpeter, *m.* saltpeter, niter; **-artig,** like saltpeter, nitrous; **-äther,** *m.* nitric ether, ethyl nitrate; **-bakterium,** *n.* nitrogen fixer; **-bildung,** *f.* nitrification; **-blumen,** *f.pl.* niter efflorescence; **-dampf,** *m.* nitrous fumes; **-erde,** *f.* nitrous earth; **-erzeugung,** *f.* niter production, nitrification; **-essigsauer,** nitrate and acetate of.

Salpeter-frass, *m.* corrosion by niter; **-gas,** *n.* nitrous oxide, nitric oxide; **-geist,** *m.* spirit of niter, nitric acid; **-grube,** *f.* saltpeter (bed) mine; **-gütemesser,** *m.* nitrometer; **-hafen,** *m.* niter pot.

salpeterhaltig, containing saltpeter, nitrous; **salpeterhaltiger Höllenstein,** *m.* mitigated silver nitrate.

Salpeter-pflanze, *f.* ruderal plant, nitrophyte; **-probe,** *f.* saltpeter test; **-salzsauer,** nitromuriate of; **-salzsäure,** *f.* nitrohydrochloric acid, aqua regia; **-sauer,** nitrate of.

Salpetersäure, *f.* nitric acid; **-anhydrid,** *n.* nitric anhydride, nitrogen pentoxide; **-äther,** *m.* nitric ether, ethyl nitrate; **-salz,** *n.* salt of nitric acid, nitrate.

Salpeter-schaum, *m.* wall saltpeter, calcareous niter; **-schwefelsäure,** *f.* nitro(syl)sulphuric acid; **-zerstörer,** *m.* destroyer of saltpeter.

salpetrig, nitrous; **salpetrige Säure,** nitrous acid; **salpetrige Schwefelsäure,** nitro(syl)-sulphuric acid.

salpetrigsauer, nitrite of; **salpetrigsaures Kalium,** *n.* potassium nitrite; **salpetrigsaures Natrium,** *n.* sodium nitrite.

Salpetrigsäure, *f.* nitrous acid; **-anhydrid,** *n.* nitrous anhydride.

Salve, *f.* volley, salute.

Salvei, *f.* sage.

Salweide, *f.* great sallow, goat willow (*Salix caprea*).

Salz, *n.*-e, salt; **-ablagerung,** *f.* salt deposit; **-ader,** *f.* salt vein; **-ähnlich, -artig,** saline, haloid, like salt; **-äther,** *m.* muriatic ether, ethyl chloride; **-bad,** *n.* salt bath; **-bedarf,** *m.* salt requirement; **-bergwerk,** *n.* salt mine; **-bildend,** salt-forming, halogenous.

Salz-bild(n)er, *m.* salt former, halogen; **-bildung,** *f.* salt formation, salification; **-bildungsfähig,** salifiable; **-blumen,** *f.pl.* efflorescence of salt; **-boden,** *m.* saline soil; **-brühe,** *f.* brine, pickle; **-decke,** *f.* cover impregnated with salts; **-drüse,** *f.* salt-secreting gland.

salzen, to salt, season.

salz-erzeugend, salt-producing; **-erzeugung,** *f.* salt production, salification; **-fähig,** salifiable; **-farbe,** *f.* basic or metallic dye; **-fleisch,** *n.* salt meat; **-fluss,** *m.* saline flux, salt rheum, eczema rubrum; **-förmig,** saliniform; **-gemisch,** *n.* salt mixture, mixture of salts; **-geschmack,** *m.* salty taste; **-getränkt,** impregnated with salt; **-glasur,** *f.* salt glaze.

Salz-grube, *f.* salt (pit) mine; **-haltig,** containing salt, salt-bearing, saline, saliferous; **-hunger,** *m.* predilection for salt.

salzig, salty, saline, briny.

Salzigkeit, *f.* saltiness, salineness, salinity.

Salz-korn, *n.* grain of salt; **-kraut,** *n.* saltwort (*Salsola kali*); **-kuchen,** *m.* salt cake; **-kupfererz,** *n.* atacamite; **-lager,** *n.* salt deposits; **-lake,** *f.* brine, pickle; **-lauge,** *f.* brine; **-lecke,** *f.* salt lick; **-liebend,** salsuginous, fond of salt; **-löser,** *m.* salt dissolver, brine mixer.

Salz-mutterlauge, *f.* bittern (in a saltworks); **-niederschlag,** *m.* deposit of salt, saline deposit; **-paar,** *n.* pair of salts; **-pfanne,** *f.* salt (brine) pan; **-pfannenstein,** *m.* pan scale; **-pflanze,** *f.* halophyte; **-quelle,** *f.* salt (saline) spring; **-reich,** rich in salt; **-salpetersäure,** *f.* nitrohydrochloric acid, aqua regia; **-sauer,** hydrochloride of, chloride of.

Salzsäure, *f.* hydrochloric (muriatic) acid; **-bindend,** fixing hydrochloric acid; **-gas,** *n.* hydrochloric acid gas, hydrogen chloride; **-lösung,** *f.* hydrochloric acid solution.

Salz-schicht, *f.*-en, layer of salt; **-schmelze,** *f.* fused salt (bath); **-siedepfanne,** *f.* salt pan; **-siederei,** *f.* salt making, saltworks; **-sole,** *f.* salt spring, brine; **-speck,** *m.* bacon; **-stein,** *m.* boiler scale; **-stoffwechsel,** *m.* inorganic metabolism; **-strauch,** *m.* Halimodendron; **-wasser** *n.* salt water, brine.

Salz-wassersumpf, *m.* saline swamp; **-werk,** *n.* saltworks, saltern; **-wiese,** *f.* salt meadow; **-wirkung,** *f.* effect of salt.

Same, Samen, *m.* seed, grain, semen, sperm, germ, source.

Samen-abfall, *m.* seed fall; harvest time; **-abführungsgang,** *m.* spermatic duct, vas deferens; **-anlage,** *f.* ovule, placenta, gemmula; **-ausführungsgang,** *m.* ejaculatory duct; **-baum,** *m.* seed tree, seed bearer; **-beere,** *f.* arillocarp; **-beet,** *n.* seedbed; **-behälter,** *m.* seminal vesicle, spermatheca; **-behandlung,** *f.* seed treatment; **-beizung,** *f.* seed disinfection.

Samen-beständig, breeding true to type, homozygotous; **-bildung,** *f.* seed formation; **-bildungszelle,** *f.* sperm-forming cell; **-bläschen,** *n.*, **-blase,** *f.* seminal vesicle; **-blatt,** *n.* seminal leaf, cotyledon; **-blättchen,** *n.* cotyledon; **-darre,** *f.* seed kiln; **-decke,** *f.* seed coat, episperm, perisperm; **-deckel,** *m.* operculum.

Samen-drüse, *f.* spermatic gland, testicle, **-eigenschaft,** *f.* property of seed; **-eikern;** *m.* mesoblast; **-eiweiss,** *n.* endosperm, albumen; **-entwicklung,** *f.* seed development; **-faden,** *m.* spermatozoid; **-fähigkeit,** *f.* maturity, ability to set seed; **-farne,** *m.pl.* Pteridospermae; **-flügelig,** wing-fruited; **-flüssigkeit,** *f.* seminal fluid; **-führend,** seminiferous.

Samen-gang, *m.* spermatic duct; **-gefäss,** *n.* spermatic vessel; **-gehäuse,** *n.* core. receptacle, seedcase, pericarp; **-haar,** *n.* hull fiber; **-haarkrone,** *f.* pappus; **-händler,** *m.* seed merchant; **-häufchen,** *n.* sorus (of ferns); **-haut,** *f.* seed coat, tegument; **-hefe,** *f.* seed yeast; **-herd,** *m.* spermatocyst.

Samen-hieb, *m.* seeding, (cutting) felling; **-holzbetrieb,** *m.* high-forest system; **-hülle,** *f.* episperm, testa, perisperm; **-hülse,** *f.* pod, husk, hull; **-jahr,** *n.* seed (fruiting) year; **-käfer,** *m.pl.* seed beetles (Bruchidae); **-kanal,** *m.* seminal tubule; **-kapsel,** *f.* capsule; **-keim,** *m.* seminal germ, germ embryo; **-kelch,** *m.* seed cup.

Samen-kern, *m.* seed kernel, sperm nucleus, endosperm; **-knospe,** *f.* ovule, seminal bud, gemmule; **-kopf,** *m.* head of spermatozoid; **-korn,** *n.* single seed, grain; **-körper,** *m.* body of spermatozoid; **-krönchen,** *n.* coronule, pappus; **-lage,** *f.* nucleus; **-lappen,** *m.* cotyledon, seed lobe; **-leiste,** *f.* placenta; **-leiter,** *m.* spermatic duct, vas deferens.

Samen-lode, *f.* seedling plant; **-mantel,** *m.* aril; **-mutterzelle,** *f.* spermatocyst, spermatoblast; **-naht,** *f.* raphe; **-patrone,** *f.* spermatophore; **-pflanzen,** *f.pl.* seed plants (Spermatophytae); **-probe,** *f.* seed test, seed sample; **-röhre,** *f.* seminal tubule; **-ruhe,** *f.* dormancy of seed; **-saft,** *m.* seminal fluid.

Samen-schale, *f.* testa, tegmen, seed coat; **-schalenbau,** *m.* seed-coat structure; **-schiessen,** *n.* going to seed; **-schildchen,** *n.* scutellum; **-schlag,** *m.* seeding (stage), felling; **-schnur,** *f.* spermatic cord; **-schopf,** *m.* seed tuft, coma; **-schuppe,** *f.* ovuliferous (seed) scale; **-schwanz,** *m.* tail of spermatozoon; **-staub,** *m.* pollen.

Samen-strang, *m.* spermatic cord; **-tasche,** *f.* spermatotheca, seminal vesicle; **-tierchen,** *n.* spermatozoön; **-tragend,** seed-bearing; **-träger,** *m.* placenta; **-untersuchung,** *f.* seed investigation, seed test; **-verbreitung,** *f.* seed dispersal; **-veredlung,** *f.* seed selection, seed amelioration; **-verfälschung,** *f.* adulteration of seeds; **-weg,** *m.* spermatic duct.

Samen-werkzeug, *n.* spermatic (male genital) apparatus; **-zapfen,** *m.* cone; **-zelle,** *f.* seminal cell, spermatozoön; **-zucker** *m.* quercitol, quercite.

sämig, thick, viscous.

sämisch, chamois, soft; **-gar,** oil-tanned, chamois; **-gerben,** *n.* chamois dressing; **-leder,** *n.* chamois leather, chamois.

Sämling, *m.* seedling.

Sämlingsmerkmal, *n.* seedling character.

Sammel-art, *f.* collective species; **-behälter,** *m.* sump; **-beine,** *n.pl.* anthophoric legs;

-biene, *f.* worker bee; **-bottich,** *m.* collecting (starting) tub; **-frucht,** *f.* syncarp; **-früchtig,** syncarpous; **-gang,** *m.* collecting duct; **-gebiet,** *n.* collecting area, watershed, drainage area; **gefäss,** *n.-e,* collecting vessel, reservoir.

Sammel-geräte, *n.pl.* collecting implements; **-glas,** *n.* preparation tube, converging lens; **-graben,** *m.* feeder drain; **-haare,** *n.pl.* collecting hairs (of bees), brush; **-körbchen,** *n.* corbiculum (of bees); **-linse,** *f.* converging (convex) lens.

sammeln, (to collect, gather, heap, lay up, assemble, accumulate, harvest.

Sammel-namen, *m.* collective name; **-nuss,** *f.* an aggregate fruit of achenes, etaerio; **-punkt,** *m.* meeting place; **-raum,** *m.* receiver, receptacle; **-referat,** *n.* collective review; **-rohr,** *n.* canaliculus; **-röhre,** *f.* canaliculus; **-schiene,** *f.* bus bar; **-schliessfrucht,** *f.* indehiscent syncarp; **-sirup,** *m.* sirup from split sugar.

Sammel-spiegel, *m.* concave mirror; **-springfrucht,** *f.* syncarpous dehiscent fruit; **-steinfrucht,** *f.* pyrenarium; **-stelle,** *f.* collecting (converging) point; **-trichter,** *m.* collecting funnel; **-zelle,** *f.* collective cell; **-zylinder,** *m.* accumulator.

Sammet, *m.* velvet; **-artig,** velvetlike, velvety; **-blatt,** *n.* velvety leaf; **-blende,** *f.* limonite; **-braun,** *n.* velvet brown; **-eisenerz,** *n.* gothite; **-erz,** *n.* cyanotrichite; **-schwarz,** *n.* ivory black; **-stoffe,** *m.pl.* pile fabric, velvet.

Sammler, *m.-,* gatherer, collector, accumulator, storage battery, condenser.

Sammlung, *f.* collection, gathering, compilation, assembly.

Sammlungsglas, *n.* -̈er, specimen glass, display glass, condensing lens.

samt, together with; ~ **und sonders,** each and all.

Samt, *m.* velvet; **-artig,** velvetlike, velvety; **-glänzend,** velvety; **-haarig,** holosericeous (silky hair).

sämtlich, all together, all, conplete, jointly, collectively,

Sand, *m.* sand.

Sandarak, *m.* sandarac, realgar; **-gummi,** sandarac (resin); **-harz,** *n.* sandarac (resin).

sand-artig, sandlike, sandy; **-bad,** *n.* sand bath; **-badschale,** *f.* sand-bath dish; **-bank,** *f.* layer of sand, arenaceous deposit; **-beere,** *f. Arbutus menziesii;* **-boden,** *m.* sandy soil.

Sand-büchsenbaum, *m.* sandbox tree (*Hura crepitans*); **-dorn,** *m.* sea buckthorn (*Hippophaë vhamnoides*); **-düne,** *f.* sand dune; **-dünengesellschaften,** *f.pl.* associations of sand dunes; **-ebene,** *f.* sandy plain.

Sandel, *m.*, **-holz,** *n.* sandalwood; **-holzgewächse,** *n.pl.* Santalaceae; **-rot,** *n.* santalin.

sand-farben, sand-colored; **-flurbestand,** *m.* sand-field vegetation; **-form,** *f.* sand mold; **-gebirge,** *n.* sandy mountains; **-geröll,** *n.* moving sand debris; **-gerüst,** *n.* sand structure; **-gewächse,** *n.pl.* arenarious plants; **-glimmer,** *m.* mica.

Sand-gras, *n.* sand grass, sand reed (*Ammophila arenaria*); **-gries,** *m.* coarse sand, gravel; **-grube,** *f.* sand pit; **-gummi,** *n.* sandarac resin, sandarac; **-guss,** *m.* sand casting; **-haargras,** *n.* lyme grass (*Elymus arenarius*); **-hafer,** *m.* lyme grass; **-haltig,** arenaceous.

sandig, sandy, arenaceous.

Sand-käfer, *m.pl.* tiger beetles; **-korn,** *n.* sand grain; **-kraut,** *n.* sandwort (Arenaria); **-läufer,** *m.pl.* tiger beetles (Cicindellidae); **-mergel,** *m.* sandy marl, lime gravel; **-myrte,** *f.* Leiophyllum; **-nelke,** *f.* sand pink (*Dianthus arenarius*); **-papier,** *n.* sandpaper; **-riedgras,** *n.* sand sedge (*Carex arenaria*); **-rohr,** *n.* sand reed (Arundo).

Sand-rücken, *m.* sand ridge, hogback; **-schicht,** *f.* layer of sand; **-schiefer,** *m.* schistous sandstone; **-segge,** *f.* sea sedge (*Carex arenaria*); **-stein,** *m.* sandstone; **-steinlager,** *n.* sandstone stratum; **-steinschiefer,** *m.* slaty sandstone; **-strahlgebläse,** *n.* sandblasting equipment; **-strahlputzen,** *n.* sandblasting.

sandte (senden), sent, was sending.

Sand-traube, *f.* bearberry; **-uhr,** *f.* sandglass, hourglass; **-uhrzelle,** *f.* hourglass type of cell; **-wespe,** *f.* sand wasp; **-wicke,** *f.* villous vetch (*Vicia villosa*); **-wüste,** *f.* sandy desert; **-zucker,** *m.* raw ground sugar.

sanft, soft, gentle, mild, smooth.

Sang, *m.* song, singing.

sanieren, to cure, restore, reclaim.

Sanikel, *m.* sanicle.

sanitär, sanitary, hygienic.

Sanität, *f.* health, hygiene, sanitation.

Sanitäts-anstalt, *f.* hygienic institute; **-kollegium,** *n.* board of health; **-pflege,** *f.* sanitation; **-polizei,** *f.* sanitary inspectors; **-wesen,** *n.* sanitary matters.

sann (sinnen), thought, was thinking.

Santel, *m.* sandal(wood).

Santoninsäure, *f.* santoninic acid.

Santonsäure, *f.* santonic acid.

Sapanholz, *n.* sapanwood.

Saphir, *m.* sapphire.

Saphirspat, *m.* cyanite.

Saponit, *n.* stealite, soapstone.

Saprämie, *f.* sapremia.

saprogen, putrefying.

Sapropel, *n.* sludge, sediment with decaying organisms.

saprophytisch, saprophytic.

Sardelle, *f.* anchovy, sardine.

Sardinenöl, *n.* sardine oil.

Sarg, *m.* coffin.

Sarkin, *n.* sarcine.

Sarkom, *n.* sarcoma.

sarkomatös, sarcomatous.

Sarsa, *f.* sarsaparilla.

Sasapalme, *f.* Nipa.

sass (sitzen), sat, was sitting.

Sassafras, *m.* sassafras.

Sassaparille, *f.* sarsaparilla.

Satinage, *f.* glazing finish.

satinieren, to satin, glaze, calender.

Satinpapier, *n.* glazed paper.

satt, (*gen.*) satisfied, satiated, saturated, deep, intensive; **es ~ haben,** to have had enough of it.

sattblau, deep (dark) blue.

Sattdampf, *m.* ̈-e, saturated steam.

Satte, *f.* bowl, dish.

Sattel, *m.*-, saddle, bridge, sella turcica, clitellum; **-bein,** *n.* saddle-shaped bone, sella trucica; **-fass,** *n.* rider cask; **-förmig,** saddle-shaped; **-fortsatz,** *m.* clinoid process; **-gelenk,** *n.* saddlelike joint; **-holz,** *n.* saddler's wood, bolster, corbel; **-lehne,** *f.* sella trucica; **-pfropfen,** *n.* saddle grafting; **-schaft,** *m.* saddle graft.

Sattel-schlange, *f.* saddle(-shaped) coil; **-stütze,** saddle pin; **-winkel,** *m.* sphenoidal angle; **-zwecke,** *f.* saddle pin.

sattgelb, deep yellow.

sättigen, to saturate, fill, impregnate, satisfy, satiate, sate.

Sättigung, *f.* saturation, satisfaction, satiety, neutralization.

Sättigungs-druck, *m.* saturation pressure; **-fähig,** capable of saturation; **-grad,** *m.* degree of saturation; **-kapazität,** *f.* saturation capacity; **-punkt,** *m.* saturation point; **-strom,** *m.* saturation current; **-verhältnis,** *n.* relative humidity of atmosphere.

sattsam, sufficient(ly), enough.

Saturations-gefäss *n.*-e, saturation vessel, saturator; **-scheidung,** *f.* purification by carbonization; **-schlamm,** *m.* sediment from carbonation.

Saturei, *f.* **-kraut,** *n.* savory.

saturieren, to saturate, carbonate.

Satz, *m.*⁻e, deposit, sediment, settlings, dregs, composition, set, charge, batch, principle, theorem, proposition, leap, jump, young (of fish), fry, price, rate, pool, stake, sentence, yeast; **-betrieb,** *m.* batch operation; **-brauen,** *n.* brewing with cold malt extract; **-krücke,** *f.* yeast rouser; **-mehl,** *n.* fecula; **-schale,** *f.* settling dish; **-weise,** intermittently, by leaps.

Satzung, *f.* statute, law, fixed rule.

Sau, *f.* ⁻e, sow, wild pig, drying kiln, blot.

sauber, clean, neat, pretty.

Säuberei, *f.* inspection, sorting.

Sauberkeit, *f.* clean(li)ness, neatness.

säubern, to clean, cleanse, inspect.

Saubohne, *f.* fodder bean, vetch, soybean.

sauer, acid, sour, tart, troublesome, hard; **-ampfer,** *m.* common sorrel, sour dock (*Rumex acetosa*); **-bad,** *n.* sour bath; **-brühe,** *f.* sour liquor; **-brunnen,** *m.* acidulous spring water; **-chromsauer,** dichromate of; **-dorn,** *m.* barberry; **-dornbitter,** *n.* berberine; **-dorngewächse,** *n.pl.* Berberidaceae; **-futter,** *n.* ensilage; **-haltig,** acidiferous; **-honig,** *m.* oxymel; **-kirsche,** *f.* sour cherry, morello cherry (*Prunus cerasus*).

Sauerklee, *m.* clover sorrel, wood sorrel (*Oxalis acetosella*); **-gewächse,** *n.pl.* Oxalidaceae; **-salz,** *n.* salt of sorrel, acid potassium oxalate; **-säure,** *f.* oxalic acid.

säuerlich, sourish, acidulous.

Säuerlichkeit, *f.* acidity.

säuerlich-stechend, sourish-turning, acid-stinging; **-süss,** sourish sweet.

Säuerling, *m.* acidulous mineral water, sour wine.

Sauermachen, *n.* acidification.

sauermachend, acidifying.

säuern, to acidify, acidulate, sour, leaven.

sauerreagierend, of acid reaction.

Sauersalz, *n.* acid salt.

Sauerstoff, *m.*-e, oxygen; **-abgabe,** *f.* loss of oxygen; **-arm,** poor in oxygen; **-ion,** *n.* anion; **-atmung,** *f.* aerobic respiration; **-atom,** *n.* oxygen atom; **-aufnahme,** *f.* oxygen absorption; **-bedürfnis,** *n.* oxygen requirement; **-bedürftig,** needing oxygen; **-bildung,** *f.* oxygen formation.

Sauerstoff-druck, *m.*-e, oxygen pressure; **-entwicklung,** *f.* evolution of oxygen; **-entziehend,** removing oxygen; **-entzug,** *m.* reduced oxygen supply; **-erzeuger,** *m.* oxygen producer; **-fänger,** *m.* a substance that absorbs oxygen, absorbent; **-frei,** free from oxygen; **-gas,** *n.* oxygen gas; **-gehalt,** *m.* oxygen content; **-gerät,** *n.* oxygen tank.

sauerstoff-haltig, containing oxygen; **-ion,** *n.* anion; **-mangel,** *m.* lack of oxygen, oxygen deficiency; **-menge,** *f.* amount of oxygen; **-messer,** *m.* eudiometer (for air); **-ort,** *m.* oxidation region; **-pol,** *m.* oxygen pole, anode; **-reich,** rich in oxygen; **-salz,** *n.* oxysalt, salt of an oxyacid.

Sauerstoff-sättigung, *f.* oxygen saturation; **-säure,** *f.* oxygen acid; **-strom,** *m.* current of oxygen; **-träger,** *m.* oxygen carrier; **-überschuss,** *m.* excess of oxygen; **-überträger,** *m.* oxygen carrier; **-verbindung,** *f.* oxygen compound; **-verbrauch,** *m.* oxygen usage; **-zufuhr,** *f.* oxygenation, supply of oxygen.

sauersüss, sour-sweet.

Sauerteig, *m.* leaven.

Säuerung, *f.* acidification, souring, leavening.

säuerungs-fähig, acidifiable; **-grad,** *m.* degree of acidity; **-mittel,** *n.* acidifying agent.

Sauer-wasser, *n.* sour water, acidulous (sparkling) water; **-wein,** *m.* sour wine, verjuice; **-werden,** *n.* souring, acetification.

Saufinder, *m.* boarhound.

Saug-ader, *f.*-n, absorbing vessel, lymphatic vessel; **-aderdrüse,** *f.* lymphatic gland; **-adersystem,** *n.* lymphatic system; **-akt,** *m.* act of absorption; **-apparat,** *m.* aspirator, suction apparatus; **-bagger,** *m.* suction dredge.

saugen, to suck, suck up, absorb.

Saugen, *n.* sucking, suction, absorption.

säugen, to suckle, nurse.

Sauger, *m.*⁻, sucker, suction apparatus, aspirator.

Säuger, *m.* mammal.

Säugetier, *n.*-e, mammal; **-gewebe,** *n.* mammalian tissue; **-tuberkulose,** *f.* mammalian tuberculosis.

Saug-fähigkeit, *f.* absorptive capacity; **-festigkeit,** *f.* resistance to suction, suction strength; **-filter,** *n.* suction filter; **-füsschen,** *n.* sucker foot; **-gefäss,** *n.* absorbent vessel; **-glas,** *n.* suction bottle, breast pump; **-haar,** *n.* absorbent hair; **-heber,** *m.* siphon; **-höhe,** *f.* suction (head), height, capillary rise.

Säugling, *m.*-e, suckling, infant.

Saug-magen, *m.* chyliferous stomach; **-napf,** *m.* suctorial disk or pore, cup-shaped sucker; **-napffangarm.** *m.* tentacle, suction tentacle; **-organ,** *n.* haustorium; **-pipette,** *f.* suction pipette; **-pumpe,** *f.* suction pump; **-rüssel,** *m.* sucker, siphon, proboscis; **-scheibe,** *f.* suctorial disk; **-scheibenranke,** *f.* tendril with adhesive disk; **-schlauch,** *m.* haustorium.

Saug-schnabel, *m.* siphon, promuscis; **-schuppe,** *f.* water-absorbing (trichome) hair; **-spitze,** *f.* collecting point; **-strahl,** *m.* jet; **-tentakel,** *n.* suctorial tentacle.

Saugung, *f.* suction, sucking.

Saug-ventil, *n.*-e, suction valve; **-wäsche,** *f.* vacuum wash; **-werkzeuge,** *n.pl.* sucking mouth parts or apparatus, haustorium; **-widerstand,** *m.* resistance to suction; **-wirkung,** *f.* suction effect; **-würmer,** *m.pl.* Trematoda; **-wurzel,** *f.* absorbing root, haustorium; **-zug,** *m.* induced draft; **-zweig,** *m.* haustorium.

Säulchen, *n.* small column, columella.

Säule, *f.* column, pillar, post, prism, pile.

Säulen-achse, *f.* prismatic axis; **-artig,** columnar, prismatic; **-förmig,** columnar, prismatic; **-hängelager,** *n.* column bracket; **-stamm,** *m.* columnar stem; **-wurzel,** *f.* stilt root, prop root; **-zelle,** *f.* columnar sclereid (cell).

Saum, *m.*-e, margin, border, fringe, seam, strip, hem, edge, selvage, fimbria.

säumen, to delay, hem, border, line out. square timber, cut, fell.

Saum-farn, *m.* common brake, bracken (*Pteris aquilina*); **-pfanne,** *f.* list pot (tin plate); **-riff,** *n.* fringing reef; **-schlag,** *m.* strip cutting; **-spiegel,** *m.* gray spiegel iron; **-topf,** *m.* list pot (tin plate); **-tracheide,** *f.* marginal ray, tracheid.

Säure, *f.* acid, sourness, acidity; **-amid,** *n.* acid amide; **-anhydrid,** *n.* acid anhydride; **-anzug,** *m.* acidproof clothing; **-artig,** acidlike; **-äther,** *m.* ester; **-ballon,** *m.* acid

carboy; **-basengleichgewicht,** *n.* acid-base equilibrium; **-behälter,** *m.* acid container; **-beize,** *f.* sour.

säure-beständig, stable toward acids, acid-resisting; **-bildend,** acid-forming; **-bildner,** *m.* acid former, acidifier; **-bildung,** *f.* acid formation, acidification; **-bindungsvermögen,** *n.* acid-combining capacity; **-dichte,** *f.* specific gravity of acid; **-echt,** fast to acid; **-eiweiss,** *n.* acid protein; **-empfindlich,** sensitive to acids; **-ester,** *m.* ester of an acid.

säure-fähig, acidifiable; **-farbstoff,** *m.* acid dye; **-fest,** acidproof, acid-fast; **-frei,** free from acid, nonacid; **-gehalt,** *m.* acid content, acidity; **-grad,** *m.* degree of acidity; **-haltig,** containing acid, acidiferous; **-heber,** *m.* acid siphon; **-löslich,** acid-soluble; **-lösung,** *f.* solution of an acid.

Säure-menge, *f.* amount of acid; **-reich,** rich in acid; **-rest,** *m.* acid residue; **-schlauch,** *m.* acid hose; **-schwarz,** *n.* acid black; **-spaltung,** *f.* acid cleavage; **-ständer,** *m.* acid cistern; **-titer,** *m.* degree of acidity; **-wechsel,** *m.* change in acidity; **-wecker,** *m.* starter, pure culture.

Säure-widerstandsfähigkeit, *f.* acid resistance; **-widerstehend,** resistant (fast) to acid; **-widrig,** antacid; **-wirkung,** *f.* action of acids; **-zahl,** *f.* acid number; **-zufuhr,** *f.* addition of acid.

säuseln, to rustle, lisp, hum.

sausen, to rush, whiz, whistle.

Schabe, *f.* scraper, scab, itch, cockroach, moth.

Schäbe, *f.* awn, refuse (chaff) of flax, scab, itch.

Schabeisen, *n.* scraper.

schaben, to scrape, shave, grate, rub.

Schabenpulver, *n.* roach powder.

Schaber, *m.* scraper.

schäbig, shabby, mean, bare, worn out, scabby, mangy.

Schabin, *n.* Dutch-metal parings (of leaf gold).

Schablone, *f.* model, pattern, template, mold, form, stencil.

schablonen-artig, -mässig, according to pattern, mechanical; **-drehbank,** *f.* copying lath; **-wesen,** *n.* routine.

Schabatte, *f.* anvil block.

Schabsel, *n.* scrapings, parings, shavings.

Schach, *n.* chess, check; **-brett,** *n.* chessboard, checkerboard.

Schacht, *m.* shaft, ravine, hollow, tunnel, depression, pit, gorge; **-abdeckung,** *f.* manhole cover.

Schachtel, *f.* box, case; **-halm,** *m.* horsetail (Equisetum); **-halmsäure,** *f.* equisetic acid; **-kraut,** *n.* horsetail (Equisetum).

schachteln, to put in a box, pack.

Schacht-ofen, *m.* shaft (furnace) kiln; **-speicher,** *m.* silo.

Schachtung, *f.* shaft(ing), excavation.

schade, unfortunate, a pity.

Schade(n), *m.* ∵, damage, injury, detriment, loss.

Schädel, *m.* skull, cranium; **-band,** *n.* cranial ligament; **-basis,** *f.* base of the skull; **-basisfraktur,** *f.* fracture of the skull base; **-boden,** *m.* floor of the skull; **-breite,** *f.* cranial breadth; **-dach,** *n.* vault of the cranium; **-decke,** *f.* scalp, skullcap.

Schädel-eingeweide, *n.* cranial viscera; **-fläche,** *f.* surface of the skull; **-fuge,** *f.* cranial suture; **-gewölbe,** *n.* vault of the cranium; **-grube,** *f.* cranial fossa; **-grund,** *m.* base of the skull; **-haut,** *f.* pericranium; **-höhe,** *f.* cranial height; **-höhle,** *f.* cavity of the cranium; **-hohlraum,** *m.* skull cavity.

Schädel-index, *m.* index of the cranium; **-kalotte,** *f.* vault of the cranium; **-kapsel,** *f.* cranium, skullcap; **-knochen,** *m.* cranium, skull bone; **-länge,** *f.* cranial length; **-naht,** *f.* cranial suture; **-öffnung,** *f.* cranial foramen.

Schädel-schuss, *m.* skull shot; **-teil,** *m.* portion of the skull; **-wand,** *f.* wall of the cranium; **-weichteile,** *n.pl.* cranial soft parts; **-wirbel,** *m.* cranial vertebra; **-wölbung,** *f.* vault of the cranium; **-wunde,** *f.* cranial wound.

schaden, (*dat.*) to do injury, damage, hurt.

Schaden, *m.* damage, injury; **-ersatz,** *m.* compensation, damages, indemnification.

schadhaft, damaged, defective, spoiled, decayed, wasted.

schädigen, to harm, injure, damage, prejudice.

Schädigung, *f.* injury, damage, harm.

schädlich, (*dat.*) injurious, harmful, noxious, dangerous, detrimental.

Schädlichkeit, *f.* injuriousness, harmfulness, perniciousness.

Schädlichmachung, *f.* rendering noxious, contamination.

Schädling, *m.* pest, destructive insect or weed.

Schädlingsbekämpfung, *f.* pest control.

schadlos, harmless, compensated; **-halten,** to compensate, indemnify.

Schaf, *n.-e,* sheep, ewe; **-bein,** *n.* bone ash, sheep bone, sheep's leg; **-blattern,** *f.pl.* ovinia (sheep pox), chicken pox; **-bock,** *m.* ram; **-darmsaite,** *f.* catgut.

schaffen, to create, produce, make, do, work, procure, provide; **einem zu ∼ geben,** to give one work to do; **zu ∼ haben,** to have something to do; **nichts damit zu ∼,** not to be concerned; **aus dem Wege ∼,** to get out of the way.

Schaffleisch, *n.* mutton.

Schaffner, *m.* manager, conductor, guard.

Schaffnerin, *f.* housekeeper, stewardess, manageress.

Schaffung, *f.* production, creation.

Schaf-garbe, *f.* yarrow, milfoil (*Achillea millefolium*); **-haut,** *f.* sheepskin, amnion; **-häutchen,** *n.* amnion; **-käse,** *m.* cheese from ewe's milk.

Schafott, *n.* scaffold.

Schaf-pocken, *f.pl.,* **-pockenseuche,** *f.* ovinia, sheep pox; **-schmiere,** *f.* sheep dip; **-schweiss,** suint, yolk (of wool); **-schwingel,** *m.* sheep's fescue (*Festuca ovina*); **-serum,** *n.* sheep serum.

Schaft, *m.* shaft, handle, scape, stalk, stem or rachis (of a feather), peduncle, shank, stock, trunk; **-formzahl,** *f.* stem form factor; **-rein,** clear-shafted, branchless, clear-boled; **-reinheit,** *f.* clearness of bole; **-reinigung,** *f.* natural pruning, self-pruning.

Schaf-waschmittel, *n.* sheep dip; **-wasser,** *n.* amniotic fluid; **-wolle,** *f.* sheep's wool.

Schagrin, *n.* shagreen.

Schakal, *m.-e,* jackal.

schal, stale, flat, insipid.

Schälarbeit, *f.* shallow plowing.

Schalbrett, *n.* concrete molding board.

Schälchen, *n.* little dish or cup, basin, capsule, cupel.

Schale, *f.* dish, basin, bowl, capsule, cup, pan, scale, carapace, shell, husk, skin, peel, rind, crust, test, cover, evaporating dish, pod.

schälen, to shell, husk, peel, pare, bark scale off.

schalen-artig, saucerlike, testaceous; **-band,** *n.* hinge ligament; **-bau,** *m.* shell structure; **-blende,** *f.* fibrous sphalerite; **-deckel,** *m.* operculum; **-drüse,** *f.* shell gland; **-eingang,** *m.* aperture; **-entwicklung,** *f.* dish development (in photography), **-form,** *f.* type of shell, shell form; **-förmig,** like a shell, in layers.

Schalen-frucht, *f.* caryopsis; **-gehäuse,** *n.* shell; **-guss,** *m.* chill casting; **-gussform,** *f.* chill; **-haken,** *m.* shell hook; **-hart,** chilled; **-hartguss,** *m.* chilled cast iron; **-haut,** *f.* periostracum; **-klappe,** *f.* shell valve; **-krebse,** *m.pl.* Mɛlacostraca.

Schalen-lack, *m.* shellac; **-lederhaut,** *f.* chorion; **-pfropf,** *m.* shell plug; **-rand,** *m.* margin of shell; **-schliesser,** *m.* adductor muscle (of mollusk shell); **-schloss,** *n.* hinge (clam); **-spalt,** *m.* cleft; **-spindel,** *f.* spindle, columella; **-träger,** *m.* dish support, tripod.

Schalfrucht, *f.* caryopsis.

Schälfurche, *f.* shallow plowing of stubble field.

schalig, scaly, foliated, testaceous, crusted, crustaceous, shelled, lamellated.

Schall, *m.* sound (mechanical waves), ring, peal, resonance, noise, echo; **-blase,** *f.* laryngeal (vocal) sac; **-brett,** *n.* lower board; **-dicht,** soundproof.

schallen, to sound, resound, ring, peal.

Schall-geschwindigkeit, *f.* velocity of sound; **-lehre,** *f.* acoustics; **-platte,** *f.* phonograph record; **-schwingung,** *f.* sound vibration.

Schallstrahler höherer Ordnung, overtones.

Schall-welle, *f.* sound wave; **-zuleitend,** sound-conducting.

Schalm, *m.* blaze.

Schälprügel, *m.* peeled billetwood.

schalt (schelten), scolded, was scolding.

Schalt-ader, *f.-n,* spurious vein; **-brett,** *n.* switchboard.

schalten, to insert, connect, rule, switch.

Schalter, *m.* manager, wicket, window, switch, circuit breaker, commutator.

Schaltiere, *n.pl.* Crustacea; **-reste,** *m.pl.* fossil shells; **-versteinerung,** *f.* fossil shell.

Schalt-jahr, *n.* leap year; **-klinkengetriebe,** *f.* ratchet drive mechanism; **-knochen,** *m.* Wormian bone; **-lamelle,** *f.* interstitial lamella; **-pult,** *n.* switchboard, control desk; **-stück,** *n.* intercalary (intermediate) piece; **-tafel,** *f.* switchboard, instrument board.

Schaltung, *f.* connection, disposal, hookup.

Schaltungsaufbau, *m.* circuit design.

Schalung, *f.* forms, sheathing.

Schalt-wirbel, *m.* interposed vertebra; **-zelle,** *f.* intercalary cell.

Schälung, *f.* shelling, peeling, excoriation, desquamation.

Schäl-wald, *m.* bark coppice; **-wunde,** *f.* injury caused by peeling; **-zahn,** *m.* deciduous tooth.

Scham, *f.* shame, modesty, chastity, genitals, pudenda.

Schambein, *n.* pubis; **-ast,** *m.* branch of the pubis; **-band,** *n.* pubic ligament; **-bogen,** *m.* arch of the pubis, **-fuge,** *f.* pubic symphysis; **-höcker,** *m.* pubic crest; **-knorpel,** *m.* interpubic cartilage; **-stachel,** *m.* pubic spine; **-verbindung,** *f.* pubic symphysis.

Scham-bogen, *m.* pubic arch; **-bogenast,** *m.* branch of pubic arch; **-drüse,** *f.* inguinal gland.

schämen, sich, *(gen.)* to be ashamed.

Scham-fuge, *f.* pubic symphysis; **-gang,** *m.* vagina; **-gegend,** *f.* pubic region; **-knochen,** *m.* pubis; **-knorpel,** *m.* cartilage of pubic symphysis.

Schamotte, *f.* fire clay, grog, chamotte; **-stein,** *m.* firebrick.

Schande, *f.* shame, dishonor, disgrace.

Schankbier, *n.* draft beer.

Schanker, *m.* chancre.

Schanze, *f.* trench, entrenchment, chance.

Schappenbohrer, *m.* shell auger.

Schar, *f.* troop, flock, herd, crowd, host, band, group, company, share.

Scharbock, *m.* scurvy; **-heilend,** antiscorbutic; **-mittel,** *n.* antiscorbutic remedy.

scharen, to flock together, assemble.

scharf, sharp, acrid, acute, severe, rigorous, pungent, corrosive, shrill, harsh, keen, well focused.

Schärfe, *f.* sharpness, acuteness, edge.

schärfen, sharpen, whet, grind, strengthen, define, increase; **-fläche,** *f.* surface of distinctness; **-tiefe,** *f.* depth of focus.

Scharf-feuer, *n.* hard (sharp) fire; **-kantig,** acute-angled, sharp-edged, square; **-manganerz,** *n.* hausmannite; **-salzig,** very salty; **-sauer,** strongly acid, very sour; **-schmeckend,** of a sharp taste, acrid, pungent, tart; **-sinn,** *m.* acuteness, discernment, acumen; **-sinnig,** clever, sagacious, ingenious, shrewd; **-winklig,** acute-angled.

Scharlach, *m.* scarlet, scarlet fever, scarlatina; **-eiche,** *f.* scarlet oak (*Quercus coccinea*).

scharlachen, scarlet.

Scharlach-exanthem, *n.* rash of scarlet fever; **-farbe,** *f.* scarlet color or dye; **-fieber,** *n.* scarlet fever, scarlatina; **-rot,** *n.* scarlet, cochineal; **-rot,** scarlet, bright red; **-wurm,** *m.* cochineal insect.

Scharnier, *n.* hinge, joint; **-stift,** *m.* hinge bolt; **-ventil,** *n.* clack (flap) valve, hinge joint, ginglymus.

Schärpe, *f.* scarf, sash, sling.

Scharpie, *f.* charpie, lint.

Scharre, *f.* rake, raker, scraper.

Scharreisen, *n.* scraper.

scharren, to scrape (off), scratch, rake.

Scharr-fuss, *m.* pes radens (Gallinacea); **-harz,** *n.* scrape resin.

Scharriereisen, *n.* scarifier, toothed chisel.

Scharr-kralle, *f.* digging claw; **-raum,** *m.* scratching room; **-vögel,** *m.pl.* scratchers; **-werk,** *n.* scraping mechanism, scraper.

Scharte, *f.* notch, gap, crack, nick, depression, indentation, fissure, dip, sawwort (Liatris, *Serratula tinctoria*).

Schartenfrass, *m.* feeding (evidenced by jagged leaf margin).

schartig, notchy, dented, nicked, jagged.

Schartigkeit, *f.* jaggedness.

Schatten, *m.* shade, shadow; **-baum,** *m.* shade(-enduring) tree; **-bedürftig,** requiring shade; **-blatt,** *n.* heliophobous leaf; **-blume,** *f.* Maianthemum; **-ertragend,** shade enduring, shade bearing.

Schatten-erträgnis, *n.* shade endurance, tolerance of shade; **-gebend,** throwing a shadow; **-holz,** *n.* shade tree; **-käfer,** *m.pl.* meal worms (Tenebrio); **-kegel,** *m.* umbra; **-liebend,** umbrosus, growing in shady places.

schattieren, to shade.

Schattierung, *f.* shading, shade, tinting, hue.

schattig, shady.

Schatz, *m.* treasure, stock, wealth, store; **-amt,** *n.* treasury.

schätzbar, capable of valuation, estimable, valuable, precious.

schätzen, to value, estimate, compute, appraise, appreciate, esteem, assess, tax.

Schatzkammer, *f.* storehouse, treasury.

Schätzung, *f.* estimate, valuation, appraisal, assessment, computation.

Schau, *f.* view, review, show; **-apparat,** *m.* attraction apparatus; **-bild,** *n.* diagram, exhibit, figure.

schaudern, to cause to shudder, shudder.

schauen, to look at, gaze, behold, examine.

Schauer, *m.* shudder, slight tremor, thrill, fit, chill spasm, shower, spectator, inspector, shed, shelter.

Schaufel, *f.***-n,** shovel, scoop, paddle, blade, vane, bucket (of turbine), palette, incisor tooth; **-bein,** *n.* sacrum; **-hirsch,** *m.* stag with palmed antlers; **-knorpel,** *m.* ziphoid (ensiform) cartilage of sternum.

schaufeln, to shovel.

Schaufelschnecken, *f.pl.* Scaphopoda.

Schaufenster, *n.-,* show window.

Schaufler, *m.* buck with palmed antlers.

Schauglas, *n.* display glass, sample glass.

Schaukel-changierung, *f.* swing-arm traverse motion; **-welle,** *f.* rocker shaft.

schaukeln, to swing, rock.

Schau-klappe, *f.* inspection door; **-linie,** *f.* line, curve in a graph; **-loch,** *n.* peephole; **-lustig,** curious.

Schaum, *m.*^{..}-e, foam, froth, lather, scum; **-ähnlich,** foamlike, foamy; **-artig,** foamy, frothy; **-beständigkeit,** *f.* foam-holding capacity; **-bildung,** *f.* formation of foam or froth; **-blase,** *f.* bubble.

schäumen, to froth, foam, sparkle, effervesce, fizz, lather, skim, scum, boil over.

Schaum-erde, *f.* aphrite; **-erz,** *n.* foamy wad; **-gips,** *m.* foliated gypsum; **-gold,** *n.* imitation (Dutch) gold; **-haken,** *m.* skimmer; **-haube,** *f.* head (brewing).

schaumig, foamy, frothy.

Schaum-kalk, *n.* aragonite; **-kelle,** *f.* skimming ladle, skimmer; **-kraut,** *n.* *Cardamine pratensis;* **-leber,** *f.* foamy liver; **-löffel,** *m.* skimming spoon, skimmer; **-los,** foamless, frothless; **-rohr,** *n.* **-röhre,** *f.* foam tube; **-schwärze,** *f.* finely powdered animal charcoal; **-schwimmaufbereitung,** *f.* flotation.

Schaum-seife, *f.* lathering soap; **-spat,** *m.* analcite; **-stand,** *m.* head (brewing); **-theorie,** *f.* foam theory of protoplasm; **-ton,** *m.* fuller's earth; **-wein,** *m.* sparkling wine, champagne.

Schau-platz, *m.* scene, stage, theater; **-sammlung,** *f.* collection for exhibition purpose; **-spiel,** *n.* spectacle, sight, play, drama; **-stellung,** *f.* exhibition; **-tafel,** *f.* diagram.

Schawatte, *n.* anvil block.

Scheck, *m.* -e, -s, check.

schecken, to dapple, spot; **-bildung,** *f.* piebald spotting, partial albinism.

scheckig, dappled, piebald, spotted, mottled, brindled.

Scheel-bleierz, *n.* scheeletite; **-bleispat,** *m.* scheeletite; **-erz,** *m.* scheelite.

Scheele's̓ches Süss, *n.* glycerol, glycerin.

scheelisieren, scheelize (treat wine with glycerin).

Scheelit, *m.* tungsten, wolframic limestone.

Scheelsäure, *f.* tungstic acid.

Scheere, *f.* scissors, shears.

Sche(e)rfestigkeit, *f.* shearing strength.

Scheffel, *m.* bushel.

Scheibchen, *n.* little disk, little slice.

Scheibe, *f.* disk, slice, cake of wax, pane of glass, honeycomb, washer, sheave, pulley, wheel, target, dial.

scheiben-ähnlich, disklike, discord; **-anker,** *m.* disk armature; **-artig,** disklike, discord; **-blei,** *n.* window lead; **-blüte,** *f.* disk (discord) flower; **-drehflieger,** *m.* **-drehflügler,** *m.* seed or fruit with Aspidospernus type of wings; **-egge,** *f.* disk harrow; **-eisen,** *n.* pig iron in disks; **-förmig,** disk-shaped, discoid; **-glas,** *n.* window glass.

Scheiben-honig, *m.* honey in combs; **-kupfer,** *n.* rose copper; **-lack,** *m.* shellac; **-pilze,** *m.pl.* Discomycetales; **-quallen,** *f.pl.* Discomedusae; **-querader,** *f.* discoid cross vein; **-reissen,** *n.* conversion into disks or rosettes; **-spule,** *f.* flanged spool; **-ständig,** implanted in the disk, central as opposed to marginal; **-wachs,** *n.* cake wax; **-zelle,** *f.* discoid cell.

scheidbar, separable, analyzable.

Scheidbarkeit, *f.* separability, analyzability.

Scheide, *f.* sheath, vagina, rostrum, boundary, border; **-bürette,** *f.* separating burette; **-erz,** *n.* picked ore, screened ore; **-fähig,** separable; **-flüssigkeit,** *f.* separating (parting) liquid; **-gefäss,** *n.* decanter; **-gold,** *n.* gold purified by parting; **-gut,** *n.* material to be separated; **-kalk,** *m.* defecation lime (in sugar refining); **-kapelle,** *f.* cupel.

Scheide-knospe, *f.* sheathed bud; **-kolben,** *m.* separating flask; **-kuchen,** *m.* liquation disk; **-kunst,** *f.* analytical chemistry; **-linie,** *f.* boundary line; **-mehl,** *n.* dust of picked ore; **-mittel,** *n.* parting agent; **-münze,** *f.* small coin.

scheiden, to separate, part, depart, analyze, decompose, pick, sort, clarify, divide, sever, divorce; **-bakterien,** *n.pl.* vaginal

bacteria; **-band,** *n.* vaginal ligament; **-blatt,** *n.* spathe, sheathing leaf; **-gewölbe,** *n.* vault of vagina, fornix; **-haar,** *n.* sheath hair; **-knospe,** *f.* adventitious bud; **-knoten,** *m.* sheath node; **-mastdarmwand,** *f.* rectovaginal wall; **-schleim,** *m.* vaginal mucus.

Scheide-ofen, *m.* parting furnace; **-pfanne,** *f.* defecating pan, clarifier; **-schlamm,** *m.* defecating slime; **-sieb,** *n.* separating sieve; **-silber,** *n.* parting silver; **-trichter,** *m.* separating funnel; **-vorrichtung,** *f.* parting apparatus; **-wand,** *f.* partition wall, septum, diaphragm; **-bildung,** *f.* wall formation (between two daughter nuclei); **-brüchig,** septifragal (dehiscence).

Scheide-spaltig, septicidal; **-wasser,** *n.* nitric acid, aqua regia; **-weg,** *m.* forked way, crossroads.

Scheidung, *f.* separation, analysis.

Scheidungsmittel, *n.* parting agent.

Schein, *m.* **-e,** appearance, pretext, luster, light, shine, bloom, document, paper, bill, certificate; **-achse,** *f.* false (cymose) spike; **-anemone,** *f.* Anemonopsis.

scheinbar, apparent, seeming, likely, plausible.

Schein-beere, *f.* sphalerocarpium, accessory fruit; **-bewegung,** *f.* apparent movement; **-dolde,** *f.* false umbel, a type of cyme.

scheinen, (*dat.*) to shine, appear, seem; es **scheint mir,** it seems to me.

Schein-fäden, *m.pl.* thread forms, pseudo threads; **-farbe,** *f.* accidental color; **-frucht,** *f.* spurious fruit; **-fruchtgehäuse,** *n.* covering of false fruit; **-fuss,** *m.* pseudopodium; **-gelenk,** *n.* false articulation (arthrosis); **-gold,** *n.* imitation gold; **-grund,** *m.* apparent reason, pretext; **-hasel,** *f.* Corylopsis, **-hefe,** *f.* mycelial cyst.

Schein-kern, *m.* false heartwood; **-kranz,** false whorl; **-malve,** *f.* Malvastrum; **-mantel,** *m.* pseudo mantle; **-nektarium,** *n.* false nectary; **-parenchym,** *n.* pseudoparenchyma; **-quirl,** *m.* false whorl; **-quitte,** *f.* Chaenomeles; **-ring,** *m.* fictitious ring, false ring; **-saftblume,** *f.* flower with false nectary.

Schein-schmarotzer, *m.* epiphyte (pseudoparasitic); **-schülferchen,** *n.* false scale; **-spiere,** *f.* Holodiscus; **-tot,** seemingly dead; **-tüpfel,** *m.* false pit; **-vererbung,** *f.* false inheritance; **-werfer,** *m.* projector, reflector, searchlight, headlight, flashlight; **-wirtel,** *m.* verticillaster; **-zwiebel,**

f. aerial tuber; **-zwitter,** *m.* pseudohermaphrodite; **-zwitterbildung,** *f.* pseudohermaphroditism.

Scheit, *n.* log, billet, block, stick.

Scheitel, *m.*-, vertex, apex, origin, summit, crown, top, parting of hair; **-abstand,** *m.* vertex distance; **-auge,** *n.* parietal (pineal) eye; **-band,** *n.* parietal bone; **-beinhöcker,** *m.* parietal eminence; **-beuge,** *f.* parietal bend, cephalic flexure; **-brechwert,** *m.* vertex refraction; **-einsenkung,** *f.* temporal depression.

Scheitel-ende, *n.* vertex; **-faktor,** *m.* amplitude factor; **-fersenlänge,** *f.* crownheel length; **-gegend,** *f.* region of the vertex; **-grube,** *f.* cephalic pit; **-höhe,** *f.* vertex capitis; **-kamm,** *m.* (external) sagittal crest; **-kanal,** *m.* canal (crossing a water divide); **-kreis,** *m.* azimuth, vertical circle; **-krümmung,** *f.* parietal curvature, forebrain flexure.

Scheitel-lappen, *m.* parietal lobe; **-linie,** *f.* vertical line; **-loch,** *n.* parietal foramen; **-naht,** *f.* parietal suture; **-platte,** *f.* apical plate, neural plate; **-pol,** *m.* cephalic pole; **-punkt,** *m.* vertex, zenith; **-recht,** vertical; **-spross,** *m.* apical shoot; **-steisslänge,** *f.* vertex-breech length, crown-rump length.

Scheitel-tangente, *f.* vertical tangent; **-tiefe,** *f.* depth of the vertex; **-wachstum** *n.* apical growth; **-wärts,** in the direction of the apex; **-wert,** *m.* peak (maximum) value, amplitude; **-windung,** *f.* parietal convolution; **-winkel,** *m.* vertical opposite angle, exterior; opposite angle; **-wirbel,** *m.* vertex whorl, parietal vertebra; **-zelle,** *f.* apical cell; **-zoid,** *m.* apical zooid.

scheitern, to suffer, wreck, be wrecked, fail, be frustrated, miscarry.

Scheitholz, *n.* split firewood.

Schelfe, *f.* husk, shell, pod.

Schellackfirnis, *m.* shellac varnish.

Schelle, *f.* clip, clamp, little bell.

schellen, to ring,

Schell-fisch, *m.* cod, haddock; **-harz,** *n.* white rosin; **-ölsäure,** *f.* shellolic acid.

schelten, to scold.

Schema, *n.* scheme, diagram, model, pattern, sketch, blank, form, schedule.

schematisch, schematic, diagrammatic.

schematisieren, to sketch, schematize.

Schemel, *m.* stool.

Schemen, *m.* shadow, phantom, delusion.

Schenkbier, *n.* draft beer.

Schenke, *f.* public house, tavern.

Schenkel, *m.*-, leg, shank, pillar, thigh, crus femur, peduncle, side, side piece; **-anhang,** *m.* trochanter; **-band,** *n.* crural ligament; **-bein,** *n.* femur; **-beinhals,** *m.* neck of the femur; **-beinknorren,** *m.* condyle of the femur; **-beinkopf,** *m.* head of the femur; **-beuge,** *f.* inguinal furrow, groin.

Schenkel-binde, *f.* crural ligament; **-bogen,** *m.* crural arch; **-dreher,** *m.* trochanter, rotator of the femur; **-gegend,** *f.* crural region; **-gelenk,** *n.* hip joint; **-hals,** *m.* neck of the femur; **-kanal,** *m.* femoral (crural) canal; **-knorren,** *m.* trochanter.

Schenkel-kopf, *m.* head of the femur; **-kreuz,** *n.* crural cross (meeting of hair lines); **-poren,** *f.pl.* gland pores on the femur; **-ring,** *m.* femoral ring, trochanter; **-rohr,** *n.* **-röhre,** *f.* elbow, bent tube, elbow pipe; **-umdreher,** *m.* rotator of the thigh, trochanter; **-wurzel,** *f.* base of femur, hip.

schenken, to pour out, give, present, retail, acquit, suckle.

Scherbe, *f.* (Scherben, *m.*), potsherd, shard, fragment, piece, crock, cupel.

Scherbel-krautwurzel, *f.* asarum, asarabacca, hazelwort.

Scherbenkobalt, *m.* native arsenic.

Schere, *f.* scissors, shears, chela, pincer, notch, nick, shafts, claw.

scheren, to shear, clip, cut, plague, torment, vex, go away, clear off, care for; **sich um etwas ~,** to trouble about something, be concerned for.

Scheren-bindung, *f.* chelation, chelate combination; **-fühler,** *m.pl.* chelicerae; **-fuss,** *m.* chelicera; **-kiefer,** *m.pl.* chelicerae; **-stahl,** *m.* shear steel; **-taster,** *m.* pincer, pedipalp; **-zange,** *f.* cutting forceps, wire cutter.

Scherfestigkeit, *f.* shearing strength.

Scherflein, *n.* mite.

Scherspannung, *f.* shearing stress, shear.

Scherungsfestigkeit, *f.* shearing strength

Scherversuch, *m.* shear(ing) test.

scherzen, to joke, jest, frolic.

Scherz, *m.*-e, joke, jest, fun, sport.

scherzhaft, humorous.

Scheu, *f.* shyness, timidity.

scheu, shy, timid, bashful.

scheuen, to shy, shun, fear, avoid, dread; **sich ~,** to be afraid of, have an aversion to.

Scheuer, *f.* barn, granary, corn crib; **-festigkeit,** *f.* abrasion resistance; **-mittel,** *n.* scouring agent.

scheuern, to scour, wash, scrub, clean, rub, chafe.

Scheuerpulver, *n.* scouring powder.

Scheune, *f.* barn, hayloft, granary, shed.

Schicht, *f.*-en, layer, stratum, bed, course, film, emulsion, coat, shift, turn, charge, batch; **-boden,** *m.* mixing place; **-ebene,** *f.* plane of stratification.

schichten, to charge, stratify, arrange in layers or beds, pile, stack; **-aufbau,** *m.* stratification; **-bau,** *m.* stratified structure; **-bindung,** *f.* connection of strata; **-glas,** *n.* laminated glass; **-gruppe,** *f.* group of strata; **-kohle,** *f.* foliated coal; **-verbindung,** *f.* combination of strata; **-weise,** in layers or strata, stratified.

Schicht-fläche, *f.* bedding plane; **-fuge,** *f.* grain (of rocks), joint of strata; **-gestein,** *n.* stratified rock; **-holz,** *n.* stacked wood, cordwood; **-mass,** *n.* stacked measure; **-nutzholz,** *n.* stacked timber, cordwood.

Schichtung, *f.* charging, piling, stratification, arranging in layers.

Schichtungsebene, *f.* plane of stratification.

Schicht-wasser, *n.* ground water; **-zahn,** *m.* milk tooth.

Schick, *m.* skill, dexterity, tact, fitness, style.

schicken, to send, happen, suit, be fit, conform, accommodate oneself, adapt, prepare; **sich** ∼, to come to pass, chance, be proper; **sich für etwas** ∼, to be adapted, suitable for something; **sich in etwas** ∼, to submit (be reconciled) to something; **geschickt,** sent, skilled, clever, suitable, fit.

schicklich, becoming, proper, fit, suitable.

Schicksal, *n.* fate, destiny, fortune, lot.

Schicksche Reaktion, *f.* Schick reaction.

Schickung, *f.* dispensation, affliction.

Schiebe-blende, *f.* sliding diaphragm; **-bühne,** *f.* movable platform or scaffold; **-dreieck,** *n.* (drafting) scaffold triangle; **-druck,** *m.* separation pressure; **-gelenk,** *n.* arthrodial joint; **-hülse,** *f.* sliding sleeve.

schieben, to shove, push, slide, slip, heave.

Schieber, *m.* slide, slider, carriage, slide plate, gate valve, slide valve, bolt, bar, shovel, pusher, damper, profiteer; **-kasten,** *m.* slide, valve chest.

Schieberohr, *n.* sliding tube or sleeve.

Schieber-pinzette, *f.* torsion or clamp forceps with sliding catch; **-ventil,** *n.* slide valve.

Schiebung, *f.* shoving, sharp practices, shifting, shearing deformation, glide, maneuver; **spezifische** ∼, shearing strain.

schied (scheiden), separated, departed.

Schieds-analyse, *f.* umpire analysis; **-richter,** *m.* umpire, arbiter, referee; **-spruch,** *m.* award, decision, arbitration.

schief, inclined, oblique, diagonal, slanting, sloping, distorted, crooked, askew, awry, amiss; **-agarkultur,** *f.* sloped-agar culture.

Schiefe, *f.* slope, inclination, obliqueness, crookedness, inclined plane.

Schiefer, *m.* slate, schist, shale, flaw; **-ähnlich, -artig,** slatelike, slaty, schistous; **-blau,** slate-blue; **-boden,** *m.* slaty soil; **-farbe,** *f.* slate color; **-gips,** *m.* foliated gypsum; **-grau,** slate-gray; **-haltig,** containing slate, schistous, slaty.

schieferig, slaty, slatelike, schistous, scaly, flaky, foliated.

Schiefer-kohle, *f.* slaty coal; **-mehl,** *n.* ground shale.

schiefern, to scale off, exfoliate.

Schiefer-stein, *m.* lithographic stone; **-talk,** *m.* indurated talc; **-ton,** *m.* slate clay, shale.

Schieferung, *f.* scaling off, exfoliation.

schief-liegend, inclined, sloping, oblique; **-nase,** *f.* deformed nose; **-winklig,** oblique-angled, tilted.

schielen, to squint, be cross-eyed.

schien (scheinen), shone, was shining, seemed.

Schienbein, *n.* shinbone, tibia; **-gräte,** *f.* extremity of tibia; **-kante,** *f.* edge of shinbone, tibial crest; **-knochen,** *m.* tibia; **-knorren,** *m.* condyle of tibia; **-kopf,** *m.* head of tibia; **-leiste,** *f.* crest of tibia; **-röhre,** *f.* medullary cavity of tibia; **-stachel,** *m.* tubercle of tibia.

Schiene, *f.* splint, rail, slat, strip, band, bar, rim, tire.

schienen, to splint; **-borste,** *f.* tibial bristle; **-grube,** *f.* tibial fossa; **-stoss,** *m.* rail joint; **-strang,** *m.* track; **-weg,** *m.* railway, tramway; **-weite,** *f.* railway gauge.

schier, sheer, pure, almost, simply, barely.

Schierling, *m.* hemlock (*Conium maculatum);* **-saft,** *m.* hemlock juice, juice of conium.

Schierlings-kraut, *n.* hemlock (*Conium maculatum);* **-tanne,** *f.* Canadian or eastern hemlock, hemlock spruce (*Tsuga canadensis).*

schiert (scheren), shears, clips.

Schiessbaumwolle, *f.* guncotton.

schiessen, to shoot, sprout, fire, dash, emit.

Schiesser, *m.pl.* runners.

Schiess-ofen, *m.* bomb oven, tube furnace; -pulver, *n.* gunpowder; -rohr, *n.,* -röhre, *f.* bomb tube; -stoff, *m.* powder; -wolle, *f.* guncotton.

Schiff, *n.*-e, ship, vessel, shuttle, galley, nave.

Schiffahrt, *f.*-en, navigation.

schiffbar, navigable.

Schiffbauholz, *n.* timber for shipbuilding.

Schiffbein, *n.* scaphoid bone; -gelenk, *n.* cuneoscaphoid articulation.

Schiff-bohrwurm, *m.* shipworm; -bruch, *m.* shipwreck.

Schiffchen, *n.* boat, little ship, shuttle keel.

schiffen, to navigate, sail.

Schiffer, *m.*-, mariner.

Schiffs-leim, *m.* marine glue; -pech, *n.* common black pitch.

Schild, *m.*-e, shield, escutcheon, carapace.

Schild, *n.*-er, badge, label, sign (board), shell; -artig, clypeate, scutate; -blatt, *n.* Peltiphyllum; -blume, *f.* Aspidistra, *Chelone obliqua.*

Schildchen, *n.* scutellum, scutiform leaf little label, shield.

Schilddrüse, *f.* thyroid gland.

Schilddrüsen-brücke, *f.* isthmus of thyroid gland; -entfernung, *f.* removal of thyroid gland, thyroidectomy; -essenz, *f.* thyroid solution; -extrakt, *n.* thyroid solution; -störung, *f.* disturbance of the thyroid gland; -wirkung, *f.* action of the thyroid.

Schilderblau, *n.* pencil blue.

schildern, to depict, sketch, portray, draw, describe.

Schilderung, *f.* description, representation.

Schild-farn, *m.* Aspidium; -förmig, shield-shaped, scutiform, peltate, thyroid; -giessbeckenmuskel, -giesskannenmuskel, *m.* thyroarytenoid muscle; -käfer, *m.pl.* tortoise beetles (Cassidinae); -kehldeckelband, *n.* thyroepiglottic ligament; -kiemer, *m.pl.* Aspidobranchia; -knorpel, *m.* thyroid cartilage.

Schild-kraut, *n. Alyssum calycinum;* -kröte, *f.* turtle; -krötenpanzer, *m.* turtle shell; -läuse, *f.pl.* scale insects (Coccidae); -patt, *n.* tortoise shell; -schlundkopfmuskel, *m.* thyrcpharyngeus muscle; -wache, *f.* sentinel; -wanzen, *f.pl.* Pentatomidae.

Schilf, *n.*-e, reed.

schilferig, scaly, lepidote, exfoliating.

schilfern, to scale off, exfoliate.

Schilf-glaserz, *n.* freieslebenite; -gräser, *n.pl.* Arundinaceae; -rohr, *n.* cane, sedge, ditch reed (*Phragmites communis*).

Schiller, *m.* play of colors, iridescence, claret; -farbe, *f.* changeable color, iridescent (schiller) color; -feder,*f.* iridescent feather; -glanz, *m.* iridescent luster.

schillerig, iridescent, opalescent.

schillern, to exhibit a play of colors, iridesce, opalesce.

schillernd, iridescent, opalescent; schillernde Färbung, *f.* fluorescence.

Schiller-seide, *f.* shot silk, changeable silk; -stoff, *m.* iridescent substance; -streifen, *m.* iridescent stripe; -wein, *m.* wine from red and white grapes mixed.

schilt (schelten), scolds.

Schimmel, *m.* mold, mildew, mustiness, gray or white horse; -artig, moldlike, moldy; -geruch, moldy smell.

schimmelig, moldy, musty, mildewed.

schimmeln, to mold, get moldy.

Schimmel-pflänzchen, *n.* little mycodermic plant; -pilz, *m.* mold fungus, mold; -pilzkultur, *f.* culture of mold; -rasen, *m.* furlike growth of mold.

Schimmer, *m.* glimmer, shimmer, glitter.

schimmern, to glisten, glitter, gleam, shine.

schimpfen, to abuse, call, scold.

Schindel, *f.* shingle, splint; -holz, *n.* wood for shingles.

schinden, to skin, flay.

Schinken, *m.* -fleisch, *n.* ham.

Schippe, *f.* shovel, spade (cards), scoop.

Schirbel, *m.* bloom, stamp of metal.

Schirm, *m.*-e, screen, cover, shelter, shade, umbrella, umbel, visor; -druck, *m.* suppression or checking by shade.

schirmen, to screen, shield, shelter, protect.

Schirm-fang, *m.* catching insects with umbrella; -fläche, *f.* covered space, shaded area; -flieger, *m.pl.* seeds or fruits with parachute wings; -förmig, umbraculiferous; -gestell, *n.* umbrella case or frame; -glucke, *f.* brooder, hover, mother; -keilschlag, *m.* shelterwood wedge system; -kraut, *n.* Trientalis; -nadel, *f.* umbellike spicule.

Schirm-pflanze, *f.* umbelliferous plant; -rand, *m.* margin of the bell (Medusa);

-rispe, *f.* umbellike panicle, corymb; **-schlag,** *m.* shelterwood felling; **-schlagbetrieb,** *m.* shelterwood compartment system; **-stand,** *m.* shelterwood; **-verjüngung,** *f.* shelterwood regeneration; **-wirkung,** *f.* screening effect.

schizogen, schizogenous.

Schizomyzeten, *pl.* bacteria, schizomycetes.

Schizostel, *m.* broken stele.

schlabbern, to slobber, overflow, chat, gossip.

Schlabber-rohr, *n.* overflow pipe; **-ventil,** *n.* check valve.

Schlacht, *f.*-en, battle.

schlachten, to kill, slaughter.

Schlacht-feld, *n.*-er, battlefield; **-haus,** *n.*⸚er, slaughterhouse, abattoir; **-hof,** *m.* packing plant.

Schlack, *m.* niter deposit.

Schlacke, *f.* slag, clinker, cinder, scoria.

schlacken, to slag, form slag, clinker; **-artig,** slaggy, scoriaceous, drossy; **-bildung,** *f.* formation of slag, scorification, **-einschluss,** *m.* slag content or inclusion; **-eisen,** *n.* cinder iron; **-form,** *f.* cinder block; **-frischen,** *n.* pig boiling; **-gang,** *m.* slag duct, cinder fall; **-halde,** *f.* slag dump; **-haltig,** containing slag or clinker.

Schlacken-herd, *m.* slag hearth; **-kobalt,** *m.* safflorite; **-lava,** *f.* scoriaceous lava; **-loch,** *n.* cinder notch, slag hole, cinder tap; **-mehl,** *n.* ground slag; **-puddeln,** *n.* pig boiling; **-reich,** rich in slag; **-rein,** free from slag; **-rösten,** *n.* roasting of slag; **-scherbe,** *f.* scorifier.

Schlacken-scherben, *m.* scorifier; **-spiess,** *m.* cinder iron, slag iron; **-spur,** *f.* slag hole, cinder (tap) notch; **-staub,** *m.* coal dust; **-stein,** *m.* slag brick; **-stich,** *m.* slag hole, cinder notch; **-zacken,** *m.* cinder (front) plate; **-ziegel,** *m.* slag brick; **-zinn,** *n.* tin extracted from slag.

schlackig, slaggy, drossy, scoriaceous.

Schlaf, *m.* sleep; **-ähnlich,** sleeplike; **-arznei,** *f.* soporific, hypnotic, narcotic; **-befördernd,** soporific; **-bewegung,** *f.* nyctitropic movement.

Schläfe, *f.* temple.

schlafen, to sleep, lie dormant.

Schläfenbein, *n.* temporal bone; **-fortsatz,** *m.* process of temporal bone, temporal apophysis; **-griffel,** *m.* styloid process of temporal bone; **-jochfortsatz,** *m.* zygomatic process of temporal bone; **-pyramide,** *f.* petrous portion of temporal bone; **-schuppe,**

f. temporal scale; **-warzenfortsatz,** *m.* mastoid portion of temporal bone.

schlafendes Auge, *n.* dormant bud or eye.

Schläfen-ecke, *f.* temporal angle; **-fläche,** *f.* temporal surface; **-flügel,** *m.pl.* alisphenoid, temporal portion of sphenoid; **-fortsatz,** *m.* temporal apophysis; **-gegend,** *f.* temporal region; **-grube,** *f.* temporal fossa; **-knochen,** *m.* temporal bone.

Schläfen-lappen, *m.* temporal lobe; **-loch,** *n.* temporal fossa; **-pyramide,** *f.* petrous section of temporal bone; **-rand,** *m.* temporal border; **-schuppe,** *f.* temporal scale; **-windung,** *f.* temporal convolution; **-zweig,** *m.* temporal branch.

schlaff, flabby, flaccid, slack, loose, soft, careless, limp.

Schlaffheit, *f.* limpness.

Schlaf-krankheit, *f.* sleeping sickness; **-mittel,** *n.* soporific, narcotic; **-mohn,** *m.* opium, poppy; **-stellung,** *f.* nocturnal position.

schläft, sleeps.

Schlaf-trank, *m.* sleeping draft; **-zimmer,** *n.* bedroom.

Schlag, *m.*⸚e, stroke, blow, impact, beat, movement, percussion, pulsation, knock, shock, kick, apoplexy, coinage, stamp, sort, cutting, area, block, plot, field, song; type.

Schlagader, *f.*-n, artery; **-ast,** *m.* arterial branch; **-gang,** *m.* arterial canal; **-haut,** *f.* coat of artery; **-kammer,** *f.* left ventricle (of heart); **-netz,** *n.* arterial plexus.

Schlagarbeit, *f.* impact work or energy.

schlagartig, sudden, in rapid succession.

schlagbar, mature, fit for cutting.

Schlag-biegefestigkeit, *f.* impact flexure strength; **-biegeversuch,** *m.* impact-bending test; **-einteilung,** *f.* distribution of fellings.

Schlagempfindlichkeit, *f.* sensitiveness to percussion.

schlagen, to strike, beat, fell, hit, knock, cut, warble, pulsate, palpitate, take root, throb; **sich** ~, to fight; **sich durchschlagen,** to get along, to get by; **Wurzel** ~, to strike (take root); **kurz und klein** ~, to knock (break) to bits; **durchschlagen,** to soak through.

schlagend, striking, impressive; **schlagende Wetter,** firedamp; **schlagender Beweis,** conclusive evidence.

Schläger, *m.* beater, fighter, batter, rapier, racket (tennis), warbler.

Schlag-festigkeit, *f.* resistance to shock, impact strength, crushing strength; -figur, *f.* percussion figure; -folge, . succession of cuttings; -gold, *n.* leaf gold; -härte, *f.* impact hardness; -hasenmühle, *f.* edgerunner mill; -holz, *n.* regular fellings; -hüter, *m.* guard of felling area; -kontrolle *f.* control of fellings; -licht, *n.* strong light, direct (sun)light, glare.

Schlag-lot, *n.* hard solder; -mühle, *f.* crusher, crushing mill, hammer mill; -ordnung, *f.* felling series; patrone, *f.* priming cartridge; -pflanze, *f.* wood plant, wildling; -pflege, *f.* tending of young growth; -probe, *f.* percussion test, impact test; -pulver, *n.* fulminating powder; -räumung, *f.* clearance of felling area; -reingung, *f.* clearing of felling area.

Schlag-saat, *f.* hempseed; -sahne, *f.* whipped cream; -sieb, *n.* precipitating sieve; -stift, *m.* firing pin.

schlägt (schlagen), strikes, beats.

Schlag-versuch, *m.*-e, impact test, plot experiment; -wasser, *n.* gush of water, bilge water; -weite, *f.* striking distance, spark distance; -werk, *n.* striking apparatus, rammer; -wetter, *n.pl.* firedamp; -widerstand, *m.* impact resistance; -wort, *n.* slogan; watchword, catchphrase; -zeile, *f.* headline; -zünder, *m.* percussion fuse.

Schlamm, *m.* mud, sludge, mire, slime, slurry, silt, ooze; -analyse, *f.* sedimentation (hydrometer) analysis.

Schlämm-analyse, *f.* analysis by elutrition; -apparat, *m.* elutriating (cleansing) apparatus.

schlämmen, to elutriate, wash, levigate.

Schlämm-fass, *n.* washing tub or tank; -flasche, *f.* elutriating flask; -fliegen, *f.pl.* Eristales.

schlammig, muddy, miry, sludgy, slimy, oozy.

Schlammherd, *m.* slime pit or tank.

Schlämm-kohle, *f.* washed coal; -kreide, *f.* prepared chalk, whiting; -peitzger, *m.* pond loach (Misgurnus); -pfännchen, *n.* scum pan; -pflanze, *f.* mud plant; -prozess, *m.* slime process; -röhre, *f.* mud tube.

Schlammschlich, *m.* washed ore slime.

Schlämm-schnecke, *f.* pond snail; -sumpf, *m.* muck swamp; -trichter, *m.* elutriating funnel.

Schlämmung, *f.* elutriating.

Schlämm-verfahren, *n.* washing process; -vorrichtung, *f.* elutriating apparatus.

schlang (schlingen), wound, twisted, was twisting.

Schlange, *f.* snake, serpent, (fire) hose, worm, coil.

schlängeln, to wind, coil, meander.

schlängelnd, sinuous, winding, serpentine.

schlangen-artig, snakelike, serpentine; -bart, *m.* snake's-beard (Ophiopogon); -gift, *n.* snake venom; -holz, *n.* snakewood, serpentwood; -kühler, *m.* spiral condenser; -rohr, *n.*, -röhre, *f.* worm, coil, spiral pipe or tube; -stein, *m.* ophite, serpentine; -sterne, *m.pl.* serpent stars (Ophiuroidea); -wurz, *f.* Virginia snakeroot (Aristolochia serpentaria); -wurzel, *f.* snakeroot, serpentaria.

schlank, slender, slim, thin.

Schlankheitsgrad, *m.* slenderness ratio.

Schlappe, *f.* defeat.

Schlappermilch, *f.* curdled milk.

Schlappohren, *n.pl.* lob ears.

Schlauch, *m.* tube, tubing, pipe, cannula, sack, utricle, ascus, hose, skin; -algen, *f.pl.* Siphoneae; -artig, saccate; -balg, *m.* utricle; -blatt, *n.* ascidiform leaf; -drüse, *f.* tubular gland.

schlauchen, to fill casks by means of hose.

Schlauch-erzeuger, *m.* ascogonium; -fasergewebe, *n.* ascogenous hyphae; -frucht, *f.* ascus fruit, utriculus; -fruchtform, *f.* ascigerous stage; -kapsel, *f.* sacellus; -keimung, *f.* tube germination; -klemme, *f.* tube clamp; -kopf, *m.* slime plug in sieve tube; -leitung, *f.* hose line.

Schlauch-pflanze, *f.* pitcher plant (Darlingtonia); -pilz, *m.* ascomycetous fungus; -spore, *f.* ascospore; -stück, *n.* tubing attachment; -tiere, *n.pl.* Coelenterata; -verbindung, *f.* hose connection; -zellen, *f.pl.* asci.

Schlauder, *f.* iron tie.

Schlaufenfadenführer, *m.* loop thread guide.

schlecht, bad, ill, poor; -bestellt, in bad condition.

schlechterdings, by all means, utterly, absolutely.

schlecht-hin, -weg, *m.* simple, merely, plainly.

Schlecht-wetter, *n.* bad weather; -wettererzeugend, producing bad weather; -wüchsig, unthrifty, badly shaped.

schleckern, to lick, lap, be dainty.

Schlegel, *m.* mallet, beetle, beater, hammer, drumstick.

Schlehdorn, *m.* blackthorn, sloe tree (*Prunus spinosa*).

Schlehe, *f.* sloe.

schleichen, to creep, crawl, slink, sneak.

schleichend, slow, creeping, lingering.

Schleich-gut, *n.* smuggled goods, contraband; **-handel,** *m.* smuggling, illicit trade.

Schleichter, *m.* reptile, creeping animal.

Schleie, *f.* tench.

Schleier, *m.* veil, haze, screen, velum, indusium, fog (in photography).

Schleierchen, *n.* indusium.

Schleier-gras, *n.* Aira; **-kraut,** *n.* Gypsophila.

schleiern, to veil, fog, cloud.

Schleifbarkeit, *f.* polishability.

Schleife, *f.* loop, noose, knot, slide, sled, sledge, float, dray, fillet.

schleifen, to grind, sharpen, polish, cut, abrade, skid, drag, trail, slide, whet; **-blume,** *f.* Iberis; **-förmig,** loop-shaped; **-kanal,** *m.* nephridial (looped) tubule; **-schenkel,** *m.* Henle's loop; **-verbindung,** *f.* anastomosis in loops.

Schleiferei, *f.* grindery, grinder's trade, pulp manufacture.

Schleif-feder, *f.* sliding spring; **-lack,** *m.* body varnish; **-material,** *n.* abrasive; **-mittel,** *n.* abrasive; **-pulver,** *n.* grinding (polishing) powder; **-rad,** *n.* grinding (polishing) wheel.

Schleifsel, *n.* **-staub,** *m.* grindings.

Schleif-stein, *m.* grinding stone, whetstone; **stoff,** *m.* ground pulp, paper pulp.

Schleifung, *f.* grinding.

Schleifweg, *m.* road slide.

Schleim, *m.* slime, mucilage, mucus; **-absonderung,** *f.* secretion of mucus; **-artig,** slimy, glutinous, mucoid; **-auswurf,** *m.* expectoration; **-bakterien,** *n.pl.* Myxobacteria; **-balg,** *m.* mucous follicle; **-band,** *n.* mucous ligament.

Schleim-bildend, slime-forming, muciparous; **-bildung,** *f.* production of (slime) mucilage; **-blatt,** mucous layer; **-drüse,** *f.* mucous gland; **-endosperm,** *n.* mucilaginous endosperm; **-epidermis,** *f.* mucilaginous epidermis; **-frucht,** *f.* fruit provided with mucilage (to eject the seed).

Schleim-gang, *m.* mucilaginous canal; **-gärung,** *f.* mucous (viscous) fermentation; **-gewebe,** *n.* mucous (mucilaginous) tissue; **-harz,** *n.* gum resin; **-haut,** *f.* mucous membrane; **-hautcarcinom,** *n.* mucous-membrane carcinoma; **-hauterkrankung,** *f.* affection of mucous membrane.

schleimig, slimy, mucilaginous, mucous, viscous; **schleimige Gärung,** *f.* milch, mucous (viscous) fermentation.

Schleimigkeit, *f.* sliminess.

Schleim-kapsel, *f.* mucous capsule; **-kork,** *m.* mucilaginous periderm; **-krankheit,** *f.* slime disease; **-kreide,** *f.* prepared chalk; **-membran,** *f.* mucous membrane; **-netz,** *n.* mucous reticulum; **-organ,** *n.* slime cells; **-papille,** *f.* club-shaped epidermal trichome containing slime or Bryophytes.

Schleim-pfropf, *m.* mucous plug; **-pilz,** *m.* slime fungus, slime mold (Myxomycetes); **-ranke,** *f.* mucilaginous thread in intercellular space of roots (orchids); **-sack,** *m.* mucous follicle; **-same,** *f.* Collomia; **-sauer,** mucate of; **-säure,** *f.* mucic acid.

Schleim-schicht, *f.* layer of mucilage; **-stoff,** *m.* mucin; **-stoffartig,** mucinlike, mucoid; **-tier,** *n.* mollusk; **-zelle,** *f.* mucilaginous cell; **-zellulose,** *f.* mucocellulose; **-zucker,** *m.* levulose.

Schleisse, *f.* splint, splinter.

schleissen, to slit, split, strip, wear (out).

Schlemmboden, *m.* diluvial soil.

schlemmen, to eat greedily, revel, carouse.

Schlempe, *f.* spent wash, vinasse, slops; **-asche, -kohle,** *f.* crude potash from beet vinasse; **-prober,** *m.* slop tester.

schlenkern, to sling, fling, swing, dangle.

Schleppbusch, *m.* brush harrow.

Schleppe, *f.* train, trail, felt board, truck.

schleppen, to trail, drag, tow, lug, skid.

Schlepper, *m.* tractor, hauler, tug, dredge.

Schleppgeissel, *f.* backward-directed cillum.

Schleppkraft, *f.* tractive force.

Schleppmühle, *f.* drag(-stone) mill.

Schlesien, *n.* Silesia.

Schleuder, *f.*-**n,** centrifuge, sling, elator; **-gebläse,** *n.* centrifugal bellows, blowpipe; blower, compressor; **-honig,** *m.* extracted honey; **-klette,** *f.* burr fruit (dispersing seed when rebounding from passing animals); **-maschine,** *f.* centrifugal machine, centrifugal.

schleudern, to sling, fling, hurl, centrifuge, hydroextract, roll, cut prices.

Schleuderwaffe, *f.* missile (weapon).

schleunig, speedy, ready, quick, immediate.

Schleuse, *f.* sluice, lock, sewer.

Schleusengas, *n.* sewer gas.

schlich (schleichen), sneaked, was sneaking.

Schlich, *m.*-e, byway, trick, concentrate, slime, schlich; **-arbeit,** *f* smelting of slimes.

schlicht, plain, simple, homely, smooth, even, sleek, fine.

Schlichte, *f.* size, dressing, blackwash, skim (white) coat, slashing.

schlichtecht, fast to sizing.

schlichten, to settle, arrange, level, adjust, smooth, plane, dress, sleek, size, blackwash.

Schlicht-leim, *m.* sizing, size; **-messer,** *n.* plane knife; **-walze,** *f.* finishing roll, roller.

Schlick, *m.* slime, silt, mud, clay, schlich; **-bank,** *f.* mudbank.

Schlicker, *m.* paste, slip, slop, dross.

schlief (schlafen), slept, was sleeping.

schliefen, to slip, creep.

Schlieren, *f.pl.* schlieren, streaks; **-faden,** *m.* striated filament; **-methode,** *f.* track method, schlieren photography.

Schliesse, *f.* pin, peg, catch, latch, anchor.

schliessen, to close, shut, lock, seal, bind, terminate, finish, conclude, reason, contract; **in sich ~,** to comprehend, include, comprise; **aus etwas ~,** to conclude from something.

Schliesser, *m.* sphincter, constrictor.

Schliess-frucht, *f.* achene, cleistocarp; **-haut,** *f.* closing membrane; **-kapsel,** *f.* carcerule; **-kopf,** *m.* rivet head.

schliesslich, final, ultimate, finally, in conclusion.

Schliess-muskel, *m.* sphincter, constrictor, adductor; **-ring,** *m.* basal cells of tubular air chamber (anneau obturateur); **-rohr,** *n.,* **-röhre,** *f.* sealed tube.

Schliessungsdraht, *m.* connecting wire.

Schliesszelle, *f.* closing cell, guard cell of stomate.

schliff (schleifen), ground, sharpened.

Schliff, *m.*-e, grinding, sharpening, smoothness, polish, grindings; *pl.* ground faces (in general); **-stopfen,** *m.* ground-in stopper.

schlimm, bad, evil, sad, severe, sore, ill, unpleasant, fatal.

Schling-baum, -strauch, *m.* wayfaring tree (Viburnum).

Schlinge, *f.* loop, noose, sling, tendril, trap, snare.

schlingen, to wind, twine, twist, creep, climb, swallow, gulp, devour.

Schling-gewächs, *n.* twiner, climber, creeper; **-läufig,** brachydodromous (with looped veins); **-pflanze,** *f.* liana, climber, twining plant; **-waffe,** *f.* snare, trap, spring.

Schlippe'sches Salz, Schlippe's salt, sodium thioantimonate.

schliss (schleissen), split, slit, wore out.

Schlitten, *m.*-, sledge, sled, sleigh, truck, sliding carriage; **-mikrotom,** *n.* sliding microtome; **-objektivwechsler,** *m.* sliding objective changer.

Schlitt-schuh, *m.* skate; **-weg,** *m.* sledge road.

Schlitz, *m.*-e, slit, fissure, slot, cleft, slash, aperture; **-blende,** *f.* slit stop; **-brenner,** *m.* batswing burner.

schlitzen, to slit, slash, slot, split, cleave, rip.

schlitzförmig, slitlike.

schloff (schliefen), crept.

schloss (schliessen), closed, locked.

Schloss, *n.* lock, snap, clasp, valve, hinge of shell, castle, palace; **-band,** *n.* hinge ligament; **-bein,** *n.* ischium.

Schlosse, *f.* hailstone.

Schlosser, *m.* locksmith, mechanic.

Schloss-feld, *n.* hinge area; **-fortsatz,** *m.* cardinal process; **-graben,** *m.* moat; **-grube,** *f.* hinge groove; **-knochen,** *m.* ischium; **-platte,** *f.* hinge plate; **-rand,** *m.* hinge line; **-zähne,** *m.pl.* hinge teeth.

Schlot, *m.* -e, **Schlotte,** *f.* flue, smokestack, soil pipe.

Schlotter, *m.* sediment from boiling.

schlottern, to hang loose, dangle, flap, shake, wabble.

Schlucht, *f.*-en, ravine, gorge, gully; **-wald,** *m.* canyon forest.

schluchzen, to sob, hiccup.

Schluck, *m.* swallow, mouthful; **-akt,** *m.* act of swallowing.

schlucken, to swallow, gulp.

Schluckung, *f.* adsorption.

Schluff, *m.* silt.

schlug (schlagen), struck.

Schlummer, *m.* slumber.

schlummern, to sleep, slumber, doze.

schlummernd₂ dormant.

Schlund, *m.* throat, pharynx, gullet, gorge, esophagus, gulf, chasm; **-bewaffnung,** *f.* pharyngeal teeth; **-bogen,** *m.* hyoid arch, pharyngeal arch, visceral arch; **-dach,** *n.* roof of pharynx; **-drüse,** *f.* pharyngeal gland; **-ganglion,** *n.* esophageal (pharyngeal) ganglion; **-gaumenbogen,** *m.* pharyngopalatine arch; **-gewölbe,** *f.* fornix of pharynx; **-höhle,** *f.* pharyngeal cavity.

Schlundkopf, *m.* upper pharynx, esophagus, buccal mass; **-gaumenbogen,** *m.* pharyngopalatine arch; **-schnürer,** *m.* constrictor of pharynx.

Schlund-kranz, *m.* corona; **-masse,** *f.* buccal mass; **-mündung,** *f.* pharyngeal opening; **-pforte,** pharyngeal opening; **-platte,** *f.* pharyngeal plate; **-ring,** *m.* pharyngeal nerve ring; **-rinne,** *f.* esophageal groove, endostyle.

Schlund-rohr, *n.* **-röhre,** *f.* esophagus, esophageal tube; **-schnürer,** *m.* constrictor of pharynx; **-schuppe,** *f.* scale in throat of corolla; **-spalte,** *f.* branchial (pharyngeal) cleft; **-spaltenorgan,** *n.* visceral cleft organ; **-tasche,** *f.* pharyngeal pouch, branchial cleft.

Schlupf, *m.* slippage.

schlupfen, schlüpfen, to slip, slide, hatch.

Schlupfloch, *n.* loophole, hiding place.

schlüpfrig, slippery, lascivious; ∼ **machen,** to lubricate.

Schlüpfrigkeit, *f.* slipperiness, lubricity.

Schlupf-wespe, *f.* ichneumon fly, **-wespenblume,** *f.* flower pollinated by Ichneumonidae; **-winkel,** *m.* lurking place, haunt.

schlürfen, to sip, lap, suck air.

Schluss, *m.*⁻e, closing, close, conclusion, end, connection, complete canopy, dense stand; **-bildung,** *f.* closing one-leaf canopy.

Schlüssel, *m.* key, screw driver, wrench, switch; **-band,** *n.* clavicular articulation.

Schlüsselbein, *n.* collar bone, clavicle; **-ausschnitt,** *m.* clavicular notch.

Schlüssel-blume, *f.* *Primula officinalis;* **-blumengewächse,** *n.pl.* Primulaceae; **-grube,** *f.* clavicular fossa; **-nummer,** *f.* key number; **-weite,** *f.* width over flats (of nut, etc.).

Schluss-ergebnis, *n.*-se, final result; **-erhaltung,** *f.* maintenance of density; **-folge,** *f.* conclusion, inference; **-folgerung,** *f.* conclusion, inference; **-gesellschaften,** *f.pl.* closed associations; **-glieder,** *n.pl.* final members; **-lockerung,** *f.* opening out of the crop.

Schluss-platte, *f.* telson, terminal lamina; **-ring,** *m.* annulus of sperm; **-stand,** *m.* close stand; **-stein,** *m.* keystone; **-unterbrechung,** *f.* interruption of contact; **-verhältnis,** *n.* degree of density of stand; **-zelle,** *f.* closing cell.

Schlutte, *f.* alkekengi (ground cherry).

Schmachtkorn, *n.* blighted grain.

Schmack, *m.* sumac.

schmacken, to treat with sumac, sumac.

schmackgar, boiled in (dressed with) sumac.

schmackhaft, palatable, savory, tasty.

schmackieren, treat with sumac, sumac.

schmal, narrow, slender, scanty, meager; **-blätterig,** narrow-leaved, angustifolious, stenophyllous.

schmälern, to narrow, reduce, curtail, abridge.

Schmal-geiss, *f.* one-year-old roe; **-kronblättrig,** stenopetalous, having narrow petals; **-lineal,** narrow-linear; **-ricke,** *f.* one-year-old roe; **-rispig,** in the form of a narrow panicle; **-seite,** *f.* narrow side, edge; **-spiesser,** *m.* knobber; **-spur,** *f.* narrow gauge.

Schmaltblau, *n.* smalt.

Schmalte, *f.* smalt.

Schmaltier, *n.* one- to two-year-old hind.

Schmalz, *n.* lard, melted fat; **-artig,** lardaceous, lardy; **-butter,** *f.* melted butter.

Schmälze, *f.* softener (of fabrics).

schmalzen, schmälzen, to grease, lard, oil.

schmalzig, lardy, lardaceous.

Schmalzöl, *n.* lard oil, oleo oil, margarine.

Schmand, Schmant, *m.* slime, sludge, ooze, cream.

schmarotzen, to live as a parasite.

Schmarotzer, *m.*-, parasite.

schmarotzerisch, parasitic.

Schmarotzer-pflanze, *f.* parasitic plant; **-pilz,** *m.* parasitic fungus; **-tier,** *m.* animal parasite.

Schmauch, *m.* smoke.

schmauchen, to smoke.

Schmeckbecher, *m.* taste (circumvallate) papilla.

schmecken, to taste, enjoy, relish, like.

Schmeckzelle, *f.* gustatory cell.

schmeichelhaft, flattering, complimentary.

schmeicheln, (*dat.*) to flatter, compliment, coax.

schmeissen, to throw, fling, hurl, dash, lash out, deposit, slam.

Schmeissfliegen, *f.pl.* Muscidae.

Schmelz, *m.* enamel, glaze, melt, melting, fusion; **-anlage,** *f.* melting plant; **-arbeit,** *f.* smelting process, enameling; **-arbeiter,** *m.* enameler; **-artig,** enamellike; **-ausdehnung,** *f.* dilation in melting.

schmelzbar, fusible, meltable.

Schmelzbarkeit, *f.* fusibility.

Schmelz-blau, *n.* smalt; **-butter,** *f.* melted butter; **-draht,** *m.* fuse wire; **-einsatz,** *m.* fuse.

Schmelze, *f.* smelting, melting, fusion, fused mass, melt, batch, ball, mill oil.

schmelzen, to melt, fuse, smelt, lignate; **geschmolzen,** melted, fused, molten.

Schmelzen, *n.* fusion, melting.

Schmelzer, *m.* melter, finer, founder.

Schmelzerei, *f.* foundry.

Schmelz-erz, *n.*-e, smelting ore; **-farbe,** *f.* enamel color, vitrifiable pigment, majolica color; **-feuer,** *n.* refinery; **-fluss,** *m.* fused mass, melt; **-flüssig,** molten; **-fortsatz,** *m.* enamel process; **-glasur,** *f.* enamel; **-grad,** *m.* melting point; **-gut,** *n.* material suitable for smelting; **-hafen,** *m.* melting pot.

Schmelz-herd, *m.* smelting furnace; **-hitze,** *f.* melting heat; **-hütte,** *f.* smelting works, foundry.

schmelzig, fusible.

Schmelz-kessel, *m.*-, melting kettle; **-küche,** *f.* laboratory; **-linie,** *f.* fusion curve; **-los,** without enamel; **-malerei,** *f.* enamel painting; **-membran,** *n.* enamel layer.

Schmelz-mittel, *n.* flux; **-ofen,** *m.* melting furnace; **-perle,** *f.* blowpipe (enamel) bead, bugle; **-post,** *f.* smelting charge, post; **-prozess,** *m.* melting (smelting) process; **-pulpe,** *f.* enamel pulp.

Schmelzpunkt, *m.*-e, melting point, fusing temperature; **-bestimmung,** *f.* melting-point determination.

Schmelz-raum, *m.*-̈e, hearth; **-schuppe,** *f.* ganoid scale; **-schupper,** *m.pl.* Ganoidei; **-stahl,** *m.* natural steel; **-stein,** *m.* mizzonite; **-temperatur,** *f.* fusing temperature.

Schmelztiegel, *m.* crucible, melting pot; **-deckel,** *m.* crucible cover, tile; **-halter,** *m.* crucible (holder) support; **-zange,** *f.* crucible tongs.

Schmelz-tröpfchen, *n.*-, blowpipe bead; **-tropfen,** *m.* drop of fused matter, blowpipe bead; **-überzug,** *m.* enamel, cuticle of enamel.

Schmelzung, *f.* fusion, melting, smelting.

Schmelzungspunkt, *m.* melting point.

Schmelz-verfahren, *n.* melting process; **-wärme,** *f.* (latent) heat of fusion; **-werk,** *n.* smeltery, enameled work; **-würdig,** suitable for smelting; **-zeug,** *n.* smelting tools; **-zone,** *f.* zone of fusion.

Schmer, *m.&n.* fat, grease, suet.

Schmerz, *m.*-en, pain, grief, suffering, sorrow; **-anfall,** *m.* attack of pain; **-bekämpfung,** *f.* fighting of pain, alleviation of pain; **-betäubend,** pain-deadening, narcotic; **-empfindlich,** sensitive to pain; **-empfindung,** *f.* sensation of pain.

schmerzen, to pain, grieve, hurt, afflict, ache, smart.

schmerz-erregend, causing pain; **-frei,** free of pain, painless; **-gefühl,** *n.* feeling of pain, painful sensation; **-haft,** painful, distressing; **-los,** painless; **-losigkeit,** *f.* painlessness; **-stillend,** deadening (alleviating) pain anodyne; **-wurz,** *f.* black bryony (*Tamus communis*).

Schmetterlinge, *m.pl.* butterflies (Lepidoptera).

Schmetterlingsblütler, *m.* papilionaceous plant (Papilionaceae).

schmettern, to dash, smash, ring, clang, crash, blare.

Schmied, *m.* (black)smith.

schmiedbar, malleable, forgeable.

Schmiedbarkeit, *f.* malleability.

Schmiede, *f.* forge, smithy; **-arbeit,** *f.* forging, smithing; **-eisen,** *n.* wrought iron, malleable iron; **-eisern,** (of) wrought iron.

schmieden, to forge, smith, frame, devise-concoct.

schmiegen, to bend, bevel, cling.

schmiegsam, flexible, pliant, supple.

Schmiegsamkeit, *f.* flexibility, pliancy.

Schmielenhafer, *m.* Aira, crincled hairgrass.

Schmier-brand, *m.* stinking smut; **-büchse,** *f.* grease cup, oil cup, lubricator.

Schmiere, *f.* grease, smear, ointment, dip.

schmieren, to lubricate, oil, grease, salve, smear, anoint, spread, butter, soap, scrawl, daub, thrash.

Schmier-fähigkeit, *f.* lubricating property; **-fett,** *n.* grease; **-fleck,** *m.* grease spot; **-hahn,** *m.* lubricating cock, grease cock.

schmierig, greasy, smeary, oily, sticky, glutinous, viscous, dirty, filthy, wet (paper).

Schmierigkeit, *f.* unctuousness, sliminess, wetness, softness, milling (in paper manufacturing).

Schmierigkeitsgrad, *m.* freeness, degree of grinding (of pulp).

Schmier-kanne, *f.* oil can; **-käse,** *m.* cottage cheese, smearcase; **-leder,** *n.* leather dressed in oil; **-masse,** *f.* lubricating paste; **-material,** *n.* lubricant; **-mittel,** *n.* lubricant, liniment, ointment; **-mittelindustrie,** *f.* lubricant industry; **-seife,** *f.* soft soap; **-stoff,** *m.* lubricant.

Schmierung, *f.* lubrication.

Schmier-vorrichtung, *f.* lubricating device; **-wirkung,** *f.* lubricating effect; **-wolle,** *f.* greasy wool.

schmilzt (schmelzen), melts.

Schminkbohne, *f.* kidney bean.

Schminke, *f.* paint, rouge.

Schmink-mittel, *n.* cosmetic; **-rot,** *n.* rouge; **-weiss,** *n.* flake white, pearl white.

Schmirgel, *m.* emery; **-leinen,** *n.* **-leinwand,** *f.* emery cloth.

schmirgeln, to rub with emery, emery.

Schmirgel-papier, *n.* emery paper; **-pulver,** *n.* emery powder; **-scheibe,** *f.* emery wheel.

schmiss (schmeissen), threw.

schmitzen, to splash, blur, whip, lash.

schmoden, to burn heaped up wood or refuse.

schmolz (schmelzen), melted, was melting.

schmoren, to stew.

Schmuck, *m.* ornament, jewelry, finery, dress.

schmuck, neat, tidy, trim, pretty.

schmücken, to adorn, trim, decorate, dress.

Schmuck-feder, *f.* **-n,** ornamental plume; **-waren,** *f.pl.* jewelry.

Schmutz, *m.* dirt, filth, smut; **-decke,** *f.* dirty layer on a filter.

schmutzig, dirty, soiled, muddy, filthy, sordid, smutty; **-rot,** cruentus, dark purplish, testaceous.

Schmutz-probe, *f.* sediment test; **-wasser,** *n.* dirty water, sewage; **-wolle,** *f.* wool in the yolk.

Schnabel, *m.*-, beak, rostrum, bill, nozzle, nose; **-artig,** beaklike, rostrate.

Schnäbelchen, *n.* little beak.

Schnabel-borsten, *f.pl.* rictal bristles; **-förmig,** beak-shaped; **-fortsatz,** *m.* coracoid process; **-haut,** *f.* integument covering the beak; **-hieb,** *m.* blow with the beak.

schnäbelig, beaked.

Schnabel-kerfen, *m.pl.* Rhynchotae; **-köpfe,** *m.pl.* Rhynchocephali; **-loch,** *n.* foramen of beak; **öffnung,** *f.* opening of the beak; **-rücken,** *m.* culmen of the bill; **-scheide,** *f.* integument (sheath) covering beak; **-spalt,** *m.* gap; **-spitze,** *f.* apex, tip of bill; **-tier,** *n.* duckbill; **-winkel,** *m.* corner of the mouth; **-zelle,** *f.* beaklike cell.

Schnaken, *f.pl.* Tipulidae.

Schnalle, *f.* buckle, clasp.

schnallen, to buckle, strap; **-brücke,** *f.* clamp connection.

schnalzen, to smack, snap.

Schnappdecke, *f.* extension of a gas mask; any cover snapped into place.

schnappen, to snap, gasp, pant.

Schnaps, *m.* spirits, spirit, dram, liquor; **-brenner,** *m.* distiller.

schnarchen, to snore.

schnattern, to cackle, chatter.

schnauben, to snort.

Schnauze, *f.* snout, muzzle, mouth, nose, nozzle, spout, beak.

Schnecke, *f.* snail, slug, worm, endless screw, volute, spiral, cochlea, lagena.

Schnecken-antrieb, *m.* worm drive; **-artig,** snaillike, circinate, helical; **-blindsack,** *m.* blind sac of cochlea; **-blütler,** *m.pl.* flowers pollinated by snails; **-deckel,** *m.* operculum; **-fenster,** *n.* fenestra (rotunda) cochlearis; **-förmig,** helicoid, spiral; **-gang,** *m.* auger, snail's pace, canal of cochlea; **-gehäuse,** *n.* snail shell, bony cochlea; **-gerollt,** circinate.

Schnecken-getriebe, *n.* worm gear; **-gewinde,** *n.* helix; **-gipfel,** *m.* summit of cochlea; **-horn,** *n.* antenna of cochlea; **-kanal,** *m.* cochlear canal; **-klee,** *m.* snail clover (*Medicago scutellata*); **-kopf,** *m.* copula cochlearis; **-linie,** *f.* helix; **-paukentreppe,** *f.* scala of cochlea; **-rad,** *m.* worm wheel; **-schale,** *f.* snail shell.

Schnecken-scheidewand, *f.* cochlear septum; **-spirale,** *f.* elongated spiral; **-treppe** *f.* scala of cochlea; **-trieb,** *m.* endless screw.

Schnee, *m.* snow; **-artig,** snowlike; **-ball,** *m.* viburnum; **-bruch,** *m.* snowbreak; **-druck,** *m.* crushing by snow; **-flocke,** *f.* snowflake; **-gips,** *m.* snowy (foliated) gypsum; **-glöckchen,** *n.* snowdrop; **-grenze,** *f.* snow line; **-huhn,** *n.* ptarmigan (Lagopus); **-wehe,** *f.* snowdrift; **-weiss,** *n.* snow white.

schneidbar, fit to be cut.

Schneidbrenner, *m.* cutting torch.

Schneide, *f.* knife edge, edge, keenness; **-kessel,** *m.* masticator.

schneideln, to lop, prune, trim, top.

Schneidelstamm, *m.* lopped tree.

Schneidelung, *f.* lopping, pruning.

Schneidelwirtschaft, *f.* lopping system.

schneiden, to cut, intersect, cleave, split, saw, prune, adulterate, gripe, mince, carve, chop.

Schneider, *m.* cutter, tailor.

Schneide-versuch, *m.* attempt at cutting; **-zahn,** *m.* incisor.

schneidig, sharp, keen, plucky.

Schneid-kante, *f.* cutting edge; **-legierung,** *f.* cutting-tool alloy; **-öl,** *n.* cutting oil.

schneien, to snow.

Schneise, *f.* forest path, ride, cleared line.

schneiteln, to lop, prune.

schnell, fast, rapid, swift, quick, sudden; **-beizverfahren,** *n.* rapid disinfection method; **-binder,** *m.* quick-setting cement; **-bleiche,** *f.* quick bleaching; **-bremsung,** *f.* rapid deceleration; **-einbettung,** *f.* rapid imbedding.

schnellen, to top, jerk, spring, snap, let fly, toss, fling, cheat.

Schnell-entladung, *f.* rapid discharge; **-färbung,** *f.* quick staining; **-flüssig,** easily fusible; **-gärung,** *f.* quick fermentation.

Schnelligkeit, *f.* rapidity, quickness, speed, velocity.

Schnell-käfer, *m.* click beetle (Elateridae); **-kochtopf,** *m.* autoclave, pressure cooker; **-kraft,** *f.* elasticity; **-kräftig,** elastic; **-laufend,** high-speed, rapid; **-lebig,** rapidly completing the life cycle; **-lot,** *n.* fusible metal, soft solder; **-methode,** *f.* rapid method, short cut; **-probe,** *f.* rapid test; **-röste,** *f.* quick retting.

Schnell-schluss, *m.* tripping mechanism (of steam turbine); **-schrift,** *f.* shorthand, stenography; **-trocknend,** quick-drying, siccative; **-verfahren,** *n.* rapid process or treatment; **-vermögen,** *n.* ability to jerk

or fly off; **-zug,** *m.* fast train, express train; **-zünder,** *m.* quick match.

Schnepfe, *f.* snipe, woodcock.

Schneppe, *f.* spout, snout, nozzle, lip.

schnitt (schneiden), cut.

Schnitt, *m.*-e, cut, section, cutting, incision, intersection, slice, edge operation, crop; **-band,** *n.* serial section, paraffin ribbon; **-brenner,** *m.* slit burner, batswing burner.

Schnittdicke, *f.* thickness of the sections.

Schnitte, *f.* cut, slice, chop, steak.

Schnitt-fänger, *m.* section lifter; **-färbung,** *f.* section staining; **-fläche,** *f.* cut surface; **-holz,** *n.* sawed timber; **-kurve,** *f.* intersecting curve; **-lauch,** *m.* chive; **-linie,** *f.* line of intersection; **-präparat,** *n.* section preparation.

Schnitt-probe, *f.* test by cutting; **-punkt,** *m.* point of intersection; **-rand,** *m.* cut edge; **-stelle,** *f.* intersection point; **-waren,** *f.pl.* draper's (dry) goods, sawn timber; **-zeit,** *f.* time of cutting.

Schnitz, *m.* cut, slice, chip, cutlet.

Schnitzel, *n.*-, slice, scrap, chip, cutlet, clipping, snip, shred; **-maschine,** *f.* slicer, shredding machine.

schnitzeln, schnitzen, to cut, chip, carve, whittle.

Schnitzer, *m.* cutter, carver, blunder.

Schnitzholz, *n.* wood for carving.

Schnüffelkrankheit, *f.* rickets.

Schnupfen, *m.* cold, catarrh, coryza.

Schnupftabak, *m.* snuff.

Schnur, *f.*-e, string, cord, line, lace, twine, tape, trim, band, umbilical cord.

schnüren, to tie up, string, lace, strap, tighten, constrict.

Schnür-kolben, *m.* flask with constricted neck; **-larve,** *f.* strobila.

Schnurlauf, *m.* small groove wheel.

Schnurborsten, *f.pl.* vibrissae.

Schnurre, *f.* rattle, joke, story.

schnurren, to buzz, hum, whir, whiz, purr.

Schnurrhaare, *n.pl.* vibrissae.

Schnurwürmer, *m.pl.* Nemertinea.

schob (schieben), pushed, shoved.

schobern, to pile, stack.

Schock, *n.* sixty, mass, lot, land tax.

Schofel, *m.* trash, refuse.

Schokolade, *f.* chocolate.

Schokoladentafel, *f.* cake of chocolate.

Scholle, *f.* clod, soil, lump, flounder, plaice, layer, stratum.

Schollenmuskel, *m.* soleus muscle.

Schöllkraut, *n.* celandine (*Chelidonium majus*).

schon, already, by this time, yet, since, indeed, surely, no doubt, after all.

schön, beautiful, handsome, fine, fair, lovely, nice, well; **bitte ~,** if you please.

Schöne, *f.* fining, isinglass.

schonen, to spare, save, preserve, protect, care for, close, inclose, manage.

schönen, to fine, clarify, clear, beautify gloss, brighten.

schonend, careful, tender, considerate, sparing.

Schön-färber, *m.* garment dyer; **-färberei,** *f.* garment dyeing; **-geistig,** aesthetic; **-grün,** *n.* Paris green.

Schönheit, *f.* beauty, fineness.

Schönheits-bedürfnis, *n.* desire for beautiful surroundings, longing for beauty; **-mittel,** *n.* cosmetic; **-wasser,** *n.* beauty wash.

schonlich, careful.

Schonung, *f.* tree nursery, closed wood.

schonungslos, unsparing, pitiless.

Schönungsmittel, *n.* fining (brightening) agent.

Schonzeit, *f.* close time, closed season.

Schopf, *m.* ̈e, tuft (of hair), (tree)top, forelock; **-bäume,** *n.pl.* trees with tufts of large leaves (palms, monocotyledons); **-blätter,** *n.pl.* crowded leaves around sex organs of acrocarpous mosses.

Schöpfbütte, *f.* pulp vat.

schöpfen, to draw, scoop, create, ladle, dip.

Schöpfer, *m.* creator, maker, author, originator, scoop, ladle, bucket, dipper.

Schöpf-gefäss, *n.* scoop, dipper, ladle, bucket; **-herd,** *m.* casting crucible; **-kelle,** *f.* **-löffel,** *m.* scoop, ladle; **-probe,** *f.* dipped (ladled) sample; **-rad,** *n.* bucket wheel; **-rahmen,** *m.* deckle.

Schopfrüssel, *m.* haustellum.

Schöpfung, *f.* creation.

Schöps, *m.* -e, wether, mutton, simpleton.

Schöpsen-fleisch, *n.* mutton; **-talg,** *m.* mutton tallow, prepared suet.

schor (scheren), sheared.

Schorf, *m.* scurf, scab, crust, eschar

Schörl, *m.* schorl.

Schörlit, *m.* pycnite variety of topaz).

Schornstein, *m.* chimney, stack, funnel, flue.

schoss (schiessen), shot, sprouted.

Schoss, *m.* lap, womb, coattail, shoot, sprig, scion, sprout; **-bein,** *n.* os pubis; **-fuge,** *f.* symphysis of pubis; **-gerinne,** *n.* channel, trough; **-knochen,** *m.* pubis.

Schössling, *m.* shoot, sprout, scion, sucker.

Schlösslings-busch, *m.* clump or cluster of coppice shoots; **-kraut,** *n.* large rosette plant.

Schosszeit, *f.* time of heading or shooting.

Schötchen, *n.* silicula.

Schote, *f.* pod, shell, husk, silique.

Schoten-dorn, *m.* acacia, black locust; **-gewächse,** *n.* leguminous plants; **-pfeffer,** *m.* red pepper, capsicum; **-pflanze,** *f.* leguminous plant.

Schott, *n.* bulkhead.

Schotter, *m.* broken stone, gravel, **-bank,** *f.* gravel bank; **-boden,** *m.* gravelly soil.

schraffieren, to cross, shade, hatch, line.

schräg, oblique, sloping, slanting, diagonal, inclined, bevel; **~ ablaufen,** to slope: **~ ablaufend,** sloping.

Schrägagar, *m.* agar slant.

Schräge, *f.* slant, slope, bevel.

schräg-gegittert, clathrate; **-kante,** *f.* bezel, inclined column; **-linie,** *f.* diagonal; **-stellbar,** inclinable; **-stellen,** to incline, tilt; **-streifen,** *m.* oblique marking; **-verengt,** obliquely contracted; **-zeile,** *f.* parastichy; **-zygomorphe Blüte,** *f.* oblique zygomorphic flower.

schrak (schrecken), became alarmed.

Schrämmaschine, *f.* coal auger.

Schramme, *f.* scratch, sore, slash, graze, scar.

Schrank, *m.* ̈e, cupboard, cabinet, case, press, closet, safe, set (of a saw).

Schranke, *f.* bar, barrier, boundary, limit; **in die Schranken treten,** to enter the lists.

Schränkeisen, *n.* saw set.

schränken, to put across, cross, set (a saw).

schränkweise, crosswise.

Schrape, *f.* Schrapper, *m.* scraper, tracer.

Schraubdeckel, *m.* screw cap, screw cover.

Schraube, *f.* screw, screw bolt, propeller; **eingelassene ~,** countersunk screw.

Schraubel, *f.* bostryx, helicoid cyme; **-wickel,** *m.* bostryx cincinnus.

schrauben, to screw, turn up, banter, mock, tease; **-artig,** spiral, helical; **-bakterie,** *f.* spirillum; **-blatt,** *n.* screwlike leaf; **-bohrer,** *m.* screw (tap), auger, twist drill; **-dreher,** *m.* screw driver; **-drehflügler,** *m.* seed or fruit with Fraxinus type of wing; **-eisen,** *n.* screw iron, screw stock, sections for screws; **-feder,** *f.* helical spring; **-förmig,** screw-shaped, (corkscrew) spiral, helical.

Schrauben-gang, *m.* thread (pitch) of a screw; **-gefäss,** *n.* spiral (element), tracheid; **-gelenk,** *n.* cochlear joint; **-gewinde,** *n.* screw thread; **-kiemer,** *m.pl.* Brachiopoda; **-klammer,** *f.* clip; **-kühler,** *m.* helical condenser or cooler; **-linie,** *f.* helical line, helix; **-loch,** *n.* screw hole; **-mutter,** *f.* nut, female screw; **-presse,** *f.* screw (fly) press.

Schrauben-quetschhahn, *m.* screw pinchcock; **-rohr,** *n.* **-röhre,** *f.* spiral tube; **-schlüssel,** *m.* screw (nut) wrench, monkey wrench; **-zieher,** *m.* screw driver.

Schraub-glas, *n.* screw-top glass tube or jar.

schraubig, acyclic, screwed; **-gewunden,** coiled.

Schraub-stock, *m.* vise; **-zwinge,** *f.* screw clamp.

Schreck, *m.* fright, terror; **-bewegung,** *f.* repulsive movement.

schrecken, to frighten, chill, startle, be afraid, alarm.

Schreck-erfahrung, *f.* experience of fright; **-farbe,** *f.* warning color; **-gespenst,** *n.* phantom of fright; **-haft,** fearful, frightened, frightening.

schrecklich, terrible, frightful, awful.

Schreckwirkung, *f.* effect of fright.

Schrei, *m.* cry, shriek, yell, shout.

Schreibart, *f.* style, spelling, method of writing.

Schreibeempfänger, *m.* teletype receiver.

schreiben, to write, mark, record.

Schreib-feder, *f.*-**n,** pen; **-fehler,** *m.* error in writing, clerical mistake; **-kies,** *m.* marcasite; **-maschine,** *f.* typewriter; **-maschinenband,** *n.* typewriter ribbon; **-materialien,** *f.* writing materials, stationery; **-papier,** *n.* writing paper; **-stift,** *m.* pencil, crayon; **-tinte,** *f.* writing ink; **-waren,** *f.pl.* writing materials, stationery; **-weise,** *f.* spelling, style.

schreien, to cry, shout, scream, shriek.

Schreien, *n.* crying, creaking.

schreiend, loud, gaudy, clamorous.

Schrein, *m.*-**e,** press, case, cabinet, chest, casket, shrine.

Schreiner, *m.* cabinetmaker, carpenter.

Schreitbein, *n.* walking leg, gressorial foot

schreiten, to step, stride, advance, proceed.

Schreit-fuss, *m.* walking leg; **-loch,** *n.* ambulacrum.

schrie (schreien), cried out.

schrieb (schreiben), wrote.

Schrift, *f.*-**en,** writing, characters, type, publication, work; **-absatz,** *m.* paragraph; **-erz,** *n.* sylvanite; **-führer,** *m.* secretary; **-giesser,** *m.* type founder; **-giessermetall,** *n.* type metal; **-gold,** *n.* sylvanite; **-granit,** *m.* graphic granite; **-guss,** *m.* type founding; **-jaspis,** *m.* jasper opal; **-leiter,** *m.* editor.

schriftlich, written, in writing.

Schrift-malerei, *f.* lettering; **-metall,** *n.* type metal; **-mutter,** *f.* type mold, matrix; **-setzer,** *m.* typesetter, compositor; **-stein,** *m.* graphic granite; **-steller,** *m.* writer, author; **-stück,** *n.* document, piece of writing; **-tellur,** *n.* graphic tellurium.

Schrifttum, *n.* literature.

Schrift-zeichen, *n.* character, letter; **-zeug,** *n.* type metal; **-zug,** *m.* written character, flourish, handwriting.

Schrill-ader, *f.* stridulate vein; **-apparat,** *m.* stridulating apparatus.

schritt (schreiten), walked, strode.

Schritt, *m.*-**e,** step, pace, stride; **-weise,** step by step, gradual(ly); **-weite,** *f.* interval (length of stride).

schroff, rough, harsh, gruff, steep, abrupt.

schröpfen, to cup, bleed, scarify.

Schrot, *f.* notch, dentation, kerf.

Schrot, *n.&m.*-**e,** cut, block, clipping, piece, small shot, groats, selvage, plumb bob, grist; **-axt,** *f.* wood-cutter's ax.

schroten, to chip, clip, cut (saw) in pieces, bruise, crush, rough-grind, shoot casks, gobble food.

Schröter, *m.* handler of barrels, woodcutter, stag beetle.

Schrot-fabrik, *f.* shot factory; **-korn,** *n* grain of shot, single shot.

Schrötling, *m.* cutting, piece, (minting) blank, planchet.

Schrot-mehl, *n.* coarse meal; **-metall,** *n.* shot metal; **-mühle,** *f.* grist mill, malt mill, bruising mill; **-sägeförmig,** runcinate; **-schusskrankheit,** *f.* shot-hole disease.

Schrott, *m.* scrap (iron), scrap metal; **-entfall,** *m.* manufacturing loss; **-roheisenverfahren,** *n.* scrap pig-iron process.

schrubben, to scrub, scour.

Schrubber, *m.* scrubber.

schrüen, to give the biscuit baking to porcelain.

Schrulle, *f.* whim, crotchet.

schrumpfen, to shrink, contract, shrivel.

schrumpfend, astringent.

Schrumpf-grenze, *f.* shrinkage limit; **-mass,** *n.* degree of shrinkage, contraction.

Schrumpfniere, *f.* atrophy of the kidney, final stage of Bright's disease, cirrhosis.

Schrumpfung, *f.* shrinking, contraction, shriveling.

schruppen, to rough, plane roughly.

Schub, *m.*ː̈e, shove, push, thrust, throw, shearing, onset, outburst, relapse; **-changierung,** *f.* sliding traverse motion; **-fach,** *n.* drawer; **-fenster,** *n.* sash window; **-festigkeit,** *f.* shearing strength, resistance to pressure; **-formänderungskurve,** *f.* shear-stress deformation curve; **-kraft,** *f.* shearing force or strength; **-kurbel,** *f.* crank; **-lade,** *f.* drawer; **-lehre,** *f.* sliding (gauge) calipers, slide rule.

Schub-spanung, *f.* shearing stress; **-weise,** by shoves, by thrusts, gradually, in batches; **-zahl,** *f.* shear coefficient.

schuf (schaffen), created.

schuften, to work hard, drudge, toil.

Schuh, *m.*-e, shoe; **-creme,** *f.* **-krem,** *f.* shoe cream, shoe polish; **-leder,** *n.* shoe leather; **-macherpech,** *n.*, **-macherwachs,** *n.* cobbler's wax; **-putzmittel,** *n.* shoe polish; **-riemen,** *m.* shoestring, shoelace; **-schmiere,** *f.* dubbing, grease; **-schwärze,** *f.* shoe blacking; **-wichse,** *f.* shoe polish.

Schul-beispiel, *n.* typical example; **-bildung,** *f.* education.

Schuld, *f.*-en, debt, fault, blame, guilt, offense, crime; **an . . . schuld sein,** to be responsible for, be to blame for.

schulden, to owe.

schuldig, (*gen.*) indebted, owing, due, guilty.

Schuldigkeit, *f.* obligation, debt, duty.

Schuldner, *m.* debtor.

Schule, *f.* school.

Schüler, *m.* scholar, pupil.

Schülfer, *m.* scaly hair, lamella.

Schülferchen, *n.* scale of peltate hair.

Schulp, *m.* cuttlebone, pen, pro-ostracum.

Schülpe, *f.* shell.

Schulpflanze, *f.* nursery transplant.

Schultasche, *f.* schoolbag.

Schulter, *f.* shoulder; **-band,** *n.* ligament of shoulder joint; **-bein,** *n.* bone of the shoulder; **-beule,** *f.* humeral callus.

Schulterblatt, *n.* scapula; **-band,** *n.* ligament of scapula; **-beule,** *f.* glenoid tubercle; **-gegend,** *f.* scapular region; **-gelenkfortsatz,** *m.* glenoid process of scapula; **-gräte,** *f.* spine of scapula; **-grube,** *f.* glenoid cavity of scapula.

Schulterblatt-hals, *m.* neck of scapula; **-kamm,** *m.* spine of scapula; **-knorpel,** *m.* scapular cartilage; **-kopf,** *m.* head of scapula; **-pfanne,** *f.* glenoid cavity; **-rand,** *m.* scapular border.

Schulter-decke, *f.* tegulae; **-ecke,** *f.* acromion; **-federn,** *n.* scapularies; **-feld,** *n.* humeral field; **-fittich,** *m.* humeral tract, parapteron; **-gelenk,** *n.* shoulder joint; **-gelenkband,** *n.* scapular ligament; **-gelenkpfanne** *f.* glenoid cavity of scapula; **-gewölbe,** *n.* roof of shoulder joint.

Schulter-gräte, *f.* spine of scapula; **-gürtel,** *m.* pectoral or shoulder girdle; **-haken,** *m.* coracoid apophysis or process; **-hakenschlüsselbeinband,** *n.* coracoclavicular ligament; **-höhe,** *f.* acromion; **-kamm,** *m.* spine of scapula; **-knochen,** *m.* scapula; **-kreuz,** *n.* shoulder cross.

Schulter-pfanne, *f.* glenoid cavity; **-queradern,** *f.pl.* nervules; **-schnabel,** *m.* coracoid apophysis; **-stück,** *n.* episternum; **-winkel,** *m.* angle of the scapula; **-zungenbeinmuskel,** *m.* omohyoid muscle.

Schund, *m.* refuse, offal, trash, rubbish.

schund (schinden), skinned.

Schüppchen, *n.* lodicule, small scale.

Schuppe, *f.* scale, flake, squama.

Schüppe, *f.* shovel, scoop.

schuppen, to scale (off), desquamate.

Schuppen, *m.* shed, barn, garage; **-artig,** scaly, squamous; **-bein,** *n.* scale of temporal bone, squamosal bone; **-bildung,** *f.* flaking; **-blatt,** *n.* scaly leaf; **-borke,** *f.* rhytidome; **-drüse,** *f.* patelliform gland.

Schuppen-flosser, *m.* squamipen; **-förmig,** like scales; **-glätte,** *f.* flake litharge; **-stein,** *m.* lepidolite. **-haar,** *n.* scalelike hair; **-hülle,** *f.* tegmen; **-narbe,** *f.* scale scar; **-tier,** *n.* scaly anteater (Manis); **-tragend,** squamiferous.

schuppig, scaly, flaky, squamous.

Schuppigkeit, *f.* scaliness.

Schur, *f.* shearing, fleece, mowing.

Schüreisen, *n.* poker, fire(hook) iron

schüren, to stir, poke (fire).

Schurf, *m* ⸚e,. scratch, hole, pit.

schürfen, to scratch, scrape, prospect.

Schürf grube, *f.* -loch, *n.* test pit.

Schürfung, *f.* scratching, scraping, abrasion.

Schür-haken, *m.* poker; -loch, *n.* stokehole (firehole).

Schurre, *f.* slide, chute.

Schurz, *m.* Schürze, *f.* apron.

schürzen, to tie, tuck up, gird up.

Schuss, *m.*⸚e, shot, blast, shooting, charge, shoot, batch, rapid motion, filling (of fabrics).

Schüssel, *f.*-n, dish, bowl, pan, cup; -artig, scutellate; -förmig, bowl-shaped; -träger, *m.* cupuliferous tree; -zinn, *n.* pewter.

Schusserbaum, *m.* Kentucky coffee tree (Gymnocladus).

Schuss-weite, *f.* range; -zeichen, *n.* hit marks, shot wound.

Schuster, *m.* shoemaker, cobbler; -pech, *n.* shoemaker's wax.

Schutt, *m.* rubbish, refuse, ruins, debris.

Schüttbeton, *m.* poured concrete.

Schütte, *f*. conduit; -krankheit, *f.* needle shedding, blight, leaf cast.

Schüttel-apparat, *m.*-e, shaking apparatus; -bewegung, *f.* shaking motion; -extraktion, *f.* rocking extraction; -frost, *m.* shivers, chill, rigor; -maschine, *f.* shaking (mashing) machine.

schütteln, to shake, agitate, churn, rock.

Schüttel-sieb, *n.* grizzly; -trichter, *m.*-, separatory funnel; -vorrichtung, *f.* mashing machine; -werk, *n.* shaking mechanism; -zylinder, *m.* shaking cylinder.

schütten, to pour, cast, shed, yield.

Schütt-gelb, *n.* Dutch pink; -gut, *n.* loose material, bulk goods; -loch, *n.* feed hole.

Schutt-halde, *f.* slope covered with rock debris; -kraut, *n.* -pflanze, plant growing on rock debris; -schlipt, *m*, rock-debris slide; -stauer, *m.* binding plant, slide stabilizer.

Schüttung, *f.* pouring, ballasting, embankment.

Schutz, *m.* protection, shelter, screen, defense; -anstrich, *m.* protective coating; -anzug, *m.* protective garment (uniform);

-beamte, *m.* guard; -beize, *f.* resist, reserve; -beizendruck, *m.* resist style; -bestand, *m.* nurse crop; -brille, *f.* goggles, protecting spectacles; -decke, *f.* protective cover or coating.

Schütze, *f.* sluice gate.

Schutzeinrichtung, *f.* protective arrangement.

schützen, to protect, guard, shelter, screen, defend; -grabenkrieg, *m.* trench warfare.

Schutz-färbung, *f.* protective coloration; -gebiet, *n.* nature reserve; -glocke, *f.* bell jar; -gürtel, *m.* shelter, (protective) belt; -holz, *n.* nurse tree, shelter wood; -impfung, *f.* protective vaccination, immunization; -kolloid, *n.* protective colloid; -kraft, *f.* protective power; -lack, *m.* protective varnish.

Schützling, *m.* protégé, charge.

schutz-los, unprotected; -mann, *m.* policeman; -mantel, *m.* windbreak, protecting jacket; -marke, *f.* trade-mark; -masse, *f.* resist (of fabrics); -massnahme, -massregel, *f.* protective measure; -mittel, *n.* preservative, preventive, prophylactic; -organ, *n.* protective organ; -papp, *m.* resist paste, reserve; -raum, *m.* air-raid shelter.

Schutz-pockengift, *n.* vaccine virus; -polyp, *m.* protective polyp; -ring, *m.*-e, guard ring; -salzlösung, *f.* protective salt solution; -scheide, *f.* protective sheet, endodermis; -schicht, *f.* protective layer; -schild, *n.* protective shield; -sekretion, *f.* protective secretion; -spross, *m.* modified shoot for protection; -stoff, *m.* protective substance, alexin.

Schutz-trichter, *m.* protecting funnel; -vorrichtung, *f.* protecting (device) contrivance; -wald, *m.* shelterwood, protection forest; -wand, *f.* safety wall, protecting screen; -wehr, *f.* weapon of defense; -werkzeug, *n.* protective organ; -wert, *m.* protective resistance; -wirkung, *f.* protective effect; -zoll, *m.* protective duty.

Schwabber, *m.* swab, mop.

schwach, weak, feeble, delicate, faint, frail, decrepit, low, dim, thin, poor, slight, light.

Schwachblasen, *n.* weak blast.

Schwäche, *f.* weakness, feebleness, infirmity.

schwächen, to weaken, enfeeble, lessen, enervate, impair, debilitate, seduce, dilute.

schwach-flaumhaarig, puberulus, slightly hairy; -herzförmig, subcordate

schwächlich, weakly, frail, delicate.

schwach-säuerlich, weakly acid; **-siedend,** gently boiling, simmering.

Schwächung, *f.* weakening.

Schwächungsmittel, *n.* depressant.

schwachwirksam, feebly active.

Schwaden, *m.* suffocating vapor, choke-damp, Glyceria; **feuriger** ~, firedamp.

Schwadenfang, *m.* hood, ventilator.

Schwalbe, *f.* swallow.

Schwalben-schwanz, *m.* dovetail; **-wurz(el),** *f.* dogbane. (*Vincetoxicum officinale*); **-wurzgewächse,** *n.pl.* Asclepiadaceae.

Schwall, *m.* swell, flood, throng, surge.

schwamm (schwimmen), swam.

Schwamm, *m.* sponge, mushroom, fungus, toadstool, spongy, growth, tinder, tutty, lot; **-artig,** spongelike, spongy, fungous; **-baum,** *m.* tree infected by fungi; **-filter,** *n.* sponge filter; **-gewebe,** *n.* spongy tissue; **-gift,** *n.* mushroom poison, muscarine; **-gummi,** *n.* spongy rubber; **-holz,** *n.* spongy wood, decayed wood.

schwammig, spongy, porous, fungous, fungoid, bibulous.

Schwammigkeit, *f.* sponginess.

Schwamm-körper, *m.-*, spongy body; **-säure,** *f.* boletic acid; **-schorf,** *m.* Spongospora scab; **-spinner,** *m.* gypsy moth; **-stoff,** *m.* fungin; **-tod,** *m.* fungicide; **-zucker,** *m.* mannitol.

Schwan, *m.-̈e,* swan.

schwand (schwinden), disappeared.

Schwand, *m.* shrinkage, loss, contraction.

Schwanenblumengewächse, *n.pl.* Butomaceae.

schwang (schwingen), swung, was swinging.

Schwang, *m.* swing, vogue.

schwanger, pregnant.

schwängern, to impregnate, saturate.

Schwangerschaft, *f.* pregnancy.

Schwängerung, *f.* impregnation, saturation.

schwank, flexible, pliable, slender, wavering.

schwanken, to hesitate, waver, fluctuate, oscillate, vary, shake, stagger, rock.

schwankend, uncertain, unsettled, unsteady; **ein Schwankender,** a variable one.

Schwankung, *f.* variation, fluctuation, vibration.

Schwankungsgrenze, *f.* limit of variability.

Schwanz, *m.-̈e,* tail, train; **-abschnitt,** *m.* caudal segment; **-anhang,** *m.* anal appen-dage, caudal furca; **-borsten,** *f.pl.* cerci, anal (caudal) bristles; **-darm,** *m.* caudal (postanal) gut; **-decke,** *f.* tail coverts; **-deckfedern,** *f.pl.* tail coverts; **-drüse,** *f.* caudal gland; **-fächer,** *n.pl.* tail (caudal) fin; **-faden,** *m.* caudal filament, tail of spermatozoon.

Schwanz-feder, *f.* tail rectrice; **-finne,** *f.* caudal fin; **-flosse,** *f.* caudal fin, uropod; **-fortsatz,** *m.* caudal appendage; **-hahn,** *m.* stopcock with an outlet through the end of the key; **-knochen,** *m.* coccyx; **-knospe,** *f.* tail bud; **-ring,** *m.* ring on a serpent's tail; **-scheide,** *f.* caudal sheath; **-schild,** *m.* pygidium.

Schwanz-segment, *n.* pygidium; **-sporn,** *m.* tail skid (of plane); **-stachel,** *m.* caudal seta; **-stern,** *m.* comet; **-stück,** *n.* telson; **-teil,** *m.* caudal part; **-wirbel,** *m.* caudal vertebra; **-wurzel,** *f.* base of tail.

schwären, to ulcerate, fester, suppurate.

Schwarm, *m.-̈e,* swarm, herd, flock, crowd, throng, cluster, colony; **-bildung,** *f.* clustering.

schwärmen, to swarm, rove, wander, migrate, stray, revel, daydream, adore, rave.

Schwärmer, *m.* rover, reveler, dreamer, visionary, enthusiast, hawk or sphinx moth, firecracker; *pl.* Sphingidae, zoospores **-blume,** *f.* flower pollinated by hawk or sphinx moth.

Schwarm-ionen, *n.pl.* exchangeable cations (in a clay particle); **-jahr,** *n.* swarm year; **-larve,** *f.* planula, hydropolyp; **-sporangium,** *n.* zoosporangium; **-spore,** *f.* swarm spore, zoospore; **-sporenkapsel,** *f.* zoosporange; **-stäbchen,** *n.* elongated swarm cell; **-zelle,** *f.* zoospore.

Schwarte, *f.* rind, skin, cortex, crust, induration, covering, scalp, slab, bark.

schwarz, black, dark, gloomy, swarthy; ~ **liegen,** be settled, be clear (of beer); **schwarzer Tod,** Black Death, bubonic plague; **schwarzes Wasser,** black mercurial lotion.

Schwarz, *n.* black, blackness; **der (die) Schwarze,** Negro.

Schwarz-beere, *f.* elderberry, melastoma; **-beinigkeit,** *f.* blackleg disease; **-beize,** *f.* black liquor, iron liquor; **-birke,** *f.* river birch (*Betula nigra*); **-blättrig,** melanophyllus, having leaves of a dark color; **-blau,** very dark blue; **-blech,** *n.* black plate; **-blei,** *n.* black lead; **-bleierz,** *n.* black lead spar; **-brache,** *f.* complete fallow.

Schwarz-braun, very dark brown; **-braun-stein,** *m.* psilomelane; **-brot,** *n.* black rye bread; **-brüchig,** black short; **-bunt,** black and white; **-dorn,** *m.* blackthorn (*Prunus spinosa*).

Schwärze, *f.* black, blacking, printer's ink, blackness, swarthiness.

Schwarzeisen, *n.* high-silicon pig iron.

schwärzen, to blacken, black, obscure.

Schwärzepilz, *m.* blackening fungus.

Schwarz-erde, *f.* black soil; **-erle,** *f.* common alder (*Alnus glutinosa*); **-färber,** *m.* dyer in black; **-farbig,** black-colored, black; **-fäule,** *f.* black rot; **-fichte,** *f.* black spruce (*Picea nigra*); **-fleckenkrankeit,** *f.* blackspot disease; **-gar,** black-tanned; **-gebrannt,** kishy; **-gelb,** very dark yellow, tawny.

schwarz-grau, very dark gray; **-grün,** atrovirens, very dark green; **-gültigerz,** *n.* stephanite, polybasite; **-käfer,** *m.pl.* Tenebrionidae; **-kernig,** black heart (malleable iron); **-kiefer,** *f.* Austrian (black) pine (*Pinus nigricans*); **-kohle,** *f.* black charcoal, black coal; **-kümmel,** *m.* nutmeg flower (*Nigella damascina*); **-kupfer,** *n.* black (coarse) copper; **-kupfererz,** *m.* melaconite; **-lauge,** *f.* black liquor.

schwärzlich, blackish.

Schwarz-manganerz, *n.* hausmannite; **-mehl,** *n.* dark-colored (rye) flour; **-pappel,** *f.* black poplar (*Populus nigra*); **-pech,** *n.* black (common) pitch; **-pulver,** *n.* black powder; **-rost,** *m.* black rust (of grain).

schwarz-rot, very dark red; **-schmelz,** *m.* black enamel; **-seher,** *m.* pessimist; **-senföl,** *n.* (black) mustard oil; **-silbererz,** *n.* **-silberglanz,** *m.* black silver, stephanite; **-specht,** *m.* black woodpecker; **-spiess-glanzerz,** *n.* bournonite.

Schwärzung, *f.* blackening, density (in photography).

Schwarz-vitriol, *m.* black vitriol (impure ferrous sulphate); **-werden,** *n.* blackening, nigrescence; **-wild,** *n.* black game, black grouse; **-wurz, -wurzel,** *f.* black discoloration, root, scorosonera, viper's grass; **-zinkerz,** *n.* franklinite.

Schwebe, *f.* suspension, suspense, sling, suspender; **-fliegen,** *f.pl.* Syrphidae; **-fliegenblumen,** *f.pl.* flowers pollinated by syrphid flies; **-flora,** *f.* phytoplankton; **-methode,** *f.* suspension method.

schweben, to hang, be suspended, be pending, hover, float.

schwebend, suspended, floating, in suspension, pending.

Schwebe-stoff, *m.-e,* suspended substance or material (or matter); **-teilchen,** *n.* suspended particle.

Schwebstofffilter, *n.* filter for suspended (colloidal) substance.

Schwebung, *f.* hovering, reverberating, swaying.

Schwebungstheorie, *f.* beat theory.

Schwefel, *m.* sulphur; **-alkohol,** *m.* carbon disulphide; **-antimonig,** thioantimonious; **-antimonsäure,** *f.* thioantimonic acid, sulphantimonic acid; **-arsenig,** thioarsenious, sulpharsenious; **-arsensäure,** *f.* thioarsenic acid, sulpharsenic acid; **-artig,** sulphur(e)ous; **-blausäure,** *f.* thiocyanic acid, sulphocyanic acid; **-bromür,** *n.* sulphur monobromide; **-chlorür,** *n.* sulphur monochloride.

Schwefelcyan, *n.* cyanogen sulphide; **-ammonium,** *n.* ammonium thiocyanate; **-kalium,** *n.* potassium thiocyanate or sulphocyanate; **-säure,** *f.* thiocyanic (sulphocyanic) acid; **-wasserstoffsäure,** *f.* sulphocyanic acid.

Schwefel-dampf, *m.* sulphur vapor; **-dunst,** *m.* sulphurous vapor; **-echt,** fast to (stoving) sulphurous acid; **-einschlag,** *m.* sulphur match, sulphuring (of casks); **-eisen,** *n.* iron (ferrous) sulphide; **-erz,** *n.* sulphur ore; **-faden,** *m.* sulphured wick, sulphur match; **-farbe,** *f.* sulphur color; **-farbstoff,** *m.* sulphur dye; **-form,** *f.* mold for sulphur, brimstone mold.

Schwefel-gallium, *n.* gallium sulphide; **-gehalt,** *m.* sulphur content; **-gelb,** sulphur-yellow; **-gerbung,** *f.* sulphur tannage; **-geruch,** *m.* sulphur odor; **-grube,** *f.* sulphur pit, sulphur mine.

Schwefel-halogen, *n.* sulphur halide; **-haltig,** containing sulphur, sulphurous; **-harnstoff,** *m.* thiourea; **-holz, -hölzchen,** *n.* sulphur match; **-hütte,** *f.* sulphur refinery.

schwefelig, of sulphur.

Schwefel-jodür, *n.* sulphur monoiodide; **-kalium,** *n.* potassium sulphide; **-kalk,** *m.* lime-sulphur; **-kalkbrühe,** *f.* lime-sulphur spraying mixture; **-kalzium,** *n.* calcium sulphide; **-kammer,** *f.* sulphur (chamber) stove; **-karbolsäure,** *f.* sulphocarbolic acid.

Schwefelkies, *m.* iron pyrites; **-gemeiner** $\sim$, pyrite.

Schwefel-kobalt, *m.* cobalt sulphide; **-kohle,** *f.* high-sulphur coal; **-kohlensäure,** *f.*

sulphocarbonic acid; **-kohlenstoff,** *m.* carbon disulphide; **-kolben,** *m.* retort for distilling sulphur; **-körnchen,** *m.pl.* sulphur granules; **-kuchen,** *m.* cake of sulphur; **-latwerge,** *f.* confection of sulphur; **-leber,** *f.* liver of sulphur, hepar; **-leinöl,** *n.* balsam of sulphur; **-milch,** *f.* milk of sulphur.

schwefeln, to sulphurize, sulphurate, fumigate, sulphur, vulcanize.

Schwefel-natrium, sodium sulphide; **-natron,** *n.* sodium sulphide; **-niederschlag,** *m.* precipitate of sulphur; **-oxyd,** *n.* sulphur oxide; **-phosphor,** *m.* phosphorus sulphide; **-quecksilber,** *n.* mercury sulphide; **-quelle,** *f.* sulphur spring; **-räucherung,** *f.* sulphur fumigation; **-regen,** *m.* sulphur rain; **-salz,** *n.* sulphur salt, sulphate.

schwefelsauer, sulphate of.

schwefelsaurer Kalk, *m.* calcium sulphate.

schwefelsaures Ammoniak, *n.* ammonium sulphate.

schwefelsaures Eisen, *n.* iron sulphate.

Schwefelsäure, *f.* sulphuric acid; **-anhydrid,** *n.* sulphuric anhydride, sulphur trioxide; **-bestimmung,** *f.* determination of sulphuric acid; **-fabrik,** *f.* sulphuric acid works; **-fabrikation,** *f.* manufacture of sulphuric acid; **-kammer,** *f.* sulphuric acid chamber.

Schwefel-schlacke, *f.* sulphur dross; **-schwarz,** *n.* sulphur black; **-silber,** *n.* silver sulphide; **-spiessglanz,** *m.* stibnite; **-stange,** *f.* roll of sulphur; **-stickstoff,** *m.* nitrogen sulphide; **-stück,** *n.* piece of sulphur; **-tonerde,** *f.* aluminum sulphide.

Schwefelung, *f.* sulphurization, sulphuring.

Schwefelungsmittel, *n.* sulphur(iz)ing agent.

Schwefel-verbindung, *f.* sulphur compound; **-verstäuber,** *m.* sulphur (pulverizator) sprayer; **-wasser,** *n.* sulphur water.

Schwefelwasserstoff, *m.* hydrogen sulphide, sulphuretted hydrogen; **-gas,** *n.* hydric sulphide; **-rest,** *m.* hydrogen sulphide residue, sulphhydryl; **-strom,** *m.* current of hydrogen sulphide.

Schwefel-weinsäure, *f.* sulphovinic acid, ethylsulphuric acid; **-werk,** *n.* sulphur refinery; **-wismut,** *n.* bismuth sulphide; **-wurz,** *f.* brimstonewort; **-wurzel,** *f.* brimstonewort (sulphurweed) root (Peucedanum); **-zink,** *n.* zinc sulphide; **-zink-weiss,** *n.* lithopone, zincolith, pigment containing chiefly zinc sulphide; **-zinn,** *n.* tin sulphide.

schweflig, sulphurous; **schweflige Säure,** sulphurous acid.

schwefligsauer, sulphite of.

Schwefligsäure, *f.* sulphurous acid; **-anhydrid,** *n.* sulphurous anhydride, sulphur dioxide; **-gas,** *n.* sulphur dioxide; **-wasser,** *n.* aqueous sulphurous acid.

Schweif, *m.*-e, tail, train.

schweifen, to stray, ramble, curve, rinse, warp, tail, bevel.

Schweifung, *f.* curve, swell, rounding.

schweigen, to be silent, hush, not to speak of.

Schweigen, *n.* silence.

schweigsam, silent, quiet, taciturn, reserved.

Schwein, *n.*-e, hog, pig, swine; **-brot,** *n.* sowbread (*Cyclamen europaeum*).

Schweinchen, *n.* little pig.

Schweine-fett, *n.* hog fat, lard; **-fleisch,** *n.* pork, **-hals,** *m.* thick neck; **-pest,** *f.* swine fever, hog cholera; **-rotlauf,** swine erysipelas; **-schmalz,** *n.* lard; **-schmer,** *n.* lard; **-seuche,** *f.* swine plague.

Schweinfurtergrün, *n.* Paris green.

Schweins-haut, *f.* hogskin, pigskin; **-leder,** *n.* hogskin, pigskin (leather).

Schweiss, *m.* sweat, perspiration, blood, yolk; **-abgabe,** *f.* perspiration; **-arbeit,** *f.* welding; **-asche,** *f.* raw potash, suint ash.

schweissbar, weldable, welding.

Schweiss-bart, *m.* icicle (weld); **-befördernd,** sudorific, diaphoretic, **-drüse,** *f.* sweat gland; **-echt,** fast to perspiration; **-eisen,** *n.* wrought iron.

schweissen, to weld, begin to melt, sweat, bleed, leak.

Schweisser, *m.* welder.

schweiss-erregend, diaphoretic, sudorific; **-fehler,** *m.* defect in welding; **-flüssigkeit,** *f.* sweat; **-gang,** *m.* sweat duct; **-gehalt,** *m.* suint content; **-gewaschen,** washed in the grease; **-hitze,** *f.* welding heat; **-hund,** *m.* bloodhound; **-kanal,** *m.* sweat duct; **-lage,** *f.* weld layer, pass of welding material.

Schweiss-loch, *n.* sweat pore; **-metall,** *m.* wrought iron; **-mittel,** *n.* sudorific, diaphoretic, flux; **-naht,** *f.* weld seam; **-prozess,** *m.* welding process; **-schmiedeeisen,** *n.* weld iron; **-stahl,** *m.* weld steel; **-stelle,** *f.* place where metal is welded; **-treibend,** diaphoretic.

Schweissung, *f.* welding, weld.

Schweiss-verfahren, n. welding process; **-wachs,** m. wax from suint, yolk wax; **-walzen,** f.pl. roughing rolls; **-wärme,** f. welding heat; **-wasser,** n. water of condensation; **-wolle,** f. wool containing suint (dried sweat of sheep in wool).

Schweiz, f. Switzerland.

Schweizerkäse, m. Swiss cheese, Gruyère cheese.

Schwelanlage, f. carbonizing plant.

schwelchen, to wither, air-dry.

Schwelchmalz, n. withered (air-dried) malt.

schwelen, to smolder, distill, carbonize at low temperature, burn slowly.

Schwelerei, f. low-temperature carbonization.

Schwelgas, n. gas from low-temperature carbonization.

schwelken, to wither.

Schwelkohle, f. coal for distilling.

schwellbar, capable of swelling, erectile.

Schwellbeize, f. swelling liquor.

Schwelle, f. sill, threshold, sleeper, beam, tie, crossbar, ledge.

schwellen, to swell, distend, increase, grow.

Schwellen-schraube, f. tie bolt or screw; **-wert,** m. threshold value, minimum stimulus needed for reaction.

Schwell-gewebe, n. erectile (cavernous) tissue; **-körper,** m. corpus (spongiosum) cavernosum, lodicule; **-kraft,** f. plumping power; **-mittel,** n. plumping agent (for leather); **-polster,** n. pulvinus.

Schwellung, f. swelling, tumefaction.

Schwellwasser, n. distension water.

Schwel-ofen, m. distilling oven, still, low-temperature carbonizing furnace; **-raum,** m. carbonizing space or chamber; **-retorte,** f. retort for low-temperature distillation; **-teer,** m. tar from low-temperature carbonization.

Schwelung, f. slow burning.

Schwel-vorgang, m. low-temperature carbonization; **-wasser,** n. water of distillation; **-werk,** n. carbonizing plant.

Schwemmboden, m. alluvial soil.

Schwemme, f. watering (place).

schwemmen, to irrigate, water, wash, flush, float, deposit.

Schwemmland, n. brook deposit, brook silt, alluvial land, delta soil; **-boden,** m. alluvial soil.

Schwemm-stein, m. (vitrified) floatstone, pumice stone; **-wasser,** n. wash (flushing) water.

Schwenkaufnahme, f. oscillating exposure.

schwenken, to wave, swing, rinse, turn about, swivel.

schwer, (dat.) heavy, stout, strong, difficult, hard, severe, serious; **das fällt ihm ~,** that is hard for him.

Schwer-achse, f. centroidal axis; **-benzin,** n. heavy benzine; **-benzol,** n. heavy benzol; **-bleierz,** n. plattnerite.

Schwere, f. heaviness, weight, severity, gravity, difficulty, hardness; **-feld,** n. field of gravity.

Schwererde, f. heavy earth, heavy spar, barite.

Schweresinnesorgan, n. sense organ of equilibrium (statocyst).

schwer-fallen, to be difficult; **-fällig,** clumsy, heavy, dull, slack; **-flüchtigkeit,** f. difficult volatility; **-flüssig,** difficulty fusible, viscous, refractory; **-flüssigkeit,** f. difficult fusibility; **-frucht,** f. heavy (grain) cereals; **-halten,** to be difficult; **-hörigkeit,** f. defective hearing, deafness; **-kraft,** f. force of gravity; **-kraftwirkung,** f. influence of gravity; **-leder,** n. sole leather.

schwerlich, hardly, scarcely, with difficulty.

schwer-löslich, difficultly soluble; **-löslichkeit,** f. difficult solubility; **-metall,** n. heavy metal; **-mut,** f. melancholy; **-punkt,** m. center of gravity; **-reiz,** m. gravity stimulus; **-schmelzbar,** difficultly fusible; **-schmelzend,** fusing with difficulty; **-schwarz,** n. weighted black; **-sieder,** m. high boiler.

Schwer-spat, m. heavy spar, barite; **-stein,** m. scheelite; **-tantalerz,** n. tantalite.

Schwert, n.-er, sword; **-blättrig,** ensifolious; **-fisch,** m. swordfish; **-förmig,** ensiform; **-fortsatz,** m. ensiform process; **-kolben,** m. sausage flask; **-lilie,** f. iris, fleur-de-lis, sword grass; **-liliengewächse,** n.pl. Iridaceae; **-schwänze,** m.pl. king crab, swordtails (Xiphosura).

schwerwiegend, weighty, serious.

Schwester, f. sister; **-art,** f. sister species, biologic species.

schwieg (schweigen), was silent.

Schwiele, f. callosity, callus, weal, weit, induration.

schwielig, callous, indurated, horny, weal-like.

schwierig, difficult, hard, fastidious.

Schwierigkeit, *f.* difficulty, trouble, obstacle.

schwiert (schwären), festers, ulcerates.

schwillt (schwellen), swells.

Schwimm-aufbereitung, *f.* flotation; **-bade-
seife,** *f.* floating bath soap; **-beine,** *n.pl.*
natatorial legs; **-bewegung,** *f.* ciliary
movement; **-blase,** *f.* air (swim) bladder;
-blatt, *n.* floating leaf.

schwimmen, to swim, float.

Schwimmer, *m.* float, swimmer.

Schwimm-fähigkeit, *f.* buoyancy; **-farne,**
m.pl. Saliviniaceae; **-flosse,** *f.* ptery-
gopodium; **-frucht,** *f.* seed or fruit capable
of floating on water for a time; **-fussast,** *m.*
exopodite; **-füsse,** *m.pl.* webfeet, pedes
natales, palmated feet, pleopods or swim-
merets (of Crustacea); **-gerät,** *n.* flotation
equipment; **-gewebe,** *n.* sclerenchyma;
-glocke, *f.* nectocalyx; **-glockenknospe,** *f.*
nectocalyx bud.

Schwimm-haut, *f.* web membrane; **-haut-
ähnlich,** weblike; **-holz,** *n.* submerged
wood; **-käfer,** *m.* water beetle (Dytiscidae);
-kiesel, *m.* floatstone; **-körper,** *m.* swimming (floating) body, float; **-kraft,** *f.*
bouyancy; **-lappen,** swimming membrane;
-methode, *f.* flotation method; **-plättchen,**
n.pl. swimming plates.

Schwimm-polypen, *m.pl.* Siphonophora;
-sand, *m.* quicksand; **-säule,** *f.* nectosome;
-stein, *m.* floatstone; **-tiere,** *n.pl.* Natatores; **-vermögen,** *n.* floating power;
-vögel, *m.pl.* Natatores; **-werkzeug,** *n.*
apparatus for swimming.

Schwindel, *m.*-, vertigo, staggers, fraud,
swindle, lot; **-haft,** fraudulent, dizzy,
deceptive; **-korn,** *n.* cubeb, coriander seed.

schwinden, to shrink, contract, dwindle,
waste, disappear, vanish, atrophy, wither.

Schwinden, *n.* shrinking, shrinkage, wasting, atrophy.

Schwind-mass, *n.*-e, amount of shrinkage,
shrinkage; **-riss,** *m.* season crack in wood;
-sucht, *f.* consumption, phthisis; **-süchtig,**
consumptive.

Schwindung, *f.* shrinkage, contraction.

Schwindungs-fähigkeit, *f.* tendency to
shrink, property of shrinking; **-loch,** *n.*
shrinkage cavity.

Schwinge, *f.* wing, swingle; *pl.* primaries.

Schwingelgras, *n.* fescue grass, fescue
(*Festuca pratensis*).

schwingen, to swing, vibrate, winnow,
swingle, balance, oscillate, wave, centrifuge.

schwingend, vibrating, vibratory, oscillating.

Schwinger, *m.pl.* halters; **-federn,** *f.pl.*
remiges; **-knopf,** *m.* halter, knob of the
halter; **-kölbchen,** *n.pl.* halters.

Schwingmesser, *n.pl.* scutching blades.

Schwingung, *f.* vibration, oscillation; **in** ∼
versetzen, to cause to vibrate, set in
oscillating motion.

Schwingungs-bewegung, *f.* vibratory (oscillatory) motion; **-bogen,** *m.* arc of oscillation; **-ebene,** *f.* plane of vibration; **-federn,**
f.pl. remiges; **-gleichung,** *f.* vibration equation; **-härchen,** *n.* vibratile cilium.

Schwingungs-knoten, *m.* node; **-mühle,** *f.*
vibratory mill; **-weite,** *f.* amplitude of
vibration; **-welle,** *f.* undulation, vibrational
wave; **-zahl,** *f.* vibration number, frequency, or rate; **-zeit,** *f.* time of vibration.

schwirren, to whiz, whir, buzz, hum,
centrifuge.

Schwirrfliegen, *f.pl.* Syrphidae.

Schwitze, *f.* sweat, sweating.

schwitzen, to sweat, perspire.

Schwitz-mittel, *n.* sudorific, diaphoretic;
-pulver, *n.* diaphoretic powder; **-röste,** *f.*
steam retting; **-wasser,** *n.* sweat (on
pipes).

Schwöde, *f.* state of being limed; **-brei,** *m.*
(leather) lime cream; **-fass,** *n.* lime vat;
-masse, *f.* (leather) lime cream.

schwöden, to lime (hides).

schwoll (schwellen), swelled.

schwomm (schwimmen), swam.

schwor (schwären), festered, ulcerated.

schwor (schwören), swore an oath.

schwören, to swear.

schwül, close, sultry, damp.

Schwüle, *f.* humidity, concretion.

Schwulst, *m.*ːe, swelling, tumor.

Schwund, *m.* atrophy, withering, loss, disappearance, shrinkage, contraction; **-er-
scheinungen,** *f.pl.* fading, contraction.

Schwung, *m.*ːe, swing, vibration, oscillation,
soaring, activity; **-bewegung,** *f.* vibratory
motion; **-decke,** *f.* tectrix; **-feder,** *f.*
pinion, remex; **-flachs,** *m.* scutched flax;
-gewicht, *n.* pendulum.

schwung-haft, swinging, soaring, lively,
sublime; **-körper,** *m.* swinging body; **-kraft,**
f. centrifugal force, vibrating power, liveliness; **-maschine,** *f.* centrifugal whirler;
-rad, *n.* flywheel, balance wheel.

schwur (schwären), festered; (schwören), swore (oath).

Schwur, *m.* ̈e, oath.

schwürig, suppurating, ulcerated.

Sclerenchymbeleg, *m.* sclerenchymatous pericycle.

Sebacinsäure, *f.* sebacic acid.

secrenieren, to secrete.

sechs, six; -atomig, hexatomic; -eck, *n.* hexagon; -eckig, hexagonal; -ender, *m.* stage of six points.

sechserlei, of six kinds, six kinds of.

sechs-fach, sixfold, sextuple; -fältig, sixfold, sextuple; -flach, *n.* hexahedron; -flächig, hexahedral; -flächner, *m.* hexahedron; -gliedrig, six(-membered)-numbered.

sechs-kantig, six sided, hexagonal; -malig, six times; -monatlich, half-yearly, semi-annual; -ring, *m.* six-membered ring; -säurig, hexacid; -seitig, hexagonal, six-sided; -strahler, *m.* hexactinellid spicule.

sechste, sixth; Sechstel, *n.* sixth.

sechs-wertig, hexavalent; -winklig, hexangular, hexagonal; -zählig, sixfold.

sechzehn, sixteen; sechzehnt, sixteenth.

sechzig, sixty.

Sectionsrähmchen, *n.* honey box.

Sedativsalz, *n.* sedative salt.

Sedimentgesteine, *n.pl.* sedimentary rocks.

Sedimentierung, *f.* sedimentation, silting.

See, *m*-n, lake.

See, *f.* sea; -ablagerung, *f.* sea deposit; -algen, *f.pl.* marine algae; -bad, *n.* seaside resort, bath in the sea; -erz, *m.* lake (iron) ore; -gang, *m.* swell; -gewächs, *n.* sea plant, marine plant, seaweed; -gras, *n* eelgrass, grassweed (*Zostera marina*); -gurken, *f.pl.* sea cucumbers (*Holothuroidea*).

See-höhe, *f.* height above sea level; -hund, *m.* seal; -igel, *m.pl.* sea urchins (Echinoidea); -igelei, *n.* sea-urchin's egg; -kabel, *n.* submarine cable; -kohl, *m.* sea kale; -krebs, *m.* lobster; -kühe, *f.pl.* sirenians, sea cows.

Seele, *f.* soul, mind, spirit, shaft, core.

Seelen-leben, *n.* life of the soul, psychic spiritual life; -ruhe, *f.* tranquillity, peace of mind, -tätigkeit, *f.* inner activity; -zustand, *m.* spiritual state, psychic condition.

See-licht, *n.* marine phosphorescence; -lilien, *f.pl.* Crinoidea.

seelisch, psychic.

See-pferdchen, *n.* sea horse; -pocken, *f.pl.* barnacles; -rosen, *f.pl.* water lilies (Nymphaea); -rosengewächse, *n.pl.* Nymphaeaceae; -schlick, *m.* sea ooze; -sterne, *m.pl.* starfishes (Asteroidea); -tang, *m.* seaweed; -walzen, *f.pl.* Holothurioidea.

Segel, *n.-*, sail, velum; -flieger, *m.pl.* glider, seed or fruits with Zanonia type of wings; -flugzeug, *n.* glider (plane); -förmig, sail-formed, veliform; -ventil, *n.* atrioventricular valve.

Segen, *m.* blessing, benediction, prosperity, abundance, yield.

segensreich, prosperous, blessed, lucky.

Segerkegel, *m.* Seger cone.

Segge, *f.* sedge, sedge grass (Carex); -moor, *n.* sedge moor.

Segment, *n.*-e, segment, somite.

Segmental-organ, *n.* excretory organ-nephridium; -trichter, *n.* nephrostome.

Segmentgrenze, *f.* limit of the segment.

Segmentierung, *f.* division into segments.

segnen, to bless, cross.

Sehe, *f.* pupil (of the eye).

Sehelement, *n.* visual element.

sehen, to see, look, appear, recognize, behold, notice, observe; zu ∼ sein, to be visible; ∼ lassen, to show, exhibit, display.

Sehen, *n.* seeing, sight, vision.

Sehenswürdigkeit, *f.* curiosity, sight, spectacle.

Seher, *m.* seer.

Seh-feld, *n.* field of vision; -grübchen, *n.* optic pit; -hügel, *n.* optic lobe, thalamus; -lappen, *m.* optic lobe; -lehre, *f.* optics; -linse, *f.* crystalline lens; -loch, *n.* pupil, optic foramen.

Sehne, *f.* tendon, sinew, tangent, fiber, chord, nerve, string, cord.

Sehneisen, *n.* fibrous iron.

sehnen, to long, yearn; -band, *n.* ligament of the tendon; -bein, *n.* sesamoid bone; -binde, *f.* tendinous fascia; -bogen, *m.* filament; -faserbündel, *n.* bundle of tendinous arch; -faser, *f.* tendinous fiber or tendinous fibers; -gallen, *f.pl.* windgalls; -gewebe, *n.* tissue of the tendon.

Sehnen-haut, *f.* aponeurosis; -klapp, *m.* sprain; -knöchelchen, *n.* sesamoid bone; -pforte, *f.* opening for a tendon; -rolle, *f.* trochlear surface; -scheide, *f.* tendon sheath; -schenkel, *m.* head or muscular attachment of a tendon; -schmiere, *f.* synovial fluid; -streif, *m.* tendinous band;

-verkürzung, *f.* shortening or contraction of the tendon; -verletzung, *f.* injury to a tendon.

Sehnerv, *m.* optic nerve.

Sehnerven-faserschicht, *f.* layer of optic nerve fibers; -kreuzung, *f.* optic chiasma; -öffnung, *f.* optic foramen; -scheibe, *f.* optic disk.

sehnig, tendinous, sinewy, fibrous.

Sehnsucht, *f.* longing, yearning, desire.

Seh-organ, *n.*-e, organ for vision; -punkt, *m.* visual point; -purpur, *m.* visual purple; -purpurbild, *n.* visual purple picture; -purpurhaltig, containing visual purple.

sehr, very, very much, very well.

Seh-rohr, *n.* periscope, telescope; -schärfe, *f.* acuteness of vision; -stäbchen, *n.* rhabdome; -störung, *f.* visual disturbance; -vermögen, visual faculty; -vorgang, *m.* process of sight; -weite, *f.* visual range; -werkzeug, *n.* organ of sight or vision; -winkel, *m.* angle of vision; -zelle, *f.* (pigmented) visual cell.

sei (sein); es sei x . . . let x be . . . .

seicht, shallow, low, flat, superficial; -gründig, shallow.

Seichtwasser-ablagerung, *f.* shallow-water formation or deposit; -bestand, *m.* shallow-water vegetation; -form, *f.* life in shallow water.

seichtwurzelnd, shallow-rooted.

Seide, *f.* silk, dodder.

Seidel, *n.* pint, half liter, tankard; -bast, *m.* mezereon (*Daphne mezereum*).

Seidenabfall, *m.* silk waste, waste silk.

seidenartig, silky; seidenartiger Glanz, *m.* silking, silky sheen.

Seiden-asbest, *m.* silky asbestos; -band, *n.* silk band; -bast, *m.* tussah silk; -bau, *m.* silk culture; -beschwerung, *f.* silk weighting; -fabrik, *f.* silk mill; -faden, *m.* silk thread; -faserstoff, *m.* fibroin; -fibrin, *n.* fibroin; flor, *m.* silk gauze.

Seiden-garn, *n.* silk yarn, spun silk; -glanz, *m.* silky luster; -haar, *n.* silky hair; -haarig, sericeous; -holz, *n.* satinwood; -industrie, *f.* silk industry; -leim, *m.* silk glue, sericin; -papier, *n.* tissue paper; -pflanzengewächse, *n.pl.* Asclepiadaceae; -raupe, *f.* silkworm.

Seiden-raupenkrankheit, *f.* silkworm disease; -raupenschmetterling, *m.* silkworm moth; -raupenseuche, *f.* silkworm epidemic; -raupenzucht, *f.* sericulture; -schrei,

m. scroop of silk; -spinner, *m.* mulberry silk moth.

Seidlitz-pulver, *n.* Seidlitz powder; -salz, *n.* Epsom salt.

seien (sein), (may)be.

Seife, *f.* soap, placer.

seifecht, fast to soaping.

seifen, to soap, lather, scour, wash; -abfälle, *m.pl.* soap scraps; -artig, soapy, saponaceous; asche, *f.* soap ashes; -bad, *n.* soap bath; -bagger, *m.* placer dredge; -balsam, *m.* soap liniment, opodeldoc; -baum, *m.* soapbark tree, quillai; -baum-gewächse, *n.pl.* Sapindaceae; -baumrinde, *f.* soapbark, quillai bark.

Seifen-bereitung, *f.* soapmaking; -bildung, *f.* formation of soap, saponification; -blase, *f.* soap bubble; -brühe, *f.* soapsuds; -erde, *f.* saponaceous clay; -ersatz, *m.* soap substitute; -erz, *n.* alluvial ore; -fabrik, *f.* soap factory; -fabrikant, *m.* soapmaker; -flocken, *f.pl.* soap flakes.

Seifen-form, *f.* soap frame; -gebirge, *n.* placer (alluvial) deposits; -gold, *n.* placer gold; -haltig, containing soap; -kessel, *m.* soap boiler; -kraut, *n.* soap plant, soapweed; -lauge, *f.* soap solution, soapsuds; -leim, *m.* soap glue, soap (paste) size; -lösung, *f.* soap solution; -probe, *f.* soap test, sample of soap.

Seifen-pulver, *n.* soap powder; -riegel, *m.* bar of soap; -rinde, *f.* soapbark; -schabsel, *n.* soap scraps; -schaum, *m.* lather; -schmiere, *f.* soap stuff; -sieder, *m.* soapmaker; -siederasche, *f.* soap ashes; -siederei, *f.* soap works; -stein, *m.* soapstone, steatite.

Seifen-stoff, *m.* saponin; -tafel, *f.* slab of soap, -täfelchen, *n.* cake of soap; -ton, *m.* saponaceous clay; -wasser, *n.* soap (suds) water; -wurzel, *f.* soapwort, soaproot; -zinn, *n.* stream tin.

seifig, soapy, saponaceous.

seiger, perpendicular.

Seiger-arbeit, *f.* liquation process; -blei, *n.* liquation lead; -dörner, *m.pl.* liquation dross.

seigern, to liquate, refine, segregate.

Seiger-ofen, *m.* liquation furnace; -schlacke, *f.* liquation slag.

Seigerung, *f.* liquation, segregation.

Seigerwerk, *n.* liquation works.

Seignettesalz, *n.* Rochelle salt, sodium potassium tartrate.

Seihe, *f.* strainer, filter; **-boden,** *m.* strainer (perforated) bottom; **-gefäss,** *n.* straining (filtering) vessel.

seihen, to strain, filter.

Seihepapier, *n.* filter paper.

Seiher, *m.* strainer, filter.

Seihe-sack, *m.* filtering bag; **-trichter,** *m.* straining funnel, strainer; **-tuch,** *n.* straining (filtering) cloth; **-vermögen,** *n.* filtering power.

Seil, *n.* cord, rope, cable, line; **-eck,** *n.* funicular polygon.

Seiler, *m.* ropemaker; **-waren,** *f.pl.* cordage.

Seil-faser, *f.* cordage fiber; **-rille,** *f.* groove for rope; **-scheibe,** *f.* rope pulley.

Seim, *m.* glutinous liquid, strained honey.

seimen, to yield a glutinous liquid, strain honey.

seimig, glutinous, mucilaginous.

sein, to be, exist, be alive; his, its; **etwas** ~ **lassen,** to leave something undone or alone.

Sein, *n.* being, existence.

seiner, of it, his, its.

seinerseits, for his part.

seinerzeit, in its (his) time, at the time.

seinige (der, die, das), his, his own.

seit, since, for; ~ **kurzem,** recently, of late; ~ **damals,** since then; ~ **lange,** for a long time, for some time; ~ **alters her,** for ages.

seitdem, since, since then, ever since.

Seite, *f.* side, face, flank, page; **nach allen Seiten,** in all directions; **zur** ~ **stehen,** to stand by, support; **meinerseits,** for my part; **von Seiten,** on the part of, on behalf of.

Seiten-achse, *f.* lateral axis; **-ader,** *f.* lateral vein; **-ährchen,** *n.* lateral floret; **-ansicht,** *f.* profile, side elevation; **-ast,** *m.* lateral branch; **-auge,** *n.* lateral eye; **-band,** *n.* lateral ligament; **-beckenbein,** *n.* lateral pelvic bone; **-blüte,** *f.* lateral flower, axillary flower; **-brustteil** (oberer), *m.* epimeron.

Seiten-druck, *m.* lateral pressure; **-eck,** *n.* lateral summit; **-ecke,** *f.* lateral summit; **-faltenhöhle,** *f.* metapleural canal; **-feld,** *n.* lateral field; **-felddrüse,** *f.* lateral gland; **-fläche,** *f.* lateral face or surface; **-flügel,** *m.* lateral wing; **-fortsatz,** *m.* lateral process; **-früchtig,** pleurocarpous.

Seiten-furche, *f.* lateral groove; **-gang,** *m.* side passage; **-graben,** *m.* side ditch; **horn,** *n* lateral horn; **-kante,** *f.* lateral edge; **-kette,** *f.* side chain; **-knospe,** *f.* lateral bud, axillary bud; **-kraft,** *f.* component (force), secondary force; **-kreislauf,** *m.* collateral circulation.

Seiten-lage, *f.* lateral position; **-länge,** *f.* length of a side; **-läppchen,** *n.* lateral (parietal) lobe; **-linie,** *f.* lateral line; **-nerv,** *m.* lateral vein; **-organ,** *n.* lateral-line organ, nervous organ; **-platte,** *f.* lateral lamina, clavicle arch; **-rand,** *m.* lateral margin; **-rohr,** *n.,* **-röhre,** *f.* side tube, branch (tube) pipe.

seitens, on behalf (of), on the part (of).

Seiten-schilder, *n.pl.* marginalia; **-schirm,** *m.* lateral shelter; **-schraube,** *f.* side screw; **-schutz,** *m.* lateral shelter; **-septum,** *n.* alar septum; **-spross,** *m.* lateral shoot; **-stachel,** *m.* lateral spine; **-ständig,** lateral; **-stechen,** pleurisy; **-strang,** *m.* lateral column.

Seiten-streifen, *m.* longitudinal stripe, sidestripe; **-stück,** *n.* sidepiece, counterpart; **-trieb,** *m.* lateral shoot; **-wand,** *f.* lateral wall; **-wandbein,** *n.* parietal bone; **-wände,** *f.pl.* quarters.

Seiten-wandknochen, *m.* parietal bone; **-wendung,** *f.* transverse movement; **-wulst,** *f.* lateral ridge; **-wurzel,** *f.* lateral root; **-wurzelig,** pleurorhizal; **-zweig,** *m.* lateral branch.

seither, since then, till now.

seitig, lateral.

seitlich, side, lateral, collateral; **-gleich,** equilateral, symmetrical.

seitwärts, sideways, laterally, aside, edgeways.

Sekante, *f.* secant.

Sekret, *n.-e,* secretion.

Sekretär, *m.* secretary, clerk, wardrobe.

Sekretbehälter, *m.* gland.

Sekretion, *f.* secretion.

sekretionshemmend, restricting secretion.

sekretorisch, secretory.

Sekretpräparat, *n.* preparation from a secretion; **-stoff,** *m.* secreted substance.

Sekt, *m.* champagne, dry wine.

Sektion, *f.* section, dissection.

Sektionalkessel, *m.* straight-tube sectional boiler.

sekundär, secondary; **sekundäre Wimperkränze,** *m.pl.* telotroch, polytroch.

Sekundär-infektion, *f.* secondary infection, **-knötchen,** *n.* secondary nodule; **-kreis,** *m.*

secondary circuit; **stellung,** *f.* secondary position; **-strahlung,** *f.* secondary radiation; **wicklung,** *f.* secondary coil.

Sekunde, *f.* second.

Sekundenuhr, *f.* watch with a second hand.

selb, selbe, same.

selber, self.

selbst, self, myself, himself, even, spontaneous, automatic; **er** ~, he himself; ~ **er,** even he.

Selbst-abnahmemaschine, *f.* Yankee paper (single-cylinder) machine; **-achtung,** *f.* self-respect, self-esteem.

selbständig, independent, self(-dependent) -reliant.

Selbständigkeit, *f.* independence, autonomy, self-reliance.

Selbst-anpassung, *f.* direct adaptation; **-ansteckung,** *f.* self-infection; **-befruchtung,** *f.* self-fertilization; **-beherrschung,** *f.* self-control; **-beobachtung,** *f.* self-observation, introspection; **-berasung,** *f.* self-sodding, establishment of a natural turf; **-bestäubung,** *f.* self-pollination; **-bewusst,** self-conscious, proud, conceited; **-biographie,** *f.* autobiography; **-binder,** *m.* reaper binder.

Selbst-differenzierung, *f.* autonomy; **-entlader,** *m.* self-dumper, car with bottom and side discharge; **-entladung,** *f.* self-discharge; **-entzündlichkeit,** *f.* spontaneous inflammability; **-entzündung,** *f.* spontaneous ignition; **-erhitzung,** *f.* self-heating; **-erregend,** self-exciting; **-erzeugung,** *f.* spontaneous generation, autogenesis; **-gärung,** *f.* spontaneous fermentation; **-gefühl,** *n.* consciousness, self-confidence or -esteem.

selbst-gemacht, self-made, homemade; **-gezüchtet,** home grown; **-gift,** *n.* autotoxin; **-hemmend,** self-retarding, irreversible; **-induktionsspule,** *f.* self-induction coil; **-infektion,** *f.* self-infection; **-kante,** *f.* selvage; **-kosten,** *f.pl.* factory or working cost, net cost; **-los,** unselfish; **-lötung,** *f.* autogenic soldering.

Selbst-mordversuch, *m.* suicidal attempt; **-redend,** self-evident; **-reinigung,** *f.* self-purification; **-schmierend,** self-lubricating; **-schrift,** *f.* autograph; **-steuerung,** *f.* autoregulation, returning to normality; **-tätig,** automatic, capable of spontaneous activity, self-acting, self-raising; **-teilung,** *f.* spontaneous division, fission; **-übung,** *f.* practice; **-umkehr,** *f.* self-reversal.

Selbst-unempfänglichkeit, *f.* self-sterility; **-unterbrecher,** *m.* automatic interrupter;

-verbrennung, *f.* spontaneous combustion; **-verdampfung,** *f.* flashing; **-verdauung,** *f.* autodigestion; **-vergiftung,** *f.* autointoxication, staling (of a culture); **-verständlich,** self-evident, of course; **-verträglich,** self-compatible; **-wendungsreaktion,** *f.* spontaneous version, turning-of-body reaction; **-wirkend,** self-acting, automatic.

Selbst-zersetzung, *f.* spontaneous decomposition; **-zerstörung,** *f.* autodestruction; **-zeugung,** *f.* spontaneous generation, abiogenesis; **-zünder,** *m.* pyrophorus, self-igniter, automatic lighter; **-zündung,** *f.* spontaneous ignition.

Selektion, *f.* selection, elimination.

selektiv, selective; **selektive Vermischung,** *f.* assortative mating.

Selen, *n.* selenium; **-ammonium,** *n.* ammonium selenide; **-blei,** *n.* lead selenide; **-bleisilber,** *n.* naumannite; **-bleiwismutglanz,** *m.* galenobismuthite; **-brücke,** *f.* selenium bridge; **-chlorür,** *n.* selenium monochloride; **-cyanid,** *n.* selenocyanate; **-eisen,** ferrous selenide; **-halogen,** *n.* selenium halide; **-haltig,** containing selenium, seleniferous.

Selenid, *n.* selenide.

selenig, selenious; **-sauer,** selenite of.

Selenigsäure, *f.* selenious acid; **-anhydrid,** *n.* selenious anhydride.

Selen-kupfer, *n.* copper selenide; **-quecksilber,** *n.* mercury selenide; **-quecksilberblei,** *n.* lehrbachite; **-salz,** *n.* selenide; **-sauer,** selenate of; **-silber,** *n.* silver selenide.

Selen-silberglanz, *m.* naumannite; **-verbindung,** *f.* selenium compound; **-wasserstoff,** *m.* hydrogen selenide; **-wasserstoffsäure,** *f.* hydroselenic acid; **-wismutglanz,** *m.* guanajuatite; **-zelle,** *f.* selenium cell.

selig, blessed, happy, deceased, late.

Sellerie, *f.* celery.

selten, rare, scarce, unusual; **seltene Erde,** rare earth.

Seltenheit, *f.* rareness, scarcity, curiosity.

Seltenheitsproblem, *n.* problem of rarity.

Selterswasser, *n.* Seltzer water.

seltsam, singular, strange, odd, curious.

Semesterring, *m.* secondary ring (in trees)

semicyclisch, semicyclic.

Semidinumlagerung, *f.* semidine rearrangement.

Semilunarklappe, *f.* semilunar valve.

semimer, semimeric.

Semmel, *f.* roll (bread).

senden, to send.

Sendung, *f.* sending, shipment, parcel (commission).

Senegawurzel, *f.* senega root.

Senf, *m.* mustard (Brassica); -gas, *n.* mustard gas; -gasspritzer, *m.* splash of mustard gas; -geist, *m.* oil of mustard; -korn, *n.* mustard seed; -mehl, *n.* ground mustard; -öl, *n.* mustard oil; -pflaster, *m.* mustard plaster; -same, *m.* mustard seed.

sengen, to singe, burn, scorch, parch.

Senk-boden, *m.* false bottom, strainer; -brunnen, *m.* dry, open caisson; -kasten, *m.* caisson.

Senkel, *m.* plumb line, plummet, lace.

senken, to sink, lower, submerge, subside, set, settle.

Senker, *m.* haustorium, layer shoot; -vermehrung, *f.* layering.

Senk-faden, *m.*∺, tentacle; -grube, *f.* cesspool, sump, catch basin; -körper, *m.* bob, sinker; -recht, perpendicular, vertical; -rechte, *f.* perpendicular line; -rücken, *m.* swayback; -spindel, *f.* hydrometer, specific-gravity spindle.

Senkung, *f.* sinking, lowering, hollow, depression, subsiding, subsidence, sedimentation, inclination, incline.

Senkungsgeschwindigkeit, *f.* velocity of settling or submergence.

Senkwaage, *f.* hydrometer, areometer.

Sennes-blätter, *n.pl.* senna leaves, senna; -strauch, *m.* senna.

Sense, *f.* scythe.

sensibel, sensible, sensitive, sensory.

Sensibilisator, *m.* sensitizer.

sensibilisierte Vira, *m.pl.* sensitized vaccines.

Sensibilisierung, *f.* sensitization.

Sensibilität, *f.* sensibility, sensitiveness.

Sensorium, *n.* sensorium, seat of sensation.

Sepalum, *n.* sepal.

separat, separate, particular, detached; -abdruck, *m.* separate impression, reprint.

separieren, to separate.

Sepia, *f.*, sepia, cuttlefish.

Septal-drüse, *f.* septal gland; -knospung, *f.* septal gemmation; -trichter, *m.* septal funnel, infundibulum.

Septikämie, *f.* septicemia.

Septikopyämie, *f.* septic pyemia.

septisch, septic.

Seradella, *f.* Ornithopus.

Seren, *n.pl.* serum.

serial, in series; seriale Beiknospe, *f.* accessor-axillary bud.

Serie, *f.* series.

serien-fremd, of a different series; -grenze, *f.* series limit; -mässig, in series; -schnitt, *m.* serial section.

Sero-diagnose, -diagnostik, *f.* serum diagnosis; -logie, *f.* serology; -logisch, serological.

serös, serous.

Serpentinieren, *n.* meandering.

Serum, *n.* Sera, serum; -agar, *n.* serum agar; -diagnose, *f.* serum diagnosis; -eiweiss, *n.* blood protein; -krankheit, *f.* serum disease; -titer, *n.* titer of serum.

Serviette, *f.* napkin.

Sesam, *m,* sesame; -bein, *n.* sesamoid bone; -knorpel, *m.* sesamoid cartilage; -kuchen, *m.* sesame-oil cake; -öl, *n.* sesame oil.

Sessel, *m.* easy chair, seat.

sesshaft, resident, sedentary, settled, stationary.

Setzbottich, *m.* settling vat.

setzen, to set, put, place, apply, plant, stack, pile, precipitate, subside, sink; sich ∼, to sit down, clarify, be deposited, settle, spawn, breed; in Gang ∼, to set in motion, set going; ∼ an, to join; in Freiheit ∼, to set free, liberate.

Setzer, *m.* setter, compositor, tamper; -fehler, *m.* printer's error; -gut, *n.* planting material; -kartoffel, *f.* seed potato; -kasten, *m.* settling tank, type case.

Setzfehler, *m.* printer's error.

Setzling, *m.* slip, cutting, layer.

Setz-phiole, *f.* flat-bottomed phial; -probe, *f.* slump test.

Setzung, *f.* settlement.

Setz-waage, *f.* level; -zapfen, *m.* suppository; -zeit, *f.* dropping, planting, or breeding time.

Seuche, *f.* contagious (infectious) disease, pestilence, epidemic.

seuchen-artig, epidemic, contagious, infectious; -fest, immune; -haft, epidemic.

Seven-baum, *m.* -kraut, *n.* savin (*Juniperus sabina*).

Sexual-hormon, *n.* sex hormone; **-zelle,** *f.* germ cell.

sexuell, sexual.

sezernieren, to secrete.

sezieren, to dissect.

S-förmig, S-shaped.

sich, himself, herself, itself, themselves, each (one) other.

Sichel, *f.* sickle, crescent, drepanium; **-borste,** *f.* falcate bristle; **-förmig,** sickle (crescent) shaped; **-förmig gebogen,** campylotropous; **-fortsatz,** *m.* falciform process; **-haar,** *n.* falcate hair.

sicheln, to cut with the sickle.

Sichelrinne, *f.* groove of falx, primitive streak.

sicher, (*gen.*) safe, secure, certain, sure, true, reliable, positive; **-stellen,** to establish.

Sicherheit, *f.* safety, security, certainty.

Sicherheits-flasche, *f.* safety bottle; **-grad,** *m.* degree (factor) of safety; **-koeffizient,** *m.* factor of safety; **-lampe,** *f.* safety lamp; **-rohr,** *n.* **-röhre,** *f.* safety tube; **-sprengstoff,** *m.* safety explosive.

Sicherheits-streifen, *m.* safety strip; **-trichterrohr,** *n.* siphon, safety tube; **-ventil,** *n.* safety valve; **-waschflasche,** *f.* safety wash bottle, **-wert,** *m.* **-zahl,** *f.* factor of safety; **-zündhölzchen,** *n.* safety match.

sichern, to secure, ensure, safeguard, guarantee; **gesichert,** secured, safe, certain.

sicherstellen, to place in safety, guarantee.

Sicherung, *f.* securing, security, safety device, fuse, insurance, protection.

Sicht, *f.* sight; **auf lange ∼,** with a view to the future, in the long run.

sichtbar, visible, perceptible, evident.

Sichtbarkeit, *f.* visibility, obviousness.

Sichtbarwerden, *n.* becoming visible.

sichten, to sight, sift, sort, classify, purify, bolt.

sichtlich, visible, evident.

Sichtung, *f.* sifting.

Sicker-fläche, *f.* phreatic (free) surface; **-graben,** *m.* trench, ditch; **-linie,** *f.* phreatic line, seepage line.

sickern, to trickle, ooze, infiltrate, percolate.

Sickerung, *f.* percolation, seepage.

Sickerwasser, *n.* infiltrated (ground) water.

sie, she, her, it, they, them.

Sieb, *n.* sieve, screen, riddle, strainer, bolter; **-artig,** sievelike cribrate; **-band,** *n.* traveling screen.

Siebbein, *n.* ethmoid bone; **-höhle,** *f.* ethmoid cavity; **-loch,** *n.* ethmoidal foramen; **-muschel,** *f.* ethmoidal turbinated bone; **-naht,** *f.* ethmoidal suture.

Siebboden, *m.* bottom of a sieve, perforated bottom.

sieben, to sift, sieve, riddle, screen, bolt.

sieben, seven; **-atomig,** heptatomic; **-blätterig,** with seven leaves, heptaphyllous; **-flächig,** heptahedral; **-gliedrig,** seven-membered; **-ring,** *m.* seven-membered ring; **-schläfer,** *m.* dormouse (*Myoxus glis*); **-spaltig,** septemfid.

siebente, seventh.

siebenwertig, septivalent, heptavalent.

Sieb-filter, *m.* spray filter; **-förmig,** sieve-shaped, sievelike; **-gefäss,** *n.* sieve tube; **-grube,** *f.* ethmoid fossa; **-knochen,** *m.* ethmoid bone; **-kurve,** *f.* sieve-analysis curve, grain-size curve; **-maschine,** *f.* sifting (screening) machine; **-mehl,** *n.* coarse flour, siftings; **-platte,** *f.* sieve (filter) plate; **-röhre,** *f.* sieve tube; **-satz,** *n.* set of sieves; **-schale,** *f.* dish with perforated bottom.

Siebsel, *n.* siftings.

Siebstaub, *m.* siftings.

Sieb-teil, *m.* conducting cells of the phloem; **-trichter,** *m.* strainer funnel; **-trommel,** *f.* revolving screen; **-tuch,** *n.* bolting cloth; **-tüpfel,** *m.* sieve plate; **-wasser,** *n.* backwater.

siebzehn, seventeen.

siebzehnt, seventeenth.

siebzig, seventy.

siech, sick(ly), infirm, weak.

Siechtum, *n.* sickliness, protracted suffering.

Siede-abfälle, *m.pl.* scum (sediment) from boiling; **-analyse,** *f.* analysis by fractional distillation; **-apparat,** *m.* boiling apparatus; **-blech,** *n.* boiling plate; **-gefäss,** *n.* boiling vessel; **-grad,** *m.* boiling point; **-grenzen,** *f.pl.* boiling range; **-haus,** *n.* boiling house; **-hitze,** *f.* boiling heat; **-kessel,** *m.* boiling (pan) vessel.

Siede-kolben, *m.* boiling (distillation) flask; **-kurve,** *f.* boiling-point curve; **-lauge,** *f.* boiling (lye) liquor.

Sied(e)lung, *f.* settlement, colony.

Siedelungsgeschichte, *f.* history of colonization.

sieden, to boil, seethe, brew, distill.

Sieden, *n.* boiling, ebullition.

Siedepfanne, *f.* boiling (evaporating) pan.

Siedepunkt, *m.* boiling point; **-bestimmung,** *f.* boiling-point determination, ebullioscopy.

Siedepunktserhöhung, *f.* boiling-point elevation.

Siederei, *f.* boiling room or house, refinery.

Siede-rohr, *n.* **-röhre,** *f.* boiling tube, boiler tube; **-röhrchen,** *n.* small boiling tube; **-salz,** *n.* common salt; **-sole,** *f.* brine; **-steinchen,** *n.* bead; **-temperatur,** *f.* boiling temperature; **-verzug,** *m.* delay in boiling; **-zeit,** *f.* boiling (period) time.

Sidotblende, *f.* Sidot's blend, luminescent ZnS.

Sieg, *m.*-e, victory.

Siegel, *n.* seal; **-erde,** *f.* terra sigillata (Lemmian bole); **-lack,** *m.* sealing wax; **-wachs,** *n.* soft sealing wax.

siegen, to be victorious, conquer, triumph.

siegreich, victorious.

sieht (sehen), sees.

sieken, to crease, seam.

Siel, *m.&n.*-e, sluice, culvert, sewer, drain; **-wasser,** *n.* sewage, drain water.

Sienaerde, *f.* sienna.

Signalzeichen, *n.* sign, symbol.

Signatur, *f.* signature, mark, stamp, brand.

signieren, to sign, brand, mark.

Sikkativ, *n.* siccative.

Silbe, *f.* syllable.

Silber, *n.* silver; **-artig,** silvery, argentine; **-ätzstein,** *m.* lunar caustic, silver nitrate; **-baum,** *m.* silver tree (Leucadendron), *arbor Dianae;* **-blatt,** *n.* silver (leaf) foil; **-blech,** *n.* silver (foil) plate; **-blende,** *f.* proustite, pyrargyrite; **-blick,** *m.* brightening (fulguration) of silver; **-bromür,** *n.* silver subbromide; **-chlorür,** *n.* silver subchloride, argentous chloride.

Silber-draht, *m.* silver wire; **-erz,** *n.* silver ore; **-essigsalz,** *n.* silver acetate; **-fahlerz,** *n.* argentiferous tetrahedrite; **-fluorür,** *n.* silver subfluoride; **-folie,** *f.* silver foil; **-führend,** silver-bearing, argentiferous; **-gare,** *f.* silver refining; **-gehalt,** *m.* silver content; **-gewinnung,** *f.* extraction of silver.

Silber-glanz, *m.* argentite, silvery luster, silver glance; **-glas,** *n.* argentite; **-glaserz,** *n.* argentite; **-glätte,** *f.* litharge; **-glimmer,** *m.* common mica; **-gold,** *n.* argentiferous gold; **-grau,** silver-gray; **-haltig,** containing silver, argentiferous; **-hell,** very

clear, bright; **-hornerz,** *n.* horn silver, cerargyrite.

silberig, silvery.

Silber-jodür, *n.* silver subiodide; **-kies,** *m.* sternbergite; **-kupferglanz,** *m.* stromeyerite; **-legierung,** *f.* silver alloy; **-lösung,** *f.* silver solution; **-lot,** *n.* silver solder, **-methode,** *f.* silver method (of flagella staining); **-münze,** *f.* silver coin.

silbern, silver.

Silber-niederschlag, *m.* silver precipitate; **-nitrat,** *n.* silver nitrate; **-nitratlösung,** *f.* solution of silver nitrate.

Silberoxyd, *n.* silver oxide; **-ammoniak,** *n.* fulminating silver; **-salz,** *n.* silver oxysalt.

Silber-oxydul, *n.* silver suboxide; **-papier,** *n.* silver paper; **-pappel,** *f.* white poplar; **-plattierung,** *f.* silver plating; **-probe,** *f.* silver assay, test for silver; **-reich,** rich in silver; **-salbe,** *f.* colloid silver ointment; **-salpeter,** *m.* silver nitrate; **-salz,** *n.* silver salt; **-sau,** *f.* silver ingot; **-schaum,** *m.* silver in thin leaves; **-scheidung,** *f.* silver refining.

Silber-schicht, *f.* layer (coating) of silver; **-schlaglot,** *n.* silver solder; **-schwärze,** *f.* earthy argentite; **-schweflig,** argentosulphurous; **-spat,** *m.* cerargyrite; **-spiessglanz,** *m.* antimonial silver; **-stahl,** *m.* silver steel; **-tanne,** *f.* silver fir; **-tiegel,** *m.* silver crucible; **-vitriol,** *m.* silver sulphate.

Silber-waren, *f.pl.* silverware; **-weiss,** *n.* silver white, white lead; **-wismutglanz,** *m.* matildite.

Silicium, *n.* silicon; **-ameisensäure,** *f.* silicoformic acid; **-äthan,** *n.* silicoethane; **-chlorid,** *n.* silicon chloride; **-eisen,** *n.* iron silicide; **-fluorid,** *n.* silicofluoride; **-fluorwasserstoff,** *m.* fluosilicic acid; **-gehalt,** *m.* silicon content; **-haltig,** containing silicon, siliceous; **-jodid,** *n.* silicon iodide.

Silicium-kohlenstoff, *m.* silicon carbide; **-kupfer,** *n.* copper silicide; **-legierung,** *f.* silicon alloy; **-magnesium,** *n.* magnesium silicide; **-methan,** *n.* silicomethane; **-oxalsäure,** *f.* silicoöxalic acid; **-oxyd,** *n.* silicon dioxide; **-säure,** *f.* fluosilicic acid; **-tetrahydrür,** *n.* silicon tetrahydride; **-verbindung,** *f.* silicon compound; **-wasserstoff,** *m.* silicon hydride.

Silikastein, *m.* silica brick.

Silikat, *n.* silicate; **-gestein,** *m.* silicate rock.

Silikoameisensäure, *f.* silicoformic acid.

Silikon, *n.* silicon.

Silizid, *n.* silicide.

Silizium, *n.* silicon.

Silo, *m.* silo, bin.

simpel, simple.

Sims, *m.*-(s)e, shelf, cornice, molding.

Simsengewäschse, *n.pl.* Juncaceae.

simultan, simultaneous.

Sinapinsäure, *f.* sinapic acid.

sind (sein), are.

singen, to sing.

Singrün, *n.* periwinkle, myrtle (Vinca).

Singulosilikat, *n.* monosilicate.

Singultus, *m.* singultus, hiccup.

sinken, to sink, subside, precipitate, fall, drop, decrease.

Sink-körper, *m.* sinker; -stoff, *m.* precipitate, sediment, deposit, material in suspension.

Sinn, *m.* mind, sense, feeling, inclination, direction; im Sinne wie, in the way that, just as; im gleichem Sinn, likewise, similarly.

Sinnebild, *n.* symbol, emblem.

sinnen, to mediate, think, speculate, reflect; gesinnt sein, to seem to be minded, disposed, inclined; gesonnen sein, to be inclined, intend; auf etwas ∼, to plan (scheme) something.

Sinnenwelt, *f.* external world.

Sinnes-apparat, *m.* sense organ; -blase, *f.* sensory vesicle; -borsten, *f.pl.* sense organs, sensory cilia; -eindruck, *m.* sense impression; -epithel, *n.* sensory epithelium; -haar, *n.* sensory cilium; -kegel, *m.pl.* sensillae basiconica; -kolben, *m.* sensory body.

Sinnes-körper, *m.* sensory body, pedicel; -körperlappen, *m.pl.* sensory lobes; -nerv, *m.* sensory nerve; -platte, *f.* sensory plate; -werkzeug, *n.* organ of sense; -zelle, *f.* sensory (tactile) cell.

sinnfällig, obvious.

Sinn-gedicht, *n.* epigram; -gemäss, accordingly, obviously; -getreu, faithful, reproduction, translation; -grün, *n.* periwinkle, myrtle (Vinca); -fällig, obvious.

sinnig, thoughtful, sensible, ingenious.

sinnlich, sensitive, sensuous, sentient, sensual.

sinn-los, senseless; -pflanze, *f.* sensitive plant (*Mimosa sensitiva*); -reich, ingenious, clever, witty; -spruch, *m.* motto, maxim, sentiment; -verwandt, synonymous; -voll, sensible, significant, ingenious; -widrig, absurd, unmeaning.

Sinter, *m.* iron dross, cinder, sinter, stalactite; -kohle, *f.* sintering coal; -metallurgie, *f.* powder metallurgy.

sintern, to sinter, trickle, drop, clinker, cake.

Sinter-quarz, *m.* siliceous sinter; -schlacke, *f.* clinker.

Sinterung, *f.* sintering.

Sinterwasser, *n.* sinter-forming water impregnated with mineral matter.

Sinus, *m.* sinus, sine; -klappe, *f.* sinus valve; -querstück, *m.* transverse portion of sinus; -satz, *m.* sine theorem.

Sipho, *m.* siphon, siphuncle.

Siphonal-düte, *f.* siphonal funnel; -öffung, *f.* siphonal opening.

siphonieren, to siphon.

Sippe, *f.* relation, tribe, kin(dred), set.

Sippen-gemisch, *n.* population; -herkunft, *f.* origin of tribe.

Sirene, *f.* siren.

Sirup, *m.* sirup; -artig, sirupy; -dichte, *f.* sirupy consistency; -dicke, *f.* sirupy consistency; -haltig, containing sirup, sirupy.

sirupös, sirupy.

Siruppfanne, *f.* sirup pan.

Sitkafichte, *f.* blue (Sitka) spruce.

Sitte, *f.* custom, usage, habit, practice. manners, morals, mode, fashion.

Sittenlehre, *f.* ethics.

sittlich, moral.

Situationsnaht, *f.* tension suture.

Sitz, *m.*-e, seat, residence, fit.

Sitzbein, *n.* ischium; -knorren, *m.* tuberosity of ischium; -stachel, *m.* spine of ischium.

sitzen, to sit, stay, dwell, perch, fit; ∼ lassen, to desert, abandon.

sitzend, sessile, sitting, perching, fixed, sedentary; -blumig, having sessile flowers.

Sitz-füsse, *m.pl.* legs of perching bird (pedes insidentes); -höcker, *m.* tuberosity of ischium; -larve, *f.* scyphula; -stachel, *m.* spine of ischium.

Sitzung, *f.* sitting, session, meeting.

Sitzungsberichte, *m.pl.* reports of sessions, proceedings, minutes.

Skala, *f.* scale, measure.

Skalen-ablesung, *f.* scale reading; -intervall, *n.* scale (interval) division; -oeder, *n.* scalenohedron; -rohr, *n.* scale tube; -teilung, *f.* scale division.

Skalp, *m.* scalp.

Skalpell, *n.* scalpel.

Skalpierung, *f.* scalping.

Skammonienharz, *n.* scammony resin.

Skapolamin, *n.* scapolamin.

Skapolith, *m.* scapolite.

Skarifikator, *m.* scarifier.

Skelett, *n.*-e, skeleton; **-material,** *n.* skeleton material; **-muskel,** *m.* skeleton muscle; **-nadel,** *f.* skeletal spicule; **-stück,** *n.* piece of the skeleton; **-teil,** *m.* portion of the skeleton.

Skizze, *f.* sketch.

skizzieren, to sketch.

Sklave, *m.* slave.

Sklerenchym, *n.* sclerenchyma.

sklerosieren, to harden, become indurated.

Skleroskophärte, *f.* scleroscope hardness.

Skonto, *m.* discount.

Skorbut, *m.* scurvy; **-ähnlich,** scurvylike.

Skorie, *f.* scoria, cinder, slag, dross.

Skorpionspinne, *f.* scorpion spider.

Skrofel, *f.* scrofula.

skrofulös, scrofulous.

Smalte, *f.* smalt.

Smaragd, *m.* emerald; **-farben,** emerald; **-grün,** *n.* Guignet's green; **-malachit,** *m.* euchroite; **-spat,** *m.* amazonite, green feldspar.

Smirgel, *m.* emery.

so, so, thus, then; ~ **ein,** such a; ~ **etwas,** such a thing; ~ . . . **wie,** as . . . as; **-viel,** so far as; ~ . . . **auch,** however; ~ . . . **denn auch,** and so; **-wie -,** anyhow; **-eben,** just; ~ **ziemlich,** pretty good; **-bald,** so soon, as soon; **-gar,** even; **um . . . , als,** the . . . , as . . . ; **-dass,** to that, in order that; **-soviel ich sehen kann,** as far as I can see.

Societät, *f.* society, company.

Sockel, *m.* pedestal, base, socket, stand.

socken, to crystallize out, contract.

Soda, *f.* soda, sodium carbonate; **kaustische** ~, caustic soda.

Soda-asche, *f.* soda ash; **-auszug,** *m.* soda extract; **-blau,** *n.* ultramarine; **-fabrik,** *f.* soda factory, alkali works; **-fabrikation,** *f.* manufacture of soda; **-haltig,** containing soda.

Soda-kristalle, *m.pl.* soda crystals; **-küpe,** *f.* soda vat; **-lauge,** *f.* soda lye; **-lösung,** *f.* soda solution; **-mehl,** *n.* sodium carbonate monohydrate; **-menge,** *f.* amount of soda.

sodann, then.

Soda-ofen, *m.* soda (black-ash) furnace; **-rückstände,** *m.pl.* soda residues; **-salz,** *n.* soda salt, sodium carbonate; **-schmelze,** *f.* black ash; **-see,** *m.* soda lake; **-seife,** *f.* soda soap; **-stein,** *m.* caustic soda; **-wasser,** *n.* soda water.

Sodbrennen, *n.* heartburn, pyrosis.

Sode, *f.* saltworks, sod.

Sodenbrot, *n.* carob bean, St.-John's-bread.

sodieren, to treat (wash) with soda.

soeben, just, just now.

sofern, so far as, inasmuch as.

soff (saufen), drank.

sofort, immediately, at once.

sofortig, immediate, instantaneous.

sog (saugen), sucked.

sogar, even.

sogenannt, so-called.

soggen, to crystallize out, precipitate in crystal form.

Sogge-pfanne, *f.* crystallizing pan; **-salz,** *n.* common salt.

sogleich, at once.

Sohl-band, *n.* gangue, matrix; **-druck,** *m.* bottom (base) pressure.

Sohle, *f.* sole, planta, bottom, floor.

Sohlen-band, *n.* plantar ligament; **-bogen,** *m.* plantar arch; **-gänger,** *m.pl.* plantigrade animals; **-leder,** *n.* sole leather; **-lederhaut,** *f.* sole corium (hoof of horse).

Sohlplatte, *f.* bottom (bed)plate, foundation (slab) plate.

Sohn, *m.*-̈e, son.

Soja, *f.* soy, soy sauce; **-bohne,** *f.* soybean, soya bean.

solange, as long as.

Sol-behälter, *m.* brine (container) cistern; **-bohrloch,** *n.* salt well.

solch, solcher, such, such a; **solch ein, ein solcher,** such a; **solche die,** such as.

Sold, *m.* pay.

Soldat, *m.* soldier.

Sole, *f.* brine, salt (water) spring; **-eindampfer,** *m.* brine concentrator; **-erzeuger,** *m.* brine mixer.

Solenhofener Platte, *f.* (Schieferstein) lithographic stone.

Solfass, *n.* brine tub.

Soll, *n.* debit; ~ **und Haben,** *n.* debit and credit.

sollen, shall, be to, be said, be supposed to, should, ought to.

Sollösung, *f.* sol dispersion.

Sollwert, *m.* theoretical (nominal) value.

Solorinsäure, *f.* solorinic acid.

Sol-pfanne, *f.* brine pan; **-quelle,** *f.* brine spring, salt well; **-salz,** *n.* spring (well) salt.

Solvenz, *n.* solvency.

Solvenzie, *f.* solvent.

solvieren, to dissolve.

solvierend, solvent, dissolving.

Sol-waage, *f.* brine gauge; **-wasser,** *n.* brine, salt water.

somit, therefore, consequently, thus, so.

Sommer, *m.* summer; **-ei,** *n.* summer egg; **-eiche,** *f.* pedunculate oak; **-flecken,** *m.* freckle; **-getreide,** *n.* summer cereals; **-grün,** deciduous.

Sommer-laubfall, *m.* summer leafdrop; **-linde,** *f.* broad-leaved linden (lime) tree (*Tilia ulmifolia*); **-spore,** *f.* temporary spore that germinates at once; **-sprosse,** *f.* freckle; **-tracht,** *f.* summer flow of honey; **-wald,** *m.* deciduous (tropophilous) forest; **-weizen,** *m.* spring wheat (*Triticum aestivum*); **-wurzelgewächse,** *n.pl.* Orobanchaceae.

sonach, accordingly, thus, so.

Sonde, *f.* sound, probe, plummet.

Sondenversuch, *m.* probe (sounding) test.

Sonder-abdruck, *m.* separate impression, reprint; **-ausgabe,** *f.* separate edition.

sonderbar, strange, peculiar, singular.

Sonder-fall, *m.* exception, exceptional case, particular case; **-gleichen,** unequaled; **-krankheit,** *f.* special disease.

sonderlich, special, particular.

Sonderling, *m.* oddity.

Sondermethode, *f.* special method.

sondern, to separate, segregate, sort, sever.

sondern, but, on the contrary.

sonders, separately; **samt und** ~, one and all.

Sonder-schrift, *f.* separate treatise; **-steigerung,** *f.* special increase; **-stellung,** *f.* separate (special) position.

Sonderung, *f.* separation.

Sonder-werk, *n.* special work; **-zweck,** *m.* special (purpose) object.

Sondierung, *f.* probing.

Sonne, *f.* sun.

Sonnen-auge, *n.* adularia, Heliopsis; **-bad,** *n.* sun bath; **-bahn,** *f.* ecliptic; **-bestrahlung,** *f.* solar irradiation; **-blatt,** *n.* heliophilous leaf; **-blume,** *f.* sunflower (*Helianthus annuus*); **-brand,** *m.* sunscald, sunburn; **-deckung,** *f.* cloudiness; **-finsternis,** *f.* solar eclipse; **-fleck,** *m.* sunspot.

Sonnen-geflecht, *n.* solar plexus; **-haft,** sunny, radiant; **-hitze,** *f.* solar heat; **-höhe,** *f.* sun's altitude; **-licht,** *n.* sunlight; **-riss,** *m.* sun crack; **-schein,** *m.* sunshine; **-schirm,** *m.* sunshade, parasol; **-spektrum,** *n.* solar spectrum; **-stein,** *m.* sunstone (aventurine feldspar).

Sonnen-strahl, *m.* solar radiation; **-strahlung,** *f.* solar radiation; **-system,** *n.* solar system; **-tau,** *m.* sundew (Drosera); **-taugewächse,** *n.pl.* Droseraceae; **-tierchen,** *n.pl.* Heliozoa; **-uhr,** *f.* sundial; **-wärme,** *f.* sun's heat, solar heat; **-wende,** *f.* solstice, heliotrope.

sonnig, sunny.

sonst, else, besides, otherwise, in other respects, usually, formerly.

sonstig, former, other, remaining.

sonstwie, in some other way.

Soorpilz, *m. Oidium albicans.*

Sorbett, *n.* sherbet.

Sorbinsäure, *f.* sorbic acid.

Sorbit, *n.* sorbitol.

Soredienanflug, *m.* soredium.

Sorge, *f.* care, concern, sorrow, anxiety.

sorgen, to care, provide, apprehend, be anxious, worry; ~ **dafür,** to assure, make possible.

sorgenvoll, full of care, uneasy.

Sorgfalt, *f.* carefulness, care.

sorgfältig, careful(ly).

sorglich, anxious, solicitous.

sorglos, careless, unconcerned, negligent, reckless.

sorgsam, careful, attentive.

sorptiv, sorptive (absorptive and adsorptive).

Sorte, *f.* sort, quality, kind, brand, type, grade, variety.

Sorten-anbauversuch, *m.* variety test; **-anfälligkeit,** *f.* varietal susceptibility; **-auslese,** *f.* select list, selection of races; **-echtheit,** *f.* purity of species; **-echtheitsprüfung,** *f.* varietal purity test; **-empfindlichkeit,** *f.* varietal susceptibility; **-wahl,** *f.* varietal selection, choice of seeds;

-wechsel, *m.* change of varieties; **-wert,** *m.* value of a variety.

sortieren, to sort, classify, brand, grade.

Sortierung, *f.* assorting, grading, classifying.

Sortiment, *n.* assortment.

sott (sieden), boiled.

Soupleseide, *f.* souple silk.

souplieren, to half boil, souple (silk).

soviel, so much, as much as, so far as; **so und soviel,** so and so much, a given amount; **soviel ich sehen kann,** as far as I can see.

soweit, as far (as).

sowie, as well as, as also.

sowohl, as well; ~ . . . **als auch,** both . . . and also, not only . . . but also.

Soya-bohne, *f.* soybean; **-bohnenöl,** *n.* soybean oil.

Sozolsäure, sozolic acid.

sozusagen, so to speak, as it were.

Spachtel, *f.* spatula; **-masse,** *f.* surfacer, filler, primer, knifing glaze; **-messer,** *n.* putty knife.

spachteln, to smooth, putty, fill up color.

Spalier-baum, *m.* trained fruit tree; **-obst,** *n.* wall (trellis) fruit; **-wuchs,** *m.* espalier growth.

Spalt, *m.* split, fissure, crevice, slit, crack, cleft, rent, gap; **-algen,** *f.pl.* Cyanophyceae; **-axt,** *f.* cleaving ax.

spaltbar, cleavable, divisible, fissile.

Spaltbarkeit, *f.* cleavability, cleavage.

Spaltbarkeitsrichtung, *f.* direction of cleavage.

Spalt-bein, *n.* biramous leg; **-bildung,** *f.* splitting process, fissure formation; **-breite,** *f.* width of slit.

Spalte, *f.* split, rift, gap, column.

spalten, to cleave, split, crack, rend, fissure.

Spalt-fläche, *f.* cleavage surface; **-frucht,** *f.* dehiscent fruit, schizocarp; **-fuss,** *m.* schizopodal leg, split foot; **-füsser,** *m.pl.* Schizopoda; **-holz,** *n.* wood for (splitting), cleavage; **-hufer,** *m.pl.* ruminants.

spaltig, split, cleavable, fissured, cracked, columned.

Spalt-körper, *m.* cleavage (substance) product; **-kronblättrig,** schizopetalous; **-lampenlicht,** *n.* slit-lamp light; **-mündung,** *f.* stoma; **-öffnung,** *f.* stomate; **-pflanze,** *f.* schizophyte, bacterium; **-pilz,** *m.* fission (schizomycetous) fungus, splitting mold; **-pilzgärung,** *f.* bacterial fermentation.

Spalt-produkt, *n.* cleavage product; **-riss,** *m.* cleavage crack; **-rohr,** *n.* slit (split) tube; **-schwimmfuss,** *m.* locate leg (pes fissopalmatus); **-stück,** *n.* detached portion, fragment; **-tüpfel,** *m.* slitlike pit.

Spaltung, *f.* cleaving, segregation, cleavage, scission, fission, division, splitting.

Spaltungs-atmung, *f.* anaerobic respiration; **-energie,** *f.* energy of splitting; **-fläche,** *f.* cleavage (plane) face; **-gärung,** *f.* cleavage fermentation; **-gesetz,** *n.* law of segregation; **-probe,** *f.* cleavage test; **-produkt,** *n.* decomposition or cleavage (fission) product; **-prozess,** *m.* cleavage process.

Spaltungs-regel, *f.* law of segregation; **-richtung,** *f.* direction of cleavage; **-stück,** *n.* fragment; **-verzug,** *m.* delayed segregation; **-vorgang,** *m.* cleavage process; **-wärme,** *f.* heat of dissociation or cracking; **-zahlen,** *f.pl.* Mendelian ratio.

Spalt-wand, *f.* schizogenous wall; **-wunde,** *f.* cleft wound.

Span, *m.*¨e, chip, shaving, splinter, boring, shred, turning.

spänen, to suckle.

Spänfass, *n.* chip cask.

Spanferkel, *n.* sucking pig.

Spange, *f.* buckle, clasp, stay bolt, bracelet, hasp.

Spangeleisen, *n.* crystalline pig iron.

spanglig, spangled, glistening, crystalline.

Spangrün, *n.* verdigris.

Spanisch, Spanish; **spanische Fliegen,** *f.pl.* Spanish flies, cantharides; **spanischer Pfeffer,** *m.* red pepper, capsicum, cayenne; **spanisches Rohr,** *n.* rattan, Spanish reed.

spann (spinnen), was spinning.

Spann, *m.* instep; **-ader,** *f.* tendon, sinew.

spannbar, ductile, tensile.

Spannbarkeit, *f.* extensibility, ductility.

Spanne, *f.* span, stretch.

spannen, to span, stretch, strain, tighten, fill (a tank), harness, increase the tension of, cock, be exciting; **gespannt,** stretched, tight, intense, excited, nervous; **spannend,** exciting.

Spanner, *m.* tensor muscle, looper moth, shiner.

Spann-fäden, *m.pl.* tension fibers; **-knorpel,** *m.* tensor (thyroid) cartilage; **-kraft,** *f.* tension, expansibility, elasticity, tonicity; **-kräftig,** elastic; **-muskel,** *m.* tensor muscle; **-riegel,** *m.* straining piece; **-rückig,** asymmetric, grooved, buttressed.

Spannung, *f.* tension, span, width, pressure, stretching, potential, voltage, stress, strain, bending.

Spannungs-abfall, *m.* voltage drop; **-dehnungs-Diagramm,** *n.* stress-strain diagram; **-differenz,** *f.* potential difference, tension difference; **-empfindlichkeit,** *f.* sensitiveness to stress or pressure; **-empfindung,** *f.* sensation of tension; **-falten,** *f.pl.* tension folds; **-grad,** *m.* degree of tension; **-los,** without tension; **-messer,** *m.* indicator, gauge, voltmeter; **-messung,** *f.* measurement of voltage.

Spannungs-prüfer, *m.* strain tester; **-reihe,** *f.* series of electrical potentials, contact (electromotive) series; **-theorie,** *f.* strain (tension) theory; **-unterschied,** *m.* difference in tension, potential difference; **-verlust,** *m.* loss of (tension) voltage; **-wechsel,** *m.* stress reversal; **-zeiger,** *m.* tension indicator, voltmeter.

Spannweite, *f.* span, width, distance, expanse of wing.

Spanversuch, *m.* glowing splinter test.

Spar-beton, *m.* lean concrete; **-brenner,** *m.* economical burner.

sparen, to save, spare, reserve, be economical.

Spar-flämmchen, *n.* **-flamme,** *f.* pilot flame.

Spargel, *m.* aspargus; **-stoff,** *m.* asparagine.

spärlich, sparse, scanty, scarce.

Spar-kalk, *m.* estrichgipsum; **-kapsel,** *f.* economy sagger; **-mittel,** *n.* sparing substance, protein sparer.

Sparren, *m.* rafter, spar.

sparrig, squarrose, with wide-spreading (processes) branches.

sparsam, sparing, economical, frugal, close.

Spartgras, *n.* esparto grass.

Sparvorrichtung, *f.* economizing device.

spastisch, spastic, spasmodic.

Spat, *m.* spar, spavin.

spät, late.

spat-artig, spathic, sparry; **-eisen,** *n.* siderite (iron); **-eisenstein,** *m.* spathic iron ore, sparry iron.

Spatel, *m.* spatula; **-förmig,** spatulate, spatula-shaped.

spateln, to smooth with a spatula.

Spaten, *m.* spade; **-pflug,** *m.* disk plow.

später, later; **-hin,** later on.

Späternte, *f.* late harvest.

spätestens, at the latest.

Spät-frost, *m.* late frost; **-herbst,** *m.* late autumn; **-holz,** *n.* summerwood.

spatig, sparry, spathic.

Spat-säure, *f.* hydrofluoric acid; **-stein,** *m.* selenite.

Spät-sommer, *m.* Indian summer, late summer; **-wirkung,** *f.* aftereffect.

Spatz, *m.* house sparrow.

Spätzahn, *m.* wisdom tooth.

spazieren, to walk, stroll, promenade.

Spazier-gang, *m.* walk, stroll; **-stock,** *m.* walking stick.

Specht, *m.*-e, woodpecker.

specifisches Gewicht, *n.* specific gravity.

Speck, *m.* lard, bacon, fat, blubber; **-ähnlich, -artig,** fatty, lardaceous; **-haut,** *f.* buffy coat.

speckig, lardy, very fat, lardaceous, heavy, amyloid.

Speck-käfer, *m.pl.* bacon beetle (Dermestidae); **-kienholz,** *n.* resinous wood; **-öl,** *n.* lard oil; **-stein,** *m.* steatite, talc, soapstone; **-steinartig,** steatitic; **-stoff,** *m.* **-substanz,** *f.* lardaceous (amyloid) substance; **-torf,** *m.* black (pitch) peat; **-tran,** *m.* train oil.

Specularit, *m.* specular hematite.

spedieren, to forward, send, dispatch.

Speer, *m.*-e, spear; **-kies,** *m.* spear pyrites.

Speiche, *f.* spoke, spike, radius.

Speichel, *m.* saliva, spittle; **-absonderung,** *f.* secretion of saliva; **-befördernd,** promoting flow of saliva, sialagogue; **-drüse,** *f.* salivary gland; **-fluss,** *m.* flow of saliva, salivation; **-flüssigkeit,** *f.* saliva; **-gang,** *m.* salivary duct; **-kasten,** *m.* saliva chamber; **-mittel,** *n.* sialagogue; **-röhre,** *f.* salivary duct; **-saft,** *m.* saliva; **-stoff,** *m.* ptyalin; **-wasser,** *n.* saliva.

Speichen-ader, *f.* radius; **-arterie,** *f.* radial artery; **-bein,** *n.* radius; **-beuger,** *m.* biceps; **-beule,** *f.* tuberosity of radius; **-kopf,** *m.* head of radius; **-strecker,** *m.* extensor of radius.

Speicher, *m.* loft, granary, warehouse, elevator; **-gewebe,** *n.* storage tissue.

speichern, to store up, accumulate.

Speicher-spross, *m.* storage shoot; **-tracheide,** *f.* storage tracheid.

Speicherung, *f.* storage, accumulation.

Speicherwurzel, *f.* storage root.

speien, to spit, vomit.

Speiköl, *n.* valerian oil.

Speise, *f.* food, nourishment, speiss, bell (gun) metal, mortar; **-apparat,** *m.* feed apparatus; **-bestandteil,** *m.* constituent of food; **-brei,** *m.* chyme; **-eis,** *n.* sherbet; **-fett,** *n.* nutrient (edible) fat; **-gang,** *m.* alimentary canal, digestive tube; **-gelb,** *n.* pale-yellow speiss.

Speise-hahn, *m.* feed cock; **-kanal,** *m.* alimentary canal; **-karte,** *f.* bill of fare, menu; **-kartoffel,** *f.* food potato, edible potato; **-masse,** *f.* ration.

speisen, to feed, eat, take food, board, charge (a battery).

Speise-öl, *n.* edible (olive) oil; **-ordnung,** *f.* diet; **-pilz,** *m.* edible fungus; **-pumpe,** *f.* feed pump; **-rest,** *m.* food particle; **-rohr,** *n.* supply pipe; **-röhre,** *f.* esophagus; **-saft,** *m.* chyle; **-salz,** *n.* common salt; **-teil,** *m.* food particle.

Speise-trichter, *m.* hopper; **-walze,** *f.* feed roll; **-zucker,** *m.* table sugar; **-zwiebel,** *f.* onion.

speisig, cobaltiferous.

Speiskobalt, *m.* smaltite.

Speisung, *f.* feeding.

Spektral-analyse, *f.* spectrum analysis; **-analytisch,** spectroscopic, spectrometric; **-apparat,** *m.* spectroscopic apparatus; **-beobachtung,** *f.* spectroscopic observation; **-bereich,** *m.* spectral region; **-bezirk,** *m.* zone in the spectrum.

Spektral-farbe, *f.* spectral color; **-gegend,** *f.* spectral region; **-linie,** *f.* spectrum line; **-probe,** *f.* spectrum test; **-rohr,** *n.* -röhre, *f.* spectrum tube; **-tafel,** *f.* spectral chart.

Spektren, *n.pl.* spectra.

Spektroskop, *n.* spectroscope.

Spektroskopiker, *m.* spectroscopist.

Spektrum, *n.* spectrum.

Spekulant, *m.* speculator.

Spelz, *m.* spelt.

Spelze, *f.* glume, husk, chaff, beard, awn.

Spelzmehl, *n.* spelt flour.

spenden, to spend, distribute.

Spengler, *m.* sheet-metal worker.

Sperbeere, *f.* serviceberry (*Pirus or Sorbus torminalis*).

Sperber, *m.* sparrow hawk.

Sperling, *m-,* sparrow.

Sperma, *n.* sperm, semen.

Spermakern, *m.* sperm nucleus.

Spermatien, *n. pl.* sperms.

spermatoide Spore, *f.* spore budding (in the ascus).

Spermatozoid, *m.* spermatozooid.

Spermien, *f.pl.* spermatozoa.

sperrbar, adjustable.

Sperr-baute, *m.* dam; **-druck,** *m.* spaced type.

Sperre, *f.* closing (of gates), closure, barring, obstruction, stoppage, embargo.

sperren, to shut up, bar, confine, close, stop, block, spread out, space, struggle, refuse, resist.

Sperr-flüssigkeit, *f.* sealing fluid; **-hahn,** *m.* stopcock; **-haken,** *m.* catch; **-holz,** *n.* plywood.

sperrig, with widespread branches, unwieldy, bulky, loose.

Sperr-klinke, *f.* catch; **-rad,** *n.* ratchet, (cog)wheel; **-schichtphotozelle,** *f.* corrected photocell; **-ventil,** *n.* stop valve; **-vorrichtung,** *f.* catch, stop; **-wasser,** *n.* sealing water.

Sperrung, *f.* opening (iris) of photometer.

Spesen, *f.pl.* charges, costs, expenses.

Spezerei, *f.* spices, grocery.

Spezial-fall, *m.*-̈e, special case; **-gebiet,** *n.* special department.

spezialisieren, to specialize.

Spezialität, *f.* specialty.

Spezial-merkmal, *n.* special characteristic; **-mutterzelle,** *f.* tetrad of cells (microspores); **-reagens,** *n.* special reagent; **-stahl,** *m.* special steel.

speziell, special, specific.

Spezies, *f.* species, herbs, drugs, samples; **-fremd,** of a different species; **-gleich,** of the same species.

spezifisch, specific; **spezifischer Bildungstrieb,** *m.* automorphosis; **spezifisches Gewicht,** *n.* specific weight (gravity, if used without units).

Spezifität, *f.* specificity.

spezifizierte Anlage, *f.* determined primordium.

Sphäre, *f.* sphere, range, province, domain.

sphärisch, spherical.

Sphärokristall, *m.* spherical crystal.

Sphen, *m.* sphene, titanite.

sphenoidisch, sphenoid.

Sphereolith, Spharulith, *m.* spherulite.

spicken, to lard, smoke, spike.

Spicköl, *n.* spike oil.

spie (speien), spat, spit.

Spiegel, *m.*-, mirror, speculum, caterpillar nest, (polished) surface, reflector, level mirror effect produced by medullary rays; **-ablesung,** *f.* mirror reading; **-bild,** *n.* reflected image, mirror image; **-bildisomer,** enantiomorphic; **-bildlich,** as a mirror image; **-blank,** highly polished; **-eisen,** *n.* specular (cast) iron, spiegel iron; **-faser,** *f.* medullary ray; **-floss,** *n.* specular (cast) iron; **-folie,** *f.* tin foil, silvering (of a mirror).

Spiegel-giesserei, *f.* plate-glass factory; **-glanz,** *m.* wehrlite; **-glas,** *n.* plate glass; **-glatt,** extremely smooth; **-gleichheit,** *f.* mirror symmetry; **-holz,** *n.* wood showing silver grain; **-holzrinde,** *f.* silver bark.

spiegelig, specular, mirrorlike.

Spiegel-karpfen, *m.* mirror carp; **-kluft,** *f.* heart-shake.

spiegeln, to reflect, shine, glitter, sparkle, be reflected.

Spiegel-narbe, *f.* mirror stigma, stigmatic surface; **-rinde,** *f.* silver bark; **-seite,** *f.* radial surface; **-skala,** *f.* mirror scale.

Spiegelung, *f.* reflection, mirage.

Spiegelzelle, *f.* areole.

Spieke, *f.* spike, spike lavender.

Spiekernagel, *m.* brad.

Spieköl, *n.* spike oil.

Spiel, *n.*-e, game, sport, play, pack of cards, working, action; **mit im Spiele sein,** to be involved, be also instrumented.

Spielart, *f.* variety, sport.

spielen, to play, sparkle, work, have play; **ins Rote** ∼, incline to red.

Spielerei, *f.* play, pastime, game.

Spiel-raum, *m.* margin, latitude, range, scope, play, elbowroom; **-waren,** *f.pl.* toys; **-zeug,** *n.* plaything, toy.

Spiess, *m.* spear, lance, spit, broach, long needle; **-bock,** *m.* brocket.

spiessen, to pierce, spear, spit.

Spiesser, Spiesshirsch, *m.* pricket.

spiessförmig, spear-shaped, hastate.

Spiessglanz, *m.* antimony, stibnite; **-artig,** antimonial; **-asche,** *f.* antimony ash; **-bleierz,** *n.* bournonite; **-blende,** *f.* kermesite; **-blumen,** *f.pl.* flowers of antimony; **-butter,** *f.* butter of antimony, antimony trichloride; **-erz,** *n.* antimony ore; **-haltig,** containing antimony; **-kermes,** *m.* kermesite; **-leber,** *f.* liver of antimony.

Spiessglanz-mittel, *n.* antimonial remedy; **-mohr,** *m.* aethiops antimonialis; **-oxyd,** *n.* antimony trioxide; **-safran,** *m.* crocus of antimony; **-schwefel,** *m.* antimony sulphide; **-silber,** *n.* dyscrasite; **-weinstein,** *m.* tartrated antimony; **-weiss,** *n.* antimony (trioxide) white; **-zinnober,** *m.* kermesite.

Spiessglas, *n.* antimony; **-erz,** *n.* stibnite; **-weiss,** *n.* antimony white.

Spiesshirsch, *m.* pricket.

spiessig, spearlike, lancelike, in long needles, badly tanned.

Spiess-kobalt, *m.* smaltite; **-lippig,** hastilabiate (spear-shaped); **-zahn,** *m.* canine tooth.

Spikblüten, *f.pl.* spike-lavender flowers.

Spiker, *m.* spike.

Spiköl, *n.* spike oil.

Spinat, *m.* spinach.

Spindel, *f.*-n, spindle, pivot, axle, arbor, hydrometer, beam, shaft, rachis, columella; **-baum,** *m.* spindle tree (Evonymus); **-bazillus,** *m.* spindle-shaped bacillus; **-faser,** *f.* spindle fiber; **-fäserchen,** *n.* small spindle fiber; **-figur,** *f.* nuclear spindle; **-förmig,** fusiform, spindle-shaped; **-glied,** *n.* rachis segment; **-presse,** *f.* screw press; **-ring,** *m.* annulus.

Spindel-waage, *f.* areometer, hydrometer; **-windung,** *f.* fusiform convolution, occipitotemporal convolution; **-zelle,** *f.* fusiform cell.

Spinnbarkeit, *f.* spinnability.

Spinndrüse, *f.* silk (spinning) gland.

Spinne, *f.* spider.

Spinell, *m.* spinel.

spinnen, to spin, twist, purr; **-gewebe,** *n.* spider web, cobweb; **-tiere,** *n.pl.* Arachnida.

Spinner, *m.* bombyx.

Spinnerei, *f.* spinning, spinning mill.

Spinn-faser, *f.* spinning (textile) fiber; **-fehler,** *m.* spinning defect; **-gewebe,** *n.* cobweb, spider web; **-lösung,** *f.* spinning solution; **-reife,** *f.* maturity, ammonium chloride index; **-schema,** *n.* spinning arrangement; **-stoff,** *m.* spinning material; **-stutzen,** *m.* gooseneck; **-topfspinnen,** *n.* spinning bucket process; **-warze,** *f.* spinneret; **-webe,** *f.* cobweb, spider web.

spinn-webenartig, cobweblike, arachnoid; **-webenhaut,** *f.* arachnoid; **-webfaden,** *m.* spider-web thread, thin thread; **-wolle,** *f.* wool for spinning.

Spionage, *f.* espionage.

Spiräe, *f.* spiraea.

Spiral-arm, *n.*-e, spiral arm (brachium); **-band,** *n.* spiral ligament; **-blatt,** *n.* spiral lamina; **-bohrer,** *m.* twist drill; **-deckel,** *m.* spiral shell; **-drehung,** *f.* spiral torsion, spiralism.

Spirale, *f.* spiral, coil, condenser.

spiral-eingerollt, convoluted; **-feder,** *f.* spiral spring; **-förmig,** spiral, helical; **-gefäss,** *n.* spiral vessel (element); **-gehäuse,** *n.* spiral shell; **-hülle,** *f.* spiral sheath.

spiralig, spiral(ly).

Spiral-kiemer, *m.pl.* Brachiopoda; **-klappe,** *f.* spiral valve; **-linie,** *f.* spiral line, spiral; **-rohr,** *n.* **-röhre,** *f.* spiral tube or pipe, worm; **-stellung,** *f.* spiral arrangement; **-tracheide,** *f.* spiral tracheid; **-verzierung,** *f.* spiral marking.

Spirillen, *n.pl.* spirilla.

Spirillose, *f.* spirillosis.

Spirituosen, *pl.* alcoholic liquors.

Spiritus, *m.* spirit(s), 95% ethyl alcohol; **-beize,** *f.* spirit mordant; **-blau,** *n.* spirit blue; **-brennerei,** *f.* distillery; **-dampf,** *m.* alcohol vapor; **-fabrik,** *f.* distillery; **-geruch,** *m.* odor of spirits; **-löslich,** soluble in alcohol; **-mischung,** *f.* alcoholic mixture; **-pumpe,** *f.* alcohol pump; **-waage,** *f.* alcoholometer, spirit level.

Spirochäten, *f.pl.* spirochetes.

Spirochätose, *f.* spirochetosis.

spiroylig, spiroylous.

Spirre, *f.* anthela.

Spital, *n.* **Spitäler,** hospital.

spitz, pointed, acute, cuspidated, sharp, acicular, stinging; **-ahorn,** *m.* Norway maple (*Acer platanoides*); **-becherglas,** *n.* sedimenting glass; **-blätterig,** acutifolious.

Spitzchen, *n.* apiculus.

Spitze, *f.* point, top, tip, vertex, apex, summit, cusp, lace, mouthpiece, counter-hook (spinning defect).

spitzen, sharpen, point, sprout; **die Ohren** ∼, to prick up one's ears; **den Mund** ∼, to purse one's lips.

Spitzen-anhängsel, *n.* tip of ventral lobe, appendage; **-aposporie,** *f.* apical apospory; **-belastung,** *f.* peak load; **-bräune,** *f.* tipburn; **-dürre,** *f.* tipburn, withertip; **-elektrode,** *f.* mucoronate electrode; **-entladung,** *f.* point discharge; **-gänger,** *m.pl.* Ungulata; **-glas,** *n.* reticulated glass; **-leistung,** *f.* peak output.

Spitzen-papier, *n.* lace paper; **-stoss,** *m.* (cardiac) apex beat; **-strom,** *m.* peak current; **-wachstum,** *n.* apical growth.

spitz-früchtig, acrocarpous (fruit is sharp-pointed); **-glas,** *n.* sedimentation glass (of tall, conical form); **-hacke,** *f.* pickax, pick; **-haufen,** *m.* couch (in brewing).

spitzig, pointed, sharp, tapering, acute.

spitz-kantig, acutangulus; **-knospe,** *f.* terminal bud; **-kolben,** *m.* tapering neck; **-kronblättrig,** acropetalous, acutipetalous; **-läufig,** acrodromous; **-malz,** *n.* chit malt; **-maus,** *f.* shrew (Sorex); **-mäuschen,** *n.pl.* Apionidae, Curculionidae; **-muschel,** *f.* pointed shell.

Spitz-röhrchen, *n.* small pointed tube; **-stachelig,** oxyacanthous; **-trichter,** *m.* tapering separatory funnel; **-wegerich,** *m.* ribwort (*Plantago lanceolata*); **-winklig,** acute-angled; **-zahn,** *m.* canine tooth.

Spleisse, *f.* splint, splinter, shiver, shard.

spleissen, to split, cleave, crack, splice.

Splint, *m.* peg, sap, pin, sapwood, splint; **-holz,** *n.* sapwood, sap, alburnum; **-käfer** *m.* cambium beetle.

spliss (spleissen), split.

Splitter, *m.*-, splint, splinter, chip, scale, fragment, shiver.

splittern, to split up, splinter, shiver, shatter.

Splitterung, *f.* splintering.

Splitterwirkung, *f.* splinter effect.

Spongioplasm, *n.* filar substance of protoplasm.

spönne (spinnen), would spin, spun, spins.

spontan, spontaneous, autogenic; **spontane Änderung,** *f.* single variation, mutation; **spontane Bewegung,** *f.* autogenic movement; **spontane Variation,** *f.* mutation.

Sporangien-frucht, *f.* sporocarpium; **-grube,** *f.* fovea; **-häufchen,** *n.* sorus.

Sporangium, *n.* sporangium; **-träger,** *m.* sporophyll, conidiophore.

Spore, *f.* spore.

sporen, to get moldy, dry, spore; **-anhäufung,** *f.* aggregation of spores; **-ausstreuung,** *f.* spore dispersal; **behälter,** *m.* spore case; **bildend,** spore-forming; **-bildung,** *f.* formation of spores, sporulation; **-bildungsvermögen,** *n.* ability to form spores; **-blatt,** *n.* sporophyll; **-entleerung,** *f.* spore dispersal.

Sporen-färbung, *f.* spore staining (stain); **-frucht,** *f.* sporocarp; **-haltig,** containing

spores; -haut, *f.* sporodermis; -hülle, *f.*
spore coat; -kapsel, *f.* spore capsule;
-kette, *f.* chain of spores; -knospe, *f.*
female organ of Chara.

Sporen-mutterzelle, *f.* spore mother cell;
-pflanze, *f.* sporophyte; -schicht, *f.* layer
or stratum of sporules or spores; -schlauch,
m. ascus; -schleuderer, *m.* elator; -tiere,
n.pl. Sporozoa; -vorkeim, *m.* prothallium;
-zelle, *f.* spore tetrad.

Sporn, *n.* Sporen, spine, spur, calcar, ergot;
-fuss, *m.* foot provided with a spur.

Sporogon, *n.* sporogonium.

Sporophyll-ähre, *f.* sporophyll axis; -höcker,
m. sporophyll primordium; -stiel, *m.*
pedicel of sporophyll.

Sporophyt, *m.* sporophyte.

Sporozen, *pl.* Sporozoa.

Sportart, *f.* type of sport.

Sportel, *f.* fee, perquisite.

spotten, to mock, ridicule, scoff.

sprach (sprechen), spoke.

Sprache, *f.* speech, language, discussion.

Sprach-eigenheit, *f.* idiom; -gebrauch, *m.*
colloquial usage; -lehre, *f.* grammar.

sprachlich, lingual, grammatical.

sprach-los, speechless, dumb; -rohr, *n.*
speaking tube; -schatz, *m.* vocabulary;
-werkzeug, *n.* vocal organs; -widrig,
ungrammatical.

sprang (springen), sprang.

spratzen, spratzeln, to spit, spurt, sp(l)utter.

Spratzkupfer, *n.* copper rain.

sprechen, to speak, talk, say, chat, converse;
jemanden zu ∼ wünschen, to wish to see
someone; jemanden ∼, to have a conference with someone; dafür ∼, to speak
in favor of, support.

Sprech-maschine, *f.* talking machine,
phonograph; -saal, *m.* hall for speaking,
forum.

Spreite, *f.* lamina, leaf blade.

spreiten, to spread (out).

spreizen, to spread, prop up, strive, resist.

spreizend, divaricate, flaring, spreading.

Spreizklimmer, *m.* climbing woody plant.

Spreng-apparat, *m.* sparger, sprinkling
apparatus, sprinkler; -arbeit, *f.* blasting;
-bohrloch, *n.* blasthole; -eisen, *n.* cracking
ring.

Sprengel, *m.* sprinkling brush, *pl.* speckles.

sprengen, to blow up, blast, explode, shoot,
burst, rupture, sprinkle, gallop, dash.

Spreng-flüssigkeit, *f.* explosive liquid;
-gelatine, *f.* explosive gelatin; -granate, *f.*
high-explosive shell; -kapsel, *f.* detonating
(blasting) cap; -kohle, *f.* cracking coal;
-kraft, *f.* explosive power (force); -kräftig,
powerfully explosive; -ladung, *f.* bursting
(explosive) charge; -loch, *n.* blasthole;
-luft, *f.* LOX, liquid oxygen explosive.

Spreng-mast, *f.* quarter mast, partial mast;
-mittel, *n.* explosive; -niet, *m.* explosive
rivet; -öl, *n.* nitroglycerin; -patrone, *f.*
explosive cartridge; -pulver, *n.* blasting
powder.

Spreng-salpeter, *m.* saltpeter blasting
powder; -schnur, *f.* fuse; -schuss, *m.* shot;
-stoff, *m.* explosive; -technik, *f.* manufacture of explosives, blasting technique;
-trichter, *m.* explosive crater.

Sprengung, *f.* exploding, explosion.

Spreng-werk, *n.* strut frame, framing;
-wirkung, *f.* explosive effect (action);
-zünder, *m.* fuse.

Sprenkel, *m.*- speckle, spot.

sprenkeln, to speckle, sprinkle, mottle, spot.

Sprenkelung, *f.* mottling.

Sprenkler, *m.* sparger, sprinkler.

sprenklig, spotted, speckled.

Spreu, *f.* chaff; -blatt, *n.* palea, chaff;
-blätterig, paleaceous, chaffy; -borstig,
fimbrillate; -fleckigkeit, *f.* aucuba mosaic;
-haar, *n.* lacinia; -schuppe, *f.* palea, chaffy
scale.

spricht (sprechen), talks.

Sprichwort, *n.* saying, proverb.

spriessen, to sprout, germinate.

Spring-bein, *n.* saltatorial leg; -brunnen,
m. fountain.

springen, to leap, spring, jump, spout,
burst, break, crack; in die Augen ∼, to
become apparent.

Spring-feder, *f.* spring; -federwaage, *f.*
spring balance; -frucht, *f.* dehiscent
syncarp (apocarp), pod, regma; -gabel, *f.*
cerci furcula; -gurke, *f.* squirting cucumber
-gurkenextrakt, *m.* elaterium; -kolben, *m.*
Bologna flask; -kraft, *f.* springiness, power
of recoil, elasticity; -kräftig, elastic,
springy; -schwänze, *m.pl.* Poduridae;
-stangen, *f.pl.* cerci.

Sprit, *m.*-e, spirit, spirits; -drucken, *n.* spirit
printing; -essig, *m.* spirit vinegar; -farbe,
f. spirit color; -haltig, containing spirit,
spirituous, fortified; -lack, *m.* spirit varnish; -löslich, soluble in spirit.

Spritz-apparat, *m.*-e, sprayer, sprinkler; -beton, *m.* gun concrete, sprayed concrete; -bewurf, *m.* rough plastering; -düse, *f.* spray nozzle, injector.

Spritze, *f.* syringe, squirt, sprayer.

spritzen, to inject, spray, spurt, sputter, squirt, throw, spout, spatter.

Spritz-flasche, *f.* wash(ing) bottle; -gurke, *f.* squirting cucumber; -guss, *m.* die casting, injection molding; -gussmasse, *f.* injection, molding compound; -kopf, *m.* spraying nozzle; -kork, *m.* sprinkler stopper; -kranz, *m.* sparger.

Spritzling, *m.* injection molding.

Spritz-loch, *n.* spiracle or rudimentary gill cleft; -mittel, *n.* injection; -nudeln, *f.pl.* vermicelli; -pulver, *n.* injecting powder; -röhre, *f.* syringe.

sprock, brittle.

spröde, brittle, short, shy, prim, friable, dry.

Sprödglanzerz, *n.* -glaserz, *n.* brittle silver ore, stephanite.

Sprödigkeit, *f.* brittleness, shortness, reserve, primness, friability.

spross (spriessen), sprouted.

Spross, *m.* Sprosse, *f.* shoot, sprout, scion, germ, offspring, spray, sprig, chit, rung, step, antler, tine, point.

Spross-achse, *f.* axis of the shoot; -anlage, *f.* shoot, primordium, plumule; -bürtige Wurzel, *f.* adventitious root; -dorn, *m.* stem thorn.

sprossen, to sprout, shoot, chit, germinate, bud, spring, descend; -bier, *n.* spruce beer; -bildung, *f.* formation of sprouts, prolification.

sprossend, proliferous.

Sprossen-extrakt, *m.* essence of spruce; -fichte, *f.* spruce fir; -kohl, *m.* broccoli, Brussels sprouts; -tanne, *f.* hemlock spruce.

Spross-folge, *f.* succession of shoots; -glied, *n.* phyton, phytomer; -keimung, *f.* sprout germination, budding.

Sprössling, *m.*-e, sprout, shoot, descendant, offspring.

spross-los, without a bud or shoot; -pilz, *m.* sprouting fungus, yeast fungus; -pilzkeimung, *f.* sprout germination; -ranke, *f.* tendril that is morphologically a stem; -spitze, *f.* stem apex; -teil, *m.* shoot.

Sprossung, *f.* budding, germination.

Sprossungsvorgang, *m.* budding process.

Spross-verkettung,*f.*(dichopodiale∼)dichotomy; -verzweigung, *f.* branching.

Spruch, *m.*̈e, saying, motto, sentence, verdict, text.

Sprudel, *m.* hot spring, fountain.

sprudeln, to bubble, spout.

Sprudel-salz, *n.* Karlsbad salt; -stein, *m.* deposit from hot springs.

Sprühelektrode, *f.* ionizing electrode.

sprühen, to emit, sprinkle, spray, spit, scintillate, drizzle, scatter.

Sprüh-entladung, *f.* spray discharge; -kupfer, *n.* copper rain; -regen, *m.* drizzle, spray.

Sprung, *m.*̈e, jump, spring, bounce, leap, crack, fissure, fault, break, discontinuity; -bein, *n.* saltatorial leg, astragalus; -bildung, *f.* cracking, fissure formation; -feder, *f.* spring; -fortsatz, *m.* apophysis of ankle joint; -gabel, *f.* taillike springing organ, cerci; -gelenk, *n.* ankle joint; -haft, by leaps and bounds; -variation, *f.* mutation, single variation; -weite, *f.* range; -zeit, *f.* time of transition.

spucken, to spit.

Spülbad, *n.* rinsing bath.

Spule, *f.* spool, quill, calamus, coil, bobbin.

Spüleimer, *m.* rinsing pail.

spulen, to wind, reel, coil, sluice.

spülen, to rinse, flush, wash, irrigate.

Spulen-filz, *m.* yarn package; -galvanometer, *m.&n.* moving-coil galvanometer; -widerstand, *m.* resistance in coil.

Spül-flüssigkeit, *f.* rinsing liquid; -gefäss, *n.* rinsing vessel.

Spülicht, *n.* dishwater, spent wash, slop.

Spül-schwelung, *f.* carbonization involving gas recirculation; -topf, *m.* rinsing jar (pot).

Spülung, *f.* rinsing, flushing, washing.

Spül-wasser, *n.* rinsing (flushing) water, dishwater; -würmer, *m.pl.* roundworms (Ascaridae).

Spund, *m.*-e, plug, bung, stopper, tongue.

spunden, to bung, cask, tongue and groove.

Spund-gärung, *f.* bunghole fermentation; -loch, *n.* bunghole; -voll, brimful; -wand,*f.* sheet-piling wall, bulkhead.

Spur, *f.*-en, track, trace, trail, scent, mark, gutter, channel, groove; -arbeit, *f.* concentration; -element, *n.* trace element.

spüren, to track, trace, trail, notice.

spurenhaft, in traces, sparingly.

Spurensuche, *f.* search for traces.

spurenweise, in traces, sparingly.

Spür-haar, *n.* tactile hair, cilium, vibrissa; **-hund,** *m.* bloodhound, pointer.

Spur-lager, *n.* step bearing, thrust bearing, hemispherical-bearing support; **-los,** trackless, without a trace; **-schlacke,** *f.* concentration slag; **-stein,** *m.* concentration matte (metal); **-weite,** *f.* track gauge.

Sputum, *n.* sputum.

S-Rohr, *n.,* **S-Röhre,** *f.* S tube, S pipe.

St., *abbr.* (Stück), piece; (Stunde), hour; (Sankt), Saint; (Stamm), stem.

Staat, *m.*-en, state.

Staatenbildung, *f.* formation of (animal) colonies.

staatlich, state, civil, national, public.

Staats-amt, *n.* public office; **-bürger,** *m.* subject, citizen; **-forstdienst,** *m.* state forest service; **-forstwirtschaft,** *f.* management of state forests; **-lehre,** *f.* political science; **-rat,** *m.* state council (councilor); **-wald,** *m.* state forest.

Stab, *m.*-e, bar, rod, stick, member, staff; **-alge,** *f.* bacillaria; **-artig,** stafflike; **-bakterie,** *f.* bacillus; **-bein,** *n.* walking leg.

Stäbchen, *n.* little rod, rod of retina, rhabdome, bacillus; **-form,** *f.* rod form; **-förmig,** rod-shaped; **-rotlauf,** bacillary erysipelas; **-schicht,** *f.* layer of rods; **-überzug,** *m.* cuticle consisting of rodlike particles; **-zelle,** *f.* rod cell.

Stab-eisen, *n.* bar iron; **-förmig,** rod-(bar-) shaped.

stabil, stable, rugged, **-bau,** *m.* stabile hive.

stabilisieren, to stabilize.

Stabilität, *f.* stability.

Stabilitäts-prüfer, *m.* stability tester.

Stab-kranz, *m.* corona radiata; **-kraut,** *n.* Artemisia; **-magnet,** *m.* magnetic rod or wand; **-stahlwalzwerk,** *n.* rod mill; **-zelle,** *f.* columnar (macro) sclereid; **-zugverfahren,** *n.* structural stress plot, graphical method.

stach (stechen), stung, pricked.

Stachel, *m.*-n, prickle, thorn, spine, sting, prong, dart; **-ästig,** acanthocladous; **-beere,** *f.* gooseberry; **-draht,** *m.* barbed wire; **-flosse,** *f.* spinous dorsal fin; **-flosser,** *m.pl.* Acanthopterygii; **-früchtig,** acanthocarpous; **-halm,** *m.* prickly stalk; **-häuter,** *m.pl.* Echinodermata.

stachelig, prickly, thorny, biting, pungent.

Stachel-käfer, *m.pl.* Mordellidae; **-kranz,** *m.* circle of spines; **-loch,** *n.* spinal foramen;

-los, free from spines; **-mohn,** *m.* prickly poppy (Argemone).

stacheln, to prick, sting, prod, spur, stimulate.

Stachel-schicht, *f.* layer of prickly cells; **-schwamm,** *m.* Hydnum; **-schwein,** *n.* porcupine; **-spitze,** *f.* dart, spike; **-spitzig,** mucronate, cuspidate; **-walzwerk,** *n.* toothed rolls.

Stadel, *m.* shed, heap, open kiln, stall; **-röstung,** *f.* stall roasting.

Stadium, *n.* stage, phase, state, stadium.

Stadt, *f.*-e, town, city; **-haus,** *n.* town hall.

städtisch, town, city, municipal.

Staffel, *f.* step, degree, rung, round.

staffieren, to equip, trim, prepare, garnish.

stagnieren, to stagnate.

stagnierend, stagnant.

stahl (stehlen), stole.

Stahl, *m.* steel; **-abfall,** *m.* steel scrap (waste); **-ähnlich,** steellike; **-arbeit,** *f.* steel process (work); **-artig,** steellike; **-arznei,** *f.* medicine containing iron; **-bandmass,** *n.* steel tape measure; **-bereitung,** *f.* steelmaking; **-beton,** *n.* steel concrete; **-brunnen,** *m.* chalybeate spring; **-draht,** *m.* steel wire; **-eisen,** *n.* open-hearth pig iron.

stählen, to steel, harden, make into steel.

Stahl-erzeugung, *f.* steel production; **-feder,** *f.* steel spring or pen; **-flasche,** *f.* steel bottle or cylinder; **-formguss,** *m.* steel casting (mold); **-gefäss,** *n.* steel receptacle; **-giesserei,** *f.* steel foundry; **-guss,** *m.* steel casting; **-gusstraverse,** *f.* cast-steel yoke or frame; **-hahn,** *m.* steel cock; **-hütte,** *f.* steelworks.

Stahl-kobalt, *m.* smaltite; **-kohlen,** *n.* conversion of wrought iron into steel by carbonization; **-kraut,** *n.* vervain; **-legierung,** *f.* steel alloy; **-mittel,** *n.* medicine containing iron; **-mörser,** *m.* steel mortar; **-probe,** *f.* steel sample; **-puddeln,** *n.* steel puddling; **-quelle,** *f.* chalybeate spring; **-rohr,** *n.* steel pipe; **-säuerling,** *m.* acidulous irion water.

Stahl-schmelzofen, *m.* steel melting furnace, open hearth; **-späne,** *m.pl.* steel (turnings) chips; **-stange,** *f.* steel bar; **-stechen,** *n.* steel engraving; **-stecherei,** *f.* steel engraving; **-stein,** *m.* siderite; **-stich,** *m.* steel engraving; **-trommel,** *f.* steel drum; **-waren,** *f.pl.* steel articles; **-wasser,** *n.* chalybeate water; **-werk,** *n.* steel mill.

stak (stecken), stuck.

Staket, *n.*-e, stockade, railing, fence; **-zaun,** *m.* railing, trellis, fence.

Stall, *m.*⸚e, stable, shed, stall, sty; **-dünger,** *m.* stable manure (dung), farmyard manure; **-fütterung,** *f.* stall feeding; **-mästung,** *f.* stable fattening; **-mist,** *m.* stable manure.

Stamm, *m.*⸚e, stem, stalk, shaft, trunk, breed, race, strain, stock, staff, tribe, stick, bole, phylum.

Stamm-abschnitt, *m.*-e, butt, log; **-analyse,** *f.* stem analysis; **-baum,** *m.* pedigree, flowsheet, phylogenetic tree; **-baumforschung,** *f.* phylogenetic investigation; **-buch,** *n.* herdbook; **-dorn,** *m.* stem thorn; **-eigen,** cauline, belonging to the stem, common.

stammeln, to stammer.

stammen, to spring, descend, originate, come; ~ **aus,** to come from; ~ **von,** to be derived from.

Stammende, *m.* butt end.

Stammes-entwicklung, *f.* development of the race, evolution; **-geschichte,** *f.* phylogeny; **-geschichtlich,** racial, relating to racial history.

Stamm-farbe, *f.* primary color; **-fremd,** of a foreign race; **-glied,** *n.* internode; **-grübchen,** *n.* lenticel; **-holz,** *n.* trunk wood, log.

stämmig, robust, strong, sturdy.

Stamm-knospe, *f.* plumule; **-körper,** *m.* parent substance or body; **-kubierung,** *f.* determining the volume of standing timber; **-lappen,** *m.* marginal or primary lobe; **-linie,** *f.* trunk (main) line, lineage; **-lösung,** *f.* standard solution, stock solution; **-reihe,** *f.* principal row; **-rest,** *m.* remnant of stem; **-riese,** *f.* timber slide; **-scheitel,** *m.* apex of stem.

Stamm-spitze, *f.* apex of stem; **-substanz,** *f.* mother substance; **-tafeln,** *f.pl.* volumetric table, flow sheets, genealogical table; **-vater,** *m.* ancestor, predecessor, progenitor; **-vegetationspunkt,** *m.* growing point of stem; **-verwandt,** kindred, cognate; **-würze,** *f.* original wort.

Stampfasphalt, *m.* tamped asphalt.

Stampfe, *f.* stamp, stamper, ram, pounding, pestle, punch, rammer.

stampfen, to stamp, tamp, punch, beat, ram, pound, pitch.

Stampfer, *m.* stamper, pestle.

Stampf-futter, *n.* tamped lining; **-haufen,** *m.* batch; **-werk,** *n.* stamp mill.

stand (stehen), stood.

Stand, *m.*-e, stand, position, level, state, place, booth, condition, height, rank, station, covert, lair; **einen in den** ~ **setzen,** to enable one.

Standard-abweichung, *f.* standard deviation; **-fehler,** *m.* standard error; **-lösung,** *f.* standard solution; **-wert,** *m.* standard value.

Stand-bild, *n.* statue; **-entwicklung,** *f.* tank development (in photography).

Ständer, *m.* pedestal, pillar, post, stand, standard, cistern, tank, container.

stand-fähig, stable, firm; **-fest,** stable, firm, rigid; **-festigkeit,** *f.* stability, rigidity, resistance; **-flasche,** *f.* a bottle for standing in a fixed place, flat-bottomed flask; **-gärung,** *f.* standing fermentation; **-gefäss,** *n.* storage vessel; **-glas,** *n.* glass (cylinder); **-haft,** steady, constant, stable, firm; **-halten,** to stand (be) firm, hold out.

ständig, stationary, permanent, fixed, constant, firm, regular.

Stand-kugel, *f.* stationary bulb; **-mörser,** *m.* mortar with firm base; **-ort,** *m.* station, stand, location, habitat, site.

Standorts-ansprüche, *m.pl.* demands made on a location; **-beeinflussung,** *f.* influence of location on plants; **-faktor,** *m.* habitat factor; **-form,** *f.* local group of individuals; **-güte,** *m.* quality of locality; **-klasse,** *f.* quality, class, grade of locality; **-veränderung,** *f.* change in type of location; **-verhältnisse,** *n.pl.* site conditions; **-verschiebung,** *f.* shifting in plant station; **-wirkung,** *f.* effect of location.

Stand-punkt, *m.*-e, viewpoint, standard, aspect; **-tropfglas,** *n.* dropping bottle; **-vogel,** *m.* sedentary bird, permanent resident; **-weite,** *f.* width of planting; **-wild,** *n.* sedentary game.

Stange, *f.*-n, stick, rod, pole, bar, perch, roll, ingot, stem, stake, staff.

Stängelchen, *n.* little stick.

Stangen-blei, *n.* bar lead; **-bohne,** *f.* climbing bean, runner; **-eisen,** *n.* bar iron, rod iron; **-gold,** *n.* ingot gold; **-holz,** *n.* pole (wood) timber; **-lack,** *m.* stick-lac; **-meter,** *m.&n.* current meter; **-riese,** *f.* pole slide; **-schwefel,** *m.* roll sulphur, brimstone; **-seife,** *f.* bar soap.

Stangen-spat, *m.* barred spar, columnar barite; **-stahl,** *m.* bar steel; **-steckschlüssel,** *m.* long-stem socket wrench; **-stein,** *m.* pycnite, columnar topaz; **-tabak,** *m.* roll tobacco; **-zinn,** *n.* bar tin.

stank (stinken), stank.

stänkern, to stink, quarrel.

Stanni-chlorid, *n.* stannic chloride; -hydroxyd, *n.* stannic hydroxide.

Stanniol, *n.* tin foil.

Stanni-oxyd, *n.* stannic oxide; -reihe, *f.* stannic series; -verbindung, *f.* stannic compound.

Stanno-chlorid, *n.* stannous chloride; -jodid, *n.* stannous iodide; -oxyd, *n.* stannous oxide; -sulfid, *n.* stannous sulphide; -verbindung, *f.* stannous compound.

Stanzabfall, *m.* stamping.

Stanze, *f.* puncher, punch, stamping, punch die.

stanzen, to stamp, emboss, punch.

Stanz-machine, *f.* punch press; -porzellan, *n.* porcelain for punching; -rohr, *n.* sample-taking cylinder.

Stapel, *m.*-, staple, warehouse, store, pile, stake, beam, heap, stack; -faser, *f.* short-fibered rayon; -gemüse, *n.pl.* bulky vegetables.

Staphylokokkus, *m.* staphylococcus.

Star, *m.* cataract, starling.

starb (sterben), died.

stark, strong, powerful, heavy, severe, thick, loud, fat, large, hard.

Stärke, *f.* starch, amylum, strength, thickness, size, depth, diameter, corpulency, vigor, force; -abbau, *m.* degradation of starch, translocation; -art, *f.* variety of starch; -artig, amyloid, amylaceous, starchy; -baum, *m.* starch tree; -bildner, *m.* leucoplast; -bildung, *f.* formation of starch; -fabrik,*f.* starch factory; -führend, amylaceous.

Stärke-gehalt, *m.* starch content; -grad, *m.* degree of strength, intensity; -gummi, *n.* starch gum, dextrin; -haltig, containing starch, starchy, amylaceous; -kleister, *m.* starch paste; -knöllchen, *n.* root tubercle; -korn, *n.* starch granule; -körnchen, *n.* starch granule.

Stärke-lösung, *f.* starch solution; -mehl, *n.* starch powder (flour); -mehlähnlich, -mehlartig, amylaceous, amyloid, starch; -mehlhaltig, containing starch; -mittel, *n.* strengthening remedy, tonic.

stärken, to starch, strengthen, thicken, refresh, restore, confirm.

stärke-reich, rich in starch; -scheide, *f.* starch sheath, endodermis; -sirup, *m.* starch sirup, glucose; -weizen, *m.* starch

wheat, emmer; -wert, *m.* starch value, amylaceous value; -zucker, *m.* glucose; -zuwachs, *m.* diameter increment.

stark-farbig, strongly colored; -faserig, strong-fibered; -holz, *n.* heavy timber; -strom, *m.* heavy current.

Stärkung, *f.* starching, refreshment, strengthening.

Stärkungsmittel, *n.* tonic.

stark-wandig, thick-walled;-wirkend,efficacious, powerful, drastic; -wirksam, powerful, highly active.

starr, rigid, stiff, stubborn, inflexible, numb.

Starre, *f.* rigor, stiffness, numbness.

starren, to stare, be numb, be stiff, be chilled, stiffen.

Starrheit, *f.* rigidity, rigor, stiffness, obstinacy.

Starr-krampf, *m.* tetanus, tonic convulsion; -krampfserum, antitetanic serum; -leinen, *n.* -leinwand, *f.* buckram; -schmiere, *f.* grease, solid lubricant; -sucht, *f.* catalepsy.

Statik, *f.* statics.

stationär, stationary.

Stationarität, *f.* principle of immobility (stationary state).

statisch, static.

statistisch, statistical.

Stativ, *n.*-e, stand, support, foot, tripod.

Statt, *f.* place, stead.

statt, instead of.

Stätte, *f.* place, room.

statten, von ~ gehen, to take place, go off, proceed; zu ~ kommen, to be of advantage or use.

statt-finden, to take place, occur, happen; -haben, to take place, occur, happen; -gehabt, previous.

statthaft, allowable, permissible, admissible, legal.

stattlich, stately, fine, splendid, portly.

Stau, *m.*-e, damming up, impounding (of water).

Staub, *m.* dust, powder, pollen; -artig, dustlike, powdery; -blatt, *n.* stamen.

staubblattvorreif, protandrous.

Staubbrand, *m.* loose smut.

Stäubchen, *n.* tiny particle, mote.

staubdicht, dustproof.

stäuben, to dust, powder, spray.

Staub-entfall, m. dust deposit; **-erde,** f. peaty humus; **-fach,** n. pollen sac; **-faden,** m. filament of anther; **-fadenröhre,** f. filament tube; **-fänger,** m. dust catcher; **-fein,** very fine, fine as dust; **-flieger,** m. spore of cryptograms, pollen grain; **-förmig,** powdery, dustlike; **-frei,** free from dust.

Staub-gefäss, n. stamen; **-gefässtellung,** f. position of stamens; **-grübchen,** n. lenticel; **-grube,** f. clinandrium, the anther bed; **-hälfte,** f. half an anther; **-haltig,** containing dust.

staubig, dusty, powdery.

Staub-kalk, m. air-slaked lime; **-kapsel,** f. pollen capsule; **-kern,** m. grain of dust; **-kohle,** f. coal dust; **-korn,** n. dust particle; **-krümmung,** f. curvature of stamen.

Stäubling, m. puffball.

Staub-masse, f. dust substance, mass of dust; **-partikelchen,** n. dust particle; **-sand,** m. very fine sand; **-sicher,** dustproof; **-sieb,** n. dust sieve; **-teilchen,** n. dust particle; **-trocken,** bone-dry, dust-free; **-übertragung,** f. transmission or conveying of pollen or dust; **-weg,** m. style of flower.

Stauchdruck, m. crushing pressure, compression.

stauchen, to knock, beat, compress, shorten, bulge, buckle.

Stauchling, m. shortened shoot.

Stauchpresse, f. bulldozer.

Stauchung, f. compression.

Stauchzylinder, m. crusher gauge.

Staudamm, m. retaining dam.

Staude, f. shrub, bush, perennial herb.

stauden-artig, shrublike, suffrutescent; **-auslese,** f. hill-selection method; **-flur,** f. perennial-herb vegetation.

stauen, to stow, dam up, restrict, congest, obstruct, choke.

Stau-kurve, f. **-linie,** f. backwater curve.

staunen, to be astonished, wonder, be surprised.

Staunen, n. astonishment, wonder, surprise.

staunenswert, wonderful, astonishing.

Staupe, f. distemper, flogging.

Stauung, f. obstruction, congestion, stopping, damming, rise of water, stowing.

Stearin-kerze, f. stearin candle; **-sauer,** stearate of; **-seife,** f. stearin soap.

Stech-apfel, m.⁼, thorn apple, stramonium; **-borste,** f. stylet.

stechen, to stick, prick, sting, pierce, puncture, stab, engrave, tap, cut, incline, spout, spire.

stechend, penetrating, stinging, piercing, pungent.

Stecher, m. pricker, proof stick (for sugar), sampler, engraver, sticker.

Stech-fliege, f. pricking house fly, stable fly; **-ginster,** m. furze, gorse, whin; **-heber,** m. thief tube, pipette; **-kolben,** n. pipette; **-kunst,** f. engraving; **-mücken,** f.pl. mosquitoes, gnats; **-palme,** f. Christ's thorn (*Paliurus*), holly (*Ilex aquifolium*); **-palmenbitter,** n. ilicin; **-pipette,** f pipette; **-probe,** f. touchstone test; **-rüssel,** m. proboscis, beak, promuscis (Hemiptera).

Steckdose, f. wall plug.

stecken, to stick, hide, stay, set, plant, fix, remain, put; ∼ **bleiben,** to be stuck, break down, remain, stand.

Steckenpferd, n. hobby, fad.

Stecker, m. wall plug, outlet.

Steckholz, n. cutting slip, dibble.

Stecklingskrankheit, f. disease of cuttings.

Steck-nadel, f. pin; **-nadelkopfgrösse,** f. pinhead size; **-rübe,** f. rutabaga; **-saat,** f. dibbled seed.

Steg, m. path, trail, crosspiece, small bridge, strap, bar, stay.

Steh-blech, n. web plate; **-bolzen,** m. staybolt; **-bütte,** f. stock tub.

stehen, to stand, be, become, fit, be (vertical) upright; **im Gegensatz** ∼, to be in contrast; **in Verbindung** ∼, to be in communication; ∼ **bleiben,** to stop.

stehen-bleibend, persistent, remaining; **-lassen,** n. allowing to stand, settling.

Steh-kölbchen, n. small flat-bottomed flask; **-kolben,** m. flat-bottomed flask.

stehlen, to steal.

Stehmähne, f. stiff (standing) mane.

Stehwasserblatt, n. dissected, submerged leaf.

steif, rigid, stiff, firm, formal, precise, awkward, inflexible.

steifborstig, hispid.

Steife, f. stiffening, starch, prop, stay, stiffness.

steifen, to stiffen, stay, starch, prop.

steifhaarig, hirsute.

Steifheit, f. stiffness, rigidity.

Steifigkeitszahl, *f.* modulus of elasticity, coefficient of rigidity.

Steif-leinen, *n.* -leinwand, *f.* buckram; -rispenhafer, *m.* stiff-panicle oats.

Steifung, *f.* stiffening, starching, sizing.

Steig, *m.*-e, path, steep trail, ladder.

Steigbügel, *m.* stapes, stirrup; -köpfchen, *n.* head of stapes; -platte, *f.* base or foot of stapes; -tritt, *m.* base or foot of stapes.

Steige, *f.* steps, ladder, hen roost.

Steigeisen, *n.* climbing iron.

steigen, to mount, climb, rise, ascend, descend, increase.

steigern, to raise, increase, enhance, auction.

Steigerung, *f.* raising, increase, rise, heightening, enhancing, comparison (grammar).

Steig-geschwindigkeit, *f.* rate of rise; -höhe, *f.* height of ascent, rise, pitch or gradient (of a screw);- höhenmethode, *f.* equilibrium method, sedimentation; -raum, *m.* space to permit rising, unfilled space above the wort; -rohr, *n.* -röhre, *f.* ascending (rising) tube, standpipe, riser.

Steigung, *f.* rise, rising, increase, ascent, incline, pitch, gradient, grade, slope.

steil, steep, precipitous, close.

Steile, *f.* steepness, declivity, precipice.

Steilhang, *m.* steep slope.

Steilheit, *f.* steepness.

Steilrohrkessel, *m.* bent-tube boiler.

Stein, *m.*-e, stone, rock, brick, calculus, concretion, matte; ∼ der Weisen, philosopher's stone.

Stein-abfälle, *m.pl.* stone chips; -ähnlich, stonelike, stony; -alaun, *m.* rock alum; -apfel, *m.* pomelike fruit in which each locule forms a stone; -arbeit, *f.* stonework, metal smelting; -artig, stonelike, stony.

Stein-auflösungsmittel, *n.* solvent for calculus; -beere, *f.* drupe; -bewohnend, lithophilous, growing on stones or rocks; -bock, *m.* steinbock, ibex; -borke, *f.* stone cork, phellem changed into sclereids; -brand, *m.* stinking smut, bunt; -brandansteckung, *f.* infection by bunt; -brech, *m.* saxifrage.

Stein-brecher, *m.* stone crusher (breaker); -brechgewächse, *n.pl.* Saxifragaceae; -brechmaschine, *f.* stone crusher; -bruch, *m.* quarry; -brut, *f.* stonebrood, pickled brood; -bühlergelb, *n.* barium (chromate) yellow; -butt, *m.* turbot; - butter, *f.* rock butter, hard sauce.

Steindruck, *m.*-e, lithograph(y); -farbe, *f.* lithographic ink.

steinern, stony, of stone.

Stein-element, *n.* stone cell, sclereid; -farbe, *f.* stone color; -flachs, *m.* mountain flax, amianthus; -frucht, *f.* stone fruit, drupe; -galle, *f.* corn; -grau, *n.* stone gray (color pigment); -griess, *m.* gravel; -grün, *n.* terre-verte (pigment); -gut, *n.* whiteware, stoneware; -hart, hard as stone; -holz, *n.* xylolith, stonewood; -huhn, *n.* rock partridge.

steinig, stony, rocky, of stone.

Stein-kanal, *m.* stone canal (Hydroductus); -kauz, *m.* screech owl, little owl; -kern, *m.* stone (in fruit), hardened endocarp; -kitt, *m.* cement for stone; -klee, *m.* melilot (*Melilotus officinalis*); -kohle, *f.* mineral coal, bituminous coal.

Steinkohlen-asche, *f.* coal ashes; -bergwerk, *n.* bituminous coal mine; -gas, *n.* coal gas; -klein, *n.* slack, culm; -schwelteer, *m.* low-temperature coal tar from bituminous coal; -schwelung, *f.* carbonization of coal; -staub, *n.* coal dust.

Steinkohlenteer, *m.* coal tar; -blase, *f.* coal-tar still; -essenz, *f.* first light oil; -kampfer, *m.* naphthalene; -präparat, *n.* coal-tar preparation, coal-tar product.

Steinkohlen-verkohlung, -verkokung, *f.* coking of coal; -zeit, *f.* Coal Age Carboniferous.

Stein-koralle, *f.* stone coral; -körper, *f.* stone cell or cluster of stone cells; -kraut, *n.* stonecrop (Sedum), Alyssum; -liebend, lithophilous; -mark, *n.* lithomarge; -meissel, *m.* stone chisel; -metz, *m.* stonemason; -mörtel, *m.* hard mortar, concrete, cement; -nuss, *f.* ivory nut; -obst, *n.* stone fruit.

Steinöl, *n.* petroleum; -haltig, petroliferous, oil-bearing.

Stein-pappe, *f.* roofing paper; -pech, *n.* stone pitch; -pilz, *m.* eatable mushroom (Boletus); -platte, *f.* stone slab, flagstone; -reich, *n.* mineral kingdom; -rösten, *n.* roasting of the regulus or matte; -salz, *n.* rock salt; -salzlager, *n.* rock-salt bed; -säure, *f.* lithic acid; -schlag, *m.* broken crushed stone.

Stein-strasse, *f.* stone road, hard road; -thylle, *f.* stone thylosis; -trift, *f.* rocky drift; -waren, *f.pl.* stoneware; -wurf, *m.* stone's throw;]-zeit, *f.* Stone Age; -zellenkork, *m.* cork made up of stone cells; -zeug, *n.* stoneware.

Steiss, *m.* rump, buttock, nates, crissum.

Steissbein, *n.* coccygeal bone; **-band,** *n.* coccygeal ligament; **-horn,** *n.* horn of the coccyx; **-krümmer,** *m.* ischiococcygeal muscle; **-wirbel,** *m.* coccygeal vertebra.

Steiss-drüse, *f.* coccygeal gland; **-feder,** *f.* anal rectrix; **-flosse,** *f.* anal fin; **-wirbel,** *m.* coccygeal vertebra.

stellbar, adjustable, movable.

Stell-bottich, *m.*-e, fermenting vat; **-bügel,** *m.* clamp.

Stelle, *f.* place, position, spot, point.

stellen, to place, put, set, adjust, regulate, arrange, stop, check, supply, furnish, place oneself, appear, stand, prove to be, pretend to be; **-weise,** in places, here and there; **-zahl,** *f.* index, position number, atomic number.

Stell-hahn, *m.* regulating cock; **-hefe,** *f.* pitching yeast.

stellig, of one digit; **einstellige Zahl,** *f.* one-digit number.

Stell-knorpel, *m.* arytenoid cartilage; **-macher,** *m.* wheelwright; **-mutter,** *f.* adjusting nut; **-ring,** *m.* slide index, clamping (adjustable) collar; **-schraube,** *f.* set-screw, adjusting screw.

Stellung, *f.* placing, situation, rank, position, arrangement, attitude, constellation, orientation, regulating, pattern (for leather).

Stellungs-isomeric, *f.* position isomerism; **-nahme,** *f.* attitude.

Stell-vertreter, *m.* deputy, substitute, representative; **-vertretung,** *f.* substitution, proxy; **-vorrichtung,** *f.* adjusting device; **-werk,** *n.* signaling device.

Stelze, *f.* stilt.

Stelzen-wurzel, *f.* stilt root, prop root; **-wurzler,** *m.* tree having prop roots.

Stelzfuss, *m.* horse with upright joints.

Stemmeisen, *n.* chisel.

stemmen, to prop, support, calk, chisel, stem, dam up, fell, cut.

Stempel, *m.*-, pistil, brand, mark, stamp, prop, imprint, stamper, die, punch, pestle, piston; **-farbe,** *f.* stamping ink; **-grube,** *f.* sensillar pit; **-holz,** *n.* small pit props; **-marke,** *f.* stamp; **-mündung,** *f.* stigma.

stempeln, to stamp, brand, mark, prop.

Stempel-träger, *m.* gynophore; **-zeichen,** *n.* stamp, mark.

Stengel, *m.*-, stalk, stem; (unterirdischer) ∼, rhizome.

stengel-artig, stalklike, cauliform; **-ausläufer,** *m.* stem runner, stolon; **-blatt,** *n.*

stem leaf, caulinary leaf; **-blattähnlich,** like a caulinary leaf; **-brenner,** *m.* anthracnose; **-fäule,** *f.* stem rot; **-gewebe,** *n.* stem tissue; **-glied,** *n.* internode of stem.

stengelig, stalked.

Stengel-knolle, *f.* tuber; **-kohle,** *f.* columnar coal; **-los,** acaulose, stemless; **-ranke,** *f.* tendril (morphologically a stem); **-spitze,** *f.* end of stalk; **-teil,** *m.* part of stem; **-treibend,** caulescent, stemmed; **-umfassend,** stem clasping, amplexicaul.

Stephanskörner, *n.pl.* stavesacre seeds.

Steppdecke, *f.* quilt.

Steppe, *f.* steppe, desert, prairie.

steppen, to quilt, stitch; **-landschaft,** *f.* steppe landscape; **-wald,** *m.* steppe forest.

sterben, to die, fade away.

sterblich, mortal.

Sterblichkeit, *f.* mortality.

Stereo-chemie, *f.* stereochemistry; **-chemisch,** stereochemical; **-isomer,** stereoisomeric; **-isomerie,** *f.* stereoisomerism; **-metrisch,** stereometric.

Sterigma, *n.* sterigma.

steril, sterile.

Sterilisation, *f.* sterilization.

Sterilisationsmethode, *f.* method of sterilization.

Sterilisator, *m.* sterilizer.

sterilisieren, to sterilize.

Sterilisierung, *f.* sterilization.

Sterilität, *f.* sterility.

Sterin, *n.* sterol.

sterisch, steric, spatial, bodily.

Sterlet, *m.* sterlet.

Stern, *m.*-e, star, asterisk, pupil (of the eye).

Sternalleiste, *f.* sternal plate.

Stern-anis, *m.* star anise (*Illicium anisatum*); **-artig,** stellate; **-band,** *n.* ciliary ligament; **-bild,** *n.* constellation; **-borste,** *f.* stellate bristle.

Sternchen, *n.* little star, asterisk.

stern-förmig, star-shaped, stellate; **-haar,** *n.* stellate hair; **-kunde,** *f.* astronomy; **-leiste,** *f.* septum of Anthozoa, radial ridge; **-physik,** *f.* astrophysics; **-rohr,** *n.* telescope; **-schnuppe,** *f.* shooting star; **-schuppe,** *f.* stellate brood scale; **-tier,** *n.* starfish; **-warte,** *f.* observatory; **-zeit,** *f.* sidereal time.

sterzeln, to ventilate.

stet, stetig, continuous, stable, constant, regular, fixed.

Stetigkeit, *f.* constancy, stability, continuity, steadiness.

stets, ever, always, continually, regularly.

Steuer, *n.*-, rudder, helm.

Steuer, *f.* tax, duty; **-amt,** *n.* revenue office, customhouse; **-feder,** *f.* rectrix; **-frei,** duty (tax) free, exempt; **-getriebe,** *n.* control mechanism; **-marke,** *f.* revenue stamp.

steuern, to control, steer, regulate, pay taxes, contribute.

Steuerung, *f.* steering, controlling, distributing gear, distribution, steering gear, automatic control.

Stich, *m.*-e, prick, puncture, stab, sting, bite, engraving, shooting pain, thrust, stitch, tinge, tapping, taphole; **im Stiche lassen,** to forsake, leave in the lurch.

Stich-abnahme, *f.* reduction in area or pass; **-auge,** *f.* taphole.

Stichel, *m.* graver, burin.

sticheln, to puncture, prick, stitch, jeer, sneer, tease.

Stichflamme, *f.* fine-pointed flame.

stichhaltig, proof, lasting, valid, sound.

Stichhaltigkeit, *f.* soundness.

Stich-kanal, *m.* puncture channel; **-kultur,** *f.* stab culture.

Stichling, *m.* three-pointed stickleback.

Stich-linie, *f.* line of stab; **-loch,** *n.* tap hole; **-pfropf,** *m.* taphole plug; **-probe,** *f.* sample at random; **-stelle,** *f.* place of injection.

sticht (stechen), stings, pricks.

Stich-verletzung, *f.* injury caused by stab; **-wein,** *m.* sample wine; **-wort,** *n.* stock phrase, catchword, cue; **-wunde,** *f.* stab wound.

Stick-dampf, *m.* chokedamp, suffocating vapor; **-dioxyd,** *n.* nitric dioxide; **-dunst,** *m.* chokedamp, suffocating vapor.

sticken, to choke, suffocate, embroider.

Stickerei, *f.* embroidery, fancywork.

Stick-gas, *n.* suffocating or nitrogen gas, carbon dioxide; **-kohlenstoff,** *m.* carbon nitride; **-luft,** *f.* close air, nitrogen; **-oxyd,** *n.* nitric oxide; **-oxydentbindung,** *f.* evolution of nitric oxyde; **-oxydul,** *n.* nitrous oxide.

Stickstoff, *m.* nitrogen; **-arm,** poor in nitrogen; **-atmosphäre,** atmosphere of nitrogen; **-aufnahme,** *f.* absorption of nitrogen; **-ausscheidung,** *f.* nitrogen elimination; **-bestimmung,** *f.* determination of nitrogen; **-dioxyd,** *n.* nitrogen dioxide; **-dünger,** *m.* nitrogenous fertilizer (manure); **-entbindung,** *f.* release of nitrogen; **-frei,** nitrogen-free, nonnitrogenous.

Stickstoff-gehalt, *m.* nitrogen content; **-gleichgewicht,** *n.* nitrogenous equilibrium; **-haltig,** nitrogenous; **-kalomel,** *n.* mercurous azide; **-kohlenoxyd,** *n.* carbonyl nitride; **-natrium,** *n.* sodium nitride; **-oxyd,** *n.* oxide of nitrogen; **-oxydul,** *n.* nitrous oxide; **-oxydulgas,** *n.* nitrous oxide gas; **-quecksilber-oxydul,** *n.* mercurous azide.

stickstoff-reich, rich in nitrogen, highly nitrogenous; **-sammler,** *m.* nitrogen-storing plant, leguminous plant; **-säure,** *f.* nitrogenous acid; **-verbindung,** *f.* nitrogen compound; **-wasserstoff,** *m.* hydrogen nitride, nitrogen hydride; **-wasserstoffsäure,** *f.* hydrazoic (hydronitric) acid.

stickt (stecken), sticks.

Stickwetter, *n.pl.* foul air, chokedamp, afterdamp.

stieben, to start, fly about like dust, disperse, scatter, drizzle.

Stiefbruder, *m.* stepbrother.

Stiefel, *m.*-, boot, barrel; **-lack,** *m.* shoe polish; **-schwärze,** *f.*, **-wichse,** *f.* shoe blacking.

Stiefgeschwister, *pl.* stepbrother(s) and stepsister(s).

Stiefmütterchen, *n.* pansy.

stieg (steigen), climbed.

Stiege, *f.* ladder, stairs, steps, score.

Stieglitz, *m.*-e, goldfinch.

stiehlt (stehlen), steals.

Stiel, *m.*-e, stalk, stem, shaft, peduncle, pedicel, stipe, handle; **-auge,** *n.* stalked (pedunculated) eye; **-blätterig,** podophyllous.

stiel-drüsig, with glandular peduncle; **-eiche,** *f.* pedunculate oak; **-fäule,** *f.* stalk rot; **-loch,** *n.* foramen; **-muskel,** *m.* pedicel muscle, adjustor muscle; **-pfeffer,** *m.* cubeb(s).

stiel-rund, terete; **-rundblättrig,** teretifolious; **-septum,** *n.* peduncular septum; **-tellerförmig,** salver-shaped; **-zelle,** *f.* stalk cell.

Stier, *m.*-e, steer, ox, bull.

stieren, to stare.

stiess (stossen), pushed.

Stift, *m.*-e, spike, peg, tag, tack, stud, pin, brad, rivet, pencil, crayon, snag, stump apprentice; **-draht,** *m.* wire for making nails.

Stift, *n.*-e, **-er,** monastery, seminary, foundation.

stiften, to tack, found, institute, establish, cause, make.

Stift-farbe, *f.* pencil color, colored, crayon; **-schraube,** *f.* stud bolt, setscrew.

Stiftung, *f.* foundation, institution, endowment.

Stigmenstellung, *f.* position of the spiracles.

Stil, *m.*-e, **Stilart,** *f.* style.

still, still, silent, quiet, calm, stagnant, inanimate, dull; **stille Wut,** *f.* dumb madness, dumb or paralytic rabies.

Stille, *f.* stillness, quietness.

stillen, to still, silence, calm, allay, quench, gratify, mitigate, stop, stay.

stillend, calming, lenitive, allaying, sedative.

still-legen, to stop, shut down; **-mittel,** *n.* sedative; **-schweigen,** *n.* silence; **-schweigend,** tacit, silent, implied; **-stand,** *m.* standstill, stop, pause, stasis; **-stehen,** to stand still, stop; **-stehend,** stationary, stagnant.

Stillung, *f.* stilling, appeasing lactation.

Stillungsmittel, *n.* sedative.

Stimm-band, *n.* vocal chord; **-bildung,** *f.* voice production, phonation.

Stimme, *f.* voice, vote, musical part, sound.

stimmen, to be in tune, tune, accord, agree, balance, vote, dispose.

Stimm-falte, *f.* fold of vocal cord; **-fortsatz,** vocal apophysis; **-gabel,** *f.* tuning fork; **-organ,** *n.* vocal organ; **-recht,** *n.* suffrage, franchise; **-ritze,** *f.* glottis.

Stimmritzen-band, *n.* true vocal cord; **-deckel,** *m.* epiglottis.

Stimmsaite, *f.* vocal cord.

Stimmung, *f.* tuning, key, humor, mood, disposition.

Stimmwerkzeug, *n.* vocal organ.

Stimulantia, *n.pl.* stimulants.

Stimulationsorgan, *n.* organ of stimulation.

stimulieren, to stimulate.

Stimulierung, *f.* stimulation.

Stink-apparat, *m.* stink gland; **-asand,** *m.* **-asant,** *m.* asafetida; **-drüse,** *f.* stink gland.

stinken, to stink, smell foul, be fetid.

stinkend, stinking, fetid.

Stink-fluss, *m.* **-flusspat,** *m.* fetid fluorspar; **-harz,** *n.* asafetida; **-kalk,** *m.* anthraconite, bituminous limestone; **-kohle,** *f.* fetid coal; **-mergel,** *m.* fetid marl; **-raum,** *m.* gas chamber; **-raumprobe,** *f.* gas-chamber test; **-schiefer,** *m.* fetid shale; **-stein,** *m.* fetid stone, bituminous limestone.

Stint, *m.*-e, smelt.

Stippe, *m.* smelt.

Stippe, *f.* stigma, small mark, speck, gravy, sauce.

Stippflecke, *m.pl.* bitter pits.

Stippstreifenkrankheit, *f.* stipple-streak disease.

Stipular-dorn, *m.* stipular spine; **-grübchen,** *n.* lenticel.

stirbt (sterben), dies, is dying.

Stirn(e), *f.* forehead, brow.

Stirn-ader, *f.* frontal vein; **-beborstung,** *f.* frontal (orbital) bristles; **-bein,** *n.* frontal bone; **-beinhöhle,** *f.* frontal sinus; **-beinnaht,** *f.* frontal suture; **-bogen,** *m.* frontal arch; **-borste,** *f.* frontal bristle; **-bucht,** *f.* frontal recess; **-ecke,** *f.* frontal angle; **-feld,** *n.* central area of head.

Stirn-fläche, *f.* end surface, face, front; **-fortsatz,** *m.* frontal process; **-fühler,** *m.* buccal tentacle; **-furche,** *f.* frontal sulcus; **-gegend,** *f.* frontal region; **-hieb,** *m.* blow with a stick or club; **-höcker,** *m.pl.* frontal tubercles; **-höhle,** *f.* frontal sinus; **-hügel,** *m.* frontal protuberance, eminence; **-kamm,** *m.* frontal crest.

Stirn-knochen, *m.* frontal bone; **-leisten,** *f.pl.* frontal ridge, spine; **-muschel,** *f.* frontal concha; **-muskel,** *m.* frontalis muscle; **-rad,** *n.* spur wheel; **-rand,** *m.* contour of the forehead; **-rinne,** *f.* sulcus; **-runzeln,** *n.* frowning; **-saugnapf,** *m.* apical sucker; **-schild,** *m.* frontal bone; **-schnabel,** *m.* frontal crest.

Stirn-schwiele, *f.* frontal callus; **-seite,** *f.* front side, front; **-stachel,** *m.* .rontal crest: **-streifen,** *m.* frontal stripe; **-vosprünge,** *m.pl.* frontal ridges; **-welle,** *f.* wave front; **-windung,** *f.* frontal convolution; **-zapfen,** *m.* frontal peg.

Stirrholz, *n.* wooden stirrer.

stob (stieben), started, gave off dust.

stöbern, to rummage, hunt about, drift, drizzle.

stochern, to stir, poke a fire.

Stöchio-metrie, *f.* stoichiometry; **-metrisch,** stoichiometric(al).

Stock, *m.*ːe, stick, staff, cane, rod, stock, block, trunk, stem, stump, body, story, floor, colony; **-abschnitt,** *m.* stump (felling) section; **-ausschlag,** *m.* stool shoot, sprout; **-bildung,** *f.* formation of colonies; **-blind,** stone-blind.

stocken, to stop, hesitate, falter, slacken, stagnate, curdle, coagulate, spoil, mold, decay, cake (paint), line with turf.

stockend, dull, stagnant, stopping.

Stock-ende, *n.* butt end; **-erz,** *n.* ore in big lumps; **-finster,** pitch-dark.

Stockfisch, *m.* stockfish, codfish; **-lebertran,** *m.* cod-liver, oil.

Stockfleck, *m.* moldy stain, mildew.

stockfleckig, spotted with mold, moldy.

Stockholz, *n.* stump wood.

stockig, stöckig, moldy, musty, stubborn, stocky, stumpy.

Stock-käfer, *m.pl.* Endomychidae; **-lack,** *m.* stick-lac; **-nutzung,** *f.* utilization of stumps; **-punkt,** *m.* solidifying point; **-roden,** *n.* extraction of stumps; **-rodung,** *f.* stump grubbing; **-rose,** *f.* hollyhock; **-schlacke,** *f.* shingling slag; **-schlagbe-trieb,** *m.* coppice system; **-sprengung,** *f.* stump blasting.

Stockung, *f.* stopping, interruption, cessation, stagnation, congestion, dry rot.

Stock-werk, *n.* story, floor, tier; **-zahn,** *m.* molar tooth.

Stoff, *m.*-e, substance, matter, subject, theme, material, cloth, fabric, stuff, pulp; **-abgrenzung,** *f.* delineation of subject matter treated; **-ableitung,** *f.* translocation; **-ansatz,** *m.* anabolism; **-aufnahme,** *f.* absorption, intake of substance; **-austausch,** *m.* exchange of material;- austritt, *m.* loss of cell content; **-bahn,** *f.* strip or width of cloth, clothing material, breadth; **-bildung,** *f.* formation of a substance; **-brei,** *m.* pulp.

Stoff-bütte, *f.* stuff chest; **-dichte,** *f.* stock density (of pulp); **-fänger,** *m.* save-all; **-gattung,** *f.* kind of material; **-gewicht,** *n.* unit weight of material, specific gravity; **-haushalt,** *m.* metabolism; **-kufe,** *f.* stuff vat.

stofflich, material.

stoff-los, immaterial, unsubstantial; **-menge,** *f.* amount of material; **-mühle,** *f.* stuff engine; **-patent,** *n.* patent; **-rahmen,** *m.* filter disk; **-teilchen,** *n.* particle of

matter; **-umsatz,** *m.* change of matter, metabolism; **-verbrauch,** *m.* consumption of material.

Stoffwechsel, *m.* metabolism; **-anomalie,** *f.* metabolic abnormality; **-bestimmung,** *f.* study of metabolic rate; **-gefälle,** *n.* metabolic gradient; **-gleichgewicht,** *n.* nutritive equilibrium; **-grösse,** *f.* metabolic rate; **-krankheit,** *f.* disease due to faulty metabolism; **-produkt,** *n.* metabolic product; **-prozess,** *m.* metabolic process; **-untersuchung,** *f.* metabolic study; **-veränderung,** *f.* metabolic change; **-vorgang,** *m.* metabolic process; **-wirkung,** *f.* metabolic effect.

Stoffzahl, *f.* number of substances.

stöhle (stehlen), would steal, were stealing, stole, steals.

Stollbeule, *f.* cap elbow.

Stolle, *f.* calk, calkin (of horseshoe).

Stollen, *m.* gangway, post, prop, gallery, drift, tunnel, loaf-shaped (currant) cake; **-holz,** *n.* pit timber, mine props, studding.

stolpern, to stumble, blunder, trip.

Stolz, *m.* pride, loftiness, vanity.

stolz, proud, lofty, arrogant.

Stomachale, Stomachalmittel, *n.* stomachic.

Stöpfel, *m.* stopper, plug, cork.

Stopfbüchse, *f.* stuffing box, packing gland.

stopfen, to stop, stuff, fill, constipate, darn, mend.

Stopfen, *m.* stopper, plug, cork.

Stopfen, *n.* stuffing, cramming.

stopfend, constipating, stuffing, anastaltic, astringent, styptic.

Stopfmittel, *n.* astringent, styptic.

Stopfung, *f.* cramming.

Stopfwerg, *n.* oakum.

Stopfzelle, *f.* tylosis.

Stoppel, *f.* stubble; **-brache,** *f.* stubble fallow; **-rückstand,** *m.* stubble remains; **-weide,** *f.* stubble pasture.

Stöpsel, *m.* stopper, plug, cork; **-flasche,** *f.* stoppered bottle (or flask); **-hahn,** *m.* stopper cock, cock stopper.

stöpseln, to stopper, cork, plug.

Stör, *m.*-e, sturgeon.

Storax, *m.* storax.

Storch, *m.*ːe, stork.

Storchschnabel, *m.* stork's-bill; **-blättrig,** gernaifolious; **-gewächse,** *n.pl.* Geraniaceae; **-kraut,** *n.* crane's-bill (Geranium).

stören, to disturb, trouble, upset, derange, interrupt, annoy, stir; **sich ~,** to be disordered.

störrig, troublesome, obstinate, refractory.

störrisch, troublesome, obstinate, refractory.

Störung, *f.* disturbance, derangement, trouble, disorder, interruption.

Störungs-entwicklung, *f.* cenogenesis; **-frei,** undisturbed, uninterrupted; **-getriebe,** *n.* mirror-effect eliminator (in rayon manufacturing); **-gleichung,** *f.* perturbation equation; **-wert,** *m.* the effect of interruption or of stimulation.

Stoss, *m.-*e, impact, impulse, push, blow, thrust, stroke, shock, collision, percussion, jolt, recoil, bump, pile, file; **-dämpfer,** *m.* shock absorber.

Stössel, *m.* pestle, rammer, stamper.

stossempfindlich, sensitive to shock.

stossen, to push, hit, ram, knock, pound, pulverize, bray, join, slot, dash, thrust, recoil, come open.

Stösser, *m.* pestle, knocker, pounder.

Stoss-fänger, *m.* shock absorber, concussion spring, pressure equalizer; **-frei,** smooth; **-ionization,** *f.* ionization by collision; **-kette,** *f.* chain of collisions; **-querschnitt,** *m.* collision area; **-reizbarkeit,** *f.* sensitiveness to shock; **-reizung,** *f.* stimulation by shock or contact; **-stellung,** *f.* position (after stimulation through shock).

stösst (stossen), pushes.

Stoss-waffe, *f.* weapon for thrusting; **-weise,** by jerks, by fits and starts, percussively, successive; **-welle,** *f.* percussion (shock) wave; **-zahl,** *f.* number of collisions; **-zahn,** *m.* tusk; **-zünder,** *m.* percussion fuse.

stottern, to stutter.

stracks, straightway, directly.

Strafe, *f.* punishment, fine, penalty.

strafen, to punish, fine, reprove, rebuke, correct.

straff, tight, tense, stretched, rigid, taut.

straffen, to tighten, stretch.

Straffheit, *f.* tightness, severity, tenseness, tension.

Strafgeld, *n.-*er, penalty, fine, forfeit.

sträflich, criminal, wrong, punishable.

straflos, unpunished, guiltless, innocent.

Strafreiz, *m.-*e, punishment stimulus.

Strahl, *m.-*en, beam, ray, jet, lightning flash, straight line, radius, ciliary process, barbule; **-apparat,** *m.* jet apparatus; **-asbest,** *m.* plumose asbestos; **-baryt,** *m.* radiated barite; **-blende,** *f.* sphalerite, **-blüte,** *f.* ligulate flower.

strahlen, to emit rays, beam, radiate; **-art,** *f.* kind of rays; **-artig,** radiating; **-band,** *m.* (ciliary) ligament; **-brechend,** refracting, refractive; **-brechung,** *f.* refraction, diffraction; **-brechungsmesser,** *m.* refractometer; **-bündel,** *n.,* **-büschel,** *m.* tuft (pencil) of rays; **-empfindlichkeit,** *f.* susceptibility to radiation.

strahlend, radiating.

Strahlen-figur, *f.* radiating figure; **-filter,** *n.* ray filter; **-förmig,** radiated, actinomorphic; **-gattung,** *f.* kind of ray; **-geflecht,** *n.* circle of cilia; **-glimmer,** *m.* striated mica; **-kegel,** *m.* cone of rays; **-körper,** *m.* ciliary body; **-kranz,** *m.* corona ciliaris; **-krone,** *f.* corona ciliaris.

Strahlen-kupfer, *n.* clinoclasite; **-messer,** *m.* radiometer, actinometer; **-nervig,** palmately veined; **-parenchym,** *n.* medullary or pith rays; **-pilz,** *m.* ray fungus (Actinomycete); **-sonne,** *f.* astrosphere; **-strom,** *n.* ray current; **-vereinigung,** *f.* fusion of rays; **-werfen,** *n.* radiation.

Strahler, *m.* radiator cell (in photography).

Strahl-erz, *n.* clinoclasite; **-fäule,** *f.* thrush; **-furche,** *f.* commissure (cleft) of the frog; **-gips,** *m.* fibrous gypsum; **-hufbeinband,** *n.* phalangosesamoid ligament.

strahlig, actinormorphic, radiate(d).

Strahl-keil, *m.* belemnite; **-kies,** *m.* marcasite; **-krebs,** *m.* canker of the hoof; **-pumpe,** *f.* jet pump, injector; **-punkt,** *m.* radiating (radiant) point; **-quarz,** *m.* fibrous quartz.

Strahlschenkel, *m.* lateral or medial segment or branch of frog (hoof); **-spitze,** *f.* point of the frog (hoof of horse).

Strahl-schörl, *m.* radiated tourmaline; **-stein,** *m.* actinolite, amianthus; **-tiere,** *n.pl.* Actinozoa, Radiata.

Strahlung, *f.* radiation.

Strahlungs-druck, *m.* radiation pressure; **-vermögen,** *n.* radiating power; **-wärme,** *f.* heat of radiation, radiant heat.

Strahlzeolith, *m.* stilbite.

Strähne, *f.* skein, hank, strand.

stramm, tight, tense, strict, robust, rigid.

Strand, *m.-*e, seashore, beach, strand; **-ablagerung,** *f.* seashore deposit; **-formation,** *f.*

littoral formation; **-gebiet,** *n.* shoreland; **-gehölz,** *n.* littoral woodland; **-gewächse,** *n.pl.* littoral plants; **-hafer,** *m.* dune grass, *Ammophila arundinacea;* **-läufer,** *m.* sandpiper; **-nelke,** *f.* sea lavender (Limonium); **-pflanze,** *f.* seaside (littoral) plant; **-sumpf,** *m.* littoral meadow.

Strang, *m.⸚e,* rope, cord, vein, halter, skein, hank, vascular strand, bundle.

Strängchen, *n.* small rope or skein.

strang-farbig, dyed in the yarn; **-förmig,** stringy, strandlike; **-gewebe,** *n.* vascular tissue; **-parenchym,** *n.* wood parenchyma; **-presse,** *f.* extruding press; **-scheide,** *f.* bundle sheath; **-verbindung,** *f.* commissural strand.

Strapaze, *f.* hardship, toil.

Strasse, *f.* street, way, road, strait.

Strassen-ausbesserung, *f.* repair of roads; **-bahn,** *f.* street railway, tramway; **-bau,** *m.* road building; **-beleuchtung,** *f.* street lighting; **-bett,** *n.* roadbed; **-kehricht,** *m.* street sweepings; **-material,** *n.* road material; **-rinne,** *f.* drain, ditch, side gutter; **-unterhaltung,** *f.* road maintenance; **-walze,** *f.* road roller.

stratifizieren, to stratify.

Stratosphärenflug, *m.* flight into the stratosphere.

sträuben, to bristle, ruffle up, resist.

straubig, sträubig, rough, coarse, rebellious, resisting.

Strauch, *m.⸚er,* shrub, bush; **-artig,** shrublike, shrubby, fruticose, frutescent; **-bestand,** *m.* shrub community; **-birke,** *f.* dwarf birch tree; **-eiche,** *f.* scrub oak.

straucheln, to stumble, fail.

Strauch-flechte, *f.* fruticose lichen; **-holz,** *n.* underwood, brushwood.

strauchig, fruticose, bushy, shrubby.

Strauch-moor, *n.* moor covered with brushwood; **-schicht,** *f.* zone of brushwood; **-steppe,** *f.* xerophytic bushland; **-werk,** *n.* shrubbery; **-wuchs,** *m.* shrubby growth.

Strauss, *m.* bouquet, bush, tuft, crest, bunch, thyrsus, ostrich, combat, strife; **-ähnlich,** thyrsoid; **-blumig,** thyrsiflorous; **-farn,** *m.* ostrich fern (Onoclea); **-gras,** *n.* Agrostis; **-graswiese,** *f.* bunch-grass meadow.

Strebe, *f.* stay, prop, strut, brace, sleeper.

Streben, *n.* tendency, endeavor.

streben, to strive, struggle, press, aspire, tend.

Strebe-pfeiler, *m.* pier, buttress; **-zelle,** *f.* supporting (prop) cell, idioblast.

strebsam, industrious, active, aspiring, ambitious.

streckbar, extensible, extendible, ductile, malleable.

Streckbarkeit, *f.* extensibility, ductility.

Strecke, *f.* distance, section, space, stretch, extent, tract, line, reach (of a river).

strecken, to stretch, spread, extend, flatten, draw out, roll, dilute, lay low, lay (lie) down; **-teilchen,** *n.* linear element.

Strecker, *m.* stretcher, extensor muscle, glass flattener.

Streck-festigkeit, *f.* resistance to stretching; **-grenze,** *f.* yield point, elastic limit; **-metall,** *n.* expanded metal; **-mittel,** *n.* diluting agent; **-muskel,** *m.* extensor muscle; **-ofen,** *m.* flattening furnace; **-sehne,** *f.* extensor tendon; **-spinnen,** *n.* stretch (tension) spinning; **-stahl,** *m.* rolled steel.

Streckung, *f.* stretching, spread, elongation.

Streckungs-mittel, *n.* diluting agent; **-wachstum,** *n.* elongation, extension.

Streckwerk, *n.* rolling mill, rolls.

Streich, *m.-e,* stroke, prank, trick, blow, stripe; **-bar,** strokable, plastic; **-bürste,** *f.* paintbrush.

Streiche, *f.* spatula.

streichen, to stroke, rub, paint, varnish, grind, whet, strike, erase, cancel, knock off, stain, sleek, card wool, nap, scrape, scourge, migrate, spawn, spread butter, move, rush, sweep over, rove, roam, pass over; **-garn,** *n.* carded yarn.

Streicher, *m.* migratory bird.

streich-fähig, easy to brush; **-farbe,** *f.* staining color; **-fläche,** *f.* striking surface; **-garn,** *n.* seine, draw net; **-holz,** *n.* match; **-hölzchen,** *n.* match; **-instrument,** *n.* stringed instrument; **-kasten,** *m.* color tub; **-kraut,** *n.* dyer's rocket; **-lack,** *m.* brushing lacquer; **-masse,** *f.* friction composition (for matches); **-muster,** *m.* stained-paper pattern; **-netz,** *n.* seine, draw net; **-ofen,** *m.* reverberatory furnace; **-stein,** *m.* hone, touchstone; **-teich,** *m.* breeding pond; **-wurzel,** *f.* superficial (tracing) root; **-zeit,** *f.* time of migration, spawning season; **-zündhölzchen,** *n.* match.

Streif, -e, Streifen, *m.-,* band, fillet, strip, stripe, stria, streak, strap, vein, belt.

streifen, to scrape, stripe, striate, streak, flute, channel, strip off, touch on, wander, graze, ramble, glide, roam, stroll.

Streifen-hügel, *m.* corpora striata; **-krank-heit,** *f.* streak (stripe) disease; **-kohle,** *f.* banded coal; **-saat,** *f.* sowing in strips; **-spektrum,** *n.* band spectrum; **-weise,** in strips.

streifig, streaked, striated, striped.

Streif-jagd, *f.* battue; **-licht,** *n.* spotlight; **-schuss,** *m.* glancing or grazing shot.

Streifung, *f.* striping, striation.

Streifzug, *m.* excursion, expedition.

Streit, *m.* dispute, quarrel, strife, contest, combat.

streiten, to contend, dispute, struggle.

Streit-fall, *m.* matter in dispute, question at issue; **-frage,** *f.* contention, disputed question, moot point.

streitig, disputed, contestable, questionable.

Streitigkeit, *f.* contest, dispute.

streng, strenge, severe, rigorous, stern, harsh, strict, stiff, hard.

strengflüssig, difficultly fusible, refractory.

Strengflüssigkeit, *f.* viscosity, refractoriness.

strenggenommen, strictly speaking, in a strict sense.

Strenglot, *n.* hard solder.

Strepto-bazillus, *m.* streptobacillus; **-kok-kus,** *m.* streptococcus; **-mykosen,** *pl.* streptomycoses; **-tricheen,** *pl.* Strepto-tricheae.

Streu, *f.* litter; **halbverweste** ∼, mulch.

Streu-blau, *n.* powder blue; **-decke,** *f.* mulch cover.

streuen, to scatter, strew, spray dust, spread.

Streu-faden, *m.* fly waste, split filament; **-frucht,** *f.* dehiscent fruit; **-glanz,** *m.* brass powder; **-gold,** *n.* gold dust; **-gräser.** *n.pl.* grasses producing hay (for litter); **-kupfer,** *n.* copper rain; **-material,** *n.* bedding material; **-nutzung,** *f.* removal of forest litter; **-pulver,** *n.* powder for strewing or dusting; **-strahlung,** *f.* scattered radiation; **-sur-rogat,** *n.* substitute for litter.

Streuung, *f.* scattering, strewing, deviation, variation.

Streuungswinkel, *m.* angle of scattering.

Streu-vermögen, *n.* scattering power; **-wert,** *m.* erratic value, extent of scattering, standard value of deviation; **-zucker,** *m.* powdered sugar.

strich (streichen), stroked.

Strich, *m.*-e, stroke, streak, line, stria, stripe, dash, grain of wood, course, direc-tion, flock, brood, flight (migration) of birds, tract, zone, region; **einen** ∼ **durch etwas machen,** to cross off.

Strichelchen, *n.* stria.

stricheln, to streak, shade, mark with little lines, dot.

Strich-farbe, *f.* streak, color of the streak; **-gitter,** *n.* simple line grating; **-kultur,** *f.* streak culture; **-punkt,** *m.* semicolon; **-punktiert,** indicated by a dot-dash line; **-vogel,** *m.* migratory bird, bird of passage.

Strick, *m.*-e, rope, line, cord, string, snare.

stricken, to knit, net, reticulate.

strickförmig, cordlike, restiform.

Strickleiter, *f.* rope ladder; **-nervensystem,** *n.* ladderlike nervous system.

Strickware, *f.* knit goods.

Striegelhaar, *n.* strigose hair.

Striemen, *m.* vitta, frontal stripe, streak.

stritt, (streiten), disputed.

strittig, questionable, contested, in dispute.

Stroh, *n.* straw; **-blume,** *f.* everlasting; **-dach,** *n.* thatched roof; **-farbig,** straw-colored; **-flachs,** *m.* raw flax; **-gelb,** straw-yellow, stramineous; **-häcksel,** *m.* chopped straw, chaff; **-halm,** *m.* (a single) straw; **-hülse,** *f.* straw envelope or cover; **-hut,** *m.*-e, straw hat.

Stroh-kessel, *m.* straw boiler; **-matte,** *f.* straw mat; **-pappe,** *f.* strawboard; **-stein,** *m.* carpholite; **-stoff,** *m.* straw pulp; **-wüch-sigkeit,** *f.* luxurious growth of straw; **-zellstoff,** *m.* straw pulp; **-zeug,** *n.* pulp.

Strom, *m.*-e, current, stream, river, flow; **-abnehmer,** *m.* brush; **-abweichung,** *f.* variation of current; **-anzeiger,** *m.* current indicator; **-art,** *f.* kind of current; **-auf-nahme,** *f.* charging rate.

Strom-bahn, *f.* course of a stream or cur-rent, circuit; **-dichte,** *f.*, **-dichtigkeit,** *f.* current density; **-durchgang,** *m.* passage of current; **-einheit,** *f.* unit of current; **-empfindlichkeit,** *f.* susceptibility to current.

strömen, to pass, stream, flow, pour.

Strom-entnahme, *f.* consumption (with-drawal) of current; **-erzeuger,** *m.* current generator; **-feld,** *n.* field of current; **-fläche,** *f.* flow plane or line; **-führend,** conducting an electric current; **-ge-schwindigkeit,** *f.* velocity of current; **-in-dikator,** *m.* current indicator; **-induktion,** *f.* induction of currents; **-kreis,** *m.* circuit; **-lauf,** *m.* flow of current.

Strom-leiter, *m.* conductor; **-leitung,** *f.* conduction; **-los,** without current; **-losigkeit,** *f.* absence of current; **-menge,** *f.* amount (strength) of current; **-messer,** *m.* ammeter, amperemeter; **-quelle,** *f.* source of current; **-richtung,** *f.* direction of current; **-richtungsanzeiger,** *m.* polarity indicator; **-schluss,** *m.* closing of circuit.

Strom-schnelle, *f.* river rapids; **-schwankung,** *f.* fluctuation of current; **-spannung,** *f.* voltage of current; **-spule,** *f.* solenoid; **-stärke,** *f.* current intensity; **-stärkemesser,** *m.* galvanometer; **-stoss,** *m.* current impulse; **-umkehrer,** *m.* current reverser; **-umkehrung,** *f.* reversal of current.

Strömung, *f.* stream, current, streaming, flowing, flow, flood, flux.

Strömungs-bild, *n.* aspect of flow, flow net; **-blatt,** *n.* flat and attenuate submerged leaf; **-messer,** *m.* current meter, flow meter; **-sinn,** *m.* sense of current perception.

Strom-unterbrecher, *m.* circuit breaker; **-verbrauch,** *m.* consumption of current; **-verlust,** *m.* loss of current; **-wandler,** *m.* current transformer; **-wechsel,** *m.* alternation; **-wechsler,** *m.* commutator; **-wender,** *m.* current reverser, commutator; **-zeiger,** *m.* current indicator.

Strontian, *m.* strontia, strontium; **-erde,** *f.* strontia, strontium oxide; **-haltig,** containing strontia, strontianiferous.

Strontianit, *n.* strontianite, natural strontium carbonate.

Strontian-salpeter, *m.* strontium nitrate; **-zucker,** *m.* strontium sucrate.

Strontium-gehalt, *m.* strontium content; **-jodid,** *n.* strontium iodide; **-karbonat,** *n.* strontium carbonate; **-salpeter,** *m.* strontium nitrate; **-wasserstoff,** *m.* strontium hydride.

strotzen, to swell (up), be swollen, be puffed up.

Strudel, *m.*-, whirlpool; **-würmer,** *m.pl.* Turbellaria.

Struktur, *f.* texture composition, structure; **-chemie,** *f.* structural chemistry.

strukturell, structural.

Struktur-farbe, *f.* structural color; **-formel,** *f.* structural formula; **-identisch,** structurally identical; **-los,** structureless, amorphous; **-veränderung,** *f.* change of structure; **-viskosität,** *f.* intrinsic viscosity.

Strumpf, *m.* stocking, hose, mantle (of gas burner); **-band,** *n.* garter; **-waren,** *f.* hosiery.

Strunk, *m.*-̈e, stump, trunk, stem, stalk, stock.

struppig, shaggy, rough, bristly, scrubby.

Struppwuchs, *m.* stunted brushwood.

Stubben, *m.* stump; **-holz,** *n.* stumps; **-rodung,** *f.* stump grubbing.

Stubbfett, *n.* stub fat.

Stube, *f.* room.

Stubenfliege, *f.* common housefly.

Stuck, *m.* Stuccatur, *f.* stucco.

Stück, *n.*-e, piece, parcel, bit, lump, fragment, number, head (of cattle), piece (of artillery); **-arbeit,** *f.* piecework.

Stückchen, *n.* particle, little piece, bit, morsel.

stückeln, to cut to pieces, cut up.

Stückenzucker, *m.* lump (crushed) sugar.

Stück-erz, *n.* lump ore; **-färbemethode,** *f.* tissue-staining method; **-farbig,** dyed in the piece; **-färbung,** *f.* piece dyeing, staining in bulk, tissue staining; **-form,** *f.* lump form, gun mold; **-grösse,** *f.* size of piece; **-gut,** *n.* piece goods, parcel, gun metal; **-holz,** *n.* half-balks, billet wood.

Stuckgips, *m.* plaster of Paris.

stückig, in pieces, patched up, lumpy.

Stück-kohle, *f.* lump coal; **-lohn,** *m.* piece wages; **-metall,** *n.* gun metal; **-ofen,** *m.* bloomery furnace; **-preis,** *m.* price by the piece; **-waren,** *f.pl.* piece goods; **-weise,** piece by piece, piecemeal.

Stuckmörtel, *m.* stucco, badigeon, plaster mortar.

Studie, *f.* study.

studieren, to study.

Studierende, *m.* student.

Studium, *n.* study.

Stufe, *f.* step, degree, rank, grade, stage, story, gradient, gradation.

stufen-artig, steplike, graduated, gradual; **-folge,** *f.* succession of steps or stages, age gradation; **-förmig,** by steps; **-gesetz,** *n.* law of stages; **-grenze,** *f.* limit of altitude line; **-leiter,** *f.* stepladder, scale; **-reaktion,** *f.* successive reaction, stepwise reaction; **-rolle,** *f.* stepped roller; **-umkehr,** *f.* reversal (in plant successions); **-weise,** in stages, in stories, stepwise, by degrees, gradually.

stufig, sturdy, regular, graduated, having steps.

Stuhl, *m.*-̈e, chair, stool, seat; **-befördernd,** aperient, laxative; **-gang,** *m.* stool, discharge from the bowels; **-lehne,** *f.* back of a chair; **-zäpfchen,** *n.* suppository; **-züchtung,** *f.* isolation of bacteria from feces by culture.

Stukkateur, *m.* stuccoworker.

stülpen, to invert, turn upside down, turn inside out, put over or upon.

stumm, dumb, mute, silent, speechless.

Stummel, *m.* stump, stub, snag, knot, end; **-beine,** *n.pl.* prolegs of caterpillar; **-füsse,** *m.pl.* parapodia, prolegs.

stümmeln, to truncate, lop before felling.

Stummelpflanze, *f.* truncated plant.

Stumpf, *m.*≃e, stump, stub.

stumpf, blunt, obtuse, flush, dull; **-eckig,** blunt-cornered; **-kantig,** blunt-edged, obtuse-angled; **-kegel,** *m.* truncated cone; **-winklig,** obtuse-angled, blunt-edged.

stumpig, stumpy, stubby.

Stunde, *f.* hour, lesson.

stünde (stehen), were to stand, would stand, stood, stands.

Stunden-glas, *n.* hourglass; **-lang,** lasting for hours; **-plan,** *m.* timetable, schedule.

stündig, of an hour's duration, for an hour.

stündlich, hourly.

Stupp, *f.* stupp, mercurial soot; **-fett,** *n.* greasy hydrocarbon mixture obtained in refining stupp, stuff fat.

stürbe (sterben), were to die, would die, died, dies.

Sturm, *m.*≃e, storm, tumult, alarm, attack; **-fest,** stormproof; **-flut,** *f.* storm tide; **-hut,** *m.* monkshood, aconite.

stürmisch, stormy, turbulent, boiling.

Sturmschaden, *m.* damage by storm.

Sturz, *m.*≃e, drop, plunge, fall, overthrow, business failure, waterfall, slab, plate; **-acker,** *m.* new-plowed land; **-bett,** *n.* tumble bay, bucket of overflow weir; **-blech,** *n.* thin plate iron.

Stürze, *f.* lid, cover.

stürzen, to plunge, overturn, hurl, throw, dump, turn up, plow for the first time, rush, dash, fall, pour, smash, tilt, ruin, tumble down; **sich ~ auf,** to attack.

Sturzflamme, *f.* reverberatory flame.

Stürzgüter, *n.pl.* goods loaded in bulk, bulk load.

Sturzregen, *m.* intense rain.

Stute, *f.* mare.

Stutenmilch, *f.* mare's milk.

Stütz-apparat, *m.*≃e, supporting apparatus, support; **-balken,** *m.* shore or prop; **-blatt,** *n.* subtending bract; **-borste,** *f.* aciculum, supporting seta.

Stütze, *f.* support, stay, prop.

stutzen, to clip, top, crop, trim, shorten, truncate, curtail.

Stutzen, *m.*-, connecting pipe, connection, socket.

stützen, to support, prop, stay, rest, lean, be based.

Stütz-fläche, *f.* supporting surface; **-frucht,** *f.* supporting crop; **-gewebe,** *n.* supporting tissue; **-hypha,** *f.* sterigma, supporting hyphen.

stutzig, startled, perplexed, nonplussed.

Stutzkäfer, *m.pl.* Histeridae.

Stütz-lamelle, *f.* supporting layer, mesogloea; **-leiste,** *f.* S-shaped membrane above cell wall in glandular cells; **-mauer,** *f.* retaining wall; **-membran,** *f.* supporting membrane; **-mittel,** *n.* supporting medium; **-organ,** *n.* supporting organ.

Stutzpflanze, *f.* truncated plant.

Stützpunkt, *m.* point of support, fulcrum.

Stutzschere, *f.* pruning shears.

Stützsubstanz, *f.* supporting (fundamental) substance.

Stutzuhr, *f.* mantel clock.

Stütz-weite, *f.* span; **-wurzel,** *f.* prop root; **-zelle,** *f.* supporting cell.

subaerisch, subaerial.

Subchlorür, *n.* subchloride.

subdural, subdural.

Suberinsäure, *f.* suberic acid.

Subformation, *f.* facies, subformation.

Subhymenialschicht, *f.* subhymenium.

subjektiv, subjective.

subkutan, subcutaneous; **-präparat,** *n.* product for hypodermic injection.

Sublimat, *n.*-e, sublimate, mercuric chloride, corrosive sublimate.

Sublimationswärme, *f.* heat of sublimation.

sublimierbar, sublimable.

Sublimierbarkeit, *f.* sublimability.

sublimieren, to sublime, sublimate.

Sublimiergefäss, *n.* sublimation vessel.

Sublimierung, *f.* sublimation.

Submaxillarisgegend, *f.* submaxillary region.

subnormal, subnormal.

subordinieren, to subordinate.

Suboxyd, *n.* suboxide.

Subphosphorsäure, *f.* hypophosphoric acid.

Subsidien, *pl.* subsidies.

Subskription, *f.* subscription.

Substanz, *f.***-en,** substance, matter, reagent; **-brücke,** *f.* connecting bridge, isthmus; **-menge,** *f.* amount of substance; **-streifen,** *m.* strip of matter; **-verlust,** *m.* loss of substance.

Substituent, *m.* substituent, substitute.

substituierbar, replaceable.

substituieren, to substitute.

Substituierung, *f.* substitution.

Substitution, *f.* substitution.

Substrat, *n.* foundation, substratum, medium.

subtrahieren, to subtract, deduct.

successiv, successive.

Suchbewegung, *f.* orientation movement.

Suche, *f.* search, tracking game, quest.

suchen, to seek, search, look for, want, try, explore; ~ **zu,** to attempt, try to.

Sucher, *m.* seeker, searcher, finder, probe.

Such-licht, *n.* searchlight; **-spindel,** *f.* exploring spindle; **-spross,** *m.* seeker shoot.

Sucht, *f.* disease, sickness, epidemic.

Sud, *m.***-e,** boiling brew(ing), gyle, decoction, mordant, batch.

Süd, *m.* south.

Süden, *m.* south.

Sudhaus, *n.* boiling (brewing) house.

südlich, south, southern.

Sud-salz, *n.* (boiled) salt; **-seifenbad,** *n.* soap bath, suds.

südwarts, southward.

Sud-werk, *n.* boiling apparatus, brewing plant; **-wesen,** *n.* brewing.

süffig, palatable, bibulous.

Suffusion, *f.* suffusion, extravasation.

Sugillation, *f.* bruise, blood extravasation.

Suhle, *f.* wallowing place, puddle.

suhlen, to wallow in the mire.

sukzessiv, successive.

Sulf-amidsäure, *f.* sulphamic acid; **-antimonig,** thioantimonious, sulphantimonious; **-antimonsäure,** *f.* thioantimonic acid, sulphantimonic acid; **-arsenig,** sulpharsenious.

Sulfat, *n.***-e,** sulphate; **-haltig,** containing sulphate.

sulfatisieren, sulphatize.

Sulfat-rest, *m.* sulphate radical; **-stoff,** *m.* sulphate pulp; **-zellstoff,** *m.* sulphate cellulose, sulphate pulp.

Sulf-carbaminsäure, *f.* thiocarbamic acid; **-hydrid,** *n.* **-hydrat,** *n.* hydrosulphide.

Sulfid, *n.* sulphide; **-schwefel,** *m.* sulphide sulphur.

sulfieren, to sulphonate.

Sulfieren, *n.* **Sulfierung,** *f.* sulphonation.

Sulfin, *n.* sulphonium; **-säure,** *f.* sulphinic acid.

Sulfit, *n.* sulphite; **-cellulose,** *f.* sulphite pulp; **-lauge,** *f.* sulphite liquor; **-verfahren,** *n.* sulphite process; **-zellstoff,** *m.* sulphite (cellulose) pulp.

Sulfkohlensäure, *f.* sulphocarbonic acid.

Sulfo-azetat, *n.* sulphoacetate; **-base,** *f.*, **-basis,** *f.* sulphur base; **-carbonsäure,** *f.* sulphocarboxylic (sulphone-carboxylic) acid.

Sulfocyan-eisen, *n.* iron (ferric) thiocyanate; **-kalium,** *n.* potassium thiocyanate; **-sauer,** sulphocyanate of, thiocyanate of; **-säure,** *f.* sulphocyanic acid, thiocyanic acid; **-verbindung,** *f.* sulphocyanate, thiocyanate.

Sulfo-gruppe, *f.* sulpho group, sulphonic group; **-harnstoff,** *m.* sulphourea; **-hydrat,** *n.* hydrosulphide; **-lyse,** *f.* sulpholysis, sulphation; **-monopersäure,** *f.* permonosulphuric acid; **-persäure,** *f.* persulphuric acid; **-salz,** *n.* thio (sulpho) salt; **-säure,** *f.* sulpho acid; **-zyanat,** *n.* sulpho (thio) cyanate.

sulfonieren, to sulphonate.

Sulfon-säure, *f.* sulphonic acid.

Sulfthiokohlensäure, *f.* thiolthionocarbonic acid.

Sulfür, *n.* sulphide.

sulfurieren, to sulphonate, sulphurize.

Sulfürschwefel, *m.* sulphur in the form of sulphide.

Sulph . . . , see SULF . . .

Sulze, Sülze, *f.* brine, jelly, gelatin, pickled meat.

Sulzfleisch, *f.* pickled meat.

sulzig, sülzig, gelatinous.

Sumbulwurzel, *f.* sumbul root.

Summa, *f.* (*pl.* **Summen**) sum.

Summand, *m.* term of a sum, item.

summarisch, summary.

Summe, *f.* sum, amount.

summen, to hum, buzz, sum up, add.

Summen-gleichung, *f.* summation equation; -satz, *m.* principle or law of sums; -wirkung, *f.* combined effect.

Summer, *m.* buzzer, vibrator.

summieren, to sum up, add.

Summierung, *f.* summing up, summarizing.

Summton, *m.* (*dial.*) hum.

Sumpf, *m.* swamp, marsh, bog, pit, sump; -beere, *f.* swampberry; -boden, *m.* swampy ground; -dotterblume, *f.* cowslip (Caltha); -gas, *n.* marsh gas; -gebüsch, *n.* bush swamp; -gesellschaften, *f.pl.* association of marshlands; -heidelbeere, *f.* bog vaccinium; -huhn, *n.* marsh hen, rail.

sumpfig, swampy, boggy, marshy.

sumpf-liebend, marsh-loving, limnodophilous, uliginose; -moor, *n.* low moor, marshy ground; -moos, *n.* bog moss (Sphagnum); -mücken, *f.pl.* Limnobiinae; -nelke, *f.* water (purple) avens (*Geum rivale*); -otter, *f.* mink; -phase, *f.* semisolid phase; -pflanze, *f.* marsh plant; -schachtelhalm, *m.* marsh horsetail (*Equisetum palustre*); -schildkröte, *f.* pond turtle.

Sumpf-schnecke, *f.* Palundina; -silge, *f.* marsh parsley (*Peucedanum palustre*); -wald, *m.* bog; -wasser, *n.* marsh water; -wasserbazillen, *m.pl.* bacilli of marsh water; -wiese, *f.* swamp meadow; -ziest, *m.* marsh woundwort (*Stachys palustris*).

Sund, *m.*-e, sound, strait.

Sünde, *f.* sin.

Superazidität, *f.* hyperacidity.

superficiell, superficial.

Super-oxyd, *n.* superoxide, peroxide; -oxydhydrat, *n.* hydrated peroxide; -phosphat, *n.* superphosphate, hypophosphate; -ponieren, to superpose, superimpose; -saturieren, to supersaturate.

Suppe, *f.* soup.

surren, to hum, buzz.

Surrogat, *n.*-e, substitute; -stoff, *m.* pulp substitute.

suspendieren, to suspend.

süss, sweet, fresh.

Süsse, *f.* sweetness.

süssen, to sweeten.

Süsserde, *f.* beryllia, glucina.

Süssholz, *n.* licorice; -saft, *m.* extract of licorice; -zucker, *m.* glycyrrhizic acid.

Süssigkeit, *f.* sweetness, suavity, sweet.

süsslich, sweetish.

Süss-mandelöl, *n.* oil of sweet almonds; -säuerlich, sourish-sweet; -stoff, *m.* sweet substance, sweetening agent, saccharine.

Süsswasser, *n.* fresh water; -bewohner, *m.* fresh-water form; -fisch, *m.* freshwater fish; -polypen, *m.pl.* Hydridae; -schwämme, *m.pl.* Spongillidae; -sumpf, *m.* fresh-water swamp.

Suturfläche, *f.* suture.

S-Wert, *m.* quantity of dissociable bases.

Syenit, *m.* syenite.

Sylvanerz, *n.* sylvanite.

Sylvesterabend, *m.* New Year's Eve.

Sylvin, *m.* sylvite; -säure, *f.* abietic (sylvic) acid.

Symbasis, *f.* agreement, parallelism.

Symbiose, *f.* symbiosis.

Symmetrie-achse, *f.* axis of symmetry; -ebene, *f.* plane of symmetry.

symmetrisch, symmetrical, symmetric.

Sympathie, *f.* sympathy.

Symptom, *n.*-e, symptom.

synchron, synchronous.

Syndikat, *n.*-e, syndicate.

Synöken, *n.pl.* commensals.

Synovialdrüse, *f.* synovial gland.

Synthese, *f.* synthesis; -prozess, *m.* process of synthesis.

synthesieren, to synthesize.

synthetisch, synthetic, artificial.

syrup . . . , see SIRUP.

Systematik, *f.* systematics, taxonomy.

systematisch, systematic; systematische Changierung, *f.* controlled variation.

systolisch, systolic.

szintillieren, to scintillate.

T

Tabak, *m.* tobacco; -asche, *f.* tobacco ashes; -bau, *m.* cultivation of tobacco; -beize, *f.* tobacco sauce; -blatt, *n.* tobacco leaf; -brühe, *f.* tobacco sauce, juice; -fabrik, *f.* tobacco factory; -kampfer, *m.* nicotianin; -rauch, *m.* tobacco smoke; -saft, *m.* tobacco juice.

tabellarisch, tabular.

tabellarisieren, to tabulate, summarize.

Tabelle, *f.* table, summary, synopsis, index, schedule, chart.

Tablett, *n.*-e, tray.

Tablette, *f.* tablet.

Tablettiermaschine, *f.* preforming press.

Tabularknospung, *f.* tabular gemmation.

Tadel, *m.* fault, blame, reproof, rebuke; **-frei, -los,** faultless, perfect, irreproachable.

tadeln, to criticize, blame, reprove, censure.

Tafel, *f.*-n, table, tablet, plate, slab, sheet, cake, pane, slate, blackboard, chart, index, lamina, lamella; **-artig,** tabular, lamellar, laminar.

Täfelchen, *n.* tablet, little table, test chart, box shake.

Tafel-farbe, *f.* local (topical) color (of fabrics); **-förmig,** tabular, lamellar, laminar; **-geschirr,** *n.* tableware (service); **-glas,** *n.* sheet glass; **-land,** *n.* tableland.

tafelig, tabular.

tafeln, to dine, feast.

Tafellack, *m.* shellac.

täfeln, to floor, wainscot, panel, inlay.

Tafel-öl, *n.* olive oil; **-salz,** *n.* table salt; **-schiefer,** *m.* slate; **-spat,** *m.* tabular spar, wollastonite; **-waage,** *f.* counter (platform) scales; **-wasser,** *n.* mineral (drinking) water; **-werk,** *n.* wainscoting; **-wurzel,** *f.* buttress root, shallow root.

Taffet, Taft, *m.*-e, taffeta.

Taftpapier, *n.* satin paper.

Tag, *m.*-e, day.

Tage-bau, *m.* surface mining, open working; **-blatt,** *n.* daily paper; **-buch,** *n.* diary, journal; **-lang,** for days, all day long; **-lohn,** *m.* daily wages; **-löhner,** *m.* day laborer.

tagen, to dawn, hold a meeting, deliberate.

Tages-anbruch, *m.* daybreak, dawn of day; **-frage,** *f.* question of the day, immediate problem; **-licht,** *n.* daylight; **-lichwirkung,** *f.* daylight effect; **-periode,** *f.* daily periodicity; **-preis,** *m.* current price.

Tages-schlaf, *m.* diurnal position; **-schwankung,** *f.* daily fluctuation; **-senkung,** *f.* depression during the day; **-stellung,** *f.* pistrophe (of plastids); **-temperatur,** *f.* diurnal temperature; **-zeit,** *f.* daytime, hour of the day; **-zeitlich,** during the day.

Tagfalter, *m.* butterfly; **-blume,** *f.* flower pollinated by butterflies.

tägig, daily; **zweitägig,** for two days.

täglich, daily, diurnal, quotidian.

Tagfauenauge, *n.* peacock butterfly.

tags, on the day, in the daytime; ∼ **darauf,** on the day after; ∼ **über,** during the day; ∼ **zuvor,** on the day before.

Tagstellung, *f.* position during the day.

tagtäglich, daily, everyday.

Tagung, *f.* session, convention.

Tagwasser, *n.* surface water; **-ableitung,** *f.* surface drainage.

Takt, *m.*-e, time (music), beat, measure, tact, stroke.

Tal, *n.*ᵘer, valley; **-becken,** *n.* circular deep valley; **-boden,** *m.* valley floor, bottom.

Tälchen, *n.* small valley, furrow.

Talecke, *f.* corner of a valley.

Taler, *m.*-, thaler (three marks).

Talg, *m.* tallow, grease, suet, sebum; **-ähnlich,** tallowlike, sebaceous; **-art,** *f.* kind of tallow; **-artig,** tallowy, sebaceous; **-baum,** *m.* tallow tree; **-brot,** *n.* tallow cake; **-drüse,** *f.* sebaceous gland.

Talgehange, *n.* slope.

talgen, to tallow, grease.

talg-gebend, producing tallow, sebiferous; **-grieben,** *f.pl.* tallow cracklings, greaves of suet.

talgig, sebaceous, tallowlike, adipose.

Talg-kerze, *f.* tallow candle; **-licht,** *n.* tallow candle; **-säure,** *f.* stearic acid; **-schmelzen,** *n.* tallow rendering; **-seife,** *f.* tallow soap; **-stein,** *m.* soapstone; **-stoff,** *m.* stearin; **-zelle,** *f.* sebaceous cell.

Talhang, *m.* valley slope.

Talk, *m.*-e, talc, talcum; **-artig,** talcose, talcous; **-erde,** *f.* magnesia, magnesium oxide; **-hydrat,** *n.* brucite.

talkig, talcose, talcous.

Talk-pulver, *n.* talcum powder; **-schiefer,** *m.* slaty talc, talcose slate; **-spat,** *m.* magnesite; **-stein,** *m.* soapstone, steatite.

Tallöl, *n.* tall oil, talloel.

Talmulde, *f.* narrow valley.

Talsand, *m.* bottom sand; **-boden,** *m.* alluvial sand soil.

Tal-schlucht, *f.* glen; **-sohle,** *f.* valley floor, bottom; **-sperre,** *f.* dam; **-weg,** *m.* line connecting lowest points of a valley; **-wert,** *m.* minimum.

Tamarindenmus, *n.* tamarind pulp.

Tambour, *m.* drum, drummer.

Tang, *m.* seaweed.

Tangens, *m.* tangent (of an angle).

Tangentenbussole, *f.* tangent compass or galvanometer.

Tangentialschnitt, *m.* tangential section.

tangieren, to touch, be tangent to.

tanken, to refuel.

Tankwagen, *m.* tank car or wagon.

Tanne, *f.* fir tree, pine.

Tannen-baum, *m.* fir tree, pine tree; **-baumhaar,** *n.* abietiform hair; **-baumkristall,** *m.* arborescent crystal; **-bestand,** *m.* silver-fir wood; **-harz,** *n.* fir resin; **-krebs,** *m.* silver-fir canker; **-zapfen,** *m.* fir cone.

tannieren, to tan.

Tannin, *n.* tannin, tannic acid; **-bleisalbe,** *f.* tannate of lead ointment; **-lösung,** *f.* tannin solution; **-salbe,** *f.* tannin ointment; **-stoff,** *m.* tannin.

Tantal, *n.* tantalum; **-erz,** *n.* tantalum ore; **-verbindung,** *f.* tantalum compound.

Tanz, *m.⸗e,* dance, brawl.

tanzen, to dance.

Tapete, *f.* tapestry, wallpaper, hanging, tapetum.

Tapeten-papier, *n.* wallpaper; **-zelle,** *f.* tapetal cell.

tapezieren, to paper, hang with tapestry.

tapfer, brave, valiant, bold.

tappen, to grope, fumble.

täppisch, awkward, clumsy.

Tara, *f.* tare (deduction).

Tarier-schrot, *n.&m.* tare shot; **-waage,** *f.* tare balance.

tarnen, to camouflage.

Tarnieren, *n.* leaching (of metals).

Tarsal-fersenbeingelenk, *n.* calcaneocuboid articulation; **-knorpel,** *m.* cartilage of the tarsus.

Tarsen-geissel, *f.* tactile flagellum of tarsus; **-glied,** *n.* tarsal joint.

tartarisieren, to tartarize.

Tartrat, *n.* tartrate.

Tartronsäure, *f.* tartronic acid.

Tasche, *f.* pocket, pouch, bursa, ventricle, bag.

Taschen-ausgabe, *f.* pocket edition; **-band,** *n.* false vocal cord; **-buch,** *n.* pocketbook; **-format,** *n.* pocket size; **-klappe,** *f.* sigmoid (semilunar) valve; **-krebs,** *m.* common crab; **-larve,** *f.* coeluma; **-lupe,** *f.* pocket magnifier (lens); **-quallen,** *f.pl.* Peromedusae; **-tuch,** *n.* pocket handerchief; **-uhr,** *f.* watch; **-ventil,** *n.* semilunar valve.

Tasse, *f.* cup, cup and saucer.

tastbar, palpable, tangible.

Tastborste, *f.* tactile bristle.

Taste, *f.* key.

Tastempfindung, *f.* sense (sensation) of touch.

tasten, to touch, grope, feel, palpate.

Taster, *m.* palpus, feeler, calipers, antenna, dactylozooid; **-endglied,** *n.* last palpal segment; **-füsse,** *m.pl.* pedipalpi; **-karpalballen,** *m.* metacarpal (touch) pad; **-zirkel,** *m.* circular calipers.

Tast-gefühl, *n.* sense of touch; **-haar,** *n.* tactile hair; **-käfer,** *m.pl.* Pselaphidae; **-körper,** *m.* touch corpuscle, tactile body; **-polyp,** *m.* tactile polyp; **-reiz,** *m.* contact stimulus.

Tast-scheibe, *f.* tactile disk; **-sinn,** *m.* sense of touch; **-spitze,** *f.* palp; **-tüpfel,** *m.* tactile pit; **-vermögen,** *n.* tactile sense; **-versuch,** *m.* tentative (preliminary) experiment; **-werkzeug,** *n.* organ of touch; **-zirkel,** *m.* calipers.

tat (tun), did, was doing.

Tat, *f.-en,* action, act, deed, fact; **in der ~,** in fact, indeed.

Tatbestand, *m.* matter of fact, state of affairs, facts.

Täter, *m.* doer, perpetrator, author.

tätig, active, busy.

Tätigkeit, *f.* activity, action, occupation, function; **in ~ treten,** to function, become active.

Tätigkeitsempfindung, *f.* sensation of action.

Tatkraft, *f.* energy, pluck.

tatkräftig, energetic.

tätlich, actual, violent.

tätowieren, to tattoo.

Tätowierung, *f.* stencil mark, tattooing.

Tatsache, *f.* fact, datum.

Tatsachenstoff, *m.* factual material.

tatsächlich, actual, real.

Tatsächlichkeit, *f.* actuality.

Tatze, *f.* paw, claw.

Tau, *m.* dew.

Tau, *n.-e,* rope, cord, cable.

taub, deaf, numb, empty, sterile, barren; **tauber Samen,** *m.* unfruitful seed.

Taube, *f.* pigeon, dove.

Taubkohle, *f.* anthracite.

Taublatt, *n.* leaf for the absorption of dew (Drosophyllum).

Taubnessel, *f.* Lamium, blind nettle.

Tauch-anlage, *f.* dipping (steeping) plant; **-beize,** *f.* disinfection by immersion, steep; **-beizverfahren,** *n.* seed steep method, seed treatment; **-brenner,** *m.* immersion heater; **-element,** *n.* plunge cell.

tauchen, to dip, immerse, plunge, steep, soak.

Taucher, *m.* diver, diving birds.

Tauch(er)kolben, *m.* plunger (piston).

Tauch-flüssigkeit, *f.* dipping fluid; **-kolben,** *m.* plunger; **-kontakt,** *m.* immersion contact; **-korn,** *n.* sinker; **-mikrotom,** *n.* immersion microtome; **-pflanze,** *f.* submerged plant; **-tasse,** *f.* suction cup, pneumatic dashpot; **-waage,** *f.* areometer, hydrometer; **-wand,** *f.* baffle, water seal; **-zylinder,** *m.* plunge cylinder.

tauen, to taw, thaw, falling of dew, condense.

taugen, to be good or fit, or of value.

tauglich, good, fit, adapted, able, qualified.

tauig, dewy.

Taumel, *m.* reeling, staggering, giddiness, intoxication, frenzy, delirium; **-käfer,** *m.pl.* whirligig beetles (Gyrinidae); **-korn,** *n.* darnel (Lolium); **-loch,** *m.* bearded darnel, cockle.

taumeln, to reel, stagger, be giddy.

Taumelscheibe, *f.* wobble plate.

Taupunkt, *m.* dew point.

Taurochol-salz, *n.* taurocholate; **-säure,** *f.* taurocholic acid.

Tau-röste, *f.* dew retting; **-rösten,** to dew ret; **-rösterreger,** *m.* dew retting agent.

Tausch, *m.* exchange, barter.

täuschen, to deceive, delude, mislead, cheat.

Täuschung, *f.* deception, delusion, illusion.

Tausch-wert, *m.* exchange value, sale value, market value; **-zersetzung,** *f.* double decomposition.

tausend, thousand.

tausenderlei, a thousand kinds; ∼ **Dinge,** a thousand different things.

Tausend-füssler, *m.pl.* centipedes (Myriapoda); **-güldenkraut,** *n.* lesser centaury (Erythraea); **-künstler,** *m.* Jack-of-all-trades; **-schön,** *n.* English daisy (*Bellis perennis*).

tausendstel, thousandth part.

tautomer, tautomeric.

Tautomerie, *f.* tautomerism.

Tau-wetter, *n.* thaw; **-wurzel,** *f.* shallow root.

Taxation, *f.* valuation, estimate, survey.

Taxe, *f.* tax, duty, rate, price, valuation.

taxieren, to estimate, appraise, tax, assess.

Technik, *f.* arts, technic, technics, skill, industry, commerce.

Techniker, *m.* technical engineer, technologist, technician.

Technikum, *n.* technical college.

technisch, technical.

Technologie, *f.* technology.

Tee, *m.* -e,-s, tea; **-kräuter,** *n.pl.* herbs (used for infusion).

Teer, *m.* tar, pitch; **-artig,** tarry; **-asphalt,** *m.* coal-tar pitch, tar asphalt; **-ausscheider,** *m.* tar separator; **-ausschlag,** *m.* tar rash; **-baum,** *m.* Scotch pine (*Pinus sylvestris*); **-bitter,** *n.* picamar; **-brennerei,** *f.* tar factory; **-dampf,** *m.* tar vapor, fumes; **-destillation,** *f.* tar distillation.

teeren, to tar, form tarry matter.

Teer-farbe, *f.* coal-tar color, aniline color; **-farbstoff,** *m.* coal-tar dye; **-frei,** tar-free; **-hefe,** *f.* tar dregs.

teerig, tarry.

Teerkessel, *m.* tar kettle.

Teerose, *f.* tea rose (*Rosa indica*).

Teer-papier, *n.* tar (red) paper; **-pappe,** *f.* tarboard; **-prüfer,** *m.* tar tester; **-rückstand** *m.* tar residue; **-säure,** *f.* tar acid; **-scheider,** *m.* tar separator; **-schwelapparat,** *m.* apparatus for distilling tar; **-schwelerei,** *f.* tar distillation; **-wasser,** *n.* tar water; **-werg,** *n.* tarred oakum.

Tegel, *m.* impure clay (of gray-greenish color, sometimes slightly marly), marl.

Teich, *m.* -e, pond, tank, pool; **-bewohnend,** stocking of ponds; **-besatz,** *m.* stock of fish in a pond; **-wirtschaft,** *f.* pond pisciculture.

Teig, *m.* -e, paste, dough; **-artig,** pasty, doughy; **-farbe,** *f.* paste color; **-form,** *f.* form of dough or paste.

teigig, doughlike, pasty, mellow.

Teigware, *f.* paste article, dye in paste form.

Teil, *m.* -e, division, part, portion, section, party, volume, element, component; **zum** ∼, in part, partly; **zum grössten** ∼, for the most part; übrigbleibender ∼, remainder.

teilbar, divisible.

Teilbarkeit, *f.* divisibility.

Teilchen, *n.-*, small part, particle, atom, molecule, element; **-anhäufung,** *f.* aggregation (accumulation) of particles; **-grösse,** *f.* grain size, size of globules; **-ladung,** *f.* particle charge; **-verteilung,** *f.* distribution (dispersion) of particles.

Teil-cylinder, *m.* schizostele; **-druck,** *m.* partial pressure, part printing.

teilen, to divide, graduate, distribute, separate, sever, share.

Teiler, *m.* divider, divisor; **-explantat,** *m.* explant of part of an organism.

Teil-fläche, *f.* incremental area; **-frucht,** *f.* diachenium, mericarp (cremocarp); **-funktion,** *f.* partial (subsidiary) function; **-furchung,** *f.* partial cleavage; **-gebiet,** *n.* branch, department; **-haar,** *n.* component hair; **-haben,** to have a share in, take part, partake of; **-haber,** *m.* participator, partner; **-haft,** (*gen.*) partaking, sharing, participating; **-haftig,** (*gen.*) partaking, sharing, participating; **-gebiet,** *n.* branch.

Teil-kraft, *f.-¨e,* component force; **-kreis,** *m.* divided circle, lower plate of transit; **-nahme,** *f.* sympathy, interest, participation; **-nehmen,** to take part, participate; **-nuss,** *f.* carcerule (*pl.* Asperifoliae); **-organisation,** *f* constituent part; **-reaktion,** *f.* partial reaction.

teils, in part, partly.

Teilschwingung, *f.* partial vibration.

Teilstrich, *m.* division, graduation mark.

Teilung, *f.* division, distribution, graduation, partition, separation.

Teilungs-bruch, *m.* partial fraction; **-ebene,** *f.* plane of division; **-fähig,** capable of dividing; **-gesetz,** *n.* law of partition; **-koeffizient,** *m.* distribution coefficient; **-pol,** *m.* division center, attraction sphere; **-prozess,** *m.* process of division; **-zahl,** *f.* dividend; **-zeichen,** *n.* mark of division; **-zustand,** *m.* state of division.

Teil-vorgang, *m.-¨e,* partial process; **-wand,** *f.* division wall; **-weise,** partly, fractional, partial(ly); **-zahl,** *f.* quotient; **-zahlung,** *f.* part payment; **-zeichnung,** *f.* detail drawing; **-zylinder,** *m.* schizostele.

Tein,-Thein, *n.,* theine.

Teint, *m.-s,* complexion.

Tekholz, *n.* teakwood.

tektonisch, tectonic.

Telefunken, *m.* radio, wireless, wireless telegraph company.

Telegraphenstange, *f.* telegraph pole.

Teleobjektiv, *n.* telephoto lens.

Teleutospore, *f.* teleutospore, resting spore (Uredinales).

Teller, *m.-*, plate, dish, palm of the hand; **-eisen,** *n.* springtrap, trap; **-fuss,** *m.* plate-shaped base; **-rand,** *m.* disk edge; **-saat,** *f.* seed sown in patches; **-ventil,** *n.* disk valve; **-zinn,** *n.* plate pewter.

Tellur, *n.* tellurium; **-alkyl,** *n.* alkyl telluride; **-blei,** *n.* lead telluride; **-erz,** *n.* tellurium ore; **-gold,** *n.* gold telluride; **-halogen,** *n.* tellurium halide.

tellurig, tellurous; **-säureanhydrid,** *n.* tellurous anhydride.

Tellur-natrium, *n.* sodium telluride; **-ocher, -ocker,** *m.* tellurite; **-oxyd,** *n.* tellurium oxide; **-sauer,** tellurate; **-säure,** *f.* telluric acid; **-schwefelkohlenstoff,** *m.* tellurium carbon disulphide.

Tellur-silber, *n.* silver telluride; **-silberblende,** *f.* sylvanite, stutzite; **-verbindung,** *f.* tellurium compound; **-wasserstoff,** *m.,* **-wasserstoffsäure,** *f.* hydrotelluric acid, hydrogen telluride; **-wismut,** *n.* bismuth telluride.

Temperatur-abfall, *m.-¨e,* drop of temperature; **-änderung,** *f.* change of temperature; **-beobachtung,** *f.* temperature observation; **-bereich,** *m.* temperature range; **-einfluss,** *m.* influence of temperature; **-erhöhung,** *f.* rise in temperature.

Temperatur-gefälle, *n.* temperature drop; **-grad,** *m.* degree of temperature; **-grenze,** *f.* temperature limit or range; **-konstanz,** *f.* constant temperature; **-messer,** *m.* thermometer, pyrometer; **-messung,** *f.* taking (measuring) of temperature; **-mittel,** *n.* mean temperature.

Temperatur-regelung, *f.* temperature regulation; **-schwankung,** *f.* variation of temperature; **-sprung,** *m.* sudden change of temperature; **-steigerung,** *f.* rise in temperature; **-veränderung,** *f.* change of temperature; **-verhältnis,** *n.* condition or state of temperature; **-wechsel,** *m.* change of temperature; **-zunahme,** *f.* increase of temperature.

Temperguss, *m.-¨e,* temper cast, malleable iron casting.

temperieren, to temper, anneal.

Temperkohle, *f.* temper carbon, graphite.

tempern, to temper, anneal.

Temper-ofen, *m.* malleableizing oven; **-roheisen,** *n.* malleable pig iron.

Tempo, *n.*-s, **Tempi,** time, measure, movement.

temporär, temporary.

Tenakel, *n.*-, tenaculum, copyholder, filtering frame.

Tenazität, *f.* tenacity.

Tendenz, *f.* tendency.

Tenne, *f.* floor (of a barn).

Tensor, *m.* tensor; ∼ **des Vektors,** tensor of vector.

Tentakel-faden, *m.pl.* filaments of tentacle; **-kranz,** *m.* circle of tentacles.

Teppich, *m.*-e, carpet, rug, tapestry, table cover.

Terbinerde, *f.* terbia earth, terbium oxide.

Terebinsäure, *f.* terebic acid.

Terephtalsäure, *f.* terephthalic acid.

Term, *m.* electron term; **-folge,** *f.* sequence of term.

Termin, *m.*-e, term, date, time.

Terminal-blüte, *f.* terminal flower; **-faden,** *m.* filum terminale; **-knospe,** *f.* terminal bud; **-körperchen,** *n.pl.* tactile organs; **-organ,** *n.* terminal organ, terminal cell (nematodes).

Terminus, *m.* term.

Termite, *f.* termite, white ant (Termes).

ternär, ternary.

Terne, *f.* tern, combination of three numbers; **-blech,** *n.* terneplate.

Terpen, *m.* terpene; **-chemie,** *f.* chemistry of terpenes.

Terpentin, *m.* turpentine; **-art,** *f.* kind (variety) of turpentine; **-artig,** like turpentine; **-firnis,** *m.* turpentine varnish; **-geist,** *m.* spirits of turpentine; **-harz,** *n.* turpentine resin; **-öl,** *n.* oil of turpentine; **-ölseife,** *m.* turpentine-oil soap; **-salbe,** *f.* turpentine ointment; **-spiritus,** *m.* oil of turpentine.

Terpin, *n.* terpinol, terpin.

Terrain, *n.* ground; **-aufnahme** *f.* surveying.

terrestrisch, terrestrial.

Tertianfieber, *n.* tertian fever.

tertiär, tertiary; **-formation,** *f.* tertiary formation.

Tesseral-kies, *m.* skutterudite, smaltite, **-system,** *n.* isometric system.

Test, *m.*-e, test, cupel, test furnace; **-asche,** *f.* bone ash; **-gift,** *n.* test toxin; **-giftdosis,** *f.* dose of test toxin.

tetanisieren, to tetanize.

Tetanotoxin, *n.* tetanotoxin.

Tetanthren, *n.* tetrahydromethylaniline.

Tetanus-antitoxin, *n.* tetanus antitoxin; **-fall,** *m.* case of tetanus; **-heilserum,** *n.* antitetanic serum, tetanus antitoxin; **-impfung,** *f.* inoculation with tetanus; **-keime,** *m.pl.* spores of tetanus bacillus.

Tetra-chlorkohlenstoff, *m.* carbon tetrachloride; **-chlorzinn,** *n.* tin tetrachloride.

Tetrade, *f.* tetrad.

Tetra-eder, *n.* tetrahedron; **-edrisch,** tetrahedral; **-edrit,** *m.* tetrahedrite; **-fluorkohlen-stoff,** *m.* carbon tetrafluoride; **-gonal,** tetragonal; **-hexaeder,** *n.* tetrahexahedron; **-jodkohlenstoff,** *m.* carbon tetraiodide; **-sporenbildung,** *f.* tetrasporeformation.

Tetrinsäure, *f.* tetrinic acid.

Tetryl, *n.* tetranitromethylaniline.

teuer, *(dat.)* dear, costly, expensive.

Teuerung, *f.* dearth, famine, increase (in price).

Teuerungszuwachs, *m.* price increment, increment in value.

Teufe, *f.* depth.

Teufel, *m.* devil.

Teufels-dreck, *m.* asafetida; **-garn,** *n.* greater dodder (Cuscuta); **-kirsche,** *f.,* belladonna, deadly nightshade (*Atropa belladonna*); **-wurz,** *f.* aconite; **-zwirn,** *m.* boxthorn (*Lycium barbarum*).

Text-abbildung, *f.* illustration (in the text); **-abschnitt,** *m.* portion of text.

Textilwaren, *f.pl.* textile goods.

Thalleiochinreaktion, *f.* thalleioquin reaction.

Thalli-chlorid, thallic chloride; **-ion,** *n.* thallic ion; **-nitrat,** *n.* thallic nitrate; **-oxyd,** *n.* thallic oxide; **-sulfat,** *n.* thallic sulphate.

Thallium-alaun, *m.* thallium alum; **-bromür,** *n.* thallous bromide; **-chlorür,** *n.* thallous chloride; **-hydroxyd,** *n.* thallic hydroxide; **-hydroxydul,** *n.* thallous hydroxide; **-oxyd,** *n.* thallium oxide; **-oxydul,** *n.* thallous oxide; **-sulfür,** *n.* thallous sulphide; **-verbindung,** *f.* thallium compound.

Thalliverbindung, *f.* thallic compound.

Thallo-bromid, *n.* thallous bromide; **-chlorat,** *n.* thallous chlorate; **-chlorid,** *n.* thallous chloride; **-fluorid,** *n.* thallous fluoride; **-ion,** *n.* thallous ion; **-jodid,** *n.* thallous iodide; **-verbindung,** *f.* thallous compound.

Thallus, *m.* thallus; **-gehäuse,** *n.* amphithecium; **-rand,** *m.* mycelial margin (type of prothallus).

Thapsiasäure, *f.* thapsic acid.

Thema, *n.* **Themen, Themata,** theme, topic, subject.

Theoretiker, *m.* theorist.

theoretisch, theoretical, speculative.

Theorie, *f.* theory.

therapeutisch, therapeutic.

Therapie, *f.* therapeutics.

Thermen, *f.pl.* warm springs, thermal waters.

thermisch, thermal.

Thermit, *n.* thermite.

Thermo-chemie, *f.* thermochemistry; **-chemisch,** thermochemical; **-dynamisch,** thermodynamic; **-elektrisch,** thermoelectric; **-elektrizität,** *f.* thermoelectricity; **-element,** *m.* thermoelement, thermocouple; **-kauter,** *m.* thermocautery.

Thermometer, *m.&n.-*, thermometer; **-einbauten,** *m.pl.* built-in thermometers; **-kugel,** *f.* thermometer bulb; **-röhre,** *f.* thermometer tube.

thermo-metrisch, thermometric; **-paar,** *n.* thermocouple; **-säule,** *f.* thermoelectric pile; **-stat,** *m.* thermostat, warm box (incubator).

These, *f.* thesis.

Thiacetsäure, *f.* thioacetic acid.

Thioäther, *m.* thio ether.

thiocyan-sauer, thiocyanate of; **-verbindung,** *f.* thiocyanate.

Thio-essigsäure, *f.* thioacetic acid; **-germaniumsäure,** *f.* thiogermanic acid.

Thionfarbe, *f.* thion dye.

Thioninlösung, *f.* thionine solution.

Thiophtalid, *n.* thiophthalide

Thiopten, *n.* thiophthene.

Thioschwefelsäure, *f.* thiosulphuric acid.

Thiosulfat-Bakterien, *n.pl.* thiosulphate bacteria.

Thomas-(fluss)eisen, *n.* Thomas low-carbon steel; Thomas ingot iron; **-mehl,** *n.* Thomas meal (fertilizer); **-prozess,** *m.* basic Bessemer process; **-stahl,** *m.* Thomas low-carbon steel.

Thoracalschüppchen, *n.pl.* tegulae.

Thorax, *m.* thorax.

Thorerde, *f.* thoria, thorium oxide.

Thoriumverbindung, *f.* thorium compound.

Thylle, *f.* tylosis.

Thymian, *m.* thyme; **-öl,** *n.* oil of thyme.

Thymochinon, *n.* thymoquinone.

Thymol-krystall, *m.* crystal of thymol; **-phtalein,** *n.* thymol phthalein.

Thymus-drüse, *f.* thymus gland; **-läppchen,** *n.* thymus lobe.

tief, deep, profound, low, dark; **-bau,** *m.* deep workings; **-blau,** deep blue; **-blick,** *m.* penetrating glance, keen insight; **-braun,** dark brown; **-druck,** *m.* low pressure, intaglio, printing with a deep edge plate; **-druckgebiet,** *n.* region of low pressure.

Tiefe, *f.* depth, deepness, profoundness.

Tief-ebene, *f.* low plain, lowland; **-eingreifend,** penetrating.

tiefen, to deepen, hollow out; **-dimension,** *f.* perspective dimension, distance; **-gestein,** *n.* plutonic rock; **-region,** *f.* region of depth; **-schärfe,** *f.* depth of focus, sharpness of shadows; **-unterscheidungsvermögen,** *n.* power of differentiating depth; **-wahrnehmung,** *f.* perception of depth.

Tieferverlagerung, *f.* deeper shifting.

tief-gehend, deep, profound; **-gipfelig,** having a low apex; **-greifend,** far-reaching, fundamental, radical, deep-seated, penetrating, thoroughgoing; **-gruben (Boden),** to subsoil; **-gründig,** deep; **-gründigkeit,** *f.* deepness or depth of soil; **-kühlung,** *f.* intense cooling, low cooling; **-land,** *n.* lowland; **-liegend,** deep-seated (-lying), deeply situated; **-rot,** deep red.

Tief-ofen, *m.* soaking-pit furnace; **-punkt,** *m.* minimum point, low ebb, rock bottom; **-rund,** concave; **-schorf,** *m.* deep scab; **-schwarz,** deep black; **-seeschlamm,** *m.* deep-sea ooze, slime; **-sinnig,** deep thinking, thoughtful, melancholic; **-stellen,** to lower; **-wurzelnd,** deep-rooted.

Tiegel, *m.-*, crucible, pot, skillet, stewpan; **-brenner,** *m.* crucible maker; **-deckel,** *m.* crucible cover; **-einsatz,** *m.* crucible charge; **-flusstahl,** *m.* crucible-cast steel; **-form,** *f.* crucible mold; **-formerei,** *f.* crucible molding; **-futter,** *n.* crucible lining; **-giesserei,** *f.* casting in crucibles; **-guss,** *m.* casting in crucibles.

Tiegel-gusstahl, *m.* crucible-cast steel; **-hohlform,** *f.* crucible mold; **-ofen,** *m.*

crucible furnace; **-untersatz,** *m.* crucible stand; **-zange,** *f.* crucible tongs.

Tier, *n.***-e,** animal; **-art,** *f.* species of animal.

Tierarznei-kunde, *f.* verterinary medicine; **-mittel,** *n.* veterinary remedy.

Tier-arzt, *m.***-e,** veterinary surgeon; **-ärztlich,** veterinary; **-beschreibung,** *f.* zoography, zoology; **-blütler,** *m.pl.* plants pollinated by animals (Zoidiogamae); **-bude,** *f.* small menagerie; **-chemie,** *f.* animal chemistry.

Tierchen, *n.* animalcule.

Tier-faser, *f.* animal fiber; **-fett,** *n.* animal fat; **-fibrin,** *n.* animal fibrin; **-garten,** *m.* zoological garden, preserve, park; **-gattung,** *f.* genus of animals; **-geographie,** *f.*, zoogeography; **-gift,** *n.* animal poison, venom; **-haft,** animallike, referring to animals.

tierisch, animal, brutish, bestial.

Tier-keim, *m.***-e,** animal germ, embryo; **-kind,** *n.* animal offspring; **-kohle,** *f.* animal charcoal; **-körper,** *m.* animal body; **-kreis,** *m.* group of animals, zodiac; **-kunde,** *f.* zoology; **-milch,** *f.* animal milk; **-öl,** *n.* oleum animale; **-pflanze,** *f.* zoophyte, phytozoic plant; **-pfropfung,** *f.* animal grafting.

Tier-reich, *n.* animal kingdom; **-säure,** *f.* zoonic acid; **-schutzverein,** *m.* society for the prevention of cruelty to animals; **-stock,** *n.* animal colony; **-versuch** *m.* experiment on an animal.

Tiger, *m.***-,** tiger; **-auge,** *f.* tigereye.

Tiglinsäure, *f.* tiglic (tiglinic) acid.

tilgen, to extirpate, destroy, eradicate, cancel, annul, amortize, exterminate, erase, delete, extinguish, pay off.

Tilgung, *f.* destruction, eradication, effacement, amortization.

Timotheebazillus, *m.* timothy-grass bacillus.

tingibel, stainable.

tingieren, to stain, dye.

Tinktion, *f.* staining.

tinktoriell, tinctorial.

Tinktur, *f.* tincture.

Tinte, *f.* ink, tint, mess.

tinten-artig, inky, like ink; **-beutel,** *m.* ink bag (Cephalopodae); **-fass,** *n.* inkstand; **-fisch,** *m.* cuttlefish, sepia (Cephalopodae); **-fischschwarz,** *n.* sepia black; **-flasche,** *f.* ink bottle; **-fleck,** *m.* inkstain, inkspot; **-gummi,** *n.* (rubber) ink eraser; **-löscher,** *m.* blotter.

tintig, inky.

tippen, to touch gently, tap.

Tisane, *f.* tisane, ptisan.

Tisch, *m.***-e,** table, board, stage of a microscope.

Tischchen, *n.* little table.

Tisch-decke, *f.* tablecloth, table cover; **-geschirr,** *n.* tableware; **-leim,** *m.* strong glue.

Tischler, *m.***-,** joiner, cabinetmaker; **-leim,** *m.* joiner's glue, glue.

Tischplatte, *f.* stage plate (of microscope).

Titan, *n.* titanium; **-chlorid,** *n.* titanium chloride or titanium tetrachloride; **-eisen,** *n.* titaniferous iron; **-eisenerz,** *n.* titanic iron ore, ilmenite; **-eisensand,** *m.* titaniferous iron sand, ilmenite; **-erz,** *n.* titanium ore; **-fluorwasserstoffsäure,** *f.* fluotitanic acid; **-führend,** titaniferous; **-haltig,** containing titanium, titaniferous; **-nitrid,** *n.* titanium nitride.

titan-reich, rich in titanium; **-sauer,** titanate of; **-verbindung,** *f.* titanium compound.

Titanofluorwasserstoffsäure, *f.* fluotitanous acid.

Titel, *m.***-,** title; **-bild,** *n.* frontispiece; **-blatt,** *n.* title page; **-kopf,** *m.* heading.

Titer, *n.* denier, titer; **-abweichung,** *f.* denier variation; **-flüssigkeit,** *f.* standard solution; **-stellung,** *f.* standardization, establishment of titer; **-welle,** *f.* denier variation.

Titrage, *f.* titration.

Titration, *f.* titration.

Titrier-analyse, *f.* analysis by titration, volumetric analysis; **-apparat,** *m.* volumetric or titrating apparatus.

titrieren, to titrate.

Titrier-flüssigkeit, *f.* test solution, standard solution; **-methode,** *f.* volumetric method.

Titrierung, *f.* titration.

titrimetrisch, titrimetric, volumetric.

Tobel, *m.***-,** hollow, gully, gorge, ravine.

toben, to rage, rave, roar.

Tobsucht, *f.* madness, delirium, mania.

Tochter, *f.***-,** daughter; **-amöbe,** *f.* daughter amoeba; **-blase,** *f.* daughter vesicle, secondary cyst; **-chromosom,** *m.* daughter chromosome; **-cyst,** *m.* daughter cyst; **-kern,** *m.* daughter nucleus; **-segment,** *m.* daughter segment.

Tod, *m.***-e,** death; **-bringend,** deadly, fatal, mortal.

Todes-dosis, *f.* lethal dose; **-gabe,** *f.* fatal dose, lethal dose; **-krampf,** *m.* death convulsion; **-strahl,** *m.* death ray; **-ursache,** *f.* cause of death.

tödlich, lethal, deadly, fatal.

Toilettenseife, *f.* toilet soap.

Tokaierwein, *m.* Tokay wine.

toll, nonsensical, mad, foolish, raving, droll, comical; **-beere,** *f.*, **-kirsche,** *f.* belladonna, deadly nightshade (*Atropa belladonna*); **-kühn,** foolhardy; **-sucht,** *f.* delirium, raving madness; **-wut,** *f.* rabies, hydrophobia; **-wutgift,** *n.* rabies virus.

Tolu-balsam, *m.* balsam of tolu; **-chinon,** *n.* toluquinone.

Toluol, *m.* toluene; **-süss,** *n.* saccharin.

Tolu-sirup, *m.* sirup of tolu; **-tinktur,** *f.* tincture of tolu.

Toluylenrot, *n.* toluylene red.

Toluylsäure, *f.* toluic acid.

Tomate, *f.* tomato.

Tomaten-fruchtfäule, *f.* tomato fruit rot; **-krebs,** *m.* tomato canker.

Ton, *m.*-e, clay.

Ton, *m.*-̈e, tone, note, sound, strain, key, tune, tint, fashion; **einfacher** $\sim$, sinusoidal sound wave, simple note.

ton-angebend, setting the fashion, leading; **-art,** *f.* kind of clay, musical pitch, nature of sound; **-artig,** clayey, argillaceous; **-aufschluss,** *m.* clay decomposition; **-aufzeichnung,** *f.* sound recording; **-bad,** *n.* toning bath; **-beize,** *f.* red liquor; **-bildnerei,** *f.* ceramics; **-boden,** *m.* clay soil; **-brei,** *m.* clay (slip) pulp.

ton-eisenhaltig, argilloferruginous; **-eisenstein,** *m.* clay ironstone.

tonen, to tone (a photograph).

tönen, to sound, resound, ring, tone, tint.

Tonerde, *f.* alumina, argillaceous earth, aluminum oxide; **-beize,** *f.* red liquor; **-haltig,** aluminiferous; **-hydrat,** *n.* alumina hydrate; **-reich,** argillaceous, rich in alumina; **-sulfat,** *n.* aluminum sulphate.

tönern, argillaceous.

ton-farbig, clay-colored; **-fenster,** *n.* sound slit; **-film,** *m.* sound-camera film; **-filter,** *n.* clay filter; **-gemisch,** *n.* sound composed of many frequencies; **-geschirr,** *n.* pottery, earthenware; **-gips,** *m.* argillaceous gypsum; **-haltig,** argillaceous; **-höhe,** *f.* pitch of a note.

tonicht, tonig, argillaceous, clayey.

tonisch, tonic.

Tonkabohne, *f.* tonka bean.

Ton-kalk, *m.* argillaceous limestone; **-kerze,** *f.* clay filter candle; **-kunst,** *f.* music, science of sound; **-lager,** *n.* clay bed; **-leiter,** *f.* scale; **-masse,** *f.* paste, clay mass; **-mergel,** *m.* clay marl; **-mühle,** *f.* clay (pug) mill.

Tönnchen, *n.* small cask, keg; **-puppe,** *f.* puparium.

Tonne, *f.* tun, cask, barrel, ton (1000 kilograms).

tonnenförmig, barrel-shaped.

Ton-papier, *n.* toned paper, tinted paper; **-platte,** *f.* toned plate; **-reiniger,** *m.* stone separator; **-retorte,** *f.* clay retort; **-schiefer,** *m.* clay slate; **-schneider,** *m.* clay (pug) mill, clay cutter.

Tonsille, *f.* tonsil.

Ton-speise, *f.* clay mortar; **-scherbe,** *f.* pottery fragment; **-steppe,** *f.* clay prairie; **-tiegel,** *m.* clay crucible; **-waren,** *f.pl.* earthenware; **-zelle,** *f.* clay cell.

Tönung, *f.* tone.

Topas, *m.*(s)e, topaz; **-fluss,** *m.* artificial topaz; **-schörlit,** *m.* pycnite, columnar topaz.

Topf, *m.*-̈e, pot, jar.

Töpfchen, *n.* small pot, mug.

Topfdeckel, *m.* lid of a pot.

Töpfer, *m.* potter.

Topferde, *f.* potting earth.

Töpferei, *f.* pottery, ceramics.

Töpfer-erde, *f.* potter's earth, clay; **-erz,** *n.* potter's ore, alquifou; **-mühle,** *f.* pottery color, ceramic color; **-geschirr,** *n.* pottery; **-gut,** *n.* potter's ware.

töpfern, earthen, made of clay.

Töpfer-scheibe, *f.* potter's wheel; **-ton,** *m.* potter's clay; **-ware,** *f.* pottery.

Topf-giesserei, *f.* casting of pots, making of crucible steel; **-glasur,** *f.* potter's varnish, earthenware glaze; **-mühle,** *f.* barrel mill; **-pflanze,** *f.* pot plant; **-pflanzenkultur,** *f.* pot-plant culture; **-scherbe,** *f.* potsherd; **-stärke,** *f.* volume; **-versuch,** *m.* pot experiment.

topisch, topical, local.

Tor, *m.*-en, fool.

Tor, *n.*-e, gate, bar.

Torf, *m.* peat, turf; **-artig,** like peat, peaty; **-asche,** *f.* peat ashes; **-boden,** *m.* peat soil; **-eisenerz,** *n.* bog iron ore; **-erde,** *f.* peaty soil; **-geschmack,** *m.* peaty flavor; **-gewinnung,** *f.* peat cutting; **-graben,** to dig out for peat making; **-kohle,** *f.* peat (charcoal) fuel.

Torf-lager, *n.* peat layer, turf bed; **-leber,** *f.* hepatic peat; **-moor,** *n.* peat moor or bog; **-moos,** *n.* peat (sphagnum) moss; **-moose,** *n.pl.* Sphagnaceae; **-mull,** *n.* ground peat, peat dust; **-stechen,** to cut (dig) turf; **-stich,** *m.* turf cutting; **-streu,** *f.* peat litter.

Torgummi, *n.* Bassora gum.

Torheit, *f.* foolishness, folly.

töricht, foolish silly.

Torkretputz, *m.* (coat of) gunite.

torquieren, to twist.

Torsions-festigkeit, *f.* torsional strength, torque; **-waage,** *f.* torsion balance; **-winkel,** *m.* angle of torsion.

Tort, *m.* wrong, injury.

Torte, *f.* tart, fancy cake.

Tosbecken, *n.* stilling basin.

tot, dead, rotten; **sich ~ stellen,** to pretend to be dead; **toter Gang,** *m.* lost motion, backlash, play; **toter Punkt,** *m.* dead point.

Totalexplantat, *m.* explant of whole organism.

totbrennen, to overburn, deadburn.

Totalitätshieb, *m.* incidental felling, damage cutting.

töten, to kill, slay, deaden (soften) colors.

Toten-blume, *f.* marigold (*Calendula officinalis*); **-farbe,** *f.* livid color, deadly pallor; **-geruch,** *m.* cadaveric odor; **-gesellschaften,** *f.pl.* dead associations; **-gräber,** *m.* burying beetle (Necrophorus); **-kopf,** *m.* death's-head, hawk moth (*Caput mortuum*), calcothar.

Töter, *m.* killer, extinguisher.

tot-gar, overrefined; **-geboren,** stillborn; **-gegerbt,** overtanned.

tötlich, deadly, mortal, lethal, fatal.

Tot-mahlen, *n.* disaggregating, overgrinding, overmilling, overbeating; **-punkt,** *m.* dead center; **-reife,** *f.* dead ripeness, black ripe.

touchieren, to touch, examine.

Tour, *f.* turn, tour, revolution, round.

Touren-zahl, *f.* number of turns; **-zähler,** *m.* speed indicator.

Tourill, *m.* bombonne.

Tournantöl, *n.* rank olive oil.

Toxamie, *f.* toxemia.

Toxicität, *f.* toxicity.

toxikologisch, toxicological.

Toxin, *n.* toxin; **-bindend,** toxin-binding.

toxisch, toxic.

Toxizität, *f.* toxicity.

Toxoid, *n.* toxoid.

Toxophoregruppe, *f.* toxophore group.

Trabant, *m.* -en, footman, satellite.

Trabeculagewebe, *n.* lacunar tissue.

Trachea, *f.* windpipe, trachea.

tracheenkieme, *f.* tracheal gill.

Tracheide, *f.* tracheid.

Tracheidensäume, *m.pl.* transfusion tissue.

Trachom, *n.* trachoma.

Tracht, *f.*-en, costume, fashion, load, prop, support, crop, charge, pregnancy, litter (puppies).

trachten, to strive, aspire, try.

trächtig, pregnant, gravid.

Trächtigkeit, *f.* pregnancy, gestation.

traf (treffen), met, hit.

Tragant, *m.* tragacanth (Astragalus); **-gummi,** *n.* gum tragacanth; **-pflanze,** *f.* Astragalus; **-stoff,** *m.* bassorin.

Trag-ast, *m.* subtending (supporting) branch; **-bahre,** *f.* stretcher, litter; **-band,** *n.* strap, suspender, suspensory bandage, truss.

tragbar, portable, fruit-bearing, productive, wearable, bearable.

Tragbarkeit, *f.* productivity, transportability.

Tragblatt, *n.* subtending leaf.

träge, lazy, idle, inactive, inert, sluggish, dull.

tragecht, fast to wearing.

Tragebalken, *m.* beam.

tragen, to bear, wear, carry, subtend, support, uphold, yield, produce, endure, suffer, be with young; **sich mit etwas** (herum) **~,** to be preoccupied with something; **Rechnung ~,** to take into account.

Träger, *m.* carrier, wearer, bearer, the atlas, supporter, truss, support, vehicle; **-frequenz,** *f.* carrier frequency (in photography, color).

Trägerin, *f.* female carrier of disease.

Trag-fähigkeit, *f.* productiveness, capacity, bearing strength, buoyancy, tonnage, load-bearing capacity; **-fläche,** *f.* airfoil; **-gas,** *n.* buoyant (supporting) gas.

Trägheit, *f.* laziness, idleness, inertness, inertia, sluggishness, inactivity.

Trägheits-mittelpunkt, *m.* center of inertia; -moment, *n.* moment of inertia; -radius, *m.* radius of gyration; -vermögen, *n.* inertia.

Trag-knospe, *f.* bearing (inflorescence) bud; -kraft, *f.* bearing power, productiveness, transverse strength, carrying capacity; -last, *f.* highest working load, peak load.

Tragödie, *f.* tragedy.

Trag-rand, *m.* basal border of wall (of hoof), margo solearis; -schale, *f.* pan, cup.

trägt (tragen), carries, wears.

Trag-vermögen, *n.* buoyancy; -weite, *f.* range, importance, significance; -zapfenreibung, *f.* journal-bearing friction; -zeit, *f.* gestation period, duration of pregnancy.

Tragzelle, *f.* stalk cell.

Trajekt, *m.*-e, path, course.

trainieren, to train.

Traktat, *m.*-e, treatise, tract, treaty.

traktieren, to treat.

Trambahn, *f.* tramway.

Trampelklette, *f.* bur fruit crushed and distributed by stamping of feet.

Tran, *m.* train oil, blubber, whale oil.

Träne, *f.* tear.

Tränen-ableitung, *f.* draining away of tears; -ableitungsgang, *m.* lachrymal passage; -bein, *n.* lachrymal bone; -drüse, *f.* lachrymal gland; -erregend, causing to weep, lachrymose; -feuchtigkeit, *f.* lachrymal fluid; -fistel, *f.* lachrymal fistula; -fluss, *m.* epiphora, dacryoma, flow of tears; -flüssigkeit, *f.* lachrymal fluid; -fortsatz, *m.* lachrymal apophysis; -furche, *f.* lachrymal groove.

Tränen-gang, *m.* lachrymal duct; -gefäss, *n.* lachrymal vessel; -grube, *f.*, -höhle, *f.* lachrymal fossa; -hügel, *m.* lachrymal protuberance (caruncle); -kamm, *m.* crest of lachrymal bone; -kanal, *m.* lachrymal canal; -knochen, *m.* lachrymal bone; -nasengang, *m.* nasal bone, nasal duct; -nasenrinne, *f.* lachrymal (nasal) groove; -punkt, *m.* lachrymal point; -rinne, *f.* lachrymal groove; -röhrchen, *n.* lachrymal canal.

Tränensack, *n.* lachrymal sac; -grund, *m.* base of lachrymal sac; -klappe, *f.* valve of lachrymal sac.

Tränen-schlauch, *m.* lachrymal duct; -see, *m.* lachrymal lake; -warze, *f.* lachrymal

papilla; -wasser, *n.* lachrymal fluid; -weg, *m.* lachrymal duct; -werkzeug, *n.* lachrymal apparatus.

tranig, resembling train oil, greasy.

trank (trinken), drank, was drinking.

Trank, *m.*-e, drink, beverage, potion, decoction.

Tränkchen, *n.* draft, physic.

Tränke, *f.* watering (place).

tränken, to give to drink, steep, soak, impregnate, suckle, saturate, water.

Tränkkessel, *m.* steeping (impregnating) vessel.

Tränkung, *f.* saturation, steeping.

Tränkungsmittel, *n.* impregnating substance.

Tran-leder, *n.* leather dressed with train oil; -schmiere, *f.* daubing; -seife, *f.* fish-oil soap.

Transformator, *m.* transformer.

Transfusionsgewebe, *n.* transfusion tissue.

Transiederei, *f.* blubber-boiling works.

Transkörper, *m.* trans substance.

Translation, *f.* transposition.

Transpeck, *m.* blubber.

Transpirationseinschränkung, *f.* retardation of transpiration.

transplantabel, transplantable.

Transplantat, *n.* graft.

transplantieren, to transplant, graft.

Transport, *m.*-e, transportation, transfer, conveyance, shipment.

Trans-porteur, *m.* transporter, carrier, conveyor, protractor; -portflasche, *f.* carboy; -stellung, *f.* transposition.

Transversal-blatt, *n.* median leaf of lateral shoot; -ebene, *f.* transverse (cross-sectional) plane; -schwingungen, *f.pl.* transversal vibrations.

Trantrester, *m.pl.* blubber residue.

Trapez, *n.*-e, trapeze, trapezium, trapezoid.

Trapezoeder, *n.* trapezohedron.

Trapezoid, *n.* trapezium.

Trapp, *m.*-e, trap(rock).

Trappe, *f.* footstep, track, trap; *m.* bustard.

trappeln, to patter, stamp, trot.

trappen, to trample.

Trass, *m.* trass, vulcanic tuff.

trassieren, to trace, mark out, draw (a bill);

trat (treten), stepped.

Tratte, *f.* draft, bill of exchange.

Traube, *f.* raceme, grape, bunch of grapes, cluster.

Trauben-abfall, *m.*-̈e, husks (of grapes); **-ähnlich,** like grapes, botryoidal; **-artig,** in clusters, racemose; **-beere,** *f.* grape; **-blei,** *n.* mimetite, pyromorphite; **-blumig,** racemiflorous; **-blütig,** racemiflorous; **-drüse,** *f.* racemose gland; **-förmig,** aciniform, racemose, in clusters; **-haut,** *f.* oveour coat, grape skin.

Trauben-kern, *m.* grape seed, grapestone; **-kirsche,** *f.* bird cherry (*Prunus padus*); **-kokkus,** *m.* staphylococcus; **-kraut,** *n.* sea wormwood (Artemisia); **-lese,** *f.* vintage; **-most,** *m.* grape must; **-saft,** *m.* grape juice; **-sauer,** racemate of; **-säure,** *f.* racemic acid; **-schimmel,** *m.* Botrytis.

trauben-tragend, grape-bearing, racemiferous; **-vitriol,** *m.* copperas; **-wickel,** *m.* botryose cyme; **-wickler,** *m.* cochylis (vine) moth (*Conchylis ambiguella*).

Traubenzucker, *m.* grape sugar; **-agar,** *m.* glucose agar; **-gelatine,** *f.* glucose gelatin; **-lösung,** *f.* solution of grape sugar.

traubig, bearing grapes, botryoidal, racemose.

trauen, (*dat.*) to trust, confide, rely, marry.

Trauer, *f.* mourning, sorrow, grief; **-birke,** *f.* weeping birch (*Betula pendula*); **-blumengewächse,** *n.pl.* Diapensiaceae; **-buche,** *f.* weeping birch; **-form,** *f.* drooping habit.

trauern, to mourn, grieve.

Trauer-spiel, *n.* tragedy; **-weide,** *f.* weeping willow (*Salix babylonica*).

Trauf, *m.* border, edge, gutter.

Traufe, *f.* eaves, drip, gutter, trough.

träufeln, to drip, drop, trickle, fall in drops, ooze.

Träufelspitze, *f.* attenuated leaf tip (providing for drainage of water).

Traufwasser, *n.* dripping (rain)water.

traulich, intimate, confidential, cordial, cozy, snug.

Traum, *m.*-̈e, dream.

traumatisch, traumatic.

träumen, to dream.

Träumerei, *f.* dreaming, reverie, musing.

traurig, sad, grieved, melancholy, depressed, wretched.

Treber, *f.* spent residue, husks, draff, brewer's grains; **-branntwein,** *m.* marc brandy.

treffen, to hit, strike, take effect, find, touch, concern, meet with, be right, provide, happen, make (preparations); **sich getroffen fühlen,** to feel hurt; **Vorkehrungen für etwas** ~, to make provisions (preparations) for something; **eine Entscheidung** ~, to come to a decision, decide upon.

Treffen, *n.* combat, engagement, action.

treffend, striking, suitable, appropriate.

Treffer, *m.* hit, success, prize.

trefflich, admirable, excellent, choice, exquisite.

Treffpunkt, *m.*-e, point of impact.

Treib-arbeit, *f.* cupellation; **-asche,** *f.* cupel ashes, bone ash; **-brühe,** *f.* old liquor; **-eisen,** *n.* white pig iron.

treiben, to drive, sprout, drift, force, propel, sublime, impel, refine, raise, work, hammer, put forth (leaves), practice, carry on, work at, stimulate, promote, circulate, ferment.

Treiben (der Knospen), *n.* bursting (of buds), gemmation.

Treiber, *m.* driver, propeller, beater, refiner.

Treibfrucht, *f.* fruit disseminated by water currents; **-laubfall,** *m.* partial leaf fall before new buds open; **-mist,** *f.* heating manure; **-pflanze,** *f.* forced (greenhouse) plant; **-samen,** *m.* seed disseminated by water currents; **-stoff,** *m.* substance that breaks the rest period.

Treib-gas, *n.* propellant gas, motor fuel; **-haus,** *n.* hothouse; **-herd,** *m.* refining hearth; **-holz,** *n.* nurse trees, driftwood; **jagd,** *f.* battue, game drive; **-kraft,** *f.* motive power; **-ladung,** *f.* propelling charge; **-mittel,** *n.* purgative, propellant, evacuant; **-ofen,** *m.* refining (cupeling) furnace; **-öl,** *n.* motor (fuel) oil.

Treib-prozess, *m.* cupellation; **-riemen,** *m.* driving belt; **-scherben,** *n.* cupel; **-schwefel,** *m.* native sulphur; **-verfahren,** *n.* method of forcing.

treideln, to tow.

trennbar, separable, divisible.

trennen, to separate, divide, sever, dissolve, resolve, decompose, disconnect.

trenn-scharf, selective; **-schärfe,** *f.* selectivity; **-schicht,** *f.* separating (abscission) layer.

Trennung, *f.* separation, division, segregation, shearing.

Trennungs-fläche, *f.* cleavage, (parting) plane, surface of separation; **-linie,** *f.* line of demarcation; **-mittel,** *n.* means of separation; **-phelloid,** *n.* periderm (Ulmus) (Acer); **-schicht,** *f.* abscission layer; **-strich,** *m.* line of separation, hyphen; **-verfahren,** *n.* separation process; **-vermögen,** *n.* separating power; **-vorgang,** *m.* separation process; **-wärme,** *f.* heat of separation or decomposition.

Treppe, *f.* staircase, stairs, scala.

Treppen-absatz, *m.* landing; **-förmig,** scalariform, ladder-shaped, stepped; **-gang,** *m.* scala (of cochlea); **-gefäss,** *n.* scalariform vessel; **-hoftüpfel,** *m.* scalariform bordered pit; **-rost,** *m.* step grate; **-stufe,** *f.* step, stair; **-tracheide,** *f.* scalariform tracheid.

Tresor, *m.*-e, treasury; **-stahl,** *m.* steel for safes.

Trespe, *f.* brome grass (Bromus).

Trester, *m.pl.* residue, grounds, husks; **-branntwein,** *m.* grape-marc brandy.

treten, to tread, step, trample, go, walk, advance, come, pass, enter, kick; **ans Licht** ~, to come to light; **an ihre Stelle** ~, to take their place.

Tretgebläse, *n.* foot blower (bellows).

treu, (*dat.*) true, loyal, faithful; **-bruch,** *m.* breach of faith, disloyalty.

Treue, *f.* faithfulness, fidelity, loyalty, sincerity.

Triakisoktaeder, *n.* triakisoctahedron.

Triazojodid, *n.* triazoiodide, iodine azide.

Tribolumineszenz, *f.* triboluminescence.

Tribüne, *f.* platform, rostrum.

Tricalciumphosphat, *n.* tricalcium phosphate.

Tricarbonsäure, *f.* tricarboxylic acid.

Trichlor-aldehyd, *n.* trichloroacetic aldehyde; **-essigsäure,** *f.* trichloroacetic acid; **-methan,** *n.* trichloromethane, chloroform; **-milchsäure,** *f.* trichlorolactic acid.

Trichromsäure, *f.* trichromic acid.

Trichter, *m.*-, funnel, cone, infundibulum, hopper, siphon; **-artig,** funnel-shaped; **-ebene,** *f.* infundibular plane; **-einlage,** *f.* filter cone; **-falte,** *f.* funnel fold; **-feld,** *n.* funnel area; **-förmig,** funnel-shaped, infundibular; **-fortsatz,** *m.* process of infundibulum; **-hals,** *m.* neck of a funnel; **-halter,** *m.* funnel holder; **-kolben,** *m.* funnel flask.

trichtern, to pour through a funnel.

Trichter-röhre, *f.* funnel tube or pipe, tube funnel; **-spalte,** *f.* infundibular fissure; **-stativ,** *n.* funnel stand; **-wandungen,** *f.pl.* funnel walls.

Tricyan-chlorid, *n.* tricyanyl chloride; **-säure,** *f.* tricyanic (cyanuric) acid.

trieb (treiben), drove, was driving.

Trieb, *m.*-e, impulse, urge, driving force, germinative power, shoot, sprout, instinct, desire, propensity; **-artig,** impulsive, instinctive; **-bewegung,** *f.* adjusting gear; **-fütterung,** *f.* stimulative feeding; **-knospe,** *f.* leaf bud; **-kraft,** *f.* motive power, moving force; **-malz,** *n.* leavening malt; **-mässig,** impulsive; **-pflanze,** *f.* perennial with short annual shoots; **-rad,** *n.*-er, driving wheel.

Trieb-rinde, *f.* cambium; **-sand,** *m.* shifting sand, quicksand; **-schraube,** *f.* coarse adjustment of microscope; **-spitze,** *f.* tip of shoot; **-stahl,** *m.* pinion steel; **-stoff,** *m.* driving substance; **-welle,** *f.* drive shaft; **-werk,** *n.* gearing, machine, mechanism, motor, transmission; **-wurzel,** *f.* main root, taproot.

triefen, to drop, gutter, trickle, water.

trifft (treffen), meets, hits.

Trift, *f.* drift, drove, herd, pasture, floating.

triften, to float, drift, pasture.

Triftholz, *n.* driftwood.

triftig, weighty, valid, adrift.

Trift-kanal, *m.* floating channel; **-pfad,** *m.* drift path; **-weg,** *m.* drift road; **-wesen,** *n.* transport by water.

Trikaliumphosphat, *n.* tripotassium phosphate.

triklin, triklinisch, triclinic.

Trimesinsäure, *f.* trimesic acid.

Trimethylamin, *n.* trimethylamine.

trinkbar, drinkable.

Trinkbecher, *m.* drinking cup.

trinken, to drink.

Trink-gefäss, *n.* drinking vessel; **-wasser,** *n.* drinking water.

Tripel, *m.* tripoli; **-erde,** *f.* tripoli powder; **-phosphat,** *n.* triple phosphate; **-salz,** *n.* triple salt.

triplieren, to triple, treble.

Trippel, *m.* tripoli.

Tripper, *m.* gonorrhea, clap; **-gift,** *n.* gonorrheal virus.

Tritol, *n.* trinitrotoluene.

Tritonkeim, *m.* Triton embryo.

tritt (treten), steps.

Tritt, *m.* tread, step, slot, track, footstep; **-gebläse,** *n.* foot blower (bellows).

Trityl, *n.* triphenylmethyl.

trivial, trivial, trite; **-name,** *f.* common (trivial) name.

trocken, dry; **-anlage,** *f.* drier installation; **-apparat,** *m.* drying apparatus, drier, desiccator; **-ästung,** *f.* lopping (pruning) of dry (dead) branches; **-batterie,** *f.* dry battery; **-beerwein,** *m.* straw wine; **-beize,** *f.* dusting, dry disinfection; **-boden,** *m.* drying loft; **-brett,** *n.* drying board; **-chlor,** *n.* dry chemicking.

Trocken-dampf, *m.* drying steam; **-dehnung,** *f.* (TD) dry elongation (DE); **-destillation,** *f.* dry distillation.

Trockene, *f.* dryness.

Trocken-element, *n.* dry cell; **-entgasung,** *f.* dry degassing; **-fäule,** *f.* dry rot; **-festigkeit,** *f.* (TF) dry strength (DS); **-filz,** *m.* drying felt; **-firnis,** *m.* siccative varnish, japan; **-frucht,** *f.* dry fruit; **-gehalt,** *m.* dry content, content of solid material; **-gerüst,** *n.* drying frame or rack; **-gestell,** *n.* drying frame or stand.

Trocken-gewicht, *n.* dry weight; **-glas,** *n.* drying glass; **-gut,** *n.* material to be dried; **-haus,** *n.* drying house; **-häutig,** dry (skinned), membranaceous.

Trockenheit, *f.* dryness, drought; **-widerstandswert,** *m.* drought resistance.

Trocken-holz, *n.* standing dry wood; **-kammer,** *f.* drying chamber or room; **-kohle,** *f.* subbituminous coal; **-legen,** *n.* **-legung,** *f.* drainage; **-liebend,** xerophilous; **-maschine,** *f.* drier, drying machine; **-mass,** *n.* dry measure; **-mauer,** *f.* dry stone wall, dry wall; **-milch,** *f.* dried (powdered) milk.

Trocken-mittel, *n.* desiccative, drying agent, siccative; **-nährboden,** *m.* desiccated nutrient medium; **-pflanze,** *f.* xerophyte; **-platte,** *f.* drying plate, dry plate; **-präparat,** *n.* dry preparation; **-probe,** *f.* dry test; dry assay; **-puddeln,** *n.* dry puddling; **-pulver,** *n.* drying powder; **-raum,** *m.* drying room or space, drier.

Trocken-reinigung, *f.* dry cleaning; **-riss,** *m.* check, seasoning crack due to drying; **-rohr,** *n.* drying tube; **-rückstand,** *m.* dry residue; **-schälchen,** *n.* drying capsule; **-schale,** *f.* drying dish; **-schleuder,** *f.* centrifugal drier; **-schrank,** *m.* drying oven, drying chamber; **-schwund,** *m.* shrinkage in drying; **-starre,** *f.* anabiosis, drought rigor.

Trocken-stube, *f.* drying room; **-substanz,** *f.* dry substance or weight, solid matter; **-system,** *n.* dry system of lenses; **-tod,** *m.*

death due to drought; **-torf,** *f.* dry peat; **-treber,** *f.* dried grains.

Trocken-tunnel, *m.* tunnel drier; **-turm,** *m.* drying tower; **-vorrichtung,** *f.* drying apparatus; **-walze,** *f.* drying roll; **-wiese,** *f.* dry meadow; **-zylinder,** *m.* drying cylinder.

Trockne, *f.* dryness.

trocknen, to dry, desiccate, season, cure, condition, wipe.

Trocknung, *f.* drying, desiccation.

Trocknungsvorlage, *f.* drying attachment.

troff (triefen), dripped, was dripping.

trog (trügen), deluded, deceived.

Trog, *m.*̈e, trough, cup, vat, hod; **-batterie,** *f.* trough battery; **-stecher,** *m.* stirrer (sugar).

T-Rohr, *n.* T tube.

Trommel, *f.* drum, tympanum; **-beinchen,** *n.* tympanic ossicle; **-darre,** *f.* drum kiln; **-fell,** *n.* **-haut,** *f.* tympanic membrane, drumhead; **-höhle,** *f.* tympanic cavity; **-mischer,** *m.* drum mixer; **-mühle,** *f.* drum mill, Alsing cylinder; **-saite,** *f.* tympanic cord; **-sieb,** *n.* cylindrical sieve.

Trompete, *f.* trumpet, tube.

Trompeten-ende, *n.* extremity of Eustachian tube; **-schlundkopfmuskel,** *m.* salpingopharyngeal muscle.

Trona, *f.* Tronasalz, *n.* trona.

Tropasäure, *f.* tropic acid.

Tropen, *f.pl.* tropics; **-frucht,** *f.* tropical fruit; **-gewächs,** *n.* tropical plant liquid, tropical vegetation; **-pflanze,** *f.* tropical-plant liquid, tropical vegetation.

tropfbar, capable of forming drops, liquid; **-flüssig,** liquid, capable of forming drops.

Tropfbarkeit, *f.* liquidity, capability of forming drops.

Tropf-behälter, *m.* dripping pan; **-bernstein,** *m.* liquid amber; **-blasse,** *f.* long star in face; **-brett,** *n.* draining board.

Tröpfchen, *n.* little drop; **-kultur,** *f.* hanging-drop culture.

Tröpfel, *m.* drips; **-fett,** *n.* drippings.

tröpfeln, to drip, trickle, form drops.

Tröpfel-pfanne, *f.* dripping pan, dripper; **-werk,** *n.* drying house.

tropfen, to drop, drip, trickle.

Tropfen, *m.-*, drop; **-flasche,** *f.* dropping bottle; **-förmig,** drop-shaped, guttiform; **-mixtur,** *f.* drops, guttae; **-registrierapparat,** *m.* drop recorder; **-weise,** drop by drop, dropwise; **-zähler,** *m.* dropping bottle, dropper, drop counter.

Tropf-flasche, *f.* dropping bottle; **-glas,** *n.* dropping glass, drop bottle, pipette; **-kante,** *f.* dripping edge; **-kasten,** *m.* save-all.

tropfsteinartig, stalactitic.

Tropf-trichter, *m.* dropping funnel; **-wasser,** *n.* drip water; **-wässer,** *n.pl.* drops; **-wein,** *m.* wine leakings, droppings.

Trophoplast, *m.* plastid.

tropisch, tropical.

Tross, *m.*-e, heavy baggage, baggage train.

trösten, to console, comfort.

Trotte, *f.* wine press.

Trottoir, *n.*-s, sidewalk.

Trotyl, *n.* trotyl, trinitrotoluene.

Trotz, *m.* defiance, insolence, scorn, spite.

trotz, in spite of.

trotzdem, nevertheless, although, notwithstanding, granted that, even though, in spite of the fact.

trotzen, (*dat.*) to bid defiance, boast (of), be obstinate, sulk, presume, oppose.

Trub, *m.* dregs, sediment.

Trübbier, *n.* beer from the sediment bag.

Trübe, *f.* turbidity, sludge, slime, cloudiness, opacity, dimness, liquid containing solid materials in suspension; **-leistung,** *f.* capacity, charge.

trübe, turbid, cloudy, dull, muddy, thick, gloomy, dreary, sad, cheerless.

trüben, to make turbid, trouble, darken, dull, cloud, make gloomy, dismal, dim, sadden; **-getrübt,** turbid, cloudy, opaque.

Trübung, *f.* turbidity, making turbid, cloudiness, dimness, blushing (lacquer).

Trübungs-erscheinung, *f.* turbidity phenomenon; **-punkt,** *m.* turbidity (cloud) point; **-stoff,** *m.* turbid substance.

Trüffel, *f.* truffle, earthnut (Tuber); **-pilze,** *m.pl.* Tuberaceae.

trug (tragen), carried, was bearing.

Trug, *m.* deception, delusion, fraud; **-bild,** *n.* phantom, illusion; **-dolde,** *f.* cyme; **-doldig,** false umbelliferous.

trügen, deceive, delude, be deceitful.

Trug-schluss, *m.*-e, false conclusion, paralogism; **-seitenständig,** only apparently lateral.

Truhe, *f.* trunk, chest.

Trümmer, *n.pl.* wreck, ruins, debris, remains, elastic rocks, fragments; **-achat,** *m.* brecciated agate; **-flur,** *f.* boulder-field

formation; **-gestein,** *n.* breccia, conglomerate; **-halde,** *f.* boulder slope, heap of rubbish; **-haufen,** *m.* heap of ruins.

Trunk, *m.*-e, drink, gulp, potion, liquor, draft.

Trupp, *m.*-s, troop, band, gang, set, flock, group, drove, grove, small cluster.

Truppe, *f.* troop, company, body, troupe, forces.

Truthahn, *m.*-e, turkey cock.

Trutz, *m.* offensive, offense; **zu Schutz und** ~, defensive(ly) and offensive(ly).

Trypanrot, *n.* trypan red.

tryptisch, tryptic.

Tsetse-Fliege, *f.* tsetse fly.

TS-Seide (Titer-Schwankungsseide), *f.* nub yarn (intentional denier variations).

T-Stück, *n.* T piece, T, tee.

Tube, Tübe, *f.* tube.

Tuberkel, *f.* tubercle; **-bazillenfärbung,** *f.* staining of tubercle bacilli; **-bazillus,** *m.* tubercle bacillus; **-bouillonkultur,** *f.* broth culture of tubercle bacillus; **-färbung,** *f.* staining of tubercle bacilli.

Tuberkulinreaktion, *f.* tuberculin reaction.

tuberkulös, tuberculous, tubercular.

Tuberkulose, *f.* tuberculosis; **-tilgung,** *f.* stamping out tuberculosis.

tubulös, tubulous, tubular.

Tubus, *m.* tube; **-aufsatz,** *m.* tube attachment; **-auszug,** *m.* drawtube; **-hülse,** *f.* outer portion; **-röhre,** *f.* drawtube of microscope; **-träger,** *m.* tube support.

Tuch, *n.*-er, fabric, cloth, handkerchief, cloth shawl; **-artig,** like cloth; **-fabrik,** *f.* cloth factory or mill.

tüchtig, capable, strong, skillful, sound, clever, efficient, proficient, thorough.

Tücke, *f.* malice, spite, trick.

tückisch, malignant, insidious.

tuff-artig, tufaceous; **-kalk,** *m.* tufaceous limestone; **-stein,** *m.* tufa, tuff.

Tugend, *f.* virtue.

Tülle, *f.* socket, nozzle, spout.

Tüllzelle, *f.* thyllus, tylosis.

Tulpe, *f.* tulip.

Tulpenbaum, *m.* tulip tree (*Liriodendron tulipifera*).

Tumefaciensgeschwülste, swellings due to *Bacterium tumefaciens,* crown gall.

tumeszieren, to tumefy, swell.

tummeln, to exercise, bestir oneself, keep moving.

Tümmler, *m.* dolphin, tumbler (pigeon), porpoise.

Tumor, *m.* tumor; **-schnitt,** *m.* section of tumor.

Tümpel, *m.*-, small pond, pool, tymp.

tun, to do, make, perform, effect, act; **zu wissen** (kund) ∼, to give notice to, inform; **sie** ∼**, als ob . . . ,** they act as if **. . . ; von sich** ∼**,** to remove, put away; **das tut nichts** (zur Sache), that is of no significance (in the matter); **es zu** ∼ **haben mit,** to deal with, have it to do with; **es ist damit nicht getan,** that does not settle it.

Tun, *n.* doings, dealings, conduct, proceeding(s).

Tünche, *f.* whitewash, plaster, parget.

tünchen, to whitewash, plaster.

Tünch-farbe, *f.* plastering color; **-schicht,** *f.* finishing coat; **-werk,** *n.* whitewashing, pargeting.

Tungstein, *m.* scheelite; **-säure,** *f.* tungstic acid.

tunken, to steep, soak, dip.

tunlich, feasible, practicable, possible, expedient, convenient.

Tunlichkeit, *f.* feasibility, practicability, expediency, convenience.

tunlichst, as far as practicable (or possible).

Tupelo, *m.* black gum, tupelo (Nyssa).

Tupf, *m.*-e, spot, dot.

Tüpfel, *m.*-, point, dot, spot, speck, pit; **gehöfter** ∼, bordered pit.

Tüpfel-farne, *m.pl.* Polypodiaceae; **-gefäss,** *n.* pitted vessel; **-gewebe,** *n.* pitted tissue.

tüpfelig, spotted, dotted, speckled.

Tüpfel-kanal, *m.* pit canal; **-methode,** *f.* ⁻pot (drop) method.

tüpfeln, to spot, dot, speckle, mottle, stipple.

Tüpfel-probe, *f.* spot (drop) test; **-raum,** *m.* pit chamber; **-schliesshaut,** *f.* closing membrane of pit; **-zelle,** *f.* pitted cell.

tupfen, to dab, spot, touch, dot, mark.

Tupfer, *m.* pledget, swab, tampon.

Tür, *f.*-e, door.

Turgor-dehnung, *f.* turgor tension; **-spannung,** *f.* turgor.

Türhüter, *m.* pylorus.

Türkensattel, *m.* sella turcica, pituitary fossa.

Türkis, *m.*-se, turquoise.

türkisch, Turkish; **türkische Bohne,** scarlet runner (*Phaseolus multiflorus*); **türkischer Weizen,** maize.

Türkischrot, *n.* Turkey red.

Türkisgrün, *n.* turquoise green.

Turm, *m.*⁻e, tower.

Turmalin, *m.*-e, tourmaline.

turmartig, turreted, like a tower.

türmen, to tower, pile up.

turm-förmig, towerlike, turreted; **-hoch,** towering; **-haus,** *n.* skyscraper.

turnen, to do gymnastics.

Turnus, *m.* turn, rotation, succession.

Türsturz, *m.* lintel beam over door.

Tusche, *f.* India ink; **-strich,** *m.* mark made with India ink; **-verfahren,** *n.* India-ink method, negative staining.

Tuschfarbe, *f.* water color.

Tuschierstein, *m.* honing (finishing) stone.

tut (tun), does.

Tute, Tüte, *f.* paper bag, assay crucible.

tuten, to toot.

tütenförmig, cone-shaped.

Tutte (Tute), *f.* assay crucible.

Typen-metall, *n.* type metal; **-molekül,** *n.* type molecule; **-muster,** *n.* standard sample; **-theorie,** *f.* type theory.

Typhoidseuche des Geflügels, fowl cholera.

typhös, typhoidal.

Typhus, *m.* typhus; **-ähnlich,** resembling typhoid; **-ausbreitung,** *f.* spread of typhoid; **-bakterien,** *f.pl.* typhoid bacilli.

Typhusbazillen-ausscheidung, *f.* secretion of typhoid bacilli; **-träger,** *m.* typhoid carrier; **-zwischenträger,** *m.* intermediate typhoid carrier.

Typhus-bazillus, *m.* typhoid bacillus; **-bekämpfung,** *f.* antityphoid measures; **-epidemie,** *f.* typhoid epidemic; **-erreger,** *m.* typhoid bacillus; **-fall,** *m.* typhoid case; **-heilserum,** *n.* curative serum for typhoid; **-infektion,** *f.* infection with typhoid; **-kranke,** *m.* typhoid patient.

Typhus-leiche, *f.* typhoid corpse; **-nachweis,** *m.* identification of typhoid; **-nährboden,** *m.* culture medium for typhoid bacillus; **-serum,** *n.* typhoid serum; **-stamm,** *m.* strain of typhoid bacilli; **-untersuchung,** *f.* typhoid investigation; **-verbreitung,** *f.* dissemination of typhoid; **-verdächtig,** suspected of typhoid; **-verschleppung,** *f.* spreading of typhoid.

typisch, typical.

Typlösung, *f.* reference solution.

Typus, *m.* type.

Tyrosin, *n.* tyrosine.

U

Übel, *n.* evil, complaint, disease, injury.

übel, evil, bad, ill; ~ **gehen,** to fare badly.

Übelkeit, *f.* sickness, nausea.

Übel-klang, *m.* dissonance; **-riechend,** smelling bad, offensive, foul, fetid; **-stand,** *m.* inconvenience, nuisance, abuse, disadvantage, drawback.

üben, to exercise, practice, drill, exert; **geübt,** skilled, experienced.

über, above, over, across, on, upon, beyond, about, against, versu̇s, higher than, more, on account of, by way of, about, concerning; ~ **und** ~, thoroughly, entirely, completely.

überall, everywhere, all over.

über-anstrengen, to strain, overexert; **-antworten,** to deliver, surrender, consign; **-äschern,** to overlime (leather).

überaus, extremely, exceedingly, excessively.

Über-bein, *n.* ganglion, node, exostosis, splint; **-bieten,** outbid, overbid, surpass, outdo; **-blasen,** to overblow, oxidize excessively; **-bleibsel,** *n.* residue, remainder, debris; **-blick,** *m.* general view, survey, synopsis, brief summary.

Überborsäure, *f.* perboric acid.

über-breiten, to cover; **-bringen,** to transmit, deliver, present; **-brücken,** to bridge over; **-chlorsauer,** perchlorate of.

Überchlorsäure, *f.* perchloric acid.

über-dauern, to outlast, survive; **-decken,** to cover over, overlap, spread over; **-deckt,** masked.

überdem, besides, moreover, in addition to.

überdestillieren, to distill over.

Überdichtung, *f.* overcompaction.

überdies, besides.

Überdruck, *m.-e,* cover printing, excess pressure, hypertonia, gauge pressure; **-artikel,** *m.* cover-print style (of fabrics).

übereilt, premature, overhasty.

überein, with one another, conformably, in agreement or accord.

übereinander, one upon another, superimposed; **-gerollt,** convolute; **-greifen,** to overlap; **-lagern,** to superimpose; **-lagerung,** *f.* superposition; **-schweissung,** *f.* lap weld.

überein-kommen, to agree, conform; **-kommen,** *n.* agreement; **-kunft,** *f.* agreement; **-stimmen,** to agree, coincide, harmonize, concur, correspond; **-stimmend,** agreeing, in accordance, comformable, corresponding; **-stimmung,** *f.* agreement, conformity.

Überentwicklung, *f.* overdevelopment.

übererregbar, overexcitable.

Überexposition, *f.* overexposure.

über-fahren, to pass (cross) over, transfer, change, drive over, convey over, run over; **-fall,** *m.* "overfall," nappe; **-fallen,** to fall upon, attack, surprise, overtake; **-fangen,** to flash, case, plate, cover (glass).

Überfärbeartikel, *m.* cross-dyed style.

überfärben, to overcolor, overstain, dye on a mordant, cross-dye, top, fill up, pad (cotton warp).

Überfärbung, *f.* overstaining, overdyeing.

über-faulen, to overferment; **-fetten,** to superfat, overstuff.

über-fliessen, to overflow; **-flügeln,** to outflank, surpass, overtop.

Überfluss, *m.⁀e,* abundance, plenty, surplus, superfluity, overflow, profusion.

über-flüssig, overflowing, superfluous, abundant, plentiful, in excess; **-fluten,** to overflow, inundate, flood; **-formen,** to mold on an inside mold (in ceramics).

Überfrucht, *f.* protecting fruit.

Überfruchtung, *f.* polyspermy, superfetation.

über-führbar, convertible, transferable; **-führen,** to convey, convert, lead over, transform, transport, change, transfer, convict, convince.

Überführung, *f.* conversion, transport.

Überführungs-zahl, *f.* transference number; **-zeit,** *f.* conversion period.

Über-fülle, *f.* superabundance, excess, repletion, plethora; **-fütterung,** *f.* forced alimentation; **-gabe,** *f.* surrender, delivery, transfer; **-gang,** *m.* transition, conversion, passage, crossing, blending (of colors), shading off.

Übergangs-epithel, *n.* transitional epithelium; **-farbe,** *f.* transition color; **-form,** *f.* transition form; **-formation,** *f.* transitory formation; **-gebiet,** *n.* transitional district; **-gegend,** *f.* region of transition; **-glieder,** *n.pl.* intermediate links.

Übergangs-klima, *n.* transitional (coast) climate; **-moor,** *n.* transition moor; **-periode,** *f.* transition period, equalization period; **-punkt,** *m.* transition point; **-stadium,** *n.* transition stage; **-stelle,** *f.* place of transition; **-stufe,** *f.* transition stage.

Übergangs-temperatur, *f.* transition temperature; **-widerstand,** *m.* resistance to conduction of electric current; **-wirbel,** *m.* transitional vertebra; **-zeitraum,** *m.* transition period; **-zelle,** *f.* transition cell; **-zone,** *f.* transition zone; **-zustand,** *m.* transition state.

übergar, overdone, overrefined, dry.

über-geben, to deliver, surrender, commit, vomit; **-gehen,** to go over, pass over, overlook, omit, change, turn, shade, overflow, be transformed.

übergerollt, convolute.

Übergewicht, *n.* overweight, excess weight.

über-giessen, to cover with, pour over, irrigate, douche, transfuse, spill; **-gipfeln,** to overtop, outgrow; **-gipsen,** to plaster, parget; **-glasur,** *f.* overglaze; **-goldung,** *f.* gilding; **-greifen,** to overlap, encroach; infringe, spread; **-greifend,** overlapping, transgressive, spreading.

Überguss, *m.* -̈e, covering, crust, icing, candy(ing).

übergut, too good, above standard.

Überhalt, *m.* maintenance (reserving) of standards.

überhalten, to leave standing, hold over, maintain.

Überhälter, *m.* standard.

überhandnehmen, to prevail, increase more and more, grow large, become too powerful.

überhauen, to overwork, overcut.

überhäufen, to overload, overwhelm, overstock.

überhaupt, generally, on the whole, at all; ∼ **nicht,** not at all; **wenn** ∼, if at all; ∼ **kein,** none at all.

überhäuten, to cover with skin, skin over.

überheben, to lift over, exempt, overstrain, excuse, boast, presume too much.

Überhetzung, *f.* excessive work, constant driving.

Über-hitze, *f.* superheat; **-hitzer,** *m.* superheater.

überhöht, increased (in geometry).

Überhöhung, *f.* increased height (of a triangle), elevation, banking up (of the outside of the curve), superelevation.

überholen, to overtake, overtop, outstrip, overhaul.

überimpfen, to inoculate, vaccinate (from one to another).

überirdisch, above the earth, superterrestrial, spiritual.

Überjodid, *n.* periodide.

Überjodsäure, *f.* periodic acid.

über-kalten, to supercool; **-kaltung,** *f.* supercooling, undercooling.

Überkieselung, *f.* silicification.

überkiesen, to cover with gravel.

überklotzen, slop-pad (fabric).

überkochen, to boil over, overboil or boil too much.

Überkohlensäure, *f.* percarbonic acid.

über-kommen, to get, receive, attack, obtain, seize; **-kompensieren,** to overbalance, overcompensate, superpose; **-krümmung,** *f.* excessive curvature; **-krusten,** to incrust; **-kühlen,** to supercool; **-laden,** to overcharge, overload, surfeit, transship.

überlagern, to cap, overlie, overlap.

Überlagerung, *f.* superposition, overlapping, superimposition.

überlandbrennen, to burn the surface of a clearcut area.

über-lappen, to overlap; **-lassen,** to leave, give up, relinquish, abandon, make over; **-lasten,** to overload, overburden, overcharge; **-lauf,** *m.* overflow, net profit, flash, spillway; **-laufen,** to run over, overrun, overflow, desert, down, annoy; **-läufer,** *m.* deserter, singler, solitary wild boar; **-laufrohr,** *n.* overflow (tube).

überleben, to outlive, survive.

über-legen, to reflect, ponder, weigh, consider, lay over; (*dat.*) superior, prevalent; **-legenheit,** *f.* superiority; **-legung,** *f.* reflection, deliberation.

überleiten, to lead over, cross, conduct over, transfuse.

Überlieferung, *f.* delivery, tradition, surrender.

überliegen, to lie over, germinate in the second year.

überlisten, to outwit, deceive.

überlöst, overgrown (of malt).

Übermacht, *f.* superior force, predominance.

übermangansauer, permanganate of.

Übermass, *n.* excess, excess height or length.

über-mässig, excessive; **-menschlich,** superhuman.

Übermikroskopie, *f.* electron microscopy.

übermitteln, to transmit, deliver.

Übermut, *m.* arrogance, insolence, presumption.

Übernahme, *f.* acceptance, assumption, taking possession or charge of.

übernähren, to overfeed, force alimentation.

über-nehmen, to accept, take over, take charge of, undertake, assume, copy, overdo, overeat; **-nehmer,** *m.* contractor; **-nommen,** (übernehmen), adapted.

übernutzen, to overwork, overcut.

überordnen, to control, superpose, place above.

überoxydieren, to peroxidize.

Überoxydierung, *f.* peroxidation.

Überpflanze, *f.* epiphyte (pseudoparasite).

Überpflanzung, *f.* graft, transplanting.

überpflatschen, to pad (fabric).

Über-produkt, *n.* by-product; **-produktion,** *f.* overproduction.

überprüfen, to check against.

überragen, to overtop, surpass, excel, tower above, transcend.

überraschen, to surprise.

überraschend, astonishing, amazing, surprising.

überreden, to talk over, persuade.

über-reichen, hand over, present; **-reichlich,** superabundant.

überreif, overripe, overdue.

überreissen, to carry over, entrain.

Überrest, *m.*-e, residue, remnant.

über-rieseln, to irrigate; **-rieselungswasser,** *n.* irrigation water.

übersäen, to strew, sow over with.

über-sättigen, to supersaturate, surfeit; **-sättigung,** *f.* supersaturation, satiety.

übersauer, too acid, too sour; **übersaures oxalsaures Kali,** *n.* potassium tetroxalate.

übersäuern, to overacidify, peroxidize.

Überschall, *m.* supersonic.

überschatten, to overshade, overshadow.

über-schätzen, to overemphasize; **-schätzung,** *f.* overrating.

über-schäumen, to froth over, foam over; **-schichten,** to cover with a layer, pour on.

Überschirmungsfläche, *f.* covered (sheltered) space.

Überschlag, *m.* calculation, estimate, covering, poultice, somersault.

überschlagen, to pass, over, omit, guess (roughly), consider, estimate, become lukewarm, fall backward, foment.

Überschlags-länge, *f.* propagation distance, guessed length; **-probe,** *f.* gap test.

überschmelzen, to superfuse, enamel.

Überschmelzung, *f.* enameling, superheating.

über-schmieren, to smear, daub; **-schreiben,** to write over, inscribe, head, label, address; **-schreiten,** to exceed, go beyond, overstep, transgress, overdraw; **-schreitung,** *f.* overstepping, transgression, exceeding; **-schrift,** *f.* inscription, heading, title; **-schuss,** *m.* excess, balance, surplus; **-schüssig,** in excess, surplus; **-schwänzen,** to sparge (in brewing).

überschwefelsauer, persulphate of.

über-schwellen, to overplump; **-schwemmen,** to overflow, submerge, flood; **-schwemmung,** *f.* flood, inundation, submersion; **-schwenglich,** excessive, boundless, exuberant, extravagant; **-seeisch,** oversea, transmarine; **-sehbar,** comprehensible; **-sehen,** to miss, supervise, overlook, oversee, survey, glance over; **-senden,** to ship, send, consign; **-setzen,** to translate, cross over, transport, overcharge; **-setzer,** *m.* translator; **-setzung,** *f.* translation, transmission; **-setzungsverhältnis,** *n.* gear ratio.

Über-sicht, *f.*-e, digest, survey, synopsis, review, summary, extract; **-sichtig,** clear, distinct, long-sighted; **-sichtigkeit,** *f.* hypermetropia, long-sightedness, clarity; **-sichtlich,** easily visible, clearly arranged.

Übersichts-bild, *n.* general view; **-spektrum,** *n.* general spectrum; **-tabelle,** *f.* tabular summary, **-tafel,** *f.* tabular statement.

übersiedeln, to emigrate, shift.

übersieden, to boil over.

übersinnlich, supersensible, abstract.

über-spannen, to overstrain, exaggerate, stretch, cover, span; **-spannt,** overstrained, overexcited, eccentric; **-spannung,** *f.* overvoltage, overstraining.

überspinnen, to spin over.

überspringen, to jump over, leap across, pass abruptly, miss, omit, intermit.

überspülen, to wash, overflow, drench, irrigate.

überständig, declining, decrepit, old, belonging to the upper story.

überstark, too much.

über-stehen, to endure, weather, overcome, project, survive, surmount; **-stehend,** standing over, supernatant; **-steigen,** to exceed, overflow, surmount; **-steiggefäss,** *n.* overflow vessel; **-strahlen,** to eclipse, illuminate, outshine; **-strecken,** to overstretch; **-streichen,** to coat, paint over, apply color.

über-streuen, to strew over, sprinkle over; **-strömen,** to flow over, overflow; **-stürzen,** to hurry, act rashly, overturn; **-stürzt,** precipitate, hasty; **-teuern,** to overcharge.

übertragbar, transferable, contagious, infectious.

Übertragbarkeit, *f.* infectiousness, transferableness.

über-tragen, to transfer, transmit, carry, apply (to); spread, transcribe, assign; **-träger,** carrier, vehicle, transmitter, transporter, transcriber; **-tragung,** *f.* transmission, transference, transfer, propagation, convection; **-treffen,** to surpass, excel, exceed; **-treiben,** to exaggerate, drive over, overdo; **-treibung,** *f.* exaggeration, excess; **-treten,** to step over, overstep, go over, transgress; **-trieben,** exaggerated, excessive, overdone.

Übertritt, *m.*-e, going over, passage.

übertünchen, to whitewash.

Übervergrösserung, *f.* supplementary magnification.

Übervermehrung, *f.* overproduction.

übervölkert, crowded, overpopulated.

über-wachen, to watch over, supervise, control, inspect, superintend; **-wachsen,** to outgrow, overtop, overtower; **-wallen,** to boil over, be occluded, heal over; **-wallung,** *f.* occlusion of wounds; **-wältigen,** to overpower, subdue, overcome; **-wiegen,** to outweigh, surpass, overbalance; **-wiegen,** *n.* predominance; **-wiegend,** dominating, dominant, preponderant(ly).

über-winden, to overcome, conquer, surmount; **-windung,** *f.* overcoming, victory, subjection; **-wintern,** to keep through the winter, hibernate; **-winterung,** *f.* hibernation; **-wipfelt,** overgrown, dominated, overtopped; **-wuchert,** overgrown with weeds; **-wucherung,** *f.* hypertrophy, healing, callus formation.

überwunden (überwinden), overcome.

Über-wurf, *m.* outer garment, roughcast; **-zahl,** *f.* surplus, greater number; **-zählig,** supernumerary, surplus.

über-zeugen, to convince, persuade; **-zeugt,** convinced, sure, certain; **-zeugung,** *f.* persuasion, conviction; **-zeugungskraft,** *f.* persuasive power.

über-ziehen, to cover, clothe, coat, case, line, incrust, lay, put on, put over; **-zieher,** *m.* overcoat; **-zug,** *m.* covering, coat(ing), incrustation, plating, crust.

üblich, usual, customary, common.

übrig, left over, remaining, residual, to spare, superfluous; **im übrigen,** after all, moreover, for the rest; **die übrigen,** the rest.

übrigbleiben, to remain (over), survive.

übrigens, as for the rest, after all, moreover, besides, however, furthermore.

übriggeblieben, residual.

übriglassen, to leave over or behind; **zu wünschen** ~, to leave nothing to be desired.

Übung, *f.* exercise, practice, use, training, drill, dexterity, routine.

Ue . . . , see Ü . . .

Ufer, *n.*-, bank, shore, beach, coast; **-flora,** *f.* shore vegetation; **-gebüsche,** *n.pl.* shore thicket; **-liebend,** riparious, frequenting river banks; **-los,** shoreless, boundless; **-nah,** inshore.

U-förmig, U-shaped.

Uhr, *f.*-en, watch, clock, hour, o'clock, meter; **-feder,** *f.* watch spring; **-federranker,** *m.* watch-spring climber; **-glas,** *n.* watch glass; **-macher,** *m.* watchmaker; **-werk,** *n.* clockwork; **-zeiger,** *m.* hand of a watch; **-zeigergegensinn,** *m.* counterclockwise direction; **-zeigersinn,** *m.* clockwise direction.

Uhu, *m.*-e,-s, eagle owl (Bubo).

Ukelei, *m.* bleak (*Alburnus lucidus*).

Ulme, *f.* elm.

Ulmen-gewächse, *n.pl.* Ulmaceae; **-krankheit,** *f.* elm disease; **-rinde,** *f.* elm bark; **-sterben,** *n.* dieback of elms.

Ulminsäure, *f.* ulmic acid.

Ulnar-arterie, *f.* cubital artery; **-kreuz,** *n.* ulnar cross (meeting of hairlines); **-rand,** *m.* cubital border.

Ultra-filter, *n.* filter for ultraviolet rays, ultrafilter; **-marin,** ultramarine; **-mikroskopisch,** ultramiscroscopic; **-rot,** infrared, ultrared; **-schall,** *m.* supersonant; **-violett,** ultraviolet; **-visible Bakterien,** *n.pl.* filterable viruses, ultramicroscopic organisms.

um, round, about, at, to, for, because of, by; **einen Tag** ~ **den andern,** every other day; ~ ... **zu,** in order to; **je mehr** ... ~ **so** (desto), the more ... the more; **meine Zeit ist** ~, my time is up; ~ **meinetwillen,** for my sake; ~ **und** ~, round about, everywhere; ~ **so mehr,** so much the more; ~ **so weniger,** so much the less; ~ **so** ... **als,** the ... than; ~ **so besser,** all the better; ~ **so** ... **je,** the ... the; ~ ... **herum,** around.

umändern, to change, alter, convert, transform.

Umänderung, *f.* transformation, conversion, change, metamorphosis.

umarbeiten, to work over, recast, rewrite, revise.

Umbau, *m.* rebuilding, reconstruction; **-erscheinung,** *f.* phenomenon of transformation.

Umbenennung, *f.* renaming.

Umbererde, *f.* umber.

umbiegen, to bend over, turn back, double down or back.

umbilden, to transform, remodel, recast.

Umbildung, *f.* transformation, metamorphosis, modification, change.

umblasen, to blow down.

umbördeln, to border, flange, edge, turn (over).

Umbra, *f.* **-erde,** *f.* umber.

umbrechen, to plough up, to turn.

umbringen, to kill, murder, destroy.

umdestillieren, to redistill, rectify.

Umdifferenzierung, *f.* redifferentiation.

umdrehen, to turn round, rotate, revolve.

umdrehend, rotatory, revolving.

Umdrehreflex, *m.* turning about reflex.

Umdrehung, *f.* revolution, turn, rotation.

Umdrehungs-achse, *f.* axis of (rotation) revolution; **-bewegung,** *f.* rotary motion; **-geschwindigkeit,** *f.* rotary velocity; **-punkt,** *m.* center of rotation; **-zahl,** *f.* r.p.m.; **-zähler,** *m.* revolution counter.

Umdruck, *m.***-e,** reprint, reimpression; **-farbe,** *f.* reprinting ink.

Umesterung, *f.* alcoholysis, interchange of ester radicals.

umfällen, to reprecipitate.

Umfang, *m.*̈**e,** circumference, girth, circuit, extent, size, compass, range, periphery; **im grossen** ~, to a great extent.

Umfangader, *f.* peripheral vein.

umfangen, to surround, embrace, encircle.

umfangreich, extensive, voluminous, spacious, wide.

Umfangsgeschwindigkeit, *f.* peripheral velocity.

umfärben, to redye.

umfassen, to contain, embrace, include, comprise, span; **in einem Blick** ~, to take in at a glance.

umfassend, comprehensive, extensive, broad.

Umfassung, *f.* spanning, embracing, envelopment, enclosure, fence.

umflechten, to twist about, weave again.

umfliessen, to flow around, encircle.

unformen, to transform, convert, change.

Umformer, *m.* converter, transformer.

Umformungsperiode, *f.* transformation period.

Umfrage, *f.* inquiry.

umfüllen, to transfer, transfuse.

Umgang, *m.*̈**e,** round, circuit, loop, turn of a spiral, rotation, volution of shell, intercourse, intimate acquaintance.

umgänglich, sociable, companionable.

Umgarnung, *f.* entanglement, maze.

umgeben, to surround, inclose, environ.

umgebogen, recurved, resupinate.

Umgebung, *f.* environment.

umgeformt, transformed.

Umgegend, *f.***-e,** surroundings, vicinity.

umgehen, to go round, go about, work, associate, avoid; ~ **lassen,** to alternate.

umgekehrt, inverse(ly), reverse, opposite, reciprocal, vice versa, conversely, on the other hand.

umgelegt, shifted, changed, turned down; **umgelegter Hals,** *m.* ringneck.

umgesetzt, converted.

umgestalten, to transform, change, remodel.

umgestaltender Reiz, *m.* metamorphic stimulus.

Umgestaltung, *f.* transformation, reform, alteration, metamorphosis, adaptation.

umgestellt, changed.

umgestülpt, inverted, overturned, everted.

umgewandelt, changed, transformed.

umgewendet, anatropous.

umgibt (umgeben), surrounds.

umgiessen, to transfer by pouring, decant, recast, pour around.

umgraben, to dig up, spade, surround with a trench.

umgreifen, to curve (span) around, clasp.

umgürten, to put a belt round, gird.

Umguss, *m.* ̈e, recasting, transfer of a liquid.

umher, around, about, here and there, on all sides, at random; **-treiben,** to wander about.

umhin, nicht ∼ **können,** to have no choice, cannot do otherwise than.

umhüllen, to cover, envelop.

Umhüllung, *f.* covering, casing, envelope.

Umhüllungshaut, *f.* investing membrane.

Umkehr, *f.* reversal, return; **-entwicklung,** *f.* reversal development (in photography).

umkehrbar, reversible, convertible.

Umkehrbarkeit, *f.* reversibility.

umkehren, to turn round, over, back, inside out, return, invert, reverse; **umgekehrt,** inverted, reverse, inverse(ly), converse(ly).

Umkehrfeld, *n.* reversing field.

Umkehrung, *f.* turning round, reversion, reversal.

umkippen, to overturn, tip over, upset.

umkleiden, to clothe, cover, change clothes.

umkommen, to perish, spoil, succumb, die.

Umkreis, *m.* circle, circuit, circumference.

umkreisen, to turn on, circle around.

umkristallisieren, to recrystallize.

umkrücken, to rake, rabble, mash.

umlagern, to surround, besiege, rearrange.

Umlagerung, *f.* rearrangement.

Umlauf, *m.* rotation, circulation, revolution, cycle.

umlaufen, to rotate, revolve, circulate.

Umlauf-pumpe, *f.* circulation pump, rotatory pump; **-zahl,** *f.* rotation number; **-zeit,** *f.* time of rotation, circulation period.

umlegbar, inclinable, reversible.

umlegen, to shift, change, relay, lay round, put on, turn down.

umliegend, surrounding.

ummanteln, to case, jacket.

umpacken, to repack.

umpfählen, to surround with poles or stakes.

umpflanzen, to transplant, reset.

umpflügen, to plow up, turn.

Umpfropfen, *n.* top grafting.

umranden, to seal.

umrandet, bordered.

umrechnen, to convert, reduce.

Umrechnung, *f.* conversion, reduction.

Umrechnungs-faktor, *m.* conversion factor; **-grössen,** *f.pl.* conversion data; **-tafel,** *f.* conversion table.

umreissen, to pull down, sketch, outline.

umringen, to encircle, surround, enclose.

Umriss, *m.* ̈e, outline, sketch, the entire margin of a leaf, contour.

Umrollung, *f.* involution, reversal of flexure.

umrühren, to stir (up), work.

ums (um das), round the, about the; (um des), for the.

Umsatz, *m.*-e, exchange, turnover, business; conversion, reaction, decomposition, transformation; **-produkt,** *n.* product of metabolism.

umsäumt, hemmed around, edged, fringed.

umschalten, to swtich over, reverse.

Umschalter, *m.* switchboard, reverser, commutator.

Umschaltungsreiz, *m.* switching stimulus.

Umschau, *f.* review, survey.

umschaufeln, to turn over with a shovel.

umschichten, to pile afresh, rearrange in layers.

umschichtig, in layers, alternately.

Umschlag, *m.* ̈e, cataplasm, wrapper, covering, sudden change, envelope, facing, hem, cover, collar, poultice, sale, alteration.

umschlagen, to apply, change, decompose, knock down, overturn, upset, poultice; **umschlagende (Sippen) Arten,** *f.pl.* ever-sporting (mutating) varieties.

Umschlagpapier, *n.* wrapping paper.

Umschlags-punkt, *m.* transition point, point of reversal; **-rand,** *m.* reflected margin; **-zahl,** *f.* titration value.

umschliessen, to surround, enclose.

umschlingen, to wind around, embrace, cling to, clasp around.

umschlossen (umschliessen), enclosed.

umschmelzen, to recast, refound, remelt.

umschreiben, to rewrite, circumscribe, transcribe.

umschroten, to cut with the saw or ax.

umschütteln, to shake (up), agitate.

umschütten, to pour into another vessel, decant.

umschwärmen, to swarm about, harass.

Umschweif, *m.* digression, roundabout way.

umschwenken, to turn round, rotate.

umschwirren, to buzz around.

Umschwung, *m.* revolution, rotation.

umsetzen, to change, change the position of, decompose, transform, exchange, convert, transpose, transplant, sell.

Umsetzung, *f.* change, conversion, double decomposition, exchange, transplantation, transposition.

Umsetzungsgeschwindigkeit, *f.* velocity (rate) of transformation.

Umsicht, *f.* prospect (round about), panorama, circumspection.

umsomehr, all the more, so much the more.

umsonst, for nothing, gratis, in vain, to no purpose.

umspannen, to surround, encase.

Umspanner, *m.* transformer.

umspinnen, to spin around, entangle.

Umspinnwalze, *f.* doffing (waste) roller.

umspulen, to rewind.

umspülen, to wash (round).

Umstand, *m.* circumstance, condition.

Umstände, *m.pl.* positions, conditions, state of affairs, ceremonies; **unter Umständen,** in certain cases, under certain circumstances; **ohne ~,** without much ado.

umständig, perigynous, surrounding.

umständlich, circumstantial, troublesome, ceremonious, intricate, detailed.

umstechen, to stir up, turn up.

umstehend, next, following, standing about.

umstellbar, reversible, transposable, invertible.

umstellen, to reverse, invert, transpose, surround.

Umstellung, *f.* transposition, permutation, inversion.

umsteuern, to reverse.

Umsteurung, *f.* reversing gear.

Umstimmung, *f.* change.

Umstimmungsmittel, *n.* alterative.

umstossen, to overthrow. throw down, abolish, annul, cancel.

Umstossung, *f.* upsetting, overthrow, canceling, reversal.

umstrahlen, to irradiate.

umstreiten, to fight about, debate, dispute.

umstritten, disputed, debated.

umstülpen, to invert, overturn.

Umstülpung, *f.* inversion, turning over.

Umsturz, *m.* overthrow, fall, downfall, ruin, subversion.

umstürzen, to overthrow.

umtauschen, to exchange.

Umtreiber, *m.* rotator muscle.

Umtriebszeit, *f.* rotation period.

umtun, to put on or around, look for, inquire.

umwachsen, to grow round, overgrow.

umwälzen, to roll over, rotate, revolutionize.

Umwälzpumpe, *f.* circulating pump, rotary pump.

Umwandelbarkeit, *f.* convertibility, transformability.

umwandeln, to convert, transform, change, inflect.

Umwandler, *m.* converter, transformer.

Umwandlung, *f.* transformation, conversion, change, metamorphosis.

umwandlungs-fähig, convertible; **-fähigkeit,** *f.* metamorphic capacity; **-geschwindigkeit,** *f.* transition velocity; **-produkt,** *n.* transformation product; **-punkt,** *m.* transition point; **-temperatur,** *f.* transition temperature; **-theorie,** *f.* transformation theory; **-wärme,** *f.* latent heat of transformation.

Umweg, *m.-e,* roundabout way, detour.

Umwehrung, *f.* circumferential reinforcement.

Umwelt, *f.* environment, world about us; **-einflüsse,** *m.pl.* environmental factors; **-faktor,** *m.* environmental factor; **-schutz,** *m.* protection against environmental influences; **-verhältnis,** *n.* relation to the external world; **-wickeln,** to envelop, coat; **-wirkung,** *f.* environmental effect.

umwenden, to turn over, invert.

Umwertungsprozess, *m.* process of revaluation.

umwickeln, to wrap round, cover, case.

umzäunen, to fence.

umziehen, to cover, draw round, wrap, change, move.

Umzug, *m.ꞏe,* procession, removal, change.

umzüngeln, to play about (of flames), envelop, surround.

unabänderlich, unalterable, unchangeable, everlasting.

unabhängig, independent.

Unabhängigkeit, *f.* independence.

un-ablässig, incessant, uninterrupted; **-absehbar,** unbounded, immense, immeasurable; **-absichtlich,** unintentional; **-achtsam,** negligent, inadvertent, careless; **-ähnlich,** unlike, dissimilar; **-anfechtbar,** incontestible, indisputable; **-angemessen,** inadequate, unsuitable; **-angenehm,** unpleasant, disagreeable; **-angeregt,** unexcited, in the normal state; **-angreifbar,** unassailable; **-annehmbar,** unacceptable.

Unannehmlichkeit, *f.* annoyance, inconvenience.

un-antastbar, not to be touched, inviolable, incontestable, intangible; **-anwendbar,** inapplicable, unsuitable; **-atembar,** irrespirable; **-aufhaltsam,** irresistible, continual; **-aufhörlich,** incessant, continuous, unceasing; **-auflösbar,** insoluble; **-auflöslich,** insoluble; **-auflöslichkeit,** *f.* insolubility.

un-ausbleiblich, inevitable; **-ausdehnbar,** inexpansible; **-ausführbar,** impracticable, unfeasible, impossible; **-ausgeglichen,** unbalanced; **-ausgemacht,** not settled, uncertain; **-ausgesetzt,** constant, uninterrupted; **-auslöschbar,** inextinguishable; **-auslöschlich,** inextinguishable.

un-beachtet, notwithstanding, unnoticed, disregarded; **-bearbeitet,** raw, crude, unwrought; **-bebaut,** uncultivated; **-bedeckt,** uncovered, open; **-bedenklich,** without hesitation; **-bedeutend,** insignificant, unimportant; **-bedingt,** unconditional(ly), absolute(ly); **-beeinflusst,** uninfluenced.

un-befangen, unbiased, unprejudiced; **-befleckt,** stainless, spotless, undefiled, immaculate; **-befriedigend,** unsatisfactory; **-befugt,** unauthorized; **-begreiflich,** incomprehensible; **-begrenzt,** infinite, unlimited; **-begründet,** unfounded, groundless; **-behaart,** hairless.

Unbehagen, *n.* discomfort.

unbehaglich, unpleasant, uneasy, uncomfortable.

Unbeholfenheit, *f.* awkwardness.

un-bekannt, unknown; **-belaubt,** bare, aphyllous, leafless, **-belebt,** inanimate, lifeless; **-belichtet,** not exposed to light; **-bemerkt,** unnoticed; **-benannt,** unnamed, abstract, indefinite, innominate.

unbenetzbar, ombrophobic (hating rain).

unbenutzt, unused.

unbepflanzt, unplanted.

unbequem, uncomfortable, troublesome, disagreeable, inconvenient.

Unbequemlichkeit, *f.* inconvenience.

un-berechenbar, incalculable; **-berechtigt,** unjustified; **-berücksichtigt,** unconsidered, disregarded; **-berührt,** untouched; **-besät,** unsown; **-beschädigt,** undamaged, unhurt; **-beschäftigt,** unemployed; **-beschränkt,** unlimited, infinite, unconditional; **-besiedelt,** unsettled; **-beständig,** unstable, changeable, fickle, labile, variable, inconstant.

Unbeständigkeit, *f.* instability.

un-bestimmt, undetermined, indefinite; **-bestimmtheit,** *f.* vagueness, uncertainty, lack of determination; **-beteiligt,** not concerned, nonparticipating; **-beugsam,** inflexible; **-bewacht,** unwatched, unguarded; **-bewaffnet,** without armature, unarmed, unaided, naked (eye).

un-beweglich, immovable, fixed; **-bewegt,** clam, motionless; **-bewohnt,** uninhabited, deserted; **-bewusst,** unknown, unaware of, unconscious of; **-biegsam,** inflexible; **-brauchbar,** useless.

und, and; ~ **zwar,** that is, to be sure.

un-dankbar, ungrateful, thankless (task); **definierbar,** undefinable; **-dehnbar,** inextensible, nonductile; **-denkbar,** inconceivable; **-denklich,** long past, immemorial, for ages; **-deutlich,** indistinct, inarticulate; **-dicht,** not tight, leaky, pervious; **-dichtigkeit,** *f.* looseness, escape, leak.

Unding, *n.* **-e,** absurdity, nonsense, nonentity.

un-durchdringlich, impermeable, impenetrable, impervious; **-durchforstet,** unthinned; **-durchführbar,** impracticable, not feasible; **-durchgängig,** impermeable, closed; **-durchlässig,** impervious, impermeable; **-durchlässigkeit,** *f.* impermeability; **-durchscheinend,** nontranslucent, opaque; **-durchsichtig,** opaque; **-durchsichtigkeit,** *f.* opacity.

uneben, uneven.

Unebenheit, *f.* unevenness, irregularity, inequality.

un-echt, false, counterfeit, not genuine, artificial, not fast; **-edel,** ignoble, base, inert, mean; **-egal,** unequal, uneven; **-egalität,** *f.* inequality, unevenness; **-eigentlich,** not literal, figurative, not real; **-empfänglich,** unreceptive, insusceptible; **-empfindlich,** rugged, resistant, indifferent, insensitive; **-empfindlichkeit,** *f.* insensibility, anesthesia.

unendlich, infinite, endless; **das geht ins Unendliche,** there is no end to that.

un-entbehrlich, indispensable; **-entbehrlichkeit,** *f.* absolute necessity; **-entdeckt,** undiscovered; **-entgeltlich,** gratuitous, free; **-entschieden,** undecided, indecisively; **-entwickelt,** undeveloped, immature; **-entwirrbar,** inextricable; **-entzündbar,** noninflammable.

un-erbittlich, inexorable; **-erfahren,** inexperienced; **-erforschlich,** inscrutable; **-erforscht,** unexplored; **-erfüllt,** unaccomplished; **-erheblich,** insignificant; **-erhört,** unheard of; **-erklärbar, -erklärlich,** inexplicable.

un-erlässlich, indispensable; **-ermesslich,** immense, immeasurable, vast; **-ermüdlich,** indefatigable; **-erregt,** unexcited, calm; **-erreichbar,** unattainable; **-erreicht,** unattained, unparalleled.

un-erschöpflich, inexhaustible; **-ersetzbar,** irreparable, irreplaceable; **-erträglich,** intolerable, unbearable; **-erwähnt,** unmentioned; **-erwartet,** unexpected.

un-fähig, incapable, unable; **-fähigkeit,** *f.* inability; **-fahrbar,** impassable.

Unfall, *m.* ⁼e, accident, disaster, misfortune.

un-fassbar, -fasslich, incomprehensible, unseizable; **-fehlbar,** infallible, unfailing, certain; **-fern,** near.

unfruchtbar, sterile.

Unfruchtbarkeit, *f.* sterility.

Unfug, *m.* disorder, mischief.

unfühlbar, imperceptible, impalpable.

ungar, not done.

ungarisch, Hungarian.

un-geachtet, notwithstanding, nevertheless, although; **-geahnt,** unsuspected; **-gebeten,** uninvited, unasked; **-gebleicht,** unbleached; **-gebrannt,** unburnt; **-gebührlich,** indecent, improper, unbecoming; **-gebunden,** uncombined, unbound, dissolute.

Ungebundenheit, *f.* ease, freedom.

Ungeduld, *f.* impatience.

ungedüngt, unfertilized.

ungeeignet, unsuited, unfit, inappropriate.

Ungefähr, *n.* chance, accident.

ungefähr, about, approximate(ly).

un-gefährdet, unharmed, safe, not endangered; **-gefährlich,** harmless; **-gefällig,** disagreeable; **-gefärbt,** undyed, unstained;

-gefleckt, immaculate; **-geflügelt,** without wings; **-gegerbt,** untanned.

un-gegliedert, inarticulate; **-gegoren,** unfermented; **-gehalten,** indignant, angry; **-gehärtet,** unhardened, soft; **-geheissen,** unasked, spontaneous, voluntary; **-geheizt,** unheated.

un-geheuer, huge, enormous, amazing; **-gehörig,** improper; **-gehörnt,** without horns; **-gekammert,** monothalamous; **-geklärt,** unsolved, not cleared; **-gekocht,** unboiled; **-gekränkt,** uninjured, not vexed; **-gekünstelt,** natural, unaffected, artless.

un-geladen, uninvited, unloaded; **-geläutert,** unpurified; **-gelegen,** inopportune; **-gelehrt,** unlearned; **-geleimt,** unglued, unsized; **-gelöscht,** unslaked (lime); **-gelöst,** undissolved.

un-gemein, extraordinary, uncommon; **-gemessen,** unlimited, unmeasured, boundless; **-gemischt,** unmixed; **-gemütlich,** uncomfortable, unpleasant; **-genannt,** unnamed, anonymous, innominate; **-genau,** inaccurate, inexact.

Un-genauigkeit, *f.* inaccuracy; **-geneigt,** unwilling, disinclined, unfriendly; **-geniessbar,** unpalatable; **-genügend,** insufficient; **-genügsam,** insatiable, greedy; **-genutzt,** unused.

un-geordnet, incoherent, unregulated, in disorder; **-geprüft,** unexamined, untried; **-gerade,** uneven, odd; **-geradzahlig,** uneven, odd (number); **-gerechnet,** not counted, not included; **-gerecht,** unjust; **-gereinigt,** unpurified; **-gern,** unwillingly; **-geröstet,** unroasted, not calcined; **-gerufen,** uncalled.

un-gesalzen, unsalted, fresh, unseasoned; **-gesättigt,** unsaturated, not satiated; **-gesäuert,** not acidified, unleavened (bread); **-gesäumt,** seamless, immediate, unhindered; **-geschält,** unpeeled, unhusked; **-geschehen,** undone; **-geschichtet,** unstratified; **-geschickt,** awkward.

un-geschlechtig, -geschlechtlich, asexual, agamic, neuter; **-geschliffen,** unground, rude, uncut, unpolished; **-geschlossen,** unclosed, open; **-gespalten,** unsplit; **-gestalt(et),** misshapen, deformed; **-gestielt,** sessile; **-gestört,** undisturbed; **-gesucht,** unsought, unaffected; **-gesund,** unhealthy, unwholesome; **-geteilt,** entire, undivided, ungraduated.

Ungetüm, *n.* ⁼e, monster.

ungeübt, inexperienced.

ungewiss, uncertain.

Ungewitter, *n.* thunderstorm.

un-gewöhnlich, unusual, extraordinary; **-gewohnt,** unaccustomed, unusual.

ungezähnelt, edentate.

Ungeziefer, *n.* vermin; **-bekämpfung,** *f.* vermin control.

ungezwungen, unconstrained, unbridled, unforced, unaffected, free, easy.

ungiftig, nonpoisonous.

Ungiftigkeit, *f.* innocuity.

Unglaube, *m.* incredulity, unbelief.

unglaublich, incredible, beyond belief.

ungleich, unequal, different, heterogeneous, unlike, dissimilar, uneven, odd, not uniform, incomparably; **-alterig,** uneven in age; **-artig,** dissimilar, heterogeneous; **-blättrig,** anisophyllous (leaves, diverse in shape or size); **-förmig,** dissimilar, unsymmetrical, irregular, different; **-gerichtet,** not parallel, opposite.

Ungleichheit, *f.* inequality, unevenness, dissimilarity.

ungleich-klappig, inequivalvate; **-mässig,** unbalanced, not uniform, dissimilar, unsymmetrical, irregular, anomalous, disproportionate; **-namig,** unlike, opposite (poles); **-seitig,** scalene (triangle); **-wimperig,** with unequal flagella; **-zeitig,** noncontemporaneous.

Unglück, *n.* misfortune, bad luck.

unglücklich, unfortunate, ill-fated, unlucky.

unglücklicherweise, unfortunately.

Unglücksfall, *m.-e,* accident, disaster.

ungültig, void, not valid.

Ungunst, *f.* disfavor, expense.

un-günstig, unfavorable; **-gut,** ill, amiss; **-haltbar,** untenable, not durable; **-heil,** *n.* hurt, harm, evil, disaster; **-heilbar,** incurable; **-heilsam,** unwholesome, noxious; **-heimlich,** uncanny, dismal, weird.

uniert, united.

unifärben, to dye (solid, uniformly) a self shade.

Unionspriorität, *f.* convention agreement, priority patent under Geneva Union.

Unistückware, *f.* plain- (self-)shade piece goods.

unitarisch, unitary.

Universal-arznei, *f.* universal remedy, panacea, cure-all; **-eisen,** *n.* flitch plate; **-fräsmaschine,** *f.* universal milling machine; **-gelenk,** *n.* universal joint; **-mittel,** *n.* cure-all, panacea.

Universität, *f.* university.

Unke, *f.* fire-bellied toad, frog.

un-kennbar, -kenntlich, indiscernible, unrecognizable.

Unkenntnis, *f.* ignorance.

unklar, confused, not clear, turbid.

Unklarheit, *f.* want of clearness, vagueness, confusion.

Unkosten, *f.pl.* charges, expenses, **-löhne,** *m.pl.* nonproductive wages.

Unkraut, *n.-er,* weed, weeds; **-streu,** *f.* litter of weeds.

unkristallisierbar, uncrystallizable.

Unland, *n.-er,* wasteland.

unlängst, of late, recently.

un-lauter, impure, ignoble, sordid; **-legiert,** unalloyed; **-leidlich,** insufferable, intolerable; **-lesbar,** illegible; **-leserlich,** illegible.

un-leugbar, undeniable, unquestionable, indisputable; **-lieb, -liebsam,** unpleasant, disagreeable; **-lösbar,** indissoluble, not solvable; **-löschbar,** slakeless, unquenchable; **-löslich,** insoluble; **-löslichkeit,** *f.* insolubility.

Unlust, *f.* dislike, displeasure, aversion.

Unmasse, *f.* great quantity.

un-massgeblich, unauthoritative; **-mässig,** intemperate, immoderate; **-menschlich,** inhuman, superhuman; **-merklich,** imperceptible; **-messbar,** immeasurable, incommensurable; **-mischbar,** immiscible; **-mischbarkeit,** *f.* immiscibility; **-mittelbar,** immediate(ly), direct(ly); **-möbliert,** unfurnished; **-modern,** old-fashioned, not modern.

unmöglich, impossible.

Unmöglichkeit, *f.* impossibility.

un-nachahmlich, inimitable; **-nachgiebig,** inflexible, unyielding; **-nahbar,** inaccessible; **-nennbar,** inexpressible; **-nötig,** unnecessary; **-nütz,** useless, unprofitable, naughty.

unordentlich, untidy, disorderly, irregular.

Unordnung, *f.* disorder, litter.

unorganisch, inorganic.

unpaar, not paired, azygous.

unpaarig gefiedert, imparipinnate.

unpaar-wertig, of odd valence; **-hufer,** *m.pl.* **-zeher,** *m.pl.* Perissodactyla.

un-parteiisch, impartial, unprejudiced; **-passend,** unfit, unsuitable; **-pässlich,** unwell, ill, indisposed; **-pressbar,** incompressible; **-pressbarkeit,** *f.* incompressibility.

Unrat, *m.* trash, refuse, dirt, garbage.

Unrecht, *n.* wrong, error, injustice, fault; ~ **haben,** to be wrong.

unrecht, wrong, false, unjust, unfair.

unrechtmässig, illegal, unlawful.

unregelmässig, irregular, zygomorphic, abnormal.

Unregelmässigkeit, *f.* irregularity, anomaly.

un-reif, unripe, immature; **-rein,** impure, unclean; **-reinheit,** *f.* impurity; **reinigkeit,** *f.* impurity; **-reizbar,** nonirritable, not sensitive; **-rentable,** not paying, unprofitable; **-rettbar,** irrecoverable, irretrievable; **-richtig,** false, erroneous, wrong, unjust.

Unruhe, *f.* unrest, disquiet, excitement, trouble, commotion, balance wheel.

unruhig, restless, unquiet, excited, troubled.

uns, us, to us, (to) ourselves.

unsachgemäss, improper.

un-sagbar, unspeakable; **-sanft,** harsh, rough; **-schädlich,** harmless, safe, innocuous; **-scharf,** not sharp, indefinite, blurred, hazy; **-schätzbar,** invaluable, inestimable; **-scheinbar,** insignificant, plain, dull.

Unschlitt, *n.* tallow, suet.

un-schlüssig, undecided, irresolute; **-schmackhaft,** insipid, tasteless; **-schmelzbar,** infusible; **-schuldig,** innocent; **-schweissbar,** unweldable; **-schwer,** easy, not difficult.

unser, our(s), of us.

unsicher, uncertain, unsafe, insecure, unsteady, unstable, dubious.

Unsicherheit, *f.* insecurity, uncertainty.

unsichtbar, invisible.

Unsinn, *m.* nonsense.

unsinnig, nonsensical, irrational, absurd, insane.

un-spaltbar, uncleavable; **-statthaft,** inadmissible, illicit; **-stet, -stetig,** variable, inconstant, unsteady, unstable, restless; **-stetigkeit,** *f.* unsteadiness, instability; **-sträflich,** blameless, irreproachable; **-streckbar,** not extensible, nonductile; **-streitig,** indisputable, unquestionable.

Unsumme, *f.* immense sum.

unsymmetrisch, unsymmetrical.

untätig, inactive, idle, unemployed, inert, dormant, indolent, nonproductive.

Untätigkeit, *f.* inactivity, indolence, idleness, inertness.

un-tauglich, unfit, useless, unsuitable; **-teilbar,** indivisible; **-teilbarkeit,** *f.* indivisibility; **-teilhaftig,** not sharing in, not participating.

unten, beneath, below, downstairs, under(-neath), at the bottom; ~ **hin,** down below; ~ **stehend,** at the bottom, underneath.

unter, under(neath), subordinate, below, among, between, during; ~ **diesem Gesichtspunkt,** from this point of view; ~ **Umständen,** under certain conditions.

unter-abteilen, to subdivide; **-abteilung,** *f.* subdivision.

Unterarm, *m.* forearm, lower arm; **-knochen,** *m.* bone of the forearm.

Unterart, *f.* subspecies, variety.

Unteraugenhöhlen-ader, *f.* infraorbital vessel; **-loch,** *n.* infraorbital foramen; **-rinne,** *f.* infraorbital groove.

Unteraugenlid, *n.* lower eyelid.

Unter-bau, *m.* foundation, substructure, underplanting; **-bauch,** *m.* hypogastrium; **-bauchgegend,** *f.* hypogastric region; **-beamter,** *m.* subordinate official; **-bewusstsein,** *n.* subconsciousness.

Unterbilanz, *f.* deficit.

unterbinden, to tie up, ligature, stop.

Unterbindung, *f.* ligature, ligation.

Unterblatt, *n.* ventral lobe, the lower part of a leaf primordium.

unterbleiben, to cease, not occur, be omitted, be left undone.

Unter-boden, *m.* subsoil; **-brechen,** to interrupt, discontinue, suspend, break, stop; **-brecher,** *m.* interrupter; **-brechung,** *f.* interruption, intermission, break, stop, suspension; **-brechungsstrom,** *m.* interrupted current, contact current.

unter-breiten, to submit, lay before; **-bringen,** to give shelter, dispose, arrange, provide; **-brochen,** interrupted, broken, discontinued, intermittent; **-bromig,** hypobromous; **-carbonisch,** subcarboniferous; **-chlorig,** hypochlorous.

unterchlorigsaures Natrium, sodium hypochlorite.

unter-des, -dessen, meanwhile, in the meantime.

Unterdistrikt, *m.* subdistrict.

Unterdruck, *m.* pressure, subatmospheric pressure, vacuum, negative pressure

unterdrücken, to suppress, repress, oppress, overtop, shade out, choke.

unterdrückt, suppressed, overtopped.

Unterdrückung, f. suppression.

untere, low(er), under, inferior.

untereinander, among (with) one another, together, mutually, reciprocally.

Untereinheit, f. subunit.

Untereinteilung, f. subdivision.

unteressigsauer, subacetate of.

Unterfaltenhöhle, f. cavity of the lower folds.

Unterfamilie, f. subfamily.

unterfangen, to venture, dare, underpin.

Unterfläche, f. lower surface, base.

Unterflügeldecken, f.pl. infra-axillary plumes.

Unterflur, f. ventral tract (pterylae).

Unterführung, f. underpass.

Unterfuss, m. sole of the foot.

Unterfutter, n. inner lining.

Untergang, m. going down, destruction, setting, fall, ruin, sinking, decline, failure.

untergärig, bottom fermenting.

Untergärung, f. bottom fermentation, underfermentation.

Untergattung, f. subgenus, subvariety, subspecies.

unter-geben, to place under, submit, commit, inferior, subordinate; -gehen, to go down, set, perish, become extinct, submerge, sink; -geklemmt, underwound (thread); -geordnet (unterordnen), of minor importance, subordinate, inferior, minor; -geschoben (unterschieben), forged, spurious, counterfeit.

Unter-geschoss, n. ground floor; -gesicht, n. lower part of the face; -gestell, n. undercarriage, substructure; -getaucht, submerged, demersed; -glasur, f. underglaze; -glasurfarbe, f. underglaze color.

untergraben, to undermine, ruin, dig in (manure).

Unter-gras, n. low-growing grass; -gräser, n.pl. diminutive grasses.

Untergräten-gegend, f. infraspinous region; -muskel, m. infraspinous muscle.

Untergrund, m. subsoil, underground, (back)ground, bottom (print), first print; -bahn, f. underground railway.

Unterguss, m. substratum (in photography).

unterhalb, below, beyond.

Unterhals, m. lower part of neck, guttural region.

Unterhalt, m. sustenance, support.

unterhalten, to support, maintain, keep, entertain, amuse, converse.

Unterhaltung, f. support, maintenance, keep, entertainment, conversation, chat.

unterhandeln, to negotiate, treat.

unterhauen, to underwork, undercut.

Unterhaut, f. derma, hypodermis, underskin; -bindegewebe, n. subcutaneous connective tissue; -gewebe, n. hypodermis, subcutaneous tissue; -zellengewebe, n. subcutaneous tissue.

Unterhefe, f. bottom yeast.

Unterhirn, n. subencephalon.

Unterholz, n. underwood.

Unterhorn, n. occipital horn (cornu) of lateral ventricle.

unter-irdisch, underground, subterranean, hypogeous; -jochen, to subdue; -jodig, hypoiodous; -jodigsauer, hypoiodite of.

Unterkiefer, m. mandible, lower jaw, inferior maxillae; -ast, m. mandibular ramus, branch of the lower jaw; -bein, n. inferior maxilla; -beuge, f. mandibular angle; -bogen, m. arch of the lower jaw; -drüse, f. submaxillary gland; -fortsatz, m. process of inferior maxilla; -gebiss, n. the lower teeth; -gegend, f. submaxillary region.

Unterkiefer-gelenk, n. temporomaxillary articulation; -grube, f. mandibular (glenoid) fossa; -knoten, m. submaxillary ganglion; -schild, m. submaxillary scale; -speicheldrüse, submaxillary salivary gland; -taster, m. maxillary palpus; -winkel, m. inferior maxillary (submaxillary) angle; -zweig, m. branch of inferior maxilla.

Unterkinn, n. submentum; -gegend, f. submental region; -lade, f. inferior maxilla.

unterkommen, to find shelter or refuge, get employment.

Unterkonoidierung, f. undercompensation.

Unterkörper, m. lower part of body, abdomen.

Unterkreideflora, f. lower cretaceous flora.

unterkriechen, to crawl under.

unterkriegen, to get the better of, conquer.

unterkühlen, to supercool.

Unterkühlung, f. undercooling, supercooling.

Unterlage, f. support, base, stand, subsoil, substratum, lining, stock in grafting; -gestein, n. underlying rock.

Unterlager, *n.* prothallus, primordial meristem, base, foundation, support.

unterlagern, to underlie.

Unterlagerung, *f.* substratum.

Unterlagsplatte, *f.* base, washer, sole plate.

Unterlass, *m.* intermission, cessation; **ohne ~,** incessantly.

unterlassen, to omit, neglect, leave off, discontinue.

Unterlauf, *m.* lower course of river.

unterlaufen, to occur (accidentally).

unterlaufen, extravasated, bloodshot.

Unterlauge, *f.* underlye.

unterlegen, to lay under, inferior, support.

Unterlegscheibe, *f.* washer.

Unterleib, *m.* abdomen, belly.

Unterleibs-beschwerde, *f.* abdominal trouble; **-eingeweide,** *n.pl.* abdominal viscera; **-entzündung,** *f.* peritonitis; **-höhle,** *f.* abdominal cavity; **-typhus,** *m.* typhoid fever, abdominal typhus.

Unterlicht, *n.* light from below.

unterliegen, to succumb, be overthrown, be overcome, lie underneath.

Unterlippe, *f.* lower lip, labium.

Unterlippen-bändchen, *n.* frenulum (frenum) of lower lip; **-bulbus,** *m.* labial bulb; **-drüse,** *f.* labial gland; **-taster,** *m.* labial palpus.

unterlöst, insufficiently grown (malt).

untermischen, to intermingle, intermix.

unternahm (unternehmen), undertook.

unternehmen, to undertake.

unternehmend, enterprising, venturesome.

Unternehmer, *m.* contractor, employer.

Unternehmung, *f.* undertaking, enterprise, attempt, venture.

unterordnen, to subordinate.

Unterordnung, *f.* suborder, subordination.

Unterpfand, *n.*¨er, pledge, security, mortgage.

unterpflanzen, to underplant.

Unterpflanzung, *f.* underplantation.

unterpflügen, to plow in.

Unter-phosphorsäure, *f.* hypophosphoric acid; **-probe,** *f.* **probeweingeist,** *m.* underproof spirit; **-rain,** *m.* lower (ventral) apterium; **-randader,** *f.* subcosta; **-rasse,** *f.* subvariety; **-redung,** *f.* conference, discourse, conversation.

Unterricht, *m.* teaching, instruction.

unterrichten, to teach, instruct.

Unterrichtsanstalt, *f.* school.

Unterrinde, *f.* lower bark or crust.

Unterrippe, *f.* lower (false) rib.

Unterrippen-gegend, *f.* hypochondriac region, upper lateral portion of abdomen.

Untersaat, *f.* undercrop.

untersäen, to undersow.

untersagen, to forbid, prohibit.

untersalpetrig, hyponitrous; **-sauer,** hyponitrite of.

Untersatz, *m.*¨e, base, support, stand, stay, saucer.

unter-schätzen, undervalue, underrate, depreciate; **-scheidbar,** distinguishable, discernible; **-scheiden,** to distinguish, differentiate, discern, discriminate, differ.

Unterscheidung, *f.* distinction.

Unterscheidungs-merkmal, *n.* differential character, characteristic sign; **-vermögen,** *n.* faculty of discrimination.

Unterschenkel, *m.* tibia, shank; **-band,** *n.* crural ligament; **-beuger,** *m.* femoral biceps; **-flur,** *f.* pteryla cruralis; **-knochen,** *m.* shank bone; **-muskel,** *m.* tibial muscle; **-raine,** *m.pl.* apteria cruralia; **-strecker,** *m.* extensor of leg; **-zuzieher,** *m.* adductor muscle of leg.

unterschieben, to push under, substitute, interpolate, forge.

Unterschied, *m.*-e, difference, distinction, discrimination, variation.

unterschiedlich, different, distinct, differential, variable.

Unterschieds-empfindlichkeit, *f.* degree of sensitiveness; **-schwelle,** *f.* differential threshold, threshold of perceptibility.

unterschlagen, to cross (arms), embezzle, intercept, suppress.

unterschlächtig, succubous; **unterschlächtige Blätter,** *n.pl.* succubous leaves (folia incuba).

Unterschläfengrube, *f.* zygomatic fossa.

Unterschlundganglion, *n.* ganglion pharyngeum inferius.

Unterschlüsselbeingrube, *f.* infraclavicular (subscapular) fossa.

Unterschnabel, *m.* lower part of beak, lower jaw of birds.

unterschreiben, to sign, subscribe.

Unterschrift, *f.* signature, subscription.

Unterschulterblatt-gegend, *f.* subscapular region; **-grube,** *f.* subscapular fossa.

Unterschwanzdecke, *f.* subcaudal feather, undertail coverts.

unterschwefelsauer, hyposulphate of.

Unterschwefelsäure, *f.* hyposulphuric acid.

unterschweflig, hyposulphurous.

unterschwefligsauer, hyposulphite of; **unterschwefligsaures Natrium,** *n.* sodium hyposulphite.

unterschwellig, subliminal (giving secondary response to stimulus).

Unterseeboot, *n.* submarine (boat).

unterseeisch, submarine.

Unterseite, *f.* lower side, bottom.

unterseits, hypo.

Untersetzscherbe, *f.* crucible stand.

untersetzt, short and stout, thickset.

Untersetzungsverhältnis, *n.* decreasing (reducing) gear ratio.

Untersippe, *f.* subtribe.

unterst, lowest, undermost, last of all.

Unterstand, *m.*-e, lower growth, foxhole.

unterständig, inferior, hypogynous, of lower growth.

unter-stehen, to stand below, venture; **-stellen,** to place under, take shelter; **-streichen,** to underline; **-stützen,** to support, assist.

Unterstock, *m.* underback.

Unterstützung, *f.* support, assistance.

Unterstützungspunkt, *m.* point of support.

untersuchen, to investigate, examine, analyze, probe.

Untersuchung, *f.* inquiry, investigation, research, examination, analysis.

Untersuchungs-chemiker, *m.* research chemist; **-ergebnis,** *n.* result of a test; **-laboratorium,** *n.* research laboratory; **-methode,** *f.* research method; **-mittel,** *n.* means of research or examination, indicator; **-richtung,** *f.* line of investigation.

unter-tan, subject to, dependent (on); **-tänig,** submissive, obedient.

Untertasse, *f.* saucer.

untertauchen, to dive, immerse, submerge.

Untertauchung, *f.* immersion, submersion.

Unterteig, *m.* underdough.

Unterteil, *m.*-e, base, under (lower) part.

unterteilen, to split up, subdivide, classify.

Unterteilung, *f.* subdivision, classification.

Untervollmacht, *f.* substitute power of attorney.

unterwärts, downward, at the base, underneath, below.

Unterwasser, *n.* tailwater, lower pool.

unterwegs, on the way, en route.

unter-weisen, to instruct, teach, **-weisung,** *f.* instruction; **-werfen,** to subject, curb.

Unterwuchs, *m.*-̈e, undergrowth.

unterwühlen, to undermine, grub up.

Unterzahn, *m.*-̈e, lower tooth.

unterzeichen, to sign, underwrite.

Unterzeug, *n.* underclothing, underwear.

unterziehen, to submit, draw (pull) under, undergo, undertake; **sich** ∼, to submit to.

Unterzungendrüse, *f.* sublingual gland.

Unterzug, *m.*-e, beam.

Untiefe, *f.* sand bar or bank (shallow place).

Untier, *n.*-e, monster.

untilgbar, inextinguishable, indelible, irredeemable.

untrennbar, inseparable.

untrinkbar, undrinkable.

untrüglich, infallible, unmistakable, certain, sure.

untunlich, not feasible, impossible.

un-überbrückbar, that cannot be bridged over, irreconcilable; **-übersteiglich,** insurmountable; **-übertrefflich,** unsurpassable, unequaled, unrivaled; **-überwindlich,** invincible.

unumgänglich, indispensable, unavoidable; ∼ **notwendig,** absolutely necessary.

un-umschränkt, unlimited, arbitrary; **-umstösslich,** irrefutable, incontestable; **-umwunden,** open, frank, plain, candid; **-unterbrochen,** uninterrupted, unbroken; **-unterscheidbar,** indistinguishable; **-untersucht,** uninvestigated.

un-veränderlich, invariable, unchangeable, constant, inalterable; **-veränderliche,** *f.* constant; **-veränderlichkeit,** *f.* constancy, unchangeableness; **-verändert,** unchanged, unaltered; **-verantwortlich,** irresponsible, inexcusable; **-verarbeitet,** unwrought, not made up in native state; **-verbesserlich,** incorrigible, unmendable; **-verbindlich,** not binding, not obligated; **-verblümt,** plain, point-blank; **-verbrennbar,** incombustible.

un-verbrüchlich, inviolable; **-verbunden,** without obligation, uncombined, unconnected; **-verbürgt,** unwarranted, unconfirmed; **-verdaulich,** indigestible; **-ver**-

dauung, *f.* indigestion; -verdichtbar, incompressible; incondensable; -verdichtbarkeit, *f.* incondensability.

un-verdient, undeserved, unmerited; -verdrossen, unwearied, persevering, patient; -vereinbar, incompatible, irreconcilable.

un-verfälscht, unadulterated, genuine, real, pure; -verfaulbar, unputrefiable, imputrescible; -verfestigt, unconsolidated; -verflüchtigt, unvolatilized; -verfroren, not frozen, impudent; -vergänglich, not perishable; -vergärbar, unfermentable; -vergesslich, unforgettable; -verglast, unvitrified.

un-vergleichbar, -vergleichlich, incomparable, unique; -verhofft, unhoped for, unexpected, unforseen; -verhohlen, unconcealed, open, unreserved; -verkäuflich, unsalable, unmarketable.

un-verkennbar, unmistakable, evident; -verkürzt, unabridged, intact; -verletzt, unhurt, uninjured, unimpaired, intact; -vermeidlich, unavoidable, inevitable; -vermengt, unmixed; -vermerkt, unperceived, unobserved; -vermindert, undiminished; -vermischt, unmixed, unalloyed, pure, unadulterated; -vermittelt, sudden(ly).

Unvermögen, *n.* inability, insolvency.

unvermutet, unsuspected, unforeseen.

Unvernunft, *f.* unreasonableness, irrationality, absurdity.

un-veröffentlicht, unpublished; -verrichtet, unperformed, unsuccessfully; -verrückbar, fixed, immovable; -verschuldet, innocently, not in debt, unmerited; -verschult, untransplanted.

un-versehens, unexpectedly; -versehrt, uninjured; -verseifbar, unsaponifiable; -versiegbar, inexhaustible; -versorgt, unprovided for; -verständig, unwise, imprudent.

un-verständlich, unintelligible, imprudent; -versteuert, duty unpaid, untaxed; -versucht, untried; -vertilgbar, ineradicable, indelible; -verträglich, incompatible, irritable, quarrelsome; -verträglichkeit, *f.* incompatibility.

un-verwandt, unrelated, unmoved, fixed; -verweilt, without delay, directly; -verweslich, imputrescible, undecaying; -verwittert, unweathered; -verwüstlich, indestructible; -verzeihlich, unpardonable, inexcusable.

un-verzüglich, immediate, instant, prompt; -verzweigt, unbranched; -vollendet, un-

finished, incomplete; -vollkommen, imperfect, defective, incomplete, submerged (of a weir); -vollkommenheit, *f.* imperfection; -vollständig, incomplete, imperfect; -vollständigkeit, *f.* incompleteness.

un-vorbereitet, unprepared; -vorhergesehen, unforeseen, unexpected; -vorsätzlich, unpremeditated, unintentionally; -vorsichtig, careless, imprudent, incautious; -vorteilhaft, disadvantageous, unprofitable; -wägbar, imponderable, unweighable.

unwahr, untrue, false, hypocritical.

unwahrscheinlich, improbable, unlikely.

un-wandelbar, unchangeable, invariable, indeclinable; -wandelbarkeit, *f.* immutability, unchangeableness; -wegsam, impassable, pathless.

unweit, not far (from).

Unwesen, *n.* disorder, confusion, monster.

unwesentlich, unessential, immaterial, accessory, accidental, unimportant.

Unwetter, *n.* stormy weather.

un-wichtig, unimportant; -widerlegbar, -widerleglich, irrefutable; -widerstehlich, irresistible; -willkürlich, involuntary; -wirksam, inactive, ineffective, neutral, inefficient, void; -wirksammachung, *f.* rendering ineffective.

unwüchsig, unthrifty.

Unzahl, *f.* immense number.

unzählbar, innumerable, countless.

unzählig, innumerable, countless.

Unze, *f.* ounce.

Unzeit, *f.* unseasonable (wrong) time.

unzeitig, untimely, immature, premature.

un-zerbrechlich, unbreakable; -zerlegbar, indecomposable, simple, indivisible; -zerreissbar, untearable; -zersetzbar, indecomposable; -zersetzt, undecomposed, simple; -zerstörbar, indestructible; -zerstört, undestroyed.

unzertrennbar, inseparable.

unzufrieden, discontented, dissatisfied.

unzugänglich, inaccessible, unapproachable.

unzulänglich, inadequate, insufficient.

un-zulässig, inadmissible; -zureichend, insufficient; -zusammendrückbar, incompressible; -zuträglich, inconvenient, disadvantageous, unwholesome.

Un-zuträglichkeit, *f.* failure.

un-zutreffend, incorrect, wrong; -zuverlässig, unreliable, uncertain, doubtful;

-zweckmässig, unsuitable, inexpedient, inappropriate; **-zweckmässigkeitslehre,** *f.* dysteleology; **-zweideutig,** clear, precise, unambiguous; **-zweifelhaft,** undoubtedly.

Upas-baum, *m.* upas tree, upas (*Antiaris toxicaria*); **-gift,** *n.* poison of upas tree.

üppig, luxuriant, plentiful, rich.

Üppigkeit, *f.* richness, luxuriance of growth.

Ur-ahn, *m.*-**en,** original ancestor, great-grand-father; **-alt,** very old, aged, ancient.

Urämie, *f.* uremia.

Uran, *n.* uranium; **-atom,** *n.* uranium atom; **-carbid,** *n.* uranium carbide; **-erz,** *n.* uranium ore.

Uranfang, *m.* prime origin, very (first) beginning.

Uran-gehalt, *m.* uranium content; **-gelb,** *n.* uranium yellow; **-glimmer,** *m.* torbernite; **-grün,** *n.* uranochalcite; **-gummi,** *n.* gummite; **-haltig,** containing uranium, uraniferous.

Urani-oxyd, *n.* uranic oxide; **-verbindung,** *f.* uranic compound.

Uranlage, *f.* original rudiment, primordium.

Urano-reihe, *f.* uranous series; **-salz,** *n.* uranous salt; **-verbindung,** *f.* uranous compound.

Uran-oxyd, *n.* uranium oxide, uranic oxide; **-oxyduloxyd,** *n.* uranosouranic oxide; **-pecherz,** *n.* pitchblende; **-sauer,** uranate of; **-strahlen,** *m.pl.* uranium rays; **-verbindung,** *f.* uranium compound.

Uratom, *n.* primordial atom.

urbar, arable, cultivated, tillable; **-machung,** *f.* cultivation, reclamation, clearing of land.

Ur-baustein, *m.* basic building material, basic unit; **-bestandteil,** *m.* ultimate (primitive) constituent; **-bewohner,** *m.* original inhabitant, native; **-bild,** *n.* prototype, original; **-bildungsstoff,** *m.* protoplasm; **-blatt,** *n.* primordial leaf; **-boden,** *m.* original soil, virgin soil.

Urdarm, *m.* primitive digestive tract or intestine; **-höhle,** *f.* primary intestinal (archenteric) cavity; **-strang,** *m.* primitive gut cord.

Ur-destillation, *f.* low-temperature distillation; **-ei,** *n.* primordial egg; **-faden,** *m.* protonema; **-farbe,** *f.* primary color; **-fels,** *m.* primitive rock; **-flosse,** *f.* primitive fin, archipterygium; **-flügler,** *m.pl.* Paleodictyoptera; **-form,** *f.* original form, prototype; **-furche,** *f.* primitive cleavage (furrow); **-gebirge,** *n.* primitive rock (mountain).

urgeschichtlich, prehistoric.

Urgeschlechtzelle, *f.* primitive spermatoblast.

Urgestein, *n.* primitive rock; **-verwitterungsböden,** *m.pl.* residuous soils derived from weathering primitive rocks.

Ur-gewebe, *n.* meristem, merismatic tissue; **-gewicht,** *n.* standard (original) weight; **-granit,** *m.* primitive granite.

Urheber, *m.* originator, author, founder.

Urin, *m.* urine; **-absatz,** *m.* urinary sediment; **-stein,** *m.* urinary calculus.

Ur-kalk, *m.* primitive limestone; **-keim,** *m.* primitive germ; **-kräftig,** very powerful.

Urkunde, *f.* record, document, voucher, title (deed).

Urlaub, *m.* leave (of absence).

Urläuter, *m.* sod oil, degras.

Urleitbündel, *n.* central cylinder.

Urlehre, *f.* master gauge.

Urmass, *n.*-**e,** standard measure or gauge.

Urmensch, *m.* first man, primitive man.

Urmeristem, *n.* promeristem.

Urmund, *m.* blastopore; **-lippe,** *f.* blastopore lip; **-ränder,** *m.pl.* lips of the blastopore.

Urnatur, *f.* primitive nature.

Urne, *f.* urn.

Urniere, *f.* mesonephros, head (primordial) kidney.

Urnieren-feld, *n.* mesonephric area; **-geschlechtsfalte,** *f.* urogenital fold; **-kanälchen,** *n.* mesonephric tubule; **-leiste,** *f.* Wolffian ridge.

Urogenitalsystem, *n.* urogenital system.

U-Röhre, *f.* U tube.

Urorgan, *n.* primitive organ.

urplötzlich, very sudden(ly).

Ur-preis, *m.* original (manufacturer's) price; **-quell,** *m.* foundation head, origin.

Ursache, *f.* cause, reason, origin.

ursächlich, causative, causal.

Urschleim, *m.* protoplasm.

urseelisch, instinctive, inherent, native.

Ursegment, *n.* primitive segment; **-höhle,** *f.* cavity of the primitive segment; **-leiste,** *f.* somite ridge; **-stiel,** *m.* primitive segment stalk.

Urspecies, *f.* original or primitive species.

Ursprung, *m.* origin, source, derivation, starting point, provenance.

ursprünglich, original, primordial, primitive, native, first, at first.

Ursprungzelle, *f.* cell of origin.

Urstoff, *m.* primary matter, element; -lehre, *f.* atomic theory.

urstofflich, elementary.

Urstoffteilchen, *n.* primordial particle, atom, molecule, ion.

Ursubstanz, *f.* original substance.

Urteer, *m.* low-temperature tar, crude tar.

Urteil, *n.*-e, judgment, sentence, decision, opinion, verdict, proposition.

urteilen, to judge, form an opinion, decide, determine.

Ur-tier, *n.* protozoon; -tierchen, *n.pl.* protozoa; -titer, *m.* original titer, titrimetric standard; -titersubstanz, *f.* standard titrimetric substance; -verkokung, *f.* low-temperature coking.

Urwald, *m.* virgin (primeval) forest; -bestand, *m.* virgin growth, primeval stand; -gebiet, *n.* region of primeval (virgin) forest.

Urwelt, *f.* primeval world.

Urwirbel, *m.* primitive vertebra, provertebra.

urwüchsig, original, native, natural, rough, blunt.

Urzelle, *f.* primitive cell, ovum.

Urzeugung, *f.* spontaneous generation, abiogenesis.

Urzustand, *m.* primitive state.

Usur, *f.* breaking down, atrophy.

Utensilien, *n.pl.* utensils, implements.

Uterusglocke, *f.* bell-shaped uterus.

Utopie, *f.* Utopian scheme or notion.

Uvinsäure, *f.* uvic acid, pyrotritaric acid.

Uwarowit, *m.* uvarovite.

V

vaccinieren, to vaccinate.

Vacheleder, *n.* neat's leather.

Vacuolen-haut, *f.* tonoplast; -höhle, *f.* peripheral cavity in stem (Equisetum); -wand, *f.* tonoplast.

vagabundieren, to rove, tramp, wander, lead a vagrant life; -vagabundierend, roving, stray.

Vaginalpalpen, *pl.* vaginal articulated appendages.

Vagus, *m.* vagus nerve.

Vakanz, *f.* vacancy, vacation.

Vakuole, *f.* vacuole.

Vakuum-filter, *m.* vacuum filter; -gärung, *f.* vacuum fermentation; -glühlampe, *f.* vacuum incandescent lamp; -meter, *n.* vacuum meter or gauge; -rohr, *n.* vacuum tube; -trockner, *m.* vacuum drier; -verdampfung, *f.* vacuum evaporation.

Vakzination, *f.* vaccination.

Vakzine, *f.* vaccine; -virus, *m.* vaccine virus.

vakzinieren, to vaccinate.

Valenz, *f.* valence, valency; -zahl, *f.* valence (number).

Valerian-öl, *n.* valerian oil; -säure, *f.* valerianic acid.

Valet, *n.*-s, farewell.

Valone, *f.* valonia.

Valuta, *f.* Valuten, value, monetary standard, fixed rate, exchange, equivalent.

Vanadin, *n.* vanadium; -bleierz, *n.* vanadinite; -säure, *f.* vanadic acid; -säureanhydrid, *n.* vanadium pentoxide.

Vanille, *f.* vanilla.

Vanillen-kampher, *m.* vanillin; -pflanze, *f.* vanilla plant.

Varec, *m.* kelp.

variabel, variable.

Variabilität, *f.* variability.

Variation, *f.* variation.

Variations-bewegung, *f.* movement of tissue; -breite, *f.* amplitude of variation; -fähigkeit, *f.* variability; -feld, *n.* variation field; -karte, *f.* variation chart; -kurve, *f.* frequency curve; -merkmal, *n.* varietal character; -rechnung, *f.* calculus of variation; -reihe, *f.* distribution of variations, frequency distribution; -weite, *f.* extent (amplitude) of variation.

Varietät, *f.* variety.

variieren, to vary.

Varixknoten, *m.* varicose knot.

Varizen, *pl.* varicose veins.

Vasal-priman, *m.* protoxylem element; -strang, *m.* vascular cord.

Vaselin, *n.* vaseline.

vaskularisiert, vascular.

Vater, *m.*⁚, father; **-land,** *n.* native land, fatherland; **-ländisch,** native, national.

väterlich, fatherly, paternal.

Vegetabilien, *pl.* vegetables, herbal drugs.

vegetabilisch, vegetable.

Vegetation, *f.* vegetation, growth.

Vegetations-bilder, *n.pl.* pictures of vegetation; **-kasten,** *m.* incubator; **-kegel,** *m.* vegetation cone; **-kuppe,** *f.* vegetative cone; **-punkt,** *m.* vegetation (growing) point; **-ring,** *m.* annual (ring) increment; **-stockwerke,** *n.pl.* layer societies.

vegetativ, vegetative.

vegetieren, to vegetate, live on, grow.

Veilchen, *n.* violet; **-gewächse,** *n.pl.* Violaceae; **-holz,** *n.* violet wood; **-keton,** *n.* violet ketone; **-stein,** *m.* iolite; **-wurz(el),** *f.* orrisroot; **-zucker,** *m.* violet jam.

Veitsbohne, *f.* kidney bean.

Veitstanz, *m.* St. Vitus's dance, chorea.

Vektor, *m.* **Radius** ∼, radius vector.

vektoriell, vectorial.

Velarfeld, *n.* velar area.

Velin, *n.* vellum; **-form,** *f.* wove mold; **-papier,** *n.* wire-wove (vellum) paper.

veloutieren, to flock paper, make velvetlike.

Vene, *f.* vein.

Venen-ast, *m.* branch of a vein; **-blut,** *n.* venous blood; **-häutchen,** *n.* choroid membrane; **-klappe,** *f.* valve of a vein; **-stamm,** *m.* trunk of a vein; **-stein,** *m.* veinstone, phlebolith; **-verästelung,** *f.* ramification of veins.

Venerie, *f.* venereal disease, syphilis.

venerisch, venereal, syphilitic.

venezianisch, Venetian; **-rot,** *n.* Venetian red.

venös, venous.

Ventil, *n.*-e, valve; **-artig,** valvelike.

Ventilation, *f.* ventilation.

Ventilator, *m.*-en, ventilator, blower, fan.

Ventilgehäuse, *n.* valve chamber.

ventilieren, to ventilate.

Ventil-sitz, *m.* valve seat; **-steurung,** *f.* poppet-valve gear.

ventral, ventral; **-furche,** *f.* ventral suture; **-schale,** *f.* ventral valve; **-schuppe,** *f.* ventral scale.

Ventrikel, *m.* ventricle.

Venüle, *f.* minute vein.

Venus-fliegenfalle, Venus's-flytrap (*Dionaea muscipula*); **-gürtel,** *m.* Cestus (*Cestum veneris*); **-haar,** *n.* maidenhair (*Adiantum capillus veneris*).

verab-folgen, to deliver, remit, hand over: **-reden,** to agree upon, appoint, fix, stipulate; **-redung,** *f.* agreement, arrangement; **-reichen,** to tender, deliver, hand over, dispense; **-reichung,** *f.* giving, application, administration; **-schieden,** to dismiss, discharge, send away, take leave.

verachten, to despise, look down upon, scorn.

verächtlich, contemptuous, scornful.

verallgemeinern, to generalize.

Verallgemeinerung, *f.* generalization.

veralten, to grow old, obsolete, stale, out of date.

veraltet, antiquated.

veränderlich, variable, changeable, unsettled, fluctuating, unstable.

Veränderliche, *f.* variable.

Veränderlichkeit, *f.* variability.

verändern, to alter, change, transform, modify, vary.

Veränderung, *f.* change, alteration, transformation, variation.

Veränderungsfähigkeit, *f.* alterability.

Verangerung, *f.* overgrowing with weeds.

verankern, to anchor, fasten, grapple, fix.

veranlagen, to organize, arrange.

Veranlagung, *f.* heredity, arrangement.

veranlagt, inclined, disposed, gifted.

Veranlagungstypus, *m.* genotype (predisposition type).

veranlassen, to occasion, give rise to, cause, induce, instigate, start, motivate, bring about.

Veranlassung, *f.* occasion, cause, instigation, inducement, motive; ∼ **geben,** to give rise to.

veranschaulichen, to illustrate, afford a view of, make clear.

veranschlagen, to estimate, appraise, value.

veranstalten, to arrange, prepare, manage.

verantworten, to answer or be responsible for, justify, vindicate.

verantworlich, answerable, responsible, accountable.

Verantwortlichkeitsgefühl, *n.* feeling of responsibility.

Verantwortung, *f.* responsibility.

verarbeiten, to digest, work (up), treat, manufacture, process, convert, manipulate.

Verarbeiter, *m.* processing plant, throwster.

Verarbeitung, *f.* working up, consumption, digestion, manufacture, treatment, processing.

verarmen, to become poor, impoverished, reduce in strength.

verarten, to degenerate.

veraschen, to ash, incinerate.

verästelt, branched, ramified.

veräthern, to etherify, alkoxylate.

veratmen, to breathe, use up by breathing.

Veratrin, *n.* veratrine.

Veratrumsäure, *f.* veratric acid.

verätzen, to corrode, cauterize.

Verätzung, *f.* erosion, cauterization.

verausgaben, to expend, spend, pay.

veräussern, to turn into cash, sell.

Verband, *m.* union, association, bandaging, dressing, bandage, binding, assemblage, alliance, connection, arrangement.

Verbänderung, *f.* fasciation.

Verband-glas, *n.* glass compound or fastening; **-holz,** *n.* framing timber; **-päckchen,** *n.* emergency kit, first-aid kit; **-schicht,** *f.* bandage layer; **-stoff,** *m.* bandaging material.

verbannen, to banish.

verbauen, to obstruct, spend in building.

Verbauung, *f.* obstruction of view, damming.

verbeissen, to suppress, browse on, stifle.

verbeizen, to overbate (leather).

Verbene, *f.* vervain, verbena.

verbergen, to hide, conceal; **-verborgen,** concealed, latent, hidden, obscure, secret.

verbessern, to make better, improve, correct, amend, revise, perfect.

Verbesserung, *f.* improvement, correction, reform.

Verbesserungs-hieb, *m.* improvement (cutting) felling, thinning; **-mittel,** *n.* corrective.

verbeugen, to bow.

verbiegen, to bend wrong, distort, curve, warp.

verbieten, to forbid, prohibit.

verbilligen, to cheapen, reduce in price.

verbinden, to unite, combine, amalgamate, bind (up), join, ally, link, connect, oblige, bandage.

verbindlich, obliging, courteous, compulsory, bound, obliged; **meinen verbindlichen Dank!,** my best thanks.

Verbindlichkeit, *f.* kindness, favor, obligation, obligingness.

Verbindung, *f.* union, compound, combination, connection, commissure, blending of colors, joining, binding, bond, communication, alliance, society, association, relation(ship), amalgamation; **in ~ mit,** in conjunction with; **in ~ stehen,** to be connected, be in communication; **in ~ treten,** to form a connection or union.

Verbindungs-balken, *m.* connecting crossbar; **-faden,** *m.* connecting fiber, median spindle fiber; **-fähigkeit,** *f.* combining ability; **-gewebe,** *n.* connective tissue; **-gewicht,** *n.* combining (equivalent) weight; **-gleichung,** *f.* equation of combination; **-glied,** *n.* connecting link; **-kanal,** *m.* connecting passage; **-klammer,** *f.* brace; **-klemme,** *f.* connector.

Verbindungs-knoten, *m.* lymphatic ganglion, spicular node; **-kraft,** *f.* combining power; **-mittel,** *n.* means of communication; **-molekül,** *n.* molecule of a compound; **-punkt,** *m.* juncture, junction; **-röhre,** *f.* connecting tube; **-schlauch,** *m.* connecting tube, nuclear spindle; **-schleife,** *f.* connecting loop; **-stamm,** *m.* communicating trunk.

Verbindungs-stelle, *f.* juncture, junction, symphysis; **-stiel,** *m.* connecting pedicel; **-strang,** *m.* commissure, connecting strand; **-streben,** *n.* affinity; **-strich,** *m.* hyphen; **-stück,** *n.* connecting piece, joint; **-stufe,** *f.* stage of combination; **-verhältnis,** *n.* combining proportion; **-wärme,** *f.* heat of combination; **-zeichen,** *n.* hyphen.

verbitten, to deprecate, object to, decline.

verblasen, to blow glass, dilute.

verblassen, to fade, discolor.

Verbleib, *m.* storage, abode, remaining.

verbleiben, to remain, continue, stay, abide.

verbleichen, to grow pale, fade, expire, pass away.

verbleien, to cover with lead.

Verbleiung, *f.* leading, lead lining.

verblenden, to blind, dazzle, infatuate, face with brick, delude.

Verblender, *m.* face brick.

verblüffen, to startle, bewilder, stagger.

verblühen, to fade, wither, cease blooming.

Verblühzeit, *f.* paracme (decline).

verblümen, to disguise.

verblümt, figurative, allegorical.

verbluten, to bleed to death, cease bleeding.

verbogen (verbiegen), crooked.

verborgen, to lend, credit.

verborgen, inconspicuous, concealed, hidden, secret; **verborgene Befruchtung,** *f.* cryptogamy.

Verbot, *n.* prohibition.

verboten (verbieten), forbidden.

verbrämen, to border, edge, trim.

verbrannt (verbrennen), burnt up, scorched, overexposed.

Verbrauch, *m.* consumption, use (of).

verbrauchen, to consume, use up.

Verbrauchs-gegenstand, *m.* article of consumption, commodity; **-stelle,** *f.* place of consumption; **-stoff,** *m.* substance of consumption.

verbraucht, worn out, used up, spent.

verbrausen, to cease fermenting, sober down, subside.

Verbrechen, *n.* offense, crime, guilt, outrage.

verbreiten, to spread, disperse, disseminate, diffuse, propagate, distribute.

verbreitern, to widen out, broaden.

verbreitet, widespread, distributed; **weit ~,** very common.

Verbreitung, *f.* distribution, range, dispersal, circulation, spreading, dissemination, propagation.

Verbreitungs-ausrüstung, *f.* equipment for dissemination; **-bezirk,** *m.* habitat, area of ramification; **-einheit,** *f.* distribution unit; **-gebiet,** *n.* range of distribution; **-geschichte,** *f.* history of distribution; **-grenzen,** *f.pl.* limits of distribution; **-mittel,** *n.* means of distribution; **-verhältnis,** *n.* distribution relationship; **-weise,** *f.* method of dissemination.

verbrennbar, combustible.

Verbrennbarkeit, *f.* combustibility.

verbrennen, to burn, scorch, singe, tan, scald, cremate, bake.

verbrennlich, combustible, inflammable.

Verbrennung, *f.* combustion, burning, incineration, cremation.

Verbrennungs-ergebnis, *n.* product of combustion; **-gase,** *n.pl.* gases of combustion; **-intensität,** *f.* intensity of combustion; **-kammer,** *f.* combustion chamber; **-(kraft)maschine,** *f.* internal-combustion engine; **-luft,** *f.* air for combustion; **-narbe,** *f.* scar from burn; **-ofen,** *m.* combustion furnace.

Verbrennungs-produkt, *n.* product of combustion; **-raum,** *m.* combustion chamber; **-rückstand,** *m.* residue on combustion (ignition); **-versuch,** *m.* combustion experiment; **-vorgang,** *m.* process of combustion; **-wärme,** *f.* heat of combustion; **-wert,** *m.* combustion value.

verbriefen, to acknowledge, confirm, secure in writing.

verbringen, to spend, pass, squander, waste, transport, remove.

verbrühen, to scald.

verbunden (verbinden), combined, obliged, indebted.

Verbund-glas, *n.* laminated glass, compound glass; **-maschine,** *f.* compound engine; **-stück,** *n.* fitting, coupling; **-verfahren,** *n.* duplex method.

verbürgen, to warrant, guarantee.

verbutten, to become stunted or dwarfed.

verbuttet, stunted, dwarfed, crippled.

Verbuttung, *f.* scrubbiness.

Verchromung, *f.* chromium plating.

Verdacht, *m.* suspicion, distrust.

verdächtig, (*gen.*) suspicious, suspected, doubtful.

verdämmen, to stunt, dwarf, encroach, suppress, dam, check.

verdämmt, choked, suppressed, dammed.

Verdämmung, *f.* encroachment.

Verdampfapparat, *m.-e,* evaporator.

verdampfbar, vaporizable, volatile.

Verdampfbarkeit, *f.* volatility.

verdampfen, to evaporate, vaporize.

Verdampfschale, *f.* evaporating dish.

Verdampfung, *f.* evaporation, vaporization.

verdampfungs-fähig, capable of evaporation; **-geschwindigkeit,** *f.* velocity of vaporization; **-punkt,** *m.* vaporization point; **-rückstand,** *m.* residue on evaporization; **-vermögen,** *n.* evaporating power; **-wärme,** *f.* (latent) heat of vaporization; **-wert,** *m.* evaporating value; **-zahl,** *f.,* **-ziffer,** *f.* coefficient of evaporation.

verdanken, to owe, be indebted to, be due to.

verdarb (verderben), spoiled, deteriorated, perished.

verdauen, to digest.

verdaulich, digestible.

Verdaulichkeit, *f.* digestibility.

Verdauung, *f.* digestion.

Verdauungs-apparat, *m.*-e, digestive apparatus; **-arbeit,** *f.* digestive work; **-dauer,** *f.* duration of digestion; **-drüse,** *f.* digestive gland; **-eingeweide,** *n.* digestive tract; **-fähig,** digestible; **-fähigkeit,** *f.* digestibility; **-flüssigkeit,** *f.* digestive fluid, gastric juice.

Verdauungs-geschäft, *n.*-e, digestive process; **-kanal,** *m.* alimentary canal, digestive tract; **-mittel,** *n.* digestive remedy; **-rohr,** *n.* digestive tract, alimentary canal; **-saft,** *m.* gastric juice; **-traktus,** *m.* digestive tract; **-verdecken,** to cover, mask, shelter, conceal; **-verlauf,** *m.* course (process), of digestion; **-vorgang,** *m.* digestive process; **-werkzeug,** *n.* digestive organ (apparatus).

verdecken, to cover, conceal, mask.

verdenken, to find fault with.

verderben, to spoil, damage, deteriorate, decay, ruin, corrupt, demoralize; **verdorben,** spoiled.

Verderben, *n.* fate, ruin.

verderblich, perishable, pernicious, destructive, corruptible, injurious.

Verderbnis, *f.*-se, depravity, deterioration, decay, corruption, destruction.

verdeutlichen, to make clear, elucidate.

verdeutschen, to translate into German, Germanize.

verdichtbar, condensable.

Verdichtbarkeit, *f.* condensability, compressibility.

verdichten, to compress, concentrate, condense, liquefy.

Verdichter, *m.* compressor.

Verdichtung, *f.* compression, consolidation, compaction.

Verdichtungsmittel, *n.* thickener.

Verdichtungs-apparat, *m.* condensing apparatus, condenser; **-grad,** *m.* degree of compression (condensation); **-hub,** *m.* compression stroke; **-wärme,** *f.* heat of compression (condensation).

verdicken, to thicken, condense, concentrate, inspissate, jell, coagulate, clot, curdle, become viscous.

Verdickung, *f.* thickening, increase in diameter.

Verdickungs-masse, *f.* secondary thickening; **-mittel,** *n.* thickening agent; **-ring,** *m.*

cambium, annual ring of trees; **-stosswelle,** *f.* compression wave.

verdienen, to earn, merit, deserve, gain, make; **sich verdient machen um,** to deserve recognition, earn, merit.

Verdienst, *n.* merit, earnings, wages, profit, deserts; **-voll,** meritorious.

verdoppeln, to double, (re)duplicate.

Verdopplung, *f.* doubling, (re)duplication.

verdorben (verderben), spoiled, foul, rotten, tainted, damaged.

verdorren, to dry up, dry, wither.

verdrängen, to displace, crowd out, shade out, supplant, drive out, remove, oust, suppress.

Verdrängung, *f.* displacement, removal, dispossession.

Verdrängungs-messer, *m.* current meter; **-prinzip,** *n.* displacement principle.

verdrehen, to distort, twist, wrench, sprain, dislocate.

Verdrehung, *f.* distortion, twisting, torsion, prevarication.

Verdrehungswinkel, *m.* torsional angle.

verdreifachen, to triple, treble.

Verdreifachung, *f.* trebling, triplication.

verdriessen, to vex, annoy, grieve.

verdriesslich, verdrossen, reluctant, grieved, vexed, loath.

verdringen, to supplant.

verdrücken, to crush, crumple, crease, overpress, devour.

Verdruss, *m.* trouble, annoyance, disgust, grief.

verduften, to evaporate, vanish.

verdunkeln, to darken, obscure, grow dim.

verdünnbar, capable of dilution, rarefiable.

verdünnen, to dilute, rarefy, weaken, attenuate, thin.

verdünnt, diluted, adulterated, dilute, rare, thin.

Verdünnung, *f.* dilution, attenuation, rarefaction, thinning.

Verdünnungs-gesetz, *n.* dilution law; **-grad,** *m.* degree of dilution; **-mittel,** *n.* diluent, attenuant.

verdunstbar, capable of evaporation, vaporizable.

verdunsten, verdünsten, to evaporate.

Verdunstung, Verdünstung, *f.* evaporation, volatilization, transpiration.

Verdunstungs-kälte, *f.* cold due to evaporation; **-schutz,** *m.* protection against evaporation or transpiration; **-wärme,** *f.* heat of vaporization.

verdursten, to die of thirst.

verdutzen, to startle, nonplus.

verecktes Geweih, *n.* completed attire, perfect head (antlers).

veredeln, to improve, raise, cultivate, breed, purify, refine, enrich, elevate, graft, ennoble, throw (yarn).

Vered(e)lung, *f.* budding, grafting, refinement, improvement, throwing, throwster.

Veredlungsverkehr, *m.* duty drawback, free import and export of goods to be finished.

verehren, to revere, respect, adore, admire.

Verehrung, *f.* veneration, devotion.

Verein, *m.-e,* union, alliance, association, society, club.

vereinbar, combinable, compatible, reconcilable.

vereinbaren, to agree upon, reconcile.

Vereinbarung, *f.* agreement, reconciliation.

vereinen, to unite.

vereinfachen, to simplify, reduce.

Vereinfachung, *f.* simplification, reduction.

vereinheitlichen, to standardize, render uniform.

vereinigen, to unite, combine, join, collect, blend, reconcile, agree.

vereinigt, united.

Vereinigten Staaten, *m.pl.* the United States.

Vereinigung, *f.* union, combination, connection, association, agreement, accord, anatomosis.

Vereinigungs-haut, *f.-̈e,* connecting membrane, conjunctiva; **-ort,** *m.* point of union, commissure; **-stelle,** *f.* junction.

Vereinsgebiet, *n.* society district.

vereintblätterig, gamophyllous (leaves united).

vereinzeln, to isolate, detach, separate, sever.

vereinzelt, isolated, solitary, scattering, sporadic(ally).

vereisen, to turn to ice, frost (refrigerators), cover with ice (road), freeze (river).

vereiteln, to frustrate, balk, thwart, defeat.

vereitern, to suppurate.

Vereiterung, *f.* suppuration.

verenge(r)n, to narrow, contract, constrict.

Verengerung, *f.* contraction, narrowing.

vererben, to bequeath, will, transmit, hand down.

vererbt, hereditary, inherited.

Vererbung, *f.* **Vererblichkeit,** *f.* inheritance, heredity, transmission.

Vererbungs-experiment, *n.* genetical experiment; **-forschung,** *f.* genetics; **-kraft,** *f.* power of transmission; **-lehre,** *f.* genetics, science of heredity; **-problem,** *n.* problem of transmission; **-regel,** *f.* law of heredity; **-studium,** *n.* inheritance study, genetics; **-substanz,** *f.* idioplasm; **-theorie,** *f.* theory of heredity; **-vorgang,** *m.* process of inheritance; **-wissenschaft,** *f.* science of heredity, genetics.

vererden, to turn to earth, oxidize.

vererzen, to mineralize.

verestern, to esterify.

verewigen, to perpetuate, immortalize.

verewigt, late, decreased.

verfahren, to proceed, act, handle, manage, deal, blunder, muddle.

Verfahren, *n.* process, method, treatment, procedure, proceeding, manner, conduct, management.

Verfahrungs-art, -weise, *f.* mode of proceeding, method, process.

Verfall, *m.* decay, ruin, decline, fall, deterioration, expiration, degeneracy.

verfallen, to decay, decline, fall, degenerate, expire; **auf etwas ∼,** to chance (hit) upon something.

verfälschen, to adulterate, debase, counterfeit, falsify.

Verfälscher, *m.* falsifier, adulterator, forger.

Verfälschung, *f.* falsification, adulteration, forgery.

verfangen, to be caught, operate, take effect, be of avail.

verfänglich, insidious, enticing, deceitful.

verfärben, to change color, fade, decrease in color, discolor.

Verfärbung, *f.* discoloration, decoloration, fading.

verfassen, to compose, write.

Verfasser(in), *m.&f.* author, writer.

Verfassung, *f.* disposition, condition, composition, constitution.

verfaulbar, putrescible, corruptible.

verfaulen, to rot, decay, putrefy, decompose.

Verfaulung, *f.* putrefying, decaying, rotting.

verfechten, to defend, advocate.

verfehlen, to miss, fail.

verfehlt, unsuccessful, miscarried, misplaced, wrong.

verfeinern, to refine, purify, improve.

verfertigen, to make, manufacture, construct, prepare, compose, fabricate.

verfestigen, to fasten, solidify by stress, strengthen, stabilize, consolidate.

Verfettung, *f.* fatty degeneration.

verfeuern, to burn (up).

verfilzen, to felt, mat.

verfilzt, matted, feltlike.

Verfilzung, *f.* felting, matting.

Verfilzungsfähigkeit, *f.* felting (matting) property.

verfinstern, to darken, obscure.

verfitzen, to tangle, perplex, embarrass.

verflachen, to flatten, become level.

Verflachung, *f.* flattening, decline.

verflechten, to interlace, interweave, involve.

Verflechtung, *f.* interweaving, implication, interlacing, entanglement.

verfliegen, to fly away, vanish, volatilize.

verfliegend, volatile, evanescent.

verfliessen, to flow away, subside, blend, pass, elapse, glide.

verflochten (verflechten), entangled, implexus, interlaced, interwoven.

verflüchtigen, to volatilize, evaporate.

Verflüchtigung, *f.* volatilization, sublimation.

verflüssigen, to liquefy, condense.

Verflüssigung, *f.* liquefaction.

Verflüssigungsmittel, *n.* liquefacient.

verfolgen, to pursue, persecute, prosecute, carry on, follow up, continue.

Verfolgung, *f.* pursuit, persecution, prosecution.

verformen, to deform, form, work.

verfrachten, to transport, ship.

Verfrachtung, *f.* transport, shipment, chartering, freighting.

verfrischen, to refine.

verfrüht, premature.

verfügbar, at one's disposal, available.

verfügen, to have at one's disposal, dispose of, order, prescribe, arrange, decide.

Verfügung, *f.* disposal, command; zur ∼ stehen, to be at one's disposal or available.

verführen, to convey, transport, mislead, corrupt.

verfüllen, to fill.

verfüttern, to feed, overfeed.

Verfütterungsversuch, *m.* feeding experiment.

vergällen, to embitter, denature.

vergangen (vergehen), gone, past.

Vergangenheit, *f.* past (times or things).

vergänglich, transient, perishable, ephemeral.

vergären, to ferment, attenuate.

Vergärungs-fähigkeit, *f.* fermentability: -grad, *m.* degree of fermentation.

vergasbar, vaporizable.

vergasen, to vaporize, reduce to gas.

Vergaser, *m.* carburetor.

vergass (vergessen), forgot.

Vergasung, *f.* vaporization, carburetion, reduction of gas, treating with gas.

vergeben, to give, confer, bestow, forgive.

vergebens, in vain.

vergeblich, vain, futile, needless.

vergegenwärtigen, to represent, picture, imagine, realize.

Vergegenwärtigung, *f.* representation, figure, graphic description.

vergehen, to vanish, pass away, perish, cease, end, subside, elapse, offend, transgress.

Vergehen, *n.* perishing, destruction, offense.

Vergeilen, *n.* etiolation.

vergelben, to turn yellow, etiolate.

vergelten, to repay, return, reward, retaliate.

Vergeltung, *f.* retaliation, return, reward.

vergesellschaften, to associate, unite with.

Vergesellschaftung, *f.* association.

vergessen, to forget.

Vergessenheit, *f.* forgetfulness, oblivion.

vergesslich, forgetful, oblivious.

vergeuden, to squander, waste, fritter away.

vergewaltigen, to offer violence, use force.

vergewissern, to assure, convince, confirm, ascertain.

vergiessen, to spill, shed, cast (run), cast badly.

vergiften, to poison.

Vergiftung, *f.* poisoning, intoxication, infection.

Vergiftungserscheinung, *f.* symptom of poisoning.

vergilben, to turn yellow, become pale, stiolate.

Vergissmeinnicht, *n.* forget-me-not (Myosotis).

vergisst (vergessen), forgets.

vergittern, to grate, lattice.

vergl., *abbr.* (vergleiche), compare.

verglasbar, vitrifiable.

verglasen, to vitrify, glaze.

Verglasung, *f.* vitrification, glazing.

Vergleich, *m.*-e, arrangement, agreement, contract, comparison, parallel.

vergleichbar, comparable.

vergleichen, to compare, check, come to an agreement, adjust, compensate, equalize.

vergleichend, comparative.

Vergleichs-fähigkeit, *f.* comparability; **-fläche,** *f.* check plat, control area; **-lösung,** *f.* standard solution; **-pflanze,** *f.* control plant; **-präparat,** *n.* comparison preparation; **-quadrat,** *n.* comparative quadrat.

Vergleichs-strich, *m.* comparative mark; **-substanz,** *f.* standard; **-verfahren,** *n.* comparison method; **-versuch,** *m.* comparative experiment; **-weise,** by way of comparison; **-wert,** *m.* comparative value.

Vergleichung, *f.* comparison.

verglichen (vergleichen), compared, equalized.

Vergliederung, *f.* articulation.

verglimmen, to cease glowing, go out.

Verglühbrand, *m.* biscuit baking (in ceramics).

verglühen, to cease glowing, cool down, fire porcelain, bake, ignite, calcine.

vergnügen, to gratify, amuse, enjoy oneself, delight.

Vergnügen, *n.* pleasure, enjoyment.

vergnügt, delighted, cheerful.

Vergnügung, *f.* pleasure, amusement, recreation.

vergolden, to gild.

vergoldet, gilded, gold-plated.

Vergoldung, *f.* gilding.

Vergoldungswasser, *n.* quickening liquid.

vergönnen, to permit, allow, grant.

vergoren (vergären), fermented.

vergossen (vergiessen), shed.

vergraben, to bury, intrench, hide in the ground.

vergrast, overgrown with grass.

vergreifen, to seize by mistake, attack, violate, embezzle, buy up (out).

vergriffen, sold out, gone, exhausted.

vergröbern, to make coarser.

vergrössern, to enlarge, increase, magnify exaggerate, raise, grow larger.

Vergrösserung, *f.* increase, enlargement, augmentation, magnification, exaggeration.

Vergrösserungs-glas, *n.* magnifying glass; **-kraft,** *f.* magnifying power; **-linse,** *f.* magnifying lens; **-tabelle,** *f.* table of magnifications.

vergrünen, to turn green, lose green color, fade.

Vergrünung, *f.* proliferation.

vergüten, to heat-treat (steel), temper, compensate, refund, make good, improve, restore.

verhaften, to arrest, apprehend.

verhagern, to become lean.

verhagert, impoverished, depleted.

Verhagerung, *f.* impoverishment, depletion.

Verhakung, *f.* interlock.

Verhalt, *m.* state of affairs, condition, behavior.

verhalten, to behave, conduct, act, be, hold back, retain, suppress; **sich ~,** to be (in a certain condition); **es verhält sich,** the case is.

Verhalten, *n.* behavior, conduct, procedure, retention, suppression.

Verhältnis, *n.*-se, relation, proportion, ratio, condition, rate, situation, connection, circumstance, means; **im ~ zu,** in comparison with.

Verhältnis-anzeiger, *m.* exponent; **-gleichheit,** *f.* equality of, proportion; **-mässig,** proportional, proportionate(ly), relative(ly), pro rata, commensurate; **-widrig,** disproportionate; **-zahl,** *f.* proportional number, ratio, coefficient factor.

Verhaltung, *f.* retention, suppression, conduct.

Verhaltungsmassregel, *f.* instruction, rule, precaution.

verhandeln, to negotiate, discuss, transact, try, sell, treat.

Verhandlung, *f.* negotiation, transaction, deliberation, proceeding, debate.

verhängen, to hang, cover over, close up, conceal, decree, pronounce.

Verhängnis, *n.* destiny, fate; **zum** ∼ **werden,** to become fatal.

verhängnisvoll, fatal, disastrous.

verharren, to abide, remain, persist.

verhärten, to harden, indurate, become sclerosed.

Verhärtung, *f.* hardening, induration, constipation.

verharzen, to become resinous, resinify, cover with resin.

verharzt, impregnated with resin, gummed.

Verharzung, *f.* resinification, gumming.

verhauen, to cut up, hack, lop, prune.

verheeren, to devastate.

verheerend, destructive.

verhehlen, to hide, conceal.

Verheidung, Verhaidung, *f.* being overgrown with heather.

Verheidungsgrad, *m.* degree of heath development.

verheilen, to heal up.

verheimlichen, to keep secret, conceal, disguise, dissemble.

verheiraten, to give in marriage, marry.

verheissen, to promise.

verhelfen, to help, assist, procure.

verhindern, to hinder, prevent.

Verhinderung, *f.* prevention, hindrance, obstacle.

verholzen, to lignify, become wood.

Verhör, *n.*-e, examination, trial, hearing.

verhornen, to become horny.

Verhornung, *f.* cornification.

verhüllen, to cover, veil, wrap up, disguise, conceal.

verhungern, to starve.

Verhungerung, *f.* starvation.

verhunzen, to botch, bungle.

verhüten, to prevent, avert, ward off.

verhütend, preventive.

verhütten, to smelt ores, treat ores.

Verhütung, *f.* prevention, prophylaxis.

Verhütungsmittel, *n.* preventive, prophylactic.

verimpfen, to transmit by inoculation or contagion.

verirren, to err, go astray.

verjagen, to drive away, expel, dislodge.

verjähren, to grow old, increase with age, grow obsolete, superannuate, lapse.

verjauchen, to form sanies, putrefy.

Verjauchung, *f.* putrefaction.

verjüngen, to rejuvenate, renovate, regenerate, reduce, constrict, narrow, taper.

verjüngt, attenuate(d), rejuvenate(d).

Verjüngung, *f.* rejuvenation, diminution, reduction, tapering off, constriction, regeneration, restocking, reproduction.

Verjüngungs-fläche, *f.* reproduction (regeneration) area; **-form,** *f.* regeneration form; **-hieb,** *m.* regeneration felling; **-knospe,** *f.* regeneration bud; **-notwendigkeit,** *f.* need for regeneration; **-schlag,** *m.* reproduction area.

verkadminieren, to plate with cadmium.

verkalben, to calve prematurely.

Verkalben, *n.* abortion in a cow.

verkalkbar, calcinable.

verkalken, to calcify, calcine, lime.

Verkalkung, *f.* calcification, calcination.

verkannt (verkennen), misunderstood, mistaken.

verkappen, to mask, disguise.

verkäsen, to become caseous.

Verkäsung, *f.* caseation.

verkäuen, to chew (up).

Verkauf, *m.*⁔e, sale.

verkaufen, to sell, dispose of.

verkäuflich, salable, marketable.

Verkehr, *m.* traffic, business, trade, commerce, intercourse, communication.

verkehren, to visit, associate, invert, reverse, pervert, transform.

Verkehrs-mittel, *n.* means of communication, conveyance; **-sicher,** safe for commerce; **-strasse,** *f.* trade route, highway; **-wesen,** *n.* traffic.

verkehrt, inverted, reversed, perverted, wrong, preposterous, absurd; ∼ **eiförmig,** obovate, obovoid; ∼ **herzförmig,** obcordate; ∼ **kegelförmig,** obconical; ∼ **lanzettlich,** oblanceolate.

verkennen, to mistake, misconstrue, misunderstand.

Verkernung, *f.* change from sapwood to heartwood.

verketten, to link together, unite.

verkettet, interlinked.

Verkettung, *f.* linking, linkage, union.

Verkettungsfähigkeit, *f.* linking capacity, ability to form chains.

Verkienung, *f.* saturation with resin.

verkieseln, to silicify.

Verkieselung, *f.* silicification.

verkiesen, to ballast, gravel.

verkitten, to cement, lute, seal with putty.

Verkittung, *f.* cementing, luting.

verklammern, to clamp, brace, interlock.

verkleben, to glue, cement, lute, apply a plaster, agglutinate, coalesce.

Verklebung, *f.* agglutination, mending, gluing together.

Verklebungs-reaktion, *f.* agglutinative reaction; **-stoff,** *m.* agglutinative substance.

verkleiden, to disguise, mask, face, case, board, line.

Verkleidung, *f.* disguise, casing, lining.

verkleinern, to reduce, diminish, narrow down, disparage, depreciate.

Verkleinerung, *f.* diminution, reduction, depreciation, detraction.

verkleistern, to paste up together, reduce to paste.

Verkleisterung, *f.* conversion into paste, pasting, clogging.

verknallen, to waste powder, detonate.

Verknäuelung, *f.* entanglement (in a knot).

verknistern, to decrepitate.

Verknisterung, *f.* decrepitation.

verknöchern, to ossify.

Verknöcherung, *f.* ossification.

verknorpeln, to become cartilaginous.

verknorpelt, cartilaginous.

Verknorpelung, *f.* chondrification.

Verknorpelungszentrum, *n.* center of chondrification.

verknüpfen, to tie, bind, join, link.

Verknüpfung, *f.* connection, linkage.

verkobalten, to plate with cobalt.

verkochen, to boil down (away), concentrate, evaporate, overboil, spoil by boiling.

verkohlen, to carbonize, turn to coal.

Verkohlung, *f.* charring, carbonization.

verkoken, to coke.

Verkokung, *f.* coking.

verkommen, to decay, degenerate.

verkoppeln, to couple, link.

verkorken, to cork.

Verkorkung, *f.* suberification.

verkörpern, to embody.

verkreiden, to calcify.

verkrümmen, to make crooked, curve, bend.

Verkrümmung, *f.* curvature.

verkrüppeln, to cripple, become deformed.

verkrusten, to become incrusted.

verkümmern, to stunt, encroach upon, spoil, be stunted, languish, degenerate.

verkümmert, rudimentary, stunted.

Verkümmerung, *f.* dwarfing, vestige, stuntedness, atrophy.

verkünden, verkündigen, to announce, proclaim, publish.

verküpen, to reduce a vat dye before dyeing.

verkupfern, to copper, copperplate.

verkuppeln, to couple.

verkürzen, to shorten, abridge, diminish, curtail, lessen, contract.

Verkürzung, *f.* shortening.

verladen, to load, ship.

Verlag, *m.-e,* publication, publishing house, funds.

Verlagerung, *f.* displacement.

Verlags-buchhändler, *m.* publisher; **-buchhandlung,** *f.* publishing house; **-handlung,** *f.* publishing company, bookstore; **-recht,** *n.* copyright.

Verlandung, *f.* deposition, delta formation.

Verlandungsbestände, *m.pl.* emergent vegetation, fresh delta facies.

verlangen, to long (for), wish (for), desire, ask, demand, require.

verlängern, to lengthen, prolong, produce, extend, protract, continue.

verlängertes Mark, medulla oblongata.

Verlängerung, *f.* prolongation, elongation, production, extension.

Verlängerungs-stück, *n.* extension piece; **-trieb,** *m.* terminal shoot, leading shoot, leader, continuation, extending shoot.

verlangsamen, to retard, delay, slow down.

Verlangsamung, *f.* retardation.

Verlass, *m.* trust.

verlassen, to leave, quit, give up, abandon, desert, depend, vacate, rely, abandoned, forsaken; **sich auf etwas ~,** to depend on something.

verlässig, verlässlich, reliable, trustworthy.

Verlaubung, *f.* frondescence, phyllody.

Verlauf, *m.* course, progress, expiration, lapse, flowing (of lacquer); **der zeitliche ~,** the progress (settlement) within a certain definite time.

verlaufen, to take a certain course, proceed, occur, expire, pass, run off, blend; **sich ~,** to lose one's way.

verlauten, to be heard, become known.

verleben, to live through, spend.

verlebt, used up, spent, decrepit.

verlegen, to shift, remove, lay, mislay, transfer, delay, obstruct, publish, misplace, establish (an equilibrium or concentration).

verlegen, spoiled, damaged, stale, embarrassed, perplexed.

Verlegenheit, *f.* perplexity, embarrassment, difficulty.

Verleger, *m.* publisher.

verleihen, to lend, invest, confer, bestow, grant.

verlernen, to unlearn, forget.

verlesen, to read (aloud) wrong, pick, select.

verletzen, to injure, damage, scratch, offend, encroach, infringe.

verletzlich, easily injured, vulnerable.

Verletzung, *f.* injury, damage, offense, wrong.

Verletzungsschmerz, *m.* pain of the injury.

verleugnen, to deny, disavow, renounce.

verlichten, to open out, thin out.

Verlichtung, *f.* gradual opening (thinning) by age.

verlieh (verleihen), lent, gave.

verlieren, to lose, get lost, subside, disappear; **verloren gehen,** to be lost; **verloren gegangen,** lost.

verliess, sich, (verlassen), relied.

verlocken, to allure, tempt, mislead, seduce.

verlohnen, to be worth.

verlor (verlieren), lost.

verioren (verlieren), lost, forlorn; **~ gehen,** to disappear, be lost, lose.

verloschen, gone out, extinct. effaced.

verlöschen, to go out, become extinguished.

verlöten, to solder (up), close by adhesion.

Verlust, *m.*-e, loss, waste, escape, leakage, damage, detriment; **-winkel,** *m.* phase angle, loss angle.

Vermächtnis, *n.* legacy, bequest.

vermag (vermögen), **er ~,** he is capable of, able to.

vermahlen, to grind.

vermännlichen, to make masculine; **sich ~,** to become masculine.

Vermännlichung, *f.* masculinization.

vermarken, to mark, demarcate.

Vermarkung, *f.* demarcation.

vermehren, to increase, augment, enlarge, multiply, propagate.

Vermehrung, *f.* reproduction, increase.

Vermehrungs-krankheit, *f.* propagation disease; **-pilz,** *m.* propagation fungus; **-tendenz,** *f.* tendency to multiply; **-trieb,** *m.* procreative impulse.

vermeidbar, avoidable.

vermeiden, to avoid, elude, evade, shirk, eliminate.

Vermeidung, *f.* avoidance.

vermeinen, to believe, suppose, imagine.

vermeintlich, supposed, pretended.

vermengen, to mix, confuse, blend.

Vermengung, *f.* mixture, confusion, blending.

Vermerk, *m.*-e, note, notice, remark.

vermessen, to measure, survey, measure inaccurately, venture.

vermessen, daring, bold, presumptuous.

Vermessung, *f.* measurement, survey.

vermieten, to let, lease, hire out.

vermilchen, to emulsify.

vermindern, -to lessen, diminish, abate, reduce, impair, decline.

Verminderung, *f.* diminution, abatement, decrease, reduction, decrement.

vermischen, to mix, dilute, adulterate, blend, alloy.

vermischt, mixed, blended, miscellaneous, adulterated, promiscuous.

Vermischung, *f.* mixing, mixture, adulteration, alloy.

vermissen, to miss.

vermitteln, to negotiate, mediate, intervene, adjust, arrange, bring about, facilitate.

vermittelst, by means of.

Vermittler, *m.* mediator, agent.

Vermittlung, *f.* mediation, intervention, interposition, adjustment, agency.

vermochte, (vermögen), was able.

vermodern, to molder, rot, decay.

vermodert, moldy, decayed.

Vermoderung, *f.* dry rot, decay, moldering.

vermöge, by virtue of, according to.

vermögen, to be able, have influence, induce.

Vermögen, *n.* ability, capacity, power, property.

vermögend, well-to-do, wealthy, capable, powerful.

vermuten, to suppose, presume, surmise, conjecture, suspect, imagine.

vermutlich, probably, likely, presumable.

Vermutung, *f.* supposition, conjecture, guess, surmise.

vernachlässigen, to neglect, disregard, ignore.

vernarben, to scar, be cicatrized, heal.

vernarbt, cicatrized.

Vernarbung, *f.* cicatrization.

Vernarbungs-gewebe, *n.* callus (traumatic) tissue; **-membran,** *f.* restitution membrane.

Vernässung, *f.* waterlogging.

vernehmen, to perceive, hear, learn, understand, examine.

Vernehmen, *n.* perceiving, hearing, understanding.

vernehmlich, perceptible, audible, intelligible, distinct.

verneinen, to deny, disavow, contradict.

verneinend, negative.

vernetzen, to cross-link.

Vernetzung, *f.* latticelike polymerization.

vernichten, to destroy, cancel, annihilate, annul.

Vernichtung, *f.* annihilation, destruction.

vernickeln, to (plate with) nickel.

Vernickelung, *f.* nickel plating.

vernieten, to rivet.

Vernunft, *f.* reason, understanding, intellect, intelligence, judgment, common sense.

vernünftig, rational, reasonable, logical, sensible.

veröden, to become waste, lay waste.

veröffentlichen, to publish, announce, advertise.

verordnen, to order, establish, institute, prescribe, decree, appoint.

Verordnung, *f.* order, regulation, decree, prescription, appointment.

verpachten, to let, lease.

verpacken, to pack (up), wrap (up).

Verpackung, *f.* packing, casking, lining.

verpassen, to miss, lose.

verpesten, to infect, poison, taint.

verpichen, to (coat with) pitch; **auf etwas verpicht sein,** to be bent (intent) on something.

verpflanzen, to transplant.

Verpflanzung, *f.* transplantation.

verpflegen, to take care of, tend, nurse, provide.

Verpflegung, *f.* provisioning, supply, nursing.

verpflichten, to oblige, pledge, bind.

Verpflichtung, *f.* obligation, duty, responsibility.

verpfuschen, to bungle, botch, spoil.

verpönen, to forbid, prohibit.

verpönt, prohibited, despised.

verpuffen, to puff (off), decrepitate, explode, detonate, deflagrate.

Verpuffung, *f.* decrepitation, explosion, detonation.

verpuppen, to pupate.

Verpuppung, *f.* pupation.

verpuppungsreif, ready to pupate.

Verputz, *m.* plaster.

verputzen, to plaster, polish, clean, squander.

verquellen, to swell (up), warp, flow away.

Verquellung, *f.* swelling.

verquicken, to amalgamate, mix.

verraten, to betray, reveal.

verrauchen, to evaporate, go up in smoke.

verrechnen, to reckon, miscalculate, be mistaken.

verreiben, to grind well, triturate, spread by rubbing.

verreisen, to travel, go on a journey, spend in traveling.

verrenken, to sprain, dislocate.

Verrenkung, *f.* dislocation, luxation.

verrichten, to do, perform, achieve, execute.

Verrichtung, *f.* performance, execution, achievement, action, business, function, daily work.

verringern, to diminish, lessen, decrease, depreciate, attenuate. reduce.

Verringerung, *f.* decrease, attenuation.

verrinnen, to run off, pass away, elapse.

verrosten, to rust.

verrostet, rusty, rusted.

verrotten, to decay, rot.

verrucht, infamous, nefarious, wicked.

verrücken, to displace, shift, disturb, remove.

verrückt, deranged, insane, crazy.

Verruf, *m.* (social) excommunication.

verrühren, to mix up by stirring.

verrussen, to become sooty or smoked.

versagen, to refuse, deny, forgo, promise, grant, fail to work, miss, function.

versägen, to saw up.

Versagen, *n.* failure.

versalzen, to oversalt, spoil, mar.

versammeln, to assemble, gather, convene.

Versammlung, *f.* assembly, meeting, convocation, congress, collection.

Versand, *m.* dispatch, export(ation), shipping; -geschäft, *n.* mail-order house, export business; -schachtel, *f.* shipping case.

Versandung, *f.* silting.

Versatz, *m.*ːe, pawning, pledging, mixing, alloy, compound.

versauern, to turn sour.

versäuern, to acidify.

Versäuerung, *f.* acidification, souring.

versäumen, to miss, delay, neglect, omit.

verschaffen, to procure, supply, provide, obtain, get, secure.

verschärfen, to sharpen.

Verschalung, *f.* form, mold.

verschäumen, to turn into foam, cease foaming.

verscheiden, to expire, pass away, die.

verschenken, to give away, retail.

verschiebbar, displaceable, sliding.

Verschiebbarkeit, *f.* ease in displacement, mobility.

verschieben, to shift, move, displace, remove, postpone, delay.

Verschiebung, *f.* displacement, shifting, slip, fluctuation, shift.

Verschiebungs-gesetz, *n.* displacement law; -strom, *m.* displacement current.

verschieden, different, differing, unlike, various deceased; -artig, different (species), various, heterogeneous; -deutlich, more or less distinct; -fach, various, different; -farbig, of different colors, versicolor, motley; -griffelig, heterostylic.

Verschiedenheit, *f.* difference, variety, diversity, variation.

verschiedentlich, different(ly), at different times, more than once, several.

verschiessen, to shoot off, discharge, shade off, fade, discolor.

verschimmeln, to mold, grow moldy.

verschimmelt, moldy.

verschlacken, to scorify, be reduced to slag or scoria.

Verschlackungsprobe, *f.* scorification assay.

verschlafen, to sleep away, oversleep.

verschlafen, sleepy, drowsy.

Verschlag, *m.*ːe, partition, compartment.

verschlagen, to board up, partition, spoil by striking, warm a little, make lukewarm, take the chill off, make a difference, drive away.

verschlagen, slightly warmed, tepid, cunning, crafty.

verschlammen, to silt up.

verschlechtern, to make worse, deteriorate, spoil, degenerate.

Verschlechterung, *f.* deterioration.

verschleiern, to veil.

verschleiert, hazy, slightly clear.

verschleimen, to obstruct with mucus.

verschleimt, mucilaginous, obstructed with mucus, sticky, slimy.

Verschleimung, *f.* gelatinization, mucilaginization.

Verschleiss, *m.* wear and tear.

verschleissen, to wear out, retail.

verschleppen, to misplace, spread, carry (off), postpone, protract.

Verschleppungsklette, *f.* seed (burr) disseminated by clinging to animals.

verschleudern, to squander, sell very cheap (below cost).

verschliessbar, capable of being closed.

verschliessen, to close, plug, stop, shut, lock, reserve.

Verschliessmuskel, *m.* sphincter muscle.

Verschliessung, *f.* closing.

verschlimmern, to make worse, deprave, deteriorate.

Verschlimmerung, *f.* change for the worse, aggravation.

verschlingen, to devour, swallow, twist, intertwine, entangle.

verschlossen (verschliessen), self-contained, (too) reserved.

verschlucken, to swallow, imbibe, absorb.

verschlungen (verschlingen), interwoven.

Verschluss, *m.* ̈e, closing, occlusion, closure, healing, compacting, stopper, fastening, shutting, locking, fastener, seal, lock, clasp, trap, shutter; **-deckel,** *m.* closing cover, operculum; **-hahn,** *m.* stopcock; **-kölbchen,** *n.* pressure flask; **-saum,** *m.* seam of closure; **-stück,** *n.* lid, stopper, plug, operculum, closure.

verschmähen, to disdain, scorn, reject.

verschmälern, to narrow, constrict, diminish.

verschmelzen, to melt, smelt, fuse, solder, blend, melt away, dissolve, merge, coalesce.

Verschmelzung, *f.* melting, smelting, fusion of parts, alloy, blending, coalescence, amalgamation, combining.

Verschmelzungspropfbastard, *m.* graft chimera.

verschmieren, to smear, stop up, lute, daub; **sich** ∼, to fog, become fouled or smeared.

Verschmierung, *f.* blurring (in X-ray).

verschmitzt, crafty, artful, cunning, subtle.

verschmolzen, (verschmelzen), fused, amalgamated, closed up.

verschmutzen, to soil, pollute, contaminate.

Verschmutzung, *f.* soiling, pollution, infection, contamination.

verschneiden, to clip, prune, cut, castrate, geld, blend, adulterate, saw up.

Verschnitt, *n.* chips, blend; **-mittel,** *n.* diluent, cutting agent, blending agent, filler; **-wein,** *m.* blended (adulterated) wine.

verschoben (verschieben), shifted, displaced, dislodged.

verschollen (verschallen), missing, forgotten, lost.

verschonen, to spare, remain immune, excuse.

verschönern, to beautify.

verschossen (verschiessen), faded, discolored.

verschränken, to cross, fold, interlace.

verschrauben, to screw up, overscrew, screw wrongly.

Verschraubung, *f.* screwing, screw cap, screw joint, coupling.

verschreiben, to prescribe, order, assign, transfer in writing, miswrite, use up in writing.

Verschreibung, *f.* prescription, written order, assignment, note, bond.

verschroben (verschrauben), confused, eccentric, queer, odd.

verschrumpfen, to shrink, get mildewed, contract, shrivel.

verschuldet, indebted, under obligation, in debt.

verschulen, to transplant.

Verschulung, *f.* removal into nursery lines.

verschütten, to spill, fill up, bury.

verschwand (verschwinden), disappeared.

verschweigen, to keep secret, suppress, conceal.

verschwellen, to swell, swell shut.

verschwenden, to waste, squander.

Verschwendung, *f.* waste, wastefulness, lavishness.

verschwimmen, to dissolve, fade away, vanish, blend.

verschwinden, to disappear, vanish; **zum** ∼ **bringen,** to make disappear.

verschwommen, indistinct, vague, blurred, blended.

verschwören, to vow, swear, curse.

versehen, to provide, supply, furnish with, perform, conduct, attend to, be mistaken in, be aware, expect, be in error.

Versehen, *n.* oversight, mistake, error.

versehen, provided, supplied.

Versehung, *f.* provision, providing with.

verseifbar, saponifiable.

verseifen, to saponify.

Verseifung, *f.* saponification.

Verseifungs-fass, *n.* saponifying tun; **-mittel,** *n.* saponifier; **-zahl,** *f.* saponification number.

verseilen, to twist to a strand.

versenden, to send away, export, transmit.

versengen, to singe, scorch, burn, parch.

versenken, to sink, lower, submerge, countersink.

versetzbar, removable, capable of being mixed.

versetzen, to mix, treat, compound, alloy, stop, obstruct, transfer, transpose, transplant, misplace, pledge, mortgage, change course, be stopped up, displace, remove, set, place, put; **eins** ~, to give a blow; ~ **mit,** to add.

Versetzung, *f.* mixing, dilution, retention, permutation, alligation, removal, change.

verseuchen, to infect.

versichern, to insure, assure, affirm, assert, make sure (of).

Versicherung, *f.* insurance, assurance, affirmation.

Versicherungsschein, *m.* insurance policy.

versickern, to ooze away, percolate.

Versickerung, *f.* seepage, percolation.

versiegeln, to seal.

versiegen, to dry up, get exhausted.

versilbern, to silver(plate).

versinken, to sink.

versinnbild(lich)en, to symbolize, represent.

versintern, to encrust, sinter.

versorgen, to provide for.

Versorgung, *f.* provision, maintenance, situation, supply.

verspäten, to be late, retard, delay.

verspätet, belated, overdue, too late.

Verspätung, *f.* delay, lateness.

verspeisen, to eat up, consume.

versperren, to obstruct.

Verspillern, *n.* etiolation.

verspotten, to mock, ridicule, tease.

versprechen, to promise, make a slip (mistake), be engaged.

verspritzen, to squirt, spill, shed.

versprochen (versprechen), promised.

Versprossung, *f.* prolification, proliferation.

versprühen, to end in a (fine) drizzle or spray.

verspüren, to feel, perceive, notice.

Verstaatlichung, *f.* acquisition by the state.

verstählen, to convert into steel, line with steel.

Verstand, *m.* understanding, intelligence, sense, comprehension, judgment.

verstanden (verstehen), understood.

verständig, intelligent, reasonable, wise, sensible.

verständigen, to inform, acquaint, agree, explain, arrange.

Verständigung, *f.* understanding.

verständlich, intelligible, clear.

Verständnis, *n.* comprehension, understanding, appreciation.

verstärken, to strengthen, concentrate, enlarge, reinforce, fortify, intensify, increase.

Verstärker, *m.* intensifier, magnifier, amplifier.

Verstärkung, *f.* strengthening, stiffening, concentration, corroboration, reinforcement.

Verstärkungs-band, *n.* strengthening (accessory) ligament; **-flasche,** *f.* Leyden jar; **-folie,** *f.* intensifying screen; **-rippe,** *f.* feather rib; **-schirm,** *m.* intensifying screen.

verstatten, to permit, allow.

verstauben, to become dusty.

verstäuben, to reduce to dust, cover with dust.

verstauchen, to sprain, strain, dislocate partially.

Verstauchung, *f.* strain, sprain, semiluxation.

verstechen, to adulterate, exchange.

verstecken, to hide, secrete, conceal.

versteckt, hidden, reserved, sly.

verstehen, to understand, comprehend, mean, grasp, agree, consent, be skilled; **das versteht sich (von selbst),** that is obvious.

versteifen, to stiffen, harden.

Versteifung, *f.* reinforcement, strut.

versteigern, to sell at auction.

Versteigerung, *f.* auction, public sale.

versteinern, to petrify, devitrify.

Versteinerung, *f.* petrification, sclerenchymatization, hardening.

Versteinerungskunde, *f.* science of fossils, paleontology.

verstellbar, adjustable, movable.

verstellen, to move, shift, misplace, bar, disguise, dissemble, obstruct, disarrange.

verstellt, pretended, insincere, fictitious.

versteuern, to pay duty (excise) on.

versteuert, duty-paid.

verstocken, to harden, grow musty, rot, grow obdurate.

verstopfen, to choke, clog, stop up, plug, obstruct, constipate; **sich** ~, to become stopped up.

verstopft, constipated.

Verstopfung, *f.* stopping up, obstruction, constipation, incrustation.

Verstopfungs-mittel, *n.* astringent; **-muskel,** *m.* obturator muscle.

verstöpseln, to cork, stopper.

verstorben, deceased, late.

verstören, to disturb, interfere with, trouble.

verstossen, to offend against, reject, cast off, repulse, divorce.

verstreben, to brace, prop.

verstrecken, to stretch.

verstreichen, to elapse, expire, fill up, stop up, spread over, obliterate.

verstreuen, to disperse, scatter.

Verstrichensein, *n.* disappearance.

verstricken, to entangle, ensnare.

verstümmeln, to mutilate, main, truncate, curtail.

Verstümmelung, *f.* mutilation, truncation.

verstummen, to grow dumb, silent.

Versuch, *m.*-e, experiment, trial, test, assay, attempt, proof, effort, research, study.

versuchen, to try, test, tempt, taste, attempt, experiment.

Versuchs-anordnung, *f.* experimental setup, instruction, method of procedure; **-anlage,** *f.* pilot plant; **-anstalt,** *f.* research institute; **-bedingung,** *f.* experimental conditions; **-dauer,** *f.* duration of experiment; **-ergebnis,** *n.* result of experiment; **-fehler,** *m.* experimental error; **-feld,** *n.* **-fläche,** *f.* experimental plot, plat; **-flüssigkeit,** *f.* experimental solution.

Versuchs-grundlage, *f.* basis of experiment; **-mensch,** *m.* subject, person experimented upon; **-methode,** *f.* experimental method; **-parzelle,** *f.* experimental plat; **-reihe,** *f.* series of tests; **-station,** *f.* experimental station; **-technik,** *f.* experimental technique; **-tier,** *n.* experimental animal; **-vorschrift,** *f.* experimental directions; **-weise,** experimentally, on approval; **-wesen,** *n.* research methods.

Versuchung, *f.* temptation.

versumpfen, to become swampy or boggy.

Versumpfung, *f.* swampiness, bogginess.

versüssen, to sweeten, edulcorate, oversweeten.

Versüssung, *f.* sweetening, edulcoration.

vertagen, to adjourn.

vertauschen, to exchange, substitute.

Vertauschung, *f.* exchange, interchange, substitution.

verte (vertatur), please turn over.

verteidigen, to uphold, support, defend, maintain.

Verteidigung, *f.* maintenance, defense, support, advocacy, protection.

Verteidigungs-drüse, *f.* rent (repugnatorial) gland; **-waffe,** *f.* weapon of defense.

verteilen, to distribute, divide, apportion, dispense, assign, allot, disseminate, disperse.

Verteiler, *m.* distributor; **-platte,** *f.* distributor plate, dividing wall, baffle plate.

verteilt, divided, distributed.

Verteilung, *f.* distribution, apportionment, division, dispersion, diffusion.

Verteilungs-einrichtung, *f.* distributing device; **-gesetz,** *n.* law of distribution; **-kurve,** *f.* distribution curve; **-satz,** *m.* law of distribution; **-stelle,** *f.* place of distribution; **-zustand,** *m.* state of subdivision.

verteuern, to raise in price.

vertiefen, to deepen, sink; **sich ∼,** to be deeply engaged, broaden.

Vertiefung, *f.* deepening, cavity, recess, niche, indentation, hollow, depression.

vertikal, vertical; **-bewegung,** *f.* vertical motion; **-ebene,** *f.* vertical plane; **-schnitt,** *m.* vertical section.

vertilgbar, exterminable, eradicable.

vertilgen, to extinguish, extirpate, eradicate, uproot, destroy, devour, annihilate.

Vertilger, *m.* destroyer, exterminator.

Vertilgungsmittel, *n.* means of eradication, destroyer.

Vertrag, *m.*-e, agreement, contract, bargain, treaty.

vertragen, to agree, be compatible, bear, carry, suffer, endure, tolerate; **sich ∼,** to get on well, agree.

verträglich, friendly, compatible, consistent.

Verträglichkeit, *f.* compatibility, tolerance.

vertrauen, (*dat.*) to confide, trust.

Vertrauen, *n.* trust, confidence.

vertrauenswürdig, trustworthy.

vertraulich, intimate, confidential.

vertraut, intimate, familiar, conversant.

vertreiben, to drive away, expel, disperse, dispel, soften, shade down, distribute.

vertretbar, replaceable, capable of being substituted, defensible.

vertreten, to replace, represent, strain, sprain, obstruct, trample.

Vertreter, *m.* representative, substitute.

Vertretung, *f.* spraining, representation, defense, agent, agency, substitution.

Vertrieb, *m.-e,* sale, market.

vertrocknen, to dry up, wither, parch.

Vertrocknung, *f.* drying up, desiccation.

vertun, to waste, squander, lavish.

verunglücken, to perish, come to grief.

Verunglückte, *m.* victim, injured one.

verunkrauten, to become weedy.

verunkrautet, weedy, infested with weeds.

Verunkrautung, *f.* overgrowing with weeds.

verunreinigen, to soil, vitiate, pollute, contaminate, adulterate.

verunreinigt, soiled.

Verunreinigung, *f.* contamination, pollution, impurity.

verunstalten, to deform, deface, disfigure.

verunstaltet, misshapen, deformed.

Verunstaltung, *f.* disfigurement, deformity.

verunzieren, to mar, disfigure.

verursachen, to cause, occasion, produce.

verurteilen, to condemn, sentence.

verviel-fachen, to multiply, reproduce; -fältigen, to multiply, reproduce; -fältigung, *f.* reproduction.

vervierfachen, to quadruple.

vervollkommnen, to perfect, improve.

vervollständigen, to complete, replenish.

Vervollständigung, *f.* completion.

verwachsen, to grow together, coalesce closer, fuse, heal up, become crooked or overgrown.

verwachsen, grown together, synanthous, healed up; mit Blättern ~, gamophyllous; ~ blätterig, gamophyllous, gamopetalous.

verwachsend, concrescent.

Verwachsung, *f.* coalescence, fusion of parts, concrescence, self-grafting.

Verwachsungsstelle, *f.* place in coalescence, place of cicatrization, suture.

verwahren, to keep, guard, preserve.

verwahrlosen, to neglect.

Verwahrung, *f.* keeping, guarding, preservation, protest.

verwalten, to manage, supervise, administer.

Verwaltung, *f.* administration, management, conduct.

Verwalzbarkeit, *f.* malleability, suitability for rolling.

verwandelbar, transformable, convertible, changeable.

Verwandelbarkeit, *f.* transformability, convertibility.

verwandeln, to transform, change, metamorphose, convert, turn.

Verwandlung, *f.* metamorphosis, transformation, modification.

Verwandlungs-fähigkeit, *f.* capability of transformation (metamorphosis); -geschwindigkeit, *f.* speed of transformation.

verwandt (verwenden), used, applied.

verwandt, related, kin, allied, cognate, similar, analogous.

Verwandte, *m.&f.* relative, relation.

Verwandtenehe, *f.* (consanguineous) marriage between relatives.

Verwandtschaft, *f.* relationship, kinship, congeniality, affinity.

Verwandtschafts-begriffe, *m.pl.* cognate ideas; -beziehung, *f.* relationship; -einheit, *f.* unity of relationship, valence; -grad, *m.* degree of relationship, affinity; -kraft, *f.* force of affinity; -kreis, *m.* family; -lehre, *f.* doctrine of affinity; -linie, *f.* line of descent; -verhältnis, *n.* hereditary relationship, comparative relationship.

verwaschen, indistinct, faded, pale.

Verwaschenheit, *f.* vagueness, indistinctness.

verwässern, to water, dilute, become weak.

verweben, to weave up, interweave.

Verwebung, *f.* interweaving, mixing.

verwechseln, to (ex)change, mistake, confuse.

verwehen, to blow away, scatter.

Verwehen, *n.* dispersion of leaves.

verwehren, to prevent, forbid.

verweiblicht, effeminate.

verweichlicht, effeminate.

verweigern, to refuse, deny, reject.

verweilen, to stay, sojourn, tarry.

verweisen, to refer, banish, reproach.

Verweisung, *f.* reference, banishment.

verwelken, to wither, fade, wilt.

Verwelkung, *f.* withering, wilting.

Verwelkungskrankheit, *f.* wilt disease.

verwendbar, available, applicable.

verwenden, to turn away, employ, apply utilize, invest.

Verwendung, *f.* use, employment, application, appropriation, intercession; **zur ∼ kommen,** to be used.

Verwendungs-fähigkeit, *f.* applicability; **-stoffwechsel,** *m.* catabolism.

verwerfen, to cast away, reject, condemn, repudiate, disperse, misplace.

Verwerfung, *f.* rejection, repudiation, dislocation, warping.

verwertbar, realizable, utilizable.

Verwertbarkeit, *f.* utilization.

verwerten, to utilize, realize, turn to account, sell.

Verwertung, *f.* utilization, realization, disposal, sale.

verwesen, to putrefy, rot, decay, decompose, administer, manage, represent.

verweslich, liable to decay, perishable.

Verwesung, *f.* decay, putrefaction, decomposition, administration.

Verwesungs-pilz, *m.* saprophyte; **-prozess,** *m.* process of putrefaction (decay).

verwichen, past, late, former.

verwickeln, to entangle, complicate, involve.

verwickelt, complicated, entangled.

Verwick(e)lung, *f.* complication, complexity, confusion, tangle.

verweigen, to weigh (out).

verwiesen, referred to, dependent on; **es sei ∼ auf,** let it be referred to.

verwildern, to grow up to weeds, run to seed.

verwildert, uncultivated, covered with weeds, wild, brutal.

Verwilderung, *f.* untilled state, becoming covered with weeds.

verwinden, to overcome, get the better of.

verwirklichen, to realize, embody, materialize.

verwirren, to tangle, bewilder, perplex, complicate, embarrass.

verwirrt, complicated, perplexed, confused, distracted.

verwischen, to blot out, efface, obliterate.

verwittern, to disintegrate, effloresce, decay, weather.

verwittert, weather-beaten, decomposed.

Verwitterung, *f.* disintegration, efflorescence, weathering.

verworfen (verwerfen), cast off, rejected, abandoned.

verworren (verwirren), confused, entangled, distracted, perplexed.

verwunden, to wound, stir up, scarify (the soil); (verwinden) twisted.

verwunderlich, astonishing, wonderful, strange.

verwundern, to astonish, surprise, wonder at; **es ist nicht zu ∼,** it is not to be wondered at.

Verwundung, *f.* wound, injury.

Verwüstung, *f.* devastation, destruction.

verzählen, to count wrong, miscount.

verzahnen, to tooth, cog, notch, indent.

Verzahnung, *f.* gearing.

verzapfen, to (join by) mortise, retail (liquors).

Verzapfung, *f.* mortise joint.

verzehnfachen, to increase tenfold.

verzehren, to consume, waste, spend.

verzeichnen, to note down, record, specify, misdraw.

Verzeichnis, *n.*-**se,** list, inventory, register, index, catalogue, invoice, specification.

Verzeichnung, *f.* distortion, specification, drafting error.

verzeihen, to pardon, excuse.

verzerren, to distort.

Verzerrung, *f.* distortion, caricature.

Verzicht, *m.* renunciation; **∼ leisten,** to waive, relinquish.

verzichten, to relinquish, waive, give up.

verziehen, to distort, warp, train badly, withdraw, delay, stay, move.

verziehen (verzeihen), forgave.

verzieren, to decorate, beautify, illustrate.

Verzierung, *f.* decoration, trimming, ornamentation.

verzinken, to coat with zinc, galvanize.

Verzinkung, *f.* galvanizing.

verzinnen, to tin.

Verzinnung, *f.* tinning.

verzinsen, to pay interest on, yield interest.

verzogen (verziehen), warped, distorted, removed, ill-bred, spoiled.

Verzögerer, *m.* restrainer, retarder.

verzögern, to delay, put off, postpone.

Verzögerung, *f.* delay, retardation, inhibition, postponement.

verzollen, to pay duty on.

verzuckern, to sugar, candy, saccharify.

Verzuckung, *f.* convulsion.

Verzug, *m.*-**e,** delay, distortion.

verzweifeln, to despair.

verzweigen, to ramify, branch.

Verzweigung, *f.* ramification.

Verzweigungsformel, *f.* inflorescence, (branching) formula.

Verzwergung, *f.* dwarfing, stunting.

vexieren, to vex, tease, puzzle.

V-förmig, V-shaped.

vibrieren, to vibrate.

Vibrionen, *f.pl.* vibriones; -art, *f.* species of vibrio.

Vieh, *n.* cattle, livestock, beast; -arzt, *m.* veterinary surgeon; -dünger, *m.* stable manure; -futter, *n.* fodder, forage; -halter, *m.* cattle breeder; -haltung, *f.* cattle rearing, cattle breeding; -mast, *f.* fattening of cattle; -pest, *f.* cattle plague; -salz, *n.* cattle salt.

Vieh-schlag, *m.* group, species or breed of cattle; -stall, *m.* cattle shed; -stand, *m.* live farming stock, cattle stock; -weide, *f.* pasture; -zucht, *f.* cattle breeding; -züchter, *m.* breeder.

viel, much, many; so ~ ich sehen kann, as far as I can see.

viel-achsig, polyaxial; -ährig, many-eared, polystachous; -ästig, very much branched, ramous; -atomig, polyatomic; -beugig, flexuous; -blättrig, polyphyllous, many-leaved; -deutig, ambiguous.

viele, many; vieles andere, many other things.

Viel-eck, *n.* polygon; -eckig, polygonal, multangular; -ehig, polygamous.

vielerlei, diverse, various, multifarious.

viel-fach, manifold, various, frequent, in many ways; -fach, *n.* multiple; -fächerig, with many partitions, multilocular; -fältig, abundant, manifold, various; -fältigkeit, *f.* variety, multiplicity; -färbbarkeit, *f.* variegation, variety of colors, polychromy; -farbig, many-colored, variegated, polychromatic; -farbigkeit, *f.* variegation, polychromy; -flach, *n.* polyhedron; -flächig, polyhedral.

Viel-flächner, *m.* polyhedron; -förmig, multiform, polymorphous; -früchtig, polycarpous; -füsser, *m.pl.* polypods (Myriapoda); -genannt, much discussed; -gestaltig, polymorphic, polyplastic; -gestellig, manifold; -gliederig, polynomial; -griffelig, polygynous, polystylous; -haarig, polytrichous.

Vielheit, *f.* multiplicity.

viel-kammerig, multichambered, polythalamous; -kapselig, many-capsuled; -kernig, multinuclear, coenocytic; -köpfig, many-headed, polycephalic; -körnig, polyspermal, multinuclear; -kronblättrig, polypetalous.

vielleicht, perhaps, possibly.

viel-linig, multilinear; -mal(s), many times, frequently; -mehr, (much) more, on the contrary, rather; -nervig, many-nerved; -rippig, multicostate; -sagend, expressive, significant; -samig, polyspermous, with many seeds; -schichtig, many-layered, stratified; -seitig, many-sided, versatile, polygonal, polyhedral; -stachelig, spinous, polyacanthaceous.

viel-teilig, multifid, multisect, polytomous, polynomial; -versprechend, very promising; -wertig, polyvalent; -wertigkeit, *f.* multivalence, polyvalence; -zellbildung, *f.* formation of a large number of cells; -zellig, multicellular; -zipfelig, laciniate.

vier, four; -atomig, tetratomic; -beinig, four-legged; -blättrig, four-leaved, quadriphyllous, tetrapetalous; -eck, *n.* quadrangle; -eckig, four-cornered, quadrangular; -eckverband, *m.* square planting.

viereinhalb, four and one-half.

viererlei, of four kinds.

vierfach, fourfold, quadruple; -chlorkohlenstoff, *m.* carbon tetrachloride.

vierfältig, fourfold, quadruple.

vier-fingerig, tetradactylous, quadridigitate; -flach, *n.* tetrahedron; -flächig, tetrahedral; -flächner, *m.* tetrahedron; -flosser, *m.* having four fins; -flügelig, tetrapterous; -flügler, *m.pl.* animal with four wings; -füsser, *m.* quadruped, tetrapod; -gliedrig, four-membered, quadrinomial; -griffelig, having four stamens.

Vierhügel, *m.pl.* corpora quadrigemina; -hirn, *n.* mesencephalon; -schenkel, *m.* superior peduncle.

vier-jährig, quadrennial; -kantig, four-sided, four-edged; -kiemer, *m.pl.* Tetrabranchiatae.

Vierlingskörper, *m.* pollen tetrad.

vier-mächtig, tetradynamous; -mal, four times; -reihig, of four series, quadriserial; -säurig, tetracid, tetrabasic, tetravalent; -seitig, rectangular, quadrilateral, tetragonal.

Vierstrahler, *m.* tetraxial spicule, tetractinal.

viertägig, every fourth day, of four days.

Viertakt, *m.* four-stroke cycle (motor).

vierte, fourth.

viertehalb, three and a half.

verteilen, to quarter.

vierteilig, in four parts.

Viertel, n.-, fourth, quarter; **-holz,** n. quartered wood; **-j hr,** n. quarter (of a year), three months; **-jahresschrift,** f. quarterly (magazine); **-tunde,** f. quarter of an hour.

viertens, fourthly, in the fourth place.

vier-wertig, tetravalent; **-wertigkeit,** f. tetravalence; **-zählig,** fourfold, quaternary; **-zehig,** with four toes.

vierzehn, fourteen.

vierzellig, quadrilocular.

vierzig, forty.

Vinylcyanür, n. vinyl cyanide.

Viole, f. violet, viol.

Violenwurzel, f. orrisroot (Iris florentina).

violettstichig, violet-tinged.

virtuell, virtual.

virulent, virulent.

Virulenz, f. virulence; **-steigerung,** f. increasing the virulence.

Virus, m. virus; **-art,** f. type of virus; **-forschung,** f. virus research.

Visceral-bogen, m. visceral arch; **-höhle,** f. visceral cavity; **-spalte,** f. visceral cleft.

Visetholz, n. fustet, young fustic (Rhus continus).

visieren, to adjust, gauge, vise.

Visitenkarte, f. visiting card.

visitieren, to search, inspect.

viskos, viscous.

Viskosität, f. viscosity.

Vitalfärbung, f. vital staining.

Vitalität, f. vitality.

Vitamin, n. vitamin; **-mangel,** m. lack of vitamins, vitamin deficiency; **-nachweis,** m. vitamin test.

vitriol-artig, vitriolic, like vitriol; **-bildung,** f. vitriolation; **-bleierz,** n. **-bleispat,** m. anglesite; **-erz,** n. vitriolic ore; **-fabrik,** f. vitriol works; **-flasche,** f. carboy; **-gelb,** n. jarosite; **-haltig,** containing vitriol; **-hütte,** f. vitriol works.

vitriolig, vitriolic.

vitriolisieren, to vitriolate, sulphate.

Vitriol-kies, m. marcasite; **-öl,** n. oil of vitriol, sulphuric acid; **-säure,** f. sulphuric acid; **-schiefer,** m. alum schist (shale); **-siederei,** f. vitriol works.

Vitsbohne, f. kidney bean (Phaseolus vulgaris).

vicinal, vicinal, neighboring.

Vlies, n. fleece.

Vogel, m.-, bird; **-amber,** m. spermaceti; **-art,** f. type (species) of bird; **-augenholz,** n. bird's-eye wood; **-beerbaum,** m. mountain ash; **-beere,** f. berry of the mountain ash; **-beersäure,** f. sorbic (malic) acid; **-blütner,** m. orthophyllous flower; **-dünger,** m. bird droppings, guano; **-dunst,** m. fine bird shot.

Vogel-ei, n. bird's egg; **-herz,** n. heart of a bird; **-kirsche,** f. bird cherry (Prunus avium); **-klaue,** f. claw of bird, talon; **-kopf,** m. sparrowwort (Passerina); **-kunde,** f. ornithology; **-leim,** m. birdlime; **-maser,** f. bird's-eye grain; **-mast,** f. quarter-mast, seed carried by birds; **-miere,** f. chickweed (Stellaria media); **-mist,** m. bird dung.

Vogel-perspektive, f. bird's-eye view; **-pest,** f. chicken typhus; **-scheuche,** f. scarecrow; **-septikämie,** f. septicemia of birds; **-serum,** bird serum; **-wicke,** f. bird's tares (Vicia cracca).

Vogt, m. overseer, warden, magistrate.

Vokal, m.-e, vowel.

Volarballen, m. volar (walking) pad; **-fläche,** f. volar (palmar) surface.

Volk, n.-er, people, nation, race, troops, men, flock, herd.

Völkerbund, m. League of Nations.

Volks-gemeinschaft, f. community (of a people); **-mund,** m. vernacular; **-nahrungsmittel,** n. staple food, chief food of the people; **-schicht,** f. social class; **-schüler,** m. pupil of elementary school.

volkstümlich, popular, national.

Volkswirtschaft, f. political economy.

Volkswirtschaftslehre, f. political economy.

voll, full, filled, replete, whole, entire, complete; **-auf,** abundantly, plentifully; **~ausgebildet,** fully developed.

Vollberichtigung, f. full correction.

vollblütig, full-blooded, plethoric.

Vollbogen, m. semicircular rail.

vollbringen, to achieve, accomplish, complete.

Volldruck, m. full pressure.

volle Brache, f. complete fallow.

vollenden, to finish, achieve, complete, perfect.

vollendet, accomplished, perfect.

vollends, wholly, entirely, altogether, moreover.

Vollendung, *f.* completion.

vollentwickelt, fully developed.

vollflächig, holohedral.

vollfüllen, to fill up.

Vollgehalt, *m.* full value.

vollgesogen (vollsaugen), filled up (by sucking).

vollhaltig, of full value, standard.

Vollheit, *f.* fullness.

Vollholz, *n.* log.

vollholzig, full-boled, cylindrical, nontapering.

Vollholzigkeit, *f.* approach to cylindrical form.

völlig, full(y), entire, complete(ly), thorough, circular.

Völligkeit, *f.* (Querschnitt) circularity (cross section).

Völligkeitsgrad, *m.* coefficient of fineness.

volljährig, of age.

vollkantig, full-edged, full-squared.

Vollkiemer, *m.pl.* Teleobranchiatae.

vollkommen, perfect, full, complete, entire, free (discharge).

Vollkommenheit, *f.* perfection.

Vollkraft, *f.* full strength, vigor, energy.

Vollmacht, *f.*÷e, full authority, power of attorney.

Vollmast, *f.* full mast.

Vollmilch, *f.* whole (unskimmed) milk.

vollmundig, full, having good body (beer).

Vollpflanze, *f.* complete plant.

Vollpipette, *f.* delivery pipette.

Vollraum, *m.* infinite body.

Vollreife, *f.* full ripeness.

Vollsaat, *f.* broadcast sowing.

vollsaugen, to suck, absorb, drink, imbibe until full.

vollschlicken, to slit.

vollspurig, of standard gauge.

vollständig, complete, entire, integral, total.

Vollständigkeit, *f.* completeness.

vollstrecken, to execute, carry out.

vollweiblich, completely feminine.

vollwertig, of full value, perfect.

vollwichtig, of full weight, weighty.

vollzählig, complete.

vollziehen, to execute, consummate, carry out, accomplish; $\sim$, **sich,** to take place.

Vollziehung, *f.* execution, fulfillment.

vollzogen (vollziehen), took place.

Vollzug, *m.* carrying out, execution.

voltaisch voltaic.

Volt-meter, *n.&m* voltmeter; **-spannung,** *f.* voltage.

Volum(en), *n.* **Volumina,** volume, contents; **-abnahme,** *f.* decrease (shrinkage) in volume;- **änderung,** *f.* change in volume; **-begrenzung,** *f.* volume limitation; **-dichte,** *f.* density by volume; **-einheit,** *f.* unit of volume.

volumetrisch, volumetric.

Volum-gesetz, *n.* law of volumes; **-gewicht,** *n.* weight of volume.

voluminös, voluminous.

Volum-prozentgehalt, *m.* volume percentage; **-teil,** *m.* part by volume; **-veränderung,** *f.* change in volume; **-verhältnis,** *n.* volume ratio; **-zunahme,** *f.* increase in volume.

Volvox, volvox; **-kolonie,** *f.* volvox colony.

vom (von dem), of the, from the.

vomieren, to vomit.

von, of, from, about, by, on upon, concerning; $\sim$ . . . **ab,** from . . . onward; $\sim$ . . . **an,** from; $\sim$ . . . **aus,** from; $\sim$ . . . **her,** from; $\sim$ **da an,** from then on; $\sim$ **Hand,** by hand; $\sim$ **neuem,** again.

voneinander, from or of one another, or each other.

vonnöten, in need, necessary; $\sim$ **sein,** to be needful.

von-seiten, on the part of; **-statten gehen,** to go on, occur, take place, progress; $\sim$ **vornherein,** from the beginning, at once; $\sim$ **vorn nach hinten,** from the front to the rear.

vor, before, in front of, for, from, of, forward, on, formerly; $\sim$ **allem,** above all; $\sim$ **einem Jahre,** a year ago; $\sim$ **kurzem,** recently; $\sim$ **allen Dingen,** first of all.

vorab, tentatively, to begin with.

Vor-abend, *m.* eve, evening before; **-ahnung,** *f.* presentiment, foreboding.

voran, before, in front; **-gegangen,** preceded; **-gehen,** to precede; **-gehend,** preceding; **-schicken,** to send on before, premise.

Voranschlag, *m.* preliminary estimate, estimated costs.

Vor-anzeige, *f.* preliminary announcement; **-arbeit,** *f.* preliminary work.

Vorarm, *m.* forethigh, forearm.

vorauf, before, on; ∼ **gehen,** to go ahead, in advance.

.oraus, before, in advance; **-bestellen,** to order in advance; **-bezahlen,** to pay in advance; **-gehen,** to go before, in advance, precede; **-gegangen,** previous, preliminary; **-haben,** to excel in something; **-nehmen,** to anticipate; **-sage,** *f.* prediction, forecast; **-sagen,** to predict; **-schauen,** to look forward, anticipate; **-schauen,** *n.* looking forward, anticipation.

voraus-schicken, to send in advance; **-sehen,** to foresee; **-setzen,** to (pre)suppose, assume; **-setzung,** *f.* provision, supposition, prerequisite, assumption, hypothesis, presupposition; **-sicht,** *f.* foresight, forethought, prospect; **-sichtlich,** prospective, presumably, expected.

Vorbackenzahn, *m.* fore molar, fore grinder.

vorbauen, to prevent, guard against.

Vorbauung, *f.* precaution.

Vorbauungsmittel, *n.* prophylactic.

Vor-bedacht, *m.* forethought; **-bedingung,** *f.* preliminary condition; **-behalt,** *m.* reservation; **-behalten,** to keep on reserve, withhold; **-behandeln,** to pretreat, prepare; **-behandlung,** *f.* preliminary treatment.

vorbei, by, past, over, done; **-fliegen,** to fly past; **-führen,** to lead past; **-gehen,** to go past, pass by; **-strömen,** to pass by.

Vor-bemerkung, *f.* preliminary remark; **-benutzung,** *f.* prior use; **-berechnung,** *f.* (preliminary) calculation.

vorbereiten, to prepare; **-vorbereitend,** preparatory.

Vorbereitung, *f.* preparation.

Vorbereitungs-hieb, *m.* preparatory cutting; **-schlag,** *m.* preparatory stage or cutting.

Vor-berg, *m.* foothill, outer hill; **-bericht,** *m.* introduction, preface; **-besprechung,** *f.* preliminary discussion; **-beugen,** to prevent, bend forward, guard against; **-beugend,** preventive, prophylactic.

Vorbeuger, *m.* pronator.

Vorbeugung, *f.* bending forward, preventative measure, prophylaxis.

Vorbeugungs-massnahme, *f.* prophylactic measure; **-massregel,** *f.* preventive measure; **-mittel,** *n.* preservative, prophylactic.

Vorbild, *n.*-er, model, pattern, standard, prototype.

vorbildich, typical, figurative.

vorbilden, to represent, typify, prepare.

Vorbildung, *f.* preparation, basic education.

vorbinden, to tie on.

Vorblatt, *n.* bract, bracteole, prophyllum.

Vorbote, *m.* early sign, preliminary symptom.

vorbringen, to utter, express, bring forward.

vordem, formerly.

vorder, front; **-ansicht,** *f.* frontal (aspect) view; **-antenne,** *f.* antennule, first antenna.

Vorderarm, *m.* forearm; **-beuger,** *m.* flexor of forearm; **-gelenk,** *n.* articulation of forearm; **-knochen,** *m.* forearm, bone of forearm; **-strecker,** *m.* triceps humeri.

Vorderbauch, *m.* epigastrium.

Vorderbein, *n.* front leg, foreleg.

Vorderbrust, *f.* chest, forebreast, prosternum; **-schild,** *m.* the sclerite between the forelegs, prosternum; **-stachel,** *m.* prosternal spine; **-stück,** *n.* prosternum.

Vorderdamm, *m.* anterior perineum.

Vorderdarm, *m.* fore intestine, stomodaeum, esophagus; **-rohr,** *n.* esophagus.

vordere, fore, forward, front, anterior.

Vorderende, *n.* anterior end.

Vorderextremitätenbezirk, *m.* fore-limb level.

Vorderfinger, *m.* forefinger.

Vorderflügel, *m.* forewing.

Vorderfuss, *m.* anterior part of foot, front leg (metatarsus); **-wurzel,** *f.* carpus, wrist, knee.

Vorderglied, *n.* anterior member, antecedent; **-masse,** *f.* anterior limb; **-massengürtel,** *m.* pectoral girdle.

Vordergrund, *m.* foreground.

Vorderhals, *m.* guttural region, throat.

Vorderhand, *f.* anterior part of hand (metacarpus).

vorderhand, for the present, for a while.

Vorderhaupt, *n.* sinciput.

Vorderhauptsbein, *n.* frontal bone.

Vorderhirn, *n.* forebrain; **-bläschen,** *n.* anterior cerebral vesicle, prosencephalon.

Vorderhorn, *n.* anterior horn.

Vorderkiefer, *m.* mandibles; **-taster,** *m.* endopodite of maxillule.

Vorderkiemer, *m.pl.* Prosobranchia; **-schnecken,** *f.pl.* Prosobranchia.

Vorderkopf, *m.* vertex, anterior portion of head; **-gebiet,** *n.* anterior region of head.

Vorderlage, *f.* anterior (antical) position.

Vorderlappen, *m.* anterior lobe.

Vorderleib, *m.* anterior part of trunk, prothorax.

Vordermittelfuss, *m.* metacarpus.

Vordermund, *m.* peristome.

Vordermuskel, *m.* anterior muscle.

Vorderpfote, *f.* forepaw.

Vorderrand, *m.* anterior margin; **-ader,** *f.* costa; **-querader,** *f.* antecubital vein.

Vorderrücken, *m.* pronotum, interscapular region.

Vordersatz, *m.* antecedent.

Vordersäule, *f.* anterior column.

Vorderschild, *m.* prescutum.

Vorderschwinge, *f.* primary, remex.

Vorderschwingkolben, *m.* prebalancer, prehalter.

Vorderseite, *f.* anterior (antical) or adaxial side.

vorderst, foremost.

Vorderstirnbein, *n.* prefrontal bone.

Vorderstrang, *m.* anterior cord.

Vorderwand, *f.* front wall, breast.

Vorderwürze, *f.* first wort.

Vorderzahn, *m.* incisor.

vordrängen, to press (push) forward.

vordringen, to push on, advance, penetrate.

vordringlich, pressing.

Vordruck, *m.* first impression, proof, form.

vordrucken, to prefix.

voreilen, to hasten on before, precede, advance.

Voreilung, *f.* advance, lead.

voreingenommen, prepossessed, prejudiced.

Voreltern, *pl.* ancestors.

vorenthalten, to withhold.

vorerst, previously, first of all, for the time being.

vorerwähnt, before-mentioned, aforesaid.

Vorfaden, *m.* protonema.

Vorfahr, *m.*-en, forefather, ancestor.

Vorfahrenreihe, *f.* line of ancestors.

Vorfall, *m.* occurrence, incident, event, prolapse, accident.

vorfallen, to occur, happen, prolapse.

vorfinden, to light upon, find; **sich** ~, to be found, be forthcoming.

Vorflügel, *m.* anterior wing.

Vorfrischen, *n.* preliminary refining.

Vorfrucht, *f.* early fruit, preceding crop (in rotation).

Vorfrühlingsblütler, *m.pl.* extremely early (prespring) blooming plants (Crocus).

Vorfühler, *m.* antennule, first antenna.

vorführen, to present, produce, bring to the front, project, demonstrate.

Vorgang, *m.*-̈e, process, reaction, proceeding, occurrence, incident, transaction, precedent, priority, event.

Vorgänger, *m.* predecessor.

vorgängig, foregoing, preceding.

vorgeben, to give advantage, pretend, allege.

Vorgebirge, *n.* promontory, foothill.

vorgeblich, pretended, supposed, would-be.

vorgebracht, brought forward.

vorgeburtlich, prenatal.

vorgeformt, preformed.

vorgegeben, above, accessible.

vorgehen, to go before, precede, lead, proceed, happen, be fast.

vorgenommen (vornehmen), undertaken.

vorgerückt, advanced.

Vorgeschichte, *f.* previous history, early history.

vorgeschichtlich, prehistoric.

vorgeschoben, advanced.

vorgeschrieben, prescribed.

vorgeschritten, advanced.

vorgesehen, provided, intended.

Vorgesetzte(r), *m.* superior, principal.

vorgestellt, imagined, conceived, introduced.

vorgestern, day before yesterday.

vorgewölbt, arched outward.

vorgreifen, to anticipate.

vorhaben, to intend, purpose, design, be engaged in, have on, reprimand.

Vorhaben, *n.* project, purpose.

vorhalten, to hold before, reproach, wear well, hold out, last, remonstrate.

Vorhand, *f.* anterior part of hand, metacarpus.

vorhanden, at hand, on hand, existing, present, ready; **-sein,** *n.* presence, existence.

Vorhang, *m.* curtain, cortina.

Vorhaupt, *n.* forehead, sinciput.

Vorhaut, *f.* prepuce; **-drüse,** *f.* preputial gland; **-geschwür,** *n.* preputial ulcer.

vorher, before, in advance, previously; **-bedenken,** to premeditate, consider beforehand; **-bestimmen,** to determine beforehand, predestine; **-gehen,** to precede, go (happen) before.

vorhergehend, preceding, previous, prior.

vorherig, preceding, previous.

Vorherrschaft, *f.* predominance, ascendancy.

vorherrschen, to prevail, predominate.

vorherrschend, dominant, prevalent.

vorhersagen, to predict, prophesy.

Vorhieb, *m.* advance cutting.

vorhielt (vorhalten), held before, upbraided.

vorhin, before, heretofore, a short time ago.

Vorhof, *m.*∸e, vestibule (of labyrinth), auricle.

Vorhofs-fenster, *n.* fenestra ovalis; **-gang,** *m.* scala vestibuli; **-kammer,** *f.* auricle; **-nerv,** *m.* nervus acusticus, vestibular nerve; **-wand,** *f.* auricular wall; **-winkel,** *m.* vestibular angle; **-wulst,** *f.* atrial swelling.

Vorhöhle, *f.* vestibule.

Vorhölzer, *n.pl.* scrub, chaparral, outskirts of forest.

Vorhut, *f.* right of first pasturage, vanguard.

vorig, former, preceding, last, previous.

Vorjahr, *n.* preceding year.

Vorkammer, *f.* auricle; **-klappe,** *f.* valve of auricle.

Vorkämpfer, *m.* champion, pioneer, advocate.

Vorkehrung, *f.* precautionary measure, provision.

Vorkeim, *m.* protonema, prothallium, proembryo; **-zustand,** *m.* protonema stage.

Vorkenntnis, *n.* previous knowledge.

Vorkenntnisse, *pl.* elementary knowledge, rudiments.

Vorkern, *m.* pronucleus.

Vorknorpel, *m.* precartilage.

vorkommen, to occur, happen, be found, take place, come forth, be admitted, come sooner, appear, seem, present itself, crop up.

Vorkommen, *n.* occurrence, presence.

Vorkommnis, *n.* occurrence, event.

Vorkost, *f.* first course, provisions.

Vorkriegszeiten, *f.pl.* prewar times.

Vorkühlung, *f.* precooling.

Vorkultur, *f.* preliminary culture.

vorküpen, to bottom with a vat dye.

Vorlack, *m.* size, pore filler.

vorladen, to summon.

Vorlage, *f.* receiver, proposal, matter, tail box.

Vorlager, *m.* prothallus, advance camp.

vorlagern, to extend in front of.

vorlassen, to admit, give precedence to.

Vorlauf, *m.* first runnings, heads.

Vorläufer, *m.* forerunner, precursor, preliminary symptom; **-spitze,** *f.* tip of developing leaf primordium.

vorläufig, preliminary, tentative, previous, provisional, meanwhile, for the present.

vorlegen, to lay before, put on, apply, display, exhibit, submit, propose, serve.

vorlesen, to read aloud.

Vorlesung, *f.* lecture.

vorletzt, next to last, last but one, penultimate.

Vorliebe, *f.* preference, predilection.

vorliegen, to lie before, be in hand, be under consideration, be present, exist.

Vormagen, *m.* antestomach, preventriculus, crop.

vormals, formerly.

Vormann, *m.* foreman.

vormännlich, protandrous.

Vormarsch, *m.* advance.

Vormast, *f.* early mast.

Vormauer, *f.* claustrum.

vormerken, to mark, note down.

Vormilch, *f.* colostrum, foremilk.

Vormittag, *m.* forenoon, morning.

Vormund, *m.* guardian, trustee.

Vormuskelgewebe, *n.* premuscle tissue.

vorn, vorne, in front, before; **von** ∼, anew, from the beginning; **nach** ∼, forward; **von** ∼ **herein,** at first, to begin with.

Vorname, *m.* first name, Christian name.

vornehm, elegant, fashionable, distinguished, first, chief.

vornehmen, to take up, undertake; **ist vorzunehmen,** must be administered.

vornehmlich, chiefly, particularly.

vornehmst, chief, foremost, main, principal.

vornherein, von ∼, at the outset, from the very beginning.

Vorniere, *f.* pronephros, head kidney.

Vornieren-gang, *m.* Wolffian duct; **-kanäl-chen,** *n.* pronephric tubule.

vornüher, head foremost.

vornumläufig, emprosthodromous.

Vornymphe, *f.* pronymph.

Vorortbahn, *f.* suburban railway.

Vorposten, *m.* outpost.

Vorprobe, *f.* preliminary test.

Vorprodukt, *n.* initial product, first runnings, intermediate (nylon).

Vorprüfung, *f.* preliminary examination.

Vorpuppe, *f.* prepupa.

vorquellen, to ooze out, spring forth.

vorraffinieren, to prerefine.

vorragen (hervorragen), to be prominent.

vorragend (hervorragend), prominent, outstanding.

Vorrang, *m.* precedence.

Vorrat, *m.*̈e, stock, store, reserve, supply.

vorrätig, in stock, on hand.

Vorrats-eiweiss, *n.* circulating protein; **-inventar,** *n.* reserve stock; **-mangel,** *m.* deficiency of growing stock; **-zelle,** *f.* store cell.

Vorrecht, *n.*-e, privilege, prerogative.

Vorrede, *f.* preamble, preface.

Vorreife, *f.* aging; **-kasten,** *m.* aging hopper.

Vorreinigung, *f.* preliminary purification.

vorrichten, to prepare.

Vorrichtung, *f.* apparatus, arrangement, device, appliance, contrivance, attachment.

vorrücken, to advance, progress, reproach.

Vorrücken, *n.* advance, forward move.

Vorsaal, *m.* vestibule.

Vorsaat, *f.* preliminary crop.

Vorsatz, *m.*̈e, anything set before, design, intention, purpose.

vorsätzlich, intentional(ly).

Vorsatzlinse, *f.* front (amplifying) lens.

Vorsatzobjektiv, *n.* front objective.

vorschalten, introduce (into a circuit), connect.

Vorschaltturbine, *f.* topping turbine.

Vorschein, *m.* appearance; **zum ～ kommen,** to appear.

vorschieben, to push forward.

vorschiessen, to shoot forth, advance, provide (money).

Vorschlag, *m.*̈e, proposal, proposition, suggestion.

vorschlagen, to propose, suggest, move.

Vorschmack, *m.* foretaste, predominance.

vorschnell, hasty, rash.

vorschreiben, to dictate, prescribe, direct, specify.

Vorschrift, *f.*-en, prescription, directions, recipe, order, command, precept, copy, specification.

vorschriftsmässig, as prescribed.

vorschrinken, to preshrink.

Vorschub, *m.* furtherance, assistance, support; ～ **leisten,** to assist, promote.

Vorschuh, *m.* upper leather, vamp.

Vorschule, *f.* preparatory school.

Vorschuss, *m.*̈e, advance of money.

vorschützen, to pretend.

Vorschwarm, *m.* first (virgin) swarm.

vorschweben, to float or hover before, be in (someone's) mind, have a recollection.

vorsehen, to provide for, take care.

Vorsehung, *f.* providence.

Vorsetzblatt, *n.* flyleaf.

vorsetzen, to put before, set before, prefix.

Vorsicht, *f.* foresight, caution, prudence, care.

vorsichtig, cautious(ly), careful(ly), prudent.

Vorsichtsmassregel, *f.*-n, precaution(ary measure).

Vorsilbe, *f.* prefix.

Vorsitz, *m.* presidency, chair.

Vorsitzende(r), *m.* president, chairman.

Vorsorge, *f.* care, foresight, attention.

Vorspannung, *f.* grid potential, initial stress.

Vorspelze, *f.* palea, palet.

vorspiegeln, to show in a brilliant light, delude, pretend.

Vorspiegelung, *f.* delusion, sham; **unter ～ falscher Tatsachen,** under false pretenses.

Vorspiel, *n.* prelude.

vorspringen, to project, leap before.

vorspringend, projecting, prominent.

Vorsprung, *m.*̈e, projection, advance, start, prominence, lead, protrusion.

Vorstadt, *f.*̈e, suburb, outskirts.

Vorstand, *m.* governing body.

vorstecken, to put on, fasten before, prefix.

vorstehen, to stand before, project, precede, direct, preside over, manage.

Vorstehende, *n.* the above.

Vorsteher, *m.* superintendent, director, manager, chief; **-drüse,** *f.* prostate gland.

Vorstehhund, *m.* pointer, setter.

vorstellen, to introduce, represent, imagine, demonstrate, personate, play, put before, advance.

Vorstellung, *f.* introduction, imagination, conception, idea, notion, representation, performance.

Vorstellungs-fähigkeit, *f.* imaginative power; **-inhalt,** *m.* content of an image.

Vorstoss, *m.*⁼e, attack, advance, projecting part, butt, joint, edging, ledge, growth from lobe (in Marchantia), spout.

vorstossen, to push forward.

Vorstufe, *f.* first step, preliminary stage.

Vorsud, *m.* first boiling.

vortäuschen, to simulate.

Vorteil, *m.* advantage, benefit, profit; **-haft,** advantageous, profitable.

Vortiegel, *m.* forehearth, lead pot.

Vortrag, *m.*⁼e, address, lecture, discourse.

vortragen, to carry before, recite, lecture on, report on.

vortrefflich, excellent, superior.

Vortreibung, *f.* projection.

vortreten, to step forward, advance.

Vortritt, *m.* precedence.

vorüber, past over, gone, done; **-fliessen,** to flow past; **-gehen,** to pass by (away); **-gehend,** passing, temporary, transient; **-kommen,** to pass, come by; **-laufen,** to walk (run) past; **-ziehen,** to pass by.

Voruntersuchung, *f.* preliminary investigation.

Vorurteil, *n.*-e, prejudice, bias.

Vorverdampfer, *m.* steaming economizer, pre-evaporator.

Vorverjüngung, *f.* preregeneration, natural reproduction.

Vorversuch, *m.*-e, preliminary experiment.

Vorwachs, *n.* bee glue.

Vorwald, *m.* outer wood.

vorwalken, to scour (cloth).

vorwalten, to prevail, predominate.

vorwalzen, to rough down, bloom.

Vorwalzwerk, *n.* roughing rolls.

Vorwand, *m.* pretext, pretense.

vorwärmen, to heat beforehand, preheat.

Vorwärmer, *m.* preheater, economizer.

vorwärts, forward, onward; **-bewegen,** to move forward; **-dreher,** *m.* pronator; **-kommen,** to get ahead, proceed; **-treiben,** to propel; **-wender,** *m.* pronator.

Vorwaschen, *n.* preliminary washing.

vorweg, before(hand); **-nehmen,** to take beforehand, anticipate.

vorweiblich, protogynous.

Vorweide, *f.* early pasture.

Vorwelt, *f.* former ages, prehistoric world.

vorweltlich, prehistoric, of primitive ages.

vorwenden, to allege, pretend.

vorwerfen, to throw before, reproach.

vorwiegen, to outweigh, prevail, dominate.

vorwiegend, predominant(ly), prevalent.

Vorwort, *n.* foreword, preface.

Vorwuchs, *m.* advance growth.

vorwüchsig, to faster growth.

Vorwurf, *m.* reproach, blame, subject.

vorzählen, to enumerate.

Vorzahn, *m.* incisor, bucktooth.

Vorzeichen, *m.* previous indication, symptom, omen, sign; **-wechsel,** *m.* change of sign.

vorzeigen, to show, expose, produce, exhibit.

Vorzeiger, *m.* bearer.

Vorzeit, *f.* antiquity, past ages.

vorzeitig, untimely, premature.

vorziehbar, preferable.

vorziehen, to draw forth, prefer.

Vorzug, *m.* preference, privilege, superiority, merit, priority, advantage, pilot train.

vorzüglich, preferable, superior, excellent.

Vorzugs-aktien, *f.pl.* preferred stock; **-temperatur,** *f.* preferred temperature; **-weise,** preferably, preeminently.

Vorzwickel, *m.* quadrate lobule, precuneus.

Vulkan, *m.* volcano; **-fiber,** *f.* vulcanized fiber.

vulkanisch, volcanic.

vulkanisieren, to vulcanize.

W

Waage, *f.* balance, scales; **in die** ~ **fallen, to be of import.**

waagerecht, horizontal.

Waagschale, *f.* pan of scales.

wabbelig, flabby.

Wabe, *f.* honeycomb.

waben-artig, honeycombed, alveolar; **-grind,** *m.* favus; **-plasma,** *n.* alveolar cytoplasm; **-theorie,** *f.* alveolar theory.

wach, awake.

Wachbewusstsein, *n.* waking consciousness.

Wache, *f.* watch, guard(house).

wachen, to be awake, guard, watch.

Wachmittel, *n.* antisoporific.

Wacholder, *m.* juniper (Juniperus); **-beere,** *f.* juniper berry; **-branntwein,** *m.* geneva gin; **-geist,** *m.* juniper spirit; **-harz,** *n.* sandarac, gum juniper.

wachrufen, to wake, call, rouse.

Wachs, *n.* wax; **-abdruck,** *m.* impression in wax.

wachsam, vigilant, watchful.

Wachs-alaun, *m.* crystallized alum; **-artig,** waxlike; **-ausscheidung,** *f.* wax secretion; **-baum,** *m.* wax myrtle, bayberry tree; **-blatt,** *n.* leaf with a waxy cuticle; **-blume,** *f.* honeywort (*Cerinthe minor*); **-boden,** *m.* wax cake; **-bottich,** *m.* roching cask; **-drüse,** *f.* ceruminous gland.

wachsen, to grow, sprout, increase.

wachsen, to wax.

wächsern, waxen, of wax.

Wachs-farbe, *f.* wax color; **-gagel,** *m.* wax (candleberry) myrtle (*Myrica cerifera*); **-gehalt,** *m.* wax content; **-glänzend,** shining like wax; **-haut,** *f.* cere; **-kerzchen,** *n.* wax match, vesta; **-kerze,** *f.* wax candle; **-kirsche,** *f.* yellow gean, yellow bigarreau; **-kohle,** *f.* pyropissite, paraffin, coal; **-kuchen,** *m.* cake of wax.

Wachs-leinen, *n.,* **-leinwand,** *f.* oilcloth; **-machen,** *n.* roching; **-motte,** *f.* wax moth; **-myrte,** *f.* wax myrtle (*Myrica cerifera*); **-papier,** *n.* wax paper; **-pflaster,** *n.* cerate; **-raum,** *m.* growing space; **-salbe,** *f.* cerate.

wächst (wachsen), grows, is growing.

Wachs-stock, *m.* wax candle (taper); **-tafel,** *f.* wax tablet; **-taffet,** *m.* oilcloth; **-tuch,** *n.* oilcloth.

Wachstum, *n.* growth.

Wachstums-achse, *f.* longitudinal (growth) axis; **-art,** *f.* type of growth; **-bedingung,** *f.* condition for growing; **-bewegung,** *f.* nutation movement; **-dauer,** *f.* duration of growth; **-drehung,** *f.* spiral growth; **-erscheinung,** *f.* growth phenomenon;

-fähig, capable of growth; **-fördernd,** growth-promoting.

Wachstums-geschwindigkeit, *f.* rate of growth; **-grösse,** *f.* extent of growth; **-hemmend,** retarding of growth; **-keim,** *m.* germ of growth; **-körper,** *m.* grain growth substance, increase in volume; **-krümmung,** *f.* growth curvature; **-kurve,** *f.* growth curve.

Wachstums-schicht, *f.* cambium; **-schnelligkeit,** *f.* rate of growth; **-stetigkeit,** *f.* active (steady) growth; **-stockung,** *f.* interrupted growth; **-verschiebung,** *f.* growth change, displacement; **-verzögerung,** *f.* delay of growth; **-vorgang,** *m.* process of growth.

Wachs-überzug, *m.* waxy covering, cuticle; **-weich,** soft like wax; **-zündholz,** *n.* wax match, vesta.

Wacht, *f.* guard, watch.

Wachtel, *f.* quail; **-hund,** *m.* spaniel; **-könig,** *m.* corn-crake, landrail; **-weizen,** *m.* cowwheat (*Melampyrum pratense*).

Wackelchangierung, *f.* oscillating traverse motion.

wackelig, shaky, tottering, rickety.

wackeln, to shake, rock, totter, wabble, be loose.

wacker, stout, brave, true, good, gallant.

Wade, *f.* calf (of the leg).

Wadel, *m.* felling time.

Wadenbein, *n.* fibula; **-beuger,** *m.* femoral biceps; **-muskel,** *m.* peroneal muscle; **-schienbeingelenk,** *n.* tibiofibular articulation; **-sprungbeinband,** *n.* external lateral ligament of ankle.

Waden-krampf, *m.⁼*e, cramp in the leg; **-muskel,** *m.* gastrocnemius muscle.

Waffe, *f.* weapon; *pl.* arms.

Waffen-dienst, *m.* military service; **-fliegen,** *f.pl.* soldier flies (Stratiomydae)· **-rüsting,** *f.* armament, arming.

waffnen, to arm.

wägbar, weighable, ponderable.

Wägbarkeit, *f.* ponderability.

Wage, *f.* balance, scales, level; **-balken,** *m.* beam of a balance; **-gang,** *m.* horizontal gallery.

Wägeglas, *n.* weighing bottle.

wagen, to venture, risk, dare, hazard.

Wagen, *m.*-, vehicle, car, conveyance, truck.

wägen, to weigh, poise, balance, ponder.

Wagen-gleise, *n.* wheel track; **-kasten,** *m.* body; **-ladung,** *f.* cartload; **-schuppen,** *m.* wagon shed; **-spur,** *f.* wheel rut, wheel track.

wag(e)recht, horizontal, level.

Waggon, *m.*-s, car, railway carriage.

Wagnerholz, *n.* wheelwright's wood, wagon stock.

Wagnis, *n.* hazard, risky enterprise.

Wagschale, *f.* balance pan.

Wägung, *f.* weighing.

Wahl, *f.*-en, choice, selection, option, election.

wählbar, eligible.

wählen, to choose, elect, select.

Wähler, *m.*-, elector, voter, selector.

wählerisch, particular, fastidious, prudish.

Wahl-recht, *n.* right to vote, suffrage; **-spruch,** *m.* motto, device; **-vermögen,** *n.* power to select; **-verwandtschaft,** *f.* elective affinity, congeniality.

Wahn, *m.* illusion, delusion, fancy, madness, folly; **-bild,** *n.* chimera, phantom, delusion, vision.

wähnen, to fancy, imagine, presume, suppose.

Wahn-kante, *f.* wane, dull (rough) edge; **-kantig,** wany, dull-edged.

Wahn-sinn, *m.* insanity, frenzy, madness, delirium; **-sinnig,** insane, crazy, mad, frantic.

wahr, true, real, genuine, correct.

wahren, to watch over, take care, preserve.

währen, to last, continue, endure.

während, during, for, while, pending, whereas.

wahrgenommen (wahrnehmen), noticed, perceived.

wahrhaft, true, genuine, real, truthful, sincere.

wahrhaftig, true, sincere, surely, really.

Wahrheit, *f.* truth, reality, fact.

Wahrheitsbeweis, *m.* factual evidence.

wahrlich, indeed, surely, truly, verily.

wahr-nehmbar, perceptible; **-nehmen,** to notice, perceive, observe, give attention to, profit by.

Wahrnehmung, *f.* perception, observation.

Wahrnehmungs-bild, *n.* perceptual image; **-kraft,** *f.* power of perception; **-urteil,** *n.* perceptive (existential) judgment; **-ver-** **mögen,** *n.* perceptive faculty; **-vorstellung,** *f.* notion by perception.

wahrsagen, to prophesy, predict.

wahrscheinlich, probably, likely, plausible.

Wahrscheinlichkeit, *f.* probability.

Wahrscheinlichkeits-rechnung, *f.* theory (calculus) of probabilities of chances; **-wert,** *m.* probable value.

Wahrspruch, *m.*-e, verdict.

Wahrung, *f.* maintaining, support.

Währung, *f.* standard, fixed value, currency.

Wahrzeichen, *n.* distinctive mark, sign, omen.

Waid, *m.*-e, woad (*Isatis tinctoria*); **-mann,** *m.* hunter, sportsman.

Wal, *m.*-e, whale.

Walch, *m.* egilops.

Wald, *m.*-er, wood, forest; **-abfindung,** *f.* cantonment of forest rights; **-ahorn,** *m.* sycamore (*Acer pseudoplatanus*); **-ameise,** *f.* red ant (Formica); **-anemone,** *f.* wood anemone (*Anemone silvestris*); **-arm,** sparsely wooded; **-bau,** *m.* silviculture; **-baulich,** silvicultural.

Wald-baum, *m.*-e, forest tree; **-beere,** *f.* cranberry (*Vaccinium myrtillus*); **-behandlung,** *f.* handling of forests; **-besitz,** *m.* forest property; **-bestand,** *m.* forest crop, stand; **-betrieb,** *m.* forest management; **-bewohnend,** growing in the forest; **-bewohner,** *m.* inhabitant of a forest.

Wald-blume, *f.* flower of the woods; **-boden,** *m.* forest soil; **-brand,** *m.* forest fire; **-dienstbarkeit,** *f.* forest servitude; **-eigentümer,** *m.* forest owner; **-erdbeere,** *f.* wild(wood) strawberry (*Fragaria vesca*); **-eule,** *f.* wood (tawny) owl.

Wald-farn, *m.* alsophila; **-feldbau,** *n.* combination of field crops and high forests; **-fläche,** *f.* wooded area; **-gärtner,** *m.* pine beetle; **-genossenschaft,** *f.* forestry society; **-gewächs,** *n.* forest plant; **-gräserei,** *f.* grass cutting in forests; **-grenze,** *f.* timber line.

Wald-hammer, *m.* range hammer; **-haselstrauch,** *m.* hazel, filbert; **-hochmoor,** *n.* high moor forest; **-hühner,** *n.pl.* grouse; **-humus,** *m.* leaf mold; **-hüter,** *m.* forest guard, woodward.

waldig, woody, wooded.

Wald-kauz, *m.* tawny owl, wood owl; **-kerbel,** *m.* wild chervil (cicely) (*Anthriscus silvestris*); **-kirsche,** *f.* wild cherry; **-komplex,** *m.* forest range; **-lücke,** *f.* gap, opening; **-mantel,** *m.* shelter belt; **-maus,** *f.*

field mouse; **-meister,** *m.* (sweet) woodruff (*Asperula odorata);* **-moor,** *n.* forest moor.

Wald-pflege, *f.* tending of forests; **-porling,** *m.* dry rot; **-rand,** *m.* edge of forest; **-rebe,** *f.* traveler's-joy (*Clematis vitalba);* **-rente,** *f.* forest rental; **-saum,** *m.* forest belt; **-simse,** *f.* bulrush (Scirpus); **-streu,** *f.* forest litter; **-teufel,** *m.* forest devil.

Waldung, *f.* forest, woodland.

Wald-verderber, *m.* injurious forest insect; **-verschlechterung,** *f.* forest deterioration; **-verwüstung,** *f.* forest devastation; **-wärter,** *m.* guard of a small beat; **-weg,** *m.* forest road; **-weide,** *f.* forest pasture; **-wertberechnung,** *f.* forest valuation; **-wolle,** *f.* pine wool; **-wollöl,** *n.* pine-needle oil.

Walfisch, *m.***-e,** whale; **-barte,** *f.* whalebone; **-sehne,** *f.* whale sinew; **-speck,** *m.* whale blubber; **-tran,** *m.* whale oil.

Walke, *f.* fulling, fulling machine.

walken, to full, mill (cloth), felt.

Walker, *m.* fuller, beetle; **-distel,** *f.* fuller's teasel.

Walkerde, *f.* fuller's earth.

Walkerseife, *f.* fuller's soap.

Walk-fett, *n.* fuller's oil; **-ton,** *m.* fuller's earth.

Wall, *m.* rampart, dike, dam, bank, shore, coast, mound, ridge.

Wallach, *m.***-e,-en,** gelding.

wallen, to bubble, simmer, boil up, undulate, be agitated.

wällen, to (let) boil, (let) simmer.

Wallnuss (Walnuss), *f.***-e,** walnut.

Wallonen-frischen, *n.* **-schmiede,** *f.* Walloon process.

Wall-rat (Walrat), *m.* spermaceti; **-stein,** *m.* dam of a blast furnace.

Wallung, *f.* boiling, ebullition, emotion, undulation, excitement.

Walnuss, *f.***-e,** walnut; **-baum,** *m.***-e,** (English) walnut tree (*Juglans regia);* **-gewächse,** *n.pl.* Juglandaceae.

Walrat, *m.* spermaceti; **-öl,** *n.* sperm oil.

Walross, *n.***-e,** walrus.

walten, to rule, govern, dispose of, manage.

Wal-tier, *n.* cetacean; **-tran,** *m.* whale oil.

Walzblei, *n.* sheet (rolled) lead.

Walze, *f.* roller, cylinder, barrel, drum, roll.

Walzeisen, *n.* rolled iron.

walzen, to roll, mill, waltz.

Walzen, *n.* rolling; **-drehzahl,** *f.* r.p.m. of roll, roller velocity; **-druck,** *m.* cylinder (roller) printing, rolling draft; **-förmig,** cylindrical; **-haar,** *n.* cylindrical hair; **-kessel,** *m.* cylindrical boiler; **-ringzahl,** *f.* number of rings, rolling speed; **-ständer,** *m.* standard; **-strasse,** *f.* rolling-mill train.

wälzen, to roll, turn about, rotate.

Walzer, *m.* waltz.

Walz-bart, *m.* burr; **-draht,** *m.* rod wire; **-fehler,** *m.* rolling defect; **-gerüst,** *n.* roll stand or frame; **-gut,** *n.* rolling stock, ore for roll crushing; **-gutwerkstoff,** *m.* industrial rolling material; **-kante,** *f.* rolling edge; **-naht,** *f.* rolling fin; **-produkt,** *n.* rolled product, sheet rubber; **-ringzahl,** *f.* number of rings, rolling speed.

Walz-sinter, *m.* mill scale; **-splitter,** *m.* sliver; **-strecke,** *f.* roll train; **-werk,** *n.* **-werksbetrieb,** *m.* rolling mill; **-walzig,** cylindrical, roller-shaped.

wand (winden), wound, was winding.

Wand, *f.***-e,** wall, partition, septum, side, coat; cheek; **-bein,** *n.* parietal bone; **-beleg,** *m.* primordial utricle; **-bewurf,** *m.* plastering, **-brüchig,** septifragal; **-dicke,** *f.* thickness of wall.

Wandelbarkeit, *f.* changeableness.

Wandel, *m.* change, mutation, alteration, conduct, behavior, trade, traffic.

wandelbar, changeable, variable, fragile, perishable.

Wandelfuss, *m.* gressorial, ambulatorial, rasorial leg.

wandellos, unalterable.

wandeln, to wander, walk, travel, trade, change, convert.

Wandelstern, *m.* planet.

Wandelung, *f.* transformation, change.

Wander-blöcke, *m.pl.* erratic blocks; **-düne,** *f.* shifting dune; **-fähigkeit,** *f.* power to migrate; **-falke,** *m.* peregrine falcon; **-flechte,** *f.* migrating lichen; **-heuschrecke,** *f.* migratory locust; **-kamp,** *m.* temporary nursery; **-knospe,** *f.* hibernacle, turion.

wandern, to travel, go, walk, wander, ramble, creep, migrate, move.

Wander-ratte, *f.***-n,** brown (Norway) rat; **-rhizom,** *m.* horizontal (traveling) rhizome; **-rost.** *m.* traveling grate; **-sand,** *m.* moving or shifting sand; **-schaft,** *m.* traveling, travels, tour; **-stärke,** *f.* transitory starch; **-staude,** *f.* (herbaceous) perennial with creeping stolons; **-tier,** *n.* migratory animal.

Wanderung, *f.* migration, traveling, trip, creeping.

Wander-versammlung, *f.* itinerant association, convention, temporary aggregation; **-vogel,** *m.* migratory bird; **-zelle,** *f.* migratory cell.

Wandler, *m.* transformer (in electricity).

Wandlung, *f.* transformation, change, metamorphosis.

Wand-malerei, *f.* mural painting; **-proto-plasma,** *n.* plasma membrane; **-putz,** *m.* plastering; **-spaltig,** septicidal; **-ständig,** parietal, marginal; **-stärke,** *f.* thickness of wall; **-tafel,** *f.* wall chart, blackboard.

wandte (wanden), turned, was turning.

Wandung, *f.* wall, partition.

Wandungs-schicht, *f.* parietal layer; **-zelle,** *f.* parietal cell.

Wandzelle, *f.* parietal (wall) cell.

Wange, *f.* cheek, gena.

Wangen-bein, *n.* cheek (malar) bone; **-bogen,** *m.* zygomatic arch; **-drüse,** *f.* buccal gland; **-fortsatz,** *m.* zygomatic process; **-gegend,** *f.* region of the cheek; **-grube,** *f.* zygomatic fossa; **-höcker,** *m.* zygomatic tuberosity; **-höhle,** *f.* buccal cavity.

Wangen-lidfurche, *f.* inferior orbitopalpebral groove, palpebromalar sulcus; **-naht,** *f.* zygomatic suture; **-platte,** *f.* gena (plate) sheath, malar portion; **-rand,** *m.* contour of the cheek; **-spalte,** *f.* fissure of the cheek; **-stachel,** *m.* genal spine.

wanken, to stagger, totter, waver.

wann, when, then; **dann und ~,** now and then.

Wanne, *f.* trough, tub, tank, vat.

Wanzen, *f.pl.* Hemiptera, (bed)bugs; **-kraut,** *n.* bugbane (Cimicifuga).

war (sein), was.

ward (werden), became.

Wardein, *m.*-e, mint warden.

Ware, *f.* ware, article, commodity; *pl.* goods, wares, merchandise.

Waren-ballenform, *f.* sarcina form; **-lager,** *n.* warehouse; **-stempel,** *m.* **-zeichen,** *n.* trade-mark.

warf (werfen), threw, was throwing.

warm, warm, hot; **-blut,** *n.* warmblood; **-blüter,** *m.pl.* warm-blooded animals, **-blütig,** warm-blooded, hematothermal; **-brunnen,** *m.* hot (thermal) spring.

Wärme, *f.* heat, warmth; **-abfuhr,** *f.* heat flow, transmission; **-abgabe,** *f* loss of

heat, heat emission; **-aufspeicherung,** *f.* storing up of heat; **-ausdehnung,** *f.* thermal expansion; **-ausstrahlung,** *f.* radiation of heat; **-behandlung,** *f.* heat treatment; **-beständig,** resistant to heat, of constant temperature; **-bildner,** *m.* heat producer; **-bildsamkeit,** *f.* forgeability.

Wärme-bildung, *f.* production of heat; **-bindung,** *f.* absorption of heat; **-durchlässig,** diathermic, conductive to heat; **-einheit,** *f.* heat unit, calorie, total heat; **-elektrisch,** thermoelectric; **-empfindung,** *f.* sensation of heat; **-entwick(e)lung,** *f.* evolution of heat; **-erzeugend,** heat-producing; **-erzeugung,** *f.* calorification, heat generation; **-gebend,** heat-yielding, exothermic; **-grad,** *m.* degree of heat, temperature.

Wärme-isolator, *m.* heat insulator; **-isolierung,** *f.* insulation of heat; **-konstanz,** *f.* constant heat; **-kraftlehre,** *f.,* **-mechanik,** *f.* thermodynamics; **-leitend,** heat-conducting; **-leiter,** *m.* conductor of heat; **-leitfähigkeit,** *f.* thermal conductivity; **-leitung,** *f.* conduction of heat; **-menge,** *f.* quantity of heat.

Wärme-messer, *m.* calorimeter; **-messung,** *f.* calorimetry; **-quelle,** *f.* source of heat.

wärmen, to warm, heat.

Wärmer, *m.* heater.

Wärme-rasse, *f.* thermal race; **-reiz,** *m.* heat stimulus; **-schutz,** *m.* thermal insulation; **-schutzmittel,** *n.* heat insulator, lagging; **-speicher,** *m.* thermal storage device; **-stau,** *m.* localization of heat; **-stauung,** *f.* stagnation, accumulation of heat; **-stich,** *m.* fever-producing puncture; **-stoff,** *m.* caloric; **-strahl,** *m.* heat ray.

Wärme-strahlung, *f.* heat radiation; **-stromdichte,** *f.* heat-flux density; **-summe,** *f.* heat sum, accumulated temperature; **-theorie,** *f.* theory of heat; **-todespunkt,** *m.* thermal death point; **-tönung,** *f.* heat tone; **-übergangszahl,** *f.* heat-transfer coefficient; **übertragung,** *f.* heat transfer; **-unterschied,** *m.* difference in heat; **-verbrauch,** *m.* heat consumption.

Wärme-vergütung, *f.* heat treatment; **-verlust,** *m.* loss of heat; **-wirkungsgrad,** *m.* thermal efficiency; **-zahl,** *f.* temperature coefficient; **-zufuhr,** *f.,* **-zunahme,** *f.* increase in heat; **-zustand,** *m.* condition of heat, thermal state.

warmlaufen, to run hot, get hot, heat up.

Wärmung, *f.* warming, heating.

Warm-wasserbeize, *f.* hot-water treatment (seed disinfection); **-wind,** *m.* hot blast.

warnen, to warn, caution.

Warte, *f.* observatory, lookout (tower).

warten, to wait, stay, attend (to), nurse; **auf sich ~ lassen,** to be long in coming.

Wärter, *m.* keeper, warder, attendant.

Wartung, *f.* attendance, nursing.

warum, why, wherefore.

Warze, *f.* wart, nipple, teat, tubercle, pin, knob.

warzen-ähnlich, wartlike, mammillary, papillary, mastoid; **-artig,** wartlike, mamillary, papillary, mastoid; **-bein,** *n.* mastoid bone; **-förmig,** wartlike, papillary; **-fortsatz,** *m.* mastoid apophysis; **-gewebe,** *n.* papillary tissue.

Warzenhof, *m.* nipple area; **-drüse,** *f.* gland of the nipple area.

Warzen-kraut, *n.* warty plant; **-pilz,** *m.* smothering fungus of coniferous seedlings; **-schwein,** *n.* wart hog.

warzig, warty, verrucose.

was, what, that, which, whatever, a fact that, how much; **~ für,** what, what a, what sort of, which; **~ auch für,** whatever kind.

Waschanstalt, *f.* laundry.

waschbar, washable, fast (color).

Wasch-bär, *m.* raccoon; **-benzol,** *n.* wash oil (benzol); **-blau,** *n.* bluing; **-bürste,** *f.* cleaning brush.

Wäsche, *f.* wash(ing), linen clothes.

waschecht, colorfast (to washing).

waschen, to wash, scour, scrub.

Wascherde, *f.* fuller's earth.

Wäscherei, *f.* laundry.

Wasch-flasche, *f.* washing bottle; **-gefäss,** *n.* washing vessel; **-gold,** *n.* placer gold; **-holländer,** *m.* washing (hollander); **-lauge,** *f.* washing liquor; **-leder,** *n.* wash leather, chamois; **-lösung,** *f.* wash(ing) solution; **-maschine,** *f.* washing machine; **-mittel,** *n.* washing agent, lotion, detergent; **-probe,** *f.* assay of washed (buddled) ore.

wäscht (waschen), washes, is washing.

Wasch-vorrichtung, *f.* washing apparatus; **-wurzel,** *f.* soapwort.

Wasen, *m.* lawn, turf, vapor.

Wasser, *n.* water; **-abfuhr,** *f.* water drainage; **-abgabe,** *f.* water loss, elimination, transpiration; **-ableitung,** *f.* drainage, diversion of water; **-abscheidung,** *f.* separation, secretion; **-absorptionsvermögen,** *n.* moisture-absorbing power; **-abspaltung,** *f.* dehydration; **-aloe,** *m.*

water soldier (*Stratiotes aloides*); **-ampfer,** *m.* water dock (*Rumex aquaticus*); **-amsel,** *f.* water ouzel.

Wasser-analyse, *f.* water analysis; **-anziehend,** hygroscopic, water-attracting; **-assel,** *f.* water sow bug, hog louse; **-aufnahme,** *f.* absorption of water; **-ausscheidung,** *f.* excretion of water; **-ausspülung,** *f.* rinsing with water; **-bad,** *n.* water bath; **-badschiessofen,** *m.* Carius tube furnace; **-bakterien,** *f.pl.* bacteria found in water; **-balg,** *m.* serous cyst.

Wasser-bauholz, *n.* wood for hydraulic works; **-baukunst,** *f.* hydraulics; **-bazillen,** *m.pl.* bacilli found in water; **-bedarf,** *m.* water requirement; **-behälter,** *m.* reservoir, cistern, tank, water back; **-beständig,** stable in (resistant to) water, waterproof; **-bewohnend,** aquatic; **-bindungsvermögen,** *n.* power of retaining water; **-blase,** *f.* vesica, pustule, bubble, water-storage cell; **-blatt,** *n.* water-shedding leaf, hydrophyllum.

Wasser-blattern, *f.pl.* chicken pox, varicella; **-blattgewächse,** *n.pl.* Hydrophyllaceae; **-blütler,** *m.pl.* hydrophyllous plants; **-bruch,** *m.* hydrocele.

Wasserdampf, *m.* steam, water vapor; **-gehalt,** *m.* steam content.

wasser-dicht, waterproof, watertight; **-dichtmachen,** *n.* waterproofing; **-drüse,** *f.* hydathode; **-echt,** fast to water; **-echtmachungsmittel,** *n.* waterproofing material; **-entziehung,** *f.* dehydration; **-faden,** *m.* hairweed (*Conferva bombycina*); **-farne,** *m.pl.* Hydropteridae; **-feder,** *f.* water violet (*Hottonia palustris*); **-fenchel,** *m.* water fennel, Oenanthe (Foeniculum); **-fest,** waterproof, watertight; **-fläche,** *f.* water level.

Wasser-flasche, *f.* water bottle; **-flora,** *f.* aquatic flora; **-frei,** anhydrous; **-früchtler,** *m.pl.* plants disseminated by water currents; **-führend,** water-bearing (strata); **-furche,** *f.* water furrow, watercourse; **-gang,** *m.* aqueduct; **-gasteer,** *m.* water-gas tar.

Wassergefäss, *n.* system, lymphatic-vessel system; **-blase,** *f.* water-vascular vesicle; **-kanal,** *m.* water-vascular canal.

Wasser-geflügel, waterfowl; **-gehalt,** *m.* water (moisture) content; **-geschwulst,** *f.* edema, hygroma; **-gewächs,** *n.* aquatic plant; **-gewebe,** *n.* water-storage (-bearing) tissue; **-gierig,** hydrophilic, hygroscopic; **-glas,** *n.* water glass, silicate of soda; **-haltend,** water-retaining (-holding); **-haltig,** containing water, aqueous, hydrous, hydrated; **-haltungsvermögen,** *n.* water-retaining power; -härtung, *f.* water hardening.

Wasser-harz, *n.* Burgundy pitch; **-haushalt,** *m.* water economy, rainfall, runoff and evaporation relations, water conservation; **-haut,** *f.* hyaloid membrane, amnion; **-hebungsvermögen,** *n.* power to raise water; **-heilkunde,** *f.* hydropathy; **-hell,** clear as water, pellucid; **-huhn,** *n.* water hen, coot.

wässerig, watery, aqueous, serous.

Wasser-immersion, *f.* water-immersion (lens); **-insekt,** *n.* aquatic insect; **-jungfer,** *f.* dragonfly; **-käfer,** *m.pl.* Hydrophilidae; **-kelch,** *m.* water calyx; **-kies,** *m.* marcasite; **-klar,** as clear as water; **-klee,** *m.* buck (bog) bean, marsh trefoil (*Menyanthes trifoliata*); **-knöterich,** *m.* knot grass (*Polygonum hydropiper*); **-kopf,** *m.* hydrocephalus.

Wasser-kraft, *f.* water power; **-kresse,** *f.* water cress; **-kristall,** *m.* rock crystal; **-kühlkasten,** *m.* water block; **-lache,** *f.* puddle of water; **-lauf,** *m.* watercourse; **-läufer,** *m.pl.* water striders, skippers; **-leben,** *n.* life in water, aquatic life; **-leitung,** *f.* water pipes, water-distributing system; **-leitungswasser,** *m.* tap water, city water.

Wasser-lilie, *f.* water lily (*Nymphaea alba*); **-linie,** *f.* water line; **-linse,** *f.* duck(meat) weed (*Lemna minor*); **-löslich,** water-soluble; **-luftpumpe,** *f.* water vacuum pump; **-lunge,** *f.* water lungs, proctal gills; **-maische,** *f.* aqueous infusion, mash; **-mangel,** *m.* scarcity of water, drought; **-mantel,** *m.* water jacket; **-mass,** *n.* water gauge.

Wasser-melone, *f.* watermelon; **-menge,** *f.* amount of water; **-milbe,** *f.* fresh-water mite (Hydrachnidae); **-moos,** *n.* alga, seaweed.

wässern, to water, irrigate, soak, hydrate.

Wasser-nabel, *m.* marsh pennywort (*Hydrocotyle vulgaris*); **-niederschlag,** *m.* precipitation of moisture; **-nuss,** *f.* water chestnut (*Trapa natans*); **-opal,** *m.* water opal, hyalite, hydrophane; **-papier,** *n.* water-leaf (paper); **-pest,** *f.* water weed; **-pfeffer,** *m. Polygonum hydropiper;* **-pflanze,** *f.* hydrophyte, aquatic plant; **-pockea,** *f.pl.* chicken pox, varicella; **-probe,** *f.* sample of water.

Wasser-reinigungsanlage, *f.* water-purification plant; **-reis,** epicormic branch, water shoot (sprout); **-reiz,** *m.* moisture stimulus; **-rest,** *m.* water residue; **-riese,***f.* flume, wet

slide; **-rispengras,** *n. Glyceria aquatica;* **-riss,** *m.* gully; **-rosengewächse,** *n.pl.* Nymphaeaceae; **-rückhaltungskraft,** *f.* ability to retain water; **-saugend,** water-absorbing.

Wasser-säule, *f.* water column; **-scheide,** *f.* water parting, watershed; **-scheu,** *f.* fear of water, hydrophobia; **-schierling,** *m.* water hemlock (*Cicuta virosa*); **-schlange,** *f.* water snake.

Wasserschlauch, *m.* bladderwort (Utricularia), water hose; **-gewächse,** *n.pl.* Lentibulariaceae.

Wasser-schluss, *m.* water seal, trap; **-schwebergesellschaften,** *f.pl.* (hydro) plankton; **-spiegel,** *m.* surface of the water, water level; **-spritze,** *f.* syringe, water sprinkler; **-stand,** *m.* water level or gauge; **-standsglas,** *n.* gauge glass; **-standshahn,** *m.* gauge cock; **-stein,** *m.* scale, incrustation, sediment.

Wasserstoff, *m.* hydrogen; **-elektrode,** *f.* hydrogen electrode; **-entwickler,** *m.* hydrogen generator; **-flasche,** *f.* hydrogen cylinder; **-frei,** free from hydrogen; **-gas,** *n.* hydrogen gas; **-gehalt,** *m.* hydrogen content; **-haltig,** hydrogenized, hydrogenous; **-hyperoxyd,** *n.* hydrogen peroxide.

Wasserstoffion, *n.* hydrogen ion; **-konzentration,** *f.* hydrogen-ion concentration.

Wasserstoff-kalium, *n.* potassium hydride; **-knallgas,** *n.* detonating gas; **-peroxyd,** *n.* hydrogen peroxide; **-reich,** rich in hydrogen; **-säure,** *f.* hydracid; **-superoxyd,** *n.* hydrogen peroxide; **-verbindung,** *f.* hydrogen compound; **-zahl,** *f.* hydrogen-ion concentration, pH numbers.

Wasser-strahl, *m.* jet of water; **-sucht,** *f.* dropsy; **-süchtig,** hydrophillic; **-suppe,** *f.* water gruel; **-talk,** *m.* brucite; **-teilchen,** *n.* water particle, molecule of water; **-treibend,** hydragogue; **-trübung,** *f.* water turbidity.

Wässerung, *f.* watering, irrigation, maceration.

wasser-unlöslich, insoluble in water; **-untersuchung,** *f.* water analysis; **-verbrauch,** *m.* consumption of water; **-verdunstung,** *f.* evaporation of water; **-verhältnis,** *n.* water relations; **-vermögen,** *n.* water-holding ability; **-versorgung,** *f.* water supply; **-verunreinigung,** *f.* contamination of water; **-vogel,** *m.-,* aquatic bird; **-vorrat,** *m.* water supply.

Wasser-waage, *f.* water level, hydrometer; **-wanne,** *f.* water (pneumatic) trough; **-wert,** *m.* water equivalent of heat capacity; **-zeichen,** *n.* watermark (of paper); **-zersetzung,** *f.* decomposition of water; **-zinkengewachse,** *n.pl.* Ceratophyllaceae; **-zufuhr,** *f.* water supply.

Wat-bein, *n.* **-fuss,** *m.* wading leg (pes vadans).

waten, to wade.

Watt, *n.* watt.

Watt, *n.*-e, shallows.

Watte, *f.* wadding, cotton wool, absorbent cotton; **-bausch,** *m.* cotton plug; **-filter,** *m.* cotton-wool strainer.

Watten-meer, *n.* shoals, shallows; **-schlick,** *m.* shoal mud.

Watte-pfropf, *m.* cotton wad, plug of cotton wool; **-verschluss,** *m.* plug of cotton wool.

wattieren, to wad, pad.

Watt-messer, *m.* wattmeter; **-stunde,** *f.* watt-hour.

Watvogel, *m.* wading bird.

Wau, *m.* weld, dyer's-weed (*Reseda luteola*); **-gelb,** *n.* luteolin; **-gewächse,** *n.pl.* Resedaceae.

weben, to weave.

Weber, *m.*-, weaver; **-distel,** *f.* fuller's teasel (*Dipsacus fullonum*).

Weberei, *f.* weaving, texture, tissue, weaving mill.

Weber-karde, *f.* fuller's teasel (*Dipsacus fullonum*); **-knecht,** *m.* shepherd spider, daddy longlegs (*Phalangium*); **-vogel,** *m.* weaver bird; **-zettel,** *m.* warp.

Web-schützen, *m.pl.* weaving shuttle; **-stuhl,** *m.* loom.

Wechsel, *m.* alternation, rotation (of crops), variation, change, exchange, joint, junction, bill of exchange, haunt, deer path, doff (in spinning).

wechselbar, changeable.

Wechsel-beanspruchung, *f.* stress reversal, changing stress; **-befruchtung,** *f.* dichogamy, bisexual impregnation; **-bewegung,** *f.* reciprocal movement; **-beziehung,** *f.* correlation, interrelation; **-blättrig,** having alternate leaves; **-fall,** *m.* vicissitude; **-farbig,** changing color, iridescent; **-fieber,** *n.* intermittent fever; **-gelenk,** *n.* movable joint, ginglymus; **-geschwindigkeit,** *f.* velocity of exchange, rate of alternation.

Wechsel-gespräch, *n.* dialogue; **-hahn,** *m.* change cock; **-handel,** *m.* banking; **-kondensor,** *m.* interchangeable (alternating) condenser; **-kurs,** *m.* rate of exchange.

wechseln, to change, exchange, alternate, vary.

Wechsel-räder, *n.pl.* change gears; **-satz,** *m.* converse, exchange principle; **-seitig,** reciprocal, mutual, alternate, opposite, interchangeable; **-spannung,** *f.* alternating voltage, alternating current; **-spiel,** *n.* fluctuation; **-ständig,** alternate; **-stein,** *m.* glazed brick (tile); **-strom,** *m.* alternating current; **-temperatur,** *f.* alternating temperature; **-tierchen,** *n.* amoeba; **-verhältnis,** *n.* reciprocal relation.

wechselwarm, with variable temperature; **wechselwarme Tiere,** *n.pl.* cold-blooded (poikilothermal) animals.

Wechsel-weide, *f.* temporary pasture; **-weise,** alternately, reciprocally; **-wiese,** *f.* temporary meadow; **-wild,** *n.* migratory game; **-wirkung,** *f.* mutual exchange, reciprocal action; **-zahl,** *f.* frequency, cycle; **-zahn,** *m.* milk tooth; **-zersetzung,** *f.* double decomposition.

Weck, *m.*-e, **Wecke,** *f.*-n, **Wecken,** *m.*-, (breakfast) roll, small loaf.

wecken, to wake, waken, rouse.

Wecker, *m.* awaker, alarm, electric bell.

Wedel, *m.*-, fan, brush, frond; **-förmig,** flabellate.

weder, neither; $\sim$ . . . **noch,** neither . . . nor.

Weg, *m.*-e, way, road, course, route, passage, direction, path, method, process, manner, means; **auf nervösem Wege,** by way of the nerves.

weg, away, far off, gone, lost; **von** . . . $\sim$, from.

weg-ätzen, to remove by caustics; **-begeben,** to go away, retire, withdraw; **-bekommen,** to get, accomplish, catch hold of, get away, get the knack of; **-brennen,** to burn off (away); **-bringen,** to remove, carry or take away; **-denken,** to imagine as absent.

Wege-bau, *m.* road-making; **-dorn,** *m.* buckthorn (*Rhamnus catharticus*).

wegen, on account of, regarding, because of.

Wegenetz, *n.* road network.

Wegerich, *m.*-e, plantain, rib grass ribwort (Plantago); **-gewächse,** *n.pl.* Plantaginaceae.

Wegfall, *m.* suppression, omission, abolition; **in** $\sim$ **bringen,** to suppress, abolish; **in** $\sim$ **kommen,** to be omitted, abolished, or suppressed.

weg-fallen, to fall off, be suppressed or omitted, cease; **-filtern,** to filter off or away; **-fressen,** to devour, eat up greedily;

-gehen, to go away, depart; **-giessen,** to pour away, pour off; **-jagen,** to chase away; **-kommen,** to get away, get lost; **-lassen,** to leave out, omit, let go; **-leitend,** efferent; **-machen,** to remove, take off.

Weg-nahme, *f.* elimination, taking away; **-nehmen,** to take away, remove; **-räumen,** to clear away; **-richtung,** *f.* direction of path or road.

wegsam, passable, accessible, penetrable.

weg-schaffen, to remove; **-sein,** to be away; **-setzen,** to put away; **-spülen,** to wash away; **-strecke,** *f.* distance; **-tun,** to put away; **-warte,** *f.* chicory (*Cichorium intybus*); **-weiser,** *m.* guide, signpost, marker; **-werfen,** to throw away, cast off, reject; **-werfend,** disdainful, disparaging; **-ziehen,** to withdraw from, depart, move.

Weh, *n.* sore, pain, grief, agony, ache; ∼ **tun,** (*dat.*) to hurt, ache, give pain, offend.

weh, woeful, painful, sore, aching.

Wehe, *f.* snowdrift.

wehen, to blow, wave.

Wehen, *f.pl.* labor pains; **-mittel,** *n.* ecbolic.

Wehr, *n.*-e, dike, dam, weir.

Wehr, *f.* defense; **-drüse,** *f.* scent (repugnatorial) gland.

wehren, (*dat.*) to restrain, keep, check, defend, resist.

wehrlos, unarmed, unprotected, inermous.

Weib, *n.*-er, woman, wife; **-chen,** *n,* female (animal).

weibermännig, gynandrian.

-weibig, -pistiled; **dreiweibig,** with three pistils.

weiblich, feminine, female, womanly, pistillate; **weibliche Keimzelle,** *f.* megaspore; **weiblicher Vorkern,** *m.* egg nucleus, ovokaryon.

Weiblichkeitsgen, *n.* gene producing femaleness.

weich, soft, tender, smooth, mellow, weak, delicate, gentle; **weicher Schanker,** *m.* soft (sore) chancre.

Weichbast, *m.* soft bast, phloem without fibers; **-insel,** *f.* island of soft bast, group of soft bast cells.

Weich-bottich, *m.* steeping tub; **-brand,** *m.* soft brick, place brick; **-braunstein,** *m.* pyrolusite; **-bütte,** *f.* steeping tank, cistern.

Weiche, *f.* flank, groin, inguinal region, softness, siding, switch.

weichen, to soften, soak, steep, yield, give way, withdraw, retreat; **-band,** *n.* inguinal ligament; **-drüse,** *f.* inguinal gland;

-gegend, *f.* inguinal region; **-platte,** *f.* iron switch.

weich-feuern, to melt down; **-floss,** *n.* porous white pig; **-flosse,** *f.* soft gill; **-flosser,** *m.pl.* Anacanthini, Malacopterygians; **-flügler,** *m.* Maladermata; **-haarig,** pubescent, pilose.

Weichheit, *f.* softness, weakness, mildness, sensibility, permeability.

Weich-holz, *n.* softwood; **-käfer,** *m.pl.* Cantharidae; **-käse,** *m.* soft cheese.

weichlich, soft, weak, tender, effeminate, delicate.

weich-machen, to soften; **-macher,** *m.* plasticizer; **-machungsmittel,** *n.* softening agent, plasticizer.

Weichsel, *f.* (saure) sour cherry; **-kirsche,** *f.* mahaleb cherry.

Weich-manganerz, *n.* pyrolusite; **-stachelig,** with soft spines or bristles; **-teil,** *m.* soft part, intestine, internal organ; **-tiere,** *n.pl.* Mollusca; **-wanze,** *f.* plant bug; **-werden,** to soften.

Weid, *m.*-e, woad.

Weid, *f.* hunting.

Weide, *f.* willow, pasture, grazing; **-bann,** *m.* closure against grazing; **-betrieb,** *m.* grass farm, pasture management; **-gang,** *m.* grazing, pastureland.

weiden, to pasture, graze, feed, browse; **-bitter,** *n.* salicin; **-bohrer,** *m.* caterpillar of goat moth; **-eiche,** *f.* willow oak; **-gebüsche,** *n.pl.* willow bushland; **-gewächse,** *n.pl.* Salicaceae; **-heger,** *m.* willow culture; **-kätzchen,** *n.* willow catkin; **-kohle,** *f.* willow charcoal; **-röschen,** *n.* willow herb.

Weiden-schorf, *m.* willow scab; **-spinner,** *m.* satin moth; **-zweig,** *m.* osier twig, wicker.

Weiderichgewächse, *n.pl.* Lythraceae.

Weidevieh, *n.* grazing cattle.

weidgerecht, skilled in woodcraft, sportsmanlike.

weidlich, hardy, lively, thoroughly.

Weidmann, *m.* sportsman, hunter; **-sprache,** *f.* sporting terms.

Weid-messer, *n.* hanger, hunting knife; **-sack,** *m.* paunch; **-werk,** *n.* woodcraft, venery, sport.

Weife, *f.* reel.

weifen, to reel, wind.

weigern, to refuse, decline.

Weihe, *f.* consecration, ordination, kite, hawk.

weihen, to consecrate, dedicate, ordain.

Weiher, *m.* pond.

Weihnachts-rose, *f.* **-wurzel,** *f.* Christmas rose (*Helleborus niger*).

Weihrauch, *m.* frankincense, incense, olibanum; **-harz,** *n.* incense resin.

weil, because, since, while.

Weilchen, *n.* little while.

Weile, *f.* while, time, leisure.

weilen, to stay, abide, tarry.

Wein, *m.*-e, wine, vine; **-ähnlich,** like wine, vinaceous; **-artig, vinous; -bau,** *m.* viniculture; **-bauer,** *m.* winegrower; **-beere,** *f.* grape.

Weinberg, *m.*-e, vineyard; **-schnecke,** *f.* edible snail.

Wein-blattlaus, *f.*-̈e, vine fretter, phylloxera; **-blume,** *f.* bouquet of wine, perfume or aroma of wine; **-blüte,** *f.* vine blossom; **-bohrer,** *m.* vine borer (*Prionus laticollis*); **-branntwein,** *m.* brandy, cognac; **-drossel,** *f.* redwing (*Turdus iliacus*).

weinen, to weep, cry.

Wein-ernte, *f.* vintage; **-erzeugend,** wine-producing; **-essig,** *m.* wine vinegar; **-farbe,** *f.* wine color; **-gar,** fermented; **-garten,** *m.* vineyard; **-gärung,** *f.* vinous fermentation; **-gehalt,** *m.* wine content; **-geist,** *m.* ethyl alcohol, **-hefe,** *f.* wine yeast.

Wein-kamm, *m.* grape pomace, rape; **-lese,** *f.* vintage; **-pfahl,** *m.* wine stake; **-probe,** *f.* sample; **-raute,** *f.* common rue; **-rebe,** *f.* grapevine; **-rebengewächse,** *n.pl.* Vitaceae; **-rebenschwarz,** *n.* Frankfort black; **-rose,** *f.* sweetbrier.

weinsauer, tartaric, vinous; **weinsaures Natrium,** *n.* tartrate of sodium.

Weinstein, *m.* tartar, hydrogen potassium tartrate; **-kohle,** *f.* black flux; **-präparat,** *n.* acid sodium sulphate; **-rahm,** *m.* cream of tartar; **-salz,** *n.* salt of tartar, potassium carbonate;

Wein-säure, *f.* tartaric acid; **-schöne,** *f.* firing for wine; **-stock,** *m.* grapevine; **-traube,** *f.* grape, bunch (cluster) of grapes; **-treber,** *f.pl.* skins of grapes; **-trester,** *m.pl.* marc of grapes.

Weise, *m.*-n, sage, philosopher.

Weise, *f.* manner, habit, custom, way, method, mood, melody; **auf diese ~,** in this way; **auf folgende ~,** as follows; **in der ~, dass,** in such a way that; **in derselben ~,** likewise, similarly.

weise, wise, prudent.

Weisel, *m.* queen bee; **-becher,** *m.* cell cupule; **-los,** queenless; **-näpfchen,** *n.*, **-wiege,** *f.*, **-zelle,** *f.* queen cell.

weisen, to show, direct, point, send, indicate.

Weiser, *m.* pointer, indicator, guide, hand; **-bestand,** *m.* indicating wood; **-formel,** *f.* indicating formula; **-methode,** *f.* indicating method.

Weisheit, *f.* wisdom, prudence, knowledge.

weiss (wissen), knows.

Weiss, *n.* white.

weiss, white, clean, blank; **weisser Fluss,** *m.* leucorrhea; **weisser Kupferstein,** *m.* white metal (copper); **weisser Leim,** *m.* gelatin; **weisser Streptokokkus,** *m.* Streptococcus albus; **weisses Eisenblech,** *n.* tin plate.

weissagen, to predict, foretell, prophesy.

Weiss-ätzung, *f.* white discharge (of fabrics); **-bad,** *n.* white liquor bath; **-baumöl,** *n.* cajuput oil; **-bier,** *n.* pale beer, weiss beer; **-birke,** *f.* white birch (*Betula alba*); **-blättrigkeit,** *f.* albinism; **-blech,** *n.* tin plate; **-blechwaren,** *f.pl.* tinware; **-bleiche,** *f.* bleaching, full bleach; **-blumig,** leucanthous, white-flowered.

Weiss-blütigkeit, *f.* leukemia; **-brennen,** *n.* calcining at white heat; **-brot,** *n.* white (wheat) bread; **-brüchig,** of white or pale fracture; **-brühe,** *f.* dégras; **-buche,** *f.* hornbeam (*Carpinus betulus*); **-buntheit,** *f.* mottling; **-dorn,** *m.* hawthorn (Crataegus).

Weisse, *f.* whiteness, white color.

weissen, to whiten, blanch, whitewash, refine.

Weiss-erde, *f.* terra alba; **-erle,** *f.* white alder; **-erz,** *n.* white ore, arsenopyrite, siderite; **-färben,** to bleach, paint (color) white; **-färber,** *m.* bleacher; **-fäule,** *f.* white rot; **-fichte,** *f.* white spruce (*Picea canadensis*); **-filzig,** white-tomentose; **-fleckenkrankheit,** *f.* white-spot disease, scleroderma; **-gar,** tawed.

weiss-gerben, to taw; **-glühen,** to raise to white heat; **-glühend,** white-hot, incandescent; **-glühhitze,** *f.* white heat; **-glut,** *f.* white heat; **-gold,** *n.* white gold; **-grau,** grayish white, canescent; **-gültigerz,** *n.* polytilite, argentiferous tetrahedrite; **-guss,** *m.* white metal; **-kalk,** *m.* pyrolignite of lime, crude calcium acetate.

weiss-kernig, white heart (of malleable iron); **-kies,** *m.* arsenopyrite; **-klee,** *m.* white clover; **-kochen,** to degum (silk);

-kohl, m. white cabbage; -kupfer, n. native copper arsenide; -kupfererz, n. cubanite.

weisslich, whitish, albescent; -grau, hoary, whitish gray.

Weisslinge, m.pl. Pieridae, whitings, whitebait.

Weiss-lot, n. soft solder; -mehl, n. white (wheat) flour; -messing, n. white brass; -ofen, m. refining furnace; -papp, m. white resist (of fabrics); -randig, white-margined; -schliff, m. white ground wood; -siedekessel, m. blanching copper; -sieden, blanch; -spiessglanzerz, n. valentinite, white antimony.

Weiss-stein, m. white metal (copper); -strahl, m. white spiegel-looking pig iron; -strahlig, white-radiated; -stuck, m. white stucco; -sud, m. blanching, blanching solution; -sylvanerz, n. sylvanite; -tanne, f. silver fir; -tellur, n. sylvanite; -tüpfelung, f. white speckling; -waren, f.pl. white (linen) goods.

Weiss-wein, m. white wine; -wollig, white-tomentose; -wurzel, f. Solomon's-seal.

Weisung, f. direction, order, instructions.

weit, wide, broad, extended, long, far, thin, distant; additional, by far, farther, moreover, considerably; ~ ab, far off; ~ bringen, to get on in the world; verschieden ~, to different degrees; ~ kommen, to get far; es zu ~ treiben, to go too far; bei weitem, by far; bei weitem nicht, by no means; von weitem, from a distance.

weitaus, by far.

weitausgebreitet, widespread, effuse, expanded.

Weite, f. distance, amplitude, wideness, width, diameter, extent.

weiten, to widen; expand, extend.

weiter, farther, further, wider, additional; und so ~, and so on, etc.; ohne weiteres, without further ado, carelessly, directly, readily.

weiter-bewegen, to move forward, advance.

weiter-befördern, to move, transport; -beförderung, f. forwarding, transport; -behandlung, f. further treatment; -bestehen, to continue to exist; -bewegen, to move forward, advance, proceed; -entwicklung, f. further development or effect.

Weiteres, n. remainder, further details, rest; ohne ~, without more ado, directly; bis auf ~, until further notice, for the present.

weiter-färben, to dye further, continue dyeing; -gerben, to retan.

weiterhin, furthermore.

Weiterungen, f.pl. difficulties, formalities, complications.

Weiter-vererbung, f. subsequent inheritance; -wachsen, n. further growth, continued growth; -züchten, to go on cultivating.

weitgehend, far-reaching, extensive, exceptional, progressive, largely.

Weithalsflasche, f. wide-necked bottle.

weithalsig, wide-necked.

weit-hin, far off, in the distance; -läufig, distant, scattered, widespread, wide, roomy, detailed; -lumig, wide-celled; -sichtig, far-sighted; -tragend, important, far-reaching; -umfassend, comprehensive, extensive.

Weitung, f. widening, width.

weit-verbreitet, widespread, prevalent; -verzweigt, widely ramified, extensive.

Weizen, m. wheat; türkischer ~, maize; -brot, m. white bread (wheaten loaf); -flugbrand, m. loose smut of wheat; -gallmücke, f. wheat midge; -griesskleie, f. middlings; -halmwespe, f. wheat-stem sawfly; -keime, m.pl. wheat germs; -kleie, f. wheat bran.

Weizen-mehl, n. wheat flour; -schrot, n. wheaten flour; -stärke, f., -stärkemehl, n. wheat starch; -steinbrand, m. bunt of wheat; -stinkbrand, m. bunt of wheat, stinking smut of wheat; -stroh, n. wheat straw.

welch, who, which, what; ~ auch immer, whoever, whatever.

welcher, which? what? who?; ~ auch (immer), whosoever; welches auch, whatsoever.

welcherlei, of what kind.

welk, withered, faded, shriveled, parched, flaccid, languid; -boden, m. withering (air-drying) floor (in brewing).

Welkekrankheit, f. wilt disease, verticillium wilt.

welken, to wilt, wither, fade, dry.

Welken, n. wilting.

welkend, wilting, marcescent.

Well-baum, m. axletree, arbor, shaft; -blech, n. corrugated (sheet) iron.

Welle, f. wave, axle, arbor, beam, shaft, undulation, fagot, bundle, bavin.

wellen, to let boil, roll, wave, corrugate; **-artig,** wavelike, undulatory; **-berg,** *m.* wave crest; **-bewegung,** *f.* undulation; **-binde,** *m.,* **-bock,** *m.* fagot-binder's press; **-brecher,** *m.* break-water; **-filter,** *n.* wave filter; **-förmig,** undulating, rolling.

Wellen-holz, *n.* fagot (bavin) wood; **-lager,** *n.* bearing; **-länge,** *f.* wave length; **-messer,** *m.* wave meter; **-schwingung,** *f.* undulation; **-stoss,** *m.* wave impulse, wave motion; **-strom,** *m.* undulatory (pulsating) current; **-tal,** *n.* wave trough, depression between two waves.

Weller, *m.* loam and straw.

wellig, undulating, wavy; ∼ **gebogen,** undulate.

Well-packpapier, *n.* corrugated paper; **-pappe,** *f.* corrugated board; **-rad,** *n.* wheel and axle, arbor wheel.

Wellung, *f.* waving, undulation.

Wellwurzel, *f.* symphytum.

Wels, *m.*-(s)e, sheatfish, silure.

welsch, foreign, Romance, Welsh.

Welt, *f.* world, society, humanity; **-all,** *n.* universe; **-auge,** *f.* hydrophane, white opal; **-ausstellung,** *f.* world's fair; **-beschreibung,** *f.* cosmography; **-bürgerlich,** cosmopolitan; **-früh,** primeval; **-gegend,** *f.* region of the world; **-gürtel,** *m.* zone; **-handel,** *m.* world commerce; **-körper,** *m.* heavenly body; **-kugel,** *f.* globe.

weltlich, mundane, temporal, worldly, secular, civil, profane.

Welt-meer, *n.* ocean; **-raum,** *m.* universal space; **-sprache,** *f.* universal language; **-stadt,** *f.* metropolis; **-teil,** *m.* continent, part of the world.

wem, to whom, whom.

wen, whom.

Wende, *f.* turning, turn, change, turning point, epoch, period, era; **-kreis,** *m.* tropic.

Wendeltreppe, *f.* spiral staircase, spiral of twining plants, *Scalaria pretiosa.*

wenden, to turn over, return, veer. cast (eyes); **gewandt,** skilled, versed.

Wendepunkt, *m.* turning point, point of reversal or inflection.

Wender, *m.* rotator muscle.

Wendestelle, *f.* turning place.

Wendezehe, *f.* hyderodactyl.

Wendezehenfuss, *m.* versatile foot.

Wendezeher, *m.pl.* plantain eaters (Musophagae).

Wendung, *f.* turning, turn, sinuosity, torsion.

Wendungszelle, *f.* basal (pivotal) cell (Nitella).

wenig, little, small, slightly few; **-ährig,** having few spikes.

weniger, less, fewer.

Wenigkeit, *f.* littleness, small quantity, smallness, trifle.

wenigköpfig, with few heads.

weniglöslich, difficultly soluble.

wenigste, least, fewest.

wenigstens, at least.

wenn, if, when, whenever, though; ∼ **auch,** although even if; ∼ **etwa,** if by chance; ∼ **schon,** though; **selbst** ∼, granted that; ∼ **gleich,** although.

wer, who, which, he who; ∼ **es auch sei,** whosoever it may be.

Werbe-gewohnheit, *f.* mode of courting; **-mittel,** *n.* means of propaganda or publicity.

werben, to strive after, aspire, make propaganda, sue, court, recruit, enlist.

Werbeschrift, *f.* propaganda article, pamphlet, catalog, advertising.

Werbung, *f.* courtship.

Werdegang, *m.* development, growth.

werden, to become, get, grow, turn, shall, will, be; ∼ **zu,** to change to.

Werden, *n.* formation, upbuilding, growth.

werfen, to throw, cast, fling, hurl, project, bring forth young, warp, throw oneself, apply oneself.

Werft, *f.* wharf, dock.

Werftkäfer, *m.pl. Lymexylon navale.*

Werg, *n.* tow, oakum; **-artig,** like tow, woolly, stupose.

Werk, *n.*-e, work, act, publication, deed, performance, mechanism; **-blei,** *n.* raw lead; **-bottich,** *m.* **-bütte,** *f.* stuff vat (for paper); **-führer,** *m.* plant manager; **-holz,** *n.* industrial wood; **-leitung,** *f.* management; **-meister,** *m.* foreman; **-probe,** *f.* sample of metal; **-silber,** *n.* silver extracted from lead ore; **-stätte,** *f.* workshop.

Werk-stein, *m.* quarry stone, freestone; **-stoff,** *m.* (industrial) material; **-stück,** *n.* piece of metal to be worked, ore to be smelted; **-tätig,** working, active, practical; **-vertriebskosten,** *f.pl.* factory selling expenses; **-zeug,** *n.* tool, instrument; **-zeugmaschine,** *f.* machine tool.

Wermut, *m.* wormwood, absinthe, vermouth; **-bitter,** *m.* absinthin; **-öl,** *n.* oil of wormwood.

wert, (*dat.*) worth, dear, esteemed, valued, honored.

Wert, *m.* value, worth, valence, merit; **-angabe,** *f.* statement of value; **-bemessung,** *f.* standardization; **-bestimmung,** *f.* determination of value or valence.

werten, to value, estimate.

wertgeschätzt, valued, esteemed.

Wertgesichtspunkt, *m.* value point of view.

-wertig, -valent.

Wertigkeit, *f.* valence.

Wertigkeits-einheit, *f.* unit of valency; **-gefühl,** *n.* sensation of appreciation.

wert-los, worthless; **-papier,** *n.* bond, security, scrip; **-sachen,** *f.pl.* valuables; **-schätzen,** to value, esteem highly; **-schätzung,** *f.* estimation, valuation; **-verhältnis,** *n.* ratio of value, relative value; **-voll,** valuable.

Wesen, *n.* being, nature, organism, essence, substance, condition, character, affairs, concern, disposition, property, manner.

wesentlich, essential, substantial, real, remarkable, material(ly), intrinsic; **im wesentlichen,** essentially; **das Wesentliche,** the essential thing.

weshalb, why, wherefore, what for.

Wespe, *f.* wasp.

Wespenbein, *n.* sphenoid bone; **-fortsatz,** *m.* sphenoid apophysis; **-höhle,** *f.* sphenoidal sinus; **-horn,** *n.* horn of the sphenoid; **-schnabel,** *m.* beak of the sphenoid; **-stachel,** *m.* spine of the sphenoid.

wessen, whose, of which.

westlich, west, western, occidental.

weswegen, why.

wett, equal, even, quits.

Wettbewerb, *m.* competition, rivalry, struggle for existence.

Wette, *f.* bet, wager, rivalry.

Wetteifer, *m.* emulation, rivalry, competition.

wetteifern, to vie, emulate, compete.

Wetter, *n.* weather, atmosphere, storm (fire) damp; **-beständig,** weatherproof; **-echt, -fest,** weatherproof, fast to exposure; **-kunde,** *f.* meteorology.

wettern, to thunder and lighten, curse and swear, storm.

Wetter-pflanze, *f.* weather-indicating plant; **-seite,** *f.* weather side; **-sprengstoffe,** *m.pl.* permissible explosives; **-stein,** *m.* belemnite; **-voraussage,** *f.* weather forecast.

Wett-kampf, *m.* contest; **-lauf,** *m.* race; **-machen,** to square up, make good; **-streit,** *m.* emulation, contest.

wetzen, to whet, grind, sharpen.

Wetzstein, *m.* whetstone, hone.

Weymuthkiefer, *f.* white pine.

wich (weichen), yielded.

Wichse, *f.* polishing wax, blacking, thrashing.

wichsen, to polish, wax, thrash.

Wicht, *m.-e,* weight, urchin.

Wichte, *f.* specific gravity.

wichtig, important, weighty.

Wichtigkeit, *f.* importance, significance.

Wicke, *f.* vetch.

Wickel, *m.-,* cincinnus, filler of cigar, roller, package.

wickeln, to wind, twist, coil, roll, wrap.

Wickel-ranke, *f.* tendril, cirrus; **-rankig,** cirrate, tendriled; **-schraubel,** *f.* cincinnus bostryx.

Wickenstroh, *n.* vetch straw.

Wickler, *m.* leaf-roller moth, tortrix.

Wicklung, *f.* wrapping, casing, envelopment, winding.

Widder, *m.-,* ram; **-stoss,** *m.* cycle of ram, water hammer.

widdern, to turn (malt).

wider, against, contrary to; **-druck,** *m.* counterpressure, reaction; **-fahren,** to happen, occur, befall; **-haarig,** crossgrained, stubborn.

Widerhaken, *m.* barbed hook; **-haar,** *n.* barbed hair; **-stachel,** *m.* glochidium.

widerhakig, glochidiate.

Widerhall, *m.* reverberation, echo.

Widerlager, *n.* **Widerlagsmauer,** *f.* abutment.

wider-legbar, refutable; **-legen,** to refute; **-leglich,** refutable.

widerlich, obnoxious, repulsive.

widernatürlich, unnatural, artificial, contrary to nature.

Widerrede, *f.* contradiction, objection; **ohne ~,** unquestionably.

Widerrist, *m.* withers (of horse); **-fistel,** *f.* fistula of the withers; **-schaden,** *m.* saddle gall.

wider-rufen, to revoke, recall, retract; **-schein,** *m.* reflection; **-setzen,** (*dat.*) to resist, oppose; **-sinnig,** absurd, contrary to common sense; **-spenstig,** stubborn, obstinate, unmanageable, unruly, rebellious, restive; **-spiegeln,** to reflect; **-spiel,** *n.* contrary, opposition; **-sprechen,** (*dat.*) to contradict; **-spruch,** *m.* contradiction, opposition.

Widerstand, *m.* resistance.

Widerstands-brücke, *f.* resistance bridge; **-einheit,** *f.* unit of resistance; **-fähig,** hardy, resistant, capable of resistance; **-fähigkeit,** *f.* power of resistance, load-bearing capacity; **-kraft,** *f.* hardiness; **-los,** offering no resistance; **-messung,** *f.* measuring of resistance; **-schaltung,** *f.* resistance (box); **-vermögen,** *n.* resisting power; **-verschiebung,** *f.* variation of resistance.

wider-stehen, to oppose, resist, be repugnant to; **-stoss,** *m.* countershock; **-streben,** to oppose, resist, be repugnant; **-strebend,** reluctantly; **-streiten,** to be contrary to, clash with, be antagonistic; **-streitend,** conflicting; **-ton,** *m.* silver heather, maidenhair (Polytrichum); **-wärtig,** disagreeable, vexatious, adverse; **-wille,** *f.* aversion, disgust, antipathy; **-willig,** reluctant, unwilling.

widmen, to dedicate, devote.

Widmung, *f.* dedication, devotion.

widrig, contrary, adverse, hostile.

wie, how, in what way, just as, as, like; ~ . . . **auch,** however; ~ **gesagt,** as has been said.

Wiebel, *m.* weevil.

Wied, *m.* woad.

Wiede, *f.* withe, willow twig.

Wiedehopf, *m.* -e, hoopoe (Upupa).

wieder, again, anew, once more, back, further; **immer** ~, again and again.

wieder-abdrucken, to reprint; **-anmeldung,** *f.* reissue, reapplication (patents); **-aufforsten,** to reafforest; **-aufleben,** to revive; **-auflebend,** revived; **-beleben,** to revive, revivify, reactivate, resuscitate, reburn (sugar); **-belebung,** *f.* recuperation, resuscitation; **-beschicken,** to reload, recharge; **-bewachsung,** *f.* revegetation; **-bewaldung,** *f.* reforestation.

Wieder-brauchbarmachen, *n.* regeneration; **-einschmelzen,** *n.* remelting; **-einsetzung,** *f.* reinstatement, restitution, reinstallment,

-erhitzen, to reheat; **-erkennen,** *n.* recognition; **-erwärmen,** to rewarm, reheat; **-erzeugen,** to reproduce, regenerate; **-erzeugung,** *f.* reproduction, regeneration; **-gabe,** *f.* reproduction, response, reply; **-geben,** to restore, return, translate, render, reproduce, project.

wieder-gewinnen, to regenerate, recover; **-gewinnung,** *f.* recovery; **-hall,** *m.* echo; **-herstellen,** to restore, cure, revive, reproduce; **-herstellung,** *f.* recovery, reinstatement; **-holbarkeit,** *f.* invariability, reproducibility, repetition, recurrence, re production; **-holen,** to repeat; **-holt,** repeated; **-holung,** *f.* repetition; **-holungsspross,** *m.* innovation shoot.

wieder-käuen, to ruminate, chew the cud, repeat over and over; **-käuend,** ruminant.

Wiederkäuer, *m.* ruminant; **-magen,** *m.* ruminant stomach.

Wieder-kehr, *f.* reappearance, return; **-kehren,** to recur, return; **-kehrend,** recurrent; **-kristallisierung,** *f.* recrystallization; **-schein,** *m.* reflection.

Wiedersehen, *n.* meeting again; **auf** ~, till we meet again, au revoir.

wieder-spiegeln, to reflect; **-strahl,** *m.* reflected ray; **-um,** again, in return; **-vereinigen,** to reunite; **-vereinigung,** *f.* recombination; **-verjüngung,** *f.* reproducing; **-wuchs,** *m.* regrowth, second growth, coppice shoot.

Wiege, *f.* cradle.

wiegen, to weigh, rock (cradle).

Wiegevorrichtung, *f.* weighing device.

wiehern, to neigh.

Wieke, *f.* pledget.

Wien, *n.* Vienna.

Wiener Ätzpulver, *n.* Vienna paste, caustic.

wies (weisen), pointed at, showed.

Wiese, *f.* meadow.

Wiesel, *n.* weasel.

Wiesen-bärenklau, *m.&f.,* cow parsnip (*Heracleum spondylium*); **-erz,** *n.* meadow ore, bog iron ore; **-flachs,** *m.* purging flax (*Linum catharticum*); **-flora,** *f.* prairie flora; **-fuchsschwanz,** *m.* meadow foxtail; **-kalk,** *m.* meadow limestone; **-klee,** *m.* red clover (*Trifolium pratense*); **-knopf,** *m.* great burnet (*Sanguisorba officinalis*); **-knöterich,** *m.* sweet dock (*Polygonum bistorta*); **-lein,** *m.* purging flax.

Wiesen-moor, *n.* meadow bog; **-platterbse,** *f.* meadow pea (*Lathyrus pratensis*); **-rispengras** ¬. Kentucky bluegrass, June grass, meadow grass (*Poa pratensis*); -salbei, *f.* meadow sage (*Salvia pratensis*); -schaumkraut, *n.* lady's-smock, cuckoo flower (*Cardamine pratensis*); -schwingel, *m.* meadow fescue (*Festuca pratensis*); -teppich, *m.* grassy carpet.

wieviel, how much, how many.

wiewohl, although.

wild, wild, savage, fierce, uncivilized, proud (flesh); wildes Fleisch, *n.* proud flesh; wildes Gestein, *n.* nonmetalliferous rock.

Wild, *n.* game; -acker, *m.* field for game in a preserve.

Wildbach, *m.* torrent; -verbauung, *f.* damming of torrents.

Wild-bahn, *f.* ride where game is found; -bret, *n.* game; -dieb, *m.* poacher.

Wilde(r), *m.* savage.

Wildente, *f.* wild duck.

wildern, to poach, revert to wild state.

wilder Wein, *m.* Virginia creeper.

Wild-frass, *m.* damage by game; -gans, *f.* bean goose; -geschmack, *m.* gamy taste; -hafer, *m.* wild oats; -hege, *f.* game preserving; -kalb, *n.* fawn; -kirschenrinde, *f.* wild-cherry bark; -leder, *n.* buckskin, deerskin.

Wildling, *m.* parent stock (on which scion is grafted), wild seedling, wild tree, animal in its wild state.

Wildnis, *f.* wilderness.

Wild-obstbaum, *m.* wild fruit tree; -park, *m.* game preserve; -pflege, *f.* game preserving; -pret, *n.* game; -recht, *n.* quarry; -reich, abounding with game; -schaden, *m.* damage by game; -schwein, *n.* wild pig, boar.

Wild-seuche, *f.* hemorrhagic septicemia of game animals; -spur, *f.* scent, track of game; -stand, *m.* covert, stock of game; -taube, *f.* wood pigeon; -verbiss, *m.* browsing by game; -wachsend, growing wild, run wild, self-sown.

will (wollen), wants to, want to.

Wille, *f.* Willen, *m.* will, volition, design, purpose, intent, pleasure; um . . . willen, for the sake of . . .

willenlos, involuntary.

Willensakt, *m.* act of volition or of will, voluntary action.

Willenstätigkeit, *f.* function of the will, voluntary action.

willfahren, to accede to, comply with.

willig, willing, ready, docile.

willkommen, (*dat.*) welcome.

Willkür, *f.* free will, free choice, arbitrary action; -bewegung, *f.* voluntary movement.

willkürlich, arbitrary, voluntary, optional, despotic.

wimmeln, to swarm, teem.

Wimmer, *m.* wavy grain, curl, gnarl.

wimmerig, curly, wavy-grained, wavy-fibered.

Wimper, *f.* cilium, lash; -apparat, *m.* ciliary apparatus; -bewegung, *f.* vibratile (ciliary) movement; -borsten, *f.pl.* short cilia; -büschel, *n.* aggregate of vibratile cilia; -epithel, *n.* vibratile (ciliary) epithelium; -feld, *n.* ciliated area; -flamme, *f.* flame cell; -furche, *f.* ciliated groove; -gürtel, *m.* ciliated girdle; -haar, *n.* ciliated hair, cilium, eyelash.

wimperig, ciliated.

Wimper-infusorien, *f.pl.* Ciliata; -kleid, *n.* ciliated covering (ectoderm); -kölbchen, *n.* flame cell; -kranz, *m.* ciliated band or circle; -muskel, *m.* ciliary muscle.

wimpernd, ciliated, ciliary, winking.

Wimper-platten, *f.pl.* comb ribs, swimming plates; -reifen, *m.* ciliated hoop, -ring, *m.* ciliated ring; -ringlarve, *f.* trochophore; -schlag, *m.* ciliary movement; -schopf, *m.* tuft of cilia; -trichter, *m.* ciliated funnel; -zelle, *f.* ciliated cell, solenocyte.

Wind, *m.*-e, wind, breeze, blast; -abtragung, *f.* wind erosion; -bestäubung, *f.* wind pollination; -blatt, *n.* leaf resistant to wind injury; -blattern, *f.pl.* chicken pox, varicella; -blume, *f.* flower pollinated by wind.

Wind-blütler, *m.* anemophylous plant; -bruch, *m.* wind breakage; -bruchfläche, *f.* area denuded by wind; -darm, *m.* colon; -dicht, airtight; -druck, *m.* blast pressure, wind pressure.

Winde, *f.* windlass, lifting jack, winch, bindweed.

winden, to wind, reel, twist, coil, wriggle.

Windengewächse, *n.pl.* twining plants (Convolvulaceae).

Windepflanze, *f.* twining plant.

Wind-erhitzung, *f.* blast heating; -fahne, *f.* vane; -fall, *m.* windfall; -flügel, *m.* ventilator, fan, fan blade; -form, *f.* twyer, tuyère; -frischen, *n.* converting, air refining, blast purifying.

Wind-früchtler, *m.* fruit disseminated by the air; -geschwulst, *f.* traumatic emphysema; -getragen, wind-borne, carried by the wind; -hafer, *m.* wild oat (*Avena fatua*); -halm, *m.* silky bent grass (*Apera spica venti*); -hund, *m.* greyhound.

windig, windy, breezy.

Wind-kasten, *m.* air chamber; -leitung, *f.* blast main; -leitungsrohr, *n.* blast pipe, air duct; -mantel, *m.* shelter belt, windbreak, wind mantle; -messer, *m.* anemometer; -mühle, *f.* windmill (turbine); -pocken, *f.pl.* chicken pox, varicella; -richtung, *f.* quarter or direction of the wind; -roller, *m.* wind disseminated (anemochorous) fruit; -röschen, *n.* wood anemone (*Anemone silvestris*).

Wind-rose, *f.* compass card, rhumb card, anemone; -rücken, *m.* windward side; -sammler, *m.* air reservoir; -schatten, *m.* lee side; -schief, warped; -schliff, *m.* plant injured by wind-blown particles; -sichter, *m.* air separator; -still, calm; -strömmung, *f.* air current, wind pressure· -treibend, carminative.

wind-trocken, wind-dried, air-dry; -trocknung, *f.* wind drying, blast (air) drying; -übertragung, *f.* transmission or conveying by the wind.

Windung, *f.* winding convolution, spiral, sinuosity, torsion.

Windungsachse, *f.* axis of convolution.

Windwurf, *m.* blowdown, windfall.

Windzug, *m.* air current, draft.

Wink, *m.*-e, sign, wink, nod, beckoning, hint.

Winkel, *m.*-, angle, corner, nook; -bein, *n.* angular bone; -bogen, *m.* arc subtending an angle; -förmig, angular; -gelenk, *n.* hinge, joint; -geschwindigkeit, *f.* circular or angular velocity; -grösse, *f.* size of an angle; -halbierende, *f.* bisector of an angle.

winkelig, angular.

Winkel-linie, *f.* diagonal; -mass, *n.* square; -messer, *m.* goniometer; -recht, rightangled, rectangular; -zug, *m.* shift, pretext, evasion; -zahn (Eckzahn), *m.* canine tooth.

winken, to wink, beckon.

Winter, *m.*-, winter; -behandlung, *f.* dormant treatment; -deckel, *m.* winter covering, operculum; -fest, hardy; -festigkeit, *f.* winter hardiness.

Wintergrün, *n.* wintergreen, ivy, periwinkle; -gewächse, *n.pl.* Pyrolaceae; -öl, *n.* wintergreen oil.

winterkahl, leafless in winter.

Winterlagerung, *f.* winter lodging.

winterlich, wintry.

Winter-linde, *f.* small-leaved lime tree; -rinde, *f.* Winter's bark (*Drimys winteri*); -rübsen, *m.* winter rape (*Brassica rapa*)· -ruhe, *f.* winter rest period; -saat, *f.* autumn-sown seed; -schlaf, *m.* hibernation; -schnitt, *m.* winter pruning; -sonnenwende, *f.* winter solstice; -spore, *f.* winter (resting) spore; -steher, *m.* plant holding seed through winter; -weizen, *m.* winter wheat.

winzig, minute, tiny, very small, puny, petty, trifling.

Wipfel, *m.*-, treetop; -pflanze, *f.* branching plant.

wipfeln, to tower, rise aloft, lop (trees).

Wippe, *f.* balancing, critical point, seesaw.

Wirbel, *m.* vertebra, vortex, whirl, eddy, vertigo, crown of the head, beak of shell; -ausschnitt, *m.* vertebral notch.

Wirbelband, *n.* vertebra ligament; -scheibe, *f.* intervertebral disk.

Wirbelbein, *n.* vertebra; -band, *n.* vertebral ligament.

Wirbel-bewegung, *f.* vortex motion; -bogen, *m.* vertebral arch; -dorn, *m.* spinous process of vertebra; -fortsatz, *m.* process of vertebra; -furche, *f.* vertebral groove; -gang, *m.* vertebral canal; -gelenk, *n.* vertebral articulation, spinal joint.

Wirbel-kanal, *m.* vertebral canal; -knochen, *m.* vertebra; -knorpel, *m.* vertebral cartilage; -kopf, *m.* head of vertebra; -loch, *n.* vertebral foramen; -los, invertebrate; -losen, *pl.* invertebrates.

wirbeln, to whirl, spin, eddy, warble, roll (of drum).

Wirbel-pfanne, *f.* vertebral fossa, cavity; -querfortsatz, *m.* transverse process of vertebra; -säule, *f.* vertebral column; -säulenband, *n.* ligament of spinal column; -säulengegend, *f.* spinal region; -strom, *m.* eddy current, whirlpool; -sturm, *m.* tornado, cyclone; -tierabteilung, *f.* group of vertebrates; -tiere, *n.pl.* vertebrates.

wirbt (werben), strives, aspires.

wird (werden), becomes, is becoming, will; es ~ mir, I feel.

wirft (werfen), throws, is throwing.

Wirk, *n.* kneading.

wirken, to effect, bring about, produce, act. work, operate, knot, weave, knit.

wirkend, acting, operative, working, efficient.

Wirkerei, *f.* knitting trade.

wirklich, actual, real, substantial, true.

Wirklichkeit, *f.* reality, actuality, truth.

wirksam, active, effective, efficient.

Wirksamkeit, *f.* activity, operation, agency' effectiveness, efficacy, efficiency, strength; **in ∼ setzen** (treten), to set going, start, take effect, throw into gear.

Wirkstoff, *m.* effective material, hormone.

Wirkung, *f.* effect, working, action, effort, operation, consequence, influence.

Wirkungs-art, *f.* mode of operation; **-bedingung,** *f.* condition of activity; **-dauer,** *f.* duration of effect; **-fähig,** capable of acting, effective; **-fähigkeit,** *f.* activity, effectiveness, efficiency; **-faktor,** *m.* responsible factor; **-gehalt,** *m.* active principle or content; **-geschwindigkeit,** *f.* rapidity of action; **-gesetz,** *n.* activity law; **-grad,** *m.* efficiency, effect.

Wirkungs-kraft, *f.*-e, active force, efficiency; **-kreis,** *m.* sphere of action; **-los,** inactive, ineffective, inefficient; **-losigkeit,** *f.* inactivity, inefficacy, inefficiency; **-richtung,** *f.* orientation of the effect; **-sphäre,** *f.* sphere of action; **-vermögen,** *n.* power of action; **-weise,** *f.* mode of action; **-wert,** *m.* efficacy.

Wirk-ware, *f.* woven goods, knit goods; **-zeit,** *f.* reaction time.

wirr, confused, tangled, disorderly.

Wirre, *f.* confusion, disorder, chaos.

Wirrseide, *f.* silk waste.

Wirt, *m.*-e, host, landlord.

Wirtel, *m.* whorl.

wirtelig, verticillate.

Wirtelpilz, *m.* whorl fungus.

Wirtsanlage, *f.* host rudiment.

Wirtschaft, *f.* economy, management, husbandry working, household exploitation, restaurant.

wirtschaften, to keep house, run a farm, manage.

Wirtschafter, *m.* manager.

wirtschaftlich, thrifty, economical, domestic, efficient, industrial.

Wirtschaftlichkeit, *f.* economy, thrift.

Wirtschafts-betrieb, *m.* household (farm) management; **-plan,** *m.* working plan; **-regel,** *f.* working rule.

wirts-hold, host-limited, preferring certain hosts; **-keim,** *m.* host embryo; **-organisator,** *m.* host organizer; **-pflanze,** *f.* host

plant; **-stet,** host-limited; **-vag,** having a wide host range, host-diversified; **-wechselnd,** heteroecious.

Wisch, *m.*-e, whisk, piece of paper, rag, litura, an obscure spot paler at one edge.

wischen, to wipe, slip away, whisk.

Wischer, *m.* wiper, cloth rubber, drawing, stump.

Wischtuch, *n.* cloth for wiping.

Wisent, *m.* European bison.

Wismut, bismuth; **-blende,** *f.* bismuth blende, eulytite; **-blüte,** *f.* bismuth ocher, bismite; **-chlorid,** *n.* bismuth trichloride; **-erz,** *n.* bismuth ore; **-gehalt,** *m.* bismuth content; **-glanz,** *m.* bismuthinite, bismuth glance; **-glätte,** *f.* bismuth litharge, blend; **-haltig,** bismuthiferous; **-jodid,** *n.* bismuth iodide.

Wismut-kupfererz, *n.* emplectite, wittichenite; **-legierung,** *f.* bismuth alloy; **-lot,** *n.* bismuth solder; **-nickel(kobalt)kies,** *m.* grunauite; **-niederschlag,** *m.* bismuth precipitate; **-nitrat,** *n.* bismuth nitrate; **-ocker,** *m.* bismuth ocher, bismite; **-oxyd,** *n.* bismuth oxide, bismuth trioxide; **-silber,** *n.* schapbachite; **-spat,** *m.* bismutite.

Wismut-sulfid, *n.* bismuth sulphide; **-tellur,** *n.* telluric bismuth, tetradymite; **-verbindung,** *f.* bismuth compound; **-weiss,** *n.* bismuth white.

wissbegierig, inquisitive, curious.

wissen, to know, understand, be able to.

Wissen, *n.* knowledge, scholarship; **-schaft,** *f.* science, learning, knowledge, scholarship; **-schaftler,** *m.* scientist; **-schaftlich,** scientific; **-schaftlichkeit,** *f.* scientific nature, scholarly method; **-schaftslehre,** *f.* theory of science.

Wissens-gebiet, *n.* field of knowledge; **-zweig,** *m.* branch of knowledge.

wissentlich, knowing, conscious, deliberate.

Witterung, *f.* weather, scent, trail.

witterungsbeständig, atmospheric corrosion-resisting.

Witterungs-kunde, *f.* meteorology; **-lehre,** *f.* meteorology; **-umschlag,** *m.* change in weather; **-wechsel,** *m.* change in weather.

Witz, *m.*-e, wit, joke, pun, sense.

wo, where, somewhere, if.

wob (weben), wove, was weaving.

wobei, whereat, whereby, in doing so, during which, as well as.

Woche, *f.* week.

Wochen-bett, n. childbed, puerperium; **-fluss,** m. lochia; **-lang,** for weeks; **-schrift,** f. weekly publication.

wöchentlich, weekly.

Wöchnerin, f. lying-in woman.

wodurch, whereby, by what means, through which.

wofern, provided, in case.

wofür, for what, for which, what for.

wog (wägen, wiegen), weighed.

Woge, f. wave, billow.

wogegen, against what, against which, in return for which, whereas.

wogen, to wave, surge, roll, move.

woher, whence, from where.

wohin, whither, where; **-gegen,** whereas, while.

Wohl, n. weal, welfare, health, prosperity, good, benefit.

wohl, well, perhaps, probably, indeed, no doubt; **so ∼ als,** as well as; **∼ aber,** however.

wohl-angebracht, well-timed, most opportune; **-auf,** now then; **-ausgebildet,** well-developed; **-bedacht,** well-considered, deliberate; **-befinden,** n. good health.

wohl-begründet, well-founded; **-behalten,** in good condition; **-bekannt,** well-known; **-beleibt,** corpulent; **-belesen,** well-read; **-besetzt,** well-filled; **-bewusst,** well-known, conscious; **-durchdacht,** well-considered; **-erfahren,** experienced.

Wohlergehen, n. welfare, prosperity.

wohl-erhalten, well-preserved; **-erwogen,** well-considered; **-fahrt,** f. welfare.

wohlfeil, cheap.

wohl-gebaut, well-built; **-gebildet,** well-informed, handsome; **-geboren,** Esquire; **-gefallen,** n. liking, pleasure.

wohl-gefällig, pleasant, agreeable; **-gelitten,** popular, much-liked; **-gemut,** cheerful, cheery; **-genährt,** well-nourished, stout; **-geordnet,** well-arranged; **-geraten,** well-done, perfect, well-bred; **-geruch,** m. pleasant odor, perfume, aroma; **-geschmack,** m. agreeable taste; **-gesinnt,** well-disposed; **-geübt,** practiced, skilled.

wohl-gewogen, well-inclined; **-habend,** well-to-do; **-klang,** m. harmony, euphony; **-klingend,** well-sounded, melodious, euphonic, musical, harmonious; **-laut,** m. harmony, euphony; **-lautend,** euphonious, melodious, pleasing to the ear; **-leben,** n. good living, luxury; **-riechend,** fragrant.

-sein, n. good health; **-stand,** m. welfare, wealth.

Wohl-tat, f. kind deed, benefit; **-täter,** m. benefactor; **-tätig,** beneficent, charitable; **-tun,** to do good, give pleasure.

Wohlverlei, m. arnica; **-wurzel,** f. arnica root.

wohl-versorgt, well-provided; **-weislich,** very wisely; **-wollen,** to be well-disposed; **-wollen,** n. kind feeling.

wohnen, to live, dwell, reside.

Wohn-bezirk, m. **-gebiet,** n. habitat, locality.

wohnhaft, living, dwelling, residing.

Wohnhaushalt, m. domestic establishment, ecology.

Wohnkammer, f. living chamber.

wohnlich, habitable, comfortable.

Wohn-ort, m.-e, dwelling place; **-röhre,** f. dwelling tube; **-sitz,** m. residence; **-stube,** f. living room; **-tier,** n. host.

Wohnung, f. dwelling, residence, habitation.

wölben, to vault, arch, crown.

Wölbung, f. curvature, vault.

Wolf, m.-ᵉe, wolf, iron lump or bloom, lupus, chafing, (**-mischer**) porcupine (mixer).

Wolfram, m. tungsten.

Wolframat, n. tungstate, wolframate.

Wolfram-bleierz, n. stolzite; **-chlorid,** n. tungsten chloride; **-draht,** m. tungsten wire; **-erz,** n. tungsten ore; **-faden,** m. tungsten filament; **-haltig,** tungsteniferous; **-lampe,** f. tungsten lamp; **-metall,** n. metallic tungsten; **-oxyd,** n. tungsten oxide; **-salz,** n. tungsten salt; **-säure · -anhydrid,** n. tungstic anhydride; **-stahl,** m. tungsten steel; **-stickstoff,** m. tungsten nitride.

Wolfs-bohne, f. lupine; **-kirsche,** f. belladonna; **-milch,** f. wolf's-milk, spurge (Euphorbia); **-milchgewächse,** n.pl. Euphorbiaceae; **-spinne,** f. wolf spider (Lycosa); **-stahl,** m. natural steel, bloom steel; **-wurz,** f. baneberry.

Wolke, f. cloud.

Wolken-angriff, m. cloud gas attack, wave attack; **-artig,** like a cloud; **bildung,** f. cloud formation; **-los,** cloudiness; **-stufe,** f. cloud level (elevation).

wolkig, cloudy, clouded.

Woll-abgang, m. wool waste; **-artig,** woolly; **-baum,** m. silk-cotton tree (Bombax); **-blumen,** f.pl. mullein flowers (verbasci).

Wolle, *f.* wool.

wollen, to intend, be about, will, wish, want.

Woll-färber, *m.* wool dyer; **-farbig,** dyed in the wool; **-faser,** *f.* woolly fiber; **-garn,** *n.* woolen yarn; **-gras,** *n.* cotton grass (Eriophorum); **-haar,** *n.* woolly hair.

wollig, woolly, lanate, laniferous.

Woll-klette, *n.* burrs which cling to wool or feathers; **-kraut,** *n.* mullein (Verbascum), high taper; **-pulver,** *n.* flock; **-schmiere,** *f.* wool yolk, suint, wool softener; **-schweber,** *m.pl.* Bombyliidae; **-schweiss,** *m.* wool in the yolk, suint, fat; **-schweiss-sasche,** *f.* potash from suint; **-schweiss-fett,** *n.* wool grease; **-staub,** *m.* flock; **-zeug,** *n.* woolen material.

womit, wherewith, by what means.

womöglich, if possible, perhaps.

wonach, whereupon, after which.

Wonne, *f.* delight, bliss, pleasure.

woran, whereon, whereat, of, against, by what.

worauf, whereupon, on which, on what.

woraus, from what, from which, whence·

worein, into which, into what.

worfeln, to winnow, fan.

worin, wherein, in which, in what.

Wort, *n.*-e, ⁼er, word, term, expression; **-ableitung,** *f.* derivation, etymology.

Wörterbuch, *n.* dictionary, glossary.

Wort-folge, *f.* order of words; **-führer,** *m.* spokesman, speaker; **-getreu,** literal; **-laut,** *m.* wording, text.

wörtlich, verbal, literal, verbatim.

Wort-register, *n.* index of words, vocabulary; **-reiz,** *m.* verbal (word) stimulus; **-schatz,** *m.* vocabulary; **-sinn,** *m.* meaning of a word; **-zeichen,** *n.* catchword, trade name.

worüber, whereat, whereof, of, over· at, upon which or what.

worum, for which; ∼ **handelt es sich,** what is it about.

worunter, under or among which or what.

woselbst, where, in which.

wovon, whereof, of what or which.

wovor, before what or which.

wozu, for what, whereto, to what, why.

Wrack, *n.* wreck, waste.

wringen, to wring.

Wucherblume, *f.* (oxeye) daisy (*Chrysanthemum leucanthemum*).

wuchern, to grow rapidly, rankly, proliferate, practice usury.

Wucherpflanze, *f.* rank weed.

Wucherung, *f.* proliferation.

wuchs (wachsen), grew, was growing.

Wuchs, *m.*⁼e, growth, habit, height, stature; **-form,** *f.* growth form.

wüchsig, thrifty.

Wuchs-kraft, *f.* growing power; **-kräftig,** (plants) having vigorous growth; **-leistung,** *f.* yield, growth increment; **-schwach,** (plants) having slow (weak) growth.

Wucht, *f.* weight, pressure, burden, force, kinetic energy.

wühlen, to root, turn up the earth, rake, agitate.

Wulst, *m.&f.*-e, swelling, pad, roll, elevation, tuberosity, convolution, bulge (thread), hump.

wulstig, swollen, puffed up, padded, tumid, torulose.

Wulstpleuren, *f.pl.* ridged (folded) pleura.

wund, chapped, wounded, sore, chafed; **-arzt,** *m.* surgeon; **-ärztlich,** surgical; **-balsam,** *m.* vulnerary balsam.

Wunde, *f.* wound, injury.

Wunder, *n.* -wonder, surprise, marvel, miracle.

wunderbar, wonderful, marvelous, miraculous.

Wunder-baum, *m.* castor-oil plant (*Ricinus communis*); **-blume,** *f.* four-o'clock, marvel-of-Peru; **-erscheinung,** *f.* miraculous phenomenon; **-kerze,** *f.* sparkler.

wunderlich, strange, singular, peculiar, odd.

wundern, to surprise, astonish, wonder, be surprised.

Wunder-netz, *n.* rete mirabile; **-pfeffer,** *m.* allspice, pimento; **-schön,** very beautiful; **-tätig,** miraculous; **-voll,** wonderful, marvelous; **-wasser,** *n.* aqua mirabilis.

Wund-fäule, *f.* rot caused by wounds; **-fläche,** *f.* injured surface, wound; **-heilgewebe,** *n.* active scar tissue; **-holz,** *n.* callus, traumatic tissue; **-infektion,** *f.* wound infection; **-klee,** *m.* kidney vetch, lady's-finger (*Anthyllis vulneraria*); **-kork,** *m.* callus, wound periderm, traumatic wood; **-krankheit,** *f.* disease caused by wounds; **-kraut,** *n.* vulnerary plant; **-pulver,** *n.* vulnerary powder.

Wund-reiz, *m.* wound stimulus; **-rose,** *f.* wound erysipelas; **-starrkrampf,** *m.* traumatic tetanus; **-stein,** *m.* copper aluminate; **-verschluss,** *m.* wound healing (covering).

Wunsch, *m.*¨e, wish, desire.

wünschen, to wish, desire.

wünschenswert, (*dat.*) desirable.

wurde (werden), became, was becoming.

Würde, *f.* dignity, honor; **-los,** undignified; **-voll,** dignified.

würdig, (*gen.*) worthy, deserving.

würdigen, to deem worthy, value, appreciate, estimate, mention duly.

Wurf, *m.*¨e, throw, cast, litter, brood.

würfe (werfen), would throw, threw, throws.

Würfel, *m.*-, cube, hexahedron, die; *pl.* dice; **-bein,** *n.* cuboid bone; **-erz,** *n.* pharmacosiderite, cube ore; **-förmig,** cubiform, cubical; **-gips,** *m.* anhydrite.

würfelig, cubical, checkered.

Würfel-inhalt, *m.* cubic contents; **-knochen,** *m.* sesamoid, cubiform bone; **-kohle,** *f.* lump coal, cobbles.

würfeln, to play at dice, checker.

Würfel-quallen, *f.pl.* Cubomedusae; **-salpeter,** *m.* sodium nitrate; **-schiefer,** *m.* clay slate, argillite; **-spat,** *m.* anhydrite; **-stein,** *m.* boracite; **-zahl,** *f.* cubic number; **-zeolith,** *m.* analcite; **-zucker,** *m.* cube sugar.

Wurf-feu(e)rung, *f.* spreader stoker; **-geschoss,** *n.* missile, projectile; **-grösse,** *f.* litter size; **-kraft,** *f.* projectile force; **-lehre,** *f.* ballistics; **-linie,** *f.* line of projection; **-mine,** *f.* trench-mortar shell or bomb; **-rauchkörper,** *n.* smoke (maroon) bomb; **-schaufel,** *f.* shovel, scoop; **-weite,** *f.* range.

Würgelpumpe, *f.* rotary pump, wing pump.

würgen, to choke, gulp, retch, strangle, slay.

Würger, *m.* strangler, slayer, murderer, butcherbird.

Wurm, *m.*¨er, worm, grub, maggot, vermin, reptile, serpent, vermiform process; **-abtreibend,** vermifuge, anthelmintic; **-ähnlich,** wormlike, vermicular; **-artig,** wormlike, vermicular; **-arznei,** *f.* anthelmintic; **-farn,** *m.* male fern; **-farnwurzel,** *f.* root of male fern; **-förmig,** worm-shaped, vermicular, vermiform; **-fortsatz,** *m.* vermiform process; **-krankheit,** *f.* vermination.

Wurm-kraut, *n.* anthelmintic herb; **-mehl,** *n.* wormhole dust, worm dust; **-mittel,** *n.* anthelmintic; **-moos,** *n.* worm moss,

Corsican moss; **-pulver,** *n.* worm powder; **-samen,** *m.* wormseed; **-samenöl,** *n.* wormseed oil; **-stich,** *m.* worm hole; **-stichig,** worm-eaten; **-tang,** *m.* worm moss, Corsican moss; **-treibend,** **-vertilgend,** anthelmintic; **-widrig,** anthelmintic.

Wurst, *f.*¨e, sausage; **-bazillus,** *m.* sausage bacillus; **-darm,** *m.* skin for sausages; **-gift,** *n.* sausage poison; **-vergiftung,** *f.* sausage poisoning.

Würze, *f.* wort, spice; **-brechen,** *n.* breaking of the wort.

Wurzel, *f.*-n, root; ~ **schlagen,** to (take) root.

Wurzel-anlauf, *m.* root swelling; **-ausläufer,** *m.* stolon; **-ausscheidung,** *f.* root secretion; **-ausschlag,** *m.* sucker; **-bakterium,** *n.* root bacterium, nitrogen fixer; **-blättrig,** rhizophilous; **-brand,** *m.* root necrosis, root rot; **-büschel,** *n.* rhizothamnium.

Würzelchen, *n.* rootlet, radicle.

Wurzel-druck, *m.* (osmotic) pressure of the root; **-erneuerung,** *f.* formation of new roots; **-exponent,** *m.* radical index; **-faser,** *f.* root fibril; **-fäserchen,** *n.* rootlet; **-fäule,** *f.* root rot; **-filz,** *m.* matting of root; **-fressend,** root-feeding; **-füsser,** *m.pl.* **-füssler,** *m.pl.* Rhizopoda.

Wurzel-geflecht, *n.* matting of the roots; **-gemüse,** *n.* root vegetable; **-gewächse,** *n.pl.* root crops; **-grösse,** *f.* radical quantity; **-haar,** *n.* root hair; **-hals,** *m.* root neck, root collar; **-haube,** *f.* root cap, pileorhiza; **-haut,** *f.* root epidermis; **-hautentzündung,** *f.* inflammation of the root membrane, alveolar periosteum; **-holz,** *n.* rootwood.

Wurzel-hülle, *f.* velamen; **-keim,** *m.* radicle; **-kletterer,** *m.* root climber; **-knöllchen,** *n.* root tubercle, nodule on roots; **-knolle,** *f.* root tuber; **-knoten,** *m.* node; **-konkurrenz,** *f.* root competition; **-körper,** *m.* root; **-krebse,** *m.pl.* Rhizocephala; **-kropf,** *m.* crown gall; **-mass,** *n.* gauge distance.

wurzeln, to take root, become rooted.

Wurzel-netz, *n.* network of roots; **-petersilie,** *f.* parsley; **-pilz,** *m.* vine-root fungus, mycorhiza; **-rinde,** *f.* epidermis of the root; **-röhrchen,** *n.* rootlet tube (in loess); **-rückstand,** *m.* remains of roots (in soil after harvest); **-scheibe,** *f.* root crown; **-scheide,** *f.* coleorhiza; **-schopf,** *m.* root tuft; **-schoss,** *m.* sucker.

Wurzel-schwamm, *m.* root-rot fungus (*Trametes radiciperda*); **-spitze,** *f.* end of a root; **-sprosser,** *m.* plant with much-branched roots; **-stock,** *m.* rootstock, rhizome; **-stoff,** *m.* radical principle; **-töter,** *m.* violet root rot; **-träger,** *m.* rhizophore; **-trieb,** *m.* sucker, root sucker, radical shoot, rootling; **-verkürzung,** *f.* root contraction; **-werk,** *n.* root system; **-zeichen,** *n.* radical sign.

würzen, to spice, season.

Würzesiedepfanne, *f.* wort boiler, brewing copper.

Würz-geruch, *m.* odor of spices; **-geschmack,** *m.* spicy taste.

würzig, spicy, aromatic.

würzlos, not spiced, not seasoned, flat.

Würz-nelke, *f.* clove; **-wein,** *m.* spiced wine.

wusch (waschen), washed, was washing.

wusste (wissen), knew.

Wust, *m.* confused mass, mess, rubbish.

wüst, waste, desolate.

Wüste, *f.* desert.

wüsten, to waste.

Wüstensteppe, *f.* semidesert.

Wut, *f.* rage, fury, rabies, madness, frenzy; **-diagnose,** *f.* diagnosis of rabies.

wüten, to rage, rave.

wütend, raging, frantic, furious.

Wut-gift, *n.* rabies virus; **-krank,** ill with hydrophobia; **-krankheit,** *f.* hydrophobia; **-seuche,** *f.* rabies.

X

X-Achse, *f.* axis of the abscissa.

xanthisch, xanthic.

x-beinig, knock-kneed.

x-beliebig, any.

xenomorph, anhedral.

Xereswein, *m.* sherry.

x-mal, a number of times.

X-Strahlen, *m.pl.* X rays, Roentgen rays.

Xylidinrot, xylidine red.

Xylochinon, *n.* xyloquinone.

Xylol, *n.* xylene.

Xylorcin, *n.* xylorcinol, xylorcin.

Xylose, *f.* xylose, wood sugar.

Y

Yamwurzel, *f.* yam.

Yerbastrauch, *m.* maté, Paraguay tea (*Ilex paraguayensis*).

Ysop, *m.* hyssop.

Ytterbinerden, *f.pl.* yterrbium earths.

Ytter-erde, *f.* yttria; **-oxyd,** ytterbium oxide; **-spat,** *m.* xenotime.

Z

Zachunöl, *n.* **Zachäusöl,** *n.* bito oil, zachun oil.

Zacke, *f.* **Zacken,** *m.* jag, prong, tooth, scallop (crenature), notch.

zacken, to jag, tooth, indent, scallop; **-blatt,** *n.* serrate leaf; **-schote,** *f.* corn rocket (Bunias).

zackig, jagged, toothed, dentated, serrated.

Zaffer, *m.* zaffer.

Zaffetika, *f.* asafetida.

Zageleisen, *n.* slab iron.

zaghaft, cautious.

zäh(e), tough, viscous, tenacious, sticky.

Zähe, *f.* tenacity.

zähfestig, tenacious.

zähflüssig, thickly liquid, viscous.

Zähflüssigkeit, *f.* viscosity.

Zähigkeit, *f.* toughness, tenacity, viscosity, stickiness.

Zahl, *f.*-en, number, cipher, numeral, figure.

Zählapparat, *m.*-e, counting apparatus.

zahlbar, payable, due.

zählebig, tenacious of life, difficult to kill.

zahlen, to pay.

zählen, to count, number, reckon, compute, calculate; ~ **zu,** to be among.

Zahlen-angaben, *f.pl.* numerical data; **-art,** *f.* kind of number; **-begriff,** *m.* conception of numbers or figures; **-beispiel,** *n.* numerical example (to show how a proposed method will work out, using actual figures); **-folge,** *f.* numerical order; **-grösse,** *f.* numerical quantity; **-mässig,** numerical(ly); **-reihe,** *f.* numerical series; **-tafel,** *f.* table of figures, multiplication table;

-verhältnis, *n.* numerical proportion; **-wert,** *m.* numerical value.

Zähler, *m.* numerator, teller, marker.

Zähl-flasche, *f.* counting bottle; **-kammer,** *f.* counting chamber.

zahl-los, numberless, innumerable, countless; **-reich,** numerous.

Zählrohr, *n.* counter.

Zahlung, *f.* payment.

Zählung, *f.* count, counting, enumeration, computation, calculation.

zahlungsfähig, solvent.

Zahlungstermin, *m.* date of payment.

Zahl-wert, *m.*-e, numerical value; **-wort,** *n.* numeral; **-zeichen,** *n.* figure, numeral sign.

zahm, tame, domestic, gentle, cultivated.

zähmbar, tamable.

zähmen, to tame, break in, domesticate, restrain, control.

Zahn, *m.*-e, tooth, tine, cog; ~ **und Triebbewegung,** *f.* coarse and fine adjustment (of a microscope).

Zahn-achse, *f.* axis of tooth; **-ähnlich,** odontoid; **-anlage,** *f.* rudiment (primordium) of tooth; **-arme,** *m.pl.* edentates; **-arzt,** *m.* dentist; **-ausbruch,** *m.* dentition; **-bein,** *n.* dentine; **-blei,** *n.* leadwort; **-bleiwurzel,** *f.* root of the leadwort; **-bogen,** *m.* dental arch; **-durchbruch,** *m.* dentition.

Zähne, *m.pl.* teeth.

zähneln, to indent, denticulate.

Zähnelung, *f.* serration.

Zahnemail, *n.* dental enamel.

zahnen, to indent, cut teeth.

Zahn-fach, *n.* alveolus; **-fächerbogen,** *m.* alveolar arch; **-faser,** *f.* dental fiber.

Zahnfleisch, *n.* gum; **-schleimhaut,** *f.* mucous membrane of gum.

Zahn-flügelband, *n.* lateral odontoid ligament; **-formel,** *f.* dental formula; **-förmig,** tooth-shaped, dentiform odontoid; **-fortsatz,** *m.* odontoid process, alveolar process; **-furche,** *f.* dental groove; **-gestalt,** *f.* shape of tooth; **-gewebe,** *n.* dental tissue; **-grube,** *f.* dental pulp cavity.

Zahn-hals, *m.* neck of tooth; **-heilkunde,** *f.* dentistry; **-höhle,** *f.* dental pulp cavity.

Zahnhöhlen-bogen, *m.* alveolar arch; **-fortsatz,** *m.* alveolar apophysis; **-gang,** *m.* alveolar canal.

zahnig, toothed, dentate, jagged.

Zahn-kanal, *m.* dentinal tubule; **-keim,** *m.* tooth germ, dental pulp; **-kitt,** *m.* dental

cement; **-knorpel,** *m.* dental cartilage; **-körper,** *m.* body of tooth; **-krone,** *f.* crown of tooth; **-lade,** *f.* alveolar part of jaw; **-latwerge,** *f.* tooth paste.

Zahn-leiste, *f.* dental ridge; **-lilie,** *f.* dogtooth violet (Erythronium); **-lücke,** *f.* gap between teeth; **-oberfläche,** *f.* surface of tooth; **-paste,** *f.* tooth paste; **-pulpa,** *f.* dental pulp; **-pulver,** *n.* tooth powder.

Zahn-rad, *n.*-er, cogwheel, gear; **-reinigung,** *f* cleaning of teeth; **-röhre,** *f.* dental tubular; **-schmelz,** *m.* dental enamel; **-schmerz,** *m.* toothache; **-stange,** *f.* rack; **-stein,** *n.* tartar (on the teeth); **-substanz,** *f.* dental substance; **-trommel,** *f.* sprocket.

Zahnung, *f.* dentition, serration, toothing.

Zahn-wall, *n.* side of dental groove; **-wasser,** *n.* tooth wash; **-wechsel,** *m.* changing of teeth; **-weh,** *n.* toothache; **-wehholz,** *n.* prickly ash (Zanthoxylum); **-weinstein,** *m* tartar on the teeth; **-wurzel,** *f.* root of tooth; **-zement,** *m.* dental cement; **-zweig,** *m.* branch of root of tooth.

zähpolen, to toughen (metal) by poling.

Zain, *m.*-e, ingot, bar, stack of wood.

zainen, to make into ingots or bars.

Zander, *m.*-, pike, perch.

Zange, *f.* pair of tongs, pliers, pincers, forceps, tweezers, palpus, maxilla.

Zängearbeit, *f.* shingling (of metal).

Zängelchen, *n.* small pincers, tweezers.

zängen, to shingle.

zangen-förmig, formed like tongues, forcipated; **-griff,** *m.* handle of tongs, pincers, or forceps; **-horn,** *n.* chelicere.

Zängeschlacke, *f.* shingling slag.

Zäpfchen, *n.* small peg or plug, uvula, cone; **-heber,** *m.* azygos uvular muscle, palatostaphylin muscle; **-kraut,** *n.* bellwort (Uvularia).

zapfen, to tap.

Zapfen, *m.* plug, spigot, tap, peg, pin, tenon, trunnion, cone; **-baum,** *m.* conifer, coniferous tree; **-förmig,** peg-shaped conical, strobiliform; **-kern,** *m.* nucleus; **-korn,** *n.* ergot; **-körper,** *m.* cone; **-lager,** *n.* bush, collar, bearing, socket; **-loch,** *n.* peg, (pivot) hole, bunghole, taphole; **-saat,** *f.* cone sowing; **-schicht,** *f.* cone layer.

Zapfen-spindel, *f.* cone axis; **-stäbchen,** *n.* cone rod; **-tragend,** coniferous; **-träger,** *m.pl.* Coniferae; **-wein,** *m.* leaked wine.

Zapfkolophonium, *n.* gum resin.

Zäpflein, *n.* uvula.

Zapon, *m.* varnish; **-lack,** *m.* varnish composed of pyroxylin and amyl acetate.

zappeln, to move convulsively, struggle, flounder, writhe, fidget.

Zarge, *f.* border, edge, rim.

zart, tender, delicate, fine, soft, fragile.

Zasel, *m.* catkin.

Zaser, *f.* fiber, filament; **-blume,** *f.* fig marigold (*Mesembryanthemum edule*).

zaserig, fibrous.

Zäsium, *n.* cesium.

Zaspel, *f.* skein, hank.

Zauber, *m.*-, spell, charm, magic, witchcraft.

Zauberei, *f.* magic, sorcery.

Zauberer, *m.* magician, juggler, wizard.

Zauberwurzel, *f.* mandrake (*Mandragora officinarum*).

zaudern, to waver, delay, hesitate.

Zaum, *m.*-̈e, bridle, rein, check.

Zaun, *m.*-̈e, fence, railing, hedge; **-grasmücke,** *f.* lesser whitethroat; **-könig,** *m.* wren; **-lilie,** *f.* spiderwort, St.-Bernard's-lily (*Anthericum liliago*); **-rübe,** *f.* Bryonia; **-wicke,** *f.* vetch (*Vicia septum*); **-winde,** *f.* bearbind, (greater) bindweed (*Convolvulus sepium*).

zausen, to tug, pull, tousle, pick.

Zebra, *n.*-e, zebra, flame effect.

Zeche, *f.* score, bill, drinking, bout, mine, mining company.

Zechenkoks, *m.* furnace (mine) coke.

zechfrei, scot-free.

Zecke, *f.* tick (insect).

Zeder, *f.* cedar (*Pinus cedrus*); **-(holz)öl,** *n.* cedarwood oil; **-tanne,** *f.* Cedrela.

zedieren, to cede, assign, transfer.

Zedrachbaum, *m.* China tree, bead tree (*Melia azedarach*).

Zedrat, *n.* candied lemon peel.

Zeh, *m.* **Zehe,** *f.* toe, digit, clove of garlic, knot, stick of ginger.

Zehen-ballen, *m.* ball of the toes; **-gänger,** *m.pl.* Digitigrada; **-gelenk,** *n.* joint of toe; **-glied,** *n.* phalanx of toe; **-haut,** *f.* interdigital membrane; **-knochen,** *m.* phalanx (bone) of toe; **-kreuzband,** *n.* plantar ligament.

Zehen-nagel, *m.* toenail; **-rücken,** *m.* dorsal surface of toe; **-seitenband,** *n.* lateral ligament of toe; **-sohle,** *f.* lower surface of toe; **-spitze,** *f.* tip of toe; **-spitzengänger,** *m.pl.*

Ungulata, Unguligrada; -strecker, *m.* extensor of the toe.

zehn, ten; **-blätterig,** decaphyllous; **-eck,** *n.* decagon; **-ender,** *m.* stag of ten points; **-fach, -fältig,** tenfold.

zehnte, tenth.

Zehntel, *n.* tenth; **-normallösung,** *f.* one-tenth normal solution.

zehntplichtig, tithable.

zehren, to eat and drink, consume, waste, make thin, shrink.

Zehrung, *f.* consumption, expenses, provisions, waste.

Zeichen, *n.* , token, sign, signal, stamp, brand, symptom, symbol, omen, mark; **-apparat,** *m.* drawing apparatus, camera lucida; **-brett,** *n.* drawing board; **-erklärung,** *f.* explanation of symbols, key to the signs; **-kreide,** *f.* crayon; **-papier,** *n.* drawing paper; **-setzung,** *f.* punctuation; **-spiegel,** *m.* camera lucida; **-sprache,** *f.* sign language; **-stift,** *m.* crayon; **-tinte,** *f.* drawing ink.

zeichnen, to draw, design, brand, sign, mark, subscribe.

Zeichner, *m.* drawer, designer, draftsman, subscriber.

zeichnerisch, graphic, diagrammatic.

Zeichnung, *f.* drawing, design, sketch, diagram, pattern, subscription, marking.

Zeigefinger, *m.* forefinger, index.

zeigen, to show, point out, exhibit, display, appear, indicate, manifest, become evident, turn out, prove, point.

Zeiger, *m.* pointer, one that shows, exponent, indicator, needle, hand, index; **-ablesung,** *f.* pointer reading; **-ausschlag,** *m.* pointer deflection; **-galvanometer,** *n.* needle galvanometer.

Zeile, *f.* line, row.

Zein, *m.* ingot, pig, bar, rod.

Zeisig, *m.*-e, siskin; **-grün,** siskin-green.

Zeit, *f.* time, epoch, period, age, season, tense; **zur** ~, at the time, at present; **vor kurzer** ~, a short time ago; **auf einige** ~, for a certain time; **nach einiger** ~, after some time; **um die** ~, about that time; **eine** ~ **lang,** for a time; **in jüngster** (neuester) ~, in most recent time(s), quite recently; **mit der** ~, in time; **längere** ~, for a fairly long time; **zur** ~, at present; **in früherer** ~, formerly.

Zeit-abschnitt, *m.* period. epoch; **-alter,** *n.* age; **-angabe,** *f.* date; **-aufnahme,** *f.* time exposure; **-begriff,** *m.* conception of time; **-einheit,** *f.* unit of time; **-epoche,** *f.* chronological era.

Zeit-folge, *f.* chronological order; **-gemäss,** timely, seasonable, up-to-date; **-genosse,** *m.* contemporary; **-gleichung,** *f.* time equation.

zeitig, opportune, early, timely, ripe, mature, seasonal, on time.

zeitigen, to mature, ripen, bring to a head.

Zeitigung, *f.* maturation, maturity.

Zeitkonstante, *f.* time constant.

Zeitlang, *f.* time; **eine** ∼, a while, for some time.

Zeitlauf, *m.* period of time.

zeitlebens, throughout life, forever.

zeitlich, temporary, temporal, earthly, per unit time, transient, periodic, timely, in time; **zeitlicher Verlauf,** *m.* progress or course within a definite given time.

Zeitlose, *f.* meadow saffron (*Colchicum autumnale*).

Zeit-mass, *n.* measure of time; **-messer,** *m.* chronometer; **-messung,** *f.* measurement of time, prosody.

Zeitpunkt, *m.***-e,** point of time, moment; **von dem** ∼ **an,** from that point on.

zeit-raubend, time-consuming; **-raum,** *m.* space of time, interval, period; **-rechner,** *m.* recorder; **-rechnung,** *f.* chronology, style; **-schätzungsvermögen,** *n.* ability to estimate time.

Zeitschr., *abbr.* (Zeitschrift), periodical.

Zeit-schrift, *f.* periodical, journal, magazine; **-sinn,** *m.* time sense; **-spanne,** *f.* length of time, time; **-staude,** *f.* perennial of short growing season; **-strecke,** *f.* distance of time, period.

Zeitung, *f.* newspaper.

Zeitungs-ausgabe, *f.* issue of a newspaper; **-wesen,** *n.* newspaper business, journalism.

Zeit-verhältnis, *n.* time relation; **-verlust,** *m.* loss of time; **-vertreib,** *m.* pastime; **-weilig,** temporary, for the time being, at times, occasionally, current, present, actual; **-weise,** temporarily, occasionally, from time to time; **-wertquotient,** *m.* time-value quotient; **-zünder,** *m.* delay-action cap; **-zwischenraum,** *m.* time interval.

zelebrieren, to celebrate.

zell-ähnlich, cell-like celluloid, cytoid; **-aufschwemmung,** *f.* cell suspension; **-bestandteil,** *m.* cell constituent; **-bildung,** *f.* cell formation.

Zellchen, *n.* cellule, small cell.

Zelle, *f.* cell, segment.

Zellelement, *n.* cell constituent.

Zellen-after, *m.* anal aperture (Infusoria); **-ähnlich,** cell-like, pseudocellular; **-anhäufung,** *f.* accumulation (mass) of cells; **-art,** *f.* type of cell; **-artig,** cell-like, cellular; **-atmen,** *n.* vesicular breathing.

Zellenbalken, *m.* cellular trabeculum; **-netz,** *n.* cellular reticulum.

zellen-bildend, cell-forming; **-bildung,** *f.* cell formation; **-drüse,** *f.* cellular gland; **-faser,** *f.* fiber; **-flüssigkeit,** *f.* cell (fluid) sap; **-folge,** *f.* cell lineage; **-förmig,** cellular, alveolar; **-fortsatz,** *m.* cellular (prolongation) process; **-frei,** cell-free; **-gang,** *m.* cellular duct.

Zellen-gehalt, *m.* cell contents; **-gewebe,** *n.* cellular tissue; **-haltig,** cellular; **-haut,** *f.* cell membrane; **-inhalt,** *m.* cell content.

Zellenkeim, *m.* cell germ; **-stoff,** *m.* cytoblastema.

Zellen-kern, *m.* nucleus; **-körper,** *m.* cellular body; **-leib,** *m.* protoplasm; **-membran,** *f.* cell membrane; **-mund,** *m.* cytostome; **-naht,** *f.* cellular suture; **-pflanze,** *f.* vascular plant; **-rad,** *n.* bucket wheel; **-saft,** *m.* cell sap (fluid); **-schale,** *f.* cell membrane.

Zellen-schalter, *m.* battery (cell) switch; **-schicht,** *f.* cell layer; **-strang,** *m.* cellular cord; **-teilung,** *f.* cell division; **-vermehrung,** *f.* multiplication of cells; **-wand,** *f.* cell wall; **-wanderung,** *f.* migration of cells; **-wandung,** *f.* cell wall; **-wucherung,** *f.* proliferation of cells; **-zapfen,** *m.* cellular cone; **-zwischensubstanz,** *f.* intercellular substance.

Zell-faden, *m.* cell filament; **-faser,** *f.* intermediate fiber; **-fläche,** *f.* tissue, cell plane; **-generation,** *f.* generation of cells; **-gerüst,** *n.* cell framework, filar substance; **-geschehen,** *n.* cell processes, cell phenomenon; **-gewebe,** *n.* tissue; **-gewebsentzündung,** *f.* inflammation of tissue cells; **-gift,** *n.* intercellular toxin.

Zell-glas, *n.* (transparent film) cellophane; **-haut,** *f.* cellophane, cellular membrane; **-höcker,** *m.* cellular protuberance; **-horn,** *n.* celluloid; **-hügel,** *m.* cellular eminence.

zellig, cellulous, celled, vesicular, honeycombed.

Zellkern, *n.* nucleus; **-teilung,** *f.* mitosis, nuclear division.

Zell-knospung, *f.* cellular budding; **-körper,** *m.* cell body, organ; **-leib,** *m.* cell body, sarc; -masse, f. cellular substance; -nest, n. group of cells.

Zelloidin, n. celloidin; -einbettung, f. embedding in celloidin.

Zellophan, n. cellophane.

Zell-pech, n. cellulose pitch; -plasma, n. cell plasma, protoplasm; -raum, m. cell space, cell cavity; -reihe, f. row of cells.

Zellsaft, m. cell sap (juice); -farbe, f. cell-sap color.

Zell-schicht, f. layer of cells; -schlauch, m. cell tube; -spalte, f. cellular fissure; -sprossung, f. cell budding.

Zellstoff, m. cellulose, paper pulp; -balken, m. trabecula; -locken, n. loose pulp; -seide, f. cellulose silk, rayon; -wechsel, m. cell metabolism.

Zell-substanz, f. cell substance; -teilung, f. cell division.

Zelluloid, n. celluloid.

Zellulose, f. cellulose; -dinitrat, n. dinitrate of cellulose; -gärung, f. fermentation of cellulose; -hülle, f. cellulose covering; -mantel, m. tunic; -verdauung, f. digestion of cellulose.

Zell-verband, m. union of cells; -verjüngung, f. cell rejuvenation; -verschmelzung, f. cell fusion; -wand, f. cell wall; -wolle, f. rayon staple, staple fiber (rayon cut and crimped like wool).

Zelt, n.-e, tent, awning, pavilion.

Zeltchen, n. lozenge, tablet.

Zement, m. cement; -artig, cementlike; -beton, m. cement concrete; -brei, m. cement slurry; -gerbstahl, m. shear steel.

zementieren, to cement.

Zementierfass, n. precipitation (cementing) vat.

Zementierung, f. cementing, cementation.

Zementrot, n. English red, Venetian red.

Zenit, m. zenith, height, climax.

zensieren, to censure, to criticize, review.

Zensur, f. censorship, certificate, report.

Zenti-gramm, n. centigram; -meter, n. centimeter.

Zentner, m.-, hundredweight, quintal, 50 kg.

zentral, central.

Zentrale, f. telephone office, center, central station, line joining two centers, power plant.

zentralisieren, to centralize.

Zentral-körperchen, n. central body, centrosome; -kreisschnitt, m. circular section

through the center; -nervensystem, n. central nervous system; -winkelständig, axial.

Zentrierblende, f. centering diaphragm.

zentrieren, to center.

Zentrierschraube, f. centering screw.

zentrifugal, centrifugal; -gebläse, n. centrifugal blower or fan; -kraft, f. centrifugal force.

Zentrifuge, f. centrifuge, separator.

Zentrifugen-schlamm, m. separator slime; -spinnen, n. pot (bucket) spinning process. -teller, m.pl. separating disks.

zentrifugieren, to centrifuge.

Zentriol, n. centriole.

zentripetal, centripetal.

zentrisch, central, concentric, symmetrical.

Zentrum, n. center, bull's-eye; kinetisches ∼, centrosphere, centrosome.

Zeolith, m. zeolite.

Zer, n. cerium.

zerarbeiten, to destroy by working, crumble, overwork.

zerätzen, to destroy with caustics.

zerbeissen, to crack, bite through, crunch.

zerbrechen, to break to pieces, shatter, smash.

zerbrechlich, fragile, brittle, breakable.

Zerbrechlichkeit, f. fragility brittleness.

zerbrochen, broken.

zerbröckeln, to crumble.

Zerbröck(e)lung, f. attenuation.

zerdrückbar, brittle.

zerdrücken, to crush, crumple.

Zerealien, f.pl. cereals.

Zerebralsystem, n. cerebral system.

Zerebrospinalflüssigkeit, f. cerebrospinal fluid.

Zeremonie, f. ceremony.

zerfahren, to crush by driving over; disconnected, confused, inattentive, thoughtless.

Zerfall, m. decomposition, breaking down, disintegration, decay.

zerfallen, to decompose, break down, disintegrate, crumble, decay, quarrel, divide.

Zerfallfrucht, f. dehiscent fruit.

Zerfalls-höhle, f. cavity; -produkt, m. decomposition product; -reihe, f. disintegration series.

Zerfaserer, *m.* kneader, pulper, stuff grinder.

zerfasern, to reduce to fibers, unravel.

zerfetzen, to cut in pieces, tear to rags, slash.

zerfleischen, to lacerate.

zerfliessbar, deliquescent.

Zerfliessbarkeit, *f.* deliquescence.

zerfliessen, to deliquesce, melt, dissolve.

Zerfliessung, *f.* deliquescence.

zerfressen, to eat away, corrode.

zerfressend, corrosive, septic.

Zerfressung, *f.* corrosion, cauterization.

zergehen, to deliquesce, melt, disperse, dissolve, dwindle, vanish.

zergliedern, to dismember, dissect, analyze, decompose.

Zergliederung, *f.* analysis, dissection, dismemberment, division, septation.

Zergliederungskunde, *f.* anatomy.

zerhacken, to cut into pieces, mince.

Zerit, *m.* cerite.

zerkleinern, to cut to small pieces, pulverize, comminute, triturate, disintegrate.

Zerkleinerung, *f.* breaking up, cutting to bits, mastication, size reduction.

zerklüften, to cleave, divide, segment, split.

Zerklüftung, *f.* fragmentation, cleavage, splitting, fissure.

zerknicken, to crack (by bending).

zerknistern, to decrepitate.

zerknittern, to crumple, rumple.

zerknittert, corrugated, crumpled up.

zerkrümeln, to stir, crumble.

zerlassen, to liquefy, dissolve, melt.

zerlegbar, decomposable, divisible, collapsible.

zerlegen, to split up, decompose, analyze, dissect, take apart, cut up, divide.

Zerlegung, *f.* decomposition, analysis, dissection.

zerlöchern, to perforate.

zermahlen, to grind fine, pulverize, mill.

zermalmen, to bruise, crush, grind.

Zermetall, *n.* cerium metal.

zermürben, to rot, grind, break up the structure.

Zernitrat, *n.* cerium nitrate.

zerpflücken, to pull apart, pluck to pieces.

zerplatzen, to burst, explode.

zerquetschen, to crush, mash, bruise.

Zerrbild, *n.*-er, caricature.

zerreibbar, friable, triturable.

zerreiben, to pulverize, triturate.

zerreiblich, friable, triturable.

Zerreibung, *f.* pulverization, trituration.

zerreissbar, capable of being torn.

zerreissen, to tear, rend, break, lacerate, rupture, wear out.

Zerreiss-festigkeit, *f.* tearing strength, tensile strength; **-probe,** *f.* rending or breaking test; **-punkt,** *m.* rupture point.

zerren, to pull, tear, tug, drag, stretch.

Zerrennherd, *n.* refining hearth.

zerrieben (zerreiben), ground, powdered.

zerrieseln, to disintegrate.

zerrissen (zerreissen), torn.

zerrühren, to mix in stirring round, beat up.

Zerrung, *f.* pulling, stretching.

zerrütten, to derange, disturb, disorder, disorganize, ruin, destroy.

zersägen, to saw up, to saw to pieces.

zerschellen, to shatter, shiver, smash.

zerschlagen, to break in pieces, batter, smash, bruise, cut up.

zerschlitzt, lacerated.

zerschmelzen, to melt.

zerschmettern, to smash, crush, shatter.

Zerschmetterung, *f.* shattering, crushing.

zerschneiden, to cut up, mince, cut into shreds, dissect.

zerschnitten, dissected; **fiederförmig ~,** pinnatisect.

zersetzbar, decomposable.

Zersetzbarkeit, *f.* decomposability.

zersetzen, to decompose, disintegrate.

zersetzlich, decomposable, unstable.

zersetzt, decomposed.

Zersetzung, *f.* decomposition, decay, disintegration.

Zersetzungs-destillation, *f.* destructive distillation; **-erscheinung,** *f.* phenomenon or effect of decomposition; **-erzeugnis,** *f.* decomposition product; **-kunst,** *f.* analysis; **-mittel,** *n.* decomposing agent; **-produkt,** *n.* decomposition product, waste product; **-prozess,** *m.* process of decomposition; **-spannung,** *f.* decomposition voltage; **-widerstand,** *m.* electrolytic resistance.

zerspalten, to cleave, split (up).

Zerspaltung, *f.* dissociation, cleavage.

zerspitzt, running into a point, pointed.

zersplittern, to splinter, scatter, shiver to pieces, break up.

Zersplitterung, *f.* shivering, splintering.

zersprengen, to burst, blast, blow up, disperse.

zerspringen, to burst, break, crack, explode.

zerstampfen, to pound, bray, trample.

zerstäuben, to reduce to dust, disperse, spray, pulverize.

Zerstäuber, *m.* sprayer, atomizer, pulverizer.

zerstäubt, sprayed.

Zerstäubung, *f.* pulverizing, fine disintegration, atomization, scattering, spraying.

Zerstäubungsapparat, *m.* spray apparatus, atomizer.

zerstieben, to be scattered as dust, disperse, spray, vanish.

zerstörbar, destructible.

Zerstörbarkeit, *f.* destructibility.

zerstören, to destroy, demolish, ruin, disrupt.

Zerstörung, *f.* destruction, demolition, overthrow, ruin.

zerstossen, to pound to pieces, bray, crush, pulverize.

zerstreuen, to disperse, dissipate, scatter, distract, disseminate, divert.

zerstreut, dispersed, distracted, absentminded, scattered, abnormal; **-blättrig,** sparsifolious; **-blumig,** sparsiflorous, with scattered flowers; **-porig,** diffuse porous.

Zerstreuung, *f.* dispersion, diversion, amusement, distraction.

Zerstreuungs-linse, *f.* dispersing or diverging lens, concave lens; **-vermögen,** *n.* dispersive power.

zerstückeln, to cut into small pieces, chip, chop up, parcel out, dismember.

zerteilbar, divisible.

zerteilen, to divide, split up, disperse, separate, resolve.

Zerteilung, *f.* division, dismemberment, separation, dissolution, resolution.

Zerteilungs-kraft, *f.* fragmentation power; **-mittel,** *n.* resolvent.

zertrennen, to separate.

Zertrennung, *f.* separation.

zertreten, to crush underfoot.

zertrümmern, to shatter, demolish, wreck.

Zertrümmerung, *f.* destruction, breaking to pieces, demolition.

Zervelatwurst, *f.* saveloy.

zerzupfen, to pick (pull) to pieces.

zessieren, to cease.

Zettel, *m.*-, slip of paper, note, handbill, label, ticket, placard, poster.

zetteln, to warp (in weaving).

Zeug, *n.*-e, stuff, material, cloth, fabric, tools, equipment, utensils, trash, yeast, pulp; **-druck,** *m.* cloth (calico) printing.

Zeuge, *m.*-n, witness.

zeugen, to beget, engender, procreate, generate, produce, demonstrate, testify, witness, give evidence.

Zeug-fabrik, *f.* cloth factory, woolen mill; **-fänger,** *m.* stuff catcher (in weaving); **-geben,** *n.* adding yeast, pitching yeast (in brewing); **-haus,** *n.* arsenal, armory; **-kasten,** *m.* stuff chest.

Zeugnis, *n.*-se, proof, witness, evidence.

Zeugsichter, *m.* pulp strainer.

Zeugung, *f.* reproduction, procreation.

Zeugungs-flüssigkeit, *f.* seminal fluid; **-mittel,** *n.* aphrodisiac; **-organ,** *n.* sexual organ; **-stoff,** *m.* semen; **-verlust,** *m.* apogamy; **-wert,** *m.* potency.

Zibebe, *f.* raisin.

Zibet, *m.* civet.

Zichorie, *f.* chicory (*Cichorium intybus*).

Zickel, *n.* kid.

Zickzack, *m.* zigzag; **-linie,** *f.* zigzag line.

Zider, *m.* cider.

Ziege, *f.* goat, she-goat.

Ziegel, *m.* brick, tile; **-brennen,** *m.* brick burning.

Ziegelei, *f.* brickyard, brick kiln.

Ziegel-erde, *f.* brick clay (earth); **-hütte,** *f.* brick kiln; **-mehl,** *n.* brick dust; **-rot,** brick-red; **-stein,** *m.* brick; **-ton,** *m.* brick clay (tile).

Ziegen-fell, *n.* goat's skin; **-käse,** *m.* goat's-milk cheese, **-leder,** *n.* goat's leather or kid; **-milch,** *f.* goat's milk; **-peter,** *m.* mumps; **-stein,** *m.* bezoar; **-talg,** *m.* goat tallow.

Ziegler, *m.* brickmaker.

zieh (zeihen), accused.

zieharm, *m.* handle, crank.

ziehbar, ductile.

Ziehbarkeit, *f.* ductility.

ziehen, to draw, pull, drag, tug, suck (breath), cultivate, dig up, grow, breed, rear, bring up, train, educate, extract; **darauf los ∼,** to pull away at; **sich zusammen ∼,** to contract; **auf sich ∼,** to draw upon oneself; **nach sich ∼,** to bring on cause, involve; **zu sich ∼,** to attract to oneself.

ziehenlassen, to allow to draw (steep) or infuse.

Ziehen, *n.* drawing, draft, traction, cultivation, education, move, twinge, twitch.

Zieh-feder, *f.* drawing pen; **-kraft,** *f.* attractive force, traction power; **-presse,** *f.* extrusion press; **-probe,** *f.* sample drawn.

Ziehung, *f.* drawing, drafting.

Ziel, *n.*-e, goal, aim, end, limit, boundary, objective, object, target, term; **-bewusst,** systematic, clear-sighted.

zielen, to aim, tend, refer to.

ziel-los, aimless; **-punkt,** *m.* goal, aim, mark, bull's-eye; **-reaktion,** *f.* purposive behavior; **-scheibe,** *f.* target, mark; **-setzung,** *f.* fixing of an aim; **-tafel,** *f.* sliding vane.

ziemen, to be fitting, become, suit.

ziemlich, suitable, moderate, considerable, fair(ly), tolerably, rather.

Zier, *f.* ornament.

Zierat, *m.* ornament, decoration, flourish, finery.

Zierbaum, *m.* ornamental tree.

Zierde, *f.* ornament.

zieren, to adorn, ornament, grace, decorate, be affected.

Zierlich, graceful, fine, elegant, pretty, neat, dainty, smart.

Zier-pflanze, *f.* ornamental plant; **-rasse,** *f.* ornamental race.

Zieselmaus, *f.* ground squirrel.

Ziest, *m.* hedge nettle (Stachys).

Ziffer, *f.* figure, numeral, digit, cipher; **-blatt,** *n.* face of clock, dial.

Zigarette, *f.* cigarette.

Zigarre, *f.* cigar.

Zigorie, *f.* chicory (*Cichorium intybus*).

Zille, *f.* Scilla.

Zimmer, *n.*-, room, chamber, apartment; **-decke,** *f.* ceiling; **-holz,** *n.* building material; **-linde,** *f.* Sparmannia; **-mann,** *m.* carpenter.

zimmern, to frame, join, timber, build, fabricate.

Zimmer-pflanze, *f.* house plant; **-tanne,** *f.* Norfolk Island pine (*Araucaria excelsa*); **-temperatur,** *f.* room temperature; **-wärme,** *f.* room temperature.

Zim(me)t, *m.* cinnamon; **weisser ∼,** canella bark.

Zimmet-aldehyd, *n.* cinnamic aldehyde; **-alkohol,** *m.* cinnamic alcohol; **-blüten,** *f.pl.* cinnamon flower, cassia bud; **-kaneel,** *m.* canella alba, canella bark; **-kassienöl,** *n.* oil of cassia; **-rinde,** *f.* cinnamon bark; **-säure,** *f.* cinnamic acid; **-stein,** *m.* cinnamon stone, essonite.

Zinder, *m.* cinder.

Zink, *n.* zinc; **-artig,** zinck$_y$; **-blech,** *n.* sheet zinc; **-blende,** *f.* zinc blende; **-blumen,** *f.pl.* flowers of zinc; **-blüten,** *f.pl.* flowers of zinc; **-butter,** *f.* zinc chloride; **-chlorid,** *n.* zinc chloride.

Zinke, *f.* prong, spike, tooth, proboscis.

Zinkeisen-erz, *n.* franklinite; **-spat,** *m.* ferriferous smithsonite; **-stein,** *m.* franklinite.

Zinken, *m.* tine, tooth, prong.

Zinkerz, *n.* zinc ore; **rotes ∼,** zincite.

Zink-fahlerz, *n.* tennantite; **-führend,** zincbearing, zinciferous; **-gekrätz,** *n.* zinc dross, oxide; **-glas,** *n.* -glaserz, *n.* siliceous calamine; **-hütte,** *f.* zinc works.

zinkig, pronged, spiked.

zinkisch, zincky.

Zink-jodid, *n.* zinc iodide; **-kalk,** *m.* zinc ash (calx); **-kiesel,** *m.* -kieselerz, *m.* siliceous calamine; **-ofenbruch,** *m.* tutty, cadmia; **-oxyd,** *n.* zinc oxide; **-pecherz,** *n.* sphalerite; **-salbe,** *f.* zinc ointment; **-salz,** *n.* zinc salt; **-schlicker,** *m.* zinc dross; **-schnitzel,** *n.pl.* zinc filings or cuttings; **-schwamm,** *m.* tutty, cadmia.

Zink-span, *m.* zink shaving or chip; **-stab,** *m.* zinc rod or stick; **-staub,** *m.* zinc dust; **-überzug,** *m.* zinc coating; **-verbindung,** *f.* zinc compound; **-vitriol,** *n.* white vitriol, sulphate of zinc; **-weiss,** *n.* zinc white; **-wolle,** *f.* flowers of zinc.

Zinn, *n.* tin; **-ader,** *f.* tin vein (lode); **-after,** *m.* tin-ore refuse; **-ähnlich,** stannous; **-artig,** tinlike, stannous; **-asche,** *f.* tin ashes; **-blatt,** *n.* tin foil; **-bromür,** *n.* stannous bromide; **-bromwasserstoffsäure,** *f.* bromostannic acid; **-chlorid,** *n.* stannic chloride.

Zinn-chlorür, *n.* stannous chloride; **-chlorwasserstoffsäure,** *f.* chlorostannic acid; **-draht,** *m.* tin wire.

Zinne, *f.* pinnacle.

zinne(r)n, of tin, pewter.

Zinn-erz, *n.* tin ore; **-feilicht,** *n.* tin filings; **-folie,** *f.* tin foil; **-gehalt,** *m.* tin content; **-gekrätz,** *n.* tin sweepings (refuse); **-gerät,** *n.* **-geschirr,** *n.* tin vessels, pewter; **-geschrei,** *n.* tin cry, crackling of tin; **-giesser,** *m.* tin founder; **-glasur,** *f.* tin glaze; **-hydroxydul,** *n.* stannous hydroxide.

Zinn-jodid, *n.* tin (stannic) iodide; **-jodür,** *n.* stannous iodide; **-kies,** *m.* tin pyrites; **-krätze,** *f.* tin refuse (dross); **-legierung,** *f.* tin alloy; **-lösung,** *f.* tin spirit (solution); **-lot,** *n.* tin solder.

Zinnober, *m.* cinnabar; **-farbe,** *f.* vermilion (color); **-spat,** *m.* crystalized cinnabar.

Zinn-oxyd, *n.* tin oxide, stannic oxide; **-oxydul,** *n.* stannous oxide; **-oxydverbindung,** *f.* stannic compound; **-pest,** *f.* tin plague; **-salmiak,** *n.* ammonium chlorostannate, pink salt; **-saum,** *m.* list of tin, selvedge.

Zinn-säure, *f.* stannic acid; **-seife,** *f.* stream tin; **-soda,** *f.* sodium stannate; **-sulfür,** *n.* stannous sulphide; **-verbindung,** *f.* tin compound; **-wolle,** *f.* mossy tin.

Zins, *m.*-(s)e, rent, interest, tribute; **-fuss,** *m.* rate of interest.

zinsen, to pay rent or interest.

Zipfel, *m.*-, tip, point, lobe, end.

zipfelig, having tips, laciniolated.

Zirbel, *f.* epiphysis; **-drüse,** *f.* pineal gland of body; **-drüsenstiel,** *m.* pedicel of pineal gland; **-kiefer,** *f.* stone pine (*Pinus cembra*).

zirculieren, to circulate.

zirka, about, nearly.

Zirkel, *m.* circle, society, (pair of) compasses.

Zirkon, *m.* zirconium, zircon; **-erde,** *f.* zirconia.

Zirkonium, *n.* zirconium.

Zirkonoxyd, *n.* zirconium oxide.

zirkulieren, to circulate.

Zirpen, *f.pl.* Cicadidae.

Zirre, *f.* cirrus.

zischeln, to whisper.

zischen, to hiss, sizzle, fizz.

Ziselieren, *n.* grape thinning.

Zisseide, *f.* cissoid.

Zisterne, *f.* cistern, tank.

Zistrose, *f.* rockrose (*Cistus crispus*).

Zitat, *n.*-e, quotation, citation.

zitieren, to cite, quote, summon.

Zitronat, *n.* candied lemon peel.

Zitronbartgras, *n.* lemon grass (*Andropogon citratus*).

Zitrone, *f.* lemon, citron.

Zitronell-al, *n.* citronellal; **-öl,** *n.* citronella oil; **-säure,** *f.* citronellic acid.

Zitronen-falter, *m.* brimstone butterfly; **-farbe,** *f.* lemon color, citron color; **-gelb,** lemon yellow, citrine; **-melisse,** *f.* lemon balm (*Melissa officinalis*); **-öl,** *n.* lemon oil; **-saft,** *m.* lemon juice; **-säure,** *f.* citric acid; **-schale,** *f.* lemon peel; **-wasser,** *n.* lemonade.

Zitrulle, *f.* watermelon.

Zitter-gras, *n.* quaking grass (*Briza media*); **-haar,** *n.* vibrating cilium; **-linse,** *f.* hairy vetch (*Vicia hirsuta*).

zittern, to tremble, flutter, shake, quiver, vibrate.

Zitter-pappel, *f.* trembling poplar, aspen (*Populus tremula*); **-pilz,** *m.* tremella, gelatinous fungus; **-rochen,** *m.* crampfish, electric ray; **-wicke,** *f.* hairy vetch (*Vicia hirsuta*); **-wurzel,** *f.* zedoary root.

Zitwer, *m.* zedoary (*Curcuma zedoaria*); **-kraut,** *n.* tarragon (*Artemisia dracunculus*); **-samen,** *m.* wormseed, santonica; **-wurzel,** *f.* zedoary root.

Zitz, *m.* chintz.

Zitze, *f.* nipple, teat.

Zitzen-bein, *n.* mastoid bone; **-förmig,** nipple-shaped, mammillary, mastoid; **-fortsatz,** *m.* mastoid process; **-tier,** *n.* mammal.

zivil, civil, moderate, reasonable.

Zobel, *m.*-, sable.

Zober, *m.*-, tub.

zog (ziehen), pulled, was pulling.

zögern, to linger, tarry, delay, hesitate.

Zögling, *m.*-e, pupil.

Zölestin, *m.* celestite.

Zoll, *m.*:e, duty, toll, custom, tariff, inch; **-amt,** *n.* custom-house.

zollbar, dutiable.

zollen, to pay duty, show (respect).

zollfrei, duty-free.

zollpflichtig, dutiable.

Zoll-satz, *m.* tariff rate; **-verschluss,** *m.* bond.

Zone, *f.* zone, region.

Zoo-chemie, *f.* zoochemistry; **-log,** *m* zoologist; **-logie,** *f.* zoology.

Zopf, *m.* ̈-e, tuft, plait, treetop; **-ende,** *n.* top end; **-holz,** *n.* top branches of tree; **-stärke,** *f.* diameter at the top; **-trocken,** top-dry; **-trocknis,** *f.* drying back of treetops, stag-headedness.

Zorn, *m.* anger, wrath, temper, passion.

Zotte, Zottel, *f.* tuft, shaggy hair, villus.

Zottel-wicke, *f.* hairy vetch (*Vicia villosa*); **-wolle,** *f.* shaggy wool.

Zotten-anhang, *m.* villous appendage; **-fuss,** *m.* base of shaggy hair; **-haut,** *f.* chorion; **-stroma,** *n.* stroma of the villi.

zottig, shaggy, matted, villous.

zu, to, at, in, for, in addition to, along with, toward, closed, too, overmuch; **um ~,** in order to, overmuch; **ab und ~,** now and then; **zum Beispiel,** for example; **zum Teil,** in part; **zum grössten Teil,** for the most part.

Zubehör, *n.* accessories, belongings, fittings; **-teile,** *m.pl.* accessories.

zubekommen, to get in addition, succeed in closing.

zubenannt, surnamed.

Zuber, *m.*-, tub.

zubereiten, to prepare, dress, cook, finish.

Zubereitung, *f.* preparation, dressing, cooking.

zubilligen, to grant, allow.

zubinden, to tie up, bandage.

zubrennen, to roast, calcine, cauterize, close by heating.

zubringen, to bring, carry, convey, pass, spend.

zubrühen, to add boiling water in mashing.

Zubusse, *f.* contribution, new supply.

Zucht, *f.* rearing, breeding, cultivation, growing, education, culture, breed, stock, discipline.

Zuchtanweisung, *f.* breeding rules.

züchtbar, capable of cultivation.

züchten, to cultivate, breed, rear, raise, grow.

Züchter, *m.* breeder, grower, cultivator.

Zucht-garten, *m.* ̈-, nursery; **-holz,** *n.* ̈-er, trees grown, artificially; **-rasse,** *f.* breed or race improved by cultivation.

Züchtung, *f.* breeding, culture, selection, rearing.

Züchtwahl, *f.* selection; **-lehre,** *f.* theory of natural selection.

zucken, to jerk, twitch, quiver, palpitate.

zuckend, quivering, convulsive, spasmodic.

Zucker, *m.* sugar; **-abbau,** *m.* breaking down of sugar; **-agar,** *m.* sugar agar; **-ahorn,** *m.* sugar maple, hard maple (*Acer saccharinum*); **-anreicherung,** *f.* increase in sugar content; **-arten,** *f.pl.* sugars; **-artig,** sugarlike, sugary, saccharine, saccharoid; **-ausbeute,** *f.* yield of sugar, rendement; **-bäcker,** *m.* confectioner; **-baryt,** *n.* barium sucrate.

Zucker-bestimmung, *f.* determination of sugar; **-bildung,** *f.* formation of sugar; **-brot,** *n.* sugar loaf, sweet cake; **-busch,** *m.* sugarbush, honeyflower (*Protea mellifera*); **-couleur,** *f.* caramel; **-dicksaft,** *m.* molasses, treacle; **-erbse,** *f.* sweet pea; **-fabrikation,** *f.* sugar manufacture; **-form,** *f.* sugar mold; **-gärung,** *f.* saccharine fermentation.

Zucker-gehalt, *m.* sugar content; **-gehalt-messer,** *m.* saccharimeter; **-gelatine,** *f.* sugar gelatin; **-gewinnung,** *f.* extraction of sugar, sugar manufacture; **-gras** *n.* sorghum; **-haltig,** containing sugar, saccharated; **-harnen,** *n.* glycosuria; **-harnruhr,** *f.* diabetes mellitus; **-hirse,** *f.* sorghum; **-honig,** *m.* old crystallized honey, treacle; **-hut,** *m.* sugar loaf.

zuckerig, sugary, saccharine.

Zuckerin, *n.* saccharin.

Zucker-kalk, *m.* sugar-lime; **-kand(is),** *m.* sugar candy; **-kessel,** *m.* sugar boiler (kettle); **-kiefer,** *f.* sugar pine (*Pinus lambertiana*); **-kohle,** *f.* charcoal from sugar; **-korn,** *n.* grain of sugar, sugarplum; **-kranke(r),** *m.* diabetic; **-krankheit,** *f.* diabetes mellitus; **-lösung,** *f.* sugar solution.

Zucker-mehl, *n.* powdered sugar; **-melone,** *f.* sugar melon; **-messung,** *f.* saccharimetry; **-mühle,** *f.* sugar mill.

zuckern, to sugar, sweeten.

Zucker,-palme, *f.* Arenga, sugar palm; **-pflanzung,** *f.* sugar plantation; **-probe,** *f.* sugar test, sample of sugar; **-rohr,** *n.* sugar cane; **-röhrchen,** *n.* sugar tube; **-rose,** *f.* red rose; **-rübe,** *f.* sugar beet.

Zuckerrüben-essig, *m.* sugar-beet vinegar; **-melasse,** *f.* beet molasses; **-saft,** *m.* sugar-beet juice; **-schnitzel,** *n.pl.* cossettes.

Zucker-ruhr, *f.* diabetes mellitus; **-saft,** *m.* saccharine juice; **-satz,** *m.* molasses; **-säure,** *f.* sacchoric acid; **-schaum,** *m.* powdered animal charcoal; **-schlamm,** *m.* lime scum (of beet sugar); **-schleuder,** *f.* centrifugal sugar; **-schotenbaum,** *m.* honey locust; **-sieden,** *n.* sugar refining, sugar boiling; **-siederei,** *f.* sugar refinery.

Zucker-spaltung, *f.* cleavage of sugar; **-stein,** *m.* granular albite; **-stoff,** *m.* saccharine matter; **-umwandlung,** *f.* sugar metabolism, sugar conversion; **-untersuchung,** *f.* examination (investigation) of sugar; **-verbindung,** *f.* compound of sugar, sucrate; **-waren,** *f.pl.* confectionery; **-werk,** *n.* confectionery.

Zuckung, *f.* spasm, quiver, convulsion.

zudem, besides, moreover.

zudrängen, to crowd, throng, intrude.

zudrehen, to turn off, shut off.

zudringlich, intruding, forward.

zudrücken, to shut, close.

zueignen, to attribute, appropriate, dedicate.

zueinander, to each other.

zuerkennen, to adjudge, award, confer.

zuerst, at first, first of all, before everybody.

Zufall, *m.* chance, accident, casualty, occurrence, attack, incident.

zufallen, to devolve upon.

zufällig, accidental, incidental, casual, chance, random.

Zufalls-gesetz, *n.* law of probability; **-kurve,** *f.* probability curve.

zufliessen, to flow in.

Zuflucht, *f.* ̈-e, refuge, shelter, recourse.

Zufluss, *m.* ̈-e, inflow, afflux, influx, fluxion, tributary; **-rohr,** *n.* supply pipe.

zufolge, by virtue of, owing to, according to.

zufrieden, content, satisfied, pleased; **-heit,** *f.* contentment; **-stellen,** to satisfy; **-stellend,** satisfactory.

zufrieren, to freeze up.

zufügen, to add, inflict.

Zufuhr, *f.* supply, importation, conveyance.

zuführen, to add, supply, introduce, feed, convey.

Zufuhrpore, *f.* dermal pore.

Zuführung, *f.* supply, importation, feed.

Zuführungsspalte, *f.* pore, external opening.

Zug, *m.* ̈-e, drawing, pulling, tug, traction, draft, train, procession, flock, stroke, line, piston drawtube, feature, progress, migration, range, passage, impulse, disposition, trait, stress; **in grossen Zügen,** generally, along general lines; **in einem Zuge,** at one pull, at once.

Zugabe, *f.* addition, extra, supplement.

Zugang, *m.* access, admittance, approach.

zugängig, accessible.

zugänglich, accessible, approachable, affable.

Zugänglichkeit, *f.* accessibility.

Zug-band, *n.* tie rod, tension member; **-beanspruchung,** *f.* tensile stress, stretching strain; **-bewegung,** *f.* pulling movement; **-dehnung,** *f.* stress strain; **-dehnungsbeziehungen,** *f.pl.* stress-strain relationships; **-druckversuch,** *m.* tensile-compression test.

zugeben, to add, accede to, allow, grant; **voll und ganz** ∼, to realize or grant fully.

zugebracht (zubringen), spent.

zugegen, present.

zugehen, to close, happen, come to pass, go up, go on, taper off, arrive.

zugehören, to belong.

zugehörig, proper, belonging, pertinent.

Zugehörigkeit, *f.* sphere of action, membership, property, belonging to.

zugekehrt, facing (something), turned toward.

Zügel, *m.* rein, bridle.

Zügelschild, *m.* frenulum.

zugemischt, admixed.

zugeschmolzen (zuschmelzen), sealed.

zugespitzt, acuminated(d), cuspidate.

Zugeständnis, *n.* concession, admission.

zugestehen, to concede, grant, admit.

zugetan (zutun), devoted, attached.

zugewandt (zuwenden), addorsed, turned toward.

Zug-faser, *f.* mantle fiber of spindle; **-festigkeit,** *f.* tensile strength; **-fisch,** *m.* migratory fish; **-frei,** free from drafts.

zugiessen, to fill up, add to by pouring.

zugig, drafty.

Zug-kanal, *m.* flue, air duct; **-kette,** *f.* draft chain; **-kraft,** *f.* tractive force, tension.

zugleich, at the same time, together.

Zug-loch, *n.* vent hole; **-luft,** *f.* current of air; **-messer,** *m.* draft gauge, drawknife; **-mittel,** *n.* attraction, vesicant; **-pflaster,** *n.* blistering plaster, vesicatory.

zugreifen, to lay hold, grab, seize.

Zug-rohr, *n.* **-röhre,** *f.* air (vent) pipe.

zugrundegehen, to go to the bottom, perish, be ruined.

zugrundelegen, to take as a basis.

Zugrundelegung, *f.* laying a foundation; **mit (unter)** ∼ **von,** taking . . . as a basis.

zugrundeliegen, to be at the bottom of, be the basis of.

Zug-salbe, *f.* resin cerate; **-spannung,** *f.* tensile stress; **-stange,** *f.* pull rod.

zugunsten, in favor of, for the benefit of.

Zuguss, *m.* infusion, pouring in.

zugute, (*dat.*) to the advantage or benefit of; ∼ **kommen,** to be to the advantage of; ∼ **kommen lassen,** to give the benefit of.

zugutemachen, to work up (ores).

zuguterletzt, last of all, finally.

zugutetun, to compensate.

Zug-versuch, *m.* tensile test; **-vogel,** *m.* bird of passage; **-wagen,** *m.* tractor; **-wirkung,** *f.* action of pulling, tension; **-wurzel,** *f.* contractile root.

zuhalten, to keep shut or closed, walk toward, make for, procure, hurry, make haste.

zuheilen, to heal up, cicatrize.

Zuhilfenahme, *f.* recourse, aid; **mit** ∼ **von,** by the aid of.

zuhören, (*dat.*) to listen, attend.

Zuhörer, *m.* hearer, auditor; **-schaft,** *f.* audience.

zuinnerst, innermost.

zukehren, to turn to, face, speak toward, close or fill up in swepping.

zukitten, to cement up, putty.

zuknöpfen, to button up.

zukommen, to come up to, be due, come to, belong; **-lassen,** to let have.

Zukrümmung, *f.* bending toward a support.

Zukunft, *f.* future.

zukünftig, future, to come, next.

Zulage, *f.* addition, increase (in salary).

zulangen, to help oneself, be sufficient.

zulänglich, sufficient.

Zulass, *m.* admission, reception.

zulassen, to admit, welcome, permit, leave closed.

zulässig, admissible, allowable.

zulaufen, to run, flock; **spitz** ∼, to run to a point, taper; ∼ **lassen,** to add, allow to run in.

zulegen, to cover up, add, provide, get, gain flesh.

zuleimen, to glue up.

zuleiten, to conduct, let in.

Zuleitung, *f.* leading in, conducting, feed pipe.

Zuleitungs-kanal, *m.* feeder; **-rohr,** *n.,* **-röhre,** *f.* inlet tube.

zuletzt, at last, finally, ultimately.

zulöten, to solder up.

zum (zu dem), at the, to the.

zumachen, to shut, close; **mach zu,** make haste.

zumal, chiefly, especially, all the more so.

zumeist, in most cases, for the most part, generally.

zumindest, at least.

zumischen, to mix with, admix.

zumuten, to expect, exact.

zunächst, nearest, next, first of all, above all.

Zunahme, *f.* increase, increment, advance growth, progress.

Zuname, *m.* surname, family name.

Zündapparat, *m.* ignition (priming) apparatus.

zündbar, inflammable.

Zündbarkeit, *f.* inflammability.

zünden, to kindle, catch fire, ignite, set on fire.

Zunder, *m.* tinder, touchwood, punk.

Zünder, *m.* lighter, igniter, match, fuse; **-satz,** *m.* fuse composition.

Zünd-flämmchen, *n.* pilot light (flame); **-funke,** *m.* spark; **-holz,** *n.* match; **-hölzchen,** *n.* match; **schwedisches Zündhölzchen,** *n.* safety match.

Zünd-hütchen, *n.* percussion cap; **-kerze,** *f.* spark plug; **-kirsche,** *f.* ignition pellet; **-masse,** *f.* igniting composition; **-mittel,** *n.* ignition agent; **-papier,** *n.* touch paper; **-pille,** *f.* primer; **-pulver,** *n.* priming powder; **-punkt,** *m.* ignition point; **-satz,** *m.* priming composition.

Zünd-schnur, *f.* fuse; **-schwamm,** *m.* amadon, German tinder, punk; **-spannung,** *f.* initial potential, ignition tension; **-stelle,** *f.* place of ignition; **-stoff,** *m.* inflammable material.

Zündung, *f.* kindling, ignition, priming.

Zündungstemperatur, *f.* ignition temperature.

Zund-waren, *f.* inflammables; **-wärme,** *f.* ignition heat.

zunehmen, to increase, grow (larger) advance, improve, swell.

Zuneigung, *f.* affection, attachment.

Zunft, *f.*-e, guild, corporation, profession, craft, fraternity, clique.

Zunge, *f.* tongue, ligule, language, pointer, needle; belegte ∼, furred tongue.

züngeln, to lick, shoot out (flames); -züngelnd, lambent.

Zungenbalg, *m.* lingual follicle; -drüse, *f.* lingual follicular gland.

Zungen-balken, *m.* tongue bar; -band, *n.* frenulum of tongue.

Zungenbein, *n.* hyoid bone; -bogen, *m.* second visceral arch, hyoid arch; -grube, *f.* inferior carotid triangle; -horn, *n.* horn of the hyoid; -kehldeckelband, *n.* hypoepiglottic ligament; -kreuz, *n.* hyoid cross (meeting of hairlines); -mittelstück, *n.* body of the hyoid; -schildmuskel, *m.* thyrohyoid muscle; -schlundmuskel, *m.* hyopharyngeal muscle; -schlundschnürer, *m.* median constrictor of pharynx; -zungenmuskel, *m.* styloglossus muscle; -zweig, *m.* branch of the hyoid.

Zungen-belag, *m.* fur of tongue; -blatter, *f.* glossanthrax; -blüte, *f.* ligulate (labiate) flower; -fleisch, *n.* lingual parenchyma (tissue); -förmig, ligulate, tongue (strap)-shaped; -fuss, *m.* base of ligule, glossopodium; -gaumenbogen, *m.* anterior pillar of fauces, glossopalatine arch; -gegend, *f.* lingual region; -grübchen, *n.pl.* glossoepiglottic fossae (valleculae); -grund, *m.* base of the tongue.

Zungen-haut, *f.* epithelium of tongue; -karbunkel, *m.* glossanthrax; -kehldeckelfalte, *f.* glossoepiglottic fold; -knochen, *m.* hyoid bone; -knorpel, *m.* cartilage of tongue; -knoten, *m.* lingual ganglion, submaxillary ganglion; -krebs, *m.* cancer of tongue, glossanthrax, blain; -loch, *n.* foramen, caecum; -los, tongueless.

Zungen-muskel, *m.* lingual muscle; -naht, *f.* raphe of tongue; -rinne, *f.* alveolar groove, lingual; -rücken, *m.* back of the tongue; -scheide, *f.* tongue sheath; -scheidewand, *f.* septum of tongue; -schleimhaut, *f.* mucous membrane of tongue; -schlundkopf, *m.* glossopharynx; -spalte, *f.* cleft of the tongue; -spitze, *f.* tip of the tongue.

Zungen-tasche, *f.* radular sac; -warze, *f.* papilla of tongue; -würmer, *m.pl.* Linguatulida; -wurzel, *f.* base of the tongue; -zäpfchen, *n.* epiglottis, uvula; -zweig, *m.* lingual branch.

Zunsler, *m.pl.* Pyralidae.

zunutze machen, sich, to use, put to use.

zuoberst, uppermost.

zuordnen, to co-ordinate, adjoin.

Zuordnung, *f.* co-ordination, association, relation.

zupfen, to pluck, pull, pick, ravel out.

Zupf-leinwand, *f.* lint; -methode, *f.* teasing with needles; -nadel, *f.* mounted needle, dissecting needle; -präparat, *n.* teased-out preparation.

zupfropfen, to cork, up, stop up.

zur (zu der), to the.

zuraten, to advise, persuade.

Zürbelkiefer, *f.* Swiss (cembra) pine.

zurechnen, to add in reckoning, ascribe, attribute, count among.

zurechnungsfähig, responsible, accountable.

zurecht, in right place, in good order; ∼ finden, to find one's way; ∼ legen, to arrange, get ready; ∼ machen, to organize, get ready, prepare; ∼ zimmern, to put into shape.

zureden, to speak to, advise, urge, encourage, persuade.

zureichen, to suffice, hand over to.

Zürgelbaum, *m.* nettle tree (Celtis).

zurichten, to prepare, convert, shape, harvest, make ready, dress, leaven, maltreat.

Zurichtmasse, *f.* sizing material.

Zurichtung, *f.* preparation, conversion.

Zurichtungskosten, *f.pl.* costs of harvesting, preparation.

zurück, back, backward, behind, in the rear; -beuger, *m.* supinator; -bilden, to form again; -bleiben, to remain (lag) behind, be late, be slow, survive; -bleibend, remaining behind, residual, laggard; -drängen, to push back, repress, restrain; -erhalten, to recover; -fallen, to fall back, relapse, be reflected, revert; -fliessen, to flow back, recede; -führbar, traceable, reducible.

zurück-führen, to lead back, trace back, reduce, be due to; -geblieben, remained behind, residue; -gebogen, reflexed, bent back; -gehen, to go back, return, recede, retrace, decline, deteriorate; -gehen, *n.* return, reversion, decline; -gekrümmt, recurved; -gerollt, revolute; -geschlagen, reduplicate(d); -gewinnen, to recover; -geworfen, thrown back, reverberated, reflected; -gewunden, retrorse; -greifen, to reach (extend) back, refer to.

zurück-halten, to keep back, repress, receive, detain; -haltend, reserved, cautious, shy; -haltung, *f.* retention; -kehren, to return, revert; -kommen, to return;

-lassen, to leave (behind); **-laufen,** to run back, recur, recoil; **-laufend,** recurrent; **-legen,** to put by, lay aside, shelve, travel; **-nehmen,** to take back, recall, retract.

Zurück-prallen, to recoil, rebound, be reflected, reverberate; **-schlagen,** to strike back, throw off; **-schnellen,** n. recovery (when bent), springback, recoil; **-setzen,** to set back, replace, neglect, slight, reduce; **-spiegeln,** to reflect; **-springen,** to jump back, run back, rebound, recoil, recede, re-enter (angle); **-stossen,** to repel, push back; **-stossungskraft,** f. power of repulsion; **-strahlen,** to reflect; **-strahlung,** f. reverberation (light).

zurück-strömen, to flow back; **-strömen,** n. reflux; **-titrierung,** f. back titration; **-treiben,** to check, drive back; **-treten,** to step back, recede, subside; **-verwandeln,** to change back; **-weichen,** n. recession; **-weisen,** to send back, refer back to, reject, decline; **-werfen,** to throw back, reflect; **-werfen,** n. reverberation (light); **-ziehen,** to return, retract, withdraw.

zurunden, to round off.

zurüsten, to equip, prepare, fit out.

zurzeit, at the time, at the present time.

zusagen, to promise, suit, agree, please.

zusagend, pleasant, suitable.

zusammen, together, jointly, all together; **-arbeit,** f. co-operation; **-backen,** to stick together, agglomerate; **-ballen,** to agglomerate, conglomerate; **-bauen,** to assemble, erect; **-brechen,** to break down; **-bruch,** m. collapse; **-drehen,** to coil together, twist; **-drehung,** f. twisting, torsion; **-drückbar,** compressible.

Zusammen-drückbarkeit, f. compressibility; **-drücken,** to compress; **-drücker,** m. compressor; **-fallen,** to fall down, collapse, synchronize, converge, coincide; **-falten,** to fold up; **-fassen,** to grasp, seize, comprehend, comprise, group, abstract, collect, summarize, condense; **-fassung,** f. summary, synopsis, compilation, comprehension; **-fügen,** to join, unite, articulate; **-geballt,** conglobate(d), agglomerated; **-gedrängt,** conferted, closely crowded; **-gedreht,** contorted.

zusammen-gefaltet, folded (up); **-gehörig,** belonging together, correlated, homologous, homogeneous, congruous; **-gelegt,** conduplicate; **-gerollt,** convolute.

zusammen-gesetzt, composite, compound, complex, complicated; **zusammengestztes Glas** n. laminated glass.

zusammen-gewachsen, grown together, anchylosed, accrete, connate, adherent; **-gezogen,** contracted; **-halt,** m. coherence, cohesion, consistency; **-halten,** to hold together, cohere, compare; **-hang,** m. connection, correlation, relationship, coherence; **-hängen,** n. to cohere, communicate, be connected; **-hängend,** connected, coherent, continuous; **-häufen,** to accumulate; **-kleben,** to stick together, agglutinate; **-kunft,** f. meeting, convention, assembly.

Zusammen-lagerung, f. assemblage; **-laufen,** to run together, congregate, converge, coagulate; **-leben,** n. companionship, association, reciprocal relations; **-legen,** to lay together, collect, fold up; **-leimen,** to agglutinate; **-leimung,** f. agglutination; **-mündung,** f. anastomosis, confluence; **-pressen,** to compress; **-reiben,** to grind (rub) together; **-rücken,** to draw together.

zusammen-rühren, to mix by stirring; **-schmelzen,** to fuse together, melt down, clinker, alloy; **-schütteln,** to shake together; **-schütten,** to pour together; **-setzen,** to compose, combine, put together, be composed, consist of; **-setzung,** f. composition, synthesis, combination, construction, compound, mixture; **-spiel,** n. interplay; **-stellen,** to place together, join, compile, group, assort; **-stellung,** f. combination, putting together, grouping, classification, compilation, juxtaposition; **-stimmen,** to agree, harmonize, vote together.

Zusammen-stoss, m. impact, collision, conflict; **-stossen,** to knock together, crush, meet, collide; **-stossend,** contiguous, adjacent; **-treffen,** to meet, coincide, concur; **-treffen,** n. anastomosis meeting; **-treten,** to appear together; **-wachsung,** f. growing together; **-wirken,** n. co-operation; **-wuchs,** m. coalescence; **-würfeln,** to jumble up, mix up.

zusammen-ziehbar, contractible; **-ziehen,** to draw together, contract; **-ziehend,** contractive, astringent; **-zieher,** m. constrictor; **-ziehung,** f. contraction, constriction, shrinking, systole.

Zusatz, m. ⁻e, addition, admixture, appendix, additive, supplement, corollary; **auf ~ von, unter ~ von,** with addition of.

Zusatz-annahme, f. additional assumption; **-excenter,** n. auxiliary eccentric, **-geräte,** n.pl. attachments; **-linse,** f. supplementary lens; **-metall,** n. alloy; **-wasser,** n. make-up water.

zuschärfen, to sharpen.

Zuschauer, *m.* spectator.

zuschieben, to push to, close, shut, pass.

Zuschlag, *m.*-̈e, increase, addition, admixture flux.

zuschlagen, to add, knock down, hit hard, slam, close up.

zuschmelzen, to close by melting, seal.

zuschneiden, to cut (out).

zuschreiben, to ascribe, dedicate, attribute, assign.

Zuschrift, *f.*-en, letter, inscription, dedication.

zuschulden, sich ~ **kommen lassen,** to become guilty of, do something wrong.

Zuschuss, *m.*-̈e, additional supply, contribution.

zuschütten, to fill up.

zusehen, to look, witness.

zusehends, visibly, obviously, noticeable.

zusetzen, to add, mix, alloy, contribute, obstruct, lose money.

Zusetzung, *f.* addition, contribution.

zusichern, to assure, promise.

zuspitzen, to point, sharpen, taper; **zugespitzt,** acuminate(d).

zusprechen, to cheer, comfort, impart by speaking, adjudge, attribute.

Zuspruch, *m.*-̈e, encouragement, consolation, call.

Zustand, *m.*-̈e, state, condition, situation.

zustande-bringen, to achieve, accomplish; **-kommen,** to come about, take place, occur, form.

zuständig, belonging to, appertaining, appropriate.

zuständlich, neutral, objective.

Zustands-änderung, *f.* change of state, change in composition or condition; **-diagramm,** *n.* phase diagram; **-form,** *f.* form or state.

zustecken, to pin together, give or hand secretly.

zustehen, to pertain, belong, be incumbent upon, become, suit.

zustellen, to close, block up, prepare, deliver, forward to.

zusteuern, to contribute, steer toward.

zustimmen, to agree, assent.

zustimmendenfalls, in case of agreement.

zustöpseln, to cork up.

Zustrebekraft, *f.*-̈e, centripetal force.

zuströmen, to pour in, stream in.

zustutzen, to trim, dress up.

zutage, to or at the surface; **oringen, bring** to light; **-fördern,** to extract, unearth, bring to light; **-kommen,** come to light, become evident; **-liegen,** to be evident, on the surface; **-treten,** to come to light, become evident.

Zutat, *f.*-en, trimming, ingredient, addition.

zuteilen, to allot, assign, apportion, distribute.

zuträglich, useful, profitable, beneficial.

zutrauen to trust in, credit with, confide in.

zutraulich, confiding, trusting.

zutreffen, to come true, agree, prove correct, happen, take place, occur.

Zutritt, *m.*-e, access, admittance, admission.

zutröpfeln, to drop (drip) in; ~ **lassen,** to add drop by drop.

zutun, to add, close, shut.

Zutun, *n.* co-operation, aid.

zuverlässig, reliable, dependable, certain, authentic.

Zuverlässigkeit, *f.* reliability.

Zuversicht, *f.* confidence, reliance, dependence, certainty.

zuversichtlich, confident, assured, positive, certain.

Zuviel, *n.* excess.

zuviel, too much (many); **mehr als** ~, more than enough.

zuvor, before, previously, beforehand, first, formerly; ~ **kommend,** anticipating, obliging; ~ **tun,** to surpass, excel, outdo.

zuvorderst, in the front rank, foremost.

Zuwachs, *m.* increase, increment, growth; **-bohrer,** *m.* increment borer; **-geschwindigkeit,** *f.* rate of growth increment; **-grösse,** *f.* growth in length; **-prozent,** *n.* increment percentage, rate of growth; **-ring,** *m.* growth ring, annual increment.

zuwachsen, to incrust, become clogged (nozzles).

zuwege bringen, to bring about, effect.

zuweilen, sometimes, now and then.

zuweisen, to allot, assign.

zuwenden, to turn to.

zuwider, against, contrary to.

zuzählen, to add, be among, reckon in with.

zuziehen, to tighten, draw shut, call in, invite, consult, incur, pull, move.

zuzüglich, with addition of.

zwacken, to pinch, tease.

zwang (zwingen), forced, was forcing.

Zwang, m. compulsion, constraint, coercion. force, pressure.

zwängen, to pinch, squeeze, force, coerce.

zwanglos, unconstrained, informal, freely, at random, irregular.

Zwangs-bestäubung, f. cleistogamy; -drehung, f. forced turning; -läufig, necessary, by necessity, enforced; -schmarotzer, m. obligate parasite; -weise, compulsory, forcible.

zwanzig, twenty.

zwanzigerlei, of twenty different kinds.

zwanzigfach, twentyfold.

zwanzigste, twentieth.

zwar, indeed, to be sure.

Zweck, m.-e, goal, object, end, aim, purpose peg, butt; mittel zum ∿, means to an end.

zweck-dienlich, serviceable, suitable, efficient, useful; -entsprechend, appropriate.

Zwecke, f. tack, brad, peg.

Zweck-haftigkeit, f. adaptiveness, suitability; -los, aimless, useless; -mässig, appropriate, suitable, expedient; -mässigkeit, f. suitability, fitness, expediency; -mässigkeitslehre, f. teleology.

zwecks, for the purpose of.

Zweck-ursache, f. final cause; -widrig, inappropriate, unsuitable, inexpedient.

zwei, two; -achsig, biaxial; -armig, twoarmed; -astig, bifurcate, bifurcated; -atomig, diatomic; -äugig, binocular.

zwei-basisch, dibasic; -blättrig, bifoliate, bipetalous; -blütig, biflorate; -brüderig, diadelphous; -deutig, ambiguous, equivocal; -einhalbfach, two-and-a-half-fold.

zweierlei, of two kinds, twofold, different; -wertig, with two valencies.

zweifach, twofold, double; -frei, bivariant; -geteilt, bipartite.

zweifächerig, two-celled, two-chambered, bilocular.

zweifachungesättigt, diethylenic, doubly unsaturated.

zweifarbig, two-colored.

Zweifarbigkeit, f. dichroism.

Zweifel, m.-, doubt, hesitation, question, uncertainty; -haft, doubtful, dubious; -los, doubtless, certain.

zweifeln, to doubt.

zweifelsohne, without doubt, doubtless.

zwei-fiederspaltig, bipinnatifid; -flügelig, dipterous, two-winged; -flügler, m.pl. Diptera.

Zweig, m.-e, twig, branch(let), sprig.

zweigabelig, dichotomous.

Zweig-ablösung, f. fall of twigs; -absprung, m. twig abscission; -blumig, flowering on the branches; -brücke, f. hyphal fusion; -ende, n. end of a branch.

zweigeschlechtig, androgynous.

Zweigeschlechtigkeit, f. monocliny, bisexuality.

zweigestaltig, dimorphous.

Zweigestaltung, f. dimorphism.

zweigipfelig, double-peaked.

Zweigipfeligkeit, f. bimodal (curve).

Zweig-kletterer, -klimmer, m. branchclimber.

zweigleisig, with double track.

Zweigleitung, f. branch line.

zweigliedrig, two-membered, biarticulate, binomial.

Zweig-lücke, f. ramular gap; -rohr, n. branch tube.

Zweigspitze, f. tip of the twig.

Zweigspitzen-dürre, f., -sterben, r. tip blight of twigs.

Zweig-steckling, m. branch cutting; -strom, m. branch current; -tragend, ramiferous, bearing branches; -vorkeim, m. secondary protonema.

zweihäusig, dioecious.

Zweihäusigkeit, f. Dioecia.

zweihiebig, two-storied.

zweihufig, cloven-footed, disulcated, bisulcous.

zwei-jährig, two years old, biennial; -keilig, bicarinate; -keimblättrig, dicotyledonous; -kernig, binuclear; -kiemer, m.pl. Dibranchia; -klappig, bivalved, bivalvous; -knöpfig, bilobed; -lappig, bilobed; -lebig, amphibious; -mächtig, didynamous.

zweimal, twice.

zweimalig, done twice, repeated.

zweimännig, diandrian.

zweimonatlich, every two months.

Zwei-paarfüssler, m.pl. Myriapoda;-phasig, two-phase; -polig, bipolar; -rad, n. bicycle; -reihig, distichous, two-rowed, two-series; -rippig, bicarinate, binervate; -samenlappig, dicotyledonous; -säurig, diacid;

-schalig, bivalve, bivalvular, conchiferous; schenk(e)lig, having two legs or branches.

zweischneidig, two edged; ~ reitend, equitant (leaves).

zwei-schnürig, straight; -seitig, bilateral, two-sided; -spaltig, doubly split, forked, bifid; -spelzig, consisting of two glumes; -sporig, bicalcarate; -ständig, dichotomous; -stärkenglas, n. bifocal lens; -stoff, m. two-component or binary (alloy); -stufig, diplocaulic, two-stage; -stündig, lasting two hours; -taktverfahren, n. two-stroke cycle.

zweite, second.

zweiteilig, bipartite, dimerous.

Zweiteilung, f. binary fission, dichotomy, bifurcation, bisection.

zweitens, secondly.

Zweiweg-hahn, m. two-way cock; -ventil, n. two-way valve.

zwei-wertig, bivalent, divalent; -zahl, f. double number, duplicate; -zählig, twofold, binate, binary; -zahn, m. bur marigold (Bidens cernua); -zehig, with two toes; -zeilig, two-rowed, two-ranked, doublespaced, distichous; -zellenstadium, n. two-cell stage; -zipfelig, bicuspidate.

Zwenke, f. false brome grass (Brachypodium).

Zwerchfell, n. diaphragm; -entzündung, f. inflammation of the diaphragm, diaphragmatitis.

Zwerg, m.-e, dwarf; -artig, dwarfish, pygmy, pumilus; -baum, m. dwarf tree; -birke, f. dwarf birch (Betula nana); -buschsteppe, f. desert scrub vegetation; -form, f. dwarfed form; -gesellschaften, f.pl. suppressed plant communities (dwarf shrubs); -haft, dwarfish; -heide, f. ling heath, dwarf-shrub heath.

Zwerg-huhn, n.-er, Bantam; -kolonie, f. dwarf colony; -männchen, n. dwarf male; -mensch, m. pigmy; -mispel, f. Cotoneaster; -palme, f. dwarf palm (Chamaerops humilis); -rost, m. cereal dwarf rust (Puccinia simplex).

Zwerg-sorte, f. dwarf variety; -steppe, f. prairie with dwarf shrubs; -strauch, m. dwarf shrub; -unterlage, f. dwarf stock (for grafting); -wuchs, m. nanism.

Zwetsche, Zwetschge, f. damson (plum) (Prunus domestica).

Zwickel, m. cuneate lobe of brain, wedge; -bein, n. Wormian bone.

zwicken, to pinch, nip; torment.

Zwickzange, f. pincers, tweezers.

Zwieback, m. biscuit, rusk.

Zwiebel, f. bulb, onion; -artig, bulbous, alliaceous; -brand, m. onion smut; -brut, f. brood bulb, bulblet; -gewächs, n. bulbous plant; -haar, n. bulbous hair.

Zwiebel-knolle, f. bulbous tuber; -kuchen, m. compressed stem portion of a bulb; -marmor, m. cipolin; -saft, m. onion juice; -schale, f. bulb scale, skin (onion); -schuppe, f. bulb scale.

Zwielicht, n. twilight.

Zwiesel, m. fork, forked branch.

zwieselig, forked, furcate.

Zwieselwuchs, m. forked growth, forking, furcation.

Zwilling, m.-e, twin.

Zwillings-achse, f. twinning axis; -bildung, f. twin formation; -doppelverbindung, f. conjugated double linkage; -kerne, m.pl. twin nuclei.

Zwinge, f. ferrule, clamp, vise.

zwingen, to constrain, force, compel, overcome.

zwingend, cogent, compelling.

Zwinger, m. enclosure, dungeon.

Zwirn, m.-e, twine, thread; -band, n. thread, tape; -deckel, m. twisting cap.

zwirnen, to twine, twist, throw silk.

Zwirnsfaden, m. (linen) thread.

Zwirnwickel, n. twisting package.

zwischen, between, among.

Zwischenband, n. copula, intervertebral ligament; -scheibe, f. intervertebral disk.

Zwischen-bau, m. intermediate culture; -bild, n. intermediate image; -blatt, n. mesenchyma; -blattseite, f. interfoliar side; -blüte, f. hermaphroditic flower; -bündel, n. intermediate bundle; -dornmuskel, m. interspinal muscle; -durch, in between, at intervals; -erzeugnis, f. intermediate product; -fach, n. interseptal chamber.

Zwischen-fall, m. incident, episode; -form, f. intermediary form; -frucht, f. crop planted between two main crops; -fruchtbau, m. cultivation of stubble crops; -furche, f. intermediate groove; -geäder, n. fine network of veins; -gelenkknorpel, m. interarticulary cartilage; -geschichtet, interstratified; -geschlecht, n. intersex; -gewebe, n. conjunctive (interstitial) tissue.

Zwischen-gleichbeinband, n. intersesamoid ligament; -glied, n. intermediate (connect-

ing) member, intermediate; **-haut**, *f.*
diaphragm; **-hirn**, *n.* midbrain, 'twixtbrain;
-kanal, *m.* interseptal (intermediary)
canal; **-kiefer**, *m.* intermaxillary bone;
-klauenband, *n.* interdigital ligament.

Zwischenknocken, *m.* lunar bone, Wormian
bone; **-band**, *n.* interosseous (interbony)
ligament; **-haut**, *f.* interosseous membrane;
-raum, *m.* interosseous space.

Zwischenknorpel, *m.* interarticular cartilage; **-scheide**, *f.* interarticular disk.

Zwischen-körper, *m.* intermediate substance; **-lage**, *f.* intermediate position
(layer), interposition; **-legen**, to interpose;
-liegend, intermediate; **-masse**, *f.* ground
substance, paramitome; **-mittelfussgelenk**,
n. intermetatarsal joint; **-mittelhand-
gelenk**, *n.* intermetacarpal joint; **-mole-
kular**, intermolecular; **-moor**, *n.* transition
moor; **-nasenschild**, *m.* internasal plate.

Zwischen-nutzung, *f.* intermediate yield;
-produkt, *n.* intermediate product; **-raum**,
m. interstice, interspace, interval; **-reak-
tion**, *f.* intermediate reaction; **-reiz**, *m.*
interposed stimulus; **-rippenfurche**, *f.*
intercostal furrow; **-rippenraum**, *m.* intercostal space; **-schalten**, to insert (between);
-scheibe, *f.* intervertebral fibrocartilage
disk; **-scheitelschild**, *m.* interparietal
plate.

Zwischen-schicht, *f.* mesenchyma, intermediate (layer) stratum; **-sehne**, *f.*
intermediary tendon; **-staatlich**, interna-
tional; **-stadium**, *n.* intermediate stage;
-ständig, intermediate; **-stein**, *m.* blue
metal (copper); **-stellung**, *f.* intermediate
position; **-strang**, *m.* intermediate cord;
-streifen, *m.* intermediate strip (layer) of
cells in lenticel; **-stück**, *n.* intermediate
part (attachment).

Zwischen-stufe, *f.* intermediary stage;
-substanz, *f.* hyaloplasm, interstitial substance; **-träger**, *m.* intermediate carrier;
-verbindung, *f.* intermediate compound;
-wand, *f.* bulkhead, partition, baffle;
-wanddrüse, *f.* intramural gland; **-wände**,
f.pl. partitions, separating walls, pseudo-
septa; **-weite**, *f.* distance between, interval.

Zwischenwirbel-knorpel, *m.* intervertebral
fiber cartilage; **-loch**, *n.* intervertebral
foramen; **-scheibe**, *f.* intervertebral disk;
-spalt, *m.* intervertebral fissure.

Zwischenwirt, *m.* intermediate host.

Zwischenwirtsvernichtung, *f.* destruction of
alternate host.

Zwischen-wuchs, *m.* diaphysis; **-zeit**, *f.*
interval, interim; **-zelle**, *f.* paraphysis,

interstitial cell; **-zellig**, intercellular;
-zellraum, *m.* intercellular space; **-ziel**,
n. intermediary goal (aim); **-zotten**, *f.pl.*
intervilli; **-zucht**, *f.* intercropping; **-zu-
stand**, *m.* intermediate state.

zwistig, discordant, in dispute.

Zwistigkeit, *f.* difference, dissension, discord.

zwitschern, to twitter, chirp, warble.

Zwitter, *m.* hermaphrodite, gynandromorph,
mongrel, hybrid, bastard; **-blüte**, *f.*
hermaphrodite flower; **-drüse**, *f.* hema-
phroditic gonad; **-gang**, *m.* hermaphroditic
duct.

zwitterig, hermaphroditic.

Zwitter-ion, *m.* amphoteric (hybrid) ion;
-reife, *f.* homogamy.

zwittrig, androgynous, bisexual.

zwo (zwei), two.

zwölf, twelve.

Zwölfender, *m.* stage of twelve points.

zwölferlei, twelve kinds of.

zwölffach, twelvefold.

Zwölf-fingerdarm, *m.* duodenum; **-flach**,
n. dodecahedron; **-flächig**, dodecahedral;
-flächner, *m.* dodecahedron; **-seitig**,
twelve-sided, dodecagonal.

zwölfte, twelfth.

Zyan, *n.* cyanogen; **-verbindung**, *f.* cyanide
compound.

Zygot, *m.* zygote.

Zygotisch, zygotic(ally).

zyklisch, cyclic.

Zykloide, *f.* cycloid.

Zyklon, *m.-e*, cyclone.

Zyklus, *m.* Zyklen, cycle.

Zylinder, *m.* cylinder; **-förmig**, cylindrical;
-kessel, *m.* shell-type boiler.

zylindern, zylindrieren, to calender.

zylindrisch, cylindrical; **zylindrische Kreuzspule**, *f.* tube.

zymogen, as an enzyme.

Zymose, *f.* zymose.

Zyper-wein, *m.* Cyprus wine; **-wurz**, *f.*
galingale.

Zypresse, *f.* cypress (Cupressus).

Zypressen-Wolfsmilch, *f.* cypress spurge
(*Euphorbia cyparissias*).

Zyste, *f.* cyst.

Zytolyse, *f.* cytolysis.

GEOGRAPHIC NAMES

Including Adjectives and Names Derived Therefrom

Aachen, *n.* Aix-la-Chapelle.

Abendland, *n.* West, Occident; **-ländisch,** Western.

Agäisches Meer, *n.* Aegean Sea, Aegean Archipelago.

Ägypten, *n.* Egypt.

Algier, *n.* Algeria.

Al(l)gäu, *n.* Algau, a district in south-western Bavaria.

Alpen, *f.pl.* the Alps.

Antiochien, *n.* Antioch.

Äquator, *m.* Equator.

Baden, *n.* Baden (grand duchy).

Basel, *n.* Basle, Bale.

Bayern, *n.* Bavaria.

Belgien, *n.* Belgium.

Birma, *n.* Burma.

Bodensee, *m.* Lake Constance.

Brasilien, *n.* Brazil.

Braunschweig, *n.* Brunswick.

Bretagne, *f.* Brittany.

Britannien, *n.* Britain.

Brüssel, *n.* Brussels.

Chinarinde, *f.* Peruvian bark.

Comersee, *m.* Lake Como.

Czeche, *m.* Czech.

Dänemark, *n.* Denmark.

Danzig, *n.* Danzig.

deutsch, German, Teuton.

Dniepr, *m.* Dnieper.

Donau, *f.* Danube.

Eismeer, *n.* Polar Sea.

Engländer, *m.* Englishman.

Estland, *n.* Esthonia.

Felsengebirge, *n.* Rocky Mountains.

Florenz, *n.* Florence.

Frankreich, *n.* France.

Franzose, *m.*-n, Frenchman.

französisch, French.

Genf, *n.* Geneva.

Genfer See, *m.* Lake Geneva.

griechisch, Greek.

Grönland, *n.* Greenland.

Grossbritannien, *n.* Great Britain.

Haag, *m.* The Hague.

Habichtsinseln, *f.pl.* the Azores.

Hansa, *f.* **Hansabund,** *m.* Hansa, Hanseatic Union or League.

Harz, *m.* **Harzgebirge,** *n.* Harz Mountains.

Hesse, *m.* Hessian.

Holland, *n.* Holland, the Netherlands.

Holländer, *m.* Dutchman.

Holsteiner, *m.* **holsteinisch,** of Holstein.

Inder, *m.* (Asiatic) Indian, Hindu; **Indianer,** *m.* (American) red Indian.

Indien, *n.* India; the Indies.

Irland, *n.* Ireland.

Island, *n.* Iceland.

Italien, *n.* Italy.

Kanadier, *m.* **kanadisch,** Canadian.

Kanal, *m.* English Channel.

Kapkolonie, *f.,* **Kapland,** *n.* Cape Colony.

Kärnten, *n.* Carinthia.

Kaukasus, *m.* Caucasus Mountains.

Kleinasien, *n.* Asia Minor.

Köln (Cöln), *n.* Cologne.

Konstanz, *n.* Constance.

Krim, *f.* Crimea.

latein(isch), Latin.

Lissabon, *n.* Lisbon.

Maas, *f.* Meuse River.

Mähren, *n.* Moravia.

Mailand, *n.* Milan.

Mainz, *n.* Mayence.

Mark, *f.* the March; **Mark Brandenburg,** (March of) Brandenburg.

Meissen, *n.* Meissen, Misnia.

Mittelasien, *n.* Central Asia.

Mittelländisches Meer, *n.* Mediterranean (Sea).

Mosel, *f.* Moselle.

Moskau, *n.* Moscow.

München, *n.* Munich.

Neufundland, *n.* Newfoundland.

Neuholland, *n.* Australia.

Neuseeland, *n.* New Zealand.

Neuschottland, *n.* Nova Scotia.

Neusüdwales, *n.* New South Wales.

Niederdeutsch, *n.* Low German.

Niederlande, *n.pl.* Netherlands, Low Countries.

niederländisch, Dutch.

Nil, Nilfluss, *m.* Nile.

Norwegen, *n.* Norway.

Nürnberg, *n.* Nuremberg.

Oberer See, *m.* Lake Superior.

Ober See, *m.* a tiny lake in Bavaria.

Ostasien, *n.* Eastern Asia, the Far East.

Ostsee, *f.* Baltic Sea.

Öst(er)reich, *n.* Austria; -Ungarn, *n.* Austria-Hungary.

Pfalz, *f.* the Palatinate.

Pole, *m.* Pole.

Polen, *n.* Poland.

Pommern, *n.* Pomerania.

Prag, *n.* Prague.

Preussen, *n.* Prussia.

Regensburg, *n.* Ratisbon.

Rhein, *m.* Rhine.

Rheinpfalz, *f.* (Rhenish) Palatinate.

Riesengebirge, *n.* part of the Sudetes.

Rumänien, *n.* Roumania.

Russe, *m.*, Russian.

Russland, *n.* Russia.

Sachse, *m.* Saxon.

Sachsen, *n.* Saxony.

Schlesien, *n.* Silesia.

Schleswig, *n.* Sleswig.

Schotte, Schottländer, *m.* Scot, Scotsman.

Schwabe, *m.*, Swabian.

Schwaben, *n.* Swabia.

Schwarzes Meer, *n.* Black Sea.

Schwede, *m.*, Swede.

Schweden, *n.* Sweden.

Schweiz, *f.* Switzerland.

Serbien, *n.* Serbia.

Sibirien, *n.* Siberia.

Spanien, *n.* Spain.

Steiermark, *f.* Styria.

Sudeten, *pl.* the Sudetes Sudetic Mountains.

Syr(i)er, *m.* Syrian.

Tirol, *n.* Tyrol.

Tscheche, *m.* Czech.

Türke, *m.* Turk.

Türkei, *f.* Turkey.

Ungar, *m.* Hungarian.

Ungarn, *n.* Hungary.

Vereinigte Staaten, *m.pl.* United States (of North America), U.S.A.

Vesuv, *m.* Mt. Vesuvius.

Vierwaldstättersee, *m.* Lake of the Four Cantons, Lake Lucerne.

Vogesen, *m.pl.* Vosges Mountains.

Voralpen, *n.pl.* the Lower Alps.

Warschau, *n.* Warsaw.

Weichsel, *f.* Vistula.

Westfalen, *n.* Westphalia.

Wien, *n.* Vienna.

Zuidersee, *m.* Zuider Zee.

Zürich, *n.* Zurich.

ABBREVIATIONS

Abbr.	*German*	*English*
a	aus, an, am	of, on, on the
a	Ar	are (100 square meters)
a.	asymmetrisch	asymmetric
A.	Alkohol	alcohol
A.	Ampere	ampere
Å	Ångström	unit(s), $1A = 1 \times 10^{-8}$ cm. $= 0.1$ my; 1 my $= 0.000001$ mm.
Ä	Äther	ether
a.a.O.	an andern Orten; an angeführten Orten, an angegeben Orten	elsewhere; in the place cited
Abb.	Abbildung	illustration, diagram, portrait, cut, figure
Abds.	Abends	in the evening, P.M.
abh.	abhängig	dependent
Abh.	Abhandlungen	papers, transactions, treatise
Abk.	Abkürzung	abbreviation
abs.	absolut	absolute
Abschn.	Abschnitt	section
absol.	absolut	absolute
abs. tr.	absolut trocken	absolutely dry
Abt.	Abteilung	department, part, portion, division
a.d.	an der	at the, on, on the, to the
a.D.	ausser Dienst	retired
Adr.	Adresse	address
Ae.	Äther	ether
Ä.E.	Angstromeinheit	angstrom unit
Aeq.	Aequivalent	equivalent
aeth.	aetherisch	ethereal
Afl.	Artillerieflieger	artillery spotting pilot
AFL	Luftfahrtabteilung	air force
Afla	Armeefliegerabteilung	army air force
A.G.	Atomgewicht	atomic weight
A.G.	Aktiengesellschaft	joint-stock company, corporation
Agfa	Aktiengesellschaft für Anilinfabrikation	Anilin Dye Corporation
Ah.	Amperestunde	ampere hour
Ak.	Akademie	academy
Akt.-Ges.	Aktiengesellschaft	joint-stock company, corporation
alk.	alkalisch	alkaline
Alk.	Alkohol	alcohol
alkal	alkalisch	alkaline
alkoh.	alkoholisch	alcoholic
allg.	allgemein	general, commonly
am	an dem	at the, to the, on the
Am.	Amerikanismus	Americanism
amk.	ammoniakalisch	ammoniacal
Amp.	Ampere	ampere
An.	Anmerkung	remark, note
anal.	analytisch	analytical

535

anerk.	anerkannt	recognized
Anfr.	Anfrage	inquiry
Ang. Angeb.	Angebot	application, offer
ang(e)w.	angewandt	used, employed, applied
Anl.	Anlage	installation, inclosure
Anm.	Anmerkung	remark, note
Ann.	Annalen	annals
anorg.	anorganisch	inorganic
ans.	an das	as the, to the, on the
Anspr.	Anspruch	requirement
Ant.	Anteil(e)	part(s)
Anw.	Anwendung	application
Anz.	Anzeiger	announcer
Anz.	Anzahl	number
AOK	Armeeoberkommando	army high command
A.P.	Amerikanisches Patent	American patent
App.	Apparat	apparatus
Arch.	Archiv	archive
Art.	Artikel	article
A.S.	Ampere Stunde	ampere-hour
asym(m).	asymmetrisch	asymmetric
At.	Atmosphäre	atmospheres
At.	Atom	atom
At.	Atom Prozent	atomic per cent
ata	atmospheres	absolute pressure
At.-G(ew).	Atom Gewicht	atomic weight
äth.	ätherisch	etheral
Atm.	Atmosphäre	atmosphere
Atm. abs. (ata.)	Atmosphäre absolut	absolute pressure in atmospheres
Atomgew.	Atomgewicht	atomic weight
atro.	absolut trocken	absolutely dry
Atü	Atmosphäre Überdruck	atmospheres absolute (excess) pressure
a.u.a.	auch under andern	also among others
Aufl.	Auflage	edition
Aufst.	Aufstellung	statement, erection
aus.	ausgeschaltet	eliminated, switched off
ausg.	(her)ausgegeben	produced, edited
Ausl.	Ausland, ausländisch	foreign, export
ausschl.	ausschliesslich	excluding, exclusive(ly)
autom.	automatisch	automatic
ä.W.	äussere Weite	outside diameter, o.d.
A.W.	Amperewindung	ampere winding
Awewa	Armeewetterwarte	meteorological observatory
Ar. A.Z.	Aufschlagzünder	percussion fuse
Az. m.V.	Aufschlagzünder mit Verzögerung	delayed-action fuse
B.	Bildung	formation, training, education, experience
B.	Beobachtung	observation
BAK	Ballonabwehrkanone	antiaircraft
Bd.	Band	volume
Bde.	Bände	volumes
B.d.F.	Bildmeldung der Flieger	photographic report by aviator
Be.	(Grade) Baume	(degrees) Baume
Bed.	Bedeutung	significance
beh.	behandeln	treat, handle, work
Beibl.	Beiblätter	supplements
Beih.	Beihefte	supplements
Bem.	Bemerkung	remark

Beob.	Beobachter, Beobachtung	observer, observation
ber.	berechnet	calculated
Ber.	Bericht(e)	report(s)
bes.	besonders	particularly
best.	bestimmt	definite, determined
Best.	Bestimmung	determination
Best.	Bestellung	order
Best.	Bestand	amount
betr.	betreffend	concerned, said, in question
bez.	beziehungsweise	or, respectively
bez.	bezogen(auf)	based on, corresponding to
bez(l).	bezüglich	with reference to
b. Geg.	bei Gegenwart	in the presence of
Bild(g).	Bildung	formation, education, experience
bisw.	bisweilen	sometimes
blf.	blätterförmig	in leaflet or flakes
Blt.	Blättchen	leaflets, lamellae
Bona	Ballonnachrichtenabteilung	balloon communication battalion
Bu. Z.	Buchner Zahl	Buchner number
b.w.	bitte wenden	please turn (page)
Bz.	Bestellzettel	order form
Bz. Bzn.	Benzol	benzene
Bzn.	Benzin	benzine
bzw.	beziehungsweise	or, respectively
C.	Celsius	centigrade
C.	elektrische Kapazität	electrical capacity
ca. cca.	circa, zirka	about, approximately, nearly
cal.	(Gramm)-Calorie	gram calorie, small calorie
Cal.	(Kilogramm)-Calorie	kilogram calorie, large calorie
calc.	calciniert	calcined
cbm	Kubikmeter	cubic meter
cbcm, ccm	Kubikzentimeter	cubic centimeter
cg.	Zentigramm	centigram(s)
Ch(m).	Chemie	chemistry
chem.	chemisch	chemical
Chem.	Chemiker	chemist
Cie.	Compagnie, Gesellschaft	company
cm	Zentimeter	centimeter
corr.	corrigiert	corrected
Cos	Kosinus	cosine
c_p.	spezifische Wärme bei konstantem Druck	specific heat at constant pressure
c_v.	spezifische Wärme bei konstantem Volumen	specific heat at constant volume
d.	der, den, des, dem, die, das	the, of the, to the, etc.
d.	rechtsdrehend	dextrorotatory
D.	Dichte	density, specific gravity
D^{16}	spez. Gew. bei 16°	specific weight at 16°
D_4^{20}	spez. Gew. bei 20° bezogen auf Wasser von 4°	specific weight at 20° with reference to water at 4°
dad. gek.	dadurch gekennzeichnet	thereby characterized
Darst.	Darstellung	preparation
d. Bl.	dieses Blattes	of this paper
dch.	durch	through, by
DD.	Dampfdichte	vapor density
DE.	Dielektrizitätskonstante	dielectric constant
De ge bo	Deutsche Gesellschaft für Bodenmechanik	German Society for Soil Mechanics

Der(iv).	Derivat	derivative
dergl.	dergleichen	the like, such, same, similar
desgl.	desgleichen	the like, such, same, similar
dest.	Destillation	distillation
deut.	deutsch	German
dg	dezigramm	decigram
dg.	dergleichen	the like, such, same, similar
d.h.	das heisst	namely, that is, that is to say, *i.e.*, which means
d.i.	das ist	that is, namely
D.I.N.	Deutsche Industrie Normen	German Industry Standards
Dipl.-Ing.	Diplom Ingenieur	graduate engineer
Diss.	Dissertation	dissertation
dm	Dezimeter	decimeter
d.m.	dieses Monats	of this month, instant
Dm.	Durchmesser	diameter
D.P.a.	Deutsche Patentanmeldung	German patent application
drgl.	dergleichen	the like, such, same, similar
D.R.P.	Deutsches Reichspatent	German State Patent
d.s.	das sind	*i.e.*, that is, namely
dsgl.	desgleichen	the like, such, same, similar
Dutz.	Dutzend	dozen
durchschn.	durchschnittlich	on the average
DVGW	Deutscher Verein Gas- und Wasserfachmänner	German Society of Gas and Water Technologists
dz	Doppelzentner (100 kg.)	hundredweight, cwt. (of 100 kilograms)
E.	Erstarrungspunkt	freezing point, solidification point
E.	elektromotorische Kraft	electromotive force
ebd.	ebenda	at the same place
edul.	entgegengesetzt dem Urzeiger laufend	counterclockwise
E.E.	Entropieeinheit	entropy unit
e.g.	zum Beispiel	for instance
Eg.	Eisessig	glacial acetic acid
e.h.	ehrenhalber	honorary
ehm.	ehemals	formerly
eig.	eigene	own
Eigg.	Eigenschaften	properties
Eigsch.	Eigenschaft	property
eig(tl).	eigentlich	properly speaking, true, especially
Einfl.	Einfluss	influence
einschl.	einschliesslich	including, inclusive of
Einw.	Einwirkung	influence, action, effect
el.	elektrisch	electric
E.L.	Einheits-Lack	unit lacquer
Elekt.	Elektrizität	electricity
elektrol.	elektrolytisch	electrolytic
EMK	elektromotorische Kraft	electromotive force, EMF
enth.	enthaltend	containing
entspr.	entsprechend	corresponding
Entsteh.	Entstehung	origin
entw.	entwickelt, entweder	developed, either
Entw.	Entwickelung	development, evolution
E.P.	Erweichungspunkt	softening point
E.P.	englisches Patent	English patent
Er.	Erstarrungspunkt, erstarrt	solidification point, solidifies
Erg. Bd.	Ergänzungsband	supplementary volume
erh.	erhitzt	heated

Erh.	Erhitzung	heating
Erk.	Erkennung	recognition, detection
Erst. P.	Erstarrungspunkt	solidification point
erw.	erwärmt	warmed, heated
e.St.	emotionelle Stellungnahme	emotional attitude
etw.	etwas	something
e.V.	emotionelle Verarbeitung	emotional working up
ev., event., evtl.	eventuell	eventual(ly), perhaps, in the event of
e. Wu	emotionelles Werturteil	emotional evaluation
exp.	experimentell	experimental
Extr.	Extrakt	extract
E.Z.	Esterzahl	ester number
f.	fast	almost
f.	fest	solid
f.	fein	fine
f.	folgende	the following, onward
f.	für	for
F.	Fahrenheit	Fahrenheit, F.
F.	Faraday's constant	number of coulombs per gram equivalent of an ion
F.	Fusionspunkt	fusion point, melting point, m.p.
Fam.	Familie	family
Farb.	Farben	colors
farbl.	farblos	colorless
Farbw.	Farbwerke	dyeworks
ff., fff.	sehr fein	very fine
ff., f.f.	und folgende	and following
F.f.	Fortsetzung folgt	to be continued
F.i.D.	Faden in Dampf	thread in vapor
Fig.	Figur	figure
fl.	flüssig	liquid, fluid
Fl.	Flüssigkeit	liquid, fluid
Flak.	Flugabwehrkanone	antiaircraft
Fll.	Flüssigkeiten	liquids, fluids
folg.	folgend	following
F.P., Fr.P.	französisches Patent	French patent
frakt.	fraktioniert	fractionated
frbl.	farblos	colorless
F.T.	Funkentelegraphie	radiotelegraphy
F.Z.j	Farbzahl gegen Jod	color number as compared to iodine
g	Gramm	gram(s)
G.	Gesellschaft	company
Gasentw.	Gasentwicklung	evolution of gas
gbr.	gebräuchlich, gebraucht	used commonly
gbr.	gebräunt	burned
G.E.	Gewichtseinheit	imperial weight, unit of weight, standard of weight
geb.	gebildet	formed, educated
geb.	geboren	born
geb.	gebunden	bound
gef.	gefunden	found
Gef. P.	Gefrierpunkt	freezing point
geg.	gegen	against
Gegenw.	Gegenwart	presence
gegr.	gegründet	founded
gek.	gekocht	boiled

gel.	gelöst	dissolved
gelat.	gelatinös	gelatinous
gem.	gemahlen	ground, powdered pulverized
gem.	gemischt	mixed
geolog.	geologisch	geological
ges.	gesamt	total
ges.	gesetzlich	by law
ges(ätt).	gesättigt	saturated
ges. gesch	gesetzlich geschützt	patented, protected by law
Ges.	Gesellschaft	company, society
geschm.	geschmolzen	molten, melted
gest.	gestorben	died
gew.	gewöhnlich	usual, ordinary
Gew.	Gewicht	weight, gravity
Gew.-T.	Gewichtsteil	part by weight
gew. Temp.	gewöhnliche Temperatur	general temperature
g.g.	gegen	against
G.G.	Gasgewinde	gas thread
Ggw.	Gegenwart	presence
Gl.	Gleichung	equation
GM.	Goldmark	gold marks
G.m.b.H.	Gesellschaft mit beschränkter Haftung (Haftpflicht)	company with limited liability, limited (liability) company
g-Mol.	grammolekül	gram molecule
gr	Gramm	gram(s)
gründl.	gründlich	entirely, fundamentally, basically
Gz.	Gefühlszustand	disposition
h.	heiss	hot
h.	hoch	high
H.	Heizwert	calorific value
H.	Härte	hardness
H.	Höhe	height, altitude
H.	Henry	henry (elec.)
ha.	Hektar	hectare
Hal, Hlg.	Halogen	halogen
Hauptwrk.	Hauptwirkung	main action
H.D.	Hochdruck	high pressure
Hekt	Hektoliter	hectoliter
H. Entw.	H-Entwicklung	hydrogen (evolution development)
herg.	hergestellt	produced
Herst.	Herstellung	production, construction, manufacture
HK	Hefner-Kerze(n)	Hefner candle(s)
hl	Hektoliter	hectoliter
Hl.	Halbleder	half leather
Hlw.	Halbleinwand	half cloth
hrsg.	herausgegeben	edited
i.	in	in
I.	Elektrische Stromstärke	strength of electrical current
i. allg.	im allgemeinen	in general
i. B. auf	in Berechnung auf	calculated on the basis of
ibid.	ibidem	in the same place
I. G. Farben	Interessengemeinschaft der Farbenindustrie	German Dye Trust
i.J.	im Jahre	in the year
inakt.	inaktiv	inactive
Inaug. Diss.	Inaugural Dissertation	thesis for doctor's degree
Ind.	Industrie	industry

Inh.	Inhalt	content, capacity
inkl.	inklusiv	inclusive, including
insb.	insbesondere	in particular
Inst.	Institut	institute
i.U.	intellektuelle Unterlage	intellectual base
i.V.	im Vakuum	in a vacuum
I.W.	innere Weite	inside diameter, width in the clear
I.W.v.	im Werte von	amounting to
J.	Journal, Jahrbuch, Jahresbericht	journal, annual report
J.	Jahr	year
Jahrg.	Jahrgang	year
Jb	Jahrbuch	annual
Jg.	Jahrgang	year's set
J.Z.	Jodzahl	iodine number
k	kaiserlich	imperial
k	kalt	cold
k.	königlich	royal
K	Konstante	constant
K.	Kalorie	calorie
Ka.	Kathode	cathode
Kal, kcal	Kilogramm Kalorie	kilogram calorie
Kap.	Kapitel	chapter
Kg., kg	Kilogramm	kg. kilogram(s)
kgl.	königlich	royal
Kl.	Klasse	class
km	Kilometer	kilometer
k.M.	kommenden Monats	of next month
Kn.	Knoten	knot
Koeff., Koeffiz	Koeffizient	coefficient
kompr.	komprimiert	compressed
konst.	konstant	constant
konz	konzentriert	concentrated
kor(r).	korrigiert	corrected
Kp.	Kochpunkt, Siedepunkt	boiling point
Kp 10	Kochpunkt bei 10 mm Quecksilberdruck	boiling point at 10 millimeters of mercury pressure
Kr.	Kran	crane, hoist
Kr.	Krystallographie	crystallography
krist.	kristallisiert, kristallinisch	crystallized, crystalline
Krist.	Kristallisation	crystallization
krit	kritisch	critical
Kryst.	Krystallographie	crystallography
	Krystall(e)	crystal(s)
	Krystallisation	crystallization
k.T.	konkrete Tatbestände	concrete facts
kub.	kubisch	cubic
Kub. Gew.	Kubik Gewicht	weight per m³ in tons = density
KW., kW	Kilowatt	kilowatt
Kwst.	Kilowattstunde	kilowatt hour
KW.-stoff	Kohlenwasserstoff	hydrocarbon
l.	lies	read
l.	löslich	soluble
l	Liter	liter
l.	links	left
l.	linksdrehend	levorotatory
L	Lösung	solution

L.	Selbstinduktionskoeffizient	inductivity (elec.)
lab.	labil	labile, unstable
landw.	landwirtschaftlich	agricultural
langj.	langjährig	for many years
Lebensl.	Lebenslauf	career
Legg.	Legierungen	alloys
leichtl.	leichtlöslich	easily soluble
lfd.	laufend	current, running, consecutive, regular
lfd. Nr.	Laufende Nummer	serial number, current number, running number
Lfg.	Lieferung	issue, number, part
lg.	lang	long, in length
linksdr	linksdrehend	levorotatory
l.J.	laufenden Jahres	of the current year
ll.	leicht löslich	easily (readily) soluble
lösl.	löslich	soluble
Lösl.	Löslichkeit	solubility
Lösungsm.	Lösungsmittel	solvent
Lsg.	Lösung	solution
Lsgg.	Lösungen	solutions
lt.	laut	in accordance with, as per inside diameter, width in the clear
l.w.	lichte Weite	inside diameter, width in the clear
Lwd. Lw.	Leinwand	linen, cloth, canvas
m.	mit	with
m.	Minute	minute
m	Meter	meter
m.	Meta	meta
M	Mark	mark(s)
M.	Masse	mass
M.	Molekulargewicht	molecular weight
M.	Monat	month
mA	Milliampere	milliampere
magn(et)	magnetisch	magnetic
m.A.n.	meiner Ansicht nach	in my opinion
m.a.W.	mit anderen Worten	in other words
max.	maximum	maximum
m.b.H.	mit beschränkter Haftung (Haftpflicht)	with limited liability, limited
M.D.	Mitteldruck	intermediate pressure
m.E.	meines Erachtens	in my opinion
Me	Methyl, Metall	methyl, metal
M.E.	Mache-Einheit	Mache unit
M.E.	Münze Einheit	coinage
mechan.	mechanisch	mechanical(ly)
met.	metallurgical	metals, metallurgy
metall.	metallisch	metallic
Meth.	Methode	method
mg	Milligramm	milligram
m.G.	mit Goldschnitt	with gilt edges
M.G.	Molekulargewicht	molecular weight
Mill.	Million	million
min.	minimal, minimum	minimum
Min.	Minute(n)	minute(s)
mitt.	mittels	by means of
Mitt.	Mitteilung	communication, report
Mk	Mark	mark(s)
mk.	mikroskopisch	microscopic

mkr.	mikroskopisch	microscopic
ml	Milliliter	milliliter
Mm, mm.	Millimeter	millimeter
mögl.	möglich	possible
mol.	molekular	molecular
Mol.	Molekül(e), Molekul	molecule(s)
Mol.·Gew.	Molekulargewicht	molecular weight
Mol.·Refr.	Molekularrefraktion	molecular refraction
Mol. W.	Molekularwärme	molecular heat
Monatsh.	Monatshefte	monthly number (of a publication)
MOTO, moto	Monatstonnen(metric)	tons per month
mul	mit dem Urzeiger laufend	clockwise
m.W.	meines Wissens	to the best of my knowledge, as far as I know
mx.	Maximum	maximum
n.	nach	after
n.	neutrɪl	neutral
n.	nördlich	northern
n.	normal	normal
n.N.	Gesamtwirkungsgrad	total (over-all) efficiency
n.	Nutzeffekt, Wirkungsgrad	efficiency
N.	nachts	at night, P.M.
N.	nachmittags	afternoon, P.M.
N.	Leistung	output, power factor, load, hp.
Nachf.	Nachfolger	successors
nasz.	naszierend	nascent
Naturv.	Naturvorkommen	natural occurrence
N.D.	Niederdruck	low pressure
Nd.	Niederschlag	precipitate
Ndd.	Niederschläge	precipitates
Ne.	effektive Leistung	effective (output) horsepower
neutr.	neutralisiert	neutralize
n.F.	neue Folge	new series
N.F.	Neue Folge	new series
n.J.	nächstes Jahr	next year
NK.	Normalkerze	standard candle power
nl.	nicht löslich	not soluble
Nm.	nachmittags	afternoon, p.m.
n.M.	nächsten Monats	of next month, proximo
Nm.	mechanischer Wirkungsgrad	mechanical efficiency
No.	Numero, Nummer	number
norm.	Normen	standards
Norw.P.	norwegisches Patent	Norwegian patent
Nr., Nro.	Nummer, Numero	number
Nt	thermischer Wirkungsgrad	thermal efficiency
Ntf.	Naturforscher	scientific investigator
Nw	wirtschaftlicher (Nutzeffekt) Wirkungsgrad	economical efficiency
o., od.	oder	or
o.	oben	above
o.	ohne	without
o.	ordinär	ordinary grade
o.	ortho	ortho
O.	Ost	east
O.D.	optisches Drehungsvermögen	optical rotation
o. dgl., o. drgl.	oder dergleichen	or the like, or similar
OH.Z.	Hydroxylzahl	hydroxyl number
opt.	optisch	optical

Ord.	Ordnung	order
org.	organisch	organic
Oxd.	Oxydation, Oxydieren	oxidation
oxdd.	oxydierend	oxidizing
p.	para	para
p.	pro	per
P.Ä.	Petroleumäther	petroleum ether
PE.	Passeinheit	unit of fit
Pf.	Pfund	pound
Pf.	Pfennig	pfennig
Pf.	Pferd(e)	horse, horsepower
Pfl.	Pflanze	plant
pH	Wasserstoffexponent	hydrogen exponent
phys.	physikalisch	physical
phys(ik)	physikal, physikalisch	physical
P.K.	Pferdekraft	horsepower
Pkt.	Punkt	point
pl.	Plural	plural
p.m.	pro Minute	per minute, per min.
pr., prakt.	praktisch	practical, applied
prim.	primär	primary
Prod.	Produkt	product
Pol. grad.	Polymerizationsgrad	degree of polymerization
Proz.	Prozent, prozentig	per cent, percentage
Prüflsgg.	Prüflösungen	testing solutions
PS.	Postskriptum	postscript
P.S.	Pferdestärke	horsepower
P.Se	effective Pferdestärke	effective horsepower
P.Sh.	Pferdestärkestunde	horsepower-hour
P.Si	Indizierte Pferdestärke	indicated horsepower
q	Quadrat	square
Q.	Wärmemenge	heat quantity
Q.	Elektrizitätsmenge	electrical quantity
qcm	Quadratcentimeter	square centimeter
qdm	Quadratdecimeter	square decimeter
qm, qM	Quadrat Meter	square meter
qmm	Quadratmillimeter	square millimeter
Q.S.	Quecksilber-stand, -säule	mercury column
qual.	qualitativ	qualitative
quant.	quantitativ	quantitative
r.	Radius	radius
r.	rechtsdrehend	dextrorotatory
R.	Réaumur	Réaumur
R.	elektrischer Widerstand	electrical resistance
rac.	racemisch	racemic
RaEl.	Radium element	radium element
raff.	raffiniert	refined
rd.	rund	about, approximately, nearly
Rd., Red.	Reduktion	reduction
redd.	reduzierend	reducing
Ref.	Referate	reports, abstracts
Rep.	Report	report
resp.	respektive	respectively, or, or rather
Rk.	Reaktion	reaction
Rkk.	Reaktionen	reactions
rm	Raummeter	cubic meter

RM	Reichsmark	mark(s)
R.P.	Reichs Patent	state (imperial) patent
R.T.	Raumteil	part by volume
s.	siehe	see
s.	symmetrisch	symmetric(al)
s.	Sekunde	second
S.	Säure	acid
S.	Seite	page
S.	Sekunde	second
s.a.	siehe auch	see also
Sa.	Summa	together, total
SA	Sonder-Abdruck	reprint
s.a.S.	siehe auch Seite	see also page
Schmp., Schmpt.,	Schmelzpunkt	melting point
Sch.P.		
schm.	schmelzend, schmilzt	melting, melts
schr.	schriftlich, schreiben	in writing, to write
Schw.	schweizerisch, schwedisch	Swiss, Swedish
schwerl.	schwerlöslich	difficultly soluble
sd.	siedend	boiling
s.d.	siehe dies	see this, which see
s.d.	siehe dort	see there
Sd. Sdp.	Siedepunkt	boiling point
sec.	Sekunde, sekundär	second, secondary
s.g.	sogenannt	so-called
s.G.	spezifisches Gewicht	specific gravity (weight)
sied.	siedend	boiling
sk.	Sekunde	second
sl.	schwer löslich	difficultly soluble
sll.	sehr leicht löslich	very easily (readily) soluble
Sm.	Schmelzpunkt, schmilzt	melting point, melts
s.o.	siehe oben	see above
sof.	sofort, sofortigen	immediate
sog., sogen.	sogenannt	so-called
spec., spez.	specifisch	specific
spez.	speziell	especially
spez. Gew.	spezifisches Gewicht	specific gravity (weight)
spezif.	spezifisch	specific
Sp. G.	spezifisches Gewicht	specific gravity (weight)
Spl.	Supplement	supplement
sp. V.	spezifisches Volumen	specific volume
sp. W.	spezifische Wärme	specific heat
SR.	Schapper-Riegler Wert	Schopper-Riegler value
SR.	Skala Réaumur	Réaumur scale
s.S.	siehe Seite	see page
SS.	Säuren	acids
St.	Stahl	steel
St.	Stunde	hour
St.	Stück	each, in number
std., stdg.	stündig	for hour(s)
Std.	Stunde(n)	hour(s)
Stde.	Stunde	hour
Stdn.	Stunden	hours
Str.	Strasse	street
s.u.	siehe unten	see below
subcut.	subkutan	subcutaneous, hypodermic
subl.	sublimiert	sublimes
Subst.	Substanz	substance
s.W.	sperzifische Wärme	specific heat

swl.	sehr wenig löslich	very difficultly soluble
s.w.u.	siehe weiter unten	see below
Syst. No.	System Nummer	system number
SZ.	Säurezahl	acid number
s.Z., s. Zt.	seiner Zeit	in due time, at that time, then
t.	Tonne(n)	ton(s)
t°	Celsiusgrad	centigrade
T.	Tonnen	tons
T.	Tausend	thousand
T.	Teile	parts
T°	absolute Temperature	absolute temperature
Tab.	Tabelle, Tausend	table, thousand
TATO, Tato	Tagestonnen	tons per day
techn.	technisch	technical
Temp.	Temperatur	temperature
Tempp.	Temperaturer	temperatures
tert.	tertiär	tertiary
Tfl.	Tafel	table
tg.	Tangente	tangent
t/h	Stundentonnen	tons per hour
tkm.	Tonnenkilometer	tons per km.
tl.	teilweise löslich	partly soluble
Tl(e)	Teil(e), Gewichtsteil(e)	part(s), part(s) by weight
Tragk.	Tragkraft	carrying capacity, load
Trp.	Tropfpunkt	drip point
u.	und	and
u.	unten	below
u.	unter	under, among
U.	Unverseifbares	unsaponifiable (substance)
U.	Umdrehung	revolution
u.a.	unter andern	among others, moreover
ü.a.	über alle	over all
u.a.a.	und an anderen Orten	and elsewhere
u.a.m.	und andere mehr	and others
u.a.m.	und anderes mehr	and so forth, and so on
u.ä.m.	und ähnliches mehr	and the like, and so on
u.a.O.	und andere Orte	and elsewhere
u.a.O.	unter anderen Orten	among other places
u.a.s.	und andere solche	and others
übsch	überschüssig	in excess
u.d.f.	und die folgende	and those following
u.dgl.	und dergleichen	and the like
u.dgl.m.	und dergleichen mehr	and the like
u.E.	unseres Erachtens	in our opinion
u.e.a.	und einige andere	and some others
Uebsch	Überschuss	excess
u.f.	und folgende	and the following, onward
U.F.	Unterfamilie	subfamily
u.ff.	und folgende	and the following, onward
umkr.	umkristallisieren	recrystallize
U./M., Uml/Min.	Umlaufungen pro Minute	revolutions per minute
Umwandl.	Umwandlung	transformation, conversion
ung.	ungefähr	about, approximately
ungel.	ungelöst	undissolved
unges.	ungesättigt	unsaturated
unl., unlösl. ul.	unlöslich	insoluble
uns.	unsymmetrisch	unsymmetric
Unters.	Untersuchung	examination, investigation

unveränd	unveränderlich	unchangeable, invariable, constant
U.O.	Unterordnung	suborder
U.p.M.	Umlanfungen pro Minute	revolutions per minute
u.s.f.	und so fort	and so on, and so forth, etc.
u.s.w.	und so weiter	and so forth, and so on, etc.
u.U.	unter Umständen	on occasion, under certain conditions
u.v.a.	und viele andere	and many others
uvsf.	unverseifbar	nonsaponifiable
u.Z., u.Zers.	unter Zersetzung	with decomposition
u. zw.	und zwar	that is, namely
v.	vormals	formerly
v.	von	from, of
V.	Vorkommen	presence, occurrence
V.	Volt	volt(s)
V.	vormittags	in the forenoon
Vak.	Vakuum	vacuum
Vak. Exs.	Vakuumexsikkatur	vacuum desiccator
vb.	verbessert	revised
Vbb.	Verbindungen	compounds
v. Chr.	vor Christi	before Christ, B.C.
V.d.Ch., VDCH.	Verein deutscher Chemiker	Association of German Chemists
V.d.I., V.D.I.	Verein deutscher Ingenieure	Association of German Engineers
ver., verb.	verbessert	revised, improved
ver.	vereinigt	united
Verb.	Verbindung	compound
Verbb.	Verbindungen	compounds
verbr.	verbraucht	consumed, used
Verd.	Verdünnung	dilution
verd.	verdünnt	dilute, diluted
Verf.	Verfasser	author
Verf., Verfahr.	Verfahren	process
Verff.	Verfahren	methods
Vergl.	Vergleich	comparison
Vergr.	Vergrösserung	magnification
vergl.	vergleiche	refer, compare, see
vergr.	vergrössert	enlarged, magnified
Verh.	Verhältniss, Verhältnis	condition, proportion, ration
Verh.	Verhalten	behavior
verk.	verkürzt	abbreviated
verkl.	verkleinert	reduced
Verl.	Verlag	publishing house, publisher
Vers.	Versammlung	meeting
Vers.	Versuch	assay, test, experiment, trial
Verss.	Versuche	experiments, tests
verw.	verwandt	related
Vf.	Verfasser	author
vgl.	vergleiche	compare, see, refer
vgl. a.	vergleiche auch	see also
v.H.	vom Hundert, Prozent	per hundred, per cent
Vhdl.	Verhandlungen	transactions
Vh. Z.	Verhältniszahl	proportional number
v.J.	vorigen Jahres	of last year
v.J.	vom Jahre	of the year
v.M.	vorigen Monats	of last month, ultimo
Vm.	vormittags	in the forenoon
Vol.	Volum, Volumen	volume
Vol.-Gew.	volumetrisches Gewicht	volumetric weight (specific gravity)

Vol. T.	Volumenteil	part by volume
vor.	vorig	former, preceding
Vork	Vorkommen	occurrence
vorm.	vormittags	in the forenoon
vorm.	vormals	previously, late, formerly
Vp(n)	Versuchsperson(en)	experimental person
V. St. A.	Vereinigte Staaten v. Amerika	U.S.A.
v.T.	von Tausend, 0/00, pro Mille	per thousand
v.u.	von unten	from beneath, from below
V.Z.	Verseifungszahl	saponification (number) value
w.	warm	warm, hot
W	Widerstand	electrical resistance
W.	Wolfram	tungsten
W.	Wasser	water
W.	Watt	watt(s)
wässr.	wässerig	aqueous, hydrous
W.E.	Wärmeeinheit	heat unit, calorie
Wewa	Wetterwarte	meteorological observatory
wf.	wasserfrei	anhydrous
Wirk.	Wirkung	action, effect
wiss.	wissenschaftlich	scientific
wl.	wenig löslich	difficultly soluble, only slightly soluble
wlösl.	wasserlöslich	water-soluble
w.o.	weiter oben	above
Wrkg.	Wirkung	effect, action
W.S.	Wassersäule (Druck)	pressure
wss.	wässerig	watery, aqueous, hydrous
Wssb.	Wasserbad	water bath
Wu	Werturteil	evaluation
z.	zu, zum, zur	at, to, for, by; at the, for the
Z.	Zeile	line
Z.	Zeitschrift	journal, periodical
Z.	Zeit, Zoll	time, inch
Z.	Zeitschrift	journal
za	zirka	about, approximately, nearly
zahlr.	zahlreich	numerous
z.B.	zum Beispiel	for example, for instance
z.b.V.	zur besonderen Verwendung	for special use
z.E.	zum Exempel	for example, for instance
Zeitschr.	Zeitschrift	publication, periodical, journal
zerfl.	zerfliesslich	deliquescent
zers.	zersetzend	decomposing
Zers.	Zersetzung	decomposition
z.H.	zu Händen	for the attention of, care of
zlo., zl.	ziemlich löslich	fairly soluble
Zle.	Zeile	line
zll.	ziemlich leicht löslich	fairly easily soluble
Zp.	Zersetzungspunkt	decomposition point
z.T.	zum Teil	partly, in part
Ztg.	Zeitung	journal, newspaper
Ztr.	Zentner	hundredweight (50 kg.)
Ztrbl.	Zentralblatt	journal
Ztschr.	Zeitschrift	journal, periodical
Zus.	Zusatz	addition
Zus.	Zusammensetzung	composition
zus.	zusammen	together, totaling
Zus.-P.	Zusatspatent	addition to a patent

z w.	zwar	true, no doubt
z w.	zwischen	between
z wl.	ziemlich wenig löslich	rather difficultly soluble, only slightly soluble
Zyl.	Zylinder	cylinder
z.Z., z.Zt.	zur Zeit	at the time, at present, acting

APPENDIX

ABBREVIATIONS OF PERIODICALS

A., Ann., Annalen der Chemie. Liebig's Annals of Chemistry.

Ann. Phys., Ann. d. Phys., Annalen der Physik. Annals of Physics.

A. Pth., Archiv für experimentelle Pathologie und Pharmakologie.

A. Spl., Liebigs Annalen Supplementbände.

B., Ber., Berichte der deutschen chemischen Gesellschaft.

Berg-Hütt.-Jahr., Berg-und Hüttenmännisches Jahrbuch.

Ber. Sächs. Ges., Berichte über die Verhandlungen der Sächsischen Gesellschaft der Wissenschaften.

C., Chemisches Centralblatt, chemisches Zentralblatt.

Ch. App., Chemische Apparatur.

App. B., Der Apparatebau.

Chem. Fabr., (Die) Chemische Fabrik.

Chem. Ztrlbl., Chemisches Zentralblatt.

Ch. I., Chem. Ind. Chemische Industrie.

Ch. Z.: Chem-Ztg., Chemiker-Zeitung.

C. Min., Zentralblatt für Mineralogie, Geologie und Paläontologie.

D.A.B., Deutsches Arzneibuch.

N.S.B.D.T., Nationalsozialistischer Bund Deutscher Technik.

Dingl. J. Dinglers polytechnisches Journal.

D. Landw. Ges. Mitteilungen der Deutschen Landwirtschafts-Gesellschaft.

D. Zuckerind., Deutsche Zuckerindustrie.

Elektroch. Z., Elektrochemische Zeitschrift.

ETZ, Elektrotechnische Zeitschrift.

Fortschr. Miner., Fortschritte der Mineralogie, Kristallographie und Petrographie.

Frdl., Friedländers Fortschritte der Teerfarbenfabrikation.

Gas., Das Gas- und Wasserfach.

Giess. Z., Giesserei-Zeitung.

Glastechn. Ber., Glastechnische Berichte.

GWF, Gas -und Wasserfach.

H., Zeitschrift für physiologische Chemie (Hoppe-Seyler).

J., Jahresbericht über die Fortschritte der Chemie und verwandter Teile anderer Wissenschaften.

Jahrb. Phot., Jahrbuch der Photographie and Reproduktionstechik.

Jahrb. Rad., Jahrbuch der Radiotivität und Elektronik.

J. Gasb., Journal für Gasbeleuchtung und Wasserversorgung.

Journ. prakt. Chem., Journal für praktische Chemie.

J. pr.: J. Pr. Ch., Journal für praktische Chemie.

J. techn. ökonom. Ch., Journal für technische und ökonomische Chemie.

Keram. Rdsch., Keramische Rundschau.

Koll. Beih., Kolloidchemische Beihefte.

Koll, Z., Kolloid-Zeitschrift.

Korrosion u. Metallschutz, Korrosion und Metallschutz.

Lieb. Ann., Liebigs Annalen der Chemie.

M., Monatshefte für Chemie und verwandte Teile anderer Wissenschaften.

Met. Erz, Metall und Erz.

Mitt. Materialpr., Mitteilungen aus dem Materialprüfungsamt Berlin-Dahlem.

Mitt. tech Versuchsanst Berlin, Mitteilungen der technischen Versuchsanstalt Berlin.

Monatsh.: Monatsh. Chem., Monatshefte für Chemie und verwandte Teile anderer Wissenschaften.

Naturw., Die Naturwissenschaften.

N. Jb. Min., Beilagebd., Neues Jahrbuch für Mineralogie, Geologie und Paläontologie; Beilagebände.

Oest. Ch. Z., Österreichische Chemiker-Zeitung.

(Der) Papierfabrikant. 140 Oranienstrasse, Berlin, Germany (the paper manufacturer.)

P.C.H., Pharmazeutische Zentralhalle für Deutschland.

Pharm. Ztg., Pharmazeutische Zeitung.

Ph. Ch., Zeitschrift für physikalische Chemie.

Phys. Z., Physilkalische Zeitschrift.

Pogg. Ann., Annalen der Physik und Chemie herausgegeben von Poggendorff.

Schweiz. min. petrogr. Mitt., Schweizerische mineralogische und petrographische Mitteilungen.

Schw. J., Schweiggers Journal für Chemie und Physik.

Seifens. Z., Seifensieder-Zeitung.

Sprechsaal, Sprechsaal für Keramik-Glas-Email, Fach-und Wirtschaftsblatt für die Silicat Industrien.

St. E., Stahl und Eisen.

Thermoch. Unters., Thermochemische Untersuchungen.

Tschermak, Tschermaks mineralogische und petrographische Mitteilungen.

V.D. Phys. Ges., Verhandlungen der Deutschen Physikalischen Gesellschaft.

Ver. Geol. Reichsanst., Verhandlungen der Geologischen Reichsanstalt (Wien).

Verh. Gewerbefl., Verhandlungen des Vereins zur Förderung des Gewerbefleisses.

Verh. phys. Ges., Verhandlungen der deutschen physikalischen Gesellschaft.

W., Annalen der Physik (formerly Wiedermann-Drude).

Wied. Ann. (Beibl.), Beiblätter zu Annalen der Physik und Chemie.

Z., Zeitschrift für Chemie.

Z. Ang.: Ztschr. angew Chem., Zeitschrift für angewandte Chemie.

Z. anorg. allg. Chem., Z. anorg. Ch., Zeitschrift für anorganische und allgemeine Chemie.

Z. Berg. Hütt. Sal., Zeitschrift für das Berg, Hütten- und Salinenwesen im preussischen Staate.

ZVDI, Zeitschrift des Vereins Deutscher Ingenieure.

Z. Elektroeh, Zeitschrift für Elektochemie.

Zentrallbl. Hütt, Walz, Zentralblatt der Hütten und Walzwerke.

Z. Instrum., Zeitschrift für Instrumentenkunde.

Z. Metallk., Zeitschrift für Metallkunde.

Z. Phys., Zeitschrift für Physik.

Z. phys Ch., Zeitschrift für physikalische Chemie.

Z. tech. Physik, Zeitschrift für technische Physik.

Z. Unters. Nahr., Zeitschrift für Untersuchung der Nahrungs- und Genussmittel.

Z. El.; Ztschr. Elektrochem., Zeitschrift für Elektrochemie und angewandte physikalische Chemie.

Ztschr. f. d. ges. Textil-Industrie, Zeitschrift für die gesamte Textil-Industrie.

Z. Kryst., Z. Kr., Zeitschrift für Kristallographie.

Ztschr. prakt. Geol., Zeitschrift für praktische Geologie mit besonderer Berücksichtigung der Lagerstättenkunde.

Z. Ver. d. Zuckerind., Zeitschrift der Wirtschaftsgruppe Zuckerindustrie.

CHEMICAL ELEMENTS

This table lists only elements whose German names (or symbols) differ from the English.

Atomic number Ordnungszahl	German Name of Element	English Name of Element	Symbol
1	Wasserstoff	Hydrogen	H
4	Beryllium	Beryllium, glucinium	Be
5	Bor	Boron	B
6	Kohlenstoff	Carbon	C
7	Stickstoff	Nitrogen	N
8	Sauerstoff	Oxygen	O
9	Fluor	Fluorine	F
11	Natrium	Sodium	Na
13	Aluminium	Aluminum	Al
14	Silizium	Silicon	Si
15	Phosphor	Phosphorus	P
16	Schwefel	Sulphur	S
17	Chlor	Chlorine	Cl
18	Argon	Argon	A
19	Kalium	Potassium	K
20	Kalzium	Calcium	Ca
22	Titan	Titanium	Ti
24	Chrom	Chromium	Cr
25	Mangan	Manganese	Mn
26	Eisen	Iron	Fe
27	Kobalt	Cobalt	Co
29	Kupfer	Copper	Cu
30	Zink	Zinc	Zn
33	Arsen	Arsenic	As
34	Selen	Selenium	Se
35	Brom	Bromine	Br
40	Zirkon	Zirconium	Zr
41	Niobium	Columbium	Cb (Nb)
42	Molybdan	Molybdenum	Mo
47	Silber	Silver	Ag
50	Zinn	Tin	Sn
51	Antimon	Antimony	Sb
52	Tellur	Tellurium	Te
53	Jod	Iodine	I
55	Caesium	Cesium	Cs
57	Lanthan	Lanthanum	La
59	Praseodym	Praseodymium	Pr
60	Neodyn	Neodymium	Nd
69	Thulium	Thulium	Tm (Tu)
71	Lutetium,	Lutecium	Lu
73	Tantal	Tantalum	Ta
74	Wolfram	Tungsten	W

Atomic number Ordnungszahl	German Name of Element	English Name of Element	Symbol
78	Platin	Platinum	Pt
80	Quecksilber	Mercury	Hg
82	Blei	Lead	Pb
83	Wismut	Bismuth	Bi
85	Alabamin	Alabamine	Ab
86	Emanium	Radon (nitron)	Rn (Nt, Em)
89	Aktinium	Actinium	Ac
92	Uran	Uranium	U

For elements not shown in this table, German spelling is the same as English spelling.

ELECTRICAL SYMBOLS

Unit	German	English	Ger. Symbol	U.S. Symbol
Volt	Spannung	Potential	U or E	V or E
Ampere	Stromstärke	Current	I	I
Ohm	Widerstand	Resistance	R	R
Coulomb	Elektrizitätsmenge	Charge	Q	Q
Farad	Elektrische Kapazität	Capacity	C	C
Joule	Elektrische Arbeit	Work	A	W
Watt	Elektrische Leistung	Rate of doing work	N	P
Henry	Selbstinduktion	Inductance	L	L

THERMODYNAMIC SYMBOLS
ACCORDING TO DIFFERENT AUTHORS

R. Luther, *Zeitschrift für Elektrochemie*, 1906, Vol. 12, p. 97.

Author	Symbol for Energy	Symbol for Heat	Symbol for Work
Clausius	dU	dQ	dW
Gibbs	d	dH	dW
Helmholtz	dU	dQ	dA
Sackur	dU	dQ	dA
Maxwell	dE	W	A
van't Hoff		Q	F
Nernst	U	Q	A
Duhem	dU	dQ	d
Planck	dU	Q	A
Helm	dE	dQ	dA
Haber	dU	q	A
Lewis and Randall	E	q	A

UNITS AND CONVERSIONS

The Metric (International Standard) System

The value of units is given by their prefixes:

T Tera	$= 10^{12}$	h Hecto	$= 10^2$	m Milli	$= 10^{-3}$
G Giga	$= 10^9$	D Deca	$= 10^1$	μ Micro	$= 10^{-6}$
M Mega	$= 10^6$	d Deci	$= 10^{-1}$	n Nano	$= 10^{-9}$
k Kilo	$= 10^3$	c Centi	$= 10^{-2}$	p Pico	$= 10^{-12}$

Thus,

$$1 \text{ megawatt} = 10^6 \text{ watts} = 1{,}000 \text{ kilowatts}$$
$$1 \text{ kilopound} = 10^3 \text{ pound} = 1{,}000 \text{ pounds}$$
$$1 \text{ hectoliter} = 10^2 \text{ liters} = 100 \text{ liters}$$
$$1 \text{ decigram} = 10^{-1} \text{ gram} = 0.1 \text{ gram}$$

Temperatures

$$C/10 = (K - 273)/10 = (F - 32)/18 = (R - 460)/18$$

0 C =	32 F =	273 K =	492 R
100 C =	212 F =	373 K =	672 R
0 F =	−17.8 C		

Temperature Scales
C = centigrade
F = Fahrenheit
R = Rankine
K = Kelvin

Weights

i kilogram = 2.2 pounds	= 0.001 metric ton
0.373 = 1	= 0.00373
1,000 = 2,205	= 1

For water at 4 C. (Greatest density):

1 liter = 1,000 cubic centimeters = 1.000 kilogram = 2.205 pound
1 cubic meter = 1 ton

Barrels

1 barrel of alcohol = 50 gallons = 1.87 hectoliters
petroleum = 42 gallons = 1.58 hectoliters
salt = 280 pounds = 127 kilograms
cement = 376 pounds = 171 kilograms

Densities

1 gram per milliliter = 1 gram per cubic centimeter = 1 kilogram per liter
= 1 ton per cubic meter = 62.4 pounds per cubic foot = 8.35 pounds per gallon

Some obsolete density scales are still occasionally found; if N = reading of the corresponding hydrometer scale, actual densities are

Balling, heavier than water: $200/(200 - N)$
 lighter than water: $200/(200 + N)$
Bates, 60 F: $(1,000 - 2.78 N)/1,000$
Baumé, 12.5 C, heavier than water: $145.88/(145.88 - N)$
 lighter than water: $145.88/(135.88 + N)$
Baumé, 15 C, heavier than water: $146.3/(146.3 - N)$
 lighter than water: $146.3/(136.3 + N)$
Baumé rational scale, 15 C, heavier than water: $144.3/(144.3 - N)$
Baumé 17.5 C, heavier than water: $146.78/(146.78 - N)$
 lighter than water: $146.78/(136.78 + N)$
Beck, heavier than water: $170/(170 - N)$
 lighter than water: $170/(170 + N)$
Brix, heavier than water: $400/(400 - N)$
 lighter than water: $400/(400 + N)$
Cartier, heavier than water: $136.8/(126.1 - N)$
 lighter than water: $136.8/(126.1 + N)$
Gay-Lussac, heavier than water: $100/(100 - N)$
 lighter than water: $100/(100 + N)$
Twaddell: $(0.5 N + 100)/100$

Volumes

1	= 0.01	hl = 1,000 cm^3	= 0.264 U.S. gal	= 61 in^8	= 0.035 ft^3
3.785	= 0.03785	= 3,785	= 1	= 231	= 0.1337
0.016	= 0.00016	= 16.39	= 0.0043	= 1	= 0.00058
28.32	= 0.283	= 28,320	= 7.48	= 1,728	= 1

Lengths

1	m	= 1,000 mm	= 39.37 in	= 3.28 ft	= 1.093 yd
0.0254		= 25.4	= 1	= 0.0835	= 0.028
0.305		= 305	= 12	= 1	= 0.333
0.9144		= 914.4	= 36	= 3	= 1

Areas

1	m²	= 1,000 cm²	= 1,550 in²	= 10.76 ft²	= 1.196 yd⁹
0.00065		= 6.45	= 1	= 0.007	= 0.00077
0.093		= 929	= 144	= 1	= 0.111
0.836		= 8,361	= 1,296	= 9	= 1

Velocities

1	m/sec	= 60	m/min	= 3.28	ft/sec	= 196.85	ft/min
0.0167		= 1		= 0.055		= 3.281	
0.305		= 18.3		= 1		= 60	
0.005		= 0.305		= 0.0167		= 1	

Pressures

1 kg/cm²	= 14.22 lb/in²	= 735.6 mm Hg	= 28.96 in Hg	= 10 water	= 32.84 ft/water
1.0333	= 14.7	= 760	= 29.92	= 10.33	= 33.92
0.07	= 1	= 51.71	= 2.036	= 0.7	= 2.31
0.0345	= 0.491	= 25.4	= 1	= 0.345	= 1.13
0.0305	= 0.4335	= 22.4	= 0.88	= 0.022	= 1
1.3596	= 19.34	= 1,000	= 39.37	= 13.6	= 44.64

In engineering usage, 1 atmosphere (atm) = 1 kilogram per square centimeter. Use of the term "atmosphere" with reference to the standard pressure of 760 millimeters of mercury is misleading.

1 ounce per square inch = 44 millimeters of water
1 pound per square foot = 4.88 kilogram per square meter
1 torr = 1 millimeter of mercury at 0 C
Atmospheres gauge = absolute atmospheres + 1
Pounds per square inch gauge = pounds per square inch absolute + 14.7

Low absolute pressures may be measured in microns of mercury; 1 micron = 0.001 millimeter

Micron (μ) and millimicron (mμ) as used in physical chemistry.
Pressure gradients:

1 millimeter of mercury per meter = 0.012 inches of mercury per foot
83.3 = 1

Heat and energy

1 kilocalorie per kilogram × C = 1 pcu per pound × C = 1 British thermal unit per pound × F. Specific heats, therefore, are numerically equal in the British and in the Standard system.

1 pcu per pound = 1 kilocalorie per kilogram = 1 calorie per gram = 1.8 British thermal units per pound

1 pcu per hour × square feet × C = 1 British thermal unit per hour × square foot × F = 4.88 kilocalories per hour × square meter × C

1 kilocalorie per second × square centimeter = 3,600 kilocalories per hour × square centimeter = 13,272,000 British thermal units per hour × square foot

1 kilocalorie per second × square centimeters × C = 3,600 kilocalories per hour × square centimeter × C = 2,903,000 British thermal units per hour × square foot × inches × F

1 British thermal unit per hour $\times$ square foot $\times$ foot $\times$ F =
1 pcu per hour $\times$ square foot $\times$ foot $\times$ C = 12 British thermal units per hour $\times$ square
foot $\times$ inch $\times$ F
= 0.00413 calories per second $\times$ square centimeters $\times$ centimeters $\times$ C
1 kilocalorie per meter $\times$ second $\times$ C = 2,420 British thermal units per foot $\times$ hours $\times$ F
1 kilocalorie per cubic meter = 0.112 British thermal unit per cubic foot
1 British thermal unit per pound = 0.555 kilocalories per kilogram
100 % boiler rating = 9,080 kilocalories per square meter $\times$ hours $\times$ F
1 HP = horsepower = 0.746 kilowatthours
1 PS = Pferdestärke = 75 meters $\times$ kilograms per second = 0.736 kilowatts
1 kilowatt = 1.36 PS = 102 meters $\times$ kilograms per second
1 meter $\times$ kilograms per second = 9.81 watts
1 kilowatt hour = 3,415 British thermal units
1 kilocalorie = 427 meters $\times$ kilogram
1 standard ton of refrigeration = 228,000 British thermal units
1 standard commercial ton of refrigeration = 12,000 British thermal units per hour =
288,000 British thermal units per 24 hours

Miscellaneous units

1 kilocalorie per cubic meter $\times$ C = 0.0624 British thermal unit per cubic foot $\times$ F
16 = 1
1 kilocalorie per cubic meter $\times$ hours $\times$ C4 = 0.0351 British thermal unit per square foot
28.5 = 1 $\times$ hours $\times$ F4
1 kilocalorie per square meter $\times$ hours $\times$ C = 0.205 British thermal unit per square foot $\times$
hours $\times$ F
488 = 1
1 kilocalorie per square meter $\times$ hour $\times$ centimeter = 0.936 British thermal unit per
square foot $\times$ hours $\times$ inch
1.07 = 1
1 kilocalorie per meter $\times$ hours $\times$ C = 0.672 British thermal unit per foot $\times$ hours $\times$ F
2.71 = 1
1 C per meter = 0.549 F per foot
1.82 = 1
1 kilocalorie per square meter $\times$ hours $\times$ C = 0.205 British thermal unit per square foot $\times$
hours $\times$ F
4.88 = 1
1 Hz = (Hertz) = 1 cycle per second

Viscosities

1 poise = 100 centipoises = 1 gram per centimeter $\times$ second =
0.000 006 72 pounds per feet $\times$ second
1 centipoise = 2.42 pounds per foot $\times$ hours
1 kilogram $\times$ second per square meter = 0.205 pound $\times$ second per square foot
4.88 = 1
1 kilogram per meter $\times$ hour = 0.672 pound per foot $\times$ hour
1.49 = 1
1 kilogram = 0.980 665 $\times$ 10⁶ Dyn
1 Dyn = 1.0197 $\times$ 10⁻⁶ kilogram

MEASUREMENTS

Are   100 square meters; 119.6 square yards; or 0.02471 acre.
At.   Atmosphäre (English atmosphere or atmospheres absolute pressure),
commonly the metric unit, 1 kilogram per square centimeter or 14.22
pounds per square inch (735.5 millimeters of mercury); as compared to
the English system of 14.70 pounds per square inch (760 millimeters of
mercury).

Atü	Atmosphäre Überdruck; atmospheres pressure above normal air pressure; or gauge pressure (to be distinguished from atmospheres absolute given above as atm).
Centimeter	$\frac{1}{100}$ meter; or 0.3937 English inch.
Cubic centimeter	0.0610 cubic inches or 0.0338 U. S. fluid ounces.
Elle	(Switzerland) 60 centimeters (23.62 English inches).
Fuss	Foot (usually 12 Zoll); Prussian, 1.03 English feet; Switzerland, 0.98ɔ English feet. (May also be literal translation of English foot.)
Gram	15.43 grams or 0.0322 avoirdupois ounce.
Hectare	100 Ares, land area measure, 2.47 English acres.
Hectoliter	100 liters; 26.42 U. S. gallons.
Kanne	1 liter.
Kilogram	1,000 grams; 2.205 avoirdupois pounds.
Kilometer	1,000 meters (0.6214 English miles).
Ligne	Line; Switzerland, 0.082 English inch; Bavaria, 0.080 inch (as compared to French Ligne, 0.089 inch).
Linie	Bavarian (*see* Ligne)
Liter	(1,000 cubic centimeters) 61.02 cubic inches; 1.057 U. S. quarts; or 0.2642 U. S. gallon.
Meile	Prussian mile (24,000 Prussian Füsse), 7.53 kilometers; league (4.68 English miles).
Meter	Metric meter (39.37 English inches).
Milligram	$\frac{1}{1000}$ gram; 0.01543 grain.
Millimeter	$\frac{1}{1000}$ meter; or 0.03937 English inch.
Morgen	Prussian land area measurement (0.63 English acre).
Pferdstärke	Metric horsepower of 75.00 kilogram meters per second (542.47 foot pounds per second) as compared to English horsepower of 76.04 kilogram-meters per second (550.00 foot-pounds per second).
Quintal	100 kilograms (220.46 English pounds).
Stab	1 meter.
Stere	1 cubic meter.
Strich	1 millimeter
Tonne	1,000 kilograms (2,204.62 English pounds).
Viertel	(Switzerland) 15 liters.
Zoll	Prussian inch ($\frac{1}{12}$ Fuss), 1.03 English inches; Switzerland, 1.181 inches. (May also be literal translation of English inch.)

ADDENDUM

abbaufähig, degradable; **bakteriel ~,** biodegradable; **biologisch ~,** biodegradable.

Abbau-produkt, *n.* catabolite; **-stoffwechsel,** *m.* catabolism.

Abbeizmittel, *n.* paint remover.

Abbildung, *f.* mapping; **latente ~,** latent image; **optische ~,** optical mapping.

Abbildungs-fehler, *m.* (optical) aberration; **-funktion,** *f.* mapping function; **-gleichung,** *f.* imaging equation; **-schärfe,** *f.* image definition; **-system,** *n.* imaging system.

Abblendung, *f.* stopping down.

Abbrand, *m.*⁻e, burn-up.

abbrechen, to truncate.

Abbrechfehler, *m.* truncation error.

Abbruch-linie, *f.* fault line, fault outcrop; **-reaktion,** *f.* termination reaction; **-zone,** *f.* fault zone.

Abdampfen der Trennflüssigkeit, bleeding, column bleeding.

Abdeckschablone, *f.* printing mask.

Abdruckverfahren, *n.* method of copying. impression method, replica method.

Abfall der Schallintensität, attenuation of sound; **~ des Stromes,** decay of current.

Abfall-beseitigung, *f.* waste disposal; **-erz,** *n.* tailings; **-verbrennungsofen,** *n.* incinerator; **-verwertung,** *f.* waste treatment; **-wirtschaft,** *f.* waste management; **-zeit,** *f.* release time, break time, decay time, fall time; **~ eines Impulses,** pulse decay time.

Abflachung, *f.* oblateness, flattening.

Abflussnetz, *n.* drainage pattern.

Abfrage-impuls, *m.* interrogation pulse; **-modus,** *m.* interrogation mode.

abfühlen, to sense, scan, trace.

Abfühl-impuls, *m.* read pulse, read-out pulse; **-stellung,** *f.* sensing position.

Abgabe, *f.* read-out.

abgehen, to be deducted.

abgeplatteter Kern, deformed nucleus.

abgeschirmt, screened.

Abgeschlagenheit, *f.* exhaustion, lassitude, fatigue.

abgeschlossene Schale, closed shell; **gegen Luft abgeschlossenes System,** airtight system; **in sich abgeschlossen,** self-contained.

Abgeschlossenheit, *f.* closure.

abgeschrägt, tapered.

Abgleich-indikator, *m.* null indicator, null detector; **-netzwerk,** *n.* balancing network.

Abgleitungsdecke, *f.* nappe.

Abgussmassen, *f.pl.* casting compounds, molding compounds.

abhängig, linear ~, linearly dependent.

abhängiger Betrieb, on-line operation.

abhören, to intercept, monitor, tap.

Abitur, *n.* graduation from high school.

Abkappschaltung, *f.* clipping circuit.

Abkippgeschwindigkeit, *f.* stalling speed.

Abkling-konstante, *f.* damping factor; **-kurve,** *f.* decay curve, decay characteristic; **-periode,** *f.* decay period; **-quote,** *f.* decay rate, rate of disappearance.

Ablage der Belege, document stacking.

Ablauf, *m.*⁻e, effluent: **-rohr,** *n.* downcomer (in distillation tower), down-pipe, downspout, waste pipe; **-walze,** *f.* delivery roll.

Ablaufs- und Planungsforschung, *f.* operations research.

Ablebensversicherung, *f.* straight life insurance.

Ableitung, *f.* dumping, lead (electrical).

Ableitungs-draht, *m.* shunt wire; **-sonde,** *f.* discharge probe; **-strom,** *m.* leakage current; **-widerstand,** *m.* leakage resistance.

Ablenkastigmatismus, *m.* deflection astigmatism.

Ablenker, *m.* deflector.

Ablenk-fehler, *m.* deflection aberration; **-feld,** *n.* deflector field; **-generator,** *m.* sweep generator, time-base generator; **-geschwindigkeit,** *f.* sweep velocity, time-base velocity; **-registrierung,** *f.* deflection registration.

Ablenkung, *f.* sweep; **~ mit Kappe,** capped deflection.

Ablenkungsvervielfacher, *m.* **optischer ~,** optical deflection multiplier.

Ablenkverzeichnung, *f.* deflection distortion.

Ablichtung, *f.* photocopy.

Ablösung von Elektronen, detachment of electrons.

Ablösungsfonds, *m.* sinking fund, redemption fund.

Abminderungsfaktor, *m.* diminution factor.

Abnutzungsprüfapparat, *m.* abrasion tester.

Abplattung, *f.* ellipticity, oblateness.

abplatzen, to peel.

Abquetschwalze, *f.* squeegee roll.

Abrechnungsstelle, *f.* clearing house.

Abregnungsbezirk, *m.* (atomic) fall-out region.

Abreiss-kontakt, *m.* arcing contact; **-zündung,***f.* make-and-break ignition.

Abrissbruch, *m.* fracture.

Abrollwalze, *f.* take-off roll.

Abschälblende, *f.* stripping aperture, stripping orifice.

Abschattierung von Banden, shading of bands, degradation of bands.

abschiessen, to launch.

Abschirm-dublett,*n.* screening doublet; **-faktor,** *m.* screening factor; **-kabel,** *n.* shielded cable; **-konstante,***f.* screening constant; **-korrektur,***f.* screening correction; **-zahl,***f.* screening number.

Abschlämmen, *n.* elutriation.

Abschlussbilanz, *f.* closing balance.

Abschmelzelektrode, *f.* consumable electrode.

Abschneide-frequenz, *f.* cutoff frequency; **-radius,** *m.* cutoff radius.

Abschnittkarte, *f.* stub card.

abschnüren, to pinch off.

Abschreibungssatz, *m.* depreciation allowance.

Abschwächung,*f.* attenuation, fading.

Absolut-fahrtmesser, *m.* true air speed indicator; **-filter,** *n.* constant bandwidth-type filter.

Absorptions-grad, *m.* absorption rate, absorptance; **-kante,***f.* absorption edge, absorption limit; **-koeffizient,** *m.* absorption coefficient; **-kontinuum,***n.* absorption band; **-kristallspektrum,** *n.* crystal absorption spectrum; **-querschnitt,** *m.* absorption cross section; **-röntgenspektrum,** *n.* X-ray absorption spectrum; **-spektroskopie,** *f.* absorption

spectroscopy; **-sprung,** *m.* absorption jump, absorption discontinuity; **-übergang,** *m.*-e, absorption transition.

Abspiel-fehler, *m.* playback loss; **-geräusch,** *n.* needle noise, surface noise.

Abstandsfaktor, *m.* spacing factor.

Abstäubung, *f.* sputtering.

absteigende Differenz, backward difference.

abstillen, to wean.

abstimmen, to collate.

Abstimm-filter, *n.* compensating filter; **-stab,** *m.* tuning wand.

Abstossungspotential, *n.* repulsion potential.

Abstreichmesser, *n.* doctor blade.

Abstreifmesser, *n.* doctor knife.

Abströmungsstrahl, *m.* slipstream.

absuchen, to scan, sweep.

abtasten, to scan, sample, sense, pick off, palpate.

Abtast-geschwindigkeit,*f.* scanning rate, scanning speed, spot speed; **-schlitz,** *m.* scanning slit; **-spannung,** *f.* sweep voltage, scanning voltage; **-verzerrung,***f.* tracking (error) distortion.

Abtönfarbe, *f.* tint, tinting color.

Abtragung, *f.* ablation.

Abtriebflüssigkeit, *f.* purging fluid.

abtupfen, to dab, swab, blot.

Abwasserlast, *f.* pollution load.

Abwehr-körper, *m.* antibody; **-stoff,** *m.* antitoxin, antibody.

Abweichung, *f.* **mittlere quadratische ~,** standard deviation; **~ vom Reziprozitätsgesetz,** reciprocity failure.

ab Werk, f. o. b.

Abwertung, *f.* devaluation, depreciation.

Abzählen, *n.* batching (of quantities).

Abzahlungssystem, *n.* installment plan.

abzugsfähig, deductible.

Abzugsschrank, *m.* fume hood.

Abzweig-dose, *f.* junction box; **-kasten,** *m.* junction box; **-schaltung,** *f.* ladder network.

Abzweigungsverhältnis, *n.* branching ratio.

Abzweigwiderstand, *m.* shunt resistance.

achten, darauf ~, to pay attention to.

Ackerkrume, *f.* topsoil.

Additionstheorem, *n.* addition theorem.

Additivität, *f.* additivity.

Aderpresse, *f.* tourniquet.

Adhäsionskultur, *f.* hanging-drop culture.

adjungiert, adjoint.

Adjunktion, *f.* adjunction.

Adsorptions-analyse, *f.* adsorption analysis; **-isotherme,** *f.* adsorption isotherm; **-platte,** *f.* adsorption plate; **-säule,** *f.* adsorption column; **-zentrum,** *n.* adsorption site, binding site.

Aelotropie, *f.* aeolotropy.

Aerosolsprühreagens, *n.* aerosol reagent.

Affinoren, *m.pl.* affinors.

affin zusammenhängend, affine-connected.

Agarschrägfläche, *f.* agar slant.

Agrarprodukt, *n.* agricultural product, farm product.

ähnliches, and the like, similar thing.

Ähnlichkeits-geometrie, *f.* geometry of (general) similarity; **-gesetz,** *n.* law of similarity; **-lehre,** *f.* homeopathy; **-regel,** *f.* similarity rule; **-satz,** *m.* similarity theorem.

Akten-notiz, *f.* memorandum; **-zeichen,** *n.* (patent) application number.

Aktiniden, *f.pl.* actinide elements; **-reihe,** *f.* actinide series.

Aktivierung durch Deuteronen, deuteron-induced activity.

Aktivierungs-analyse, *f.* activation analysis; **-detektor,** *m.* activation detector; **-enthalpie,** *f.* enthalpy of activation; **-entropie,** *f.* entropy of activation; **-wärme,** *f.* heat of activation.

Aktivkohle, *f.* activated charcoal.

aktuelle Verharzungsprodukte, *n.pl.* existent gum.

akustischer Zweig, acoustic (frequency) branch.

Akzeptionswert, *m.* acceptance value.

Akzeptor-niveau, *n.* acceptor level; **-störstelle,** *f.* acceptor impurity.

akzessorischer Parameter, irreducible constant (of a differential equation).

aleatorisch, random.

Alkaliatom, *n.* alkali atom.

Alkalihalogenid-kontinua, *n.pl.* continuous spectra of alkali halides; **-kristall,** *n.* alkalihalide crystal; **-schicht,** *f.* alkali-halide film.

Alkalimetallion, *n.* alkali-metal ion.

Alkohol-sucht, *f.* dipsomania; **-vergiftung-** *f.* alcoholism, alcohol poisoning.

Akrylfaser, *f.* acrylic fiber.

Alleinfutter, *n.* complete feed.

allerwenigst, least of all.

Allgemein-bestrahlung, *f.* whole-body irradiation; **-gebrauch,** *m.* routine use; **-infektion,** *f.* systemic infection.

Allgruppenspender, *m.* universal (blood) donor.

Allradantrieb, *m.* four-wheel drive.

Allrichtungs-mikrofon, *n.* omnidirectional microphone; **-schallquelle,** *f.* simple sound source; **-signal,** *n.* omnisignal.

alphanumerisch, alphanumeric.

Alpha-strahler, *m.* alpha emitter; **-teilcheneinfang,** *m.* alpha-particle capture; **-zerfall,** *m.* alpha decay.

ambulatorisch, ambulatory, outpatient.

Ammoniumdihydrophosphat, *n.* ammonium dihydrogen phosphate.

amorphe Unterlage, amorphous substratum.

Amphidromie, *f.* amphidromy; **-punkt,** *m.* amphidromic point.

amphoter, amphoteric.

Amplituden-analysator, *m.* kick-sorter- **-regelung,** *f.* gain control, amplitude regulation.

Analogdigitalwandler, *m.* analog-to-digital converter.

Analogiemaschine, *f.* analog computer.

Analogrechner, *m.* analog computer; **elektronischer ~,** electronic analog computer.

Analysensichter, *m.* analytical separator.

Anbaugerät, *n.* add-on unit, unitized equipment.

Anbinden vor dem Farben, tie dyeing.

anderen, zum ~, secondly.

anders gesagt, in other words.

Anderswertigkeit, *f.* being of different valence.

Andrück-rolle, *f.* tension roll; **-walze,** *f.* tension roll.

Aneinanderreihung, *f.* sequencing.

anelastisch, inelastic.

Anfachungsstadium, *n.* initial state.

Anfahrzeit, *f.* start-up time.

anfalls-artig, paroxysmal; **-kalender,** *f.* seizure chart.

Anfangs-bedingung, *f.* initial condition; **-durchschlag,** *m.* initial breakdown; **-fehler,** *m.* inherited error; **-kristallisation,** *f.* incipient crystallization; **-potential,** *n.* starting potential; **-stück,** *n.* initial part; **-vorspannung,** *f.* initial bias; **-wertaufgabe,** *f.* initial-value problem.

Anfärbung, *f.* staining.

Anfeuchter, *m.* humectant.

angeregt, excited.

angeschlossenes Gerät, on-line equipment, on-line unit.

Angewohnheit, *f.* habit, addiction.

Angewöhnung, *f.* habituation.

Anhaltpotential, *n.* stopping potential.

Anhänger, *m.* trailer.

anharmonisch, anharmonic.

Anharmonizität, *f.* anharmonicity.

Anharmonizitätskonstante, *f.* constant of anharmonicity.

anheimfallen, to be subject to.

Anionenaustauscher, *m.* anion exchanger; **-harz,** *n.* anion-exchange resin.

Ankristallisation, *f.* nucleation.

Anlage, *f.* design.

Anlagerungs-polymerisation, *f.* addition polymerization; **-term,** *m.* trapping level; **-wahrscheinlichkeit,** *f.* attachment probability.

anlaufend, incident, incoming.

Anlaufsrechnung, *f.* preliminary calculation.

anleiten, to introduce.

Anlockstoff, *m.* attractant.

anmutig, delightful.

Annahme-kurve, *f.* acceptance boundary, acceptance line; **-wahrscheinlichkeit,** *f.* acceptance probability.

Anoden-belastung, *f.* anode loading; **-dunkelraum,** *m.* anode dark space; **-gebiet,** *n.* anode region; **-glimmlicht,** *n.* anode glow; **-katodenverstärker,** *m.* anode-cathode follower; **-plasmatemperatur,** *f.* anode-plasma temperature.

anomalistisch, anomalistic.

Anpassung, *f.* matching operation, habituation; **-sfaktor,** *m.* fudge factor.

anpeilen, to take a bearing.

Anregungs-band, *n.* excitation band; **-bedingung,** *f.* excitation condition; **-energie,** *f.* excitation energy; **-fehler,** *m.* excitation defect; **-potential,** *n.* appearance potential; **-spannung,** *f.* exciting voltage; **-stärke,** *f.* work function; **-stoss,** *m.*-e, excitation collision; excitation shock; **-übertragung,** *f.* excitation transfer.

Ansatz, *m.* trial solution (math.); **in ~ bringen,** to take into account.

Anschluss-block, *m.* terminal block, connection block; **-gleis,** *n.* railway siding; **-schnur,** *f.* extension cord; **-stecker,** *m.* plug; **-stelle,** *f.* connection point; **-wert,** *m.* power requirement.

anschwellend, intumescent.

Ansprechzeit, *f.* response time; **~ eines Relais,** pick-up time.

ansteuern, to energize, drive, trigger.

Ansteuerung, *f.* drive, excitation, selection; **-skontrolle,** *f.* selection check.

Anstiegs-funktion, *f.* ramp function; **-zeit,** *f.* rise time.

Anströmgeschwindigkeit, *f.* slip velocity.

antarktisch, antarctic.

Anthropotechnik, *f.* human engineering.

Antiautomorphismus, *m.* antiautomorphism.

antibindend, antibonding.

Antidröhnmittel, *n.* sound absorbent.

Antiferro-elektrika, *n.pl.* antiferroelectrics; **-elektrisch,** antiferroelectric; **-elektrizität,** *f.* antiferroelectricity; **-magnetisch,** antiferromagnetic; **-magnetismus,** *m.* antiferromagnetism.

Antiflussspatgitter, *n.* antifluorite lattice.

Antikathodenleuchten, *n.* anticathode luminescence.

Antischleiermittel, *n.* antifogging agent.

Antiteilchen, *n.* antiparticle.

Antizentrum, *n.* anticenter.

Antriebs-drehzahl, *f.* driving speed; **-moment,** *n.* driving torque.

Anwachskurve, *f.* growth curve.

anwuchsverhindernder Anstrich, antifouling paint.

Anzeige, *f.* display, readout; **einzeilige ~,** in-line readout.

anzeigepflichtig, reportable, certifiable, notifiable.

Apertur-begrenzung, *f.* aperture limitation; **-blende,** *f.* aperture stop; **-winkel,** *m.* angular aperture.

Aplanate, *m.pl.* aplanatic systems.

Apparat, *m.* machine; **im ~ gefärbt,** package-dyed.

Approximation im Mittel, mean approximation.

äquianharmonisch, equianharmonic.

Äquidensitometrie, *f.* isodensitometry.

äquidistant, equidistant.

Äquivalenzverbot, *n.* exclusion principle.

Arbeiterin, *f.* female worker.

Arbeitsdrehbuch, *n.* scenario, shooting script.

Arbeitsgang eines Rechners, computer run.

Arbeits-gemeinschaft, *f.* task force; **-kosten,** *f.pl.* labor and machinery costs; **-kraftkosten,** *f.pl.* labor costs; **-planung,** *f.* operations scheduling; **-rückstand,** *m.* backlog; **-schicht,** *f.* shift; **-stellung,** *f.* on position, operating position; **-unfähigkeit,** *f.* disability.

Argonhochstrombogen, *m.* high-current argon arc.

armierter Beton, reinforced concrete.

Arsen-blüte, *f.* arsenite; **-gitter,** *n.* arsenic lattice (structure); **-trisulfid,** *n.* arsenic trisulfide.

Arzneimittelsucht, *f.* drug addiction.

asche-arm, low-ash, having a low ash content; **-frei,** ashless, ashfree.

Addendum   563

Aschen-boden, *m.* podsol; **-salz,** *n.* potash; **-schmelzpunkt,** *m.* ash-fusion temperature.

asphärisch, aspherical.

Astatisierung, *f.* astatization.

Asthenosphäre, *f.* asthenosphere.

Asymmetriefehler, *m.* (optical) coma.

Asymptoten-abbildung, *f.* asymptotic image; **-brennweite,** *f.* asymptotic focal length.

Asymptotik, *f.* asymptotic behavior.

Atem-frequenz, *f.* respiratory rate; **-kapazität,** *f.* breathing capacity.

Äthermitbewegung, *f.* ether drift.

Äthylendiamintartrat, *n.* ethylene diamine tartrate.

Äthylsulfat, *n.* ethyl sulfate.

Atomabstand, *m.* interatomic distance.

Atome auf Zwischengitterplätzen, interstitial atoms.

Atom-formfaktor, *m.* atomic scattering factor; **-gewichteinheit,** *f.* atomic-weight unit; **-hüllenniveau,** *n.* atomic level.

Atomionen-anteil, *m.* fraction of atomic ions; **-bildung,** *f.* production of atomic ions.

Atom-kraftwerk, *n.* atomic power plant, nuclear power plant; **-kugel,** *f.* atomic sphere; **-leitfähigkeit,** *f.* atomic conductivity; **-meiler,** *m.* nuclear pile or reactor; **-müll,** *n.* radioactive wastes; **-rakete,** *f.* nuclear rocket; **thermische ~,** thermonuclear rocket; **-rand,** *m.* atom surface; **-regen,** *m.* radioactive fall-out; **-strahl,** *m.* atomic beam; **-widerstand,** *m.* atomic resistance; **-zertrümmerung,** *f.* atom smashing, nuclear fission.

Attrappe, *f.* mock-up, dummy.

Ätz-bild, *n.* etch pattern; **-druck,** *m.* discharge printing; **-figur,** *f.* etch figure; **-punkt,** *m.* etch pit.

auch, wie dem ~ sei, however that may be.

Aue, *f.* flood plain.

Aufbau-mechanismus, *m.* metabolism; **-mittel,** *n.* restorative; **-stoff,** *m.* (detergent) builder; **-zeit,** *f.* time of formation, rise time, buildup time, breakdown time, ionization time.

Aufdampfschicht, *f.* evaporated film.

Auffang-anode, *f.* collector plate; **-diode,** *f.* catching diode; **-elektrode,** *f.* target or collecting electrode.

Auffinden, *n.* retrieval; **~ eines Information,** information retrieval.

Aufgabeboden, *m.* feed tray or plate (in distillation).

aufgedampft, evaporated, vapor-deposited.

aufgespalten, split, cloven, extended (dislocation).

Aufheizpastenkathode, *f.* self-heating oxide cathode.

Aufheller, *m.* brightener (textiles), brightening agent, whitening agent, fill-in light, booster light, klieg light; **optische ~,** optical brightener; **-schirm,** *m.* reflecting screen.

Aufhellungsdicke, *f.* clearing thickness.

Aufkocher, *m.* reboiler.

Auflagedruck, *m.* stylus force, tracking force.

Auflicht, *n.* vertical illumination, incident light; **~ Elektronenmikroskop,** direct-light electron microscope.

auflösbarer Abstand, resolving distance.

auflösungsbegrenzender Faktor, factor limiting resolution.

Aufmerksamkeitsreflex, *m.* psychomotor reflex.

Aufnahme-abstand, *m.* shooting distance; **-gerät,** *n.* recorder, record unit, tape recorder; **stereofonisches ~,** binaural recorder; **-kopf,** *m.* recording head; **-röhre,** *f.* camera tube, pickup tube.

aufnehmen, to record, consume, accept, acquire, accommodate, house.

aufpolymerisieren, to graft, graft polymerize.

aufschlussreich, informative.

Aufsetzen, *n.* touchdown (of an aircraft).

aufsteigende Differenz, forward difference.

Auftastimpuls, *m.* gating pulse.

auftauchen, to appear.

auftragen, to plot, coat, face, protract (in geometry), charge (a furnace), wear out (clothing).

Auftragwalze, *f.* applicator roll.

Auftriebs-verfahren, *n.* hydrostatic weighing method (to determine the density of a sample); **-wasser,** *n.* upwelling.

aufwalzen, to roller-coat.

Aufwind, *m.* updraft.

Aufzugshebel, *m.* shutter cocking lever.

Auge, im ~ haben, to have in mind; **ihm werden die Augen übergehen,** he will be surprised.

Augen-höhe, *f.* eye level; **-schärfe,** *f.* visual acuity.

Ausbeute, *f.* efficiency; **-matrix,** *f.* efficiency matrix; **-messung,** *f.* yield measurement; **-tensor,** *m.* efficiency tensor.

Ausdehnungs-messer, *m.* extensometer, dilatometer; **-verflüssiger,** *m.* expansion liquefier.

ausdrücken, to eject.

Ausfall-häufigkeit, *f.* failure rate; **-zeit,** *f.* down time.

Ausfaulgrube, *f.* septic tank.

ausflecken, to retouch, spot.

Ausführungsform, *f.* embodiment.

Ausgabe, *f.* output, readout; **-druck,** *m.* printout.

Ausgang, *m.* $\ddot{}$-e, output; **ausgeglichener** $\sim$, balanced output; **einseitiger** $\sim$, unidirectional output; **sinusförmiger** $\sim$, sine wave output.

Ausgangs-wert, *m.* baseline value; **-zustand,** *m.* parent or initial state.

ausgeglichene, $\sim$ **Bewegung,** smoothed motion; $\sim$ **Konstante,** adjusted constant; $\sim$ **und Störbewegung,** mean and eddy motion.

ausgelöst, liberated.

ausgeschlossene Werte, rejected values.

Ausgleichs-bad, *n.* compensating bath; **-rechnung,** *f.* calculation of most probable value(s); **-schicht,** *f.* equalizing layer; **-tiefe,** *f.* compensation depth.

Ausgleichswert, *m.* adjusted value; **Ausgleichswerte der kleinsten Quadrate,** adjusted values of least squares.

Ausguss, *m.* $\ddot{}$-e, talus.

Aushärtung, *f.* cure, curing.

Aushärtungs-mittel, *n.* curing agent, **-zustand,** *m.* degree of cure.

Ausheilen von Gitterfehlern, annealing of lattice imperfections.

ausklammern, to factor out.

Auskopierpapier, *n.* printing-out paper.

auslaufend, reflected, outgoing.

Ausläufer, *m.* tail.

Auslauf-feld, *n.* delivery zone; **-rahmen,** *m.* delivery frame.

Auslaugung, *f.* elution.

Auslegerbalkenbrücke, *f.* cantilever bridge.

Auslegeschrift, *f.* examined (German) patent application.

ausleuchten, to illuminate.

auslochen, to erase.

Auslöschung, *f.* quenching.

Auslöse-elektron, *m.* triggering electron; **-funktion,** *f.* trigger function; **-impuls,** *m.* stimulus.

Auslöser, *m.* shutter release.

Auslösezeit, *f.* time of liberation.

Auslösungsursache, *f.* triggering agency.

Ausnagung, *f.* erosion.

auspolstern, to pad.

ausprüfen, to debug, check out.

Ausrüstungsmaschinen, *f.pl.* textile finishing machinery.

Aussage, affine geometrische $\sim$, affine geometric sentence; **dualisierte** $\sim$, dual or reciprocal sentence.

Ausscheidungsmittel, *n.* diuretic.

Ausschlag, *m.* decision.

Ausschlämmen, *n.* elutriation.

Ausschliessungsprinzip, *n.* (Pauli) exclusion principle.

Ausschluss, *m.* rejection; **-chromatographie,** *f.* exclusion chromatography.

Ausschreibung, *f.* invitation to bid, request for a proposal.

Ausschwingen, *n.* decay, dying down, dying out.

Aussenstehender, *m.* outsider.

ausserhalb des Systems, off-line.

aussteuern, to modulate.

austarieren, to tare, calibrate.

Austasten, *n.* palpation.

Austastspannung, *f.* blackout voltage.

Austastung, *f.* pulse sampling, gating, blanking.

Austauschbeschränkung, *f.* exchange narrowing.

Austauscher, *m.* (ion) exchanger; **-wirkungsgrad,** *m.* exchanger efficiency.

Austausch-glocke, *f.* bubble cap; **-kraft,** *f.* exchange force; **-ladung,** *f.* exchange charge; **-mischkristall,** *m.* substitutional solid solution; **-term,** *m.* exchange term; **-vermögen,** *n.* exchange capacity; **-wechselwirkung,** *f.* exchange interaction.

Austritts-arbeit, *f.* work function; **-fenster,** *n.* exit window; **-geschwindigkeit,** *f.* escape velocity; **-öffnung,** *f.* orifice.

Auswahl, *f.* selection, sampling, alternative; **bewusste** $\sim$, controlled sampling; **zufällige** $\sim$, random sampling.

Ausweich-frequenz, *f.* alternative frequency; **-hafen,** *m.* emergency airport.

Auswerte-impuls, *m.* gating pulse.

auswerten, to evaluate.

auszahlen, to pay out, disburse.

auszählen, to count out, sort, tabulate.

Auszieh-hilfsmittel, *n.* exhausting agent; **-kopf,** *m.* extruder head; **-verfahren,** *n.* exhaust method (of dyeing).

Auszugsfilter, *n.* color separation filter.

autobarotrop, autobarotropic.

Autobarotropie, *f.* autobarotropy.

Autofriedhof, *m.* used car dump, auto junk yard.

Autoionisation, *f.* autoionization.

Autoradiographie, *f.* radioautography.

Axialstromturbine, *f.* axial-flow turbine.

azentrisch, acentric.

Backzeit, *f.* cure time, curing time.

Bäderbehandlung, *f.* balneotherapy, spa treatment.

Bahndrehimpuls, *m.* orbital angular momentum; **-operator,** *m.* orbital angular momentum operator; **-quadrat,** *n.* square of the orbital angular momentum.

Bahn-form, *f.* shape of orbit; **-höhe,** *f.* orbit height, orbit altitude; **-moment,** *m.* orbital moment; **-verfolgungsnetz,** *n.* space tracking network; **-zustand,** *m.* -e, orbital state.

Bake, *f.* beacon.

Balgenauszug, *m.* bellows extension.

Balken-biegung, *f.* deflection of a beam; **-darstellung,** *f.* bar graph, bar chart, histogram; **-diagramm,** *n.* bar chart, histogram.

Ballenpresse, *f.* baling machine.

Balligkeit, *f.* crown, convexity.

Ballung, *f.* package, packing, bundle, bunching; ~ **von Ausgangsimpulsen,** burst of output pulses; **überkritische** ~, overbunching; **unterkritische** ~, underbunching.

Band, gefülltes ~, filled band; **nicht besetztes** ~, unoccupied band; **verbotenes** ~, energy gap.

Band-ablage, *f.* tape file; **-abstand,** *m.* -e, energy gap; **-aufnahme,** *f.* tape recording.

Bandbreit, *f.* bandwidth, tapewidth.

Bandeinheit, *f.* tape deck.

Bänderung, *f.* banding, foliation, lamination, veining, ribboning.

Bänderungslinien, *f.pl.* lines of foliation.

Band-generator, *m.* van de Graaff generator; **-geschwindigkeit,** *f.* tape speed; **-schleifmaschine,** *f.* belt sander; **-spieler,** *m.* tape recording player; **-theorie,** *f.* band theory; **-vorschub,** *m.* tape feed; **-zuführung,** *f.* tape feed.

bankig, thickly bedded.

Barboteur, *m.* bubbler.

Bargeld, *n.* cash (in hand), ready money.

Barium-boratglas, *n.* barium borate glass, **-titanattyp,** *m.* barium titanate type.

baroklin, baroclinic.

Baroklinievektor, *m.* baroclinicity vector.

barotrop, barotropic.

Barotropie, *f.* barotropy.

baryzentrisch, barycentric.

Basal-stoffwechsel, *m.* basal metabolism; **-zelle,** *f.* basal cell, basilar cell.

Basis-ebene, *f.* datum plane; **-komma,** *n.* radix point; **-linie,** *f.* base line, reference line; **-vektor,** *m.* unit-cell vector, base vector; **-zentriert,** base-centered.

Bastelbuch, *n.* do-it-yourself manual, how-to-do-it book.

Bauch-endoskopie, *f.* laparotoscopy; **-raumeröffnung,** *f.* laparotomy.

Baueinheiten, *f.pl.* (computer) hardware.

Bau-element, *n.* component, module, unit, package; **-elemente,** *n.pl.* (computer) hardware; **-gruppe,** *f.* subassembly; ~ **für digitale Technik,** digital module; **-kastenkonstruktion,** *f.* unit, unitized, modular, or building-block construction; **-modell,** *n.* mockup.

bauschiges Garn, bulked yarn, textured yarn.

Bauschung, *f.* bulking.

Bau-stein, *m.* unit (in chemistry); **-teile,** *n.pl.* (computer) hardware.

Beatmung, *f.* artificial respiration.

Beatmungsgerät, *n.* respirator.

Bedeckungsgrad, *m.* degree of coverage.

Bedienungs-element, *n.* control element, operating control, control; **-fehler,** *m.* operating error; **-pult,** *n.* control panel; **-sicher,** fool-proof.

Befehl, *m.* -e, instruction, order.

Befehls-feld, *n.* instruction array; **-folge,** *f.* control sequence.

Beflocken, *n.* flocking, coating with flock.

begebbar, negotiable.

Begleitmineralien, *m.pl.* accessory minerals.

begriffen, in Bewegung ~, in motion.

Beharrungs-kraft, *f.* inertia; **-zustand,** *m.* state of inertia.

behelfsmässig, improvised, temporary, emergency.

Behinderung, *f.* handicap, obstruction; **körperliche** ~, physical disability.

Beifutter, *n.* supplement, supplementary feed.

Beigeschmack, *m.* foxy flavor, foxy taste (of wine).

Beilfüsser, *m.pl.* pelecypods, *Pelecypoda.*

bekanntgeben, to announce.

Belastung, *f.* stress.

Belebungsanlage, *f.* activated sludge plant.

Beleg, *m.* document.

Beleuchtungsstärke, *f.* illuminance, illumination, brightness.

Belieben, je nach ~, as you like, according to taste.

bemängeln, to quibble.

Bemessung, *f.* rating, sizing, proportioning, design.

Benetzungsmittel, *n.* wetting agent.

Beobachtungs-abstand, *m.* viewing distance; **-daten,** *n.pl.* observational data; **-gleichung,** *f.* equation of observation; **-korrelation,** *f.* observational correlation; **-schirm,** *m.* viewing screen, **-unabhängigkeit,** *f.* observational independence.

Berechnung, *f.* costing; ~ **von Trennstufe zu Trennstufe,** tray-to-tray calculation.

Berechtigung, *f.* justification.

bereinigter Fehler, adjusted error.

Bereitschafts-arbeitsweise, *f.* standby mode; **-kernspeicher,** *m.* immediate access core store.

Berg-fläche, *f.* peak area; **-höhe,** *f.* peak height; **-rutsch,** *m.* rock slide, landslide; **-zug,** *m.* mountain range.

Berstscheibe, *f.* rupture disk.

Berufs-hygiene, *f.* occupational hygiene; **-krankheit,** *f.* occupational disease; **-verhalten,** *n.* professional conduct.

beruhigter Stahl, killed steel.

Beruhigungsmittel, *n.* tranquilizer.

Berührungs-transformation, *f.* contact transformation; **-zwilling,** *m.* contact twin, juxtaposition twin.

Beschäftigungs-behandlung, *f.* occupational therapy; **-schaden,** *m.* occupational injury.

bescheiden, sich mit etwas ~, to rest content with.

beschichten, to coat.

Beschleunigungsanlage, *f.* accelerator; ~ **für hohe Energien,** high-energy (particle) accelerator.

Beschleunigungskriechen, *n.* accelerated creep.

beschränkte Variable, bounded variable.

Beschränkung, *f.* constraint.

Beschreibung, *f.* (patent) specification, disclosure.

beschriften, to mark.

Beschussteilchen, *n.* bombarding particle.

Beschwerdebild, *n.* clinical symptoms.

Besetztton, *m.* busy signal.

Besetzungsverbot, *n.* exclusion principle; ~ **der vollbesetzten Quantenzustände,** exclusion principle of occupied electron states.

Besetzungs-vorschrift, *f.* occupation rule; **-zahl,** *f.* occupation (phonon) number, population.

Bestands-daten, *n.pl.* inventory data; **-karte,** *f.* balance card, bin card; **-überwachung,** *f.* stock control.

Bestrahlungs-erholung, *f.* radiation annealing; **-krankheit,** *f.* radiation sickness; **-rate,** *f.* (radiation) dosage; **-schaden,** *m.* radiation damage; **-stärke,** *f.* irradiance.

Bestückung, *f.* ~ **mit,** use of; ~ **mit instrumenten,** instrumentation; ~ **mit Transistoren,** transistorization.

Betatronstrahlung, *f.* betatron radiation.

Betazerfall, *m.* beta decay.

betören, to delude.

Betracht, in ~ **ziehen,** to take into consideration.

betreffen, to attack, strike.

Betrieb, *m.* establishment.

Betriebs-lehre, *f.* farm management; **-mittel,** *n.* working capital; **-unterbrechung,** *f.* downtime, shutdown, interruption of operation; **-wasser,** *n.* process water.

betroffen, struck, concerned.

Bett-flasche, *f.* hot water bottle; **-lägerig,** bedridden, confined to bed; **-ruhe,** *f.* bed rest.

beuchen, to kier boil.

Beuch-fass, *n.* kier; **-flotte,** *f.* kiering liquor.

Beugungs-diagramm, *n.* diffraction pattern; **-reflex,** *m.* diffraction spot; **-saum,** *m.'*-e, diffraction fringe; **-stripping,** *f.* diffraction stripping; **-tensor,** *m.* deflection tensor.

beulen, to buckle.

beweglichkeits-geregelt, mobility-controlled; **-gleichung,** *f.* mobility equation; **-tensor,** *m.* mobility tensor.

Bewegung, wirbelfreie ~, potential motion, streamline motion.

Bewegungen, ungeordnete ~, random walk.

Bewegungs-drang, *m.* hyperkinesis, hyperactivity; **-energie,** *f.* kinetic energy; **-funktion,** *f.* locomotor function; **-gruppe,** *f.* translation group.

Bewertungsfunktion, *f.* weighting function.

Bewitterungsdauer, *f.* exposure time.

bezogene Dichte, *f.* specific gravity, relative density.

Bezug, in ~ **auf,** referring to, with reference to.

Bezugs-linie, *f.* reference line, base line; **-punkt,** *m.* reference point, datum; **-system,** *n.* frame of reference; **-zeitraum,** *m.* base period.

Biege-schwingung, -welle, *f.* flexural wave.

Biegungsschwingung, *f.* flexure mode.

bieten, sich nichts ~ **lassen,** not to put up with.

Bild-empfang, *m.* facsimile reception; **-fehler,** *m.* image aberration, distortion.

Bildfeld-grösse, *f.* width of field; **-winkel,** *m.* lens angle, angle of aperture; **-wölbung,** *f.* curvature of field.

Bild-format, *n.* picture size, image size; **-mässig,** imagewise.

Bildpunkt, *m.* picture element; **hellster** ~, highlight.

Bild-röhre, *f.* picture tube, camera tube; **-schirm,** *m.* screen, viewing screen; **-sender,** *m.* video transmitter, facsimile transmitter; **-sucher,** *m.* view finder; **-suchfunktion,** *f.* image-seeking function.

Bildungs-dauer, *f.* formative time; **-energie,** *f.* energy of generation.

Bild-verstärker, *m.* video amplifier, image intensifier; **-wand,** *f.* motion picture screen, projection screen.

Bilinear-form, *f.* bilinear form; **-skalar,** bilinear scalar.

Bimetallaktinometer, *m.* bimetal actinometer.

Bindigkeit, *f.* covalence.

Bindungs-eigenschaft, *f.* bond property; **-energie,** *f.* `cohesive energy, binding energy; **-wertigkeit,** *f.* covalence.

Biometrie, *f.* biometrics.

Bipotentialgleichung, *f.* bipotential equation.

Biprismaversuch, *m.* biprism method.

Bivektor, *m.* bivector.

Bläschenkammer, *f.* bubble chamber.

Blasen-destillation, *f.* distillation in pot stills; **-säule,** *f.* bubble-tray column.

Blasenstahl, *m.* blister steel.

Blas-folie, *f.* blown film; **-form,** *f.* blow mold.

Blättchen, *n.* thin layer.

blaugrün, cyan.

Blauspiegel, *m.* blue-light mirror.

Blei-boratglas, *n.* lead borate glass; **-datierungsmethode,** *f.* lead dating method; **-halogenid,** *n.* lead halide; **-silikatglas,** *n.*-er, lead silicate glass; **-strahlenschutzschicht,** *f.* lead shielding; **-sulfidtyphalbleiter,** *m.* lead sulfide semiconductor.

Blenden-ausschnitt, *m.* shutter opening; **-einstellung,** *f.* stop setting; **-paar,** *n.* pair of diaphragms; **-system,** *n.* collimation system; **-wert,** *m.* f-stop, stop; **-zahl,** *f.* stop number, f-number.

Blind-anteil, *m.* reactive component; **-belastung,** *f.* reactive load.

Blindelement, *n.*-e, dummy (fuel) element.

Blinden-hund, *m.* seeing-eye dog; **-schrift,** *f.* Braille.

Blindflug, *m.* automatic instrument flying, blind flying.

Blitz-beleuchtung, *f.* flash illumination; **-kopiergerät,** *n.* photocopier; **-lampe,** *f.* flash bulb; **-leuchte,** *f.* flash gun; **-photolyse,** *f.* flash photolysis; **-röhre,** *f.* electronic flash; **-schlag,** *m.* bolt of lightning; **-schutz,** *m.* lightning protection.

blockierend, blocking.

Block-länge, *f.* block size; **-polymerisation,** *f.* bulk polymerization; **-relaxation,** *f.* block relaxation; **-schachtelung,** *f.* block nesting.

Blödigkeit, *f.* imbecility, stupidity.

Blut-bahn, *f.* blood stream, circulation; **-befund,** *m.* hematological findings, blood picture; **-bild,** *n.* blood picture; **-gruppenabstimmung,** *f.* blood matching; **-gruppenbestimmung,** *f.* blood typing.

Blutsenkungs-apparat, *m.* sedimentometer; **-geschwindigkeit,** *f.* blood sedimentation rate, erythrocyte sedimentation rate; **-rörchen,** *n.* blood sedimentation tube.

Blutserum, *n.* blood serum; **-kultur,** *f.* seroculture.

Blut-spenden, *n.* blood donation; **-spiegel,** *m.* blood level; **-strömung,** *f.* flow of blood, circulation; **-titer,** *m.* agglutination titer; **-transfusion,** *f.* blood transfusion; **langsame ~,** drip transfusion; **-versorgung,** *f.* blood supply; **-weg,** *m.* blood system, circulation, blood stream; **-wert,** *m.* blood count; **-zelle,** *f.* hemocyte, hematocyte, blood cell.

Boden-bewegung, *f.* ground movement; **-decke,** *f.* blanket of soil, regolith, mantle; **-eis,** *m.* anchor ice, bottom ice, fossil ice; **-höhe,** *f.* plate height; **-reibung,** *f.* bottom friction; **-rollen,** *n.* ground roll; **-vorbereitung,** *f.* soil conditioning; **-wind,** *m.* surface wind.

Bogen-bildung, *f.* arcing; **-diagramm,** *n.* arc plot; **-entladung,** *f.* arc discharge; **-entladungskontinuum,** *n.* arc-discharge continuum; **-länge,** *f.* arc length; **-mass,** *n.* radian measure; **-plasma,** *n.* high-temperature plasma; **-säule,** *f.* arc column; **-spektrum,** *f.* arc spectrum; **-zündung,** *f.* arc ignition.

Bohrloch-schiessen, *n.* borehole shooting, well shooting; **-untersuchung,** *f.* borehole logging.

Bohr-profil, *n.* well log; **-schablone,** *f.* jig.

Bolometerstrahlungsmessung, *f.* bolometer detection.

Bombage, *f.* crown, swell.

Bombierung, *f.* cambering (of a tire), crown, camber.

Bonität, *f.* credit, solvency.

Bortrifluoridzähler, *m.* boron trifluoride counter.

Bortrimethylzähler, *m.* boron trimethyl counter.

Boten-RNS, *f.* messenger RNA, m-RNA.

Brachystochrone, *f.* brachistochrone.

Brandausbreitungsgeschwindigkeit, *f.* flame spread, burning rate.

Brandungsschwebung, *f.* surf beat.

Brechertyp, *m.* breaker type.

Brechungsanteil des Potentials, refractive potential.

Brechungsindexrealteil, *m.* real part of the refractive index.

Brechungsmesser, *m.* refractometer.

Brechzahlmesser nach Abbe, Abbe refractometer.

Breite in der Ekliptik, latitude in ecliptic.

Bremse, *f.* moderator.

Brems-feldröhre, *f.* retarding field tube; **-gitter,** *n.* suppressor grid; **-länge,** *f.* slowing-down length; **-leistung,** *f.* brake horsepower; **-potential,** *n.* retarding potential; **-prozess,** *m.* slowing-down process; **-querschnitt,** *m.* stopping cross section; **-rakete,** *f.* retro-rocket; **-substanz,** *f.* moderator; **-vermögen,** *f.* stopping power.

Bremsung, *f.* braking, retardation, deceleration; **~ von Neutronen,** moderation of neutrons.

Brennbarkeits-probe, *f.* flammability test, burning test; **-verzögerer,** *m.* fire retardant.

Brennfleck-ausdehnung, *f.* disk of confusion (radius); **-charakteristik,** *f.* focal-spot characteristic.

Brennkraftmaschine, *f.* internal combustion engine.

Brennkreis, *m.* caustic circle.

Brennlackierung, *f.* baked-enamel finish.

Brennpunktsabstand, *m.* focal distance.

Brennstoff-kreislauf, *m.* fuel cycle; **-zelle,** *f.* fuel cell.

Brettschaltung, *f.* breadboard circuit.

Briede, *f.* adhesion (in medicine).

Brinell-härte, *f.* Brinell hardness; **-kugel,** *f.* ball penetrator (Brinell).

bringen, mit sich ~, to bring with it; **soweit ~,** to get so far as.

Brombenzol, *n.* bromobenzene.

Brownsche Bewegung, *f.* Brownian motion.

Bruch, *m.* fraction; **-ablenkung,** *f.* fractured deflection; **-fläche,** *f.* fault plane, fracture surface; **-landung,** *f.* crash landing; **-linie,** *f.* fault line.

Brückenmethode, *f.* bridge method.

Brumm, *m.* hum, ripple; **-abstand,** *m.* signal-to-hum ratio; **-faktor,** *m.* ripple ratio, ripple factor.

Brutreaktor, *m.* breeder reactor; **schneller ~,** fast breeder.

Bruttosozialprodukt, *n.* gross national product.

bügelfrei, no-iron; **bügelfreie Ausrüstung,** *f.* wash and wear finish, drip-dry finish.

Bundel, *n.* beam; **-erzeugungssystem,** *n.* beam-producing system; **-ung,** *f.* collimation, bunching, focusing.

Bündelverbreiterung (durch Eigenladung), *f.* (space-charge) beam spreading.

Buntsandstein, *m.* Bunter sandstone, Lower Triassic (period).

Bunt-heit, *f.* chrominance; **-metall,** *n.* nonferrous metal.

Bürsten-auftrag, *m.* brush coating; **-druck,** *m.* brush printing.

Büschel, *m.* hand (of tobacco), pencil (of rays).

Bussole, *f.* compass.

Büttenleimung, *f.* tub-sizing.

Cadmium-arsenid, *n.* cadmium arsenide; **-selenid,** *n.* cadmium selenide.

Calciumfluorid, *n.* calcium difluoride.

Cäsiumchlorid, *n.* cesium chloride; **-gitter,** *n.* cesium chloride lattice (structure).

Cäsiumlichtbogen, *m.* cesium arc.

Charakteristik, *f.* characteristic (curve); **quadratische ~,** square-law characteristic.

Charakteristikenverfahren, *n.* characteristics method.

charakteristische Daten, characteristics.

Chelatharz, *n.* chelating resin.

Chelierung, *f.* chelation.

Chemiefaser, *f.* man-made fiber, synthetic fiber.

Chemiolumineszenzkontinuum, *n.* chemiluminescence continuum.

chemische Bindung, chemical bond.

Chlorgehalt, *m.* chlorinity, chlorine content.

Chromalaun, *n.* chrome alum; **eingebettetes ~,** diluted chromium alum.

Chromatographie, *f.* chromatography; **absteigende ~,** descending chromatography; **aufsteigende ~,** ascending chromatography; **zweidimensionale ~,** bidirectional chromatography.

Chromosphäre, *f.* chromosphere.

COBOL-Sprache, *f.* COBOL, common business-oriented language.

Code, *m.* code; **korrigierbarer ~,** error-correcting code, self-correcting code; **prüfbarer ~,** error-detecting code, self-checking code.

Codeumsetzer, *m.* code converter.

codieren, to code, encode.

Conradsonzahl, *f.* Conradson carbon residue.

Corioliskraft, *f.* Coriolis force.

Coronaentladung, *f.* corona discharge.

Coroniumlinie, *f.* coronium line.

Cristobalitgitter, *n.* cristobalite lattice.

cumulusartig, cumuliform.

Dach-kantprisma, *n.* ridge prism, penta prism; **-rinne,** *f.* gutter; **-winkel,** *m.* roof angle.

daherrühren, to originate, come from.

dahin-leben, to vegetate; **-siechen,** to waste away.

Dammriff, *n.* barrier reef.

Dämm-wert *m.* sound damping factor; **-zahl,** *f.* sound damping factor.

dämpfen, to attenuate.

Dämpferspule, *f.* damping coil.

Dampf-hals, *m.* riser; **-kamin,** *m.* riser.

Dampfkompressions-kältemaschine, *f.* compressed-vapor refrigerator; **-system,** *n.* compressed-vapor system.

Dampf-maschine, *f.* steam engine; **-phasenchromatographie,** *f.* vapor phase chromatography; **-quelle,** *f.* steam vent, fumarole.

Dämpfungs-ausgleich, *m.* attenuation equalization; **-eigenschaft,** *f.* damping characteristic; **-mittel,** *n.* sedative, **-widerstand,** *m.* loss resistance; **-zylinder,** *m.* dashpot.

darangehen, to set to work.

daraufhin, to this end; **-arbeiten,** to work away at it.

Darm-einlauf, *m.* enema; **-lehre,** *f.* enterology; **-spiegel,** *m.* proctoscope.

darstellen, to represent, present, display.

darstellende Geometrie, descriptive geometry.

Darstellungs-raum, *m.* space of representation; **-theorie,** *f.* representation theory.

Datei, *f.* file.

Daten-gruppe, *f.* string; **-kanal,** *m.* data line, data channel; **-reduktion,** *f.* data reduction; **-speicherung,** *f.* data storage; **-verarbeitung,** *f.* data processing; **-verdichtung,** *f.* data reduction.

Datumsgrenze, *f.* date line.

Dauer des Anwachsens, time of growth.

Dauer-betrieb, *m.* continuous operation; **-dosis,** *f.* maintenance dose; **-entladung,** *f.* steady discharge; **-festigkeit,** *f.* endurance limit; **-koronadurchbruch,** *m.* steady corona; **-tropfinfusion,** continuous intravenous drip, slow drip infusion.

Daumenlutscher, *m.* thumb sucker.

Deckenbeleuchtung, *f.* top lighting.

Deck-falte, *f.* fold carpet, thrust fold, recumbent fold; **-gestein,** *n.* cap rock; **-kraft,** *f.* covering power; **-operation,** *f.* symmetry operation (of the lattice); **-vermögen,** *n.* covering power.

Defekt-elektron, *m.* hole (in electron valence band); **-halbleiter,** *m.* p-type semiconductor, hole conductor.

Definitionsbereich, *m.* domain of definition.

defokussiert, out-of-focus.

Deformations-schwingung, *f.* bending vibration, deformation vibration; **-verteilung,** *f.* strain distribution.

Deformierbarkeit, *f.* deformability (of nuclei).

Deformierung, *f.* deformation.

Dehnungs-bereich, *m.* zooming range; **-gesetz,** *n.* Hooke's law; **-grenze,** *f.* (apparent) yield point, yield strength, elastic limit, elongation limit, proof stress, offset yield stress; **-messer,** *m.* strain gage; **-messstreifen,** *m.* wire strain gage, resistance strain gage; **-modul,** *m.* modulus of elasticity (in tension); **-spannung,** *f.* tensile strain; **-welle,** *f.* dilatational wave; **-zahl,** *f.* reciprocal of the modulus of elasticity, strain coefficient.

Deklinationstiden, *f.pl.* declination tides.

Deltafunktion, *f.* delta function.

dem, wenn ~ so ist, if that be true; **~ ist so,** that is true.

Demagnetisierungsfaktor, *m.* demagnetizing factor.

Depot-fett, *n.* depot fat; **-Präparat,** *n.* sustained-release preparation; **-wirkung,** *f.* depot effect.

desensibilisierende Farbe, desensitizing dye.

Destillationsrückstände, *m.pl.* bottoms.

determinierende Gleichung, indicial equation.

Deuteronenbildung, *f.* deuteron formation.

Deuteronphotoeffekt, *m.* deuteron photodisintegration.

Devisenkurs, *m.* rate of foreign exchange.

Dezil, *n.* decile.

Dezimaldarstellung, *f.* decimal notation.

Dezimalzahl, *f.* decimal number; **dual dargestellte ~ ,** binary ordered decimal number.

Dia, *n.* slide, transparency, diapositive; **-betrachter,** *m.* slide viewer; **-bildwerfer,** *m.* slide projector; **-gerät,** *n.* slide projector; **-glasplatte,** *f.* slide glass, cover glass.

Diagonalisieren, *n.* diagonalization, diagonalizing.

Diamantgitter, *n.* diamond lattice (structure).

Diastrophismus, *m.* diastrophism.

Diät, *f.* diet, regimen; **ausgeglichene ~ ,** balanced diet; **eiweissarme ~ ,** low-protein diet; **eiweissreiche ~ ,** high-protein diet.

Diawechselschieber, *m.* slide changer.

Dichte-abfall, *m.* decrease or slope of the density; **-anisotropie,** *f.* density anisotropy; **-funktion,** *f.* density function; **-gepackt,** close-packed; **-zahl,** *f.* specific gravity.

Dickengradient, *m.* thickness gradient.

dickleibig, corpulent, stout, obese.

Diederklassen, *f.pl.* dihedral classes.

dienen, to be of use, be used.

Dienst-alter, *n.* seniority, years of service; **-frei,** off-duty; **-habend,** on-duty.

Differentialfilter, *m.pl.* balanced filters.

Differenzenschema, *n.* array of differences.

Differenz-methode, *f.* paired sample t-test; **-rechnung,** *f.* calculus of differences; **-tonbildung,** *f.* intermodulation.

Diffusions-kreis, *m.* circle of confusion; **-sprung,** *m.* diffusional jog; **-tensor,** *m.* diffusion tensor; **-weg,** *m.* diffusion path.

Digital-ablesung, *f.* digital read-out; **-analogwandler,** *m.* digital-to-analog converter; **-anzeige,** *f.* digital display, digital read-out.

Digitalisierungsrate, *f.* digitizing rate.

Digitalrechner, *m.* digital computer.

Digyre, *f.* diad axis, two-fold axis of symmetry.

Digyroide, *f.* diad axis of the second sort.

Diode, *f.* diode; **heisse ~** thermionic diode.

Dipoldipol-verbreiterung, *f.* dipole-dipole broadening; **-wechselwirkung,** *f.* dipole-dipole interaction.

Dipol-näherung, *f.* dipole approximation; **-zeile,** *f.* linear array.

direktgekoppelt, on-line.

Diskont-satz, *m.* discount rate, bank rate; **-wert,** *m.* discounted value.

Diskrepanz, *f.* discrepancy.

Diskriminante, *f.* discriminant.

Diskriminatorfenster, *n.* analyzer window.

Dispersions-farbe, *f.* emulsion paint; **-terme,** *m.pl.* dispersion terms.

dissoziativ, dissociative.

Dissymmetrie, *f.* dissymmetry.

Distributivgesetz, *n.* distributive law.

Divergenztechnik, *f.* divergent-beam technique.

Donatoren-niveau, *n.* donor level; **-wanderung,** *f.* donor migration.

Dopen, *n.* doping.

Doppel-aufnahme, *f.* double exposure; **-bifilargravimeter,** *m.* double-bifilar gravimeter; **-bildsehen,** *n.* diplopia, double vision; **-blendenmethode,** *f.* double-slit method; **-integral,** *n.* double integral; **-kristall,** *m.* bicrystal.

Doppel-leerstelle, *f.* double vacancy, double void, vacancy pair; **-prinzipal,** *m.* double diapason; **-prisma,** *n.* biprism; **-randschicht,** *f.* double barrier layer; **-röntgenblitzrohre,** *f.* double X-ray flash tube; **-scheibenspule,** *f.* pancake coil; **-schicht,** *f.* double layer; **-sehen,** *n.* diplopia, double vision; **-spitzenwert,** *m.* peak-to-peak;

-streuversuch, *m.* double-scattering experiment; **-verhältnis,** *n.* cross ratio; **-zugriff,** *m.* dual access.

Dosen-höhe, *f.* dose level; **-stärke,** *f.* dose rate.

Dosiertank, *m.* metering tank.

Dosisleistung, *f.* dose rate.

Dosis-Wirkungskurve, *f.* dose-response curve.

Dotierung, *f.* doping; **~ mit Eigendonatoren,** native-donor doping; **~ mit Fremddonatoren,** foreign-donor doping.

Dotierungs-atom, *n.* doping (dopant) atom; **-ion,** *n.* doping (dopant) ion; **-mittel,** *n.* doping agent, dopant.

Douben, *n.* dubbing.

Draht-heftmaschine, *f.* stapler; **-potentiometer,** *n.* wire-wound potentiometer; **-wendelleiter,** *m.* helical conductor.

drakonitisch, draconitic.

Drall, *m.* spin; **-geber,** *m.* twister, twisting device; **-stabilisiert,** spin-stabilized.

Dreh-bandkolonne, *f.* spinning band column; **-feder,** *f.* torsion spring; **-fläche,** *f.* surface of revolution; **-geschwindigkeit,** *f.* angular velocity of rotation; **-impedanz,** *f.* cyclic impedance.

Drehimpuls, *m.* angular momentum; **-matrixelement,** *n.* angular-momentum matrix element; **-operator,** *m.* angular-momentum operator; **-quantenzahl,** *f.* azimuthal quantum number.

Dreh-inversionsachse, *f.* rotary inversion axis; **-körper,** *m.* solid of revolution; **-kristallmethode,** *f.* rotating crystal method; **-melder,** *m.* selsyn, synchro, synchro drive; **-momentverstärker,** *m.* torque amplifier; **-reaktanz,** *f.* cyclic reactance; **-regler,** *m.* variable control; **-schwingung,** *f.* torsional mode; **-spiegelachse,** *f.* rotary alternating axis; **-symmetrie,** *f.* rotational symmetry; **-transformator,** *m.* adjustable transformer, converter, induction regulator.

Drehungskoma, *m.* rotation coma.

Drehungstendenz, *f.* twist liveliness; **Garne ohne ~,** yarns without twist liveliness, nontorque yarns.

Drehungsverzeichnung, *f.* rotational distortion.

Drehzahlgeber, *m.* tachometer.

Dreibein, *n.* trihedral; **begleitendes ~,** moving trihedral.

Dreieck-modulationssystem, *n.* delta modulation system; **-schaltung,** *f.* delta circuit, delta connection.

Dreierstoss, *m.* ¨-e, three-body collision.

Drei-körperkräfte, *f.pl.* three-body forces; **-ladungsträgermodell,** *n.* three-carrier model.

dreiparametrige Wellenfunktion, three-parameter wave function.

Addendum

Dreiphononen-prozess, *m.* three-phonon process; **-wechselwirkung,** *f.* three-phonon interaction.

Dreistrahlproblem, *n.* three-beam problem.

dreiteilen, to trisect.

Drift-geschwindigkeit, *f.* drift velocity; **-kraft,** *f.* drifting force.

Drill, *m.* torsion, twist.

Drillingskristall, *m.* triplet crystal.

Drillschwingung, *f.* twisting vibration.

Drillung, *f.* permanent angle of twist.

Drillungskristall, *m.* twister crystal.

Dringlichkeitssignal, *n.* priority signal.

dritteltägig, terdiurnal, three times daily; **dritteltägige Welle,** eight-hourly wave.

Drossel-kette, *f.* low-pass filter; **-stelle,** *f.* constriction.

Druck-abfall, *m.* pressure drop; **-bild,** *n.* printing format; **-dichtebeziehung,** *f.* pressure-density relation; **-kammer,** *f.* pressure chamber; **-koeffizient,** *m.* pressure coefficient; **-schablone,** *f.* printing screen.

Druck-schwingung, *f.* compressional vibration; **-sieb,** *n.* screen stencil; **-spaltung,** *f.* compressive cleaving; **-taste,** *f.* push button; **-wasserreaktor,** *m.* pressurized water reactor; **-welle,** *f.* shock wave; **-zwillingsbildung,** *f.* compressive twin formation.

Drudenfuss, *m.* pentagram.

Drüsen-balg, *m.* follicle; **-erkrankung,** *f.* adenopathy; **-unterfunktion,** *f.* glandular insufficiency.

Dualzahl, *f.* binary number.

Dublettabstand, *m.-e,* doublet spacing.

Dungertablette, *f.* prilled fertilizer.

Dunkel-entladung, *f.* dark discharge; **-feldbeleuchtung,** *f.* dark-field illumination; **-feldüberprüfung,** *f.* dark-field examination.

dünne Folie, thin film; **dünne Metallschicht,** thin metal layer or film.

Dünn-filmkapillarsäule, *f.* coated open tubular column; **-schichtchromatographie,** *f.* thin layer chromatography.

Dünnschnitt, *m.* thin section; **-verfahren,** *n.* microtomy.

Dunst-atmosphäre, *f.* haze atmosphere; **-glocke,** *f.* haze canopy, smoggy bowl.

durchatmen, to breathe deeply.

Durchblutung, *f.* blood circulation, supply of blood to.

Durchbruch-chromatogramm, *n.* breakthrough chromatogram; **-feldstärke,** *f.* breakdown field; **-spannung,** *f.* breakdown voltage.

Durch-dringungszwilling, *m.* penetrating twin; **-führungselektrode,** *f.* lead-through electrode; **-führungsfeld,** *n.* feed-through panel; **-gelassenes Licht,** transmitted light; **-griff,** *m.* transconductance, penetration factor; **-haltevermögen,** *n.* persistence.

Durch-lassgrad, *m.* transmittance; **-lässigkeit,** *f.* transmission coefficient; **-lassspannung,** *f.* forward voltage; **-lassstrom,** *m.* forward current; **-laufchromatographie,** *f.* continuous flow chromatography, elution analysis, elution chromatography; **-licht,** *n.* transmitted light; **-sacken,** *n.* sagging; **-schlag,** *m.* breakdown.

durchschlagen, sich ~, to get along, get by.

Durchschlagfeldstärke, *f.* dielectric strength.

Durchschlags-bedingung, *f.* (dielectric) breakdown condition; **-kanal,** *m.* breakdown filament; **-strom,** *m.* spark current.

Durchschneidungssprung, *m.* intersection jog.

Durchschnitt zweier Mengen, section of two sets.

Durchsenkung, *f.* vertical deflection.

Durchstrahlungsspektrograph, *m.* transmission spectrograph.

durchtunneln, to tunnel.

duroplastisch, thermosetting.

eben, flat.

Ebenenpaar, *n.* pair of planes.

Echo-anzeige, *f.* blip; **-dämpfung,** *f.* return loss; **-entstörung,** *f.* echo suppression; **-impuls,** *m.* echo pulse, blip; **-technik,** *f.* sonar technique; **-zacken,** *m.* echo amplitude.

Echtzeit-basis, *f.* real-time base; **-rechnersystem,** *n.* real-time computer system.

Eckfrequenz, *f.* square-wave frequency, cutoff frequency.

Edelgas-bogen, *m.* arc in rare gases; **-kontinua,** *n.pl.* continuous rare-gas spectra.

Effektgarn, *n.* novelty yarn.

Effektivitätszahl, *f.* figure of merit.

Effektiv-strom, *m.* root mean square (r.m.s.) current; **-wert,** *m.* root mean square (r.m.s.) value.

Effekt-lampe, *f.* spotlight; **-scheinwerfer,** *m.* spotlight.

Egalfärbung, *f.* level dyeing.

Egalisier-fähigkeit, *f.* leveling power; **-farbstoff,** *m.* leveling dyestuff; **-mittel,** *n.* level-dyeing assistant.

Eich-invarianz, *f.* gage invariance; **-substanz,** *f.* gage substance; **-transformation,** *f.* gage transformation.

Eigen-vektor, *m.* characteristic vector; **-viskosität,** *f.* internal viscosity; **-wechsel,** *m.* promissory note; **-wertaufgabe,** *f.* characteristic-value problem.

eigentlich orthogonal, proper orthogonal.

Eigen-bewegung, *f.* characteristic motion; **-frequenz,** *f.* characteristic frequency; **-gesetzlichkeit,** *f.* autonomy; **-grösse,** *f.* characteristic variable; **-halbleiter,** *m.* intrinsic semiconductor; **-ladung,** *f.* space charge; **-magnetisch,** self-magnetic; **-periode,** *f.* characteristic period; **-schutzbedingungen,** *f.pl.* fail-safe conditions; **-schwingung,** *f.* mode; **-sinn,** *m.* obstinacy, stubbornness; **-stabilisierung,** *f.* self-stabilization; **-symmetrie,** *f.* characteristic symmetry.

Eignungsprüfung, *f.* aptitude test.

Eilösung, *f.* ovulation.

Einbau-fläche, *f.* panel plane; **-instrument,** *n.* panel instrument; **-koeffizient,** *m.* distribution coefficient; **-teil,** *n.* package.

Einbetten, *n.* encapsulating, potting.

Einbettmaterial, *n.* encapsulating compound, potting mixture.

Einbettungsmittel, *n.* mounting medium, embedding material.

Einbruchs-becken, *n.* trough; **-feld,** *n.* depression; **-kessel,** *m.* caldera; **-meer,** *n.* ingression sea; **-phase,** *f.* transgressive phase; **-tal,** *n.* rift valley.

eindeutig, single-valued, unique.

Eindeutigkeit, *f.* uniqueness; **umkehrbare ~,** one-to-one correspondence.

Eindrings-härte, *f.* indentation hardness; **-tiefe,** *f.* penetration depth, skin depth.

eineindeutige Zuordnung, one-to-one correspondence.

einfach, ~ abgeschlossene Schale, single-closed shell; **-frei,** univariant; **~ zusammenhängend,** simply connected.

Einfach-filter, *n.* one-layer filter; **-ionisation,** *f.* single ionization; **-schicht,** *f.* monolayer; **-streuung,** *f.* single scattering.

Einfallen, *n.* implosion.

Einfang, *m.* capture; **-frequenz,** *f.* capture frequency; **-querschnitt,** *m.* capture cross section; **-strahlung,** *f.* capture radiation.

Einfriertemperatur, *f.* second order transition temperature.

Einfühlungsvermögen, *n.* empathy.

Einführungsbohrloch, *n.* injection borehole, injection well.

einfüllen, to bag, pack in bags.

Eingabe-speicher, *m.* input store; **-streifen,** *m.* input tape; **-werk,** *n.* input device.

Eingangs-daten, *n.pl.* input data; **-fehler,** *m.* inherited error.

eingebettete Kristalle, diluted crystals.

eingefroren, frozen in.

eingegabelt, bracketed.

eingehen, auf etwas näher ~, to consider something in more detail.

eingipfelig, unimodal.

Eingliederungsmöglichkeit, *f.* compatibility.

Eingriff, *m.* operation, surgical intervention, surgery.

Eingriffsfunktion, *f.* influencing function.

Einheits-bauweise, *f.* modular design; **-funktion,** *f.* unit function; **-kugel,** *f.* unit sphere; **-matrix,** *f.* identity matrix; **-tensor,** *m.* unit tensor, identity tensor; **-wurzel,** *f.* root of unit; **-zelle,** *f.* unit cell.

Einhüllbedingung, *f.* condition of enveloping.

Einhüllende, *f.* envelope.

Einkristall-faden, *m.* whisker, single-crystal filament; **-oberfläche,** *f.* single-crystal surface; **-probe,** *f.* single-crystal specimen.

Einlagerungen, *f.pl.* added impurities.

Einlagerungs-fremdatome, *n.pl.* interstitial impurities; **-mischkristall,** *m.* solid solution; **-verbindung,** *f.* inclusion compound.

Einlassschlitz, *m.* intake port.

Einlauf, *m.* intake, enema.

einlaufende Kugelwelle, incoming spherical wave.

einlegen, to deposit, invest.

Einniveauformel, *f.* single-level formula.

Ein- oder Zweikreisgoniometer, *n.* one- or two-circle goniometer.

einohrig, monaural.

Einpegelung, *f.* level adjustment.

einregeln, to zero, adjust, regulate.

einreihen, to sequence.

einsacken, to bag, pack in bags.

Einsatz, *m.* participation; **-forschung,** *f.* operations research; **-zeit,** *f.* arrival time.

einschalig, of one sheet (geom.).

Einschichtpolarisator, *m.* one-layer polarizer.

Einschienenbahn, *f.* monorail.

Einschliessungssatz, *m.* inclusion theorem.

Einschlussverbindung, *f.* clathrate complex, inclusion complex.

Einschnüreffekt, *m.* pinch effect.

Einschub, *m.* plug-in unit; **-baustein,** *m.* plug-in module, plug-in assembly.

Einschwing-frequenz, *f.* natural frequency; **-impuls,** *m.* transient pulse; **-verlauf,** *m.* transient response; **-zeit,** *f.* transient period, response time, buildup time.

Einseitenband, *n.* single sideband.

einseitig unendlich, semi-infinite.

Einsetzen, *n.* onset.

Einsparung, *f.* cost savings.

Einsprung, *m.* entry; **-stelle,** *f.* entry point.

Einstellentfernung, *f.* focal range; ~ **nah auf unendlich,** hyperfocal distance.

Einstellung, *f.* focusing, setting.

Einstellungsperiode, *f.* induction period, initial period.

Einstellzeit, *f.* relaxation time, adjustment time, response time, transient period.

Einteilchen-modell, *n.* single-particle model; **-niveau,** *n.* single-particle level; **-schalenmodell,** *n.* single-particle shell model; **-übergang,** *m.*˜**-e,** single-particle transition; **-wellenfunktionen,** *f.pl.* single-particle wave functions.

eintragen, to plot, post, mark on.

Einwegflasche, *f.* no-return bottle.

einzeilig, in-line.

Einzel-berg, *m.* butte; **-elektron,** *n.* lone electron; **-matrix,** *f.* idempotent or unit matrix; **-probe,** *f.* spot check; **-schrittverfahren,** *n.* single-step method; **-stoss,** *m.*˜**-e,** single collision; **-stück,** *n.* item; **-versetzung,** *f.* single dislocation.

Einzwirnung, *f.* twist take-up.

eisen-frei, iron-free; **-gekapselt,** ironclad; **-oxydschicht,** *f.* iron oxide layer; **-reihe,** *f.* iron group.

Eis-keim, *m.* sublimation center (in ice formation); **-scholle,** *f.* ice floe; **-spalte,** *f.* crevasse.

Eiweissstoffwechsel, *m.* protein metabolism.

Ektohormon, *n.* pheromone.

e-Kurve, *f.* exponential curve.

Elastizitäts-gesetz, *n.* elasticity law; **-grenze,** *f.* elastic limit; **-probe,** *f.* stretch test; **-theorie,** *f.* theory of elasticity.

Elationswirkungsquerschnitt, *m.* elation cross section.

Elektret, *m.* electret.

elektrodenlos, electrodeless.

elektrodisch, electrodic.

Elektrodynamik, *f.* electrodynamics.

Elektrofilter, *n.* electrostatic precipitator.

elektrokalorisch, electrocaloric.

Elektrolumineszenz, *f.* electroluminescence.

elektrolytisch aufgebracht, electrolytically deposited.

elektromechanisch, electromechanical.

Elektron, *n.* **auslösendes** ~, triggering electron.

Elektronelektronzusammenstoss, *m.* electron-electron collision.

Elektronen, Stoss zwischen ~, electron-electron collision.

Elektronen-affinitätsspektrum, *n.* electron-affinity spectrum; **-anlagerung,** *f.* electron attachment; **-anregung,** *f.* electronic excitation; **-aufnehmer,** *m.* electron acceptor; **-ballung,** *f.* electron bunching.

Elektronen-beugung, *f.* electron diffraction; **-beschuss,** *m.* electron bombardment; **-blitz,** *m.* electron burst, electronic flash, strobe; **-bündel,** *n.* electron beam; **-bündelung,** *f.* electron focusing; **-defektstelle,** *f.* electron vacancy; **-donator,** *m.* electron donor; **-einfang,** *m.* electron capture; **-emittierendes Metall,** metallic electron emitter; **-empfang,** *m.* electron capture.

Elektronen-entladung, *f.* electron discharge; **-falle,** *f.* electron trap; **-fänger,** *m.* acceptor; **-gasstatistik,** *f.* electron-gas statistics; **-geräte,** *n.pl.* electronic equipment; **-gittermodell,** *n.* electronic-lattice model; **-hülle,** *f.* electron cloud; **-interferenz,** *f.* electron interference; **-interferometrie,** *f.* interferometry of electrons.

Elektronen-kanone, *f.* electron gun; **-konfiguration,** *f.* configuration of electrons; **-kontinua,** *n.pl.* continuous electronic spectra; **-ladung,** *f.* electronic charge; **-laufzeit,** *f.* electron transit time; **-lawine,** *f.* electron avalanche; **-leitfähigkeit,** *f.* electronic conductivity, n-type conductivity; **-lücke,** *f.* electron vacancy, hole; **-masse,** *f.* electron mass; **-schleuder,** *m.* electron accelerator, electron gun.

Elektronen-spektrum, *n.* electron spectrum; **-spinresonanz,** *f.* electron-spin resonance; **-statistik,** *f.* electron statistics; **-stossspektrum,** *n.* electron-impact spectrum; **-strahl,** *m.* electron beam; **-strahlkatode,** *f.* electron gun; **-strahlröhre,** *f.* cathode-ray tube; **-streuung,** *f.* electron scattering; **-strom,** *m.* electronic current.

Elektronen- und Gitterkomponente, *f.pl.* electronic and lattice components.

Elektronen-vervielfacher, *m.* photomultiplier; **-wechselwirkung,** *f.* electron interaction.

Elektronion-rekombination, *f.* electron-ion recombination; **-wandrekombination,** *f.* electron-ion wall recombination.

Elektronneutronwechselwirkung, *f.* electron-neutron interaction.

Elektronphononwechselwirkungs-energie, *f.* electron-phonon interaction energy; **-parameter,** *m.* electron-phonon interaction parameter.

Elektrophorese, *f.* electrophoresis; **trägerfreie** ~, free electrophoresis, moving boundary electrophoresis.

Elektrostriktion, *f.* electrostriction.

elektrostriktive, electrostrictive.

Elementar-bereich, *m.* unit cell; **-faden,** *m.* monofil, monofilament; **-ladung,** *f.* unit or electronic charge; **-teilchen,** *n.* elementary particle; **-teilchentheorie,** *f.* elementary divisor theory; **-zelle,** *f.* elementary (lattice) cell, unit cell.

Element- und Verbindungshalbleiter, *m.* element and compound semiconductor.

Ellbogen-freiheit, *f.* elbow room; **-nerv,** *m.* ulnar nerve, elbow nerve.

Elliptizität, *f.* ellipticity.

Eloxalverfahren, *n.* anodizing process.

eloxieren, to anodize.

Elutions-mittel, *n.* eluent; **-vermögen,** *n.* developing power, eluting power, elutive power; **-wirkung,** *f.* developing power, eluting power, elutive power.

Emanationsabgabe, *f.* radioactive emission, emanation of radiation.

Emaniervermögen, *n.* emanating power.

Emissions-bande, *f.* emission band; **-fähigkeit,** *f.* emission capability; **-kontinuum,** *n.* continuous emission spectrum; **-kristallspektrum,** *n.* emission spectrum of crystals; **-kurs,** *m.* issue price, par, rate of issue; **-steuerung,** *f.* emission control.

emittierende Thoriumschicht auf Wolfram, thoriated tungsten emitter.

Empfängnis-regelung, *f.* birth control; **-verhütung,** *f.* contraception.

Empfindlichkeit, *f.* sensitivity, response; **lichtelektrische ~,** photoelectric sensitivity, photoelectric response, photoresponse.

Empfindlichkeits-grenze, *f.* sensitivity limit; **-mass,** *n.* sensitivity measure; **-spitze,** *f.* peak response; **-wert,** *m.* speed rating (film).

Empfindungskälte, *f.* frigidity.

empirisch bestimmt, empirically determined.

empor-quellen, to well up; **-richten,** to raise up.

Emulsionspolymerisat, *n.* emulsion polymer.

enantiomorph, enantiomorphic.

Endbildleuchtschirm, *m.* final-image luminescent screen.

Endlos-faden, *m.* continuous filament; **-garn,** *n.* continuous filament yarn.

endogen, endogenous.

Endomorphismus, *m.* endomorphism.

endovenös, intravenous.

Endübertrag, *m.* carry-over.

Endvergrösserung, *f.* final magnification.

Energie-abstand, *m.* energy gap; **-bandstruktur,** *f.* energy-band structure; **-bandverbreiterung,** *f.* energy-band broadening; **-bilanz,** *f.* energy balance; **-freigabe,** *f.* energy release; **-frequenzbeziehung,** *f.* energy-frequency ratio; **-haushalt,** *m.* energy balance; **-impulssatz,** *m.* energy-momentum theorem; **-lückenmodell,** *n.* energy-gap model.

Energie-niveaudiagramm, *n.* energy-level diagram; **-satz,** *m.* law of conservation of energy; **-schale,** *f.* energy shell; **-schwelle,** *f.* energy

threshold, energy barrier; **-sprung,** *m.* energy gap; **-stromdichte,** *f.* energy flux density; **-strömung,** *f.* energy flow; **-technik,** *f.* power engineering; **-termverschiebung,** *f.* energy shift; **-verbrauch,** *m.* energy dissipation; **-zone,** *f.* energy (band) gap.

Energiezustand, *m.* energy state; **~ des Elektrons,** electronic energy state; **~ geringer Anregungsenergie,** low-energy state.

Energiezuwachs, *m.* gain of energy.

Engpass, *m.* bottleneck.

Entaktivierung, *f.* deactivation.

Entartung der Energieniveaus, degeneracy of energy levels.

Entbindungs-anstalt, *f.* maternity hospital, lying-in hospital; **-schock,** *m.* post-partum shock; **-tisch,** *m.* delivery table.

entchloren, to dechlorinate.

Entfernungs-kreis, *m.* distance circle; **-messer,** *m.* range finder.

Enthalpie, *f.* enthalpy.

Entionisierung, *f.* deionization.

Entionisierungszeit, *f.* clearing time (of counter), deionization time.

Entkopplungs-kondensator, *m.* neutralizing capacitor; **-kreis,** *m.* antiresonant circuit; **-schaltung,** *f.* decoupling circuit.

Entladeverzug, *m.* time lag (in discharge).

Entladungs-nachglimmen, *n.* discharge afterglow; **-plasma,** *n.* low-temperature plasma; **-strecke,** *f.* discharge gap.

Entlüftungsventil, *n.* air bleeding valve.

Entmagnetisierung, *f.* demagnetization.

Entmischung, *f.* separation.

Entmischungs-textur, *f.* segregation texture, separation texture; **-vorgang,** *m.-e,* separation process.

Entnahme-leitung, *f.* intake pipe; **-stelle,** *f.* sampling point.

Entölungsvorgang, *m.-e,* crude oil recovery process.

entriegeln, to unlock, unlatch, unblock, release.

Entropiedichte, *f.* entropy density.

Entsalzungsanlage, *f.* desalination plant.

Entschäumer, *m.* antifoaming agent; defoamer.

Entscheidungs-bereich, *m.* preference region; **-gehalt,** *m.* information content; **statistische ~-theorie,** decision theory.

entschlüsseln, to decode.

entseuchen, to decontaminate, disinfect.

Entspannungs-temperatur, *f.* annealing temperature, annealing point; **-versuch,** *m.* stress relaxation test.

Entspiegelung, *f.* dereflection.

Addendum 575

entsprechend, dem ~, corresponding to that, accordingly.

entstören, to screen.

entstört, interference-free, screened.

Entwicklung, *f.* expansion (in mathematics).

Entwicklungs-dose, *f.* developing tank; -satz, *m.* expansion theorem; -stand, *m.* state of the art; -stillstand, *m.* arrested development; -theorie, *f.* theory of evolution, -zyklus, *m.* life cycle.

Entwöhnungsbeschwerden, *f.pl.* withdrawal symptoms.

Entwurf, *m.* draft, plan.

Entziehungserscheinung, *f.* withdrawal symptoms.

Ephemeriden, *f.pl.* ephemerides.

Epikutantest, *m.* patch test.

Episit, *m.* predator; -ie, *f.* predation.

epitaxial, epitaxial; ~ abgelagert, epitaxially deposited; ~ gewachsen, epitaxially grown.

Epitaxialschicht, *f.* epitaxial layer; schwach dotierte ~, lightly doped epitaxial layer.

Erb-faktor, *m.* gene; -rückschlag, *m.* throwback, reversion.

Erdabplattung, *f.* earth's oblateness.

Erdalkali-atom, *n.* alkaline-earth atom; -halogenid, *n.* alkaline-earth halide; -kontinua, *n.pl.* continuous alkaline-earth spectra; -salz, *n.* alkaline-earth salt.

Erdbeben-messer, *m.* seismograph; -strahl, *m.* seismic ray; -warte, *f.* seismological observatory; -welle, *f.* seismic wave.

Erd-ferne, *f.* apogee; -fliessen, *n.* solifluction; -floh, *m.* garden flea hopper; -gezeit, *f.* earth's bodily tide; -magnetfeld, *n.* geomagnetic field; -magnetisch, geomagnetic; -nähe, *f.* perigee.

Erfahrung, *f.* vor aller ~, *a priori;* nach der ~, *a posteriori.*

Ergodensatz, *m.* ergodic hypothesis.

erhöht, enhanced.

Erhebungsformular, *n.* questionnaire.

Erhaltungs-chirurgie, *f.* conservative surgery; -dosis, *f.* maintenance dose; -grenze, *f.* survival level; -satz, *m.*-e, conservation law.

Erholungserscheinung, *f.* recovery process.

Erkenntnisfunktion, *f.* cognitive function.

erneut, again, renewed.

erregen, to energize.

Erreger, *m.* pathogen, causative organism.

Ersatz-empfänger, *m.* emergency receiver; -kreis, *m.* equivalent circuit.

Erscheinungsspannung, *f.* appearance potential.

erschlagen, to kill.

Erstarren, gerichtetes ~, normal freezing.

Erstarrungs-beginn, *m.* initial set; -ende, *n.* final set.

erste, als erster, as the first.

erwarb (erwerben), he acquired; er erwirbt, he acquires.

Erweichungs-punkt, *m.* softening point; -temperatur, *f.* heat distortion temperature.

erweiterte Methode der ebenen Wellen, augmented plane-wave method.

Erzeugende einer Klasse, generating element of a class.

Erzeugung, *f.* activation.

Erzeugungsoperator, *m.* production operator.

e. s. E. (elektrostatische Einheit), electrostatic unit, esu.

euklidisch-affin, Euclidean affine; -geometrisch, Euclidean.

Evektion, *f.* evection.

Evektionstides, *f.pl.* evectional tides.

Expansionsmaschine, *f.* expansion engine; abwechselnd wirkende ~, reciprocating expansion engine.

Exponentialröhre, *f.* variable-mu tube.

Extrapolationsformel, *f.* extrapolation formula.

extraterrestrisch, extraterrestrial.

Exzitonenniveau, *n.* exciton level.

Facharzt, *m.* specialist; ~ für Altersleiden, gerontologist; ~ für Geburtshilfe, obstetrician; ~ für Magen- und Darmleiden, gastroenterologist.

fachen, to double, fold, ply.

Fächer-mulde, *f.* synclinorium; -sattel, *m.* anticlinorium, compound arch.

Fachzwirning, *f.* doubling, ply doubling.

Faden-abszess, *m.* stitch abscess; -galvanometer, *n.* string galvanometer; -kristall, *m.* whisker; -transistor, *m.* filamentary transistor.

Fahr-strahl, *m.* radius vector; -weise, *f.* operating mode.

Faktorenzerlegung, *f.* factoring, factorization.

Faktorgruppe, *f.* factor group.

Faktorisierungsmethode, *f.* factorization method.

Fall-beschleunigung, *f.* gravitational acceleration; -geschwindigkeit, *f.* settling rate.

Fälligkeits-datum, *n.* due date; -tag, *m.* maturity day.

Fall-richtung, *f.* direction of dip, line of dip; -rohr, *n.* downcomer; -schirmjäger, *m.* parachutist, paratrooper; -streifen, *m.* virga;

-wasser, *n.* condenser water; **-winkel,** *m.* dip angle, slant.

Falsch-draht, *m.* false twist; **-licht,** *n.* stray light.

falschphasig, out-of-phase.

Falt-kamera, *f.* folding camera; **-molekülmethode,** *f.* convolution molecule method.

Faltung von Funktionen, folding (convolution) of functions.

Faltungsintegral, *n.* convolution integral.

Fang-anode, *f.* collecting anode, gathering anode; **-gitter,** *n.* suppressor grid; **-stelle,** *f.* trap; **-stoff,** *m.* getter.

Farb-abweichung, *f.* chromatic aberration, color difference; **-auszug,** *m.* color separation; **-beständigkeit,** *f.* color fastness; **-bildner,** *m.* color former; **-bildröhre,** *f.* color picture (television) tube.

Farbenempfindlichkeit, *f.* dye sensitivity.

Farb-fernsehempfänger, *m.* color television receiver; **-film,** *m.* color film; **-gitter,** *n.* color grating, color grid; **-grenze,** *f.* visibility threshold; **-raster,** *m.* color screen; **-ringsystem,** *n.* colorcycle system; **-schlierenverfahren,** *n.* color schlieren method; **-teilauszug,** *m.* color separation; **-überzug,** *m.* paint film; **-valenz,** *f.* color stimulus; **-werte,** *m.pl.* tristimulus values; **-zentrum,** *n.* color center.

faseraffin, fiber-reactive.

Faser-band, *n.* sliver; **-brücke,** *f.* filament; **-optik,** *f.* fiber optics; **-vlies,** *n.* fiber fleece, bonded fabric, nonwoven fabric; **-zusammenballung,** *f.* pilling.

Fassbauch, *m.* pot belly.

Fastebene, *f.* peneplain.

Faul-gas, *n.* digester gas, sludge digestion gas; **-schlamm,** *m.* digested sludge, activated sludge (sewage).

faulnisverhindernd, anti-fouling.

Faulung, *f.* (sewage) digestion.

Feder-konstante, *f.* spring constant; **-wolke,** *f.* cirrus cloud, mare's tail.

Federungs-vermögen, *n.* resilience; **-widerstand,** *m.* compliance.

Fedorowscher Tisch, *m.* universal stage (of a microscope).

Fehl-abgleich, *m.* misalignment; **-anpassung,** *f.* mismatch, misfit, mismating; **-atmung,** *f.* respiratory failure.

Fehler einer Ausgleichung, adjustment residual.

Fehler-abgleichsmethode, *f.* compensation of error; **-ausgleichung,** *f.* adjustment of errors; **-beseitigung,** *f.* debugging; **-ellipsoid,** *f.* ellipsoid of error; **-erkennung,** *f.* error detecting,

fault recognition; **-ermittlungsprogramm,** *n.* diagnostic control program.

Fehler-fortpflanzung, *f.* propagation of error; **-fortpflanzungsgesetz,** *n.* law of propagation of error; **-funktion,** *f.* aberration function, error function; **-matrix,** *f.* error matrix.

Fehlernte, *f.* crop failure.

Fehler-orthogonalität, *f.* orthogonality of error; **-quadratmethode,** *f.* least-squares method; **-suche,** *f.* trouble-shooting, fault finding; **-unterdrückung,** *f.* debugging; **-verteilung,** *f.* error distribution.

Fehl-ordnung, *f.* disorder, defect; **-ordnungsstreuung,** *f.* disorder scattering; **-schlagen,** to fail; **-stelle,** *f.* defect, imperfection, flaw, hole.

Fein-bereichsbeugung, *f.* fine-range diffraction; **-gleitung,** *f.* microslip, fine slip.

Feinheitsnummer, *f.* denier, count, gage.

Fein-mechanik, *f.* precision mechanics; **-strahlanordnung,** *f.* high-resolution camera.

Feinstruktur, *f.* fine structure; **-aufspaltung,** *f.* fine-structure splitting; **-dublett,** *n.* fine-structure doublet.

Feld, *n.* array; **erregtes ~,** induced field; **quellenfreies ~,** source-free solenoidal field.

Feld-abhängigkeit, *f.* field dependence; **-blende,** *f.* field stop; **-desorption,** *f.* field desorption; **-emission,** *f.* field emission.

Feldemissions-mikroskop, *n.* field-emission microscope; **-quelle,** *f.* field-emitter source.

Feldionenmassenspektroskopie, *f.* field-ion mass spectrometry.

Feld-linie, *f.* line of force; **-sprung,** *m.* field change; **-wanderung,** *f.* field drift.

Felsschutt, *m.* detritus, rock debris, scree.

Fern-betätigung, *f.* remote control; **-fokuskathode,** *f.* telefocus cathode; **-gas,** *n.* manufactured gas; **-messgerät,** *n.* telemetering instrument; **-ordnung,** *f.* long-range order; **-schreiber,** *m.* teleprinter, telewriter.

Fernseh-bild, *n.* television picture; **-empfang,** *m.* television reception; **-telephon,** *n.* videophone.

Fernübertragung, *f.* remote transmission.

Ferro-elektrika, *n.pl.* ferroelectrics; **-elektrizität,** *f.* ferroelectricity; **-magnetika,** *n.pl.* ferromagnetics.

festamorph, solid amorphous.

festangeschlossene Geräte, on-line equipment.

Festigkeit, elektrische ~, dielectric strength.

Fest-kapital, *n.* fixed assets; **-komma,** *n.* fixed point.

Festkörper, *m.* solid; **-modell,** *n.* model of solid; **-physik,** *f.* solid state physics; **-schaltung,** *f.* solid state circuit.

festsitzend, sessile.

Feststellschraube, f. set screw.

Feststellung, f. verification.

Feststoffrakete, f. solid-propellant rocket.

feucht-adiabatisch, moist adiabatic.

Feucht-haltemittel, n. humectant; **-labilität,** f. hygroscopic instability.

Feuerkugel, f. fireball.

fibrillieren, to beat (pulp), grind.

Film-druck, m. film screen printing, screen printing, silk screen printing; **-klammer,** f. film clip; **-klebestelle,** f. splice; **-lochkarte,** f. aperture card; **-schablone,** f. screen; **-schicht,** f. emulsion coating; **-schichtträger,** m. film base, film support; **-streifen,** m. badge.

Filtrierhilfsmittel, n. filter aid.

Finanz-jahr, n. fiscal year; **-period,** f. fiscal period.

Fixpunkt, m. fixed point, set point, bench mark; ~ **der Inversionsachse,** fixed point of the inversion axis.

Flachdruck, m. planographic printing, photolithography.

Fläche, abwickelbare ~, developable surface; ~ **allgemeiner Lage,** face in general position.

Flächen-ausdehnung, f. surface area; **-ausmessung,** f. planimetering; **-diode,** f. junction diode; **-indizes,** m.pl. Miller indices; **-krümmung,** f. curvature of a surface; **-normale,** f. normal of a surface; **-polarisator,** f. sheet polarizer.

Flächenstück, n. surface element, unit area; **orientiertes** ~, oriented surface.

Flächen-symmetrie, f. plane symmetry; **-treu,** of equal area, area-preserving, equivalent; **-transistor,** m. junction transistor; **-zentriert,** face-centered; **-zentrierung,** f. centered face.

Flammen-emissionskontinuum, n. flame-emission continuum; **-spektrum,** n. flame-emission spectrum; **-tulpe,** f. upturned flame, inverted flame; **-werfer,** m. flame thrower.

flamm-festmachen, to flameproof; **-schutz,** m. fire retardant, flame retardant.

Flaschen, in ~ **füllen,** to bottle.

fleck-echt, spot resistant; **-effekt,** m. patch effect; **-geschwindigkeit,** f. scanning speed; **-mittel,** n. spot remover; **-verzerrung,** f. deflection aberration.

fliegende Untertasse, flying saucer.

Fliess-bett, n. fluid bed, fluidized bed; **-erde,** f. soil flow, solifluction; **-figuren,** f.pl. flow figures, slip bands; **-mittel,** n. mobile phase, solvent; **-mittelfront,** f. solvent front; **-schicht,** f. fluid bed, fluidized bed; **-spannung,** f. yield point; **-staubkontakt,** m. fluid catalyst.

flimmern, to shimmer, flicker.

Flocken-ausrüstung, f. flock finish; **-muster,** n. flocked design.

Flockungsmittel, n. flocculent.

Flüchtigkeit, f. fugacity.

Fluchtliniennomogramm, n. alignment nomogram.

Flügel, m. flyer; **-flächenbelastung,** f. wing load; **-spinnmaschine,** f. flyer spinning frame; **-zwirnmaschine,** f. fly twister.

Flug-regler, m. autopilot, **-sicherung,** f. air traffic control; **-widerstandskraft,** f.-e, drag.

Flugzeit-messung, f. time-of-flight measurement; **-methode,** f. time-of-flight method.

Flugzeug, n. aircraft; ~ **für kurze Start- und Landebahnen,** short take off and landing aircraft (STOL).

Fluoreszenzausbeute, f. fluorescence yield.

Fluorimetrie, f. fluorimetry.

Fluorkohlenstoffharz, n. fluorocarbon resin.

flüssiger Erdkern, liquid core.

Flüssiggas, n. liquefied petroleum gas, LPG.

Flüssigkeits-eingabeort, m. injection port; **-masse,** f. bulk liquid; **-spiegelreflexion,** f. liquid mirror reflection.

Flüssigkristall, m.-e, liquid crystal.

Flussspatgitter, n. fluorite lattice.

Flussvektor, m. flow vector.

Flüstergalerie, f. whispering gallery.

Fokusdifferenz, f. depth of focus.

Fokussierungs-bedingung, f. focusing condition; **-fehler,** m. focusing defect.

Folge, f. progression (in math), sequence (in operations), succession, consequence, series, corollary.

Folge-frequenz, f. repetition rate; **-krankheit,** f. sequela, secondary disease; **-regler,** m. servomechanism.

Folgesteuerelement, n. sequencer.

Folgesteuerung, f. sequence control, sequential control, sequencing, cascade control, automatic sequence control, series control.

Folgesteuerungsmechanismus, m. servomechanism.

Folien-blasverfahren, n. blown tubular film method; **-strangpresse,** f. sheet extruder; **-verformung,** f. sheet forming.

Fontäneeffekt, m. fountain effect.

Formalismus, m. formalism.

Form-beständigkeit, f. shape retention, dimensional stability; **-deutversuch,** m. Rorschach test; **-gerecht,** full-fashioned; **-pressen,** n. compression molding; **-schwingung,** *f.* contour vibration; **-zahl,** *f.* form quotient.

Forscherblick, *m.* searching eye (of a scientist).

FORTRAN-Sprache, *f.* FORTRAN (formula translator) language.

fortschreiben, to update.

Fortwaschen, *n.* ablation.

fossilführend, fossiliferous.

fotoleitend, photoconductive.

Foulard, *m.* padding machine, padder; **-färbung,** *f.* pad dyeing.

Fraktionieraufsatz, *m.*¨-e, fractionating column.

Freieelektronennäherung, *f.* free-electron approximation.

freie Weglänge, free path; **freier Fall,** free fall; **Freiheitsgrad des freien Elektrons,** electronic mode.

freilaufend, freewheeling.

Fremdatom, *n.* impurity atom; **-zusatz,** *m.*¨-e, addition of impurities.

Fremd-diffusion, *f.* diffusion of one substance in another; **-feld,** *n.* stray field; **-halbleiter,** *m.* extrinsic semiconductor; **-kapital,** *n.* borrowed capital; **-licht,** *n.* stray light; **-ling,** *m.* xenocryst; **-störstelle,** *f.* impurity.

Frequenz-gang, *m.* frequency response; **-gleichung,** *f.* frequency equation; **-unabhängig,** independent of frequency; **-wobbler,** *m.* sweep generator.

Fress-neigung, *f.* scuffing tendency; **-zone,** *f.* scoring zone.

Fritfliege, *f.* frit fly.

Fühler, *m.* sensing element, sensor, probe; **eingebauter ~,** in situ sensing element.

Füll-faktor, *m.* filling factor, space factor; **-grad,** *m.* filler loading, filler content; **-konstante,** *f.* bulk factor.

Fundamentaltensor, *m.* fundamental tensor.

Funkbildübertragung, *f.* facsimile.

Funken-kontinuum, *n.* spark-discharge continuum; **-überschlag,** *m.* sparkover; **-verhindernd,** spark suppressing.

Funkmesstechnik, *f.* radar.

Funksprechgerät, *n.* radio telephone.

Funkstelle, *f.* radio station.

Funktional-ableitung, *f.* functional derivative; **-determinante,** *f.* functional determinant; **-differentialgleichung,** *f.* functional differential equation.

Funktionen, singuläre ~, irregular functions; **zugeordnete ~,** associated functions.

Funktions-papier, *n.* graph paper; **-störung,** *f.* malfunction; **-trieb,** *m.* input table; **-zweig,** *m.* branch.

Fusion, *f.* merger.

Fusspunkt des Lotes, foot of a perpendicular.

Fusspunktkurve, *f.* pedal locus.

Gabelblitz, *m.* forked lightning.

Gadolinium-anthrachinon, *n.* gadolinium anthraquinone; **-nitrobenzol,** *n.* gadolinium nitrobenzene.

Gallium-antimonid, *n.* gallium antimonide; **-arsenid,** *n.* gallium arsenide.

Galvanispannung, *f.* galvanic current.

galvanomagnetisch, galvanomagnetic.

Gamowfaktor, *m.* barrier penetration factor.

Gang, *n.* cycle, loop, operation, response.

ganze Funktion, integral function.

ganzrational, rational integral.

ganztägige Welle, diurnal wave.

Gas-anzeichen, *n.* gas show; **-behandlung,** *f.* gas treatment; **-chromatographie,** *f.* gas chromatography; **-entladungsplasma,** *n.* gas discharge plasma; **-entlösungspunkt,** *m.* bubble point; **-führungssystem,** *n.* gas-inlet system; **-kältemaschine,** *f.* gas refrigerating machine; **-nebel,** *m.* gas nebula.

Gebär-mutterhals, *m.* cervix; **-station,** *f.* maternity ward.

Geber, *m.* transducer, pickup, transmitter.

Gebiets-bewirtschaftung, *f.* district planning; **-kollokation,** *f.* domain collocation.

Gebirgs-druck, *m.* rock pressure; **-schlag,** *m.* rock burst.

Gebrauchsfähigkeitsprüfung, *f.* performance test.

gebündelt, focused, narrowed, collimated, bunched.

Geburten-beschränkung, *f.* birth control, family planning; **-regelung,** *f.* birth control, family planning; **-rückgang,** *m.* declining birth rate; **-ziffer,** *f.* birth rate.

Gedächtnis-schwund, *m.* loss of memory; **-stützend,** mnemonic; **-verlust,** *m.* amnesia.

Gedanken-flucht, *f.* mental aberration; **-lesen,** *n.* mind reading; **-übertragung,** *f.* telepathy.

gedruckte Schaltung, printed circuit.

Gefällezuführung, *f.* gravity feed.

Gefäss-darstellung, *f.* angiography, vasography; **-dilatation,** *f.* vasodilatation; **-reich,** vascularized, rich in blood vessels; **-verengend,** vasoconstricting; **-versorgung,** *f.* vascularization.

Gefrier-kern, *m.* freezing nucleus; **-punkterniedrigung,** *f.* freezing-point depression; **-trocknung,** *f.* freeze drying, lyophilization.

Gegenanzeige, *f.* contraindication.

Gegen-induktivität, *f.* mutual inductance; **-ion,** *m.* counter-ion; **-kopplung,** *f.* (negative) feedback.

gegenphasige Bereiche, antiphase domains.

Gegenphasigkeit, *f.* phase opposition.

Gegen-sprechanlage, *f.* intercom; **-sprechbetrieb,** *m.* duplex operation; **-strahlung,** *f.* atmospheric radiation; **-stromaustauscher,** *m.* countercurrent exchanger; **-taktschaltung,** *f.* push-pull connection; **-taktwellenwiderstand,** *m.* odd-mode impedance.

gegenübersehen, sich ∼, to confront.

gegenüberstellbar, opposable.

gegenüberstellen, to compare, correlate.

Gegenwalze, *f.* nip roll.

Gehirnwassersucht, *f.* hydrocephalus.

Geiger-Müller-Zähler, *m.* Geiger-Müller counter.

Geisterbild, *n.* TV ghost.

Geländearbeit, *f.* field operation (earth-moving, excavation, etc.).

Gelbildungszeit, *f.* gel time.

Gelchromatographie, *f.* gel chromatography, gel permeation chromatography, GPC.

Gelierungszeit, *f.* gel time.

Gemein-kosten, *f.pl.* fixed costs, indirect costs, overhead; **-löhne,** *m.pl.* indirect labor costs.

gemeinsam benutzen, to share.

Gemeinsames, *n.* things in common.

Genbestand, *m.* genetic complement.

General-bass, *m.* basso continuo; **-schalter,** *m.* master switch.

genommen, streng ∼, strictly speaking.

Genussmittel, *n.* stimulant.

Genveränderung, *f.* gene change, mutation.

geochemisch, geochemical.

Geochronologie, *f.* geochronology.

Geodäsie, *f.* geodesy.

geodätisch parallel, geodesic parallel.

Geoid-bestimmung, *f.* geoid determination; **-undulation,** *f.* geoid warping.

geostrophisch, geostrophic.

geozentrisch, geocentric.

Geraden, windschiefe ∼, skew lines.

Geradenbüschel, *n.* family of lines.

geradlinig, straight-lined, linear.

Geräteausstattung, *f.* hardware (computers).

Geräusch-abstand, *m.* signal-to-noise ratio; **-bekämpfung,** *f.* noise abatement, noise control; **-dämpfung,** *f.* soundproofing; **-pegel,** *m.* noise level.

Gerüst-schwingung, *f.* skeletal vibration; **-substanz,** *f.* (detergent) builder.

Gesamt-drehimpulsquantenzahl, *f.* total angular momentum quantum number; **-krümmung,** *f.* total curvature; **-leuchtkraft,** *f.* overall luminosity; **-querschnitt,** *m.* total cross section; **-reflexion,** *f.* integral reflection; **-schrittverfahren,** *n.* total step method; **-schwankung,** *f.* variation; **-wirkungsquerschnitt,** *m.* total cross section.

Geschlechtskrankeit, *f.* venereal disease.

geschweifte Klammer, brace.

Geschwindigkeits-abhängigkeit, *f.* velocity dependence; **-auflösung,** *f.* velocity resolution; **-fokussierend,** velocity focusing; **-raum,** *m.* velocity space; **-selektor,** *m.* velocity selector.

gesellschaftsfeindlich, antisocial.

Gesichtstäuschung, *f.* optical illusion.

Gestammel, *n.* stammering.

Gestotter, *n.* stuttering.

Gesundbeter, *m.* faith healer.

Gewässerüberwärmung, *f.* thermal pollution.

Gewebe-streckmaschine, *f.* tenter frame, tenter, stretching frame; **-streichmaschine,** *f.* coater.

Gewerbehygiene, *f.* industrial hygiene.

Gewinn-faktor, *m.* gain factor; **-spanne,** *f.* profit margin.

gezeiten-erzeugend, tide producing; **-rechenmaschine,** *f.* tide-computing machine.

g-g-Kerne, *m.pl.* even-even nuclei.

Giessharz, *n.* casting resin.

Gitter-abstand, *m.* grating space, lattice distance; **-baustein,** *n.* lattice element; **-blende,** *f.* grating diaphragm.

Gitterenergie, *f.* lattice energy; **-berechnung,** *f.* calculation of lattice energy.

Gitter-fehler, *m.* lattice imperfection or defect; **-fehlstelle,** *f.* lattice imperfection; **-formel,** *f.* grating formula; **-kennlinie,** *f.* grid characteristic; **-komplex,** *m.* lattice complex; **-kreis,** *m.* grid circuit; **-leerstelle,** *f.* lattice vacancy; **-leitfähigkeit,** *f.* lattice conductivity; **-lücke,** *f.* lattice vacancy; **-messung,** *f.* grating measurement.

Gitter-parameter, *m.* lattice parameter; **-punkt,** *m.* grid point, lattice point, lattice node; **-relaxation,** *f.* lattice relaxation; **-schneidetechnik,** *f.* ruling technique; **-schwingung,** *f.* lattice vibration; **-spektrometer,** *m.* grating spectrometer; **-sperrspannung,** *f.* cutoff voltage, cutoff bias; **-stichprobenverfahren,** *n.* grid sampling; **-störung,** *f.* lattice imperfection; **-vorspannung,** *f.* grid bias.

Gitterwärme, *f.* lattice heat; **-leitfähigkeit,** *f.* lattice thermal conductivity.

Gitter-welle, *f.* lattice vibration, lattice wave, lattice vibrational wave; **-zellenvolumen,** *n.* unit cell volume (of a lattice).

Glanzwinkel, *m.* glancing angle.

Glas-hauswirkung, *f.* greenhouse effect; **-keramik,** *f.* pyroceramic, vitroceramic, devitrified glass; **-perlwand,** *f.* beaded screen; **-temperatur,** *f.* glass transition point.

Glättung, *f.* smoothing.

Gleiboden, *m.* gley soil.

gleichbleibender Zustand, steady-state condition.

Gleichgeschlechtlichkeit, *f.* homosexuality.

Gleichgestaltigkeit, *f.* isomorphism.

Gleichgewichts-feldstärke, *f.* equilibrium field; **-lage,** *f.* equilibrium position; **-leuchtdichte,** *f.* equilibrium luminance.

gleichhändig, ambidextrous.

Gleichlauf, *m.* synchronization, tracking; **-abstimmung,** *f.* ganged tuning; **-impuls,** *m.* synchronizing pulse; **-schaltung,** *f.* lock-in circuit; **-schwankungsrate,** *f.* flutter rate; **-zustand,** *m.* ganged condition.

Gleichlichtstrahlung, *f.* steady radiation.

gleich-mässig stetig, uniformly continuous; **-phasig,** in-phase; **-schalten,** to synchronize, coordinate; **-setzen,** to treat alike, compare, equate; **-setzung,** *f.* equalization, equating.

Gleichstromprozess, *m.*-e, uniflow method.

Gleichungs-system, *n.* system of equations; **-typ,** *m.* type of equation.

Gleichverteilungssatz, *m.* law of equipartition.

Gleit-band, *n.* ¨-er, slip band; **-bewegung,** *f.* slip motion; **-drahtpotentiometer,** *n.* slidewire potentiometer; **-ebene,** *f.* glide plane, slip plane; **-entladung,** *f.* sliding discharge; **-fläche,** *f.* slip surface; **-komma,** *n.* floating point; **-richtung,** *f.* glide plane; **-spiegelebene,** *f.* glide plane, slip plane; **-spiegelung,** *f.* glide reflection; **-sumpf,** *m.* sliding load (electrical); **-zeit,** *f.* gliding work time; **-zone,** *f.* slip zone.

Gleyboden, *m.* gley soil.

Gliedziffer, *f.* link relative (in statistics).

Glimm-dauer, *f.* afterglow; **-entladung,** *f.* glow discharge; **-entladungskontinuum,** *n.* glow-discharge continuum; **-röhre,** *f.* glow-discharge tube, neon tube.

Glocken-boden, *m.* bubble cap plate, bubble tray; **-isolator,** *m.* petticoat insulator.

glühelektrisch, thermionic.

Glühelektronenquelle, *f.* thermionic electron source.

Glühemissions-eigenschaften, *f.pl.* thermionic emission properties; **-konstante,** *f.* thermionic constant.

Glüh-kathodenentladung, *f.* hot-cathode discharge; **-sonde,** *f.* hot probe; **-zeit,** *f.* time of ignition.

Glutwolken, *f.pl.* hot avalanche.

gnomonisch, gnomonic.

Goldzusatz, *m.* gold doping, addition of gold.

Graben, *m.* rift valley.

Gradations-änderung, *f.* change of gamma, variation of gamma; **-kurve,** *f.* characteristic curve, H and D curve, Hurter and Driffield curve.

Graphit-bogen, *m.* graphite arc; **-schichtstruktur,** *f.* graphite-layer structure.

Grasfangbox, *f.* lawn sweeper.

Gratifikation, *f.* bonus, gratuity, gratification.

Gratlinie, *f.* edge of regression.

Grau-keil, *m.* neutral wedge, grey wedge, density wedge; **-strahlung,** *f.* grey radiation.

Graupel, *m.* soft hail.

Gravimetrie, *f.* gravimetry.

Gravitations-erregung, *f.* gravitational excitation; **-feld,** *n.* gravitational field, attraction.

gravoidelastoide Wellen, gravitational-compressibility waves.

Grenz-albedo, *n.* albedo limiting value; **-amplitude,** *f.* oscillation amplitude limit; **-auflösung,** *f.* limit of resolution; **-beweglichkeit,** *f.* limiting mobility; **-empfindlichkeit,** *f.* limiting sensitivity; **-energie,** *f.* boundary energy; **-fall,** *m.* borderline case.

Grenzfläche, *f.* boundary; **Streuung an Grenzflächen,** boundary scattering.

grenzflächen-aktiv, surface-active; **-aktive Stoffe,** surfactants, surface-active agents; **-bedingung,** *f.* boundary condition; **-reibung,** *f.* boundary-layer friction; **-schicht,** *f.* boundary layer; **-spannung,** *f.* interfacial tension; **-welle,** *f.* boundary wave.

Grenz-frequenz, *f.* threshold frequency, cutoff frequency; **-geschwindigkeit,** *f.* limiting velocity; **-kohlenwasserstoffe,** *m.pl.* paraffinic hydrocarbons, alkanes; **-menge,** *f.* limiting set; **-radius,** *m.* boundary radius; **-schicht,** *f.* boundary layer; **-schmierung,** *f.* boundary film lubrication; **-schwingung,** *f.* marginal vibration; **-strahl,** *m.* limiting ray.

Grenzübergang, *m.* passage to the limit; **sukzessiver ~,** iterated limit.

Grenz-wächter, *m.* limit selector; **-wellenlänge,** *f.* threshold wavelength, wavelength limit; **-widerstand,** *m.* boundary resistance, critical resistance; **-zone,** *f.* fringe area.

Grobwaschmittel, *n.* heavy-duty detergent.

Grössen-verteilung, *f.* size distribution; **-wahn,** *m.* megalomania, delusion of grandeur.

Gross-kreis, *m.* great circle; **-winkelkorngrenze,** *f.* large-angle grain boundary.

Grund, zu ~ richten, to ruin.

Grund-absorption, *f.* fundamental absorption;

-baustein, *m.* mer, monomeric unit; **-gebiet,** *n.* basic region; **-gesamtheit,** *f.* population; **-gitter,** *n.* host lattice; **-molekül,** *n.* mer, structural unit; **-operation,** *f.* unit operation; **-prozess,** *m.* unit process; **-punkt,** *m.* basic (fundamental) point; **-rauschen,** *n.* background noise.

grund-sätzlich, fundamental; **-sätzliches,** *n.* principles; **-schwärzung,** *f.* base density; **-stellung,** *f.* normal position; **-translationsvektor,** *m.* unit-cell vector; **-trieb,** *m.* natural impulse, instinct; **-viskosität,** *f.* intrinsic viscosity; **-zustand,** *m.* ground state.

Grün-fläche, *f.* green belt; **-siegel,** *n.* green seal.

Gruppen-algebra, *f.* group algebra; **-arbeit,** *f.* teamwork; **-auswahl,** *f.* stratified sampling; **-behandlung,** *f.* group therapy; **-geschwindigkeit,** *f.* group velocity; **-summen,** *f.pl.* subtotals; **-theoretische Behandlung,** group theoretical treatment.

Gültigkeits-bereich, *m.* region of validity; **-grenze,** *f.* limit of validity.

gummiert, rubber-lined, rubber-covered.

Gummi-faden, *m.* elastic thread, rubber thread; **-futter,** *n.* rubber backing; **-garn,** *n.* elastic yarn; **-linse** *f.* zoom lens.

Gussschablone, *f.* template.

gut, so   wie, practically.

Güte-daten, *n.pl.* efficiency data; **-faktormesser,** *m.* Q-meter, quality factor meter; **-grad,** *m.* figure of merit; **-kontrolle,** *f.* quality control; **-test,** *m.* quality test; **-zahl,** *f.* figure of merit.

Gyro-frequenz, *f.* gyro frequency; **-magnetisches Verhältnis,** gyromagnetic ratio.

Haar-entfernungsmittel, *n.* depilatory; **-kristall,** *m.* whisker; **-schuppen,** *f.pl.* dandruff.

Habitus-ebene, *f.* habit plane; **-wirkung,** *f.* habit effect.

Hacker, *m.* doffer comb; **-kamm,** *m.* doffer comb.

Haft-elektron, *n.* trapped electron; **-festigkeit,** *f.* bond strength; **-glas,** *n.* contact lens; **-kleber,** *m.* contact adhesive; **-linse,** *f.* contact lens; **-niveau,** *n.* trap level; **-pflicht,** *f.* liability; **-pflichtversicherung,** *f.* liability insurance; **-stelle,** *f.* trap, trapping site.

Hakenkreuz, *n.* swastika.

Halbaddierwerk, *n.* half adder.

Halbbild, *n.* (television) field, frame; **-frequenz,** *f.* frame frequency.

Halb-empirisch, semiempirical; **-gruppe,** *f.* semigroup.

Halbierungs-linie, *f.* bisectrix; **-punkt,** *m.* midpoint.

halbklassisch, semiclassical.

Halbleiter, *m.* semiconductor; **~ mit Defektelektronenleitung,** p-type semiconductor, de-

fect semiconductor, hole conductor; **~ mit Eigenleitfähigkeit,** intrinsic semiconductor.

Halbleiter-kristall, *m.* semiconducting crystal; **-oberfläche,** *f.* semiconductor surface.

Halb-periode, *f.* half cycle; **-satz,** *m.*:e, clause; **-schattenschleier,** *m.* penumbral blur; **-tägig,** semidiurnal; **-ton,** *m.* halftone, continuous tone; **-versetzung,** *f.* half-dislocation.

Halbwertsbreite, *f.* half-width; **~ der Interferenzen,** half-width of interference maxima.

Halbwertsschicht, *f.* half-value layer.

Haltbarkeit, *f.* shelf life, storage life.

Haltung, *f.* keeping, breeding, rearing.

Hand, an die ~ geben, to suggest; **von der ~ weisen,** to reject; **an ~ derer,** by means of which.

Handlocher, *m.* key punch.

Hangschutt, *m.* talus.

Hantelmodell, *n.* dumbbell model.

Hardware, *f.* hardware.

Harmonikafaltung, *f.* accordion pleating, accordion folding.

Härtegrad, *m.* contrast, gradation (of photographic negative density), (photographic) paper grade.

härten, to cure.

Härter, *m.* curing agent, hardener, activator.

Härtezeit, *f.* setting time.

Hartmetallschneide, *f.* tipped bit.

häufend, cumulative.

Haufen-schichtwolke, *f.* stratocumulus cloud; **-wolke,** *f.* cumulus cloud.

Häufigkeit, *f.* abundance, incidence; **-squotient,** *m.* incidence rate.

Häufungspunkt, *m.* limiting point, point of accumulation, bottleneck.

Haupt-achsentransformation, *f.* principal axis transformation; **-film,** *m.* main film, feature film; **-idealring,** *m.* principal ideal ring; **-krümmungsrichtung,** *m.* direction of principal curvature; **-minor,** *m.* principal minor; **-normalenvektor,** *m.* principal normal; **-programm,** *n.* feature film, full-length film; **-quantenzahl,** *f.* principal quantum number; **-satz der Wärmelehre,** law of thermodynamics; **-schlusswicklung,** *f.* series winding; **-sequenzstern,** *m.* star of principal sequence; **-stichwort,** *n.*-e, **·er,** descriptor; **-stromwicklung,** *f.* series winding.

Hautwirkung, *f.* skin effect.

heften, to staple, baste, tack.

Heftmaschine, *f.* stitching machine, stapler; **~ für Drahtheftung,** stapler.

Heftzwecke, *f.* thumbtack.

Heilweise, *f.* therapy, treatment.

Heiss-dampfreaktor, *m.* high-temperature steam reactor; **-fixierung,** *f.* heat setting, thermosetting; **-leiter,** *m.* thermistor; **-leitfähigkeit,** *f.* pyroconductivity; **-lötstelle,** *f.* hot junction.

Heizfaden, *m.* **thorierter ~,** thoriated filament; **~ mit Oxydschicht,** oxide-coated filament.

Heiz-tischmikroskop, *n.* hot-stage microscope; **-verfahren,** *n.* curing method; **-zeit,** *f.* curing time.

helfen, sich zu ~ wissen, to know how to manage.

Helium-ionenstoss, *m.* helium-ion collision; **-schicht,** *f.* helium film; **-wellenfunktion,** *f.* helium wave function.

Hell-bezugswert, *m.* albedo; **-feldbild,** *n.* bright-field image.

Helligkeits-ausbeute, *f.* luminosity; **-koeffizient,** *m.* luminance factor; **-wert,** *m.* brightness level.

herauf, bis ~ zu, up to.

heraus-heben, to factor out; **sich ~,** to cancel out; **-schleudern,** to eject, expel, emit; **-schneiden,** to intercept; **-suchen aus,** to sort out from.

Herd-gebiet, *n.* focal region; **-tiefe,** *f.* focal depth.

hermitisch, Hermitian.

Herpolhodiekegel, *m.* herpolhode.

Herz-ausstoss, *m.* cardiac output; **-belastung,** *f.* cardiac stress; **-frequenz,** *f.* heart rate; **-leistung,** *f.* cardiac output; **-schlagzahl,** *f.* pulse rate; **-stillstand,** *m.* cardiac arrest.

Hetero-ladung, *f.* heterocharge; **-polar,** heteropolar.

Hilfe, zu ~ nehmen, to use.

Hilfs-antrieb, *m.* servo drive; **-betrachtung,** *f.* auxiliary consideration; **-blitz,** *m.* fill-in flash; **-motor,** *m.* servo motor.

Himmels-lichtpolarisation, *f.* skylight polarization; **-mechanik,** *f.* celestial mechanics; **-richtunge,** *f.pl.* compass bearings.

Hinterflanke, *f.* trailing edge.

Hintergrund, in den ~ treten, to recede, step back.

Hirn-achse, *f.* brain stem; **-hautentzündung,** *f.* meningitis; **-strombild,** *n.* electroencephalogram.

Hitzehärtung, *f.* heat curing.

hochangeregter Zustand, highly excited state.

Hochbauschgarn, *n.* bulky yarn.

hoch-beanspruchbar, heavy duty; **-belastbar,** heavy duty.

Hochdruck-bogen, *m.* high-pressure arc; **-förderung,** *f.* crash program; **-glimmentladung,** *f.* high-pressure glow discharge.

Hoch-frequenzentladung, *f.* high-frequency discharge; **-frequenzleistung,** *f.* radio-frequency power; **-gespannt,** highly stressed; **-ionisiert,** highly ionized; **-nebel,** *m.* fracto-cumulus cloud; **-ohmig,** high-resistivity, high-impedance; **-spannungsanlage,** *f.* high-voltage set.

Höchstfrequenz, *f.* ultrahigh frequency; **-welle,** *f.pl.* microwaves.

Höchstgeschwindigkeit, *f.* speed limit.

Hoch-stromkohlebogen, *m.* high-current carbon arc; **-tonlautsprecher,** *m.* high-frequency loudspeaker, tweeter; **-vakuumdurchschlag,** *m.* high-vacuum breakdown; **-wert,** *m.* Y coordinate, latitude, northing (geodesy and surveying); **-widerstandsfähig,** high-tenacity.

hohe Atmosphäre, upper atmosphere.

Höhen-bestimmung, *f.* height determination; **-linie,** *f.* contour line; **-regler,** *m.* treble control; **-verteilung,** *f.* vertical distribution.

Hohl-anode, *f.* hollow anode; **-kathodenentladung,** *f.* hollow-cathode discharge; **-leiter,** *m.* waveguide; **-seide,** *f.* bulking yarn.

Hohlraum-bildung, *f.* cavitation; **-feld,** *n.* cavity field; **-resonator,** *m.* cavity resonator; **-resonatorröhre,** *f.* resonant cavity tube, magnetron; **-strahlung,** *f.* black-body radiation.

Hohlstelle, *f.* hollow.

Holographie, *f.* holography.

Homogenisierung, *f.* homogenization.

Homomorphismus, *m.* homomorphism.

Homöoladung, *f.* homocharge.

homöopolar, homopolar.

Hör-gerät, *n.* hearing aid; **-schwelle,** *f.* audibility threshold.

Hub-scheibenwelle, *f.* cam shaft; **-schrauber,** *m.* helicopter; **-volumen,** *n.* swept volume.

Hülle, *f.* closure, shell.

Hüllfläche, *f.* enveloping surface.

Hüllwerkstoffe, *m.* canning material, cladding material.

Hybridbindung, *f.* hybrid binding.

Hybridisierung, *f.* hybridization.

hydrierende Spaltung, hydrogenolysis.

Hydroraffination, *f.* hydrogen refining.

Hyperbelbahn, *f.* hyperbolic orbit.

Hyperboloid, *n.* hyperboloid.

Hyperfeinstruktur, *f.* hyperfine structure; **-multiplett,** *n.* hyperfine-structure multiplet; **-operator,** *m.* hyperfine-structure operator.

Hyperfläche, *f.* hypersurface.

hypergeometrisch, hypergeometric.

hyperkomplex, hypercomplex.

Addendum

Hysterese, *f.* hysteresis; -verluste, *m.pl.* eddy current loss.

Hysteresis, *f.* hysteresis; -schleife, *f.* hysteresis loop.

Ich, *n.* ego.

ideal fehlgeordnet, ideally imperfect (crystal).

identifiziert, identified.

Identitätsoperator, *m.* identity operator.

immer mehr, ever more.

Immunitäts-forschung, *f.* immunology; -reaktion, *f.* immune response, immune reaction.

Immunkörperspiegel, *m.* antibody titer.

Impedanz, *f.* impedance; -höhe, *f.* impedance level; -spule, *f.* reactance coil.

Impf-kristall, *m.* seed crystal; -kultur, *f.* vaccine culture; -serum, *n.* vaccine.

Imponiergehaben, *n.* display.

Impuls, falscher ~, spurious pulse; rechteckiger ~, square pulse; scharf begrenzter ~, sharply peaked pulse.

Impuls-abfallzeit, *f.* pulse decay time; -abstand, *m.* pulse spacing; -abtrennung, *f.* pulse clipping; -änderung, *f.* momentum change; -betrieb, *m.* pulsed operation; -dichte, *f.* counting rate; -dichtefunktion, *f.* momentum density function; -dichtemesser, *n.* counting rate meter; -erzeugung, *f.* pulse generation.

Impuls-fluss, *m.* momentum flux; -folge, *f.* pulse train, pulse sequence; -former, *m.* pulse shaper; -frequenzmesser, *m.* (counting) rate meter; -geber, *m.* pulse generator; -grösse, *f.* pulse amplitude; -kugel, *f.* momentum sphere; -raum, *m.* momentum space; -reihe, *f.* pulse train.

Impulsübertragung, *f.* momentum transfer; Stoss mit ~, momentum-transfer collision.

Impulsübertragungsreaktion, *f.* impulsive reaction.

Impuls- und Energieaustausch, *m.* momentum and energy exchange.

Impulsverteilung, *f.* momentum distribution.

Indifferenzbereich, *m.* doubtful region.

Indikatorenmethode, *f.* tracer method.

Indium-antimonid, *n.* indium antimonide; -selenid, *n.* indium selenide; -tellurid, *n.* indium telluride.

Indizes, *m.pl.* subscripts (and superscripts).

Indizierung, *f.* indexing.

Induktionsheizung, *f.* induction heater.

Induktivität, *f.* inductance.

ineinander-schachteln, to nest; -schiebbar, telescoping.

inelastisch, inelastic.

infinitäres Verhalten, asymptotic behavior.

Informations-dichte, *f.* recording density; -element, *n.* bit; -erschliessung, *f.* information retrieval; -wähler, *m.* data selector.

Infra-rotbeseitigung, *f.* infrared removal; -schall, *m.* infrasonics; -schwerewelle, *f.* infragravity wave.

·Inhomogenitätskorrektion, *f.* inhomogeneity correction.

inkaufnehmen, to make allowance for.

Inklinations-kompass, *m.* dip circle; -messer, *m.* inclinometer.

inkohlen, to carbonize, coalify, coke.

Inkohlungsgrad, *m.* coalification index, rank (of coal).

inkompatibel, incompatible.

Inkompatibilität, *f.* incompatibility.

Inkompatibilitätstensor, *m.* incompatibility tensor.

Inkreis, *m.*-e, inscribed circle.

innenzentriert, (cubic) body-centered.

Insektenpuppe, *f.* chrysalis.

Inselmodell, *n.* island model.

Insuffizienzgefühl, *n.* inferiority complex.

Instrumentenanflug, *m.* instrument approach.

Integrabilitätsbedingung, *f.* integrability condition.

Integral-begriff, *m.* concept of the integral; -beziehung, *f.* integral relation; -darstellung, *f.* integral representation; -gleichung, *f.* integral equation; -invariant, *m.* integral invariant; -satz, *m.*-e, integral theorem.

Integrand, *n.* integrand.

Integrator, *m.* integrator.

Integrieranlage, *f.* differential analyzer.

integrierbar, integrable.

Integritätsbereich, *m.* integral domain, domain of integrity.

Integrodifferentialgleichung, *f.* integrodifferential equation.

Intensitäts-anomalie, *f.* intensity anomaly; -bereich, *m.* intensity region; -maximum, *n.* maximum intensity; -schwächung, *f.* intensity decrease; -summensatz, *m.* intensity sum rule.

Interferenz-apparatur, *f.* diffraction camera; -aufnahme, *f.* interference photograph; -bild, *n.* interference pattern; -doppelbrechung, *f.* interference in double refraction; -frequenzmesser, *m.* heterodyne frequency meter; -spektrogramm, *n.* interference spectrogram; -streifen, *m.* interference fringe.

Inter-kombination, *f.* intercombination; -polationsformel, *f.* interpolation formula.

Intervallschachtelung, *f.* nest of intervals.

Invariante, *f.* invariant.

Invarianzprinzip, *n.* principle of invariance.

Inversions-schicht, *f.* inversion layer; -zentrum, *n.* center of inversion.

invertierbar, invertible.

Involutionssystem, *n.* involution system.

Inzidenzgeometrie, *f.* geometry of coincidence.

Ionen-austausch, *m.* ion exchange; -bindung, *f.* ionic bond, electrovalent bond; -bremsfeld, *n.* ion-retarding field; -falle, *f.* ion trap; -gitter, *n.* ion lattice; -kette, *f.* ion chain; -rumpf, *m.* -e, ion core; -sättigungsstrom, *m.* ion saturation current; -strom, *m.* ion current; -wanderungsgeschwindigkeit, *f.* ion-drift velocity.

Ion-Ion-Rekombination, *f.* ion-ion recombination.

Ionisations-energie, *f.* ionization energy; -gleichgewicht, *n.* ionization balance; -grad, *m.* ionization constant; -kammer, *f.* ionization chamber; -kontinuum, *n.* ionization continuum; -stufe, *f.* ionization stage.

ionisierte Störstelle, ionized impurity.

Ionisierungsausbeute, *f.* ionization efficiency; -kurve, *f.* ionization yield.

Ionisierungsbruchteil, *m.* ionization fraction.

Ionisierungspotential, *n.* ionization potential; ~ durch Variationsmethode, variational ionization potential.

Ionisierungs-querschnitt, *m.* ionization cross section; -spannung, *f.* ionization voltage; -stärke, *f.* total ionization; -strahlung, *f.* ionizing radiation.

Ionisierungs- und Anregungswahrscheinlichkeit, *f.* probability of ionization and excitation.

Ionisierungswelle, *f.* ionizing wave.

Ionosphärenschall, *m.* ionosphere sound.

Irrelevanz, *f.* ambiguity.

Irrenheilkunde, *f.* psychiatry, psychotherapy.

Irr-fahrt, *f.* random walk; -strahl, *m.* stray light.

Isentropenanalyse, *f.* isentropic analysis.

isentropisch, isentropic.

isobar, isobaric.

isoelektronisch, isoelectronic.

Isohypsenplan, *m.* isohyps map.

Isolatoroberfläche, *f.* insulator surface.

Isolierschicht, *f.* insulator.

isometrisch Konsistenzkarte, isometric consistency chart.

Isomorphismus, *m.* isomorphism.

isoperimetrisch, isoperimetric.

Isoporenfokus, *m.* isoporic focus.

isostatisch, isostatic.

isotaktisch, isotactic.

isotherm, isothermal.

Isotopen-anreicherung, *f.* isotope enrichment; -effekt, *m.* isotope effect; -ersetzung, *f.* isotope replacement; -häufigkeitsmessung, *f.* isotopic-abundance measurement; -indikator, *m.* tracer isotope; -trennvorgang, *m.*-e, isotope-separation process.

Isotopie-effekt, *m.* isotope effect; -spin, *m.* isotopic spin; -verschiebung, *f.* isotope shift.

Isotropie, *f.* isotropy.

Ist-anzeige, *f.* indicated value; -grösse, *f.* actual size; -menge, *f.* actual quantity; -wert, *m.* real value, actual value; -zeit, *f.* real time.

Iterationsverfahren, *n.* iteration method.

iteriert, iterated.

Ja-Nein-Entscheidungen, *f.pl.* fail-pass indications.

Kabel-masse, *f.* sheathing compound; -schuh, *m.* terminal.

Käfig-effekt, *m.* cage effect; -läuferasynchronmotor, *m.* squirrel-cage induction motor; -wicklung, *f.* squirrel-cage winding.

Kaliglimmer, *m.* muscovite, potash mica.

Kalium-bifluorid, *n.* potassium bifluoride; -boratglas, *n.*-er, potassium borate glass; -niobat, *n.* potassium niobate.

Kaliumphosphat, *n.* potassium phosphate; primäres ~, potassium dihydrogen phosphate.

Kaliumtantalat, *n.* potassium tantalate.

Kalkabnahme, *f.* decalcification.

Kalkspatinterferometer, *m.* calcite interferometer.

Kalotte, *f.* spherical surface.

Kalottenfläche, *f.* impression, indentation (Brinell test).

kaltaushärtbar, cold-cured, cold-hardening, cold set.

Kälte-maschine, *f.* refrigerating machine, refrigerator; -mittel, *n.* refrigerant, cooling agent; -schlaf, *m.* hibernation; -schutzmittel, *n.* antifreeze; -sprödigkeit, *f.* low-temperature brittleness; -viskosität, *f.* low-temperature viscosity.

Kalt-leiter, *m.* positive-temperature-coefficient (PTC) resistor; -luftdom, *m.* cold dome; -verformung, *f.* cold work; -verstreckt, cold-worked, cold-drawn.

Kamin, *m.* riser, flue; -stummel, *m.* riser.

Kammlänge, *f.* crest length.

Kanalbildung, *f.* channeling.

Kanalstrahl-entladung, *f.* canal-ray discharge; **-ionenquelle,** *f.* canal-ray discharge ion source; **-röhre,** *f.* canal-ray tube.

Kanten-kräuselung, *f.* stress curling; **-schema,** *n.* Deslandres table.

Kapazität, *f.* capacitance.

Kapazitäts-diode, *f.* varactor, variable-capacitance diode; **-frei,** noncapacitive; **-faktor,** *m.* capacity ratio.

Kapazitron, *n.* capacitron.

Kapillar-aszension, *f.* capillary rise; **-chromatographie,** *f.* open tubular column chromatography; **-elektrometer,** *m.* capillary electrometer; **-niveauschwingung,** *f.* capillary level oscillation.

Kapitalbegegnungsmethode, *f.* capital anticipation method.

Kappazahl, *f.* kappa number.

Kar, *n.* glacial amphitheatre, cirque; **-niveau,** *n.* cirque belt.

Karbonatisation, *f.* carbonatization (in geochemistry).

Karbonatisierung, *f.* carbonatization (in geochemistry).

karbonisieren, to carbonate, carbonize (textiles).

Karbonisieren, *n.* carbonation.

Karies, *f.* caries, tooth decay; **-erzeugend,** cariogenic.

Karrotage, *f.* logging.

Karte, *f.* card; ~ **mit Kantenlochung,** edge punched card.

Karten-abfühler, *m.* card reader; **-ablage,** *f.* card stacker; **-abtaster,** *m.* card reader; **-locher,** *m.* card punch; **-mischer,** *m.* collator; **-netz,** *n.* map grid; **-satz,** *m.* card deck.

Kartiergerät, *n.* plotter, plotting machine.

Kartograph, *n.* plotter, plotting machine.

kaschieren, to back, coat.

kaschierte Gewebe, backed fabric, reinforced fabric.

Kaschierungsmittel, *n.* laminating material.

Kaskaden-entmagnetisierung, *f.* cascade demagnetization; **-konstante,** *f.* cascading constant; **-übergang,** *m.*-e, cascade transition.

Kastenleiter, *m.* rectangular waveguide.

Katastrophenhilfe, *f.* disaster relief.

Kater, *m.* hangover.

Kathoden-ausdehnung, *f.* area of the cathode; **-berechnung,** *f.* cathode evaluation; **-dunkelraum,** *m.* cathode dark space; **-glimmlicht,** *n.* cathode glow; **-mechanismus,** *m.* cathode mechanism; **-polarisation,** *f.* cathodic polarization; **-verstärker,** *m.* cathode follower.

Kationenaustauscher, *m.* cation exchanger; **-harz,** *n.* cation-exchange resin.

Kausalitätsforderung, *f.* causality requirement.

Kaustik-fläche, *f.* caustic surface; **-spitze,** *f.* caustic tip.

Kegel, *m.* taper; **-achsenaufnahme,** *f.* cone-axis photograph; **-fallpunkt,** *m.* pyrometric cone equivalent, softening point of the cone; **-stoffmühle,** *f.* jordan; **-strahlröhre (Kestral-Röhre),** *f.* cestral tube.

Kehrbild, *n.* inverted image.

Kehrichthaufen, *m.* junk pile.

Kehrwertintegration, *f.* reciprocal integration.

Keilstreifen-Technik, *f.* wedge-tip technique.

Keimbildung, *f.* nucleation.

Kenn-frequenz, *f.* assigned frequency; **-grösse,** *f.* characteristic number, characteristic value, characteristic quantity, parameter, dimensionless number.

Kenntnis nehmen, to take notice of.

keramische Körper, ceramics, refractory material.

Keramisierungsprozess, *m.*-e, ceramming process.

Kerb-empfindlichkeit, *f.* notch sensitivity; **-schlagbiegversuch,** *m.* notch impact bending test.

Kern, anthropogener ~, man-made nucleus.

Kern-ausrichtung, *f.* nuclear alignment; **-bildung,** *f.* nucleation; **-brennstoffbedarf,** *m.* nuclear fuel demand; **-entmagnetisierung,** *f.* nuclear demagnetization; **-ferromagnetismus,** *m.* nuclear ferromagnetism; **-fremdes Feld,** extranuclear field; **-grösse,** *f.* nuclei size; **-indexmethode,** *f.* kernel-index method; **-kopplungskonstante,** *f.* nuclear coupling constant; **-kraftwerk,** *n.* nuclear power plant.

Kernladungs-verteilung, *f.* nuclear charge distribution; **-zahl,** *f.* nuclear charge.

kern-magnetische Kopplung, nuclear magnetic coupling; **-magneton,** *n.* nuclear magneton.

Kern-mitbewegung, *f.* motion of the nucleus; **-moment,** *m.* nuclear moment.

Kernphoto-reaktion, *f.* photonuclear reaction; **-wechselwirkung,** *f.* photonuclear interaction.

Kernprozessstreuphase, *f.* nuclear phase shift.

Kernquadrupol-kopplung, *f.* nuclear quadrupole coupling; **-resonanz,** *f.* nuclear quadrupole resonance.

Kernreaktor, *m.* nuclear reactor, nuclear pile.

Kernresonanz, *f.* nuclear resonance; **-fluoreszenz,** *f.* nuclear-resonance fluorescence.

Kern-schalenmodell, *n.* nuclear-shell model; **-schichtmethode,** *f.* core method; **-spaltung,** *f.* nuclear fission; **-spaltungsfragment,** *n.* fission fragment; **-spin,** *m.* nuclear spin; **-suszeptibilität,** *f.* nuclear susceptibility; **-umwandlung,** *f.* nuclear transmutation; **-zerfall,** *m.* nuclear decay; **-zertrümmerung,** *f.* nuclear disintegration.

Kescher, *m.* insect net.

Kettbaum, *m.* warp beam; **-färberei,** *f.* beam dyeing.

Ketten-abbrecher, *m.* chain terminator; **-bruchdarstellung,** *f.* continued-fraction representation; **-leiter,** *m.* ladder network; **-matrix,** *f.* iterative matrix; **-methode,** *f.* iterative method; **-schaltung,** *f.* cascade connection, ladder network; **-startreaktion,** *f.* chain initiation; **-wachstum,** *n.* chain propagation.

Kilopond, *n.* kp, kilogram-weight or kilogram-force, kgf.

Kinder-arzt, *m.* pediatrician; **-betreuer,** *m.* baby-sitter.

Kindes-alter, *n.* infancy, childhood; **-entführung,** *f.* kidnapping.

Kinematographie, *f.* cinematography.

Kipp-ablenkung, *f.* sweep deflection, horizontal deflection; **-frequenz,** *f.* sweep frequency, relaxation frequency; **-kreis,** *m.* time-base circuit, sweep circuit; **-last,** *f.* buckling load; **-schaltung,** *f.* flip-flop circuit, sweep circuit; **-schwingung,** *f.* wagging vibration; **-teiler,** *m.* multivibrator.

Kissenverzeichnung, *f.* pincushion distortion.

Klamm, *f.* canyon, gorge.

Klammerrelation, *f.* bracket relation.

klang-getreu, orthophonic; **-regler,** *m.* tone control.

Klär-anlage, *f.* sewage treatment plant, clarification plant, sewage disposal plant; **-schlamm,** *m.* sludge.

Klassensumme, *f.* class sum.

Klassifikation, *f.* classification.

Klebe-band, *n.*—**-er,** tape, adhesive tape; **-lade,** *f.* splicer.

Kleb-festigkeit, *f.* bond strength: **-freitrocknung,** *f.* tack-free drying time.

Klebrigmacher, *m.* tackifier.

Kleinbild-dia, *n.* 35-mm slide; **-film,** *m.* 35-mm film, miniature film.

Kleinfilm, *m.* 35-mm film, miniature film.

Kleinformatkamera, *f.* 35-mm camera.

Kleinwesen, *n.* small being.

Kleinwinkel-korngrenze, *f.* small-angle grain boundary; **-streuung,** *f.* small-angle scattering; **-streuversuch,** *m.* small-angle scattering experiment.

Klemmeffekt, *m.* pinch effect.

Klimaanlage, *f.* air conditioner; **mit ~ versehen,** air-conditioned.

Klinke, *f.* pawl, telephone jack.

Klopfbremse, *f.* anti-knock agent.

Knebelpresse, *f.* tourniquet.

Knick-band, *n.* kink band; **-bruch,** *m.* greenstick fracture; **-punktchlorung,** *f.* breakpoint chlorination.

Knoten-linie, *f.* nodal line; **-satz,** *m.* zero rule.

Knotte, *f.* nodule.

Knüpfstelle, *f.* crosslinking site.

Koagulationszeit, *f.* clotting time.

koaxial, coaxial.

Kochbeuche, *f.* kier boiling.

Kode, *m.* code; **korregierbarer ~,** error-correcting code: **prüfbarer ~,** error-detecting code.

Kode-erzeugung, *f.* code generation; **-muster,** *n.* coded pattern; **-wähler,** *m.* code selector.

Koerzitivfeld, *n.* coercitive field.

Kohärenzbegriff, *m.* concept of coherence.

Kohäsionseigenschaft, *f.* cohesive property.

Kohle-bogen, *m.* carbon arc; **-hülle,** *f.* envelope of carbon.

Kohlen-entgasungsanlage, *f.* coal carbonization plant, by-product coke plant; **-kammer,** *f.* carbon button (microphone); **-reifung,** *f.* coalification.

Koinzidenzschaltung, *f.* coincidence circuit.

Koksrückstand nach Conradson, Conradson carbon residue.

Kolben-abstand, *m.*—**-e,** piston clearance; **-blasenströmung,** *f.* plug flow; **-blitz,** *m.* flashbulb; **-maschine,** *f.* reciprocating engine; **-strangpresse,** *f.* ram extruder.

Kolk-bildung, *f.* cratering; **-tiefe,** *f.* crater depth.

kollabieren, to collapse, deflate.

Kollektivmodell, *n.* collective model; **~ der Elektronen,** collective electron model.

kollimierend, collimating.

Kollineation, *f.* collineation.

Kollodiumschicht, *f.* collodion film.

Kollokation, *f.* collocation.

Kolmatierung, *f.* silting up, filling up, aggradation.

Kometenbahn, *f.* cometary orbit.

Komma, bewegliches ~, floating decimal point.

kommutativ, commutative.

Kompatibilitätsbedingung, *f.* compatibility condition.

Komplementablenkungsreaktion, *f.* complement fixation test.

Addendum 587

Komplementärmenge, f. complementary set.

komplex konjugiert, complex conjugated.

Komplex-bildner, m. complexing agent, sequestering agent; -bildung, f. complexing reaction.

Kompressions-modul, n. bulk modulus; -zentrum, n. center of compression.

Konfigurations-entropie, f. configurational entropy; -raum, m. configuration space; -wechselwirkung, f. configuration interaction.

konfluent hypergeometrisch, confluent hypergeometric.

konforme Abbildung, conformal mapping.

Kongruenz-annahme, f. assumption of congruence; -satz, m. congruence theorem.

Konjugationslinie, f. joint.

Konjunktivbruch, m. compression fault.

Konkavgitter, n. concave grating.

Konormale, f. conormal.

Konservenmusik, f. canned music.

Konsistenzmass, n. measure of consistency.

Konsonant, m. consonant; stimmhafter ~, voiced consonant; stimmloser ~, unvoiced consonant.

Konstantan, n. constantan.

Konstanzelement, n. element of constancy.

Kontakt, m. catalyst; -draht, m. whisker; -gift, n. catalyst poison; -glas, n. contact lens; -korrosion, f. galvanic corrosion; -menge, f. catalyst mass; -potential, n. contact potential; -spitze, f. contact whisker.

Kontinental-rand, m. ̈-er, continental margin; -verschiebung, f. continental drift.

Kontinuum, n. continuum.

Kontinuumsmodell, n. continuum model.

kontragredient, contragredient.

Kontrastwiedergabe, f. contrast rendition.

kontravariant, contravariant.

Konturierungsbohrung, f. field development well.

Konvention für die Summation, summation convention.

konvergent, convergent.

Konvergenz im Mittel, convergence in mean.

Konvergenz-gebiet, n. region of convergence; -kreis, m. circle of convergence.

Konzeptionsverhütung, f. contraception.

Koog, m. koog, diked land, polder.

Koordinationsgitter, n. coordination lattice.

Kopf-hörer, m.pl. headset, headphones; -produkt, n. forerun; -stein, m. cobblestone.

Kopiervorlage, f. material to be copied.

Koppelgetriebe, n. linkage.

Kopplung kurzer Reichweite, short-range coupling; ~ nächster Nachbarn, nearest-neighbor coupling.

Kopplungs-matrix, f. dynamic or coupling matrix; -parameter, m. coupling constant.

Körnelung, f. speckle (in diffraction patterns).

Kornflächenätzung, f. contrast etching.

Korngrenz-diffusion, f. grain-boundary diffusion; -energie, f. energy of grain boundary.

Körnigkeit (des Films), f. grain (of the film).

Körnungsgesetz, n. law of size distribution.

Kornverfeinerung, f. grain refining.

Korona, f. corona; ~ der Zündung, preonset corona.

Koronadurchbruch, m. pulse corona.

Koronadurchschlag, m. einmaliger ~, burstpulse corona.

Korona-entladung, f. corona discharge; -linie, f. coronal line.

Körper, m. field (math.); idealelastischer ~, Hookean solid.

körper-festes System, body system; -stösse, m.pl. body collisions.

Korrelations-einfluss, m. correlation effects; -koeffizient, m. correlation factor.

Korrosionshärtemessung, f. measurement of hardness by corrosion.

Kosmonaut, m. space man, astronaut.

kovalent, covalent.

kovariant, covariant.

Kovariante, f. covariant.

Krack-anlage, f. cracking unit or plant; -verfahren, n. cracking (of hydrocarbons).

Kräfte-paar, n.-e, couple; -zerlegung, f. resolution of forces.

Kraft-feld, n. force field; -netz, n. power line.

Kranken-bild, n. clinical picture; -blatt, n. medical record; -geschichte, f. case history; -wagen, m. ambulance.

Kranzarterie, f. coronary artery.

Kräuselmarken, f.pl. ripples, ripple marks, wave lines.

Kreditoren, m.pl. accounts payable.

Kreisel-frequenz, f. gyrofrequency; -kompass, m. gyrocompass; -molekül, n. top molecule.

Kreis-frequenz, f. angular frequency; -funktion, f. trigonometric function; -lochblende, f. circular aperture; -prozess, m. circulation process, cycle; -versetzung, f. circular dislocation.

Kreuz-see, m. choppy sea; -stromboden, m. cross-flow tray; -tisch, m. cross-table.

Kreuzungspunkt, m. crosspoint, crossover point.

Kriechen, n. surface leakage, creeping; ~ dün-

ner Flüssigkeitsschichten, film creep; ter-
tiares ~, accelerated creep.

Kristall-bereich, m. crystal domain; -be-
reichswand, f. domain wall.

Kriställchenflüssigkeit, f. crystal liquid, liquid
crystal.

Kristall-einbettung, f. dilution of a crystal;
-fehler, m. imperfection of a crystal.

Kristallfeld, n. crystalline field; -aufspaltung, f.
crystalline field splitting.

Kristall-gitterskala, f. crystal-lattice scale;
-hyperfeinstruktur, f. crystal hyperfine structure.

kristalline Flüssigkeit, liquid crystal.

Kristall-kollimator, m. crystal collimator;
-monochromator, m. crystal monochromator;
-morphologie, f. crystal morphology; -per-
iodizität, f. crystal periodicity.

Kristall-plättchen, n. crystal wafer; -platte, f.
crystal slab; Anreissen der ~, wafer scribing.

Kristall-pulver, n. powdered crystal; -quanten-
zahl, f. crystal quantum number; -term, m. crystal term; -triode, f. crystal triode; -wachstum, n.
crystalline growth; -wechselwirkung, crystalline field interaction; -ziehen, n. crystal pulling,
crystal growing.

kritisches Verhältnis, critical rate.

Krümmungs-kreis, m. circle of curvation; osculating circle; -linie, f. line of curvature.

krumpfen, to shrink.

Krustengestein, n. crustal rocks.

kryomagnetisch, cryomagnetic.

Kryostat, n. cryostat.

Kryotechnik, f. cryogenics.

kubisch, ~ dichtest, cubic close-packed; ~
flächenzentriert, face-centered cubic; ~ raum-
zentriert, cubic body-centered.

Küchenabfällen, m.pl. kitchen middens.

Kugel-blitz, m. ball lightning; -druckhärte-
prüfer, m. ball tester; -druckversuch, m. indentation test; -flächenfunktion, f. surface
harmonics; -funktion, f. spherical function;
-funktionsentwicklung, f. spherical harmonic
analysis; -gestaltsfehler, m. spherical aberration; -graphit, m. nodular (spheroidal) graphite;
-koordinaten, f.pl. spherical coordinates.

Kugelpackung, f. packing of the spheres;
dichteste ~, close-packed structure.

Kugel-pyranometer, m. spherical pyranometer;
-schreiber, m. ball-point pen.

Kühl-aggregat, n. refrigerator; -falle, f. cold
trap; -körper, m. heat sink; -patrone, f. cooling
device, cartridge; -platte, f. heat sink.

Kühlungskoeffizient, m. cooling coefficient;
bei konstanter Entropie, isentropic cooling
coefficient.

Külbel, m. parison.

Kunststoff, technischer ~, engineering plastic.

Küpenfarbstoffe, m.pl. vat dyes.

Kurs-fehler, m. tracking error; -funkfeuer, n.
radio range; -winkel, m. magnetic azimuth,
route angle.

Kurven-anpassung, f. curve fitting; -darstel-
lung, f. plot, graph; -integral, n. contour integral; -körper, m. cam (math.); -lineal, n. French
curve; -schar, f. family of curves.

kurzbrennweitig, short-focus.

Kürze, der ~ halber, for the sake of brevity, for
short.

kurz-kämmig, short-crested; -reichweiten-
grenze, f. short-range limit; -reichweitig,
short-range; -schlussventil, n. bypass valve;
-strahlung, f. short-wave radiation; -wellige
Grenze, short-wavelength limit; -zeichen, n.
symbol.

Küstenbauten, m.pl. coastal construction.

Kybernetik, f. cybernetics.

Ladestelle, f. entry point.

Ladung-Masse Verhältnis, n. charge-to-mass
ratio.

Ladungs-bild, n. electrostatic image, charge pattern; -invarianz, f. charge independence; -mul-
tiplett, n. charge multiplet; -speicherung, f.
charge storage; -spin, m. charge spin;
-transport, m. charge transport; -übertragung,
f. charge transfer; -unabhängigkeit, f. charge
independence; -verformung, f. charge distortion;
-verteilung, f. charge distribution; -verviel-
fachung, f. multiplication of charge; -zahl, f.
charge number.

Lage-beziehung, f. topological relation;
-gruppe, f. position group.

Lagenholz, f. plywood.

Lager-spiel, n.-e, bearing clearance, bearing
play; -stätte, f. (oil) reservoir, pool.

Lamellen-rohr, n. finned or ribbed tube; -röhre,
f. lamellar tube; -technik, f. vane technique.

laminares Modell mit Verzweigungen,
branched laminar model.

Lande-bahn, f. runway; -klappe, f. landing flap.

lange, noch ~ nicht, not for some time, far from
it, anything but.

Länge in der Ekliptik, longitude in ecliptic.

längentreu, length-preserving, isometric.

Längenübertragung, f. transfer of the length.

Lang-spielplatte, f. long-playing record; -welle,
f. long wave.

Lanthaniden, f.pl. lanthanide elements, lan-
thanides; -reihe, f. lanthanide series.

Läppchenprobe, f. patch test.

Lärm-bekämpfung, *f.* noise abatement, noise control, anti-noise campaign; **-belastung,** *f.* noise pollution; **-hintergrund,** *m.* background noise; **-stärke,** *f.* noise level.

Laser, *m.* laser; **kontinuierlicher ~,** continuous wave laser; **-gas,** *n.* lasing gas; **-welle,** *f.* laser mode.

Last, zur ~ legen, to charge with.

Laster, *n.* vice, addiction.

laufen lassen, to develop, chromatograph.

Läufer-geschwindigkeit, *f.* rotor speed; **-wicklung,** *f.* rotor winding.

Lauf-feldröhre, *f.* traveling-wave tube; **-fläche,** *f.* tread; **-geschwindigkeit,** *f.* migration rate; **-mittel,** *n.* mobile phase; **-richtung,** *f.* development direction; **-strecke,** *f.* length of run.

Laufzeit, *f.* travel time, time of flight, transit time, propagation time, time delay, development (chromatogram) time; **-methode,** *f.* time-of-flight technique; **-spektrometer,** *m.* time-of-flight spectrometer.

Lautsprecher, *m.* loudspeaker.

Lavastrom, *m.*-e, lava flow.

Lawinen-durchschlag, *m.* avalanche breakdown; **-schwankung,** *f.* avalanche fluctuation.

Lebens-gemeinschaft, *f.* symbiosis; **-hülle,** *f.* biosphere.

Leckleitwert, *m.* leakage conductance.

Lecksucher, *m.* leak detector.

Leer-lauf, *m.* idle running, idling, no-load operation; **-präparat,** *n.* placebo; **-stelle,** *f.* vacancy.

Leerstellen-paar, *n.* vacancy pair; **-sprung,** *m.* vacancy jog.

Leerwert, *m.* background.

legiertes Motorenöl, doped lube oil.

Lehr-automat, *m.* teaching machine; **-maschine,** *f.* teaching machine.

Leichen-beschauer, *m.* coroner; **-besichtigung,** *f.* post-mortem examination; **-schauhaus,** *n.* morgue.

Leimung, *f.* in der Masse, internal sizing.

Leistungs-charakteristik, *f.* performance characteristic; **-faktor,** *m.* power factor; **-reaktor,** *m.* nuclear power plant; **-reserve,** *f.* standby power; **-verlust,** *m.* power loss; **-verstärker,** *m.* high-gain amplifier.

Leitelement, *n.* tracer element.

Leiter-bild, *n.* wiring diagram; **-platte,** *f.* (printed) circuit board; **-polymere,** *n.* ladder polymer.

Leitfähigkeit, *f.* conductance.

Leitfähigkeits-abfall, *m.* conductivity decay; **-elektronen,** *n.pl.* conductance electrons; **-zähler,** *m.* conductivity counter.

Leitungs-band, *n.* conduction band; **-eigenschaft,** *f.* conduction property; **-elektron,** *n.* conduction electron; **-stromdichte,** *f.* conduction-current density.

Leitweg, *m.* routing.

Lenzen, *n.* dumping.

letzter, als ~, as the last one; **~ Hand,** at last.

Leuchtelektron, *n.* valence electron.

Leuchtstoff, *m.* fluorescent or phosphorescent material; **-lampe,** *f.* fluorescent lamp.

Lichtausbeute, *f.* luminous efficiency, light output.

Lichtbeständigkeitsprüfer, *m.* fade-o-meter.

Lichtbogen-ofen, *m.*-, arc furnace; **-physik,** *f.* arc physics.

Licht-figur, *f.* asterism.

Lichtfleck, *m.* light spot; **feststehender ~,** stationary light spot.

licht-gehärtet, photocured; **-geschwindigkeitsmessung,** *f.* velocity of light measurement; **-kanone,** *f.* laser; **-quellenspalt,** *m.* light-source slit; **-schnitt,** *m.* light intersection; **-sondentechnik,** *f.* light-probe technique; **-spiel,** *n.* motion picture; **-stärke,** *f.* luminosity, luminous intensity, lens speed, f stop; **-steuerung,** *f.* light modulation; **-strom,** *m.* luminous flux; **-weg,** *m.* optical path.

Liefergrad, *m.* volumetric efficiency.

liegen, etwas ~ lassen, to let a thing lie (be).

Linearbeschleuniger, *m.* linear accelerator.

linearisiert, linearized.

Linearisierung, *f.* linearization.

linear unabhängig, linearly independent.

Linienblitz, *m.* streak lightning.

Linienbreite, *m.* line width; **gesamte ~,** integral line width.

Linien-dichte, *f.* line density; **-dipol,** *n.* line dipole; **-form,** *f.* line shape; **-höhe,** *f.* peak height; **-profil,** *n.* profile of a line; **-schreiber,** *m.* plotter; **-umkehr,** *f.* reversal dip; **-verbreiterung,** *f.* line broadening.

Linkssystem, *n.* left-handed system.

Lithium-boratglas, *n.*-er, lithium borate glass; **-silikatglas,** *n.*-er, lithium silicate glass; **-tantalat,** *n.* lithium tantalate.

Löcher-leitfähigkeit, *f.* hole conductivity, p-type conductivity; **-spektrum,** *n.* hole spectrum.

Lochkarte, *f.* punched card.

Lochkarten ablochen, to keypunch.

Lochstreifen, *m.* (punched) paper tape, punched tape.

Lock-mittel, *n.* attractant; **-stoff,** *m.* attractant; **-wirkung,** *f.* attractant action.

logarithmisch-normale Verteilung, logarithmiconormal distribution.

Lohn-abzug, $m.$-e, payroll deduction; **-kosten,** $f.pl.$ labor cost; **-steuer,** $f.$ withholding tax.

lokal eben, locally flat.

Lokalisierungssatz, $m.$ localization theorem.

Longitudinalwelle, $f.$ longitudinal wave.

Löslichmachung, $f.$ solubilization.

löschen, to blank, clear, erase, reset.

Lösch-impuls, $m.$ erase signal; **-kontakt,** $m.$ reset contact; **-kopf,** $m.$-e, erase head, erasing head.

Loschmidtsche Zahl, $f.$ Avogadro's number, Loschmidt's number.

Löschtaste, $f.$ cancel key, manual override key, reset button, selector key, clearing key.

Löschung, $f.$ quenching.

Lösungs-effekt, $m.$ solvent effect; **-verbesserer,** $m.$ solubilizer; **-vermittler,** $m.$ solubilizer.

Lotabweichung, $f.$ plumb-line deflection.

Lötbad, $n.$ solder dip.

Lot-richtung, $f.$ plumb line, vertical; **-schwankung,** $f.$ deflection of the vertical.

Loxodrome, $f.$ loxodromic line.

Lues, $f.$ syphilis.

Luft-aufnahme, $f.$ aerial photography, photogrammetry.

Luftberg, $m.$ air peak; **Durchbruchzeit des ~,** air peak time.

Luft-bild, $n.$ aerial photograph; **-druckwelle,** $f.$ barometric variation; **-entladung,** $f.$ air discharge; **-leuchten,** $n.$ air glow; **-molluskel,** $n.$ aerial mollusk; **-polster,** $n.$ air space; **-rektifikationsanlage,** $f.$ air rectifier; **-spalt,** $m.$ air gap; **-streuung,** $f.$ Rayleigh scattering; **-verflüssigungsmaschine,** $f.$ air liquefier; **-verpesterung,** $f.$ air pollution; **-verschmutzung,** $f.$ air pollution; **-verunreinigung,** $f.$ air pollution.

Lumineszenzanregung, $f.$ luminescence excitation.

Luvseite, $f.$ windward side; **auf der ~,** to the windward.

Magerkohle, $f.$ semianthracite.

Magnesiumantimonid, $n.$ magnesium antimonide.

Magnet-band, $m.$ magnetic tape; **~ für Tonaufzeichnung,** audio tape; **-bandspeicher,** $m.$ tape store, magnetic tape store; **-feld,** $n.$ magnetic field; **-feldröhre,** $f.$ magnetron.

magnetisches Zeichen, magnetic character.

Magnetisierung, $f.$ magnetization.

Magnetkartenspeicher, $m.$ magnetic card memory; **~ mit beliebigem Zugriff,** magnetic card random access memory.

Magnetkernspeicher, $m.$ magnetic-core memory or storage.

Magnetkern-speicherung, $f.$ magnetic-core storage; **-wähler,** $m.$ core switch.

Magnetkies, $m.$ pyrrhotite, magnetic pyrites, FeS.

Magnet-kissen, $n.$ magnetic cushion; **-kopf,** $m.$ magnetic head; **-plattenspeicher,** $m.$ magnetic-disk memory.

Magneto-meter, $m.$ magnetometer; **-tellurik,** $f.$ magnetotellurics, magnetotelluric method.

Magnet-spule, $f.$ magnet coil, solenoid, trip coil; **-tonband,** $n.$ magnetic tape recording; **-verstärkerkippschaltung,** $f.$ magnetic amplifier flipflop circuit.

Mahlgrad, $m.$ freeness (of pulp).

Mahlung, $f.$ grinding, crushing, milling, beating (of pulp).

Mahlzustand, $n.$ freeness (of pulp).

Majorante, $f.$ majorant, upper bound.

Makro-ablauf, $m.$ macroaction; **-smat,** $m.$ macrosmatic animal.

Manganknolle, $f.$ manganese nodule or concretion, halobolite.

Mangel-elektron, $n.$ electron vacancy, positive hole; **-haftigkeit,** $f.$ deficiency, defectiveness, faultiness, inadequacy; **-leiter,** $m.$ deficit semiconductor, p-type conductor, hole conductor; **-leitung,** $f.$ hole conduction, p-type conductivity or conduction.

Manufakt, $n.$ artifact.

maritim, maritime; **maritimes Erdöl,** offshore oil.

Marke, $f.$ ticket, label, make; **bis zur ~ auffüllen,** to adjust volume to the mark.

Markierungs-bit, $n.$ flag bit, mark; **-leser,** $m.$ tagging reader, labeling reader; **-zeichen,** $n.$ flag bit, mark.

Markscheider, $m.$ surveyor (land or mine).

Marquardt'sche Masse, Marquardt paste or cement.

Mars-kanäle, $n.pl.$ Martian canals; **-monde,** $n.pl.$ Martian moons.

Marsupialer, $n.pl.$ marsupials, marsupial mammals.

Maschen-drahtfüllkörper, $m.pl.$ mesh packing; **-weite,** $f.$ mesh size, mesh opening, screen aperture; **-zahl,** $f.$ mesh, number of meshes (per unit length).

Maschinencode, $m.$ machine code, computer code, absolute code; **-programm,** $n.$ object program, target program.

Maschinen-fehler, *m.* machine error, hardware failure, machine fault; **-komma,** *n.* machine point; **-nutzzeit,** *f.* machine-available time; **-rüstzeit,** *f.* machine setup time.

maschineschreiben, to typewrite.

Massbestimmung, *f.* mensuration, metric determination.

Masse, *f.* body (of ceramics), batch, material, compound; **scheinbare ~,** effective mass, apparent additional mass.

Massen-anteil, *m.* weight fraction; **-anziehung,** *f.* gravitation, gravitational attraction; **-bremsvermögen,** *n.* mass stopping power; **-einheit,** *f.* unit of mass; **-gebirge,** *n.* massif; **-komponente,** *f.* bulk component.

Massenkorrektur, *f.* mass correction: **~ für Austausch,** exchange mass correction.

Massen-kraft, *f.* inertial force, gravitational force; **-kreuzung,** *f.* polycross; **-mässig,** quantitative; **-schwächungskoeffizient,** *m.* massextinction coefficient; **-speicher mit beliebigem Zugriff,** random access mass memory; **-spektrometrisch,** mass-spectrometric; **-spektroskopie,** *f.* mass spectroscopy; **-synchrometer,** *m.* mass synchrometer; **-wechsel,** *m.* population fluctuation; **-zahl,** *f.* mass number.

Massflüssigkeit, *f.* titrant, standard solution.

Massiv, *n.* massif.

massiver Polyäthylen, bulk polyethylene.

Masslösung, *f.* titrant, standard solution.

Mass-stabshöhe, *f.* scale height; **-zahl,** *f.* numerical value, coefficient of measure, numerical measure.

Mastzelle, *f.* mast cell, mastocyte.

Materialkonstante, *f.* material constant, physical property.

mathematisch negativ, clockwise; **in mathematisch negativem Sinn,** clockwise.

Matrixdrucker, *m.* matrix printer, mosaic printer, dot printer, wire printer.

Matrizenform, *f.* matrix formulation.

Matrizen-RNS, *f.* messenger RNA (ribonucleic acid).

Mattkohle, *f.* cannel coal.

Matur, *n.* graduation from high school.

Maturant, *m.* high school graduate.

Maulbeerkeim, *m.* morula.

Maximum, *n.*-a, maximum; **~ zu Untergrund,** peak-to-background.

mechanisch-kalorischer Effekt, mechanocaloric effect.

Medusen, *f.pl.* Hydrozoa, hydrozoans.

Meeres-kunde, *f.* oceanography, oceanology; **-optik,** *f.* marine optics.

Meerwasserentsalzung, *f.* desalination or desalting of sea water.

Mehrbereichsöl, *n.* multigrade oil.

mehrdeutig, many-valued, ambiguous.

Mehrelektrodensystem, *n.* multielectrode system.

mehrfach geladen, multiply charged.

Mehrfach-auslegung, *f.* redundant design; **-austausch,** *m.* compound crossing-over; **-gleitung,** *f.* multiple slip; **-nebenwiderstand,** *m.* universal shunt, Ayrton shunt; **-pendel,** *n.* multiple pendulum; **-schicht,** *f.* multilayer; **-schunt,** *m.* universal shunt, Ayrton shunt; **-streuung,** *f.* plural scattering; **-verdampfer,** *m.* multipleeffect evaporator.

Mehrjährigkeit, *f.* perennation.

Mehrkörper-kräfte, *f.pl.* many-body forces; **-problem,** *n.* many-body problem.

Mehr-lochkern, *m.* multiaperture core, transfluxor; **-schichtenfilter,** *n.* multilayer filter; **-schichtstoffe,** *m.pl.* multilayer composites (in plastics); **-stellenverfahren,** *n.* multiplace method; **-stufenentmagnitisierung,** *f.* multiple-stage demagnetization; **-teilchenwellenfunktion,** *f.* multiparticle wave function; **-teilig,** multipartial, multipart, multisectional; **-zweckschneideöl,** *n.* multipurpose cutting oil.

Mendelvererbung, *f.* particulate inheritance.

Menge, *f.* set, collection, aggregate; **Ableitung einer ~,** derived set or aggregate; **leere ~,** empty set.

Mengen-bilanz, *f.* material balance; **-faktor,** *m.* multiplicity factor; **-lehre,** *f.* set theory.

meridional, meridional, tangential (in optics); **-transport,** *m.* meridional flux.

Merkmalsänderung, *f.* clinal variation.

Merkurdurchgang, *m.*-e, mercury transit.

Mero-eder, *m.* merohedron; **-edrie,** *f.* merohedrism; **-edrischer Zwilling,** merohedral twin.

meromorph, meromorphic.

Mesomerie, *f.* mesomerism, resonance (in chemistry).

Mesonatom, *n.* mesonic or mesic atom.

Mesonenerzeugung, *f.* meson production.

Mesonniveau, *n.* mesonic level.

Mesonpaar-dämpfung, *f.* meson-pair damping; **-term,** *m.* meson-pair term.

Mesonterm, *m.* mesonic term.

Mesozoikum, *n.* Mesozoic.

Mess- und Versuchswerte, *m.pl.* data.

Mess-blende, *f.* orifice, orifice plate, sharp-edged orifice, slit limiter (in optics); **-brücke,** *f.* resistance or measuring bridge; **-düse,** *f.* metering nozzle; **-einrichtung,** *f.* measuring device, system, unit, or set-up.

Messerspitze, *f.* pinch, knife point, point of a knifeful (about 0.5–1 gram).

Mess-fahne, *f.* surveyor's flag; **-fehlergrenze,** *f.* error limit; **-flasche,** *f.* graduate; **-fühler,** *m.* sensor, detector, measuring probe; **-glas,** *n.* graduate; **-kette,** *f.* surveyor's chain; **-kolben,** *m.* volumetric flask; **-körper,** *m.* specimen; **-kunde,** *f.* surveying, metrology; **-lauf,** *m.* test run; **-lösung,** *f.* titrant, standard solution; **-plan,** *m.* schedule of tests; **-prisma,** *n.* refractometer prism; **-punkt,** *m.* test point, experimental point; **-warte,** *f.* control panel or room; **-wert,** *m.* experimental value, measurement or test result, test value, datum; **-zahl,** *f.* numerical or measured value; **-ziffer,** *f.* index number; **-zweig,** *m.* measuring arm.

Metachromasie, *f.* metachromatism.

Metadichlorobenzol, *n.* m-dichlorobenzene.

Metall-atom, *n.* metallic atom; **-beize,** *f.* metallic mordant (in dyes); **-drahtentladung,** *f.* exploded wire, exploding wire discharge; **-drahtentladungskontinuum,** *n.pl.* exploded wire continuum.

Metallierung, *f.* metalation.

Metallisierung, *f.* metallization.

Metall-keramik, *f.* cermet, metal-ceramic, ceramet; **-organisch,** organometallic; **-salzkontakt,** *m.* metal-to-salt contact; **-schicht,** *f.* metal film; **-schmelze,** *f.* molten metal; **-spritzen,** *n.* sputtering, metallization, metal spraying.

Metastabilität, *f.* metastability.

Metazöl, *n.* metacoel.

Meteor-licht, *n.* meteoric light; **-schweif,** *m.* meteor trail.

Methode des schnellsten Abstiegs, method of fastest descent, method of steepest descent.

Methode des steilsten Abfalls, method of steepest descent.

metonisch, metonic.

Metrik, *f.* metric.

Mickerfett, *n.* mesenteric fat.

Mikro-bar, *n.* microbar; **-barograph,** *m.* microbarograph; **-baustein,** *m.* microelement, micromodule, chip; **-bruch,** *m.* microcrack; **-dehnung,** *f.* microstrain; **-element,** *n.* microelement, single-component wafer; **-kristall,** *m.* microcrystal; **-kristallin,** microcrystalline; **-photo,** *n.* photomicrograph; **-photometer,** *m.* microphotometer; **-pipette,** *f.* micropipette; **-riss,** *m.* microcrack; **-röhre,** *f.* microtube.

Mikroröntgen-bild, *n.* microradiograph; **-strahl,** *m.* microbeam of X-rays.

Mikro-schieferung, *f.* microfoliation; **-schnitt,** *m.* microsection; **-schwärzungsmessung,** *f.*

microdensitometry; **-seismen,** *f.pl.* microseisms; **-skala,** *f.* microscale.

Mikroskop-heiztisch, *m.* hot stage; **-kühltisch,** *m.* cold stage; **-tisch,** *m.* microscope stage.

Mikro-textur, *f.* microstructure; **-wachs,** *n.* microcrystalline wax.

Mikrowellen-ausbreitung, *f.* microwave propagation; **-bereich,** *m.* microwave region; **-durchschlag,** *m.* microwave breakdown; **-entladung,** *f.* microwave discharge; **-hohlraum,** *m.* microwave cavity; **-interferometrie,** *f.* microwave interferometry; **-messung,** *f.* microwave measurement.

Mikrowellenresonanz, *f.* microwave resonance; **-absorptionsmethode,** *f.* microwave resonance absorption method.

Mikrowellentechnik, *f.* microwave technique or engineering, ultra-high frequency engineering.

Mikro-zonenschmelzen, *n.* microzone melting; **-zotten,** *f.pl.* microvilli.

Milch-glas, *n.* frosted glass, opal glass; **-strassensystem,** *n.* galactic system; **-strassensysteme,** *n.pl.* island universes.

Millival, *m.* and *n.* milliequivalent (in chemistry), milligram-equivalent weight.

Mimesie, *f.* mimesis, pseudosymmetry.

Mimikrie, *f.* camouflage (in biology), mimicry.

Mindest-arbeit, *f.* minimum work; **-suchzeit,** *f.* minimum access time.

Mineral-anhäufung, *f.* mineral aggregate; **-ausbildung,** *f.* mineralization; **-boden,** *m.* subsoil; **-dünger,** *m.* mineral fertilizer; **-entstehung,** *f.* mineral genesis; **-gang,** *m.* mineral vein or feeder; **-lösung,** *f.* mineralizing solution; **-öl,** *n.* mineral oil, petroleum, crude oil, rock oil; **-wachs,** *n.* mineral wax, ozocerite.

minerogen, minerogenic.

Minimal-kurve, *f.* minimal curve; **-polynom,** *n.* minimal polynomial.

Minimumstrahl-definition, *f.* definition of minimum beam; **-kennzeichnung,** *f.* marking of minimum beam.

Minorante, *f.* minorant, lower bound.

Minoritätsträger, *m.* minority carrier.

Misch-arbeit, *f.* collating operation; **-äther,** *m.* mixed ether.

Mischbarkeitslücke, *f.* miscibility gap.

Mischbindungstyp, *m.* mixed bond type.

mischen, to collate, merge.

Mischkristall-bildung, *f.* mixed-crystal formation; **-reihe,** *f.* series of mixed crystals, series of solid solutions.

Misch-oktanzahl, *f.* blending octane number, blending value; **-polymer,** *n.* copolymer, mixture of different polymers; **-polymerisat,** *n.* co-polymer; **-polymerisation,** *f.* copolymerization, cross-polymerization; **-probe,** *f.* mixed melting point test.

Mischungsweg, *n.* mixing length.

Missklang, *m.* dissonance, discord.

missliebig, unpopular.

Misspickel, *m.* arsenopyrite, mispickel.

Mit-arbeiter, *m.* fellow worker, employee, staff member, detail man (a drug salesman), drug sales representative, medical representative; **-bewegung,** *f.* dragging.

Mitesser, *m.* blackhead.

Mit-fällung, *f.* coprecipitation; **-gefaltet,** infolded; **-gerissen,** entrained; **-hörer,** *m.* monitor, fellow listener; **-laufend,** on-line, in-line.

Mitleidenschaft, *f.* sympathy, compassion; **in ~ ziehen,** to involve.

Mitnehmer, *m.* azeotrope former.

Mitosegift, *n.* mitotic poison.

mitreden, to join in a discussion.

Mit-reissen, *n.* entrainment, carry-over; **-schleppen,** to entrain, carry along; **-schwingungsgezeit,** *f.* co-oscillational tide; **-sprechen,** to join in a discussion.

Mittagshöhe, *f.* meridional height.

Mittelalter, *n.* Middle Ages, Mesozoic Era.

Mittellot, *n.* normal bisector.

mittelquadratischer Fehler, root-mean-square error.

Mittelschenkel, *m.* common limb (in geology), center limb; **-bruch,** *m.* anticlinal fault.

Mittelung, *f.* averaging.

Mittelwasser, *n.* mean tide.

Mittelwert, quadratischer ~, root-mean-square value.

Mittelwertsatz, *m.* law of averages.

Mittenabstand, *m.* center-to-center distance, distance between successive rulings (on diffraction gratings).

mittlere freie Weglänge, mean free path.

mittlere quadratische Abweichung, *f.* root-mean-square deviation.

Mittlersubstanz, *f.* transmitter substance.

Mizelle, *f.* micella, micelle.

Modellierung, *f.* simulation, mockup.

Moderator-kreislauf, *m.* moderator loop or circuit; **-vergiftung,** *f.* moderator poisoning.

Modul, *m.* diametral pitch (of a gear), ratio (as used in chemical industry, e.g., SiO_2/Al_2O_3 in moles).

Modulargleichung, *f.* modular equation.

Modulfunktion, *f.* modular function.

Mole, *f.* breakwater.

Molekular-gefüge, *n.* molecular structure; **-sieb,** *n.* molecular sieve; **-strahlmethode,** *f.* molecular-beam method.

Molekülbahnmethode, *f.* method of molecular orbitals.

Molekülbildung, *f.* molecule formation; **scheinbare ~,** pseudomolecule formation.

Molekül-emissionskontinuum, *n.* continuous molecular emission spectrum; **-gasion,** *n.* molecular gas ion; **-ionisationskontinuum,** *n.* continuous molecular ionization spectrum; **-komplex,** *n.* molecular cluster; **-rekombinationsspektrum,** *n.* molecular recombination spectrum; **-zustand,** *m.:-e,* molecular state.

Molsieb, *n.* molecular sieve.

Molybdängruppe, *f.* molybdenum group.

Molybdatophosphorsäure, *f.* phosphomolybdic acid.

Moment, rückdrehendes ~, restoring moment.

Momentanleistung, *f.* instantaneous power.

Momentverschluss, *m.* automatic shutter.

Momentwert, *m.* magneton.

Monats-binde, *f.* sanitary napkin; **-wechsel,** *m.* monthly allowance.

Mond-bahn, *f.* lunar orbit; **-finsternis,** *f.* lunar eclipse; **-hof,** *m.* lunar halo; **-knoten,** *m.* lunar node; **-länge,** *f.* moon's longitude; **-scheibe,** *f.* lunar disk; **-sichel,** *f.* crescent of the moon; **-umlauf,** *m.* lunar circuit.

Moneren, *f.pl.* Monera, monerans.

mono-atomar, monatomic; **-chromatfilter,** *m.* monochromatic filter; **-chromatisierung,** *f.* monochromatization; **-chromator,** *m.* monochromator; **-eder,** *n.* pedion; **-energetisch,** monoenergetic.

monogen, monogenic.

Monogyre, *f.* monogyre, one-fold axis.

monoklin, monoclinic.

Monomer, *n.* monomer.

Monomere, *n.* monomer.

Monopolübergang, *m.* monopole transition.

Monostyrol, *n.* styrene monomer.

monoton, monotonic, monotonically; **~ fallend,** monotonically decreasing.

monotone-Welt, monotonic model, monotonic universe.

Monotonie, *f.* monotonicity, monotony.

Montage-gerüst, *n.* erection frame or structure, erecting scaffolding; **-strasse,** *f.* assembly line.

Moossteppe, *f.* tundra.

Moränen-girlanden, *f.pl.* festooned moraines; **-kuppe,** *f.* morainic hill; **-schutt,** *m.* glacial fill, morainic debris; **-schuttboden,** *m.* glacial soil; **-zug,** *m.* morainal dams or lobes.

Morgan-Einheit, *f.* morgan.

morphologisch, morphologic.

Morulabildung, *f.* morulation.

Mosaikstruktur, *f.* mosaic structure.

Motorantrieb, *m.* motor or engine drive; **mit ~,** motor- or engine-driven.

Motor-armatur, *f.* motorized valve; **-drehzahl,** *f.* engine speed.

Motorik, *f.* motoricity.

Motor-roller, *m.* motor scooter; **-titrierstand,** *m.* motorized (automatic) titrator.

mulden-artig, bowl-shaped, trough-shaped, synclinal; **-berg,** *m.* synclinal mountain; **-bildung,** *f.* downfolding; **-fächer,** *m.* synclinorium; **-flügel,** *m.* synclinal limb.

Mülldeponie, *f.* dump site, garbage pit.

Müllerscher Gang, Müller's duct.

Multiplett, *n.* multiplet; **-aufspaltung,** *f.* multiplet splitting.

Multiplikations-faktor, *m.* reproductive factor; **-theorem,** *n.* multiplication theorem.

Multiplikatorenbereich, *m.* domain of multipliers.

Multiplikatorquotientenregister, *m.* multiplier-quotients register.

Multipol-entwicklung, *f.* multipole expansion; **-ordnung,** *f.* multipolarity; **-potential,** *n.* multipole potential; **-strahlung,** *f.* multipole radiation; **-strahlungsübergang,** *m.*-e, multipole transition probability; **-übergang,** *m.*-e, multipole transition.

Multi-polyaddition, *f.* copolyaddition; **-polykondensation,** *f.* copolycondensation; **-polymerisation,** *f.* copolymerization.

Multivektor, *m.* multivector.

Multivibratorschaltung, *f.* multivibrator circuit; **bistabile ~,** flip-flop circuit.

Mumienpuppe, *f.* obtected pupa.

Mund-zu-Mund Beatmung, mouth-to-mouth resuscitation.

Mündungskorrektion, *f.* mouth correction, orifice correction.

Muskelerschlaffung, *f.* muscular relaxation.

Muster, *n.* prototype, sample solution (in chemistry); **-aussetzer,** *m.* designer, draftsman; **-betrieb,** *m.* pilot plant; **-blatt,** *n.* hand sheet (in paper technology); **-brennstoff,** *m.* reference fuel; **-färbung,** *f.* sample dyeing; **-fertigung,** *f.* pilot production; **-zieher,** *m.* sampler, sampling device.

Mutantenstamm, *n.* mutant strain.

Mutations -auslösend, mutagenic, mutagenous;

-auslösung, *f.* induction of mutation; **-fähigkeit,** *f.* mutagenicity; **-verzögerung,** *f.* mutational lag or delay.

Mutatorgen, *n.* mutator gene.

mutieren, to mutate.

Mutter-gestein, *n.* source rock; **-kern,** *m.* parent nucleus, precursor; **-kornvergiftung,** *f.* ergotism; **-kristall,** *m.* mother (host) crystal; **-kultur,** *f.* stock culture; **-substanz,** *f.* parent substance, host; **-tier,** *n.* dam.

Myon, *n.* muon, mu meson.

Myonen-einfang, *m.* muon capture; **-paarerzeugung,** *f.* muon-pair production; **-zerfall,** *m.* muon decay.

Myzelstrang, *m.* rhizomorph.

Nabelpunkt, *m.* umbilical point.

Nach-ahmer, *m.* mimic; **-ausgabe,** *f.* post-edition (of a machine translation).

Nachbar-befruchtung, *f.* geitonogamy; **-zahl,** *f.* number of neighbors.

Nach-bildung, *f.* simulation, modeling, imitation, replica, copy, reproduction, forgery; **-brunst,** *f.* metestrus, metestrum; **-entladung,** *f.* after-discharge; **-fermentation,** *f.* resweat (of tobacco); **-formen,** to copy; **-führen,** to update, pan (with a camera); **-gerade,** little by little, at last.

Nach-giebigkeit, *f.* resilience, yield; **-glimmen,** *n.* afterglow; **-guss,** *m.* sparge liquor, second wort, second cast, copy; **-hirn,** *n.* myelencephalon, marrowbrain; **-kühler,** *m.* aftercooler, subcooler; **-kühlkreislauf,** *m.* residual heat removal loop; **-kultur,** *f.* subculture; **-kur,** *f.* after-treatment; ladungsmenge, *f.* refueling replacement batch; **-leuchten,** *n.* afterglow; **-maturation,** *f.* postaging or reaging (of tobacco).

Nachrichten-kanal, *m.* communication or information channel; **-verarbeitung,** *f.* information or data processing; **-verkehr,** *m.* communications.

Nachspeisung, *f.* make-up feed, reactor core isolation cooling.

Nachthimmelslicht, *n.* nocturnal airglow, night sky luminescence, night sky light.

Nachwärmeabfuhr, *f.* residual heat removal.

Nachweissgrenze, *f.* detection limit.

Nachwirkungseffekt, *m.* aftereffect.

Nachzerfallswärme, *f.* decay heat.

Nachzucht, *f.* offspring, progeny.

Nadelöhr, *n.* pinhole.

nähern, sich -, to converge.

Näherung, empirische ~, trial-and-error method; **schrittweise ~,** stepwise approximation.

Näherungs-lösung, *f.* approximation; -verfahren, *n.* approximate method.

Nahordnung, *f.* short-range order.

Nahrungsaustausch, *m.* nutrient exchange, trophallaxis.

Narkotikum, *n.* narcotic, anesthetic.

Nasskompressionsmaschine, *f.* wet-compression machine.

Natriumniobat, *n.* sodium niobate.

Naturbenzin, *n.* casinghead gasoline.

Nebel-abscheider, *n.* mist eliminator, demister; -kammer, *f.* cloud chamber; -linie, *f.* nebular line.

Neben-achse, *f.* minor axis (of an ellipse), conjugate axis (of a hyperbola); -kühler, *m.* ancillary cooler, side-stream cooler; -funktion, *f.* tributary function; -klasse, *f.* coset (in math); -komplex, *m.* coset (in math); -maximum, *n.* secondary maximum; -meer, *n.* border sea; -schleuse, *f.* emergency air lock.

Neben-schluss, *m.* shunt, bypass, leak, sink; -setzung, *f.* juxtaposition; -sprechen, *n.* crosstalk, near-end crosstalk; -strom, *m.* side flow, bypass flow, induction current; -symmetrieebene, *f.* secondary symmetry plane; -wirkung, *f.* side effect; -zeit, *f.* downtime, idle time, auxiliary process time.

negativer Logarithmus, *m.* cologarithm.

Neigung, *f.* grade (of a road), obliquity, trend, fall, declivity, tilt, offset, hade, descent.

Neigungs-fehler, *m.* tilt error; -korngrenze, *f.* tilt boundary; -messer, *m.* clinometer, inclinometer, gradiometer, tiltometer; -schiessen, *n.* dip shooting; -winkel, *m.* dip (in geology), side rake or back rake (in machine tools), rake, angle of depression.

Nenn-weite, *f.* nominal width, diameter, or size; -wert, *m.* rated value, rating, face value.

Neonverflüssigungsmaschine, *f.* neon liquefier.

Neosilikat, *n.* island silicate.

Nerv, *m.* snap (in rubber).

Nervengeflecht, *n.* nerve plexus, neuroplexus.

Netz-ebene, *f.* atomic plane; -ebenenabstand, *m.‑e,* interplanar spacing, interlattice plane distance.

Netzer, *m.* wetting agent.

Netzplantechnik, *f.* network technique, project planning.

Netzpolymer, *n.* network polymer, crosslinked polymer.

netzwerk-ändernd, network-modifying; -bildend, network-forming

Neu-definition, *f.* redefinition; -eichung, *f.* recalibration, restandardization, manufacturer's calibration.

neuordnen, to edit.

Neutralisationszahl, *f.* neutralization number.

Neutralisierung, *f.* neutralization.

Neutronen-abschirmung, *f.* neutron shielding; -aktivierungsanalyse, *f.* neutron-activation analysis; -ausfluss, *m.* neutron leakage or escape; -bestrahlung, *f.* neutron radiation; -beugung, *f.* neutron diffraction; -dosisleistung, *f.* neutron dose rate; -fluss, *m.* neutron flux; -gift, *n.* nuclear poison, neutron poison, reactor poison; -leerstelle, *f.* neutron vacancy; -nachweis, *m.* neutron detection; -polarisation, *f.* neutron polarization.

Neutronenquerschnitt, *m.* neutron cross section; ~ bei elastischer Streuung, elastic neutron cross section.

Neutronenresonanzenanregungsstärke, *f.* strength of neutron resonance.

Neutronenresonanz-linie, *f.* neutron-resonance line; -messung, *f.* neutron-resonance measurement.

Neutronen-strahl, *m.* neutron beam; -vervielfachung, *f.* multiplicity of neutrons.

n-Halbleiter, *m.* n-type semiconductor, excess semiconductor, n-type conductor.

nicht-abzählbar, nondenumerable, uncountable; -additiv, nonadditive; -beschränkt, nonbounded; -eisenmetalle, *n.pl.* nonferrous metals; -ellipsoidal, nonellipsoidal; -entartet, nondegenerate; -euklidisch, non-Euclidean; -gleitfähig, sessile; -kommutativ, noncommutative; -kreisförmigkeit, *f.* out-of-roundness; -konservativ, nonconservative; -kugelförmig, aspherical.

nicht-linear, nonlinear; -linearität, *f.* nonlinearity; -lokal, nonlocal; -polar, nonpolar; -primitiv, nonprimitive; -separierbar, nonseparable; -supraleitend, nonsuperconducting; -unterscheidbar, indistinguishable; -zentralsymmetrisch, noncentrosymmetric.

Niederdruck-entladung, *f.* low-pressure discharge; -säule, *f.* low-pressure column.

Nieder-frequenzlongitudinalwelle, *f.* low-frequency longitudinal wave; -schlagsprognose, *f.* precipitation forecast; -spannungsbogen, *m.,* -voltbogen, *m.* low-voltage arc.

Nieseln, *n.* drizzle.

Niton, *n.* radon.

Nitratbeize, *f.* nitrate mordant.

Nitromethan, *n.* nitromethane.

Niveau-fläche, *f.* equipotential surface; -linie, *f.* equipotential line, contour; -schema, *n.* level scheme; -verbreiterung, *f.* level broadening.

n-Leiter, *m.* n-type conductor, electron conductor.

Nomogramm, *n.* nomogram.

Nomographie, *f.* nomography.

596 Addendum

Nordlicht, *n.* aurora borealis; **-spektrum,** *n.* auroral spectrum.

Normalbündel, *n.* normal congruence.

Normale, *f.* normal, perpendicular.

Normalelektrode, *f.* standard electrode.

Normalenrichtung, *f.* normal direction.

normal-glühen, to normalize (in metallurgy); **-prozess,** *m.* ordinary (normal) process; **-schwingung,** *f.* normal mode; **-strahler,** *m.* standard radiator; **-teiler,** *m.* invariant subgroup, self-conjugate subgroup; **-uhr,** *f.* master clock.

Normblatt, *n.* specification, standard sheet.

Normenentwurf, *m.* tentative standard, preliminary specification.

normierbar, normable (functions).

normierte Eigenfunktionen, normalized eigenfunctions.

Normzustand, *m.* standard or normal state, state under normal or standard conditions of temperature and pressure; **physikalischer** ~, NTP or normal temperature and pressure conditions, i.e., $0°$ C and 760 torr; **technischer** ~, conditions of $20°$ C and 1 kp/cm² (735.6 torr).

Not-abfahren, *n.* emergency shutdown (of reactor); **-abschaltung,** *f.* emergency shutdown, scram.

Note, *f.* grade, mark, remark.

n-Tensid, *n.* nonionic surfactant, tenside, or detergent.

n-Typ-Halbleiter, *m.* n-type semiconductor.

Nukleinsäure, *f.* nucleic acid.

Nukleonenbreite, *f.* nucleon width.

Nukleonnukleonstreuung, *f.* scattering of nucleons.

Nuklid, *n.* nuclide; **betastabiles** ~, betastable nuclide.

Null-abgabe, *f.* zero release (of radioactivity); **-darstellung,** *f.* null representation; **-dimensionel,** zero-dimensional; **-dimensionale Fehlordnung,** point defect; **-durchgang,** *m.* zero crossing; **-einsteuerung,** *f.* zero fill; **-element,** *n.* null element.

nullen, to reset, zero.

Null-feder, *f.* zero spring.

Nullinie, *f.* neutral axis, elastic axis, neutral fiber, null line, baseline, reference line, band center (in spectroscopy), band origin.

Null-moment, *n.* zero moment; **-operator,** *m.* null operator.

Nullpunkt-druck, *m.* zero-point pressure; **-energie,** *f.* zero-point energy, energy of absolute zero; **-entropie,** *f.* zero-point entropy; **-unruhe,** *f.* zero-point motion.

Null-reichweite, *f.* zero range; **-stelle,** *f.* zero, zero position; **-teiler,** *m.* zero divisor.

Numerus, *m.* antilogarithm.

nutzbare Reflexordnungen, *f.pl.* available orders of reflection.

Nutzeffekt, *m.* coefficient of performance.

Nutz-Stör Verhältnis, *n.* signal-to-noise ratio, S/N ratio.

Oberdurchschnitt, *m.* average of averages.

Oberfläche, spezifische ~, specific surface area (in chemistry).

Oberflächenenergieparameter, *m.* surface-energy parameter.

Oberflächenfilm, *m.* surface film; **-bildung,** *f.* film formation.

Oberflächen-inhalt, *m.* surface area; **-leitfähigkeit,** *f.* surface conductivity; **-rauhigkeit,** *f.* surface roughness; **-rekombinationsgeschwindigkeit,** *f.* surface recombination velocity; **-verunreinigung,** *f.* surface contamination; **-wanderung,** *f.* surface migration; **-widerstand,** *m.* surface impedance; **-zustand,** *m.*:e, surface state.

Ober-gruppe, *f.* class of classes, larger class (in statistics); **-lastig,** top-heavy.

Objektbereich, *m.* specimen region, commercial sector.

Objektivpolschuh, *m.* objective pole shoe.

Objekt-tisch, *m.* specimen stage; **-träger,** *m.* specimen holder; **-treu,** object preserving; **-verschmutzung,** *f.* object fouling.

Offenbandhalbleiter, *m.* open-band semiconductor.

Offenlegungs-schrift, *f.* unexamined (German) patent application; **-tag,** *m.* date on which patent application is opened to public inspection.

Öffnungs-fehler, *m.* spherical aberration; **-winkel,** *m.* wedge or included angle.

Oktaeder-struktur, *f.* octahedron structure; **-symmetrie,** *f.* octahedral symmetry.

Oktanwert, *m.* octane number or rating.

Oktanzahl, *f.* octane number; **mit hoher** ~, high-octane; **-verbesserer,** *m.* antiknock additive.

Oktopol-anregung, *f.* octupole excitation; **-übergang,** *m.*:e, octupole transition.

Öldämpfer, *m.* oil dashpot.

Olfaktorius, *m.* olfactory nerve.

Öl-kohle, *f.* carbon deposit (in engines); **-lacke,** *f.* oil slick; **-pest,** *f.* oil pollution; **-russ,** *m.* lampblack; **-teppich,** *m.* oil slick; **-tröpfchen,** *n.* oil drop.

Operatoren-bereich, *m.* operator domain; **-kalkül,** *n.* operational calculus.

Operator-isomorphie, *f.* operator isomorphism; **-rechnung,** *f.* operator manipulation.

Opferanode, *f.* sacrificial anode.

optimieren, to optimize.

Optimierung, *f.* optimization.

optische Dicke, optical path.

optisch leer, optically nonabsorbent (in spectroscopy).

Ordinarius, *m.* professor.

Ordinate, *f.* axis, e.g., **X-Ordinate,** i.e., X-axis.

Ordination, *f.* ordination, prescription (in medicine).

Ordnungs-domäne, *f.* ordering domain; **-grad,** *n.* degree of order; **-parameter,** *m.* order parameter.

Ordnungs-Unordnungs Umwandlung, *f.* order-disorder transformation or transition.

Organisationsprogramm, *n.* executive program, master routine, main program.

orientierbar, orientable.

orientiert, oriented, aligned.

orientierte, ~ Aufwachsung, epitaxial growth; **~ Keimbildung,** oriented nucleation.

Orientierungs-fehlordnung, *f.* disorder of orientation; **-güte,** *f.* quality of orientation; **-häufigkeit,** *f.* orientation frequency; **-unordnung,** *f.* disorder orientation.

originäre Strategie, pure strategy.

Orogenese, *f.* orogenesis.

orogenetisch, orogenetic.

Ortbeton, *m.* poured-in-place concrete.

Ort der Synthese, position of synthesis; **andern Orts,** elsewhere.

Orthodichlorbenzol, *n.* o-dichlorobenzene.

orthogonalisiert, orthogonalized.

Orthogonalisierungs-prozess, *m.* orthogonalization process; **-verfahren,** *n.* orthogonalization method.

Orthogonalitäts-methode, orthogonality method; **-relation,** *f.* orthogonality relation.

Orthogonalsystem, normiertes ~, orthonormal system.

Orthopolarenverfahren, *n.* orthopolar method.

Ortho- und Parawasserstoff, *m.* ortho- and parahydrogen.

Orts-bestimmung, *f.* position determination, localization; **-beziehung,** *f.* topology, topological relation; **-dosis,** *f.* local dose, local dosage; **-koordinate,** *f.* space coordinate; **-kurve,** *f.* locus; **-lexikon,** *n.* gazetteer; **-name,** *m.* place-name; **-treue,** *f.* philopatry, site-attachment.

Oszillator, *m.* oscillator; **-stärke,** *f.* oscillator strength.

Oszillographentechnik, *f.* oscillographic technique.

Otto-kraftstoff, *m.* fuel for spark-ignition engines; fuel for Otto-cycle engines, motor gasoline; **-motor,** *m.* gasoline engine, spark-ignition engine, Otto-cycle engine.

Oxalin, *n.* imidazole, glyoxaline.

Oxäthylierung, *f.* ethoxylation.

Oxdiazol, *n.* oxadiazole.

Oxeton, *n.* dihydroxyketone.

oxy-, hydroxy- (chemical prefix).

oxydiert, oxidized.

Oxydkathode, thermionische ~, oxide-coated thermionic cathode.

Oxydkohle, *f.* oxidized coal, oxy coal.

oxydüberzogen, oxide-coated.

Oxyduleisen, *n.* ferrous iron.

Ozon-abbau, *m.* ozonolysis; **-betrag,** *m.* ozone content; **-kontinua,** *n.pl.* continuous ozone spectra.

Ozonosphärenschall, *m.* ozonosphere sound.

Ozon-radiosonde, *f.* ozone radiosonde; **-spaltung,** *f.* ozonolysis; **-zerstörung,** *f.* ozone annihilation.

Paar-bildung, *f.* pair production, pairing, pair creation; **-erzeugung,** *f.* pair creation; **-umwandlung,** *f.* pair conversion.

Paarungsenergie, *f.* pairing energy.

Paarvernichtung, *f.* pair annihilation.

Paläomagnetismus, *m.* paleomagnetism.

Paläozoikum, *n.* Paleozoic.

Palynologe, *m.* palynologist.

Palynologie, *f.* palynology (study of fossil pollens).

Panzeraktinometer, *m.* shielded actinometer.

Papier-band, *n.* paper tape, punched paper tape, perforated tape; **-lochband,** *n.* punched paper tape, perforated tape; **-streifen,** *m.* punched paper tape, paper tape, perforated tape; **-streifeneinführung,** *f.* paper threading.

Paraffin-ausscheidung, *f.* cloud point (in oils); **-charakter,** *m.* paraffinicity; **-gatsch,** *m.* slack wax, crude scale wax.

Parallel-arbeit, *f.* time-shared operation; **-gegenkopplung,** *f.* shunt feedback; **-lauf,** *m.* concurrent flow.

Paramagnetismus, *m.* paramagnetism.

Parameter-darstellung, *f.* parametric representation; **-linie,** *f.* parameter curve; **-stellung,** *f.* parametric representation.

Parametrisierungstechnik, *f.* parametrization technique.

Parawasserstoff, *m.* parahydrogen.

Paraxialbahn, *f.* paraxial orbit.

Parazustand, *m.* para state.

Pardelkatze, *f.* ocelot.

Parität-änderung, *f.* parity change; **-erhaltung,** *f.* parity conservation; **-ziffer,** *f.* parity digit.

Pariwert, *m.* par value.

Partialbruch-regel, *f.* partial-fraction rule; **-zerlegung,** *f.* decomposition of a fraction into partial fractions.

Partial-querschnitt, *m.* partial cross section; **-tide,** *f.* partial tide; **-wellenlösung,** *f.* partial wave solution.

partielle Integration, *f.* integration by parts.

Partikelgrösse, *f.* grain size, particle size, granulation.

Passlehre, *f.* gage, jig, template.

Passungsrost, *m.* fretting corrosion.

Pastellstift, *m.* crayon.

Pause, *f.* intermission.

PBC-Vektor, *m.* periodic bond chain vector, PBC-vector.

Peilanlage, *f.* direction-finding installation.

Pendelhärte, *f.* pendulum hardness; **-prüfgerät,** *n.* pendulum hardness tester, pendulum sclerometer.

Pendelschlaghärteprüfung, *f.* pendulum hardness test.

Pendeln, *n.* hunting, cycling, cyclic variation, swinging.

Pendeluhr, *f.* pendulum clock.

Pendelung, *f.* hunting, swinging, oscillation.

Penetrationszwilling, *m.* interpenetration twin.

Penetron, *n.* meson.

Pentan, *n.* pentane.

perfundiert, perfused.

Perioden-parallelogramm, *n.* periodic parallelogram; **-uhr,** *f.* harmonic dial.

Periodizitäts-bedingung, *f.* periodicity condition; **-volumen,** *n.* periodic volume.

Perlit, *m.* perlite (mineral); pearlite (component of steel).

Perl-polymerisation, *n.* bead polymerization; **-polymerisat,** *n.* bead polymer.

Perlschnurblitz, *m.* bead or chain lightning.

Perltransistor, *m.* bead transistor.

Perm, *n.* Permian.

Petroleum, *n.* kerosine, naptha (N.B. Current usage refers to naphtha with a boiling range of about 150–270° C at atmospheric pressure).

Pfeilwinkel, *m.* sweep angle.

Pflanzengummi, *n.* vegetable gum, sizing gum.

Pflichtenblatt, *n.* specification.

Pfropfenströmung, *f.* plug flow.

Pfropf-grad, *m.* degree of grafting; **-kopolymer,** *n.* graft copolymer; **-polymerisat,** *n.* graft polymer; **-strömung,** *f.* plug flow.

Phagen-behandlung, *f.* bacteriophage treatment; **-loch,** *n.* plaque.

Phän, *n.* phen.

Phasen-änderung, *f.* phase transition, phase change; **-beziehung,** *f.* phase relation; **-diagramm,** *n.* phase or equilibrium diagram; **empfindlich,** phase-sensitive; **-glitter,** *n.* phase grating; **-grenze,** *f.* phase interface.

Phasenkontrast-bild, *n.* phase-contrast image; **-verfahren,** *n.* phase-contrast method.

Phasen-raum, *m.* phase space; **-regler,** *m.* interfacial level controller; **-übergang,** *m.ʽe,* phase transition; **-umformung,** *f.* phase transformation; **-umkehrung,** *f.* phase inversion; **-umwandlung,** *f.* phase transformation, change of state.

Phasenumwandlungs-intervall, *n.* phase transition interval; **-punkt,** *m.* phase transition point.

Phasen-ungleichgewicht, *n.* phase unbalance; **-verschiebung,** *f.* phase shift; **-vertauschung,** *f.* phase reversal; **-welle,** *f.* de Broglie or electron wave; **-winkelanalyse,** *f.* phase-shift analysis.

Pheromon, *n.* pheromone.

phosphatieren, to phosphatize, Parkerize.

Photo-ablösung, *f.* photodetachment; **-absorptionsband,** *n.* photoabsorption band; **-anregungsquerschnitt,** *m.* photoexcitation cross section; **-auslösung,** *f.* photoproduction; **-blitzkondensator,** *m.* photoflash capacitor; **-dielektrisch,** photodielectric; **-dissoziationskontinuum,** *n.* continuous spectrum of photodissociation.

Photo-effekt, *m.* photodisintegration, photoelectric effect; **-elektromagnetisch,** photoelectromagnetic; **-element,** *n.* photoelectric cell, photocell; **-galvanomagnetisch,** photogalvanomagnetic; **-ionisation,** *f.,* **ionisierung,** *f.* photoionization.

Photoionisierungs-ausbeute, *f.* photoionization efficiency; **-querschnitt,** *m.* photoionization cross section.

Photo-lampe, *f.* photoflood lamp; **-leiter,** *m.* photoconductor; **-leitfähigkeit,** *f.* photoconductivity; **-leitung,** *f.* photoconduction; **-leitungsempfindlichkeit,** *f.* photoconductive sensitivity; **-magnetisch,** photomagnetic.

Photonenabsorption, *f.* photon absorption, photoelectric absorption.

Photo-platte, *f.* photographic plate; **-schicht,** *f.*

Addendum

photocathode; -spaltung, f. photofission; -spannung, f. photovoltage (photovoltaic effect).

Photostrom-abfall, m. photocurrent decay; -anregung, f. photocurrent stimulation.

Photo-verstärker, m. photomultiplier; -zelle, f. photoelectric cell.

physikalische Atmosphäre (atm), normal atmosphere or atmosphere (1.0332 kgf/cm² = 760 torr) (cf. technische Atmosphäre).

piezoelektrisch, piezoelectric.

Piezo-modul, m. piezoelectric modulus; -kristall, m. piezoelectric crystal, piezocrystal.

Piezotropie, f. piezotropy.

Pilzvertilgungsmittel, n. fungicide.

Pion, n. pion, pi meson.

Plagieder, n. pentagonal icositetrahedron.

planen, to plan, scheme, project, design, plot.

planetarische, planetary; ~ Nebel, planetary nebula.

Planimeterkurve, f. planimeter trace.

planlos anordnen, to randomize.

planparallel, plane parallel.

Planungsforschung, f. operations research.

planvoll, carefully planned.

Plasma-brenner, m. plasma torch; -einschluss, m. cytoplasmic inclusion; -kugel, f. plasma sphere; -schwingung, f. plasma oscillation; -spaltungsreaktor, m. fission plasma reactor; -strahl, m. plasma beam; -wechselwirkung, f. plasma interaction.

plastische Ableitung, plastic shear, shear strain.

plastische Verformung durch Abgleiten, accommodation kink or kinking (in crystals).

plastischer Spannungszustand, plastic stress.

plastischer Zustand, plastic state.

Platinreihe, f. platinum group.

Plättchen, n. wafer, slab, slice (of a crystal), chip, die (semiconductor).

Platte, f. wafer (semiconductor).

Platten-adresse, f. disk address; -arbeitsdatei, f. disk work file; -gleichung, f. plate equation; -halter, m. plateholder; -paketsystem, n. (Berkeley) grid system; -speicher, m. disk memory, disk storage; -spieler, m. phonograph.

Plattierung, f. cladding, hardfacing, veneering (of wood).

plattiger Habitus, laminar, platy or micaceous habit.

Platz-ersparnis, f. space saving; -verteilung, f. space sharing; -wechsel, m. interchange of sites.

p-Leitfähigkeit, f. p-type conductivity.

p-Leiter, m. p-type conductor or semiconductor, hole semiconductor or conductor, hole-conducting semiconductor.

Plutonylion, n. plutonyl ion.

pn-Kontakt, m. p-n junction.

pnpn-Transistor, m. p-n-p-n transistor.

pn-Übergang, m. p-n junction, p-n transition.

Polabstand, m. colatitude, polar distance, pole clearance.

Polardiagramm, n. polar diagram.

Polare, f. polar (line), polar curve (in aerodynamics).

Polarisationsnachweis, m. polarization detection.

Polarisierbarkeit, f. polarizability.

Polarisierbarkeitstensor, m. polarizability tensor.

polarisierende Wirkung, polarizing power.

Polar-koordinat, n. polar coordinate; -kreis, m. Arctic Circle; -licht, n. northern lights.

Polarographie, f. polarography.

Polarstern, m. North Star.

Polhodie, f. polhode, moving centrode; -kegel, m. moving cone of instantaneous axes, moving axode, polhodic cone.

Poller, m. mooring post, bollard, bitt, snubbing post, trunnion.

Pol-verschiebung, f. polar wandering, shifting of the pole; -versetzung, f. pole dislocation.

Polychroismus, m. polychroism.

Polyederabbildung, f. polyhedral projection.

Polyenfettsäure, f. polyunsaturated fatty acid.

polygonale Versetzung, f. polygonal dislocation.

Polygonisierung, f. polygonization.

Polygonzugverfahren, n. point-slope method.

polykristallin, polycrystalline.

Polymer, n., Polymere, n., Polymeres, n. polymer.

Polymer-einheit, f. polymer structural unit; -gen, n. polymeric gene.

Polymerisat, n. polymer.

Polymerisationsgrad, m. degree of polymerization.

Polymolekularität, f. polydispersity.

Polynom, n. polynomial.

PONA-Analyse, f. PONA (paraffins, olefins, naphthenes, aromatics) analysis.

Pond, n. p, gram-weight or gram-force (as distinguished from mass), gf; Kilopond, n. kp (kilogram-weight or force), kgf.

Poren-grössenverteilung, f. pore size distribution; -leitfähigkeit, f. pore conductivity; -mes-

sung, *f.* porometry; **-raum,** *m.* pore space or volume.

Positronstrahler, *m.* positron emitter.

Post-leitzahl, *f.* zip code number; **-scheckkonto,** *n.* post office checking account.

Postulat, *n.* postulate.

Potential-berg, *m.* potential hill; **-emission,** *f.* potential liberation.

Potentialform-abhängig, shape-dependent; **-unabhängig,** shape-independent.

Potential-gebirge, *f.* electric image; potential image; **-gefälle,** *n.,* **-gradient,** *m.* potential gradient; **-sprung,** *m.* potential jump, step, or relief; **-tiefe,** *f.* potential well depth; **-topf,** *m.* potential well; **-verteilung,** *f.* potential distribution; **-wall,** *m.* potential barrier.

Potenz-achse, *f.* radical axis; **-ebene,** *f.* radical plane.

potenzieren, to raise to a power, exponentiate.

Potenz-papier, *n.* log-log paper; **-punkt,** *m.* radical center; **-produkt,** *n.* power product; **-reihe,** *f.* power series.

Prachtkleid, *n.* courtship coloration.

Prädissoziation, *f.* predissociation.

Prägervorrichtung, *f.* embossing device.

Prägung, *f.* imprinting.

Präkambrium, *n.* Pre-Cambrian.

Praktikant, *m.* trainee, probationer.

Präparat, *n.* specimen, product, compound, (microscope) slide; **-befestigung,** *f.* specimen mounting; **-halter,** *m.* slide holder.

Präzessionsaufnahme, *f.* precession diffraction pattern.

Präzisionswert, *m.* precision value.

prellen, to chatter, vibrate, bounce, thump, click, bruise.

Prellerscheinung, *f.* relay chatter.

prellfrei, bounce-free.

Prell-kraft, *f.* resiliency; **-schuss,** *m.* ricochet; **-schwingung,** *f.* chatter vibration; **-stoss,** *m.* bump.

Prellung, *f.* contusion, bruise.

Prellzeit, *f.* bounce time.

Pressling, *m.* slug, (glass) blank, molding.

Primär-impuls, *m.* primary pulse; **-strahl,** *m.* primary ray.

Primaten, *n.pl.* primates.

Prinzip-bild, *n.* schematic diagram; **-schaltbild,** *n.* basic circuit diagram, **-schnitt,** *m.* diagrammatic section.

Prismenbinokular, *n.* prism binocular.

Probekörper, *m.* sample (specimen).

Proben-einlassheizung, *f.* injection port heat (on chromatograph); **-plättchen,** *n.* sample coupon.

Probiermethode, *f.* trial-and-error method; **-rechnung,** *f.* trial-and-error calculation.

Produkt, äusseres ~, outer or cross product.

Produktdarstellung, *f.* product representation.

Produktionsstruktur, *f.* plant balance (e.g., in a petroleum refinery).

Produktraum, *m.* product space.

Proferment, *n.* proenzyme, enzyme precursor.

Programm, *n.* routing, program; **-bearbeiter,** *m.* programmer, coder; **-gesteuerte Ausspeicherung,** *f.* memory or code dump.

Programmierhilfen, *f.pl.* software.

Programm-wandler, *m.* program converter; **-zeitschachtelung,** *f.* program time sharing.

Projektion, *f.* projection.

projektiv, projective.

Projektivität, *f.* projectivity.

Propin, *n.* propyne, methylacetylene; **-säure,** *f.* propynoic acid.

Proportionalitätsannahme, *f.* assumption of proportionality.

Proportionalzählrohr, *n.* proportional counter tube.

Propyläther, *m.* propyl ether.

Protaktinium, *n.* protactinium.

Protektorgummi, *m.* tread rubber.

proterozoisch, proterozoic.

Protokollprogramm, *n.* automonitoring routine, tracing routine.

Protonelektronmassenverhältnis, *n.* proton-electron mass ratio.

Protonen-präzessionsfrequenz, *f.* proton precession frequency; **-spin,** *m.* proton spin; **-stoss,** *m.*-e, proton collision; **-streuung,** *f.* proton scattering.

Prüf-last, *f.* test load; **-liste,** *f.* check list; **-locher,** *m.* verifier, control punch; **-taste,** *m.* test pushbutton or key.

Pseudo-abschnitt, *m.* dummy section; **-datei,** *f.* dummy file, dummy data set; **-einkristall,** *m.* pseudosingle crystal; **-euklidisch,** pseudo-Euclidean; **-morphie,** *f.* pseudomorphy; **-satz,** *m.* dummy record; **-skalar,** pseudoscalar, **-sphäre,** *f.* pseudosphere; **-tensor,** *m.* pseudotensor.

p-Typ-Halbleiter, *m.* p-type semiconductor, defect semiconductor, hole conductor.

p-Typ-Leiter, *m.* hole conductor, p-type conductor, defect conductor, hole-conducting semiconductor.

p-Typ-Leitung, *f.* p-type conduction or conductivity, hole or defect conduction.

Puffer-behälter, *m.* surge tank, buffer; -flasche, *f.* trap; -gen, *n.* buffering gene.

Pulsfrequenz, *f.* pulse rate.

pulsierend, throbbing, pulsating, pulsed.

Puls-reaktor, *m.* pulsed reactor; -wellenlaufzeit, *f.* pulse wave velocity (in medicine).

Pult, *n.* console, lectern.

Pulverglühanode, *f.* powder anode.

Pumpzeit, *f.* pump-down time.

Punkt-abbildung, *f.* point-to-point focusing (X-rays); -dipol, *m.* point dipole.

Punktfehl-ordnung, *f.* point defect; -stelle, *f.* point imperfection or defect.

Punkt-flächentransformation, *f.* point-surface transformation; -förmiger Brennpunkt, point focus; -gitter, *n.* point lattice; -gruppe, *f.* point group.

Punktkernnäherungsmethode, *f.* point-kernel method.

Punktlage, *f.* point position, position; allgemeine ~, general position (in crystallography).

Punkt-lichtquelle, *f.* point source of light; -mutation, *f.* gene or point mutation; -ordnung, *f.* arrangement or array of points; -quelle, *f.* point source; -störstelle, *f.* point defect or imperfection; -transformation, *f.* point transformation; -wolke, *f.* scatter or dispersion diagram; -zahl, *f.* score.

Pupinisierung, *f.* coil loading, pupinization, series or lumped loading.

Pupin-kabel, *n.* coil-loaded cable; -spule, *f.* loading or Pupin coil.

Puppenstadium, *n.* pupal stage.

Purpur, *m.* magenta (in color photography).

Putzbewegungen, *f.pl.* grooming behavior.

PVC-Band, *n.* poly(vinyl chloride) tape.

Pyramiden-oktaeder, *n.* triakisoctahedron, trisoctahedron, pyramidal octahedron; -tetraeder, *n.* triakistetrahedron, tristetrahedron, pyramidal tetrahedron.

Pyritoeder, *n.* pyritohedron, pentagonal tetrahedron.

Pyroelektrizität, *f.* pyroelectricity.

Quadratausgleich, kleinster ~, least-squares adjustment.

Quadrate, Methode der kleinsten ~, method of least squares.

quadratische Kennlinie, square-law function.

quadratisierter Kristall, squared crystal.

Quadratsumme, *f.* sum of squares.

Quadratsummendurchschnitt, *m.* mean square.

quadrierbar, squarable.

Quadrupol-intensität, *f.* quadrupole intensity; -kopplungsterm, *m.* quadrupole coupling term; -moment, *n.* quadrupole moment; -quadrupolkopplung, *f.* quadrupole-quadrupole coupling; -schwingung, *f.* quadrupole vibration; -strahlung, *f.* quadrupole radiation; -übergang, *m.* quadrupole transition.

Quantelung, *f.* quantization.

Quanten-bahn, *f.* quantum orbit or path; -elektrodynamik, *f.* quantum electrodynamics; -mechanik, *f.* quantum mechanics; -mechanisch, quantum-mechanical; -sprung, *m.* quantum jump; -stoss, *m.* photoimpact.

quantisiert, quantized.

Quantisierung, *f.* quantization.

Quantor, *m.* quantifier.

Quartilsabstand, *m.* quartile deviation.

quasigeostrophische Näherung, quasi-geostrophic approximation.

Quasigleichgewichts-effekt, *m.* quasi-equilibrium effect; -verteilung, *f.* quasi-equilibrium distribution.

Quasi-impuls, *m.* quasi-momentum; -neutralität, *f.* quasi-neutrality; -stationär, quasi-stationary, quasi-static; -statisch, quasi-static.

Quasi-spiegelung, *f.* quasi-symmetry; -stetig, quasi-continuous; -teiler, *m.* quasi-divisor; -vielfaches, *n.* quasi-multiple.

Quaternisierungsmittel, *n.* quaternizing agent.

Quecksilber-dampfstrom, *m.* mercury-vapor stream; -höchstdrucklampe, *f.* high-pressure mercury-vapor lamp; -kontinuum, *n.* continuous mercury spectrum.

Quelldichte, *f.* source density, divergence (of a vector field).

quellenfrei, source-free, solenoidal.

Quellschicht, *f.* source layer.

Quellungsdruck, *m.* imbibition pressure (in botany).

Quer-beziehung, *f.* cross-correlation; -dehnung, *f.* transverse strain.

Querdehnungs-ziffer, *f.* Poisson's ratio; -zahl, *f.* Poisson's ratio.

Quer-drift, *f.* cross drift; -gleitung, *f.* cross slip; -kontraktionskoeffizient, *m.* Poisson's ratio; -rechnen, *n.* cross-checking; -sattel, *m.* transverse anticline; -schwingung, *f.* lateral oscillation; -stromboden, *m.* cross-flow tray or plate.

Quer-tal, *n.* transverse valley, cross valley; -verbindung, *f.* cross connection, cross-linkage, cross-linking; -**verweisung,** *f.* reference; -**verwerfung,** *f.* transverse fault, cross fault; -**zahl,** *f.* Poisson's ratio.

Quetsch-falte, *f.* squeezed or compressed fold; -**fuge,** *f.* nip (in rolls); -**fuss,** *m.* pinched base.

Quibinärcode, *m.* quibinary code.

quinär, quinary.

Quirl, *m.* curl (of a vector function).

Quote, *f.* portion, quota, proportionate share, ratio, dividend.

Q-Welle, *f.* Q wave, Love wave.

Q-Wert, *m.* nuclear reaction energy, Q factor, Q, figure of merit.

Radial-eigenfunktion, *f.* radial eigenfunction; -**integral,** *n.* radial integral; -**schwingung,** *f.* radial mode; -**strom,** *m.* radial flow.

Radio-echo, *n.* radio echo; -**frequenzstrahlung,** *f.* radio-frequency radiation.

radiogen, radiogenic.

Radio-indikator, *m.* radioactive tracer; -**widerstand,** *m.*-e, radio resistor.

Raketen-abwehrgeschoss, *n.* antimissile missile; -**abwehrsystem,** *n.* antimissile system; -**blitz,** *m.* rocket lightning.

Randbedingung, *f.* boundary condition; ~ **der Periodizität,** periodic boundary condition.

Rand-behandlung, *f.* boundary treatment; -**dichte,** *f.* boundary density.

Rand-effekt, *m.* edge effect (in xerography).

Rändelknopf, *m.* knurled knob.

Rand-fläche, *f.* boundary surface, interface; -**gebiete,** *n.pl.* fringe areas; -**integral,** *n.* contour integral; -**kollokation,** *f.* boundary collocation; -**lochkarte,** *f.* edge-punched or edge-notched card; -**problem,** *n.* boundary problem; -**punkt,** *m.* frontier point; -**schicht,** *f.* boundary or surface layer; -**verschmiert,** tapered, having a diffuse edge.

Randwert-aufgabe, *f.,* -**problem,** *n.* boundary-value problem.

Rangzahl, *f.* rank.

Raster, *m.* grating, raster, grid, scanning pattern, unmodulated light spot, scan or scanned area (in television), mosaic (in photocathode tube), engraved roll; -**blende,** *f.* scanning diaphragm; -**elektronenmikroskop,** *n.* scanning electron microscope; -**feinheit,** *f.* image definition; -**impuls,** *m.* scanning pulse; -**markierung,** *f.* graticule marking; -**mikroskop,** *n.* scanning microscope; -**platte,** *f.* grid board; -**punkte,** *m.pl.* halftone dots (in photoengraving), lock-points.

Rasterung, *f.* scanning (in television), picture definition, embossing.

Rastpolkurve, *f.* herpolhode, fixed centrode.

Ratenzahlung, *f.* installment payment.

Rationalitätsgesetz der Flächenindizes, law of rational indices.

Räuber, *m.* predator; -**tum,** *n.* predation.

Rautiefe, *f.* peak-to-valley height.

Raum-anordnung, *f.* spatial arrangement; -**artig,** spacelike; -**ausdehnungskoeffizient,** *m.* cubic expansion coefficient; -**belastung,** *f.* space velocity; -**bild,** *n.* stereoscopic picture; -**drehung,** *f.* space rotation; -**erfüllung,** *f.* efficiency of space filling; -**fahrt,** *f.* space flight; -**fahrzeug,** *n.* spaceship, spacecraft; -**fokussierung,** *f.* space focusing; -**geschwindigkeit,** *f.* space velocity; -**gitter,** *n.* three-dimensional lattice, space lattice; -**gruppe,** *f.* space group.

Raumgruppen-symbolik, *f.* space-group symbols; -**tabelle,** *f.* table of space groups.

Raum-krümmung, *f.* space curvature; -**kurve,** *f.* space curve.

Raumladungs-anhäufung, *f.* space-charge accumulation; -**begrenzt,** space-charge limited; -**detektor,** *m.* space-charge detector; -**einfluss,** *m.* space-charge effect; -**konstante,** *f.* space-charge factor, perveance; -**schicht,** *f.* space-charge layer; -**verzerrt,** space-charge distorted; -**verzerrung,** *f.* space-charge distortion.

Raum-spiegelung, *f.* space reflection; -**spirale,** *f.* helix; -**transformation,** *f.* space transformation; -**welle,** *f.* space wave, sky wave, atmospheric wave, reflected wave, spherical wave, propagating wave; -**winkel,** *m.* solid angle; -**winkelmass,** *n.* steradian measure; -**zentriert,** body-centered.

Rauschen, *n.* noise, static, background; **schmalbandiges ~,** narrow-band noise; **weisses ~,** white noise.

Rausch-gift, *n.* addictive drug, dope, narcotic, intoxicant; -**kennlinie,** *f.* noise characteristic; -**messung,** *f.* noise measurement; -**spannung,** *f.* noise voltage.

Reaktions-geschwindigkeitskonstante, *f.* reaction rate constant; -**kinetik,** *f.* reaction kinetics; -**träge,** inert, unreactive, slow-to-react, inactive; -**weg,** *n.* reaction channel; -**weise,** *f.* reaction, course of reaction, reaction behavior; -**zeit,** *f.* response time, reaction time.

Reaktivitäts-ausbruch, *m.* reactivity excursion; -**hub,** *m.* excess reactivity; -**rückführung,** *f.* reactivity feedback; -**störfall,** *m.* reactivity accident; -**stoss,** *m.* reactivity surge.

Reaktor, *m.* reactor, nuclear reactor; **Einkreissiedewasserreaktor mit Zwangsumlaufkühlung,** single-cycle forced-circulation boiling-water reactor; -**aufwärmspanne,** *f.* reactor enthalpy rise; -**aktivierung,** *f.* reactor activation; -**baulinie,** *f.* reactor system.

Reaktorbecken, *n.* refuelling cavity, reactor wall; **-flutung,** *f.* refuelling cavity flooding, reactor wall flooding.

Reaktor-behälter, *m.* reactor vessel.

Reaktordruckgefäss, *n.* reactor pressure vessel; **~ mit Einbauten,** reactor pressure vessel with internals.

Reaktor-fahrt, *f.* reactor operation, reactor run; **-gitter,** *n.* reactor lattice; **-hohlraum,** *m.* reactor cavity.

Reaktorkern, *m.* (nuclear) reactor core; **-auslegung,** *f.* reactor core design.

Reaktor-kuppel, *f.* containment building dome; **-schnellabschaltsystem,** *n.* reactor scram system.

Rechen-anlage, *f.* computer; **-automat,** *m.* automatic calculating machine; **-blatt,** *n.* nomograph, nomogram, alignment chart; **-folge,** *f.* sequencing, computing sequence; **-grösse,** *f.* operand; **-löcher,** *m.* calculating punch; **-maschine,***f.* calculating machine, calculator; **-schaltung,***f.* setup for calculating machine; **-scheibe,** *f.* circular slide rule; **-werk,** *n.* arithmetic unit or organ.

rechnen, damit zu ~ haben, to have to take into account.

rechner-abhängig, on-line; **-eingabe,** *f.* computer input; **-merkmal,** *n.* computer feature; **-unabhängig,** off-line.

Rechnungsformular, *n.* calculation sheet.

Rechteck-darstellung, *f.* histogram; **-geber,** *m.* squarer.

Rechts-ansicht,*f.* right-side view; **-asymmetrie,** *f.* negative skewness (of the frequency curve); **-drall,** *m.* right-handed twist or lay; **-gängig,** right-handed; **-gerichtet,** right-handed; **-gewinde,** *n.* right-handed thread; **-herum,** to the right, with right-handed rotation; **-system,** *n.* right-handed system; **-vielfaches,** *n.* right multiple; **-wert,** *m.* X coordinate, departure, easting (in surveying and geodesy).

Rechtwinkelnomogramm, *n.* right-angle nomogram.

Reduktionsschema, *n.* reduction scheme.

Reduzibilität, *f.* reducibility.

Referenzellipsoid, *n.* reference ellipsoid.

Reflektanz, *f.* reflectance.

Reflexe, *n.pl.* reflections.

Reflexion, *f.* reflection, reflex, echo or reradiation (in radar); **reguläre ~,** specular reflection.

Reflexions-dickenmesser, *m.* backscatter thickness gage; **-gitter,** *n.* reflection grating; **-grad,** *m.* reflectance, reflection factor, reflectivity, total reflection factor, reflection coefficient (in optics, normal incidence); **-lichthof,** *m.* reflection halation; **-koeffizient,** *m.* reflection coefficient or factor, total reflection factor; **-kugel,** *f.* sphere of reflection; **-maser,** *m.* reflection-type cavity maser; **-messung,***f.* reflectometry, measurement of reflectance; **-mikroskop,** *n.* reflected-light microscope; **-polarisator,** *m.* reflection polarizer; **-prüfung,** *f.* reflection-type radiometric materials testing; **-schwärzungsmesser,** *m.* reflection densitometer; **-seismik,***f.* reflection shooting (in geophysics); **-vermögen,** *n.* reflecting power, reflectivity, (in optics, oblique incidence), reflectance, reflection factor or coefficient.

Reflex-klystron, *n.* reflex klystron; **-reichtum,** *m.* reflection abundance; **-stoff,** *m.* retroreflecting material.

Regel-antrieb, *m.* variable-speed drive; **-lage,** *f.* regular position; **-losigkeit,** *f.* randomness.

Regelungsvorgang, *m.* regulation process.

Regenerierbarkeit, *f.* regenerability.

Regeneriermittel, *n.* regenerant.

Regien, *f.pl.* overhead expenses.

Regiepult, *n.* mixing desk (in radio).

Registerwerk, *n.* recording unit or output.

Regressionslinie, *f.* regression line.

Reib-echtheit, *f.* resistance to abrasion, fastness to rubbing, crock resistance (of textiles); **-korrosion,** *f.* fretting corrosion; **-rad,** *n.* friction disk; **-rost,** *m.* fretting corrosion; **-scheibe,** *f.* friction wheel.

Reibungs-elektrizität, *f* static electricity, triboelectricity; **-kraft,** *f.‥e,* frictional force; **-schicht,** *f.* friction layer; **-wert,** *m.* coefficient of friction; **-zunge,** *f.* radula.

Reichweite, *f.* range of transmission, outer or cantilever arm, coverage, operating span; **~ der Protonen,** proton range; **kleine ~,** short range; **tatsächliche ~,** actual range; **wirksame ~,** effective range.

Reichweiten-flug, *m.* maximum flight range; **-messung,** *f.* range measurement; **-streuung,** *f.* range straggling.

Reihe, an die ~ kommen, to take one's turn.

Reihen-entwicklung, *f.* series expansion; **-experiment,** *n.* serial experiment; **-umfang,** *m.* size of distribution (in statistics).

reinerbig, homozygous.

Reinhaltung,*f.* pollution control; **~ der Luft,** air pollution control.

Reinkohle, *f.* low-ash coal, clean coal, cleaned coal, ash- and moisture-free coal, pure coal substance.

Reinstkohle, *f.* super coal, ultraclean coal (in Germany, under 0.5% ash).

Rein-transmissionsgrad, *m.* internal transmittance (in glass); **-viskos,** Newtonian.

Reissdehnung, *f.* elongation at break.

Reiz-antwort, *f.* stimulus response; **-mengengesetz,** *n.* reciprocity law, Bunsen-Roscoe reciprocity law.

Rekombinations-koeffizient, *m.* recombination coefficient; **-kontinuum,** *n.* recombination continuum or band; **-wahrscheinlichkeit,** *f.* recombination probability; **-zentrum,** *n.* recombination center or trap.

Rektifikationsteil, *m.* enriching section (in distillation).

rektifizier-bar, rectifiable; **-teil,** *m.* enriching section (in distillation); **-zone,** *f.* enriching section.

Rekursion, *f.* recursion.

Rekursionsformel, *f.* recursion formula.

Relais, *n.* relay, **-abfallzeit,** *f.* relay release time; **-beben,** *n.* simultaneous earthquake; **-betrieb,** *m.* relay operation; **-röhre,** *f.* thermionic relay, cold-cathode tube; **-satz,** *m.* relay group, relay set.

relativistisch, relativistic.

Relativverschiebung, *f.* relative displacement.

Relaxations-effekt, *m.* relaxation effect; **-entfernung,** *f.* relaxation distance.

Rennkraftstoff, *m.* racing fuel.

Renormalisierung, *f.* renormalization.

Replika-Technik, *f.* replica plating.

Reservat, *n.* nature reserve, reservation.

Residualgebiet, *n.* refuge, refugium.

Resistanz, chemische ~, chemical durability (of glass).

Resolvente, *f.* resolvent.

Resonanz-band, *n.*-**er,** resonance band; **-frequenzänderung,** *f.* resonant frequency variation; **-photon,** *n.* resonance photon; **-übertragung,** *f.* resonance transfer.

Resorptionsquote, *f.* rate of absorption (of drugs).

Rest, *m.*-**e,** remainder term (in math.), group (in chem.), moiety (in chem.), radical (in chem.); **-kern,** *m.* residual nucleus; **-klasse,** *f.* coset, residue class; **-klassengruppe,** *f.* quotient group, factor group; **-klassenring,** *m.* residue class ring; **-meristem,** *n.* intercalary meristem; **-spannung,** residual stress, residual voltage; **-varianz,** *f.* residual variance, mean square error, residual error; **-widerstand,** *m.* residual resistance.

Retardierungskorrektur, *f.* retardation correction.

retuschieren, to retouch.

Reversionspendel, *n.* reversible pendulum.

Revier, *n.* territory; **-gesang,** *m.* territorial song.

Revisionsstillstand, *m.* inspection shut down, inspection outage.

Rezeptur, *f.* formulation, recipe.

Rezidiv, *f.* relapse.

Reziprozitätstheorem, *n.* reciprocity theorem.

Richtgrösse, *f.* elastic constant.

Richtungs-doppelfokussierung, *f.* two-directional focusing; **-durchschlag,** *m.* directional breakdown; **-feld,** *n.* vector field; **-fokussierend,** direction focusing; **-fokussierung,** *f.* directional focusing; **-konstante,** *f.* trend constant; **-krümmung,** *f.* curvature of the direction; **-unschärfe,** *f.* direction uncertainty; **-verteilung,** *f.* directional distribution.

Riesen-molekül, *n.* macromolecule, giant molecule; **-wuchs,** *m.* gigantism.

Righeit, *f.* rigidity.

Ring-analyse, *f.* structural group analysis, ring analysis; **-bildung,** *f.* aromatization; **-brennpunkt,** *m.* ring focus; **-fläche,** *f.* torus, ring surface; **-gitter,** *n.* ring grating; **-kern,** *m.* toroidal core; **-körper,** *m.* torus; **-mechanismus,** *m.* ring mechanism; **-schluss,** *m.* cyclization, ring closure; **-strömung,** *f.* annular flow; **-wulst,** *f.* torus, ring.

Rippelwelle, *f.* ripple.

Rippenrohr, *n.* finned tube.

Ripströmung, *f.* rip current.

Rissbildung, *f.* crack growth.

Risschenbildung, *f.* crazing.

Risskeimbildung, *f.* crack nucleation.

Ritz-gerät, *n.* stylus recorder; **-härte,** *f.* scratch resistance, sclerometric hardness.

Rizinoleat, *n.* ricinoleate.

Rizinusöl, *n.* castor oil.

Roboter, *m.* robot.

Rodel, *m.* toboggan, bobsled.

Roh-benzin, *n.* straight-run gasoline; **-braunkohle,** *f.* raw lignite; **-dichte,** *f.* apparent density, bulk density, bulk weight; **-kaffee,** *m.* green coffee; **-kristall,** *m.* crystal blank; **-öluntersuchung,** *f.* crude oil assay, crude oil evaluation.

Rohrbündelwärmeaustauscher, *m.* shell-and-tube heat exchanger.

Röhren-erhitzer, *m.* tubular heater, tubestill heater, pipestill; **-radius,** *m.* tube radius.

Rohr-entladung, *f.* pipe discharge; **-feld,** *n.* bank of tubes (in a heater); **-post,** *f.* pneumatic-tube installation; **-schelle,** *f.* pipe saddle, pipe hanger, pipe clamp, wall hook, pipe strap; **-strahl,** *m.* hollow beam; **-zucker,** *m.* cane sugar.

Roll-grenze, *f.* plastic limit (in soil mechanics); **-tabak,** *m.* twist tobacco.

Addendum

Röntgenabsorptions-kontinuum, *n.* X-ray absorption band; **-spektrum,** *n.* X-ray absorption spectrum.

Röntgenbeugungs-bild, *n.* X-ray diffraction pattern; **-methode,** *f.* X-ray diffraction method.

Röntgenbild, *n.* radiograph, X-ray photograph, X-ray pattern.

Röntgenblitz, *m.* X-ray flash; **-interferenz,** *f.* X-ray flash interference; **-röhre,** *f.* X-ray flash tube; **-zeitdauer,** *f.* X-ray flash time.

Röntgen-durchleuchtungsanlage, *f.* fluoroscope, radioscope; **-durchstrahlung,** *f.* fluoroscopy; **-fluoreszenzspektroskopie,** *f.* X-ray emission spectroscopy; **-gruppe,** *f.* diffraction group; **-heizaufnahme,** *f.* hot X-ray diffraction pattern; **-kontrastdarstellung,** *f.* endoradiography.

röntgenographisch, radiographic.

Röntgenschirmbildaufnahme, *f.* fluorography.

Röntgenstrahlen, Beugung von ~, X-ray diffraction.

Röntgenstrahlenkristalldichtemethode, *f.* X-ray crystal density method (XRCD method).

Röntgen-strahlquelle, *f.* X-ray source: **-streudiagramm,** *n.* X-ray diffraction diagram or pattern; **-term,** *m.* X-ray level.

Rostebene, *f.* grid plane.

Rot, *n.* **erster Ordnung,** first-order red.

Rotalixdrehanodenröhre, *f.* Rotalix tube.

Rotaryverfahren, *n.* rotary drilling.

Rotation, *f.* curl (in mathematics).

Rotations-absorptionsfrequenz, *f.* rotational absorption frequency; **-bandenspektrum,** *n.* rotational band spectrum; **-ellipsoid,** *n.* ellipsoid of revolution; **-elliptisch,** spheroidal; **-fehlordnung,** *f.* rotation disorder; **-freiheit,** *f.* rotational freedom; **-spektrum,** *n.* rotational spectrum; **-viskosimeter,** *n.* rotational viscometer.

Rotliegenderuptiva, *n.pl.* igneous rocks of the Lower Permian.

Rotliegendes, *n.* Rotliegendes (Lower Permian), Rotliegende stage.

Rottange, *m.pl.* red algae, Rhodophyta.

Rotverschiebung, *f.* red shift.

Rubidiumstrontiumalter, *n.* rubidium-strontium age.

Rück-beeinflussung, *f.* feedback; **-bindung,** *f.* back donation; **-diffusionsverlust,** *m.* back diffusion loss; **-drehung,** *f.* inverse rotation.

rückenspaltig, loculicidal.

Rück-formung, *f.* recovery of shape; **-führöl,** *n.* cycle oil, cycle stock; **-kehrkurve,** *f.* edge of regression; **-koppelnd,** regenerative; **-kopplung,** *f.* regeneration reaction, retroaction, feedback,

reactive or regenerative coupling; **-kopplungsschaltung,** *f.* feedback circuit; **kühler,** *m.* recirculation cooler.

Rücklauf, *m.* recycle, flyback (in TV), backstroke, return stroke, kickback, return motion, reverse travel, reflux; **-rohr,** *n.* downcomer, return pipe, downpipe, downtake, downspout.

Rück-leitung, *f.* return circuit or conductor, return piping; **-spulen,** to rewind; **-spülwasser,** *n.* backwash water; **-standshöchstmenge,** *f.* tolerance value.

Rückstell-bit, *n.* reset bit; **-knopf,** *m.* reset button; **-taste,** *f.* resetting key.

Rückstossstreamer, *m.* recoil streamer.

Rückstrahl-aufnahme, *f.* back-reflection pattern; **-optik,** *f.* retro-reflecting optical unit.

Rückstreuung, *f.* back scattering; **-strom,** *m.* backwash, reflux, backflow.

rückwärts gestreut, back-scattered.

Rück-wirkung, *f.* feedback, reactive effect, regeneration; **-wirkungsfeld,** *n.* reaction field.

Ruhe-druck, *m.* stagnation pressure; **-masse,** *f.* rest mass.

Ruhenergie, *f.* rest energy.

Ruhe-potential, *n.* rest potential, open-circuit potential; **-spore,** *f.* resting spore, hypnospore.

rühren, daher ~, to come from, be due to.

Rumpfisomerie, *f.* core isomerism.

runden, to round off, truncate.

Rundlauf, *m.* whirling arm, concentric, circular catwalk.

Runzelbild, *n.* wrinkle or frost image.

Russzahl, *f.* smoke number.

R-Wert, *m.* discrepancy factor.

Saatelementreaktor, *m.* seed core reactor.

Saiten-gravimeter, *m.* string gravimeter; **-näherung,** *f.* string approximation.

Säkular-gleichung, *f.* secular equation, characteristic equation; **-verzögerung,** *f.* secular retardation.

Salzgehalt, *m.* salinity; **-diagramm,** *n.* salinity diagram.

Salz-haushalt, *m.* salt balance; **-kohle,** *f.* salty coal.

Samenstiel, *m.* seed-stalk, funicle.

Sammel-kristall, *m.* polycrystal; **-kristallisation,** *f.* accretive crystallization.

Sandpflanzen, *f.pl.* sand plants, psammophytes.

Sandsackmodell des Atomkerns, sandbag model of the nucleus, statistical model of Bohr's nucleus.

Saprobie, *f.* saprobiont.

Sarosperiode, *f.* saros.

Satellit, *n.* satellite.

Satellitenreflex, *m.* satellite reflection.

Sattel-füllkörper, *m.* saddle packing (for absorbers); **-punkt,** *m.* saddle point.

Sattelpunkts-konfiguration, *f.* configuration of saddle point; **-lage,** *f.* saddle point position.

Sättigungsmagnetisierung, *f.* saturation magnetization.

Sauerstoff-oktaederferroelektrikum, *n.* oxygen-octahedron ferroelectric; **-verschiebung,** *f.* oxygen displacement; **-vorrat,** *m.* oxygen supply.

Saug-düse, *f.* suction nozzle, venturi tube; **-fähigkeit,** *f.* suction capacity (of a pump); **-wert,** *m.* osmotic value.

Säulen-rekombination, *f.* columnar recombination; **-widerstand,** *m.* column resistance.

Saum, *m.* boundary.

Sayresche Vorzeichenbeziehung, *f.* Sayre's sign relation.

Schablonendruck, *m.* screen printing.

Schadensfall, *m.* accident, loss, failure, break, case of damage.

Schadinsekt, *n.* insect pest, harmful insect.

Schädlichkeitsschwelle, *f.* danger threshold.

Schädlingsbekampfungsmittel, *n.* pesticide.

Schadstoff, *m.* pollutant.

schaffen machen, to busy, bother, concern.

Schälchen, *n.* planchet, boat (in chemistry).

Schalen-abschluss, *m.* closure of shell; **-modell,** *n.* shell model; **-verteilung,** *f.* shell distribution.

Schall-beugung, *f.* sound diffraction; **-brechung,** *f.* sound refraction; **-bündel,** *n.* sound beam; **-dämpfer,** *m.* muffler; **-mauer,** *f.* sonic barrier; **-quant,** *n.* phonon, sound quantum; **-quantenentropie,** *f.* phonon entropy.

Schallquelle, *f.* source of sound, sound radiator; **pneumatische ~,** air gun source (in geophysics).

Schalt-bild, *n.* circuit or wiring diagram; **gedrucktes ~,** printed circuit; **-bogen,** *m.* switch arc; **-neuron,** *n.* interneuron, relay cell; **-plan,** *m.* circuit diagram; **-tafel,** *f.* patch panel, plugboard, switchboard, distribution panel.

Schärfe, *f.* keenness, pungency, harshness, acrimony, exactness, sharp definition, acuity, resolving power, stringency, bite (of tobacco).

Schatten-bild, *n.* shadow image, silhouette; **-läufer,** *m.* skiodrome; **-mikroskopie,** *f.* shadow-projection microscopy.

Schaubild, *n.* flow chart, flow diagram, graph, perspective view, operational chart.

Schaufel-dynode, *f.* focused dynode, **-verviel-**

facher, *m.* focused multiplier phototube, focused photomultiplier.

Schauglas, *n.* gage glass, sight glass, inspection glass.

Schaukelschwingung, *f.* wagging, wagging vibration.

schaumbar, expandable, foamable.

Schaum-beton, *m.* aerated concrete; **-bildenvermögen,** *n.* foaming ability, foamability; **-bildner,** *m.* foaming agent; **-gold,** *n.* tinsel, Dutch metal; **-gummi,** *n.* foam rubber; **-öl,** *n.* antifroth oil, defoamer; **-mittel,** *n.* foaming agent; **-schläger,** *m.* egg beater; **-verhüter,** *m.* antifoaming agent; **-wert,** *m.* lather value; **-zahl,** *f.* lather value.

Scheibchen, *n.* slice, wafer (of semiconductor); **quaderförmiges ~,** die (of semiconductor).

Scheinadresse, *f.* dummy address (in data processing).

scheinbare Masse, effective mass.

Scheindiffusionskoeffizient, *m.* eddy diffusivity.

Schein-leitfähigkeit, *f.* eddy conductivity; **-periode,** *f.* spurious period; **-reibung,** *f.* eddy viscosity, phantom friction; **-struktur,** *f.* apparent structure; **-symmetrisch,** pseudosymmetric; **-tod,** *m.* anabiosis.

Scheinwerferlicht, *n.* searchlight beam, floodlight.

Scheinwiderstand, *m.* impedance.

Scheitelwinkel, *m.* crest angle, vertex angle, crown angle.

Scherbeanspruchung, *f.* shear strain.

Scheren-bildung, *f.* chelation; **-schwingung,** *f.* scissor vibration; **-verbindung,** *f.* chelate.

Scher-feld, *n.* shear region; **-gefälle,** *f.* rate of shear, shear gradient; **-geschwindigkeit,** *f.* shear rate; **-schwingung,** *f.* shear mode, shear vibration.

Scherungs-bruch, *m.* shear fracture; **-instabilität,** *f.* shearing instability; **-schwingung,** *f.* shear mode, shear vibration.

Scheuerwirkung, *f.* scouring action.

Schicht endlicher Dicke, finite slab.

Schicht-aufname, *f.* sectional radiography; **-baugruppe,** *f.* wafer module; **-dicke,** *f.* film thickness; **-dickenmessung,** *f.* film-thickness measurement; **-durchhärtung,** *f.* emulsion hardening (in photography); **-element,** *n.* sandwich; **-höhe,** *f.* bed height (of catalyst); **-linie,** *f.* contour line, isohypse; **-strömung,** *f.* laminar flow; **-struktur,** *f.* layered structure; **-träger,** *m.* film base (in photography); **-transistor,** *m.* junction transistor.

Schichtung, *f.* striation, lamination, bedding, stacking.

Schicht-wachstum, *n.* film growth; **-wolke,** *f.* stratus cloud.

Schief-hermitisch, skew-hermitian; **-körper,** *m.* skew field; **-symmetrisch,** skew-symmetrical.

Schill, *m.* shell rock, coquina, pike perch (*Lucioperca lucioperca L.*)

Schirm-bildaufnahme, *f.* fluorography; **-faktor,** *m.* shielding factor; **-gitter,** *n.* screen grid.

Schlag eines Blitzes, stroke of lightning; **-bohrung,** *f.* cable drilling; **-reihenfolge,** *f.* stroke order (lightning); **-seite,** *f.* list (of a ship); **-sieb,** *n.* vibrating screen, shatter box; **-spaltung,** *f.* impact cleaving; **-wort,** *n.* keyword, heading.

Schlammbelebung, *f.* sludge activation.

Schlamm-belebungsverfahren, *n.* activated-sludge process; **-fressend,** limivorous.

Schlämmputz, *m.* slurry plaster.

Schlängelbewegung, *f.* undulating movement.

schlauchlos, tubeless.

Schlauchpumpe, *f.* peristaltic pump, hose pump, flexible tube pump.

Schlechtseite, *f.* no-go side (of a gage).

Schleifenoszillograph, *m.* loop oscillograph, bifilar oscillograph.

Schleifring, *m.* slip ring.

Schlepp-gas, *n.* carrier gas; **-mittel,** *n.* azeotrope former.

Schleuderfrucht, *f.* ballistic fruit.

Schleudern, *n.* centrifugal action, sideslip, skid, sliding, slippage, slipping.

Schleuse, *f.* airlock, refueling slot (in a nuclear reactor), transfer canal (in a nuclear reactor).

Schleusenschwenkkammer, *f.* transfer canal tilting device.

Schleusrohr, *m.* fuel transfer tube (in a nuclear reactor).

Schliere, *f.* cord (in glass), streak.

Schlierenblende, *f.* schlieren diaphragm.

schlimm d(a)ran sein, to be badly off.

Schlingenkurve, *f.* lemniscote.

Schlingern, *n.* rolling, roll, rolling motion.

Schlüsselwort, *n.* index or key word.

Schmelz-druck, *m.* melting pressure; **-kontakt,** *m.* fused catalyst; **-tropfen,** *m.* flaming drippings (in flammability testing); **-wärme,** *f.* melting heat; **-zone,** *f.* displacement spike, melting zone.

Schmiegebene, *f.,* **Schmiegungsebene,** *f.* osculating plane.

Schneiden-methode, *f.* Foucault knife-edge test; **-spektrograph,** *m.* wedge spectrograph, Seemann spectrograph.

Schnell-ablassventil, *n.* fast drain valve, dump valve, jettison valve; **-abschaltbefehl,** *m.* scram signal; **-abschaltung,** *f.* scram, fast shutdown, reactor trip, emergency shutdown; **-alterungstest,** *m.* accelerated aging test; **-brüter,** *m.* fast breeder (nuclear reactor).

Schnellschluss, *m.* reactor scram, fast shutdown, trip, emergency shutdown; **-ablassbehälter,** *m.* scram dump tank.

Schnitt-bildentfernungsmesser, *m.* split-field range finder; **-punkt,** *m.* intercept.

Schnüffel-kontrolle, *f.* sniffing check; **-leitung,** *f.* gas sampling line.

schnüffeln, to sniff.

Schoopieren, *n.,* **Schoopisieren,** *n.* sputtering, metallization.

Schöpfprobe, *f.* bottle sample, silt sample, sample taken with a water bottle.

schöpferisch, productive, creative.

Schottky-Fehlordnung, *f.* Schottky defect or disorder; Schottky vacancy.

Schottky-Leerstelle, *f.* Schottky vacancy or defect.

Schräg-bedampfung, *f.* shadow casting; **-schrift,** *f.* italics; **-verzahnung,** *f.* helical gears or gearing.

Schrauben-achse, *f.* screw axis; **-lehre,** *f.* micrometer; **-textur,** *f.* spiral texture; **-versetzung,** *f.* screw dislocation; **-wachstum,** *n.* spiral growth.

Schraubungssinn, *m.* direction of screw rotation.

Schreiber, *m.* recorder.

Schreib-spitze, *f.* stylus, nib; **-weise,** *f.* notation (in data processing).

Schreitschlepper, *m.* walking machine.

Schritt-grösse, *f.* step size; **-haltend,** on-line, real-time.

Schrittmacher, *m.* pacemaker; **-wechsel,** *m.* pacemaker wandering.

Schritt-motor, *m.* stepping motor; **-weite,** *f.* step size.

Schrumpfung, *f.* shrinkage, shortening.

Schub-kraft, *f.* pushing force, thrust (of propeller or jet); **-mittelpunkt,** *m.* shear center; **-modul,** *m.* shear modulus, rigidity modulus; **-rakete,** *f.* take-off rocket; **-spannung,** *f.* shear stress, transverse stress, viscous stress, viscous shearing stress; **-spannungshypothese,** *f.* maximum shear theory, Guest's theory; **-vektor,** *m.* polar vector, thrust vector; **-verformung,** *f.* shear strain; **-viskosität,** *f.* shear viscosity.

Schüttgewicht, *n.* bulk density, apparent density, piled density, powder density.

Schüttung, *f.* filling, fill, ballast.

Schütt-volumen, *n.* bulk factor (in plastics), bulk volume, apparent volume, volume per unit weight, e.g., cu. ft./lb.; **-wichte,** *f.* apparent density, bulk density.

Schutz-gas, *n.* blanketing or cover gas (in a reactor), inert gas, protective gas; **-gitter,** *n.* screen grid (in electronics); **-stelle,** *f.* security or guard digit; **-zahl,** *f.* gold number (in chemistry).

Schwächung, *f.* attenuation, fading, damping, reduction, diminution, lowering; **~ des Querschnitts,** contraction of cross section.

Schwächungsgesetz, *n.* extinction law; **-koeffizient,** *m.* attenuation coefficient.

Schwaden, *m.* streamer (of gas or smoke), cloud of gas or smoke produced by gunfire, blasts or explosions, swath, window.

Schwallströmung, *f.* slug flow.

Schwankung, *f.* oscillation, amplitude variation.

Schwankungsquadrat, *n.* square fluctuation.

Schwanzbildung, *f.* tailing, tail formation (in chromatography).

schwarze Strahlung, black-body radiation.

Schwarzstrahler, *m.* black-body radiator.

Schwärzungs-dichte, *f.* density (in photography); **-fleck,** *m.* spot; **-keil,** *m.* density wedge; **-kurve** *f.* characteristic curve (in photography), Hurter-Driffield curve, exposure-density curve; **-messer,** *m.* densitometer.

Schwarz-Weiss-Gitter, *n.* black-and-white lattice.

Schwebemethode, *f.* flotation method, temperature gradient method, Millikan's method, oil-drop experiment.

Schweben, *n.* levitation; **freies ~,** levitation, suspension in space.

Schwebeschmelzen, *n.* im Magnetfeld, levitation melting in a magnetic field.

Schwebstoff, *m.* suspended matter, aerosol.

Schwebstoffe, *n.pl.* suspended load, silt load, silt.

Schwebstoff-messer, *m.* turbidimeter; **-schöpfer,** *m.* silt sampler, suspended load sampler.

Schwebung, *f.* beat, beat vibration, beating, whine, wow.

Schwebungs-dauer, *f.* beat period, beat cycle; **-frequenz,** *f.* beat frequency; **-summer,** *m.* heterodyne, heterodyne oscillator, beating oscillator; **-zahl,** *f.* note frequency, beat frequency.

Schwefeldioxyd, *n.* sulfur dioxide.

Schweissbrenner, *m.* welding torch.

Schwellenergie, *f.* energy threshold.

Schwellen-gesetz, *n.* threshold law; **-messung,** *f.* threshold measurement; **-potential,** *n.* threshold potential.

Schwellenwert der Wellenlänge, threshold wavelength.

Schwellenwertkurve, *f.* threshold field curve.

Schwelteerpech, *n.* tar pitch from low-temperature carbonization.

Schwelung, *f.* dry distillation, destructive distillation, low-temperature carbonization.

Schwenk-kurve, *f.* rocking curve; **-verfahren,** *m.* oscillating crystal method; **-filmspektrometer,** *n.* oscillating film spectrometer; **-keil,** *m.* deviating prism.

Schwereabscheider, *m.* settler.

Schwerentflammbarkeit, *f.* flame resistance, flame retardance, flame-retarding characteristic.

Schwerbenzin, *n.* naptha, heavy gasoline, mineral spirits.

Schwere-anomalie, *f.* gravity anomaly; **-beobachtung,** *f.* gravity observation; **-formel,** *f.* gravity formula; **-karte,** *f.* gravity contour map, gravimetric map; **-losigkeit,** *f.* weightlessness, zero gravity; **-netz,** *n.* gravity network; **-vermessung,** *f.* gravity survey; **-welle,** *f.* gravitational wave, gravity wave.

Schwerfeld, *n.* field of gravity.

Schwerpunkts-bewegung, *f.* center-of-mass motion; **-system,** *n.* center-of-gravity system; **-verschiebung,** *f.* displacement of the center of mass.

Schwimmbeckenreaktor, *m.* swimming pool reactor.

Schwindungszugabe, *f.* shrinkage allowance.

Schwingmühle, *f.* vibratory mill.

Schwingungs-bauch, *m.* loop (of oscillation or standing wave), antinodal point, antinode; **-dämpfer,** *m.* oscillation or vibration damper, dashpot, attenuator; **-energie,** *f.* energy of vibration; **-festigkeit,** *f.* dynamic strength, resistance to vibration, fatigue strength, reversed fatigue strength; **-freiheitsgrad,** *m.* vibrational degree of freedom; **-gleichung,** *f.* wave equation; **-instabilität,** *f.* oscillatory instability; **-kreis,** *m.* resonant or tuned circuit, oscillatory circuit, tank circuit; **-möglichkeit,** *f.* oscillation possibility; **-period,** *f.* torsional period (in polymer testing); **-risskorrosionsneigung,** *r.* fatigue (or vibration) corrosion cracking susceptibility; **-schreiber,** *m.* oscillograph; **-spektrum,** *n.* vibrational spectrum; **-tilger,** *m.* attenuator, vibration absorber; **-überlagerung,** *f.* superposition of vibrations; **-wandler,** *m.* vibration transducer; **-zustand,** *m.*-e, vibrational state.

Schwitzablauf, *m.* foots oil (in wax sweating).

Sechsering, *m.* sixfold ring.

Sechskantmutter, *f.* hexagonal nut.

Sediment-aufnehmend, geophagous (organisms); **-decke,** *f.* sedimentary cover.

See-aal, *m.* conger, grayfish; **-adler,** *m.* osprey; **-spiegel,** *m.* lake level or surface; **-wetterdienst,** *m.* maritime meteorological service; **-wind,** *m.* sea breeze, onshore wind.

segmentkernig, polymorphonuclear.

Seh-schwelle, *f.* visual threshold; **-stäbchen,** *n.* optical rod.

sei, es ~ denn, dass, except if, unless . . .

Seichtwasserwelle, *f.* shallow-water wave.

Seifenblasen-gasmengenmesser, *m.* soapbubble flow meter; **-modell,** *n.* soap-bubble model.

Seifenfilmströmungsmesser, *m.* soap-bubble flow meter.

Seileckkonstruktion, *f.* construction of the funicular (link) polygon.

Seite, zur ~ setzen, to put aside; **von anderer ~,** on the part of others; **von verschiedenen Seiten,** on the part of various individuals.

Seiten-turm, *m.* stripper, stripping column; **-wind,** *m.* cross-wind; **-zentriert,** face-centered.

Sektion, *f.* autopsy, post-mortem examination.

Sektions-befund, *m.* autopsy findings; **-chef,** *m.* department head.

Sektorfeld, *n.* sector field; **abgehacktes ~,** cutoff sector field.

Sekundärdurchbruch, *m.* secondary burst.

Sekundärelektronen-emission, *f.* secondary electron emission; **-resonanz,** *f.* secondary electron resonance; **-vervielfacher,** *m.* photomultiplier.

Sekundärstrahlung, *f.* secondary radiation.

Selbst-abstossung, *f.* self-repulsion; **-adjungiert,** self-adjoint; **-adjungierte Gleichung,** self-adjoint equation.

selbständig, autonomous, independent, separate, self-sustained, self-maintained.

selbständige, ~ Einheit, off-line equipment; **~ Entladung,** self-sustaining discharge; **~ Funktion,** self-consistent function.

Selbst-anlasser, *m.* self-starter, automatic starter; **-anschluss,** *m.* automatic (telephone) connection; **-ausrichtend,** self-aligning, self-orienting; **-austausch,** *m.* self-exchange; **-diffusion,** *f.* self-diffusion; **-energiediagramm,** *n.* self-energy diagram, **-gang,** *m.* automatic feed, self-feed, automatic operation; **-löschend,** self-extinguishing; **-prüfung,** *f.* self-checking, self-verification; **-steuerung,** *f.* self-control, automatic control; **-stoss,** *m.* self-collision; **-umkehr,** *f.* self-inversion.

Selbstung, *f.* self-fertilization, autogamy.

Selbst-verstümmelung, *f.* autotomy; **-vorspannung,** *f.* self-bias.

Selektivität, *f.* selectivity.

Selen-gitter, *n.* selenium lattice (structure); **-sperrschichtphotozelle,** *f.* selenium-barrierlayer photovoltaic cell.

Selfkante, *f.* selvage, selvedge.

Senke, *f.* sink, trough, valley, dip, depression; **~ für Leerstelle,** vacancy sink.

Senkwaage, *f.* plumb, sounding lead, densitometer.

separierbar, separable.

Serien-ablesung, *f.* serial readout; **-aufnahme,** *f.* serial radiography; **-fertigung,** *f.* mass production; **-linie,** *f.* diagram line; **-motor,** *m.* serieswound motor, production engine; **-rechner,** *m.* serial digital computer; **-zugriff,** *m.* serial or sequential access.

Serigraphie, *f.* silk screen printing.

Servo-mechanismus, *m.* servomechanism; **-motor,** *m.* servomotor; **-schleife,** *f.* servoloop.

Sessel-Wanne Isomerie, *f.* chair-boat isomerism.

Sexuallockstoff, *m.* sex attractant.

Shockley-Versetzung, *f.* Shockley dislocation.

Sicherheits-einrichtung, *f.* engineered safeguard, safety feature; **-erdbeben,** *n.* maximum potential earthquake; **-grenze,** *f.* confidence limit, safe limit; **-hülle,** *f.* containment (building or shell of reactor); **-schwelle,** *f.* confidence level, level of significance; **-stab,** *m.* safety, scram or shut-down rod (of reactor).

sicherlich, surely, certainly.

Sicherung, *f.* significance (in statistics), safety bolt; **~ gegen Aufschwimmen,** levitation safeguard (in reactor).

Sichtbarmachung der Flecke, the spots are revealed (in chromatography).

Sichtmesser, *m.* visibility meter.

Sicker-bewegung, *f.* percolation; **-verlust,** *m.* leakage.

siderisch, sidereal.

Siede-analyse, *f.* boiling range analysis, distillation analysis; **-beginn,** *m.* initial boiling point, incipient boiling; **-endpunkt,** *m.* final boiling point; **-kennziffer,** *f.* average boiling point; **-kühlung,** *f.* boiling cooling; **-kurve,** *f.* distillation curve; **-perle,** *f.* boiling bead (in chemistry); **-schwanz,** *m.* heavy tails, heavy ends, boiling tail; **-wasserreaktor,** *m.* boiling-water reactor.

Siemens-Martin Stahl, *m.* open-hearth steel.

Silberhalogenid, *n.* silver halide.

Silitstabofen, *m.* Silit (type of silicon carbide)-resistor-equipped furnace.

silizisch, silicic.

Simulant, *m.* malingerer.

Simulationsteste, *m.* malingering test.

simulieren, to simulate, muse, brood, feign (illness), sham, malinger.

Simultanrechner, *m.* time-shared computer.

Singulett-system, *n.* singlet system; **-zustand,** *m.*-e, singlet state.

Sink-geschwindigkeit, *f.* free-fall velocity, sedimentation velocity; **-nadelviskosimeter,** *m.* penetrometer, melt-viscometer; **-stoff,** *m.* sludge, settlings.

Sinterkathode, *f.* powder cathode.

Sinus-bedingung, *f.* sine condition; **-transformation,** *f.* sine transform.

Sirte, *f.* whey.

sistieren, to stop.

Skalarfeld, *n.* scalar field.

Skolopalorgan, *n.* scolopale.

Söderberg-Elektrode, *f.* self-baking electrode, Soederberg electrode.

Software, *f.* software.

Soll-bahn, *f.* stable orbit; **-kreis,** *m.* equilibrium orbit, synchronous orbit; **-kreissprengung,** *f.* stable orbit break-up; **-phase,** *f.* charged particle equilibrium phase; **-teilchen,** *n.* equilibrium particle, phase-stable particle; **-wert,** *m.* desired value, rated value, set level, set point, command variable, face value, reference input.

Solvatation, *f.*, **Solvatisierung,** *f.* solvation.

Sonden-ausdehnung, *f.* probe area; **-charakteristik,** *f.* probe characteristic; **-technik,** *f.* probe technique.

Sonder-druck, *m.* reprint; **-rechenstab,** *m.* special slide rule.

Sondierung, *f.* sounding, logging (of an oil well).

Sonnen-batterie, *f.* solar battery; **-energie,** *f.* solar energy; **-fackel,** *f.* solar flare; **-ferne,** *f.* aphelion; **-kontinuum,** *n.* sun continuum; **-korona,** *f.* solar corona; **-nähe,** *f.* perihelion; **-photosphäre,** *f.* solar photosphere.

Sortenabbau, *m.* deterioration of strains.

Sortiment, *n.* assortment, product mix; **-vereinigung,** *f.* consolidation of product mix.

Soxhlethülse, *f.* Soxhlet extraction cartridge.

Sozial-amt, *n.* social welfare office; **-beamter,** *m.* welfare worker; **-beiträge,** *m.pl.* social insurance contributions; **-denkend,** public-spirited, charitable; **-einrichtungen,** *f.pl.* social services; **-fürsorge,** *f.* social welfare work; **-raum,** *m.* recreational facilities.

Spalt-algen, *f.pl.* blue-green algae; **-bar,** fissionable; **-bombe,** *f.* fission bomb; **-edelgas,** *n.* inert or noble fission gas.

Spalten-index, *m.* column index; **-matrix,** *f.* column matrix.

Spalterwartung, *f.* **asymptotische** ∼, iterated fission expectation.

Spalt-höhe, *f.* slit height; **-kollimation,** *f.* slit collimation; **-korrosion,** *f.* intercrystalline corrosion, crevice corrosion, cleavage brittleness, weld decay; **-neutron,** *n.* fission neutron.

Spaltprodukt, *n.* fission product, fragment; **-aufbau,** *m.* fission product build-up.

Spaltrohr, *n.* collimator; **-motor,** *m.* canned motor.

Spaltstoff, *m.* fissionable material, nuclear fuel; **-stab,** *m.* fuel rod.

Spaltungs-generation, *f.* filial generation; **-gesetz,** *n.* Mendel's second law (law of segregation); **-grad,** *m.* severity of cracking; **-querschnitt,** *m.* fission cross section.

Spalt-weite, *f.* spacing, gap width, clearance; **-zone,** *f.* reactor core.

Spann-beton, *m.* prestressed concrete; **-en,** *n.* gripping, chucking, holding, clamping, stretching; **-gerät,** *n.* stud tensioner; **-packung,** *f.* stretchwrap.

Spannungs-dehnungsbeziehung, *f.* stress-strain relation; **-feld,** *n.* stress field; **-koeffizient,** *m.* thermal expansion coefficient; **-regelröhre,** *f.* voltage-regulator tube; **-rissbeständigkeit,** *f.* resistance to environmental stress cracking; **-risse,** *m.pl.* stress cracking, stress crazing; **-stoss,** *m.* voltage pulse; **-teiler,** *m.* voltage divider; **-tensor,** *m.* stress tensor; **-zusammenbruch,** *m.* voltage collapse.

Spannweite, *f.* range (in statistics); ∼**-F-Test,** *m.* substitute F-test; ∼**-F-Wert,** *m.* substitute F-ratio; ∼**-Test,** *m.* range test, G-test.

Spatprodukt, *n.* scalar triple product, parallelepipedal product.

Speichelamylase, *f.* salivary amylase or ptyalin.

Speicher, *m.* memory (in data processing), store, storage; **-auszug,** *m.* memory dump; **-bit,** *n.* memory bit; **-paket,** *n.* memory stack, store stack; **-stoff,** *m.* reserve substance or material.

Speicherung, *f.* retention (in medicine).

spektral, spectral; **-apparat,** *m.* spectroscopic apparatus; **-steuerung,** *f.* spectral shift control.

Spektralverteilung, *f.* spectral distribution; **Mittelwert über die** ∼, spectral average.

Spektrograph, *m.* spectrograph.

Spektroskopie, *f.* spectroscopy.

spektroskopisch, spectroscopic.

Spenderbakterie, *f.* donor bacterium.

Sperre, *f.* gate (in television).

Sperreaktion, *f.* gaping reaction.

Sperren, *n.* gaping.

sperr-frei, without depletion layers, nonrectifying; **-gas,** *n.* seal gas; **-gitter,** *n.* barrier grid; **-kennlinie,** *f.* blocking characteristic.

Sperrschicht, *f.* depletion layer, barrier film,

barrier layer, blocking layer; **-breite,** *f.* junction (depletion layer) width; **-effekt,** *m.* photovoltaic effect, barrier-layer effect, Becquerel effect; **-element,** *n.* p-n junction cell, photovoltaic cell; **-kapazität,** *f.* depletion-layer capacitance, p-n junction capacitance, barrier-layer capacitance; **-temperatur,** *f.* junction temperature; **-theorie,** *f.* barrier-layer theory.

Sperr-spannung, *f.* inverse voltage, biasing potential, gate voltage; **-strom,** *m.* reverse current, cutoff current.

Sperrung, *f.* blocking, rejection, stoppage, barring, interlocking, blackout, embargo.

Sperr-verlust, *m.* loss in reverse direction; **-vorrichtung,** *f.* catch, locking device; **-vorspannung,** *f.* reverse bias; **-zeit,** *f.* off-period, closing time, curfew.

spezifische Oberfläche, specific surface area.

spezifischer Abbrand, specific burnup, irradiation level.

spezifischer Widerstand, resistivity.

spezifisches Gewicht, specific gravity (N.B. No units); density or specific weight (with units, e.g., g/ml).

sphäroidal, spheroidal.

Spicken, *n.* spiking.

Spickung, *f.* implant.

Spiegel-bildfunktion, *f.* mirror-image function; **-ebene,** *f.* mirror plane; **-kern,** *m.* mirror nucleus; **-punkt,** *m.* mirror point.

Spiegelungs-achse, *f.* imaging axis; **moment,** *m.* parity; **-symmetrie,** *f.* symmetry of reflection.

Spiel, *n.* clearance, backlash, working cycle, free space, tolerance.

spielend leicht, very easy.

Spielraum, *m.* clearance, allowance, backlash, tolerance, margin, free space, windage.

Spin-Abfangtechnik, *f.* spin trapping.

Spin-abhängigkeit, *f.* dependence on spin; **-ausrichtung,** *f.* spin alignment; **-austauschwechselwirkung,** *f.* exchange interaction.

Spinbahn-kopplung, *f.* spin-orbit coupling; **-wechselwirkung,** *f.* spin-orbit interaction.

Spin-drehimpuls, *m.* spin angular momentum; **-dublett,** *n.* spin doublet; **-eigenzustand,** *m.*-e, spin eigenstate; **-elektron,** *n.* spin electron.

Spinellzwilling, *m.* spinel twin.

Spin-gitterrelaxation, *f.* spin-lattice relaxation; **-matrix,** *f.* spin matrix; **-moment,** *n.* spin moment; **-multiplett,** *n.* spin multiplet.

Spinodale, *f.* spinodal curve.

Spinoperator, *m.* spin operator.

Spinor-feld, *n.* spinor field; **-komponente,** *f.* spinor component.

Spinrichtung, *f.* spin direction.

Spin-Spinwechselwirkung, *f.* spin-spin interaction.

Spinumklapp-prozess, *m.* flop-over process, umklapp process; **-streuung,** *f.* spin flip scattering.

Spinumklappung, *f.* spin flip, spin inversion.

Spinwellenmethode, *f.* spin-wave method.

Spiral-bahnspektrometer, *m.* spiral-orbit spectrometer; **-furchung,** *f.* spiral cleavage; **-nebel,** *m.* spiral nebula; **-quelle,** *f.* spiral source.

Spitzen-abstand, *m.* peak separation; **-diode,** *f.* point contact diode; **-flächentransistor,** *m.* point-junction transistor; **-gleichrichter,** *m.* point-contact rectifier; **-kontakt,** *m.* point contact; **-last,** *f.* peak load; **-strom,** *m.* point discharge current; **-transistor,** *m.* point-contact transistor; **-wert,** *m.* peak value.

Spitze-Platte-Entladung, *f.* point-to-plane discharge.

Spitze-Spitze-Zündstrecke, *f.* point-to-point spark gap.

Splitt, *m.* crushed stone, loose gravel.

Sprachdeutlichkeit, *f.* intelligibility.

Sprache, zur ~ kommen, to come under discussion.

Sprachenübersetzung, automatische ~, automatic language translation, machine translation.

Spratzen, *n.* sputtering (in metallurgy).

sprechen, zu ~ kommen, to come under discussion.

Sprechstunde, *f.* office hour, calling hour, consultation hour.

Sprechstundenhilfe, *f.* receptionist, nursesecretary.

Spreng-mittel, *n.* blasting agent, disintegrant (in tablet making), disintegrating agent; **-plattieren,** *n.* explosive cladding.

Spring-kamera, *f.* self-erecting folding camera; **-stift,** *m.* bouncing pin (in octane rating of gasoline).

Spritz-ampulle, *f.* disposable syringe; **-metallisieren,** *n.* sputtering, metallization.

Sprödbruch, *m.* brittle fracture.

Spross-knolle, *f.* stem tuber; **-konidie,** *f.* blastospore; **-pflanzen,** *f.pl.* cormophytes; **-system,** *n.* stem system.

sprudelnd, effervescent, ebullient, fizzing.

Sprüh-kranz, *m.* sparger ring, ring sparger; **-verteilerring,** *m.* sparger ring, spray ring.

Sprung, *m.* jog, dislocation jog, rebound, recoil, step, saltus, transition; **-bildung,** *f.* jog formation, kink formation; **-distanz,** *f.* jump distance; **-erscheinung,** *f.* skip phenomenon; **-frequenz,** *f.* transition frequency; **-haft,** discontinuous, discrete, erratic, jumpy, jumplike, by steps, sudden, unsteady, spasmodic; **-linie,** *f.* jog line (in crystals); **-mechanismus,** *m.* jump mechanism; **-punkt,** *m.* point of discontinuity, discontinuity, transition point, critical temperature, transition temperature; **-schicht,** *f.* discontinuity layer; **-stelle,** *f.* point of discontinuity, discontinuity, jump discontinuity; **-temperatur,** *f.* transition temperature.

Spuckgrenze, *f.* flooding point (in distillation).

spülen, to purge, sweep.

Spulenstromversorgung, *f.* coil-current supply.

Spül-gas, *n.* purging, rinsing, scavenging or recycle gas; **-mittel,** *n.* scavenging medium; **-öl,** *n.* flushing oil; **-pumpe,** *f.* scavenger pump; **-stein,** *m.* sink; **-ung,** *f.* scouring, scavenging, drilling mud, drilling fluid.

Spur, auf die ~ kommen, to get a clue; **-abstand,** *m.* track pitch.

Spuren-analyse, *f.* trace analysis; **-finder,** *m.,* **-sucher,** *m.* tracer; **-verunreinigung,** *f.* traces of impurity.

Spuren von Sternen, prongs of stars.

Stabbündel, *n.* rod cluster.

Stabilitäts-bedingung, *f.* stability condition; **-regel,** *f.* stability rule.

Stab-leistung, *f.* rod power, linear specific power; **-teilung,** *f.* rod lattice pitch.

Stachel-länge, *f.* spike length; **-tragend,** spiniferous.

Staffelbild, *n.* histogram, bar chart.

Staffelei, *f.* easel.

Stamm-baumverzweigung, *f.* cladogenesis; **-blütigkeit,** *f.* cauliflory; **-form,** *f.* primitive form; **-substanz,** *f.* parent substance.

Stampfgewicht, *n.* bulk density, compacted density.

Stand der Technik, state of the art; **im Stande sein,** to be able.

Standard-affinität, *f.* free energy; **-fehler-berechnung,** *f.* calculation of standard errors; **-nährboden,** *m.* basic culture medium.

Ständerpilze, *m.pl.* club fungi, basidiomycetes.

Stapelfehler, *m.* stacking fault, stacking disorder; **-ebene,** *f.* stacking-fault plane; **-energie,** *f.* stacking-fault energy.

Stapel-fehlordnung, *f.* stacking disorder, stacking fault; **-fermentation,** *f.* bulk fermentation, natural sweat (of tobacco); **-folge,** *f.* stacking sequence; **-operator,** *m.* stacking operator; **-ordnung,** *f.* stacking order.

Stapelung, *f.* stacking, storing.

Startschleuder, *m.* catapult.

Station, *f.* station, stop, hospital ward.

Stationärbehandlung, *f.* in-patient treatment.

stationäres Kriechen, steady-state creep.

Stationsarzt, *m.* house physician.

statistisch verteilt, randomly distributed.

Statoakustikus, *m.* auditory nerve.

Staub-beutel, *m.* anther; **-fliessverfahren,** *n.* fluid or fluidized process.

Stau-druck, *m.* velocity head, dynamic head, impact pressure; **-rohr,** *n.* impact tube, static tube, Pitot tube; **-strahltriebwerk,** *n.* ram-jet engine.

stecken, sich dahinter ~, to hide behind something.

Steck-scheibe, *f.* blank, blind; **-schnur,** *f.* patchcord; **-tafel,** *f.* patchpanel, plugboard, pegboard.

Stehspannung, *f.* breakdown voltage, maximum voltage that insulation can withstand, maximum permissible alternating-current voltage.

Steigrohr, *n.* gas offtake pipe.

Steinpflanze, *f.* lithophyte.

Stelle, an ~, in place of; **~ der Bestimmtheit,** regular point (of a differential equation).

Stelleinrichtung, *f.* servo.

stellen, dahin gestellt bleiben, it is open to doubt; **dahin gestellt sein lassen,** to leave uncertain.

Stell-motor, *m.* servomotor; **-öl,** *n.* flux oil.

Stempeltechnik, *f.* replica plating.

Stengelknoten, *m.* node, joint (in botany).

Sterbeziffer, *f.* death rate, mortality rate.

Stereogrammbeschreibung, *f.* stereogram description.

stereographisch, stereographic.

Stern mit vielen Spuren, multiprong star.

Stern-bedeckung, *f.* occultation; **-bildung,** *f.* star formation; **-haufen,** *m.* stellar cluster; **-punktklemme,** *f.* neutral terminal; **-schnuppe,** *f.* meteor; **-spannung,** *f.* Y-voltage, star voltage; **-system,** *n* galaxy; **-tag,** *m,* sidereal day; **-zwilling,** *m.* stellate twin.

Sterz, *m.* uropyge, uropygium, tail, plow handle.

Steuer-gitter, *n.* control grid; **-stabbank,** *f.* control rod bank; **-werk,** *n.* control unit.

Stichprobe, *f.* sample (in statistics).

Stichproben-erhebung, *f.* sampling, sample survey; **-fehler,** *m.* sampling error; **-funktion,** *f.* statistic, sample function; **-umfang,** *m.* sample size.

Stich-tag, *m.* target date, cutoff date, deadline, keyday; **-wahl,** *f.* random choice, second ballot; **-wort,** *n.* keyword, identifier.

Stickstoff-bakterien, *f.pl.* nitrifying bacteria; **-entzug,** *m.* denitrogenation.

Stiefmutter, *f.* stepmother, cruel mother.

stiefmütterlich, stepmotherly, unkind, biased; ~ **behandeln**, to treat cruelly or shabbily, neglect badly, give Cinderella treatment.

Stillstandzeit, *f.* shutdown time, downtime, outage time, time of dwell, idle time.

Stockpunkt, *m.* freezing point, setting point, pour point, point of congelation, solidification point; **-erniedriger**, *m.* pour point depressant.

Stoff-auflöser, *m.* pulper (in paper making); **-austausch**, *m.* mass transfer; **-durchgangszahl**, *f.* overall mass transfer coefficient; **-grösse**, *f.* material constant, physical constant; **-transport**, *m.*, **-übergang**, *m.*, **übertragung**, *f.* mass transfer.

Stoffwechsel, abbauender ~, anabolism; **aufbauender** ~, catabolism; **erhöhter** ~, hypermetabolism; **-schlaken**, *f.pl.* metabolic wastes.

Stoffwert, *m.* physical characteristic.

Stoppuhr, *f.* stop watch.

Stör-atom, *n.* impurity atom, disturbing atom; **-bandleitung**, *f.* impurity band conduction.

Storchschnabel, *m.* pantograph, geranium.

Störfall, *m.* incident, accident; **-analyse**, *f.* accident or fault analysis.

Stör-feld, *n.* interference field; **-niveau**, *n.* impurity level, defect state; **-phase**, *f.* distortion phase; **-schall**, *m.* noise, masker; **-sendung**, *f.* jamming.

Störstelle, *f.* defect, imperfection, point imperfection, impurity; ~ **im Kristallgitter**, lattice defect.

Störstellen-atom, *n.* impurity atom; **-beweglichkeit**, *f.* defect mobility; **-diffusion**, *f.* impurity diffusion; **-fotoleitfähigkeit**, *f.* impurity photoconductivity; **-halbleiter**, *m.* impurity or extrinsic semiconductor, hole semiconductor, p-type semiconductor; **-platz**, *m.* impurity or defect site; **-profil**, *n.* doping or impurity profile.

Stör-stoff, *m.* contaminant; **-stoss**, *m.* burst of interference; **-strahlung**, *f.* spurious emission.

Störung, *f.* imperfection, defect, fault, perturbation, upset.

Störungen, *f.pl.* **statistische** ~, random disturbances.

Störungs-berechnung, *f.* perturbation calculation; **-energie**, *f.* perturbation energy; **-methode**, *f.* perturbation method; **-rechnung**, *f.* perturbation calculation; **-sucher**, *m.* lineman (in telephony), troubleshooter; **-theorie**, *f.* perturbation theory; **-unempfindlich**, perturbation insensitive; **-unterdrückung**, *f.* noise suppression; **-wert**, *m.* lattice disturbance parameter, lattice distortion value.

Störwellenmethode, *f.* distorted-wave method.

Stoss-approximation, *f.* impulse approximation; **-dämpfung**, *f.* collision damping; **-dämpfungsverbreiterung**, *f.* collision broadening;

-dosis, *f.* loading dose, massive dose or priming dose (in pharmacology); **-durchschlag**, *m.* impulse breakdown; **-einfluss**, *m.:*-e, effect of collision(s).

stossen, ~ **auf**, to come upon.

Stoss-entaktivierungswahrscheinlichkeit, *f.* collision-deactivation probability; **-häufigkeit**, *f.* collision frequency; **-ionisation**, *f.* impact ionization; **-ionisationswahrscheinlichkeit**, *f.* impact-ionization probability; **-matrix**, *f.* collision matrix; **-parameter**, *m.* impact parameter; **-querschnitt**, *m.* collision cross section; **-rohr**, *n.* shock tube; **-spannung**, *f.* impulse voltage, surge voltage, stress produced by impact.

Stoss-spannungsbeanspruchung, *f.* impulse voltage stress; **-stärke**, *f.* collision strength, shock strength; **-strom**, *m.* transient current; **-tank**, *m.* surge tank; **-therapie**, *f.* loading, massive or priming therapy; **-übergangswahrscheinlichkeit**, *f.* collision-transition probability; **-verbreiterung**, *f.* impact broadening; **-verlust**, *m.* loss of momentum; **-vervielfachung**, *f.* collisional multiplication; **-weise**, pulsating, spasmodic, intermittent, vibratory; **-zahl**, *f.* pulse count, impact number.

Stosszeit, mittlere ~, mean free time.

Strahl-antrieb, *m.* jet propulsion, jet engine; **-bündelung**, *f.* focusing, beam concentration, beam forming; **-dichte**, *f.* radiance, radiant intensity; **-effekt**, *m.* Munroe effect; **-einschnürung**, *f.* vena contracta, contraction of jet.

Strahlen-belastung, *f.* radiation exposure; **-chemie**, *f.* radiochemistry; **-messer**, *m.* radiometer, flux meter; **-schutz**, *m.* radiation protection; **-schutzlabor**, *n.* health physics laboratory; **-tierchen**, *n.pl.* radiolarians; **-zersetzung**, *f.* radiolysis, radiolytic decomposition.

Strahler, *m.* emitter, radiator, antenna, radiating system.

Strahl-erhaltung, *f.* beam survival; **-flugzeug**, *n.* jet plane; **-jäger**, *m.* jet fighter plane; **-sauger**, *m.* ejector; **-strom**, *m.* jet stream; **-triebwerk**, *n.* jet engine.

Strahlungs-bilanzmesser, *m.* radiation balance meter; **-breite**, *f.* radiation width; **-diagramm**, *n.* radiation chart; **-einfang**, *m.* radiative capture; **-frei**, radiationless; **-glied**, *n.* radiation term; **-induziert**, radiation-induced; **-korrektur**, *f.* radiative correction; **-lebensdauer**, *f.* radiative lifetime; **leistung**, *f.* radiation efficiency; **-los**, nonradiative, radiationless.

Strahlungs-messgerät, *n.* radiation detection instrument, radiation meter; **-messinstrument**, *n.* radiation instrument; **-normal**, *n.* radiation standard; **-rekombination**, *f.* radiative recombination; **-scheinleitung**, *f.* radiation conductivity; **-strom**, *m.:*-e, radiation flux; **-übergang**, *m.* ̈-e, radiative transition; **-übergangswahr-scheinlichkeit,** *f.* radiative transition probability; **-überschuss,** *m.* radiation surplus.

Strang-presse, *f.* extruder, auger, plodder (in soap industry), **-tabak,** *m.* rod tobacco.

Strass, *n.* paste, easily fusible glass.

Strassenoktanzahl, *f.* road octane.

Streamer vor der Zündung, preonset streamer.

Strecke, *f.* line segment; **zur ~ bringen,** to kill.

Strecken-krümmung, *f.* curvature of a line; **-weise,** by sections, here and there; **-zug,** *m.* straightedge.

Streifen, *m.* tape, ribbon, slip, fringe.

streifender Einfall, grazing incidence.

streifen-gesteuert, tape operated; **-leser,** *m.* tape reader; **-locher,** *m.* tape perforator; **-prüfer,** *m.* tape verifier.

Streu-amplitude, *f.* scattering amplitude; **-bereich,** *m.* reproducibility, repeatability, scatter, spread, spread band, zone of dispersion; **-faktor,** *m.* scattering factor; **-feldabschirmung,** *f.* stray field screening; **-koeffizient,** *m.* scattering coefficient; **-kontinuum,** *n.* scattering continuum; **-länge,** *f.* scattering length, Fermi intercept; **-matrix,** *f.* scattering matrix; **-phase,** *f.* phase shift; **-präparat,** *n.* powder mount (in X-ray technology); **-querschnitt,** *m.* scattering cross section; **-stoss,** *m.* scattering collision.

Streuung, *f.* dispersion (in statistics); **~ in grossem Winkel,** large-angle scattering.

Streuungs-querschnitt, *m.* scattering cross section; **-verhalten,** *n.* scedasticity, dispersion; **-zerlegung,** *f.* variance analysis.

Streu-weglänge, *f.* scattering length; **-winkel,** *m.* scattering angle; **-zentrum,** *n.* scattering center.

Strichfokus, *m.* linear focus.

Striemen, *m.* band of secondary slip.

Strippreaktion, *f.* stripping reaction.

Strom-änderung, *f.* current change; **-arbeit,** *f.* electric energy, Joule heat; **-brecher,** *m.* baffle; **-dichte,** *f.* flux; **-falle,** *f.* flux trapping; **-linie,** *f.* streamline; **-linienformig,** streamlined.

stromlos, dead, deenergized; **stromlose Fläche,** surface of no motion.

Strom-messer, *m.* fluxmeter; **-spannungscharakteristik,** *f.* current-voltage characteristic; **-stabilisierung,** *f.* current stabilization; **-stabilisierungsdiode,** *f.* corrector; **-tätigkeit,** *f.* stream activity, (meteor) shower activity.

Strömung, küstenparallele ~, longshore current.

Strömungs-abriss, *m.* stall; **-doppelbrechung,** *f.* flow birefringence; **-führung,** *f.* flow configuration; **-gleichung,** *f.* flow equation; **-lehre,** *f.* hy-

drodynamics, fluid dynamics, aerodynamics; **-maschine,** *f.* jet engine, turbomachinery; **-uhr,** *f.* flowmeter; **-umlenkung,** *f.* flow reversal.

Strom-verdrängung, *f.* skin effect; **-vergrösserung,** *f.* current gain; **-vervielfachung,** *f.* current multiplication.

Strudelpunkt, *m.* spiral point.

struktur-abhängig, structure-dependent; **-bindung,** *f.* structural bond; **-empfindlich,** structure-sensitive; **-faktor,** *m.* structure factor; **-lehre,** *f.* tectology; **-schema,** *n.* block diagram or scheme; **-viskosität,** *f.* structural viscosity (of pastes); **-vorschlag,** *m.* trial structure.

Stück, grosse Stücke halten, to think a great deal (of him).

stückweise glatt, piecewise smooth.

Studentisierung, *f.* studentization.

Studentsche Verteilung, Student's distribution, t distribution.

Student-Test, *m.* Student's test, t test.

Stufen-funktion, *f.* step function; **-länge,** *f.* step length; **-prozess,** *m.* step process; **-übergang,** *m.* step junction; **-versetzung,** *f.* edge dislocation; **-ziehen,** *n.,* **-ziehverfahren,** *n.* rate growing (of crystals), deep drawing in steps (in metallurgy).

Stufozahl, *f.* colorimetric index number.

Sturmflut, *f.* tidal flood.

Stützpunkt, *m.* check point.

Sub-harmonische, *f.* subharmonics; **-keim,** *m.* subnucleus.

Substanzformel, *f.* empirical formula.

Substitutionsgrad, *m.* degree of substitution.

Subtraktionssubstitution, *f.* substitution by subtraction (in crystallography).

Suchverfahren, *n.* searching method or procedure.

Sulfataschenmethode, *f.* sulfated ash method.

Sulfitablauge, *f.* spent sulfite liquor.

Sulfoseife, *f.* sulfonic soap, black soap.

Summationsformel, *f.* summation formula.

Summen-formel, *f.* empirical formula, summation formula, gross formula; **-häufigkeit,** *f.* cumulative frequency; **-satz,** *m.* sum rule; **-trieb,** *m.* adding unit; **-verteilung,** *f.* cumulative frequency distribution, probability function.

summiert, summed.

Super-benzin, *n.* premium grade gasoline; **-elastisch,** superelastic; **-multiplett,** *n.* supermultiplet; **-novaüberrest,** *m.* supernova remnants; **-positionsprinzip,** *n.* superposition principle.

Supra-fluid, *n.* superfluid; **-fluidität,** *f.* superfluidity; **-flüssig,** superfluid; **-leitend,** superconductive; **-leiter,** *m.* superconductor; **-leitfähig-**

Addendum

615

keit, *f.* superconductivity; **-leitungsübergang,** *m.*-e, superconductive transition.

Suszeptibilität, *f.* susceptibility.

Suszeptibilitätsmaximum, *n.* susceptibility maximum.

Symbollöschtaste, *f.* symbol clearing key.

Symmetrie, *f.* symmetry; **-eigenschaft,** *f.* property of symmetry.

Symmetrierung, *f.* balancing.

Symmetriesymbolik, *f.* symmetry symbols.

Symmetrisierung, *f.* symmetrization.

symplektisch, symplectic.

Synchronabtastung, *f.* synchronous scanning.

Synchroskopmethode, *f.* triggered oscilloscope method.

Syngonie, *f.* crystal system.

Syzygien, *f.pl.* syzygies.

Szintillation, *f.* scintillation.

Szintillations-abfallzeit, *f.* scintillation decay time; **-spektrometer,** *m.* scintillation spectrometer; **-zähler,** *m.* scintillation counter; **-zählrohr,** *n.* photomultiplier counter; **-zählung,** *f.* scintillation counting.

Tabak-behälter, *m.* tobacco case; **-folie,** *f.* tobacco sheet, reconstituted tobacco sheet; **-haufen,** *m.* tobacco pile.

Tablette, *f.* pellet, fuel pellet, preform, billet, biscuit.

Tablettensäule, *f.* pellet stack, column of pellets.

Tachodynamo, *m.* **Tachogenerator,** *m.* tachoalternator.

Tag, zu Tage liegen, to lie exposed; **zu Tage treten,** to appear.

tagblühend, hemeranthic.

Tages-bedarf, *m.* daily requirement; **-gang,** *m.* diurnal variation.

Tagundnachtgleiche, *f.* equinox.

Tagung, *f.* meeting, conference, congress.

Taifun, *m.* typhoon.

Takt-geber, *m.* clock, master clock; **-gerät,** *n.* timing unit; **-impuls,** *m.* synchronizing or timing pulse.

Tangentenabbildung, *f.* tangent image formation.

Tangentialebene, *f.* tangential plane.

Tank, *m.*-e, -s, tank (also military), container, fuel tank (automobile); **-abwehr,** *f.* **-en,** antitank defense; **-anhänger,** *m.* tank trailer.

tanken, to refuel, take in fuel, fill up.

Tank-säule, *f.* gasoline pump; **-stelle,** *f.* filling station, service station, gasoline station; **-wagen,** *m.* tank car; **-wart,** *m.* service station attendant.

Tantalat, *n.* tantalate.

Tapetenschicht, *f.* tapetum.

Targetstrom, *m.* target current.

Tarntracht, *f.* cryptic coloration.

Taschenlampe, *f.* flashlight.

Tastatur, *f.* keyboard, keybank.

Tastenlocher, *m.* keypunch, key card punch, keyboard perforator.

Tastverhältnis, *n.* duty cycle, keying ratio, pulse width to repetition ratio, pulse duty factor.

Tato, tons per day.

Tauch-pumpe, *f.* submersible pump; **-rührwerk,** *n.* plunger-type stirrer; **-sieder,** *m.* immersion heater.

Tauscherharz, *n.* ion exchange resin.

Tauschspule, *f.* transducer.

Technik, *f.* engineering sciences, technology, dexterity, technique.

Technikum, *n.*-en, -a, school of engineering, technical school, pilot plant.

Technikumsmassstab, *m.* pilot-plant scale.

technisch, industrial, engineering, applied, commercial, specialized.

technische, ~ Atmosphäre (at), metric atmosphere (1 kgf/cm² = 0.967841 normal atmosphere = 735.559 mm Hg) (cf. **physikalische Atmosphäre**); **~ Einzelheiten,** technicalities; **~ Geologie,** engineering geology; **~ Hochschule,** institute of technology, polytechnic, technical college; **~ Unterlagen,** engineering data; **~ Zeichnungen,** engineering drawings.

technischer Chemiker, chemical engineer.

technisches, ~ Eisen, commerical iron; **~ Können,** technical know-how.

technisieren, to mechanize.

Teigigwerden, *n.* assumption of a pasty state.

Teig-knetmaschine, *f.* dough kneading machine; **-mischer,** *m.* blender; **-waren,** *f.pl.* farinaceous products, noodles, paste products.

Teilareal, *n.* disjunction, discontinuity.

Teilbogen, *m.* fragmentary arc, isolated arclet, partial arc.

Teilchen-beschleuniger, *m.* particle accelerator; **-bild,** *n.* particle aspect; **-grösse,** *f.* particle size; **-kern,** *n.* nucleus; **-nachweis,** *m.* particle detection; **-stoss,** *m.* particle impact; **-strom,** *m.* particle flow; **-zahl,** *f.* number of particles.

Teil-folge, *f.* subsequence; **-gebietsmethode,** *f.* partial domain method; **-gitter,** *n.* sublattice; **-menge,** *f.* subset; **-reihe,** *f.* subseries; **-schmierung,** *f.* mixed lubrication.

Teilungs-faktor, *m.* divisor; **-vermehrung,** *f.* scissiparity.

Teilversetzung, *f.* partial dislocation.

Tektosilikat, *n.* framework silicate.

Telegrafengleichung, *f.* telegraph equation.

Telephonzentrale, *f.* telephone exchange.

Telephotometrie, *f.* telephotometry.

Telomere, *n.* telomer.

Temperatur-abhängigkeit, *f.* temperature dependence; **-beeinflussung,** *f.* temperature effect; **-entropiediagramm,** *n.* temperature-entropy diagram; **-leitfähigkeit,** *f.,* **-leitvermögen,** *n.,* **-leitzahl,** *f.* thermal diffusivity; **-schichtung,** *f.* thermal stratification; **-skala,** *f.* temperature scale; **-wechselbeständigkeit,** *f.* thermal shock resistance.

Temperierung, *f.* attemperation, temperature regulation.

Tensid, *n.* surfactant, tenside, detergent, surface-active agent.

Tensor-algebra, *f.* tensor algebra; **-bedingung,** *f.* tensor condition; **-dichte,** *f.* tensor density.

tensoriell, tensorial.

Tensoroperator, *m.* tensor operator.

Teppichboden, *m.* floor covering.

Term, *m.* (optical) level; **-anzahl,** *f.* level numbers; **-beeinflussung,** *f.* level displacement; **-dichte,** *f.* level density; **-kontinuum,** *n.* quasicontinuum of levels; **-lage,** *f.* term value; **-schema,** *n.* level diagram; **-schemata,** *pl.* level schemes; **-struktur,** *f.* level structure.

Terz, *f.* third (music); **grosse ~,** major third; **kleine ~,** minor third.

Terzett, *n.* trio.

Test-benzin, *n.* white spirits, solvent naphtha, mineral turpentine; **-teilchen,** *n.* test particle.

Tetraedersymmetrie, *f.* tetrahedral symmetry.

texturbehaftet, with preferred orientation.

Texturröntgenaufnahme, *f.* X-ray diffraction diagram of textured specimen.

Thallium-halogenid, *n.* thallous halide; **-sulfid,** *n.* thallous sulfide.

theoretische Trennstufenhöhe, height equivalent to a theoretical plate (HETP).

thermische Bewegung, thermal agitation.

Thermo-diffusion, *f.* thermodiffusion; **-dynamik,** *f.* thermodynamics; **-emissionsenergieumformer,** *m.* thermionic energy converter; **-kraft,** *f.* thermoelectromotive force, thermoelectric power, thermoelectric potential; **-magnetisch,** thermomagnetic; **-plastbandaufzeichner,** *m.* thermoplastic tape recorder; **-spannung,** *f.* thermoelectromotive force, thermal e.m.f.; **-stabilisiert,** thermostatically controlled.

thesaurieren, to hoard.

Thetafunktion, *f.* theta function.

Thio-harnstoff, *m.* thiourea; **-plaste,** *m.pl.* polysulfide polymers.

Tholeiitgang, *m.:*-e, tholeiite dyke.

Tief-bau, *m.* underground working, underground excavation, deep level mining, drift mining, underground engineering; **-druck,** *m.* gravure printing.

Tiefen-karte, *f.* bathymetric chart; **-stufe,** *f.* gradient; **-wasser,** *n.* bottom water; **-zirkulation,** *f.* deep-water circulation.

Tief-kühlung, *f.* deep-freezing, quick-freezing; **-strahler,** *m.* floodlight; **-temperaturelemente,** *n.pl.* cryogenic or supraconductive elements; **-temperaturforschung,** *f.* cryogenics; **-temperaturpulverkamera,** *f.* low-temperature powder camera.

Tiefung, *f.* deep-drawing, indentation, cupping, depression, deepening.

tiegelfrei, floating (zone melting).

Tierzucht, *f.* animal breeding.

tippen, to typewrite.

Titandioxydrutil, *n.* titanium dioxide rutile.

Titelzeile, *f.* headline.

Titer-abnahme, *f.* denier decrease (in textiles); **-lösung,** *f.* titrant.

Todesrate, *f.* death rate, mortality rate.

tödliche Dosis, lethal dose; **mittlere~~,** median lethal dose, MLD 50.

Toleranzdosisleistung, *f.* tolerance dose rate.

Tomograph, *m.* tomograph, laminograph.

Tomographie, *f.* tomography, body section radiography.

Ton-abnehmer, *m.* phonograph cartridge; **-arm,** *m.* pick-up arm.

Tonband, *n.* recording tape; **-aufnahme,** *f.* tape recording; **-gerät,** *n.* tape recorder, tape set; **-löschgerät,** *n.* tape eraser.

Ton-blende, *f.* bass-treble control, tone control; **-kopf,** *m.* magnetic head (in tape recorder), soundfilm head.

Tonnenverzeichnung, barrel distortion.

Ton-rolle, *f.* capstan (in tape recorder); **-spur,** *f.* sound track.

Topftiefe, *f.* well depth.

Topotaxie, *f.* topotaxy.

Toprückstand, *m.* reduced crude, topped crude, long residue.

Toroidkondensator, *m.* toroidal condenser.

Torr, *n.* torr (unit of pressure; a standard atmosphere has a pressure of 760 torr).

Torschaltkreis, *m.* gate or gating circuit.

Torsionmodul, *n.* torsion modulus.

Torsions-dehnungsmessstreifen, *m.* torsion

Addendum

strain gage; **-kräuselung,** *f.* twist curling (of yarn); **-schwingung,** *f.* torsional wave.

Totalixröhre, *f.* totalix tube.

Tot-speicher, *m.* read-only memory, fixed memory; **-wasser,** *n.* still water, stagnant water; **-zeit,** *f.* dead time.

Träger, *m.* substrate, base, backing, girder, beam, stay, bracket; **-auffüllung,** *f.* carrier replenishment; **-bahn,** *f.* backing web, substrate; **-beweglichkeit,** *f.* carrier mobility; **-bündel,** *n.* carrier beam; **-dichte,** *f.* carrier density; **-diffusionslänge,** *f.* carrier diffusion length; **-durchlaufzeit,** *f.* carrier transit time; **-einfang,** *m.* carrier trapping; **-erzeugung,** *f.* carrier production or generation; **-falle,** *f.* carrier trap; **-gas,** *n.* carrier gas; **-kristall,** *m.* support crystal; **-lebensdauer,** *f.* carrier lifetime; **-nachlieferung,** *f.* carrier support; **-punkt,** *m.* base point.

Trägheits-gesetz, *n.* law of inertia; **-lenkung,** *f.* inertial guidance; **-prinzip,** *n.* Newton's first law of motion, law of inertia; **-welle,** *f.* inertial wave.

Tragöse, *f.* lifting lug, ear.

Tragpratze, *f.* support lug, supporting bracket.

Traktrix, *f.* tractrix.

Trampeltier, *n.* dromedary.

Transfluxorlogik, *f.* transfluxor logic.

Transformationsmatrix, *f.* transformation matrix

Transistorgatter, *n.* transistor gate.

transjugiert, transjugated (in mathematics).

Translationsgitter, raumzentriertes ~, body-centered cubic lattice.

Transmissionsquerschnitt, *m.* transmission cross section.

Transpluto, *m.* trans-plutonian planet.

transponiert, transposed.

Transport-satz, *m.* transport theorem; **-weglänge,** *f.* transport mean free path.

Transurane, *n.pl.* transuranium elements.

transversal, transverse.

Transversalitätsbedingung, *f.* transversality condition.

transzendent, transcendental.

Trapez-regel, *f.* trapezoidal rule; **-verzerrung,** *f.* trapezoidal or keystone distortion.

Traubenhaut, *f.* uvea, uveous coat.

Treiberimpuls, *m.* driving or control pulse.

Treib-mittel, *m.* driving motor, motive fluid, fuel, working fluid, blowing agent (for plastics), foaming agent; **-stoff,** *m.* fuel, motor fuel, propellant.

Trenn-analyse, *f.* discriminatory analysis (in statistics); **-fläche,** *f.* joint plane (in geology);

-rohr, *n.* separation column; **-säule,** *f.* separation column; **-schärfe,** *f.* resolution, sharpness of separation, selectivity (in data processing); **-schleuder,** *m.* centrifuge separator.

Trennung, *f.* discrimination (in statistics).

Trennungswand, *f.* dividing wall, partition, separation barrier or membrane.

Trennvermögen, *n.* resolving power.

Treppen-diagramm, *n.* histogram; **-gitter,** *n.* echelon, echelon grating, Michelson echelon; **-kar,** *n.* stepped cirque; **-kurve,** *f.* stepped curve.

treten, in Erscheinung ~, to appear.

Trichroismus, *m.* trichroism.

Trickfilm, *m.* stunt film, animated cartoon, cartoon film.

Triederwinkel, *m.* trihedral angle.

Triel, *m.* dewlap, wattles.

Triftstrom, *m.* drift current.

trigonometrisch, trigonometric.

Trigyre, *f.* trigyre, three-fold axis.

trigyrisch, trigyric, trigonal.

Trikarbonsäurezyklus, *m.* tricarboxylic acid cycle, Krebs cycle.

Trimere, *n.* trimer.

Trimm, *m.* trim, adjusting, trimming.

Trimmerkondensator, *m.* trimmer, trimming capacitor.

Trimmstab, *m.* shim rod (in reactor).

Trimmung, *f.* shimming, control; **chemische ~,** chemical shim.

Trimorphie, *f.* trimorphism.

triözisch, trioecious.

Tripel-punkt, *m.* triple point; **-punktsdruck,** *m.* triple pressure.

Triplett-spektrum, *n.* triplet spectrum; **-zustand,** *m.* triplet state.

Trochoide, *f.* trochoid.

trocken-adiabatisch, dry-adiabatic; **-eis,** *n.* dry ice; **-kompressionsmaschine,** *f.* dry compression machine; **-stoff,** *m.* desiccant, drying agent.

Trommel-kamera, *f.* drum camera; **-speicherspur,** *f.* drum store channel.

Tröpfchenmodell, *n.* liquid-drop model.

Tropfen, *m.* drip, trickle, gob (of glass); **-abscheider,** *m.* drop separator, mist extractor, demister; **-wachstum,** *n.* droplet growth.

Tropfpunkt, *m.* Ubbelohde drop point, dropping point.

TRT Technik, *f.* SRS technique (in chromatography).

Trübungs-faktor, *m.* turbidity factor; **-titration,** *f.* turbidimetric titration.

Tüpfel-platte, *f.* spot test plate; **-reaktion,** *f.* spot reaction, spot test.

Turbine, *f.* turbine.

Turbinen-antrieb, *m.* turbine drive; **-luft-strahlmotor,** *m.* turbojet engine, **-stau-strahlwerke,** *n.pl.* turboramjet engine; **-strahltriebwerk,** *n.* turbojet engine.

turbinieren, to centrifuge.

Turbo-aufladung, *f.* turbo-supercharging; **-mischer,** *m.* turbomixer, impact mixer.

Turbulenz-energie, *f.* eddy energy, energy of turbulence; **-fluss,** *m.* eddy flux; **-koeffizient,** *m.* eddy viscosity coefficient; **-transport,** *m.* eddy flux.

Typen-beschränkung, *f.* simplification; **-haus,** *n.* standardized building; **-schild,** *n.* name plate.

Typhomologe, *f.* type-homologous curve.

Typisierung, *f.* standardization of types.

überabzählbar, non-enumerable, uncountable.

Überbeanspruchung, *f.* overstressing, overvoltage, overload.

Überbrückung, *f.* by-pass.

übereinanderliegend, superposed, superjacent, stacked.

Übereinstimmung von Schicht und Unterlage, epitaxy.

übererlaubt, superallowed.

Überfahren, *n.* override, overrun, overtravel, overshoot; **~ der Samariummulde,** samarium valley override.

Überfall, *m.* weir, discharge, hasp (of a lock); **-anruf,** *m.* emergency call.

überfällig, overdue.

Überflutungsgrenze, *f.* flooding point (in distillation).

Überführungs-wärme, *f.* heat of transfer; **-zahl,** *f.* transport number.

Übergang, *m.*-e, junction; **~ innerhalb einer Schale,** intrashell transition.

Übergangs-bereich, *m.* transition region; **-forschungsprogramm,** *n.*-e, provisional or tentative research program; **-metall,** *n.* transition metal; **-wahrscheinlichkeit,** *f.* transition probability; **-zeit,** *f.* transit time; **-zustand,** *m.*-e, transient state.

Übergitter, *n.* superlattice.

Überhitzung, *f.* superheating.

Überhöhungsfaktor, *m.* advantage factor.

Überkippung, *f.* tilting over, canting, overturn, overthrust, reverse fault.

Überkorrektion, *f.* overcorrection.

Überkreuz-vererbung, *f.* criss-cross inheritance; **-züchtung,** *f.* criss-crossing.

überkritisch, supercritical.

überlagern, to overlay (in data processing), cover (in mathematics).

überlagert, superimposed.

Überlagerungs-empfänger, *m.* superheterodyne (radio) receiver; **-prinzip,** *n.* principle of superposition; **-satz,** *m.* superposition theorem.

Überlappung, *f.* overlap, overlapping, transvariation (in statistics); **~ der Ladungsdichte,** overlap charge density.

Überlappungsbereich, *m.* transition region.

Überlastbarkeit, *f.* overload capacity.

Überlaufbit, *n.* overflow bit.

Übermännchen, *n.* super-male.

übernormal, supernormal.

Überregelungsfaktor, *m.* overshoot ratio.

Übersäen, *n.* overseeding.

Überschall-flug, *m.* supersonic flight; **-knall,** *m.* sonic boom.

Überschlag, *m.* flashover.

Überschussleiter, *m.* n-type semiconductor.

überschwerer Wasserstoff, tritium.

Überschwingung, *f.* overshoot.

Übersetzungsfehler, *m.* ratio error (of transformer).

Überspielen, *n.* rerecording.

Übersprechen, *n.* crosstalk.

Überströmweg, *m.* by-pass.

Überstruktur, *f.* superlattice, superstructure; **-gitter,** *n.* superlattice; **-reflex,** *m.* superlattice reflection; **-umwandlung,** *f.* superlattice transformation.

Überstunden, *f.pl.* overtime.

Überträger, *m.* vector (in bacteriology).

Übertragung, *f.* carrying (over).

Übertragungs-band, *n.* transmission band; **-datenverarbeitung,** *f.* transfer data processing; **-prinzip,** *n.* principle of transfer; **-verhältnis,** *n.* transfer ratio; **-weise,** *f.* mode of transmission.

Überwachung, *f.* monitoring, surveillance, check, observation, policing.

Überwachungsprogramm, *n.* supervisory program, tracing program, monitor program, sequence checking program.

überwiegend, overriding.

Überzugaktivierung, *f.* coating activation.

Überzugsleitfähigkeit, *f.* coating conductivity.

Ultra-ionisierung, *f.* ultraionization.

Ultra-kurzwelle, *f.* ultra-high-frequency wave; **-rotsperre,** *f.* infrared block.

Ultraschall, *m.* ultrasonics, ultrasonic sound beam; **-abschwächung,** *f.* ultrasonic attenuation; **-baustein,** *m.* ultrasonic device; **-dicken-messgerät,** *n.* ultrasonic thickness measuring instrument; **-rissprüfer,** *m.* ultrasonic flow detector; **-umformer,** *m.* ultrasonic transducer.

Ultra-schwerewelle, *f.* ultragravity wave; **-strahlung,** *f.* cosmic radiation; **-weich,** ultrasoft.

um einen Zentimeter, by 1 centimeter.

Umesterung, *f.* transesterification.

Umgebung, *f.* neighborhood, medium, surroundings, ambiency.

Umgebungs-belastung, *f.* environmental impact, environmental exposure; **-gefährdung,** *f.* environmental hazard; **-leitung,** *f.* by-pass line; **-schaltung,** *f.* by-pass connection, shunt switch; **-temperatur,** *f.* ambient temperature.

Umhüllende, *f.* envelope, enveloping curve.

Umhüllung, *f.* jacket.

Umkehr-formel, *f.* inversion formula; **-funktion,** *f.* inverse function; **-integral,** *m.* inversion integral; **-satz,** *m.* inversion theorem; **-schalter,** *m.* reversing switch.

Umkehrung, *f.* inversion; **~ einer Operation,** inverse of an operation (in mathematics); **~ einer Reihe,** reversion of a series (in mathematics); **~ eines Theorems,** converse of a theorem (in mathematics).

Umklappwiderstand, *m.* resistance to the Barkhausen effect.

Umladebehälter, *m.* cask (for radioactive material).

Umladung, *f.* charge exchange, reloading, transshipment.

Umlauf, *m.* circuit, recycle; **-integral,** *n.* contour integral; **-speicher,** *m.* circulating memory or store.

Umlaufsrelation, *f.* circuital relation.

Umlenkblech, *n.* baffle.

umlenken, to turn around, turn back.

Umlenkplatte, *f.* baffle.

Umluft, *f.* recirculated air.

Ummagnetisierung, *f.* magnetization reversal.

umordnen, to rearrange, transpose, redistribute.

Umordnung, *f.* interaction, rearrangement.

Umordnungsstoss, *m.*,-e, rearrangement collision.

umpolen, to reverse polarity.

Umpolschalter, *m.* reversing switch.

Umrechner, *m.* translator, decoder.

Umrichter, *m.* transverter, frequency changer, inverter, converter.

Umriss-diagramm, *n.* contour diagram; **-fühler,** *m.* profile tracer; **-tastung,** *f.* profile tracing; **-zeichnung,** *f.* outline drawing, sketch.

Umsatzstatistik, *f.* sales analysis.

Umschlagrelais, *n.* throw-over relay, kipp relay, switching relay.

Umschlagsintervall, *n.* transition interval.

Umschlagzeit, *f.* transit time (of a relay).

umsetzbar, metabolizable.

Umsetzung, *f.* reaction; **doppelte ~,** double decomposition.

Umwandlerausbeute, *f.* converter efficiency.

Umwandlung erster Ordnung, first-order transformation.

Umwandlungswärme, *f.* heat of transition.

Umweganregung, *f.* indirect excitation.

umwelt-angepasst, adapted to environment; **-bedingt,** environmental; **-schaden,** *m.* environmental damage; **-schadstoff,** *m.* environmental pollutant; **-schutz,** *m.* environmental protection.

Umweltseinflüsse, *m.pl.* environmental factors.

Umwelt-verschmutzer, *m.* polluting plant, polluter; **-verseuchung,** *f.* environmental pollution; **-verunreinigung,** *f.* pollution; **-vorschrift,** *f.* antipollution regulation.

unabhängig, off-line; **unabhängiges System,** off-line system.

Unabhängigkeitsgesetz, *n.* Mendel's third law (law of independent assortment).

unabzählbar, uncountable.

unauffällig, unobtrusive, inconspicuous, attracting no attention.

unaufgelöst, unresolved, undissolved.

Unbestimmte, *f.* variable (in algebra).

Unbestimmtheitseffekt, *m.* uncertainty effect.

unbeträchtlich, inconsiderable, negligible.

Unbrunst, *f.* anoestrum, anoestrus.

Undulationstheorie, *f.* undulation theory.

unedler, less noble, less positive, less electropositive.

unedles Potential, electronegative potential.

uneigentlich, improper.

uneinheitlich, nonuniform(ly), inhomogeneous(ly), polydisperse.

unelastisch, inelastic.

ungerade-gerade-Kern, *m.* odd-even nucleus.

ungerade Kontrolle, odd control, imparity check.

ungeradwertig, of odd valence.

ungerichtet, nondirectional, random; **ungerichtete Geschwindigkeit,** random velocity.

ungleicherbig, heterozygotic.

Ungleichung, *f.* inequality.

Ungleichungsmethode, *f.* inequality method.

Uniformitätsgesetz, *n.* Mendel's first law (law of dominance of hybrids).

unitär, unitary; **-ähnlich,** unitary similar.

Universal-drehtisch, *m.* universal stage (of microscope); **-gelehrter,** *m.* polymath.

Unkrautvertilgungsmittel, *n.* weed killer.

unlöschbare Speicherung, non-erasable storage or memory.

unrelativistisch, nonrelativistic.

Unrundheit, *f.* out-of-roundness.

unscharf, diffuse.

Unschärfe, *f.* diffusiveness, uncertainty; **-bedingung,** *f.* uncertainty condition; **-beziehung,** *f.*, **-relation,** *f.* uncertainty relation, uncertainty principle, Heisenberg's uncertainty principle.

unstarr, nonrigid.

Unstetigkeit, *f.* discontinuity.

Unstetigkeits-fläche, *f.* surface of discontinuity; **-stelle,** *f.* point of discontinuity.

Unsymmetriegrad, *m.* degree of asymmetry.

Unteralgebra, *f.* subalgebra.

Unterbrust, *f.* dewlap.

Unterdrückungsspannung, *f.* cutoff voltage.

untere Integrationsgrenze, lower limit of integration.

Unterfrequenz, *f.* subharmonic.

Untergitter, *n.* sublattice.

Untergrund, *m.* background; **-strahlung,** *f.* background radiation; **-streuung,** *f.* background scattering.

Unter-gruppe, *f.* subgroup; **-harmonische,** *f.* subharmonic; **-korrektion,** *f.* undercorrection; **-kühlt,** supercooled; **-lage,** *f.* substrate, backing.

Unterlagen, *f.pl.* data, information, documentation, records, dossier; **-herstellung,** *f.* manufacture of substrates.

unterliegen, keinem Zweifel ~, it cannot be doubted.

Untermenge, *f.* subset.

Unternehmensforschung, *f.*, **Unternehmungsforschung,** *f.* operations research.

Unter-programm, *n.* subprogram, subroutine; **-raum,** *m.* subspace; **-satz,** *m.* console.

Untersetzungsverhältnis, *n.* scaling factor, reduction ratio, step-down ratio.

Unter-struktur, *f.* substructure; **-wasserschallanlage,** *f.* underwater sound installation; **-wind,** *m.* downdraft, forced draft, undergrate blast.

unumkehrbar, irreversible.

unvernetzt, uncrosslinked.

unvollständig, partial.

Uranbrenner, *m.* uranium pile or reactor.

Uranylradikal, *n.* uranyl radical.

Urbild, *n.* inverse image, preimage.

Urdarmdach, *n.* chorda-mesoderm.

Ureizelle, *f.* oogonium.

Urharnsack, *m.* allantois.

Urhirn, *n.* archencephalon.

Ursamenzelle, *f.* spermatogonium.

ursprünglich, primeval.

Ursprungsänderung, *f.* change of origin.

Vagusstoff, *m.* vagus hormone, acetylcholine.

Vakuumpolarisationsdiagramm, *n.* vacuum polarization diagram.

Val, *m.* and *n.* equivalent weight, gram-equivalent (in chemistry).

Valenz, *f.* rank (e.g., of a matrix); **-bindungsmethode,** *f.* valence-bond method; **-gesteuert,** valency-controlled; **-schwingung,** *f.* stretching vibration; **-winkel,** *m.* bond angle.

Vanadationen, *n.pl.* vanadate ions.

Variabilitäts-index, *m.* measure of dispersion (in statistics), standard deviation; **-koeffizient,** *m.* coefficient of variation.

Variations-ableitung, *f.* variation derivative; **-verfahren,** *n.* variation principle; **-wellenfunktion,** *f.* variational wave function.

Varioptik, *f.* zoom lens.

Vektorensatz, *m.* vector set.

Vektorgebilde, *n.* vector space.

Vektor-körper, *m.* vector field; **-raum,** *m.* vector space; **-zerläger,** *m.* resolver.

Verarbeitungseinheit, *f.* processor (for data).

Verarmung, *f.* depletion.

Verätherung, *f.* etherification.

Verätherungsgrad, *m.* degree of etherification.

Verband, *m.* lattice structure (in mathematics).

verbiegbar, deformable.

Verbiegung, *f.* buckling.

Verbindung, *f.* joint, link.

Verbleibwahrscheinlichkeit, *f.* nonleakage probability (of a reactor).

verborgen, latent.

Verbreiter, *m.* vector, transmitter.

Verbreiterung, *f.* broadening.

Verbrennungs-wärme, *f.* heat of combustion; **-wert,** *m.* heating value, calorific value, gross or upper heating value.

Verbund-lager, *n.* babbitt bearing; **-lochkarte,** *f.* dual punch card; **-träger,** *m.* composite beam; **-werkstoffe,** *n.pl.* composite materials, clad materials.

vercoden, to code, encode.

Verdampferkühler, *m.* waste heat boiler.

Verdampfungs-analyse, *f.* thermal volatilization analysis; **-keim,** *m.* evaporation nucleus; **-wärme,** *f.* heat of evaporation, heat of vaporization.

Verdichtungsstossleuchten, *n.* shock-wave luminescence.

verdingen, to let out on hire.

Verdrahtung, *f.* wiring, harnessing, interwiring.

Verdrängungskolben, *m.* displacer piston.

Vered(e)lung, *f.* purification, shift toward a more positive potential (in electrochemistry), finishing, converting (paper).

Vered(e)lungs-stoff, *m.* additive, **-verfahren,** *n.* refining process.

Verein, *m.* partially ordered set, ordered set (in math.).

Vereinbarungssymbol, *n.* declarator.

Vereinheitlichung, *f.* unification.

Vereinigungsmenge, *f.* union of sets.

Vereinzelung, *f.* singulizing, **~ der Brennelemente,** fuel element singulizing.

Vereisung, *f.* glaciation, icing, freezing.

Veresterung, *f.* esterification.

Verfahren, ~ der quadrierten Wurzeln, Graeffe's root-squaring method, Graeffe's method; **~ der streifenden Abbildung,** Wetthauer test.

Verfahrens-fehler, *m.* error of approximation, procedural bias, truncation error; **-forschung,** *f.* operations research; **-schema,** *n.* process flow sheet; **-technik,** *f.* process engineering, chemical engineering, unit operations; **-zeit,** *f.* process time.

verfälscht, biased (in statistics).

Verfälschung, *f.* bias, regular error (in statistics).

verfälschungssicher, tamperproof.

verfeinerte Phase, raffinate phase (in extraction).

Verfeinerung, *f.* refinement, improvement, raffinate.

Verfestigung, *f.* work-hardening.

Verfestigungs-ansteig, *m.* work-hardening or strain-hardening coefficient; **-kurve,** *f.* work-hardening curve.

Verformung, *f.* deformation.

Verformungs-bruch, *m.* ductile fracture; **-geschwindigkeit,** *f.* strain rate; **-mechanismus,** *m.* mechanism of deformation; **-zone,** *f.* zone of deformation.

Verfügung, zur ~ stellen, to make available.

vergleichen, to match (in data processing).

Vergleichs-folge, *f.* collation sequence; **-funktion,** *f.* comparison function; **-spannung,** *f.* refer-

ence voltage, criterion of failure (in strength of materials), maximum utilizable strength; **-streubereich,** *m.* reproducibility.

Verhüttung, *f.* smelting, metallurgical operations.

Verjüngung, *f.* contraction, narrowing.

Verklonung, *f.* clonal selection.

Verknüpfung, *f.* combination.

Verlagerungsspannung, *f.* biasing voltage.

verlängert-rotationsellipsoidisch, prolate, spheroidal.

Verlegung, *f.* transfer, shift, removal, relocation, siting, rerouting, postponement; **~ im Meer,** offshore siting; **~ in der Stadt,** urban siting.

Verlustfaktor, *m.* dissipation factor, acoustic dissipation factor, loss tangent, dielectric loss coefficient, loss factor, dielectric power factor.

Vernetzer, *m.* crosslinking agent (in polymers).

vernetzte Polymere, *n.pl.* crosslinked polymers, network polymers.

Vernetzung, *f.* crosslinking, crosslinkage (of polymers).

Vernetzungs-grad, *m.* degree of crosslinkage; **-kleber,** *m.* crosslinking adhesive.

Vernichtungsstrahlung, *f.* annihilation radiation.

Verpuffungstemperatur, *f.* deflagration temperature.

verriegeln, to bolt up, block, cut off, close, lock, interlock, latch.

Verrohrung, *f.* casing (in wells), pipework.

Verrückung, *f.* displacement; **innere ~,** intrinsic displacement.

Verschiebung der Absorptionskanten, absorption edge shift.

Verschiebungs-faktor, *m.* shift factor; **-feld,** *n.* displacement field, biased field; **-konstante,** *f.* permittivity of free space or vacuum.

Verschiedenheitsfaktor, *m.* diversity factor, diversity ratio.

Verschlüsselung, *f.* coding, code, encoding.

verschmutzungsreduzierend, soil-resistant.

Verschnitt-mittel, *n.* cosolvent, adulterant, extender; **-öl,** *n.* compounded oil.

verschränkt, twisted, crossed, interlaced.

verschwunden, disappeared.

Verseifung, *f.* hydrolysis.

Versenkungs-bohrung, *f.* disposal well; **-tiefe,** *f.* depth of burial.

versetzen, to permute (in mathematics), dislocate.

Versetzung, *f.* dislocation; **~ von Bildpunkten,** relief displacement; **eingeschnürte ~,** pinching dislocation.

Versetzungs-ätzgrube, *f.* dislocation etch pit; **-aufspaltung,** *f.* dislocation splitting; **-beweglichkeit,** *f.* mobility of dislocations; **-bewegung,** *f.* dislocation motion; **-dichte,** *f.* dislocation density; **-kern,** *m.* dislocation kernel; **-knoten,** *m.* dislocation node; **-krater,** *m.* dislocation crater; **-linie,** *f.* dislocation line.

Versetzungsmodell der Zwillingsbildung, dislocation model of twinning.

Versetzungs-netzwerk, *n.* dislocation network; **-schleife,** *f.* dislocation loop; **-sprung,** *m.* dislocation jog; **-stärke,** *f.* strength of dislocation; **-stufe,** *f.* dislocation step; **-trichter,** *m.* dislocation crater; **-verteilung,** *f.* dislocation distribution; **-wald,** *m.* dislocation forest; **-wanderung,** *f.* dislocation migration; **-wechselwirkung,** *f.* interaction of dislocations; **-zentrum,** *n.* dislocation center.

Verseuchung, *f.* infection, contamination.

verspannter Kristall, strained crystal.

verspannungsfreies Gitter, strain-free lattice.

Versprödung, *f.* embrittlement.

verstärkte Konstruktion, ruggedized construction (in electronics).

Verstärkung, *f.* amplification, transmission gain, ruggedization.

Verstärkungs-faktor, *m.* amplification factor; **-gerade,** *f.* enrichment line (in distillation diagram).

versteckte Zone, latent zone (in crystals).

Verstellung, *f.* motion, movement, repositioning, adjustment, setting.

Verstimmung, *f.* detuning, mistuning.

Versuchsschleife, *f.* experimental loop, loop.

vertauschbar, interchangeable.

Vertauschungs-matrix, *f.* permutation matrix (in crystals); **-regel,** *f.* commutation rule.

Verteiler, *m.* header, manifold.

Verteilungs-chromatographie, *f.* partition chromatography; **-funktion,** *f.* partition function; **-koeffizient,** *m.* distribution coefficient, partition coefficient; **-zahl,** *f.* distribution number, partition ratio.

Vertikalstrom, *m.* air-earth current.

verträgliche Verteilungsfunktion, congruent distribution function.

Verunreinigung, *f.* contaminant, crud (in reactor), admixture, adulterant, lattice impurity, pollutant, pollution; **eingebaute ~,** lattice impurity; **~ durch Oberwellen,** contamination by harmonics.

Verunreinigungs-leerstellenpaar, *n.* impurity-vacancy pair; **-stoff,** *m.* contaminant.

Vervielfältiger, *m.* multiplier, copying machine.

Verwachsung, *f.* intergrowth, intercrescence (in crystals).

Verwachsungs-ebene, *f.* composition plane; **-fläche,** *f.* composition surface; **-gesetz,** *n.* law of intergrowth.

Verweil-gefäss, *n.* hold tank; **-zeit,** *f.* holding time, retention time, dwell time, residence time, lifetime, dwell, hold-up time.

Verwerfung, *f.* fault (in geology), distortion.

Verwerfungsstruktur, *f.* shift structure.

Verwitterungsschicht, *f.* weathered layer.

verzerrt, strained, biased; **verzerrtes Gitter,** strained lattice.

Verzerrung, *f.* deformation strain, strain (in crystals), aberration, bias (in statistics).

Verzerrungs-energie, *f.* strain energy; **-tensor,** *m.* deformation tensor; **-verbreiterung,** *f.* distortion broadening.

Verzögerung, *f.* deceleration.

Verzögerungs-stufe, *f.* delay cascade; **-zeit,** *f.* time lag, lag time, delay time.

Verzugsspeicher, *m.* delay line (in acoustics).

Verzunderung, *f.* scaling (in metallurgy), oxidation.

Verzweigung, *f.* branching, fork, branch, exit.

Verzweigungs-modell, *n.* branching model; **-programm,** *n.* branching program or routine; **-punkt,** *m.* branch point; **-struktur,** *f.* lineage structure; **-verhältnis,** *n.* branching ratio.

Vielfach-stoss, *m.-e,* multiple collision; **-streuung,** *f.* multiple scattering; **-zwilling,** *m.* multiple twin.

Vielfarbenbilderzeugung, *f.* color imaging.

Vielkeimbildung, *f.* multiple nucleation.

Vielkörper-kraft, *f.-e,* many-body force; **-problem,** *n.* many-body problem.

Vielkristall, *m.* polycrystal.

viellappig, multilobar.

Vielling, *m.* polycrystal.

vielschichtig, multilayered.

Vielschlitzmagnetron, *n.* multicavity magnetron.

Vierer-kette, *f.* four-fold chain (in crystallography); **-vektor,** *m.* four-vector, world vector.

Vierfachkette, *f.* four-fold chain.

Vier-Kugel Apparat, *m.* four-ball tester.

Viernetzlaufzeitmethode, *f.* four-gauze-shutter method.

Viertelflächner, *m.* tetartohedron.

vierteltägige Welle, six-hourly wave.

Vierundzwanzigflächner, *m.* pentagonal icositetrahedron.

Vinylaliphat, *n.* aliphatic vinyl compound.

Virialsatz, *m.* virial theorem.

virtuell, apparent, not actual, possible.

Viskosimeter, *n.* viscometer.

Viskositäts-dichtenverhältnis, *n.* kinematic viscosity; **-messer,** *m.* viscometer; **-verhältnis,** *n.* relative viscosity, ratio of viscosities; **-zahl,** *f.* viscosity number, intrinsic viscosity.

Vitrokeram, *n.* pyroceramic.

Vlies, *n.* nonwoven fabric, nonwoven.

Vogelzug, *m.* bird migration.

Voll-insekt, *n.,* **-kerf,** *m.* imago, adult insect; **-linear,** fully linear; **-reduzible,** completely reducible.

Vollständigkeitsrelation, *f.* completeness relation.

Vollwaschmittel, *n.* heavy-duty detergent.

Voltametrie, *f.* voltametry, voltametric titration.

Voltammetrie, *f.* voltammetry.

Volumen-effekt, *m.* volume effect; **-ionisierung,** *f.* volume ionization; **-leitung,** *f.* volume conduction.

Voluminosität, *f.* bulkiness.

Vorabprüfung, *f.* preliminary test.

Vorbeben, *n.* foreshock.

vorbilden, to preshape, educate.

voreilig, premature.

Vorentladung, *f.* predischarge.

Vorfertigung, *f.* prefabrication.

Vorfluter, *m.* main canal or ditch (in sewerage systems), outfall ditch, draining canal, receiving body of water.

Vorgänger, *m.* precursor.

vorgespannt, prestressed (concrete, glass), biased (grid).

vorhandener Gum, vorhandenes Harz, existent gum.

vorhersehen, to foresee.

vorkritischer Zustand, *m.* precriticality.

Vorläufer, *m.* precursor.

Vormagnetisierung, *f.* magnetic bias.

Vorrangprogramm, *n.* priority program or routine.

Vorspannung, *f.* bias voltage, prestress, preload.

Vorspannungseffekt, *m.* bias effect.

Vorsteuerventil, *n.* pilot valve, servovalve.

Vorstufe, *f.* precursor.

Vortiefe, *f.* foredeep.

Vorvakuumpumpe, *f.* forepump, backing pump, rough-vacuum pump.

Vorwähler, *m.* preselector.

Vorwärtsstreuung, *f.* forward scattering.

Vorzeichenbestimmung, *f.* sign determination.

Vorzugs-ebene, *f.* preferred plane; **-richtung,** *f.* preferred direction.

Vulkanologie, *f.* volcanology.

Wachstums-fehler, *m.* growth defect; **-grube,** *f.* growth pit; **-kegel,** *m.* cone of growth; **-spirale,** *f.* growth spiral; **-stufe,** *f.* growth step; **-treppe,** *f.* growth step; **-verzögerung,** *f.* growth retardation.

wahlfrei, optional, elective, at random, random (in statistics).

wahlfreier Zugriff, random access.

wahlweise, selective, by choice, at will, optional.

Wahrheitsfunktion, *f.* function of formal logic.

Wahrscheinlichkeits-hügel, *m.* probability hill (of two random variables); **-verteilung,** *f.* probability distribution.

Walzen-lager, *n.* roller bearing, journal box; **-spalt,** *m.* nip.

Walz-plattierung, *f.* roll-bonded cladding; **-textur,** *f.* sheet texture, rolling texture (in crystallography).

Wamme, *f.* dewlap.

Wandeffekt, *m.* wall effect.

Wander-feldröhre, *f.* traveling-wave tube; **-fläche,** *f.* migration area; **-marke,** *f.* floating mark.

wandernde, ~ **Schicht,** moving layer; ~ **Welle,** progressing wave.

wandernder Lichtfleck, flying spot.

Wanderosion, *f.* scour (in geology).

Wanderungs-geschwindigkeit, *f.* drift velocity; **-verlust,** *m.* migration loss.

Wanderwelle, *f.* traveling wave.

Wandladung, *f.* wall charge.

Wandladungsdichte, *f.* wall-charge density.

Wandler, *m.* converter, transducer; **-verlust,** *m.* transducer loss.

Wandlung, *f.* conversion.

Wandrekombination, *f.* wall recombination.

Warmabstellung, *f.* hot standby (reactor).

Wärme, zugeführte ~, added or supplied heat.

Wärmeäquivalent, mechanisches ~, mechanical equivalent of heat, Joule's equivalent.

Wärme-abfuhrleistung, *f.* heat removal capacity; **-austauscher,** *m.* heat exchanger, recuperator; **-belastung,** *f.* heat load, heat removal rate, thermal stress; **-dämmung,** *f.* heat insulation, thermal insulation, insulation; **-dämmzahl,** *f.* heat transmission resistance; **-dehnzahl,** *f.* thermal expansion coefficient; **-diagramm,** *f.*

temperature-entropy diagram, thermal diagram; -**durchgangszahl**, *f.* overall heat transfer coefficient, coefficient of heat transfer; -**durchschlag**, *m.* thermal breakdown; -**einschliessung**, *f.* thermal confinement; -**fluss**, *m.* heat flow or flux; -**haushalt**, *m.* heat balance.

Wärme-inhalt, *m.* heat content, enthalpy; -**kapazität**, *f.* heat capacity; -**kraftlehre**, *f.* thermodynamics; -**lehre**, *f.* thermodynamics, heat technology, science of heat; -**leitung**, *f.* thermal conduction; -**leitungsgleichung**, *f.* heat conduction equation, Biot-Fourier equation; -**messfarbstift**, *m.* temperature-indicating crayon, Tempilstick, -**pol**, *m.* heat pole; -**rekristallisation**, *f.* recrystallization in hot-worked material; -**rückvermischung**, *f.* back-mixing of heat; -**schalter**, *m.* thermal switch.

Wärme-tauscher, *m.* heat exchanger; -**tönung**, *f.* heat effect, heat of reaction; -**übergabe**, *f.*, -**übergang**, *m.* heat transfer; -**undichtigkeit**, *f.* heat leak; -**wechsel**, *m.* thermal cycling; -**wellen zweiter Art**, second sound; -**wert**, *m.* heat value, caloric value, calorific value, heat of combustion; -**wirkung**, *f.* thermal effect; -**zufuhr**, *f.* heat input; -**zustandsgrösse**, *f.* entropy.

warmfest, heat-resistant, thermostable.

Warmriss, *m.* thermal crack, heat crack.

warmrissig, hot-short.

Warmsprödigkeit, *f.* hot-shortness, brittleness when hot.

Warngerät, *n.* monitor, warning device.

Warnungssignal, *n.* danger signal.

Warteschlange, *f.* waiting line, line-up, queue.

Warteschlangenproblem, *n.* queuing problem.

Wartung, *f.* maintenance, upkeep, servicing, care.

wartungsfrei, maintenance-free.

Warwenton, *m.* varved clay.

Wasch-hilfsmittel, *n.* builder, detergent auxiliary; -**kraft**, *f.* detergency, detergent power; -**mittelverstärker**, *m.* detergent builder, -**produkt**, *n.* eluate.

Wasser-aufbereitung, *f.* water treatment, water purification; -**auszug**, *m.* aqueous extract; -**bau**, *m.* hydraulic engineering; -**bleiocker**, *m.* molybdite; -**bombe**, *f.* depth charge; -**druckprobe**, *f.* hydraulic test, hydrostatic test; -**druckprüfung**, *f.* hydrostatic test; -**dunst**, *m.* water vapor; -**findepapier**, *n.* water indicator paper; -**glanz**, *m.* moiré; -**glocke**, *f.* liquid seal; -**haushalt**, *m.* water balance; -**himmel**, *m.* water sky; -**kraftlehre**, *f.* hydrodynamics; -**kraftwerk**, *n.* hydroelectric installation; -**messer**, *m.* water meter, water gage; -**pfropfen**, *m.* slug of water; -**schlag**, *m.* water hammer, water shock; -**spalte**, *f.* water stoma; -**stabilisiert**, water stabilized.

Wasserstoff-abspaltung, *f.* dehydrogenation; -**ähnlich**, hydrogen-like; -**bombe**, *f.* hydrogen bomb; -**brüchigkeit**, *f.* hydrogen embrittlement; -**brücke**, *f.* hydrogen bond or linkage; -**brückenbindung**, *f.* hydrogen bond; -**entziehend**, dehydrogenating; -**entzug**, *m.* dehydrogenation; -**lichtbogen**, *m.* hydrogen arc; -**sprödigkeit**, *f.* hydrogen embrittlement; -**unterschuss**, *m.* hydrogen deficiency.

Wasser-uhr, *f.* water meter; -**verdrängung**, *f.* (water) displacement.

Wechsel-maschine, *f.* fuel handling machine (for reactor); -**richter**, *m.* inverted rectifier, current inverter, inverter, dc to ac converter, chopper, vibrator; -**rohr**, *n.* refueling tube.

Wechselstrom-bogen, *m.*-**en**, alternating-current arc; -**brücke**, *f.* alternating-current bridge; -**komponente**, *f.* alternating-current component of current.

Wechselwirkung, *f.* interaction, correlation, interplay.

Wechselwirkungs-aufspaltung, *f.* interaction splitting; -**bereich**, *m.* interaction range; -**gesetz**, *n.* Newton's third law (of motion); -**länge**, *f.* interaction mean free path.

Wechselwirt, *m.* alternate host.

Weck-amine, *n.pl.* analeptic amines; -**mittel**, *n.* stimulant; -**reaktion**, *f.* arousal reaction.

Wedelschwingung, *f.* wagging, wagging vibration.

Wegdifferenz, *f.* path difference.

Weglänge, mittlere freie ~, mean free path.

Weglaufen, *n.* drift; ~ **der Frequenz**, frequency drift; ~ **von Absorberstaben**, absorber rod runaway.

Wegmesser, *m.* hodometer, odometer, perambulator.

Weicheisen, *n.* soft iron.

Weichtierkunde, *f.* malacology, study of molluscs.

weiter, alles weitere, everything further; **des weiteren**, furthermore.

Weit-schweifigkeit, *f.* redundancy; -**winkeldiagramm**, *n.* wide-angle diagram.

Welle, ebene ~, plane wave.

Wellen-anfachung, *f.*, -**anregung**, *f.* wave generation; -**fläche**, *f.* wave front; -**funktion**, *f.* wave function; -**gleichung**, *f.* wave equation; -**kamm**, *m.*-**e**, wave crest.

Wellenlängen-abhängigkeit, *f.* dependence on wavelength; -**grenze**, *f.* wavelength limit; -**präzisionsmessung**, *f.* wavelength precision measurement.

Wellen-leiter, *m.* wave guide; -**mechanisch**, wave mechanical; -**paket**, *n.* wave packet; -**steilheit**, *f.* wave steepness; -**vektor**, *m.* wave vector; -**zahl**, *f.* wave number.

Welt-gittertätigkeit, *f.* world thunderstorm activity; **-zeit,** *f.* Greenwich mean time.

Wendel, *f.* spiral, helix, helical fin, traveling-wave helix; **-abtastung,** *f.* helical scanning.

Wendeperiode, *f.* hunting period.

Wenigborster, *m.pl.* bristle-footed worms, *Oligochaeta.*

Werkbank, *f.* workbench.

Werkzeug, *n.* implement, cutting tool, mold, die; **-halter,** *m.* tool holder, die block; **-lehre,** *f.* tool gage; **-macher,** *m.* toolmaker, diesinker; **-stahl,** *m.* tool steel; **-tasche,** *f.* kit, tool bag, tool roll.

Wertevorrat, *m.* range of values.

Wert-funktion, *f.* value function; **-ziffer,** *f.* significant digit; **-zoll,** *m.* ad valorem duty.

Westdrift, *f.* westward drift.

Wetter-front, *f.* synoptic front, meteorological front; **-mast,** *m.* meteorological tower; **-zone,** *f.* synoptic zone.

Wichtung, *f.* weighting.

Wichtungsfaktor, *m.* weighting factor.

Wickelbehälter, *m.* strip-wound (for steel) or wire-wound (for concrete) vessel.

Widersachertum, *n.* antagonism.

Widerstand, *m.* drag, strength (of materials), impedance, opposition, reluctance; **abgestufter** ~, stepped resistance; **induktiver** ~, inductive resistance, inductance; **magnetischer** ~, magnetic resistance, reluctance; **reiner** ~, nonreactive resistance; **schädlicher** ~, parasitic drag or resistance (in aviation); **scheinbarer** ~, impedance, apparent resistance; **winkelfreier** ~, resistance with zero phase angle.

Widerstandsänderung, *f.* resistance variation; ~ **im Magnetfeld,** magnetoresistance.

Widerstandsanomalie, *f.* resistance anomaly.

Widerstands-beiwert, *m.* resistance coefficient; **-faktor,** *m.* impedance factor; **-gerade,** *f.* load line; **-kette,** *f.* voltage divider, potentiometer; **-körper,** *m.* external drag body, baffle, damper; **-linie,** *f.* resistance line; **-messer,** *m.* ohmmeter, electric resistance meter; **-satz,** *m.* decadic resistor, standard resistance; **-übergang,** *m.* resistive transition; **-ziffer,** *f.* resistance coefficient.

wieder-aufarbeiten, to reprocess, rework; **-auffinden,** to retrieve; **-einbringzeit,** *f.* payout period; **-gabe,** *f.* playback.

Wiederholstreubereich, *m.* repeatability.

Wiederholungs-fehler, *m.* repetitive error; **-zwilling,** *m.* repeated twin.

Wiedervereinigungs-gesetz, *n.* recombination law; **-koeffizient,** *m.* recombination coefficient.

Wiederzünden, *n.* reignition.

wieviel, der, die, das wievielte? what day? what number? which?

willkürliche, ~ **Verteilung,** randomization; ~ **Zahl,** arbitrary number.

Wilsonkammer, *f.* (Wilson) cloud chamber.

Wind-gleichung, wind equation; **-kanal,** *m.* wind tunnel.

Windsee, kurzkämmige ~, short-crested sea.

Windstau, *m.* (wind) pressure.

Windwirklänge, *f.* fetch.

Winkel-abhängigkeit, *f.* angular dependence; **-flussdichte,** *f.* angular particle flux density; **-funktion,** *f.* trigonometric function; **-treu,** equiangular, isogonal, conformal, angle-preserving; **-verteilung,** *f.* angular distribution.

Wippe, *f.* rocker, bascule, balance, trigger pair, yoke, pivoted detent, whip (in electrical engineering).

Wirbel-bett, *n.* fluid or fluidized bed; **-bö,** *f.* whirling squall, **-frei,** irrotational, potential; **-röhre,** *f.* vortex tube; **-schicht,** *f.* fluidized or fluid bed; **-schichtverfahren,** *n.* fluid or fluidized bed process, fluidization; **-stabilisierung,** *f.* whirl stabilization.

Wirbelungsenergie, *f.* eddy energy, energy of turbulence.

Wirbel-welle, *f.* rotational wave; **-wert,** *m.* vorticity.

Wirken, *n.* activity.

Wirkfaktor, *m.* power factor.

wirksame Windbahn, fetch.

Wirkstoff, *m.* active substance, biocatalyst, additive, dope.

Wirkungsquantum, *n.* Planck's constant, quantum of action.

Wirkungsquerschnitt, *m.* cross section (in physics); ~ **für Anregung,** excitation cross section; ~ **für Haftung,** trapping cross section; ~ **für Kernspaltung,** fission cross section; ~ **für Spalteinfang,** fission capture cross section.

wirtschaftlich, profitable.

Wirts-kristall, *m.* host crystal; **-wechsel,** *m.* host alternation.

Wismutselenid, *n.* bismuth selenide.

Wissen, meines Wissens, to my knowledge.

Wogenwolke, *f.* billow cloud.

wohin auch, wherever.

Wölbung, *f.* arch, crowning, camber, buckling, vaulting, convexity, kurtosis (in statistics).

Wölbungsverhältnis, *n.* camber ratio.

Wolframato-kieselsäure, *f.* silicotungstic acid; **-phosphorsäure,** *f.* phosphotungstic acid.

Wolfram-bandlampe, *f.* tungsten filament lamp; **-einkristall,** *n.* single crystal of tungsten; **-trioxyd,** *n.* tungsten trioxide.

Wolken-entladung, *f.* cloud discharge; **-säen,** *n.* cloud seeding.

wonach, according to which.

Wuchsstoff, *m.* growth stimulant, growth-promoting substance.

Wurtzit-gitter, *n.* wurtzite lattice; **-struktur,** *f.,* **-typ,** *m.* wurtzite structure.

Wurzel-grösse, *f.* root element; **-ortskurve,** *f.* root locus; **-verzweigung,** *f.* root branching.

Xanthogenatkunstseide, *f.* viscose rayon.

Xanthogensäure, *f.* xanthic acid.

X-Einheit, *f.,* **XE,** X-unit, XU, Siegbahn X unit.

Xenon-blasenkammer, *f.* xenon bubble chamber; **-bogenlampe,** *f.* xenon arc lamp; **-hochdruckbogen,** *m.* xenon high-pressure arc; **-reaktivitätsreserve,** *f.* xenon override; **-schwingung,** *f.* xenon instability; **-vergiftung,** *f.* xenon poisoning (of reactor).

Xenotin, *m.* xenotine.

Xerochasie, *f.* xerochasy.

Xerodruck, *m.* xerographic or electrostatic printing.

Xerographie, *f.* xerography.

X-Platte, *f.* horizontal or X plate, horizontal deflector, horizontal deflection plate.

X-Schaltung, *f.* lattice type connection, lattice network, X-quadripole.

Xylamon, *m.* teredo.

Xylem, *n.* xylem.

Xylit, *m.* xylitol.

Xylit, *m.* *(n.)* xylite, lignite.

Xylylsäure, *f.* xylic acid.

X-Y-Schreiber, *m.* X-Y plotter.

Ylem, *n.* ylem, primordial plasma.

Ylid, *n.* ylide; **-reaktion,** *f.* ylide reaction.

Yohimbin, *n.* yohimbine; **-säure,** *f.* yohimbic acid.

Yohimbosäure, *f.* yohimbic acid.

Youngscher, **~ Elastizitätsmodul,** **~ Modul,** Young's modulus of elasticity, Young's modulus, modulus of elasticity.

Yukawa-Potentialtopf, *m.* Yukawa well.

Yukawa-Wechselwirkung, *f.* Yukawa interaction.

Yukon, *n.* yukon, nuclear pi-meson, Yukawa meson.

Yulescher Abhängigkeitskoeffizient, coefficient of association (in statistics).

Zahl, *f.* constant.

Zahldiamant, *m.* counting diamond.

Zahlen-anzeiger, *m.* digital indicator; **-material,** *n.* numerical data; **-mittel,** *m.* number-average.

Zähler, *m.* counter, meter, tally.

Zählgas, *n.* counter gas.

Zähligkeit, *f.* fold symmetry, multiplicity.

Zähl-körper, *m.* number field; **-rohr,** *n.* counter tube, radiation counter, counter.

Zählrohr-auflösungszeit, *f.* counter resolving time; **-aufnahme,** *f.* diffractogram; **-goniometer,** *n.* X-ray goniometer with counter.

Zähl-statistik, *f.* counting statistics; **-werk,** *n.* counter, register, integrating device, meter.

Zähnelung, *f.* denticulation.

Zänozoikum, *n.* Cenozoic.

Zehnerpotenz, *f.* power of ten, order of magnitude.

Zeichen-automat, *m.* plotter; **-dreieck,** *n.* set square, square (in drafting); **-erkennung,** *f.* character recognition; **-gerät,** *n.* plotter; **-kette,** *f.* string (in data processing); **-lesbarkeit,** *f.* legibility of characters, intelligibility of characters; **-maschine,** *f.* drafting machine (numerically controlled); **-schärfe,** *f.* image sharpness.

Zeilen-drucker, *m.* line printer; **-index,** *m.* line index; **-matrix,** *f.* row matrix; **-summenprobe,** *f.* check column method.

zeit-abhängig, time dependent; **-angabe,** *f.* time symbol, e.g., min.; **-artig,** timelike; **-auflösungsvermögen,** *n.* time resolution; **-gesetz,** *n.* overall rate of reaction; **-geteilt,** time-shared; **-gleichung,** *f.* equation of time (difference between mean and true solar time); **-kanalanalysator,** *m.* time-channel analyzer.

zeitlicher Ablauf, time sequence.

Zeitlupe, *f.* slow-motion camera, high-speed photography.

Zeitlupen-anordnung, *f.* slow-motion arrangement; **-kamera,** *f.* slow-motion camera; **-photographie,** *f.* high-speed photography (for low-speed projection).

Zeit-reaktion, *f.* slow reaction, long-duration reaction; **-schachtelung,** *f.* time sharing; **-skala,** *f.* time scale.

Zeitstand-festigkeit, *f.* creep resistance, creep strength; **-kriechgrenze,** *f.* creep limit, creep strength; **-versuch,** *m.* long-time creep test, creep-rupture test.

Zeit-teilung, *f.,* **-verteilung,** *f.* time sharing; **-verzögerung,** *f.* time lag.

Zelleib, *n.* cell body.

Zelleinschluss, *m.* cell inclusion.

Zellenmethode, *f.* cellular method.

Zell-forschung, *f.* cytology; **-gummi,** *n.* foam rubber; **-kernlehre,** *f.* nuclear cytology; **-membran,** *f.* nuclear membrane.

Zenitflut und Nadirflut, tide for zenith and nadir.

Zentimeterwelle, *f.* centimeter wave.

Zentral-bewegung, *f.* central force motion; **-feld,** *n.* central field; **-feldnäherung,** *f.* central-field approximation; **-symmetrisch,** centrosymmetric, central; **-wert,** *m.* median, ordinary water stage (in hydraulics).

Zerfalls-akt, *m.* disintegration event; **-energie,** *f.* disintegration energy, decay energy; **-konstante,** *f.* decay constant; **-leuchten,** *n.* decay luminescence; **-schema,** *n.* decay scheme.

Zerfallsperre, *f.* flame arrestor.

Zerfalls-wahrscheinlichkeit, *f.* decay probability; **-weg,** *m.* decay channel, decay path; **-weglänge,** *f.* decay mean free path; **-wert,** *m.* demulsibility number or index; **-zweig,** *m.* decay branch.

Zerhacker, *m.* chopper, vibrator; **-feder,** *f.* synchronous reed.

zerlegen, to resolve, factor.

Zerlegevorgang, *f.* breakdown or dismantling procedure.

Zerlegung, *f.* factorization, partition, disintegration, resolution, dismantling; **spektrale ~,** spectral dispersion.

Zerreissdiagramm, *n.* stress-strain diagram.

Zerschneidung, *f.* dissection.

zerstäubt, sputtered.

Zerstäubung, *f.* sputtering.

Zerstrahlung, *f.* (pair) annihilation.

Zezidie, *f.* plant gall.

Ziehachse des Kristalls, draw axis of crystal.

ziehen, in Betracht ~, to take into account.

Zieh-flotationsverfahren, *n.* draw-flotation method; **-geschwindigkeit,** *f.* drawing or pulling rate (speed); **-kristall,** *m.* pulled crystal; **-technik,** *f.* pulling technique.

Ziffern-rechner, *m.* digital computer; **-mässig,** numerical, mathematical.

Zilie, *f.* cilium.

Zinkblendegitter, *n.* zincblende lattice.

Zinkblendetyp, *m.* zincblende structure; **-halbleiter,** *m.* zincblende-type semiconductor.

Zinkselenid, *n.* zinc selenide.

Zirkonate, *n.pl.* zirconates.

zirkumpolar, circumpolar.

Zirp-laut, *m.* stridulation; **-organ,** *n.* stridulating organ.

Zischmechanismus, *m.* hissing mechanism.

Zölom, *n.* coelom; **-sack,** *m.* coelomic sac.

zonal gemittelt, zonally averaged.

Zonarbau, *m.* zoning.

Zonen-index, *m.* zone index; **-nivellierung,** *f.* zone leveling; **-raffination,** *f.* zone refining, zone purification; **-reinigen,** *n.* zone refining; **-schmelzen,** *n.* zone melting; **-verband,** *m.* crystal zones, zone assembly; **-verbandsgesetz,** *n.* zone law; **-zeit,** *f.* regional time.

zufällige Schrittfolge, random walk.

Zufälligkeit, *f.* randomness.

Zufälligkeitstest, *m.* test of randomness.

Zufalls-abweichung, *f.* random deviation; **-auswahl,** *f.* random sampling, random selection; **-bewegung,** *f.* random walk; **-fehler,** *m.* unbiased error, random error; **-grösse,** *f.* random variable; **-koinzidenz,** *f.* chance coincidence; **-paarung,** *f.* random breeding; **-stichprobe,** *f.* random sample; **-stichprobenfehler,** *m.* random sampling error; **-tafel,** *f.* table of random numbers; **-weg,** *m.* random walk.

Zuflussboden, *m.* feed tray or plate (in distillation).

Zuführer, *m.* feeder, connecting pipe, feeder pipe, belt pawl, feeding mechanism, inlet jumper.

zugeordnet, associated with.

Zug-messer, *m.,* **-messgerät,** *n.* tension dynamometer, traction dynamometer, tensiometer; **-richtung,** *f.* direction of migration.

Zugriffszeit, *f.* access time, read-out time.

zugrunderichten, to ruin.

Zugspaltung, *f.* tension cleaving.

Zulaufboden, *m.* feed tray or plate (in distillation).

Zünd-bedingung, *f.* condition for ignition; **-beschleuniger,** *m.* cetane number improver, ignition accelerator; **-elektrode,** *f.* ignition electrode.

Zunder, *m.* scale, oxide layer, hammer scale, cinder.

Zünd-schwellenerniedrigung, *f.* threshold lowering; **-spannung,** *f.* ignition threshold; **-stoff,** *m.* detonation agent, primer, igniter, fuel.

Zuordner, *m.* sequencer, interpreter, allocator.

zurückgestreut, back-scattered.

Zurückkriechen, *n.* reverse creep.

zurückverwandeln, to reconvert, retransform.

Zusammen-drückungsmodul, *n.* compressibility; **-fliessen,** *n.* coalescence; **-führen,** to compile, merge.

zusammenschliessen, sich ~, to join.

Zusammentragegerät, *n.* collator.

Zusatz-einheit, *f.* auxiliary unit, slave unit; **-gerät,** *n.* peripheral equipment; **-programm,** *n.* alternative program; **-spannung,** *f.* additional boosting voltage; **-speicher,** *m.* extended memory.

Zustands-diagramm, *n.* diagram of state; **-dichte,** *f.* density of state; **-gleichung,** *f.* equation of state; **-integral,** *n.* partition function; **-schaubild,** *n.* phase or equilibrium diagram; **-summe,** *f.* partition function.

zutreffend, striking, suitable, appropriate, conclusive.

Zuverlässigkeitsfaktor, *m.* reliability factor.

Zuwachs, *m.* buildup, accretion, extension; **-faktor,** *m.* build-up factor.

Zwangskraft, *f.* reaction, reactive force, reaction of constraints.

Zwei-achsenschreiber, *m.* X-Y plotter; **-deutigkeit,** *f.* ambiguity; **-dimensional,** two-dimensional.

Zweielektronen-, dielectronic.

Zweierkette, *f.* two-fold chain.

Zweiersystem, *n.* binary system, binary notation system.

Zweifachkette, *f.* two-fold chain.

Zweiflächner, *m.* dihedron.

zweigeisselig, biflagellate.

zweigespalten, bifid.

Zweikörper-formalismus, *m.* two-body formalism; **-kraft,** *f.*̈-e, two-body force; **-problem,** *n.* two-body problem.

Zweikreis-goniometer, *n.* two-circle goniometer; **-reaktor,** *m.* dual-cycle reactor.

zweischalig, of two sheets.

Zweischichten-gitter, *n.* two-layer lattice; **-struktur,** *f.* two-layer structure.

Zweistoffsystem, *n.* binary system.

Zweistrahl-betatron, *n.* double-ray betatron; **-problem,** *n.* two-beam problem.

Zwei-stufenprozess, *m.* two-stage process; **-wellenmikroskopie,** *f.* two-wavelength microscopy.

zweiwertige Logik, binary logic.

zwei-zackig, two-pronged; **-zählige Achse,** two-fold axis; **-zonenmodell,** *n.* two-zone model.

Zwillings-arten, *f.pl.* geminate species; **-bau,** *m.* twin structure; **-bildung,** *f.* twinning; **-ebene,** *f.* twinning plane, twin face; **-grenze,** *f.* twin boundary; **-kristall,** *m.* twin; **-stellung,** *f.* twin position; **-streifen,** *m.* twin band; **-streifung,** *f.* twin striation; **-versetzung,** *f.* twinning dislocation; **-verwachsung,** *f.* twinning, twin formation.

zwischen-atomar, interatomic; **-behälter,** *m.* surge tank, intermediate tank or container; **-beschleuniger,** *m.* interaccelerator; **-gefäss,** *n.* surge drum, accumulator.

Zwischengitter-atom, *n.* interstitial (atom); **-atombildung,** *f.* interstitial formation; **-atomwanderung,** *f.* interstitial migration; **-legierung,** *f.* interstitial alloy; **-lücke,** *f.* vacancy; **-mechanismus,** *m.* interstitial mechanism; **-paar,** *n.* interstitial pair; **-platz,** *m.* interstitial site; **-sprung,** *m.* interstitial jog; **-wanderung,** *f.* interstitial migration.

Zwischen-haftniveau, *n.* intermediate trap level; **-kern,** *m.* compound nucleus, compound core; **-kopie,** *f.* intermediate; **-kristallin,** intercrystalline; **-original,** *n.* master; **-phase,** *f.* intermediate phase; **-raum,** *m.* gap, interstitial space, opening, hole, distance, play, clearance, backlash, allowance, spacing, separation, intermediate space; **-reflux,** *m.* internal reflux; **-schale,** *f.* subshell; **-schicht,** *f.* interface; **-sockel,** *m.* adapter; **-speichern,** to buffer, store temporarily, save, dump; **-stecker,** *m.* adapter; **-wasser,** *n.* intermediate water.

Zwitterrind, *n.* freemartin.

zyklisch-invers, cyclic-inverse.

zyklometrisch, inverse circular.

Zyklotron, *n.* cyclotron; **-resonanzexperiment,** *n.* cyclotron resonance experiment; **-umlauffrequenz,** cyclotron frequency.

zylindersymmetrisch, cylindrically symmetric.

Zytokinese, *f.,* **Zytoplasmateilung,** *f.* cytokinesis.